HANDBOOK OF RESEARCH ON WALDORF EDUCATION

Waldorf Education: An all-round, balanced approach to education that is equally concerned with intellectual-cognitive and artistic-creative learning. A practice- and experience-based pedagogy. Non-selective and open to all children and young people; offering a stress-free, secure learning environment across 12 grades; embedded in a community of students, teachers, and parents. An alternative education that has been successfully practiced for over a century.

The first Waldorf School was founded in Stuttgart, Germany, in 1919. Today, Waldorf Education is practiced in all countries and cultures around the world: in over 1,000 schools, more than 2,000 kindergartens, and numerous centers for special needs education. This makes Waldorf Education the most prevalent alternative approach to teaching. And yet, despite the success and (now empirically validated) recognition that Waldorf schools enjoy, the theory underlying them remains controversial. Within the academic debate, Waldorf Education is seen as ideologic and unscientific.

This publication sets out to bring clarity to this debate: Renowned researchers explain and discuss Waldorf Education's foundations in relation to the current discourse on education and core disciplines such as theory of knowledge, anthropology, developmental psychology, learning theory, and the theory of professions. This scientific inquiry into Waldorf Education is breaking new ground, casting light on its fascinating humanistic ideal and holistic potential.

Jost Schieren is the Dean and Director of the Institute for School Pedagogy and Teacher Training, Department of Education, Head of the Master of Arts in Pedagogy with a focus on Waldorf Pedagogy/School and Teaching, and Head of the Graduate School in Waldorf Pedagogy, at Alanus University, Germany.

HANDBOOK OF RESEARCH ON WALDORF EDUCATION

Edited by Jost Schieren

NEW YORK AND LONDON

Designed cover image: Chalk image: Nola Bunke
Boy with Prism Image: Angelika Lonnemann
Classroom image: Charlotte Fischer

First published in English 2023 by Routledge
605 Third Avenue, New York, NY 10158

and by Routledge
4 Park Square, Milton Park, Abingdon, Oxon, OX14 4RN

Routledge is an imprint of the Taylor & Francis Group, an informa business

© 2023 selection and editorial matter, Jost Schieren; individual chapters, the contributors

Translations completed by:
Karin Di Giacomo, Front matter, Contributors, Epilogue, and chapters 1 through 4;
Margot Saars, chapters 5 through 9, and cover materials

The right of Jost Schieren to be identified as the author of the editorial material, and of the authors for their individual chapters, has been asserted in accordance with sections 77 and 78 of the Copyright, Designs and Patents Act 1988.

All rights reserved. No part of this book may be reprinted or reproduced or utilised in any form or by any electronic, mechanical, or other means, now known or hereafter invented, including photocopying and recording, or in any information storage or retrieval system, without permission in writing from the publishers.

Trademark notice: Product or corporate names may be trademarks or registered trademarks, and are used only for identification and explanation without intent to infringe.

Published in German by Beltz Juventa 2016

Library of Congress Cataloging-in-Publication Data
Names: Schieren, Jost, 1963- editor.
Title: Handbook of research on Waldorf education / edited by Jost Schieren.
Description: New York : Routledge, 2023. | Includes bibliographical
references and index. | Identifiers: LCCN 2022036579 | ISBN 9781032034706 (Hardback) |
ISBN 9781032034683 (Paperback) | ISBN 9781003187431 (eBook)
Subjects: LCSH: Waldorf method of education. | Anthroposophy.
Classification: LCC LB1029.W34 H36 2023 | DDC 371.39/1--dc23/eng/20220825
LC record available at https://lccn.loc.gov/2022036579

ISBN: 978-1-032-03470-6 (hbk)
ISBN: 978-1-032-03468-3 (pbk)
ISBN: 978-1-003-18743-1 (ebk)

DOI: 10.4324/9781003187431

Typeset in Bembo
by KnowledgeWorks Global Ltd.

CONTENTS

Introduction   1
Jost Schieren

   1 Critique [academic criticism] from the perspective of educational science 1
   2 Empirical turnaround 3
   3 Waldorf education in academic context 4
   4 Issues of reception 6
   5 Research colloquium "Waldorf Education and Educational Science" 7

CHAPTER 1
Epistemology   **13**

Introduction   15
Jost Schieren

Epistemological Foundations of Waldorf Education   17
Johannes Wagemann

   1 Introduction 17
   2 Background in the history of cognition and science 18
   3 Rudolf Steiner's epistemology 25
   4 Relevance of Steiner's epistemology in the philosophy of education 38

CHAPTER 2
Anthropology   **49**

Introduction   51
Jost Schieren

Pedagogic Anthropology in Educational Science and Waldorf Education 53
Christian Rittelmeyer

> 1 *On the concept of pedagogic anthropology 53*
> 2 *Problems of classical anthropologies illustrated in the example:*
> *"Sensualism" vs. "Rationalism" 54*
> 3 *Questioning the search for "The Human Being": The emergence*
> *of historic pedagogic anthropology 58*
> 4 *Anthropologies in educational science and the study of the human being*
> *in Waldorf education: Differences and possible rapprochements 61*

Freedom as an Anthropological Perspective: On the Concept of Man
in Waldorf Education 68
Jost Schieren

> 1 *Historic pedagogic anthropology 68*
> 2 *Waldorf education 70*
> 3 *Soul observation in the work of Herbert Witzenmann 73*
> 4 *Perceiving and thinking 74*
> 5 *Terminology of Waldorf education 77*
> 6 *Summary and outlook 80*

The Study of Man and Educational Practice 85
Albert Schmelzer

> 1 *Introduction: Good practice—Anachronistic ideology? 85*
> 2 *Rudolf Steiner's pedagogic anthropology 85*
> 3 *On the transformation of Waldorf education's pedagogic*
> *anthropology into teaching practice 87*
> 4 *The motif 87*
> 5 *Methodic consciousness 89*
> 6 *Conclusion 91*

CHAPTER 3
Developmental Psychology **95**

Introduction 97
Albert Schmelzer

Attempts to Understand the Development of Children, Adolescents,
and Adults 101
Christian Rittelmeyer

> 1 *Fundamental aspects of an interdisciplinary discourse 101*
> 2 *Developmental psychology "insights" in historic review 103*
> 3 *Possibilities of a critical discourse on the topic "Waldorf education and developmental*
> *psychology": Illustrated by the example of developmental theories 108*

Discussion of Rudolf Steiner's Developmental Psychology 119
Albert Schmelzer

    1 The 1980s 119
    2 The 1990s 122
    3 Newer publications 122
    4 Conclusion 124

Approaches to Substantiating the Concept of Seven-Year Cycles
of Development in Waldorf Education 128
Peter Loebell

    1 Introductory remarks 128
    2 The development of the child as the basis for Waldorf education 128
    3 The transition around the seventh year of life 130
    4 Learning in the second seven-year cycle 134
    5 Transition to the third seven-year cycle 136
    6 Summary: The concept of the seven-year cycles as a foundation for education 140

Waldorf Education and Developmental Psychology in Early Childhood 145
Walter Riethmüller

    1 The concept of development in Waldorf education 145
    2 The concept of "I" 146
    3 Imitation and modeling 148
    4 Surroundings and the formation of self 149
    5 Connections among the development of body, soul, and spirit 150
    6 The child as co-creator of his/her life world: Development as dialog 151
    7 Attachment research 152
    8 Conclusion 152

The Rubicon as a Developmental Phenomenon in Middle Childhood 158
Axel Föller-Mancini and Bettina Berger

    1 History of the term Rubicon 158
    2 Child development in the light of spiritual science 160
    3 The Rubicon as a watershed moment in the second seven-year cycle 162
    4 Excursus: The Rubicon and Oevermann's crisis typology 166
    *5 Rubicon—Middle childhood: Perspectives from developmental
      psychology and anthropology 168*

Adolescence and the Findings of Brain Research 176
Wenzel M. Götte

    1 Introduction 176
    2 Remarks on problems in interpreting the results of neuroscience research 177
    3 Neuroscience research findings relevant to pedagogy 178
    4 Select examples from brain research 182

Contents

5 On the reception of neuroscientific studies 189
6 Areas of potential discourse 193
7 Conclusion and outlook 195

CHAPTER 4
Learning Theory

203

Introduction
Peter Loebell

205

Learning from the Perspective of Educational Science
Wolfgang Nieke

209

1 Our learning concept model is imported from psychology 209
2 Reasons for needing a new definition of the concept of learning
   from a perspective of educational sciences 211
3 Five approaches to a new definition of learning from the perspective
   of educational sciences 213
4 Reasons for learning: Motivation, interest, relevance 218
5 Learning—A cultural science perspective, illustrated by the example
   of learning resistance and equal opportunity 219
6 Learning and teaching 220
7 Learning in freedom 221
8 Learning with the group and against it 222
9 An educated state of being as a result of learning 224
10 Human learning: Independent of content or category-specific? 225
11 Pedagogical consequence: Learning requires meaning and generates it 228

Waldorf Education and Learning Research: Convergences and Differences
Peter Loebell

234

1 Waldorf education in the context of different learning theories 234
2 Learning in the context of Waldorf education 237
3 Summary and outlook 251

Learning in Waldorf Education
Jost Schieren

257

1 Learning theories 257
2 Rudolf Steiner's teachings on imagination 258
3 Disposition and condition 259
4 Imagination and will 260
5 Case study: Agricultural internship 261
6 Aspects of learning 261
7 "Mother Holle" 266
8 Summary 267

Contents

CHAPTER 5
The Art of Teaching   **269**

Teaching Approaches in Waldorf Education   271
Wilfried Sommer

>   *1 Introduction 271*
>   *2 Connections and divisions in educational theory 273*
>   *3 The model of main lesson teaching in Waldorf schools 277*
>   *4 Main lesson teaching as performative education 295*
>   *5 Conclusion 299*

The Waldorf Curriculum: Curriculum, Teaching Plan, or Guideline?   303
M. Michael Zech

>   *1 Curriculum and teacher autonomy in Waldorf education 303*
>   *2 Concept continuity and heterogeneity 305*
>   *3 Attempt at defining the Waldorf curriculum in terms of education science 309*
>   *4 The future of the curriculum and of curriculum development in*
>   *Waldorf schools 314*

CHAPTER 6
Theory of Professions   **319**

Introduction   321
Walter Riethmüller

The Professional Image of the Waldorf Grades Teacher   323
Walter Riethmüller

>   *1 Outline of recent research 323*
>   *2 The Waldorf grades teacher from the point of view of professions theory 325*
>   *3 The grades teacher principle 327*
>   *4 The concept of authority in Waldorf education 329*
>   *5 Reflections from the point of view of professions theory 330*
>   *6 Outlook and conclusions 332*

Teacher Competencies and Professional Success: Ex-post Findings from
Dirk Randoll's Waldorf Teacher Study   337
Jürgen Peters

>   *1 Problem, goals, and method 337*
>   *2 General findings 338*
>   *3 Competences and professional success 340*
>   *4 The link between competences and resilience 343*
>   *5 Conclusion 344*

Contents

The Teacher's Path of Development: Toward Mindfulness in Education 346
Albert Schmelzer

    1 Introduction 346
    2 Personal competences in the education science discourse 346
    3 Anthroposophically oriented education as a path of development 348
    4 Personal qualities and skills worth striving for 348
    5 How to practice? 350
    6 Conclusion 353

CHAPTER 7
Education Science and Waldorf Education/Education Reform **357**

Introduction 359
Peter Loebell

Challenges to Education Science Posed by Waldorf Education as Education Reform 363
Wolfgang Nieke

    1 Education science—The link among orientational, conditional,
      and transformative knowledge 363
    2 School climate as a shared orientational pattern 367
    3 Teachers' mindfulness toward students in Waldorf schools 369
    4 Waldorf education is more than and different from education reform 370

Education Reform and Waldorf Education: Interpreting a Historically
Difficult Relationship 374
Volker Frielingsdorf

    1 Introduction 374
    2 Waldorf education and education reform: What they have in common 375
    3 Differences between Waldorf education and education reform 379
    4 Five theses on the relationship between Waldorf education and education reform 384
    5 Constructive forms of future cooperation 385

Central Motifs in Education Reform and Waldorf Education 391
Peter Loebell

    1 Education reform and Waldorf education: Common topics 391
    2 Essential features of Waldorf education 396
    3 Summary: Waldorf education—A searching movement 407

CHAPTER 8
Waldorf Education and Anthroposophy **413**

Education Science and Waldorf Education 415
Wolfgang Nieke

Contents

1 *Waldorf education and anthroposophy 415*
2 *What is fascinating about Waldorf education? 415*
3 *Points of mutual rejection 416*
4 *Possible meeting points 417*

How Can Steiner's Pedagogical Esotericism Be Open for Discussion?: Theses on
Avoidable Obstacles to Discourse   419
Johannes Kiersch

1 *Obstacles to discourse 420*
2 *Esotericism between public discourse and secret space 422*
3 *Helpful questions 423*

Anthroposophy and Waldorf Education: A Field of Tension   428
Jost Schieren

1 *The worldview problem 429*
2 *Anthroposophy and science 430*
3 *Anthroposophy in Waldorf education 432*
4 Epoché *or the renunciation of anthroposophy 433*
5 *Worldview as a cognitive challenge 434*
6 *The teacher's self-development 435*
7 *Conclusion 435*

The Anthroposophic Understanding of History from the Point of View
of Waldorf Education, Education Science, and History Teaching   438
M. Michael Zech

1 *Problem description 438*
2 *The significance of cultural history in Steiner's time 442*
3 *Steiner's approach to cultural history 443*
4 *The importance of the history of culture and consciousness in anthroposophy 447*
5 *The background of Steiner's historical theory 448*
6 *The self-location of anthroposophy and Waldorf education 453*
7 *History in the Waldorf school 453*
8 *History teaching in Waldorf schools 456*

CHAPTER 9
Individual Topics   463

Intercultural Education and Waldorf Education: An Inspiring Encounter   465
Albert Schmelzer

1 *Starting point and research questions 465*
2 *Intercultural versus transcultural education? 466*
3 *Objectives 467*
4 *Ways of dealing with cultural diversity 468*

5 Goals 469
6 Interim observation 469
7 The Intercultural Waldorf School in Mannheim 470
8 Conclusion 473

Religious Education in Waldorf Schools in the Context of the Current Pedagogical Discourse 475
Carlo Willmann

1 Introduction 475
2 Religion between plurality and individualism 476
3 Current discussions on religious education 477
4 General religious education in Waldorf schools 484
5 Perspectives 491

Waldorf Education and Media: Human and Technological Development in Contrast 496
Edwin Hübner

1 Introduction 496
2 "A Silicon Valley school that doesn't compute" 496
3 Basic questions 497
4 Definitions of media 497
5 A phenomenological approach to media 498
6 Side effects 499
7 Direct and indirect media education 499
8 Basic gestures of human development 499
9 Direct and indirect media education in childhood and youth 500
10 Direct media education 501
11 Curriculum for the media form "image" 502
12 Curriculum for the media form "sound" 503
13 Curriculum for the media form "script" 503
14 Curriculum "Understanding electronic devices" 504
15 Curriculum "Sensible media use" 505
16 Underlying paradigms 505
17 Anthropologic media education compared to other approaches 506
18 Transhumanism and the anthroposophic image of the human being 507

School Autonomy and Collaborative Governance as Constitutive Elements of Waldorf Schools 513
M. Michael Zech

1 Introduction 513
2 History of collaborative governance 514
3 Regional, national, and international collaboration of Waldorf institutions 518
4 The parents 519
5 The students 520
6 Quality assurance tools 520

Contents

7 *Conferences 521*
8 *The function of internal publications 522*
9 *The Association of Waldorf Schools' Research Institute 522*
10 *The funding challenge 522*
11 *Republican and democratic 524*
12 *Administrative structures 525*
13 *Faculty meetings 527*
14 *Outlook 528*

Epilogue	532
Volker Frielingsdorf and Christian Boettger	
Contributors	535
Index	538

INTRODUCTION

Jost Schieren

At present, Waldorf schools number among the best-known and most widespread institutions that emerged from a background of Reform pedagogy. In Germany alone, there are currently about 236 Waldorf schools and more than 500 Waldorf kindergartens; worldwide more than a thousand schools operate in more than 27 countries. In particular, China has been considered the *boom country* of Waldorf education in the last years. There is no school movement founded during the times of Reform pedagogy that comes even close to such a wide distribution other than Montessori facilities, which are even more numerous.[1]

Waldorf schools profit especially from the growing interest in private schools, ever since the first alarming PISA *[Programme for International Student Assessment]* results were available. In Germany, the educational policy measures in response to these findings included continuous achievement level surveys and shortening the middle school years. Such measures further raised the interest in private schools. Parents who send their children to Waldorf schools hold Waldorf education to be less focused on one-sided academic achievement and therefore a less stressful type of school. These parents perceive Waldorf schools to offer the students greater freedom for individual development, while encouraging them to make versatile use of such developmental opportunities. Further well-known characteristics of Waldorf education are as follows: emphasis on crafts and artistic-musical activities, geared to balance out a one-sided cognitive education; non-graded report cards; commitment to a constant person of reference during the so-called classroom-teacher period of the first eight years; learning in groups with different achievement levels; absence of school year repetition; learning epochs and early instruction in a foreign language.

As a matter of course, Waldorf schools have become a part of German and international (private) school systems. In spite of this overall successful and positive development, it must be noted that educational science has either barely acknowledged the educational concept of Waldorf education or harshly passed judgment on its theoretical foundations. The position of educational science toward Waldorf education ranges from ignorance to sharp criticism, with the former being most often the unspoken basis for the latter.

1 Critique [academic criticism] from the perspective of educational science

The 1970s saw a surge of newly founded Waldorf schools; it was only thereafter, in the 1980s, that educational scientists issued extensive, basic critiques of Waldorf education, which remain relevant to this day. In 1985, Klaus Prange issued a book with the punchy title *Education in Anthroposophy* (Prange 2000). From the viewpoint of educational science, Prange described [Waldorf education] as an ideologically biased, dogmatic pedagogy, aiming at indoctrination, which he saw as its fundamental flaw. In his dissertation "The occult worldview of Waldorf education," (Ullrich 1986) Heiner Ullrich provides a detailed assessment of anthroposophy as the underlying teaching of Waldorf education. He concluded

DOI: 10.4324/9781003187431-1

1

that anthroposophy was a pre-modern, i.e., pre-enlightenment mystical worldview that fails to measure up to the standards of current scientific thought. In another part of his book, he states: "In contrast to conscious, methodical self-discipline, to the plurality and openness of modern scientific thinking, Steiner and his disciples purport to dogmatically know or behold a well-ordered cosmos as an eternally unchangeable truth [...]. Their form of thinking equals a degenerated philosophy, an ideology [...]. In the development of his occult science of Anthroposophy, Steiner entirely succumbed to the perils of such thinking. Here, Neo-Platonism with its pre-modern, dogmatic-speculative bent merges seamlessly into Theosophy's consciously re-mythologizing cosmic view" (Ullrich 2011, p. 109).

The position outlined by both authors today remains authoritative in educational science. Academia's ideology critique still governs the current discussion about Waldorf education. Anthroposophy is deemed to be the problem of Waldorf education. In his latest publication "Waldorf Education. A Critical Introduction," Heiner Ullrich again emphatically repeats his criticism (Ullrich 2015).

On one hand, he acknowledges the practical success of Waldorf education: "Waldorf schools can definitively be deemed successful" (Ibid., p. 172). On the other hand, this testimony to the acknowledged success of Waldorf education is counterweighted, based on a diagnosis of the ideological imprint characterizing Waldorf education: "Its encompassing foundation lies in Rudolf Steiner's anthroposophy, in its concept of the human being and its worldview. These determine not only educational and teaching methods but impact in manifold, interconnected ways including lesson plan contents and teaching topics. There is no other school culture stemming from the time of classic Reform pedagogy that bears such a deep ideological stamp as does Waldorf education" (Ullrich 2015, p. 173). In his critical introduction, Ullrich again and again reiterates this core criticism. He repeatedly states that anthroposophy constitutes not only the background of an overall positive pedagogical movement, but that it is also a dominant factor in all aspects of Waldorf education.

According to Ullrich, Waldorf education is through and through shaped by anthroposophical ideology. Here it should be noted that academia appears to accord considerably more weight to the ideological ballast of Waldorf education than the scientifically no less incommensurable "cosmic education" of Maria Montessori. Montessori's "child-centered" pedagogy is taught in many of its public schools, relatively unburdened by theoretical criticism. Also, in educational science seminars, the Montessori concept is dealt with in neutral, cognition-based, and overall benign terms. However, the theoretical impositions of anthroposophy have so far generally barred educational science from academic access to Waldorf education. It is alone due to the broad esteem in which parents hold Waldorf schools that they have been granted an existence in the legally protected enclaves of international private school systems.

The [anthroposophical] theory behind Waldorf education is portrayed as grossly unscientific and irrational even in fact-oriented academic presentations that aim for neutrality. Andreas Lischewski in his "Milestones in pedagogy" (Lischewski 2014), for example deals with Waldorf education only in a few paragraphs in which he cites in rapid sequence the concept of "the four bodies," which unfold in a fixed "seven-year rhythm" and the developmental principle of the "I" as being "Reincarnation and Karma." This treatment may be attributable to the brevity of the section, yet it is apparent that such fragments of thought and conceptual notions can hardly suffice for a valid theoretical position, even as many Waldorf schools employ the same descriptions in their promotional brochures and on their websites.

Further examples of educational science's views on Waldorf education include the "Lexikon der Pädagogik" *[Dictionary of pedagogy]* by Heinz-Elmar Tenorth and Rudolf Tippelt. They write: "Waldorf education is acknowledged for its child-centered work and its autonomous forms in the organization of time and topics; yet at the same time it has been criticized for its anthroposophical indoctrination" (Tenorth, Tippelt 2007, p. 762). As their only bibliographical reference here, they mention Prange's "Education in anthroposophy." In Ehrenhard Skiera's authoritative monograph "Reformpädagogik in Geschichte und Gegenwart" *[Reform pedagogy in historic and present times]*, we read—after a quote from Rudolf Steiner—the following sentence: "That is totalitarian ideology in purest form. It tends to pull everything under its spell and to reject all critics. As long as its mission remains unfulfilled, such totalitarianism only displays open-mindedness so it can integrate and adapt other ideas to serve its own ends as a strategy of a gradual takeover" (Skiera 2009, p. 264). Such statements draw a sharp and definitive line between the position of educational science and any theoretical claims of Waldorf education. In fact, a debate on the subject is impossible, because the freighted term *totalitarianism* touches upon the sensitive, untouchable canon of post-war German values.

However, apart from his criticism of anthroposophical theory, Skiera describes the practice of Waldorf education neutrally and in great detail, in many passages, even according to its distinction. Moreover, the first edition of his book on Reform pedagogy clearly displays on its cover a Waldorf picture that is used for introducing the alphabet. In this vein, he concludes: "The critical view set forth here may appear to suggest a negative judgment on the practice of Waldorf education. But that does is not necessarily so. For example, one can acknowledge various achievements of Alchemy (e.g., the invention of porcelain) without being convinced of its theoretical premises or of the expediency of its overall approach. Waldorf education consistently translates its concept of the human being into educational practice and thus definitely evidences desirable factors *[desiderata]* of modern pedagogy in its approaches and results" (Skiera 2009, p. 265). Skiera then lists a few central aspects of Waldorf educational practices that fall under these "desiderata": the significance of authority in schools, building of values, aesthetic and wholistic development, aspects of inclusiveness, and others.

Overall, the attitude of academia entails that in the framework of liberal educational politics Waldorf education can claim a place in the private school landscape and occasionally also may inspire the field of public education. But the greater part of its success rests on reliable approval from the side of privileged middle-class parents, who are far removed from average societal standards. Meanwhile, the theoretical foundations of Waldorf education remain completely excluded from academic discussion.

2 Empirical turnaround

On one hand, academia largely rejects or ignores the theoretical foundations of Waldorf education, yet on the other hand, in the last 15 years, the educational practice in Waldorf schools has become subject to extensive empirical research. By now, more than 223 empirical studies on Waldorf education have been conducted nationally and internationally (Peters 2013, p. 3). Thus, Waldorf schools count among the best-researched schools within the larger context of Reform pedagogy. The distinct increase in empirical studies over the last 25 years is illustrated by the graphic below, taken from the thesis of Jürgen Peters (Böhle, Peters 2011; Peters 2013, p. 6):

Number of empiric studies in Waldorf schools 1980–2010

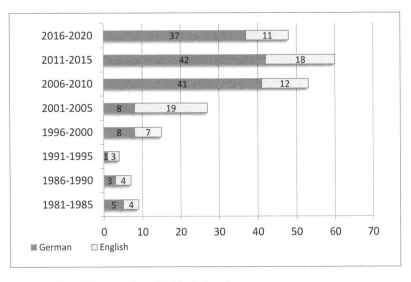

Figure 0.1 Frequency of empiric research on Waldorf education

The empiric studies of Heiner Ullrich deserve notice, as he pursues an ongoing interest in Waldorf education research, notwithstanding his theoretical criticism. In cooperation with Werner Helsper, he provided a comprehensive study on the so-called classroom-teacher time period (Helsper, Ullrich, et al. 2007). Numerous scientific works of his students offer further contributions: Till-Sebastian Idel researched biographies of Waldorf students (Idel 2007), Gunter Graßhoff (Graßhoff 2008), Katharina Kunze (Kunze 2011), and Davina Höblich (Höblich, Graßhoff 2006) have published research pertaining to the above-cited classroom- teacher study. Heiner Ullrich and his circle pursued mainly qualitative research, which is complemented by numerous quantitative studies by Dirk Randoll, as well as further qualitative works by Heiner Barz. These two authors conducted comprehensive research on Waldorf graduates (Barz, Randoll 2007) and studies on the Waldorf teacher profession (Randoll 2013; Barz 2013), as well as a joint study with Sylvia Liebenwein on school quality in Waldorf schools (Liebenwein, Barz, Randoll 2012). Moreover, by now, a number of international empirical studies are available: Great Britain (Woods, Ashley, Woods 2005), Sweden (Dahlin 2007), USA (Gerwin, Mitchell 2007), and Switzerland (Randoll, Barz 2007).

All in all, most of these studies are giving Waldorf schools a relatively positive evaluation. Among other findings, there appeared no evidence for the indoctrination motive postulated by Klaus Prange. Rather, the graduate study conducted by Barz and Randoll finds no evidence among the surveyed graduates that they did in fact experience any indoctrination (Randoll, Barz 2007, p. 133).

Measured by the gauge of empirical educational research, Waldorf schools are internationally competitive and Waldorf students show a high degree of identification with their school (Liebenwein, Barz, Randoll 2012, p. 50). Waldorf teachers evidence apparently a high identification with their profession as well, even though they are earning less than a public-school teacher, nor do they enjoy public-servant benefits *[status]*. Waldorf teachers are highly motivated and at the same time experience less danger of burnout (Randoll 2013).

Are Waldorf schools then the "Blissful Isles" in a more-or-less stressful educational landscape that is governed by economic constraints? Certainly not. The joyous liveliness and colorful radiance of Waldorf schools is, rather, indebted to an economic selection mechanism among other factors. This is not intentionally initiated by the schools themselves, but results from state legislated private-school sector laws, which stipulate that private schools can only partially rely on public funding. Accordingly, Waldorf parents have to come up with a school fee, the amount of which is tied to their income level and averages about 160 euros per child and month (Koolmann 2014, p. 5). Waldorf schools therefore have become a type of "client-school" that offers a protected educational space for children of college-educated parents, who pursue comprehensive educational aspirations and individualistic blueprints for the life of their children. These parents see Waldorf education as protecting their child from the dissociative tendencies of modern-day society and its vacillating values.[2]

A first exception of this bourgeois "island-world" of Waldorf education is the Intercultural School in Mannheim (www.fiw-mannheim.de), which operates as a Waldorf school in a hot-spot neighborhood of the city.

It is encouraging to note that more school projects of this kind are being founded. Moreover, it deserves attention that the bourgeois imprint on Waldorf education is largely a German, i.e., European phenomenon (as a result of states' educational politics). Internationally, many Waldorf school projects are demonstrating that Waldorf education can work very successfully in areas where circumstances are marked by poverty and distress; such projects providing social therapeutic and basic educational services are operating in African townships, in the Favelas of Brazil, in Palestine, Haiti, and Eastern Europe.

3 Waldorf education in academic context

The strong increase in empirical research on Waldorf education brought with it a marked change in Waldorf teacher education. Waldorf education is likely the only type of private school in the world that maintains its own teacher training, which in Germany is currently funded with over ten million euros annually, funded by Waldorf schools' contributions. Until 2006, Waldorf teacher education was nearly exclusively provided in Waldorf teacher seminars, which offered fundamental full-time study courses for classroom teachers, who then were issued specific types of teaching certificates that were only valid for teaching at Waldorf schools and varied depending on the policies in each state of the German Federal Republic. In addition, university graduates in specific academic subjects could earn supplementary Waldorf qualifications and then teach at the Waldorf high school level. The largest German Waldorf teacher seminars are located in Stuttgart, Mannheim, and Witten-Annen. Of these, the Freie Hochschule Stuttgart *[Independent (Waldorf) University Stuttgart]* has been accredited by the state of Baden-Württemberg. Altogether there are ten independent locations for full-time Waldorf teacher education in Germany, and more than 25 seminar facilities offering part-time and on-the-job training courses.

Waldorf teacher training has undergone distinct changes since 2007. Since that time, the Alanus Hochschule für Kunst und Gesellschaft *[Alanus University of Arts and Social Sciences]* in Alfter, close to Bonn, offers a teacher training program in art, leading to the German First State Exam for Teachers with Waldorf teacher credentials. At the same time, its part-time study program leading to a master's degree in pedagogy received accreditation, offering teacher qualifications for graduates from other disciplines. This master's program includes a focus area on Research on Pedagogic Practice, addressing educators who are already teaching. Furthermore, a part-time study program for master's degree in special education was accredited in Alfter, as well as a bachelor's study program in childhood pedagogy in 2011. Further degree programs—offering bachelor of arts and master of fine arts in education for teachers at high- and integrated schools—received accreditation in 2011. All these study programs share profile traits that are characteristic of Waldorf education while engaging in a dialog among Waldorf education, various types of Reform pedagogy, and general educational science.

With its educational science degree programs, Alanus University aims at liberating Waldorf education from its narrow ideological frame and monolithic image and at providing its students with a broad forum for discourse. Within the larger context of successful institutional accreditation, the German Council of Science and Humanities in 2010 conferred the right to award doctorates to the Alanus department of educational studies. As part of this academically oriented development based on the Bologna Process, the teacher seminars in Stuttgart and Mannheim also developed and accredited BA and MA programs for Waldorf education with various areas of focus. Since 2015, the Stuttgart Waldorf College has offered an international, English-language MA program in Waldorf education. First professorships for Waldorf education were established in 2008.

This development within Waldorf education led also to a new culture in the fields of science and research. Already in the 1980s, Stuttgart college initiated a colloquium with Waldorf educators and educational scientists, making Waldorf education more visible to the public through regular publications and by contributing to discussions (Bohnsack, Kranich 1990; Bohnsack, Leber 1996). This colloquium circle included from the academic educational sciences side the following professor emeriti: Fritz Bohnsack (University of Essen), Horst Rumpf (Goethe University, Frankfurt), Harm Paschen (University of Bielefeld), Karl Garnitschnig (University of Vienna), Bo Dahlin (University of Karlstad), and lately also professors Wolfgang Nieke (University of Rostock), Jochen Krautz (Bergische University Wuppertal), and Guido Pollack (University of Passau).

Further contributors to the discourse between academia and Waldorf education are Peter Schneider and his professorial thesis describing Rudolf Steiner's epistemology as a theoretical foundation of Waldorf education (Schneider 1982), Heiner Barz, who, in his study, also explores the epistemic foundations of Waldorf education (Barz 1994), and further the works of Christian Rittelmeyer on school architecture (Rittelmeyer 1996), on aesthetic perception (Rittelmeyer 2005), and a body-oriented pedagogic anthropology (Rittelmeyer 2002) based on empiric psychology and hermeneutics. Horst Philipp Bauer and Peter Schneider published a two-volume anthology giving insight into the perspective of educational science on Waldorf education titled "Waldorf Education, Perspectives of a Scientific Dialog" (Bauer, Schneider 2006), and in 2010, Harm Paschen issued his "Educational Science Approaches to Waldorf Education" (Paschen 2010).

The scientific online magazine RoSE (Research on Steiner Education) has been published semi-annually since 2010 by Alanus University and the Rudolf Steiner University/College in Oslo (www.rose-journ.com). Its contributions are selected in a peer-reviewed process according to strict criteria and are generally published in bilingual (German and English) form. The Network of European Academic Steiner Teacher Education (ENASTE) deserves mention here, whose members are academically oriented Waldorf Teacher Training Institutions in Norway, Sweden, France, the Netherlands, Switzerland, Austria, and Germany. In 2015, a third International Congress for Education took place at ENASTE's Vienna headquarters, where educational scientists with or without Waldorf qualifications gathered to address issues regarding teacher education (Congress 2011: The Future of Teacher Education), pedagogic anthropology (Congress 2013: The Educator's View of the Human Being. Consequences for Schools and Teacher Education), and finally present-day challenges facing educational processes (Congress 2015: Transformations. Education in a Rapidly Changing World).

All these publications, initiatives, research projects, and institutional developments show that Waldorf education has been undergoing fundamental changes in the 21st century. During its history, spanning nearly one century, it was mainly focused on expansion through founding new schools and on establishing its educational practice. In this process, the self-definition of Waldorf education was largely affirmative, relatively uncritical, and marked by a reliance on Rudolf Steiner's educational writings under avoidance of academic science in its pedagogic source material. But now, since the beginning of the 21st century, a profound shift has occurred toward an increased scientific orientation and a research-based, open dialog with representatives of general educational science. A reflex-like rejection of critical voices from that direction no longer prevails, but now such critique has become open to debate and is being included in professional discourse. Volker Frielingsdorf's work "Waldorf Education in Educational Science" (Frielingsdorf 2012) affords us a well-founded and thoroughly researched review of the scientific literature published since the founding of Waldorf education. Interestingly, of the approximately 800 listed scientific titles on Waldorf education, 350 have been published in the first decade of this century alone (Frielingsdorf 2012, p. 69). This tendency toward a growing number of scientific publications on Waldorf education has continued and even increased in the last few years.

4 Issues of reception

Notwithstanding these newer developments, Waldorf education has dwelled over decades in a sort of grubby esoteric corner. Even to this day, educational science does not accord academic validity to the theoretical underpinnings of Waldorf education. In the context of an (eventually rejected) institutional accreditation process for the Mannheim Free University, the German Council for Sciences and Humanities concluded in 2011 that there was danger "in establishing an institution of higher learning on the foundation of a specific, ideologically freighted pedagogy, i.e., an unscientific theory of education."[3] The scientific deficit of Waldorf education exists not only in the perception of the established academic system, nor is it caused merely by a narrow concept of science, as Waldorf defenders like to assert, but it is in fact also self-generated.

Many followers of anthroposophy are deeply engaged in their work in the fields of medicine, agriculture, Waldorf education, special education, and art therapy. The successful development and distribution of Waldorf education rested on the enthusiasm and commitment of many people who felt the pedagogical impulse of Rudolf Steiner to be humanistic and particularly well suited to foster the development of children and adolescents. But an evaluation of Waldorf education cannot happen on even grounds with the academic sciences if it relies on educational practice alone (as the assessment of the Council for Science and Humanities suggests).

In the past, a lack of basic institutional capability and infrastructure prohibited the development of a theoretically valid account of Waldorf education and of a corresponding culture of research. Moreover, a somewhat unfortunate culture of apodictic apologetics has sprung up as a result of teachers experiencing the deep meaning and fertile effectivity of Waldorf education in their daily work, while this pedagogical approach was subjected to fundamental scientific criticism. On the level of scientific theory, this kind of approach hardly produced any convincing lines of reasoning. But it did generate a highly self-affirmative, prolific secondary literature on anthroposophical Waldorf education, which, however, was of only limited use in attracting educational scientists of renown and engaging them in a discourse on the topic. A spiral of futile arguments and counterarguments ensued, which inhibited any discourse.

The one-sided recourse to the work of Rudolf Steiner, the founder of Waldorf education, also proved to be unproductive. Until his death in 1925, Rudolf Steiner developed Waldorf education as a sort of "work in progress." He developed the teacher trainings and the fundamentals of Waldorf education unsystematically and only verbally in many public lectures, often in answer to special situations and conditions of his time. He did not leave any systematic writings on Waldorf education, but he rather lectured and talked about Waldorf education, directing special focus toward a pedagogic motivation and inspiration of Waldorf teachers. In his eyes, the pedagogic excellence of Waldorf schools is less substantiated by scientific theories and cognition or by institutional systemic aspects, but rather it is contingent upon the quality of real-life teaching practice and the competence of Waldorf teachers, who are encouraged to bring a wealth of innovative impulses to their work and, first of all, to meet their students in a spirit of loving attention. Without any doubt, Steiner succeeded in sparking high enthusiasm for the pedagogic impulse of Waldorf education in the first staff of teachers and in many generations of Waldorf teachers after that. Rudolf Steiner's main concern was that Waldorf schools should not be allowed to become ideological schools. Again and again, he firmly pointed out that anthroposophy should not be permitted to influence the curriculum content of the schools. (See Schieren's contribution in Chapter 8.)

5 Research colloquium "Waldorf Education and Educational Science"

A valid scientific base for the theory of Waldorf education has notably not yet been sufficiently established, in spite of dynamic and pro-scientific developments that occurred particularly in the 21st century. The 2011 verdict of the Council for Science and Humanities, namely that Waldorf education is a non-scientific educational system, has weighty consequences—not only academically, but also politically and legally. It impacts access to accreditation, teaching- and school permits, and to public funds. These factors strike at the core of Waldorf education (at least in Germany).

The work of this research colloquium, which started in 2011, resulted in the book presented here. This round table was initiated and sponsored by Walter Riethmüller (Pedagogic Research Unit at the Federation of Independent Waldorf Schools) and Jost Schieren (Alanus University). The colloquium's core group includes—other than the two initiators—Christian Boettger (Research Unit for Pedagogy at the Federation of Independent Waldorf Schools), Wenzel Götte (Free University Stuttgart), Peter Loebell (Free University Stuttgart), Albert Schmelzer (Alanus University), and Wilfried Sommer (Alanus University). Christian Rittelmeyer (em. University Göttingen) participated in the sessions of this colloquium as a guest and advisor. Sophie Pannitschka as a research associate of Alanus University supported the work organizationally.

This research colloquium set itself the goal of proactively fostering the dialog between Waldorf education and educational science. The discourse did not primarily address the fundamental questions of whether Waldorf education or anthroposophy are scientifically sound, nor did it center around the issue whether or not the *current scientific community* favors an overly narrow concept of science that results in a wholesale disregard for Waldorf education and anthroposophy, based on a time-specific, reductionistic scientific paradigm. While such debates on principles may be rewarding in regard to content, they often tend to polarize the positions and rarely lead to mutual understanding or rapprochement. In single scientific disciplines such as educational science, fundamental reflections on scientific paradigms are generally of minor importance. It is in the sub-disciplines of each science that the concrete field of scientific practice unfolds. Therefore, the research colloquium primarily focused on these sub-disciplines of educational science. They first clarified central themes and directions of discourse for specific areas of educational science. In the next step, they compared them with themes and positions adopted by Waldorf education so as to then discuss them.

Their work attended more closely to the following sub-disciplines of general educational science: epistemology, anthropology, developmental psychology, learning theory, methodology, professions theory, and Waldorf education in the historic context of Reform pedagogy and educational science. The field of tension between anthroposophy and Waldorf education furnished a separate topic of discussion. Each of the core members prepared and moderated one of these topics as well as a few chosen singular topics such as intercultural pedagogy, media education, religious studies pedagogy, and school autonomy. In addition to the core group, specially invited guests attended the sessions of the research colloquium. Their respective contributions are included in this book.

The core group chose focal topics for discourse according to specific viewpoints as previewed in the following paragraphs:

Epistemology (Coordinator: Jost Schieren): While Rudolf Steiner presented his esoteric teachings mainly in lecture form, he developed his own epistemology referencing Goethe's concept of scientific cognition (Steiner 1979) in his early philosophical work after 1886, which moreover encompasses his philosophy of freedom (Steiner 2005). Steiner saw in his early works the seed of his later anthroposophy; however, this aspect of his writing has rarely received due recognition. Steiner's epistemology is well suited as a basis for scientific discourse, since it offers an explicitly philosophical and thus rational framework.

Anthropology (Coordinator: Jost Schieren): A firm concept of the human being is a key characteristic of Waldorf education. The introductory lectures that Steiner gave in Stuttgart in 1911 marked the founding of Waldorf education. In these lectures, he presented his anthroposophical anthropology (Steiner 1980), his understanding of the human being, and his concept of child and youth development as the essential educational foundations of Waldorf education. So far, there have been only sketchy attempts at reconciliation between anthropological positions of Waldorf education on one hand and scientifically propounded pedagogic anthropology on the other.

Developmental Psychology (Coordinator: Albert Schmelzer): Based on its anthropological understanding, Waldorf education purports to align its pedagogic practice—in both curriculum and didactic methodology—along the development of the child and youth. Steiner introduced a much-discussed concept with his seven-year development cycle. The full understanding of this concept—and how it carries over to research findings in modern developmental psychology—awaits discussion.

Learning Theory (Coordinator: Peter Loebell): Waldorf education does not have an explicit learning theory. Nevertheless, its teaching-and-learning practice can be matched to key tenets of learning theory.

General Methodology (Coordinator: Wilfried Sommer): On the level of everyday educational practice in the Waldorf school, the impression may arise that Waldorf education follows a type of recipe approach that implements certain forms of methodology and didactics (main lesson blocks, non-graded report cards, etc.) without much theoretical understructure. This chapter discusses the differentiated theoretical foundation of Waldorf education from the level of general methodology and establishes that Waldorf education is fit to enter into discourse with representatives of current didactic theory.

Professions Theory (Coordinator: Walter Riethmüller): Waldorf teachers are known for their professional understanding that is both categorical and very deep. Waldorf classroom teachers in particular evidence high professional ethics, which guides their teaching practice. This topic is now open for discussion based on recently available valid scientific research presented in empiric studies (Helsper, Ullrich, et al. 2007; Peters 2013; Randoll 2013).

Waldorf Education in the historic context of reform pedagogy and educational science (Coordinator: Peter Loebell): This chapter deals with the historic research dimension of educational science demonstrating the position of Waldorf education in the historical context of Reform pedagogy and general educational science.

Waldorf Education and Anthroposophy (Coordinator: Wenzel M. Götte): Since its inception, Waldorf education has been haunted by the general suspicion and accusation that it is governed by ideology and

Introduction

dogmatism. This topic is therefore given its own chapter, resolutely posing the question in what way and to what degree anthroposophy shapes and influences Waldorf education.

Singular Topics: Since there is already a vivid exchange on specific curriculum subjects between regular school pedagogy and Waldorf education, the chosen topics in this section (intercultural education, media pedagogy, the pedagogy of religion, and school autonomy) do not include such subject-specific methodology. The selection covers a representative range of fields where Waldorf education implements new developmental impulses and focal points that may prove of interest to educational science.

This publication does not claim to furnish a scientific basis for Waldorf education, nor does it discuss whether or not Waldorf education is scientifically valid. Rather, this book aims at a comprehensive scientific approach to Waldorf education. This process reveals congruences as well as differences with central tenets of general educational science. This is true for every scientific discussion on equal footing. The central goal of this publication is to contribute to an approach to Waldorf education that does not merely dismiss it with the rather chauvinistic sounding verdicts of *pre-* or *non-scientific* but gives serious consideration also to its theoretic foundations in scientific research. Ultimately, even an established academic discipline like educational science cannot afford to remain disinterested and overlook an internationally successful pedagogic concept that has been established for decades and continues to spread. In the long run, academia will not be able to keep disregarding Waldorf education with its explicit theoretical foundations nor hold it in contempt. This publication wishes to help start a broad, open, scientific dialog around Waldorf education within the context of general educational science.

A cordial thank you to all those involved in the work of the research colloquium and to all authors for their congenial and productive cooperation. Thank you also for the general financial support of the Pädagogische Forschungsstelle beim Bund der Freien Waldorfschulen *[Pedagogic Research Unit at the Federation of Independent Waldorf Schools]* and of the Software AG Foundation, which made this project possible. Further thanks go to Sophie Pannitschka, who has been with the projects since its inception and thoughtfully facilitated communication in between the colloquium's sessions. Volker Frielingsdorf and Angelika Wiehl are thanked for their thorough and intensive proofreading, especially Angelika Wiehl, who shepherded the book through the last phases of editing with great dedication and care. A grateful acknowledgment to Beltz Publishing and Frank Engelhardt for their spontaneous willingness to support such an extensive publishing venture. The final and particular thank you goes to Christian Boettger, the manager of the Pedagogic Research Unit at the BdFWS; from the beginning, he gave attention and support to this project with his deep personal engagement, fine sense of tact, extraordinary communication skills, and great enthusiasm.

Notes

1 In this regard, it is however important to note that Montessori schools in Germany are mostly part of the public school system, while Waldorf schools are organized exclusively as private schools.

2 See Heiner Ullrich: "Evaluating the studies on parent professions shows that former Waldorf students continue to come mostly from the academically educated higher middle class" (Ullrich, Strunk 2012, p. 72). Ullrich bases his assessment on the graduate study of Barz and Randoll (2007). However, this study relies on cohorts from the 1990s at most. The Association of Independent Waldorf Schools has commissioned a study conducted by Steffen Koolmann and Lars Petersen that is currently underway at Alanus University.

3 Position in regard to accreditation of the founding process of the Free University Mannheim. Accessible online at www.wissenschaftsrat.de/download/archiv/pm_0511.pdf (last accessed January 2016).

References

Barz, Heiner (1994): Anthroposophie im Spiegel von Wissenschaftstheorie und Lebensweltforschung. Zwischen lebendigem Goetheanismus und latenter Militanz. *[Anthroposophy as reflected in Science Theory and life environment research. Between contemporary Goethean thought and latent militarism.]* Weinheim: Deutscher-Studien verlag.

Barz, Heiner (2013): Unterrichten an Waldorfschulen: Berufsbild Waldorflehrer: Neue Perspektiven zu Praxis, Forschung, Ausbildung. *[Teaching at Waldorf schools: Professional profile of Waldorf teachers: New perspectives on practice, research and training.]* Wiesbaden: VS.

Barz, Heiner/Randoll, Dirk (2007): Absolventen von Waldorfschulen. Eine empirische Studie zu Bildung und Lebensgestaltung ehemaliger Waldorfschüler. *[Waldorf school graduates. A study on their culture and way of life.]* Wiesbaden: VS.

Bauer, Horst Philipp/Schneider, Peter (Eds.) (2006): Waldorfpädagogik. Perspektiven eines wissenschaftlichen Dialoges. *[Waldorf education: Perspectives of a scientific dialog.]* Frankfurt am Main: Peter Lang.

Böhle, Petra/Peters, Jürgen (2011): Empirische Forschungen an Waldorfschulen im deutschsprachigen Raum, Teil 2. *[Empiric research on Waldorf schools in German speaking areas, part 2]*. In: RoSE, Research on Steiner Education, Online Journal Vol. 2, No. 1 (2011). www.rosejourn.com.

Bohnsack, Fritz/Kranich, Ernst-Michael (Eds.) (1990): Erziehungswissenschaft und Waldorfpädagogik. Der Beginn eines notwendigen Dialogs. *[Educational science and Waldorf education. Opening a necessary dialog.]* Weinheim, Basel: Beltz.

Bohnsack, Fritz/Leber, Stefan (Eds.) (1996): Sozial-Erziehung im Sozial-Verfall: Grundlagen, Kontroversen, Wege. *[Social education in the midst of social decay: Basic factors, controversies, pathways.]* Published by F. Bohnsack und St. Leber. Weinheim, Basel: Beltz.

Dahlin, Bo (2007): The Waldorf School – Cultivating Humanity? A report from an evaluation of Waldorf schools in Sweden. Karlstad: University Press.

Frielingsdorf, Volker (2012): Waldorfpädagogik in der Erziehungswissenschaft. Ein Überblick. *[Waldorf education in educational science. An overview.]* Weinheim, Basel: Beltz.

Gerwin, Douglas/Mitchell, David (2007):Survey of Waldorf Graduates – Phase II. New Hampshire: The Research Institute for Waldorf Education.

Graßhoff, Gunter (2008): Zwischen Familie und Klassenlehrer. Pädagogische Generationsbeziehungen jugendlicher Waldorfschüler. *[Between family and classroom teacher. Generational relations in the education of young Waldorf students.]* Wiesbaden: VS.

Helsper, Werner/Ullrich, Heiner, u.a. (Eds.) (2007): Autorität und Schule. Die empirische Rekonstruktion der Klassenlehrer-Schüler-Beziehung an Waldorfschulen. *[Authority and school. An empiric reconstruction of the relationship between classroom teachers and students at Waldorf schools.]* Wiesbaden: VS.

Höblich, Davina/Graßhoff, Gunter (2006): Lehrer-Schüler-Beziehungen an Waldorfschulen. Chancen und Risiken einer auf Vertrauen und Nähe basierenden Beziehung. *[Teacher-student relations in Waldorf schools. Opportunities and risks of relationships based on trust and closeness.]* In: Schweer, Martin K. W. (Publ.) (2006): Bildung und Vertrauen. Frankfurt am Main: Peter Lang.

Idel, Till-Sebastian (2007): Waldorfschule und Schülerbiographie. Fallrekonstruktionen zur lebensgeschichtlichen Relevanz anthroposophischer Schulkultur. *[Waldorf schools and student biography: Case reconstruction on the relevance of anthroposophical school culture for students' life-history.]* Wiesbaden: VS.

Koolmann, Steffen (2014): Sozialökonomische Analyse im freien Bildungswesen. *[Socio-economic analysis within the private school sector.]* In: Kullak-Ublik, Henning (2014): BdFW Jahresbericht 2014. In: www.waldorfschule. de/fileadmin/downloads/jahresberichte/Jahresbericht_2014.pdf.

Kunze, Katharina (2011): Professionalisierung als biographisches Projekt: Professionelle Deutungsmuster und biographische Ressourcen von Waldorflehrerinnen und Waldorflehrern. *[Professional development as a biographic project: Professional interpretation patterns and biographical resources of Waldorf teachers.]* Wiesbaden: VS.

Liebenwein, Sylva/Barz, Heiner/Randoll, Dirk (2012): Bildungserfahrungen an Waldorfschulen. Empirische Studie zu Schulqualität und Lernerfahrungen. *[Educational Experiences at Waldorf schools. Empirical study on school quality and learning experiences.]* Wiesbaden: VS.

Lischewski, Andreas (2014): Meilensteine der Pädagogik. *[Milestones in pedagogy.]* Stuttgart: Kröner.

Paschen, Harm (Ed.) (2010): Erziehungswissenschaftliche Zugänge zur Waldorfpädagogik. Diskussion paradigmatischer Beispiele zu epistemischen Grundlagen, empirischen und methodischen Zugängen und Unterrichtsinhalten. *[Access to Waldorf education for pedagogic science. A discussion of paradigmatic examples for epistemic foundations, methodological approaches, and lesson content.]* Wiesbaden: VS.

Peters, Jürgen (2013): Arbeitsbezogene Verhaltens- und Erlebensmuster von Waldorflehrern im Zusammenhang mit Arbeitsbelastung und Berufszufriedenheit – Eine empirische Untersuchung. *[Work-related patterns in experience and behavior of Waldorf teachers in connection with workload and professional contentment – An empirical study.]* Inaugural Dissertation an der Alanus Hochschule in Alfter bei Bonn.

Prange, Klaus (2000): Erziehung zur Anthroposophie. Darstellung und Kritik der Waldorfpädagogik. *[Education in anthroposophy. Portrayal and critique of Waldorf education.]* Bad Heilbrunn: Klinkhardt.

Randoll, Dirk/Barz, Heiner (2007): Bildung und Lebensgestaltung ehemaliger Schüler von Rudolf Steiner Schulen in der Schweiz. Eine Absolventenbefragung. *[Education and way of life of former students of Rudolf Steiner schools in Switzerland. A survey of graduates.]* Frankfurt am Main: Peter Lang.

Introduction

Randoll, Dirk (2013): Ich bin Waldorflehrer: Einstellungen, Erfahrungen, Diskussionspunkte – Eine Befragungsstudie. *[I am a Waldorf teacher: Attitudes, experiences and points for discussion.]* Wiesbaden: VS.

Rittelmeyer, Christian (1996): Der Schulbau als Sozialpartner des Kindes. Ein Bericht über den Zusammenhang von Baugestaltung und Schülerverhalten. *[School architecture as a social factor in the life of a child. A report on the connection between building design and student behavior.]* Hannover: Wilhelm-Ernst Barkhoff Institut.

Rittelmeyer, Christian (2002): Pädagogische Anthropologie des Leibes. Biologische Voraussetzungen der Erziehung und Bildung. *[Pedagogic anthropology of the body. Biological preconditions for education and inculturation.]* Weinheim, Munich: Juventa.

Rittelmeyer, Christian (2005): Über die ästhetische Erziehung des Menschen. Eine Einführung in Friedrich Schillers pädagogische Anthropologie. *[On the aesthetic education of the human being. An introduction to Friedrich Schiller's pedagogic anthropology.]* Weinheim, Munich: Juventa.

Schneider, Peter (1982): Einführung in die Waldorfpädagogik. Konzepte der Humanwissenschaften. *[Introduction to Waldorf education. Concepts of the humanities.]* Stuttgart: Klett-Cotta.

Skiera, Ehrenhard (2009): Reformpädagogik in Geschichte und Gegenwart. Eine kritische Einführung. *[Reform pedagogy in history and present times. A critical introduction.]* Munich: Oldenbourg.

Steiner, Rudolf (1979): Grundlinien einer Erkenntnistheorie der Goetheschen Weltanschauung. Mit besonderer Rücksicht auf Schiller (1886). *[A Theory of Knowledge Based on Goethe's World Conception with special consideration of Schiller.]* Rudolf Steiner Gesamtausgabe 2. Dornach: Rudolf Steiner Verlag.

Steiner, Rudolf (1980): Allgemeine Menschenkunde als Grundlage der Pädagogik. *[The general study of man as a foundation of pedagogy.]* GA 293. Dornach: Rudolf Steiner Verlag.

Steiner, Rudolf (2005): Die Philosophie der Freiheit. Grundzüge einer modernen Weltanschauung (1918). *[The Philosophy of Freedom. Outline of a modern world concept.]* GA 4. Dornach: Rudolf Steiner Verlag.

Tenorth, Heinz-Elmar/Tippelt, Rudolf (Eds.) (2007): Lexikon der Pädagogik. *[Dictionary of pedagogy.]* Weinheim, Basel: Beltz.

Ullrich, Heiner (1986): Waldorfpädagogik und okkulte Weltanschauung. Eine bildungsphilosophische und geistesgeschichtliche Auseinandersetzung mit der Anthropologie Rudolf Steiners. *[Waldorf education and occult worldview. A critical analysis of Rudolf Steiner's Anthroposophy in historic and cultural perspective.]* Weinheim, Basel: Juventa.

Ullrich, Heiner (2011): Rudolf Steiner. Leben und Lehre. *[Rudolf Steiner. Life and teaching.]* Munich: Beck.

Ullrich, Heiner (2015): Waldorfpädagogik. Eine kritische Einführung. *[Waldorf education. A critical introduction.]* Weinheim, Basel: Beltz.

Ullrich, Heiner/Strunk, Susanne (2012): Private Schulen in Deutschland: Entwicklungen – Profile – Kontroversen. *[Private schools in Germany: Developments – profiles – controversies.]* Wiesbaden: VS.

Woods, Philip/Ashley, Martin/Woods, Glenys (2005): Steiner Schools in England. Bristol: University of West of England.

CHAPTER 1

Epistemology

INTRODUCTION

Jost Schieren

Rudolf Steiner, the founder of Waldorf education, is known in public discourse as an esotericist and life reformer. This attribution is understandable, as the largest part of his entire works, which is extant in more than 350 volumes, consists of transcripts and notes based on his lectures on esoteric topics. His actual writings fill only 30 of these volumes, mostly a few early publications of a philosophical nature. In 1882, Karl Julius Schröer, academic instructor of the young Rudolf Steiner, invited him to prepare for publication Goethe's writings on natural science within the framework of "Kürschner's Deutsche National-Literatur" editions (*Kürschner's German National Literature*). Steiner complied this invitation in the years between 1884 and 1897, publishing four volumes with his *Introductions to Goethe's Writings on Natural Science* (Steiner 1987). Steiner's first independent philosophical work *Goethe's Theory of Knowledge: An Outline of the Epistemology of His Worldview* (Steiner 2003) was published in 1886. It contains Steiner's acknowledgment of Goethe's epistemological approach in empirical natural science and his efforts to generate an appropriate form of epistemology for each type of natural phenomenon. In 1892 followed *Truth and Science* (Steiner 2010), an expanded version of his dissertation submitted at the University of Rostock, in which Steiner discusses the philosophy of Kant and post-Kant developments and presents his own epistemology.

The year 1894 marks the publication of his main work, *The Philosophy of Freedom*, which was reissued in revised and expanded form in 1918; this is the version still in print today (Steiner 1995). In this work, Steiner outlines an ethical-oriented concept of freedom based on his epistemology. Other than a few more philosophical writings (Steiner 1983, 1985, 2000), his later publications and lectures all focus on esoteric aspects of his approach, which he named *Anthroposophy* and he conceived to be a spiritual science. In public perception and in the presentation of many of Steiner's followers, this esoteric aspect of his work is dominant. Therefore, Steiner is viewed essentially as an esoteric author, and anthroposophy is considered a teaching on metaphysical consciousness. As a result, educational science has pigeonholed the theoretical understructure of Waldorf education as an esoteric, meta-physical, and dogmatic system that lacks scientific validity (Prange 1985, 2000; Skiera 2003, 2010; Ullrich 2015).

In contrast, this publication aims at making the theory of Waldorf education accessible to scientific investigation. The philosophical work of Steiner offers a useful foundation for such endeavors. Steiner himself considered his epistemology to provide a valid basis for anthroposophy, which he developed later. However, this view is critically examined in Hartmut Traub's comprehensive study *Philosophy and Anthroposophy* (Traub 2011). On one hand, Traub acknowledges anthroposophy is rooted in the philosophical approaches of Spinoza, Goethe, and especially Fichte and thus stands on a philosophical basis of its own. But in Traub's view, Steiner's own derivation of anthroposophy from his early philosophical

DOI: 10.4324/9781003187431-3

thought is unconvincing and also constitutes a constrictive anthropological reinterpretation. This chapter on epistemology deals with the question of whether Steiner's philosophical work indeed offers a suitable basis for anthroposophy and Waldorf education.

References

Prange, Klaus (1985): Erziehung zur Anthroposophie. Darstellung und Kritik der Waldorfpädagogik. *[Education in anthroposophy. Portrayal and critical review of Waldorf education].* 3rd ed. with new afterword. Bad Heilbronn: Klinkhardt.

Skiera, Ehrenhard (2003, 2010): Reformpädagogik in Geschichte und Gegenwart. Eine kritische Einführung. *[Reform pedagogy in historic and modern times—a critical introduction].* 2nd ed., reviewed and corrected. Munich: Oldenburg.

Steiner, Rudolf (1983): Von Seelenrätseln. *[Riddles of the soul].* Rudolf Steiner, complete works vol. 21 (GA 21). Dornach: Rudolf Steiner Verlag.

Steiner, Rudolf (1985): Die Rätsel der Philosophie in ihrer Geschichte als Umriss dargestellt. *[The riddles of philosophy—A historic outline.].* GA 18, Dornach: Rudolf Steiner Verlag.

Steiner, Rudolf (1987): Einleitung zu Goethes naturwissenschaftlichen Schriften. *[Goethean science]* GA 1. Dornach: Rudolf Steiner Verlag.

Steiner, Rudolf (1995): Die Philosophie der Freiheit. Grundzüge einer modernen Weltanschauung. Seelische Beobachtungsresultate nach naturwissenschaftlicher Methode. *[The philosophy of freedom—The basis for a modern world conception].* GA 4. Dornach: Rudolf Steiner Verlag.

Steiner, Rudolf (2000): Friedrich Nietzsche. Ein Kämpfer gegen seine Zeit. *[Friedrich Nietzsche, fighter for freedom].* GA 5. Dornach: Rudolf Steiner Verlag.

Steiner, Rudolf (2003): Grundlinien einer Erkenntnistheorie der Goetheschen Weltanschauung mit besonderer Rücksicht auf Schiller. Zugleich eine Zugabe zu Goethe's "Naturwissenschaftlichen Schriften" in Kürschners Deutscher National-Literatur. *[The theory of knowledge implicit in Goethe's world-conception: Fundamental outlines with special reference to Schiller. Also published as an addendum to Goethean Science in Kürschner's German National Literature].* GA 2. Dornach: Rudolf Steiner Verlag.

Steiner, Rudolf (2010): Wahrheit und Wissenschaft. Vorspiel einer Philosophie der Freiheit. *[Truth and science: Prelude to a philosophy of freedom].* GA 3. Dornach: Rudolf Steiner Verlag.

Traub, Hartmut (2011): Philosophie und Anthroposophie. Die philosophische Weltanschauung Rudolf Steiners – Grundlegung und Kritik. *[Philosophy and Anthroposophy. The philosophical world concept of Rudolf Steiner. Fundamental principles and critique].* Stuttgart: Kohlhammer.

Ullrich, Heiner (2015): Waldorfpädagogik. Eine kritische Einführung. *[Waldorf education. Introduction and critique].* Weinheim, Basel: Beltz.

EPISTEMOLOGICAL FOUNDATIONS OF WALDORF EDUCATION

Johannes Wagemann

1 Introduction

One of the special characteristics of Waldorf education is that it is based on an explicitly formulated epistemological concept, namely Rudolf Steiner's epistemology and anthroposophy (Frielingsdorf 2012). This cannot be taken for granted, since pedagogical approaches often rely directly on religious or ethical worldviews and political or scientific paradigms without critical review or philosophical substantiation. Independent of any apparent practical success, which may be evidenced qualitatively or quantitatively, the validity of any educational concept is essentially gauged by insight and acceptance of its pedagogic-philosophical structure of meaning. Any pedagogy runs the danger of being accused of tying itself to an irrational worldview and thus furthers the polarization of adherents and skeptics, if it lacks a comprehensible philosophical foundation. In particular, alternative forms of education are confronted with such accusations, since the public perceives them to diverge from the norm. But this should not obfuscate the fact that even educational approaches that are socially accepted as "normal" are trying to take a stance against "confessional pedagogy" (Fatke, Oelkers 2014, p. 8). However, they are themselves neither unbiased nor neutral in their worldview (Kiersch 2011, p. 430) and thus are under the same obligation of philosophical substantiation. The question, whether a pedagogical system or approach is meaningful or not and worthy of implementation, can only be decided by way of a conscious investigation of its foundational philosophic understructure.

Pedagogic practice does in fact always—even if only implicitly—rely on a specific epistemic attitude or epistemology (Brezinka 1978) and its corresponding concept of the human being (Meinberg 1988). Indeed, all educational attitudes, methods, and concrete measures can in the final analysis also be interpreted as specific assessments of the human capacities for insight and learning and of suitable steps toward their development. The only question here is, how this assessment in each case comes about, what it entails, and how it can be substantiated or justified. Waldorf education has frequently been attacked, particularly in regard to its justification matrix (Prange 2000; Ullrich 2012).[1] Therefore, it appears necessary to deal with these questions as thoroughly as possible and to come up with corresponding answers. To this end, this article first offers a background outline of the history of science and cognition, as relevant to an understanding of this topic. This is a necessary step for the later clarification of Steiner's epistemology and its relation to both philosophy and science from a historic perspective. Against this backdrop, the development of Steiner's epistemology will be reconstructed, starting with the transformation of Johann Wolfgang Goethe's scientific methodology and Johann Gottlieb Fichte's philosophy. On this basis, we go on to demonstrate how Steiner's epistemology

DOI: 10.4324/9781003187431-4

transcends these concepts and how it relates to present-day philosophy and scientific understanding. The following key themes of educational philosophy are brought into focus:

- *The cognoscibility of the world* (relation between epistemology and ontology)
- *The process character of cognition* (developmental character of knowing and consciousness)
- *The cognoscibility of knowing* (reflexivity, autology, and freedom as perspectives of development)

This structure aims at conveying an understanding of the epistemic basis of anthroposophy in a systematic historic analysis and at scrutinizing how far this basis is relevant to Waldorf education in terms of its educational philosophy.

2 Background in the history of cognition and science

The explicit epistemic foundations of Waldorf education are—as stated—on hand; however, that does not mean that they are easily understood and that their acceptance is a given. Rather the opposite appears to be true, and Steiner's epistemology and anthroposophy seem to require explanation and substantiation in turn. In particular, academic circles feel easily irritated by the mere term *Erkenntniswissenschaft* (the science of knowing) and find it presumptuous in view of the methods and results of academic philosophy and science.[2] On one hand, the methodological status of Steiner's epistemology in relation to the present-day concept of science remains to be clarified. On the other hand, pedagogic debates favor the use of scientific findings as "secular" and "anti-dogmatic" means of justification (Fatke, Oelkers 2014; Ullrich 2015, p. 14). Therefore, it seems appropriate to take a wide approach and to focus first on the topic of science: What is science and how did it develop into the prototype of arriving at modern epistemic insight? But his question cannot be duly considered without looking at the topic of science in the larger historic context of human consciousness. This first, more general, section is designed to facilitate an evaluation of Steiner's epistemology in the larger context of the history of consciousness and cognition, enabling the reader to contextualize Steiner's epistemology within its closer historic matrix of society and philosophy, as Zander (2007) and Traub (2011) have attempted to do. Only against such a backdrop can we arrive at a cogent assessment of the charge that Steiner supposedly cobbled together anthroposophy from sundry parts of other esoteric traditions and intellectual approaches.[3]

Science as we know it today is a relatively recent phenomenon in the history of human consciousness. It is barely 500 years old, if we consider Copernicus and Galileo as the first representatives of modern natural science. Generally speaking, *the striving for knowledge and insight* has a way older tradition that loses itself in the illiterate darkness of prehistoric times and can therefore even be considered "a basic anthropological constant" (Nühlen 2010, p. 7).[4] Max Scheler considers the striving for knowledge as the driving force behind all education and characterizes it as *Love*: "ever insatiably thirsting for any closer union and resonance with the world soul" (Scheler 1925, p. 12). While this sentence may sound somewhat flowery and idealistic today, it does implicitly contain a fundamental premise of all—also scientific—cognition: It is only meaningful to strive for "union and resonance with the world soul" if one is separated from the world soul/essence and experiences it at least temporarily and partially as an "adverse reality" (*Widerfahrnis*) (Kamlah 1972) or something "alien" (Waldenfels 2006) or a "crisis" (Oevermann 2008). Indeed, without this premise, all striving for knowledge—in the sense of an integrating acquisition—appears unnecessary. Many thinkers considered that which is alien, problematic, or unrecognized as the necessary point of departure for all processes of cognition: from Plato and Aristotle, who saw the origin of philosophy in astonishment and wonder in the face of the "inexplicable" over Descartes, who tried to eliminate prejudice through radical doubt down to C.S. Peirce, John Dewey, and also Rudolf Steiner.[5]

This fact has twofold consequences for a conceptual determination of science.

If science is understood as an overcoming of ignorance, its definition will rest mainly on the path or method for acquiring knowledge, not only on the *contents* of the respective fields of knowledge.

The key question here is not whether knowledge is sought, but *how* knowledge is pursued. Science defines itself primarily by its methodology, not by the area of cognition. We can even state: Only the method of the approach defines, whether something is an object of science. Depending on interest, angle of inquiry, and the respective method used, very different facets of any phenomenon can be accessed. For example, regarding a piano performance of a sonata by Brahms, we can investigate its physical-acoustic effects, its music-theory-related aspects, and finally the performance's artistic expression. Depending on the researchers' angle of inquiry, they arrive at different findings, and portals of insight open up toward completely different phenomena.

Thus, science presents itself as a special path in the methodic quest for knowledge; the continuous refinement of its methodology leads also to an ever more finely differentiated field of scientific disciplines.

The cultural history of humanity so far consisted mainly of pre-scientific phases, so it is reasonable to assume that the *conscious distance* to the world, which is, as stated, a pre-condition for science, was in those early epochs not present, or only in first traces. Therefore "the innate, primordial striving for a wholistic understanding of life within and without" must have been satisfied in different ways (Witzenmann 1987, p. 47). When the human being experiences confrontation with the world in whatever form or intensity, he tries to overcome these challenges within the range of his possibilities and to thus establish new relationships with the world. These confrontations may consist of the necessity to survive in wild nature, of navigating the oceans to make new discoveries, and, finally, they may also lead to questions about the relation between mind and matter. These various forms of conquests and relationships always also imply a drive toward the development of consciousness and cognition beyond that of securing one's mere survival. In that vein, we can also understand not only modern science but also magical hunting rituals, alchemical practice, mystical contemplation, and religious cultus as *epoch-specific methods* for attaining "union and resonance with the world soul" (Scheler 1925). Stepping back from the science-centrism of our era and examining its historic matrix, the apodictic chasm between pre-scientific forms of consciousness and modern science begins to narrow; the following statements reflect this fact: "The belief in science is the dominant religion of our time" (Weizsäcker 1990, p. 3). "And most educated people publicly submit to the power of scientific opinion and profess their faith in *[scientific]* orthodoxy" (Sheldrake 2012, p. 39).

These assessments, pronounced by two modern natural scientists, throw into relief a strange mixture of religious and scientific states of mind. Consequently, more ancient forms of thinking should no longer simply be dismissed as "flawed modes of thinking that precede later, i.e., modern thought processes" (Barz 1994; Steenblock 2000). Rather, research should focus more on the relationship between pre-scientific attitudes and practices of cognition and those of contemporary science. Even though they differ in form and concrete expression, yes, appear even incompatible, both these approaches can be understood as "cultural forms of expression" (Witzenmann 1987, p. 46) of the same basic human striving to overcome the mental separation of self and world. The following text shall investigate this ambivalent relationship in more depth.

2.1 *On the relationship between more ancient and modern forms of consciousness*

Jean Gebser (2010) describes how humankind first emerged from the embracing matrix of nature by developing structures of magical consciousness. The human being becomes painfully aware of being helpless, when faced with the powers of nature and finding himself under their spell. His answer lies in magical rituals and counter-spells. He gains power over the animal through hunting magic, which he first symbolically depicts and then symbolically enacts, using the image he created. At that time, as in principle in all following epochs, he developed a concentration of psychic energy on the inner mental level and externalized it in ritual painting and action to gain power over nature; Gebser calls this process the "externalization of inner powers" (Gebser 2010, p. 89). The collective anticipation of hunting success lends it objective character, thereby facilitating conscious union with the world and control over the hunt's outcome. After the successful hunt, there is a second part of the ritual in which the drawings are erased step-by-step; this reveals that the purpose of the ritual is not only viewed as an instrument for success, but that its meaning lies rather in a mental rebalancing, an appeasement of nature, atoning for the sacrilegious act of killing. The balance in the natural order that was disturbed by human action is being restored and the act of killing is integrated into the web of life.

This gesture of cultural expression is embedded in a state of mind that is still un-individualized and pre-rational, but it nevertheless corresponds to a basic *structure of separating and conjoining,* which can be shown to factor into the further development of consciousness and finally also into the emergence of modern science. This process can be broken down into several steps: The starting point is a differentiating experience (e.g., hunger), which, however, is not immediately translated into action along a stimulus-response scheme. Rather, first a mental connection is established in a ritual that "permits abstract planning," before it is practically "experimentally" implemented. If success ensues, the experience of separation (sacrilege) necessitates a re-connection with nature as a "theoretical integration," analogous to the process of arriving at an "individual scientific finding." This background of fundamental structures offers an understanding of several authors, who pointed out that more ancient and primordial forms of consciousness do not merely disappear and give way to newer ones, but that they—at first subconsciously—continue to exert influence (Gebser 2010; Habermas 1985; Jung 1957; Weizsäcker 1990; Witzenmann 1987).

According to the analogy indicated above, nowadays the influence of magical thinking can be demonstrated in contemporary power politics, in science-credos, and in the modern enthrallment with technology.[6] This shows that the specific forms and levels of consciousness development can give birth to the culture of an entire epoch, while they also, in their subconscious continuance, can further lead to the downfall of a culture. Gebser calls them *efficient* or *deficient* effects of various forms of consciousness (Gebser 2010).

Alchemy, a discipline historically closely associated with modern natural science, presents a similarly ambivalent relationship between rational, scientifically trained consciousness and its more ancient forms (Wagemann 2015b). While the procedural and material aspects of alchemistic practice can certainly be seen as precursors of today's chemistry and pharmacology, their pre-rational entanglement with the researcher's consciousness meets categorical repudiation (Tetens 2013; Ullrich 2015). However, the true alchemists directed their efforts not toward the material transmutation of lead into gold or to inventions like porcelain (Skiera 2010, p. 265), but, rather, their labors centered on the mystical and spiritual goal of raising their own consciousness (Hitchcock 1857; Silberer 1914). In analogy to magical hunting spells, the material activities in the context of a pantheistic mindset served the alchemists as true symbolic expressions of inner, mental processes, here aiming at a mystical communion with God. Once again, we meet here the same motif of historic consciousness: the theme of reunion with a world that had been experienced as separated. The object-oriented material symbology of alchemy expresses the targeted mental processes as follows: "(after purification, smelting, etc.), the bad metal assumes the nature of gold, i.e., of divine nature, if it is tinged with the philosopher's stone."

"The volatile essence that rises up when it is warmed in the 'vessel,' i.e., in the human being, is the soul that rises into higher strata; distilled down in a rain-like process, [...] it each time carries with it a divine gift for the thirsty material aspect of man" (Silberer 1914, p. 213). If we follow along the structure of a hunting ritual, we see here a reversal: The first step consists of the volatilization and ascent of the human soul, reintegrating the "bad metal" (that corresponds to the result of killing), which fell out of the divine order. The second step then deals with man's ability to in turn bring something to the material world: a condensing "distillation" of the "divine gift" in an individual process of cognition or action (analog to ritual painting). However, this individual act again sets the human being apart from "divine nature," externalizes and descends to the "bad" plane, so a continuous repetition of this cyclical operation is necessary.

This alchemical example leads beyond the processes of volatilization and distillation and establishes a structural correspondence to today's science. The above reference to hunting magic hints at a structural analogy to the processes of ascent and descent that compares to the dynamics of science as it is practiced today, which means with the relationship between theories and empiric data. The "God" or "gold" of today's science corresponds to its store of theoretical knowledge, which it seeks to increase and to secure; the "impure adept" or "bad metal" resembles raw data before their interpretation (Wagemann 2015b). From a perspective of science theory, the acquisition process of knowledge can be understood as an interplay of induction (general embedding of specific data sets, conjoining) and deduction (hypothetic cases deduced from general laws, separation). It is thus directed at outer, objective things but is in fact impossible without or outside of the consciousness of the researcher (Hayward 2007). Structurally speaking, the modern researcher follows the same pattern of (inductive) ascent and (deductive) descent that corresponds to the above-outlined practices and expressions of pre-rational levels of consciousness.

2.2 Efficiency of modern scientific mindsets

The examples from magic and alchemy, with their implicit structural references to modern consciousness, served to support the hypothesis of a continuous pattern in the development of human consciousness.

Now it is warranted to take closer look at the characteristics that distinguish modern scientific consciousness from its predecessors. As already mentioned above, science *defines itself* mainly through its methodology, in relative independence of its topics. Important here is the reflexive formulation, which indicates that the act of definition proceeds not implicitly and factually but is consciously carried out as an explicit and expressive achievement. On the developmental path of science, it is important to know what to do, in order to arrive at new, as yet unfamiliar knowledge. Already in the 13th century, Roger Bacon distinguished between different ways of arriving at knowledge: knowledge transference from authorities, justification in debate, or experimental, scrutinizing experience. He favored the certainty and autonomy achieved through one's own experience (Lay 1981). For Newton, this approach did not seem to oppose his religious beliefs and his practice of alchemy—it is a phenomenon indicating a free-flowing transition in consciousness as has been documented for a number of researchers down to Isaac Newton (Steenblock 2000); it illustrates the hypothesis of a continuous developmental motif that takes on varying forms of expression. Already the medieval mystics and alchemists defined their work as methodological, but the history of science points to an additional element, namely the ever-increasing distance and thus complete disenchantment of the world in respect to its metaphysical connections (Horkheimer, Adorno 2006). With increasing awareness of what precisely a scientist has to do to arrive at valid results, he also understands ever more clearly what he must not do, for example, drawing on explanatory patterns that rely on unobservable (according to the methodological paradigm) metaphysical entities such as the "philosopher's stone" or "God."[7] The interplay of polar methodological aspects, the scientists' systematic tightening of methodological control, and also the systematic weakening of metaphysical, non-objective, subjective influences—all these factors elucidate the success story of modern science, which started with the natural sciences but soon spread to all other fields of knowledge.

Helmut Kiene (2001) traced this process over four centuries, starting with Galileo Galilei (1564–1642), illustrated in the form of the four paradigmatic pillars of empirical research that developed over that time span.

This development starts with Francis Bacon's (1561–1626) call for abandoning sporadic observation and making it the questionable source of speculative-dogmatic theories; instead, he demanded, scientists should set up intentional, controlled experiments in order to investigate phenomena systematically. The experimenting scientist consciously operates in opposition to natural phenomena and isolates through his interventions effects that he can control and whose patterns are at best presented in mathematical form. For Bacon, this form of methodical scientific research represented a so-to-say *internalized use of tools*: "Neither the naked hand nor the understanding left to itself can effect much. It is by instruments and helps that the work is done, which are as much wanted for the understanding as for the hand. And as the instruments of the hand either give motion or guide it, so the instruments of the mind supply either suggestions for the understanding or cautions" (Bacon 2013, p. 31). His approach provided a universal cornerstone in the self-definition of natural science; the question about causal connections between phenomena guided the next steps.

A first answer to this question was furnished by David Hume (1711–1776), who proposed that for scientific purposes a phenomenon should not only occur once but must be repeatable, so that it can be observed as often as needed (Hume 1904). This approach was supposed to eliminate the danger of attributing importance to subjective, metaphysically oriented interpretations of single, concomitant incidents, which could be confused with the actual causal factors. Indeed, the simultaneous occurrence of two phenomena cannot be taken to indicate a causal connection. The simple replicability of a phenomenon alone did not suffice but needed to be complemented by another methodological element, developed by John Stuart Mill (1806–1873): that of "Comparative Control." If a researcher introduces into the second of two identical experiments a third factor, which then generates a certain effect that was not observable in the first experiment, there is a great probability that this third factor alone caused that effect (Mill 2002). Here the control of the scientist is again heightened in the artificial setup of a random number of "identical experiments" and the arbitrary addition or withholding of experimental causal factors. A final step, particularly when dealing with data related to human beings, consists of randomizing the match-up between human research subjects and specific experimental conditions, which is supposed to eliminate the influence of hidden factors (e.g., age, gender). Ronald Fisher (1890–1962) introduced the paradigm of randomization that permits a previously unattainable identification and elimination of erroneous correlation of data and cause-effect connections (Fisher 1935).

Randomization thus became a standard criterion for empiric research—both under laboratory and field conditions—for widely different disciplines (biology, psychology, social sciences, economics), which also function as reference points for modern educational science.

Three aspects of this developmental outline of today's empirical science are of interest here. The first two of those will be covered in the following pages, and the third aspect in the next subchapter.

First, each of these steps, embedded in their historic development phase, separates (or distances) the human being and the world—a dynamic that has been shown to also be true for more ancient forms of consciousness. Second, we can discover a new tendency in the specific mode of awakening scientific cognition as compared to older forms of consciousness. This innovative tendency is connected, as already indicated, to the faculty of performing the processes of conjoining and separating—no longer in a ritual dream state, but in a state of increasing waking consciousness—and to the ability of implementing them ever more stringently and consistently. The first pioneers of natural science had no recourse to authorities or traditions that could have pointed to specific procedures. Their unanswered questions led them onto their own original path that would lead them to reliable answers, which means that they were neither adopted nor invented.[8] Hence, conscious man's own goal-oriented activity is strengthened in respect to the world that he seeks to understand. Yet at the same time, his self-involvement in regard to content and experience is systematically eliminated. It is no coincidence that at the origin of modern science's success story stood physics and its subdiscipline of mechanics, because methodological distance and control could be most easily established by using material objects that could be fixed in time and space, quantified, and abstracted from daily use. While the researcher becomes increasingly active and autonomous in this process, he paradoxically creates ever more distance to his own self. As he grows in self-assurance, the scientist acts within an ever more rigid, mechanistic world, while gradually erasing the pre-rational consciousness of an unbreakable bond with a wholistic life world.[9]

Indeed, the ideal of methodological objectivity entails eliminating all inappropriate involvement, particularly the researcher's subjectivity.

While consciousness still continues to develop through separating and reconnecting the human being and the world, this dynamic has shifted toward separation, i.e., distancing.[10] On one hand, this approach implicates a growing awareness in the process of scientific cognition, but on the other hand, this approach isolates the human being from all traditional ways of generating meaning. He scores gains in objectivity and certainty of cognition but pays for it with the loss of his primordial connection with nature. Gebser (2010) describes this change in consciousness as a transition from the magical *unity* and entanglement with nature, through mythical *polarity*, whose poles complement each other in a dynamic relationship, to rational *duality*, whose sides (subject/object, true/false) always directly oppose one another.

2.3 Deficiency of the modern scientific mindset

Along with the stark duality of object and subject and its concomitant loss of an innate embedment in nature and of spiritual sense-perceptiveness, characteristic flaws have begun to take shape in the approaches of modern consciousness. The consistent leitmotif of man's connection with the world now must find different forms of expression. So, the third aspect of the development as described above consists of the transference of scientific methodology from material objects—that it was originally targeting—to phenomena like life, consciousness, and society. The success of the leading disciplines in research and technology, i.e., chemistry and physics, has caused not only its methodology to become the chosen standard for the life- and social sciences as well as for the humanities, but these also adopted their materialistic ontology (Rey 1908).[11] Actually, in the framework of their program for enlightenment, the natural sciences had intended to secure the reliability of cognition only through its methodology, independent of metaphysical references.

Yet while the focus on the material realm offered methodological certainty and technical success, a different metaphysical dependence sprung up: the belief that in the final analysis everything is material and subject to identical mathematical and methodological approaches (Hayward 2007). The old joke comes to mind, where a drunkard searches for something at night, crawling around in the circle of light shed by a lantern. A helpful policeman asks him what he was looking for, and he answers that he lost his keys. The policeman asks whether he was sure to have lost the keys right there in the cone of light, and the drunkard answers: "No, it was over there where it is dark, but here I at least can see something" (Weizenbaum 1978). Drunk on the certainty of success, the wish to look for answers exclusively in the light of standard methods of the natural sciences appears understandable, especially in view of the developments presented above. But such limitation does not guarantee that the key that was lost in the dark—the original connection to nature—will be found that way. The results generated by the methodology of physics or chemistry are on the material level, according to their "aspect character" (Wagenschein 1995, p. 12), their "bias of perspective" (Gebser 2010). The nonmaterial realm related to either the world (God, cosmos) and the human being (soul, spirit) eludes this approach and therefore excluded from scientific investigation.[12]

The connection with the immaterial, spiritual realms is now relegated to private opinion, while for millennia it moved the experience and thinking of humanity and has brought forth many cultures. At best, science deals with nonrational, incomprehensible spheres of experience as distant, exotic research objects; the scientist tries to approach them in the same methodological style of intellectual subjugation as any other topic of interest.[13] Today's science seeks to keep such topics as far away as possible from its own narrow methodological and theoretical domain. Ever since Kant's criticism of introspection and mysticism (Kant 1974) and his "casting out of the irrational" (Böhme, Böhme 1985, p. 187), rational consciousness has tried to secure its own ground. But that which has been cast out continues to exert influence from the underground, be it in the form of an unknowable *thing in itself* (Kant) or in the form of the subconscious (Freud) that is not directly accessible, but governs the psyche and hence muddles up science's claim on absolute sovereignty.

At the latest with Emil du Bois-Reymond's "Ignorabimus," it has become apparent that the security attained by drawing up insurmountable barriers to cognition leads only to a dead end. He asserted that consciousness must have purely material causes, yet he considered it impossible to ever find out *how* consciousness arises from physical processes in the brain (Bois-Reymond 1927). Today's attempts to answer this question according to materialistic identity theory have again set off a relapse into older mindsets, even though they are now clad in the glittering new garment of a complex scientific theory. Hans Flohr for example makes the following assumptions: "1. That states of consciousness are identical with representational conditions of a higher order; 2. that representations of a higher order are instantiated by a special class of assemblies; 3. that the formation of such assemblies requires a binding mechanism, that facilitates large and relatively stable assemblies; 4. that this binding brings about a special type of synapsis, the NMDA synapsis" (Flohr 2002, p. 55). Or very simply stated by Wolf Singer "You are your brain, what else?" (Singer 2009). Yet, assuming an identity of material (neurological processes) and mental aspects of consciousness (phenomenon-oriented cognition) is irreconcilable with the scientific approach, which is characterized by incorruptible analysis and precise differentiation of phenomena in its methodology, as the natural sciences had claimed originally (Wagemann 2010). As demonstrated in the example of the hunting ritual, assumptions like that indicate a magical mindset, in which mental occurrence (anticipation of successful hunt), representation (drawing and symbolic kill of the prey), and that which is being represented (actual process of the hunt), are inextricably interwoven (Chalmers 1995; Horkheimer, Adorno 2006, p. 16).[14] If we follow identity theory, the semiotic triangle (of meaning—symbol—object) would conflate in at least two aspects, i.e., the mental occurrence (meaning) and its neural representation (symbol). Moreover, if the identity-theoretical approach is coupled with skeptical constructivism, as in the case of prominent brain researchers and neuro-philosophers (Roth 2013; Singer 2009), the question arises in how far we can even speak of real things and processes in a real world[15]: "Our life resembles the life in a prison cell. The windows to the outer world are our sense organs. We only perceive what they transmit to us. In this process, the inflowing reality is falsified by the translation tricks of the sense organs and the nervous system. [...] For the organism, the sense organs are the only sources of information about his environment" (Lathe 2009, p. 45). This quote is taken from a current textbook; it illustrates what kind of knowledge is deemed today to be scientifically reliable and therefore pedagogically legitimate. The methodological self-confidence of natural science is unaware of overstepping its self-imposed boundaries and turns into an illusory sense of certainty, which in final consequence leads to a fundamental uncertainty in the human faculty of cognition. The scientist either resigns himself to shy away from the boundaries of the methodologic cone of light, or he transgresses this boundary without safety nets and falls back into patterns that are more ancient in respect to the history of cognition. It is doubtful that this approach offers a suitable frame of reference for educational science or pedagogical practice. The third part of this chapter deals with the question whether in this situation today there is a third path for human cognition.

2.4 Separating and conjoining as a fundamental pattern in the development of human consciousness

In summary, this investigation has so far resulted in an incomplete and ambivalent sketch of the faculty of contemporary human cognition. Modern natural science profoundly imprints all people of our times in their view of the world and of self, and even those who do not work in the field of science are impacted. Thus, it has become (so to speak): "The absolute organ of culture, and the history of natural science is actually the history of humanity" (Bois-Reymond in Steenblock 2000, p. 162). On one hand, following the reasoning demonstrated above, the development of human consciousness is seen to logically result in scientific cognition that in its own assessment is alone the epitome of true knowledge. On the other hand, the supremacy of the natural sciences' theory of knowledge is cast into doubt by the fact that a rigorous pursuit of its approach to cognition ends at its own boundaries and thus becomes a reactionary approach in regard to its programmatic claim to enlightenment.[16] If it ignores these boundaries, it involuntarily reproduces thought and behavior patterns from older, irrational strata of consciousness that were thought to be surmounted long ago and do not serve the striving for knowledge either.

No matter, if the scientific mainstream approach presents itself as resigned and abstemious or sure of its success and productive, we can detect epistemological structures in its applied methodology that are also fundamental for more ancient types of consciousness in era-specific forms. The approach in this chapter differs from the "Dialectics of Enlightenment," identified within the Critical Theory of the Frankfurt School as a flawed "back-flip of enlightenment into mythology" (Horkheimer, Adorno 2006,

p. 33). Rather, our approach here is characterized by the attempt to trace a basic pattern of consciousness development as it oscillates between efficiency and deficiency. Horkheimer and Adorno regarded the motive of social dominance as immanent in all forms of enlightenment; such motive in its isolation leads by necessity to alienation and destructiveness. This view remains phenomenologically incomplete without the basic intention of "union and resonance" (Scheler 1925, p. 12). The main focus here is not on a critical attitude, turning "against naturalism or the 'scientific worldview'" (Windelband 1957, p. 583), but rather on understanding this worldview as a stringent—though not final—historic phenomenon of realization and consciousness.

All epoch-specific types of cognition and consciousness are based on a characteristically weighted proportion of separation and conjoining processes in the relationship between the human being and the world (Wagemann 2018). Apparently, historic development starts with an instinctual, passive bond with which the human being wrestles in order to emancipate himself and to grow beyond it. In this process, he moves toward a waking, active detachment, in which he is looking—though increasingly unsuccessfully—for the lost connection with the world. Science, in particular natural science, can be understood as the current phenotype of this motive in the development of human consciousness. As such, it is a work in progress that shows traits of a flawed, excessive rationality that no longer—or probably not yet—understands itself and thus reverts to older forms of consciousness. On the other hand, various alternative approaches indicate that science is not fixed in its current form and may still carry in it the seeds of unrealized paradigmatic potentials (Lommel 2009; Sheldrake 2012; Witzenmann 1983). The fundamental change in consciousness, brought about by the development of the new era's science, does not preclude its appropriate continuation and the development of new scientific forms of cognition. Maybe we can even state: *Hopefully* people in coming centuries will experience a similar, fundamental turning point in consciousness as we have in regard to pre-Copernican times.

3 Rudolf Steiner's epistemology

3.1 Goethe and Fichte—separation and conjunction becoming explicit

So far we investigated the motifs of separating and conjoining in the context of the history of consciousness; Johann Wolfgang Goethe made this motif the foundation of his nature research: "If the whole of existence is an eternal separating and conjoining, it follows that the human being in his contemplation of awesome states [of nature] will at times separate and at other times conjoin" (Goethe 1977, p. 35). Goethe's conclusion offers two possible interpretations: On one hand, the human being is part of the whole of existence that comprises separation and conjunction and thus acts correspondingly. On the other hand, he realizes (contemplates) existence precisely in his activities of separating and conjoining, expressing himself through these two processes. The first of these perspectives leads from being to man, corresponding to a *realistic* viewpoint (being determines consciousness), while the second perspective leads from man to being, which corresponds to an *idealistic* viewpoint (consciousness determines being). In his ambiguous conclusion, Goethe implicates an interpenetration, a union of being and knowing, that obviously posits him in opposition to the idea of a strict separation of being and knowing of subject and object, which was prevalent at his time, as it is still today (Heisenberg 1968; Weizsäcker 1990). Here is another illustration of Goethe's perspective of a reciprocal relationship between man and world: "If the eye were not sun-like, how could it ever perceive the sun; if God's own power dwelled not in us, how could the divine blissfully delight us?" (Goethe 1982, vol. 3, p. 88)

A key principle emerges here and in the aphorism cited above: the one favored by Empedocles (495–435 BCE) and later by Neoplatonism: it is the idea of "realizing like with like," be it through similar forms of process (separating, conjoining) or likeness in respect to particular aspects of the human being ("eye," "the indwelling power of the Divine") in relation to the world ("Sun," "the Divine"). Anaxagoras (499–428 BCE) claims in contradiction that a premise for realization lies in precisely the otherness of an object from its subject in respect to that which is to be realized or known. According to him, it is the very difference between, e.g., a cold hand and warm liquid that enables knowing in the form of sense perception. However, the seeming contradiction between the standpoint of Empedocles and the Anaxagorean principle in Goethe's concept can be resolved: In regard to being, the human being not only conjoins but also separates; the latter process is characterized precisely by differences, divergences, and disparities.

Furthermore, we can recognize the Anaxagorean principle of differentiation also in semantic differences between the verbs *perceive* (distance) and *delight* (confluence).[17] From Goethe's perspective both principles could summarily be described as follows: That of Empedocles appears as separation within conjunction; the two elements (object and subject) are alike in certain respects yet remain different (otherwise no knowledge could be attained). The principle of Anaxagoras appears as "conjunction within separation" insofar as subject and object stand in relationship to each other (conjoining), which is caused precisely by their difference.

All those, who are fixated on the intellectual routines of today's scientific institutions and are convinced that these are superior to any other forms of cognition, will accord little value to such "mind games" (Prange 2005, p. 91), which seems to rely just on the speculations of pre-Socratic philosophers, alchemists, and mystics and their traditional principles (Kutschera 2008; Skiera 2010; Ullrich 2015). However, the deliberations outlined in Section 2 of this chapter may have shed light on the fact that a study of the development, history, and types of scientific approaches to knowledge may after all lead to a clarification of the genesis and peculiarities of natural science cognition, if seen in the historic perspective of separating and conjoining principles. The equivalency principle of Empedocles (to know like through like) illustrates here that in all epochs, the light of consciousness determines how the human being perceives the world—just as the "sun" is perceived with the "eyes"—and how he can arrive within this framework at an epoch-specific consciousness of himself. This is in particular valid for science, which has been affirmed over the last centuries by various sociologists and philosophers of science, for example, Thomas P. Kuhn (1997) and his concepts of *normal science* and *paradigm shift* as well as Ludwig Fleck (1980) in terms of his *style of thought* and of the *thought collective*. Karl Popper's critical insight that "all observation is theory-laden" also belongs within this context, an idea that indeed had been already discovered by Goethe.[18] On the other hand, the Anaxagorean principle of differentiation in the form of increasing separation of subject and object gains ever more importance as *the* condition for seeking any new knowledge at all.

The first section of this chapter already dealt with the view that a confrontation between man and world forms the point of departure for all striving for knowledge, and various philosophers were already discussed in this context.

Furthermore, a concrete methodological aspect of modern natural science, namely that of gauging tool and measuring activity, can also illustrate the relevance of Goethe's principle (Empedoclean/Anaxagorean) for the philosophy of science. When we measure the length of a table, for example, two kinds of activities can be distinguished, that is, a process of aligning and one of counting. Aligning an instrument to the task presupposes, that there just is such a measuring instrument that can be distinguished from the table, e.g., a measuring stick (separation). This tool is then held with its zero point to an edge of the table so that they are directionally aligned in the same way toward the distance to be measured (conjoining). The count starts by departing from the zero point in specific steps, determined by a unit of measurement such as inches or centimeters (separation). The counting steps end, where the measuring stick meets the opposite edge of the table (conjoining) and the length of the table is now determined by reading off the unit mark on the stick. Any however complicated measuring process and each collection of quantitative data can, in the last analysis, be reduced to this same logical procedural structure (Wagemann 2010). At the same time, Goethe's approach offers a synthetic-analytical, separating and conjoining methodology that can be recovered for the humanities. For example, hermeneutic circles approach a text with more or less conscious preconceptions and try to understand each of its parts. They will succeed in some parts more than in others, resulting in a more differentiated perspective and a need for modifying the preconceptions (separation, analysis).

Based on inconsistencies and the attempt to overcome contradictions, the horizon for understanding widens (conjoining, synthesis) and allows for a new approach to the text, which in turn will be—again temporarily—improved. Altogether, this results in an endless, but optimistically assessable, cognitive process in respect to the art of text interpretation.

Even more than the content of Goethe's natural science research or his aesthetic production, it was the universality and the potential of his method that inspired the young Rudolf Steiner to develop his own methodology for the field of consciousness research. Defying all critical speculation, Goethe's method does not represent a regression into older forms of consciousness, because it can be consciously controlled and it contains the basic structural pattern of cognition—of separating and conjoining—in explicit form, corresponding to the new era's consciousness (Witzenmann 1987).[19]

Goethe strove for immanence in the sense of an experimental integration of consciousness and being, while he did not aim at magical unity nor a mythic state that enmeshes and binds the subject into dependency, more or less annihilating his individuality. The immanence he seeks is rather a methodically guided process—along the lines of Bacon's activity criterion—toward a state of awareness that perceives the essential nature within an empirical phenomenon (Schieren 1998; Steiner 1987). Hence, Goethe's approach reaches even beyond the logical duality of subject and object, which ever since Aristotle has been elevated to a fundamental tenet of rational cognition, while it simultaneously demarcates its limitations. Goethe does not connect subject and object in abstract terms, like in a syllogism of formal logic, but from the vantage point of an intuitive power of judgment which he understands as a differentiation and integration of two juxtaposed forms of cognition. Steiner reconstructs this methodological principle using some correspondence between Goethe and Schiller, in which Goethe refers to a lost continuation of his essay titled "The experiment as mediator between subject and object" (Steiner 1987, p. 187): Initially the scientist faces the raw, empiric phenomenon that appears still unordered and void of relationships. If he would adhere rigidly to his empiric perspective, he would have to contend himself with the mere collection of data and their archiving. Every activity, however minimal, toward ordering raw data already signals an anti-empirical intervention of the scientist in regard to the raw data—albeit an unavoidable one, because without it there would be no science to speak of, but only random data collection. The viewpoint, under which the data are arranged and then analyzed, cannot be determined by the data themselves but only by scientific reason. The researcher attempts to rationally apply explanatory patterns to the data and to detect the causes of phenomena—mostly in the form of abstract principles and quantifiable laws. While it is of note that pure empiricism can only arrive at separate, unconnected phenomena, which is unsatisfying to the cognitive interest, there is also an issue with one-sided rationalism, which inserts invalid explanatory patterns into the phenomenal realm. In opposition to both the empiric stasis in facing a world that we can experience as relational and to the rationalistic transgression beyond it, the methodology of Goethe takes form as a balancing approach that lingers in the realm of accessible phenomena and develops further there.

This power of intuitive judgment does indeed differentiate between the two basic epistemic approaches within the respective epistemic paradigms and between two basic epistemic states: the raw phenomenon, void of relations, and the archetypal phenomenon that is brought to light through human involvement and intuition. In the first approach, the scientist experiences himself in differentiating opposition (Anaxagorean), and the latter (Empedoclean approach) connects him with the world. According to Goethe, experimental success does not derive from simply counting and abstract alignment of phenomena in the sense of a merely regulative, non-experiential principle (Kant 1974, p. 472, B 537); rather, success depends on a *transformation of the scientist's mode of perception* so that in his mind he looks for lawful connections and finds them as constitutive forces in the world that appears to his senses. Goethe's approach to cognition does not set a research goal of finding "a basic tenet [...] but a basic phenomenon" (Heisenberg 1968, p. 244). A rational principle (e.g., the law of gravity) can be viewed apart from a concrete percept (e.g., a falling apple), which may seem to suggest a transcendental ontology (e.g., belief in the existence of imperceptible fields or particles); yet this type of suggestion cannot arise in respect to an archetypal phenomenon (Weizsäcker 1990, p. 459). For this, it not only appears within human cognition, but then at the same time also as a valid lawful pattern of the world.

In differentiating two epistemic, immanent, observable process types on the object side of the subject/object polarity, Goethe achieves integration between empiricism and rationalism (in regard to epistemology) or between realism and idealism (in regard to ontology). In its explicit consideration of man's active cognition and faculty of experience, which implies a connection between being and thinking that can be systematically developed, Goethe's methodology can be characterized as a logically three-fold approach: In the experiment, the *subject* mediates between the *isolated phenomenon* and the *archetypal phenomenon* (Urphänomen) by adopting suitable perspectives of cognition (Goethe 1982). We today owe to Gotthard Günther's transclassical logic the knowledge that a trivalent view for the first time allows the complete formal description of mental processes and developments, because it transcends the inner bivalent structure of everyday rational consciousness that is organized in dualities (true-false, object-subject) (Günther 1978). Goethe's insights were guiding lights for Steiner, precisely because of this process-quality, even though Steiner did not choose the path of formal logic but oriented his work along Goethe's immanent-phenomenological approach, which he expanded. Indeed, such an expansion was needed, because Goethe's blind spot lay in the object of thought itself.

In contemplation, his mind distanced and juxtaposed itself in regard to specific phenomena, as he worked toward a unitive, luminous recognition of archetypal phenomena in his research on outer nature, but he avoided applying this methodological thought to itself in a reflexive way.

It was in the work of the philosophers of idealism, particularly those of Johann Gottlieb Fichte, that Steiner found philosophical ideas that could inspire him in his endeavor of formulating a self-referencing theory of knowledge. Philosophers like Fichte, Schelling, and Hegel developed holistic approaches, based on recognizing a teleological purpose of humanity and the spiritual aspect of the world. They pitched these approaches against the increasing influence of technology and of industrialization, which set in toward the end of the 18th century, and against the concomitant alienation of life from its natural origins. It is interesting that Fichte fully grasps the very aspect central to the transformation toward scientific and technological consciousness: an unshakeable self-assurance and self-confidence in one's own dynamic mental powers, which we already identified above as Bacon's initial spark for success in natural science research. That marks Fichte as a child of his time. Only, Fichte does not direct these dynamic mental forces into external, physical-empirical experimentation but turns them entirely and reflexively toward thought itself, in order to derive everything else therefrom. This is the "fact-act [...] which does not—and cannot—occur within the constraints of an empirical view of our consciousness, but that actually forms the basis of all cognition and that alone makes it possible" (Fichte 1794, pp. 3–4). While the non-empirical, absolute subject—in positioning itself as the origin of all consciousness—identifies itself as complete and free, the everyday "I" emerges from that self only through self-limitation of its action. Compared to self-positing, the process of self-limitation appears as an act of *opposing something* and only through this act can the "I" differentiate itself from "not-I," the empirical subject from the object. The example of the magical-ritualized drawing in hunting spells comes to mind as well as the natural-science experiment both being incremental manifestations of this principle. Because the origin for such differentiation is found alone in the (absolute) "I," this "I" includes also its object as its one and only result. Fichte talks in this regard about the "creative power of imagination" (Fichte 1794, p. 321) that is imbued with a potency that renders it downright world-generative. The empiric subject that defines itself in opposition to the (unconsciously self-generated) world of objects overcomes this obstacle in steps by reflecting on his own opposing and originally self-positing action. With every step toward overcoming a barrier through self-reflection, a new and higher obstacle takes form, which in turn must be penetrated and thus conquered through self-reflectively heightened consciousness. According to Fichte, cognition occurs as a "process of self-knowledge of the mind, that arises from the ground of sensory perception" (Windelband 1957, p. 510).

Steiner expressed many critical reservations in respect to Fichte's philosophy (Steiner 1987); however, he honored above all the impulse, in Fichte's conscious, self-guided thought process to understand himself in his mental activity, and to grasp that this was a secure source of scientific cognition: "Fichte here discovered something where he perceived himself as entirely independent of any other field of existence. A God could create me, but he would have to rely on me to recognize myself as 'I.' I bestow upon myself the consciousness of self. In this I realize a knowing, a recognition that I did not receive, but one that I created. Thus, Fichte established a fixed point of absolutely certainty for his world concept" (Steiner 1985, p. 181). True, this "certainty" is not entirely missing in Goethe's conceptual approach either, insofar as Goethe always made sure of his own acts of separation and conjoining as aspects of his methodological processes. However, as we have stated, Goethe was not prone to explicitly think about his own cognition, i.e., making it, rather than natural phenomena, the object of his deliberations. But it was precisely Fichte's "power to awaken oneself into being" that interested Steiner (Steiner, 1984, p. 32). Nevertheless, he had to distance himself from Fichte in regard to methodology, because the latter's method was dialectic, deductive, and therefore ultimately abstracting; this was not a suitable approach for his phenomenological cognitive findings (Traub 2011; Veiga 1989; Wagemann 2012). Fichte conceded that the (absolute) "I" cannot be logically deduced—which is "why philosophy is compelled to make the 'I' the point of departure" (Fichte 1794, p. 297); yet he developed his theory of science along strictly logical-transcendental principles, not phenomenological-observational ones. Nonetheless, Fichte's approach also shows some resonance with Goethe's pheno-practical processes of separating and conjoining: The self-limitation in juxtapositioning the self corresponds to separation, while the self-positing of the "I" and its reflexive ascendancy to self-contemplation resonates with the principle of conjoining. Just as Goethe did not arrive at a clear awareness in regard to a heightening of the subject pole, Fichte lacked a clear differentiation in regard to the object pole, which he wholesale considered a figment of creative imagination.[20] Both Goethe and Fichte conceptually transcended Kant's idea of "the thing in and of itself" but they took different paths: Goethe phenomenologically verifies the essence (archetypal phenomenon) through sense-perception, while Fichte binds all being back to an absolute "essential 'I'" that is now only determined by action.

Goethe's and Fichte's concepts are portrayed here in somewhat overstated form for purposes of reconstructing Steiner's epistemology in a context of the historic development of consciousness and philosophy; this review leads to the following conclusion: Both in their methodology and their object range, the two approaches complement each other. They both emphasize aspects that had grown apart in the history of cognition and they offer first attempts to reintegrate them. In the early phases of consciousness evolution, the human being did not differentiate between *perception and thought*, experience and reflection, yet in the course of further development these processes increasingly differentiate and grow ever more apart from each other. However, they cannot be fully separated. In his immanent methodology, Goethe emphasizes the *reflective (content-oriented) aspect of perception* and thus he arrives via the isolated phenomenon and then its transformation by the archetypal phenomenon, which for him is the only real being. Fichte's philosophy centers in the fact-act, the *perceptible (act-) aspect of thinking*, and develops a concept of thought as an actively self-referencing, self-creating being. But in approaching what can ultimately only be perceived through introspection and meditation, Fichte persists in an abstract-deductive methodology. Overcoming their deficiencies, an integration of these two approaches—heightened opening to the world (Goethe) and heightened consciousness in action (Fichte)—could result in a new synthesis of thought and perception on a higher level of consciousness (Wagemann 2018).

The approaches of Goethe and Fichte are logically trivalent, but in the ontological understanding of the value positions, they remain one-sided and thus incomplete. Goethe makes precise distinctions on the object side of the subject-object polarity (empirical phenomenon—archetypal phenomenon) but does not differentiate the subject side; Fichte makes precise distinctions on the subject side (empirical I—absolute I) but does not differentiate the object part of the polarity. With this, both transcend the bivalent subject-object split, which is a mark of *common sense* in scientific circles to this day, but neither of them arrives at a complete, general solution. Yet, a differentiation of both poles, subject and object, their process-oriented integration and genetic observation would lead to an ontologically complete and phenomenologically expanded science of consciousness that would be both logical and anthropologically trivalent.[21]

3.2 Steiner's transformation of Goethe's and Fichte's concepts

Accordingly, we will first demonstrate how Steiner grasps and transforms Goethe's and Fichte's approaches and thus integrates them. Next, we will show how Steiner's concept develops its distinct original features by either building on or leaving behind aspects of their work.

From Goethe as a representative of a pantheistic-immanent philosophical worldview, Steiner takes over his experimental methodology that sees the archetypal phenomenon in any specific object.[22] In the experimental process, accidental constraints are eliminated through repetition and reduced to necessary constraints for a series of experiments, in which the archetypal phenomenon can emerge in the consciousness of the scientist. Once the scientist has grasped this archetypal phenomenon, either image-like or as a form mental movement or expressed as a formula, he will be able to *see* it also under less favorable, natural conditions—even where unschooled eyes see nothing at all. The archetypal phenomenon thus acts as a medium that directs the attention toward lawful connections and is the key to unveiling the wholeness of being. The archetypal phenomenon can only be experienced in its connective, relational effects as it emerges in thought—yet any isolated phenomenon can only provoke that experience but cannot substantially contribute to it. But this means that the scientist must have actually envisioned the archetypal phenomenon—that is, as a primordial image (archetype) or idea—already, before he becomes aware of its effects in sensory phenomena. The archetypal phenomenon guides the attention of the researcher, leading him up to its sensory appearance. In fact, Steiner's key innovation in this regard consists of bringing the *principle of gaze-direction* (as a methodically positive turnaround from theory-laden approaches) into full consciousness and stringently applying it to non-sensory phenomena (Steiner 2003, p. 40; Witzenmann 1986, p. 45). As a poet, i.e., in aesthetic respects, Goethe constantly focuses on the non-sensory dimension of the human being and world—be it metaphorically ("The soul of man is like the waters") or lyrically ("Wanderer's Nightsong"; Witzenmann 1987), but he does not extend this focus to his phenomenological research.[23]

From Fichte, as a radical representative of new age self- and action consciousness, Steiner seized the inspiration to place the point of departure for his epistemology in the fact-act [*Tathandlung*] of the "I." In thinking and thought-reflection, the "I" understands itself as a necessary premise for all being. Because nothing but the "I" can consciously comprehend and actively create itself. But if it goes no further, it soon loses sight of the world in its becoming and ceasing. In believing that it can exteriorize everything that exists, it bloats itself in its imagination from a necessary to a supposedly sufficient premise for all (conscious) being. Steiner's crucial innovation here concerns his observation that the ego is by no means "monologizing with itself alone" (Steiner 1985, p. 182) and is not only capable of discursively distinguishing itself conceptually from the world and uniting itself with it. The action of the "I" is originally and potentially free, but this potential for freedom realizes itself precisely in contact and interchange with the releasing structural conditions of the world. It is only in the dynamic interchange between the "I" and pre-predicative structural components and in their mediation that we realize the subjects and objects of our everyday consciousness, which we then, in hindsight, can analyze intellectually.[24]

Here Steiner moves beyond Fichte's concepts—first by turning the absolute, pre-predicative, and pre-conscious "I" from a postulated invisible, transcendental factor into a potential object of empirical self-observation (Steiner 1958b; mental observation; Witzenmann 1989b, p. 77: "Observing our Observation"). Second, Steiner clarifies the "impulse," which remains obscure in Fichte's conception: The impulse that the empirical "I" has to suffer—as if it were externally inflicted—is actually caused by the "I"'s activity itself (Fichte 1794, p. 173). How and why does the empirical "I" manage to produce this impulse from within itself and at the same time suffer from its impact? It appears more logical and phenomenologically verifiable to view the *alien* (Waldenfels 2006), *crisis-like* (Oevermann 2008) or *purely perceptible* not as a product of thought, but as a structural component that is conveyed by the sense-organs "without my active cooperation" and to trace its influence within structure formation (Steiner 1958b, pp. 22, 41; Witzenmann 1989a, p. 22).

At the same time, the unrestrained cognitive activity of the "I" is necessary for arriving at the connections that cannot be perceived sensory. Yet the insight gained—and experienced as success—in the individual thought process cannot alone account for the task of the "I" in initiating thought, its effort and exertion, and its probing motion in trying to arrive at cognitive connections.

Because *what* we realize is produced and realized in our thinking, but it relies on its own independent laws. These constitutive laws of reality Steiner calls *concepts*, albeit not in its common meaning.[25] Using Goethe's terminology we could also speak of an archetypal phenomenon. Concepts can be accessed through thought, but at the same time they elude our subjective-manipulative willfulness as they determine their own coherence exclusively from within themselves and thus are able to offer the missing interrelations within the realm of the observable. They are elements of reality.[26]

So far, we can summarize Steiner's transformative work in his epistemology as follows: He brought Goethe's scientific methodology to a mental/spiritual level by focusing on mental, not sense-perceptible phenomena; he brings Fichte's philosophy down to a level of phenomenal concretization, differentiation, and releasing it from ego-centric one-sidedness. Before we elaborate further, the connection of this first outline to the preparatory remarks in Section 2 shall be clarified. Remembering the paradoxical structure in the history of consciousness, we call to mind that the attempts to bridge the chasm between I and world are at first efficient in their epoch-specific perspectives of consciousness and cognition; but when they are stringently applied, their effects revert to deficiencies, and thus they come up against their own boundary.

This boundary can only be crossed by a transformation in the consciousness of the epoch, which means this process in turn consists of acts of cognition, i.e., consciousness that require ever-new forms and means of expression. In view of the flawed paralysis of the scientific mindset that rigidly focuses on a narrow, rationalistic concept of the subject/object split, Goethe's and Fichte's concepts offer outlines for an increasingly differentiating shift of focus of the researcher toward the subtle structures within object and subject and their development potential, be it by way of Goethe's phenomenological differentiation of the object or Fichte's dialectic differentiation of the subject. Both their concepts point to the possibility of recognizing the paradox in the history of consciousness to be an expression of the process structure of human cognition: the realization of the world (Goethe) and the self-apprehension of the human self (Fichte). The transformation in consciousness necessary for this turn could only be accomplished by Steiner, as he released the one-sidedness of the subject-object split and integrated both approaches in his epistemology "after the methodology of natural science" (Steiner 1958b). This "after" is meant both in the temporal sense of a historic demarcation and also in the sense of a positive connection to the natural science method ("according to"). In his theory of knowledge, Steiner connects over to the core of scientific consciousness, a core that could further be developed methodologically; but at the same time—in order to do justice to his range of focus—he distances himself from the object-centric perspective and discipline-specific methodological doctrine of the natural sciences (Steiner 1989; Veiga 2011).

The object of Steiner's epistemology is however not an object in the usual sense; it can be neither apprehended through sense perception nor instrumentally measured nor defined in its boundaries through discursive-abstract thinking. Steiner deals here with cognition itself as an in-dwelling process in consciousness, not to be confused with its attendant corporeal-material epi-phenomena nor its intellectual (psychological/philosophical) modeling. This is not a matter of everyday cognition predicated on subject and object, which would only be a self-forgotten echo of its generative process. The existence of this generative process has to this day been mostly overlooked or remains hotly contested (Janich 2009); it has long been perceived merely as an implicit, transcendental process that brings forth apodictic results in cognition and consciousness, subject and object. Yet, meanwhile, transpersonal psychology (Assagioli 1992), psychological meditation research (Lutz et al. 2009), and introspection research (Petitmengin et al. 2013; Wagemann 2020; Wagemann, Weger 2015a) all point toward the possibility that human consciousness can indeed expand and differentiate itself in view of its own development. From a philosophical perspective, Charles S. Peirce's teaching on threefold categories and his continuum concept may serve as guiding ideas, which synergistically offer a picture of cognition and reality that oscillates between separating and conjoining (Peirce 1988).

3.3 Separating and conjoining as the basis for the process of cognition

Within this field, where so far little research has been done, Steiner's methodological claim elicits the question where and how a solid point of departure can be found that assures insight in a form that does not lag behind the accomplishments of empirical research. As we demonstrated above, human consciousness cannot be bracketed out of the scientific research process, which leads to the question how it still can articulate itself in the aftermath of pre-scientific and recent scientific forms of expression? It must find new forms that are more explicit and foundational in respect to earlier stances and exceed them in methodological clarity and certainty. Does Steiner's phenomenology of consciousness offer an "empirical base" that could function as a reliable gauge for gaining insight regarding cognition? Famously, Popper indicated that even the simplest observation is theory-laden and thus interpretative. The endeavor of logical empiricism, to give a solid foundation[27] to the natural sciences through basic observation and measurement, crashed and burned in the face of this argument.[28] Hence, theories cannot be built from generalizations of empirical statements but, to the contrary, they engender them. Popper correctly concluded that all solid research must start with a critical inventory and review of theoretical concepts that guide its observations. Even so, Popper limited himself in his concept to the context of logical justification of theoretical statements and categorically excluded from his considerations any cognitive-psychological matrix (context of discovery) within which they developed. But it is precisely the epoch-specific, sociocultural perspective of the researcher that determines what is logical and what is not (alchemistic tingeing with the philosopher's stone or a quantum-physical interpretation of reality). With this in mind, we can state that the specific mode of consciousness plays a key role in the development of science—beyond all "objectively compelling," merely bivalent logic.

Taking into account these considerations on the theory of science, we can show that Steiner's epistemology can indeed be understood as a *system of descriptive basic statements*. These basic statements are post-empiricist because their development includes the causative role of concepts that guide the direction of research. They are post-rationalistic statements, because they do not stop at the logical meaning of the terms, but use them to focus on mental forms of activity and states of experience. Steiner's epistemology makes use of "theory" in order to stimulate specific forms of mental activity and their immanent observation. Yet, mental activity and its observation are pre-predicative contents of consciousness and therefore "theory-free." This ambivalence that oscillates back and forth between thinking and observing is already contained in nominalization of theory in the original Greek verb *theorein* (to observe, behold, contemplate). Here Wittgenstein's ladder may come to mind, which is to be tossed after successful use, because in regard to the "achievement," it appears now "nonsensical" but is of course methodologically necessary in the overall context (Wittgenstein 1963, p. 115). While we can thus arrive at basic statements, these are themselves non-verbal but constitute the meta- and sub-verbal realizations of "*fundamental meditative experiences*" (Witzenmann 1989b, p. 75). They can be verbalized in a sense of a pheno-practical experience finding gaze-directing expression, and they redirect the attention to this experience again. This process does not exhaust itself in rational, logical, or illogical verbal contents but articulates itself in the form of action-specific criteria for determining consciousness and its further development.

3.3.1 Total difference as drawing of boundaries

Steiner begins his phenomenological account of the cognitive process by describing the state of non-recognition set in the context of sense-perception—a relatively non-flamboyant philosophical approach.[29]

However, he is not content with mentioning this state to forthwith abandon it, but rather he describes how it develops as a relation between a receptive form of mental activity and its corresponding structural component: If we completely hold back any interpretative thought activity,[30] for a short time we perceive only a disconnected mass of discrete phenomena.[31] At first, these are singular rifts within otherwise structured sets of perception. Our experience of the coherence of things and contexts is interrupted by precisely such rifts, gaps, or void spots in our conscious awareness of the phenomenal world—especially, if we notice them, get interested in them, or are bothered by them. Such a situation arises, for example, when an approach that seemed plausible at first, suddenly does not work anymore, and we are irritated by what we see, or better: by what we do *not see*. Once, when I was out walking after a rain shower, I thought I saw a puddle in the half shade under the shrubbery. But *when I looked closer,* it turned out to be a broken pane of glass with irregular edges. The mental state under discussion here—or better: that, which obstructs it—emerged *exactly between* seeing the puddle and said glass pane; it occurs in that moment, when I actually saw *nothing,* while definitively encountering "something." This state of mind began with a latent restlessness that gradually expanded into a state of feeling "cast back into isolation." In the versatility of our routines, one could also say in our ignorance, our everyday consciousness skips over such irritations—often so quickly that they do not even register in our awareness. But, if we notice them, we find ourselves in a pre-predicative transitional state[32] of our experience (and in this regard a sharp focus of attention is of help, aided by suitable "theoretical" concepts). This state that is usually only noticed at the edge of our awareness, expands, and takes over our entire frame of mind when we encounter situations like shock, fright, or when we are startled up from deep sleep. In any case, the relation to the world, which—more or less consciously—slipped away, marks a "point zero" in our cognition as a total difference between one's own mental activity and the as-yet unrecognized potential object of awareness. In such moments, neither the proximal sensory stimulus nor one's own frame of mind is in any way helpful for recognizing connections; therefore, there is not only a relation of difference, but also one of equivalency: That which is intrinsically disconnected, the relinquished self, is posited against that which—without him—is equally disconnected, i.e., the pure percept.

A reminder of the Anaxagorean and Empedoclean principles of cognition is expedient here (the difference vs. equivalency of cognition), as we encounter it now in even more exaggerated form than in Goethe's approach, occurring in pre-subjective and pre-objective modes.

While this state of experience and its juxtaposition to an unknown factor "X" is not yet involved in any activity of conceptual assessment, it can be seen negatively as a demarcation of boundaries; positively it can be regarded as a safe point of departure for cognition, since it appears unconditional, unfalsifiable, and therefore methodologically reliable (Steiner 1958a; Witzenmann 1986).[33] In reference to the science-theory debate outlined above, this could be called a *first pheno-practical basic statement.* It is unconditional insofar as that which is perceptible enters into the field of our attention without *subjective contribution*, and because there is *no conceptual addition* braided into its beholding. We articulate this statement in a quasi-sub-verbal experiential transition through this state of mind; it would be possible to direct the gaze by saying: "All this, I am not" (Witzenmann 1989b, p. 75). This statement outweighs the one-sided empiristic as well as the rationalistic viewpoint and at the same time constitutes in its immediacy a clear theoretical conceptualization and its own suspension in pheno-practical realization, because in this state one knows without words or mediation that one experiences it.[34]

While rigid insistence on a subject-object relation causes one-sidedness, Steiner's approach expands the view toward the origin of their relationship, as we shall demonstrate in the following pages. In the perspective of educational philosophy, this first basic concept articulates our innate ability to distance ourselves as a condition for an individual and emancipative development that is oriented toward freedom. One can here speak of freedom *from* all kinds of things, also from a connection that is externally determined, but this freedom can only realize itself fully, when it is made conscious.

3.3.2 Universalization of individual cognition

Continuing further along the lines of Steiner's exposition, Fichte's "I" moment or cognition's self-defining articulation comes into play.

Indeed, the opportunity of making a new beginning depends on the total difference between one's own mental being and, better, *not-being,* which involves both. Within the aggregate of disconnected discrete phenomena, we can comprehend ourselves as the point from where we can leave this state. Grasping this opportunity means an inversion of mental activity from a self-limiting, receptive form to a creative and productive one. Its first effect is nothing else than a self-proclamation and self-empowerment (Steiner 1958a, 2003). In tearing itself away from the focus on disconnected phenomena and, as it were, pulling itself out of the swamp by its own bootstraps, mental activity establishes for itself a first but crucial connection.[35] In its inner (self) connectivity, mental activity in principle identifies itself as a portal for any relational connection (with the world)—which, however, does not yet in any way intimate the sought-after relation to content.

The examples of picture puzzles, other ambiguous situations, and of artistic processes can systematically illustrate how a new beginning "from nothing" can emerge in the decision of changing one's perspective, transiting through the suspension state of leaving the old without already perceiving the new, which we also can practice and realize in everyday or biographical crisis situations. The important factor is ever the transition from a receptive-suffering attitude to one of initiative and action. The initially emerging individual "thinking act" aims at conjoining with a universal "thought content," which at the same time is potential world-content (Steiner 2003; Witzenmann 1983, p. 52).[36] The eventual occurrence or non-occurrence of insight, in its superficiality or depth, will determine if and how we were successful in accessing the contentual web of relationships via choosing a suitable form of mental activity. In this transitional process, we can phenomenologically distinguish among (a) *transformation* of receptive activity into a creative one, (b) *orientation* of the creative activity toward contentual connectivity, and (c) *insight* into the autological nature of coherence.

The aspect of individual activity in this phase of the cognitive process is here characterized first, yet Steiner's terms of *imagination, inspiration,* and *intuition* used in anthroposophical contexts imply a gradually increasing evidential validity in regard to mental activity (Steiner 1989; Wagemann 2013b).

Witzenmann refers here to "steps of reciprocal determination" (Witzenmann 1985, p. 116). Appropriate meditative practices can bring the various phases of this process into conscious awareness; subconsciously, they occur in all everyday processes of thought and cognition. Their regular occurrence in the cognitive process is not dependent on outer factors nor on conceptual interpretation but is only contingent upon the degree of formal development of individual activity; thus, these phases can summarily be described as a *second pheno-practical basic statement.* Indeed, one can describe them as increasing alignments or qualitative equivalences of individual and universal cognitive activities. In the perspective of science theory, this usually subconscious process can be understood as the first part of the principle of measurement within the field of natural science, which was explained above as *alignment* (Wagemann 2004, 2010): At the beginning of his cognitive process, the scientist in search of insight differentiates himself from that which he can perceive ("table that is to be measured") and aligns himself with a conceptual point of reference ("zero-point of the measuring stick").

This basic anthropological principle of separating and conjoining/aligning is, from a scientific perspective, initially projected from the outside onto an instrumental procedure. By making it explicit in the cognitive process, this principle can be expanded into scientific fields beyond the natural sciences, as we shall further demonstrate. For educational philosophy, this insight into the primordial nature of the human power to initiate and transform is relevant indeed, since the undifferentiated sensory stimulus in no way contains predetermination or reliance on alien factors yet any content relies only on one's own original efforts. The experience of a principally free initial and transitional ability that can be temporarily distracted by extrinsic motivation but cannot be manipulated at its core, along with the ability to distance oneself, constitutes the second freedom philosophical aspect of Waldorf education.

While above we were talking about freedom *from* heteronomous determination, here we can speak of freedom *to* self-determination (autonomy).

3.3.3 Total coherence and evidence

Steiner describes the goal of the transition outlined above as the third phase of the cognitive process. In the framework of science theory, it appears useful to deal with transition as a distinct phase, since it also provides the basis for the fourth phase. We find here on one hand the characteristic aspects—now heightened into full actualization—of the first phase and on the other hand the enabling conditions for the latter. Beyond that, we deal here, like in the first phase, with a state of experience and activity that is both independent in phenomenological and constitutive-logical regard.

Again, we can only paradoxically point toward this state, but no longer in a sense of "neither (something) ... nor (nothing)" but in a sense of "both ... (individual) ... and also (universal)." In said state, which Steiner terms intuition,[37] there is nothing that is not determination and reciprocal determination.[38] The stream of individually determining mental activities (start, creation, search) pours itself, as it were, into the ocean of universal self-determination (autology), yet it does not dissolve into it but rather perceives the backflow of the actualized cognitive content (reciprocal determination).[39] This ever-moving and simultaneously restful continuity, nowhere interrupted, forms a complementary state in regard to the total difference between the emptied gaze of thought and the pure percept and can therefore be termed "total coherence."[40] The concept of total coherency corresponds to the Empedoclean equivalency principle, except that here we do not experience a confrontative juxtaposition of discrete singularities, but a unitive, living, mutual penetration of determining and redetermining activity. The different far-Eastern traditions of meditation strive for complete and formless merging of individuality into universality (Nirvana, Satori); bringing this state of mind into conscious awareness in the context of a modern path of cognition, we must always take into consideration also the aspect of *separation within the conjunction*. Separation here means to maintain (a certainly expanded) individual consciousness within the process of conjoining.

From the perspective of Steiner's phenomenology of consciousness, the "formless" (arupa-loka) of Buddhism (Fritsch-Oppermann 2000, p. 187) can be understood as the absence of all imagined individualized or concrete form, which, however, does not necessarily lead to a regressive absorption of individual consciousness (Wagemann 2013b). Rather, this state is characterized by the "I" and light-infused primordial experience of universal creative power, which provides connectivity to all conscious structures (things, Gestalt formations, beings, situations and events, thoughts, feelings, etc.).[41] In this sense, we can recognize today's magical-mythical forms of expression—but also rationally deficient ones (e.g., identity theories)—as a reminiscing search for the experience of total coherency that, however, avoids an active, conscious access to this state.

In the perspective of science theory, total coherency can be held up as a *third pheno-practical basic statement*; it is pre-theoretically primordial by nature and accessible through meditative consciousness research. Like the two previous ones, we can point to it by theoretical-gaze-directing considerations (as we tried to do), but it defies every verbal-theoretical abstraction in its existential, experiential character. We articulate this basic statement in meta-verbal form, so to speak, because all verbalization is informed by its potential meaning; as we transit this primordial epistemological state, we could possibly verbalize it as "This all am I" in order to guide the attention in this direction (Witzenmann 1989b, p. 75). This statement is relevant for educational philosophy, expressing man's own, basic faculty to unite with everything. In distinction to purely natural beings, the intuitive faculty of the human being enables him to be *interested* in everything beyond the boundaries specific to his species (e.g., also in glass panes under bushes and how they are recognized); he can turn his attention to everything and appropriate everything. "Appropriating" here does not mean a dominating, exploitative, destructive behavior, but rather that which Scheler calls "love for essential being," in continuance of the initial quote (Scheler 1925, p. 12).[42] In Steiner's words: "In the higher regions of the meta-sensory realm the human being will gain something, which is not given to him but only something that he generates himself: the love for the world he lives in" (Steiner 1993, p. 212).

In this love lies the source of a freedom *in* reality and community, and thus the blueprint for harmonious relationships, for a peace that is grounded not in an elimination of differences but in an encounter in universality.

Before proceeding to the last phase of the cognitive process, a short review of the previous phases is called for.

a. The initial state is characterized by an absolute deficiency of connection, which cannot be cured from within itself. This deficiency, or more precise, the total difference between the emptied gaze of thought and the pure percept, emerges in the cognitive process as a transition to a new, constitutive framework from a no-longer consistent approach that has become partially or entirely obsolete.

b. The resolution of this tension initially consists of a reversal of the emptied gaze of thought (abstinent self) toward the production of a thinking act (expressive self) that in turn incrementally unfolds a thought content (internalizing self[43]).

c. When the thinking act is in a state of full unfoldment, it corresponds qualitatively to the full potential of a thought content. The actual moment of insight (evidence) emerges in this target phase of the thought process, but the original state of deficiency is in fact not yet remedied. Indeed, the thought content (e.g., glass pane) is not only autologically inter-connected and connected to all other thought contents, but it also points beyond these connections to various fields of perception, in which, e.g., glass panes can be detected.

To counter a popular misconception, we here emphasize that the thought content "glass pane" (like all other thought contents) cannot have been formed through abstraction of previously perceived glass panes (or other similar objects), provided that means a generalizing grouping of similar characteristics (e.g., "transparent," "smooth," "reflecting,") as for example done by Piaget and Inhelder (1999). In fact, the epistemically unprocessed stimulus does not evidence any such similarities, characteristics of object-related segmentations that rather can solely be cognitively apprehended as belonging to a meaning structure. The sensory-perceptual stimulus is *too rich* in potential interpretation (Popper 1989), viz, *too poor* in its own meaning content (Foerster 1998; Laurence, Margolis 2001) and therefore its ordering principles cannot be derived from within itself.

Any presumably derived meaning, any ordering principle, must have been (subconsciously) added before.[44] For such an addition to be possible, an "autological level of reality with objective meaning structures" (Oevermann 2008, p. 17) is needed. In complement to the pheno-practical experience of "evidence," this also represents a logical reason for a realism of universalia, which has been propounded by Steiner and other philosophers in various forms and intensity (Oevermann 2008; Peirce 1988; Platon 2002; Popper 1989).[45]

3.3.4 Conceptual individualization and experiment

The last phase of the cognitive process deals with this act of adding that which is conceptual to that which is perceptible.[46] At the same time, such an addition signifies the *sighting* of that, which can be perceived; so—in polarity to the thinking act—we can call it an act of observation. This is possible, because the thought content, in itself logically complete and determined, can point beyond itself toward a potential determination of that which is perceptible. This is necessary to bring about a concrete observable result for the just initiated cognitive act.[47]

If we, e.g., are searching for a screwdriver, it is not enough merely to think of it. However, we must *intentionally seek* and explore a perceptual field to find it.[48] If we get distracted and forget about the screwdriver, the focused search turns into bumbling about without a plan. But even when we stay focused on our search, some things may come into view that at first may seem suitable but under closer scrutiny prove to be not screwdrivers (e.g., cooking spoons, pencils). The sighting orientation toward perceptible raw stimuli must be continued by adapting the general meaning structure to these as a further condition of structure formation. This dynamic adapts itself to the conditions of perception and occurs within the variability range of the object's meaning (all possible types and forms of screwdrivers).

Whether the metamorphotic variation of lawfulness in a concrete situation actually leads to the observation of a screwdriver depends on the one hand on the extent to which the searcher is able to update its concept; if he does not know of a certain variant of this tool (for example, a cordless electric screwdriver), he cannot find it, even if one would lie right in front of him. On the other hand, the success of observation largely depends on that which is sighted and perceptible, in interaction with the conceptual search process. If the perception allows the concept to attach itself to certain points (e.g., handle, blade, blade tip, size, material), the latter will be fitted into the perceptual field: We actually see a screwdriver.[49]

The steps of this transition process can be summarized as follows:

1. Orientation of the actualized concept toward that which is perceptible (intentionality)
2. Adaptation of the concept to that which is perceptible (metamorphosis)
3. Incorporation of the concept into a perceptual field (inherence) (Witzenmann 1983, p. 42)

This example of describing the act of observation shall serve to illustrate that we deal here with an observable process within human consciousness itself, just like in the previous phases. Insofar as we can reach a meditative observational awareness of this object-oriented consciousness, we also gain the ability to follow our own actions within that context and to concomitantly shape them consciously. However, this means—as variously indicated above—that the quality and reliability of our insight lies in our own hands, instead of relying on supposed physiological processes or transcendental doctrines.[50] Hence, in the last analysis, the success of observation depends on how a concept can be incorporated into a field of perception. In the example above, of the supposed puddle under the bushes, the concept "puddle" served to intentionally attend to a field of perception and could be briefly adapted metamorphically, so that the short, but in fact false, impression emerged of an actual, existing puddle.

If I had walked on with this erroneous understanding in mind, this prejudice would have persisted and the assessment of the situation would have remained fixed *before* waiting for a complete integration of concept and percept. But pausing I noticed that the perceptual stimuli of the "puddle" could not sufficiently individualize and incorporate this concept and that it could therefore not be fixed to a consistent individual case. In other words, the cognitive experiment "puddle" failed and was repeated in all its phases again with the concept "glass pane." Obviously, the character of our cognitive behavior is a determining factor for either *true failure* or *inadequate success*. We can either follow—with firm attention—the transition from a universal concept through to the individualized form and wait until we reach a point of sufficient certainty or we can interrupt, i.e., distort, this process arbitrarily and prematurely for subjective reasons (e.g., lack of interest, favorite or compulsive ideas, political motives). In the case of a successful experiment, which can also include an interim failure, the mutual fit of concept and percept is expressed *without my intervention* and might, therefore, be considered objective. Since theoretically permeated objectivity is not a premise of experimental cognitive behavior but rather is its result, we can thus formulate here the *fourth pheno-practical basic statement*: The "theoretical" (conceptual) tentative draft directs the experimenters' attention to a perceptual field, is transformed according to its conditions, and adapts to fit into that framework—to the degree that the percept can at all be integrated into the conceptual contexts. The actual, process-oriented criterion for manifest reality entails the conscious (meditative) tracking of the concept's individualization in interplay with the percept and its universalization in conceptual context.

Complementing the second basic statement, which involves scientific measurement viewed as an alignment (individual to universal autology), the fourth basic concept allows us to observe the aspect of distancing.[51] True, the step-by-step process of transition leads from universal to individualized conceptualization and thus to an integration of concept and percept. Yet, in this process, the vivid, active cooperation of the researcher increasingly turns into a receptively abstemious attitude of attentiveness, corresponding to the gradual paralytic narrowing of universal variability toward a discrete case.

The sober, observant ascertainment of concept and percept in actual conjunction corresponds here to the methodological ideal of experimental objectivity, which forms the anthropological basis of the second part of the measuring principle (the "counting"). Here, objectivity, i.e., the attentive distance between observer and "thing," does not relate to the outer correspondence of things (e.g., in aligning a specific scaling mark on the measuring with the edge of the table), but it relates to the structural formation of a thing itself as an inner correspondence of concept and percept. If the cognitive process results in the subject's gain of the concrete object, it can paradoxically lead anew to its loss, if we continue to pursue the conceptually guided observation. The addition of further qualifiers (e.g., "Phillips," "long," "red") enriches the structural field of the object at first. Yet with the appearance of any unexpected details, it reaches the boundaries of the generic concept's range of conceivability and dissolves in front of our eyes: The purely perceptible appears to us again in its full, non-conceptual peculiarity (Phase 1). We no longer see a screwdriver, but only an inexplicable something shimmering through its transparent grip ... (Phases 2–4 are again repeated).

With this open end, the (structure-) phenomenological analysis of the cognitive process reconnects with its beginning and thus emphasizes its *cyclical Gestalt, which involves at the same time a dimension of unlimited development.* Cognition starts with perceptible boundaries, transcends those in the act of thinking and perceiving, and advances to new boundaries to be challenged by them in turn. The fourth phase of the cognitive process is relevant for educational philosophy insofar as the intentional *development potential of human consciousness* is reflected in this never-ending, continuous process of overcoming limitations. In no way can one say that this process would lead "also to an unbounded theory of knowledge" implying also "an exaggerated concept of human existence" (Ullrich 2015, p. 130). We must distinguish the functional boundaries of cognition, because they again and again can be overcome, from those absolute, (in principle) insurmountable boundaries drawn by Kant. The term *boundaries* is only meaningful, if we assume that *something* lies beyond them. It is crucial to distinguish the assumption that this something is transcendental in nature and unknowable, from the view that it is something not yet recognized at a given time. In the latter approach, the concept of boundary is phenomenologically verifiable, functional, and development-oriented, while the first approach appears in contrast speculative, dogmatic, and eventually un-pedagogical. Aside from that, the assertion of absolute boundaries of cognition contradicts the "historicity of the human self-concept," which is developed here and that even critics of Waldorf education emphasize (Ullrich 2015, p. 129). Against this backdrop, the assumption of insurmountable cognitive boundaries is relativized as a dogma that is prejudiced by epoch-specific views.

In contrast, Steiner's phenomenological analysis of the cognitive process leads to an "optimistic assessment of the human cognitive potential" (Frielingsdorf 2012, p. 89); this is foundational for the pedagogical motif that individual development proceeds through gradually increasing emancipation from heteronomous determination and illusion: "The general interplay of separation and conjunction takes form in the human being as decomposition and recomposition of reality. This realization, however, can only be that of a free being and will in turn set that being free if its outcome is not just to be received but must be sought and found and created according to the respective type of consciousness" (Witzenmann 1987, p. 68).

4 Relevance of Steiner's epistemology in the philosophy of education

The core aspects regarding educational philosophy have already been presented in the context of its epistemological development. We shall once more summarize them briefly and add some explanatory remarks. The fundamental and authentic cognoscibility of the world and the human being forms an indispensable basis for Waldorf education. It results from the equivalence of the basic mental gestures of separating (restraining) and conjoining (producing) carried out in the cognitive process with the character of the structural components of reality (percept, concept) as well as with their relational forms of separation (decomposition) and conjunction (recomposition) co-performed by humans. Man and world can be known; they are neither illusionary constructs of a supposedly pre-formed, in itself unknowable, reality, nor are they forms of an "absolute knowledge" (Prange 2000, p. 174), which should be dogmatically pronounced and faithfully accepted;[52] rather, that recognition of world and man is a process that is actively participatory and formative, and whose cognitive illumination becomes itself a constitutive part of reality. According to Steiner's epistemology, which transitions into an expanded, immanent ontology, the human being arises as a co-creator of reality by overcoming the ever-present initial limitations of cognition and thus increasingly determines his own development toward an ever more conscious conjoining with reality.

This development is sparked by a functional, radically effective process of drawing boundaries, which exempts the human being in the initial phase of the cognitive dynamics from any determining mental context and thus challenges him again to produce new, original connectivity. If he takes up this challenge, the recognizer (also acting from cognition) pronounces his freedom in self- and world-creative conjoining power, evidenced in the mental generation of universal possibilities. In the mindful and experimental devotion of the possible to the unrealized world, he cautiously examines, whether and how far new realities (material, mental, pedagogical, social, etc.) can emerge in this way. The human being makes himself fully at home in the world only in the process of this individual development toward ever more consciousness; only then can he—increasingly free—creatively shape his life in the world, in the community with other people and other creatures.

The motifs implied here of the human faculty for cognition and its potential for development can only unfold fully in the course of one's own progress in developing meditative consciousness. Yet, the phenomenology of cognition outlined here does demonstrate that a genuine cognoscibility of knowing is also contained in these developmental possibilities. In the context of Waldorf education, children and youths are of course not to be prompted toward a spiritual training path—that decision one can only make as an adult; but the pedagogic attitudes and actions of the educators are tasked with furthering the students' innate freedom in developing their minds and to safeguard their health as best they can. This also includes fostering an optimistic mindset aiming at self-responsible attitudes toward recognizing; this requires the educators' insight into the connection between cognitive and developmental processes—an insight that, as shown, is already attainable with an untrained mind and that does not constitute any occult knowledge. This cognitive attitude's central motif lies in the pedagogical significance of situations evidencing differentiation or coherency, which are important for development toward emancipation (Oerter, Montada 2003) and salutogenesis (Antonovsky 1997).

Moreover, the paragraphs above demonstrate that the charge of a regressive relapse into pre-scientific forms of consciousness is unjustified. Steiner's epistemology and the structure phenomenology that follows on from it appear methodologically as a stringent expression of the consciousness-genetic motif of separating and conjoining, which we developed in Section 2. A historic version of this motif appears in the science paradigm of the new age, which its proponents defend against "irrational attacks." This dynamic often overlooks two necessary distinctions, namely what is being defended and against what this defense is mounted.

What actually must be defended is the efficient basics of a mental attitude in modern science, yet a mere defense (rather than further development) of its previous forms always holds the danger of falling back into one-sided reductionism and materialism. Yet it seems reactionary and pedagogically counterproductive to defend a flawed approach that narrows and ontologizes the goal of fostering cognition and the original emancipatory motives of scientific development. On the other hand, in this defense against the irrational, no distinction is made between pre-rational and post-rational attitudes in consciousness (Gebser 2010) and everything that is not rational is lumped together in one bin (Prange 2000, p. 62; Ullrich 2015, p. 126). Indeed, it is understandable from the viewpoint of rationalism that everything unlike itself is labeled as a potential danger; but the historic nature of all forms of consciousness demands that we recognize the relativity of our own, current position in view of further, future-oriented development. The rationalistic adherence to absolute boundaries of cognition is in that regard no better than the suspected fact of absolute knowledge, a suspicion that cannot be proven in view of the process character of cognition, its fallibility, its respective time-bound results, and considering that its forms might be outdated. This is of course also true for the representations of anthroposophy that—according to Steiner—may in the far future "only be recounted like memories, such as we today tell stories and fairy tales" (Steiner 1995, p. 96).

Against this background stands the fact that Steiner's statements on pedagogical topics are time- and situation-specific and are issued in a conceptual framework leaning on Theosophy, which does not appear directly compatible with his epistemological work. Even so, Steiner emphasizes that he did not abandon the basic ideas of his epistemology in his later publications, but that he only applied them to the field of spiritual experience (Steiner 2003, p. 139); this suggests a distinction between the epistemological core of Waldorf education and its time-specific forms of expression. If the view remains fixated on traditional forms of expression (that need to and can be modernized and transformed), Waldorf education may indeed appear as abstruse, and its understructure of anthroposophy may seem like a confused mass of idealistic philosophy and theosophical teachings. However, we can present the basic educational philosophy of Waldorf education also in a form that connects over to present-day conventions in scientific thought and language, but only if we dig deeper into the basic structure of the cognitive process in phylo-, onto-, and actual-genetic development.

This is not a "hasty recourse to abstract and far-fetched justifications of early works on the theory of cognition" (Kiersch 2011, p. 435), but it clears a path for exposing the foundational structure of Waldorf education in order to enable new and authentic forms of expression. To be sure, this is not contrary to using traditional anthroposophical concepts such as "etheric body" and "astral body" in an experimental-heuristic approach for the purpose of developing new facets of pedagogic practice (Kiersch 2011; Rittelmeyer 2011, p. 345). This approach corresponds to the method of guiding attention to meta-sensory ranges of phenomena, which Steiner introduced in his foundational works. Yet one must keep in mind that there is a danger of speculative reification of subtle phenomena and therewith dogmatism, analogous to a materialistic ontology that relies on atoms and chemical elements.

Moreover, the "high heuristic value" (Kiersch 2011, p. 436) of Steiner's ideas and observations may be practically demonstrated in the success of Waldorf education, but, from a scientific viewpoint, this appears relatively worthless, as long this approach does not also furnish consistent strings of justification in the context of educational philosophy.

Given this situation, a key to the scientific understanding of anthroposophy and Waldorf education may well be found within Steiner's works on epistemology and anthroposophy because in his early works both these topics use the same consistent methodology albeit in modified forms: "The difference lies essentially in the emphasis of expression" (Witzenmann 1993, p. 148). We can speak of "observation of the soul" in the sense of Steiner's "Philosophy of Freedom" (Steiner 1958b), as long as the attention is primarily on mental activity and its interaction with structural components of concept and percept. When the researcher shifts his attention away from his own activity and to the "ontological" and thus "essential" contents of cognition, to their ways of appearing and affecting the world, then his transition to "intuitive observation" or "spiritual science" is complete (Steiner 1989, p. 115). Accordingly, this cognitive process—which we presented in the second part in its phenomenological aspects—can also assume anthropological accentuation, namely by interpreting its process states, or phases, as expressions of the anthropological constitutional layers which determine them (Wagemann 2010). In this way, we can connect the initial epistemic state of cognitive crisis—experienced as total difference—with the decomposing nature of the physical body's organization, particularly of the sense- and nerve-related processes (Section 3.3.1).

In confrontation with the physical aspect, the mind builds its own sphere of experience through functional distinction and the power of mental initiative and creativity; we can understand it in its subjective form as a sphere of the soul (Section 3.3.2). Meta-subjective contexts of cognition occur within consciousness in total coherency; at the same time, they also function as potential meta-objective epistemological tools and can be interpreted as man's spiritual level of existence. The individualization of a concept, which is actively accompanied and carried out by the recognizer, again emphasizes the soul level and leads to a recognizing integration of the bodily mediated raw material of sense perception (Section 3.3.4). This indicates the way in which a meditative-phenomenological analysis of the epistemological process can lead to an authentic, conceptually consistent understanding of the threefold organization of the human being into body, soul, and spirit that Steiner presents in his anthroposophical works (Weger, Wagemann 2015b). The above-outlined subtle structure of both transition phases that highlight the level of the soul lends itself also to interpretation along the lines of Steiner's spiritual anthropology. We already pointed out that cognition's unfolding developmental stages of soul and spirit (transformation—alignment—insight) are connected with those of meditative states (imagination—inspiration—intuition) (Section 3.3.2). These stages are not relegated to a "background world" (Ullrich 2015, p. 2), but they take place in consciousness and can primarily be experienced biographically as stages of a soul- and spirit-based transformation of corporeality; that is why at the same time they also reflect their functional differentiation into three levels (astral, etheric, and physical bodies: Steiner 1989). As we turn our attention toward the physically transmitted sense stimulus (act of observation), we pass through the same sequence (orientation—adaptation—integration) but now in reverse order (Section 3.3.4). An overview of these relationships is illustrated in Figure 1.1. These levels of being are no abstract categories with clear demarcation lines, but they mutually permeate each other according to function and transitional dynamics.[53]

Gaining precise and comprehensive insight into the epistemological foundations of Waldorf education is a necessary condition for understanding it properly, for fair evaluation and for working with it authentically. This addresses not so much content of abstract knowledge as rather an earnest and optimistic orientation toward the developmental potentials of one's own, specific consciousness as well as human cognition in general. Such work requires a willingness to apply concepts of learning "theory" in the sense of working hypotheses that can kindle awareness.

Unless we apply these concepts to our own cognition, they remain in the realm of mere theory; in our pedagogic and social interactions, we must turn them into focal points for pheno-practical observation. This type of work results in effective pedagogical images, facilitated by conscious development and self-education in the cognitive life of the educator (Steiner 1907). Each teacher carries in his or her mind—consciously or subconsciously—an image of the human cognitive potential, and they live and express it in their actions; this image has inescapable effects. Accordingly, Bertolt Brecht recommends to never fully finish the images we make of people and their potentials, because they too are continually developing and changing (Brecht 1967). Therefore, in this sense, the most appropriate image that teachers can bestow upon children and youths is the image of their own living example, expressed in their own, open-ended consciously developing cognitive life.

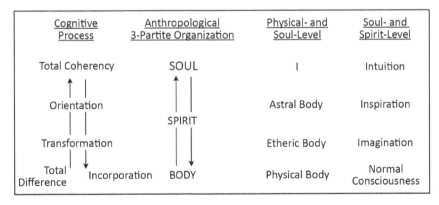

Figure 1.1 Illustration of the structural connection among epistemological process, ontological layers, and levels of meditative consciousness

Notes

1 For an overview of the criticism of the foundations of Waldorf education, see Frielingsdorf (2012).

2 "The anthroposophical variant of cognition [does] not [...] constitute an expansion of scientific research, but in its last consequence a transgression" (Ullrich 2015, p. 138); "Anthroposophie und ihr fragwürdiger Wissenschaftscharakter" *[Anthroposophy and its questionable scientific character]* (Ullrich 2015, p. 144).

3 "Steiner's philosophy and world concept in itself is nothing truly original, but a more or less willful re-working of pre-existent thought inventories" (Traub 2011, p. 786).

4 "All human beings naturally strive for knowledge" (Aristoteles 1994, p. 37). "Basic theme of all human striving [...]: the unfolding of consciousness" (Gebser 2010, p. 71).

5 Aristoteles 1994, 982 b11; Descartes 2007; Dewey 1910; Peirce 1983; Platon 2002 (Theaitetos 155d); Steiner 1958b.

6 "Not only our machines and our technology, but also today's power politics in the last analysis have their roots in magical thinking: nature, the environment and 'others' have to be dominated so that they do not overpower man; this fear of being forced to dominate the outer world in order not to be crushed by it, is particularly symptomatic for our epoch" (Gebser 2010, p. 96).

   "The Ritual offers rules for right behavior toward those superhuman powers, on which we all have to depend throughout our entire lives. For the most part, the modern human being can no longer understand these rules. He can no longer – not even playfully – shuttle into a state of consciousness that is typical for a human being that believes firmly in such powers. Yet he could quite easily find an analogy in his own belief in natural laws and in his readiness to follow instruction manuals that he receives together with any piece of modern technology. [...] If you do not learn to push the right lever, you will never learn to drive. If you not learn to recite the correct magic incantation at the right moment, the demons will never obey you" (Weizsäcker 1990, p. 8).

7 For many modern physicists, there is also no contradiction between their mystical beliefs and science. However, they generally separate their scientific work from their concept of the world and of life (Dürr 1986).

8 Johannes Kepler refers to the "thorny thicket of experiments, [...] through which I wedged myself" (Kepler 1922, p. 60).

9 Steenblock speaks in this context of a "desecration of the cosmos by turning it into a world-machine" and "a loss of competency of theology" (Steenblock 2000, p. 154).

10 Physics is the peculiar investigation of nature by man, who at first found himself inseparably and unquestionably entangled in it. In physics, the human being sets himself constructively apart from nature in a peculiar process that separates and forms subject and object alike. This process changes nature as it appears to us and also ourselves, as we narrow our perspective—which rests on questionable premises—to that of an observer and that permits only a one-sided view of a rigid "physical image of nature, as if this were the only true, real and actually correct view of the world. Yet, this is merely a projection, an aspect, a way of seeing, yes, the result of a [research] methodology" (Wagenschein 1995, p. 12).

11 "Methodology and ontological premises of the inorganic natural sciences – especially physics (of the 19th century) – are being transferred wholesale to apply to all of reality" (Windelband 1957, p. 583).

12 "[Science], in its wish to escape the superstitious fear of nature, has revealed nature's objective powers and causative forces to be hiding places for chaotic materials, cursing its influence on humanity as slavery, until the subject in theory had become a single unbounded, empty authority. All the power of nature was perceived merely as undifferentiated resistance for the abstract powers of the subject" (Horkheimer, Adorno 2006, p. 9).

13 For example, religious sciences, research into mysticism, esoteric subjects, and opinion research.

14 "The experience of transcendence is rooted in the survival of older types of consciousness within a newer form of cognition" (Witzenmann 1987, p. 53).

15 "The real world per definition is inaccessible to me. My brain does not have contact with the outer world. The totality of my experiential world a pure construct of the brain" (Roth 2013, p. 128).

16 "Bringing existing dogmas into question is not unscientific, but actually is part of science's essential nature. Science is rendered creative through a spirit of open-minded research." "I am convinced that the natural sciences, regardless of their success, are hampered by outdated belief systems" (Sheldrake 2012, pp. 41, 44).

17 An earlier version of an integration of both principles of knowledge is found in the writings of Albinos, an intermediate Platonist (who lived in the 2nd century CE): "The Demiurge (world creator) plants all principles into the ground of the soul, so that she can gain knowledge of everything. In the soul, the Demiurge conjoins the indivisible and divisible aspect of being; the principles of sameness and of difference. That is how knowledge is gained of the Like through Like and the Unlike through the Unlike" (Deuse 1983, p. 87).

18 "Because a mere looking at an object alone cannot further our insight. All seeing blends over into observation, all sense perception into contemplation, all contemplation into a process of connecting, and so we can say that whenever we look at the world, theorize into it" (Goethe 1982, vol. 3, p. 79).

19 This finding is reinforced by Goethe's dislike of the romantic art of his time, which he characterized, e.g., as a flight from the past, subjective rhapsodizing, and a "weakly form of contemplation" (Heisenberg 1968, p. 242).

Epistemological Foundations of Waldorf Education

20 "There is no other reality than that of intuitive perception, and none other can exist" (Fichte 1794, p. 521).

21 "The transition from classic Aristotelian thought to a new and more comprehensive theoretical level of consciousness requires a metamorphosis of the soul in the whole human being. A non-Aristotelian logic must correspond to a trans-Aristotelian type of man, and the latter in turn must correspond to a new dimension of human history" (Günther 1978, p. 114).

22 By the way, here lies a fundamental difference to the philosophical phenomenology in Husserl's tradition, which also focuses on "the things" but then attempts to behold the eidetic laws of their nature through a liberation "from all fetters [of being] and experiential valences," in a process of "eidetic abstraction" (Husserl 1999, pp. 424, 314; Wagemann 2010).

23 "There is only one sector that Goethe can be accused of leaving blank: He needed nature as a mediating force and did not elevate introspectively the process of thinking itself to become an object of contemplation." Yet implicitly, in his concept of art, Goethe strives for reflexive introspective activity (Schieren 1988, pp. 219ff).

24 Here too, Fichte lacks clear insight into the contents of the "I"'s activity. "He never got through to that" (Steiner 1958a, p. 81).

25 "Thought engenders concepts and ideas. We cannot express in words what 'concept' means. Words can only call man's attention to the fact that he has concepts" (Steiner 1958b, p. 38).

26 "But it remained unrecognized that thinking comprises at the same time both objective and subjective factors, and that absolute reality is conveyed by integrating perception with concept" (Steiner 1958b, p. 174).

27 "Science is a system of sentences that has been constructed according to experience. Verification consists through 'protocol sentences', which are those sentences that contain the original protocol of, e.g., a physicist or a psychologist" (Carnap 1931–1932, p. 437).

28 "Observation always is 'observation in the light of theories'" (Popper 1989, p. 31). "We cannot express scientific statements that do not reach far beyond the 'ground of unmediated experiences' that we can know with certainty" (*Transcendence of Statements*).

29 "How we determine where to begin lies beyond cognition nor is it cognitive in itself. But we must search for it right before we engage in the cognitive process, so that already the next step taken by the human being is cognitive activity" (Steiner 1958a, p. 49).

30 "Complete self-deprivation of expression [*Vollständige Entäußerung unseres Selbstes*]" (Steiner 2003, p. 27); "Pure content of observation" (Steiner 1958b, p. 23); "Emptied gaze of thought [*Denkblick*]" (Witzenmann 1985, p. 10).

31 "Disconnected aggregate" (Steiner 2003, p. 46); "Immediately received image of the world" (Steiner 1958a, p. 49); "Perception" (Steiner 1958b, p. 34); "Pure content of observation" (Steiner 1958b, p. 41).

32 Steiner also speaks of an "exceptional state" (Steiner 1958b, p. 25).

33 Without reference to Steiner or Witzenmann, Waldenfels states: "The working boundary is […] not something that can be fixed in time, it also is not 'nothing' because without it there would be no distinction between this and that, nor between self and other" (Waldenfels 2006, p. 26).

34 "Our Theory of Knowledge […] surmounts one-sided empiricism and one-sided rationalism by integrating them both on a higher level. In this way, it does justice to both approaches. The empirical viewpoint is satisfied, because we show that all cognitive contents in regard to any phenomenon can only be obtained through the direct contact with that object itself. The rationalist view is satisfied by our approach as well, because we explain thinking as the necessary and only conveyor of knowledge" (Steiner 1958a, p. 88).

35 In analogy, Waldenfels speaks of a "preference within difference" (Waldenfels 2006, p. 27).

36 "We have to imagine two things: first, that we actively cause the appearance of the ideational world and secondly, that at the same time this product of our creative action is based on its own laws" (Steiner 2003, p. 51).

37 "Intuition is a word that in everyday life is often incorrectly used to denote an unclear, uncertain insight into something, for a sort of hunch that at times hits upon something true, but whose validity so far cannot be proven. What is meant here, of course, has nothing to do with this kind of intuition. In this context here, Intuition signifies an insight of highest, most luminous clarity, whose validity is in the fullest sense conscious to him who has it" (Steiner 1989, p. 357).

38 "Since intuition is an active process in the human spirit, it is also a spiritual perception that does not rely on any sense organ. It is a kind of perceptive awareness in which the individual himself is active; it is self-generated activity that is simultaneously perceived. With intuitive thought, the human being enters a spiritual world as the one who also perceives. What he encounters within this world as perception, like the spiritual world of his own thinking, the human being recognizes as spiritual perceptual world" (Steiner 1958b, p. 181).

39 Witzenmann here also uses the term "evidences" (Witzenmann 1985, p. 13).

40 "The extraordinary disposition of the human mind to think about everything in the difficult, nearly incomprehensible form of a continuum, can only be explained, if we assume that each of us in our own true nature is also a continuum" (Peirce 1988, p. 398).

41 "Within the human being, the 'wisdom of the outer world' turns into inner wisdom" (Steiner 1989, p. 416).

42 The quote goes on as follows: "a strange love – a love that is like an ardent thirst and at the same time factual, value-oriented, of highest objectivity, since this love approves in final goodness everything that unfathomably emerged from nothingness; this love suffers all that we cannot praise or admire and still blesses kindly what we must suffer. Therefore, it is part of education to learn not to despise anything fully and to know that one is held securely in the innermost center of being" (Scheler 1925, pp 12ff.).

43 Plato: The remembrance of archetypal images (Plato 2002, Menon 81c–d, Phaeton 72e–77a).

44 "It is precisely this basic mistake that flaws many current scientific endeavors; they believe they are reflecting pure experience, while they actually only lift those concepts into awareness that they themselves have injected beforehand" (Steiner 2003, p. 39ff.).

45 Witzenmann speaks of a "reality-constituting concept of universalia" (Witzenmann 1994, p. 111).

46 "This content is brought by thinking toward perception from the world of concepts and ideas of the human being" (Steiner 1958b, p. 66).

47 Steiner indicates the act of observation as such in his foundational works but did not describe it with the same thoroughness as the thinking act. Therefore, the presentation of this phase relies mainly on Witzenmann's detailed findings.

48 This also is the root of the method of gaze-direction.

49 "The full reality of a thing reveals itself to us in the moment of observation through an integration of concept and percept. A percept gives individual form to a concept, and provides a connection to this concrete percept" (Steiner 1958b, p. 75).

50 "Hardly anyone noted so far that this reality is first being created in the process of cognition and therefore cannot be found through cognition" (Steiner 2003, p. 137).

51 Regarding the history of consciousness, the development of the natural science paradigm is mirrored here (Sections 2.2 and 2.3).

52 Skiera speaks even of a "paradigmatic totalitarianism in purest form" (Skiera 2010, p. 264).

53 Wagemann (2013a, 2015a) presents further studies on Waldorf education motifs, making them accessible through a structural-phenomenological hermeneutic approach. More general empirical-introspective studies on mental action can be found in Wagemann, Edelhäuser, and Weger (2018) and Wagemann (2020).

References

Antonovsky, Aaron (1997): Salutogenese. Zur Entmystifizierung der Gesundheit. *[Salutogenesis. De-mystifying health, German expanded edition].* Deutsche erweiterte Ausgabe. Ed. von A. Franke. Tübingen: dgvt.

Aristoteles (1994): Metaphysik. *[Metaphysics].* Ed. von B. König. Hamburg: Meiner.

Assagioli, Roberto (1992): Psychosynthese und transpersonale Entwicklung. *[Psychosynthesis and transpersonal development].* Paderborn: Junfermann.

Bacon, Francis (2013): Große Erneuerung der Wissenschaften. *[Great renewal of the sciences].* Ed. von K.-M. Guth. Berlin: Contumax.

Barz, Heiner (1994): Anthroposophie im Spiegel von Wissenschaftstheorie und Lebensweltforschung: zwischen lebendigem Goetheanismus und latenter Militanz. *[Anthroposophy in the mirror of scientific theory and lifeworld research: between live Goetheanism and latent militancy].* Weinheim: Deutscher Studienverlag.

Böhme, Gernot/Böhme, Hartmut (1985): Das Andere der Vernunft. Zur Entwicklung von Rationalitätsstrukturen am Beispiel Kantp. *[The 'other' dimension of reason. On the development of reality structures in the example of Kant].* Frankfurt am Main: Suhrkamp.

Bois-Reymond, Emil du (1927): Über die Grenzen der Naturerkenntnip. *[On the limits of knowing nature].* Bielefeld: Velhagen and Klasings.

Brecht, Bertolt (1967): Notizen zur Philosophie 1929–1941. *[Notes on philosophy].* In: Hauptmann, Elisabeth, ed. (1967): Bertolt Brecht. Gesammelte Werke. Schriften zur Politik und Gesellschaft. Band 20 *[Collected works – writings on politics and society. Vol. 20].* Frankfurt am Main: Suhrkamp.

Brezinka, Wolfgang (1978): Metatheorie der Erziehung. Eine Einführung in die Grundlagen der Erziehungswissenschaft, der Philosophie der Erziehung und der praktischen Pädagogik. *[Meta-theory of education. Introduction to the foundations of educational science, of the philosophy of education and of practical pedagogy].* Munich: Ernst Reinhardt.

Carnap, Rudolf (1931–1932): Die physikalische Sprache als Universalsprache der Wissenschaft. *[Physical language as the Lingua Franca of science].* In: Erkenntnis *[In: Cognition 2].* 2, pp. 432–465.

Chalmers, David (1995): Facing up to the problem of consciousness. In: *Journal of Consciousness Studies* 2 (3), pp. 200–219.

Descartes, René (2007): Die Prinzipien der Philosophie. *[Principles of philosophy].* Ed. von C. Wohlers. Hamburg: Meiner.

Deuse, Werner (1983): Untersuchungen zur mittelplatonischen und neuplatonischen Seelenlehre. *[Studies on mid-and neo-Platonic concepts of the soul]*. Mainz: Akademie der Wissenschaften und der Literatur.

Dewey, John (1910): How We Think. Boston: Heath & Co.

Dürr, Hans-Peter (1986): Physik und Transzendenz. Die großen Physiker unseres Jahrhunderts und ihre Begegnung mit dem Wunderbaren. *[Physics and transcendence. The great physicists of our century and their encounters with the miraculous]*. Bern: Scherz.

Fatke, Reinhard/Oelkers, Jürgen (2014): Das Selbstverständnis der Erziehungswissenschaft: Geschichte und Gegenwart. *[The self-concept of educational science: in history and prresent times]*. In: Zeitschrift für Pädagogik, Beiheft 60. Weinheim: Beltz.

Fichte, Johann Gottlieb (1794): Grundlage der gesammten Wissenschaftslehre. *[Foundations of the entire doctrine of scientific knowledge]*. Leipzig: C.E. Gabler.

Fisher, Ronald (1935): The Design of Experiments. London: Oliver and Boyd.

Fleck, Ludwik (1980): Entstehung und Entwicklung einer wissenschaftlichen Tatsache. *[Origination and development of a scientific fact]*. Frankfurt am Main: Suhrkamp.

Flohr, Hans (2002): Die physiologischen Grundlagen des Bewusstseinp. *[The physiological foundations of consciousness]*. In: Elbert, Thomas and Nils Birbaumer, eds. (2002): Enzyklopädie der Psychologie. Biologische Grundlagen der Psychologie. *[In: Encyclopedia of psychology: biological foundations of psychology. Vol.6]*. Bd. 6. Göttingen: Hogrefe, pp. 35–86.

Foerster, Heinz von (1998): Entdecken oder Erfinden. Wie lässt sich Verstehen verstehen? In: Gumin, H. and H Meier (1998): Einführung in den Konstruktivismus. *[Discovery or innovation. How can we understand understanding?]*. *[In: Introduction to constructivism. 4th ed.]*. 4. Auflage. Munich: Piper, pp. 41–88.

Frielingsdorf, Volker (2012): Waldorfpädagogik in der Erziehungswissenschaft. Ein Überblick. *[Waldorf education and educational science. An overview]*. Weinheim and Basel: Beltz Juventa.

Fritsch-Oppermann, Sybille (2000): Christliche Existenz im buddhistischen Kontext. Katsumi Takizawas und Seiichi Yagis Dialog mit dem Buddhismus in Japan. *[Christian existence in a Buddhist context. Katsumi Takizawa's and Seiichi Yagi's dialog with Buddhism in Japan]*. Hamburg: Lit Verlag.

Gebser, Jean (2010): Ursprung und Gegenwart. Erster Teil: Die Fundamente der aperspektivischen Welt. Beitrag zu einer Geschichte der Bewusstwerdung. *[The ever-present origin. Part 1]*. Schaffhausen: Novalip.

Goethe, Johann Wolfgang (1977): Schriften zur Naturwissenschaft (Auswahl). *[Selected writings on natural science]*. Ed. von M. Böhler. Stuttgart: Reclam.

Goethe, Johann Wolfgang (1982): Naturwissenschaftliche Schriften. Bd.1-5. *[Writings on natural science. Vol. 1–5]*. Ed. von R. Steiner. Dornach: Rudolf Steiner Verlag.

Günther, Gotthard (1978): Idee und Grundriss einer nicht-Aristotelischen Logik. Die Idee und ihre philosophischen Voraussetzungen. 2. Auflage. *[Idea and outline of a non-Aristotelian logic. The idea and its philosophical prerequisites. 2nd ed.]*. Hamburg: Meiner.

Habermas, Jürgen (1985): Die Verschlingung von Mythos und Aufklärung: Horkheimer und Adorno. In: derp. (1985): Der philosophische Diskurs der Moderne. Zwölf Vorlesungen. *[The entanglement of mythos and enlightenment: Horkheimer and Adorno. In Id. (1985): the philosophical discourse in modern times. Twelve lectures]*. Frankfurt am Main: Suhrkamp, pp. 130–157.

Hayward, Jeremy (2007): Methodik und Validierungsverfahren der Wissenschaft. *[Scientific methodology and validation procedures]*. In: Hayward, Jeremy W. and Francisco J. Varela, eds. (2007): Gewagte Denkwege. Wissenschaftler im Gespräch mit dem Dalai Lama. *[In: Gentle Bridge. Conversations with the Dalai Lama]*. Munich: Piper, pp. 21–44.

Heisenberg, Werner (1968): Das Naturbild Goethes und die naturwissenschaftlich-technische Welt. *[Reflections of the natural philosophy of Goethe]*. In: Physikalische Blätter 24/6, pp. 241–247.

Hitchcock, Ethan (1857): Remarks upon alchemy and the alchemists. Indicating a method of discovering the true nature of hermetic philosophy. Boston: Crosby, Nichols & Co.

Horkheimer, Max/Adorno, Theodor (2006): Dialektik der Aufklärung. Philosophische Fragmente. *[Dialectics of enlightenment. Philosophical fragments. 16th ed.]*. 16. Auflage. Frankfurt am Main: Fischer.

Hume, David (1904): Traktat über die menschliche Natur. Ein Versuch die Methode der Erfahrung in die Geisteswissenschaft einzuführen. *[Treatise on human nature. At attempt to introduce the experimental method of reasoning into moral subjects]*. Ed. von T. Lipps. Hamburg: Leopold Vosp.

Husserl, Edmund (1999): Erfahrung und Urteil. Untersuchungen zur Genealogie der Logik. *[Experience and judgment. Studies on the genealogy of logic]*. Ed. von L. Landgrebe. Hamburg: Meiner.

Janich, Peter (2009): Kein neues Menschenbild. Zur Sprache der Hirnforschung. *[No new concept of man. On the language of brain research]*. Frankfurt am Main: Suhrkamp.

Jung, Carl Gustav (1957): Bewusstes und Unbewusstep. *[Conscious and unconscious]*. Frankfurt am Main: Fischer.

Kamlah, Wilhelm (1972): Philosophische Anthropologie. Sprachkritische Grundlegung und Ethik. *[Philosophical anthropology. Fundamental conceptual critique and ethics]*. Mannheim: Bibliographisches Institut.

Kant, Immanuel (1974): Kritik der reinen Vernunft. *[Critique of pure reason]*. Ed. von W. Weischedel. Frankfurt am Main: Suhrkamp.

Kepler, Johann (1922): Grundlagen der geometrischen Optik (im Anschluss an die Optik des Witelo). *[Optics: paralipomena to Witelo]*. Leipzig: Akademische Verlagsgesellschaft.

Kiene, Helmut (2001): Komplementäre Methodenlehre der klinischen Forschung. *[Complementary methodology of clinical research]*. Berlin: Springer-Verlag.

Kiersch, Johannes (2011): Waldorfpädagogik als Erziehungskunst. *[Waldorf education as the art of education.]*. In: Uhlenhoff, Rahel, ed. (2011): Anthroposophie in Geschichte und Gegenwart. *[Anthroposophy in history and present times]*. Berlin: Berliner Wissenschaftsverlag, pp. 423–476.

Kuhn, Thomas (1997): Die Struktur wissenschaftlicher Revolutionen. *[The structure of scientific revolutions. 14th ed.]*. 14. Auflage. Frankfurt am Main: Suhrkamp.

Kutschera, Ulrich (2008): Lobenswerte Bemühungen: Nichts in den Geisteswissenschaften ergibt einen Sinn, außer im Lichte der Biologie. *[Laudable efforts: nothing in the humanities makes sense other than in the light of biology]*. In: Laborjournal 15/6, pp. 32–33.

Lathe, Wolfgang (2009): Nervensystem und Sinnesorgane. Grundwissen und Prüfungsvorbereitung. Reihe Abiturhilfen. 3., akt. Auflage. *[Nervous systems and sense organs. Basic knowledge and exam preparation. Series Graduation Aids. 3rd updated ed.]*. Mannheim: Duden.

Laurence, Stephen/Margolis, Eric (2001): The poverty of the stimulus argument. In: *British Journal for the Philosophy of Science* 52 (2), pp. 217–276.

Lay, Rupert (1981): Die Ketzer. Von Roger Bacon bis Teilhard. *[From Roger Bacon to Teilhard]*. Munich: Langen Müller.

Lommel, Pim van (2009): Endloses Bewusstsein. Neue medizinische Fakten zur Nahtoderfahrung. *[Infinite consciousness. New medical facts regarding near-death experiences]*. Düsseldorf: Patmos.

Lutz, Antoine/Slagter, Heleen/Rawlings, Nancy/Francis, Andrew/Greischar, Lawrence/Davidson, Richard (2009): Mental training enhances attentional stability: neural and behavioral evidence. In: *Journal of Neuroscience* 29 (42), pp. 13418–13427.

Meinberg, Eckhard (1988): Das Menschenbild der modernen Erziehungswissenschaft. *[The concept of the human being in modern educational science]*. Darmstadt: Wissenschaftliche Buchgesellschaft.

Mill, John Stuart (2002): A System of Logic. Honolulu: University Press of the Pacific.

Nühlen, Maria (2010): Erwachsenenbildung und die Philosophie. Historischer Rückblick und die Herausforderung für die Zukunft. *[Adult education and philosophy. Historic review and the challenge for the future]*. Berlin: Lit.

Oerter, Rolf/Montada, Leo (2003): Entwicklungspsychologie. *[Developmental psychology]*. Weinheim: Beltz.

Oevermann, Ulrich (2008): "Krise und Routine" als analytisches Paradigma in den Sozialwissenschaften (Abschiedsvorlesung). *["Crisis and routine" as an analytical paradigm in the social sciences]* at http://www.ihsk.de/publikationen/Ulrich-Oevermann_Abschiedsvorlesung_Universitaet-Frankfurt.pdf (accessed: October 2015).

Peirce, Charles S. (1983): Phänomen und Logik der Zeichen. *[Phenomenon and logic of signs]*. Ed. Pape, H. Frankfurt am Main: Suhrkamp.

Peirce, Charles S. (1988): Naturordnung und Zeichenprozess. *[Natural order and semiotic process]*. Ed. Pape, H. Frankfurt am Main: Suhrkamp.

Petitmengin, Claire/Remillieux, Anne/Cahour, Beatrice/Carter-Thomas, Shirley (2013). A gap in Nisbett and Wilson's findings? A first-person access to our cognitive processes. In: *Consciousness & Cognition* 22 (2), 654–669.

Piaget, Jean/Inhelder, Bärbel (1999): Die Entwicklung des räumlichen Denkens. *[The development of spatial thinking]*. Stuttgart: Klett-Cotta.

Platon (2002). Platons Philosophie. Gesamtausgabe in drei Bänden. *[Plato's collected works in three volumes]*. Ed. F. Kutschera. Paderborn: Mentis.

Popper, Karl (1989): Logik der Forschung. 9. Auflage. *[Logic of scientific discovery. 9th ed.]*. Tübingen: J. C. B. Mohr.

Prange, Klaus (2000): Erziehung zur Anthroposophie. Darstellung und Kritik der Waldorfpädagogik. 3. Auflage. *[Education in anthroposophy, portrayal and critique of Waldorf education. 3rd ed.]*. Bad Heilbrunn: Klinkhardt.

Prange, Klaus (2005): Curriculum und Karma. Das anthroposophische Erziehungsmodell Rudolf Steiners. *[Curriculum and karma. Rudolf Steiner's anthroposophical model of education]*. In: Forum Demokratischer Atheistinnen. *[In: Forum of democratic atheist women]*. Mission Klassenzimmer. Zum Einfluss von Religion und Esoterik auf Bildung und Erziehung. *[Mission classroom. On the influence of religion and esoterics on character development and education]*. Aschaffenburg: Alibri, pp. 85–100.

Rey, Abel (1908): Die Theorie der Physik bei den modernen Physikern. *[The modern physicists and their theory of physics. Reviewed by R. Eisler]*. Ed. von R. Eisler. Leipzig: Klinkhardt.

Rittelmeyer, Christian (2011): Gute Pädagogik – fragwürdige Ideologie. Zur Diskussion um die anthroposophischen Grundlagen der Waldorfpädagogik. *[Good pedagogics – questionable ideology. A contribution to the discussion around the anthroposophical foundations of Waldorf education.]*. In: Loebell, Peter, ed. (2011): Waldorfschule heute. Eine Einführung. *[Waldorf school today. An introduction]*. Stuttgart: Freies Geistesleben.

Roth, Gerhard (2013): "Das Gehirn nimmt die Welt nicht so wahr, wie sie ist." *["The brain does not perceive the world as it is"]*. In: Eckoldt, Matthias, ed. (2013): Kann das Gehirn das Gehirn verstehen? Gespräche über Hirnforschung und die Grenzen unserer Erkenntnip. *[Can the brain understand the brain? Conversations about brain research and the limits of cognition]*. Heidelberg: Carl-Auer, pp. 117–141.

Scheler, Max (1925): Die Formen des Wissens und der Bildung. *[The forms of knowledge and character development)* Bonn: F. Cohen.

Schieren, Jost (1998): Urteilskraft. Methodische und philosophische Grundlagen von Goethes naturwissenschaftlichem Erkennen. *[Judgment in beholding. Methodological and philosophical foundations of Goethe's Theory of Knowledge]*. Düsseldorf: Parerga.

Sheldrake, Rupert (2012): Der Wissenschaftswahn. Warum der Materialismus ausgedient hat. *[The science delusion. Why materialism is outdated]*. Munich: O. W. Barth.

Silberer, Herbert (1914): Probleme der Mystik und ihrer Symbolik. *[Problems of mysticism and its symbolism]*. Wien and Leipzig: H. Heller & Co.

Singer, Wolf (2009): "Sie sind doch Ihr Gehirn, wer sonst?" *["You are just your brain, what else?"]*. In: Spektrum der Wissenschaft, 9/2009, pp. 74–78.

Skiera, Ehrenhard (2010): Reformpädagogik in Geschichte und Gegenwart. Eine kritische Einführung. 2. Auflage. *[Reform pedagogy in history and present times. An introduction and critique. 2nd ed.]*. Munich: Oldenbourg.

Steenblock, Volker (2000): Arbeit am Logos. Aufstieg und Krise der wissenschaftlichen Vernunft. *[Working on logos. Rise and crisis of scientific reason]*. Münster: Lit Verlag.

Steiner, Rudolf (1907): Die Erziehung des Kindes vom Gesichtspunkte der Geisteswissenschaft. *[The education of the young child from the perspective of the humanities]*. In: Steiner, Rudolf, ed. (1987): Lucifer – Gnosis. Grundlegende Aufsätze zur Anthroposophie und Berichte aus den Zeitschriften «Luzifer» und «Lucifer – Gnosis» 1903–1908. Rudolf Steiner GA 34. Dornach: Rudolf Steiner Verlag, pp. 309–348.

Steiner, Rudolf (1958a): Wahrheit und Wissenschaft. *[Truth and science]*. (1892) GA 3. Dornach: Rudolf Steiner Verlag.

Steiner, Rudolf (1958b): Die Philosophie der Freiheit. Grundzüge einer modernen Weltanschauung. Seelische Beobachtungsresultate nach naturwissenschaftlicher Methode. *[The philosophy of freedom]* (new edition 1918). GA 4. Dornach: Rudolf Steiner Verlag.

Steiner, Rudolf (1984): Vom Menschenrätsel. *[The riddle of man]*. (1916) GA 20. Dornach: Rudolf Steiner Verlag.

Steiner, Rudolf (1985): Die Rätsel der Philosophie in ihrer Geschichte als Umriss dargestellt. *[The riddles of philosophy]*. (1914) GA 18. Dornach: Rudolf Steiner Verlag.

Steiner, Rudolf (1987): Einleitungen zu Goethes naturwissenschaftlichen Schriften. Zugleich eine Grund- legung der Geisteswissenschaft (Anthroposophie). *[Goethe's theory of knowledge. An outline of the epistemology of his world view]*. (1926). GA 1. Dornach: Rudolf Steiner Verlag.

Steiner, Rudolf (1989): Die Geheimwissenschaft im Umriss. *[An outline of occult science]*. (1909). GA 13. Dornach: Rudolf Steiner Verlag.

Steiner, Rudolf (1993): Wie erlangt man Erkenntnisse der höheren Welten. *[Knowledge of higher worlds and how to attain it]*. (1918) GA 10. Dornach: Rudolf Steiner Verlag.

Steiner, Rudolf (1995): Das Johannes-Evangelium. *[The gospel of Saint John]*. (1908) GA 103. Dornach: Rudolf Steiner Verlag.

Steiner, Rudolf (2003): Grundlinien einer Erkenntnistheorie der Goetheschen Weltanschauung. *[The Theory of Knowledge Implicit in Goethe's World Conception]*. (1924) GA 2. Dornach: Rudolf Steiner Verlag.

Tetens, Holm (2013): Wissenschaftstheorie. Eine Einführung. *[Theory of science. An introduction]*. Munich: C. H. Beck.

Traub, Hartmut (2011): Philosophie und Anthroposophie. Die philosophische Weltanschauung Rudolf Stei- nerp. Grundlegung und Kritik. *[Philosophy and anthropology. Rudolf Steiner's philosophical worldview. Foundation and critique]*. Stuttgart: Kohlhammer.

Ullrich, Heiner (2012): Waldorfpädagogik und okkulte Weltanschauung. *[Waldorf education and occult worldview]*. In: Volker Frielingsdorf, ed. (2012): Waldorfpädagogik kontrovers. Ein Reader. Weinheim and Basel: Beltz, pp. 286–298.

Ullrich, Heiner (2015): Waldorfpädagogik. Eine kritische Einführung. *[Waldorf education. An introduction and critique]*. Weinheim and Basel: Beltz.

Veiga, Marcelo da (1989). Wirklichkeit und Freiheit. Die Bedeutung Johann Gottlieb Fichtes für das philosophische Denken Rudolf Steiners. *[Reality and freedom. The significance of Johann Gottlieb Fichte for Rudolf Steiner's philosophy]*. Dornach: Gideon Spicker.

Veiga, Marcelo da (2011): Zum wissenschaftlichen Selbstverständnis der Anthroposophie Rudolf Steiners. *[On the scientific self-concept of Rudolf Steiner's anthroposophy]*. In: Research on Steiner Education 2 (2), pp. 109–114.

Wagemann, Johannes (2004): Beginn eines Gesprächs über Rudolf Steiners Philosophie der Freiheit. *[Start of a dialog on Rudolf Steiner's philosophy of freedom]*. In: Beiträge zur Weltlage 35 (150), pp. 46–58.

Wagemann, Johannes (2010): Gehirn und menschliches Bewusstsein. Neuromythos und Strukturphänomenologie. *[Brain and human consciousness. Neuro-myth and structural phenomenology]*. Aachen: Shaker.

Wagemann, Johannes (2012): Die philosophische Weltanschauung Rudolf Steiners (Rezension zu Traub 2011). *[The philosophical word concept of Rudolf Steiner (Critique regarding Traub 2011)]*. In: *Anthroposophie* 2012/1 (Nr. 259), pp. 75–79.

Wagemann, Johannes (2013a): Entwurf eines sozialanthropologischen Strukturmodells pädagogischen Erkennens und Handelns. *[Outline of a socio-anthropological structural model of pedagogic thinking and acting.]*. In: *Research on Steiner Education* 3 (2), pp. 28–53.

Wagemann, Johannes (2013b): Strukturmerkmale anthroposophischer Meditation. *[Structural characteristics of anthroposophical meditation]*. In: *Die Drei* 4/2013, pp. 23–35.

Wagemann, Johannes (2015a): Shared Intentionality: conception and consequences in terms of waldorf education. In: *Research on Steiner Education* 6 (1), pp. 44–56.

Wagemann, Johannes (2015b): Mystik als "Protowissenschaft" immanenter Bewusstseinsforschung. *[Mysticism as a proto-science of immanent consciousness]*. In: *Research on Steiner Education* 6 (2), pp. 68–77.

Wagemann, Johannes (2018): The confluence of perceiving and thinking in consciousness phenomenology. *Frontiers in Psychology* 8, Art. 2313, doi: 10.3389/fpsyg.2017.02313

Wagemann, Johannes (2020): Mental action and emotion – what happens in the mind when the stimulus changes but not the perceptual intention. In: *New Ideas in Psychology* 56, doi: 10.1016/j.newideapsych.2019.100747.

Wagemann, Johannes/Edelhäuser, Friedrich/Weger, Ulrich (2018): Outer and inner dimensions of the brain-consciousness relation – refining and integrating the phenomenal layers. In: *Advances in Cognitive Psychology* 14 (4), pp. 167–185, doi: 10.5709/acp-0248-2.

Wagenschein, Martin (1995): Die pädagogische Dimension der Physik. *[The pedagogical dimension of physics]*. Aachen: Hahner Verlag.

Waldenfels, Bernhard (2006): Grundmotive einer Phänomenologie des Fremden. *[Basic themes of a phenomenology of the unknown]*. Frankfurt am Main: Suhrkamp.

Weger, Ulrich/Wagemann, Johannes (2015a): The challenges and opportunities of first person inquiry in experimental psychology. In *New Ideas in Psychology* 36, pp. 38–49.

Weger, Ulrich/Wagemann, Johannes (2015b): The behavioral, experiential and conceptual dimensions of psychological phenomena: body, soul and spirit. In: *New Ideas in Psychology* 39, pp. 23–33.

Weizenbaum, Joseph (1978): Die Macht der Computer und die Ohnmacht der Vernunft. *[The omnipotence of computers and the impotence of reason]*. Frankfurt am Main: Suhrkamp.

Weizsäcker, Carl F. von (1990): Die Tragweite der Wissenschaft. 6. Auflage. *[The Import of science. 6th ed.]*. Stuttgart: Hirzel.

Windelband, Wilhelm (1957): Lehrbuch der Geschichte der Philosophie. *[Textbook of the history of philosophy]*. Ed. von H. Heimsoeth. 15. Auflage. Tübingen: Mohr/Siebeck.

Wittgenstein, Ludwig (1963): Tractatus logico-philosophicus. Logisch-philosophische Abhandlung. Frankfurt am Main: Suhrkamp.

Witzenmann, Herbert (1983): Strukturphänomenologie. Vorbewusstes Gestaltbilden im erkennenden Wirklichkeitenthüllen. Ein neues wissenschaftstheoretisches Konzept. *[Structural phenomenology. Pre-conscious gestalt formation in the cognitive revealing of reality]*. Dornach: Gideon Spicker.

Witzenmann, Herbert (1985): Verstandesblindheit und Ideenschau. Die Überwindung des Intellektualismus als Zeitforderung. *[Blind reason and vision. Overcoming intellectualism as a challenge of our time]*. Dornach: Gideon Spicker.

Witzenmann, Herbert (1986): Die Voraussetzungslosigkeit der Anthroposophie. Eine Einführung in die Geisteswissenschaft Rudolf Steiners. *[The unconditionality of anthroposophy. Introduction into the spiritual science of Rudolf Steiner]*. Stuttgart: Freies Geistesleben.

Witzenmann, Herbert (1987): Goethes universalästhetischer Impuls – die Vereinigung der platonischen und aristotelischen Geistesströmung. *[Goethe's universal-aesthetic impulse – the conjoining of Platonian and Aristotelian streams of thought]*. Dornach: Gideon Spicker.

Witzenmann, Herbert (1989a): Sinn und Sein. Der gemeinsame Ursprung von Gestalt und Bewegung. Zur Phänomenologie des Denkblicks. Ein Beitrag zur Erschließung seiner menschenkundlichen Bedeu- tung. *[Meaning and being. The common origin of gestalt and motion. On a phenomenology of thoughtful beholding. A contribution to understanding its significance for the science of man]*. Stuttgart: Freies Geistesleben.

Witzenmann, Herbert (1989b): Was ist Meditation? 2. Auflage. *[What is meditation? 2nd ed.]*. Dornach: Gideon Spicker.

Witzenmann, Herbert (1993): Das Rebenschiff. Sinnfindung im Kulturniedergang. *[The ship of grapes. Finding meaning in the decline of culture]*. Dornach: Gideon Spicker.

Witzenmann, Herbert (1994): Die Kategorienlehre Rudolf Steiners. *[Rudolf Steiner's teachings on categories]*. Dornach: Gideon Spicker.

Zander, Helmut (2007): Anthroposophie in Deutschland: Theosophische Weltanschauung und gesell-schaftliche Praxis 1884-1945. *[Theosophical worldview and social practice 1884–1945]*. Göttingen: Vandenhoek & Ruprech.

CHAPTER 2

Anthropology

INTRODUCTION

Jost Schieren

Waldorf education is based—more than nearly any other pedagogic practice—on a differentiated and complex concept of man. When in 1919 Rudolf Steiner followed the prompting of industrialist Emil Moll and founded the first Waldorf school in Stuttgart, he held 14 lectures for the teaching staff on "The General Study of the Human Being as the Foundation for Pedagogy" (Steiner 1980). In these and many further lectures, which still today remain authoritative for Waldorf education, Steiner repeatedly emphasized that the essential aspect of Waldorf educational practice and for each teacher lay in acquiring an appropriate and living understanding for the developing human being. The entire system of Waldorf education and teaching practice at Waldorf schools should rest on the anthropological considerations he developed, their internalization, and fruitful realization. From a scientific perspective, Steiner's so-called anthroposophical concept of the human being does however contain many impositions. With concepts like *reincarnation* and *karma,* pre-birth and post-death aspects of human existence are integrated. It uses unconventional terms like *etheric body* and *astral body,* whose content cannot be verified within the framework of empirical research.

Steiner often talks about "essential being" and "patterns of law" and thus evokes the supposition that his statements hold a direct claim to absolute truth. While they are important for Waldorf education and imprint some milieu aspects of Waldorf education, such and other statements have led to a judgment that Waldorf education as a whole is ideological and dogmatic. Waldorf education is considered an essentialistic pedagogy based on a *[peculiar]* concept of man, which runs counter to the modern demand for rational humility and openness in cognition, for plurality and life designs that contain multiple perspectives; from this viewpoint, Waldorf education works with rigid categories, cookie-cutter concepts, and confining, corset-like ideas of human development. Those educational scientists who at all deal with Waldorf education (Prange 2000; Skiera 2010; Ullrich 2015), have *universally* passed this stern judgment, which currently defines the discussion. Yet, undisturbed by this critique, generations of Waldorf teachers worldwide continue to be inspired and motivated in their daily pedagogical work by the anthroposophical foundations of Waldorf education (Randoll 2012).

In turn criticizing academic anthropology, the Waldorf educator Ernst-Michael Kranich states: "Quite obviously there is distance between pedagogic anthropology and pedagogic practice. The anthropological concepts do not cross over into the concrete spheres of teaching and educating. They belong to the sphere of theory, from where one rarely transitions successfully to the reality of *[practical]* education" (Kranich 1999, p. 10). Assuming Kranich's criticism is correct, a curious contradistinction results between a scientifically valid academic anthropology that lacks practical relevance and simultaneously ascribes ideological diffidence to Waldorf education on one hand, and an anthropology of Waldorf education, on the other hand, that is rated as unscientific yet proves fertile in the practice of

DOI: 10.4324/9781003187431-6

Waldorf education. No matter what perspective is taken, the discussion between academic educational science and Waldorf education is stalled, mainly expressed in opposing stances regarding theory and practice. The verdict "successful practice and obscure theory" will not and cannot move Waldorf education into the focal point of scientific discourse.

This publication attempts to lift the dialog beyond the current paralysis and to establish a base of compatibility for scientific discourse. Anthropology as a core concept for Waldorf education is of vital importance for this endeavor.

Christian Rittelmeyer's article starts out from the Kantian differentiation between sensualism and rationalism; he then shows how the more recent anthropological discussion attributes a much higher value to sensualism than historic educational concepts did. Yet the pedagogically relevant connection between sensual-physiological and rational-mental aspects of the human being remains anthropologically unsolved. In this respect, Waldorf education offers interesting starting points for discussion. In order to expand the understanding of the human being and its development, Rittelmeyer advocates employing Steiner's concepts not as fixed truths, but as instruments for observation in a heuristic sense.

Jost Schieren discusses the positions of contemporary historic-pedagogic anthropology, which rejects any form of an authoritative concept of man. He outlines a concept of man—specific to Waldorf education—that leaves development open-ended and contains the ethos of individual freedom. From a phenomenological-functional perspective, he portrays the complex and seemingly ideological concepts of the anthroposophical study of man.

In an internal study with a Waldorf teacher college, Albert Schmelzer pursues the question of how teachers incorporate the specific anthropological impulses of Rudolf Steiner into their teaching practice.

Deeper questions take shape such as: How productive is Steiner's anthroposophy for pedagogical practice? and Does the use of these concepts lead to an ideological imprint? His article describes the results of this study.

References

Kranich, Ernst-Michael (1999): Anthropologische Grundlagen der Waldorfpädagogik. *[Anthropological foundations of Waldorf education]* Stuttgart: Freies Geistesleben.

Prange, Klaus (2000): Erziehung zur Anthroposophie. Darstellung und Kritik der Waldorfpädagogik. 3., um eine Nachschrift vermehrte Auflage. *[Education in anthroposophy. Portrayal and critique of Waldorf education 3rd ed., with postscript addition]* Bad Heilbrunn: Klinkhardt.

Randoll, Dirk (2012): Ich bin Waldorflehrer: Einstellungen, Erfahrungen, Diskussionspunkte – Eine Befragungsstudie. *[I am a Waldorf teacher: Attitudes, experiences, points for discussion – A survey]*. Wiesbaden: Springer VS.

Skiera, Ehrenhard (2010): Reformpädagogik in Geschichte und Gegenwart. Eine kritische Einführung. 2., durchges. u. korr. Auflage. *[Reform pedagogy in history and present times. A critical introduction. 2nd reviewed and corrected edition]* Munich: Oldenburg.

Steiner, Rudolf (1980): Allgemeine Menschenkunde als Grundlage der Pädagogik. *[The study of the human being as a foundation of pedagogy]* Rudolf Steiner, GA 293. Dornach: Rudolf Steiner Verlag.

Ullrich, Heiner (2015): Waldorfpädagogik. Eine kritische Einführung. *[Waldorf education. A critical Introduction]* Weinheim: Beltz.

PEDAGOGIC ANTHROPOLOGY IN EDUCATIONAL SCIENCE AND WALDORF EDUCATION

Christian Rittelmeyer

1 On the concept of pedagogic anthropology

Pedagogic anthropology—what is it all about? When teachers try to adapt their style of teaching and lesson contents to the surmised learning capacity of the students, consciously or unconsciously their assessment is *always* based on certain assumptions concerning the life environment of their students and, in a narrower sense, their learning capabilities; thus they follow a—stable or situational/temporary—specific concept of the human being that has guiding function. The same is true for parents, who form more or less detailed ideas about the best ways to support the education of a child and about which social, mental, emotional, and motivating factors should be the focus of their educational efforts. Probably they want to contribute to the development of their children toward becoming self-directed and responsible members of society: This desire, too, rests on a culturally specific concept of the human being that may be more or less conscious or possibly fragmentary. It is the task of pedagogic anthropology to bring such action-orienting concepts of the human being to light.

It seems to me that this task can in no way be limited to purely descriptive analysis, if it also wants to fulfill a mandate of illuminating and guiding pedagogical practice. Indeed, no pedagogical action is beyond such normative concepts of man. A merely descriptive anthropology that does not inquire about the aims of education would be fulfilling only half of its mandate.

The issue here is not an "ought – is" dichotomy, nor to derive pedagogic directives from the analysis of pedagogical concepts of man. Rather, pedagogic anthropology aims at reflexively anchoring anthropologically based maxims of action in the pedagogic discourse of modern times (Wulf, Zirfas 1994, p. 14ff.). From my perspective that means, i.e., to relate to anthropologically based maxims that were historically developed in Europe and were culturally accepted, such as a broad, all-round education (instead of a specialized one); such as adjusting educational practices to the child's environment (e.g., the developmental state of children); fostering education through encouragement and praise (rather than threats and punishments); and to relate to the principle of a development-appropriate "call to self-directed action" (instead of compliance and other-directedness). Do certain anthropological tenets support these maxims that have formed in the course of the history of pedagogic thought—or are they ignoring or even combatting them? When we contemplate—with closer intent—the seemingly natural way of how we deal with youths, we start to realize that our guiding pedagogical concepts often rest on unrecognized and unspoken anthropological premises. The Dutch educational scientist Martinus Jan Langeveld illustrated this, for example, with simple questions such as: Should ten-year-olds children be allowed to marry or not? Are they anything else than only incomplete adults? In our current culture, we would probably answer the first question more often with a "no" and with a "yes"

DOI: 10.4324/9781003187431-7

to the second. But it is a known fact that other cultures and eras would answer very differently—and have answered differently—because they had and have developed different ideas about "the nature of the child" and what factors are supportive or obstructive to the child's development (Ariès 1975; Arnold 1980; deMause 1980). In his phenomenological, interdisciplinary "Studies on the Anthropology of the Child" (1964), Langeveld attempted to provide a scientific foundation for such anthropological convictions that normally remain below the threshold of awareness. He designed the studies with a sense of respect and consideration for specific characteristics of the life environment of the child. The importance of anthropological analyses and reflections also comes into focus when we consider certain cultural trends of our times—which undoubtedly put their stamp on our concept of man. That applies, for example, to the currently prevalent tendency of analogizing the human being and machine (for example, when brain researchers speak of "hard-wiring brain cells" of "neural hardware" or when they declare their colorful pictures of the brain metabolism to be a direct expression of the efficacy of the human mind; see also critiques of this approach in Gehring 2004; Rittelmeyer 2012). There is a call for pedagogic anthropology to diagnose contemporary issues as a critical discipline of enlightenment.

All focused, thoughtful, and consciously designed ways of interacting with youths are subject to these action-guiding ideas about the human attributes and should be researched in the framework of pedagogic anthropology. But strangely enough, even though it always played an important role in pedagogy. Anthropology has never emerged as an independent discipline within the educational sciences (like school-, social-, and preschool pedagogy, adult education, didactics, and general pedagogy). The possible reason for this may lie in the fact that—while the role of anthropology is undisputed—the positions developed within its framework have always been under controversial debate and were frequently under suspicion of ideology. (For example, in regard to the anthropological assumptions of the pedagogic classic Jean-Jacques Rousseau on the distinct "nature" of the genders in his educational novel *Emile*, published in 1762.) Before addressing this controversy, I would like to first illustrate this discourse with a historic example that is still relevant in our time, namely the distinction between feeling/sensing and thinking *[empiricism vs. rationalism?]* as two basic faculties of man.

Can we meaningfully relate academic pedagogic anthropology to the anthropological assumptions that—at least in their original core ideas—are ascribed to Waldorf education? This question must be answered within the context of this discourse.

2 Problems of classical anthropologies illustrated in the example: "Sensualism" vs. "Rationalism"

In his *Critique of Pure Reason*, Immanuel Kant described a distinction that later became significant for pedagogy: "Our knowledge springs from two fundamental sources of our mind – the first is the capacity to receive an impression (receptivity for impressions), the second is the faculty to recognize an object through these impressions (spontaneity of generating concepts) [...].

Let us call our mind's receptivity for impressions – as far as they can be pinned down – *sense receptivity*, then, in juxtaposition, let us call the faculty to self-generate concepts, or spontaneous cognition, *rational understanding*. [...] Neither of these faculties is preferable to the other. Without sense receptivity (intuition), there would be no perceptible object; without rational understanding, no thought of an object could arise. Thoughts without content are empty. Sense receptivity *[intuition]* without concepts is blind. Therefore, it is just as necessary to make one's concepts sensible (i.e., add the object to the intuition) as it is to make these intuitions intelligible (i.e., to conjoin them with concepts). Also, these two faculties or powers cannot exchange their functions. Cognition cannot intuit, the senses cannot think. Only through their conjunction can understanding arise. But that is no reason for obfuscating the part that each play; to the contrary, there is great reason for separating and carefully distinguishing one from the other" (Kant 1967, p. 94ff.).

This stark distinction between "sensualism" and "rationalism" *[sensing and thinking]*, which certainly is also an anthropological statement, has influenced pedagogy probably more deeply than

Pedagogic Anthropology in Educational Science and Waldorf Education

many educational scientists realize. Again and again, arguments flare up against a school that is too "heady," which focuses too much on knowledge and intellectual abilities; in opposition, demands are raised to give more attention to the sense-oriented *[sensory/intuitive]* aspect of the human being. It is instructive for our topic, to take a closer, exemplary look at such trends from historic and anthropological perspectives. This discussion took place with particular perspicuity in the 1980s: At that time, everyone talked about "learning through all the senses" (Rittelmeyer 2001). After classic experts of this field of research enlightened us regarding the meaning of the senses (Straus 1956), about "sensualism" (Michel, Wieser 1977) or the "ignored senses" (Rumpf 1981), numerous works followed, for example, on the "stimulus of the senses" (Maelicke 1990), on "unfolding of the senses" (Kükelhaus, zur Lippe 1984), on "sensory awareness" (zur Lippe 1987), on "the waning senses" (Kamper, Wulf 1984), or on "sensory work" (Hoffmann-Axthelm 1987). Educational scientists called for a "change of mind" *[in German this is a pun: "a chance of sense"]* (Beck and Wellershoff 1989) or for "sensory comprehension" (Hierdeis, Schratz 1992)—obviously these calls were quite successful: "sensory learning landscapes" were constructed everywhere, where the children could—in the most varied arrangements—smell, taste, hear, and touch and where they could exercise their sense of equilibrium on wobble boards and other contraptions. A book called *Sinn-Salabim* (Ackermann, Urfer, Müller, Dominik 1993) contained instructions for playful sensory training: hand- and foot training, exercises for toe- and fingertips, auditory and visual experiences—all this was part of the program. A secondary school in Düsseldorf announced: "School your senses, instead of being cool" and in 1998 it implemented a project facilitating touching-, hearing-, and spatial experiences. The magazine *Spielraum* (2/1994) *[Play Space]* urged in a literal sense of the word: "Come back to your senses." "Sense-ations everywhere" was the name of the "Project Panorama for Educating the Senses." Even the furniture company Hülsta gave tips in its catalog—interspersed with sales offers for children's furniture—how a child can train its sense of taste by eating fruit, how its visual and olfactory faculties could be improved by closing its eyes and concentrating on smells, how the sense of touch can be trained with an old sofa cushion, and how sorting nails and screws can school the visual abilities. Nearly all pedagogic conventions at that time took up the topic in one way or another.

Horst Rumpf described all this as unreflected allotria. "The well-meaning demand for learning by involving all the senses is in need of clarification, lest it should fall – prompted also by the teaching aid industry – into a didactic hubbub of the senses that confuses bustle with *[real]* life" (Rumpf 1994, p. 5).[1]

Numerous pedagogues follow these trends like a historic mental grammar, but it should be evident that such historic trends result most often from certain *unrecognized* anthropological concepts—in this case concepts of the human being that arise for a time and require rehabilitating various forms of sensory education that are—in fact or seemingly—lacking in the governing forms of education and teaching. As an aside, due to their foundation in their own, specific pedagogical anthropology, Waldorf schools always maintained a balanced culture of sensory and intellectual education, while the pedagogic landscapes all around had "lost their senses." Eventually, deeply rooted anthropological convictions took a stance against this one-sided cognitive orientation—even outside of educational science: An interesting consequence of Kant's distinction obviously was culturally habituated.

These historic vacillations between sensualism and rationalism have been followed more or less blindly; as a matter of fact, at the time—faced with the "allotria of the senses" described above and to break free from said vacillations—I voiced the opinion that we needed an "anthropologically oriented reflection on an education of the senses and of the entire bodily aspect; I called for a reflection on what kind of meaning such an education might have for human development and on what kind of a relationship might exist between sensory and mental activity" (Rittelmeyer 2001, p. 193ff.).[2] In fact, it is interesting that many pedagogues are of the anthropologically largely specious opinion that the two basic forms of human cognition proclaimed by Kant have lost their balance, impoverishing the sensual side of the human being in favor of his intellectual side. Yet, frequently the counter-movement suspends the intellect to a considerable extent, in favor of a rich diversity in sensory experience. But how can both sides move into a pedagogically sound educational connection? And are the two positions anthropologically plausible distinctions at all? Should we not regard them as interpretations that were formed by cultural and historic factors, as cultural *constructions* that we should rather review critically than accept prematurely?

Friedrich Schiller's *Letters on the Aesthetic Education of Man* present a classical theoretical outline that answers the first question (1989; also detailed reference in Rittelmeyer 2005). Schiller's attempt to elucidate the concept and educational meaning of aesthetics in regard to sensualism and rationalism can be considered a succinct classical example of a pedagogical anthropology. Thinking about the *elementary constitutive conditions* of man, as the author did in his 11th letter, we realize that on one hand not only the human being continuously changes, but also that something about him remains constant at least over certain periods of time. The first pertains to his ever-changing state of being, the latter to his person, his identity. Only by constantly changing, the human being *exists*, only in remaining unchanged, *he* exists. Both forms of existence are based on elementary constitutive conditions, which Schiller calls "drives." The force that ever strives to change he calls the sense drive, the force that aims at bringing constancy into all changes (e.g., through concepts), is the form drive. Schiller discusses the problems arising from the predominance of one or the other drive in the actual life of man: On one hand *wildness*, when the sense drive dominates all rational principles (e.g., when we act in affect but later regret it) or on the other hand *barbarianism*, when the form drive prevails over the sense-related needs of the human being (as when cities are bombed, which actually goes against moral conscience but is being justified as a necessary act of war strategy). We shall not further elaborate on this discussion here.

While only sporadically attainable, the harmony of both drives leads the human being to experience his purpose as a being that is, so to speak, equally sensual and rational; only then he reaches a state of "real and active determinability" (Schiller 1989, letters 19–21), i.e., a state of inner freedom: He is neither compelled by the sensual needs nor the "violent usurpation of the rational force." Indeed, this state of harmony is the aesthetic experience. It relies on the awakening of the human play drive (for Schiller, the human being is only truly human when he plays), i.e., an experience, where an observed object *[percept]* appears inwardly as useful, beautiful, rich in content or expressiveness, while mind does not yet know *how* this impression is generated. Through this process, imagination ("direct appearance of a beautiful object") and the rational mind ("what is it that appears so beautiful to me") enter into an open-ended play.[3]

In the *Letters* (1989), Schiller not merely references the aesthetics developed by Immanuel Kant in his "Critique of the Power of Judgment" (1790), which also proclaimed that the beautiful is—as the letter writer puts it—completely infertile in regard to cognition and mind-set. It is entirely up to each individual what such an aesthetic state produces in terms of cognition and mind-set (Schiller 1989, 21st letter). Rather, Schiller quite obviously refers to Kant's differentiation between sensualism and rationalism, as mentioned previously.

We can pose the critical question: But is this distinction still tenable from today's perspective—or should it be understood as a *historic*, meaning an anthropological Gestalt that is definitively subject to questions? (Schmidt 1982) Phenomena, like the "allotria of the senses" just described, seem to indicate that the distinction is certainly not unrealistic. And in human action and experience, when observed from a phenomenological perspective, the two antagonists—rational thought and sensory experience of one's world or corporeality—are clearly identifiable. When, for example, a young woman says goodbye to her lover at the train station, embracing and caressing him, and when she then sits alone, introspectively, by the train window and thinks once more about the experiences of being together and when she already looks forward to their next meeting—then sensual experience and rational thought can be recognized in their specific phenotype within the real world. The wish arising in the train, to soon again experience the sensory presence of the beloved, does indicate in fact that the retrospective mental imagination of an experienced and expected meeting does not feel sufficient, even though contemplating it makes conscious what happened here. In such real-life situations, sensing and thinking, the efficacy of sense- and form-drive, are of course never so clearly distinguishable, as portrayed in the ideal-typical philosophical speculations of Kant and Schiller—Schiller points that out again and again in the *Letters* (Schiller 1989). But can we from today's scientific perspective—in particular from the angle of sense-oriented science—uphold this speculative distinction of sensualism and rationalism, which in fact represents a basic anthropological Gestalt? Doubts are in order here. An example shall illustrate one reason for such a skeptical attitude. Twelve-year-old children are shown vertical and slanted triangles standing on their tip. The researchers ask them to describe what they see. All of them describe triangles—some added: "They cannot stand like this" or "they will fall right away."

Special instruments are used to measure their eye movements while they regard the figures. When we visually observe an object, we can only see a small part of the vision field sharply and must therefore visually *palpate* the objects with rapid eye movements (so-called saccades). These eye movements are registered as movement-sensations via receptors in eyeballs and head, so that the visual perception in truth always is also a perception of our self-generated movements, it is intermodal and synesthetic (on the following example: Rittelmeyer 1994, p. 16).

Figures 2.1a, 2.1b, 2.2a, and 2.2b are selected from a larger series of graphs and show some typical eye-motoric patterns of the children. These are eye movements performed within the first 20 seconds after first seeing the respective figure. The numbers indicate fixation points, where the movement rested for a short period of time—the respective detail comes into clearer relief. In Figure 2.1a the number 1 marks the start; dotted lines with arrows mark jumps in the eye movement that extend beyond the figure. After 20 seconds, about 30 such jumps occurred.

Let us first discuss the vertically aligned triangles: In this figure, the children did not follow the geometric outline, rather, their eye movements sweep away from the triangle's center of gravity to the right and to the left, so that the lines of their movement to the fixation points resemble "rods of balance" (Figure 2.1a) or the children move their eyes intensely, e.g., up and down the imaginary middle axis of the triangle, as if they were looking for a firm or stabilizing axis of this figure (Figure 2.1b). In other cases, the fixations occur in the center part of the triangle. If the triangle, like a slanting figure, stands on a diagonally aligned tip, there are for example distinct fixative motions in the direction of the expected fall or movements reaching far into the opposite direction; here and there we also find nearly perpendicular figures "built up" besides the actual figure (Figure 2.2a and 2.2b). Here, too, we find a (certainly unconscious) active and constructive engagement of the child with the form it sees. The Gestalt is not reflected passively, as in a mirror; seeing is not just a receptive act. Rather, every child accesses the object actively and in different ways! Obviously, the children in this case experience—and grapple with—an issue of the figure's instability or balance. Yet, why should they deal in an eye-motoric stabilizing way with seemingly unstable figures, if they would not simultaneously have

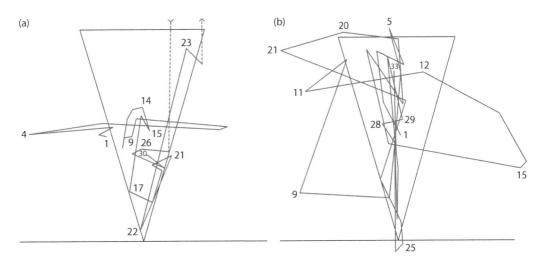

Figures 2.1a and 2.1b Typical eyemotoric patterns of children

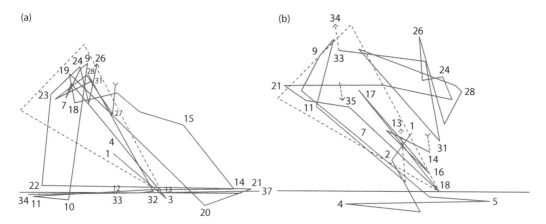

Figures 2.2a and 2.2b Typical eyemotoric patterns of children

a sense of their own equilibrium problems? At first, one could object that the physical sense-organ for equilibrium resides in the inner ear (vestibule-receptors), which is not being stimulated since the child sits quietly, without moving. Psychological research has however shown that irritations of the sense of equilibrium can also be provoked visually, i.e., though the optical sense. At this point, let us remember that each of the senses never works in isolation, but that they always mutually influence each other (and this is of great importance for an anthropologically based theory of the senses); we therefore speak of synesthetic and intersensory qualities of the human sensory organization. Rudolf Steiner already pointed to this fact, in a nearly visionary way, in his anthropology of the senses. (For more detail on this, see: Rittelmeyer 2002.) The motoric tracking diagrams shown above may suggest the following suppositions: The figures, which appear unstable, provoke (or irritate) the inner sense of equilibrium of the children, which happens naturally, in nearly imperceptible, undramatic ways, probably never reaching each individual child's threshold of consciousness, and only manifests in the child's feeling, a gestalt that draws attention and activates the soul's mood. Meanwhile we come to understand that in the act of apparently "pure seeing," more factors are involved, such as the sense of self-generated movement and the sense of balance (and as we can infer other senses as well).

This example is just a small mosaic piece within a research genre that has become ever more expansive in the last years, termed *Embodied Cognition*, *Embodiment Turn*, or *Embodied Cognitive Action*.

Embodied Cognition denotes the insight that all our cognitive processes, even very abstract thoughts, are rooted in elementary body processes. The body processes that support or even generate cognition are registered via internal bodily sensors (such as receptors for equilibrium, life functions, or self-generated movements) so that sensing can no longer be strictly distinguished from thinking and vice versa. While Schiller's dualistic anthropology can certainly appear plausible from an experiential-analytical and phenomenological perspective, it does generate problems from the viewpoint of modern embodiment research. From this double perspective, we certainly can come to a much more differentiated critical assessment of any "allotria of the senses" that went astray and no longer bears the marks of any anthropological reflection. It is of utter importance to develop the senses also as intuitive organs—in my understanding, that has ever been a central concern of Waldorf education.

3 Questioning the search for "The Human Being": The emergence of historic pedagogic anthropology

What can pedagogic anthropology now learn summarily from this somewhat detailed proto-typical example of an anthropological "essence-determination" of man? In my assessment, it is most important to understand that anthropological categories and concepts like *sensuality* and *rationality* are in principle always to be questioned; we cannot claim general validity for them. That does not at all mean that they cannot serve as conceptual orientations for a meaningfully conceived pedagogic approach. However, because they in turn can again be questioned based on newer research, critical analyses of ideology, intercultural confrontations changes in social mentality and other developments, such concepts should be interpreted within certain contexts, maybe as meaningful criteria for contemplation, but not as "essential characteristics of man." Pedagogic anthropology today assumes exactly this general position: It defines itself largely as historic anthropology (Gebauer 1989; Wulf 1997; Wulf 2004; *Magazine Paragrana*). Christian Wulf, a main representative of this direction, writes: "The claim of pedagogic anthropology to make statements about the human being or the child or educator, was never – and can in principle never be – validated. Such claims to universality have to be qualified historically, culturally and epistemologically, otherwise they appear as illicit fiction and phantasms implying entitlement to power and dominance" (Wulf 2004, p. 40). Even today we can still find anthropological categories set as absolutes; categories that were typical for many classical theories of this scientific field are seen to be caused by missing or flawed reception of insights from systems theory, hermeneutics, structuralism, and post-modern theories. This unenlightened position understood "pedagogic anthropology frequently as a positive anthropology that wanted to establish foundations for education as well as cultural and personal development" (ibid.). Since then, the humanities underwent a process of dissolving seemingly solid frames of references and thus ushered in change in relatively fixed concepts of the "nature of the human being," the "nature of the child," etc., leading to historically transforming conceptualizations. Historic pedagogic anthropology is therefore searching not so much for "essential features" but rather for such historically changing or interculturally varying concepts and their effects on pedagogic practice. "Anthropological thinking is an unavoidable part of pedagogy" and can therefore be identified in classical educational concepts of Rousseau, Campe, Kant, Goethe, and down to Wilhelm von Humboldt and Schleiermacher (Wulf 1996).[4] Yet, this new anthropology understands itself to be a "normal anthropology," but an interdisciplinary, self-examining cultural science that does not aim at formulating authoritative maxims for action (Wulf 2004, p. 40; Wulf, Zirfas 1994, p. 22). In an enlightening review of several new publications on the topic, Heinz-Elmar Tenorth, the educational scientist from Berlin, put this basic thesis into these words: "Talking about the 'Nature of Man' or the 'Purpose of Man' proved problematic, because it implies the fallacious argument that there is something like a meta-temporal, normative knowledge of the 'essence of man,' that would be directly relevant and serve as a guiding principle, e.g., for pedagogues" (Tenorth 2000, p. 907; similar also Kamper 1995).

It was not in the framework of historic anthropology that this critical position was developed. It had already been foreshadowed in classical historic pedagogy of the postwar era, when controversies erupted among representatives of, e.g., rather philosophical, cultural-anthropological, or psychological concepts of man, i.e., representatives of so-called aspect- or "regional anthropologies in distinction to a more comprehensive, interdisciplinary contemplation of man."[5] As an example, we will here highlight several of these authors. One of the best-known older representatives of a humanities-oriented anthropology is certainly Otto Friedrich Bollnow, who concerned himself with elementary pedagogic phenomena, which he calls "existential," such as admonishment, encounter, emotional security, trust, and engagement (Bollnow 1956); but Theodor Adorno also attributed to him a "jargon of peculiarity" because of his style of language (Adorno 1964, p. 23). The echo of existentialism, which was *en vogue* at the time, is unmistakable; it probably contributed to exactly that choice of these "existential phenomena."

Andreas Flitner saw pedagogic anthropology as a study of educational actions and situations fueled by the question as to what this can teach us about the "essential being of man" (Flitner 1963). In contrast to Bollnow, he called for attention to research that was conducted in neighboring disciplines such as psychology, e.g., former and current studies on child development. He thought that basic concepts of pedagogic anthropological thought would lack substance without taking that research into consideration. Yet he also warned against following "fad anthropologies" (among others of that time, for example, the much-discussed "constitutive biogenetic law," i.e., the position that the child's ontogenesis is a shortened replica of phylogenesis). Moreover, Flitner criticized not only the adoption of naïve, positivistic developmental concepts, but also that of certain "layered models" (body and spirit; instinctual drives and rationality; unconscious and conscious; It, I, and Super-ego) gleaned from theories of that time that varied in quality.

Here we can discern clear beginnings of an interdisciplinary reflexive anthropology, which was however not formulated until much later, especially by the French sociologist Pierre Bourdieu (Bourdieu, Wacquant 2006). This term not only denotes a critically analyzing discipline of educational science; but it also is not defined by a continuous reflexive critique of one's own position—which its protagonists may have more trouble realizing. Maybe it will take two decades before we again should inquire into "the essential nature of man," because by then new perspectives may have opened up in this regard.[6] The term "reflexive anthropology" denotes also a cognitive method that is supposed to reveal the dialectics of social and mental structures. Accordingly, phenomena of human social action are to be understood neither as just individually motivated activities nor, in structural interpretation, as merely socially formed or socialized activities. In Bourdieu's view, we can rather speak of an incorporation of social structures by active individuals, who also shape them; structure and individual constitution often appear empirically as homologue, i.e., one cannot be meaningful investigated without the other. Indeed, individualistic concepts of anthropology must appear somewhat naïve from such a perspective.

Interesting enough, Werner Loch distinguished the "Question for a Concept of Man" from the "Question of Anthropology" (Loch 1965). In his view, the first of these questions is concerned with a "unified, normative image of man," while the latter question addresses a pedagogical framing of this essence: "What does pedagogy actually see of the human being? How does the human being figure in pedagogical concepts?" Pedagogy, like other research-oriented disciplines (such as psychology), always arrives at the insight that the human being appears in ever-new forms, as an ever-new phenomenon, e.g., in form of the historical change in the concept of "youth" or as new insights into early childhood and its peculiar features, as discovered in psychological research. In pedagogy, the anthropological approach "registers the change in education via the change in the human being." Here too we can recognize early, preliminary forms of a position that is then refined in the framework of a newer historic anthropology and becomes the dominant habit of thought.

Finally, Heinrich Roth popularized this focus on changeable concepts of man; he demanded and also fostered the so-called realistic turnaround in the educational sciences, i.e., the consideration of the findings of the empirical human and social sciences that had been disregarded by many educational scientists in the 1950s and 1960s. Many empiricists experienced philosophical anthropology as a sort of armchair speculation that had lost view of the real phenomena in education.

"Faced with the tremendous amount of material, whose full scope still awaits review, that the empiric sciences presented in regard to the human being, it seems to me anachronistic, to still contemplate philosophically on the nature of the human being par coeur *[through heart-centered thinking]* and by means of pure reason. Rather, we must take into account the material on the human being, which the empirical sciences have furnished" (Roth 1965, p. 207). Heinrich Roth was later—I think, not quite unjustly—reproached for a tendency to psychologize anthropology.

These examples illustrate that even in their highly varying viewpoints on "the human being" alone, the classical anthropological authors have promoted the conviction that it is not so easy to establish an anthropological foundation for practical pedagogy. The anthology of characteristic texts, published by Christoph Wulf and Jörg Zirfas in 1994, opens up vivid and precise views into these controversies and positions (Zirfas 1998). Also, these older texts contain already numerous indicators that call for anthropology to function as an open question, whose answers require cautious restraint in proclaiming authoritative "Concepts of Man." In a study conducted in 1964, the philosopher and educational scientist Jürgen-Eckhard Pleines stated that there is "a crisis of the anthropological rationale for pedagogy." He criticized the "untenable metaphysical idea [...] that there could be a universal or individual essential nature of man," impervious to the change of times, that persisted as a self-sufficient "I" even in the face of all the variability of inner and outer conditions (Pleines 1976, p. 210).

In 1982, the educational scientist Hans Scheuerl presented his historic overview of positions in pedagogic anthropology and therein ascertained that, for many people, pedagogic anthropology, which

Pedagogic Anthropology in Educational Science and Waldorf Education

so far had been oriented either biologically/aesthesiologically (Adolf Portmann, Helmuth Plessner) or philosophically (Andreas Flitner, Werner Loch, and Theodor Ballauff), had become for many a questionable point of reference, due to the "realistic turnaround" with its alignment toward the social sciences. Nonetheless, the anthropological question, he said, "remains fundamental for all pedagogic understanding"; therefore the interest in "images that the human being has formed and forms of himself can never be 'final' or 'obsolete' in the context of education and educational science" (Scheuerl 1982, p. 7). Consequently, it is certainly of importance for the reception of academic pedagogic anthropology by representatives of Waldorf education, to critically acknowledge the classics of this genre, even though they are sensitized differently regarding anthropological questions and therefore also worthy of reading. This slowly emerging position of historic anthropology is currently dominant, although it is not shared in all circles of educational science[7] and received quite critical commentary (Tenorth 2000).

A corresponding variety of topics are covered by the "Commission for pedagogic anthropology in the German Association of Educational Science" (DGfE): Conventions topics range from "the Education of the Body" *[also another meaning in German: "the formation of the body"]* (Bilstein, Brumlik 2013) and "Metamorphoses of Space, Educational Science Research and Chrono-topology" (Liebau, Miller-Kipp, Wulf 1999) over "Transformations of Time. Educational Science Studies on Chronotopology" (Bilstein 1999) to "Aisthesis, Aesthetics. Between Perception and Consciousness" (Mollenhauer, Wulf 1996).

The same is true for topics and contributions in the interdisciplinary professional magazine *Paragrana* that informs, aside from presenting the convention reports just mentioned, also on theories and research initiatives in the field of historic anthropology. The titles of their issues are, e.g., "Sound (*acoustic*) Anthropology. Performativity – Imagination – Narration" (Schulze 2007), "Body-machines – Machine-bodies" (Köpping, Wulf, Papenburg 2005), "Theories of the Performative" (Fischer-Lichte, Wulf 2001), "Metaphors of the Impossible" (Wulf 2000), "Beyond" (Kasten, Wulf 1998), or "the Man" (Lenzen, Mattenklott 1997).

The articles in these magazine issues and the contributions at aforementioned conventions describe ideas, research projects, theorems, observations, and contemplated experiences often in form of essays. The atmosphere at the conventions is characterized by great openness for the variety of these anthropological studies and perspectives and also allows room for, generally, constructive critical discussions. Is a dialog possible between these new and earlier forms of anthropological positions of the educational sciences on one hand and anthroposophy-based Waldorf schools on the other? I do not believe a viable dialog (though possible) can be achieved through analyzing points of commonality, such as Helmuth Plessner's "layer theory" (plants, animals, humans as steps in the development of organic life) or his concept of the "positionality of the eccentric form" (Plessner 1965, p. 288) or Arnold Gehlen's concept of the "plasticity of the human being" or Bollnow's "Existential Phenomena" (Mertens 1998). At the core of the issue lies a much more fundamental question.

4 Anthropologies in educational science and the study of the human being in Waldorf education: Differences and possible rapprochements

In 1919, Rudolf Steiner, the founder of Waldorf schools, explained in a lecture on the topic "The Independent School and the Threefold Order *[of the Body Social]*": "The challenge at present is to anchor the school fully in a freedom of life and spirit. Only the understanding of the young person and his individual potential shall determine the contents of teaching and education. True anthropology shall be the foundation of education and practical pedagogy in the classroom. The question to be asked is not: What should the human being know and what skills does he need for the existing social order; rather, the question should be: What is the human being's potential and how can it be developed? The *it* becomes possible, to enrich the social order with ever new powers emerging in the upcoming generation. Then the social order will always harbor the kind of life that the newly entering, mature human beings create; but then, the existing social organization will not be able to shape the next, budding generation according to its will" (Steiner 1977, p. 28).

It is a genuinely anthropological approach, to base school education and learning on a deeper insight into the developing child, i.e., to shape his learning behavior according to "the understanding of the young person and his individual potential," rather than deriving it primarily from outer guidelines. But how can we recognize, e.g., the individual potential of the human being, how can we acquire the decreed faculty of the "recognition of man's nature"? Steiner bases his study of the human being on a radically new anthropology, only specific to Waldorf education; he does not take recourse to the insights of developmental psychology or even developmental biology. In his foundational work *The Education of the Child from the Point of view of Spiritual Science* (1907), he propounds: "The child's nature shall simply be described – without programs or demands. The educational perspectives will naturally arise from the essence of the developing human being" (Steiner, 1907, p. 9f.).

This "hidden nature of man" characteristically encompasses the interplay of various "parts of essential being": The physical body with life- and formative powers, also called the etheric body, which is present not only in then human being but also in animals and plants; the astral body, with characteristic emotional, feeling-powers, which is also present in animals; and finally, the "I-body" that is only typical for the human being. Within the framework of this contribution, we cannot go into further detail on the manifold pedagogical considerations, such as the approximate seven-year rhythms in the child's development. It is not expedient here to discuss the long-term transformation of these "bodies" into higher links of essential being, nor can we take a closer look at their relation to Steiner's theory of the temperaments and his ever-new perspectives in contemplating that theory again and again throughout his lectures (Leber 1993). From a perspective of traditional anthropology, it may still be acceptable to speak of the "nature of the child" (as also in Kranich 2003); yet it remains questionable, if the *[three?]* "higher" links of essential being can be scientifically validated. From the perspective of historical anthropology, concepts like "links of essential being" or "nature of man" would be rejected and attributed to traditional anthropology, which is scientifically no longer tenable and moreover a metaphysical position (Ullrich 1991).

On the other hand, it is precisely this new discipline of *historic* pedagogic anthropology—and its openness just described—that offers the opportunity for a discussion on anthropological concepts that are typical for Waldorf education, if only a scientifically acceptable ingress were presented. Such an ingress could for example consist of describing the above-mentioned theory of the links of essential being not as an absolute truth, but to present it as a possible, heuristically interesting view of the human being. A demonstration of the practical application of such theories, e.g., in classroom didactics, could show how these concepts may prove insightful in respect to cognition theory and pedagogically fruitful. It is strange, for instance, that a critical article by the sociologist and educational scientist Dietmar Kamper has gone nearly unnoticed up to now, though he is a member of the founding circle of historic pedagogic anthropology (Kamper 1994).

The author references Immanuel Kant's *Anthropology from a Pragmatic Point of View,* where it says in the introduction: "A teaching on the cognition of man (anthropology) can, in systematic regards, be either biologically or pragmatically stratified." In Kamper's view, Kant himself wanted to see "the physiological cognition of man, namely what nature makes of man, complemented by a pragmatic cognition of the human being, i.e., an understanding of what he, as a freely acting being, can or shall make of himself. Up to today, this concept of a double anthropology of man's 'is and ought' has not been realized. Either each side has been dealt with separately and without relation to the other, or one was subsumed into the other, so that one or other of the sides was never given due consideration. However, if both points of view are deemed valid—seeing the human being as nature made him and seeing him in relation to his own being, i.e., his spirit, then we arrive at the desideratum of an anthropology that maintains a twofold view of the human being—i.e., as a being of nature *and* of spirit. Its fundamental methodological challenge would lie in mastering the difference between the two approaches" (Kamper 1994, p. 193). He added also that Kant referred a few years later, in his "Lectures on Pedagogy," to anthropology in precisely that double aspect of man, which is a foundational prerequisite for pedagogic practice. I have the impression that Kamper's stated problem remains unsolved; there is still no

Pedagogic Anthropology in Educational Science and Waldorf Education

pedagogic anthropology that looks at the biological and mind-soul activity of the human being in a substantial context, not only a correlative one. Gernot Böhme's *Anthropology from a Pragmatic Point of View* (Böhme 1985) follows up on Kant's question in treating the history of reason as the psychological and sociological genesis of rational man, i.e., in the sense of historic anthropology. Kant's so-called physiological side comes into focus in the "embodiment" theme, which so far has been misunderstood, together with other, so far repudiated, concepts like the "other of reason," i.e., nature, imagination, and the irrational. For Boehme, the scientification of our world is disastrously effective in practice, since it causes essential human experiences to fade from the field of awareness. But what is addressed here is philosophical regional anthropology, and not pedagogic issues. Yet, with its issues, it touches upon then "wholistic" didactics of Waldorf schools.

In my work *Pedagogic Anthropology of the Body* (2002), I attempted for the first time to connect the research findings of life sciences with the pedagogical thought of the humanities; but this too constitutes only an attempt, not an explicit anthropology. It appears, however, of importance that this book has incorporated numerous suggestions of Rudolf Steiner (e.g., from his theory of the senses) and his students (like those stemming from the so-called Goethean natural sciences), thus affirming their heuristic value for an anthropology along the lines of Kamper's conceptual framework. Yet it is also true that many phenomena of man's biological nature—such as the earlier indicated judgment process through synesthetic perception—most likely are more ubiquitous than historic anthropology would like to acknowledge.[8] But that does not mean that this—or Boehme's—book intends to offer any "determination of the nature of man." Rather, it focuses on the development of anthropological viewpoints that are always necessary for pedagogical practice, but which must ever again be tested to reflect new scientific findings, practical experiences, ethical orientations, and intercultural perceptions. Or maybe the teaching on the "concept of man," presented by anthroposophical anthropology, is not meant to offer a fixed image of man, as it seems at first. Could it be that categories like "links of the essential nature," developmental cycles, and other concepts of Waldorf anthropology should be understood in the same way as historic anthropology understands categories like history, history of cognition, and cultural formation: as concepts that specifically facilitate our perception of the living change "of mankind" and its inexhaustible manifold phenomenology?

Notes

1 See also Bilstein (2011), Wulf, Poser, Kamper (1995), Wulf, Kamper, Trabant (1993).
2 See examples for this in Buck/Kranich (1995) and Gadamer (1979).
3 The American culture critic Jeremy Rifkin in his book *The Age of Access* (2000) already references Schiller when he calls for rehabilitation of the play and of beautiful appearances, set in contrast to a rationalistic and economically operationalized state of society, which by now influences (e.g., through "customer loyalty") everyday human relationships. "Play for playing's sake is the highest form of human freedom – and freedom is nothing you can buy" (Rifkin 2000, p. 356).
4 Even more comprehensive and going back to Plato: Scheuerl (1982).
5 On these various perspectives, see then classic anthropology series by Gadamer, Vogler (1972).
6 In her book on Embodiment Research, Sabine C. Koch goes from the assumption that certain meaning-conveying motions of the human being deal with "invariants in a sense of universal semantic characteristics" – as, e.g., elementary motions/gestures of "approaching" or "avoiding" (Koch 2011, p. 6).
7 See, e.g., the Biologically Oriented Anthropology of Max Liedke and his team (Adick, Krebs 1992; Liedke 1972; Uher 1995).
8 Regarding the example of architecture perception, see also Rittelmeyer (2013).

References

Ackermann, Liselotte/Urfer, Renate/Müller, Bernhard/Dominik, Jost (Eds.) (1993): Sinn-Salabim. Tasten – Hören – Sehen: Spiele und Theaterprojekte für Kinder. *[Sense-alabim. touching – hearing – seeing]* Zürich: Verlag an der Ruhr.

Adick, Christel/Krebs, Uwe (Eds.) (1992): Evolution, Erziehung, Schule. Beiträge aus Anthropologie, Entwicklungspsychologie, Humanethologie und Pädagogik. *[Evolution, education, school. Contributions from anthropology, developmental psychology, human ethology, and pedagogy]* Erlangen: Univ.-Bibliothek.

Adorno, Theodor W. (1964): Jargon der Eigentlichkeit. *[Jargon of authenticity]* Frankfurt am Main: Suhrkamp.

Ariès, Philippe (1975): Geschichte der Kindheit. *[History of childhood]* Munich: Hanser.

Arnold, Klaus (1980): Kind und Gesellschaft in Mittelalter und Renaissance. Beiträge und Texte zur Geschichte der Kindheit. *[Child and society in the Middle Ages and Renaissance. Contributions and texts on the history of childhood]* Paderborn: Schöningh.

Beck, Johannes/Wellershoff, Heide (1989): Sinnes Wandel. Die Sinne und die Dinge im Unterricht. *[Changing the senses. The senses and objects in the classroom]* Frankfurt am Main: Scriptor.

Bielefeld, Jürgen (Ed.) (1986): Körpererfahrung: Grundlage menschlichen Bewegungsverhaltens. *[Body experience: Foundations of human motoric behavior]* Göttingen: Hogrefe.

Bilstein, Johannes (Ed.) (1999): Transformationen der Zeit. Erziehungswissenschaftliche Studien zur Chronotopologie. *[Transformations of time. Educational science studies on chronotopology]* Weinheim: Beltz.

Bilstein, Johannes (Ed.) (2011): Anthropologie und Pädagogik der Sinne. *[An anthropology and pedagogy of the senses]* Opladen: Budrich.

Bilstein, Johannes/Brumlik, Micha (Ed.) (2013): Die Bildung des Körpers. *[The formation of the body]* Weinheim: Beltz.

Böhme, Gernot (1985): Anthropologie in pragmatischer Hinsicht. *[Anthropology in pragmatic perspective]* Frankfurt am Main: Suhrkamp.

Bollnow, Otto Friedrich (1956): Das veränderte Bild vom Menschen und sein Einfluss auf das pädagogische Denken. *[The changed concept of the human being and its influence on pedagogic thought]* In: Bollnow, Otto Friedrich (Ed.) (1956): Erziehung wozu? *[Education for what?]* Stuttgart: Kröner, S., pp. 35–47.

Bollnow, Otto Friedrich (1965): Die anthropologische Betrachtungsweise in der Pädagogik. *[The anthropological approach in pedagogy]* Essen: Neue Deutsche Schule.

Bourdieu, Pierre/Wacquant, Loic J.D. (2006): Reflexive Anthropologie. *[Reflexive anthropology]* Frankfurt am Main: Suhrkamp.

Braun, Walter (1989): Pädagogische Anthropologie im Widerstreit. Genese und Versuch einer Systematik. *[Pedagogic anthropology in controversy]* Bad Heilbrunn: Klinkhardt.

Brooks, Charles V.W. (1991): Erleben durch die Sinne. *[Sensory awareness]* Munich: dtv.

Buck, Peter/Kranich, Ernst-Michael (Eds.) (1995): Auf der Suche nach dem erlebbaren Zusammenhang. *[In search of experienceable connection]* Weinheim and Basel: Beltz.

deMause, Lloyd (Ed.) (1980): Hört ihr die Kinder weinen. Eine psychogenetische Geschichte der Kind- heit. *[Do you hear children crying? A psycho-genetic history of childhood]* Frankfurt am Main: Suhrkamp.

Dreitzel, Hans-Peter (1992): Reflexive Sinnlichkeit. Mensch, Umwelt, Gestalttherapie. *[Reflexive sensuality. Man, environment, gestalt therapy]* Köln: EHP.

Fischer-Lichte, Erika/Wulf, Christoph (Eds.) (2001): Theorien des Performativen. *[Theories of the performative]* Paragrana. Internationale Zeitschrift für historische Anthropologie 10, iss. 1. *[International magazine for historic anthropology]* Berlin: Akademie.

Flitner, Andreas (1963): Die pädagogische Anthropologie inmitten der Wissenschaften vom Menschen. *[Pedagogic anthropology within the humanities]* In: Flitner, Andreas (Ed.): Wege zur pädagogischen Anthropologie. *[Pathways to pedagogic anthropology]* Heidelberg: Quelle & Meyer, pp. 218–226.

Gadamer, Hans-Georg/Vogler, Paul (Eds.) (1972): Neue Anthropologie: Biologische Anthropologie. 2 Bände. *[New anthropology: Biological anthropology. 2 vol.]* Munich: dtv.

Gadamer, Hans-Georg/Vogler, Paul (Eds.) (1973): Neue Anthropologie: Kulturanthropologie. *[New anthropology: Cultural anthropology]* Munich: dtv.

Gadamer, Hans-Georg/Vogler, Paul (Eds.) (1975): Neue Anthropologie: Philosophische Anthropologie. 2 Bände. *[New anthropology: Philosophical anthropology. 2 vol.]* Munich: dtv.

Gadamer, Hans-Georg (Ed.) (1979): Der Mensch ohne Hand oder die Zerstörung der menschlichen Ganzheit. *[The human being without hands or the destruction of human wholeness]* Munich: dtv.

Gebauer, Gunter (Ed.) (1989): Historische Anthropologie. Zum Problem der Humanwissenschaften heute oder Versuche einer Neubegründung. *[Historic anthropology. On the problem of the humanities today or attempts for a new rationale]* Reinbek bei Hamburg: Rowohlt.

Gehring, Petra (2004): Es blinkt, es denkt. Die bildgebenden und weltbildgebenden Verfahren der Neurowissenschaft. *[It blinks, it thinks. The processes of creating images and world concepts in neuroscience]* In: Philosophische Rundschau 51, iss. 4, pp. 273–293.

Gerner, Berthold (1986): Einführung in die pädagogische Anthropologie. 2. Auflage. *[Introduction to pedagogic anthropology. 2nd ed.]* Darmstadt: Wissenschaftliche Buchgesellschaft.

Hamann, Bruno (2005): Pädagogische Anthropologie. Theorien – Modelle – Strukturen. Eine Einführung. 4. Auflage. *[Pedagogic anthropology. Theories – models – structures. An introduction. 4th ed.]* Frankfurt am Main: Peter Lang.

Hierdeis, Helmwart/Schratz, Michael (Eds.) (1992): Mit den Sinnen begreifen. *[Comprehension through the senses]* Wien: Österreichischer Studienverlag.

Hoffmann-Axthelm, Dieter (1987): Sinnesarbeit. Nachdenken über Wahrnehmung. *[Sensory work. Thoughts on perception]* Frankfurt am Main and New York: Campus.

Kamper, Dietmar (1994): Neue Ansätze zu einer pädagogischen Anthropologie. *[New Approaches toward a pedagogic anthropology]* In: Wulf, Christoph and Jörg Zirfas (Eds.): Theorien und Konzepte der pädagogischen Anthropologie. *[Theories & concepts of pedagogic anthropology]* Donauwörth: Ludwig Auer, pp. 193–206.

Kamper, Dietmar (1995): Anthropologie, pädagogische. *[Anthropology, pedagogic]* In: Lenzen, Dieter and Klaus Mollenhauer (Eds.) (1995): Enzyklopädie Erziehungswissenschaft 1. *[Encyclopedia of educational science 2nd ed.]* Stuttgart: Klett, pp. 311–316.

Kamper, Dietmar/Wulf, Christoph (Eds.) (1984): Das Schwinden der Sinne. *[Waning of the senses]* Frankfurt am Main: Suhrkamp.

Kant, Immanuel (1787/1967): Kritik der reinen Vernunft. *[Critique of pure reason]* Hamburg: Meiner.

Kant, Immanuel (1790): Kritik der Urteilskraft. *[A critique of judgment]* Berlin and Libau: Lagarde and Friedrich.

Kant, Immanuel (1977): Anthropologie in pragmatischer Hinsicht. *[Anthropology from a pragmatic point of view]* In: Weischedel, Wilhelm (Ed.): Kant, Immanuel: Schriften zur Anthropologie, Geschichtsphilosophie, Politik und Pädagogik. *[Immanuel Kant: Writings on anthropology, historic philosophy, politics and pedagogy]* Edition of works vol. XII. Frankfurt am Main: Suhrkamp, pp. 395–690.

Kasten, Ingrid/Wulf, Christoph (Eds.) (1998): Jenseits. [Beyond] Paragrana. Internationale Zeitschrift für historische Anthropologie 7. *[International magazine for historic anthropology 7, issue 2.]* Berlin: Akademie.

Koch, Sabine C. (2011): Embodiment. Der Einfluss von Eigenbewegung auf Affekt, Einstellung und Kognition. *[The influence of self-generated motion on feelings, attitude and cognition]* Berlin: Logos.

Köpping, Klaus-Peter/Wulf, Christoph/Papenburg, Bettina (Eds.) (2005): Körpermaschinen – Maschinen-körper. *[Body machine – machine body]* Paragrana. Internationale Zeitschrift für historische Anthropologie 14, iss. 2. Berlin: Akademie.

Kranich, Ernst-Michael (2003): Der innere Mensch und sein Leib. Eine Anthropologie. *[The inner person and his body]* Stuttgart: Freies Geistesleben.

Kükelhaus, Hugo/zur Lippe, Rudolf (1984): Entfaltung der Sinne. *[Unfolding the senses]* Frankfurt am Main: Fischer-Taschenbuch.

Kükelhaus, Hugo (1986): Fassen, Fühlen, Bilden. *[Grasping, feeling, forming]* Köln: Gaia.

Langeveld, Martinus Jan (1964): Studien zur Anthropologie des Kindes. 2. Auflage. *[Studies on the anthropology of the child]* Tübingen: Niemeyer.

Lassahn, Rudolf (1983): Pädagogische Anthropologie. Eine historische Einführung. *[Pedagogic anthropology. A historical introduction]* Heidelberg: Quelle and Meyer.

Leber, Stefan (1993): Die Menschenkunde der Waldorfpädagogik. *[The study of the human being in Waldorf education]* Stuttgart: Freies Geistesleben.

Lenzen, Dieter (1989): Anthropologie, historische. *[Anthropology, historic]* In: Lenzen, Dieter (Ed.): Pädagogische Grundbegriffe, Band 1. *[Basic pedagogic concepts. Vol.1]* Reinbek: Rowohlt, pp. 78–82.

Lenzen, Dieter/Mattenklott, Gert (Eds.) (1997): Der Mann. *[Man]* Paragrana. Internationale Zeitschrift für historische Anthropologie 6, iss. 2. Berlin: Akademie.

Liebau, Eckart/Miller-Kipp, Gisela/Wulf, Christoph (Eds.) (1999): Metamorphosen des Raums. *[Metamorphoses of space]* Weinheim: Beltz.

Liechti, Martin (2000): Erfahrungen am eigenen Leibe. Taktil-kinästhetische Sinneserfahrung als Prozess des Weltbegreifens. *[Body experiences. Tactile-kinesthetic sense-experience as a process of understanding the world]* Heidelberg: Winter.

Liedke, Max (1972): Evolution und Erziehung. Ein Beitrag zur integrativen Pädagogischen Anthropologie. *[Evolution and education. A contribution to pedagogic anthropology]* Göttingen: Vandenhoeck & Ruprecht.

Lippitz, Wilfried/Plaum, Jürgen (1981): Tasten, Gestalten, Genießen. *[Touching, forming, enjoying]* Königstein: Scriptor.

Loch, Werner (1965): Der pädagogische Sinn der anthropologischen Betrachtungsweise. *[The pedagogic meaning of the anthropological approach]* In: Bildung und Erziehung 18, iss. 3, pp. 164–180.

Löscher, Wolfgang (Ed.) (1994): Vom Sinn der Sinne. *[The meaning of the senses]* Munich: Don-Bosco.

Maelicke, Alfred (Ed.) (1990): Vom Reiz der Sinne. *[On the stimulation [also: lure] of the senses]* Weinheim: VCH.

Marotzki, Winfried/Masschelein, Jan/Schäfer, Alfred (Eds.) (1998): Anthropologische Markierungen. Herausforderungen pädagogischen Denkens. *[Anthropological markings. Challenges of pedagogic thought]* Weinheim: Beltz.

Meinberg, Eckart (1988): Das Menschenbild der modernen Erziehungswissenschaft. *[The concept of the human being in modern educational science]* Darmstadt: Wissenschaftliche Buchgesellschaft.

Mertens, Gerd (1998): Die Bedeutung der Bioanthropologie Gehlens und Plessners für die Pädagogik. [The pedagogic significance of Gehlen's and Plessner's bio-anthropology] In: Marotzki, Winfried Jan Masschelein and Alfred Schäfer (Eds.) (1998): Anthropologische Markierungen. Herausforderungen pädagogischen Denkens. [Anthropological markings. Challenges of pedagogic thought] Weinheim: Beltz, pp. 45–54.

Michel, Karl Markus/Wieser, Harald (Eds.) (1977): Kursbuch 49. Sinnlichkeiten. [Sensualisms] Berlin: Kursbuch.

Mollenhauer, Klaus/Wulf, Christoph (Eds.) (1996): Aisthesis, Ästhetik. Zwischen Wahrnehmung und Bewusstsein. [Aisthesis, aesthetics. Between perception and consciousness] Weinheim: Beltz.

Pieper, Hans-Joachim (1993): Die Sinnhaftigkeit der Sinne. [Meaningfulness of the senses] In: Pädagogische Rundschau 47, iss. 6, pp. 637–657.

Pleines, Jürgen-Eckhardt (1976): Über die anthropologische Betrachtungsweise in der modernen Pädagogik. [On the anthropological approach in modern pedagogy] In: Pleines, Jürgen-Eckhardt (Ed.): Mensch und Erziehung. [Man and education] Kastellaun: Henn, pp. 187–210.

Plessner, Helmuth (1965): Die Stufen des Organischen und der Mensch. Einleitung in die philosophische Anthropologie. 2. Auflage. [Stages of organic development and the human being. An introduction to philosophic anthropology] Berlin: De Gruyter.

Plessner, Helmuth (1980): Die Einheit der Sinne. Grundlinien einer Ästhesiologie des Geistes. In: Plessner, Helmuth (Ed.): Gesammelte Schriften Band 3. [The unity of the senses. An outline of an aesthesiology of the spirit, in: Plessner, Helmuth: CW vol. 3] Frankfurt am Main: Suhrkamp, pp. 7–315.

Rifkin, Jeremy (2000): Access. Das Verschwinden des Eigentums. [The age of access. The disappearance of possessions] Frankfurt am Main and New York: Campus.

Rittelmeyer, Christian (1994): Schulbauten positiv gestalten. Wie Schüler Farben und Formen erleben. [Positive school architecture. How students experience forms and colors] Wiesbaden and Berlin: Bauverlag.

Rittelmeyer, Christian (2001): Wozu Lernen mit allen Sinnen? [Learning with all the senses: Why?] In: Bildung und Erziehung 54, iss. 2, pp. 193–206.

Rittelmeyer, Christian (2002): Pädagogische Anthropologie des Leibes. Biologische Voraussetzungen der Erziehung und Bildung. [Pedagogic anthropology of the body. Biological premises of education] Munich and Weinheim: Juventa.

Rittelmeyer, Christian (2005): "Über die ästhetische Erziehung des Menschen." Eine Einführung in Friedrich Schillers pädagogische Anthropologie. [On the aesthetic education of man. An Introduction to Friedrich Schiller's Pedagogic Anthropology] Munich and Weinheim: Juventa.

Rittelmeyer, Christian (2012): Vom Nutzen und Nachteil der Gehirnforschung für die Pädagogik. [On the usefulness and shortcomings of brain research for pedagogy] In: Bilstein, Johannes and Micha Brumlik (Eds.): Die Bildung des Körpers. [The education (also: formation) of the body] pp. 233–246.

Rittelmeyer, Christian (2013): Architektur. [Architecture] In: Wulf, Christoph and Zirfas, Jörg (Eds.): Handbuch Pädagogische Anthropologie. [Handbook of pedagogic anthropology] Wiesbaden: Springer.

Roth, Heinrich (1965): Empirische Pädagogische Anthropologie. [Empirical pedagogic anthropology] In: Zeitschrift für Pädagogik [Magazine for pedagogy] 11, iss. 3, pp. 207–221.

Roth, Heinrich (1966/1971): Pädagogische Anthropologie. 2 Bände. [Pedagogic anthropology, 2 vol.] Hannover: Schroedel.

Rousseau, Jean-Jacques (1962/1971): Emile oder über die Erziehung. [Emile or on education] Paderborn: Ferdinand Schöningh.

Rumpf, Horst (1981): Die übergangene Sinnlichkeit. [Ignored sensuality] Munich: Juventa.

Rumpf, Horst (1994): Mit allen Sinnen lernen? Vorschläge zur Unterscheidung. [Learning with all the senses? Suggestions for distinctions] In: Musik und Bildung [Music and education] 26, iss. 2, pp. 5–9.

Scheuerl, Hans (1982): Pädagogische Anthropologie: eine historische Einführung. [Pedagogic anthropology: A historic introduction] Stuttgart: Kohlhammer.

Scheurle, Hans-Jürgen (1984): Die Gesamtsinnesorganisation. [The wholistic organization of all the senses] Stuttgart and New York: Thieme.

Schiller, Friedrich (1989): Über die ästhetische Erziehung des Menschen in einer Reihe von Briefen. Zuerst veröffentlicht [On the aesthetic education of the human being in a series of letters. First published] in "Die Horen" (1795). In: Schiller, Friedrich (Ed.): Sämtliche Werke. Band 5. Erzählungen, theoretische Schriften. [Collected works (CW) vol. 5. Tales, theoretical writings] Munich: Hanser, pp. 570–669.

Schmidt, Horst-Michael (1982): Sinnlichkeit und Verstand. Zur philosophischen und poetologischen Begründung von Erfahrung und Urteil in der deutschen Aufklärung. [Sensuality and reason. On the philosophical and poetological rationale of experience and judgment in German enlightenment] Munich: Fink.

Schulze, Holger (Ed.) (2007): Klanganthropologie. Performativität – Imagination – Narration. [Sound anthropology. Performativity – imagination – narration] Paragrana. Internationale Zeitschrift für historische Anthropologie. [Paragrana – International magazine for historic anthropology] 16, iss. 2. Berlin: Akademie.

Serres, Michel (1993): Die fünf Sinne. [The five senses] Frankfurt am Main: Suhrkamp.

Pedagogic Anthropology in Educational Science and Waldorf Education

Steiner, Rudolf (1907): Die Erziehung des Kindes vom Gesichtspunkte der Geisteswissenschaft. *[The education of the child from the point of view of spiritual science]* In: Steiner, Rudolf (Ed.) (1987): Lucifer – Gnosis. Grundlegende Aufsätze zur Anthroposophie und Berichte aus den Zeitschriften «Luzifer» und «Lucifer – Gnosis» 1903–1908. Rudolf Steiner GA 34. Dornach: Rudolf Steiner Verlag.

Steiner, Rudolf (1977/1919): Freie Schule und Dreigliederung. *[Independent school and the threefold organization]* In: Steiner, Rudolf (Ed.) (1977): Aufsätze über die Dreigliederung des sozialen Organismus und zur Zeitlage 1915–1921. *[Essays on the threefold organization of the body social and on contemporary issues 1915–1921]* GA 24. Dornach: Rudolf Steiner Verlag, pp. 27–33.

Straus, Erwin (1956): Vom Sinn der Sinne. *[On the sense of the senses,* 2nd *ed.]* 2. Auflage. Berlin: Springer.

Tenorth, Heinz-Elmar (2000): "Vom Menschen" – Historische, pädagogische und andere Perspektiven einer "Anthropologie" der Erziehung. *[On the human being – Historic, pedagogic and other perspectives of an anthropology of education]* In: *Zeitschrift für Pädagogik* 46, iss. 6, pp. 905–925.

Uher, Johanna (Ed.) (1995): Pädagogische Anthropologie und Evolution. *[Pedagogic anthropology and evolution]* Erlangen und Nürnberg: Univ.- Bibliothek.

Ullrich, Heiner (1991): Waldorfpädagogik und okkulte Weltanschauung. Eine bildungsphilosophische und geistesgeschichtliche Auseinandersetzung mit der Anthropologie Rudolf Steiners. 3. Auflage. *[Waldorf education and occult worldview. An educational-philosophical and historic-cognitive discussion of Rudolf Steiner's anthroposophy. 3rd ed.]* Weinheim, Munich: Juventa.

Wagner, Hans-Josef (2002): Wilhelm von Humboldt: "Anthropologie und Theorie der Menschenkenntnis." *[Anthropology and the theory of human nature]* Darmstadt: Wissenschaftliche Buchgesellschaft.

Wulf, Christoph (Ed.) (1992): Miniatur. [Miniature] Paragrana. Internationale Zeitschrift für historische Anthropologie 1, iss. 1. Berlin: Akademie.

Wulf, Christoph (1996): Anthropologisches Denken in der Pädagogik 1750–1850. *[Anthropological thought in pedagogy]* Weinheim: Beltz.

Wulf, Christoph (Ed.) (1997): Vom Menschen. Handbuch der Historischen Anthropologie. *[On man. Handbook of historic anthropology]* Weinheim: Beltz.

Wulf, Christoph (Ed.) (2000): Metaphern des Unmöglichen. *[Metaphors of the impossible]* Paragrana. Internationale Zeitschrift für historische Anthropologie 9, iss. 1. Berlin: Akademie.

Wulf, Christoph (2001): Einführung in die Anthropologie der Erziehung. *[Introduction to anthropology of education]* Weinheim and Basel: Beltz and Gelberg.

Wulf, Christoph (2004): Anthropologie, pädagogische. *[Anthropology, pedagogic]* In: Benner, Dietrich and Jürgen Oelkers (Eds.): Historisches Wörterbuch der Pädagogik. *[Historic dictionary of pedagogy]* Weinheim and Basel: Beltz, pp. 33–57.

Wulf, Christoph/Kamper, Dietmar/Trabant, Jürgen (Eds.) (1993): Das Ohr als Erkenntnisorgan. *[The ear as a cognitive organ]* Paragrana. Internationale Zeitschrift für historische Anthropologie 2, issues 1–2. Berlin: Akademie.

Wulf, Christoph/Poser, Hans/Kamper, Dietmar (Eds.) (1995): Aisthesis. [Aisthesis] Paragrana. Internationale Zeitschrift für historische Anthropologie 4, iss. 1. Berlin: Akademie.

Wulf, Christoph/Zirfas, Jörg (Eds.) (1994): Theorien und Konzepte der pädagogischen Anthropologie. *[Theories and concepts of pedagogic anthropology]* Donauwörth: Auer.

Wulf, Christoph/Zirfas, Jörg (Eds.) (2013): Handbuch pädagogische Anthropologie. *[Handbook of pedagogic anthropology]* Wiesbaden: Springer.

Zirfas, Jörg (1998): Die Frage nach dem Wesen des Menschen. Zur pädagogischen Anthropologie der 60er Jahre. *[Inquiry into human nature. On pedagogic anthropology in the sixties]* In: Marotzki, Winfried Jan Masschelein and Alfred Schäfer (Eds.) (1998): Anthropologische Markierungen. Herausforderungen pädagogischen Denkens. *[Anthropological markings. Challenging pedagogic thought]* Weinheim: Beltz, pp. 55–81.

Zur Lippe, Rudolf (1987): Sinnenbewusstsein. Grundlegung einer anthropologischen Ästhetik. *[Sensory awareness. Foundations for an anthropological aesthetics]* Reinbek: Rowohlt.

FREEDOM AS AN ANTHROPOLOGICAL PERSPECTIVE
On the Concept of Man in Waldorf Education

Jost Schieren

Abiding by a long scientific tradition, pedagogic anthropology asks habitually: What is Man? And: Why and to what aim should he be educated? All pedagogic action—consciously or unconsciously—is based on and guided by a concept of man; it was and is the task of pedagogic anthropology to bring such concepts or assumptions into conscious awareness and to reflect upon them critically. In this endeavor, it has to examine its own claim, namely whether it indeed operates descriptively and which parameters define the descriptive approaches to man. Or does it operate normatively and dare to stipulate a goal image of the *ideal* human being and thus stigmatize divergences and flaws? In the Renaissance, the *subject* was discovered; enlightenment emphasized rational perspectives while the German classical period worked with ideal types in their concept of the human being up to Rousseau, who presented the idea of natural goodness of the human being; going through all these stages, occidental thought has slowly developed a basic concept, which understands the human being as subject-centered, rationally oriented, and as striving for autonomy. In fact, European humanism is at the same time a *human-centered* approach that seems to construct a universally valid concept of man, essentially creating a mirror image of his own cultural paradigms, puzzle-like, through transcendental-philosophical self-reflection.

However, this ideal typology of universal man, inspired by one's own reflected image, overlooks all that, which falls outside the categories of reflection, subject, and autonomy—the *Other*. This *Other* may appear as differences in consciousness or culture, as embodiments, natural phenomena, or in animal forms—and up to today it has been enslaved with power and might, embattled, exploited, polluted, and, at best, *educated*. But it is always rational, autonomous man's claim to power, which tries to form the world in his image and measure. Michel Foucault has firmly taken a stand against this approach. As Nietzsche speaks of the death of God, so Foucault speaks of ending and dying, of the death of man as a human being: "We do not need to get upset about the end of the human being; it is only a special case of a much more general process of dying. I do not mean the death of god here, but the death of the subject, of the subject as the origin and basis of knowledge, of freedom, of history" (Foucault 2001, vol. 1.).

1 Historic pedagogic anthropology

According to Foucault, contemporary pedagogic anthropology (which can no longer be termed current) is of central referential importance (Zirfas, 1998, p. 6). Since the 1990s, it defines itself now as a *historic-cultural anthropology* (Wulf 2009; Wulf, Kamper 2002; Wulf, Zirfas 1994, 2014; Zirfas 2004); this new anthropology no longer asks "What is man?" but rather: "How is the human being perceived in different historic and cultural perspectives?" Historic anthropology does not presume to make *authoritative* statements about the human being. With this stance, it critiques previous traditions of anthropological thought, such as philosophical (Gehlen 1993; Plessner 1981; Scheler 1976) or phenomenological approaches (Bollnow 1965; Langeveld 1964; Nohl 1929) or those that are trying to integrate various scientific disciplines (biology, psychology, sociology, etc.), like the work of Heinrich Roth (Roth 1966–1971). These traditional anthropological approaches have one thing in common: their object, i.e., the human being, is not yet lost; and while they operate with open-ended questions, they still go from the assumption that one could possibly come up with answers. Meanwhile, such assumptions have been systematically dismantled. Wulf writes: The claim of pedagogic anthropology, to furnish valid statements about *the* human being, *the* child, or *the* educator, has not been—and in principle cannot be—fulfilled. Such universalistic claims are in need of historic, cultural, and epistemic relativization, otherwise they would appear to be illicit fiction and phantasms that denote claims to power and dominance (Wulf 2002, p. 17). Historic Anthropology therefore is always a *negative pedagogic anthropology* (Liebau 2012; Wimmer 1998), because it does not claim to come up with normative, "positive" characteristics of man, such as language or thought, because such criteria "lead to deviances from the norm being classified as 'inhuman'" (Liebau 2012, p. 3).

Accordingly, Wimmer points out: "In view of this critique, Anthropology can no longer be conceived as a positive or even normative science, nor as an integrative science or a philosophical anthropology – it can only constitute a deconstruction of thought structures, in which it discredited itself" (Wimmer 1998, p. 92).

When historic anthropology makes statements about the human being, they have only heuristic, not determinative, function, which is why Zirfas speaks of a "heuristic pedagogic anthropology" (2004, p. 34).

New fields of research and reflection open up for anthropological thought, as statements that favored generalities and basic principles about the nature of the human being are abandoned. On one hand, systematic reflection and criticism of historic, sociological, cultural, and political affairs, in view of currently existing anthropologies, present a wide area of research. Research topics are coming into focus that so far have been quite neglected. These topics refer to structures and areas that indeed cannot be subsumed into the enlightenment ideals of rationality, autonomy, reflection, and subjectivity; they are beyond the reach of such ideals, and thus they also cannot be directly contained by such terms. The brothers Hartmut and Gernot Böhme call it the "*Other* of Reason" (Böhme, Böhme 1983) and write: "The *Other* of Reason: Seen from the perspective of reason it is that which is irrational, ontologically that which is unreal, morally it is that which is indecent, and logically that which is illogical. The *Other* of reason is, content-wise, that which is nature, the human body, imagination, desire, feelings – or better: all that which reason has not been able to appropriate" (ibid., p. 13). This shift is not new—the representatives of the romantic movement already turned their back on the rationality demands of the classic and enlightenment periods. In anthropology, this shift of perspective results mainly from ethical concerns. Indeed, no repetition of the romantic movement is intended: "The issue is not the re-enchantment of the world nor complete enlightenment, but a way of thinking that can experience its own boundaries in aware perception. The impulse to want it all crashes against the acknowledgement that there is no 'all,' namely that its presence is not enforceable and that it does not yield to anything" (Kamper 1995, p. 14).

Previously, the educational discussion largely neglected these anthropological aspects; it was heavily weighted toward rationality and cognition. But these anthropological factors are now newly coming under consideration, referencing the "corporeal, historic, subjective and cultural aspects of man" (Liebau et al. 2003, p. 7). It is remarkable that a stronger interest in cultural education ensued after the discourse of historic anthropology—also as a result of constraining educational views of PISA and OECD.

In particular, there is more weight given to topics of the human body, man's corporeality (Zirfas 2004, p. 85ff.), and to the sphere of perception and the human senses, while paying attention to phenomena of unavailability and contingency (Wuchterl 2011).

2 Waldorf education

What is Waldorf education's position against the backdrop of this more recent anthropological discussion? First, let it be noted that it does not appear in this discussion at all, which from an outside perspective seems astonishing, because at first glance the educational practice in Waldorf schools seems to attend quite comprehensively to all fields of interest and research within current pedagogic anthropology—certainly more so than the public school system, which is under pressure from a political system that fell prey to the materialistic economic dictate to produce faster results, higher achievements, and to comply with demands for continuous evaluation and testing. The actual educational program of Waldorf education contains surprisingly many topics that are being discussed in the more recent anthropological discourse and that are also called for in the name of cultural education. The following aspects shall serve as examples:

Social Aspects: Waldorf schools are known to make an effort to do particular justice to every single student's personality. Individual student assessment reports replace normative (graded) evaluation procedures. School years cannot be repeated. Characteristically, no selection is performed based on achievement. The individual learning process of each student is taken into account. Moreover, within the teacher's collegium, hierarchical structures are eliminated so that it operates on a basis of equality in communication, reminiscent of Habermas's "authority-free discourse" (Habermas 1981). Priority is given to the concept of a community of students, parents, and teachers (Bohnsack, Leber 1996).

Corporeal Aspects: Physical learning plays a central role in Waldorf education; it was one of the first and is to this day one of the few pedagogic approaches that involve the body in the process of learning. The development and education of the senses and experiential learning are core aspects of early childhood Waldorf education reaching into the school years. The ideal of each Waldorf school is to actively engage a school physician in its teacher collegium; this in fact shows that the attentive observation of bodily processes is an integral part of the Waldorf pedagogic concept. Moreover, the arts and crafts are accorded the same importance as cognitive subjects.

Emotional Aspects: External observers often regard Waldorf education as a feel-good, cuddly, or fun type of pedagogy. From the perspective of an academic track high school with selective achievement criteria this may well appear to be the case. Having stated that, Waldorf education can overall demonstrate above-average graduation results. It distinguishes itself in giving strong consideration to the emotional needs of the students and in striving to establish an atmosphere of learning that is both positive and motivating. The much-maligned Doctrine of the Temperaments (Ullrich 2015, p. 115) does not aim at categorizing and typecasting students, as so many critics assume, but serves the goal of perceiving individual emotional moods and dispositions so they can be taken into consideration.

Cultural Aspects: On one hand, Waldorf education is a product of European culture with notable references to ideas of the classics and of idealism. On the other hand, its curriculum reflects the high importance Waldorf education places on the involvement with other cultures. After decades of functioning, rather like a European export product, Waldorf education has by now developed a relatively high autonomous profile in more than 30 countries and is certainly able to adapt to and integrate itself into other cultures. In Israel, for example, Waldorf schools operate in Jewish, Islamic, and Christian contexts, each with distinct characteristics. In Asian countries as well, there are Waldorf schools with noticeable Hindu or Buddhist backgrounds. Moreover, several Waldorf schools in the United States and also South America operate within indigenous populations. There is hardly any other European concept of pedagogy that has spread so broadly across different cultures. Meanwhile the first intercultural Waldorf schools are also appearing in Germany. This is a rather late development, which is less due to Waldorf pedagogic concepts, than to the legal and economic constraints in Germany and many other countries that required Waldorf schools to operate there exclusively as tuition-based private schools. These constraints resulted in an unwanted yet unavoidable selection of parents, who are privileged in their social status and educational background.

Other aspects indicative of a closeness to topics of current historic pedagogic anthropology and cultural education include: the integration of rituals into daily school life, an aesthetic design of lesson plans, learning environment and school facilities (Rittelmeyer 1994, 2013), the overall performative understanding of lesson design (Sommer in Chapter 5), and also includes the (not necessarily verbal) honoring and acknowledgment of reflexively transparent structures of knowledge—*tacit knowing* (Polanyi 1985).

In fact, in some text passages issued by scientific circles in the sphere of historic anthropology and cultural education, the diction sounds remarkably similar to statements of Rudolf Steiner. There is talk of "the process character of all educational activity" (Liebau et al. 2003, p. 8) and we read that "education always deals with change, with a becoming and that which is becoming" (ibid.). Correspondingly, Steiner says in reference to the development of Waldorf education: "In fact, it is of central importance that we can draw on the life-filled observation of the becoming [*developing*] human being for devising not only our methods of instruction but also, above all, for creating our lesson plans and setting educational goals" (Steiner 1998, p. 167). And Liebau writes: "The corporeal aspect [*of the child's development*] provides the foundation for pedagogic action. [...] The body states (such as waking, sleeping; consciousness, rapture, dream; health, illness, etc.) are always tied in with visible or invisible motion and conscious or unconscious perception. Sensory perceptions, feelings, thought and judgment processes are constitutive parts of human action. [...] The dimension of corporeality points to the unity of body, soul and spirit" (Liebau 2012, p. 31). The foundational anthropological deliberations of Rudolf Steiner in his lectures on "The General Study of Man as the Foundation for Pedagogy" (Steiner 1980) orbit around very same body of topics.

Yet, even though Waldorf education touches upon many central topics of contemporary historic pedagogic anthropology and cultural education, it has either been ignored in the scientific discussion or critically rejected. Here a strange ambivalence comes into view: The praxis of Waldorf education by now offers a rather successful alternative to common public schools that has proven its worth for more than ninety years. Next to Montessori pedagogy, it has developed worldwide into one of the most widespread reform pedagogical models. However, its theoretical background, particularly its fundamental anthropological concepts, continues to be highly controversial. The discourse within educational science meanwhile deals with the practice of Waldorf education on an empiric basis. Yet within the general scientific discourse, the verdict of ideological orientation (Prange 1985; Ullrich 1986) remains unchanged and recently was once again reiterated in identical phrasing by Heiner Ullrich (Ullrich 2015). A comparatively high acceptance of Waldorf educational practice is irreconcilably juxtaposed to a withering critique of its theory. Largely, this appears to be based in the claim to universal validity and truth, which Rudolf Steiner and also many of his followers seem to connect with anthroposophy.

Still at the beginning of the 20th century, these kinds of claims to universality were customary in German academic philosophy; such claims constituted a regular, accepted form of argumentative defense of one's own theses; in our time, this form of argument has become obsolete and inacceptable. The media tried to deal with this dilemma by writing about possible options such as "Waldorf schools without Steiner" (Centmayer 2007)[1] or "Waldorf light" (Schröder 2013).[2] However, this brings up the question, whether we lose the actual core substance of Waldorf education when we distance ourselves from the founder of Waldorf education and thus from the concept of the human being in anthroposophy, which provides the foundation for Waldorf education. Therefore, let us pose the reverse question: Can we not consider Waldorf education's science-abstinence and its immunity to scientific discourse regarding its theoretic foundations more as a habitual stance, rather than a structurally immanent aspect? Is it not possible to foster both critical *and* discourse within educational science in reference to the theory that underlies Waldorf education?

2.1 On the concept of the human being in Waldorf education

At a first look at the concept of the human being in Waldorf education, as it is offered to the public (e.g., via internet in the self-presentations of some Waldorf schools or also in the pedagogy textbooks on teaching practice in the higher grades of academic track high schools), we often gain the impression that it is a highly complicated, hermetic concept that is very difficult to understand. Without further explanations or details, they often talk about a "wholistic" or "three-partite" concept of man that is composed of body, soul, and spirit. Then we encounter the terms *physical body, etheric body, astral body,* and *Self* or *Self-body.* Concepts such as *reincarnation* and *karma* are mentioned as anthropological base categories and constitute unreasonable impositions in the light of educational science.[3] Faced with the challenge of discussing anthroposophy or Waldorf education in the context of contemporary anthropological theories, such portrayals of the concept of the human being in Waldorf education are highly prone to misunderstanding; they appear misleading and, in that form, ultimately unworthy of discussion. But neither writings and lectures of Waldorf education's founder, Rudolf Steiner, nor the publications of his students prove to be helpful in that respect. Anthroposophy, as established by Rudolf Steiner, presents itself as a metaphysical model for explaining the world, which claims universal dominion of insight on the basis of initiatic knowledge that cannot be verified. Anthroposophy offers authoritative essentialist and ontological thought patterns, which form the foundation for the orthodox mindset within the tradition of Waldorf education. Throughout Waldorf literature, there is talk of the *being-ness* of man, of *cognitive essence,* of *developmental laws,* etc., without any recourse to scientific reasoning. From a perspective of historic anthropology, the extant theoretic framework of Waldorf education and its anthropological concepts must appear anachronistic and largely impervious to critical self-reflection. This is in fact the current state of discourse from a perspective of educational science (Prange 1985, 2000; Skiera 2003; Ullrich 1986, 2015).

Any rapprochements and acknowledgments clearly refer to the practice of Waldorf education, which occasionally wrests positive remarks even from avowed critics. As a summary of his latest publication, which presents the ideological contamination of Waldorf education in rich detail, Ullrich writes: "By all means, Waldorf schools may be deemed successful" (Ullrich 2015, p. 172). Then he acknowledges "the manifold forms of furthering sensory capacities and artistic abilities" (Ullrich 2015, p. 174) and "the specific significance of an aesthetic approach to the world" for "an individual process of development" (ibid.); Skiera (2003, p. 265) follows along a similar line of argument.

2.2 Capacity for freedom

How can we approach the issue of partial acknowledgment of educational practice vs. a comprehensive criticism of the theoretical understructure of Waldorf education? Among the many variants and interpretations of Rudolf Steiner's anthroposophy that provide the theoretical background for Waldorf education, so far the most established and best known is that of a theosophical-metaphysical spiritual vision. In regard to this approach, critics and followers of anthroposophy are not far apart. Helmut Zander has presented a comprehensive critical analysis of anthroposophy (Zander 2007). He sees in Steiner's work a mainly eclectic and mystically charged rehash of existing spiritual schools, especially from the sphere of Theosophy, which is dressed up by Steiner's claim to genuine initiatic knowledge. In Zander's assessment, the practical applications of anthroposophy (agriculture, medicine, Waldorf education) are merely attempts to spread theosophical teachings through civilization and to popularize them. Steiner's followers defend anthroposophy against this historicizing and deconstructive criticism by trying to prove Zander's errors in reception and interpretation and by emphasizing the authenticity of the initiate Rudolf Steiner. In this process, they evidence the same metaphysical universalism of which Zander accuses Steiner. Thus, both sides, the critics of Steiner and his followers, feed off the same Steiner image, just with reversed valences.

This discussion pays hardly any attention to the fact that Steiner's works traditionally produced also other variants and interpretations than solely that of Steiner as a dogmatic esotericist. Up to the end of the 19th century, Steiner's early works are essentially epistemological in nature and focus on critique of cognition. On the basis of a meticulously developed theory of cognition, he created his *Philosophy of Freedom* (see Wagemann in Chapter 2). In his early works, the essential core of Steiner's thought is the perspective of a capacity for freedom of the human being. The entire anthroposophical approach is aligned toward this core, which provides at the same time the basic orientation for all thought and action in Waldorf education. This idea of freedom is generally not brought into sharp relief—not even within the internal anthroposophical discourse. What is rather cast into the foreground (in part also by anthroposophists) is the teaching of a spiritual world. This constitutes a grave problem in regard to the reception of Steiner's work, which is perpetuated by critics and followers alike. If, in fact, anthroposophy would be at its core a doctrine of an existing—one has to add: *self-existent*—spiritual world, it would not offer much that is new. It would indeed be eclectic, because spiritually oriented concepts of the world have always been around.

The special characteristic of anthroposophy lies in Steiner's approach of connecting a spiritually oriented worldview with the dimension of human freedom. In a certain sense, Steiner has coined a new concept of spirit. He writes in his early work *Goethe's Theory of Knowledge: An Outline of the Epistemology of His Worldview*: "The cosmic matrix has poured itself fully into the world; it has not retreated from the world in order to direct it from outside, it powers the world from within; this matrix energy has not withheld itself from the world. Thought, and with it the human personality, is its highest form of manifestation within the reality of an ordinary life" (Steiner 1924, p. 98). This does not align with a classical metaphysical worldview. At its core, this is a statement that there is no spiritual essence that exists in and of itself outside of human consciousness processes. One might object that this may be epistemologically valid, but ontologically a spiritual essence does exist just like the creation that surrounds us—at least in anthroposophical views. But this argument itself is exactly the problem, because Steiner's epistemology aims fundamentally at overcoming the so-called naïve realism, i.e., the belief in a reality that exists without the participation of human cognition. Reality exists only insofar as the processes of human cognition constitute it. However, Steiner did not conceive of this construction of reality as a purely subjective act like constructivism does. While it depends on the individual, free act of human thinking, thought itself does not only have subjective significance for Steiner; rather, it is able to transmit an inter- and trans-subjective experience of reality.

In reference to the natural world, of evident reality, this line of argumentation generally is acceptable to most Anthroposophists and is probably not unknown to them. In reference to an assumed spiritual world, however, anthroposophical and Waldorf circles often afford themselves exactly that naïve realism, which Steiner so vehemently tried to overcome. The belief in a spiritual world that exists in and of itself lets them relapse into old concepts of spirituality. This is a naïve spiritual realism that actually was thought to be obsolete already in the era of enlightenment.[4] Moreover, the spiritual reality that Steiner variously describes has by now become an experience in the consciousness of modern man.

This conscious, autonomous approach is anchored in the method of soul introspection that Steiner developed in *Philosophy of Freedom* (1918). It is an observation of the experiences of the soul in the process of thinking. This is the reference point for Witzenmann, whose work receives little acknowledgment within anthropological circles. His work is fundamentally concerned with rendering Steiner's epistemological approach fertile for a new understanding of spirit.

3 Soul observation in the work of Herbert Witzenmann

Witzenmann reasons that anthroposophy is not primarily concerned with *contents* of consciousness, but rather with the *form* of consciousness. He speaks of "overcoming intellectualism" and writes: "The intellect itself likes to make use of thought processes for supplying communications about the spiritual world – unknown to itself – to satisfy emotional needs. The intellect uses procedural data that issue from the same source, whose origins lie outside of its understanding, in the interest of individual or group advantages." This kind of intellectual endeavor produces "neither individual nor cultural progress. A new kind of consciousness is not achieved by gathering information about the spiritual world, but only by gaining insight through one's own thoughtful observation" (Witzenmann 1998, p. 168). Here he exacts a high degree of autonomy and individualization in the discussion of Steiner's writings, which has so far found little consideration in the anthroposophical movement. The text-abiding, meditatively oriented study of Steiner's work is so far deemed to be the valid paradigm for its reception.

For Witzenmann, the essential leverage point in Steiner's work is his productive concept of reality, which also proves of significance for Waldorf education. Reality comes into existence only in the process of human cognition by joining perception and conceptual thinking. For this to occur, the ontological dimension of the world must annihilate itself, so to speak, within the organization of the human being.

Witzenmann describes the human sensory-nervous organization as a spirit-annihilating organ produced by ontological evolution; as such it dissolves the connective web of the world, confronting the human being with alienation, with the nothingness of sensory perception so that he can attain freedom, from where he can newly constitute reality in the process of cognition.[5] The sensory organization of the Human Being thus leads to a sort of point zero, upon which human cognition can unconditionally build. Steiner outlines in his *Philosophy of Freedom* that there are two different points of reference: on the one side perceptions, facilitated by the sensory organization, and on the other side the self-generated process of thinking. Introspective soul observation and meditative practice allow the human being to deal with these two poles of the human cognition process—perceiving and thinking—and to become aware of a new, freedom-based origination of the world and one's existence.

4 Perceiving and thinking

Both poles, perceiving and thinking, present each a different form of qualification. According to Witzenmann, dispositions (predispositions or tendencies of reality) are formed in the process of perceiving, in the encounter with the world. They are the result of the participation of human cognition in factual reconstruction, i.e., in the construction of distinct world designs; in this process of forming predispositions, concepts and ideas emerging from corresponding perceptions are integrated and individualized. In this vein, Witzenmann propounds that the dispositions (predispositions of reality) are "the result of co-individualizing concepts (*universalia*) concomitant with their metamorphosis-like adaptation to the conditions that present themselves in form of perceptions, which they can permeate" (Witzenmann 1988, p. 10). Accordingly, dispositions are formed in every encounter with the world that involves cognition. In this process, we experience the qualities inherent in the phenomena of the world. This aspect touches upon a central core of Steiner's thinking: Goethe's concept of knowledge.

4.1 Goethe's concept of knowledge or method of cognition

One characteristic of Goethe's approach to knowledge is his critical rejection of a self-absorbed and prejudiced formation of concepts. He finds fault with concepts that are more subject-oriented than object-oriented. In his essay "The Experiment as a Mediator between Subject and Object," he writes: "As soon as man becomes aware of the objects around him, he regards them in reference to himself. [...]. This very natural way of observing and assessing things seems to be as easy as it is necessary, and yet the human being is exposed to a thousand errors in this process, which often cause him embarrassment and embitterment in life" (Goethe 1988b, vol. 13, p. 10). With his everyday notions, man blocks himself from perceiving reality and from access to the world. "Man indeed gains more enjoyment in a thing—or better said, he *only* enjoys a thing if he imagines it and it fits into his sensibilities, and no matter how high he raises his own thought above common notions, however well he purifies it, it will usually ever remain just one type of notion" (Goethe 1988b, vol. 13, p. 15).

Goethe's critique of this kind of conceptualization concurs with the philosophy of Kant. On September 18, 1831, he writes in a letter to privy counselor Schultz: "I thank critical philosophy for making me aware of myself, that is an immense gain" (Goethe 1988a, vol. 4, p. 450). While he acknowledges Kant for successfully overcoming naïve realism, he then qualifies "but he never arrives at the object" (ibid.). With this statement, he gives expression to a limit of conceptualization that Kant himself perceived as well: "Laws are not inherent in the phenomena themselves, but only relative to the subject in whom the phenomena appear, insofar as he (the subject) is endowed with a mind; phenomena do not exist in and of themselves either, but they only exist relative to the same subject insofar as it is endowed with senses. Phenomena alone are only notions of things which exist in a state of being unknown, no matter what they may be in and of themselves. Yet as mere notions, they are not subject to any nexus law but alone that which dictates the force of interconnectivity" (Kant 1974, vol. 3, p. 156). Kant here expresses his conviction that human cognition cannot reach beyond itself and is subject to its own limitation. In this view, reality is merely a subjective mirror of one's own conceptualizations. Goethe also recognized this problem. Yet he did not stop there but wanted to transcend the self-relevance of human cognition. In that he distinguishes himself from Kant. Goethe was of the opinion that human cognition transcends its self-directed reflexivity by questioning his theoretic-conceptual matrix, breaking free from it and strengthening the capacity for observation and intuition.

Human cognition, in Goethe's sense, can transcend itself and develop into an organ of intuition; only then can it open up to the object side of the polarity, to that which is *other* (as described above). Goethe calls this process "intuitive judgment" (Schieren 1998) and he points out "that through the process of intuitively perceiving ever-creative nature, we become worthy of the mental participation in its creations" (Goethe 1988b, vol. 143, p. 30). Intuitive consciousness, in Goethe's sense, leads to genuine congress with the world, beyond self-reflectivity and subject-centeredness of the imagination. Thus, Goethe broadens the ideals of rationality and reason of the age of enlightenment. He is here concerned with precisely "that which lies beyond reason, the *other of reason*" (Böhme, Böhme 1983). At the same time, Goethe voices his criticism of the ideas of enlightenment, which, in his view, paid the price of losing the world for gaining the freedom of the subject. He writes about Schiller: "Schiller had joyfully absorbed Kant's philosophy of elevating the individual (subject) so high by seemingly constraining it. This philosophy facilitated the development the extraordinary gifts with which nature had endowed his (Schiller's) being, and at the peak of feeling freedom and self determination he was ungrateful toward the great mother, who certainly had not treated him shabbily" (Goethe 1988b, vol. 10, p. 539). In this view of Schiller's ideal of autonomy and individuality, Goethe preempts a core argument in Foucault's critique of enlightenment's ideas.

Rudolf Steiner squarely placed Waldorf education in a direct tradition of Goethean consciousness that relies on intuition and focuses on the world (Schieren 2010). Exploring the world and participating in it are a central motif. In Waldorf schools, children and adolescents are to be led toward a productive encounter with the world—that is, the didactic horizon—by integrating the cognitive participation in the construction of the phenomena of the world into their spectrum of abilities. Essentially, all special subject-specific didactic and methodological approaches of Waldorf education are designed to achieve this goal (e.g., focus on experience, perception, activity, aesthetic-creative approaches). Waldorf education is less concerned with accumulating abstract knowledge and concepts than with fostering of abilities that are being practiced in direct experiential contact with the world's phenomena.

4.2 *Thinking pole*

Yet, there is another part of the polarity—that of thinking—which is of importance in Steiner's epistemology of cognitive participation in reality. This is opposite to the pole of perceiving, it does not deal with encountering the world, but rather with the subject aspect in the process of cognition.

Here, too, there is a point zero of sorts, which must be the unconditional foundation of any unfurling into freedom. Tying in with Fichte's *fact-act*, Steiner delineates in *Philosophy of Freedom* that thinking depends solely on the individual thinker's impulse to act. Thinking must be brought forth individually. Nobody's insight can be obtained from outside (without one's own doing), but it is always the result of one's own activity (which may well be *stimulated* from without). Without such (self-willed) activity, no insight or learning can occur. This pertains to the one side *(of this polarity)*.

Moreover, thought activity based on individual impulses transcends itself when encountering self-evident thought contents ("concepts" in Steiner's terminology) in the process of thinking. This imbues the thought process with its content-related meaning. Steiner assumes that thinking is not entirely determined by history, biography, or culture, but that every concept actualized in the thought process represents at its core a valid, trans- and intersubjective gestalt, though that core may actually not have fully emerged yet. Steiner here assumes a conceptually realistic position and distances himself from a nominalist attitude. Mathematics can serve as an example for this inner lawfulness of thinking. Individual human thought is imprinted in a relatively universal way by conceptual contents, which Witzenmann refers to as conditions (we can also call them conditions of cognition). The insights, which the human being gains, are on one hand individual achievements that can only emerge through one's own thinking activity. They are instrumental (in the sense of "conditions") for manifesting the space of individual consciousness, which serves as an orientation for all human thinking and acting; they also are the basis for the evident restful self-indwelling that is intrinsic to human consciousness. Consciousness can only restfully dwell in itself insofar as in every thought process the individual act of thinking stands in interchange with a corresponding immanent, universal thought content. (This is the basis of Steiner's version of essentialism.) Witzenmann summarily describes the abilities that emerge at both sides of the thought-perception polarity as follows: "Our dispositional freedom arises from involvement of the individual consciousness in its penetration by perceptions; it is a birth 'into matter.' It is self-generation in co-creation with thought contents. Our conditional freedom is formed through the impact that our individual (i.e., conditioned) processes have on universal consciousness [*spirit*] that means through receiving it into one's own sphere of being. Thus, this freedom is a freedom in spirit [*consciousness*]" (Witzenmann 1988, p. 13).

4.3 Pedagogic relevance

The qualifications formed at the two poles of *perceiving and thinking* can be more clearly categorized in the context of a quote from Steiner's *Theosophy*. We read there: "If we want to understand the essence of a human being, we must know [...] two things about him: first, how much of the eternal has been revealed in his being, and secondly, how many treasures of the past he carries in him" (Steiner 1922, p. 52). This quote suggests that the entire complexity of a human being can be understood by considering these two aspects alone. At first, that must seem reductionist in its approach. However, if we indeed examine these two aspects more closely, it becomes apparent that they do not contain firmly delineated definitions; they rather open up a wide field for attentive observation. The concern here is not a rigid determination of what defines a being human, but a cognitive orientation that allows itself to be inspired by two perspectives: One perspective ("treasures of the past") already points to the pole of perception mentioned above, it leads to the creation of reality and participation in the world. In accordance with constructivism theories, the world potential here too is creatively unlocked. Each encounter with the world poses an existential/cognitive riddle to the human being that must be solved by penetrating it with one's own thinking. Man forms concepts to infuse, with their help, his perceptions and thus create a web of connectivity. In contrast to constructivism, this process offers contents to perceptions, but they are not forced upon perception. In a Goethean sense, we can become aware of the qualitative essence of world phenomena in the light of each respective concept. Witzenmann here speaks of inherencies that are immanent in concepts within perceptions. In this cognitive process, dispositions are formed, which are capacities for understanding and acting that emerge in and with the help of the respective object spheres. Those are the "treasures of the past" that Steiner refers to, because behind each cosmic understanding and each capacity for action stretches a learning path of practice, which has been traversed biographically. Learning at Waldorf schools is grounded in experience, practice, and projects, and it aims in this regard at facilitating valid encounters with the world that engender a treasure trove of understanding and orientation. Especially, the artistic classes in Waldorf education guide and encourage the students to experiment with ever new ingresses into the world so that they are not limited by cultural, milieu-related, or habitual patterns of thought and imagination; the actual challenge of cognition that opens up via the sphere of awareness and the gates of the senses can be fully met as it thus is safeguarded from undermining limitations. No human being can avoid the historic, biographical, psychological, cultural, etc., imprints that everyone experiences, and of course en- and acculturation always involve the adoption of positive, desirable values and worldviews. But there also exists, aside from these participatory cultural encounters with the world, a genuinely individual layer of world experiences, which Witzenmann calls "dispositions" and which Waldorf education definitely takes into account in the educational process.

The *revelation of the eternal*, as it is termed in Steiner's quote, is to be categorized as belonging to the thought side of the perceiving/thinking polarity. Not the encounter with the world stands in the foreground, but here the concern is the subject itself. Soul observation *(intuitive introspection)* affords a view into the depth of human consciousness. Within an idealistic conceptual understanding of thinking, the possibility of an autonomous creation on the level of ideas takes shape. This means a conceptual-realistic sphere of immanent concepts, with which the individual thinking faculty engages intuitively. This process gives rise to *conditions* that represent the individual human capacities for understanding and thinking, and form the matrix within which one's own insights, individual impulses, and value orientations emerge. It is important to consider here that not only rational cognitive aspects are addressed, when we direct our attention to the inner realm of the human being and speak of *thinking*. Rudolf Steiner's concept of thought is not limited to intellectual aspects; rather it includes also emotions, sensations, moods, and aspects of will and motivation. Why does Steiner designate *thinking* as the central force in the inner life of man and subsume feeling and will into that force? The reason can be found in the fact that in Steiner's understanding, the conscious, free appropriation of the self is most developed in thinking (see Fichte's *fact-act*) and can therefore be addressed more clearly in the process of education.

In a pedagogic context, Waldorf education is concerned with inner individual life motifs of a human being, which are often biographically hidden from even one's own awareness; these motifs are supposed to be addressed in manifold ways during the developmental process in *(Waldorf)* schools. At its best, pedagogy serves to guide the child toward a deeper understanding of self, toward a fundamental moral-ethical orientation and leads to an idealistically inspired development of that motif, which generates the power to realize individual life goals.

5 Terminology of Waldorf education

Against the backdrop of Steiner's concepts of cognition and freedom so far delineated, we will take a fresh look at the initially quoted terms as used in anthroposophy and Waldorf education. Steiner considers the human being under three different aspects: body, soul, and spirit.

The term *body* points to the traits physically inherited in the context of the natural stream of evolution. It entails purely biological, physiological processes as well as the material aspect of the body.

The term *soul* pertains basically to nothing metaphysical, or pre-natal or after-death matters, but Steiner uses it to denote the psyche, the inner realm of the human being. For Steiner, the core characteristic of soul-related aspects is self-generated activity, as it surfaces in the process of thinking; however, he broadens the meaning of the term to include feelings and will.

Spirit for Steiner is that dimension of thinking that transcends the soul aspect; it touches upon an immanent sphere of concepts and ideas, with which it enters into a cognitive-reasoning exchange.

This tripartite organization of the human being into a physical body that is given *(inherited)* a soul with self-generated activity and an immanent spiritual part should be understood as a purely phenomenological and functional description without normative connotations. The organization of the human being into so-called members of being, which describes a further differentiation of these three parts on a higher level, can be understood along the same lines.

5.1 Phenomenological-functional anthropology

Steiner uses the term *physical body* to describe the purely material, the matter aspect of man. The term *etheric body* signifies the life processes that permeate the material aspects. Contrary to common notions that life processes are to be understood as epiphenomena of material forces, Steiner understands the life force to be a factor of its own, which acts upon and organizes material phenomena. The term astral *body* pertains to the human capacity for feeling and the process of sensing, based on the sense-organs, which infuse the physical dimension with bodily life force that enables various sense perceptions. The fourth member in this scheme is deemed to be the human "*I,*" the self, which can think and thus can produce autonomous creations of consciousness. The "I" is active in the realm of the soul where it engenders a further differentiation of soul processes: *the sentient soul,* the *intellectual soul,* also the *mind soul* and the *consciousness (spiritual) soul.*

The sentient soul results from thought that directs its attention and observation toward various sense-perceptions and identifies the qualities inherent in their awareness (red, blue, sweet, bitter, loud, major, minor, scratchy, soft, etc.).

The sentient soul denotes the first member or link of the soul. It has to rely on data and information communicated through the sensory body and it qualifies those. This soul aspect is developed to the degree that attention is guided toward sense perception through one's own initiative or through cultural participation (e.g., in education).

Steiner calls the second member of the soul the intellectual or mind soul. It is functionally developed when thought activity is not alone focused on the qualification of sense perceptions, but is used purposefully to care for one's existence. In this sense, the entire array of civilization's technical resources is an achievement of the mind soul, which settles into its existence through thought activity. The next dimension Steiner calls the consciousness (spiritual) soul, since the human being here employs thought activity not only to serve purpose or intent but also enters into the treasures of the mind's immanent consciousness itself. Steiner also connects specific cultural achievements with each soul dimension, which makes it easier to understand this subject area: The so-called epoch of the consciousness soul begins with the dawning of the new age after the end of the middle ages; in this era, mankind began freeing itself from the authority of state and church, which until then was unquestioned; modern science was conceived in that epoch and the human being discovered increasingly the power and significance of autonomous reason.

Beyond the realm of the soul, Steiner also characterizes the spiritual realm with three subcategories, which, however, are subject to self-development alone and are therefore irrelevant for the pedagogic process. The realm of the soul, too, is essentially distinguished by self-generated activity, which is why the child's or adolescent's individuality is treated with a certain reserve and a high measure of respect within Waldorf education. If we intervene too directly and forcefully, Steiner writes, "We only disturb the educational process. We educate by behaving in such a manner that our conduct facilitates the children educating themselves" (Steiner 1988, p. 163).

This glossary of anthropological terms in Waldorf education presented so far should, to start with, be seen as a phenomenological description of the human being. In stark distinction to commonly held contemporary views issuing from the reigning scientific paradigm, Steiner does not make the basic assumption that the material-physical aspect is the universal operative cause of life, sentience, and consciousness processes. Steiner treats all dimensions initially as autonomous, just as they appear. One can judge this as a paradigmatic prejudication, but it is, formally seen, on the same level as the reverse assumption of a causative materialistic force.

5.2 Reincarnation and karma

Let us now turn our attention to the concepts of *reincarnation* and *karma,* which appear equally problematic. These terms prove to be an immense, paradigmatically burdened stumbling block for Waldorf education, particularly in pedagogic contexts. It is useful to approach these terms against the background of the discourse on personality theories. Waldorf education proceeds from the assumption of an autonomous core of the personality. It inherently does not preclude hereditary, neurophysiological, behavioristic, sociological, interaction-based or other factors, which influence human personality development. Beyond that, Waldorf education in fact regards the human "I" as an entelechy, which entails the potential for self-realization. In Waldorf education, as generally practiced within the teacher collegia, an essential aspect of the work consists of an attentive observation of children and adolescents based on comprehensive, holistic understanding. A central concern is to consider unique individual traits, predispositions, and talents of each student. In this context, reincarnation is nothing else but a basic pedagogic axiom, viewing the essential personality of a human being as immanent without any other external cause. This genuine core of the personality manifests itself in the thought process. There is an interchange between the individual generative activity of thought (soul) and a self-restive content (spirit) providing the foundation for a core personality in the human being, which is independent of hereditary factors and autonomously integrates socialization experiences. The concern of pedagogy, cannot consist of determining if this personality core is embodied (how, when, where?)—that would be certainly be an encroachment. The basic pedagogic attitude of the teachers alone is critically important, as they entertain the possibility that such an autonomous personality core exists, so that they may respect it and possibly thus facilitate its emergence.

In regard to the two poles mentioned before—perceiving and thinking—the reincarnation aspect belongs more to the side of thinking, of the individual capacity for cognition, because it reflects the genuine uniqueness of the personality. In anthroposophy, karma is not understood as a deterministic or fatalistic concept of fate. The perspective of karma is attributable more to the side of the perceiving pole, as presented above, and marks the way how the human being encounters the world, what kind of challenges he meets and what nascent skills he acquires. Indeed, the abilities to participate in the world, and to profit from encountering it, vary individually, which Steiner understands as a previously practiced participation in reality, which is solely achieved by one's own creativity. The human being retains the imprints of experiences with the phenomena of the world, and these determine, furthermore, his individual encounters with the various world spheres and his closeness or distance to them. Since the world has gifted man (because of then-participation in its construction) with abilities, the relationship here is one of affection, characterized by *warmth* and *love*. Human beings treasure and love the world aspects that engender their faculties, just like a musician appreciates his instrument and the athlete his sports equipment. The line of thought outlined so far can be illustrated as follows (Table 2.1):

On one side of this qualifying scheme *(perception pole)*, the human being develops *faculties* as he/she encounters the world and is lovingly inclined toward those world spheres, where the *treasures of the past* emerge in form of dispositions—at any rate this would be the metaphor of the pertinent pedagogic undertone in this respect. Here, we come across conditions, encountered by everyone in the process of development, that are karmic in nature according to anthropological understanding. In the pedagogic context, that means to facilitate positive, loving encounters with the world that give the young students courage and strength to gain specific abilities for action and insight in the respective world spheres through repeated and persistent practice.

Table 2.1 Developmental polarities in the perspective of Waldorf education

Judgment in beholding (Goethe)	Intuitive (soul) perception (Steiner)
Zero point: perception	Zero point: thought
Productive creation of reality	Productive self-creation
Inherence	Intuition
Disposition	Condition
Treasures of the past	Revelations of the eternal
Faculties/Love	Insight/Light
Karma	Reincarnation

On the other side of the qualifying scheme, i.e., where the human being arrives at insights as a result of his own creative thinking, valid and value-forming aspects emerge. The apt metaphor for this type of insight is *Light*. Ideals and fundamental beliefs emerge here, that illuminate a permanent core of the personality regardless of all variabilities. Whether or not reincarnation actually occurs—this question remains completely open. It is, however, of pedagogic significance, whether a fundamental core of the human personality is considered possible or not. Only to that degree, is reincarnation of any import for the concept of the human being in Waldorf education. Against this backdrop, Waldorf education is particularly concerned that the students should develop a faculty of valid and autonomous judgment throughout their education. Every young human being is challenged to find within their own inner being a gauge of certainty for social, moral, and aesthetic judgments, which shape being and doing. Another essential feature is the formation of youthful idealism. Within the current societal context, this developmental process often has a sobering and disappointing effect on young people, at times leading to tendencies of detached sarcasm or even cynicism. However, it should be precisely the educational goal of a school to graduate young people with strong ideals, who are motivated to actively realize these ideals to the benefit of society. The pedagogic concept of Waldorf education places great importance on supporting students in their development of autonomous individual ideals.

6 Summary and outlook

This article starts with a portrait of central positions in current historic pedagogic anthropology, which refrain from any statements about the inner nature of man, both in descriptive as in normative perspective. It sees its major task in the critique and analysis of explicit as well as implicit historic and contemporary anthropological thought. It thus sees itself as a deconstructive, negative anthropology. Historic pedagogic anthropology rejects unjustified generalized statements about the human being and opens up new areas of research beyond established anthropological topics such as subject, autonomy, rationality, etc.; rather, this approach pulls into consideration non-verbal, meta-reflexive, and corporeal-sensory aspects. In this context, research within the wider area of cultural education plays a critical role.

In this anthropological discussion, Waldorf education is not included, because it is viewed as a form of pedagogy that relies on an essentialistic, metaphysical-dogmatic concept of man. Both critics and followers of Waldorf education are responsible for that kind of interpretation. This article questions the validity of this view in consideration of Steiner's epistemological approach.

Contrary to popular allegation, Steiner does not advocate a closed system of an absolutist epistemological approach, but he follows Goethe in challenging a quasi-religious belief in the dominance of intellectual rationalism, as enlightenment had proclaimed it. Steiner does agree with the philosophy of enlightenment in his critique of naïve realism. He propounds a concept of creative realism, insofar as he understands reality to be the result of a co-creative act of cognition. Reality therefore always has process character and is never finite. In that sense, achievements of cognition are always temporary. Steiner's anthropological concept of individual freedom is based on a possibility of participation in reality through conscious thought. While this constitutes a positive statement, it nevertheless does not contradict the critique of essentialism, since the human being carries within himself only a predisposition to freedom but is not compelled to realize it; moreover, the concept of freedom refutes any kind of normativity that is injected from the outside.

Waldorf education rests on Steiner's epistemology and philosophy of freedom insofar as it seeks to foster and support through its didactic and methodological approaches the individually productive process of cognition in co-creating reality. The two poles of thinking and perceiving are unconditionally exposed in the interest of an active encounter with the world and valid self-realization; they are schooled and integrated into concrete pedagogic practice. Current research has so far given scanty consideration to Waldorf education's focus on central topics of contemporary historic pedagogic anthropology, such as aspects of corporeality, culturality, and emotionality.

Waldorf education uses terms that appear rather problematic; they are extricated from their esoterically ornamented interpretation and newly interpreted within the context of Steiner's philosophy.

The so-called members of being are understood as a functional-phenomenological type of anthropology. Steiner viewed the entire organization of the human being as an evolutionary and functional orientation toward the thought process and the point of freedom that is contained therein. Steiner does not simply introduce esoteric and other concepts by defining them, but his statements are based on observations and thus phenomenologically sound. The various aspects (members) he describes are to be understood as pure functional forms inherent in being human, i.e., in man's freedom. They only exist insofar as they are or were individually and culturally realized. On the level of the *physical body*, an emancipatory concept of evolution comes into play, as Bernd Rosslenbroich (Rosslenbroich 2014) outlined. Steiner described the *etheric body* as a corporeal form of thinking and understood and qualified the *astral body*—transitioning into the *sentient soul*—also as a form of thinking that is oriented toward sensory beholding in gestures of attention. The *intellectual soul* (mind soul) makes use of the thought process, while the *spiritual soul* is that aspect which has become self-aware of thinking.

In this sense, we must understand thinking as the power that is constitutive for the human being. Therefore, Waldorf education can be described as a pedagogy of thought unfoldment; here it is crucial to define the concept of thought not too narrowly as rational. Steiner includes in his description of thought all the individual-autonomous processes of the mind such as attention, observation, feeling, and the will. Certainly, Steiner's idea-realism presents a controversial point, where he assumes that ideas and concepts, which actualize in human thought, do not originate in subjective or cultural and historic factors alone, but that they are pervaded by their own principles or laws, as the example of mathematics shows; in the process of thinking, such inherent principles are experienced as insights.

Naturally, many questions and research issues remain unanswered in this attempt to reconnect Waldorf education with Steiner's epistemological approach of his early writings, and they await future attention and work. Examples are Steiner's complex teachings on the senses and on development—especially in view of his thesis that powers, which are bound up in the corporeal etheric body at first, after school age eventually become available in form of free powers of intelligence. Moreover, a wide field opens up for research to be done not only in human sciences but especially also in natural science, as Steiner's numerous statements come into focus pertaining to the interconnection of corporeal-physical processes (in respect to nutrition, also blood, nerves, etc.) with phenomena of the mind or psyche. Regardless of these open issues, the thoughts here presented are meant to contribute to a critical-constructive interpretation of Waldorf education's storehouse of anthropological theory that has so far received no due recognition.

Notes

1 In connection with the founding initiative for a public Waldorfschule in Hamburg-Wilhelmsburg, the article demanded to adopt only "the methods of Waldorf education" without including the fundamental aspects of Steiner's teachings (Maurer 2014; Sonnberger 2012; Ulrich 2012).

2 Within the world of Waldorf education, however, this term is not being used. These words were [falsely] put into the mouth of a speaker for the Association of Independent Waldorf Schools during the founding initiative for a Waldorf school in Hamburg-Wilhelmsburg. Information concerning the planned opening of this public school that works with elements of Waldorf education are available at the website of the Association for Fostering Intercultural Waldorf education in Hamburg e.V. (at www.waldorfwilhelmsburg.de).

3 The internet description of the Waldorf kindergarten in Frankenthal reads: "The concept of man in anthroposophy, which forms the understructure of Waldorf education, sees man as a tri-partite being that is composed of body, soul and spirit. The pedagogic practice relies on this holistic understanding of the tripartite human being, the four members of being and the developmental stages of man. This concept of man includes the ideas of reincarnation and karma, which constitute possibly the most essential differences to traditional pedagogy. The spiritual 'substance' of man is immortal; it lives and develops in ever-new incarnations. Human beings are self-responsible for their fate and it is their task to accordingly shape their life here on earth" (www.waldorfkindergarten-frankenthal under "pedagogy" menu. Last accessed July 1, 2014).

4 Ullrich accuses Steiner of precisely that kind of pre-enlightenment mythology: "Contrary to conscious, methodical self-constraints, to plurality and transparency of modern science, Steiner and his followers claim dogmatic visionary knowledge of a well-ordered cosmos as if it were an eternal, unchangeable truth. [...] Their form of thought is a degenerative philosophy and worldview. [...] Steiner fully succumbed to the dangers of such an approach in developing the anthroposophical 'secret science.' Here, the premodern, dogmatic-metaphysical speculation of Neoplatonism bleeds over into the consciously re-mythologizing explanation of the world, as Theosophy presents it" (Ullrich 1988, p. 28; Ullrich 2011, p. 1100). This accusation is wrongly directed at Steiner but certainly can be deemed just for the majority of Steiner exegeses by anthroposophical authors.

5 See also this quote: "In the unsurpassed, artful conception of a human sensory-nervous system, the creative cosmos reduces itself back to its original state. Pure perceptions, facilitated by out sensory organs, represent the unordered material mandate of our own self-actualization. In that process we become creative to the degree that we can master this task of self-actualizing in our thinking; we newly create the world that undid itself. Regarding the creation of reality, we ourselves are the creators of our individual life" (Witzenmann 1988, p. 10).

References

Böhme, Hartmut/Böhme, Gernot (1983): Das Andere der Vernunft. Zur Entwicklung von Rationalitätsstrukturen am Beispiel Kants. *[The other of reason. On the development rationality structures in the example of Kant]* Frankfurt am Main: Suhrkamp.

Bohnsack, Fritz/Leber, Stefan (1996): Sozialerziehung im Sozialverfall: Grundlagen, Kontroversen, Wege. *[Social education within social disintegration: Fundamentals, controversies, pathways.]* Weinheim and Basel: Beltz.

Bollnow, Otto Friedrich (1965): Die anthropologische Betrachtungsweise in der Pädagogik. *[The anthropological mode of observation in pedagogy]* Essen: Neue Deutsche Schule Verlagsgesellschaft.

Centmayer, Dieter (2007): Waldorfschule ohne Steiner. *[Waldorf schools without Steiner]* In: Erziehungskunst, H. 2007, 10, p. 1142–1143.

Foucault, Michel (2001): Dits et Ecrits. Schriften in vier Bänden. *[Writings in four volumes]* Frankfurt am Main: Suhrkamp.

Gehlen, Arnold (1993): Der Mensch. Seine Natur und seine Stellung in der Welt. *[The human being. His nature and position within the world.]* Complete Works, vol. 3. Ed. by Karl-Siegbert Rehberg. Frankfurt am Main: Klostermann.

Goethe, Johann Wolfgang v. (1988a): Goethes Briefe und Briefe an Goethe. *[Letters from and to Goethe]* Hamburger Ausgabe. 6 Bände. *[Hamburg edition, 6 volumes.].* Ed. by Karl Robert von Mandelkow. Munich: Beck.

Goethe, Johann Wolfgang v. (1988b): Goethes Werke. *[Goethe's works]* Hamburg Edition. Vols. 14. Ed. by Erich Trunz. 11th. printing. Munich: Beck.

Habermas, Jürgen (1981): Theorie des kommunikativen Handelns. *[The theory of communicative action]* Vols. 2. Frankfurt am Main: Suhrkamp.

Kamper, Dietmar (1995): Unmögliche Gegenwart. *[Impossible presence]* Munich: Fink.

Kant, Immanuel (1974): Kritik der reinen Vernunft. *[A critique of pure reason]* In: Kant, Immanuel (1974): work edition. 12 volumes. Vols. 3 and 4. Ed. by Wilhelm Weischedel. Frankfurt am Main: Suhrkamp.

Langeveld, Martinus J. (1964): Studien zur Anthropologie des Kindes. *[Studies on the Anthropology of the Child]* Tübingen: Niemeyer.

Liebau, Echart/Bilstein, Johannes/Peskoller, Helga/Wulf, Christoph (Eds.) (2003): Natur: Pädagogisch-anthropologische Perspektiven. *[Nature: Pedagogic anthropological perspectives]* Weinheim: Beltz.

Liebau, Eckart (2012): Anthropologische Grundlagen [Anthropological basics] In: Handbuch Kulturelle Bildung. *[Handbook of cultural education].* Eds. by Bockhorst, Hildegard, Vanessa-Isabelle Reinwand-Weiss and Wolfgang Zacharias. Munich: Kopaed, pp. 29–35.

Maurer, Mathias (2014): Traditionen über Bord werfen. Ein staatlich-waldorfpädagogischer Schulversuch in Hamburg. Im Gespräch mit Christiane Leiste. *[Breaking with traditions. A Waldorf education and public-school experiment. In conversation with Christiane Leiste]* Erziehungskunst *[The Art of Education]* Vol. 5, pp. 14–17.

Nohl, Herman (1929): Pädagogische Menschenkunde. *[The study of man in pedagogy]* In: Handbuch der Pädagogik II. *[Handbook of pedagogy II].* Eds by Nohl, Herman and Ludwig Pallat. Langensalza: Belt.

Plessner, Hellmuth (1981): Die Stufen des Organischen und der Mensch. *[Steps in the development of organic factors and of man]* Gesammelte Schriften. *[Collected works]* Vol. 4. Eds. by Günter Dux, Odo Marquard, Elisabeth Ströker. Frankfurt am Main: Suhrkamp.

Polanyi, Michael (1985): Implizites Wissen. *[Implicit knowledge]* Frankfurt am Main: Suhrkamp.

Prange, Klaus (1985): Erziehung zur Anthroposophie. Darstellung und Kritik der Waldorfpädagogik. *[Education in anthroposophy. Portrait and critique of Waldorf education.]* Bad Heilbrunn: Klinkhardt.

Prange, Klaus (2000): Erziehung zur Anthroposophie. Darstellung und Kritik der Waldorfpädagogik. *[Education in anthroposophy. Portrait and critique of Waldorf education.]* 3., um eine Nachschrift vermehrte Auflage. *[3rd edition with added postscript]* Bad Heilbrunn: Klinkhardt.

Rittelmeyer, Christian (1994): Schulbauten positiv gestalten. Wie Schüler Formen und Farben erleben. *[Positive school design. How students experience form and color]* Wiesbaden: Bauverlag.

Rittelmeyer, Christian (2013): Einführung in die Gestaltung von Schulbauten. *[Introduction to school design]* Frammersbach: Farbe und Gesundheit. *[Color and health]*

Rosslenbroich, Bernd (2014): On the Origin of Autonomy. A New Look at the Major Transitions in Evolution. Heidelberg, New York: Springer Cham.

Roth, Heinrich (1966/1971): Pädagogische Anthropologie. 2 Bände. *[Pedagogic anthropology. 2 volumes]* Hannover: Schroedel.

Scheler, Max (1976): Die Stellung des Menschen im Kosmos. *[The human place in the cosmos]* In: Scheler, Max (1976): Späte Schriften. *[Late works.]* Gesammelte Werke. Bd. 9. *[Collected works, vol.9].* Ed. by Manfred S. Frings. Bern, Munich: Bouvier.

Schieren, Jost (1998): Anschauende Urteilskraft. Methodische und philosophische Grundlagen von Goethes naturwissenschaftlichem Erkennen. *[Judgment in beholding. Methodological and philosophical foundations of Goethe's theory of knowledge in the natural sciences.]* Bonn: Parerga.

Schieren, Jost (2010): Die goethesche Bewusstseinshaltung der Waldorfpädagogik. *[The Goethean stance of consciousness in Waldorf education]* In: Erziehungswissenschaftliche Zugänge zur Waldorfpädagogik. *[In: Access to Waldorf education through educational science].* Ed. by Paschen, Harm. Wiesbaden: Springer VS.

Schröder, Axel (2013): Widerstand gegen staatliche Waldorfschule in Hamburg. Kritik entzündet sich an überholten pädagogischen Konzepten. *[Resistance against the public Waldorf school in Hamburg. Critique sparked by obsolete pedagogical concepts]* Radiobeitrag Deutschlandfunk vom 08.03.2013. *[Radio broadcast; Deutschlandfunk of August 3rd, 2013].* Online at: www.deutschlandfunk.de/widerstand-gegen-staatliche-waldorfschule-in-hamburg.680.de. html?dram:article_id=236845 (last accessed: January 2016).

Skiera, Ehrenhard (2003): Reformpädagogik in Geschichte und Gegenwart. Eine kritische Einführung. *[Reform pedagogy in history and in present times. A critical introduction]* Munich: Oldenburg.

Sonnberger, Heike (2012): Schulexperiment: Ein bisschen Regelschule, ein bisschen Waldorf. *[School experiment: A bit of public schooling, a bit of Waldorf education]* In: Spiegel online of 9/19/2012. At www.spiegel. de/schulspiegel/schulversuch-in-hamburg-waldorfpaedagogik- an-staatlicher-schule-a-856778.html (Last accessed: January 2016).

Steiner, Rudolf (1918): Die Philosophie der Freiheit. Grundzüge einer modernen Weltanschauung. Seelische Beobachtungsresultate nach naturwissenschaftlicher Methode. *[The Philosophy of Freedom. Outline of a modern worldview. Results of soul observation in the methodology of natural science.]* Berlin: Philosophisch-anthroposophischer Verlag.

Steiner, Rudolf (1922): Theosophie. Einführung in die übersinnliche Welt- und Menschenbestimmung. *[Theosophy: An introduction to the supersensible knowledge of the world and the destiny of man]* Stuttgart: Der Kommende Tag.

Steiner, Rudolf (1924): Grundlinien einer Erkenntnistheorie der Goetheschen Weltanschauung mit besonderer Rücksicht auf Schiller *[An outline of the epistemology of Goethe's worldview with special reference to Schiller].* Stuttgart: Der Kommende Tag.

Steiner, Rudolf (1980): Allgemeine Menschenkunde als Grundlage der Pädagogik. Vierzehn Vorträge, gehalten in Stuttgart vom 21. August bis 5. September 1919. *[The general study of man as the basis for pedagogy. 14 lectures held in Stuttgart between August 21 and September 5, 1919]* Rudolf Steiner GA 293. Dornach: Rudolf Steiner Verlag.

Steiner, Rudolf (1988): Geistige Wirkenskräfte im Zusammenleben von junger und alter Generation. Pädagogischer Jugendkurs. Dreizehn Vorträge, gehalten in Stuttgart vom 03. bis 15. Oktober 1922. *[Spiritual forces of action in the coexistence of young and old generations. Pedagogical Youth Course. Thirteen lectures held in Stuttgart from October 3 to 15, 1922.]* Rudolf Steiner GA 217. Dornach: Rudolf Steiner Verlag.

Steiner, Rudolf (1998): Idee und Praxis der Waldorfschule. Neun Vorträge, eine Besprechung und Fragenbeantwortungen zwischen dem 24. August 1919 and 29. Dezember 1920 in verschiedenen Orten. *[Idea and practice in Waldorf schools. Nine lectures, a review and answers to questions between August 24, 1919 and December 29, 1920, held in various locations]* GA 297. Dornach: Rudolf Steiner Verlag.

Ullrich, Heiner (1986): Waldorfpädagogik und okkulte Weltanschauung. Eine bildungsphilosophische und geistesgeschichtliche Auseinandersetzung mit der Anthroposophie Rudolf Steiners. *[Waldorf education and occult worldview. An educational-philosophical and historic-intellectual approach to the anthroposophy of Rudolf Steiner]* Weinheim, Munich: Juventa.

Ullrich, Heiner (1988): Wissens chaft als rationalisierte Mystik. Eine problemgeschichtliche Untersuchung der erkenntnistheoretischen Grundlagen der Anthroposophie. *[Science as rationalised mysticism. A historic-critical study of the epistemological foundations of anthroposophy]* In: Neue Sammlung *[New collection]* vol. 28, issue. 2, pp. 168–194.

Ullrich, Heiner (2011): Rudolf Steiner. Leben und Lehre. *[Rudolf Steiner. Life and teachings]* Munich: Beck.

Ullrich, Heiner (2015): Waldorfpädagogik. Eine kritische Einführung. *[Waldorf education. A critical introduction]* Weinheim: Beltz.

Ulrich, Friederike (2012): Schul-Kooperation. Hamburg gründet erste staatliche Waldorfschule. *[School cooperation. Hamburg founds the first public Waldorf school]* In: Hamburger Abendblatt dated 9/19/2012. Online at: www.abendblatt.de/hamburg/hamburg-mitte/article 2403251/Hamburg-gruendet-erste-staatliche-Waldorfschule.html (last accessed: October7, 2014).

Wimmer, Michael (1998): Die Kehrseiten des Menschen. Probleme und Fragen der Historischen Anthropologie. *[The other sides of man. Problems and questions of historic anthropology]* In: Anthropologische Markierungen. Herausforderungen pädagogischen Denkens. *[Anthropological markings. Challenges of pedagogic thought].* Eds by Marotzki, Winfried, Jan Masschelein and Alfred Schäfer. Weinheim: Deutscher Studien Verlag, pp. 85–112.

Witzenmann, Herbert (1988): Der Urgedanke. *[Primordial thought]* Krefeld: Gideon Spicker.

Witzenmann, Herbert (1998): Ein Weg in die Zukunft. Texte zum Wiederlesen. *[A path into the future. Texts for reading again]* Dornach: Verlag am Goetheanum.

Wuchterl, Kurt (2011): Kontingenz oder das Andere der Vernunft. Zum Verhältnis von Philosophie, Naturwissenschaft und Religion. *[Contingency or the other of reason. On the relations between philosophy, natural science and religion]* Stuttgart: Steiner.

Wulf, Christoph (2002): Die Wendung zur historisch-pädagogischen Anthropologie. *[The shift toward historic pedagogic anthropology]* In: Wigger, Lothar (Ed.) (2002): Forschungsfelder der Allgemeinen Erziehungswissenschaft. *[Areas of research in general educational science]* Opladen. Zeitschrift für Erziehungswissenschaft *[Magazine for educational science].* Nr. 1, 5. Jg., inserted issue, pp. 5–8.

Wulf, Christoph (2009): Anthropologie: Geschichte, Kultur, Philosophie. *[Anthropology: History, culture, philosophy]* Köln: Anaconda.

Wulf, Christoph/Kamper, Dietmar (2002): Logik und Leidenschaft. *[Logic and passion]* Berlin: Reimer.

Wulf, Christoph/Zirfas, Jörg (1994): Theorien und Konzepte der pädagogischen Anthropologie. *[Theories and concepts of pedagogic anthropology]* Donauwörth: Auer.

Wulf, Christoph/Zirfas, Jörg (2014): Handbuch Pädagogische Anthropologie. *[Handbook of pedagogic anthropology]* Wiesbaden: Springer VS.

Zander, Helmut (2007): Anthroposophie in Deutschland. Theosophische Weltanschauung und gesellschaftliche Praxis. *[Anthroposophy in Germany. Theosophical worldview and societal practice]* 2 volumes. Göttingen: Vandenhoeck & Ruprecht.

Zirfas, Jörg (1998): Die Frage nach dem Wesen des Menschen. Zur pädagogischen Anthropologie der 60er Jahre. *[The question of man's essential nature. On pedagogic anthropology in the sixties]* In: Anthropologische Markierungen. Herausforderungen pädagogischen Denkens. *[Anthropological markings. Challenges to pedagogic thought].* Eds. by Marotzki, Winfried, Jan Masschelein and Alfred Schäfer. Weinheim: Deutscher Studien Verlag, pp. 55–84.

Zirfas, Jörg (2004): Pädagogik und Anthropologie. *[Pedagogy and anthropology]* Stuttgart: Kohlhammer.

THE STUDY OF MAN AND EDUCATIONAL PRACTICE

Albert Schmelzer

1 Introduction: Good practice—Anachronistic ideology?

Currently, the Waldorf school movement is in a paradoxical situation: On one hand, the discussions in public as well as educational science circles issue numerous positive evaluations of practical Waldorf school education, while, on the other hand, its Anthroposophic-anthropological foundations are emphatically rejected as being mythological, dogmatic, anachronistic, in short: unscientific.[1] Facing this situation, Waldorf education must meet a double challenge:

First, it is vital to take a closer look at the status, and thus also at the function, of Anthroposophical anthropology within the philosophy of science: Is this about a rigid, metaphysical determination of the essence of man? Or can the anthroposophical study of man be viewed as a possible, heuristically stimulating perspective of the human being, not conceptualized as an educational science theory but as a foundation for pedagogical practice?

These questions direct us to look at the second task: It is vital to ask how concepts of the Anthroposophical study of man relate to concrete classroom instruction at Waldorf schools. Do they simply constitute a superstructure or do motifs of pedagogic anthropology penetrate into the educational practice?[2]

The following article will pursue both lines of questioning. Part one attempts to outline how Rudolf Steiner sketched out the character and function of anthroposophy, as he conceptualized it, and its relation to the educational science of his time. The second part presents the results of a first exploratory survey, which the author conducted at the Intercultural Waldorf School Mannheim. This study investigates in what way a motif from Steiner's lectures on pedagogic anthropology, *The Study of Man* (Steiner 1973a), is transformed into teaching practice.[3]

2 Rudolf Steiner's pedagogic anthropology[4]

As literal translation suggests, anthroposophy is generally understood to mean "wisdom pertaining to man," which provides, upon closer study, a plethora of associative topics, laid down in the writings and lectures of Rudolf Steiner and published in a most copious, complete edition of his works that is difficult to overview. Steiner himself was quite unhappy with such an understanding of anthroposophy. Anthroposophy was not supposed to be "gray theory" but "true life"; if it is "*made* into grey theory, then it is often not at all a *better,* but a *worse* theory than others. But it [*anthroposophy*] actually only becomes theory, if it is changed to become that, if it is killed" (Steiner 1976, p. 56).

DOI: 10.4324/9781003187431-9

Accordingly, he places the concept *(anthroposophy)* in a different matrix of understanding: Not "wisdom pertaining to man" is the correct interpretation of the word *anthroposophy*, but *"the conscious awareness of him/her being human"* (Steiner 1965, p. 76). Here it becomes clear that Rudolf Steiner saw anthroposophy as an individual path of awakening into one's own humanity. A similar idea is expressed in the now popular phrase: "Anthroposophy is a path of knowledge to guide the spiritual in the human being to the spiritual in the universe" (Steiner 1976, p. 14).

This gives a different significance to the ideas presented by Steiner: They are an expression of *his* personal, individual cognition efforts, and experiences; they are not meant to express empirically validated scientific theories. His approach is fertile insofar, as it can inspire and motivate other individuals to construct their own worldview.

The Waldorf pedagogue Johannes Kiersch has shown in a foundational article in how far the perspective broached here is significant for understanding Steiner's pedagogic anthropology (Kiersch 2014). Steiner was not concerned with creating yet another theory of educational science—that seemed to him entirely unnecessary as well. In fact, he acknowledged the educational science of his time and never concealed the fact that he integrated important elements of Reform pedagogy into the Waldorf concept (Steiner 1994, p. 84).

In fact, Steiner was convinced that there had to be a different approach to pedagogic anthropology besides that of educational science—a view of the human being that could lead to an art of education: "And so we attempted [...] to lay the groundwork for an anthropology, an educational science, that can develop into an art of education [...]" (Steiner 1980, p. 25).

In 1917, in his work *Riddles of the Soul*, (Steiner 1983) Steiner developed a theoretical framework for this approach. There he expounds that scientific anthropology relies on cognitive processing of sensory data, while the concept of the human being developed by anthroposophy "is painted with a very different brush" (ibid., p. 32 pp); both approaches, he writes, complement each other and could converge in a common "Philosophy of the Human Being."

Tracing the significance of this statement, it becomes necessary to look at concepts that are used within the Anthroposophical study of man. In this connection, Steiner speaks of "living concepts" and Kiersch pointed out the context within which we can understand this statement (Kiersch 1994, p. 75ff; 2014, p. 60): Living concepts are "perspective-like" and open up a view for those who have not yet arrived; they guide the attention to a specific direction, they have a pointer character. Thus, they are not definitions, but only approximations, like poetic metaphors and that which Goethe described as "symbolical thought forms" (Kiersch 2014, p. 61). They are in this sense *open* concepts. Such concepts require artistic means of expression, such as ordering phenomena into specific serial arrangements or a composition along the principles of polarity and progression. Consequently, living concepts call for a certain type of apprehension: gentleness, quiet introspection, and a meditative way of dealing with them. Therefore, Steiner expected Waldorf teachers to deal with these concepts as a practice in their teaching activities. The point is to first study the concept of man, to then meditate on it and finally to "internalize" [remember] it, which means to intuitively realize them in pedagogic practice (Steiner 1993, p. 52).

However, the pointer to the heuristic function of the concepts in Steiner's teacher training course "The General Study of Man" does not imply that Anthroposophically oriented anthropology can be dismissed as irrational or mythical, in short: unscientific. Rather, its position in the historic tradition of philosophical anthropology can certainly be determined in precise ways, as remains to be shown in several examples. Furthermore, Christian Rittelmeyer's question is valid, whether the central concepts of Anthroposophical anthropology should not be understood in a similar way "as the categories of the historic dimension, the history of the human mind, the cultural formation in historic anthropology: as concepts that help us learn to perceive precisely that living changes in the human beings, their inexhaustible manifold and varied phenomenology" (Rittelmeyer in Chapter 2).

After this contemplation on the character and function of an anthroposophically oriented anthropology, we will now, in a second step, look at its transformation into educational practice.

3 On the transformation of Waldorf education's pedagogic anthropology into teaching practice

In view of the discrepancy between predominantly positive assessments of Waldorf education and the overall deprecating attitude in regard to its anthropology, as outlined in the introductory section of this article, Christian Rittelmeyer recommended to examine the transformation of Steiner's anthropological concepts into Waldorf teaching practice (Rittelmeyer 2011). He writes: the question arises, if an investigation of "practice-related school phenomena could not lead to an understanding of the initially rejected foundations of Waldorf education that would be different than initially surmised" (ibid. p. 330). The author followed this recommendation; in Fall 2012 he initiated a first research project at the Intercultural Waldorf School in Mannheim Neckarstadt, investigating the transfer of a teaching practice motif from Steiner's pedagogic anthropology. The study was set up as follows: The author chose a motif from Rudolf Steiner's lectures on *The Study of Man* and presented it to the teacher's college of the elementary and middle-school levels at the Intercultural Waldorf School Mannheim-Neckarstadt.

It was agreed that the teachers would study this theme over the next three weeks. After that time span, the author conducted with them nine non-standardized individual interviews, which he started with the twofold question: "Did you study this theme and, if yes, in how far has this process influenced your teaching practice?"

The following paragraphs will introduce the theme (motif) and assign it a position within the context of educational science and the history of philosophy. A report follows with examples of answers. An inquiry into the experiment's relevance for the current discourse concludes this section. It should be restrictively noted that the study's design reflects its narrow character. We neither pursued the general question whether the teachers align their classroom teaching along Steiner's *Study of Man,* nor is there any systematic investigation into the comparative character of this process. Rather, this is an exploratory case study, designed to document how a small group of Waldorf teachers created transfers between a theme of the *Study of Man* and their classroom teaching practice.

4 The motif

In the second lecture of *The Study of Man*, Steiner outlines foundational elements of a pedagogic psychology of learning. Here, he first emphasizes that pedagogy should by necessity be founded on psychology and points in this connection to the extensive influence of Friedrich Herbart's pedagogic psychology.[5] This short side note conceals a long and intensive involvement with Herbart. In numerous passages, totaling of 233 pages of his work, Steiner refers to the views of this highly influential pedagogue of the second half of the 19th century. While this discourse cannot be covered extensively in the context of this article, some references may be useful.

Steiner recognizes the central importance of Herbart for the school system in Austria and Germany (Steiner 1998, p. 23). Herbart's pedagogy, he writes, is helpful for disciplining the mind (ibid., p.237) and had been an "excellent pedagogy for older times" (Steiner 1966, p. 34). Even so, in Steiner's opinion, Herbart fell prey to one-sided intellectualism, as evidenced in his statement "The formation of the sphere of thought is the essential part of education (quoted according to Blättner 1980, p. 234). The root cause, according to Steiner, lies in Herbart's psychology, which in Steiner's opinion is essentially a psychology of imagination" (Steiner 1998, p. 26). In Steiner's view, Herbart's mode of thinking is permeated by the "unconscious belief that the true life of the soul consists of the representational faculty's process of mutual restraints and support, and that which surfaces as feeling and will only exists in the motions of the imaginative *[representational]* life" (ibid., p. 27). Accordingly, Herbart called for educating the emotions and the will, yet he only outlined principles suitable for educating the intellect (ibid., p. 25); for Steiner, Herbart's worldview did not account for *action* (Steiner 1968, 256 pp).

Therefore, it is not surprising that Steiner uses an approach that gives equal weight to the power of will as an antipole to the power of representation *(imagination).* In this context, Steiner makes reference to Schopenhauer, who, in Steiner's view, had intuited that the will bears within it the seed of a reality that would take form in the future (Steiner 1973a, p. 34). This terse reference also conceals an intense engagement. Especially toward the end of the 19th century, Schopenhauer's ideas constituted an important point of reference in philosophical discourse. During his employment at the Goethe-Schiller Archive in Weimar, Steiner edited a twelve-volume edition of Schopenhauer's works, which was published in 1894 (Schopenhauer 1894). An indicator of how important this philosopher was for Steiner may be the fact that in his writings and lectures there are 812 pages within 129 presentations that refer to Schopenhauer. Among other things, Steiner describes how Schopenhauer accepted one and only one "unified reality": the will represented the "sole *[exclusive]* ground *[cause]* of the world" (Steiner 1973b, pp. 178, 230). He does not consider this world-cause to be "an all-wise and all-benevolent being, but a blind urge or will" (Steiner 1998, p. 206). This urge does not exist only in the human soul, for example in the sexual drive, but also in his corporeality, that is, in breath and heartbeat; it is the unquestionable cause of the entire phenomenal world. Schopenhauer was the first thinker in the history of philosophy, as Hans-Joachim Störich notes, who directed the attention toward the "dark depth, which lies beneath the surface of man's conscious awareness" and with that, he "cleared the way for a philosophy and psychology of the subconscious" (Störich 1973, p. 186).

These few hints may suffice to make clear that Steiner integrated *(diametrically opposed,)* polar approaches in his pedagogic psychology in order to thus include the full scope of the life of the soul (Schieren 2012). Thereby Herbart's thoughts directly influenced, through his students Tuiskon Ziller and Wilhelm Rein, the pedagogic discourses up into Steiner's time (Blättner 1980, p. 250). Via Nietzsche and the reform pedagogues that came after him, Schopenhauer's approach led to an emphasis on the significance of developing the will and—as in the movement for art education and work-oriented schools—to concrete first steps in that direction (ibid., p. 259).

Steiner's thumbnail sketch of his pedagogic psychology in the second lecture on "The General Study of Man" reflects the above outlined integration of polar approaches that pit the representational faculties on one hand against the will on the other. The author elucidated this integration at the conference as follows:

The point of origin concerning the psyche are attitudes of sympathy and antipathy, which are primordial phenomena of the life of the soul. Antipathy appears as a force of limitation: The human being confronts the world. In contrast, sympathy is a force for binding himself to the world: The world and I become confluent. These primordial phenomena give rise to the development of basic concepts for a pedagogic psychology, arranged in form of two series in polar opposition to each other.

First, *antipathy* heads the series that contains the elements of representation, memory, concept. As the human being cognitively confronts the world, these three elements are expressions of an increasing degree of antipathy: *representation* is the production of an inner image that forms as a result of certain sensory impressions; the image imprints itself upon *memory* and the *concept* is based on an inner notion acquired since early childhood, which underlies the concrete representation. This outlook by necessity references the past—the respective world phenomenon has to already exist before it becomes then object of cognition.

As we turn our attention toward the antipole headed by *sympathy*, we find ourselves immersed in a completely different sphere. The first element here is the *will*. We identify with the will, it has existential character, we become confluent with it. In fact, the will expresses itself in its elementary form as physical activity: for example, when we chop wood, whittle, dance, or make music, we are fully immersed in this activity. In this sense, will is not an image, but a seed and thus oriented toward the future (*teleological*); each activity has a reflexive effect on the person performing it, developing faculties, which contain growth potential. If the will is enhanced, imagination emerges. In particular, the transition from will to imagination is demonstrated beautifully by children at play. Sitting at the beach, they create a sand pile. Quickly, that becomes a castle, then they add a moat, fetch seashells for adornments and erect a banner, protect the castle with dikes and so on. Imagination grows out of activity.

No artistic process contains its result ahead of time in the imagination. Rather, the opposite is the case—from the willing process something emerges that is new, without preconception, unforeseen.

As the will activity of the imagination is now further increased and penetrates the senses, it gives rise to what Steiner calls "common imagination": the intensive life in a sensory percept, a color or a sound, which permeates the entire human being with its quality.

At the conference, following in the vein of the second lecture of *The Study of Man*, the author thus portrayed the two polar streams within the life of the soul: one stream of *cognition*, based on antipathy, i.d. distance and one stream of the *will,* of activity and experience; this stream is based on sympathy, on identification. The teachers involved committed to studying this motif for the next three weeks and to ask themselves how far this study influenced their teaching practice. The statements made in the ensuing interviews are presented in the next chapter.

5 Methodic consciousness

In response to the introductory question, all interviewed teachers affirmed that they had dealt with the indicated motif, however, in varying ways; its relevance for teaching practice was emphasized. The following facets came to the fore: In particular, in the lower classes, teaching practice starts with the gesture of sympathy, which is will-infused activity. Form drawing in the first and second grades, in particular, shows this very clearly. "At the beginning, the point is to experience the form [drawn on the blackboard], then the children sit there, in wonder, dreaming themselves into the form; they are delighted and look forward to the form, are also quiet as a mouse [...]. And then we detach step by step – the form is now drawn with the hand in the air, the children are allowed to trace along the lines of the form on the blackboard, we help with the hand in the air, then the form is traced with a finger onto the table, then with the fingers onto a sheet of paper, then we take the pencil and draw it on the sheet." This description emphasizes how the teacher successively guides the students through the phase of initial identification in sympathy and wonder toward their own drawing, which presumes indeed an already contoured imagination/representation. Of particular interest in this context is the statement of a teacher, who integrated into these steps the process of drawing with a finger in a bowl filled with fine sand: "When sand-painting, I just noticed they are quite different there. As if they were dissolving *[or: melting]* a bit [...]. And the children also said: 'Oh, it looked so pretty in the sand and it isn't working out in the notebook.'" Obviously, the sensual feeling of sand running through the fingers creates a rather dream-like atmosphere, which is different from copying the form on the blackboard, which demands greater alertness and, especially with mirror images, a greater power of imagination.

In arithmetic, too, the starting point is a physical *experience* of numbers: The teacher drops marbles into a bowl and all count quietly in their mind. Or below the table, the teacher strikes a horseshoe with a nail, or the children tap each other on the back. With such experiential elements, they can sympathetically delve into a sensory experience and all engage fully. A different situation is the introduction of a mathematical sign, e.g., the plus sign, which has an abstract effect. Particularly, a teacher reports the more dreamy children come and ask: "What is that cross supposed to be?" The concern here is to provide guidance toward this *conceptual element* with a certain patience.

But it also happens that some children will volunteer the respective concept if their experience is sufficiently intense. That may happen, for example, when children, fully immersed in imitating (the teacher's example), are stomping or walking rhythmically and suddenly, a child exclaims: "Oh, but this is the series of five!"

Another teacher describes how their storytelling at the end of main lesson brings the students into intense contact with the stream of imagination: "At that point they can one more time delve deeply [into their imagination], and they do love that [...]. I am lucky to have a class that loves stories; they still are waiting for them every day!" This teacher adds that she is telling her stories in free speech, because she noticed that "a great number of children do not really connect" if she just reads the tales out loud. The "antipathic" gesture ensues the following day: The students retell the story from memory and thus revisualize the experience of the previous day; this means that they are engaged in the activity of representation.

In the first grammar (language) lessons of the third grade, the pendular movement between experience to cognition also plays a role. A teacher describes how first teachers and students "do crazy stuff" like jumping down from a table—i.e., engaged in the element of will—and then the term "do-word" is introduced. Students learn about the qualities of different word types in the same way; they also experience the terms *verb, noun,* and *adjective.* In the following years, the class revisits these different qualities on various occasions. Finally, there comes a moment when the students can demonstrate to what degree they really understand this subject matter: when the verb-derived nouns are introduced. A boy raised his hand and said, "Yes, this is a do-word, but it is no longer doing, it has turned into something else!"

These examples demonstrate how the work on living concepts can sometimes stretch over [several] years. This aspect is especially important for a classroom teacher of the sixth grade. Studying the second lecture of *The Study of Man*, a classroom teacher reports that it has made him newly aware of the main lesson design and he illustrates this below with an example from geography class in the sixth grade.

One topic of this lesson main lesson block is the landscape of Norway, but this remains a secret at first. Rather, the teacher tells a story of a fictitious class trip starting out from the Hamburg port. He describes the ship they take, the landing at the coast, the hike along a wide river, and the discovery that this river has no obvious source. The next day, the teacher asks: "Where have we been?" The students relate what they remembered from the previous day, and what caught their attention. In this context, the question emerges: How can there be a river that has no source? After a while, a student raises her hand: "I believe that I have been there once with my parents. That is no river, that is the ocean." That is how we introduce the concept of *fjord*, not as an abstract learning subject, but brought forth from an inner process of one's own experience, in which imagination participates.

Many more statements from the interviews could be brought up; they all point in the same direction. Studying the themes of the second lecture of Steiner's *Study of Man* led the teachers to renew their *conscious awareness* of a certain methodology and to *apply* it into practice with *more attentiveness*: From the connection with a phenomenon through will and emotion, the conceptual element develops though an experiential process.

A review of these cited statements is evidence of the fertility of Steiner's pedagogic psychology for Waldorf teaching practices. These examples illustrate how, based on the polarity of identification and distancing, the various learning processes start with an engagement of the *will*, of action and active experience of a phenomenon to then arrive at *cognition*. Physical activity plays an important role regarding the willing process: sand tracing in form drawing, rhythmic stomping, and walking/running in arithmetic, jumping off the table as an aid in experiencing the word-type of verbs. The activity can also become internalized—then it appears as imagination and becomes the basis for the inner elaboration of stories and tales that the children can consciously "dive into." Moreover, intense sensory experiences are of great importance in this context: the senses of touch, motion, or equilibrium when sand drawing, jumping, walking, and listening attentively to the sound of the horseshoe when working with numbers.

Out of this stream of the will, cognition emerges. Starting from an experience of wonder in form drawing, the teacher guides the students step-by-step toward contoured imagination: The children first absorb the teacher's story in a dream-like way; in retelling the story, it then is remembered and thus more firmly imprinted upon their memory. Experiencing a rhythm through stomping or hand-clapping teases out the concept of number. The following structure of learning processes emerges as a result:

will	*cognition*
(bodily) activity	representation
imagination	memory
sensation	concept

Thus, there is an interplay of bodily activity, imagination, and sensation on one hand, and representation, remembering, and conceptualization on the other, all functioning in such a way that, to follow the famous dictum of Kant here, what emerges are not "empty" concepts or "blind" ideas, but thoughts that are saturated with experience.

One cannot help but draw various connections over to the discourse in educational science. One line connects over to pedagogic phenomenology, which honors sensation as the starting point for learning processes (Rumpf 1981), relies on the experimental and playful dimension of (not only) child-related learning processes (Meyer-Drawe 1982, p. 21), and sees learning as an event composed of active and passive elements, interactivity and unavailability, planning, and surprise (Göhlich, Zirfas 2007, p. 47).

A second reference points to experience-based learning according to John Dewey, who has very recently experienced a new reception in German-speaking pedagogy (Bittner 2001; Oelkers 2011). An essential component of this approach appears to be that learning is seen as an active process, starting with concrete experiences, which involve questioning, explorations, discoveries, and thinking. However, here learning appears more as a cognitive process, possibly giving the impression that an understanding of teaching practice at Waldorf schools might better be approached via the theory of performativity (Fischer-Lichte 2012). Because from the perspective of that theory, learning appears as an artistic process with a lively interaction of the physical presence of the actors: the elements of space, sensations, and specific atmosphere, the rhythm of the event and the gradual dawning of meaning. In this process, the boundary between teachers and students becomes permeable—it becomes a threshold that both are crossing, in order to enter into a space of shared experience. Likewise, the boundary between subject and object dissolves; those involved in the pedagogic process enter into a direct participation, e.g., in storytelling, through stimulation of the powers of fantasy and imagination; they together dive into the direct experience of phenomena and then can regain their distance to them through the process of reflection (Fischer-Lichte 2012, p. 53).

6 Conclusion

The results of this study allow us to ascertain certain aspects. The study was designed, as already pointed out, to be a first exploration of topics that so far have not been subject to research; it does not permit general statements concerning the relevance of Steiner's "General Study of Man" for teaching practice. Moreover, it does not constitute, in a strict sense, empirical research employing a scientific methodology, but it rather presents an illustration for the potential fruitfulness of Steiner's pedagogic psychology for practical classroom instruction: The *(case study)* example showed how the teachers involved were inspired in their teaching practice—after brief study within the framework of the conference—by a motif from Steiner's *Study of Man* and how they reflected on their pedagogic activity against this backdrop.

It does not appear farfetched to suppose that the transition from anthropological foundations to practical classroom instruction is eased through Steiner's "living" concepts and their composition; those who study this approach can build up inner vision, from where they can look at everyday phenomena. For the teachers involved, this anthroposophically oriented anthropology appeared not as other-worldly theory or constrictive dogma, but as a source of orientation and inspiration. Furthermore, the results invalidated, in the example of at least one motif, the claim that the study of the human being according to Steiner is to be viewed as pre-scientific (Ullrich 1986, 2015), mythical (Prange 1985), or even the product of a "totalitarian metaphysic" (Skiera 2003). Rather, we could hint at the science theory context of Steiner's pedagogic psychology and to cross reference it with present-day discourses in current educational science.

Notes

1 Prange (1985), Ullrich (1986, 2015), Skiera (2003); see also in this regard Rittelmeyer (2011), Schieren (2015).

2 The empirical study published by Dirk Randoll under the title "I Am (a) Waldorf Teacher" (Randoll 2013) has substantiated that 82.1% of Waldorf teachers attribute great or very great significance to anthroposophy in their professional work (ibid., p. 72). However, this study did not examine in how far there is a concrete relationship between dealing with motifs from Rudolf Steiner's pedagogic anthropology and practical classroom instruction.

3 These 14 lectures, which Rudolf Steiner held between August 21 and September 5, 1919, in Stuttgart, were published under the title *The General Study of Man as the Foundation for Pedagogy* (1973b); they constitute the Intensive Training course together with several talks—held on the same days—titled *The Art of Education. On Methodology and Didactics* (Steiner 1966) and *Seminar Reviews and Lesson Plan Lectures* (Steiner 1978). With this Intensive Training course, Steiner prepared the first Waldorf teachers for their pedagogic task; thus, they represent an essential cornerstone of anthroposophical pedagogy.

4 On Steiner's pedagogic anthropology in relation to the anthropologies of modern educational science, see Wiehl (2015, p. 98ff).

5 On the pedagogic psychology of Herbart and on Steiner's discussion of this theme, see also Wiehl (2015, p. 115ff).

References

Bittner, Stefan (2001): Learning by Dewey? John Dewey und die deutsche Pädagogik 1900–2000. *[John Dewey and German pedagogy 1900–2000]* Bad Heilbrunn: Klinkhardt.

Blättner, Fritz (1980): Geschichte der Pädagogik. *[History of pedagogy]* Heidelberg: Quelle and Meyer.

Fischer-Lichte, Erika (2012): Performativität. Eine Einführung. *[Performativity. An introduction.]* Bielefeld: Transcript.

Göhlich, Michael/Zirfas, Jörg (2007): Lernen. Ein pädagogischer Grundbegriff. *[Learning. A basic concept of pedagogy]* Stuttgart: Kohlhammer.

Kiersch, Johannes (1994): "Lebendige Begriffe" – Einige vorläufige Bemerkungen zu Denkformen der Waldorfpädagogik. *[Living Concepts – Some preliminary remarks on the thought forms of Waldorf education]* In: Bohnsack, Fritz/Kranich, Ernst-Michael (Ed.) (1994): Erziehungswissenschaft und Waldorfpädagogik. *[Educational science and Waldorf education]* Weinheim and Basel: Beltz.

Kiersch, Johannes (2014): "Mit ganz andern Mitteln gemalt." Überlegungen zur hermeneutischen Erschließung der esoterischen Lehrerkurse Steinerp. *[Painted by very different means. Reflections on the hermeneutic interpretation of Rudolf Steiner's esoteric teacher training courses]* In: Demisch, Ernst-Christian et al. (Eds.) (2014): Steiner neu lesen – Perspektiven für den Umgang mit Grundlagentexten der Waldorfpädagogik *[Reading Steiner with new eyes – Perspectives for dealing with foundational texts of Waldorf education]* Frankfurt am Main: Peter Lang, pp. 55–70.

Meyer-Drawe, Käte (1982): Lernen als Umlernen. *[Learning as re-learning]* In: Lippitz, Wilfried (Ed.) (1982): Lernen und seine Horizonte. Phänomenologische Konzeptionen menschlichen Lernenp. *[Learning and its horizons. Phenomenological conceptions of learning]* Frankfurt am Main: Cornelsen, pp. 19–43.

Oelkers, Jürgen (2011) (Ed.): John Dewey. Demokratie und Erziehung. *[John Dewey. Democracy and education]* Weinheim: Beltz.

Prange, Klaus (1985): Erziehung zur Anthroposophie. Darstellung und Kritik der Waldorfpädagogik. *[Education in anthroposophy. Portrait and critique of Waldorf education]* Bad Heilbrunn: Klinkhardt.

Randoll, Dirk (2013) (Ed.): "Ich bin Waldorflehrer": Einstellungen, Erfahrungen, Diskussionspunkte – Eine Befragungsstudie. *[I am a Waldorf Teacher: Attitudes, Experiences, Points of Discussion – A Survey Study.]* Wiesbaden: Springer VS.

Rittelmeyer, Christian (2011): Gute Pädagogik – fragwürdige Ideologie? *[Good pedagogy – Questionable ideology?]* In: Loebell, Peter (Ed.) (2011): Waldorfschule heute. Eine Einführung. *[Waldorf school today – an introduction]* Stuttgart: Freies Geistesleben, pp. 327–347.

Rumpf, Horst (1981): Die übergangene Sinnlichkeit. Drei Kapitel über die Schule. *[Ignored sensuality. Three chapters on the subject of school]* Munich: Juventa.

Schieren, Jost (2012): Das Lernverständnis der Waldorfpädagogik. *[The understanding of learning in Waldorf education]* In: RoSE – Research on Steiner Education, Vol. 3, Number 1, pp. 75–87.

Schieren, Jost (2015): Das Menschenbild der Waldorfpädagogik. *[The concept of man in Waldorf education]* In: Bauer, Horst Philipp/Schieren, Jost (2015): Menschenbild und Pädagogik. *[The concept of the human being and pedagogy]* Weinheim and Basel: Beltz Juventa, pp. 133–145.

Schopenhauer, Arthur (1894–1896): Werke in 12 Bänden. *[Collected works in 12 volumes]* Stuttgart: Cotta.

Skiera, Ehrenhard (2003): Reformpädagogik in Geschichte und Gegenwart. Eine kritische Einführung. *[Reform pedagogy in historic and contemporary perspectives. A critical introduction]* Munich: Oldenbourg.

Steiner, Rudolf (1965): Anthroposophische Gemeinschaftsbildung. *[Awakening to community]* Rudolf Steiner Gesamtausgabe *[Complete edition]* GA 257. Dornach: Rudolf Steiner Verlag.

Steiner, Rudolf (1966): Erziehungskunst. Methodisch-Didaktisches. Vorträge, gehalten vom 21. August bis 6. September 1919. *[Art of education. Methodical-Didactic. Lectures given from August 21 to September 6, 1919.]* GA 294. Dornach: Rudolf Steiner Verlag.

Steiner, Rudolf (1968): Die Rätsel der Philosophie. *[The riddles of philosophy]* GA 18. Dornach: Rudolf Steiner Verlag.

Steiner, Rudolf (1973a): Allgemeine Menschenkunde als Grundlage der Pädagogik. *[The study of man as a basis for pedagogy]* GA 293. Dornach: Rudolf Steiner Verlag.

Steiner, Rudolf (1973b): Goethes Naturwissenschaftliche Schriften. *[Goethe's writings on natural science]* GA 1. Dornach: Rudolf Steiner Verlag.

Steiner, Rudolf (1976): Anthroposophische Leitsätze. *[Anthroposophical leading thoughts]* GA 26. Dornach: Rudolf Steiner Verlag.

Steiner, Rudolf (1978): Die Philosophie der Freiheit. *[The philosophy of freedom]* GA 4. Dornach: Rudolf Steiner Verlag.

Steiner, Rudolf (1980): Rudolf Steiner in der Waldorfschule. *[Dear children I–III]* GA 298. Dornach: Rudolf Steiner Verlag.

Steiner, Rudolf (1983): Von Seelenrätseln. *[Puzzles of the soul]* GA 21. Dornach: Rudolf Steiner Verlag.

Steiner, Rudolf (1993): Erziehung und Unterricht aus Menschenerkenntnis. Meditativ erarbeitete Menschenkunde. *[Deeper education – Three lectures]* GA 302a. Dornach: Rudolf Steiner Verlag.

Steiner, Rudolf (1994): Erneuerungsimpulse für Kultur und Wissenschaft. *[Impulses for renewal – Seven lectures]* GA 81. Dornach: Rudolf Steiner Verlag.

Steiner, Rudolf (1998): Idee und Praxis der Waldorfschule. *[Idea and practice in Waldorf schools]* GA 297. Dornach: Rudolf Steiner Verlag.

Störich, Hans-Joachim (1973): Kleine Weltgeschichte der Philosophie. *[A little world history of philosophy]* Bd. 2. Frankfurt am Main: Fischer.

Ullrich, Heiner (1986): Waldorfpädagogik und okkulte Weltanschauung. Eine bildungsphilosophische und geistesgeschichtliche Auseinandersetzung mit der Anthroposophie Rudolf Steiners. *[Waldorf education and occult worldview. Analyzing Rudolf Steiner's anthroposophy from a perspective of educational philosophy and the history of thought]* Weinheim and Munich: Juventa.

Ullrich, Heiner (2015): Waldorfpädagogik. Eine kritische Einführung. *[Waldorf education. A critical introduction]* Weinheim, Basel: Beltz.

Wiehl, Angelika (2015): Propädeutik der Unterrichtsmethoden der Waldorfpädagogik. *[Preparatory instructions on teaching methods in Waldorf education]* Frankfurt am Main: Peter Lang.

CHAPTER 3

Developmental Psychology

INTRODUCTION

Albert Schmelzer

An essential component of Waldorf education is its claim that it is consistently guided by the development of the young person. When founding the first Waldorf school, Rudolf Steiner started with the question: What is the human being's potential and what of that can develop within? (Steiner 1982, p. 37) It was his experience as a pedagogue that led to this approach: For eight years, he worked as a private tutor for pupils and students; moreover, between 1884 and 1890, he worked as a home tutor for the four sons of the Specht family in Vienna; his particular charge was Otto, who suffered from hydrocephaly. It was doubtful if and in how far he could be educated: "Even slight mental efforts caused headaches, decrease of life force, he became pale and showed concerning mental behaviors" (Steiner 2000, p. 104). Steiner made every effort to gain maximum achievement through a minimum of stress on the physical and mental powers of the boy and succeeded in supporting him so that he could graduate, go to the university, and become a physician (Schmalenbach 2011, p. 479). Steiner remarked retrospectively that this experience provided him with "an insight into the interconnection between the spiritual, soul and physical aspects of the human being"; for him, this process constituted his "true study of physiology and psychology" (Steiner 2000, p. 105). In addition, he followed the scientific developments in pedagogy and psychology with acute interest; he also dealt intensely and critically with Herbart and his movement, which was an important factor in the Austrian system of education at the time (Wiehl 2015, p. 115ff.).

The same applies for the just emerging scientific research on child psychology or developmental psychology: He studied and commented on authors such as Wilhelm Preyer, William Stern, Alfred Adler, and Ernst Meumann. He gave all due respect to the scientific diligence of the empiric studies in particular; however, Steiner pointed out that he deemed the results of experimental psychology to be fruitless pedagogically, because they only involved the cognitive aspects of the human psyche but ignored its emotional and volitional factors (Steiner 1990, p. 82ff.).

In his little book on *The Education of the Child in the Light of Spiritual Science* that was published in 1907, Steiner does not directly comment on this body of research (Steiner 1907). Instead, he develops his approach based on his differentiated understanding of the human being.

In his view, the source of the human being's potential for self-development lies in the synergy of the three bodies: the *physical body*—materially subject to physical and bio-chemical laws, the *etheric* or *vital body*—the formative power organizing growth and vital processes, and the *astral* or *sentient body*, which is the vehicle of consciousness and of the "I" as the core of man's individuality. Steiner writes that the child's development takes form in the successive birth of these members of being *[three bodies]* in a seven-year rhythm. In the first phase, the vital body effects the physical formation and transformation of the child. During this time, he writes, it is important to provide the right outer and moral environment for the child,

DOI: 10.4324/9781003187431-11

97

because it develops through imitating and following examples. As the permanent teeth come in, part of the vital power now is freed up and becomes available for learning through the faculties of imagination, memory, and fantasy. In that phase, Steiner emphasizes, aesthetic education and pictorial instruction are of paramount significance; the child is looking for a beloved authority. As the child transitions into puberty, another birth occurs: The astral or sentient body is delivered as a vehicle for desire and pain, instinct and passion, making it possible for the young person to arrive at her/his own conclusions and judgments. Only "in the twentieth and twenty-first year," Steiner writes elsewhere does the human being become mature enough to "develop an 'I' from within him/herself" (Steiner 1983, p. 120).

In regard to the establishment and pedagogic support of Waldorf schools, Steiner variously added to this first draft and further developed his approach; up to today his developmental psychology "has remained the heart and core of the Waldorf education's pedagogic psychology – and on one side has been enthusiastically received and developed and with similar fervor attacked and opposed on the other side" (Frielingsdorf 2012, p. 102).

Christian Rittelmeyer's first essay in this section, "Attempts to Understand the Development of Children, Adolescents, and Adults," follows up on the previously presented critique regarding Waldorf education's understanding of the developmental process; the author qualifies it by pointing out that developmental psychology text books commonly the classify developmental phases by using the classical distinctions: childhood lasts until the change of teeth, when the child enters school; youth/adolescence lasts until puberty sets in; adulthood sets in after that transition is completed. Most texts, Rittelmeyer notes, see no problem in segmenting human development into phases. However, tying the developmental stages to a rigid age and especially correlating them with specific pedagogic types of interventions evokes rejection. Rittelmeyer goes on to give a historic overview of different phases as presented by academic developmental psychology and he notes that essentially four distinct approaches have emerged: cognition theories (Piaget, Kohlberg a.o.), psychoanalytically oriented theories (Erikson), biological maturation theories (Gesell), and, lately again, behavioristic approaches in substantiating concepts of learning theory or lesson methodology (Woolfalk, Ulich). According to Rittelmeyer, these theories not only show a certain one-sidedness by emphasizing partial aspects of the developing human being, but they also point to aspects of development that should be further examined: Cognitive theories center on thinking, psychoanalytic theories focus on feeling, behavioristic approaches on the formation of the will, and maturation theories emphasize physicality. This could provide an entry point for a discourse with anthropologically oriented developmental psychology. Steiner's understanding of a threefold organization of the human being into body, soul, and spirit integrates cognitive, emotional, volitional, and physical aspects, Rittelmeyer writes, and it constitutes therefore an "up to now unique and futuristic impulse in developmental psychology" (Rittelmeyer), which we must investigate heuristically as to its suitability for research.

The next article by Albert Schmelzer, "Discussion of Rudolf Steiner's Developmental Psychology," tracks the critique leveled against Steiner's approach, primarily by Heiner Ullrich, Klaus Prange, Wolfgang Schneider, Ehrenhard Skiera, and Winfried Böhm. The critique was sparked by Steiner's teaching on human development with its seven-year rhythms, which, the critics felt, considers the development of the psyche as a quasi-biological maturation process; another point of contention was the underlying doctrine of the members of being, which the critics saw as negating the unity of the person, and finally they took issue with Steiner's understanding of reincarnation and karma, which, in their perspective, leads to a deterministic view of the human being. His critics assert that within a context of the history of science, Steiner's teachings on human development are tantamount to a relapse into mythological, speculative teachings on the ages of man as propounded in antiquity and that his theoretical approach is not supported by empiric research. On the other hand, Rittelmeyer's article cites, e.g., Heiner Barz's arguments in support of core elements of Steiner's developmental psychology from a perspective of educational science: basic congruence with results of empiric research in the field of developmental psychology; close compatibility with Piaget's structuralist interaction theory in Steiner's consideration of individual learning capacity and of environmental influences. He *[Rittelmeyer]* portrays

Introduction

a resulting pedagogy, which makes an effort to create age-specific learning arrangements—far removed from being a "spectator pedagogy."

The author goes on to sketch out issues that should be examined in the interest of a fruitful continuance of the discourse: Considering the results of more recent empirical research, the question emerges whether Steiner's developmental concepts really lead to determinism; attention should be given to developing pathways to understanding the metamorphosis of corporeal forces into those of imagination and fantasy formation, which occurs at the time of the change of teeth. From a perspective of science theory, the related issue of the intersubjective validation of anthroposophical anthropology should be investigated. In conclusion, Rittelmeyer briefly points to the unsolved issue of how to contextualize Steiner's developmental psychology. His *[Steiner's]* well-documented reception of authors such as Preyer, Wundt, Freud, Ebbinghaus, Ziehen, Ament, and Lay points to the probability that his critics' claim of a mere relapse into mythological doctrine on the life stages of man cannot be upheld as such.

Peter Loebell, in his article "Approaches to Substantiating the Concept of Seven-Year Cycles of Development in Waldorf Education," deals with the aspect of potential interfaces of Steiner's developmental psychology with newer research. Here he points to cross-references to the understanding of Erikson, Piaget, Kohlberg, and the practicing pedagogue Janusz Korczak. Also, Loebell casts into relief how Steiner was not concerned with rigid age specifications, but with the portrayal of qualitatively distinct developmental phases. In the interest of such a discourse, it also appears important that Steiner noted a second, contrasting process in counterpoint to the seven-year cycle—a process of increasing individualization that draws attention to the 3rd, 9th/10th, and 12th years. In the next sections of his article, Loebell presents the transitions around the 7th and 14th years and the learning dispositions connected to these transitions; he discusses the issue of the metamorphosis of physical formative powers into the development of imaginative faculties. The article also sheds light on fact that the concept of successive births of bodies or members of being opens up the possibility of integrating the various aspects of development. Moreover, according to Loebell, the blueprint of such a general doctrine of developmental phases may permit a better detection of possible dissociations in cognitive, emotional, volitional, and physical development; Loebell also asserts that these concepts *[the three bodies, members of being, etc.]* create a protective shield against societal *[i.e., standardized, achievement-oriented]* demands and premature pedagogic actions.

These rather general articles presented above are followed by contributions that deal with specific developmental stages.

In his article "Waldorf Education and Developmental Psychology in Early Childhood," Walter Riethmüller embarks on discussing the most recent research on the first years of life up to preschool age, introducing the anthroposophical understanding of this life phase. He first deals with the concept of development, which Waldorf education infuses with a value-added dynamic regarding freedom and responsibility. Interfaces appear with Daniel N. Stern's concept of the emergent self. Only recently, Birgit Elsner and Sabina Pauen go from the assumption that the "I" already exists in the first weeks of the infant's life. According to Riethmüller, Waldorf education deals heuristically with the assumption "that the I as the core of a spiritual identity is not newly born as a blank page, but that it brings along its own destiny and manifold experiences from previous incarnations of earth" (Riethmüller), which currently still appears to pose an obstacle to a rapprochement of viewpoints *[between Waldorf- and academic pedagogy]*.

Riethmüller pinpoints further fields of discourse: the significance of imitation and modeling; the metamorphosis of physical powers into faculties of learning; the understanding of the child as a co-creator of his/her life. In particular, the latter topic shows that the respective results of research on the dialectic structure of development and of attachment research have not only received notice and were under discussion by representatives of Waldorf education but have also been introduced into the guidelines of their work.

The subsequent phase of life is the topic of Axel Föller-Mancini's and Bettina Berger's article, "The Rubicon as a Developmental Phenomenon in Middle Childhood." The authors first clarify that Steiner took Caesar's crossing of the Rubicon as a metaphor for a strengthening of the sense of "I" around the ninth/tenth year of life; then they point to the context within which Steiner's view emerged. We find this context in Steiner's references to specific psychologists, such as Wilhelm Preyer and Wilhelm Wundt and consequently also Stanley Hall, who all arrived at their viewpoints through empiric study. Next, the authors focus on Steiner's view of the Rubicon within the context of his anthropology and developmental psychology and characterize it as an upheaval of the psyche in threefold ways: as a germinating I-consciousness, as an increasing distancing from the world and the human community, and, finally, in physiological perspective, as a taking shape of "the maturation of breath." The authors take an excursion into modern socialization theory to better describe how the relationship to authority can be newly defined during this phase of life.

The last article of this chapter is Wenzel Götte's "Adolescence and the Findings of Brain Research," concerning newer findings in neuroscience research that are significant for the field of pedagogic practice. At the same time, this article contains fundamental aspects of a possible reception of brain research from a pedagogic perspective and describes how educational science and Waldorf education have so far received neuroscience research on the topic of youth and adolescence. The authors state that, so far, the two disciplines *[of pedagogy and neuroscience]* have not yet opened up a discourse on this issue. Götte provides a list of research findings that highlight the significance and relevance of neurological studies for dealing with youths and adolescents.

For example, in puberty, large parts of the cerebrum undergo massive restructuring— particularly limbic system, the physiological substrate of emotions, and the pre-frontal cortex, which is the physiological basis for the goal achievement and for moral behavior, as well as the stability of character. The factors that young people are qualitatively facing are of crucial importance during this sensitive phase, when unused brain structures are dismantled and used ones are stabilizing.

Götte succeeds in establishing plausibility regarding the value of brain research for the pedagogy of adolescence: It can foster understanding for many insufficiencies in puberty, especially as concerns boys, it highlights the significance of stimuli and suggestions offered to adolescents in this sensitive phase of life. Moreover, brain research can draw the attention to the fact that in adolescence too, cognition can be supported not only in direct ways but also indirectly, e.g., through skilled and harmonious movement.

References

Frielingsdorf, Volker (2012): Waldorfpädagogik in der Erziehungswissenschaft. Ein Überblick. *[Waldorf education and educational science. An overview.]* Weinheim and Basel: Juventa

Schmalenbach, Bernard (2011): Anthroposophische Heilpädagogik. *[Anthroposophical Remedial Pedagogy].* In: Uhlenhoff, Rahel (Ed.) (2011): Anthroposophie in Geschichte und Gegenwart. *[Anthroposophy in historic and current perspective].* Berlin: BWV, pp. 477–515.

Steiner, Rudolf (1907): Die Erziehung des Kindes vom Gesichtspunkte der Geisteswissenschaft. *[The Education of the Child in Light of Spiritual Science].* In: Steiner, Rudolf (1987) (Ed.): Lucifer – Gnosis. Grundlegende Aufsätze zur Anthroposophie und Berichte aus den Zeitschriften «Luzifer» und «Lucifer – Gnosis» 1903–1908. Rudolf Steiner Gesamtausgabe 34 *[Foundational essays on anthroposophy and reports from the magazines 'Luzifer' and 'Lucifer – Gnosis' 1903–1908. Collected Works GA 34].* Dornach: Rudolf Steiner Verlag, pp. 309–348.

Steiner, Rudolf (1982): Aufsätze über die Dreigliederung des sozialen Organismus und zur Zeitlage 1915–1921. GA 24. *[Essays on the threefold order of the body social and on current affairs 1915–1921. Collected works GA 24].* Dornach: Rudolf Steiner Verlag.

Steiner, Rudolf (1983): Erfahrungen des Übersinnlichen. Die drei Wege der Seele zu Christus. *[Experiences of the supersensible. Three paths of the soul to Christ] Collected works* GA 143. Dornach: Rudolf Steiner Verlag.

Steiner, Rudolf (1990): Erziehungskunst. Methodisch-Didaktisches. *[The art of education. On methodology and didactics] Collected works* GA 294. Dornach: Rudolf Steiner Verlag.

Steiner, Rudolf (2000): Mein Lebensgang. *[The passage of my life] Collected works* GA 28. Dornach: Rudolf Steiner Verlag.

Wiehl, Angelika (2015): Propädeutik der Unterrichtsmethoden in der Waldorfpädagogik. *[Propaedeutics of teaching methods in Waldorf education]* Frankfurt am Main: Peter Lang.

ATTEMPTS TO UNDERSTAND THE DEVELOPMENT OF CHILDREN, ADOLESCENTS, AND ADULTS

Christian Rittelmeyer

1 Fundamental aspects of an interdisciplinary discourse

In the past, Waldorf education was quite frequently accused of paying only scant attention to the findings of modern developmental psychology, while preferring the pre- and nonscientific developmental doctrines of Rudolf Steiner as a guidepost.[1] In fact, to my knowledge, there are no attempts as yet in Waldorf circles to systematically engage with the positions and research results of developmental psychology; there are, however, occasional deliberations on this topic, such as potential connections between Steiner's developmental doctrine and the cognitive developmental theory of Jean Piaget (Lindenberg 1981, p. 43). Also here and there are thoughts on enriching Anthroposophical anthropology with various findings of developmental psychology (Leber 1993) or ponderings on moral development in public and Waldorf schools along the model of Lawrence Kohlberg (Mayer 2006). Conversely, academic psychology takes no notice of Steiner's developmental teachings although certainly acknowledging in historic excursions some developmental theories, e.g. by Rousseau or Pestalozzi, that are far from scientific.[2] As far as I can ascertain, academic psychology does not take note of other differentiated—though rather phenomenologically oriented—studies in developmental psychology such as that by Hans Müller-Wiedemann (1973).

Later in this article, I want to show an example of how such ignorance can obstruct possible insights, which could diffuse many an inner-disciplinary controversy.

Which insights or theories of developmental psychology can be fruitful for Waldorf education? Where do irreconcilable differences appear to exist? How could a substantial discourse between both disciplines take shape? It is my impression that these questions can be pursued in two ways: reviewing the current authoritative works on developmental psychology (including also some "classics" that are still relevant) and examining which specific insights, scientific studies, and theories are relevant for Waldorf education in how far they are foundational for its anthropological and didactic core, whether they support it or question it. This approach is so broad in view of the huge volume of professional literature in developmental psychology that I cannot endeavor to tackle it, certainly not in the framework of this article. Nevertheless, I want to add a few remarks regarding this approach.

Waldorf circles probably do no doubt that developmental psychology has arrived at a plethora of findings that are of significant value for teachers—insights, for example, into attachment behaviors in early childhood, speech development, the genesis of social and cognitive competencies, or morphological and neurological phenomena of development. As we review the tables of contents in various text- and handbooks on this topic, we notice very different settings of priorities, but they still present a catalog of interesting topics: development of the sense organs; of body control; of the consciousness of self *[self-confidence]*; of fears and other conspicuous factors; of conscience, fantasy, motoric skills, and perception; of sexuality, language skills, intelligence, etc.

DOI: 10.4324/9781003187431-12

Unfortunately, we lack so far any book that would appeal to the interested circles of Waldorf educators by presenting the current understandings of developmental psychology—insofar as the insights promise to hold sufficient continuity—in a concise and understandable form and that introduces these findings in a way that connects closely to pedagogic practice. I will shortly return to this topic of continuity in psychological insight. Such a practice-oriented introduction to developmental psychology for Waldorf educators would have to avoid presenting insights that have short half-lives—representative illustrations in regard to such caution would be older works on developmental psychology that sold well a few decades ago but are all but forgotten by now (Oerter 1975; Schraml 1972). On the other hand, such an introduction should contain also insights and viewpoints that are rare in current introductory works and handbooks of this discipline, even though they are very important for understanding early childhood development. In this category fall, among other works, studies on interaction theory and some works with phenomenological orientation pertaining to the development of the child's faculty of speech, such as the work of Hans Ramge (1976). While there already exists a wide range of literature on the topic of psycho-linguistic development, it fails to acknowledge important contributions like the one just mentioned (Grimm 2001); most handbooks neglect to include, in particular, the topic of *child drawings*, although it is nevertheless a critical area for understanding a child's life world.

An exception is the work of the child psychologist Lotte Schenk-Danzinger (1993), which is a classic by now and didactically very well conceptualized; likewise, an exception is the handbook for qualitative developmental psychology by Günter Mey (2005). Yet there is an extensive literature on child drawing outside of the standard works on developmental psychology, which is worth consideration (Mühle 1971; Widlöcher 1993). This is similarly valid for development-oriented research reports on child and youth literature (Rittelmeyer 2009). But overall, such an ambitious publishing endeavor has not yet been realized. In the following sections, I therefore want to pursue a different path of interdisciplinary discussion in order to show that the "scientific nature" of developmental psychology is by no means uncontested. Mainly, that can be elucidated by presenting a historic review of this discipline.

The critique from the perspective of developmental psychology centers definitively on the developmental doctrine of Rudolf Steiner, which entails the (approximately) seven-year rhythm (Figure 3.1), the teachings on the threefold order of the human organism, and its underlying doctrine of the members of being (Rittelmeyer, Chapter 2). In the following passages, I attempt to show that currently we can give no substantiated answer to the question, whether the positions of contemporary developmental psychology appear compatible with Steiner's developmental doctrine with its pedagogically significant leitmotifs, and especially with the characteristic developmental phases that follow each other in approximately seven-year rhythms. Reviewing the typical outlines in text books on developmental psychology, we again and again discover concepts like *childhood, youth,* of *newborn, preschool child, school-age child,* or *adolescence,* which are more or less congruent with classic distinctions that have been known since antiquity: Childhood lasts up to the change of teeth and start of school; youth extends until puberty, and, upon full sexual maturation, adulthood follows.[3]

It is my impression that developmental psychologists today by and large find no problem with the segmentation of human development into phases or stages. Rather, they see a problem in binding these stages to strictly defined age levels, because of the distinct differences in the progression of individual development. Most of the criticism is leveled against certain representatives of maturation theory and pedagogues, who are coupling certain age-correlated development stages with specific pedagogic tasks, as if a specific development status (such as the "terrible twos") would predetermine a definite pedagogic form of intervention. Already in 1975 (p. 62ff.), Rolf Oerter provided a moderate opinion on this topic, when he emphasized that it was not possible to use certain supposed age-related phases of development as an immediate, fruitful tool for lesson didactics; the benefit of such phase-related teachings, Oerter wrote, lies rather in perceiving children as individuals that are undergoing radical qualitative change instead of seeing them as small, as yet incomplete, adults following their own developmental laws and in sensitively observing these processes.

Attempts to Understand the Development of Children, Adolescents, and Adults

1st to approximately 7th year (change of teeth)
Pedagogic guiding principle: Imitation and modeling

The child gives itself fully over to its close surroundings to form, driven by the imitative instinct, his or her own growing powers and faculties. That is why it is especially significant what happens in the child's environment ("foolish actions" lead to imitation of "foolishness").

> Anthropological leitmotif: The child is fully immersed in sense organ perception.
> Basic pedagogic orientation: The world is good.
> Around the time of the change of teeth: Birth of the body of formative forces.

Approximately 7th to 14th years (puberty)
Pedagogic guiding principle: Succession and authority

The child's soul opens to a conscious reception of the educator's own life and self-expression, based on an implicit authority. The child vaguely feels that something is alive in the educator that will also become alive within him/herself. Interest arises in the relations between things and events and human beings, which around the 9th year also extends to objective relations between objects (an awakening of the feeling of "I"). Important: regulated fantasy; images and parables; adoration and awe. The child experiences intellectual and moral powers mainly in the other person.

> Anthropological leitmotiv: Dominance of the rhythmic system.
> Pedagogic guiding principle: The world is beautiful.
> In the time of puberty: Birth of the sentient body.

Approximately 14th to 21st year
Pedagogic guiding principle: forming one's own judgment/opinion

The formation of independent reason, of abstract or formal imagination, thinking beyond sensual factors, and the power of discrimination. Respect for the thoughts of others; the young person has to develop the sense to engage in learning before judging.

> Anthropological leitmotif:
> Pedagogic guiding principle: The world is true.
> Around the 21st year: The birth of the "I"

Figure 3.1 Rudolf Steiner's approach to child development

These Waldorf pedagogic positions regarding human development and those of academic psychology, however, are by no means unchangeable factors. Especially, higher-grade Waldorf teachers increasingly have academic education that leads to them being familiar with the forms of thoughts and research that are characteristic for system science; this leads noticeably to a more acute understanding *[awake consciousness]* also regarding the insights of developmental psychology.[4] However, developmental psychology undergoes a constant change and can, as just intimated, in no way be seen as a fixed point, that offers valid "current state of research" or "canon of knowledge," from where, for example, Steiner's developmental teachings could be conclusively evaluated. This calls for some further notes which could prove helpful for an interdisciplinary discourse.

2 Developmental psychology "insights" in historic review

After World War II, developmental psychology underwent some fundamental changes in regard to key issues such as its methods of research, theories, and areas of interest. Certainly, the core of developmental psychology research consists of observing and explaining the physical, mental, and soul development of *children and adolescents*. Only recently, this discipline started to deal more distinctly with the *entire span of life*. Nevertheless, I have the impression that specific key topics or at least popular trend can be discerned in historic review. For example, the *development of the individual child* was a central focus of research in the fifties and sixties. (Arnold Gesell, Jean Piaget, René Spitz, John Bowlby, Hildegard Hetzer, Charlotte Bühler, Lotte Schenk-Danziger were important experts.) In the seventies and eighties, the additional issue emerged of *socialization effects in youth and adolescence* and became a focal point of interest and research.[5] Parallel developments in sociology gave rise to an interest in the congregational behavior of young people and their effects and to the popularity of *group dynamics* in social psychology, which drew attention to the fact that adolescent always develop within specific social contexts; without knowledge of their contexts, one cannot understand their development (e.g., Oerter 1978a,b and Peter Rudolf Hofstätter's bestseller *Group Dynamics* 1986).

Then, in the eighties and nineties, *theories of lifelong development* or the so-called *life span development* played a more and more important role.[6] Consequently, current standard works on developmental psychology generally begin—notwithstanding sections on methodology and history of the discipline—with childhood or pre-natal development and end with adulthood or occasionally even with topics such as wisdom, life experience, loss, spirituality, retirement, or death (Berk 2005; Filipp, Staudinger 2005; Oerter, Montada 1987). An approach like this is basically only useful when we look at a human life as an organic whole imbued with meaning and purpose—a thought that, as far as I can discern, has not been more stringently developed in the relevant handbooks (Berk 2005; Hasselhorn, Schneider 2007; Keller 1998; Sugarman 1995). The most recently published textbooks on developmental psychology of adulthood (Faltermaier et al. 2014) appear to distance themselves from this comprehensive biographic perspective, which anthroposophy circles also deem important.

The first volume of the monumental work *Encyclopedia of Psychology* (Schneider, Wilkening 2006, p. 36ff.) deals with developmental psychology and describes several distinctive changes that this discipline experienced in the last decades, in regard to the concepts of man, to theoretical positions, and angles of inquiry:

a. The shift from childhood research to life-span perspective, as already mentioned;
b. A shift away from general models of development toward specific approaches in information processing and then acquisition of knowledge (meaning the currently—again—controversial development of focusing on situation-specific cognitive developmental processes);
c. The transformation of theories of human developmental from normative-descriptive explanation models towards multi-causal ones (I will shortly resume this topic);
d. Abandoning the focus on children's specific competency deficits in favor of descriptions of both the competent child and the old person.

Several further changes can be added to this list of prevailing perspectives in developmental psychology. Conspicuously, there was in recent years growing interest in issues of self-competency, self-concept, or the active self; in the formation *[development]*; I and self; personal and individual accountability; relationship competency or independent; self-empowered living; and the discovery of life purpose.[7]

In retrospect, we can also discern specific areas of interest, theories, and research topics which are of nearly no import today—for example, the education-style research of the sixties and seventies (Herrmann 1966; Lukesch 1977; Schneewind, Herrmann 1980) or Anne-Marie and Reinhard Tausch's book, reprinted numerous times, on socially integrative and autocratic teaching styles, which had been of formative importance for teacher education at the time (Tausch, Tausch 1973).

I find the teaching-style research of those times quite interesting, if styles are understood as differentiating categories of observation for the behavior of parents or teachers, but not as rigid behavioral habits. The same is true for older, intuitive distinctions such as *logo-tropic* (focused on teaching content) or *paidotropic* (focused on the child) teachers (Caselmann 1949) and also for the classic descriptions of authoritarian, democratic, and laissez faire styles of education *[leadership]*, according to Kurt Lewin et al. (1939).

Attempts to Understand the Development of Children, Adolescents, and Adults

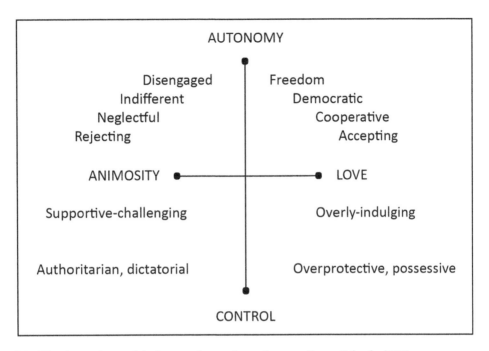

Figure 3.2 The circumplex model of maternal parenting styles according to Schaefer (1959)

The same holds especially for the empiric- and statistic-based bipolar, multi-dimensional models of autonomy vs. control and love vs. animosity in parental behavior (Schaefer 1959; Figure 3.2).

I list these examples because they allow us to recognize something of crucial importance in regard to the dialog between academic psychology and Waldorf education. Why does hardly anyone today talk about these previously much discussed options for describing parent and teacher behavior? For me, an obvious answer seems be the hypothesis: Because we have found pedagogic action to be much more complex than these categories suggest and because the empiric observation of such behavior types brought up so-called issues of reliability tests that yielded a dominant autocratic educational style in certain situations and in that they prove to be specific teachers, led at later times to different results, since the behavior of the test subjects proved to be inconstant. We draw the conclusion based on such historic analyses that categories of developmental psychology may at first appear to be scientifically well founded; however, with progressing research, they prove to be much too simply designed and moreover they may prove unreliable in long-term perspective. Therefore, we must exercise due caution in seizing upon so-called insights of developmental psychology for Waldorf education—these insights of today may be much discussed, but may possibly soon appear invalid. Of course, we must be prepared for such developments in regard to the state of research in general and assume skepticism regarding today's findings in view of the future.

It is, for example, astounding to what degree introductions to modern developmental psychology from the seventies and sixties appear outdated today, as already mentioned, and younger representatives of the discipline are most likely unfamiliar with them. Other "classics," such as the textbook for developmental psychology by Oerter and Montada, have undergone periodic deep revisions so that they could withstand the changing times. Their last edition was edited by Schneider and Lindenberger in 2012. However, here I must quote from an older edition of their standard work because it contains important research on the developmental theories of Erik H. Erickson, which are no longer included in newer editions—maybe because Erikson's theory has lost significance. In view of the frequent argument that Waldorf education should kindly use as an orientation the scientific insights of academic psychology instead of Steiner, such historically based reservations against premature proclamations of a "current state of knowledge" should be heeded in the interest of any truly critical discourse; the demand *[for a new orientation]* without such considerations is simply naïve, in my view. Therefore, a critical reception is in fact called for in regard to adopting assumptions made by developmental psychology, even more so in cases, as in the new science of brain research, where they seem to *correspond to* certain anthropological hypotheses of Waldorf education (Götte in Chapter 3).

Nevertheless, this does not mean that all research findings and theories of developmental psychology must be declared uncertain and temporary. The insight, for example, that young children are not what they long were assumed to be—passive, instinct driven, and helpless, with rather poorly developed cognitive abilities—should be noted as an important progress of scientific insight that could be naturally developed. In the 1980s and 1990s, the research on early childhood reached a new level of excellence and it essentially changes out view of the faculties of infants and young children.[8]

Therefore, earlier views of infants' competencies appear incomplete, if not faulty, from today's perspective, which provides also a historic lesson to be heeded before referring to the "newest state of scientific insight in developmental psychology." For example, we now know that the sensory faculties of infants develop much earlier than we assumed 20 years ago (Goldstein 2008, 389ff.), and that infants are not only influenced by their primary caregivers but also influence them actively, e.g., through gestures and body posture when picked up. Based on such insights, many developmental psychologists might take a skeptical approach to Rudolf Steiner's "Leitmotifs" in the seven-year cycles (Figure 3.1; Steiner 1977): Is the preschool-age child indeed "all sense organ"? Does he/she in fact need to experience the world as "good"? There are many clues that something like intense inquiries after truth can already occur during preschool age[9] and that children create thoroughly esthetic scenarios, for example in their drawings and when playing. A more thorough clarification should help us understand whether these motifs are concerned with empirical statements or normative ones, however non-dogmatic in focus, and whether they may perhaps have pedagogic value and meaning.

Developmental psychology of the 1970s and 1980s was also largely characterized by sometimes forceful and antagonistic *controversies on the validity of certain developmental theories*.[10] An extensive new field of research emerged in the 1980s and 1990s in the form of *attachment research*, which in fact goes back to famous studies from the 1940s to 1970s, conducted by René Spitz, John Bowlby, and the Robertsons (Rittelmeyer 2005). Currently, the so-called *embodiment approach* is being developed as a new area of research, that is, the analysis of physical/bodily foundations and also of cognitive competencies and achievements (Cartmill et al. 2012; Koch 2011; Rittelmeyer 2013; Simms 2008). It attests to the validity of Waldorf education's characteristic and comprehensive approach of including spirit, soul, and body in the educational process.

Aside from these additions and thematic shifts of focus, we can also observe an increasing *interdisciplinary* approach in developmental psychology: In the explanation of speech development, researchers draw on insights from linguistics (for example, the grammar theory of Noam Chomsky) (Kegel 1987), and since the 1990s, then newly popular neuroscience (brain research) plays an ever more important role for the explanation not only of cognitive achievements, but also of the child's learning competency and its general prerequisites (Giedd et al. 2009; Spitzer 2003). The explanation of the child's gifts and achievements draws on behavior-genetic theorems (Asendorpf 1993; Rittelmeyer 2002); detailed information from the fields of medicine and evolutionary biology has replaced earlier, rarely empirically based maturation theories[11] and various studies explored the interrelation between the development of the body and the soul (Lerner, Foch 1987; Gauggel, Herrmann 2008).

The massive accumulation of research studies has brought about an ever-increasing complexity and, concomitantly, a segmentation or rather specialization within the discipline—the same phenomenon can be observed in most other scientific disciplines (as also in those of psychology: differential psychology, applied psychology, social psychology, diagnostics, pedagogic psychology, etc.). In the *Encyclopedia for Psychology*, the subdiscipline of "developmental psychology" is presented in seven large volumes! By now, only specialists can keep at least a relative overview of branches such as attachment research or adolescence research; representatives of one subdiscipline often have barely any knowledge of the other branches. This particularization or splintering (Keller 1998, p. 141) brings with it a danger of no longer holding a comprehensive view of the developing human being and thus could be wrongly interpreted—a problem that was already apparent during the 1960s and 1970s in the controversies about the "correct" developmental theory.

We also need to pay attention to the *changes in methodological standards:* Most, though not all, study designs have become more complex since it became apparent to what extent mono-causal studies can produce methodologically generated artifacts. An example can demonstrate this statement: Figure 3.3 shows one of the results of a comprehensive study to investigate the effects of art instruction on various competencies of elementary-school children (Grebosz 2006). The author studied children in three Polish elementary schools: One of the schools had a profile focusing on music pedagogy; the focus area of the second school was the fine arts, while the third school offered no specific artistic curriculum. The graphic shows the change in the children's creativity scores (as determined through tests) during the time span of the first through second grade. The results in the control group (the third school) did not decline significantly and can be viewed as unchanged. Both schools with artistic focus, however, showed a significant increase in creativity test scores.

A basic problem of such studies lies in the uncertainty, whether the effect is really caused by artistic instruction or by other, unrecognized, factors. The author did introduce the socio-economic status of the parents, and also the child's gender as control variables, which qualifies her study as one of the rather high-end research endeavors. But the question comes up if parents with high educational aspirations also foster the creative faculties of their children at home and if they are more inclined to send their children to schools with special artistic profile—e.g., artistically oriented elementary schools. Studies often are designed to work with randomly segmented groups of research subjects (following the principle of coincidence) in order to deal with this problem, which however also engenders new problems that cannot be covered here. One study design that is nowadays deemed high quality is the so-called *pathway analysis*. Various possible variables (such as educational aspiration, gender, and parental socio-economic status) are introduced to enable mathematical verification of reciprocal effects between the "independent" and "independent" (e.g., creativity) variables. (Figure 3.4: The respective effectivity scores are given in percentage form; the reciprocities are indicated by two-directional arrows.)

Meanwhile, there are many examples showing that the effects that were found in mono-causal studies are disappearing when these more complex variables are taken into consideration, and that they were just methodology-engendered artifacts. For how many research findings of earlier decades and their ensuing practical recommendations may this have been true? The demand that Waldorf educators

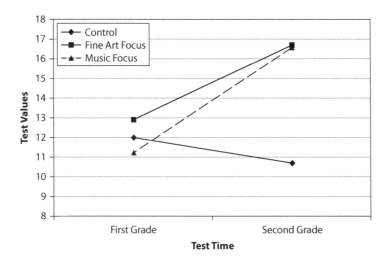

Figure 3.3 Development of creativity potential (test scores) over a one-year span

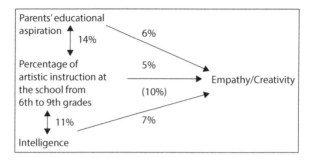

Figure 3.4 Model of a pathway analytic transfer study

should put their pedagogy on solid scientific psychological foundations must therefore at first be met with these reservations. The concern cannot be something like a blind "transfer" of positions from developmental psychology—they have various problems of their own; rather, there needs to be a thorough and critical discussion of methodologies, to find out which positions from that discipline could be of future value for Waldorf educators. I would like to show in the following example, how such discourses can certainly also be illuminating for developmental psychology.

3 Possibilities of a critical discourse on the topic "Waldorf education and developmental psychology": Illustrated by the example of developmental theories

Heidi Keller writes in her *Textbook for Developmental Psychology* that developmental theories always engender certain concepts of the human being (see also Chapter 2 on anthropology). Insight into the possible limitations that such doctrines impose on the views of the developing person has—among other factors—caused contemporary psychologists to step away from closely binding themselves to any specific theory. The four classic developmental theories (Baumgart 2007; Flammer 2005; Trautner 1991/1997) that played a major role in the post war period up to the 1980s, also in pedagogic theory development, are in today's discussion considered as rather temporary and domain-specific: the theory of cognitive development (Jean Piaget, Lawrence Kohlberg, and others) facilitated the explanation the intellectual performance capacity of children and how to foster them in ways appropriate to their development (Butzmann 2000; Elkind 1991); psychoanalytically oriented theories (Erikson 2001) were fruitful for educational counseling or for interpreting certain problems of adolescence (Berk 2005, p. 235ff; Frey, Haußer 1987; Oerter, Montada 1987); biologically oriented maturation theories (Gesell 1964) in new and research-based form assisted in the understanding of speech and brain development (Pinker 1996; Schneider, Wilkening 2006, p. 461ff.); learning and especially behavioristic theories—which are, according to Heidi Keller, experiencing a renaissance—offered explanations for concepts in learning therapy and lesson didactics (Ulich 2002; Woolfalk 2008, p. 257ff). For the marginalization and critical reception of the classic developmental theories, there are two more reasons.

First: In the last decades, numerous studies were published that gave rise to doubts about the general validity as well certain positions of these (mutually competitive) theories of human development. For example, the postulate of an egocentric orientation as being typical for small children—according to Piaget—has by now become a controversial issue.

Also, his theory of sensor-motoric intelligence being dominant up to the second year of life has turned out to be much too one-sided. In repeat studies, many of his classic experiments with children yielded divergent results. His critics found that he by and large overlooked the socializing influence of the entire life environment, to just name a few of the objections.[12] In the 1970s and 1980s, the developmental teachings of Erikson were broadly received, also in pedagogy; his theory proclaimed certain fundamental issue clusters, e.g., trust vs. mistrust in the first year or an identity diffusion in puberty, but could not always be validated through empiric studies (Oerter, Montada 1987, p. 298ff).

One representative of learning theory even claimed that the psychoanalytic work of Sigmund Freud evidenced qualities of fiction literature more than of science (Selg 1978, p. 160).

In turn, critics take a skeptical view of the behavioristic learning theory of Burrhus Skinner, which had already met with fierce criticism by linguist Noam Chomsky (1959); this skepticism is based on the fact that many phenomena cannot be explained through learning theory (as for example the peculiar child grammar of approximately three-year old children—"I have drinked the whole glass," etc.). Therefore, it became ever more questionable to refer to such theories in regard to one's *pedagogic actions.* We can see in retrospect that the attempt of some Waldorf pedagogues was not unproblematic as they searched for correspondences between Steiner's developmental teachings and the developmental theory of Piaget in particular. The same reservations are of course valid concerning the demand from the side of educational scientist that Waldorf education should take these purportedly scientific developmental theories into consideration. Common sense already tells us that, e.g., cognitive theories of development alone will hardly suffice to explain typical puberty issues, while psychoanalytic and biological theories may be helpful. The question of at what age a child is generally able to solve specific mathematical problems or understand the syntax of a language, however, may best use explanations offered by cognitive theories. It remains incomprehensible in view of such considerations, why the representatives of such theories, even at the height of their popularity, were fighting so fiercely for the correctness or even superiority of their positions. Another reason for the erosion of distinctive developmental theories has barely received notice—i.e. the question in how far discourse opportunities between Waldorf education and developmental psychology even existed, which may be interesting and illuminating for both sides to pursue.

We need therefore first take a closer look at the specific human attributes that receive special consideration from cognition and learning theories and those attributes, which are the focus of biologically and psychoanalytically oriented theories. This process can show that respective partial aspects of the developing human being are accorded one-sided emphasis, which may serve to explain many issues that have emerged in regard to the validity of these theories. While there are other socialization or developmental theories besides the four classic ones, they have never attained lasting significance in educational science as well. Here we can list the "ecological socialization" or systems theory (Bronfenbrenner 1982 and others), which studies the dynamic interaction between environment and individuality throughout life, investigating the ecological validity of positions in developmental psychology, e.g., attends to the question of school-readiness (Oerter 1978b); others on this list are the *information processing theory,* as a special variant of cognitive theories (development as a change in cognitive structures), also the *evolutionary psychology theory* in the tradition of Konrad Lorenz and Niko Tinbergen as well as Lev Vygotsky's theory of socio-cultural development and other perspectives.[13] "Constantly there emerge new interpretations of the process of human development," writes Laura Berk in her book *Developmental Psychology* (2005, p. 27). "The discoveries of earlier theories are being questioned and amended or serve as foundations for new perspectives" (ibid.). Yet it seems to me that the four classic developmental theories named above certainly do provide "foundations for new perspectives," if we take a close look at them.

They indeed offer important clues for the key conditions determining the development of adolescents: thinking (recognition, representation), feeling (their emotions, affect, etc.), and willing (*that means in more recent psychology a renewed focus on volitional aspects of action, which had long been overlooked in favor of cognitive aspects*), and on their bodily aspects, i.e., the biological aspects of development. I suspect that each of these four, factually interconnected aspects became the one-sided focus of different socialization theories. If, however, we study the mental development of the child without considering his/her physical or emotional development, we blind ourselves voluntarily and easily lose our way with possibly deleterious pedagogic consequences, going astray, e.g., due to explanations based on cognition theory and thus, narrowly focusing on a school pedagogy that is oriented toward cognitive goals. This is also true for attempts to link developmental theories of the psychoanalytic type with learning theories or learning theories with cognitive ones (Bandura 1979; Berlyne 1974). Thinking is thus given more relative significance in those developmental theories that are called cognition theories, within whose framework we study the development of cognition (in general) or, e.g., of moral discernment (in particular). Best known is Piaget's (1896–1980) theory of successive stages of mental development[14], which proved highly consequential for pedagogic theory formation. We can easily understand the fascination that was engendered, among school pedagogues in particular, by this developmental theory that seemed so well supported by numerous famous experiments with children: It seemed that Piaget's theory of stagewise development provided guidance and an answer to the question of how to align one's teaching/lesson didactics with the respective intellectual capabilities of the students.[15]

The psychoanalytic theory of development centers especially on the area of *feeling* (the emotions, affects, sympathies, antipathies). However, Freud's theory of psycho-sexual development along different phases (oral, anal, genital) has never been able to attain as prominent a significance in pedagogy or in developmental psychology as the Freud-based but significantly more comprehensive eight-stage development theory of Erik H. Erikson (1902–1994). This eight-stage theory inspired pedagogic theories on identity development and adolescence in particular. The special feature of this theory is its expansion to cover the entire life span; as already mentioned, its basic approach to proclaim specific elemental conflict constellations—so-called psycho-social crisis points—for different age spans (that are not precisely defined), which need to be resolved if the further development up to old age is supposed to proceed smoothly. According to Erikson, for example, the first year of life brings with it the primal conflict between trust and mistrust—which poses the developmental task to develop trust (mainly through and with the persons of reference). In puberty (around ages 11–17), Erikson writes, arises the conflict between a successfully proceeding identity formation (finding a positive self-image) and the diffusion of identity.[16]

This theory obviously directs acute attention to the development of the emotional problem constellations that are typical for respective stages of development and brings the affects and fears, the delights and sympathies into focus, while the cognitive or also bodily aspects are not subject to explicit or systematic reflection.

The development of the will is emphasized in classic learning theories and—this may come as a surprise—in behaviorism, which consciously bracketed out thinking and feeling functions of adolescents as an unknown "black box."[17] Instead, here the focus is on observable *actions*, which—supposedly—can be called forth as responses to positive or negative "reinforcements" in form of certain stimuli. A student's attacks on classmates, for example, can be described as the conditioned response to success experiences while acting out such aggressions. However, such theories often emphasize a more passive form of will development and not the self-driven, active form of volitional action that has recently received renewed attention (Kuhl, Heckhausen 1996, p. 361ff.). Because these behavioristic learning theories see the development of the child as a result of conditioning processes—a somewhat simplified statement—there is also no mention of stages of development. Characteristic for this critical position is the statement of the developmental psychologist Horst Nickel with learning theory orientation that there is no so-called natural development, which would need to be awaited as a prerequisite for systematic pedagogical action. "Rather," Nickel writes, "the attained level of development is always essentially the result of learning processes, since the inter-individual differences between children [...] are most of the time very significant, education and instruction in our schools can hardly be expected to rely on allegedly concurrent developmental prerequisites for any specific age group" (Nickel 1974, p. 45ff.).

Learning-theory-oriented developmental psychologists soon recognized that a strictly behavioristic approach would leave many child behaviors unexplainable (Angermeier et al. 1991; Foppa 1975) and that they therefore had to make assumptions of intervening cognitive variables between stimulus and response processes. As mentioned above, the child grammar typical for children around age three can only be explained as a self-engendered cognitive achievement and not just as imitative speech elicited by parental reinforcements.

Developmental psychologists with learning theory orientation therefore have introduced more complex theoretical outlines of childhood behavior development, in distinction from radical behavioristic notions; Albert Bandura, for example, with his social-cognitive learning theory who, among others,

Attempts to Understand the Development of Children, Adolescents, and Adults

studied the imitation behavior of children (Bandura 1979). Robert E. Sears' behavioristic development theory, too, no longer adhered to the strict black-box model and to Skinner's technological theory of learning, since it also addresses among others the emotions of adolescents (Maier 1983). While, however, developmental psychology deems behavioristic theories in particular to be too one-sided and outdated, they still crop up in pedagogic contexts again and again in form of unexamined explanation patterns.

It is interesting and perhaps no coincidence when Heidi Keller writes in her *Textbook of Developmental Psychology* (Keller 1998) that behavioristic notions are undergoing a renaissance—and this at the dawn of achievement tests (TIMMS, PISA, etc.) and establishment of fixed educational achievement standards (Ulich 2002). The dominance of behavioristic theories often occurs hand-in-hand with a technocratic understanding of education and development, which aims at reaching certain educational goals with the help of (preferably empirically validated) teaching technologies without any attention to individual processes of soul and mind that are always essential to learning processes. In conclusion, I want to emphatically point out that I indirectly deducted that there is a will focus in behavioristic theories of learning, and that the authors of these theories do not interpret them in this way. But it deserves mention that most books on developmental psychology do not address willing and will (the volitional aspect of development); also, the term *will* is not the same as *motivation*. In the 1920s and 1930s, authors such as Kurt Lewin and Narziss Ach focused intensely on the genesis of volitional action. After that time the topic has largely been forgotten and has only recently reappeared in the form of the volitional aspect of action.[18]

Finally, the bio-psychological and maturation theories place particular emphasis on bodily aspect of human development (e.g., when describing the body's physical growth in puberty and its effect on students' learning behavior).

Arnold Gesell (1880–1961), Oswald Kroh (1887–1955), Heinz Werner (1890–1964) or bestselling authors relevant to teacher education in the 1960s, such as Heinz Remplein (Rittelmeyer 2002), were classic representatives of such endogenic maturation theories. I suspect that a thorough analysis of Bernard Lievegoed's work on developmental psychology would also bring to light premises of such maturation theories—aside from the anthroposophical references (Lievegoed 1989). It was in particular Arnold Gesell (e.g., 1964), who amassed valuable material portraying the typical behavioral characteristics that children show in their respective biological stages of development. Just like many developmental psychologists and probably also pedagogues in the 1960s, Gesell adhered to a theory of endogen maturation: The child's development of soul and mind is culturally imprinted, but in its basic patterns, it follows a blueprint of genetic predispositions. This bodily aspect of human development has been rarely explicitly discussed and has only in our time regained attention due to elaborate research methods such as imaging tomography and also micro-biological behavior-genetic research methods.[19] Consequently, the "body aspect" of developmental processes are recently attracting more and more interest. In particular, the discipline of neuroscience and its research studies might become more interesting as it attends to segments and steps of brain development typical for specific age thresholds and their concomitant development phenomena of the psyche. Researchers detected fundamental changes in brain structure in certain areas, especially around the time of puberty, which in their view explained many apparently typical teenage behaviors.[20]

In conclusion, here is a summary of correspondences between anthropological aspects and different socialization theories:

- Thinking: Primary focus of cognition theories
- Feeling: Primary focus of psychoanalytic theories
- Willing: Primary focus of classic behavioristic learning theories
- Body: Primary focus of endogenetic or bio-psychological theories

In respect to the interdisciplinary discourse with Waldorf educators, I am concerned with the obvious fact that it was immensely one-sided, considering these theoretical preconceptions about the development of

Body	Soul	Mind-spirit
Neurosensory System	Representation (Antipathy)	Waking
Rhythmic System	Feeling (Antipathy/Sympathy)	Dreaming
Metabolic-Limbic System	Willing (Sympathy)	Sleeping

Figure 3.5 Rudolf Steiner: The threefold order of the human being

children and adolescents. Yet, it is even more astonishing that up until today there was no attempt to follow these theories and the clues, embedded in their one-sided perspectives, regarding the obvious need for a more comprehensive anthropological-pedagogical reflection on the developing human being. Laura Berks (2005), however, in her handbook on developmental psychology, emphasizes the need to look at the development from small child into adulthood under equal consideration of bodily, cognitive, and emotional/social phenomena; but these suggestions are not leading to a consolidated integrated theory, which also would include the acts of will, i.e., volitional aspects (Berk 2005). To me, here Rudolf Steiner's anthropological thoughts on the threefold nature of man appear to point the way—even though just heuristically initially, because their accessibility for research would first need to be examined. Figure 3.5 shows this functional threefold order of the human being, which essentially inspired me to consider the classic theories of development as described above in a critical and more comprehensive way (Steiner 1977).

The four anthropological categories are closely interwoven here, imagining/representing, feeling, and willing also classified as attributes of the soul, while waking, dreaming, and sleeping corresponding to the mental/spiritual attributes of waking, dreaming, and sleeping—attributes as they are meant here that psychology too would classify as belonging to the domain of the soul. Because sleeping in Rudolf Steiner's sense is also a toning down of consciousness while being awake, for instance, as we accomplish routine work without consciously registering what we do. When we listen to a piece of music with feelings of like or dislike, a form of dreaming occurs. Thinking about the cause for such feelings occurs in the realm of waking representation. We always have to distance ourselves somewhat, when we mentally process phenomena that, according to Steiner, indicate a kinship with antipathy.

Interestingly, corporeality here is not shown as a separate anthropological category, but as part of the organic threefold side of mind and soul activities. Also, Rohen and Lütjen-Drecoll's histological text (1982), which identifies a threefold organization also on the cellular level, demonstrates that these categories can also, from a medical science perspective, offer very reasonable insights into the human organism. If we perceive Steiner's system just as an empirically valid categorization scheme, it would certainly lead us astray. It is first of heuristic interest because of evidencing close relations with anthropological concepts that are important to developmental psychology and can be regarded as a model in this respect. Steiner's system plays an important role in Waldorf education due to its connection with the theory of development. What emerges is a principle of unbiased observation that needs to be studied to determine, whether it overly simplifies the developing child or even determines it unduly—or whether it allows us to perceive the child in more artistic and substantial perspectives. As a matter of fact, I view the attempt to establish an organic, anthropologically based connection between cognitive, emotional, volitional, and corporeal faculties as a unique and futuristic impulse in developmental psychology, especially because the theories described above are presented in such a one-sided and thus uninspired way. One might add that both the developmental teaching of Steiner and the threefold system need to be examined to see how the findings of so-called ecological socialization research can figure in the understanding of manifest influences of the respective culture, of peer relations, or socio-economic circumstances and living conditions of the developing child, who also co-creates these environments in self-empowered and individual ways.

Notes

1 Ullrich (1986, p. 101; 2002, p. 191), Frielingsdorf (2012, p. 10ff), Kranich, Ravagli (1990, p.166ff).
2 Trautner (2003, p. 15), Oerter, Montada (1987, p. 25), Thomas, Feldman (2002).
3 Mietzel (2002), Oerter (1978a,b), Hasselhorn, Schneider (2007, pp. 131ff); for historical reference on that topic see also Reinert (1976).
4 Loebell (2004), Lutzker (1996), Götte (2005); Marti (2006); see also the following articles in Chapter 3 of this handbook.
5 Erikson (2001), Ausubel (1979), Markefka, Nave-Herz (1989), Schumann-Hengsteler, Trautne (1996), Asendorpf (1999), Fend (2001), Alt (2005), Silbereisen, Hasselhorn (2008).
6 Baltes, Brim (1983), Lerner, Foch (1987), Oerter (1978a), Langenmayr, Schubert (1987), Kruse, Schmitz-Scherzer (1995), Hendry, Kloep (2002), Hasselhorn, Schneider (2007).
7 Asendorpf (2005), Filipp, Staudinger (2005), Hendry, Kloep (2002), Greve (2000).
8 Keyword: "the competent infant" (Hasselhorn, Silbereisen 2008; Markefka, Nauck 1993; Papousek 1994; Stern 1994; see also the LOGIK longitudinal study with children: ages 3–13: Weinert 1998).
9 Keyword: "The Philosophizing Child" (Neißer 2012; Neumann, Horster 1992).
10 Jeran Piaget, Sigmund Freud, Erik H. Erikson and others (Baumgart 2007; Trautner 1991/1997, vol. 1).
11 Keller (1993), Touwen (1993), Holle (1988), Kohnstamm (1990), Maier et al. (1994), Markowitsch (1996).
12 Billmann-Mahecha (1990), Trautner (1991/1997), Smith (1996), Modgil, Modgil (1987), Katzenbach, Steenbuck (2000).
13 Garz (2006), Miller (2000), Wuketis (1995), Tillmann (2006), Hurrelmann (2008), Keller (1998, pp. 121ff), Hasselhorn, Schneider (2007, pp. 26ff), Ahnert (2013).
14 On this theory and its reception in educational science and its critical discussion see: Trautner (1991/1997), Flammer (2005), Modgil, Modgil, Brown (1983), Sime (1978), Smith (1996), Katzenbach, Steenbuck (2000), Siegel, Brainerd (1978).
15 Furth (1973), Butzmann (2000), Piaget (2003), Elkind (1991), Ulich (2002, pp. 502ff).
16 For an overview see: Erikson (2001), Flammer (2005), Trautner (1991/1997), Thomas, Feldman (2002).
17 See especially also Burrhus Frederic Skinner (1957, 1971), Trautner (1991/1997), Flammer (2005).
18 One of the few exceptions is the textbook by Oerter (1975); for more detail see also: Kuhl, Heckhausen (1996, pp. 361ff).
19 Call to mind the distinct resonance that certain "brain researchers" like Manfred Spitzer experienced in pedagogic circles, or the "embodiment approach," which we already mentioned, but also the ever newly sparking debate on behavioral genetics: Are—and to what extent—"talents" the result of nature or nurture—are talents learned or inherited? (Bilstein, Brumlik 2012; Rittelmeyer 2002).
20 Götte Chapter 3; Ramsden et al. 2011; Strauch 2004; Bennett, Baird 2006; Giedd et al. 2009; Johnson et al. 2009; Tiemeier et al. 2010.

References

Ahnert, Lieselotte (2013): Theorien der Entwicklungspsychologie. *[Theories of developmental psychology]* Berlin: Springer VS.

Alt, Christian (Ed.) (2005): Kinderleben – Aufwachsen zwischen Familie, Freunden und Institutionen. *[Child's life – Growing up among family, friends and institutions]* Wiesbaden: Springer VS.

Angermeier, Wilhelm F./Bednaz, Peter/Hursh, Stevem (Eds.) (1991): Operantes Lernen. Ein Handbuch. *[Operant learning. A handbook].* Munich: Reinhard.

Asendorpf, Jens (1993): Entwicklungsgenetik der Persönlichkeit des Kindes. *[Developmental Genetics of Child Personality]* In: Markefka, Manfred/Nauck, Bernhard (Eds.) (1993): Handbuch der Kindheitsforschung. *[Handbook of childhood research]* Neuwied: Luchterhand, pp. 17–30.

Asendorpf, Jens (1999): Keiner wie der andere. Wie Persönlichkeitsunterschiede entstehen. *[No one is like another. On the genesis of personality differences]* 2., durchges.und aktual. Auflage. *[2nd revised and updated edition]* Dreieich: Edition Wötzel.

Asendorpf, Jens (Ed.) (2005): Soziale, emotionale und Persönlichkeitsentwicklung. Enzyklopädie der Psychologie C 5. vol3. *[The development of social aspects, emotions, and the personality. Encyclopedia of psychology, chapter 5. Vol. 3].* Göttingen: Hogrefe.

Ausubel, David (1979): Das Jugendalter. *[The age of youth.]* 6th edition. Munich: Juventa.

Baltes, Paul B./Brim, Orville G. (Eds.) (1983): Life-Span Development and Behavior. Vol. 5. New York: Academic Press.

Bandura, Albert (1979): Sozial-kognitive Lerntheorie. *[Social-cognitive learning theory].* Stuttgart: Klett-Cotta.

Baumgart, Franzjörg (Ed.) (2007): Entwicklungs- und Lerntheorien. 2. Auflage. *[Theories of development and learning. 2nd edition.]* Bad Heilbrunn: Klinkhardt.

Bennett, Craig M./Baird, Abigail A. (2006): Anatomical Changes in the Emerging Adult Brain. In: Human Brain Mapping 27, pp. 766–777.

Berk, Laura E. (2005): Entwicklungspsychologie. 3., aktual. Auflage. *[Developmental psychology, 3rd updated edition.]* Munich: Pearson Studium.

Berlyne, Daniel E. (1974): Konflikt, Erregung, Neugier. Zur Psychologie der kognitiven Motivation. *[Conflict, excitement, curiosity. On the psychology of cognitive motivation]* Berlin: Klett.

Billmann-Mahecha, Elfriede (1990): Egozentrismus und Perspektivenwechsel. *[Egocentrism and change of perspective]* Göttingen: Hogrefe.

Bilstein, Johannes/Brumlik, Micha (Eds.) (2012): Die Bildung des Körpers. *[The development of the body]* Weinheim und Basel: Beltz.

Bronfenbrenner, Urie (1982): Die Ökologie der menschlichen Entwicklung. 2. Auflage. *[The ecology of human development. 2nd edition]* Stuttgart: Fischer.

Butzmann, Erika (2000): Sozial-kognitive Entwicklungstheorien in der Praxis. *[Social-cognitive theories of development in praxis context]*. Weinheim: Deutscher Studienverlag.

Cartmill, Erica A./Beilock, Siar/Goldin-Meadow, Susan (2012): A word in the hand: action, gesture and mental representation in humans and non-human primates. In: Philosophical Transactions of the Royal Society B U (Biological Sciences) 367, pp. 129–143.

Caselmann, Christian (1949): Wesensformen des Lehrers. *[Teachers' styles of being]* Stuttgart: Klett.

Chomsky, Noam (1959): Verbal Behavior by B. F. Skinner. In: Language 35, pp. 26–58.

Elkind, David (1991): Das gehetzte Kind. Werden unsere Kleinen zu schnell groß? *[The hurried child. Are our little ones growing up too fast?]* Hamburg: Kabel.

Erikson, Erik H. (2001): Identität und Lebenszyklus. Drei Aufsätze. *[Identity and Life Cycle. Three Essays.]* Frankfurt am Main: Suhrkamp.

Faltermaier, Toni/Mayring, Philipp/Saup, Winfried/Strehmel, Petra (2014): Entwicklungspsychologie des Erwachsenenalters. 3. Auflage. *[Developmental psychology of adulthood. 3rd edition]* Stuttgart: Kohlhammer.

Fend, Helmut (2001): Entwicklungspsychologie des Jugendalters. 2., durchgesehene Auflage. *[Developmental psychology of childhood. 2nd reviewed edition]* Opladen: Leske + Budrich.

Filipp, Sigrun-Heide/Staudinger, Ursula (Eds.) (2005): Entwicklungspsychologie des mittleren und höheren Erwachsenenalters. Enzyklopädie der Psychologie C5 Band 6, *[Developmental psychology of adult middle and old age. Encyclopedia of psychology C5 volume 6]* Göttingen: Hogrefe.

Flammer, August (2005): Entwicklungstheorien. 3., korrigierte Auflage. *[Developmental theories. 3rd and revised edition]* Bern: Huber.

Foppa, Klaus (1975): Lernen, Gedächtnis, Verhalten. Ergebnisse und Probleme der Lernpsychologie. 9. Auflage. *[Learning, memory, behavior. Findings and issues of the psychology of learning. 9th edition]* Köln: Kiepenheuer & Witsch.

Frey, Hans-Peter/Haußer, Karl (Eds.) (1987): Identität. Entwicklungen psychologischer und soziologischer Forschung. *[Identity. Developments in psychological and sociological research]*. Weinheim: Enke.

Frielingsdorf, Volker (2012): Waldorfpädagogik in der Erziehungswissenschaft. Ein Überblick. *[Waldorf education and educational science. An overview]*. Weinheim: Beltz Juventa.

Furth, Hans (1973): Piaget für Lehrer. *[Piaget for teachers]*. Düsseldorf: Schwann.

Garz, Detlef (2006): Sozialpsychologische Entwicklungstheorien. 3., erweiterte Auflage. *[Developmental theories in social psychology. 3rd revised and updated edition]*. Wiesbaden: Springer VS.

Gauggel, Siegfried/Herrmann, Manfred (Eds.) (2008): Handbuch der Psychologie. Bd. 8. Handbuch der Neuro- und Biopsychologie. *[Handbook of psychology. Vol. 8. Handbook of neuro- and bio-psychology]*. Göttingen: Hogrefe.

Gesell, Arnold (1964): Das Kind von Fünf bis Zehn. 5. Auflage. *[The child age five to ten. 5th edition]*. Bad Nauheim: Christian.

Giedd, Jay/Lalonde, Francois/Celano, Mark/White, Samantha/Wallace, Gregory/Lee, Nancy/Lenroot, Roshel (2009): Anatomical brain magnetic resonance imaging of typically developing children and adolescents. In: Journal of American Academic Child Adolescent Psychiatry 48, pp. 465–470.

Götte, Wenzel M. (Ed.) (2005): Hochbegabte und Waldorfschule. *[Highly gifted children and Waldorf education]*. Stuttgart: Freies Geistesleben.

Goldstein, Eugen Bruce (2008): Wahrnehmungspsychologie. *[The psychology of perception]*. 7. Auflage. *[7th edition]*. Berlin: Spektrum.

Grebosz, Katarczyna (2006): Der Einfluss musikalischer Ausbildung auf die Entwicklung der Psyche von Kindern. Eine empirische Untersuchung an drei unterschiedlichen Grundschulen in Polen. *[The influence of music education on children's psychological development. An empirical study conducted at three different elementary schools in Poland]*. Dissertation: Universität Salzburg.

Greve, Werner (Ed.) (2000): Psychologie des Selbst. *[The psychology of the self]*. Weinheim: Beltz.

Grimm, Hannelore (Ed.) (2001): Sprachentwicklung. Enzyklopädie Psychologie. Serie Sprache. Band 3. *[Speech development. Encyclopedia of psychology. Series speech. Vol. 3]*. Göttingen: Hogrefe.

Attempts to Understand the Development of Children, Adolescents, and Adults

Hasselhorn, Marcus/Schneider, Wolfgang (Eds.) (2007): Handbuch der Entwicklungspsychologie. *[Handbook of developmental psychology]*. Göttingen: Hogrefe.

Hasselhorn, Marcus/Silbereisen, Rainer (Eds.) (2008): Entwicklungspsychologie des Säuglings- und Kindesalters. Enzyklopädie der Psychologie C5 Band 5. *[Developmental psychology of the infant and young child. Encyclopedia of psychology C5 vol. 5]*. Göttingen: Hogrefe.

Hendry, Leo B./Kloep, Marion (2002): Lifespan Development: Resources, Challenges and Risks. London: Thompson Learning

Herrmann, Theo (Ed.) (1966): Psychologie der Erziehungsstile. *[Psychology of educational styles]*. Göttingen: Hogrefe.

Hofstätter, Peter Rudolf (1986): Gruppendynamik. Kritik der Massenpsychologie. Vollständig erweiterte und überarbeitete Neuausgabe. *[Group dynamics A critique of mass psychology. Completely revised and updated new edition]*. Reinbek bei Hamburg: Rowohlt.

Holle, Britta (1988): Die motorische und perzeptuelle Entwicklung des Kindes. *[The motoric and perceptual development of the child]*. Munich: Psychologie Verlags Union.

Hurrelmann, Klaus (Ed.) (2008): Handbuch Sozialisationsforschung. 7. Auflage. *[Handbook of socialization research. 7th edition]*. Weinheim: Beltz.

Johnson, Sara B./Blum, Robert/Giedd, Jay (2009): Adolescent maturity and the brain: the promise and pitfalls of neuroscience research in adolescent health policy. In: Journal of Adolescent Health 45, p. 216–221.

Katzenbach, Dieter/Steenbuck, Olaf (Eds.) (2000): Piaget und die Erziehungswissenschaft heute. *[Piaget and educational science today]*. Frankfurt am Main: Lang.

Kegan, Robert (1982): Die Entwicklungsstufen des Selbst. *[The developmental stages of the self]*. Munich: Kindt.

Kegel, Gerd (1987): Sprache und Sprechen des Kindes.3.Auflage. *[Language and speech activity of the child. 3rd edition]*. Opladen: Springer VS.

Keller, Heidi (1993): Psychologische Entwicklungstheorien der Kindheit. Versuch einer evolutionsbiologischen Integration. *[Theories of psychological development in childhood. Attempt of an evolutionary-biological integration]*. In: Markefka, Manfred/Nauck, Bernhard (Eds.) (1993): Handbuch der Kindheitsforschung. *[Handbook of childhood research]*. Neuwied: Luchterhand, pp. 31–44.

Keller, Heidi (Ed.) (1998): Lehrbuch Entwicklungspsychologie. *[Textbook developmental psychology]*. Bern: Huber.

Koch, Sabine (2011): Embodiment. Der Einfluss von Eigenbewegung auf Affekt, Einstellung und Kognition. *[The influence of autonomous motion on affect, attitude, and cognition]*. Berlin: Logos.

Kohnstamm, Rita (1990): Praktische Kinderpsychologie. 3., korrigierte und erweiterte Auflage. *[Practical child psychology. 3rd revised and expanded edition]*. Bern: Huber.

Kranich, Ernst-Michael/Lorenzo Ravagli (1990): Waldorfpädagogik in der Diskussion. Eine Analyse erziehungswissenschaftlicher Kritik. *[Waldorf Education under Discussion. An analysis of educational criticism]*. Stuttgart: Freies Geistesleben.

Kruse, Andreas/Schmitz-Scherzer, Reinhard (Eds.) (1995): Psychologie der Lebensalter. *[The psychology of the ages of man]*. Darmstadt: Steinkopff.

Kuhl, Julius/Heckhausen, Heinz (Eds.) (1996): Motivation, Volition und Handlung. Enzyklopädie der PsychologieC 4 Band 4. *[Motivation, volition, and action. Encyclopedia of psychology C4 vol. 4]*. Göttingen: Hogrefe.

Langenmayr, Arnold/Schubert, Ulrich (1987): Lebenslaufanalyse. *[Life span analysis]*. Göttingen: Hogrefe.

Leber, Stefan (1993): Die Menschenkunde der Waldorfpädagogik. *[The study of man in Waldorf education]*. Stuttgart: Freies Geistesleben.

Lerner, Richard/Foch, Teryll T. (Eds.) (1987): Biological-psychological interactions in early adolescence. Hillsdale/London: Lawrence Erlbaum.

Lewin, Kurt/Lippit, Ronald/White, Ralph K. (1939): Patterns of aggressive behavior in experimentally created social climates. In: Journal of Social Psychology 10, pp. 271–299.

Lindenberg, Christoph (1981): Die Lebensbedingungen des Erziehens. Von Waldorfschulen lernen. *[The life context of education. Learning from Waldorf schools]*. Reinbek bei Hamburg: Rowohlt

Lievegoed, Bernard C. J. (1989): Entwicklungsphasen des Kindes. 4. Auflage. *[Developmental phases of the child. 4th ed.]*. Stuttgart: Mellinger.

Loebell, Peter (2004): Ich bin, der ich werde. Individualisierung in der Waldorfpädagogik. *[I am, who I am becoming. Individualization in Waldorf education]*. Stuttgart: Freies Geistesleben.

Lukesch, Helmut (1977): Elterliche Erziehungsstile. Psychologische und soziologische Bedingungen. *[Parenting styles. Psychological and sociological conditions]*. Stuttgart: Kohlhammer.

Lukesch, Helmut (1977): Erziehungsstile. Pädagogische und psychologische Konzepte. *[Education styles. Pedagogic and psychological concepts]*. Stuttgart: Kohlhammer.

Lutzker, Peter (1996): Der Sprachsinn. *[The sense of speech]*. Stuttgart: Freies Geistesleben.

Maier, Henry William (1983): Drei Theorien der Kindheitsentwicklung. *[Three theories of child development]*. Munich: UTB/Harper & Row.

Maier, Karin/Ambühl-Caesar, Gioia/Schandry, Rainer (1994): Entwicklungspsychophysiologie. *[Developmental psycho-physiology]*. Weinheim: Psychologie Verlags Union.

115

Markefka, Manfred/Nauck, Bernhard (Eds.) (1993): Handbuch der Kindheitsforschung. *[Handbook of childhood research]*. Neuwied: Luchterhand.

Markefka, Manfred/Nave-Herz, Rosemarie (Eds.) (1989): Handbuch der Familien- und Jugendforschung, Band 2: Jugendforschung. *[Handbook of family and youth research, vol. 2: Youth research]*. Neuwied: Luchterhand.

Markowitsch, Hans (Ed.) (1996): Grundlagen der Neuropsychologie. *[Fundamentals of Neuro-Psychology]*. Enzyklopädie der Psychologie C1 Band 1, *[Encyclopedia of psychology C1 vol. 1]*. Göttingen: Hogrefe.

Marti, Thomas (2006): Wie kann Schule die Gesundheit fördern? *[How can school foster health?]*. Stuttgart: Freies Geistesleben.

Mayer, Michaela Christine (2006): Soziomoralischer Kompetenzvergleich von Regel- und Waldorfschülern nach Grundlagen des Kohlberg-Modells. *[Comparison of socio-motoric competency in students of public and Waldorf schools on the basis of the Kohlberg Model]*. Dissertation an der Philosophischen Fakultät der UniversitätPassau. *[Dissertation at the Philosophical Department of the University Passau]*.

Mey, Günther (Ed.) (2005): Handbuch qualitative Entwicklungspsychologie. *[Handbook of qualitative developmental psychology]*. Köln.

Mietzel, Gerd (2002): Wege in die Entwicklungspsychologie. Kindheit und Jugend. 4. Auflage. *[Inroads into developmental psychology. Childhood and youth. 4th edition]*. Weinheim: Beltz.

Miller, Patricia (2000): Theorien der Entwicklungspsychologie. *[Theories of developmental psychology]*. Heidelberg/Berlin: Spektrum Akademischer Verlag.

Modgil, Sohan/Modgil, Celia (Ed.) (1987): B. F. Skinner. Consensus and Controversy. New York: FalmerPress.

Modgil, Sohan/Modgil, Celia/Brown, Geoffrey (Eds.) (1983): Jean Piaget. An Interdisciplinary Critique. London: Routledge.

Mühle, Günther (1971): Entwicklungspsychologie des zeichnerischen Gestaltens. 4. Auflage. *[Developmental psychology of creative drawing. 4th edition]*. Berlin: Springer.

Müller-Wiedemann, Hans (1973): Mitte der Kindheit. Das neunte bis zwölfte Lebensjahr. *[Mid-childhood. Age nine to twelve]*. Stuttgart: Freies Geistesleben.

Neißer, Barbara (2012): Kinder philosophieren. *[Children do philosophize]*. Münster/Berlin: Lit.

Neumann, Karl/Horster, Detlef (1992): Philosophieren mit Kindern. *[Philosophizing with children]*. Opladen: Leske + Budrich.

Nickel, Horst (1974): Entwicklungspsychologie des Kindes- und Jugendalters. Band I. 2. Auflage. *[Developmental psychology of childhood and youth. Vol. 1, 2nd edition]*. Bern: Huber.

Oerter, Rolf (1975): Moderne Entwicklungspsychologie. 15. Auflage. *[Modern developmental psychology. 15th edition]*. Donauwörth: Auer.

Oerter, Rolf (1978a): Entwicklung und Sozialisation. Kindheit – Jugend – Alter. *[Development and socialization. Childhood – youth – old Age]*. Donauwörth: Auer.

Oerter, Rolf (1978b): Zur Dynamik von Entwicklungsaufgaben im menschlichen Lebenslauf. *[On the dynamics of developmental challenges in the human life span]*. In: Oerter, Rolf (Ed.): Entwicklung als lebenslanger Prozess. *[Development as a lifelong process]*. Hamburg: Hoffmann und Campe, pp. 66–110.

Oerter, Rolf/Montada, Leo (Eds.) (1987): Entwicklungspsychologie. 2. Auflage. *[Developmental psychology. 2nd edition]*. Weinheim/Munich: Psychologische Verlags-Union.

Papousek, Mechthild (1994): Vom ersten Schrei zum ersten Wort. Anfänge der Sprachentwicklung in der vorsprachlichen Kommunikation. *[From the first scream to the first word. Beginnings of speech development in pre-speech communication]*. Bern/Stuttgart: Huber.

Piaget, Jean (2003): Meine Theorie der geistigen Entwicklung. *[My theory of cognitive development]*. Weinheim: Beltz.

Pinker, Steven (1996): Der Sprachinstinkt. Wie der Geist die Sprache bildet. *[The speech instinct. How the mind forms speech/language]*. Darmstadt: Wissenschaftliche Buchgesellschaft.

Ramge, Hans (1976): Spracherwerb und sprachliches Handeln. *[Gaining speech competency and speech action]*. Düsseldorf: Schwann.

Ramsden, Sue/Richardson, Fiona M./Josse, Goulven/Thomas, Michael/Ellis, Caroline/Shakeshaft, Clare/Seghier, Mohamed/Price, Cathy (2011): Verbal and non-verbal intelligence changes in the teenage brain. In: Nature 479, pp. 113–116.

Reinert, Günther (1976): Grundzüge einer Geschichte der Human-Entwicklungspsychologie. *[Basic outline of a history of human developmental psychology]*. In: Balmer, Heinrich (Ed.): Die Psychologie des 20. Jahrhunderts. Band 1. *[20th century psychology. Vol.1]*. Zürich: Kindler pp. 862–896.

Rittelmeyer, Christian (2002): Pädagogische Anthropologie des Leibes. *[Pedagogic anthropology of the body]*. Weinheim: Juventa

Rittelmeyer, Christian (2005): Frühe Erfahrungen des Kindes. Ergebnisse der pränatalen Psychologie und der Bindungsforschung. Ein Überblick. *[Early childhood experiences. Results of pre-natal psychology and attachment research. An Overview]*. Stuttgart: Kohlhammer.

Rittelmeyer, Christian (2009): Was sollen Kinder lesen. Kriterien, Beispiele, Empfehlungen. *[What are children supposed to read. Criteria, examples, recommendations]*. Stuttgart: Kohlhammer.

Rittelmeyer, Christian (2013): Leibliche Erfahrung und Lernen. Über den Sinn einer allseitigen Sinnesbildung. *[Body experience and learning. On the meaning of a comprehensive education of the senses]*. In: Hildebrandt-Stramann, Reiner/Laging, Ralf/Moegling, Klaus (Eds.): Körper, Bewegung und Schule. Teil 1: Theorien, Forschungen und Diskussion. *[Body, movement, and school. Part 1: Theories, research, and discussion]*. Immenhausen: Prolog, pp. 36–53.

Rohen, Johannes W./Lütjen-Drecoll, Elke (1982): Funktionelle Histologie. *[Functional histology]*. Stuttgart, New York: Schattauer.

Schaefer, Earl S. (1959): A circumplex model for maternal behavior. In: Journal of Abnormal and Social Psychology, 59, pp. 226–235.

Schenk-Danzinger, Lotte (1993): Entwicklungspsychologie. 22. Auflage. *[Developmental psychology. 22nd edition]*. Wien: Österreichischer Bundesverlag.

Schneewind, Klaus/Herrmann, Theo (Eds.) (1980): Erziehungsstilforschung. *[Education Style Research]*. Stuttgart: Kohlhammer.

Schneider, Wolfgang/Wilkening, Friedrich (Eds.) (2006): Theorien, Modelle und Methoden der Entwicklungspsychologie. Enzyklopädie der Psychologie C5. Band 1. *[Theories, models and methods of developmental psychology. Encyclopedia of psychology C5. Vol. 1]*. Göttingen: Hogrefe.

Schraml, Walter J. (1972): Einführung in die moderne Entwicklungspsychologie. *[Introduction to modern developmental psychology]*. Stuttgart: Klett-Cotta.

Schumann-Hengsteler, Ruth/Trautner, Hanns Martin (Eds.) (1996): Entwicklung im Jugendalter. *[Development in youth]*. Göttingen: Hogrefe.

Selg, Herbert (1978) (Ed.): Zur Aggression verdammt? 5. Auflage. *[Condemned to be aggressive? 5th edition]*. Stuttgart: Kohlhammer

Siegel, Linda/Brainerd, Charles (Eds.) (1978): Alternatives to Piaget: Critical Essays on the Theory. New York: Academic Press.

Silbereisen, Rainer/Hasselhorn, Marcus (Eds.) (2008): Entwicklungspsychologie des Jugendalters. Enzyklopädie der Psychologie C5 Band 5. *[Developmental psychology of youth. Encyclopedia of psychology C5, vol. 5]*. Göttingen: Hogrefe.

Sime, Mary (1978): So sieht ein Kind die Welt. Piaget für Eltern und Erzieher. *[How a child sees the world. Piaget for parents and educators]*. Olten: Walter.

Simms, Eva (2008): The Child in the World. Embodiment, Time, and Language in Early Childhood. Detroit: Wayne State University Press.

Skinner, Burrhus F. (1957): Verbal Behavior. New York: Appleton.

Skinner, Burrhus F. (1971): Erziehung als Verhaltensformung. Grundlagen einer Technologie des Lernens. *[Education as behavior formation. Fundamentals of a technology of learning]*. Munich: Keimer.

Smith, Lesli (Ed.) (1996): Critical Readings on Piaget. London: Routledge.

Spitzer, Manfred (2003): Lernen: Gehirnforschung und die Schule des Lebens. *[Learning. Brain research and the school of life]*. Heidelberg: Spektrum.

Stapf, Karl-Heinz/Herrmann, Theo/Stapf, Aiga/Stäcker, Karl Heinz (1972): Psychologie des elterlichen Erziehungsstils. *[The psychology of parenting styles]*. Stuttgart/Bern: Huber.

Steiner, Rudolf (1977): Die Erneuerung der pädagogisch-didaktischen Kunst durch Geisteswissenschaft. *[The renewal of education]*. GA 301. Dornach: Rudolf Steiner Verlag.

Stern, Daniel (1994): Tagebuch eines Babys. Was ein Kind sieht, spürt, fühlt und denkt. 5. Auflage. *[Diary of a baby. What a child sees, senses, feels, and thinks. 5th edition]*. Munich: Piper.

Strauch, Barbara (2004): Warum sie so seltsam sind. Gehirnentwicklung bei Teenagern. *[Why they are so weird. Brain development in teenagers]*. Berlin: Berliner Taschenbuch Verlag.

Sugarman, Leonie (1995): Life-Span Development: Concepts, Theories and Interventions. London: Routledge.

Tausch, Reinhard/Tausch, Anne-Marie (1973): Erziehungspsychologie. 7. Auflage. *[Educational psychology. 7th edition]*. Göttingen: Hogrefe.

Thomas, Robert/Feldman, Birgit (2002): Die Entwicklung des Kindes. 2. Auflage. *[Child development. 2nd edition]*. Weinheim: Beltz.

Tiemeier, Henning/Lenrot, Roshel/Greenstein, Deanna/Tran, Lan/Pierson, Ronald/Giedd, Jay (2010): Cerebellum Development during Childhood and Adolescence: A Longitudinal Morphometric MRI Study. In: Neuroimage 49, pp. 63–70.

Tillmann, Klaus-Jürgen (2006): Sozialisationstheorien. 14. Auflage. *[Socialization theories. 14th edition]*. Reinbek bei Hamburg: Rowohlt.

Touwen, Bert (1993): Physische Entwicklung und motorische Fähigkeiten. *[Physical development and motoric faculties]*. In: Markefka, Manfred/Nauck, Bernhard (Eds.) (1993): Handbuch der Kindheitsforschung. *[Handbook of childhood research]*. Neuwied: Luchterhand, pp. 239–251.

Trautner, Hanns Martin (1991/1997): Lehrbuch der Entwicklungspsychologie. Band 1: Grundlagen und Methoden, Band 2: Theorien und Befunde. *[Basics and Methods, Vol.2: Theories and Findings]*. Göttingen: Hogrefe.

Trautner, Hanns Martin (2003): Allgemeine Entwicklungspsychologie. 2. Auflage. *[General Developmental Psychology. 2nd edition]*. Stuttgart: Kohlhammer.

Ulich, Dieter (2002): Zur Relevanz verhaltenstheoretischer Lernkonzepte für die Sozialisationsforschung. *[On the relevance of theoretic-behavioristic concepts of learning for socialization research]*. In: Hurrelmann, Klaus/Ulich, Dieter (Eds.) (2002): Handbuch der Sozialisationsforschung. *[Handbook of socialization research]*. Weinheim: Beltz, pp. 57–70.

Ullrich, Heiner (1986): Waldorfpädagogik und okkulte Weltanschauung. Eine bildungsphilosophische und geistesgeschichtliche Auseinandersetzung mit der Anthropologie Rudolf Steiners. *[Waldorf education and occult worldview. An exploration of Rudolf Steiner's anthropology from a perspective of educational philosophy and the history of science]*. Weinheim: Juventa.

Ullrich, Heiner (2002): Befremdlicher Anachronismus oder zukunftsweisendes Modell? *[Strange anachronism or futuristic model?]*. In: Hansen-Schaberg, Inge/Schonig, Bruno (Eds.) (2002): Waldorf-Pädagogik. *[Waldorf education]*. Baltmannsweiler: Schneider, pp. 181–215.

Weinert, Franz E. (Ed.) (1998): Entwicklung im Kindesalter. *[Development in childhood]*. Weinheim: Psychologie Verlags Union.

Widlöcher, Daniel (1993): Was eine Kinderzeichnung verrät. 2. Auflage. *[What a child's drawing tells us. 2nd edition]*. Frankfurt am Main: Fischer Taschenbuch.

Woolfalk, Anita (2008): Pädagogische Psychologie. 10. Auflage. *[Pedagogic psychology. 10th edition]*. Munich: Pearson.

Wuketis, Franz (1995): Die Entdeckung des Verhaltens. Eine Geschichte der Verhaltensforschung. *[The discovery of behavior. A history of behavioral research]*. Darmstadt: Wissenschaftliche Buchgesellschaft.

DISCUSSION OF RUDOLF STEINER'S DEVELOPMENTAL PSYCHOLOGY

Albert Schmelzer

The following article presents the discussion of Rudolf Steiner's developmental psychology in educational science circles since the 1980s, outlining the basic structure of argumentation, as presented by various contributions.[1] This review brings up the issue of the context, within which emerged Steiner's understanding of child development and its anthropological foundations. Finally, we identify issues resulting from the line of arguments here presented, which will need further exploration in scientific research on Waldorf education.

1 The 1980s

In the 1980s, the Waldorf school movement experienced progressive expansion that brought with it a new phase of critical discussions within educational science pertaining to Waldorf education (Frielingsdorf 2012, p. 42ff.). The main publications on the topic of developmental psychology were presented by Heiner Ullrich (1982, 1986), Etta Wilken (1983), Kallert et al. (1984), Heiner Barz (1984), and Klaus Prange (1985).

It was Klaus Prange—then teaching at Bayreuth University—who voiced the most radical critique in his book *Education in Anthroposophy* (Prange 1985). This critique was fueled, not least, by Steiner's concept of development. According to Prange, Steiner's view of development followed along a figure of thought that is known in projective geometry as a *line at infinity*, "where beginning and end coincide, where rise and fall are the same, so that all is given simultaneously.[…] The future means returning home, not an open sea of possibilities but an arrival at port" (ibid., p. 90). Prange claims to base his view on Steiner's understanding of reincarnation and karma: "the course of life returns to that, which was always karmically constellated" (ibid., p. 91). Therefore, Prange argues, "Steiner implies that development does not bring anything new – it is always but a variation of the old and basically same pre-recorded movie, which is playing over and over again" (ibid.). Prange deduces that Waldorf education, therefore, is concerned "not with the unfoldment and exploration of something substantially new, but rather with regressive processing" (ibid.) and that the principle of "authority that always already knows better than the learner her/himself" entirely permeates the system of Waldorf education. According to Prange, the "education toward freedom" as touted in anthroposophy is therefore a deception, because Waldorf's instructional and educational goal is not the individual formation of judgment and opinion, but an opaque "indoctrination of an esoteric ilk" (ibid.).

Besides Steiner's concept of development, Prange critically examines his characterization of the developmental phases of the child (ibid., p. 86). Steiner, Prange writes, introduces "a strangely stationary model of the course of development" (ibid.). It may be plausible that the child at first learns by imitation, adopting speech and movement from the immediate surroundings, yet, in Prange's view,

DOI: 10.4324/9781003187431-13

there is little convincing evidence "that imitation is everything, and that imitation, as Piaget has shown, does not contain already the first signs of cognitive and emotional structures" (ibid., p. 85).

Prange's most polemic criticism is aimed at the hypothesis of the metamorphosis of powers. He still portrays in an objective manner Steiner's view of formative powers that are at first body-bound but undergo a transformation at the time of the change of teeth, when they become available to the child as cognitive faculties, but he has nothing but mockery for the opinion of Waldorf pedagogue Rudolf Grosse, who speculated that the formation of the adult set of teeth might give a clue as to how mental faculties may be developed: "We can understand how a man thinks by looking into his mouth" (ibid., p. 88). Here, Prange writes, we see "exactly that circular figure of thought that is immune to all critique, which is the substratum of anthroposophy as a whole: It 'proves' what it already knows and 'observes' what it thinks to be so" (ibid., p. 89).

This sentence is a typical example of Prange's main line of argument: He alleges that Steiner uses an auto-suggestive method of cognition. Steiner—according to Prange—identifies the "result of cognition with the experiential process of looking, observing and discerning, as if it were the same thing. [...] He draws conclusions from the reality of the process of imagining to the reality of the cognate. [...]"

Also: he (Steiner) thinks: "If we enter into something by imagining, living or thinking it, then the experience of the imagined [process or thing] becomes proof of its reality" (ibid., p. 59).

Clearly, against the foil of Prange's view, anthroposophy is to be categorized as irrational and unscientific and appears as a myth that is unsubstantiated and cannot be substantiated either, which leads to a pedagogy of subtle indoctrination and determinism in regard to young people.

Prange's publication resulted in a fiery controversy that used the forum of the *Zeitschrift für Pädagogik [Journal of Pedagogy]* (vol. 4, 1986) for the debate between him and Johannes Kiersch, the co-founder of the Institute for Waldorf education in Witten-Annen (Kiersch 1986). Essentially this controversy revolved around the issues of cognitive theory as delineated above, so there is no need to further attend to it in this context. It seems remarkable how the remedial education pedagogue Etta Wilken, in stark contrast to Prange, does not regard Steiner's teachings on reincarnation as a cause for determinism but views it as an outright guarantor of the "invulnerability of the I" (Wilken 1983, p. 53); in her article, which appeared in the Journal *Sonderpädagogik [Journal for Special Education]*, she otherwise limits herself to a description of Steiner's developmental teachings and refrains from passing judgment.

Three educational scientists from Frankfurt—Heide Kallert, Eva Maria Schleuning, and Christa Ellert—also do not take issue with the idea of a pre-existent [pre-incarnational] individuality of the child, but they point in this context to the "creative spirit" that is inherent in the child and must be awakened in the process of education (Kallert et al. 1984, p. 642). They write that Steiner here "thinks along the same lines as many reform pedagogues, who insisted that the immaturity of the child is not to be judged as a deficiency" (ibid.).

Besides Prange, the educational scientist Heiner Ullrich from Mainz has also presented a critique of Steiner's developmental psychology, which was broadly received after it was published. In an essay written as early as 1982 (Ullrich 1982) and then in a revised version of his doctoral thesis titled "Waldorf Education and Occult Worldview" (Ullrich 1986), he describes Steiner's developmental teachings and reduces them basically to three pillars: the doctrine of the four members of being, the principle of the metamorphosis of the bodies of man in a regular seven-year rhythm, and the law of the preservation of energy that causes the powers that are initially organically body-bound to not disappear "but to urge into manifestation on another level" (ibid., p. 109).

His critique is sparked mostly by the concept of the seven-year cycle of development and we can summarize it as follows: According to Ullrich, the teaching of the seven-year cycles is not empirically supported, but it views the development of the psyche as a pre-determined, so-to-speak biological maturation process and is thus in danger of relying on a laissez-faire pedagogy that is just letting the child grow and neglects specific learning arrangements. Moreover, the seven-year cycle doctrine is in Ullrich's perspective too undifferentiated, as it does not consider cultural and individual differences and postulates the synchronicity of cognitive, emotional, motivational, and social development.

Ullrich's critique has—remarkably—found some opposition in educational science circles. Already in 1984, in his book *The Waldorf Kindergarten*, Heiner Barz called attention to the parallels between Steiner's developmental theory and Piaget's phases of the cognitive development of the child. Barz recognizes "fundamental congruities" of Steiner's theories with "the results of empiric studies in developmental psychology research" (Barz 1984, p. 104). Barz writes that Jean Piaget observed his own children and those at the Maison des Petits in Geneva, conducted innumerable interviews with children, and thus arrived at a theory of developmental phases that resembles Steiner's doctrine "in both their stage boundaries (thresholds at age 7 and between age 12 and 14) as well as in their descriptive characteristics of each phase" (ibid.).

Barz further remarks that Steiner is unfairly dealt with by portraying his view as a mere theory of maturation. In agreement with Waldorf pedagogue Christoph Lindenberg, Barz writes that Steiner is more concerned with describing "typical learning dispositions of the child," than with "a one sided biodeterminism of development; instead Steiner focuses on the *interplay or synergy* of the child's learning opportunities and the behavior and teachings of the adults around them" (ibid., p. 111; Lindenberg 1979, p. 176). In this process, influences from the environment are of crucial importance, writes Barz: "Waldorf education approaches the fundamental issue in developmental psychology, that of maturing or learning *[nature vs. nurture]* pedagogy with a model of reciprocal effects, which is no different from Piaget's 'structuralist theory of interaction'" (ibid., p. 112). Barz therefore finds no justification for equating developmental phase models with "spectator pedagogy." As presented above, both Steiner and Piaget unceasingly stressed the significance of stimuli and suggestions, especially in the sensitive phases of learning.

In conclusion, we can so far summarize that in the 1980s fierce, often polemic controversies erupted around Steiner's theory of development. These controversies circled mainly around the following questions: Is Steiner's concept of development based on a deterministic concept of man or else can we view the concept of a reincarnating spiritual individuality as a guarantor for the invulnerability of the I? Does Waldorf education have an indoctrinating effect or can it be seen as an Education for Freedom? Does the concept of the seven-year cycles, at least in rough outline, correspond to empirical findings? Can it serve as a basis for an age-specific pedagogy? Or else is it a speculative model that is educationally counterproductive, because it suggests a quasi-biological maturation process, postulates transitions that are too rigid, and gives scant consideration to cultural and individual differences?

These controversies also bring up the issue of contextualizing Steiner's theory of development. Heiner Ullrich opines in this regard that Steiner's teaching of the seven-year cycles constitutes a regress to the mythic hebdomad teachings, which we can already find in Greek antiquity in Solon's work and are further reflected in the 5th-century pseudo-Hippocratic treatise "Peri Hebdomadon"; the influence of Hebdomad doctrines can further be traced through medieval thought up to Luther and Shakespeare. Ullrich speculates that Steiner's reception of the seven-year cycle scheme was perhaps stimulated by a corresponding annotation in Helena Petrovna Blavatsky's second volume on the *Anthropogenesis of Her Secret Doctrine* (Ullrich 1986, p. 118). With this opinion, Ullrich shifts the context of Steiner's developmental theory into a prescientific realm of classical cosmological speculations; Ullrich writes: "they *[Steiner's developmental teachings]* basically constitute an anachronistic regress into traditional world views that rely on numbers mysticism and mythology, as we find it, e.g., in the thinking of antiquity regarding the human existence" (ibid., p. 118). Therefore, according to Ullrich, these teachings "cannot really be fruitfully discussed in the disciplinary realm of scientific psychology" (ibid., p. 113).

Interestingly, Klaus Prange suspects another source of Steiner's teaching—especially as regards Steiner's comments on the ninth year of life, when the child takes not only a receptive but also a questioning stance toward its environment: "Steiner picked up the teaching of the second round of 'the terrible twos' propounded by the developmental psychology of his time and appropriated and integrated it for his anthroposophy" (Prange 1985, p. 109). Other than that, Steiner passed over the developmental psychology of his time, Prange asserts, and he mentions in this context Wilhelm Wundt, Sigmund Freud, Alfred Binet, Edward Lee Thorndike, and Hermann Ebbinghaus (Prange 1985, p. 19).

2 The 1990s

At the beginning of the 1990s, Ernst Michael Kranich, lecturer at the Seminar for Waldorf Education in Stuttgart and Lorenzo Ravagli published a book that they considered to be "an analysis of scientific critique" (Kranich, Ravagli 1990). In this publication, Kranich discusses Prange's book *Education in Anthroposophy* (1985) and proves how he distorted and truncated Steiner's ideas in his portrayal. For example, he simply ignored Steiner's numerous comments on the needs for autonomous judgment formation in youth (ibid., p. 27). Moreover, Kranich shows that Steiner did in fact study Wundt and Freud and also knew Ebbinghaus (Kranich, Ravagli 1990, p. 14).[2] Ravagli offers a very detailed review of Ullrich's book *Waldorf Education and Occult Worldview* together with an overview of various critiques and discussions of his writing. In reference to developmental psychology, Ravagli raises the question whether if Ullrich's verdict against age-phase models may not also apply to important streams of thought in modern developmental psychology, and whether Ullrich himself might have fallen prey to "a reductionist and monopolistic concept of science" (Kranich, Ravagli 1990, p. 168). Furthermore, he (Ravagli) points out that Steiner himself always meant the thresholds of the seven-year cycles to just be an approximation (ibid., p.173; Steiner 1986, p. 79); there just is no "rigid schematism of seven-year cycles" (ibid.).

Regardless, Heiner Ullrich and Klaus Prange (Prange 1992) reiterated their positions in later years]; Ullrich was particularly productive, writing several contributions on Waldorf education (Ullrich 1992, 1994, 1995), which were published in anthologies on reform pedagogy (Ullrich 1996, 1998) representing Waldorf education, without any change in his verdict on Steiner's developmental theory.

Wolfgang Schneider voiced further criticism of Steiner's teachings in his dissertation "The Concept of Man in Waldorf Education," which appeared in the series *Freiburger Theologische Studien [Freiburg Theological Studies]* published by Herder. The heuristic pivot point of his broadly conceived philosophic-theological exploration is the concept of man *[the person]*, which he pursues throughout his analysis of anthroposophy and Waldorf education. He presents Steiner's understanding of the threefold organization of the human being into different "bodies" and criticizes the lack of empiricism in this approach. Referring back to Ullrich, Schneider accordingly finds Steiner's developmental teachings "peculiar, if seen in a perspective of developmental psychology" (Schneider 1991, p. 132). In addition—so Schneider writes—Steiner holds the view that any development in this world only mirrors previous incarnations and earlier evolutionary stages. Thus, in Schneider's opinion, Steiner sees the human being already as pre-determined in childhood.

Schneider goes on to say that such an anthropology and developmental doctrine results in a dogmatic form of education; the teacher must educate the child in (strict) accordance with Steiner's developmental model, "i.e., only those aspects may be fostered which are considered appropriate to these specific phases– even though these phases appear more than questionable in the perspective of today's developmental psychology" (ibid., p. 280).

Schneider arrives at a scathing verdict: "This schematic doctrine of educational phases and its transference into specific educational and instructional measures [...] prevents by necessity a truly *personal* meeting of teacher and student and thus a person-specific education. [...] The central focus of such an education is not the *individual person* of the child, but a postulated *generality,* which is both unsubstantiated and non-personal in its essential traits" (ibid., p. 281).

Schneider's view amounts to a fundamental criticism of Waldorf education and he presented it largely without references to the pedagogic deliberations of Steiner or to the practice of Waldorf education. His dissertation at first drew no attention but—as the following shall show—its influence is unfolding up into most recent times.

3 Newer publications

There were several educational science publications after the year 2000 that touch upon the developmental psychology approach of Waldorf education, but the basic critical tone of that discussion changed, in fact, very little. In another book, titled *Outlandish Anachronism or Futuristic Model? The free Waldorf school in pedagogic discourse and educational science research*, Ullrich reiterated his already known allegations: Steiner had not conceptualized his approach with reference to the "contemporary discourse in developmental psychology." Rather he took recourse to "the archaic system of the ages of man, which had been of greatest importance in European Mediterranean culture, before the emergence of a scientific study of man" (Ullrich 2002, p. 190). According to Ullrich, there could be no constructive discussion of such a "soul-oriented anachronism within the disciplinary framework of a modern-empirical science approach in developmental psychology, even if Steiner's stage *[phase]* model appears to show superficial correspondences to the concepts of Jean Piaget or Oswald Kroh" (ibid., p. 191).

Against the backdrop of such a verdict, it appears somewhat astounding that in the further course of his presentation he attests to a "high degree of stimulation" in Waldorf-specific methodology, especially referencing block-lessons in the natural sciences; as a reason, he cites that Waldorf education focuses characteristically "not primarily on the structure of the discipline of physics, chemistry or biology, *but rather on the cognitive and emotional development of the students,* and their *age-specific* approaches to nature" (ibid., p. 197; italics emphasis by the author of this article). A few pages earlier, Ullrich had declared Steiner's developmental psychology as "not fit for constructive discourse."

Also, in his most recent publication titled *Waldorf Education. A Critical Introduction* (Ullrich 2015), Ullrich holds fast to his above-described notions on developmental psychology in Waldorf education. Yet, in this book, he is at the same time well able to acknowledge various aspects of Waldorf education and takes note of an increasingly constructive discussion, which he attributes to the "dialog with educational scientists that was first instigated by Waldorf pedagogues and has been intensifying since about two decades, as well as the empiric research on Waldorf schools that has meanwhile gained traction" (Ullrich 2015, p. 13). But in regard to developmental psychology, he references his 1986 dissertation "Waldorf Education and Occult Worldview" and reiterates his former points of view.

A monograph on reform pedagogy published by Ehrenhard Skiera (Skiera 2003/2010) contains further remarks on Steiner's developmental psychology. Skiera states—in line with Wolfgang Schneider's (1991) thoughts—that "anthroposophy abrogates the concept of the person as the epitome of unique individuality [...]" (Skiera 2003/2010, p. 264). Skiera argues that anthroposophy nullifies the boundaries between birth and death and thus "expands the radius of action into infinity so that it entirely ceases to function as a possible horizon of action" (ibid.); on the other hand, he writes, the "wholeness" of the person is fragmented into different bodies that wage war with each other inside the human being.

Furthermore—according to Skiera—anthroposophy does not acknowledge any development driven "by one's own power, own drive, own determination," but rather development needs the "agency of a 'being' who is already more highly evolved (i.e., closer to the spiritual realm), which acts upon the lower being or member of being" (ibid., p. 265) In Skiera's view, anthroposophy teaches that the human being and with him/her all of creation, hangs on the silken thread of entities—good ones as well evil ones, divine or Luciferic —with whom he has to wrestle constantly (ibid.).

However, Skiera holds the opinion that his adverse attitude toward anthroposophy does not necessarily lead to a negative assessment of the *educational practice* of Waldorf schools. "One can certainly acknowledge specific achievements of alchemy (example: the invention of porcelain) without believing its theoretical premises or the usefulness of its overall approach" (ibid.).

In the process of Waldorf education's consistently transposing its concept of man into practical education, it does certainly point to "desiderata of 'modern' pedagogy," such as, for example, "the significance of authority in the educational process," the "value of a continuous educational process (no repeating of grades), the meaning of reliable value orientations and structures" and the "worth of an aesthetic permeation of the environment and life at school."

How specifically such designs can be transferred into the context of a different pedagogic theory would need to be examined; according to Skiera, Waldorf education "in any case is worth the effort to explore such a transfer, also from a pragmatic perspective" (ibid., p. 266).

Winfried Böhm, in his brief monograph "Reform Pedagogy. Montessori, Waldorf and other Teachings," (Böhm 2012) refers to Wolfgang Schneider's criticism and agrees with it. In Böhm's perspective, Waldorf education cannot fulfill its claim of being a person-centered pedagogy, because the anthroposophical worldview is too deterministic and does not view the child "primarily as an independent person, but only as a mirror of another" (ibid., p. 102), and in the final analysis, the child remains "subjected to an anonymous cosmic law of life" (ibid., p. 103).

Against the backdrop of the fierce criticism voiced by Ullrich, Skiera, and Böhm, the remarks of the Swiss Psychologist August Flammer on Steiner's developmental teachings appear astoundingly unagitated. In the fourth, completely revised and updated edition of his foundational work *Developmental Theories. Psychological Theories of Human Development*, Flammer briefly presents the seven-year cycle doctrine of Waldorf education's founder and, without going into detail, he points to its occidental roots, which later resurfaced in the works of philosopher and theologian Romano Guardini (Guardini 1954). He also remarks that this system of developmental phases is "not necessarily derived from empiric study; it rather reflects the cultural organization (which is, however, not coincidental) [...] e.g. the sequence of school types in our society" (Flammer 2009, p. 53). Of course, there are "even biological inter-individual variances, which do not strictly correspond to the chronological age" (ibid.). But, Flammer writes, we must consider "that Steiner was not a psychologist and that he wanted this system to merely provide a rough guideline for educators" (ibid.).

In 2007, Helmut Zander published his monumental work *Anthroposophy in Germany*. While it was written from a perspective of cultural history, there are two remarks worth mentioning that he makes in regard to Steiner's developmental theory. The first of these remarks pertains to Ullrich's charge of a rigid categorization of age groups. Zander comments that Steiner often "was prudent enough to understand the age-thresholds as approximations" (Zander 2007, vol. 2, p. 1404) and cites Steiner at least once in this connection (Steiner 1977, p. 22).

The other remark pertains to the context within which Steiner formulated his concept of developmental psychology. Zander points out that the notion "of the seven-year steps has already been formulated in antiquity" (Zander 2007, p. 1404), for example by Solon, but that we just need to consult an encyclopedia of pedagogy dating from the time after World War I, to find "a nearly ubiquitous presence of teachings on the ages of man, particularly in contemporary developmental psychology" (ibid., p. 1405). Zander quotes a passage from a Pedagogic Encyclopedia from the year 1913: "We can hold fast to the seven…which was sacred in antiquity [...] even as we consider the facts" (ibid., p. 1405; Willmann, Roloff 1913, vol.1, p. 1042). The passage goes on to present the seven-year cycles of development, understood as relative approximations, "which, also in many practical details, could have been written by Steiner" (ibid.). Therefore, Zander feels "nearly certain" that Steiner "drew his inspiration from some place in this treasure trove *[of thought]* from the turn of the century" (ibid.), an opinion that still awaits concrete substantiation.

4 Conclusion

First, we must note that up to now there has been no real change in educational science's critique of the developmental theory that underlies Waldorf education. Essentially the positions today are the same as those voiced in the 1980s; Wolfgang Schneider's fundamental critique joined those voices by asserting that Waldorf education obstructed a person-centered education. This persistence is particularly baffling, since empirical research refuted at least the accusation of indoctrination. The first *Study of Waldorf Graduates,* conducted in 1981, showed that Waldorf students retrospectively did not feel that they were influenced to adopt any specific worldview or even anthroposophy (Hofmann et al. 1981); these findings were substantiated also by the comprehensive work published by Heiner Barz and Dirk Randoll in 2007 under the title *Graduates of Waldorf Schools. An empiric study on education and life design* (Barz, Randoll 2007).

On the other hand, the field of discussion is wide open. In fact, educational scientists themselves—first among them Barz—have refuted some of the criticism leveled against Steiner's developmental psychology. They counter addressed the supposed lack of empirical support, the alleged rigidity of

Steiner's system and his presumably precise, adamant fixation of age phases, as well as the opinion that his teachings simply constitute a maturation theory, which logically leads to a form of "spectator pedagogy." These topics require a differentiated portrayal of Rudolf Steiner's thoughts and the consideration of more recent findings in empirical research, including also the meanwhile very nuanced critique and acknowledgment of Piaget's work. This is similarly true for the view that Steiner paid no—or too little—attention to inter-individual and intercultural differences, a view that has as yet not been contested.

Also, we need to consider Prange's remark that the child is not only an imitating being during the first seven years of life; the same consideration is needed for this author's question of how we can understand and specifically substantiate the doctrine of the metamorphosis of powers, which are at first body-bound and then mutate into representational and imaginative faculties and the connection of this process with the change of teeth.

Of particular significance is the question, how to conceptualize development. Prange, Schneider, Skiera, and Böhm hold the opinion that Steiner's understanding of development results in determinism, because the overlay is formed by the doctrine of karma and reincarnation. In their view, Steiner's teaching entails that learning is just imitation, that it denies any self-empowered activity of the developing child, and that from an anthroposophical perspective, the human being is just a puppet on silken strings that are moved by spiritual beings (Skiera 2003/2010, p. 265). Supposedly, in Steiner's system, the person is abrogated as an epitome of individuality by expanding the perspective into after-death and pre-birth realms and also by postulating the existence of various "bodies" (ibid., p. 264).

These issues present a challenge to Waldorf education to thoroughly portray Rudolf Steiner's pedagogic anthropology and its perspective on reincarnation and karma; in this endeavor, the focus must be on the weight and significance that Steiner's work attributes to terms such as "individuality" and "person." Furthermore, to meet this challenge, Waldorf education will need to show that alongside the stepwise development in seven-year phases there is a counter-rhythmic tendency of individualization, which most critics obviously overlooked: Steiner mentions eruptions of a heightened I-consciousness as a Rubicon experience (Föller-Mancini, Berger in Chapter 3) not only in years 9/10 but in the 3rd, 5th, 12th, and 18th years of life (Loebell in Chapter 3). Steiner's overall body of work shows that he moved beyond the outline he presented in 1907 in his essay "The Education of the Child from the Perspective of Spiritual Science" (Steiner 1907).

These critics point to an interesting issue when they say that Steiner's developmental theory is too undifferentiated; that it postulates the synchronicity of cognitive, emotional, motivational, and social development, which de facto does not occur that way (Ullrich 1986, p. 112). The question comes up, if this postulate really presents a disadvantage. Could we not see Steiner's concept as a developmental model that integrates aspects of development, which are otherwise often presented as segmented, and could it not offer a foil against which de-synchronizations could be analyzed more easily (Rittelmeyer, Loebell in Chapter 3)?

Contextualization plays a significant role in assessing the status of Steiner's developmental psychology. Ullrich assigns it to number-mystical speculations of the Hebdomad doctrine in antiquity; however, Zander thinks that Steiner borrowed from developmental psychology of his time. Prange however holds that Steiner ignores the developmental psychology of his time—other than the theory of the "Second Terrible Twos" around the ninth year (Prange 1985, p. 109). That obvious divergence shows that here lies another important task for further research. Such research has to examine which important influences Steiner was exposed to at different times, as he conceptualized his developmental teachings, and which ideas he integrated and which ones he rejected.

On this topic, Axel Föller-Mancini and Bettina Berger (Chapter 3) presented the first results, which indicate that Steiner studied the emerging discipline of experimental psychology, spearheaded by Wilhelm Wundt, with great intensity (Steiner 1901). Likewise, Steiner thoroughly reviewed the work of child psychologists Wilhelm Ament and of Wilhelm August Lay, who propound a similar phase model of age development as Steiner. In this connection, researching Steiner's library does prove helpful.

Albert Schmelzer

An examination of his library, which contained more than 9000 books, shows clearly that Steiner was broadly cognizant of the human science of his time. Contrary to Prange's opinion that Steiner did not study authors such as Wundt, Freud, or Ebbinghaus, Steiner's library contains nine works by Wilhelm Wundt, i.a. his *Natural Science and Psychology* (Leipzig 1903, 5th edition), which was extensively worked through—two books by Ebbinghaus, i.e., his *Outline of Psychology* (Leipzig 1908) with underlined and marked passages; his library also contains books by Freud, whose work *The Psychopathology of Everyday Life* (Berlin 1904) Steiner verifiably studied and worked through.

Such examples prove that some of the issues raised can indeed be solved. Finally, we hope research will proceed swiftly and that the future discourse between educational science and Waldorf education will be less polemic and characterized more by an atmosphere of mutually productive curiosity.

Notes

1 Up to now, there are two studies that look at Steiner's pedagogy in the mirror of its critics: the work of Ludger Kowal-Summek (2001) and that of Volker Frielingsdorf (2012). Their findings pertaining to developmental psychology are reflected in this article.
2 See also Steiner (1968, p. 513), Steiner (1980, p. 131), Steiner (1974, p. 131).

References

Barz, Heiner (1984): Der Waldorfkindergarten. Geistesgeschichtliche Ursprünge und entwicklungspsychologische Begründung seiner Praxis. *[The Waldorf kindergarten. Intellectual sources and justification of its practice in a developmental psychology perspective].* Weinheim und Basel: Beltz.
Barz, Heiner/Randoll, Dirk (2007): Absolventen von Waldorfschulen. Eine empirische Studie zu Bildung und Lebensgestaltung. 2. Auflage. *[Waldorf school graduates. An empirical study on education and life design. 2nd edition].* Wiesbaden: VS.
Böhm, Winfried (2012): Die Reformpädagogik. Montessori, Waldorf und andere Lehren. *[Reform pedagogy. Montessori, Waldorf and other teachings].* Munich: Beck.
Flammer, August (2009): Entwicklungstheorien. Psychologische Theorien der menschlichen Entwicklung. 4. Auflage. *[Theories of development. Psychological theories of human development. 4th edition].* Bern: Huber.
Frielingsdorf, Volker (2012): Waldorfpädagogik in der Erziehungswissenschaft. *[Waldorf education in educational science].* Weinheim und Basel: Beltz Juventa.
Guardini, Romano (1954): Die Lebensalter. *[The ages of man].* Würzburg: Werkbund.
Hofmann, Ulrike/von Prümmer, Christine/Weidner, Dieter (1981): Bildungslebensläufe ehemaliger Waldorfschüler. *[Educational biographies of former Waldorf students].* Stuttgart: Pädagogische Forschungsstelle beim Bund der Freien Waldorfschulen.
Kallert, Heide/Schleuning, Eva-Maria/Illert, Christa (1984): Der Aufbau der kindlichen Persönlichkeit in den Entwicklungslehren von Maria Montessori und Rudolf Steiner. *[The organization of the child's personality in the developmental theories of Maria Montessori and Rudolf Steiner].* In: Zeitschrift für Pädagogik, 30, pp. 633–645.
Kiersch, Johannes (1986): Wie lässt sich die Pädagogik Rudolf Steiners verstehen? Bemerkungen zu einem vorläufigen Versuch über ein ungelöstes Problem. *[How can we understand the pedagogy of Rudolf Steiner? Remarks on a tentative solution to an unsolved problem].* In: Zeitschrift für Pädagogik 32, 4, pp. 543–550.
Kowal-Summek, Ludger (2001): Die Pädagogik Rudolf Steiners im Spiegel der Kritik. 2. Auflage. *[Rudolf Steiner's pedagogy in the mirror of its critics. 2nd edition].* Herbolzheim: Centaurus.
Kranich, Ernst-Michael/Ravagli, Lorenzo (1990): Waldorfpädagogik in der Diskussion. Eine Analyse erziehungswissenschaftlicher Kritik. *[Waldorf education in discussion. An analysis of the critique from the side of educational science].* Stuttgart: Freies Geistesleben.
Lindenberg, Christoph (1979): Rudolf Steiner. In: Scheuerl, Hans (Ed.) (1979): Klassiker der Pädagogik.Bd. II. *[Classics of pedagogy. Vol. II].* Munich: Beck, pp. 170–182.
Prange, Klaus (1985): Erziehung zur Anthroposophie. Darstellung und Kritik der Waldorfpadagogik. *[Education for Anthroposophy. Presentation and criticism of Waldorf pedagogy].* Bad Heilbrunn: Klinkhardt.
Schneider, Wolfgang (1991): Das Menschenbild der Waldorfpädagogik. *[Waldorf education's concept of man].* Freiburg: Herder.
Skiera, Ehrenhard (2003/2010): Reformpädagogik in Geschichte und Gegenwart. Eine kritische Einführung. *[Reform pedagogy in historic and contemporary perspective. A critical introduction].* Munich: Oldenbourg.

Steiner, Rudolf (1907): Die Erziehung des Kindes vom Gesichtspunkte der Geisteswissenschaft. *[The education of the child in the perspective of spiritual science].* In: Steiner, Rudolf (Ed.) (1987): Lucifer – Gnosis. Grundlegende Aufsätze zur Anthroposophie und Berichte aus den Zeitschriften «Luzifer» und «Lucifer – Gnosis» 1903–1908. Rudolf Steiner Gesamtausgabe 34. Dornach: Rudolf Steiner, pp. 309–348.

Steiner, Rudolf (1968): Die Rätsel der Philosophie. *[Riddles of philosophy].* GA 18. Dornach: Rudolf Steiner Verlag.

Steiner, Rudolf (1974): Das Hereinwirken geistiger Wesenheiten in den Menschen. *[The influence of spiritual beings upon man].* GA 102. Dornach: Rudolf Steiner Verlag.

Steiner, Rudolf (1977): Die Erneuerung der pädagogischen-didaktischen Kunst durch Geisteswissenschaft. *[The renewal of education]* [Translator's note: Literal translation = The renewal of the art of pedagogy and methodology through spiritual science]. GA 301. Dornach: Rudolf Steiner Verlag.

Steiner, Rudolf (1980): Individuelle Geistwesen und ihr Wirken in der Seele des Menschen. *[Individual spiritual beings and their influence on the human soul].* GA 178. Dornach: Rudolf Steiner Verlag.

Steiner, Rudolf (1986): Gegenwärtiges Geistesleben und Erziehung. *[Education and modern spiritual life].* GA 307. Dornach: Rudolf Steiner Verlag.

Steiner, Rudolf (1897): Wilhelm Preyer. Gestorben am 15. Juli 1897. *[Wilhelm Preyer. Deceased on July 15, 1897].* In: Steiner, Rudolf (Ed.) (1989): Methodische Grundlagen der Anthroposophie. Gesammelte Aufsätze 1884–1901. *[Methodological foundations of anthroposophy. Collected essays 1884–1901].* GA 30. Dornach: Rudolf Steiner Verlag, pp. 346–359.

Steiner, Rudolf (1901): Moderne Seelenforschung. In: Steiner, Rudolf (Ed.) (1989): Methodische Grundlagen der Anthroposophie. Gesammelte Aufsätze 1884–1901. *[Methodological foundations of anthroposophy. Collected essays 1884–1901].* GA 30. Dornach: Rudolf Steiner Verlag, pp. 462–469.

Ullrich, Heiner (1982): "Ver-Steiner-te" Reformpädagogik. Anmerkungen zur neuerlichen Aktualität der Freien Waldorfschulen. *[Reform pedagogy turned to stone. Comments on the new popularity of free Waldorf schools].* [Translator's note: In German 'Steiner' means loosely: "the one who works with stone," so this is a wordplay on Steiner's name] In: Neue Sammlung 22, pp. 539–564.

Ullrich, Heiner (1986): Waldorfpädagogik und okkulte Weltanschauung. Eine bildungsphilosophische und geistesgeschichtliche Auseinandersetzung mit der Anthroposophie Rudolf Steiners. Weinheim und Munich: Juventa.

Ullrich, Heiner (1992): Kleiner Grenzverkehr. Über eine neue Phase in den Beziehungen zwischen Erziehungswissenschaft und Waldorfpädagogik. *[Small border traffic. On a new phase of relationships between educational science and Waldorf education].* In: Pädagogische Rundschau, 46, 4, pp. 461–480.

Ullrich, Heiner (1994): Rudolf Steiner. A neo-romantic thinker and reformer. In: Prospects: The quarterly review of comparative education. UNESCO. International Bureau of Education. Paris. XXIV (3/4), pp. 555–572.

Ullrich, Heiner (1995): Vom Außenseiter zum Anführer der Reformpädagogischen Bewegung? Betrachtungen über die veränderte Stellung der Pädagogik Rudolf Steiners in der internationalen Bewegung für eine Neue Erziehung. *[From outsider to leader of the reform pedagogy movement. Reflections on the changed status of Rudolf Steiner's pedagogy within the international movement for a new type of education].* In: Vierteljahresschrift für wissenschaftliche Pädagogik *[Scientific Pedagogy Quarterly],* 71, pp. 284–297.

Ullrich, Heiner (1996): Rudolf Steiner und die Waldorfschule. *[Rudolf Steiner and the Waldorf school].* In: Seyfarth-Stubenrauch, Michael and Ehrenfried Skiera (Eds.) (1996): Reformpädagogik und Schulreform in Europa. Grundlagen, Geschichte, Aktualität. *[Reform pedagogy and school reform in Europe. Foundations, history, relevance today].* Vol. 2: Schulkonzeptionen und Länderstudien. Baltmannsweiler: Schneider, pp. 253–267.

Ullrich, Heiner (1998): Freie Waldorfschulen. *[Independent Waldorf schools].* In: Kerbs, Diethart and Jürgen Reulecke (Eds.) (1998): Handbuch der deutschen Reformbewegungen. 1880–1933. *[Handbook of German reform movements 1880–1933].* Wuppertal: Hammer, pp. 411–424.

Ullrich, Heiner (2002): Befremdlicher Anachronismus oder zukunftsweisendes Modell? Die Freie Waldorfschule im pädagogischen Diskurs und in der erziehungswissenschaftlichen Forschung. In: Hansen-Schaberg *[Outlandish anachronism or futuristic model? Independent Waldorf schools in pedagogic discourse and in education science research].* In: Inge and Bruno Schonig (Eds.) (2002): Waldorf-Pädagogik. Baltmannsweiler: Schneider.

Ullrich, Heiner (2015): Waldorfpädagogik. Eine kritische Einführung. *[Waldorf education. A critical introduction].* Weinheim und Basel: Beltz.

Wilken, Etta (1983): Waldorfpädagogik und anthroposophische Heilpädagogik. *[Waldorf education and anthroposophical remedial pedagogy].* In: Sonderpädagogik, 13, 2, pp. 49–64.

Willmann, Otto/Roloff, Ernst M. (1913): Lexikon der Pädagogik I. *[Encyclopedia of pedagogy I].* Freiburg: Herder.

Zander, Helmut (2007): Anthroposophie in Deutschland. *[Anthroposophy in Germany].* Göttingen: Vandenhoeck & Ruprecht.

APPROACHES TO SUBSTANTIATING THE CONCEPT OF SEVEN-YEAR CYCLES OF DEVELOPMENT IN WALDORF EDUCATION

Peter Loebell

1 Introductory remarks

An essential cornerstone of Waldorf education is the continuous orientation toward the development of the growing human being from birth to maturity. Generally, teacher education places high priority on scientific study and research compliant with recognized science standards such as plurality, verifiability, transparency, scientific-based orientation, and repeatability of the line of reasoning; however, we can also understand pedagogy as an art that should be value-oriented and unfolds in concrete encounters of human beings with each other.

Waldorf schoolteachers base their daily practice not only on current scientific findings, but first of all on their own understanding of the child's development, which is shaped by their personal life experience. The physician and educator Janusz Korczak offers a very convincing example; based on an academic degree, he developed the elements of his pedagogy through practical activity and always checked his insights against the children's perception. "'I take a child from his home to come along with me and then bring him/her back,' Korczak said [...]. At age 14, it was a completely changed child that emerged from Korczak's cocoon" (Lifton 1990, p. 189). Korczak was not familiar with the concept of the seven-year cycle, but in his everyday pedagogic practice, he used the noticeable changes, which occur approximately every seven years in a young person's life, to orient himself (Loebell 2015). Furthermore, Waldorf education recognizes the significance of additional developmental aspects, which, according to Rudolf Steiner, repeatedly intersect and modify the sequenced phases that each span approximately seven years.

All developmental steps manifest in highly differentiated form due to special individual and life environment conditions. This gives rise particular challenges for pedagogy, as the understanding of an age-appropriate developmental level forms an indispensable measuring gauge for fostering individualization.

2 The development of the child as the basis for Waldorf education

2.1 The seven-year cycles

Already in his brief, but foundational work *The Education of the Child from the Perspective of Spiritual Science*, Rudolf Steiner first outlines the theoretical basis of what was later to become Waldorf education (Steiner 1907). On a few pages, he develops his concept of the human members of being (physical body, etheric body, astral body, and "I" or ego) and outlines the thesis that human development occurs in three stages or "birth processes" which occur in sequential seven-year intervals. Approximately seven years after the first, physical, birth, there ensues a profound developmental step, which Steiner also calls "the release of the etheric body." In contrast, the changes in body and soul that occur during puberty around the 14th year are considered indicators for the "birth of the astral body." In his later lecture cycles and conferences, Steiner repeatedly affirmed this understanding of a seven-year rhythm. It is considered a cornerstone of Waldorf education. In another context, Steiner mentions also an "birth of the I" taking place around the 21st year of life (Steiner 1985, p. 146).

However, Steiner also points out that the timing of the transitions that he describes may differ according to individual development and gender. More important that precise age designations are in his opinion the characteristic physical and soul-related changes that occur during the time, when the child goes to school: The change of teeth relates to the "birth of the etheric body" and puberty to the "birth of the astral body." A textbook for developmental psychology points out "that Steiner was no psychologist and with his system he only wanted to provide a rough guidepost for education" (Flammer 2009, p. 53). In fact, most of Steiner's statements regarding development in childhood and youth are linked with concrete suggestions for pedagogic action.

2.2 Moments of I-awareness in the continuous flow of development

Obviously, the human biography is not only shaped by certain long-term developmental phases but also influenced by other endogenous and exogenous factors. Steiner therefore issued various differentiations in reference to the first two seven-year cycles and their transitions, pointing to additional important events in human development. "For example, we observe a distinct developmental break in the time between birth and the change of teeth, approximately around the third year of life, when the child enters the phase of developing for the first time a distinct sense of self ('I')" (Steiner 1998, p. 46). While the human 'I' does not fully mature until age 21—as indicated earlier—it here becomes clear that the core of identity, which Steiner calls *Wesenskern*, shows a much earlier dynamic: As soon as it is born, the child appears as a unique individuality. Then, the experience of self finds expression around age three in a meaningful use of the first personal pronoun: "In the 3rd year, children start to use pronouns like *my* and *your*, and finally the I-form" (Largo 2012, p. 47).

On April 16, 1912, Steiner gave a lecture in Stockholm in which he took the view that in the life of a human being there were two different strands of development that overlay each other. On one hand, we can discern a natural sequence of changes within the human organization, occurring in seven-year stages: "Thus the first seven years appear as a period of imitation followed by the second seven years that are characterized by looking up to authorities, and the third seven-year cycle brings with it a budding of ideals, which would bring the human being into full consciousness of the 'I'" (Steiner 1994, p. 123). Here Steiner also expresses the opinion that the human being cannot reach freedom through these natural processes alone. A crosscurrent of developmental dynamic is necessary, an "inner development" in which "the consciousness of our 'I' comes to maturation, starting at the most tender age of childhood and creating its own independent path through life" (ibid., p. 122).

According to this thesis, the biological course of development is intersected already in the 3rd year of life by the crosscurrent of human individuality, which expresses itself in an increased I-awareness at that early stage. Similarly, Steiner draws attention to a special event around the age of nine/ten: "As the child approaches the age of nine, we will be able to observe a great change in this/her development" (Steiner 1998, p. 47). In another pedagogic lecture, he says that we can discern three smaller time segments within every seven-year cycle (ibid., p. 254).

Steiner emphasizes that the learning behavior of the child undergoes changes as early as the third and fifth years of life; and he repeatedly mentions developmental steps in the ninth/tenth and the twelfth year (Steiner 1987, 1982, p. 95).

In this connection, he even speaks of a complete "overhaul in human nature between the change of teeth and puberty"; Steiner notes that this important life transition starts "for most children approximately between year 9 and 10" (Steiner 1982, p. 109). At that age, the children experience themselves as an identity apart from the outer world. This change in consciousness does not occur in form of a question arising but manifests as a change in behavior toward the teacher or educator (ibid., p. 109). According to Steiner, around age 12, in pre-puberty, we must expect that the above-mentioned overhaul will lead to other important changes in the cognitive development of youths.

In the third seven-year cycle, as well, we can observe developmental rifts that evidence the effects of a self-cognizant I. By the 17th year, most girls and boys have completed puberty. That results in the developmental challenge of "reclaiming and permeating the body as an instrument of the soul" (Götte, Loebell, Maurer 2009, p. 242). Young people can develop their identity through the emerging ability to form judgment and thus enhance their ability to authentically present themselves to their environment. After the 18th year, toward the end of their school education, it becomes ever more important for the young person to connect the subjective with the objective dimensions, to fill his/her own actions with meaning, and to achieve moral autonomy. Around this time, we can frequently observe a change in the developmental process. Around age 18.5, the young adult makes a distinct move toward professional orientation, a step which at the same time frequently results in a "natural" separation from the parental home (ibid., p. 339).

3 The transition around the seventh year of life

3.1 Learning through imitation and exploration in the first seven-year cycle

Steiner holds the view that the learning behavior of children passes through developmental phases of fundamental changes that he calls "birth processes." So, he proceeds from the assumption that children up to age seven primarily learn by imitating the actions and attitudes of persons in their surroundings.

Their development is obviously not dependent on biological maturation processes only. On one hand, it depends on external conditions for imitation, whether a child achieves, aside from maturity, also the ability and readiness for cognitive learning in a school context. On the other hand, children avail themselves of opportunities for imitation in individually very different ways and at different times (Largo 2012). For example, the upright body posture characteristic for man is not acquired by instinct but by imitation. It is only in the course of the first seven years that children adopt the typical walking patterns of adults, also by imitation (ibid.). Therefore, the children would not be able to acquire this basic ability without a suitable environment. But even under comparable conditions, body motion develops in very different variations (Largo 2012, p. 35).

At approximately the age of 9–14 months, i.e., in the time when they learn to walk upright and without help, most children also start to utter the first purposeful words, mostly by doubling syllables (*mama, papa*), and they comprehend that their utterances have a meaning. Also, at about age one, they comply with simple spoken commands. At approximately 24 months of age, children independently start to connect two words. While these milestones of speech development can occur at various age points, they nevertheless show up in basically the same sequence in contrast to early forms of forward motion (Largo 2012, p. 34).

Thinking is awakened by speaking due to the relationships that can be autonomously established between various conceptual contents. Children now can express very different semantic relationships (Grimm, Weinert 2002, p. 532). Between approximately month 18 and month 24, when the first 50 words are being learned, a strong dynamic in speech development commences: new words are learned on a daily basis—by the fourth year that can amount to about 3000 words, which means on average four new words are added each day. At the same time, children master most sentence constructions of their mother tongue and pay attention to grammatical rules. They already avoid many mistakes, and the mistakes they still make mostly follow a certain logic (Petermann, Niebank, Scheithauer 2004, p. 157).

Generally, four- to five-year-old children have a command of the main sentence constructions in their language. But it is only in year six that they gain the ability to find new ways within for organizing the available words in a subconscious process of re-organization (Grimm, Weinert 2002, p. 534).

This also makes it possible for the six-year-old to spontaneously self-correct her/himself. Incidentally, the entire process of speech acquisition depends on corresponding stimuli from the surroundings.

While imitation, as Steiner describes it, plays a great role in the learning process during the first years of life, there can be no doubt that learning at every age is essentially driven by curiosity, by an urge to explore, which first manifests in small children as the exploration of their own body, then of the closer, and finally the farther environment. Remo Largo differentiates between *object-oriented* and *social learning* (imitative behaviors) (Largo 2012). A varied, stimulus-rich environment is of highest significance for the development of sensory perception. Also, we know today that explorative behavior is closely connected to the quality of attachment the child could establish during the first years of life with the persons closest to him/her—mostly with the mother (Zimmermann 2004, p. 54). *Attachment* is loosely defined as a strong emotional bond with familiar adults (mostly parents or surrogate parents) that the child turns to for protection, comfort, or help (Hopf 2005, p. 29).

3.2 The child's development around the seventh year of life

At around age seven, children generally are characterized by various attributes and abilities that we consider prerequisite for starting school (Tent 2001, p. 607). These include:

- Physical characteristics such as body measurements and proportions, ossification (bone formation), dentition (change of teeth), general health, and motoric skills;
- Cognitive indicators such as command of language and sensory competency, understanding instructions and symbol comprehension as well as memory for arbitrary, abstract forms, capacity for differentiated perception (analysis), formation of sound- and writing figures from different elements (synthesis), psycho-motoric coordination dealing with quantities, amounts, numbers and relations, fantasy, formation of concrete concepts, beginnings of specific processes of thought and pertaining to invariances in quantities;
- Motivational characteristics such as spontaneous interest and curiosity, readiness for achievement (taking on tasks), refraining from spontaneous gratification of wants, attention and concentration, systematic approach to fulfilling tasks, self-control, tolerance for failure, and acceptance of criticism;
- Characteristic of social behavior such as the readiness to detach from persons of reference, readiness for contact with strangers, emotional stability in the face of unpleasantness, responsiveness when addressed in the group, independence.

Steiner paraphrases the developmental process underlying these developmental options and emerging abilities as "the birth of the etheric body." He emphasizes that around the seventh year the formative powers, which were until then engaged in the formation of the (physical) body, become increasingly available for processes of conscious thinking and thus form the basis for cognitive learning. The human being now activates "those formative powers that previously had transformed the body and its organs into a more complete and perfect configuration" (Kranich 1999, p. 133). The loss of one's baby teeth is considered a visible signal that the formation of the physical body and its organs has come to completion (Kranich 1999, p. 125). Only when the adult set of teeth in its double symmetry has come in can most children grasp the directionality of numbers and letters and can correctly reproduce them. For example, "the mirrored writing of five- to six-year-old children [...] corresponds to a normal phase in the achievement of writing competency [...]. At around age seven, most children have internalized our customary direction of writing and gained certainty in the orientation of numbers and letters" (Fischer 2012, p. 25).

In regard to cognitive traits, Jean Piaget's description of concrete, operational thinking is considered a particular signpost for the developmental stage in the seventh year of life. Most children can now combine, separate, and order different elements in their own imagination, as long as they deal with objects that can be experienced through the senses or with thoughts about such objects. Moreover, they can now understand that certain attributes of an object (for example, its quantity or weight) can remain the same, even if other features change—Piaget speaks in this connection of conceptual schemata. By now, Piaget's findings have undergone repeated revision, for example, it has been shown that cognitive achievements occur at a significantly earlier age than Piaget assumed, if only we simplify the tasks presented to the child. But: "Many of these simplified tasks only apply to intuitive understanding, while Piaget had assumed a conceptual and reflexive behavior" (Flammer 2009, p. 159).

The structural characteristics of the child's thought process stood at the center of scientific interest for a long time, but research in developmental psychology has focused since the 1980s more on change in category-specific contents of the child's concepts (Sodian 2002). Nevertheless, some of Piaget's important insights still remain valid even today: There are inherited conceptual schemata as well as those that are actively constructed. Even if some of the achievements described by Piaget obviously occur earlier than he assumed, and even though some of these achievements do not correspond at all to the stage he designated for them, his differentiation of the various form of representation remains a valuable contribution (Flammer 2009, p. 170). A child's general readiness to achieve and a tendency to solve tasks that are chosen by him/herself or assigned by an adult count among the motivational traits indicative of school readiness.

At this age, the child develops a "sense for assignments." That includes "the growing certainty that assignments are meaningful, have significance, and can be enticing as a potential source of joy" (Schmid 1996, p. 227). Also, still until about age 9, most children are convinced that they can reach all goals, if only they work hard enough or learn long enough (Flammer 1995, p. 39). This establishes the prerequisite for persistent dedication to a task and to learning itself.

3.3 Maturity, competency, and readiness at the start of school

The term *school maturity* refers to the genesis of those attributes and traits that are prerequisite for the start of school. There is no controversy regarding a maturation process in the narrower sense, indicated by body characteristics as mentioned above. Height, bone solidification, and the onset of the change of teeth are biological processes that are largely independent of environmental and educational influences with exceptions only in extreme cases. Here the concept of maturation is justified and applies in full. Yet, at the same time as certain physical characteristics appear, we can observe also other cognitive and motivational phenomena as well as new competencies in social behavior.

The concept of school maturity has by now largely been replaced, because it suggests the idea of maturation that could be understood to imply that a seven-year-old child would inherently be ready to start school without needing any outer support. But that is not the case. For example, the language competency of school-age children from certain strata of the population often does not suffice to meet the schools' demands. Therefore, the term "school competency" has prevailed since the 1970s. School competency refers to what the surroundings expect of the child, rather than what it becomes in and of its own (Schenk-Danzinger 2002, p. 2203).

This concept is therefore particularly suited to detect developmental deficits and, if needed, to mobilize special measures for educational support. However, Schenk-Danzinger points out that this term also entails some problems, because the schools' requirements for newly enrolling students are often ambiguous; they can differ from one institution to the next—yes, even from teacher to teacher. In that sense, the competencies that the child should have acquired before starting school are entirely determined by external demands.

In contrast, the term *school readiness* moves the subjective component of the child into the foreground. It addresses "the child's feelings, dispositions, interests and attitudes toward school and is of equally crucial importance for the child's success in the first years of school" (Schenk-Danzinger 1988, p. 33). A child is considered ready for schooling when it has exhausted the range of learning opportunities offered during preschool age and when she/he demands new organizing principles for dealing with the world. The term "school readiness" highlights another component: It is the child him/herself who gains a more or less clear *consciousness* of his/her own abilities and wants to test them in the framework of learning processes the school offers. It seeks new challenges and is prepared to accept assignments from the teacher.

The three different approaches reveal three different dimensions that are obviously significant for development:

- The concept of *school maturity* points to endogen, corporeal processes that rely on inner development patterns within the changing human being, such as growth and body proportions, loss of baby teeth as well as motoric skills.
- The concept of *school competency* focuses on demands from the environment, which the child has to fulfill within the framework of its role in society. That addresses, first of all, the soul-related components required for a successful start of school: operational thinking, motivation for learning, readiness to solve problems, and ability to interact in groups.
- *School readiness* refers to the child's experience of her/himself as the subject of his/her own learning processes: The human spirit in its self-efficacy experiences itself as the author of the efforts it makes toward acquiring skills and understanding.

Currently we can observe a strong tendency in *[German]* educational politics to move the start of school to an earlier age, so that in many German states children would start school not at six to seven years, but as early as age five; on the other hand, the application process for a delayed school start for one's child has become increasingly difficult or has been abolished altogether (Puhani, Weber 2006, p. 3). Within the anthropological strictures relevant to Waldorf education, we can say that in children who are too young, the etheric body is employed for cognitive learning before it has matured sufficiently. There are in fact empirical studies that permit the conclusion that such a premature engagement can have negative effects on the learning achievements of children. Furthermore, the "probability of attending a Gymnasium (in contrast to those who attend Real- or Integrated schools) is by about 12 percent higher for children that started school at a later age (ibid., p. 26)." [Translator's note: *Gymnasium* is an academically oriented type of German high school; *Real* and *Integrated* (Haupt) schools are school types oriented toward professional trade or vocational careers within the German school system.] Barchmann and Kinze note: "The increasing age alone has a stabilizing effect on the ability to concentrate and on the child's general attitude toward work" (Barchmann, Kinze 1989, p. 231).

3.4 Synchronism

If the birth of the etheric body is supposed to be a prerequisite for the developmentally appropriate start of school, we must ask whether the three approaches agree regarding the timing of developmental changes: Does the endogen maturation process lead the child to be internally prepared and able to meet the challenge of attending school? Obviously, the development of children and adolescents is not only a continuous process—for example, in gaining specific types of knowledge—but also a discontinuous one, when maturation progresses quickly or new faculties emerge in a short span of time in form of developmental breakthroughs. The Psychology of the 20th century has variously described developmental stages. The respective researchers focused on certain aspects of development, such as cognition (Piaget), morality (Kohlberg), or developmental tasks (Havighurst). Based on an anthroposophical understanding of man being composed of body, soul, and spirit, the desynchronization of the various dimensions of development can be examined in more differentiated ways. The distinction of the above-described three criteria for the start of school offers that opportunity.

Since the 1970s, the concept of school maturity has been complemented or even replaced by the other two terms—*school competency* and *school readiness*. This could indicate that, since then, characteristics of body, soul, and spirit development in school-ready children are often no longer occurring in chronological connection. As a matter of fact, studies related to the start of school have increasingly indicated that the various dimensions of development are progressing at a different pace. Research showed that many children present an awakened intellect and preparedness for achievement already before school age, which seems to justify an earlier start of school. Yet these children frequently lack other characteristic of body and soul that could be considered prerequisites for the start of school. "It is not rare to observe a severe *dissociation*, a disparity in the different levels of development: The child is just about ready for school on an intellectual level, but physiologically, soul-wise and socially he/she is not ready for it – not by a long shot. Other forms of dissociation also occur, for example when intellectual maturity lags behind an earlier maturation of the physical body" (Patzlaff, Saßmannshausen 2005, p. 33).

Public elementary schools try to level out dissociations of different development dimensions as much as possible by offering special preparatory classes to get ready for school. Even though, within the framework of the school-ready child, public elementary schools should offer wholistic support to children, in reality, the primary focus is on fostering preliminary skills for school learning in the areas of language and numbers competency. Waldorf schools, in contrast, focus on giving children the time to develop their abilities through play and handicrafts. This approach corresponds to the insight in developmental psychology research that early, age-inappropriate fostering does not lead to improvement in school learning and achievement. "Meaningful learning consists of self-determined action, through which the child can prove itself. When children learn to read due to their own volition, they experience reading as a self-acquired skill that improves their sense of self-worth. If, however, a child learns reading because it is made to read, reading becomes something that others demand, and the child's sense of self-worth will suffer from it" (Largo 2012, p. 227).

4 Learning in the second seven-year cycle

4.1 *The significance of authority*

According to Steiner, the learning behavior of children starts to change in the seventh year of life. "The institution of school only is possible, because children around six or seven years of age are ready to learn from unknown teachers, or, to exaggerate a bit, teachers only exist, because children ask for them" (Largo 2012, p. 140). In Steiner's view, two core principles govern the learning process at this stage: First, the need for visual instruction that stimulates the child's own fantasy and imagination and, second, the need for authoritative guidance from competent educators. As a matter of fact, authority is once again considered indispensable in education, ever since many experiences showed "that a teacher, who has no authority, cannot meaningfully carry out his profession" (Heymann 2006, p. 6). "Authority in this connection does not just refer to a certain status that a pedagogue holds due to his office, but rather it refers to a special kind of interpersonal relationship: the person that is an authority for others enjoys their respect, is held in high regard, is taken seriously and on this basis such an authority is granted the right to give guidance, leadership and make decisions that are honored by others—at least within the possibly limited context, in which their authority is acknowledged" (Heymann 2006, p. 7).

Overall, the personality of a teacher, who is accepted by children and youths, is characterized by the following attributes: The teacher

- is considered a model for a child seeking an orientation.
- communicates clear structures, rules, and instructions for work, without requiring lengthy discussions.
- gives truthful support to students and takes them seriously.
- cultivates an authentic relationship with young people, without hurting them personally.
- can also answer questions that diverge from the actual subject matter of the class.
- is interested in the students (Riedl 2006, p. 12).

These characteristics correspond largely to what, in parental context, we call an "authoritarian style of education" (Rheinberg et al. 2001, p. 290).

4.2 Growing independence

Can we today still assume that children up to age 14 feel the need to be guided by adult authority—even as we observe that they are increasingly independent in our times? They have learned to use age-specific offers of the media, consumer- and leisure-industries with ever-growing independence and competency and therefore children today are considered to be "active agents within in their life world."

On one hand, there can be no doubt that increasing emancipation has always been a driving force in childhood development. On the other hand, children are afforded also a type of independence "in order to gradually release the adults from the often-cumbersome duties of being caretaker, guardian, helper, supporter and supervisor" (Göppel 2002, p. 42). Accordingly, it seems appropriate, to carefully determine differentiations in the concept of independence. In this vein, Rülcker distinguishes

- *functional independence*, which accords more availability and value to the human being in the sense of a more flexible and less complicated adaptability, from
- *productive independence*, which is aligned with the idea of increasing emancipation, the pursuit of one's own interests and increasing one's radius of action.

Göppel adds another type under the keyword "resigned independence," which means the mere feeling of "there is nothing I can do but..." (ibid., p. 43). He suggests making a distinction between independence types that are "option- and enjoyment-oriented" and those that are "duty-oriented and governed by the reality principle, which is more concerned with the responsible completion of assignments and tasks" (ibid., p. 48).

Based on these suggestions, we can differentiate independence by using four different qualities—if we omit the resigned type:

Independence	Functional: Availability	Productive: Increasing emancipation
Option- or	Adaptation to consumer offers;	Definition of one's own needs;
enjoyment-oriented	Gratification through rewards	Self-directed leisure activity
Duty- or reality orientation	Transfer of responsibility by adults	Self-commitment, responsibility

Figure 3.6   Forms of independence in children and youths according to Göppel (2002)

This diagram shows that we need a highly differentiated evaluation of independence in the development of young people.

- The combination of functionality with option- or enjoyment-oriented independence leads largely to an outer-directedness of the child and satisfies the needs of the soul only superficially and possibly deceptively.
- Functionality in connection with a duty- or reality-oriented independence means that children have to take on tasks with a high level of responsibility, e.g., because they have to contribute to their family's basic necessities of life because their parents being overburdened.
- Productivity in the sense of increasing emancipation in connection with option- or enjoyment-oriented independence can point to the growing autonomy that sets in with the transition to adolescence and youth.
- Productive, duty-, and reality-oriented independence means that the young person accepts tasks based on his/her own insights and completes them responsibly.

The boundaries between these different qualities are, in reality, not always unambiguous. Nevertheless, there is a need for a differentiated evaluation of the obviously increasing independence in young people and it would be a mistake to assume their independence in general, which would make the guidance of a reliable adult educator appear obsolete.

4.3 *The transition to adolescence*

At age nine to ten, with the beginning of the turn-around or push in mental development, as described above, children overcome the last effects of childish imitation. They take a more distanced attitude in perceiving worldly phenomena, which now in turn have a much more direct impact on their feelings. The turn-around, which began at age 9 to 10, reaches a new stage in pre-puberty: In this time—around the 11th year for girls and around year 12–13 for boys—important events occur in their social life and the possibility emerges, to more strongly direct one's own thoughts. Increasingly, the students try now to look beyond the surface of world phenomena. While they derive joy from the variety of self-created images simply through their appearances, now their desire awakens to gain their own insights into the relationships between cause and effect. Phenomenology is more than just recognizing and ordering phenomena; rather, its main concern is the question of causality.

Since the first Waldorf School was founded, one of the essential characteristics of its profile is the arrangement that a classroom teacher pedagogically accompanies the children during the first eight grades and teaches them personally every morning in main lesson blocks on most subjects. Steiner justified this long-lasting responsibility of one central teacher personality in various lectures: "There is nothing more useful than being able to provide the child between ages 7 and 8 with content in the form of images so that you can later, maybe between ages 13 and 14, refer to them in some form. That is precisely the reason, why we try at the Waldorf schools to leave the children as long as possible in the care of one teacher. When the children start school around age 7, they are entrusted to the care of a teacher. As the children progress through the grades, this teacher stays with them as long as possible. This is good, because this way the things that that the child received seed-like can again and again be re-used as contents in educational instruction" (Steiner 1979, p. 63).

It stands to reason that one teacher cannot always accompany the child over the entire eight-year time span. Not only many causes—such as pregnancy, illness, transfer to another school, professional re-orientation—lead to a change in classroom teachers. But also, the high demands on the pedagogical and subject-oriented competency of classroom teachers—particularly in grades 7 and 8—have led Waldorf schools make the appropriate duration for a classroom teacher's commitment a subject for discussion. The concept of Waldorf education allows each school to find the solution to this challenge, for example:

- modification of the classroom teacher concept through a middle-school-level teacher's college
- increasing proportional transfer of main lesson blocks to high-school-level teachers
- continuity of classroom-teacher care with strongly modified methodology and a fundamentally different attitude toward adolescents

5 Transition to the third seven-year cycle

5.1 *Puberty—the birth of the astral body*

Physiological changes between ages 10 and 14—such as an enormous growth of the lungs and a change in respiration form the physiological basis for an augmented experience of one's own feelings (Kranich 1999, p. 187). Moreover, the appearance now changes, due to an emergence of more distinct personal facial features. Just as in growth, girls go through the changes of puberty generally earlier than boys.

At the time of their first menstruation, girls are usually approximately 10–16 years old; on average, menarche occurs between ages 12.5 and 13, when the peak of the physical growth phase has already passed (Largo, Czernin 2011, p. 28). Most boys experience their biological maturity in form of the first ejaculation two years later, at age 15. The profound body changes result in the young person experiencing their own self and body as something alien. The adolescents compare their own characteristics and abilities with those of their peers, recognize peculiarities, distance themselves from others, and search for their own goals and ideals. Often a profound sense of insecurity accompanies such increased self-reflection. Due to accelerated physical growth, young people often experience themselves a being heavy and clumsy. On the other hand, their direct perception of physical strength also triggers stronger intensity in dealing with external reality. Waldorf education goes from the assumption that the experience of cause-effect relations in the mechanics of their own bone structure gives rise to the adolescents' need for a causal understanding of natural phenomena (Kranich 1999, p. 204).

A definite turn toward friends of same age and gender now replaces the attachment to parents and teachers, and the first romantic partnerships are formed. All the processes described here occur within the context of profound psychological and social changes and typical developmental challenges (Oerter, Montada 2002, p. 271), such as:

- building newer, deeper relationships with peers of both gender;
- accepting the changes in their own body and appearance;
- acquiring gender-specific behavior and social behavior;
- forming a closer relationship with one "best" male or female friend;
- separating from the parents (becoming independent from parents);
- thinking about their own education and later choice of profession;
- imagining what a future relationship or family might be like;
- coming to know themselves and to know how others see them;
- developing their own worldview;
- planning their life and striving to achieve realistic goals.

Waldorf education rests on the assumption that there is a close connection between somatic and psychological development, which means we must not consider the processes of maturation and learning as isolated from each other: physical changes give rise to challenges and conditions for the learning process: pedagogy in turn can also have an effect on biological maturity. That is also true for puberty. Already as early as 1977, a study found that female students of public middle and high schools reach menarche on average at 12 years and 7 months of age, which is distinctly earlier than Waldorf students, who enter menarche at the average age of 13 years and 3 months (Matthiolius, Schuh 1977).

5.2 Competence to judge

According to Piaget, the recognition of moral norms proceeds between years 6 and 13 in three stages (Schenk-Danzinger 1988, p. 122):

- In *simple moral realism*, it is the fact of punishment that morally qualifies an action; for example, the young child arrives at the understanding that it is wrong to steal because then one gets punished.
- The child reaches the stage of *heteronomous morals* when it understands that it has to avoid an undesirable action (e.g., stealing), because an authority prohibits that action. (However, newer studies found that already at four years of age, the child may reject an immoral act because of the consequences it has for others concerned and not because of an authority's opinion (Montada 2002, p. 632).
- Finally, *autonomous morals* encompass the evaluation of a behavior based on one's own social responsibility: Accordingly, one should not steal because otherwise no one would be able to trust anyone else and the human community would suffer.

In his particularly influential model of moral development, Kohlberg describes three qualitatively different levels (partly congruent with those of Piaget) with two stages each (Hascher, Althof 2004, p. 65; Montada 2002, p. 635):

a. Pre-conventional level

   ♦ Heteronomous morality: one obeys rules, because when we break them, we get punished.
   ♦ Individualism, goal-consciousness, and exchange: One obeys rules if they serve anyone's interests; also, just is what is fair.

b. Conventional level

   ♦ Mutual expectations, relationships, and interpersonal conformity: One tries to meet expectations of other persons (close to oneself). Important here is the wish to behave well in the sense of complying with accepted rules and authorities, in order to maintain important social relationships.
   ♦ Social system and moral conscience: Once accepted, one must fulfill duties; one obeys laws, insofar as they do not contradict other social obligations. Thus, one acts in compliance with a given system of law and order, which regulates the rights, obligations, and claims of all people.

c. Post-conventional level

   ♦ The stage of the social contract and of individual rights: One is aware that there is a multitude of agreed-upon—largely group specific—values and rules that one must follow in the interest of social justice. Moreover, certain rights (such as human rights) are considered inalienable.
   ♦ The stage of universal ethical principles: one follows ethical principles out of one's own insight, recognizing them as binding and oriented on universal justice; if any laws violate such principles, then, when in doubt, one acts in accordance with such universal ethics.

Kohlberg does not set up a correspondence between the six stages of moral development with any specific age level. According to Steiner, the particularly important time for the formation of moral consciousness lies between the 13th and 15th years of life. Newer findings in brain research confirm his views: The pre-frontal cortex, which enables the conscious formation and application of moral values, is the last brain area that is myelinated and thus rendered fully functional: "The frontal cortex is that cortical area, whose tendrils connecting it to other brain areas are the last ones to be sheathed by myelin in the course of life. This process of myelination of tendrils to and from the frontal cortex is only completed at the time of puberty or even – in parts – later than that" (Spitzer 2002, p. 352). The prefrontal cortex regulates social behavior, evaluations, and the formation of long-term values, and so Spitzer concludes "that ethics (in the strict sense of reflection on the principles of moral behavior) cannot be taught in the lower grades [...] Even in seventh grade, there can as yet be no real discussion on ethical values" (ibid., p. 353).

5.3 Acceleration

In general, puberty has accelerated since the time between 1900 and 1980 by an average of two years (from 15.6 to 13.2 average menarche age). This tendency appears to have stagnated since 1962 (with an average menarche age of 12.5 years) or even shows some reversal (Knußmann 1996, p. 207). Nevertheless, "the acceleration [...] signifies a shortening of childhood. It causes an earlier hormonal re-structuring. In the realm of the psyche that means a change in worldview. The psychologically immature adolescents are facing special problems. Often, they do not know how to deal with the onslaught of new desires, needs, body sensations and fantasies, which their maturing bodies urge upon them" (Schenk-Danzinger 2004, p. 258).

Also, when dealing with adolescents, we can frequently experience that the different dimensions of puberty development—e.g., bodily, psychological, and sociological aspects—are not happening all at the same time (Fend 1990). Adolescents are often overestimated by their surroundings and met with increased social demands by others, because their early physical development makes them appear more mature. Often, they are expected to arrive at competent judgments, a faculty, which, according to Steiner, only emerges through the birth of the astral body. If the young person is too early—i.e., before age 12—required to form their own critical judgments, they can, in Steiner's view, not yet arrive at that through the powers of the astral body but must take recourse to the realm of the etheric body.

In that case, the adolescent is not yet prepared to accept the judgment of others with love and to examine it in a spirit of good will (Steiner 1982, p. 108).

The acceleration of puberty and the ensuing social expectations also engender long-term effects: "The analysis of long-term studies shows that those who went through puberty earlier are still at age 38 more responsible, cooperative and self-confident, more controlled and better adjusted than their peers of the same age. However, they were also more conventional, conforming and showed less humor. People who went through puberty later, were in comparison to others of the same age more impulsive, less balanced, yet also more playful, inventive and more insightful in regard to themselves, even at the age of 38" (Oerter, Montada 2002, p. 281).

5.4 Causality

Waldorf education considers the formation of autonomous judgment to be closely connected with understanding causality. In an early work on cognition theory, Steiner developed this concept employing the throwing-parable—when something, e.g., a ball, is being thrown, three factors must come together—i.e., the smooth motion of the push, even acceleration of the fall, and the resistance of air (Kranich 1997, p. 25). This results *by necessity* in a specific effect. The objective law of nature therefore entails "not only that a process happened under certain conditions, but also that it had to happen. One gained the *insight* that it had to occur because of the nature of the action observed" (Steiner 2003, p. 91).

Modern natural science in general is not primarily concerned with causal understanding, but with the order of phenomena, so that certain results can be systematically predicted. We can assume a regular pattern when these predictions come true and we can apply them in technical processes. The concern in this case is primarily the control of nature.

In Waldorf education, an understanding of the principle of causality presupposes that we can internally create the various phenomena through our own *[representational? imaginative?]* activity; only then can we fully arrive at an insight as an individual experience. Such insight can only form through the self-engendered creative activity of thinking. The adolescent "receives the phenomena into his representational world and re-experiences internally that, which he/she has perceived. [...] In this process a special sphere is forming in the inner world of the young person: an inner space of recognition and truth" (Kranich 1997, p. 53).

The kind of thought that is searching for causality penetrates the web of interconnected energies, which can explain the apparent phenomena, even though these are not available for direct sense perception. He who creates in this way the phenomena of the world out of himself so as to compare them with perceived reality does not only pierce the surface of phenomena with his mind: Rather, he recreates them from within and thus he does a reality check as to how much his own idea formation is appropriate. Those who want to train themselves in this activity will notice that they have to overcome their own prejudices and habits of thought to arrive at an appropriate judgment. According to Steiner, this striving toward one's own, internally generated judgment evidences the soul dimension of the birth of the astral body.

While an understanding of causality already has been detected in infants (Rauh 2002), that observation obviously deals with a different, basic form of perceiving contiguity. Moreover, many studies with three- or four-year-old preschool children show that they can recognize and predict the regular sequence of causes and effects in physical events (Goswami 2001). Goswami uses four principles to examine the question of whether the thinking of small children follows generally recognized criteria of causality:

- The *priority principle* means that causes must either precede the effects or occur simultaneously with them (Goswami); this knowledge seems to exist at the latest at three years of age.
- The *co-variation principle* is the second criterion for assessing causality. It means: "If an effect can be re-traced to several possible causes, the actual cause is the one which occurs together with the effect regularly and predictably" (ibid., p. 178).
- The *principle of time contiguity* refers to closeness in time and space of various events, which are staged as possible causes and effects. The events must not only co-variate in these cases, but they must also "be connected to each other through a contiguous chain of mediating events" (ibid., p. 180).
- The *principle of similarity* forms the fourth criterion, which applies when there is no information about time contiguity or co-variation.

The study design for exploring causal understanding in children consists of specially staged events, in which the research subjects are—partly intentionally—deceived.

In no case did the study focus on the understanding of cause-and-effect relations in real physical processes, but that is exactly the meaning of the causality principle that Steiner refers to in his statements about the competency of judgment in adolescents. An understanding of causality in the sense of Waldorf education is only possible when the transition to adolescence starts around the 12th year of life. We here want to emphasize that the concern is not to teach the students relations in natural science differently from what the curriculum of public school provides. Rather, the concern is to develop a completely transparent concept of causality, so that the adolescents can replace their habitual thoughts of co-variation with an actual, autonomously formed judgment concerning cause-effect relationships.

6 Summary: The concept of the seven-year cycles as a foundation for education

Obviously, the possible benefit that the seven-year concept offers for understanding development lies in its differentiated and carefully thought-out balance between normative and descriptive components: Each human being has the right to be seen in his own unique development without prejudice; however, we can discover individual and cultural idiosyncrasies only when we hold expectations of normal change processes. Steiner himself differentiates the qualities of various processes that occur in the development in children and adolescents:

- An endogenous, linear maturation process that unfolds—with individual variations—in seven-year cycles. These cycles each lead to the emancipation of the members of being as Steiner describes them, first with the physical birth, then at the beginning of the change of teeth, next with the onset of puberty, and finally with the emancipation of the young adult.
- Exogenous influences from the surrounding, especially through the effects of an education, which stresses imitation in the first seven-year cycle, emphasizes following an authority between the 7th and 14th years, and, after puberty, primarily targets the formation of autonomous judgment.
- Important, singular rifts in the linear process of development occur especially in the third and ninth year of life, e.g., through crisis-like moments in conscious self-perception. These breaks consist of mostly unexpected, events that are experienced without preparation and can also occur simultaneous with illnesses; they lead often to profound changes in psyche and body.

The concept of the seven-year cycles can only find meaningful consideration in pedagogy within the context of the other endo- and exogenous influences on child development. The metaphor of birth, which Steiner uses in connection with the seven-year-cycle transitions, entails the image of an organism that matures within a protective sheath to emancipate itself at an endogenously triggered

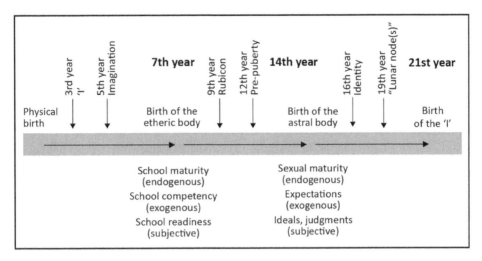

Figure 3.7 Development of children and adolescents—Linear process and point-like events

point in time. In this sense, the pedagogic benefit of the seven-year concept does not rely on an empiric proof of certain developmental stages at accurately fixed points in time. We can understand Steiner's references in regard to children and adolescents rather as heuristic pointers for drawing pedagogues' attention to specific conditions:

- Respect for the endogenous developmental progress while simultaneously attending to the support and assistance needed;
- Consideration of possible dissociation of various dimensions of development and assessment, and whether compensatory measures are indicated;
- The need for a protective sphere for the developing young person so as to avoid pre-mature, excessive demands and damages;
- The protective sphere that pedagogy should create before each transition into the next phase is established—according to Steiner—by adults who should serve as role-models for imitation during preschool years, and should provide the "beloved authority" figure for school-age children.

The effect of such educator personalities can open up the opportunity for children to fully form the powers of their not-yet-emancipated members of being, who are still in need of protection. This view is today substantiated by experiences and research findings in the areas of psychology and neurobiology. The neurobiologist Joachim Bauer states in his book on mirror neurons that the "interpersonal relationship between learners and instructors is of pre-eminent importance" (Bauer 2006, p. 122). Moreover, he emphasizes "that personal instruction, demonstration and modeling by teachers is a crucial component of learning and teaching" (ibid., p. 123).

Neurobiologist Gerald Hüther holds the view that schools should create an atmosphere of challenge, protection, and trust: "Only under the sensitive protection and competent guidance provided by adult 'models' can children recognize the full range of manifold creative opportunities and use them resourcefully to thus develop their own abilities and possibilities even further. Only in this process can the frontal cortex produce the child's own, inner image of self-efficacy and self-motivation that can be employed for all ensuing learning processes" (Hüther 2007, p. 54).

Manfred Spitzer alerts us to the significant role of adults' behavior for the moral development of young human beings: "Just as children in kindergarten need the right language input in order to learn to speak correctly, so adolescents need the right surroundings on all levels of their community in order to test their actions; they need the right models to evaluate their actions through model learning and they need enough free space to experiment with their own behaviors" (Spitzer 2002, p. 354). Other than synchronicity of various development dimensions and creation of a protective atmosphere characterized by challenges and trust, there are several other factors—as described above—that should be considered:

- The tension between expecting age-appropriate unfoldment of development and taking into account individual possibilities and needs;
- Safe attachment and support for speech development during the first seven-year cycle;
- Careful diagnosis regarding the right age for the start of school and support for individual school readiness;
- Creating an authoritative, reliable relationship between students and teachers during the second seven-year cycle;
- Fostering productive, dutiful, and reality-oriented self-reliance;
- Supporting the understanding of causality and autonomous competence of judgment in the transition to young adulthood.

Protective "mother-sheaths" for the vulnerable, not yet emancipated powers of the as-yet unborn members of being are—according to Steiner—the life- and development spheres that adults create through their competent, responsible pedagogic action. In this sense, the seven-year cycles can be understood as developmental phases with individual, historic, and cultural variation that pedagogues must perceive sensitively and accompany responsibly. The determination of an exact time for the end of each transition is less important than the harmonious synchronism of the development in body, soul, and spirit. If we take seriously the various dates that Rudolf Steiner mentions, we find that the birth processes of the etheric and astral bodies are long-term developments that have already started years before the 7th or 14th years in age and that still continue on past these dates.

References

Barchmann, Harald/Kinze, Wolfram (1989): Kinder mit guten und schlechten Konzentrationsleistungen im Vergleich. *[A comparison of children with good or bad concentration achievements].* In: Psychologie in Erziehung und Unterricht; yr. 36, pp. 229–232.
Bauer, Joachim (2006): Warum ich fühle, was du fühlst. Intuitive Kommunikation und das Geheimnis der Spiegelneurone. *[Why I feel what you feel. Intuitive communication and the secret of mirror neurons].* Munich: Heyne.
Fend, Helmut (1990): Vom Kind zum Jugendlichen. Der Übergang und seine Risiken. Entwicklungspsychologie der Adoleszenz in der Moderne. Bd. 1. *[From childhood to adolescence. The transition and its risks. Developmental psychology of adolescence in modern times, vol. 1].* Bern: Huber.
Fischer, Jean-Paul (2012): Rätsel Spiegelschrift. In: Gehirn und Geist *[The puzzle of mirrored writing. In: Brain and Mind].* issue 12/2012, pp. 22–25.
Flammer, August (1995): Kontrolle, Sicherheit und Selbstwert in der menschlichen Entwicklung. *[Control, security, and self-worth in human development].* In: Wolfgang Edelstein (Ed.) (1995): Entwicklungskrisen kompetent meistern. *[Competent mastery of developmental crises].* Heidelberg: Asanger, pp. 35–42.
Flammer, August (2009): Entwicklungstheorien. Psychologische Theorien der menschlichen Entwicklung. 4. Auflage. *[Developmental theories. Psychological theories of human development].* Bern: Huber.
Goswami, Usha (2001): So denken Kinder. Einführung in die Psychologie der kognitiven Entwicklung. *[How children think. Introduction to the psychology of cognitive development].* Bern: Huber.
Göppel, R. (2002): Frühe Selbstständigkeit für Kinder – Zugeständnis oder Zumutung? *[Early autonomy for children – concession or imposition?].* In: Datler, Wilfried, Annelinde Eggert-Schmid Noerr and Luise Winterhager-Schmid (Eds.) (2002): Das selbständige Kind. *[The independent child].* Gießen: Psychosozial-Verlag.
Götte, Wenzel M./Loebell, Peter/Maurer, Klaus-Michael (2009): Entwicklungsaufgaben und Kompetenzen. Zum Bildungsplan der Waldorfschulen. *[Developmental tasks and competencies. On the curriculum of Waldorf schools].* Stuttgart: Freies Geistesleben.
Grimm, Hannelore/Weinert, Sabine (2002): Sprachentwicklung. *[Speech Development].* In: Oerter, Rolf and Leo Montada (Eds.) (2002): Entwicklungspsychologie. 5. Auflage. *[Developmental psychology. 5th edition].* Weinheim, Basel: Beltz, pp. 517–550.

Hascher, Tina/Althof, Wolfgang (2004): Vom Egozentrismus zur Empathie. Moral und Werte in der Pubertät. *[From Egocentrism to empathy. Morals and values in puberty]*. In: Magazin Schüler (2004): Aufwachsen. Die Entwicklung von Kindern und Jugendlichen. *[Growing up. The development of children and adolescents]*. Seelze: Verlag Friedrich, pp. 62–66.

Heymann, Hans Werner (2006): Autorität im Schulalltag. *[Authority in daily life at school]*. In: Pädagogik, yr. 58, 2/2006, pp. 6–9.

Hopf, Christel (2005): Frühe Bindungen und Sozialisation. *[Early attachments and socialization]*. Weinheim, Munich: Juventa.

Hüther, Gerald (2007): Resilienz im Spiegel entwicklungsneurobiologischer Erkenntnisse. *[Resilience in the mirror of developmental neuro-biological research]*. In: Opp, Günther and Michael Fingerle (Eds.) (2007): Was Kinder stärkt. Erziehung zwischen Risiko und Resilienz. *[What makes children stronger. Education between risk and resilience. 2nd edition]*. 2. Auflage. Munich and Basel: Ernst Reinhardt, pp. 45–56.

Knußmann, Rainer (1996): Vergleichende Biologie des Menschen. 2. Auflage. *[Comparative human biology. 2nd ed.]* Stuttgart: Gustav Fischer.

Kranich, Ernst-Michael (Ed.) (1997): Unterricht im Übergang zum Jugendalter. Anregungen zur Bewaltigung einer schwierigen Aufgabe. *[Teaching in the transition to adolescence. Suggestions for coping with a difficult task]*. Stuttgart: Freies Geistesleben.

Kranich, Ernst-Michael (1999): Anthropologische Grundlagen der Waldorfpädagogik. *[Anthropological foundations of Waldorf education]*. Stuttgart: Freies Geistesleben.

Largo, Remo (2012): Kinderjahre. Die Individualität des Kindes als erzieherische Herausforderung. 23. Auflage. *[The years of childhood. The individuality of the child as an educational challenge. 23rd edition]*. Munich: Piper.

Largo, Remo/Czernin, Monika (2011): Jugendjahre. Kinder durch die Pubertät begleiten. 2. Auflage. *[The years of adolescence. Accompanying children through puberty]*. Munich/Zürich: Piper.

Lifton, Betty Jean (1990): Der König der Kinder. Das Leben von Janusz Korczak. 2. Auflage. *[King of Children. The life and death of Janusz Korczak. 2nd edition]*. Stuttgart: Klett-Cotta.

Loebell, Peter (2015): Der Entwicklungsgedanke bei Janusz Korczak. *[The concept of development in the work of Janusz Korczak]*. In: Bartosch, Ulrich, Agnieszka Maluga, Christiane Bartosch and Michael Schieder (Eds.) (2015): Konstitutionelle Pädagogik als Grundlage demokratischer Entwicklung. Annäherungen an ein Gespräch mit Janusz Korczak. *[Constitutional pedagogy as a basis for democratic development. Approaching a conversation with Janusz Korczak]*. Bad Heilbrunn: Klinkhardt, pp. 207–215.

Matthiolius, Hanno/Schuh, Christa (1977): Der Einfluss der Erziehung auf die Akzeleration des Menschen (am Beispiel des Menarchetermins). In: Beiträge zur Erweiterung der Heilkunst. *[The influence of education on the acceleration of human development (demonstrated through the example of the menarche onset) [In: Contributions for an expansion of the healing arts]. Vol. 30, pp. 129–140.*

Montada, Leo (2002): Die geistige Entwicklung aus der Sicht Jean Piagets. *[The mental development from the point of view of Jean Piaget]*. In: Oerter, Rolf and Leo Montada (Eds.) (2002): Entwicklungspsychologie. 5. Auflage. *[Developmental psychology. 5th edition]*. Weinheim, Basel: Beltz.

Oerter, Rolf/Montada, Leo (2002): Entwicklungspsychologie. *[Developmental psychology]*. Weinheim: Beltz.

Patzlaff, Rainer/Saßmannshausen, Wolfgang (2005): Leitlinien der Waldorfpädagogik für die Altersstufe von 3 bis 9 Jahren. *[Waldorf pedagogic guidelines for the age group from three to nine years]*. Stuttgart: Pädagogische Forschungsstelle beim Bund der Freien Waldorfschulen.

Petermann, Franz/Niebank, Kay/Scheithauer, Herbert (2004): Entwicklungswissenschaft. Entwicklungspsychologie – Genetik – Neuropsychologie. *[Developmental science. Developmental psychology – genetics – neuropsychology]*. Berlin, Heidelberg: Springer.

Puhani, Patrick A./Weber, Andrea M. (2006): "Fängt der frühe Vogel den Wurm? Eine empirische Analyse des kausalen Effekts des Einschulungsalters auf den schulischen Erfolg in Deutschland." *[Does the early bird catch the worm? An empirical analysis of the causal effect the age of school begin has on school success in Germany]*. Diskussionspapiere der Wirtschaftswissenschaftlichen Fakultät der Universität Hannover. *[Discussion papers of the science department at the University of Hannover]*. Online under: www.wiwi.uni-hannover.de/Forschung/Diskussionspapiere/dp-336. pdf.

Rauh, Hellgard (2002): Vorgeburtliche Entwicklung und frühe Kindheit. *[Pre-natal development and early childhood]*. In: Montada, Leo and Rolf Oerter (Eds.) (2002): Entwicklungspsychologie. 5. Auflage. *[Developmental psychology. 5th edition]*. Weinheim, Basel: Beltz.

Rheinberg, Falko/Bromme, Rainer/Minsel, Beate/Winteler, Adi/Weidenmann, Bernd (2001): Die Erziehenden und die Lehrenden. *[Educators and teachers]*. In: Krapp, Andreas and Bernd Weidenmann (Eds.) (2001): Pädagogische Psychologie *[Pedagogic psychology]*. Weinheim: Beltz, pp. 271–355.

Riedl, Silke (2006): "Diese Klasse ist nicht zu unterrichten." Autoritätsprobleme in einer Hauptschulklasse aus der Sicht der Schülerinnen und Schüler. *["I cannot teach this class" Authority issues in a [Hauptschule-] classroom from a student perspective]*. In: Pädagogik, 58, 2, pp. 10–13.

Schenk-Danzinger, Lotte (1988): Entwicklung – Sozialisation – Erziehung. Schul- und Jugendalter. *[Development – socialization – education. School-age and adolescence]*. Stuttgart, Wien: Österreichischer Bundesverlag.

Schenk-Danzinger, Lotte (2002): Entwicklungspsychologie. Völlig neu bearbeitet von Karl Rieder. 1. Auflage. *[Developmental psychology. Completely updated by Karl Rieder. 1st edition]*. Wien: Österreichischer Bundesverlag.

Schmid, Peter (1996): Verhaltensstörungen aus anthropologischer Sicht; 3. Auflage *[Disruptive behaviors from an anthropological perspective]*. Bern, Stuttgart, Wien: Haupt.

Sodian, Beate (2002): Entwicklung begrifflichen Wissens. *[Development of conceptual knowledge]*. In: Oerter, Rolf and Leo Montada (Eds.) (2002): Entwicklungspsychologie; 5. Auflage *[Developmental psychology. 5th edition]*. Weinheim, Basel: Beltz, pp. 443–468.

Spitzer, Manfred (2002): Lernen. Gehirnforschung und die Schule des Lebens. *[Learning. Brain Research and the school of life]*. Heidelberg, Berlin: Spektrum.

Steiner, Rudolf (1907): Die Erziehung des Kindes vom Gesichtspunkte der Geisteswissenschaft. *[The education of the child from a perspective of spiritual science]*. In: Steiner, Rudolf (Ed.) (1987): Lucifer – Gnosis. Grundlegende Aufsätze zur Anthroposophie und Berichte aus den Zeitschriften «Luzifer» und «Lucifer – Gnosis» 1903–1908. Rudolf Steiner GA 34. Dornach: Rudolf Steiner Verlag, pp. 309–348.

Steiner, Rudolf (1979): Die Kunst des Erziehens aus dem Erfassen der Menschenwesenheit. 7 Vorträge in Torquay 1924 *[The Art of Education from a Conception of the Essential Being of Humanity 1924. 7 lectures at Torquay 1924]*. GA 311. Dornach: Rudolf Steiner Verlag.

Steiner, Rudolf (1982): Die pädagogische Praxis vom Gesichtspunkte geisteswissenschaftlicher Menschenerkenntnis. 8 Vorträge in Dornach 1923. *[Pedagogical praxis from the viewpoint of a spiritual science's knowledge of the human being. Eight lectures at Dornach 1923]*. GA 306. Dornach: Rudolf Steiner Verlag.

Steiner, Rudolf (1985): Esoterische Betrachtungen karmischer Zusammenhänge. 5. Band. 16 Vorträge in Prag, Paris und Breslau 1924. *[Esoteric observations of karmic relationships. Vol. 5. 16 lectures in Prague, Paris, and Bratislava 1924]*. 239. Dornach: Rudolf Steiner Verlag.

Steiner, Rudolf (1987): Die gesunde Entwickelung des Menschenwesens. Eine Einführung in die anthroposophische Pädagogik und Didaktik. 16 Vorträge und Fragenbeantwortungen in Dornach 1921/22. *[The healthy development of the human being. An introduction to anthroposophical pedagogy and didactics. 16 lectures with questions and answers in Dornach 1921]* GA 303. Dornach: Rudolf Steiner Verlag.

Steiner, Rudolf (1994): Erfahrungen des Übersinnlichen. Die Wege der Seele zu Christus. 14 Vorträge in verschiedenen Städten 1912 *[Experiences of the supersensible. Three paths of the soul to Christ. 14 lectures in various cities 1912]* GA 143. Dornach: Rudolf Steiner Verlag.

Steiner, Rudolf (1998): Idee und Praxis der Waldorfschule. 9 Vorträge an verschiedenen Orten 1919–1920. *[The Waldorf school and its spirit in idea and practice. 9 lectures in different locations 1919–1920]*. GA 297. Dornach: Rudolf Steiner Verlag.

Steiner, Rudolf (2003): Grundlinien einer Erkenntnistheorie der Goetheschen Weltanschauung *[Ouline of a theory of knowledge implicit in Goethe's world conception]*. (1886). GA 2. Dornach: Rudolf Steiner Verlag.

Tent, Lothar (2001): Schulreife und Schulfähigkeit. *[School maturity and school competency]*. In: Detlef H. Rost (Ed.) (2001): Handwörterbuch Pädagogische Psychologie. 2. Auflage. *[Handbook of pedagogical psychology. 2nd edition]*. Weinheim: Beltz, pp. 607–615.

Zimmermann, Peter (2004): Bindung und Beziehung. Emotionale Wurzeln als Basis kindlicher Entwicklung. *[Attachment and relationship. Emotional roots as a basis for childhood development]*. In: Schüler (2004). Aufwachsen. Die Entwicklung von Kindern und Jugendlichen *[Growing up. The development of children and youths]*, Seelze: Friedrich.

WALDORF EDUCATION AND DEVELOPMENTAL PSYCHOLOGY IN EARLY CHILDHOOD

Walter Riethmüller

This article gives an overview of core dimensions of Waldorf education's understanding of earliest and early childhood development in order to bring it into dialog with essential research findings of modern developmental psychology. To achieve this goal, we describe fundamental aspects of Waldorf education for preschool age children and then compare them with the results of attachment research, in particular. This process brings up very interesting commonalities, which may provide a good basis for further research.

1 The concept of development in Waldorf education

The discourse between developmental psychology and Waldorf education has long suffered from the circumstance that outsiders—in particular those with previous scientific education—have a difficult time in approaching Rudolf Steiner's occasionally unwieldy views in regard to the child's development in the first years of life (0–2 years) and in early childhood (3–6 years) (Schneider, Lindenberger 2012). For example, it may appear strange that development is supposed to occur in seven-year rhythms. It also may sound strange when there is talk of various "births," of some "higher members of being," which are supposed to take place around the 7th, 14th, and 21st years of life, and, at those points in time, allegedly cause the release of certain powers, which from then on are supposedly available for other purposes such as learning and the acquisition of new skills.

According to Steiner, this is true for the time around the seventh year of life, when a metamorphosis of powers occurs, forces that were first bound up in the formation of the physical body are morphing into soul faculties, which are now available for a new stage of learning and educational influence, differing distinctly from the previous phase. Up to full emancipation at age 21, this view asserts, there are altogether three "births" that take place, each of which confers the possibility for qualitatively new steps of development (Loebell 2011a,b; Steiner 1976).

Educational scientists have repeatedly critically questioned and discussed this concept (Loebell 2011a,b; Ullrich 2015). In this connection, Christian Rittelmeyer's suggestion is helpful, that we should first accept Steiner's statements as working hypotheses, in order to then examine them experientially (Rittelmeyer 2010). This would also take into account that Steiner himself sees the seven-year rhythm as being intersected by an individual process of soul development, which can again and again irritate the original constellation of harmonious body- and soul-development (Steiner 1994). Therefore, Steiner's system certainly does not entail any rigid scheme (Loebell in Chapter 3).

Waldorf education should attentively follow the research in developmental psychology regarding child development issues. This offers us the opportunity to compare its findings with Steiner's statements,

DOI: 10.4324/9781003187431-15

to critically examine them, and, if indicated, integrate the revised results into the fundus of Waldorf education's scientific knowledge.

For example, the discourse on salutogenesis and its consequences for pedagogy influenced the study by Thomas Marti (2010) as well as the "Guidelines of Waldorf Education for Children Ages Three to Nine," authored by Rainer Patzlaff and Wolfgang Saßmannshausen (Patzlaff, Saßmannshausen 2007). Through this process, Waldorf educational pedagogy and educational practice for preschool age children can be modernized, re-substantiated, and infused with new life. The appeal to Jean Piaget's theory of cognitive development of the child, which Christoph Lindenberg endeavored decades ago (Lindenberg 1981), could be updated as well and might contribute to modifying and differentiating the explanations of pedagogical principles of Waldorf education.

With an understanding of development that appears conclusive for an entire course of life—as outlined above—the anthroposophical-anthropological view differs significantly from modern developmental psychology, which does not know a comparable, generally applicable concept of development (Rittelmeyer in Chapter 3). Speaking from a perspective of Waldorf education, Kranich made a distinction between the concept of *development,* which leads from a lower to a higher stage, and the concept of transmutation, which goes beyond a mere change and entails the unfoldment of the child's latent potential through learning processes (Kranich 1989, Munich: 96). Kranich follows Hegel in responding to the inquiry into the acting principle in the process of development by pointing to an inner determination, which emerges in the transmutation process; when we further extend this point of view logically, according to Kranich, it brings up the issue of a pre-existing destiny (ibid., p. 123). Kranich further elaborates: "We can only understand the changes in childhood and adolescence as a form of development, if we notice that an inner principle of human essence manifests itself in these changes" (ibid.).

Here we can only hint at this dimension, which imbues Waldorf education with a logical conclusiveness that is generally lacking in the perspective of modern developmental psychology. That perspective contains manifold theories, which Rittelmeyer discusses in his article, and which are more or less able to withstand scrutiny, showing various degrees of effective half-life duration; however, they allow for highly varying modes of interpretation, depending on the operative paradigm (Schenk-Danzinger 2002, p. 27).

Conclusiveness, however, should not be confused with rigidity of with a presumed "fixation of seemingly unchangeable laws and tasks of development embedded in the nature of the child," a reproach that Heiner Ullrich leveled against Waldorf education, when he alleged that Waldorf education ignores the social context in regard to the dramatic changes in modern childhood (Ullrich 2010, p. 108).

In contrast, Peter Loebell presents a precise rendering of Waldorf education's concept of development. It rests on the basic assumption that every person "is an individual human being destined for freedom, i.e., responsibility, with his/her own specific needs regarding education and development" (Loebell 2010, p. 216). According to Kranich, this teleological energy becomes apparent in self-motivated action or in the will to learn, in wanting to achieve something that is not yet in one's range of abilities. This purposeful energy constantly renews itself and gives "direction and strength for every step the 'I' makes in its effort to find itself" (ibid.); it is also the force, we might add, "that strives to go beyond any state, once it is reached" (Kranich, p. 124).

2 The concept of "I"

In the perspective of Waldorf education, we cannot really understand early childhood development and the forces that drive it without a concept of "I" as an active force that is operative from birth on, e.g., in the imitation process.

In modern developmental psychology research, Daniel N. Stern's described differentiated developmental phases and characteristics that occur during the formation of the "Self"; his work brings up and orientates the question about the agency of the "I" in regard to imitation behavior in early childhood (Dornes 1993; Stern 1992). More recently, Elsner and Pauen also attest to the existence of an "I" already in the first weeks of an infant's life: "Various findings indicate that the 'I' already exists in the first weeks of life, in so far as children can differentiate between their own self and their surroundings. For example, proprioception allows an infant, when perceiving touch, to distinguish, whether that touch originated from within or came from the outside. The 'I' is connected with an awareness of controlling one's own actions (later also thoughts), i.e., the human being experiences him/herself already very early as an acting subject" (Elsner, Pauen 2012, p. 179).

But acknowledging the differentiation between one's own body and the surroundings as a telltale sign for the "formation of the I" (ibid., p. 180) falls short of the mark. Obviously, we can detect "I-presence" already extremely early, in the very first hours of life. From a perspective of psychotherapy, Hilarion G. Petzold described the moment of the first eye contact between mother and child as a process of mutual recognition of "I" and "Thou"; this eye contact steadies continuously in the course of the first three months of life and marks the origin of the primary attachment modality, which fundamentally shapes the child's identity throughout the further course of life (Riethmüller 2012).

Anthroposophy goes from the assumption that the "I" as the core of a spiritual identity is not born afresh without imprint, like a blank page, but that it brings along its own destiny and highly varying experiences from previous incarnations, starting a new incarnation with certain intentions. Indeed, this assumption is a cornerstone of anthroposophy's view of development and can make the dialog with the world of academia very difficult. On the other hand, we could also treat this assumption as a heuristically valuable hypothesis and further examine the highly variable intentionality in the approach to the world that we can already observe in infants and small children in their obviously different processing of environmental stimuli; we can ask ourselves if we might explain this variable intentionality not merely with hereditary and environmental influences after all, but also with our very own, personal modus that we bring with us into this life (Leber 1989, p. 140ff.).

We could at least experiment with viewing the quality and intensity of infant- and baby-behaviors as energetic states, whose variability, intensity, and constancy might be understood as expressions of an "I." In research on temperament, for example, research scientists tried to use these characteristics to create an inventory of life expressions and behaviors according to "color hues" and to systematize them.[1]

It is certainly worth discussing, whether we already want to accord a certain cognitive quality to "'I'-behavior" that infants and small children exhibit in controlling their own actions (Elsner, Pauen 2012). Rather, the individually distinct direction, intensity, and stability of life- and behavior-expressions can serve to describe the existence of an "I," as researchers—the so-called baby watchers—have painstakingly done in various ways, mainly for the past three decades.[2]

Describing development from a perspective of individuality does not dismiss other factors that also can cause, foster, or hinder development. However, this perspective makes it possible to indicate an educational goal the "I" strives to reach. "We also can understand development as a movement of the human 'I' toward itself" (Loebell 2010, p. 239). This perspective also makes it unnecessary, to evaluate the significance of a later stage of development compared to an earlier one, since its benchmarks are independent of ideological, social, and individual notions of value: Describing development from such a perspective that focuses on the individual does indeed also mean depicting and trying to understand a dynamic process that ultimately never remains static but undergoes constant change (ibid., p. 217).

In focusing on the "I" as the crucial force, which drives development, we ensure that the attention of Waldorf education cannot and must not rigidly fixate on any concept, whatever it may be; even if it is obviously perceived as doing so in the pedagogic practice of Waldorf schools and in early childhood education—also in Waldorf kindergartens and day nurseries; if rigidity of that kind occurs, it is rightly criticized (Stapf 2003, p. 230).[3]

Waldorf education's concept of development can be termed *transactional*. Transactional models share the core assumption "that the human being and his/her surrounding form a wholistic system, within which the subject of development and its environment actively interpenetrate and mutually influence each other." Changes in one aspect cause changes in other aspects and/or in the whole system, and they have retroactive effects.

"All people are constantly developing, not only children and adolescents. All of us gain new knowledge, new insights, modify our self-image and our image of the world, change our attitudes and normative convictions, etc." (Montada, Lindenberger, Schneider 2012, p. 34f.). In the following section, we shall demonstrate Waldorf education's transactional understanding of development illustrated by the example of its underlying concept of imitation.

3 Imitation and modeling

In Rudolf Steiner's early, short publication on pedagogy, *The Education of the Child in the Perspective of Spiritual Science* (1907), he describes his foundational concept of the "seven-year cycles" as qualitatively distinguishable biographical phases in childhood and youth; he was concerned with characterizing the child's inherent powers in accessing the world in such a way that, on one hand, the outward-directional dynamic is brought to bear and, on the other hand, we also come to understand the forces that impact the developing child from the surroundings, which it has to process (Steiner 1976).

According to Steiner, in approximately the first seven years of life, imitation and modeling are the "magic words describing how the child enters into a relationship with the world" (ibid., p. 21). From early childhood to about seven years of age, it is imitation that Steiner views as the driving force in the way that the child meets the model—i.e., in the widest sense, the "right physical surrounding" (ibid.); Steiner describes this process as effectively permeating also the physiological development and the "formative building" of the body (ibid., p. 22). Steiner used the example of brain development to clarify this dynamic effect and the findings of current neurophysiological research support his view, such as Thomas Fuchs, who in his studies goes so far as to call the brain "the organ of the person" (Fuchs 2013, pp. 185ff.).

In this connection, it is particularly remarkable how Steiner characterizes the small child's bond with the world while he/she is still "all sense-organ." In various lectures on pedagogy, Steiner again and again revisits and describes this theme and emphasizes his understanding—strange as it was at the time to scientific physiology and its body of knowledge—that the eye "is a sense organ in which the will is operative" (Steiner 1975, p. 96); "the will and nothing else forms the inner image" (ibid.). For Steiner, every sense organ harbors an inner activity of a volitional nature: "and this kind of *[unconscious]* volition effectually and intensely pervades the entire body of the small child, up to the change of teeth" (ibid.). In Steiner's view, the eye is oriented toward the world and serves the inner processing of perceptions in "nervous activities," which are more-or-less concentrated in the head region.

Likewise, he considers the entire physical organism in the first years of life to be a sense organ, i.e., the child is "all eye," just as it still is "all ear," "all taste," etc. According to Steiner, everything that the child sees and perceives—persons, their way of moving, their facial expressions, actions, objects, forms, and colors—it participates in by imitation, which directly engenders bodily processes, e.g., a change in the circulatory function or breathing rhythm, causing long-term effects, if similar experiences occur frequently. From the side of Waldorf education, it was in particular Ernst-Michael Kranich, who employed this broad understanding of the child as a sense organ and brought the process of learning to stand upright and walking into focus, using and critically acknowledging pertinent scientific findings. He describes how the entire skeletal organization undergoes a complete change in this process and could be understood as a representation of the child's I-directed efforts. Thus, the entire process of acquiring an upright posture carries the imprint of the "I" (Kranich 1999, pp. 74ff.; 2003, pp. 19ff.). Peter Loebell follows up on this view and points out that "it is not the acquisition of upright posture itself that is innate to the child, but the faculty of imitation" (Loebell 2010, p. 229). He goes on to clarify that the origin of this *[up-righting]* process lies in the "essence of the child's 'I' itself, while the toddler's disposition and the circumstances of his/her life world are merely necessary but not sufficient conditions" (ibid.).

Loebell holds that in early childhood, perception is still overlaid by subjective impression. The child sees more than just objects, movements, etc.; it also simultaneously perceives its meaning. Here we can gain insight into a pedagogic remark Steiner makes in regard to acting foolishly or committing immoral acts around the child (Steiner 1976, p. 22), because the child cannot directly and simultaneously perceive the intent; effects of such behavior can penetrate down to the physical level, which in turn may cause behavioral dispositions of their own later in life or even engender tendencies for becoming prone to certain illnesses in adulthood.

Steiner cites the example of a choleric father, who lets his emotions rip in front of the child. While the child cannot yet have an inner understanding of the emotional event, he/she still feels that there is something immoral (wrong) about it, "absorbing not only the outer image of the behavior, but also the entire moral value implicit in the outburst. When I give way to anger, this permeates down into the blood organization of the child, and if the angry outbursts repeat, they gain expression in the child's circulatory function. The child's bodily organization reflects my expressive behavior in his/her surrounding" (Steiner 1965, p. 49f.).

Steiner's remarks on the potential long-term effects of interpersonal imitative relationships find substantiation in recent studies within the context of attachment research. From a psychotherapeutic perspective, Hilarion G. Petzold described in detail such late effects that are caused by damaging factors in early childhood (Petzold 1997). So far, there are no Waldorf pedagogical studies available regarding long-term damages caused by (negative) modeling behaviors in early childhood. A broadly designed study, involving not only biographical effects of school experiences but also and particularly those in the first years of life, remains therefore an important desideratum in research on early childhood development.

4 Surroundings and the formation of self

Waldorf kindergarten practice traditionally puts special emphasis on the design of the environment in order to offer children a stimulus-rich atmosphere for self-formation. Furthermore, Steiner pointed out that all education has to be self-education and that teachers and educators "only constitute the surroundings of the child as it is educating itself" (Steiner 1975, p. 131). He adds to this remark suggestions for appropriate behaviors in educators: helpful for a thriving development of the child are educators, who experience "joy in and with their surroundings," also "serene facial expressions and especially honest, upright love that is in no way forced" (Steiner 1976, p. 26). In this context, Steiner stressed the effect of the surroundings on the formation of the organs of the physical human body—if they are "directed into the correct channels of development, if they receive the right impressions from their surroundings" (ibid., p. 22).

This strong emphasis on the effects the (social) environment has on the child and his/her will for self-development may explain why Waldorf education remains skeptical in regard to early booster-programs, which were mostly instituted after the "PISA shock." In particular, the demand that children should at an early age already reflect on their actions and experiences and assess their effect on the social surroundings (Fthenakis 2003a,b) is contrary to Waldorf education's approach to the early childhood learning process (Patzlaff, Saßmannshausen 2007).

Just so, Waldorf education is not entirely alone in this view. The educational scientist Ludwig Liegle summarizes his reservations regarding such early booster-programs as follows: "Children have a hundred languages. This view of the child was coined by Loris Malaguzzi; under the name of Reggio-Pedagogy, his concepts spread across the whole world and have become nearly a matter of course here, entering into the vocabulary and thoughts of many educators. If now three-, four- and five-year-old children produce ten or twenty of their one hundred languages (ways of communication) and surprise and delight us adults with them, should we then ask our children to reflect on the significance that the just-produced language – let us say number 19 of the 100 – has for them and their learning process? Are we willing, obliged or allowed to ask our children to think about their 100 languages? Will they still produce the same language varieties, if and even though we organize them right away into drawers of their methodological learning competency?" (Liegle 2006, p. 107).

Instead of thus exposing children already at preschool age to the dangers of early intellectualism, Waldorf kindergartens try to give fair consideration to the child's own learning efforts and to create stimulus-rich surroundings, which correspond to the actual developmental needs at this age.

5 Connections among the development of body, soul, and spirit

Waldorf education understands the development of the child as a synergy of forces in body, soul, and spirit. Ernst-Michael Kranich describes this connection as follow: "Physical development unfolds in closest context with that of the soul/spirit. Both inter-penetrate in a wholistic process. Today, this wholeness is generally subdivided into early childhood psychology and into anatomy/developmental physiology of childhood. This approach gives the impression of two processes – on one hand the development of soul and spirit and on the other hand, that of the body which give barely a hint of their inner inter-connectedness. This dualism hides the basic fact that changes in the child's body are expressions of something pertaining to soul and spirit" (Kranich 1999, p. 76). The view of Waldorf education may be summarized as follows: In the first seven years of life, the powers of learning are always also the formative forces of the body. The latter, however, would be weakened by a premature stimulation of the intellect. Therefore, Waldorf education rejects an early appeal to intellectual powers, because the child can only be considered truly school-ready around six years of age, after the completion of the formative body processes (Steiner 1976, pp. 21ff.).

In this context, Steiner states that only after the change of teeth should and can we meaningfully "from outside, educationally" influence these formative powers (Steiner 1976, p. 26f.). Ernst-Michael Kranich described this relationship as follows: "the powers, which were so far engaged in the active formation of the child's organism are now undergoing a metamorphosis in regard to their area of activity. [...] They henceforth become active in the soul, in the consciousness of the child" (Kranich 1999, p. 125f.).

In Waldorf education, these newly released powers are now employed in the first years of school, for example, in form drawing. Seen from a perspective of developmental psychology, these thoughts may be difficult to follow, since they contradict all current efforts geared at mandating an early start of school, which is meant to make early use of the children's learning capacities. Waldorf education has used and still uses the term "school maturity" but that has widely given way to the concept of school competency, which entails that individual transitions from early childhood to school age should be actively designed, so that the child can early on develop certain learning competencies (Griebel, Niesel 2003).

Waldorf education has specific reasons for basing its assessment on phenomena such as free memory capacity, ability for free imagination, etc. in order to determine the child's abilities and potential for explicit learning. In this wholistic assessment process, physical phenomena play an important role—e.g., the re-organization of the incoming adult teeth, body control, and fine-motoric coordination. More recently, developmental psychology has shown that the great majority of children can demonstrate complicated fine-motoric skills like tying shoelaces only at the age of six or seven and learn to ride a bicycle mostly between five and six years of age (Schneider, Hasselhorn 2012, p. 189) or also that they show a distinct increase in memory achievement—especially in free memorization—between year six and seven (ibid., p. 194); however, while these findings do not explain the connection among the development of body, soul, and spirit, they at least draw attention to the fact that time around the sixth/seventh year of life marks a crucial threshold in childhood development. Lotte Schenk-Danzinger offers an overview of the behavioral changes from early childhood to the school age, which supports this line of thought (Schenk-Danzinger 2002, pp. 212ff.).

In turn, these findings also bolster the experience, which has been again and again proven valid in practical Waldorf education, that at this age the development of the child's form recognition, -memory and -drawing awakens new possibilities of realization, which we can consider evidence for the metamorphosis of corporeal and soul/spirit competencies (Kranich 1999, pp. 129ff.).

However, so far, we lack valid empirical data that can substantiate the metamorphosis-like interconnection of powers that are released after the physical body is formed and then become available for learning. A research group around Rainer Patzlaff has tried to remedy this deficiency in the last years. A broadly designed survey of Waldorf students, who began school at an early or at a normal age, endeavored to evaluate their development in the first two years of school. The results do at least point to the same metamorphic connection, where forces that [– on an unconscious level –] formed the physical body are being transmuted into capacities for conscious form building, as Steiner outlined and Kranich described in detail.[4]

Further research on this topic is necessary, so that Waldorf education may rely on substantiated empirical data, when explaining its pedagogical practice.

Obviously, Steiner's concept of the synergy of forces suggests also a proximity to the results of salutogenetic research. This has already been demonstrated in regard to fostering health support in schools (Marti 2010) and also in regard to "school-age and health support" in kindergartens.[5]

6 The child as co-creator of his/her life world: Development as dialog

We would interpret Steiner too narrowly if we reduced his basically multi-perspective views to an exclusive concern with creating a meaningful and stimulating environment that meets the child's efforts toward self-development. If we heed the concept of development characterized above, we must, to a great extent, reckon with individual forces of development that are triggered by encountering the actual "world" and engaging with it. In short, whenever child development occurs, it always happens in form of a dialog with persons and surroundings and thus involves a certain "pressure to adapt." Therefore, we should also understand Steiner's remarks on sense-organ qualities to include intentionality, which gives direction to every perception: One does not only look, one looks at something, one does not only hear, one listens to something, one touches something specific, etc. Thus, since the beginning of his/her life, the human being is not merely a passive recipient of messages from the world; he/she turns in an intentionally selective way to the various sense impressions pertaining to his/her own corporeality or surroundings (Leyendecker 1997).

Today's childhood research focuses in that respect primarily on detecting early childhood competencies. The "competent infant" who explores the world with and "the scientist in the crib" have by now become well-known terms.[6] Various handbooks on childhood research repeatedly offer, and offered, updates on this dynamic branch of research in form of comprehensive introductions or outlines.[7] Research studies on early childhood competencies acknowledge the child as a co-creator of his/her own educational and developmental processes. Especially during phases of calm wakefulness, the infant appears as an attentive explorer, who increasingly integrates the findings of his explorations into his experiential universe and thus expands the spectrum of his abilities (Schäfer 1995, 2003).

The understanding of *imitation*, which was formerly defined more narrowly, referring usually to the active confluence with a model, has expanded due to this change in perspective of the infant as an active and attentive agent in engaging with his environment. Observation and research regarding the interaction between infant and an attachment figure—usually the mother—in various areas of competency led to a new quality in perspective. Daniel N. Stern has described a dialog-like sequence in the interactions of infant and mother as a process of mutual attunement, climax, and relaxation, corresponding in some ways to the script of a classic drama (Stern 1991). In this kind of attentive interaction, both actors did not only carefully and contingently comply with the script, but they also learned from each other as well, i.e., the mother also undergoes a change. This process also clarified that the roles of model and imitator could switch: In her caring attention, the mother also imitated the infant by responding to and amplifying his behaviors in sound and facial expression, which then could initiate a stimulating dialog or exert a calming influence on the infant.

It was primarily Mechthild Papoušek, who successfully used this dialog-focused approach in her research. Exploring childhood speech development addresses in this respect not only the significance of the infant's pre-lingual sound utterances for speech development but emphasizes also its importance for the scope and effect of dialoging behavior regarding impulse formation and further language development of the child.[8]

Waldorf education understood these findings as a stimulus for expanding and enriching the internal discussion in Waldorf circles with the newest results of research (Patzlaff, Saßmannshausen 2007; Riethmüller 1999, 2001, 2007).

7 Attachment research

The recognition of attachment theory, as established by John Bowlby and Marie Ainsworth, and its manifold valuable research findings, is particularly significant for the dialog between developmental psychology and early childhood Waldorf education.[9] Thomas Fuchs called it [attachment theory] "the probably most significant psycho-biological model of the child's organismic social development" (Fuchs 2013, p. 197). This applies also to Waldorf education, especially in regard to the conclusions that can be drawn for its educational practice.

Of particular interest is the characterization of four types of attachment, determined by the "strange situation test" (Elsner, Pauen 2012, p. 180f.), because the respective attachment behavior can be considered a fully validated predicator for later verbal, cognitive, social, and moral development regarding early childhood and the first years of school. These early attachment experiences characterize and modify, for example, brain structures and functions (Fuchs 2013, p. 197).

Even more important for Waldorf education, whose approach always strives to consider the effects of pedagogic actions on the whole biographical development of the human being, are research studies exploring the [long-term] effects of early attachment behavior far into the time of puberty and beyond.[10] The effects of attachment behaviors in infancy are of uncontested significance at least for early childhood development and we cannot overstate its importance: "The child's curiosity, his/her interest, learning and craving to understand, his/her conquest of the world, development and competencies, […] all these root in fundamental attachment and autonomy experiences and draw their energy from there. The child's attachment experiences and his self-engendered creative processes are inextricably connected" (Liegle 2006, p. 93; Schenk-Danzinger 2002, p. 129). Earliest childhood attachment behavior is therefore without doubt of great biographical significance (Gebauer, Hüther 2014).

This field of research offers important impulses for Waldorf education so that it no longer needs to accept Steiner's statements on the fundamental significance of early childhood imitation behavior as mere hypotheses of heuristic value. While Steiner in his time still lacked substantiation through empirically valid data, today the research on biographical effects of early childhood behavior offers a body of valuable research findings in at least a few partial areas. This is, for example, true for the long-term significance of the infant's eye-contact behavior in its relevance for identity formation later in life (Riethmüller 2012). Attachment research findings of this kind are particularly valuable to Waldorf education, since they help substantiate and differentiate central assumptions of its own, traditional concept of development.

8 Conclusion

Developmental psychology, especially in some of its sub-disciplines, offers highly valuable research findings and interpretive approaches for Waldorf education. In the endeavor of initiating its own research, Waldorf education can now use these research findings of developmental psychology on one hand in its pedagogic practice—*against the background of its own foundations and experiences*—and on the other hand it can now fruitfully use it in the confrontation with different points of view to reflect on its own positions and *thus strengthen, modify, or even revise them. This also allows us to understand many of Rudolf Steiner's statements on development and education in the earliest years of childhood until the beginning of school as an inspiration for research-oriented attention.*

Notes

1. For overview and recognition of temperament research, see first Zentner (1998); then Asendorpf (2003), Oerter (2002), Riethmüller (2004), Rittelmeyer (2010).
2. For a summary update of the pertinent research until 1990, see Dornes (1993); for more recent research, see Keller (2003).
3. Ullrich (2015) critiques the Waldorf system in general seeing it as a closed system; in regard to media education in Waldorf education, see also Ullrich (2010).
4. McKeen, Patzlaff, Rawson (2004), Patzlaff, Boeddecker, Schmidt (2006), Patzlaff, Schmidt (2007).
5. Patzlaff, Boeddecker, Schmidt (2006), Patzlaff, Saßmannshausen (2007), Kardel et al. (2007).
6. Stern (1992, 1991), Dornes (1993, 1997), Gopnik, Kuhn, Meltzoff (2000).
7. Markefka, Nauck (1993), Keller (2003), Baacke (1999), Hurrelmann, Bründel (2003).
8. Papoušek (1994), Papoušek/Papoušek (1995), Keller (2003), Tomasello (2006).
9. See overview in Grossmann et al. (2003), Grossmann, Grossmann (2004), Rittelmeyer (2005), Ahnert (2008).
10. Schölmerich (1996); first results that need to be evaluated with caution in Keller (1997a,b), Hopf, Nunner-Winkler (2007), Grossmann, Grossmann (2014), Fuchs (2013, p. 199).

References

Ahnert, Lieselotte (Ed.) (2008): Frühe Bindung. Entstehung und Entwicklung. 2. Auflage. *[Early attachment, origin, and development. 2nd edition].* Munich: Reinhardt.

Asendorpf, Jens B. (2003): Temperament. In: Keller, Heidi (Ed.) (2003): Handbuch der Kleinkindforschung. 3., korr., überarb. u. erw. Auflage. *[Handbook of early childhood research. 3rd corrected, updated and expanded edition].* Berlin: Huber, pp. 775–814.

Baacke, Dieter (1999): Die 0 bis 5 Jährigen. Einführung in die Probleme der frühen Kindheit. *[Children age 0 to 5. An introduction to problems in early childhood].* Weinheim, Basel: Beltz.

Dornes, Martin (1993): Der kompetente Säugling. Die präverbale Entwicklung des Menschen. *[The competent infant, Pre-verbal human development].* Frankfurt am Main: Fischer.

Dornes, Martin (1997): Die frühe Kindheit: Entwicklungspsychologie der ersten Lebensjahre. *[Early childhood: Developmental psychology of the first years of life].* Frankfurt am Main: Fischer.

Elsner, Birgit/Pauen, Sabine (2012): Vorgeburtliche Entwicklung und früheste Kindheit. *[Pre-natal development and earliest childhood].* In: Schneider, Wolfgang and Ulman Lindenberger (Eds.) (2012): Entwicklungspsychologie, 7. vollständig überarbeitete Auflage. *[Developmental psychology. 7th, fully updated edition].* Weinheim, Basel: Beltz, pp. 159–185.

Fthenakis, Wassilios E. (Ed.) (2003a): Elementarpädagogik nach PISA. Wie aus Kindertagesstätten Bildungseinrichtungen werden können. 2. Auflage. *[Elementary pedagogy after PISA. How daycare centers can become educational institutions. 2nd edition].* Freiburg: Herder.

Fthenakis, Wassilios E. (2003b): Zur Neukonzeptualisierung von Bildung in der frühen Kindheit. *[On a new conceptualization of early childhood education].* In: Fthenakis, Wassilios E. (Ed.) (2003): Elementarpädagogik nach PISA: Wie aus Kindertagesstätten Bildungseinrichtungen werden können. 2. Auflage. *[Elementary pedagogy after PISA. How daycare centers can become educational institutions. 2nd edition].* Freiburg: Herder, pp. 18–37.

Fuchs, Thomas (2013): Das Gehirn – ein Beziehungsorgan. Eine phänomenologisch-ökologische Konzeption. 4. Auflage. *[The brain – a relational organ. A phenomenological-ecological concept. 4th edition].* Stuttgart: Kohlhammer.

Gebauer, Karl/Hüther, Gerald (Eds.) (2014): Kinder brauchen Wurzeln. Neue Perspektiven für eine gelingende Entwicklung. 8. Auflage. *[Children need roots. New perspectives for successful development. 8th edition].* Ostfildern: Patmos.

Gopnik, Alison/Kuhn, Patricia/Meltzoff, Andrew (2007): Forschergeist in Windeln. Wie Ihr Kind die Welt begreift. 6. Auflage. *[The scientist in the crib. What early learning tells us about the mind? 6th edition].* Munich: Piper.

Götte, Wenzel M. (Ed.) (2005): Hochbegabte und Waldorfschule. Grundlagen, Aufgaben, Anregungen. *[Highly gifted children and the Waldorf school. Foundations, challenges, impulses.].* Stuttgart: Freies Geistesleben.

Griebel, Wilfried/Niesel, Renate (Eds.) (2003): Die Bewältigung des Übergangs vom Kindergarten in die Grundschule. *[Managing the transition from kindergarten to elementary school].* In: Fthenakis, Wassilios E. (Ed.) (2003): Elementarpädagogik nach PISA. Elementarpädagogik nach PISA: Wie aus Kindertagesstätten Bildungseinrichtungen werden können. 2. Auflage. *[Elementary pedagogy after PISA. How daycare centers can become educational institutions. 2nd edition].* Freiburg: Herder, pp. 136–151.

Grossmann, Karin/Grossmann, Klaus E. (2004): Bindung. Das Gefüge psychischer Sicherheit. *[Attachment. The feeling of psychic security]*. Stuttgart: Klett-Cotta.

Grossmann, Klaus E. (2008): Theoretische und historische Perspektiven der Bindungsforschung. *[Theoretical and historical perspectives in attachment research]*. In: Ahnert, Lieselotte (Ed.) (2008): Frühe Bindung. Entstehung und Entwicklung. 2. Auflage. *[Early attachment, origin, and development. 2nd edition]*. Munich: Reinhardt, pp. 21–41.

Grossmann, Klaus E./Grossmann, Karin (2014): Das eingeschränkte Leben. Folgen mangelnder oder traumatischer Bindungserfahrungen. *[Consequences of deficiency or trauma in attachment experiences]*. In: Gebauer, Karl and Gerald Hüther (Eds.) (2014): Kinder brauchen Wurzeln. Neue Perspektiven für eine gelingende Entwicklung. 8. Auflage. *[Children need roots. New perspectives for successful development. 8th edition]*. Ostfildern: Patmos, pp. 35–63.

Grossmann, Klaus/Grossmann, Karin/Kindler, Heinz et al. (2003): Die Bindungstheorie: Modell, entwicklungspsychologische Forschung und Ergebnisse. *[Attachment theory: Model, developmental psychology research and findings]*. In: Keller, Heidi (Ed.) (2003): Handbuch der Kleinkindforschung. 3., korr., überarb. u. erw. Auflage. *[Handbook of early childhood research. 3rd, corrected, updated, and expanded edition]*. Bern: Huber, pp. 223–282.

Honig, Michael-Sebastian (1999): Entwurf einer Theorie der Kindheit. *[Outline of a theory of childhood]*. Frankfurt am Main: Suhrkamp.

Honig, Michael-Sebastian/Lange, Andreas/Leu, Hans Rudolf (Eds.) (1999): Aus der Perspektive von Kindern? Zur Methodologie der Kindheitsforschung. *[Form the perspective of children? On the methodology of childhood research]*. Weinheim, Munich: Juventa.

Hopf, Christel/Nunner-Winkler, Gertrud (Eds.) (2007): Frühe Bindungen und moralische Entwicklung. Aktuelle Befunde zu psychischen und sozialen Bedingungen moralischer Eigenständigkeit. *[Early attachments and moral development. New findings on psychic and social conditions for moral autonomy]*. Weinheim, Munich: Juventa.

Hurrelmann, Klaus/Bründel, Heidrun (2003): Einführung in die Kindheitsforschung. 2. vollst. überarb. Auflage. *[Introduction to childhood research. 2nd fully updated edition]*. Weinheim, Basel: Beltz.

Kagan, Jerome (1987): Die Natur des Kindes. *[The nature of the child]*. Munich: Piper.

Kardel, Telse/McKeen, Claudia/Patzlaff, Rainer/Saßmannshausen, Wolfgang (2007): Leitlinien der Waldorfpädagogikfür die Kindheit von 3 bis 9 Jahren. Teil II. 2. überarb. Auflage. *[Guidelines of Waldorf education for children between ages 3 to 9. Part II. 2nd. updated edition]*. Stuttgart: Pädagogische Forschungsstelle beim Bund der Freien Waldorfschulen.

Keller, Heidi (Ed.) (1997a): Handbuch der Kleinkindforschung. 2., vollst. überarb. Auflage. *[Handbook of early childhood research. 2nd fully revised edition]*. Bern: Huber.

Keller, Heidi (1997b): Eine evolutionsbiologische Betrachtung der menschlichen Frühentwicklung. *[Early human development in the perspective of evolution biology]*. In: Zeitschrift für Pädagogik 43, pp. 113–128.

Keller, Heidi (Ed.) (1998): Lehrbuch Entwicklungspsychologie. *[Textbook of developmental psychology]*. Bern: Huber.

Keller, Heidi (Ed.) (2003): Handbuch der Kleinkindforschung. 3., korr., überarb. u. erw. Auflage. *[Handbook of early childhood research. 3rd fully revised edition]*. Bern: Huber.

Keller, Heidi/Gauda, Gudrun/Miranda, Delia (1985): Die Entwicklung des Blickkontaktverhaltens im ersten Lebensjahr. *[The development of eye-contact behavior in the first year of life]*. Zeitschrift für Entwicklungspsychologie und pädagogische Psychologie 17, pp. 258–269.

Kranich, Ernst-Michael (1989): Anthropologie – das Fundament der pädagogischen Praxis. *[Anthropology – the foundation of applied pedagogy]*. In: Bohnsack, Fritz and Ernst-Michael Kranich (Eds.) (1989): Erziehungswissenschaft und Waldorfpädagogik. Beginn eines notwendigen Dialogs. *[Educational science and Waldorf education. Beginning a necessary dialog]*. Weinheim, Basel: Beltz, pp. 96–139.

Kranich, Ernst-Michael (1999): Anthropologische Grundlagen der Waldorfpädagogik. *[Anthropological foundations of Waldorf education]*. Stuttgart: Freies Geistesleben.

Kranich, Ernst-Michael (2003): Der innere Mensch und sein Leib: Eine Anthropologie. *[The inner person and his body: an anthropology]*. Stuttgart: Freies Geistesleben.

Leber, Stefan (1989): Die menschliche Individualität. *[Human individuality]*. In: Bohnsack, Fritz and Ernst-Michael Kranich (Eds.) (1989): Erziehungswissenschaft und Waldorfpädagogik. Beginn eines notwendigen Dialogs. *[Educational science and Waldorf education. Beginning a necessary dialog]*. Weinheim, Basel: Beltz, p.140–184.

Leber, Stefan (1993): Die Menschenkunde der Waldorfpädagogik. *[The study of man in Waldorf education]*. Stuttgart: Freies Geistesleben.

Leyendecker, Birgit (1997): Die Entdeckung der subjektiv relevanten Handlungsangebote. *[Discovering subjectively relevant options for action]*. In: Keller, Heidi (Ed.) (1997): Handbuch der Kleinkindforschung. 2., vollst. überarb. Auflage. *[Handbook of early childhood research. 2nd fully revised edition]*. Bern: Huber, pp. 509–514.

Liegle, Ludwig (2006): Bildung und Erziehung in früher Kindheit. *[Formation and education in early childhood]*. Stuttgart: Kohlhammer.

Lindenberg, Christoph (1981): Die Lebensbedingungen des Erziehens. *[Life circumstances of education]*. Reinbek bei Hamburg: Rowohlt.

Lintz, Martin (Ed.) (1999): Von der Würde des Kindes. Die Kindheit verstehen und schützen. *[On the dignity of the child. Understanding and protecting children].* Stuttgart: Freies Geistesleben.

Loebell, Peter (2010): Die Signatur der menschlichen Entwicklung als Grundlage der Waldorfpädagogik. *[The signature of human development as a foundation of Waldorf education].* In: Paschen, Harm (Ed.) (2010): Erziehungswissenschaftliche Zugänge zur Waldorfpädagogik. *[Educational science approaches for accessing Waldorf education].* Wiesbaden: VS, pp. 215–244.

Loebell, Peter (2011a): Die Jahrsiebte in der menschlichen Entwicklung. *[The seven-year cycles in human development].* In: Loebell, Peter (Ed.) (2011): Waldorfschule heute. Eine Einführung. *[Waldorf schools today. An introduction].* Stuttgart: Freies Geistesleben, pp. 97–108.

Loebell, Peter (Ed.) (2011b): Waldorfschule heute. Eine Einführung. *[Waldorf schools today. An introduction].* Stuttgart: Freies Geistesleben.

Markefka, Manfred/Nauck, Bernhard (1993): Handbuch der Kindheitsforschung. *[Handbook of childhood research].* Berlin: Luchterhand.

Marti, Thomas (2010): Wie kann Schule die Gesundheit fördern. Erziehungskunst und Salutogenese. *[How can the school foster health? The art of education and salutogenesis].* Stuttgart: Freies Geistesleben.

McKeen, Claudia/Patzlaff, Rainer/Rawson, Martyn (2004): Früheinschulung und veränderte Kindheit – ein Zwischenbericht. *[The lowering of school age and the changes in childhood: An interim report].* In: Erziehungskunst 2004, 5, pp. 515–522.

Montada, Leo/Lindenberger, Ulman/Schneider, Wolfgang (2012): Fragen, Konzepte, Perspektiven. *[Questions, concepts, perspectives],* In: Schneider, Wolfgang and Ulman Lindenberger (Eds.) (2012): Entwicklungspsychologie, 7. Vollständig überarbeitete Auflage. *[Developmental psychology, 7th fully updated edition].* Weinheim, Basel: Beltz, pp. 27–60.

Oerter, Rolf (2002): Temperament und Persönlichkeit. *[Temperament and personality].* In: Oerter, Rolf and Leo Montada (Eds.) (2002): Entwicklungspsychologie. 5., vollst. überarb. Aufl., *[Developmental psychology. 5th fully updated edition].* Weinheim, Basel: Beltz, pp. 210–212.

Oerter, Rolf/Montada, Leo (Eds.) (2002): Entwicklungspsychologie. 5., vollst. überarb. Aufl. *[Developmental psychology. 5th fully updated edition].* Weinheim, Basel: Beltz.

Papoušek, Mechthild (1994): Vom ersten Schrei zum ersten Wort. Anfänge der Sprachentwicklung in der vorsprachlichen Kommunikation. *[From the first scream to the first word. Beginnings of language development in pre-lingual communication].* Bern: Huber.

Papoušek, Hanus/Papoušek, Mechthild (1995): Vorsprachliche Kommunikation: Anfänge, Formen, Störungen und psychotherapeutische Ansätze. *[Pre-lingual communication: Begin, forms, disturbances and psychotherapeutic approaches].* In: Petzold, Hilarion G. (Ed.) (1995): Die Kraft liebevoller Blicke. Psychotherapie und Babyforschung. Vol. 2. *[The power of loving eye contact. Psychotherapy and baby research].* Paderborn: Junfermann, pp. 123–141.

Paschen, Harm (Ed.) (2010): Erziehungswissenschaftliche Zugänge zur Waldorfpädagogik. *[Educational science ways of access to Waldorf education].* Wiesbaden: VS.

Patzlaff, Rainer/Boeddecker, Doris/Schmidt, Martina (2006): Einschulungsalter und Gesundheitsentwicklung. Ein Forschungsprojekt des IPSUM-Instituts. *[School enrollment age and health development. A research project of the IPSUM Institute].* In: Erziehungskunst 2006, 5, pp. 531–543.

Patzlaff, Rainer/Saßmannshausen, Wolfgang (2007): Leitlinien der Waldorfpädagogik für die Kindheit von 3 bis 9 Jahren. Teil I. 2., überarb. Auflage. *[Guidelines of Waldorf education for children from 3 to 9 years of age. Part I., 2nd updated edition].* Stuttgart: Pädagogische Forschungsstelle beim Bund der Freien Waldorfschulen.

Patzlaff, Rainer/Schmidt, Martina (2007): Einschulungsalter und Gesundheitsentwicklung. Zwischenbericht zum Forschungsprojekt des IPSUM-Instituts. *[School enrollment age and health development. Interim report on a research project of the IPSUM Institute].* In: Erziehungskunst 2007, 10, pp. 1113–1119.

Patzlaff, Rainer/McKeen, Claudia/von Mackensen, Ina/Grah-Wittich, Claudia (Eds.) (2010): Leitlinien der Waldorfpädagogik für die Kindheit von der Geburt bis zum dritten Lebensjahr. *[Guidelines of Waldorf education for children from birth to three years of age].* Stuttgart: Pädagogische Forschungsstelle beim Bund der Freien Waldorfschulen.

Petzold, Hilarion G. (Ed.) (1995): Die Kraft liebevoller Blicke. Psychotherapie und Babyforschung. Vol. 2. *[The power of loving eye contacts. Psychotherapy and baby research].* Paderborn: Junfermann.

Petzold, Hilarion G. (Ed.) (1997): Frühe Schädigungen – späte Folgen? Psychotherapie und Babyforschung. *[Early damages – late consequences? Psychotherapy and baby research].* Vol. 1. 2. Auflage. Paderborn: Junfermann.

Riethmüller, Walter (1999): Der Dialog mit der Welt in der Entwicklung des Kindes. *[The dialog with the world in child development].* In: Lintz, Martin (Ed.) (1999): Von der Würde des Kindes. Die Kindheit verstehen und schützen. *[On the dignity of the child. Understanding and protecting childhood].* Stuttgart: Freies Geistesleben, pp. 48–66.

Riethmüller, Walter (2001): Begegnung mit der Individualität des Kindes. *[Meeting the individuality of the child].* In: Erziehungskunst 2001, 12, pp. 1355–1363.

Riethmüller, Walter (2004): Temperamente in der Diskussion. *[Temperaments in discussion].* In: Erziehungskunst 2004, 7/8, pp. 774–786.

Riethmüller, Walter (2005): Kindheitsforschung (Vorschulalter) und Hochbegabung. *[Childhood research (pre-school age) and highly gifted children].* In: Götte, Wenzel M. (Ed.) (2005): Hochbegabte und Waldorfschule. Grundlagen, Aufgaben, Anregungen. *[Highly gifted children and Waldorf schools. Foundations, challenges, impulses].* Stuttgart: Freies Geistesleben, pp. 391–454.

Riethmüller, Walter (2007): Wie kommt das Kind zur Sprache? *[How does the child approach language?].* In: Erziehungskunst 2007, 1, pp. 11–16.

Riethmüller, Walter (2012): Modalitäten der Selbst- und Identitätsbildung in der frühen Kindheit am Beispiel des Blickkontakts. *[Modalities of self- and identity-formation in early childhood, illustrated by the example of eye contact].* In: Basfeld, Martin/Hutter, Walter (2012): Identitätsbildung im pädagogischen Prozess. Ein interdisziplinäres Forschungskolloquium. *[Identity formation in the pedagogic process. An international research colloquium].* Baltmannsweiler: Schneider, pp. 139–158.

Rittelmeyer, Christian (2005): Frühe Erfahrungen des Kindes. Ergebnisse der pränatalen Psychologie und der Bindungsforschung. Ein Überblick. *[Early experiences of the child. Findings from pre-natal psychology and attachment research. An overview.].* Stuttgart: Kohlhammer.

Rittelmeyer, Christian (2010): Die Temperamente in der Waldorfpädagogik. Ein Modell zur Überprüfung ihrer Wissenschaftlichkeit. *[The temperaments in Waldorf education. A model for testing their scientific viability].* In: Paschen, Harm (Ed.) (2010): Erziehungswissenschaftliche Zugänge zur Waldorfpädagogik. Wiesbaden: VS, pp. 75–100.

Schäfer, Gerd E. (1995): Bildungsprozesse im Kindesalter. Selbstbildung, Erfahrung und Lernen in der frühen Kindheit *[Educational processes in childhood. Self-education, experience and learning in early childhood].* Weinheim, Basel: Beltz.

Schäfer, Gerd E. (2003): Was ist frühkindliche Bildung? *[What is early childhood education?].* In: Schäfer, Gerd E. (Ed.) (2003): Bildung beginnt mit der Geburt. Ein offener Bildungsplan für Kindertageseinrichtungen in Nordrhein-Westfalen. *[Education starts at birth. An open plan for education in child day care centers in North-Rhine-Westphalia].* Weinheim, Basel: Beltz, pp. 10–42.

Schenk-Danzinger, Lotte (2002): Entwicklungspsychologie. Völlig neu bearbeitet von K. Rieder. *[Developmental psychology. Completely revised and updated edition by K. Rieder].* Wien: öbv et hpt.

Schneider, Wolfgang/Hasselhorn, Marcus (2012): Frühe Kindheit (3-6 Jahre). *[Early childhood (years 3–6)].* In: Schneider, Wolfgang/Lindenberger/Ulman (Ed.) (2012): Entwicklungspsychologie, 7. vollständig überarbeitete Auflage. *[Developmental psychology. 7th completely revised and updated edition].* Weinheim, Basel: Beltz, pp. 187–209.

Schneider, Wolfgang/Lindenberger, Ulman (Eds.) (2012): Entwicklungspsychologie, 7. vollständig überarbeitete Auflage. *[Developmental psychology. 7th completely revised and updated edition].* Weinheim, Basel: Beltz.

Schölmerich, Axel (1996): Frühe Kindheitserfahrungen und Eintritt in die Reifezeit. *[Early childhood experiences and transition to adolescence].* In: Schumann-Hengsteler, Ruth and Hanns M. Trautner (Eds.) (1996): Entwicklung im Jugendalter. *[Development in youth].* Göttingen: Hogrefe, pp. 41–56.

Stapf, Aiga (2003): Hochbegabte Kinder. Persönlichkeit, Entwicklung, Förderung. *[Highly gifted children. Personality, development, fostering].* Munich: Beck.

Steiner, Rudolf (1965): Der pädagogische Wert der Menschenerkenntnis und der Kulturwert der Pädagogik. Zehn Vorträge, gehalten in Arnheim vom 17. bis 24. Juli 1924. 3. Auflage. GA 310. *[The Pedagogical Value of a Knowledge of the Human Being and the Cultural Value of Pedagogy CW 310]* Dornach: Verlag der Rudolf Steiner-Nachlassverwaltung.

Steiner, Rudolf (1975): Die pädagogische Praxis vom Gesichtspunkte geisteswissenschaftlicher Menschenerkenntnis. Die Erziehung des Kindes und jüngeren Menschen. Acht Vorträge, gehalten in Dornach vom 15. bis 22. April 1923. GA 306. *[Pedagogical praxis from the viewpoint of a spiritual-scientific knowledge of the human being. The education of the child and young human beings CW 306].* Dornach: Rudolf Steiner Verlag.

Steiner, Rudolf (1976): Die Erziehung des Kindes vom Gesichtspunkte der Geisteswissenschaft. 1907. Einzelausgabe. *[The education of the child from the perspective of spiritual science].* Dornach: Rudolf Steiner Verlag

Steiner, Rudolf (1994): Erfahrungen des Übersinnlichen. Die drei Wege der Seele zu Christus. Vierzehn Vorträge, gehalten zwischen Januar und Dezember 1912 in verschiedenen Städten. GA 143. 4., neu durchges. Auflage. *[Experiences of the supersensible. Three paths of the soul to Christ CW 143]* Dornach: Rudolf Steiner Verlag.

Stern, Daniel N. (1991): Tagebuch eines Babys. Was ein Kind sieht, spürt, fühlt und denkt. *[What a child sees, senses, feels, and thinks].* Frankfurt: Piper.

Stern, Daniel N. (1992): Die Lebenserfahrung des Säuglings. *[The interpersonal world of the infant].* Stuttgart: Klett-Cotta.

Stern, Daniel N. (2000): Mutter und Kind. Die erste Beziehung. 4. Auflage. *[Mother and child. A primer of the first relationship].* Stuttgart: Klett-Cotta.

Tomasello, Michael (2006): Die kulturelle Entwicklung des menschlichen Denkens. *[The cultural origins of human cognition]*. Frankfurt am Main: Suhrkamp.

Ullrich, Heiner (2010): Das Konzept der Kindheit – ein aktuelles Problem der Waldorfpädagogik. *[The concept of childhood – a current problem of Waldorf education]*. In: Paschen, Harm (Ed.) (2010): Erziehungswissenschaftliche Zugänge zur Waldorfpädagogik. *[Educational science ways of accessing Waldorf education]*. Wiesbaden: VS, pp. 101–123.

Ullrich, Heiner (2015): Waldorfpädagogik. Eine kritische Einführung. *[Waldorf pedagogy. A critical indroduction.]* Weinheim, Basel: Beltz.

Zentner, Marcel R. (1998): Die Wiederentdeckung des Temperaments. Eine Einführung in die Kinder- und Temperamentsforschung. Überarb. und erw. Neuausgabe. *[The rediscovery of temperament. An introduction to research on temperaments and the child. Revised and expanded new edition]* Frankfurt am Main: Fischer.

THE RUBICON AS A DEVELOPMENTAL PHENOMENON IN MIDDLE CHILDHOOD

Axel Föller-Mancini and Bettina Berger

In the public discourse on the character of Waldorf education, several prominent terms are in circulation that seem to fulfill an explanatory function. Quite a few people today connect expressions such as *eurythmy*, *main lesson blocks*, or *learning without being graded* with core themes of Waldorf education. Among these terms, we find also a more-or-less diffuse idea of the Rubicon, which parents discuss in internet chat rooms as a crisis occurring before puberty (Blaß 2013).

This article attempts first a historical classification of the term, then it proceeds to identify it as a corollary of the developmental concepts in anthroposophy and spiritual science, as set forth by Rudolf Steiner after approximately the year 1907. This shall highlight the main aspects of the child's upheaval that the founder of anthroposophy connected with the Rubicon. An excursion into modern socialization theory is then designed to bring into relief the requirements, as Steiner emphasized them, for the pedagogical support of children age 8–11. Finally, we accord the Rubicon concept a position within developmental psychology's current discourse on middle childhood.

1 History of the term *Rubicon*

In historic times, the Rubicon was a border river that separated the roman province of Gallia Cisalpina from the Italian mainland. In the year 49 bc, Julius Caesar and his army crossed the Rubicon, defying the directives of the Roman senate. This act signified a declaration of war to the Roman senate, marking a point of no return. Cesar commented on this with the famous phrase *alea iacta est* (the die is cast). Since then, the expression *crossing the Rubicon* has been established as a metaphor for an act that can bring about great changes and appears highly risky. In the area of science, the term has risen to prominence twice: in Rudolf Steiner's developmental teachings that he propounded from 1919 on and in the psychological theory of action by Heckhausen and Gollwitzer (1987).

The Rubicon model of action phases explores the cognitive prerequisites for the transition from a decision made to its translation into action. The first (pre-decisional) phase in this process is of crucial importance, characterized by the evaluation of the risk involved. At any point in time, the assessment phase concludes successfully, initiating the realization of action, which then has to live with the risks of unrecognized determinants (Achziger, Gollwitzer 2009, p. 151).

Steiner, too, uses the term *Rubicon* because he can derive from its historic references a metaphoric construct that is suitable for the description of the time of said human development [*middle childhood*]. In middle childhood,[1] around the ninth or tenth year, he sees a break in development that leads to a deepened sense of "I." Once the child has lived through this stressful time, he/she would never again—figuratively speaking—return to the place from where he/she set out: that sphere of early childhood mentality, where he/she imitated the adult world. The child has here reached a structural-cognitive, "caesarean" point of no return, which gives direction to further, successive identity formation processes. Moreover, we can find cross-references between the Rubicon and the concept of a second age of defiance (the second "terrible twos") that emerged at the beginning of the 20th century in early empirical developmental psychology. Prange claims in his book *Education in Anthroposophy* that Steiner appropriated this concept and "anthroposophically integrated" it (Prange 1985, p. 109).

Zander repeats this reproach, referencing Prange (Zander 2007, vol. II, p. 1045). However, neither author presents any substantiation for this criticism. Therefore, we want to add here a few remarks on this topos.

It has been established that Rudolf Steiner has studied the newly forming discipline of psychology and reviewed its pertaining literature from the 1880s up to the first decade of the 20th century. All his publications bear evidence of this fact. Already in "Goethe's theory of knowledge, an outline of the epistemology of his worldview" (Steiner 2011), Steiner gives a draft overview of the ubiquitous empirical efforts toward an understanding and systematic explanation of processes in the human soul and spirit. Steiner notes that in these efforts, psychology increasingly loses touch with a unified concept of the soul. He holds that these empirical efforts longer allow a successful differentiation between psychic and cognitive (noetic) achievements, leading to an erosion in the understanding of the "I-centered" identity of the human being. Darwinism gained traction and, with it, the idea of development was considered more and more under evolutionary biological premises. Steiner followed the publications of a few psychologists, such as Wilhelm Preyer (1841–1897), who did share the evolutionary concept of Darwinism but vehemently rejected some of its materialistic consequences. Preyer held onto a concept of the soul, which we should not simply regard as an epiphenomenon of purely biological processes. His systematically directed observations of infants led him to postulate that phylogenetically it was the reason that generates language and that in the human ontogenesis the newborn brings along "into the world much more reason than talent of speech" (Preyer quotes after Eckardt 1989, p. 37). Preyer held the view that reason is innate as a formative power and then crystallizes out into distinct faculties as we engage with our physical body and our surroundings (Preyer 1989, p. 271; Preyer quotes after Eckardt 1989, p. 37). In his obituary for Preyer, Steiner acknowledged his approach as a significant contribution to psychology (Steiner 1989a–c, p. 346ff.). Preyer's book *The Soul of the Child,* published in 1882, is until today deemed a groundbreaking work in empirical child psychology.

The essay "Modern Soul Research" (Steiner 1989a–c) then represents Steiner's attempt to track several main currents in empirical psychology after the turn of the century. In this endeavor, he of course also refers to experimental psychology and its main representative, Wilhelm Wundt. Steiner here makes an inconspicuous side note that demonstrates his thorough attention to the charismatic power that this new science exerted from its home at the Leipzig Institute that Wundt had established. Students from all parts of the civilized world arrived in Leipzig learning the new methodologies under Wundt's guidance. And they disseminated these modern psychological research methods everywhere.

In Copenhagen and Jassy, in Italy and America, they taught experimental psychology in the spirit of the researcher of Leipzig (Steiner 1989a–c, p. 468). Among these students was also the American psychologist and pedagogue Granville Stanley Hall (1844–1924). Hall had stayed in Germany for four years, studying and conducting research in Wundt's laboratory. After his return to the United States, he sought to apply what he had learned. He developed a method that appeared suitable to collect and systematically process large amounts of data gained by psychological observation. He succeeded in devising the questionnaire. Hall is considered the father of survey studies (Kreppner 1998, p. 130). With this newly created instrument, he conducted the first large-scale studies on various aspects of child development. In particular, his students analyzed the steps the child makes in the process of identity formation. They gave detailed descriptions of the abundant phenomena observed, then systematically processed the data, and categorized them according to behavior types, which allowed them to slowly develop a phase model of child development based on these data. Hall's theory distinguishes four phases (Cizek et al. 2005, p. 8) that lead the small child toward later autonomy as a young adult: early childhood (0–4 years), childhood (4–8 years), youth (8–12 years), and adolescence (11/13–22/25 years). The phases of youth and adolescence are phases of radical change, partly marked by grave tensions on a soul level. Moreover, Hall had gained the impression that in this time of development each individual unconsciously reenacts important motifs of human history. This concept has gained popularity as the "theory of biogenetic recapitulation" (Cizek et al., ibid.) and Steiner propounded a spiritual version of this theory.

Hall's studies were influential and in turn set impulses for German empirical psychology. He published his work "Some aspects of the early sense of self" in the United States (1898), which was then translated into German and published there in 1903 (Hall 1903).

The studies of Oswald Kroh (1887–1955) demonstrated outstanding reception of Hall's work. He was a psychologist who wanted to use the new insights also for the benefit of pedagogy. Mainly, he tried to employ the knowledge about the phases of development for the profit of education and lesson method-ology. Also, Kroh tried to clarify the concept of recapitulation that Hall had postulated. The first sense of "I," that stirs in the two- to three-year-old child, is on one hand marked by the child saying "I" and on the other hand by the phase of defiance (the *terrible twos*) that constitutes a first impulse for setting external boundaries. According to Kroh, this phase returns again in a different form during the transi-tion from the second to the third level of school readiness (Kroh 1928, p. 93ff.).

In the first phase of school attendance, the elementary school child around age seven lives in a world of fantastic realism and analogies, while in the second phase around age ten, it arrives at a more con-scious attitude (naïve realism), and the third phase is characterized by the child acquiring a critical atti-tude, accompanied by all indications of a second phase of defiance. Kroh called this phase in the child's development "critical realism" (Bergius 1959, p. 138; Kroh 1928, p. 100; Trautner 1997, p. 34). At the same time the 10-, 11-, or 12-year-old child—these dates depend on the individual—goes through the second period of defiance and makes "a turn inward" (Bergius 1959, p. 138).

Since the beginning of the 20th century, developmental psychology thus has offered a detailed concept of phases, based on empirical studies and not on the historically customary, traditional, and rigid idealiza-tion of phases. Sensitive moments of detachment around the age of pre-puberty are addressed here, which we can describe as transitional phenomena. Kroh repeatedly emphasizes the time around the tenth year of life: "The critical attitude of children in that age bracket does not even exempt statements and remarks of teachers in class and is connected to the fact that the 10-year-old child increasingly turns away from direct, given phenomena and starts to pay attention to the relationships forming the context of such phenomena. Yes, we can say that now phenomena draw less interest while the relations between phenomena become more interesting" (Kroh 1928, p. 100). In the same place, he says: "The awareness of the self-worth shows that 10- to 12-year-old children have developed the ability not only of evaluation bestowed upon them and their peers, but also that of determining the imagined or actual un-worthiness of adults" (ibid.).

In the context of historic term analysis, we must see a connection between the "second phase of defi-ance" and the Rubicon concept. Indeed, there is a factual as well as structural connection. However, professional literature assigns the authorship regarding the second phase of defiance to Kroh alone.[2] Kroh began his scientific career in 1921 with his first publication "The Phases of Development in Middle Childhood." Even that early in his career, he intended the phase model to benefit pedagogy. This article quotes Kroh's first more extensive monograph, "Psychology of Children of Elementary School Age," which did not appear until 1928. Steiner, who died in 1925, could no longer study this new psychological theory, even though he probably followed its early stages through Hall.

Therefore, we can conclude that Steiner did not derive the concept of the Rubicon from that of the second phase of defiance, contrary to the speculations of Prange and Zanders.

2 Child development in the light of spiritual science

The Rubicon concept was already implicit in Steiner's developmental theory with its concept of phases that he laid out relatively. Already in 1907 Steiner clearly points to a pedagogy derived from spiritual science (Loebell in Chapter 3). On one hand that kind of pedagogy must answer questions generated by the science-driven push for renewal. On the other hand, Steiner found it deplorable that many suggestions for reform coming from very different areas of knowledge and life remained superficial, which he attributed among others to the dominance of the materialistic paradigm. For him, that held equally true for pedagogical concepts and reform initiatives pertaining to schools and in-class instruction. According to Steiner, the materialistic mode of interpretation derives from the postulate that sensory observation is the only source for verifiable and replicable insights (Steiner 1992, p. 10). We can certainly include in this critique all possible extensions of the human observation capacity such as technical measuring instruments and observation tools. But Steiner's critique aims not primarily at the observation process and the data it furnishes, because these bring to light aspects of the percepts (here: the human being) that cannot be repudiated; rather, the verdict—inherent in the materialistic approach—that all structural attributes of a living being are basically explainable by material components is, according to Steiner, pivotal for the materialistic world. That means that appearance, structure, accessibility, and explanation all remain on the same ontological (material) level.[3] This line of thought implies that any changes in the development of a living being are effects caused by the interplay of merely sensory forces. In contrast, Steiner describes a fourfold entity in human development that unfolds over time, changes in that process, and thus gains the possibility of "I"-development (personal identity).

The physical body of the human being is subject to physical and biochemical laws, insofar as it contains these material components. Man shares this existential dimension with large parts of non-organic nature.

But according to Steiner, the physical components cannot—so-to-speak "from below"—explain the ordered living substances and their meaningful interplay. He attributes a specific ontological dynamic to the formative power as an organic formative principle, a power that he called "etheric." The *etheric* or *life body* is the formative power that harmonizes physical processes and safeguards their functional organic unity. This level man shares with plants and animals that are equally endowed with living bodies that unfold in time and space.

Steiner calls the third member of the human being the *sentient* or *astral body* as the quintessential realm of the soul. Animals share in this functional level as well. In this realm of consciousness, we observe phenomena like sensations, passion, joy, grief, desire, and striving (Heusser 2011, p. 169; Steiner 1992, p. 13). The list of these phenomena primarily points to states of need, sensitivities, and implicit goals that serve self-preservation (Wandschneider 2014, p. 178). This is the realm of the soul, which can be described quantitatively but does not yet comprehend itself. It expends itself in subject matters of psychic states.

Lastly, Steiner determines the "I" as a member of being that no other creature shares with humankind. As a thinking consciousness, the "I" is spirit or "spirit soul" (Thomas Aquinas, Beck pp. 138 ff.) and enables the unity of consciousness. However, there are great individual variances from person to person. While every healthy adult can call him/herself "I," the individualization of I-functions in form of cognitive faculties and transformative forces relies on the initiative of each person. The structure of "I"-consciousness reveals itself to be utterly identical with self-unfoldment in the medium of cognition (Steiner 1992, p. 16). In the process of thinking, the human being generates the ordered, conceptual connections that allow him/her to interpret the phenomena of this world and also of his own existence.

The four members of the human being are each in need of their own form of description. It is understood that a higher form of consciousness can unfold when it rests upon a lower level. A person, for example, who has the ability to differentiate between the flavors of different coffee varieties thus has the opportunity to make a choice and subsequently form and act on an intention (volitional act). Here, perception precedes the volitional act timewise, but that volitional step is not caused by that perception (one can just passively experience interesting subjective perceptions without an ensuing action). Volitional acts thus form their own class of soul processes and we need to investigate them as to their specific order and lawful patterns (Heusser 2011, p. 170). This is similarly true for the other levels: the living organism (physical-etheric). Psychic organization (astral) and "I" (conscious thinking) each are based on the level below their own, but they unfold their essence in this basis according to their own dynamic.

The didactic approach of Steiner's inaugural pedagogic publication *The Education of the Child in the Perspective of Spiritual Science* that appeared in 1907 proves now to be the result of developmental constraints that govern the four levels or members of the human being (Steiner 1992). Here two factors join together: the endogenous development of the individual and the external, modifying behavior of the educators (exogenous effect). Steiner orders the endogenous dynamic into seven-year rhythms, which is only meant in the sense of an ideal-type, and which certainly are subject to variances specific to each individual. In the development up to young adulthood, there occur three "births" in seven-year cycles within the soul and spirit framework of the human being. The time between physical birth and school age is still strongly dedicated to the formation of the physical organism: the development of the sensory system, of the brain, and motoric faculties. According to Steiner, it is the etheric body that is closely associated with the physical body, which participates most vitally in this formative development. The etheric organization changes around age seven, as evidenced visibly in the change of teeth. In Steiner's view, the etheric body now is no longer bound so closely to the physical organization: It becomes available to support the awakening cognitive faculties of the child. While children learn mainly through imitation until school age, they now look to adults as representing an order that they can accept. Children now no longer accept the authority of adults in their surroundings without question. The children, who just started school, increasingly take a critical stance toward the adults they relate to most closely and they experiment with many different behaviors in this process. According to Steiner's model, the young person enters puberty around age 14. Steiner attributes the soul-upheaval during this time to the liberation (or birth) of the astral body, which harbors conscious emotionality. Finally, at approximately 21 years of age, occurs the actual birth of the "I," of full selfhood. The powers of cognition and will are now unfolded and enable young adults to navigate the course of their own life.

Steiner draws our attention to a second factor, i.e., the educational influences that modulate the endogenous development processes of the child. He describes the pedagogic attitude as that of sheltering accompaniment: In early childhood up to elementary school age, the activities and affinities of the children fluctuate strongly and their adult persons of reference should keep close track of such proclivities and process them in such a manner, that the emergent bio-psychic impulses can fully unfold. At the same time, it is of concern to protect the children from stimulation and influences, which they are not yet able to process due to their constitution not being yet fully formed: "Just as we must protect the unborn child from physical influences of the eternal world, so we should not expose the etheric body before the change of teeth to forces that are equivalent to the physical environment's impressions on the physical body. Accordingly, the astral body should only be exposed to the respective influences after puberty has set in" (Steiner 1992, p. 20).

From 1919 on, Steiner developed a wealth of thoughts on pedagogy, schools, and class instruction (Ruef 2012; Selg 2011) based on these two contra-directional pedagogical principles—those *supportive* to the effects resulting from bio-physical endogenous development and those *sheltering from unwholesome influences*. Transforming Steiner's seed idea of a sheltering or protective function to apply to one of the discourses in modern educational science, we can join Oevermann in speaking of a "prophylactic-therapeutic task for the persons of reference" (Oevermann 1996b, p. 158). In the context of such a pedagogic self-concept, we must take note of the unavoidable crises in the process of development and socialization and moderate them as needed.

3 The Rubicon as a watershed moment in the second seven-year cycle

Steiner's treatise *The Education of the Child in the Perspective of Spiritual Science* (Steiner 1907, 1992) can rank as the opening of a depiction of human development from birth to adolescence as viewed by spiritual science. At any rate, this essay constitutes neither a humanities-oriented "scientific study," nor can it claim to be in any way exhaustive. We should rather understand this treatise as a pointer to a field of phenomena, to which every reader can partially connect his/her own life experience in retrospect: a field that usually is subject to different kinds of interpretation.

In his explanatory approach to human development, Steiner frequently refers to force fields that are themselves of non-material, super-sensible origin, even though they bring forth effects in time and space. He cannot "prove" their existence, but he only refers to arguments of plausibility; his methodology does not rely on charisma but proposes empirical and theoretical replicability. Within the framework of phase development with its three births—referencing soul and spirit—a watershed moment occurs in the middle of the second seven-year cycle. Steiner indicates various points in time when this happens. Most of the time he speaks of the ninth/tenth year of life, but there are numerous other quotes where he rather speaks about a *time span* that very well may extend into the 11th year of life (Selg 2011, p. 17). He also does not preclude the eighth year from being the point in time when the Rubicon event begins.[4]

Against the backdrop of the released etheric body and the possible psychic differentiations offered by that model, Steiner describes the core event he is concerned with in threefold ways:

1. as germinating self-awareness or a more spiritualized recurrence of the "I"-impulse that began in the second or third year of life (Ruef 2012, p. 26; Steiner 1994, p. 128),
2. as restructuring the relationships with the social and the phenomenal world, and
3. from a physiological perspective, as the formative development of the rhythmic system ("respiratory maturity").

In the following sections of this article, we shall follow up on these three essential points of view, which Steiner repeatedly referenced in numerous publications. Apparently, Steiner understands the term Rubicon to mean a crisis that always occurs in the course of normal human development.[5] The Rubicon occurs in the context of a personal experience of unfolding selfhood. Müller-Wiedemann described this as "manifest activity of the 'I' between childhood and youth, when for the first time in the course of human life the child's emotional life unfolds in between past and future and wants to create its own experience" (Müller-Wiedemann 1999, p. 31). In this process, the child becomes conscious of relationships he/she experienced in the first seven-year cycle.

Now contrasting experiences may dawn of a seemingly more detached kind of existence. Both a diffusely felt past and a sense of self that is cast into sharper relief lead the child to question his/her own existence. Before this point in time, the children did not dwell on their own past nor their future. According to Müller-Wiedemann this process sets in approximately between the 9th and 12th years of life (ibid.)

This means, in regard to relationships, that simultaneously the drive to imitate is fading, which entangled the child in non-conceptional learning processes during the first seven-year cycle. The imitation drive thus forms the structural matrix that embeds the somewhat symbiotic relationship between the small child and the persons he/she relates to most closely. Once the imitation impulse wanes, the constraints of the interactional matrix must also change. The child must build substitute structures for both imitation as a principle of learning and for the symbiotic relationship with the primary caregivers and educators. Ideally this would result in an increase in autonomy alongside an expansion of the sphere of life. In Steiner's words: "The aftereffects of the imitation drive gradually disappear and something visibly happens for the child [...]: a special relationship arises for the child to his or her own self" (Steiner 1998a, p. 172).

The relationship with the child's reference persons also changes and the status that the child attributed to parents and educators remains no longer unquestioned. Natural authority, transmitted in the quality of living relationships, suddenly collapses in view of the child's changed inner world. In early childhood, the statement holds true: "There is the person of authority. It gives me the world. I gain a view of the cosmos through this authority" (Steiner 1979a,b, p. 45). In contrast, the child now asks: "Is this the right figure of authority for me? Does this person really provide me with a true image of the world?" (ibid.)

Outwardly, a new relationship with the self is established and Steiner describes it as "a considerable strengthening [...] and consolidation of the sense of self" (Steiner 1980, p. 16), a new "configuration of 'I' consciousness" (Steiner 1994, p. 128) or a "growing felt awareness of self" (Selg 2011, p. 21). For the first time, the child meets the world as a "Thou"—"the other person *as* someone different and independent" (ibid., p. 27).[6]

According to the descriptions, there are also fundamental changes that occur in the child's relationships with the world of phenomena: "At the time, when the 'I' awakens around the age of nine, the human being separates himself from the natural surroundings and matures into the ability to draw objective comparisons between natural phenomena" (Steiner 1998a, p. 173f.).

From here, Steiner enters into extensive didactic deliberations, which were then translated into practical Waldorf education. Summarily we can say that this is an attempt to transpose a developmental event, as determined through spiritual science, into educational practice, which is a classic motif in pedagogic psychology (Krapp, Prenzel, Weidenmann 2006, p. 5f.). Thus, Steiner's concept of the Rubicon delineates a boundary: Before the Rubicon threshold, the teacher orients his or her teaching style on the child's experience of oneness (the child's identification with the social and the phenomenal world). In this process, it is helpful for the teacher to use emotionally vivid language and pictorial narratives. *After* the Rubicon threshold, the teacher can introduce the child, e.g., not only to the plant or animal kingdoms, but also to mathematics and language, employing new methods of presentation and new concepts.

This means that the transposition *[of theoretical insight into teaching practice]* is interconnected with the emerging cognitive faculties of the child—and this includes primarily also the pedagogically guided formation of concepts. We can here reference Piaget's genetic theory of cognition and his theorem of the concrete-operational phase in middle childhood (age 8–12): Sensory appearance no longer dominates in determining constancy or comparability of objects and their various forms of presentation, but the child is already more significantly oriented toward conceptual criteria, even if he or she cannot yet express this achievement verbally (Piaget 1973, 38ff.). This heightened inner flexibility affects the degree of complexity in the *adoption of viewpoints* within a social context. At the time of their first school enrollment, children are able to imagine what a person thinks about others or about themselves. They are then also capable of "sequentially coordinating the perspective of one person with that of another, e.g., the father wants to go on a walk with his child because the child enjoys it" (Bischof-Köhler 2011, p. 346). But only around age ten, the child can conceive of simultaneous, interconnected perspectives. That means, at that point, the child can take the viewpoint of a second person, extrapolate from there the perspectives of other participants, and evaluate them if needed (Bischof-Köhler 2011, ibid.; Selman 1984).

Likewise, we observe changes in the child that are related to the Rubicon crisis that Steiner speaks of on two levels: (a) the behavior of the child toward its social surroundings and (b) the behavior of the child toward the world of phenomena, which include mental object representations and the connection to reality; children redefine objects that so far were part of their inner world and release them for example from magical contexts.[7] Yet according to Steiner, it is the renewed relationship to the self that drives this restructuring process. The deepened sense of self gives rise to these changes. Steiner correlates this process with a restructuring on the physical level.

According to Steiner's concept of development, the formation of the organism dominates the first seven-year cycle. The formative powers of the etheric body are tied to the physical organism and enable maturation of its sensory organization. The child develops based on all kinds of sensory experiences, embedded in their corresponding emotional matrix (parent-child relationship). For Piaget, this is the phase of sensory-motor development (Piaget 1973, p. 102). With the beginning of the second seven-year cycle and the concomitant release of the formative powers, the body's rhythmic processes now increasingly develop and synchronize. The physician Selg summarizes Steiner's view as follows: "With the rise of the rhythmic system to the center of organic life processes, the different rhythms have to find their own balance and center, facilitated by the heart nexus in breath- and blood-circulation. Due to the generally dominant head organization (i.e., the nervous-sensory system), the breathing processes supersede in their functional importance the cardio-vascular rhythms until middle childhood. However, according to Steiner then these (breath) processes connect with the blood circulation, and adapt to it, [...] which finally results in finding an individual equilibrium" (Selg 2011, p. 40).

However, this coordination process of physiologically fine-tuning the relationship between breath- and heart frequencies (approximately 18 breaths correspond to about 72 heartbeats in an adult) does not just harmoniously happen by itself. For Steiner, it constitutes a process of physiological crisis, an "inner battle within the organism" (Steiner, quoted by Selg 2011, p. 41), which we should regard as the "bodily correlate" of an upheaval in soul and spirit that calls for pedagogic support (Steiner 1989a–c, p. 110).[8] Moreover he holds the view that between years 7 and 14 the "rhythmic system" acts as a functional unit of development, which bestows new means of expression on the child and should be addressed pedagogically, in particular by means of music, movement, and speech (Steiner 1987, p. 159).

Aside from such suggestions for didactic approaches, Steiner considers it necessary that the adults involved should review their attitude toward the nine- or ten-year-old child. While the child changes and initiates a new adjustment in his or her relationship to authority, the adults must adjust their attitude accordingly. The asymmetrical relationship that had stayed intact since birth begins to gradually dissolve in middle childhood. In the asymmetrical (parent-child) relationship, the child could follow and learn through imitation; he or she experienced the order set by authority, inherent in the quality of this relationship as universally valid. As the child detaches from this order, he or she also starts to see authority in a different light; the child's soul forces are being released and urge the question, whether the order represented by parental authority is an authentic, lived reality—or not. The child can find stability in this crisis, if the persons of reference illuminate a higher order within their social life and reality.

The adult can then communicate with the child by referencing this higher order in form, content, and in authentic self-disclosure; she can point beyond herself to a world of the sublime, of the ground of being. Steiner explained this seemingly religious figure of thought in practical terms: "In the self-same phase of life between ages 9 and 10, when children learn to properly distinguish themselves from their surroundings, it is of supreme importance for their entire future moral life that they can attach themselves to some teacher or educator deserving of their highest respect and sense for true authority" (Steiner 1998a, p. 264). A little further on he continues: "The entire moral-spiritual education depends on the child going through a phase of reverence at this point in life" (ibid., p. 265).

The focus here is not on the person of reference as such and certainly not on establishing an uncritical and thus dangerous, disempowering sense of authority, as one might object; rather, Steiner is merely concerned with an education that includes references to an immanent transcendence,[9] which shall illuminate the soul of the child, yet whose rationale can the child only question intellectually after adolescence starts.[10] An educator should interact with a child in such a way that it "develops a feeling like: the super-sensory world 'has his back,' he is leaning into this support. The teacher does not just randomly speak his mind, but he appears as a messenger of then divine" (Steiner 2010, p. 106).

The person of reference serves as a stabilizing and orienting factor during the identity crisis and thus becomes the mediator between the child's subjectivity and a higher level of reality, which he or she can autonomously relate to in later life.[11]

Here it becomes apparent, of course, how broadly Steiner defines the educational task of the pedagogue. He is in charge not only for the transmission of universal values but also for compensatory support during the developmental crisis of middle childhood. Helsper (Helsper et al. 2007, 74ff.) critically reviewed this lofty claim and the resulting charismatic concept of authority; the concept of pedagogical authority in Waldorf education remains still today unbroken tradition and is strongly advocated, but it runs counter to current societal trends and points to a "reflexive rollback of modern concepts" (ibid.).

4 Excursus: The Rubicon and Oevermann's crisis typology

Sociology offers a new approach in research that appears suitable to further illumine the concept of the Rubicon beyond what we presented so far. It offers a new interpretation and conceptualization of Steiner's views on the pedagogic-therapeutic support function for overcoming authority problems that come up during the Rubicon crisis. In the following section of this article, we therefore want to outline Oevermann's crisis typology, which also offers coping strategies that the human being can activate when the crisis occurs. Wagner (Wagner 2001, 2004a, 2004b) gives a detailed presentation of Oevermann's theoretical approach in his work on "Structural Socialization Theory." We take the following deliberations from there.

According to Wagner, Oevermann analyzes three structurally distinguishable types of crises that human subjects can experience. Correspondingly, there are three distinctly different approaches to alleviating these crises by ameliorating, improving, and fully overcoming them. The following typology applies:

a. *The traumatization crisis*: Within the framework of this type, a person's life is confronted by externally triggered or internally experienced events and can no longer uphold the routines that his or her actions followed up to this point. One cannot *react* to this class of experiences (Wagner 2004b, p. 38). The intensity of such a raw crisis has or can have traumatizing effects—it can be like a natural disaster, highly stressful to the soul as well as the body. Accordingly, the person hit by this type of crisis can only counter it with a certain psychic effort and/or needs the support of other people to get through it.

b. *The crisis of decision:* This type of crisis occurs when the subject must choose between different options that are unavoidable results of their contextual actions. In practical life, a person has to deal rationally with objectively given issues, to take action or maybe just not act upon them, and therefore the individual is always forced to make decisions. This includes decisions with unknown effects on the future. These may be wide-ranging decisions, because they generate in the long term *a point of no return*, for example, the decision to marry *this* or another partner or to conceive a child and carry it to term. Correspondingly it is true that in this kind of crisis it is impossible to *not* make a decision (ibid., p. 39).

c. *The unforced crisis:* It arises in the individual's space of relative freedom and one can, according to Oevermann, allocate it to the category of aesthetic experiences (ibid., 39f.). One meets such a crisis, e.g., when faced with a new challenge and putting up with incalculable consequences if one accepts that challenge. An example would be quitting a secure job in order to take on a very difficult kind of professional task that, however, may offer new options. Only later, in retrospect, will the person be able to assess if that decision to accept this challenge that was not prompted by compelling necessity had negative or positive effects. This attests to something new entering through a sphere of heightened awareness and prompts a decision, even though there is a risk factor involved. Because the intensity of awareness transcends that of everyday life, this moment is comparable to the moment of opening up to the field of aesthetic experience (Oevermann 1996a, p. 46; Wagner 2004b, p. 40).

The developing human being goes repeatedly through significant experiences that originate in the sphere of the body and yet are closely connected to the experiences of the adults that raise him or her. While going through such experiences, children may find that eventually a change in their relation to self, along with a change in relationship with their surroundings, and thus open up new scopes of action. Expanded spheres of action generally only become accessible, if the person lets go of structures that had so far been familiar and reliable.

Along with the gradual detachment from old structures arises the opportunity to stepwise develop one's own identity. Insofar as these crisis experiences are inextricably connected with each individual's development, i.e., pertaining to the ontogenesis of body and soul, we can here speak of "ontogenetic emancipatory crises" (Wagner 2004b, 368ff.). While various schools of psychological thought present these phenomena in conceptually different terms, the significance of emancipatory processes in the course of human development is undisputed—that means there is broad consensus in regard to this abstract fact. From a psychoanalytical point of view, Oevermann determines the following emancipatory crises: pregnancy/birth, detachment from the early symbiotic relationship between mother and child, the oedipal crisis, the period of latency (school, middle childhood) and adolescence (ibid.). Since these emancipatory crises arise unavoidably from the endogenous dynamic, they represent the traumatization crisis type, and the individual has no powers of decision over them. The individual cannot make a decision to avoid the challenges of these gradual detachment processes. Such an attempt would only harm the individual due to the consequences that an aborted emancipation process incurs on the development of one's identity. Therefore, socialization theory does not look for strategies to avoid these crises, but it analyzes the psychological prerequisites for dealing with these unavoidable challenges.

In this analysis, Oevermann presents three conditions that he considers pivotal for mastering the emancipatory crises; in his view, the first two factors are closely tied in with primary experiences of ontogenesis and form a basis for lasting dispositions of the psyche. These factors are (a) *conviction,* (b) *belief,* and (c) *knowledge.*

Convictions, in the sense Oevermann uses the term here, are habit formations that are deeply anchored in personal life experiences. They emerge from the sphere of symbiotic relationships, which means they are closely connected to the first bonding structures of early childhood patterned by the mother-child dyad. Later on, convictions emerge from aspects of "inner-family bonding" (Wagner 2004b, p. 31) and the experiences with *peer groups:* "All these sequential pauses in the course of development offer protection and free spaces for experimentation. After going through a sufficient number of such crises without questions or problems, the respective convictions will become parts of the individual's inner landscape as biographical sediments of these experiences; only if later in life extreme crises of change occur, will the individual be able to drastically modify such convictions or even give them up altogether" (Oevermann 2000a,b, as quoted by Wagner 2004, p. 3).

Thus, convictions also allow us to detect affective and cognitive patterns that originated in primary relationship experiences. They are visceral and difficult to grasp consciously; they elude comprehensive objectification. In the event of a crisis, successful symbiosis (or in attachment theory terminology: secure bonding; Grossmann, Grossmann 2009) activates the conviction, e.g., that one can turn to other people for support. In order for this to become a pattern that can be easily reproduced, the individual needs to have more deeply anchored biographical experiences that one can trust other people (Kißgen 2009, p. 98).

While convictions grow out of attachment structures, *belief* is generated by the unavoidable processes of emancipation and detachment; belief itself is a child of crisis and also significantly contributes to overcoming it. Oevermann thus presents a concept of belief that is open to functional interpretation both as secular and religious in a narrower sense. After succeeding in forming a symbiotic relationship, the child moves step by step toward emancipation. Attachment research has shown that emancipation proceeds more successfully to the degree that deeply trusting primary bonds had been established (Faix 2004, p. 278). Even so, this process is so fraught with conflict partly because the child builds up feelings of guilt as it lets go of the protective parental sphere. The often clearly visible ambivalence, e.g., in nearly simultaneous behavior patterns of rejection and clinging, is a possible sign of such guilt feelings. *After enjoying the symbiotic relationship*, the child experiences guilty entanglement as a paradoxical dynamic, which it cannot yet grasp or define rationally with its mental faculties. This calls for a dissolution of tension through a third, synthesizing force. Since the child apparently cannot find such a harmonizing force within his or her world, where he experiences the unsolvable dilemma of wanting to leave what he loves at same time as wanting to keep it; so, the child turns elsewhere for a solution. Oevermann here puts forward belief as a factor that comes into play: "The belief in a higher power, which we could call a supreme spiritual power spirit, which offers the believer at the same time hope for reconciliation and reliability – no matter what the concrete content of the specific beliefs. So, belief here is the polar complement of conviction and just as indispensable for overcoming crises" (Oevermann 2000a,b, as quoted by Wagner 2001, p. 199). This sketch of a sociological-religious approach interprets crisis events in individual development as a source of transformation and brings up *religion* or "binding back" to that which was seemingly lost. It appears significant that Oevermann presents his concept of belief in a neutral way, i.e., open to either religious, content-specific, or secular-functional interpretation.[12] That means that the individual is free to choose the concrete interpretation of *spirit, power,* or *authority,* while at the same time biographically constellated socialization factors certainly also play a role.

Finally, there is no overcoming of any crisis without a stock of *knowledge* that the individual can use. Oevermann here does not tie the concept of knowledge to that of crisis, as he did with *conviction* and *belief.* Rather he moves knowledge into a sphere of routine or habit (Oevermann 2000a,b; Wagner 2001, p. 200f.). Knowledge springs from experience, insofar as one can over time derive from these experiences "tested claims" that can gain societal acceptance as being generally valid. In the event of a crisis, human subjects take recourse to such knowledge, or we can also say: Without established routines, it would be impossible to overcome the crisis; because if then crisis would overthrow everything that the individual held once to be true, this would lead to a moment of despair. We must add here that the possibility of taking recourse to the sphere of knowledge and routine is certainly contingent upon the person's degree of maturity and therefore age-specific. In this context, it appears even more significant that adults who care for the child can provide them with "substitute interpretations,"[13] making the child feel more secure. Substitute interpretations convey elements of knowledge that do not originate in the child's own experience but are borrowed from other contexts and made available to the child by pedagogical authority.

As we compare the two approaches regarding crisis in middle childhood, the following structural elements emerge: Structural Socialization theory describes the emancipatory dynamic as an ontogenetically unavoidable and indispensable event, because the autonomy of the developing person can only be evoked in the field of tension between the poles of symbiosis and detachment. Yet the crises are of equal importance to development: The probationary dynamic, in which the person is caught up, fosters the development toward an autonomous self. Oevermann considers primary relationship experiences highly significant for successfully overcoming these watershed crises. Positive early relationships engender the conviction that, on principle, one can always overcome a crisis. However, due to the structurally embedded traumatizing aspect within every identity crisis, another factor must enter the picture here, which can give rise to such trust. The individual can develop a belief in transcendence, so to speak, through substitute interpretations by significant others, parents, or persons of reference.

Steiner, on the other hand, considers the Rubicon, as described here, as an ontogenetic development event and he sees it as eminently important for the process of identity formation. His view also expresses itself in a softer focus on puberty and adolescence, which we need to regard critically in light of the most recent research. That said, Steiner considers the first years of life as a highly significant time span for child development. If everything unfolds as it should, the sheath of the dyadic relationship gives the child a sense that the world it was born into is true, good, and beautiful.[14] Education then has the task of instilling in the child a primordial sense of the world as his or her home. As a result, the child feels safe, which is the prerequisite for exploring the world. For Steiner, the time of the Rubicon presents a challenge to the skills of the educator. Once again, the pedagogue here becomes a representative of a "higher order." He can point to the stabilizing force of transcendence in the way he comports him/herself and in his authentic bearings and thus provide orientation for the child. In contrast to Oevermann, however, Steiner regards the religious connection as spiritual-realistic, not only as functional.

5 Rubicon—Middle childhood: Perspectives from developmental psychology and anthropology

So far, we attempted to make clear that the Rubicon marks a watershed in child development, characterized by psychic, cognitive, and—in the broadest sense—also organismic features; according to Steiner, this represents an overall dynamic that drives identity development in the phase between approximately the 8th and 11th years of life.

While research in developmental psychology has not explicitly adopted Steiner's Rubicon concept; there are nevertheless connections in content and structure between the two streams of theory construction.

Couching the Rubicon-related phenomena listed above in the terminology of developmental psychology, we could along with Erikson speak of an emerging sense of one's own identity, which initially is subjected to scrutiny. However, Erikson clearly places this identity formation to take place during the phase of youth (Erikson 2000; Marcia 1980).

In contrast, the term *self-concept* is a related phenomenon in developmental psychology, which already begins in earlier childhood (Unzner 2009, p. 13) and entails "a person's thoughts, feelings, evaluations in regard to him or herself" (ibid.; Roebers 2007). The emergence of the self-concept already in early childhood has been suggested by empirical findings; for example, children regard their bodies as a hindrance already in the second year. Only shortly after that they recognize themselves in the mirror and in videos or pictures and they demonstrate understanding of feelings and the intentions of other people. "With growing cognitive abilities, the child's self-concept further differentiates out in the course of childhood and after about 10 years of age it stabilizes sufficiently" (Unzner 2009, p. 13).

In the professional literature, a change in self-concept is more often seen as a proof of reaching a state of development that is attributed to middle childhood. Kathleen Dwyer, for example, states: "Also during middle childhood, children's self-concepts and their conceptions of others become more comprehensive, so that they increasingly focus on inner traits and encompass generalities across behaviors. With a more solid sense of self, children are increasingly able to regulate their own behaviors" (Dwyer 2005, p. 3).

Fegert, who allocates middle childhood in the time between ages 7 and 11/12, also sees the reasons for a changing self-concept in an ever-wider range of the child's internal and external activities. In Fegert's view, "multiple new experiences in various life contexts and new interaction with many different individuals, such as with teachers or peers they meet in clubs or organizations, etc.," are causal factors in this process of change. Fegert here highlights a first distinction between *ideal self* and *real self*. While the small child still could experience a sense of oneness, school-age children now become able to compare their own self with their social surroundings and thus clearly develop the ability to differentiate (Fegert 2010, S. 11). An originally heterogenous image of self gradually changes through their own awareness of their motoric skills (physical self-concept), academic learning, and through social contexts. Fegert, therefore, notes a typical decrease in self-worth that starts with school age and can reach puberty (ibid.).

When the child starts to have mixed feelings in middle childhood, this experience is regarded as another instant of soul crisis. The child experiences simultaneous, contradictory emotions, which can result from the tension between authentic feelings and social expectations (ibid., p. 12). That said, Fegert also puts emphasis on the tenth year as sort of marking the median of middle childhood: From the tenth year on, he observes a clear improvement in the strategies and then the child devises for regulating emotions. From the year on, the child increasingly works on:

- Strategies to elicit social support
- Strategies for solving specific functional problems
- Strategies to avoid problems

These strategies generally aim at reaching emotional self-sufficiency (ibid.).

The research field of middle childhood has recently elicited growing attention, instead of being just one developmental phase among others. In 2011, the magazine *Human Nature* issued a special edition on this topic. From a cross-cultural and evolution-theoretical perspective, this edition presented contributions on physiological correlates and the cultural and ecological variability of that time period (Campbell 2011).

The newest studies attribute to middle childhood a prominent role for the individual's future biographical development. The authors' collective around Marco Del Giudice[15] comes to this conclusion not only because of the psychic, motoric, and social impulses presented above, which occur more and more frequently around ages 6–12, but also because of biological and endocrinological processes. For quite a while, research has demonstrated that, after the vehement phase of early infancy, the cortisol levels stay practically constant throughout life, while the adrenal androgens increase during ages 6–12 (Stolecke 1997, p. 103): "This physiological and autonomous biological sign of physical maturity is called *Andrenarche*, which qualitatively continues into the phase of puberty" (ibid.).

During this developmental phase, according to Del Giudice, the adrenarche has a regulatory function that acts as an intermediary between individual biographical experiences and genetic dispositions (Del Giudice 2011, p. 5; West-Eberhard 2003). In particular, what drives this process is the adrenal gland hormone, which only the higher primates and the human species can produce.

In girls, the production of the adrenal 17-ketosteroid marks the beginning of adrenal maturation around the ninth year of life. At that point in time, the blood levels of the prohormone dehydroepiandrosterone (DHEA) and its sulfated form (DHEAS) are measurably on the rise (Del Giudice 2011, p. 4). Six to twelve months later the pubarche sets in, i.e., the beginning of pubic hair growth triggered by the transformation of DHEA into the male sexual hormone testosterone. This hormone is still present at birth, but then rapidly disappears to only resume production in middle childhood. As yet, its function appears largely unclear.

Middle childhood is—also from an anthropological perspective—a time when children go through a successive emancipatory process in regard to their primary persons of reference and attachment, while not yet showing signs of physical sexual maturity (in contrast to other mammals); that means an additional window in time is available to them for developing their personality, in which they can give expression to the impulses of selfhood as outlined above. That said, many cultures assign children of this age co-responsible tasks such as procuring and preparing food and caring for younger siblings. We cannot presume a specific one been instrumental in clarifying the timeline for this process, as we are now used to seeing in western cultures of technological character.

Attachment research has clarified how important this time is in setting the course for the health of the human being later in life. Svenja Zellmer, for example, points to the interrelationship between resilience and attachment in the time span between preschool age and middle childhood (Zellmer 2007).

We can here also cite the studies of Mary Jane West-Eberhard (2003, 129ff.) that describe the middle childhood as a switch point that sets the course relevant for development. For here, this *developmental switch* is an event category that generates a lot of environmental information offering the respective individual different paths for development. The individuals going through this phase, which is particularly sensitive to change, are deemed particularly vulnerable and in need of [pedagogic] support, because the changes at this time have fundamental effects on further course of development.

Here we can detect that in the context of modern research, Steiner's concept of the Rubicon is being refreshed. The Rubicon impulses are now differently accentuated as developmental switches, impulses of biographical identity formation, and a physiological expression of a transformative process in pre-puberty, and at the same time they are topics in middle childhood research.

It remains a task for future empiric research to show how far the Rubicon concept requires further inferences about preventing and proper handling of this crisis, in view of its thorough anthropological and humanitarian understructure.

Notes

1 Middle childhood—often called *juvenility* in Anglo-Saxon language areas—is a phase of development that attracts increasing interest from researchers. Today there is a more differentiated view of the latency period, as described in psychoanalytic texts in the sense of a psycho-sexual retardation in development between years 6 and 12. In middle childhood, the young person meets active challenges of extrinsic and intrinsic nature, which are highly significant for the development of the child's personality. However, the date ranges for middle childhood are not always uniform. They vary between the 6th and 8th years of life (entry) and the 11th and 12th years of life (exit and beginning of pre-puberty) (Ahrend 2002, p. 17).

2 Montada, Oerter (2008), Cizek et al. (2005), Steinebach (2000), Trautner (1997), Bergius (1959).

3 This kind of scientific concept can be described as "ontological naturalism" (Ziegler 2014, p. 9). It differs by its rigid reference to everything material from "methodological naturalism" (ibid., p. 10ff.), whose methodological trajectory is also empiristic but initially does not categorically exclude any dimensions of reality. Methodological naturalism generally assumes a lawfully structured world and bases its approach on a hypothetical realism (ibid.).

4 "Some children reach this point in time already before the ninth year, others reach it later but on average the moment I want to talk about begins with the ninth year" (Steiner 1990, p. 96). This quote substantiates that Steiner's more frequent references to the ninth or tenth year of life constitute an average date range that should in no way not be made into dogma.

5 Steiner frequently uses the term *crisis* or *watershed moment* to characterize the Rubicon (Steiner 1986, p. 205). In a different context, he talks about "life change" and "life metamorphosis," which occur in connection with the change of teeth or later with the beginning of puberty (Steiner 1981, p. 41; see also Selg 2011, p. 35). We call Steiner's understanding of crisis "norm-conforming" [or *normal*], because he obviously understands it as an integral part of regular ontogenesis. These are generalized attributions, which are also valid, if the child's subjective experience of this crisis is not—or only weakly—developed.

6 Here we have to take note that Steiner views then changing "I – Thou" relationship merely in regard to the child's relation to adults. But that falls short of the mark. Modern studies on middle childhood explore the importance of peer relationships among six- to twelve-year-old children as relevant socialization factors beyond asymmetric constellations *[i.e., adult/child configurations]* "because peers are not a given part of the surroundings, like parents, but peer relations are characterized by free choice on both sides and can end, if there is strife or discontent. Thus, peer relations present a challenge: children have to negotiate the rules of togetherness on their own, voice their interests but also notice and consider the wishes of their friends" (Traub 2006, p. 198).

7 Within a sequence of events, the animistic (magical) worldview attributes motives and intentions to inanimate objects. This tendency can persist up to school age and then it is relatively quickly replaced by an understanding of causality (Bischof-Köhler 2011).

8 In a study by Breithaupt, Bestehorn, Zerm, and Hildebrandt (1980), the researchers determined and compared the individual relationship between breath- and heartrates in 47 boarding school students aged 6–13 and a group of 50 adults. We can summarize the findings as follows: "We could find a similar coordination of relative frequencies both in adults and students; however, the students did not yet show an inter-individual normative relation between those frequencies, while in adults a 4:1 proportional frequency prevails. Rather, the findings show that a broader spectrum of preferred whole-numbered frequencies exists in the students, while some variances occur dependent on time of day and age. Especially striking is the observation that average proportional values are higher during sleep (topo-tropic stage) than during waking (ergo-tropic) phases. Due to the lack of an interindividual 'normal' values in the age group under observation we cannot apply a unified concept of 'normal' frequency proportions within this age-span, even though on some age levels there occurred a more intense frequency coordination during tropho-tropic sleep phase" (ibid. p. 405). Another study by Cysarz et al. found a dependency of the heart's mid-range frequency during childhood development: "In young children it registers at about 100 heartbeats per minute, while during the tenth year, it slows to about 90 beats. Accordingly, also the rhythm of the heartbeat changes – it is more rigid in small children because the higher frequency rate narrows the range of the rhythm. After the 10th year, the quality of the heart rhythm becomes comparable to that of an adult" (Cysarz 2008, p. 3; see also in more detail Cysarz et al. 2013).

9 This figure of thought connects human actions with transcendental dimensions of reality and gives it pedagogical expression; it also exists in other cultures such as the Chinese one: "Through the true and authentic [quality of human action] that which is divine and transcendent takes on human-like qualities. Expressed in Being, the heavens move closer to the earth and lend human form to the immanence of transcendence, signifying a connection and real-ness for man, his emotions and situations; on the other hand it also offers man a comprehensible model for transcendence in everyday life, which implicitly means: the foundation of morality" (Yang 2004, p. 114).

10 Steiner's writings on authority in a pedagogic context reveal that authority for him is a dynamic concept; analyzing the relationship between the child and adults, he arrives at his views on appropriate relationships with authority. This relationship undergoes qualitative changes, because the child is engaged in the process of becoming an autonomous person. That means the relationship with authority must change as well. An overall authoritarian understanding of education would allow for this dynamic. Steiner's understanding of authority is explicitly non-static and is close to today's educational science theorem of "interactional authority" (also called "pedagogical authority"), which presupposes a relationship of mutual recognition. The child's recognition of the authority figure is based on the assumed competency this person demonstrates in diverse areas of life ("epistemic authority" according to Bochenski 1974). That means: "The actual authority lasts only as long

as such a relationship between the one who acknowledges and the acknowledged person. As soon as one of the interacting partners dissolves the relationship, the dynamic of authority ends as well" (Latzko 2012, p. 578).

11 Such a relationship results in the concept of authority for Hegel as well: "The coincidental is supposed to give rise to the necessary and the human awareness of that which is ephemeral should be rooted in an awareness of the eternal, reflected in feeling, thinking, and action; the ephemeral factor is generally called authority" (Hegel 1983, p. 223).

12 Oevermann's religious sociology approach follows Max Weber in referencing a "probationary dynamic," which everyone must face in life. Biographically, the three types of crises are unavoidable events. This way of proving oneself is the individual aspect of overcoming a crisis (Wohlrab-Sahr 1984, p. 20).

13 Concerning the term *substitute interpretation*, derived from the terminology of therapeutic professions, and on its transformation into pedagogic action, see Oevermann (1996b, pp. 152ff.).

14 "The educator has to act in such a way that he does not merely describe the true, good and beautiful to the child but embodies it as a lived reality. All teaching must essentially consist of modeling this for the child. Teaching has to be an art, not just consist of theoretical content" (Steiner 1979a,b, p. 221). If we translate that into the terminology of structural socialization theory, it says that through artful representation of objective structures of meaning and through the surrogate (modeled) interpretations of the educator, the child learns step-by-step to take hold of the world.

15 Del Giudice, Angeleri, Manera (2009), Colle, Del Giudice (2011), Del Giudice (2011). Middle childhood is here regarded globally as "the developmental switch point in human life history" (Colle, Del Giudice 2011).

References

Achziger, Anja/Gollwitzer, Peter M. (2009): Rubikonmodell der Handlungsphasen. In: Brandstätter, Veronika (Ed.) (2009): Handbuch der Allgemeinen Psychologie: Motivation und Emotion. Göttingen: Hogrefe, pp. 151–156.

Ahrend, Christine (2002): Mobilitätsstrategien zehnjähriger Jungen und Mädchen als Grundlage städtischer Verkehrsplanung. Münster: Waxmann, pp. 17–54.

Bergius, Rudolf (1959): Entwicklung als Stufenfolge. In: Thomae, Hans (Ed.) (1959): Handbuch der Psychologiein 12 Bänden. Band III: Entwicklungspsychologie. Göttingen: Hogrefe. pp. 105–151.

Bischof-Köhler, Doris (2011): Soziale Entwicklung in Kindheit und Jugend. Bindung, Empathie, Theory of Mind. Stuttgart: Kohlhammer.

Blaß, Simone (2013), online unter: www.t-online.de/eltern/schulkind/id_62832594/vorpubertaet-so-beginntdie-phase-der-pubertaet.html (Last accessed: September 2014).

Bochenski, Joseph Maria (1974): Was ist Autorität? Einführung in die Logik der Autorität. Freiburg: Herder.

Breithaupt H./Zerm, F.-J./Bestehorn, H.-P./Hildebrandt, G. (1980): Über die Frequenzbeziehung von Puls und Atmung im Kindesalter. In: Monatsschrift für Kinderheilkunde 128, 1980, pp. 405–411.

Campbell, Benjamin (2011): An Introduction to the Special Issue on Middle Childhood. In: Human Nature, September 2011, 22, 3, pp. 247–248.

Cizek, Brigitta/Kapella, Olaf/Steck, Maria (2005): Entwicklungstheorie II. Adoleszenz. Österreichisches Institut für Familienforschung. No.49, 2005. Online unter: www.oif.ac.at/fileadmin/ OEIF/Working_Paper/wp_48_entwicklungstheorie_1.pdf (Last accessed: Mai 2016).

Colle, L./Del Giudice, M. (2011): Patterns of Attachment and Emotional Competence in Middle Childhood. In: Social Development, 20, 2011, pp. 51–72.

Cysarz, Dirk/Linhard Maijana/Edelhäuser, Friedrich/Längler, Alfred/Van Leeuwen, Peter/Henze, Günter/Seifert, Georg (2013): Symbolic Patterns of Heart Rate Dynamics Reflect Cardiac Autonomic Changes during Childhood and Adolescence. In: Auton Neurosci, 2013 Nov, 178 (1–2), pp. 37–43.

Cysarz, Dirk (2008): Comparison of respiratory rates derived from heart rate variability, ECG amplitude, and nasal/oral airflow. Online: https://pubmed.ncbi.nlm.nih.gov/18855140/(Last accessed: October 2022).

Del Giudice, Marco/Romina Angeleri/Valeria Manera (2009): The Juvenile Transition: A Developmental Switch Point in Human Life History. In: Developmental Review, 29, 2009, pp. 1–31.

Del Giudice, Marco (2014): Middle Childhood: An evolutionary developmental synthesis. In: Child Development Perspectives, 2/2014, pp. 1–8.

Dwyer, Kathleen (2005): The Meaning and Measurement of Attachment in Early and Late Childhood. In: Human Development, 48, 2005, pp. 155–182.

Erikson, Erik (2000): Identität und Lebenszyklus. 18. Auflage. Frankfurt am Main: Suhrkamp.

Faix, Wilhelm (2004): Bindung als anthropologisches Merkmal. Die Bedeutung der Eltern-Kind-Beziehung als Prävention für eine gesunde Persönlichkeitsentwicklung aus biblischer und entwicklungspsychologischer Sicht und gemeindepädagogische Folgerungen. In: Hille, Rolf and Herbert Klement (Eds.) (2004): Ein Mensch – was ist das? Zur theologischen Anthropologie. Wuppertal: Brunnen, pp. 260–289.

Fegert, Jörg M. (2010): Das Selbstkonzept als Leitbild der Therapie? Vortrag auf dem ADHS Gipfel in Hamburg am 06.02.2010. Online at: www.uniklinik-ulm.de/fileadmin/Kliniken/Kinder_ Jugendpsychiatrie/ Praesentationen/fe_ADHS_HH_Selbstkonzept06_02_10.pdf (Last accessed: Mai 2015).

Grossman, Klaus/Grossmann, Karin (2009): Die Erfassung psychischer Sicherheit und Unsicherheit in der mittleren Kindheit. Unterschiede in der ‚Konstruktiven Internalen Kohärenz' als ein Merkmal sicherer und unsicherer Bindungsqualitäten. In: Julius, Henri, Barbara Gasteiger-Klipcera and Rüdiger Kißgen (Eds.) (2009): Bindung im Kindesalter. Diagnostik und Interventionen. Göttingen: Hogrefe, pp. 139–174.

Hall, Granville Stanley (1898): Some Aspects of the Early Sense of Self. In: The American Journal of Psychology, Vol. IX, 1898, pp. 351–395.

Hall, Granville Stanley (1903): Ausgewählte Beiträge zur Kinderpsychologie und Pädagogik. Altenburg: Oskar Bonde.

Heckhausen, Heinz/Gollwitzer, Peter Max (1987): Thought contents and cognitive functioning in motivational versus volitional states and mind. In: Motivation and Emotion, 11/1987, pp. 101–120.

Hegel, Georg Wilhelm Friedrich (1983): Entwürfe über Religion und Liebe. In: ibid. (1983): Frühe Schriften. Theorie Werkausgabe Vol.1, Frankfurt: Suhrkamp, pp. 223–256.

Helsper, Werner/Ullrich, Heiner/Stelmaszyk, Bernhard/Hoblich, Davina/Grashoff, Gunther/Jung, Dana (2007): Autoritat und Schule. Die empirische Rekonstruktion der Klassenlehrer-Schuler-Beziehung an Waldorfschulen. [Authority and School. The Empirical Reconstruction of the Class Teacher-Schooler Relationship at Waldorf Schools].Wiesbaden: Springer VS.

Heusser, Peter (2011): Anthroposophische Medizin und Wissenschaft. Beiträge zu einer integrativen medizinischen Anthropologie. Stuttgart: Schattauer.

Kißgen, Rüdiger (2009): Diagnostik der Bindungsqualität in der frühen Kindheit – Die Fremden – Situation. In: Julius, Henri, Barbara Gasteiger-Klipcera and Rüdiger Kißgen (Eds.) (2009): Bindung im Kindesalter. Diagnostik und Interventionen. Göttingen: Hogrefe, pp. 92–105.

Krapp, Andreas/Prenzel, Manfred/Weidenmann, Bernd (2006): Geschichte, Gegenstandsbereich und Aufgaben der Pädagogischen Psychologie. In: Krapp, Andreas and Bernd Weidenmann (Eds.) (2006): Pädagogische Psychologie. Weinheim: Beltz, pp. 1–32.

Kreppner, Kurt (1998): Vorstellungen zur Entwicklung der Kinder: Zur Geschichte von Entwicklungstheorien in der Psychologie. In: Keller, Hans (1998): Lehrbuch zur Entwicklungspsychologie. Bern: Huber, pp. 212–246.

Kroh, Oswald (1928): Die Psychologie des Grundschulkindes in ihrer Beziehung zur kindlichen Gesamtentwicklung. Langensalza: Beyer & Söhne.

Latzko, Brigitte (2012): "Autorität." In: Sandfuchs, Uwe, Wolfgang Melzer, Bernd Dühlmeier and Adly Rausch (Eds.) (2012): Handbuch Erziehung. Stuttgart: Klinkhardt, pp. 577–581.

Marcia, James E. (1980): Identity in adolescence. In: Adelson, J. (Ed.) (1980): Handbook of Psychology. New York: Wiley and Sons, pp. 159–187.

Montada, Leo/Oerter, Rolf (2008): Entwicklungspsychologie. Weinheim: Psychologie Verlag.

Müller-Wiedemann, Hans (1999): Mitte der Kindheit. Das neunte bis zwölfte Lebensjahr. Beiträge zu einer anthroposophischen Entwicklungspsychologie. 5. Auflage. Stuttgart: Freies Geistesleben.

Oevermann, Ulrich (1996a): Krise und Muße. Struktureigenschaften ästhetischer Erfahrung aus soziologischer Sicht. Frankfurt am Main: Unveröffentlichtes Manuskript.

Oevermann, Ulrich (1996b): Theoretische Skizze einer revidierten Theorie professionalisierten Handelns. In: Combe, Arno and Werner Helsper (Eds.) (1996): Pädagogische Professionalität. Untersuchungen zum Typus pädagogischen Handelns. Frankfurt am Main: Suhrkamp, pp. 70–182.

Oevermann, Ulrich (2000a): Wissen, Glaube, Überzeugung – Ein Vorschlag zu einer Theorie des Wissens aus krisentheoretischer Perspektive. Frankfurt am Main: Unveröffentlichtes Manuskript.

Oevermann, Ulrich (2000b): Überlegungen zur Integration und Synthese der begrifflichen und methodischen Instrumentarien der Forschungen im Sonderforschungsbereich/FK 435 "Wissenskultur und gesellschaftlicher Wandel." Frankfurt am Main: Unveröffentlichtes Manuskript.

Piaget, Jean (1973): Einführung in die genetische Erkenntnistheorie. Frankfurt am Main: Suhrkamp.

Prange, Klaus (1985): Erziehung zur Anthroposophie. Darstellung und Kritik der Waldorfpädagogik. Bad Heilbrunn: Klinkhardt.

Preyer, Wilhelm Thierry (1882): Die Seele des Kindes: Beobachtungen über die geistige Entwicklung des Menschen in den ersten Lebensjahren. Leipzig: Grieben.

Preyer, Wilhelm Thierry (1989): Die Seele des Kindes. Eingeleitet und mit Materialien zur Rezeptionsgeschichte versehen von Georg Eckardt. Berlin, Heidelberg, New York: Springer.

Roebers, Claudia M. (2007): Entwicklung des Selbstkonzepts. In: Hasselhorn, Marcus and Wolfgang Schneider (Eds.) (2007): Handbuch der Entwicklungspsychologie. Göttingen: Hogrefe, pp. 381–391.

Ruef, Mona (Ed.) (2012): Rubikon. Entwicklungsschritte im 9./10. Lebensjahr. Eine Sammlung aus Werken von Rudolf Steiner. Dornach: Verlag am Goetheanum.

Selg, Peter (2011): "Ich bin anders als du." Vom Selbst- und Welterleben des Kindes in der Mitte der Kindheit. Dornach: Ita Wegmann.

Selman, Robert L. (1984): Die Entwicklung des sozialen Verstehens. Frankfurt am Main: Suhrkamp.

Steinebach, Christoph (2000): Entwicklungspsychologie. Stuttgart: Klett-Cotta.

Steiner, Rudolf (1907): Die Erziehung des Kindes vom Gesichtspunkte der Geisteswissenschaft. *[The education of the child in the light of spiritual science]*. In: Steiner, Rudolf (1987): Lucifer – Gnosis. Grundlegende Aufsätze zur Anthroposophie und Berichte aus den Zeitschriften «Luzifer» und «Lucifer – Gnosis» 1903-1908. Rudolf Steiner Gesamtausgabe 34. *[Lucifer-Gnosis: Foundational essays on anthroposophy and reports from the periodicals 'Lucifer' and 'Lucifer-Gnosis' 1903–1908]*. Dornach: Rudolf Steiner Verlag, pp. 309–348.

Steiner, Rudolf (1979a): Anthroposophische Menschenkunde und Pädagogik. GA 304a. *[Anthroposophical knowledge of the human being and pedagogy]*. Dornach: Rudolf Steiner Verlag.

Steiner, Rudolf (1979b): Erziehungs- und Unterrichtsmethoden auf anthroposophischer Grundlage. GA 304. *[Methods of education and teaching based on anthroposophy]*. Dornach: Rudolf Steiner Verlag.

Steiner, Rudolf (1980): Die Welt des Geistes und ihr Hereinragen in das physische Dasein. GA 150. *[The world of the spirit and its extension into physical existence]*. Dornach: Rudolf Steiner Verlag.

Steiner, Rudolf (1981): Anthroposophische Pädagogik und ihre Voraussetzungen. GA 309. *[Anthroposophical pedagogy and its prerequisites]*. Dornach: Rudolf Steiner Verlag.

Steiner, Rudolf (1986): Was wollte das Goetheanum und was will die Anthroposophie? GA 84. *[What did the Goetheanum intend and what should anthroposophy do?]*. Dornach: Rudolf Steiner Verlag.

Steiner, Rudolf (1987): Die gesunde Entwicklung des Menschenwesens. Eine Einführung in die anthroposophische Pädagogik und Didaktik. GA 303. *[The healthy development of the human essence. An introduction to anthroposophical pedagogy]*. Dornach: Rudolf Steiner Verlag.

Steiner, Rudolf (1989a): Die Kunst des Erziehens aus dem Erfassen der Menschenwesenheit. GA 301. *[The renewal of pedagogic-didactical art through spiritual science]*. Dornach: Rudolf Steiner Verlag.

Steiner, Rudolf (1989b): Methodische Grundlagen der Anthroposophie. GA 30. *[Methodical foundations of anthroposophy]*. Dornach: Rudolf Steiner Verlag.

Steiner, Rudolf (1989c): Die pädagogische Praxis vom Gesichtspunkte geisteswissenschaftlicher Menschenerkenntnis. GA 306. *[Pedagogical praxis from the viewpoint of a spiritual-scientific knowledge of the human being]*. Dornach: Rudolf Steiner Verlag.

Steiner, Rudolf (1990): Erziehungskunst. Methodisch-Didaktisches. GA 294. *[The art of education, methodology, and didactics]*. Dornach: Rudolf Steiner Verlag.

Steiner, Rudolf (1992): Die Erziehung des Kindes vom Gesichtspunkte der Geisteswissenschaft. *[The education of the child in the light of spiritual science]*. Dornach: Rudolf Steiner Verlag.

Steiner, Rudolf (1994): Die Sendung Michaels. GA 194. *[The mission of Michael]*. Dornach: Rudolf Steiner Verlag.

Steiner, Rudolf (1998a): Idee und Praxis der Waldorfschule. GA 297. *[The Idea and practice of the Waldorf school]*. Dornach: Rudolf Steiner Verlag.

Steiner, Rudolf (2010): Der pädagogische Wert der Menschenerkenntnis und der Kulturwert der Pädagogik. GA 310. *[The pedagogical value of a knowledge of the human being and the cultural value of pedagogy]*. Dornach: Rudolf Steiner Verlag.

Steiner, Rudolf (2011): Grundlinien einer Erkenntnistheorie der Goetheschen Weltanschauung. Mit besonderer Rücksicht auf Schiller. 5. Auflage. GA 2. *[An outline of the epistemology of Goethe's world view, with special consideration of Schiller]*. Basel: Rudolf Steiner Verlag.

Stolecke, Herbert (1997): "Androgene" *[Androgenes]* In: Stolecke, Herbert (Ed.) (1997): Endokrinologie des Kindes und Jugendalters. *[Endocrinology of childhood and adolescence]* Berlin, Heidelberg, New York: Springer

Traub, Angelika (2006): Kontinuität und Kompensation. Die Bedeutung von Familie und Gleichaltrigen (Peers) für Persönlichkeit und Problemverhalten in der mittleren Kindheit. *[Continuity and compensation. The significance of family and peers for personality and problem behavior in middle childhood]* In: Diskurs Kindheits- und Jugendforschung 1, 2006, pp. 197–216.

Trautner, Hanns Martin (1997): Lehrbuch der Entwicklungspsychologie. Vol. II. Göttingen: Hogrefe.

Unzner, Lothar (2009): Identitätsentwicklung unter dem Blickwinkel der Bindungsforschung. *[The development of identity in the perspective of attachment research]* In: Dobslaw, Gudrun and Theo Klauß (2009): Identität, geistige Behinderung und seelische Gesundheit. *[Identity, mental disabilities, and wellbeing of the soul]* Materialien der DGSGB, Band 19. Kassel: Materialien der DGSGBS, pp. 13–22.

Wagner, Hans-Josef (2001): Objektive Hermeneutik und Bildung des Subjekts. *[Objective Hermeneutics and the Formation of the subject]* Weilerswist: Velbrück Wissenschaft.

Wagner, Hans-Josef (2004a): Sozialität und Reziprozität. Strukturale Sozialisationstheorie I. *[Sociality and reciprocity. Structural socialization theory, vol. I]* Frankfurt am Main: Humanities Online.

Wagner, Hans-Josef (2004b): Krise und Sozialisation. Strukturale Sozialisationstheorie II. *[Crisis in socialization. Structural socialization Theory, vol. II]* Frankfurt am Main: Humanities Online.

Wandschneider, Dieter (2014): Geist als Höchstform und Überschreitung materiellen Seins. *[Spirit as the highest form and transcendence of material existence]* In: Weinzirl, Johannes and Peter Heusser (Eds.) (2014): Was ist Geist? *[What is spirit?]* Wittener Kolloquium Humanismus, Medizin und Philosophie. Vol.2. Würzburg: Königshausen und Neumann, pp. 175–191.

West-Eberhard, Mary Jane (2003): Development Plasticity and Evolution. Oxford and New York: Oxford University Press.

Wohlrab-Sahr, Monika (1984): Religion und Religionslosigkeit. Was sieht man durch die soziologische Brille? *[Religion and Having No Religion. What do we see through the lenses of sociology?]* In: Heimbach-Steins, Marianne (Ed.) (1984): Religion als gesellschaftliches Phänomen. Soziologische, theologische und literaturwissenschaftliche Annäherungen. *[Religion as a societal Phenomenon. Approaches from sociology, theology and literary science]* Münster: LIT, pp. 11–26.

Yang, Yousheng (2004): Immanente Transzendenz. Eine Untersuchung der Transzendenzerfahrung in der antiken chinesischen Religiosität mit Berücksichtigung des Konfuzianismus. *[Immanent Transcendence. An exploration of transcendent experience in ancient Chinese religiosity with special consideration of Confucianism]* Tübingen: Schriften der Universität Tübingen.

Zander, Helmut (2007): Anthroposophie in Deutschland. Theosophische Weltanschauung und gesellschaftliche Praxis 1884–1945. *[Anthroposophy in Germany. Theosophical world view and societal practice 1884–1945]* Vol. II. Göttingen: Vandenhoeck & Ruprecht.

Zellmer, Svenja (2007): Kontinuität der Bindung: Bindungsentwicklung vom Vorschulalter bis zur mittleren Kindheit. *[Continuity of attachment: Attachment development from preschool to middle childhood]*. Saarbrücken: AV Akademikerverlag.

Ziegler, Renatus (2014): Wissenschaftsphilosophie, Naturalismus und übersinnliche Erkenntnis. Teil I: Analyse und Konsequenzen. *[Philosophy of science, naturalism, and meta-sensory cognition. Part I: Analysis and consequences]* In: RoSE – Research on Steiner Education. Vol. 5, No.1/2014, pp. 1–2.

ADOLESCENCE AND THE FINDINGS OF BRAIN RESEARCH

Wenzel M. Götte

1 Introduction

Over the last decades, brain research has developed a fascinating dynamic (Blakemore 2012).[1] The results of this research impacted numerous areas of science and life, including the theory and practice of pedagogy. Here, the insights gained in brain research touch upon two areas in particular: Foundational sciences of pedagogy such as developmental psychology, learning theories, aspects of pedagogic anthropology, and—of special interest to Waldorf education—the attempts of neurobiologists to develop a new view of the human being, i.e., a new concept of the human being (Das Manifest 2004 *[The Manifesto 2004]*; a critique of the latter, see "Memorandum" 2014).

Waldorf education claims to base its pedagogic views—down to their concrete practice—on a special "understanding of the human being," i.e., the anthroposophical concept and study of man (Kranich 1999b, 2003, p. 203): "We must first gain a true insight into human nature before we can establish true pedagogy," wrote Rudolf Steiner, the founder of Waldorf education, in 1922 (Steiner 1961, p. 283). Steiner here points to a—certainly controversial—peculiarity of Waldorf education. For Steiner, "true insight into human nature" is a kind of anthropology that "comprehends the human being in all aspects of body, soul, and mind/spirit" (ibid.).

This also means that insights from the neurosciences, in particular from brain research, belong to a field of natural science, which is of eminent importance to Waldorf education in respect to its foundations. In fact, brain research does not only produce findings, e.g., concerning physiological-anatomical phenomena of brain development but also provides insights into associated psychological factors, which in turn are relevant to pedagogical practice. Waldorf education will need to deal with this "new concept of the human being" as presented in the "Manifesto" mentioned above, the somatic aspect being explicitly viewed as an integral part of their concept of the human being and bearing implications for pedagogical action. Therefore, we will start with some preliminary remarks, calling attention to the issue of an overly naïve adoption of insights from brain research, in particularly in regard to the possible consequences for a concept of the human being that is foundational for any type of pedagogy (Section 2).

But our main focus will turn to other questions, because we must at least come to know about a few relevant research studies and their methodologies before we turn to a more profound discussion. Therefore, we will discuss here the following questions and topics:

Some examples shall illustrate brain research's relevance for pedagogy. These examples stem from the area of neuroscience research on adolescence, a branch that was very highly developed mainly in the United States; therefore, American research papers furnish most of the referenced literature (Section 3 and 4).

Next, we must clarify how educational science and Waldorf education have so far received these findings and what conclusions are to be drawn from that reception (Section 5).

In this process it is important to see how far Waldorf education and educational science could possibly enter into a discourse on these topics. Conceivably, perspectives gained in brain research could assist in building bridges, instead of only perpetuating differences (Section 6).

Finally, the conclusion attempts to draw attention and focus to the contributions that these examples offer for the theory and practice of pedagogy (Section 7).

2 Remarks on problems in interpreting the results of neuroscience research

In dealing with brain research, we encounter some problems for reasons that the following paragraph will spell out. The concern here is not only on intellectual reception, but a few researchers aim also at transposing these findings into pedagogical practice (Bauer 2007; Roth 2011; Singer 2006; Spitzer 2006). This aim, however, not only requires educators to inform themselves on research results, but also, and first of all, to reflect on the anthropological implications of these results in regard to the underlying concept of the human being. Some researchers call for a new concept of the human being, which would reduce the human subject to brain processes, which eliminates man as a spiritual/mental entity and "unmasks" the idea of freedom as an epi-phenomenal illusion about the reality of monocausal, physiologically determined processes (Pauen 2004a; Pauen, Roth 2008). Such a new concept would have grave consequences in regard to attitudes and actions—not only in pedagogy. Two factors caution us to be highly thoughtful, when we deal with such reasoning, because we have to assume that such a concept of the human being forms the understructure of every type of pedagogy (Meinberg 1988) and that it acts as a sort of "hidden curriculum" factor.

It is important here that the latter is already subconsciously being accepted, when we adopt any specific terminology. Brain research in particular offers many examples of a technologized terminology (Roth 2007), which opens a gate for ideas of what is doable or efficient or should be optimized.

Notably many—also well-known—neuroscientists feel the need to barge into discussions on pedagogical issues. They actively voice their opinions on a broad range of topics and point to, e.g., new, presumably improved, forms of learning, often with a certain claim to absoluteness. For example, well-known neuroscientists have commented on topics of learning psychology, giftedness research, methodology and organization of teaching practice, on issues of attachment- and intelligence research, etc. Among them are researchers like Gerhard Roth, Gerald Hüther, Manfred Spitzer in Germany and in the United States since a long time the researcher Jay Giedd, who also, in particular, publishes on the topic of youth research.

The specific, demonstrably largely subconscious, effects that the personality or attitude of an educator or teacher *[has in the student]* show how careful we have to be in interpreting the findings of neuroscience research and in drawing conclusions in regard to the concept of the human being in pedagogical practice.[2] For this reason, authors from various branches of science have submitted alternate concepts for interpreting neuroscientific findings, striving to be alert to and to avoid the dangers of cerebral-centrism or neuroconstructivism (Fuchs 2008).[3] Thomas Fuchs writes from the perspective of a psychiatrist (and this is equally valid for a pedagogue): "The *ethical* consequences of certain body-soul theories are pivotal for assessing whether they are a positive factor in medical-therapeutic practice, or whether they pose a problem. Psychiatrists may find it unacceptable in practice to assume that the options of autonomy and freedom of action are just an illusion that are useful to the patient, or that intersubjectivity can be reduced to an exchange of programs between bio-machines that process information" (Fuchs 2008, p. 259).

Especially, regarding the anthropological foundations of Waldorf education, it would be of precarious consequence for pedagogic action to eliminate an ontologically real subject or "I." In pedagogy, i.e., in a particularly intense relationship between human beings, the view of the brain offered by Thomas Fuchs appears to yield a comprehensive and profound analysis. He sees the brain as a "relational organ" that is connected with the entire bodily experience and the life world of the human being, an organ that is connected also with the subject or "I" of man himself and is essential to the dignity of the human being in body, soul, and spirit.

We must however point out a difference in regard to the perspective of Waldorf education. Fuchs emphasizes that the mind/soul, spirit, and the body of man form an unbreakable unity and are interconnected. Without being able to go into a further line of reasoning here, we want to stress that accepting the individuality of the human being as a reality that reaches beyond this life on earth is a core element of Waldorf education (Götte 2006, 87ff.; Leber 1993, 154ff.). Waldorf philosophy regards the brain as a physical substrate of all attributes and characteristics such as consciousness, thinking, feeling, willing, and the activity of the "I," which it itself is not a productive but an enabling factor; in other words, the brain constitutes only a necessary but not sufficient condition for these soul- and spirit-connected phenomena.

To some extent, this understanding (of the brain's function) outlined above appears already in the work of Hans Jonas (1987) as well as Karl Popper (1997) and John Eccles (1982). In most recent times, the molecular- and neurobiologist and physician Joachim Bauer "rediscovered" the "self" as an agency of possible freedom (Bauer 2015).

Here we cannot further discuss the substantiation and pedagogical consequences of an anthropology that assumes the pre- and post-existence of spiritual individuality, but we shall hold space for the idea of a spiritual identity.

Neuroscientific study of the brain has many facets that are of particular interest for learning research (Blakemore, Frith 2006; Spitzer 2006). We will now look at a small but substantial area of newer research: The exploration of developmental reorganization in the brain during puberty. Here again, we have to make a choice, because we cannot follow each of the manifold directions in this field.

3 Neuroscience research findings relevant to pedagogy

Some select research findings on brain development during adolescence shall serve to show which insights could be fruitful for the theory and practice of pedagogy.

3.1 *Preliminary remarks on procedures*

The following presentation of some facts that pertain to brain development calls to mind that any narrow focus on specific brain areas and their function does neglect the wholistic oneness of an individual's corporeality. Today we deem the localization theorem largely outdated, along with its one-sided focus on single specific brain areas. The brain as an organ is part of an infinitely intricate web that forms a nexus of connections within itself and at the same time with the whole body. This limitation does appear appropriate here, since these cases are meant to sufficiently clarify important insights of developmental psychology that are relevant to pedagogic action.

This article focuses on only two aspects in regard to this localization. First, it has been demonstrated that damage to certain brain areas (e.g., through lesions) leads to the loss of certain functions (e.g., loss of speech recognition, active speech, deliberate behavior management, and vision). But this implies neither that these areas produce the respective functions, nor that they are the only causative factor. We also have taken into consideration that once a brain area is damaged, not all of its functions can be transferred to another area of the brain, in spite of the so-called plasticity of the brain.

Furthermore, it seems justified to make the analog inference that a particular brain area cannot fulfill its functions later in life, if it has not properly matured in the course of childhood development. This viewpoint is of particular significance to pedagogues, since it brings up important questions and insights for the development of, e.g., cognitive and social functions:

- Should we rather wait for the *[natural]* development of certain brain areas and the maturation of their functions, or is it useful to accelerate this process through early training?
- Should children, e.g., go through learning programs in foreign languages or mathematics, before the brain has fully developed the areas responsible for cognitive achievements?

- May we expect adolescents to show specific adult behaviors, while they are still in the process of developing the brain functions for impulse control, drive management, and deferred gratification?
- Should we treat girls differently than we treat boys, who generally reach full development of such functions only at a later age?
- At which stage in the developmental process should we pose certain challenges and demands?
- Is the knowledge of how to stimulate the development of competencies a sufficient reason to also in fact carry out such stimulation?
- Could a mathematical education in early childhood possibly constitute a damaging mental overload?

3.2 On the development of research methodology

While many areas of adolescent hormonal development have been subject to research, offering a budding systematic approach, neuroscientific research of adolescence is still characterized as a science that is fragmented into many distinct facets and that furnishes some fundamental insights in standalone studies; however, these findings hardly avail us a systematic, comprehensive order and overview of these phenomena. In contrast, the methods of brain research have developed at lightning speed. Especially methods like magnetic resonance tomography (MRT) or the functional MRT (fMRT) with high resolution capacity enable us to observe the living brain without invasive procedures or damaging radiation. Longitudinal observational studies with children and adolescents—conducted over the span of many years with the same subjects—have thus become possible. These methods allow us to gain an understanding of long-term processes in brain development.

Since these methods have been employed, especially since the 1980s, a plethora of new insights resulted that are relevant for pedagogy, in particular also insights into the development and modes of operation of the brain in childhood and adolescence. The well-respected researcher Roshel K. Lenroot highlights the potential of such studies in comparison to earlier animal experiments or postmortem studies. He emphasizes that now we can observe long-term changes and identify factors that bring about certain kinds of development (Lenroot, Giedd 2006, p. 719). He also offers a detailed overview of research methods and the stages of brain development.

Earlier, researchers assumed that the brain was all practically fully equipped in the embryonic stage, and the only changes that could still happen occurred in its synaptic architecture and in the area of myelinization. This view assumed that the nervous system of grown-ups did not experience any neurogenesis. Today we regard this view as outdated in many respects. After proving that neurogenesis does occur in adult song birds (Barnea, Pravosudov 2011), scientists showed that it also happens in the hippocampus of mammals, e.g., mice and likely also in human beings,[4] depending on their activities and behaviors such as alcohol abuse. This also proved yet again the plasticity of the brain.

A few more recent findings are interesting to pedagogues, among others the discovery of the neuronal foundations of imitation by Giacomo Rizzolatti and his team (Rizzolatti et al. 2006). The insights into mirror neurons offered a plethora of new findings for behavior research, for understanding the physical basis of imitation and for areas of psychopathology; researchers succeeded in proving the existence of mirror neurons in the human being (Mukamel et al. 2010). Just as an aside, this discovery may be most significant for the pedagogy of early childhood, in particular. We are familiar with the phenomenon of imitation and how the behavior of adults—even down to body posture—can make an impression on children. (For dramatic examples see Nitschke 1968.) As we now know, the child's observations of behaviors in the surroundings trigger the same neuronal activities in the brain as if they themselves actually engaged in that activity (we may think, e.g., of modeled language); therefore, we can assume that it has profound effects within the child's organism, which extend into imprinting the physical body, its anatomy, and the psyche.

The issue of lifelong brain development has also become a subject of longitudinal studies with individuals from childhood to adulthood.[5] Only then could researchers arrive at an insight, which replaced a traditional, dogmatized concept: The brain's development does not end at age 10–12, but it undergoes an anatomical upheaval at the age of puberty and continues to stay in constant reorganization for quite a while after that—not only by means of the so-called synaptic plasticity of the brain. The thorough study of these processes brought facts to light, which are of great significance for understanding or the developments during adolescence in two respects: For once, such study furnished insights into the physical, structural, and physiological changes within the brain and also clarified over what time spans these changes take place. Second, we can now develop a new understanding for the changes that adolescents undergo regarding their capabilities and behaviors. Let us illustrate how in fact many researchers themselves deal critically with these results by citing here the statements of the most well-known representative of adolescent brain research. When questioned in how far it is justified to draw conclusions from the understanding of physiological processes for mental processes and developments, Jay N. Giedd answered: "The connection between these structural changes and behavioral changes is only beginning to be elucidated" (Giedd 2004, p. 83). Such caution should also be exercised in regard to drawing parallels between the maturation processes and functions in certain brain areas and specific age brackets. Most recent studies show that such connections have only contingent *[and thus limited]* validity (Brown et al. 2012, p. 9).

Also, there is a generally critical assessment regarding the transfer and incorporation of neurobiological insights into current pedagogical practice and knowledge (Becker 2006).

3.3 *The reorganization of the brain in adolescence*

Before taking a closer look at some details, we shall offer an overview highlighting focal points of adolescent brain development in the following sections and also outline some issues and insights that emerge in connection with the research findings presented here.

Since the 1990s, neuroscience research has provided the fundamentally new insight that the brain undergoes a *massive re-organization* during puberty (Giedd et al. 1999).[6]

- The reorganization applies to a large part of the cerebrum, particularly the limbic system and the prefrontal cortex, and also to the cerebellum. This reorganization offers developmental possibilities to the adolescents, but at the same time exposes them to some dangers. In an interview, Jay N. Giedd remarked: "Those adolescents, who train their brain by learning to order their thoughts, to understand abstract concepts, and to control their impulses, lay the neuronal foundations for lifelong benefits from such discipline". In his opinion, this is an argument for adolescents training their brain with as many of such activities as possible: "You are hardwiring your brain in adolescence. Do you want to hardwire it for sports and playing music and doing mathematics – or for lying on the couch in front of the television?" (Giedd 2002a).
- Also, brain research supplies a strong argument for the controversial view that in puberty there are certain "windows of development" or developmentally sensitive phases. Brain physiology has demonstrated that such windows of development exist, particularly in the development of vision (Singer 2006, p. 14) and the changes during puberty point to this fact as well (Blakemore, Frith 2006, 45ff.).

Around the 11th to 12th year of life, new structures begin to develop in the brain's organization. There is, however, an issue in assessing causal relations: As already mentioned, we cannot simply presume the fact that the studies of cases with *[brain]* lesions, which reveal certain functional deficits, at the same time signify that these functions are actualizing only through the maturation of the respective brain areas, i.e., naturally occur in certain phases of development.

The studies by David H. Hubel and others do show that there are developmental windows that must be utilized, if we want to develop the functions—here: seeing/vision—at all (Hubel 1989, 197ff.). If the sensitive time span passes unutilized, the function of seeing cannot be established later.

The most significant issue is, however, if and in how far appropriate stimuli and targeted training can bring about maturation and possibly accelerate it. Probably, we can assume reciprocal effects. Certainly, a stimulus-response dynamic in the sense of "use it or lose it" is an essential factor to the development of the brain and its reorganization. In regard to pedagogy, this issue has two implications: First, it is not certain that early challenges (like those posed by learning programs for babies) are really beneficial for development. Likewise, it still remains unclear whether such early challenges may be harmful. Second, many studies that focus on adolescence show that adolescents cannot yet draw on certain faculties before they have naturally developed and matured. Can we conclude that we should not even try to deal with that issue? Hardly. There is the possibility that the interaction between stimulus and natural maturation processes could be productive. Foremost, the knowledge of this issue inspires us to deal in an understanding way with the peculiarities of adolescent behavior.

One argument still deserves consideration. Studies show that stimulating an early development of cognitive faculties is possible, but that later on such children recalibrate to the same level as those who got a later start; this suggests that such faculties might develop with less effort if they are called up at a later age, after the neuronal foundations are already established and available (Pauen 2004b, 521ff.; Stern 2004, 531ff.).

- As referenced above, Giedd's findings show that the adolescents' qualitative focus on their own activities or those of their educator's choosing—their type and methods (content and quality)—are of crucial importance and demonstrate the relevance of such activities, because of their effect on the brain, which is in the process of restructuring and reorganizing and is therefore particularly sensitive.
- Physiologically, the reorganization of the brain is due to erasing imprints that are not—or are no longer—useful, i.e., the dismantling of grey matter along with a simultaneous buildup of white matter in the brain, which stabilizes the function of active synaptic structures. Therefore, this process does not lead to any increase in overall brain volume, which may have led to the earlier, erroneous view that the brain is already fully developed at that time.
- This development extends also to the cerebellum. The insight comes into ever clearer focus that the cerebellum's range of functions reaches—contrary to earlier views—far beyond the steering function of the body's motoric responses. More and more studies show the connection between the cerebellum and certain areas of the cerebral cortex, which are regarded as a substrate of mental processes. Research supplies ever more substantiation for the hypothesis that dexterity development is connected to thought formation processes and language skills, meaning that the cerebellum is also of significance for mental processes and faculties.
- These insights lead to the pedagogical question: Should we not offer adolescents around the time of puberty an especially rich and appropriate movement program that is prone to foster skillful, elegant body movements and musicality?
- Likewise of importance is the insight that intelligence (IQ) is not a constant. Especially in puberty, the IQ can move up- or downward (Ramsden et al. 2011). This invites pedagogues to conclude that during this time, teaching didactics and methods are of particular import, as are the types of extracurricular activities outside of school.
- The onset of puberty limits the time of new development in the part of the brain called the retrograde prefrontal cortex, which is responsible for executive frontal cerebral functions (Förstl 2004).[7]
- However, the time span of this development differs according to anterograde gender-specific factors: In the female gender, it lasts until the approximate age of 19. In male individuals, it extends up to the mid-20s and partially even longer than that. Keeping this in mind, we can find explanations for the behavioral changes in adolescents and also for the time-differences in mental and social maturation of the genders. These findings should lead to pedagogical consequences, they establish a new basis from where we can understand adolescents and their gender-specific developmental differences. This may possibly be an indicator for the reasons why boys show a slower development in their social behavior than girls, who mature earlier in that respect and it may also explain why boys today often constitute the "problem group." For pedagogy, the further question arises: Are

there new arguments for a gender-specific form of education and instruction or at least for a way of socializing that is appropriately adjusted?

- Precise knowledge of the physiological substrate is helpful for a deeper understanding of the students' psychological development; that means the knowledge and consideration of the processes in the prefrontal cortex and in the limbic system, and specifically also in the *nucleus accumbens*, the part of the brain that is assigned to the so-called gratification system. A problem lies in the fact that the controls of the pre-frontal cortex mature a bit later than the function of *nucleus accumbens*. Yet, activities such as learning or social behaviors are dependent on the development of a balanced interplay between control, the ability to adopt other perspectives (pre-frontal cortex) and emotions or instinctual drives (limbic or meso-limbic system) (Bauer 2015). Successful learning, for example, always requires a form of behavioral "asceticism"—refusing to be distracted by tempting diversions or keeping to higher level goals (ibid.).
- We can come to a more comprehensive understanding of adolescent behavior by studying Rudolf Steiner's references to teachers' content-related preparation for the instruction of adolescents. Steiner placed great value on teachers gaining in-depth knowledge of the adolescents' "inner psychological landscape" and on observing them keenly (Götte 2011; Götte et al. 2009; Steiner 1986, p. 83).
- The physiological changes are associated with changes in thought structures directed toward hypothetical and deductive thinking, logical stringency, and formal-operative thought patterns. Around the 12th year, the brain is being imprinted for life as the organ that is instrumental for our "I" in directing the basic functions of our soul, mind, emotions, and actions. The pedagogically relevant question arises: How should we didactically plan our teaching activity in the light of these insights? Should we foster intellectual learning before this phase in order to stimulate corresponding development in the brain—or else should we only ramp up our efforts at a time when the brain has naturally developed a basis for such learning?[8]

Practical Waldorf education has always favored the latter option. With all due caution, we might come to understand, why Steiner called for avoiding any one-sided, premature cognitive development. It is only in puberty that brain structures are developed, which allow for a meaningful abstract comprehension of natural science and causality-based methods in the learning process. Steiner's approach rather follows the maxim, "Cultivate and utilize that which is naturally developing: Do not pull on the blade of grass to make it grow faster."

The combination of attachment- and brain research substantiates that in childhood stable emotional and social attachments are necessary for proper brain development (Hüther 2003). We must ask: Is this, possibly in other form, also true for the time of puberty? This could correspond to Steiner's meaning of the term *authority*. We may assume that stable relationships with caregivers and educators are important in this chaotic phase of reorganization, which starts around the 12th year; however, such relationships must be adapted to this beginning phase of development geared more and more toward self-directedness and autonomy (Bauer 2015). Only now the brain structures develop, which form the basis for inner-directed social behavior and for independent learning and thought processes. The cybernator receives his steering wheel, which he first must learn how to use. [(Translator's note: Reference to a Super Nintendo game called Cybernator.]

These studies brought to light new insights into the reasons, why adolescents behave so differently, especially in regard to risk-taking. Male adolescents in particular tend to test the limits of their powers and possibilities, getting into dangerous, exciting situations that are barely controllable anymore.

4 Select examples from brain research

The following section of this article presents select examples from studies exploring one area of brain changes (in particular in the cerebellum) during adolescence and covers other areas more in form of an annotated open list. This approach was chosen because of the overwhelming number of studies, which we cannot all cover in the same detailed way. This also applies to the scientific findings. We will preface these examples with some facts on the overall maturation of the brain, with focus on the development of the prefrontal cortex.

4.1 The development of the brain and of the prefrontal cortex

The development of myelinization (white matter) is of particular interest. The fatty sheath around the axons considerably increases the speed of neural signals. From childhood on and throughout puberty, the volume of white matter increases continuously. Myelin also impacts other functions: "Myelin does not only maximize the speed of transmission but also modulates the timing and synchrony of the neuronal firing patterns that create functional networks in the brain" (Giedd et al. 2009, p. 2). This also affects the speed and efficiency of mental processes.

Interestingly, white and grey brain matter develop differently in respect to volume: "Whereas WM (white matter) increases during childhood and adolescence, the trajectories of GM (gray matter) volumes follow an inverted U-shaped developmental trajectory" (Giedd et al. 2009, p. 3). This dynamic explains why the brain volume does not grow in puberty.

The increase in white matter roughly balances out the decrease in grey matter. Involved here are the prefrontal cortex, the temporal lobes, the cerebellum, and the corpus callosum. Gray matter first increases, its density grows in pre-puberty, and then it decreases again (around 11–16/17 years of age). Studies show both increase *and* decrease, with the decrease being interpreted as the loss of less important neuronal connections, simultaneously with the stabilizing increase of more important ones.

This reorganization renders mental processes more efficient and safer; i.e., around puberty we can reach complex cognitive achievements more and more effectively and there is an increase in our control over emotions, thought formation, and actions (executive functions). Presumably, this is a process called *synaptic pruning*, i.e., unused synaptic connections are dismantled and thus the efficiency of the newly acquired synaptic relationships grows.[9] More recent studies (Brown et al. 2012, 1693ff.) show that, e.g., the average thickness of the cortex decreases with age in a linear fashion (between age 3 and 20) and matures relatively late until approximately age 20. In contrast, the total cortical surface increases until about 12.3 years of age and then again decreases somewhat. With the stricture of longer-lasting brain plasticity and the somewhat varying maturation times in different brain areas, we can say that around this time span we establish the "final" architecture of the mature, adult brain.

Timewise, the maturation of gray matter in primary sensory-motoric areas predates the development in areas of a higher order, i.e., the dorsal-lateral prefrontal cortex and other areas (Giedd et al. 2009, p. 3).

This developmental time lag occurs in various areas. Again and again, we hear that this has effects on the development of mental, higher functions such as memory and object perception, which later relate to such elementary functions as maturation of motoric and perceptual areas (Lenroot, Giedd 2006, p. 723). Among the relatively late events in the brain's structural development is the maturation of the prefrontal cortex (gauged by the thickness of the gray matter). The studies of Joacquin Fuster (Fuster 1989) and, later, others have shown that here we find the physical substrate for planning and organizing, for designing one's own life as well as for stern commitment to set goals.

Moreover, here we also find the basis for formative elements of one's personality, which are particularly important for living one's life: moral behavior, strength of character, and many other personality attributes.[10]

To round out the picture, the focus on maturation of white brain matter shows that it plays an important role in the development of cognitive, emotional, and social functions and, last but not least, in the motoric development during childhood and adolescence.[11]

There are many more insights from brain research that are interesting to pedagogy. Let me just mention two more examples before taking a closer look at some select phenomena, because these examples could also prove significant for the issue regarding "windows of development."

4.1.1 Working memory

Research shows that the effectivity of working memory is connected to maturation of a certain area in the prefrontal cortex. Here, too, it proves true that, before reaching maturity, children cannot or can only barely accomplish certain achievements and tasks. Children and adolescents, for example, cannot easily solve any so-called manipulative tasks. These tasks entail memorizing a given fact and then processing the task on the basis of that memory. This is an important competency for many areas of life, such as the organization of one's daily schedule or solving mathematical problems (Crone 2011, 56ff.; Crone et al. 2006).

In this context, the prefrontal cortex (particularly the dorsolateral prefrontal cortex) plays an important role. As already described, this area only matures in adolescence. Only after approximately age 12, do the achievements of adolescents slowly calibrate to adult levels. This insight is significant not only because it holds relevance for practical classroom instruction (e.g., task selection; complexity of the teacher's presentation) and for the demands placed on the students regarding a more complex mental organization; this finding is also significant because apparently here too it is only a specific development in the brain that functionally enables certain achievements.

4.1.2 Visual perception

Visual perception, too, or more precisely its processing in regard to assessing, e.g., distance or tilt of objects, develops only around the 12th year of life far enough that it comes up to par with adult perception. This depends on the connection now possible of purely visual perception and cognitive processing (estimates, assessments) (Nardini et al. 2010). Studies have demonstrated that adults reduce uncertainty in assessing visual objects (distance, tilt, incline, etc.) by synthesizing and integrating different sources of information. While this is already possible around age eight, this faculty only develops fully around age 12. This is not only true for the faculty of seeing, but also for other sense perceptions. We reach the optimal stage "by a weighted averaging of estimates, in which each estimate is weighted in proportion to its relative reliability" (ibid., p. 1). Let us mention here that this development—especially when focusing on only one sense modality—can also lead to errors, since a child may perform better than the average. This brings up the interesting question for art education, as to how these insights might be usefully applied in designing an age-appropriate curriculum.

There is an asymmetric development (accelerated maturation) in feeling-associated brain areas in the limbic system compared to that in the prefrontal cortex (relatively delayed maturation Giedd et al. 2015b), which means that adolescents have difficulties with action- and impulse control, struggle with assessing the consequences of their own actions, and have trouble with focused thinking and moral behavior.[12] This development and growth is in part due to an increase in synapse formation and in part to ongoing, progressive myelinization of the nerve-pathways (increase in the speed of signal transmission). While at first the synapse density in the prefrontal cortex rises, we later find a process of synaptic elimination, a reduction in synaptic density, which however enables a surge in efficiency and fine-tuned calibration of neuronal processes.[13]

As the prefrontal cortex, specifically the dorsolateral prefrontal cortex, matures, we associate the executive functions mentioned above with their development. Lenroot and Giedd write: "Notably late to reach adult levels of cortical thickness is the dorsolateral prefrontal cortex, involved in circuitry subserving control of impulses, judgment, and decision-making. The implications of late maturation of this area have entered educational, social, political and judicial discourse in matters ranging from whether minors are cognitively mature enough to qualify for the death penalty to the age at which teenagers should be allowed to drive" (Lenroot, Giedd 2006, p. 723).

Associating complex functions, as those mentioned above, is as generally widely accepted. However, most researchers view this association with some caution. Issuing an important warning against a hasty association of *brain-behavior-relationships,* researchers emphasize: "In these debates, there is a tendency

Adolescence and the Findings of Brain Research

to overestimate our understanding about the relationships between brain biology and behavior or cognition, especially on an individual basis. [...] Nonetheless, correlations have been identified between some aspects of brain structure size and functional capacity. Several studies have shown that there are correlations of brain structural measures with IQ on both whole-brain and regional levels" (Lenroot, Giedd 2006, 723ff.).

The interconnection between prefrontal cortex and limbic system further develops— as mentioned above—at a slow pace. That means, only now the neurobiological basis develops for self-directed action and consciously controlled operations in the outlined fields of behavior. The faculty of abstract thinking grows, along with the possibility to see oneself in the perspectives of others (perspective transfer), not only leading to the possibility of better behavior control and more mature social behaviors but also to new problems in emotional processing (Bauer 2015; Rosso et al. 2004, 355ff.; Yurgelun-Todd, Killgore 2006, 194ff.).

Even when the brain reaches its final volume around age 14, its inner reorganization generally continues until the end of school age (18–19), yes, even may proceed into the early 20s.[14] This provides a good example for a different take on the connection between mental faculties and the physical-organismic basis: We can *also* understand it as the maturation of certain organs (here: the brain) results in the *possible access of conscious, self-directed individuality* in the sense of a mutually reciprocal effects, i.e., we can choose—or not—to support and foster the organic maturation process through learning and educational measures, and, reciprocally, the organ's development also promotes new learning abilities. If it is not met with challenges, the organ's development may possibly remain incomplete, just like in the locomotor system (Hüther 2004; Spitzer 2004, 165ff. and 330ff.).

Two facts here are of high interest for pedagogy: First, we have to assume that our everyday knowledge of changes in the abilities and behaviors of adolescents are based on corresponding changes in the adolescent brain and, therefore, we have to consider the possibility that we cannot just expect and demand certain behaviors but that we need to understand that the physiological foundations must first develop in the process of further brain maturation. Second, closer examination of these phenomena shows that we are dealing here with a development that follows different timelines according to gender (sexual dimorphism; Section 4.3).

It is important for teachers to know about these processes. We not only can adopt very different behaviors and attitudes toward these adolescents, if we know just how very intensely they are engaged in their inner struggle in regard to these processes; but also we can more responsibly try to choose and present contents and methods, if we know that in all our teaching we help imprint this adolescent's brain, its final form, and future possibilities.[15]

4.2 Excitation and inhibition

More recent research has tried to trace back nonlinear behavioral changes in adolescence to changes in brain structure, in particular to the asynchronistic development of different brain areas as described above. It is very important for decision-making behavior, if we can take one action and desist from another one. For example, if we can exercise emotional control when experiencing aggression, we will not respond with (possibly even stronger) aggression of our own or even violent behavior; if we can manage our reaction and curb our own aggressive attitude. This ability also plays a role in choosing between short-term success or reward and a goal we can only reach in the long term (Roth 2011, 55ff.).[16] For adolescents, this *[self-control]* is often sufficient for deciding between learning and "going disco" or other entertainments.

Brain research has found evidence that such processes may actively involve two sectors of the brain. One sector is the middle limbic system, which also acts as a substrate for feelings and emotional assessments. Specifically, it is the *nucleus accumbens*, the part of the *ventral striatum* that is activated here, whose functions are also known as the "reward system."

Furthermore, this also plays a role in addictive behavior[17] and in risk-taking (risk-related behavior).[18] One theory assumes that this brain area is highly active in adolescence and that other areas, like the pre-frontal cortex, which did not mature at the same rate, can only exercise weak control functions, which is why adolescents tend toward risky behavior and brush aside efforts that are demanded of them in favor of emotional actions that they find more desirable.

Another theory assumes that this (reward) system still is relatively weak and therefore the satisfaction they strive for can only be reached through heightened stimulation. They must hear music at an ever-higher volume, movies must offer ever more exciting action, drinking alcohol must end up in excessive binge-drinking, etc. One study concludes that only further research could help solve this problem.[19] Some studies show that 12-year-old adolescents and those a little older have as yet not developed a mature inhibition area (ventrolateral prefrontal cortex) for recognizing risks and regulating risk-taking; therefore, these adolescents are not yet able to "curb risky processes as well as adults can." This is par-ticularly true after approximately the 12th year of age; by age 18, the respective brain area develops far enough for the inhibiting effect reaching the same level as that in an adult.[20]

Brain areas such as the orbito-frontal, the dorsolateral frontal, and the somatosensory cortex are involved in the connections between emotions and the capacity for assessing the short- and long-term consequences of a decision. Studies of patients suffering from damages to their orbito-frontal cortex revealed a problem insofar as they increasingly made decisions that led to short-term gratification, and they even could give an intellectual assessment of long-term consequences, but they could not align their actions accordingly (Crone 2011, 103ff.; Damasio 1994). The respective brain areas only reach maturity in the process of development that extends from adolescence up to young adulthood. "For teenagers it is therefore still difficult to gain a full overview of the long-term effects of their actions. They are more invested in a chance for short-term gratification than in making a safe decision" (Crone 2011, 1134ff.).

Part of the basal ganglia stimulate actions by being receptive to gratifications, even if they are only imagined. This part is controlled through connections to the prefrontal cortex (impulse control; Fuchs 2008, p. 213). Considering the "belated" maturation of this part, we can understand how adolescents—whose prefrontal cortex has not yet fully developed—still have ample room to make decisions that are motivated by anticipated rewards. That is how they arrive at risky decisions for seemingly senseless ventures that test boundaries and promise particularly great kicks while they pose potentially high risks to health or even their life. It is not that adolescents cannot intellectually comprehend such risks—they simply are prone to act in a risky way even though they know about the dangers (Steinberg 2005).

4.3 Different brain development in girls and boys

We shall now shed some light on another aspect that we already briefly mentioned: the sexual/gender gap: the gender-specific development of some of the brain areas in boys and girls, and the consequences of such a gap. The differently timed development in boys and girls counts among the most important insights of neurophysiology. While this process is completed in girls by the end of their schooling—i.e., around age 18—it takes much longer in boys, up to their mid-20s or partly even until the end of the second decade of life. Every teacher dealing with age cohorts knows this scenario: In the 8th and 9th grades both boys and girls age 13–14 are sitting in class together, and the girls are often already young women, who—though not always—show a much more reasonable behavior and some self-confidence. Here, too, we deal with a distinctive fact of brain development.

Total brain volume on average reaches its developmental peak in girls around age 10.5, in boys this peak occurs around age 14.5. That means, in girls, the development of grey matter is maximized one to three years earlier than in boys.[21]

However, the interpretation of this sexual dimorphism is notably quite difficult. The phrase "size matters" is ambiguous in regard to its contents. What researchers always emphasize is that size (volume/

surface area) cannot yet securely be taken as a determinant of the package, i.e., the neuronal density per unit and other factors. Size alone does not permit us to simply make inferences about intelligence or qualities of behavior.

The National Institutes of Health (NIH) conducted the largest study on this topic in 2007 and found unequivocal gender-specific differences in development as regards volume and timing. But the question about density remained open. The study showed that total brain volume not only differed within a certain range of averages, but also that the maximum brain size was reached at different times: According to this study, girls reach their maximum on average around 10.5 years of age, while boys reach it on average around 14.5 years. This brain-volume-related difference is greater than the development in body size, which this study factored out. On the other hand, the study found that male and female brain development gradually converged in later adolescence and youth (around 22 years) (Raznahana et al. 2010). On the basis of these findings in regard to gender-specific timing of development in the prefrontal cortex and also the limbic system (in particular in the amygdala)—and with all necessary caution—we can therefore draw the conclusion as to why inhibitory functions vs. affective impulses are earlier operative in girls than in boys.[22]

Due to such findings, we can yet surmise that the behavioral difference in gender-specific development also is a phenomenon reliant on brain maturation. For pedagogy, this brings up two consequences: First, that we should deal differently with the two genders in school as well as at home; second, that in co-educational schooling there is possibly a kind of beneficial pedagogic effect that girls may have on the behavior of boys. The reverse may also engender positive effects. Therefore, in this phase of development would not necessarily be a good course of action to separate the genders into different classes.

4.4 The cerebellum—views, symptoms, development

While the anatomy of the cerebellum was relatively well researched already early on, the understanding of its functions was very limited (Thompson 1990, 24ff.). Essentially, scientists saw this part of the brain as the steering center for motoric processes. Two areas of research changed this understanding profoundly: on one hand, classic lesion research and on the other hand, studies on neuronal connections with structures both in the cortex and in the limbic system.

Lesion research showed that in the case of malformations and illness, deficiencies and changes occur not only in the area of motor skills, but also in emotional behavior, in speech competency and many cognitive functions. The researchers even described and named a special type of illness: the "cerebellar cognitive affective syndrome" (CCAS; Schmahmann 2004). Since then, ever-new aspects are coming into view, in particular regarding cognitive functions[23]; meanwhile, research arrived at recognizing intense circular interconnections with cortical structures. In particular, longitudinal studies served to observe the development of the cerebellum and the consequences of changes across longer time spans, which in turn became possible by employing new technologies such as fMRT (Tiemeier 2010, 63ff.). Anatomical studies, image-generating technology, and neuropsychological research all have variously supported the observation of activities in the cerebellum during motoric activities and likewise during cognitive efforts (Stoodley 2012).

Overall, the view seems outdated that holds cerebellar functions to be mostly limited to apply to motoric skills; at least we can see more and more support for the hypothesis that the cerebellum involves multifunctional processes in interacting with the cerebral cortex and other brain areas. The following statement bolsters this new understanding:

> The cerebellum has traditionally been associated with balance, motor control and the ability to learn complex motor sequences. However, a growing body of literature indicates that the cerebellum also plays a prominent role in higher cognitive functions. For instance, cognition but also emotion regulation is affected in patients with vascular and degenerative cerebellar disease.[24]

Again, the developmental aspect is of interest to the topic. Obviously, the cerebellum develops not only in childhood, but throughout the years up to adulthood as well. Like the development in the frontal and prefrontal areas, the cerebellum reaches its peak of development in girls on average at 11.8 years; boys are an average of 15.6 years old when they reach the same point in development, with the volume in boys being 10%–13% larger. These findings have been substantiated since 1996 (Caviness et al. 1996, 726ff.).

We also want to point to further aspects that most likely connect over to the functions of the cerebellum and encourage a stronger focus on its development. Researchers suspect that the development of vision and the understanding of time—that means also the understanding of grammatical forms (tenses, verb-conjugation)—are connected with cerebellum development. The findings so far suggest that there is a connection between temporal and spatial concepts and that both hemispheres of the cerebellum play an important role in linking memories (past) with the present or future time (Oliveri et al. 2009).

Already in 2004, the psychologist and professor for teaching- and learning-research at the Swiss Federal Institute of Technology in Zurich (ETH Zürich), Elsbeth Stern, wrote: "Among the interesting findings of newer brain research is the realization that that we cannot limit ourselves to observing the cerebral cortex, when we study higher mental processes that are unique to human beings. That also means, for example, that the cerebellum's function does not only [...] extend to regulating the equilibrium, but that it is also involved in sophisticated, complex processes of learning and thinking. Psychological learning research furnishes mounting evidence for close connections between physical activity and thinking, e.g., in gesticulation. It is to be expected that merging the findings of psychology and brain research will lead to an intermediate development of integrative theories, linking thought and behavior" (Stern 2004, 531ff.).

In an interview, Jay N. Giedd summarized this already in 2003 and thus pointed to a direction where we may find interesting ideas for our pedagogical practice. He stated that the cerebellum is hardly subject to genetic controls, but is especially open to influences from the surroundings. This is particularly true for the changes in adolescence. This development goes on until the early 20s. True, the cerebellum is in charge of muscular movement and coordination. However, just as we know that it originates graceful movement and makes one into a good dancer or athlete, likewise "we now know it is also involved in coordination of our cognitive processes, our thinking processes. Just like one can be physically clumsy, one can be kind of mentally clumsy. And this ability to smooth out all the different intellectual processes to navigate the complicated social life of the teen and to handle mental processes smoothly and gracefully instead of lurching through them, [...] seems to be a function of the cerebellum" (Giedd 2002b).

From all these pointers, we can draw the following conclusion: This area of the brain depends in its development particularly on external influences and is much less predetermined by genetics; it undergoes intense development during adolescence, and we should pay special attention to it, because all depends on how its unfoldment is constellated at this time. The interactions between cognitive and movement areas indicate an interconnected web of effects between movement skills and thought- and speech processes, which certainly should be subject to further research. (See an overview of research topics in Beaton, Marien 2010.)

It looks like it is not only important that adolescents move, but also *how* they move. The notion arises that movements requiring skillfulness, i.e., elegant, flowing, coordinated movements, logical, i.e., choreographically meaningful body expressions—these all could also be beneficial for developing such skillfulness in thinking and speaking. In practical terms, certain types of movement would be predestined for practicing such movement, such as dance, athletic disciplines such as running or swimming, and eurythmy in Waldorf schools.

In practice, this has long been intuitively implemented. Already Rudolf Steiner saw a connection here, considering for example knitting, form drawing (learning to draw complex forms) and eurythmy to be beneficial for the development of thinking competency. In regard to needlework and knitting for girls *and* boys, he remarked on the significance of skillful finger movement for the development of thinking: "Our finger movements are to a high degree also the teachers for elasticity of our thinking"

(Steiner 1987, p. 24). For children, who are weak in mathematics, he recommended extra lessons in gymnastics and eurythmy in order to strengthen their abilities (Steiner 1984, p. 93, 1987, p. 141).

The brain only offers opportunities for development. However, the surroundings must stimulate and make use of these opportunities. Summarizing some of the previously presented findings and facts, in the time after approximately 11–12 years, generally after the sixth grade, a task emerges that we must attend to: we must cultivate physical movement skills in adolescents and, in a parallel process, we must stimulate their thought activity in such a way that it permeates and, most importantly, develops a variety of cognitive processes so they can arrive at full comprehension. In Waldorf schools, for example, the first block lesson in physics is taught in 6th grade, the first one in chemistry in 7th grade; but in that time, the students also need to study history in order to develop, e.g., causal thinking with new methodological understanding (Steiner 1990, 113ff., 1993, p. 75). But this is only a beginning in fulfilling this developmental task. The actual focus will have to emerge in the transition to senior high school and the following years. It is frequently assumed that quality and efficiency of cognitive achievements change and reach a new stage by developing combinatory thought processes, proportionality, probability thinking, and arriving at logical conclusions or the ability to isolate variables.[25] We may assume that the movement activities outlined above have a supportive effect here.

At any rate, it will be of interest also to pedagogues to follow further developments in brain research especially in these areas.

5 On the reception of neuroscientific studies

A considerable part of literature, both from the side of Waldorf education and from the educational science, takes a skeptical stance toward brain research and questions the usefulness of its findings. This is a problem, already recognized by Eveline Crone, which has sprung from a naïve overestimation of such brain research findings and their unqualified interpretation as well as generalization. Crone speaks of "Neuro-myths" that, in the wake of the "triumphal victory march of educational neuroscience," led to faulty interpretations of brain research (Crone 2011, p. 90).

This skepticism applies in part to the validity of studies (transferability of animal research) and how their results can be used in pedagogic practice; it often elicits statements like: "This is just old knowledge in a new form. Indeed, some insights about the behavior and competency of children and adolescents are commonly known and not new at all." But it is easy to overlook the accompanying cognitive gains that come with the insights on the reasons for certain behaviors, abilities, and inabilities, and how they are connected to facts of physiological development. We can learn here to understand them as based on natural processes and thus to take them into consideration.

Also, pedagogy's reception of neuroscientific research findings does actually encounter some obstacles. We must realize the difficulty of attempting to connect three disciplines that each are highly complex: first, the insights of biological brain development; second, developmental psychology's understanding of adolescent development; and third, the experiences and questions emerging from pedagogical practice. This outlines a challenge for interdisciplinary research, which so far still remains largely unmet.

We can illustrate the difficulties of such a bridging task in a simple example: The most frequently asked questions that guide neuroscientific research stem from a non-scientific field. For example, research aims at exploring certain brain areas and their functions that are of preeminent importance for mathematical thinking. But that is only possible through the intersubjective communication of experiences that can only be accessed through introspection.

5.1 Examples from educational science developmental psychology

Only around the middle of the last century did educational science in Germany focus more intensely on the findings of brain research and their consequences for pedagogy. Timewise, we can locate the beginning of this increased focus around the end of the 1990s and the beginning of the 21st century, as evidenced, e.g., in the articles published in 2002 in *Zeitschrift für Pedagogy [Magazine for Pedagogy]*. The majority of the examples given are drawn from contributions in this magazine.

The work of Manfred Spitzer was particularly essential for the reception of brain research by pedagogic experts, in politics and in the public; it was this author, whose efforts led in 2004 to founding the Transfer Center for Neurosciences and learning (ZNL), which mainly focused on neurodidactics. Close cooperation with the government of Baden-Württemberg supported this activity.

A notable contribution was Christian Rittelmeyer's work *Pedagogic Anthropology of the Body* (Rittelmeyer 2002, 127ff.). In part of his work, he explores the interaction between brain development and environment. He found that a variety of factors influence structurally formative processes in brains of children down to zyto-architecture: not only social connections, in particular the relationships with parents, but also, e.g., the spatial design of rooms. Rittelmeyer accentuates the significance of "living concepts" that stimulate brain development in a variety of ways, e.g., through music and especially also child's play; he also points to the problem of media effects. This approach includes the (whole) body and the milieu in regard to the development of brain function and performance and thus shows that a critical involvement of neuroscientific research holds the possibility of fruitful contributions to pedagogic issues.

In 2004, the *Zeitschrift für Erziehungswissenschaft [Magazine for Educational Science]* (ZfE col. 50, issue 4) presented a series of articles by various authors on the topic of brain research. Ulrich Herrmann spoke for a cautious reception of brain research regarding organization in processes of learning and understanding. However, this cannot replace the teachers' practical organization of learning environments, etc. Gerald Hüther develops his theory of the brain's social structuring, which he later developed more fully, and the connected insights on trust and security's positive impacts on learning processes, as well as the negative influence of fear and stress. In Gerald Roth's article, he emphasizes the central significance of active self-engagement in learning processes and he develops a list of five factors that play an important role in learning (motivation of the educator, the student's individual cognitive and emotional predispositions for learning, among others).

Anna Katharina Braun and Michaela Meier summarize a series of brain research findings and make a case for interdisciplinary research in the areas of educational science, developmental psychology, and neurosciences. Sabina Pauen explores the question: What contributions did neuroscience research make on the topic of "windows of development"? She substantiates her thesis with the example of visual learning development and the corresponding phases in brain development. She here poses the important question: What kind of conclusions we can draw "given the knowledge of critical windows of development"? Her own conclusion is that this is an issue of values. Elsbeth Stern's article points out that knowledge of the history of science and of cognitive psychology might help teachers to build a storehouse of discipline-specific pedagogic knowledge but that this information is largely general and cannot replace the teachers' actual work of methodologically preprocessing knowledge contents for learning. Still, only performance tests can ascertain actual progress in learning, which makes it so difficult "to research the kind of learning that generates meaning and understanding." Yet, an exciting issue remains to be solved in the future: which activities unfold in the brain during the learning process?

In 2006, Annette Scheunpflug and Christoph Wulf, both educational scientists, published a supplemental issue of the *Magazine for Educational Science* (ZfE) containing 14 articles from the disciplines of educational science, neuroscience, philosophy, and psychology (Scheunpflug, Wulf 2006). Nicole Becker's (educational science) article took a particularly in-depth look at a topic that she had already covered in her dissertation "The Challenge of Neuroscience for Pedagogy" (Becker 2006). She clarifies that the onset of a reception *[by neuroscience]* is to be seen in the larger context of the thematically more general question, whether biological insights were at all relevant (Becker 2006, p. 172; Rittelmeyer 2002). One of her chapters covers the development of specific methodological approaches substantiated by neuroscience (Becker 2006, 181ff.). She is particularly critical of transferring the findings based on animal experiments to pedagogical theory and practice. Many educational scientists share Becker's critique, opposing an euphoric overestimation, especially in regard to the views of some neuroscientists:

While the relationship between neurosciences and educational science was strengthened through an increased reception of the former by the latter, critical analyses show that it is too early, and possibly questionable in principle, to try to shape linear deductions from the findings of brain research into directives for educational action "because the application and 'transfer possibilities' of neuroscience for educational research are consistently overestimated" (ibid.). Becker concludes with an appeal for working toward "subject knowledge and subject expertise" within the educational sciences, in order to be able to react "with sovereignty to the statements and challenges of the neuro sciences" (Becker 2006, p. 211).[26]

Only lately did developmental psychology mention or integrate the insights about adolescence. The substantial work, *Developmental Psychology of Adolescence*, by Helmut Fend (Fend 2000), for example, did not yet mention any of the discussed research, while he discusses hormonal processes in detail and more extensively than usual. Flammer and Alsaker's *Developmental Psychology of Adolescence* (2002) also does not contain any references to brain research, except for a brief remark of the "hypothesis" that brain development occurs in episodes. While Sabina Pauen in her work *Developmental Psychology of Childhood and Adolescence* does reference newly developed research methods, she gives no contentual information about *[brain research and]* adolescence (Pauen 2008). Oerter and Montada present a brief introduction to this topic by Rolf Oerter and Eva Dreher (Oerter, Montada 2008, p. 286). This reference to developmental psychology is meant to show that the discipline is poised to integrate neuroscientific findings, but that it is overall still in the early stages of a comprehensive reception.

Moreover, a review of educational science literature shows that there are several interesting popular science presentations that are helpful for understanding and relevant to pedagogy on the subject of the research findings and their consequences, which we will outline in the following paragraphs, for example, the book by Barbara Strauch, science editor of *The New York Times*, *Why Are They So Weird? What's Really Going on in a Teenager's Brain?* (Strauch 2007). Another work written in a popular science style was published by the neuroscientist Eveline Crone, *Brain in Puberty. How Children Become Adults* (Crone 2011). This book, as well, contains a wealth of pedagogical references. That is also true for a book written in 2005 by two researchers, Sarah-Jayne Blakemore and Uta Frith, *The Learning Brain – Lessons for Education* (German edition 2006). Joachim Bauer's newest publication, *Self-Regulation. The Restoration of Free Will* (Bauer 2015), deserves special recognition. He connects essential brain development processes with facts of developmental physiology and gives many suggestions that are useful and valuable for pedagogues and scientific pedagogy.

In summary, we can say: While many brain researchers try to make the results of their studies fruitful for pedagogy and often, nearly like proselytizing missionaries, plead in favor of integration, representatives of educational science take positions that are not even remotely unified.

Critical comments are prevalent. Generally, it is acknowledged that there need to be more thorough investigations to establish whether a transfer from neuroscientific research to pedagogy is legitimate.

So far, however, it is rare to meet an optimistic attitude pertaining to the fruitfulness of this research—except for the views expressed by representatives of "neuro-pedagogy" (Gyseler 2006), which is pretty much a fringe phenomenon. The following section will have the task to show that a similarly oscillating attitude prevails in circles of Waldorf education.

5.2 Waldorf education and brain research

Waldorf education bases its educational practice on an anthropology that gives the same weight to somatic aspects as to mental and spiritual ones. Human development involving all three areas *(body, mind/soul, and spirit)* is the foundation of the Waldorf-specific *Study of Man*. Let us just mention here two aspects that are among others important for understanding this approach. First, Waldorf education always strives to see the person as a whole, i.e., always involving the three members of the human being *(body, emotions/soul, mind/spirit)* and recognize both their distinctiveness and inner differentiation as also their interconnection. Second, the aspects of soul and spirit are taken to be real and essential to man, in contrast to today's common understanding (Rittelmeyer 2011, 327ff.).[27] This leads to a very differentiated structure of the personality, as Rudolf Steiner variously described it, and as it was incorporated into the anthropological foundations of Waldorf education (Leber 1993).

To understand Waldorf education's approach to the implications of brain research presented here, we would need to further discuss these views; however, in the framework of this article that is not possible. At any rate, with its claim to anthropological substantiation, Waldorf education will have to face the challenge of dealing with the progress made in brain research. We will briefly outline the way this was handled up to now. In 1993, Stefan Leber, in his standard work for Waldorf educators, had already dedicated a short chapter to the topic of the nervous system (Leber 1993, 428ff.). From the perspective of Rudolf Steiner's anthropology, he presented somatic facts, among others on the topic of radical changes in adolescence and the spirit and soul aspects of brain development.

Puberty is here considered the threshold, when the prefrontal cortex reaches maturity and the human being can gain full mastery of its instrument, the brain; also, it is viewed as the point in time when free powers of judgment develop in highly diverse areas. This corresponds with Steiner's stance that "at this age the central theme for pedagogy is the formation of the power of judgment" (Steiner 1979, p. 178). Certainly, this shows clearly how Waldorf educational programs regard the facts of somatic development as connected with areas of mental and soul-development.

From my own experience, I can say that, in the 1970s, the Waldorf teacher seminar in Stuttgart already offered courses and lectures that included findings of brain research.

Overall, it is deemed true that representatives of Waldorf education have occasionally dealt with the topic *[of brain research findings]*, mainly in issues of the magazine *Erziehungskunst [The Art of Education]*. Andreas Neider published a collection of articles in the volume *Who Structures the Human Brain? Brain Researchers' Questions Concerning the Human Understanding of Self"* (Neider 2006); in this volume, representatives of Waldorf education—among others—address fundamental questions. This collection also contains articles by Gerald Hüther, giving an expose of his theory of the brain as a social construct and by Ernst-Michael Kranich, who describes the mental activity of the individuum as a structure-building element of the brain.

Recently, Thomas Marti wrote a paper which he closed with the remark: "Up to now I have never yet encountered a single conclusion of brain research – in the narrower sense of it being a natural science – that, e.g., could lead to making schools more humane. [...] Therefore, we would be well advised to respond to the conclusions of brain research with at least some measure of critical caution" (Marti 2012, 51ff.).

Several prominent representatives of brain research itself sparked off reflections on fundamental philosophical issues such as: Who directs thinking and behavior—the brain or an "I"? Is the equation "brain = mind/spirit" a valid one? Who forms the brain—genes, environment, or a spiritual individuality? Is there free will? And if not, what about human responsibility for actions taken? Do we need a new concept of the human being? In particular, the "Manifesto" (2004), mentioned above, gave rise to this kind of discussion. Most authors from the field of Waldorf education focus their discussions of such topics.

Bernd Kalwitz, who works as a school physician at a Waldorf school, was (as far as I am informed) the first person who dealt with the topic of adolescence and brain development in a 2008 issue of the magazine *Erziehungskunst* (Kalwitz 2008); in his contribution he included several important findings that reflected the—then current—state of research.

He aimed at awakening understanding for adolescents, who go through turbulent times due to the brain's reorganization during puberty. However, Kalwitz did not present a critical review of the findings of brain research in his article. As far as I can see, his approach did not find any further resonance. Hormonal changes, which were the focus also in articles on developmental psychology, still drew more attention. It would therefore be desirable for Waldorf education to advance the discussion on neuroscience research as well. The field that here opens up to a possible discourse with academic educational science has, so to speak, just been cleared, but not yet ploughed and planted. This results in open perspectives for such a dialog.

Axel Ziemke noted that neuroscientific research has yielded barely any suggestions for methodology, didactics, and general pedagogy. Much *[of what brain research offered]* has been known for a long time (Ziemke 2008, 31ff.). Rather, the impression arises that the studies served to "provide a foundation for pedagogy through brain research" (ibid., p. 39). Moreover, one could only interpret the findings and validate them in educational practice by including insights from the fields of psychology and social science. Ziemke also points to the methodological gaps in the "Manifesto" mentioned above. These gaps probably limited the scope of research for a long time. On the other hand, the author certainly deems this research to contribute to the understanding of pedagogically relevant phenomena.

5.3 Connections between educational science and Waldorf education for adolescents

So far, educational scientists have barely commented on Waldorf education's concept of the human being in adolescence as portrayed in the writings of Waldorf education; consequently, we find no references to the anthropological facts presented therein, even though Steiner himself held a number of lectures on the topic and Waldorf educators issued a series of publications as well (Götte 2009, 214ff.; id. 2011). A few examples may illustrate the level of such sporadic remarks from the side of educational science.

A tentative overview regarding a potential discourse between educational science and Waldorf education on the topic of "brain research and adolescence" shows that:

- a discourse between educational science and Waldorf education was to date virtually non-existent;
- educational science itself aims to communicate with then fields of brain research, with developmental psychology and other sciences, aside from the exchanges among the various disciplines within educational science;
- Waldorf education also seeks connection with developmental psychology, anthropology, and neuroscience, but rarely attempts to communicate about educational science's reception of adolescence research and brain research, respectively. This results in a communication triangle that can be called nearly classic, in which the connection between two corner points is (nearly completely) absent. This corresponds to the general situation as we have known it for many years. (On this topic see the insightful works by Frielingsdorf 2012a and 2012b.)

Ehrenhard Skiera (2010, 233ff.) and Heiner Ullrich (1987, 76ff., 2011, 128ff.) are among the very few who attempted to address this issue. The approaches that, for example, Leber (1993) presented remained entirely unconsidered. Most recently, Ullrich published a resume of his research on Waldorf education (Ullrich 2015). In this work, he emphasizes the relation of the anthropological foundations in the description of the curriculum, which aims at the "genetic" stages of development in children and adolescents impacting the inner soul development, but he does not discuss the descriptions of bodily development presented for example by Kranich (1999a, 2003) or Leber (1993). But this aspect is an essential part of the theory of development at the foundation of Waldorf education (Götte et al. 2009; Loebell 2011; Maris, Zech 2006).

6 Areas of potential discourse

There are a few issues that were newly introduced in the field of discussion due to recent insights offered by neuroscience. These are questions that Waldorf education can ask for the purpose of self-reflection. They might also be suitable for the discourse with academic pedagogy. This list may be expanded and the questions could be posed more succinctly.

I tried to use a small sample from the plethora of newer findings of neuroscience in order to demonstrate that through such ideas, we can not only arrive at new causal connections for insights that represent partly old pedagogic knowledge, but that also new insights can be won this way.

We could not engage here in a further exploration of issues that underlie the phenomena discussed here. However, this will prove necessary in the future. The discussion around the "members of being" in Waldorf education—here especially the astral body and the "I"—would need to find a new approach in relation to brain research. The "concept of beingness" *[Wesensbegriff]* meets even sharper criticism than usual from the side of educational science; educational science itself needs to deal also with these questions: Are all the mental functions, each decision, really supposed to be the work of the "author" brain? It seems to me unavoidable to pose the question, so much frowned upon, by asking: What is the nature of the human being, his constitution of soul and mind/spirit, and their relationship with the physical body; this is particularly important in view of the challenging development in neuroscience, which drained the meaning out of concepts like *spirit* and *soul*. The incremental reduction of the human being to physical-mechanistic functional units, and the respective methods for their programming, unavoidably poses such questions for all those responsible for education and formative guidance.

We could break down educational science literature's fixation on criticizing the doctrines of the so-called Hebdomad or the temperaments regarding the discussion around Steiner's phases of development. While it is true that Steiner himself highlighted these doctrines—especially in his written work *The Education of the Child in the Light of Spiritual Science* (Steiner 1987), in his lectures, he provided essential expansions and differentiations and, in particular, also new approaches to the understanding of the human nature that differs from the one outlined above. Just one example: Steiner variously emphasizes the importance of the timespan in the 12th—14th year of life. That means, he not only viewed the "classic" 7-year cycles as important segments of development, but also the so-called Rubicon watershed thresholds around years 9–10 and during the time of sexual maturation (puberty) around years 12–14, which we have variously discussed above. Based on neuroscience's theories of developmental phases, we could also begin a new discussion relating these to Steiner's system described above.

Steiner regards the 12th year of life as the time when an intellectual understanding of causality begins to mature (Steiner 1993, p. 75), a process that the teachers' instructions should gradually expand from then on up to the 12th grade. From that age on, Steiner considers the development of thinking as the core educational task, so that it can be used in the formation of one's own ability to reason, discern, and judge. This faculty of judgment should receive training, but in such a form "that the formation of their own judgment, this inner independence, appears like an ever-new awakening. Any indoctrination that we give after puberty from the outside, is an act of tyranny toward the student and enslaves him" (Steiner 1979, p. 178). We showed above that this approach harmonizes with research findings on the underlying maturation and development of the brain. Steiner remarks on this topic (ibid., p. 76): "The students must now develop a fascination with riddles, a deep and intense interest in nature, the cosmos and the world and must now comprehend causes, effects, goals and intentions. They should make use of the powers that are now available for this endeavor, otherwise these faculties are in danger of degenerating."

One question opening up for discussion concerns Waldorf education's relatively late focus—compared with public school curricula—on the natural sciences and their methods. Another topic for discussion could also lie in the question that we already touched upon earlier, whether, in view of the brain's restructuring phase after the age of 12, a new form of educational guidance would be meaningful and qualitatively different from the teaching style that Steiner recommended up to that time, which he marked with the term *authority*, which today carries connotations that are critically viewed. The complexity of the brain restructuring process, the still immature mastery of faculties, etc., all that indicate that during adolescence, there is a certain destabilization in behavior, relationships to the world and thinking, which possibly calls for such guidance that, while not authoritarian, should be based on understanding.

Furthermore, we face a question about the significance of esthetic and practical education for the development of, e.g., cognitive faculties—now with added consideration of neuroscientific insights (Rittelmeyer 2010). Is the great significance that Waldorf schools place on such instruction not yet or not *quite* up to date? Is it a matter of the form in which these classes are conducted? Are there really any transfer effects *[from physical to mental processes]* and, if so, what kind? Can't we substantiate the developmental value of these areas of education on the basis of the facts just described, even if no transfer effects occur (or are observable)? As shown above, brain research here too offers approaches to substantiation. Maybe we can thus eventually explain such a controversial sentence by Steiner as: "Between ages 14 and 15 and 20 and 21, the teacher must meet his students with panache and a certain spark that mainly serves to enliven the imagination; because, while the children develop the tendency to judge from within themselves, their judgment of us, the educators, emerges from the realm of imagination" (Steiner 1993, p. 82). Waldorf education can thus find new arguments not only for gymnastics, sports, exercise, and dance, but also for the significance of Eurythmy. One connection may be of particular interest: the relationship between sexuality/love and the cognitive processes in adolescence, which Steiner repeatedly emphasized (Steiner 1969, p. 241, 1986, pp. 73 and 135).

7 Conclusion and outlook

We could add in manifold ways to the insights presented above. This article is concerned with demonstrating that we can learn to understand the reasons for the possibilities and limits of behavior and achievements of adolescents, and thus gain new insights into their faculties, abilities, and inabilities and their interconnections to the brain's maturation processes.

We can deduce pedagogic consequences from such facts. We just cannot assume that adolescents, who appear and look like adults, are in fact already fully grown up (developmental psychology is long familiar with this phenomenon under the keyword *acceleration*). It is pedagogically helpful for the evaluation of the educator's role and task to understand what cannot yet be accomplished and what is possible on the basis of inner (organismic) developmental processes. The educator must develop this understanding and also fulfill the task of supporting adolescents in meeting their developmental challenges, which they have to master on their own ("Developmental tasks"; Götte et al. 2009). Other tasks of adolescents that are in need of pedagogical support issue from the surroundings, especially also those that adults ask them to fulfill in school and trainings (ibid.). The aim here is not to develop a mechanical image of the effects of brain development and their consequences. Rather, the concern is to develop an attitude toward adolescents that springs from understanding and consideration of the physical developmental steps and the resulting connected dispositions in mind and psyche.

Let us point out that pedagogy in Waldorf schools can also find a new substantiation for their curriculum from insights of brain research. Parts of the effort to systematically and stepwise develop the power of judgment between age 12 and the 12th grade (Rauthe 1990) are also found in numerous assignments of age-specific internships, of yearlong projects in eurythmy classes that complement sports activities, etc.

It would be an interesting research project to examine the correspondences between the developmental steps postulated in the anthroposophical study of the human being (not only focusing on the seven-year cycles!) and the respective lesson contents and methods with those known in brain research. Such studies are already available regarding other organic-physiological facts.

On one hand, I want to advocate for discussing the findings of neuroscience. Waldorf education in particular can gain important elements and perspectives for its own anthropologically based pedagogy. This is also true for educational science and developmental psychology. Through critical thoughtfulness, we must overcome the fear of amateurish interpretations of neuroscientific findings.

I deem this to constitute an outright scientific duty, particularly for the type of pedagogy of Waldorf schools: According to its own self-concept, its pedagogy should be based on a comprehensive understanding of the human being and development.

Waldorf education understands itself as a pedagogy that is based on anthroposophical anthropology. Its founding spirit, Rudolf Steiner, continuously studied anatomy, physiology, psychology, and the beginnings of brain research and incorporated their findings into the foundations of his pedagogy. Scientific progress in these fields now demands a substantiation and further development of an anthropologically based pedagogy and also the ongoing discussion of continuously unfolding insights from the field of neuroscience. We need to investigate biological phenomena and their implications for pedagogy, which could become mutually beneficial in Waldorf education's discourse with corresponding initiatives from the side of educational science.

I definitely do not agree with the occasionally propounded view that the neurosciences or brain research cannot contribute to pedagogical issues or cannot bring anything new to the discussion or offer no fruitful suggestions for educational practice. Of course, we do know that adolescents become "difficult" in puberty. But—plainly said—did we know that adolescents often have no choice and most importantly, why is that so? Did we know what amount of time the brain needs to develop into adult maturity? We knew that there are different timelines for the psychological maturation of boys and girls—all practicing educators know that from their own experience. But did we know, e.g., that this developmental difference spans several years, is evident also in the brain's development (gender-based dimorphism), and did we know that boys have to deal with this process four to five years longer than girls?

In writing this article, it became clear that it is not necessary to adopt the ideological judgment of neurocentrist, brain-fixated views in order to acknowledge the distinct benefits that the findings of brain research can offer to developmental psychology (not only pertaining to adolescence). But there is definitely a lack of a systematic presentation in this field. It is, for example, difficult to gain an overview of the important facts and simultaneously compile relevant and valid findings distilled from the flood of individual papers on this topic.

In conclusion, let me cite a lovely quote from a research scientist in this field, Eveline Crone: "As we saw in this chapter, adolescence is fortunately not only a time when we have to resign ourselves to waiting until the difficult brain of the teenager calms down again, because also in this time this difficult adolescent brain offers a full range of possibilities to develop into a unique individuality" (Crone 2011, p. 185).

Notes

1 A graph presented by Blakemore shows how the number of papers on "developmental neuroimaging" alone increased between 1996 and 2010: from 200 to about 1500. Tendency: exponential growth (Blakemore 2012).
2 In this connection, see the Rosenthal-Jacobson experiment (Rosenthal, Jacobson 1971) and others like it. In contrast, Aronson, Wilson, Akert (2008) offer a critical perspective.
3 Here see also Bauer (2015), Hüther (2006); for an anthroposophical point of view, see Heusser (2011).
4 Karolinska Institutet (2004), Bergmann, Frisén (2013), Spalding et al. (2013).
5 For comprehensive overviews see: Lenroot, Giedd (2006, p. 718ff.), Giedd et al. (2009), Giedd, Keshavan, Paus (2008, p. 947ff.).
6 For an overview of current state of research, see Giedd et al. (2009); Lebel, Beaulieu (2012, p. 5964).
7 The term *executive functions* describes those mental processes that steer actions by establishing goals, planning, and how one anticipates, deals with problems, arrives at decisions, sets priorities, and controls disruptive emotional impulses.
8 This same question comes up in regard to Piaget's phases of intelligence development.
9 In Giedd's et al. (2009) paper this is still an open issue. Today "synaptic pruning" is regarded as an established fact.
10 See also the presentation of the famous case study on Phineas Gage in Damasio (1994).
11 Nagy et al. (2004, p. 1227ff.), Barnea-Goraly et al. (2005, p. 1848ff.).
12 Strauch (2007, p. 197ff.), Casey, Getz, Galvan (2008, p. 62ff.).
13 See also Giedd (2004, p. 77ff.), Gogtay et al. (2004), Giedd et al. (2004, p. 817ff.), Morasch (2007, p. 476ff.).
14 Fuster (1989), Lebel, Beaulieu (2012, p. 10937ff.), Giedd et al. (1999, p. 273ff.), Giedd (1997, 1999, p. 273ff., 2004).
15 This also true, even in older age, if this organ retains a high "plasticity."
16 Roth specifies that the dorsal part of the anterior cingulate cortex plays the most significant role in risk-taking behavior.
17 Giedd et al. (2015a), gives an overview on addictive behavior and mental illness in adolescence.
18 Bjork et al. (2004, p. 1793ff.), Casey et al. (2008, p. 62ff., 2010, p. 225ff.), Sturman, Moghaddam (2011, p. 1471ff.), Somerville et al. (2011, p. 2123ff.).

19 However, this study is based on only a small number of subjects: Involved were 12 adolescents ages 12–17 and 12 young adults ages 22–28 (Bjork et al. 2004, p. 1793ff.).
20 Galvan et al. (2006, p. 6885ff.); on "Go/No-Go" experiments see Crone et al. (2006) and Crone (2011, p. 62ff.).
21 For further details, see Lenroot, Giedd (2006, p. 718ff) and Giedd et al. (2009, p. 3).
22 On these findings, see the overview by Strauch (2007); furthermore Killgore et al. (2001), Blakemore, Choudhury (2006, p. 296ff.), Bramen et al. (2011, p. 636ff.); variously, researchers have also explained this phenomenon by referencing the earlier development of the amygdala in girls, raising earlier and more easily triggered fears around risky decisions.
23 Fawcett, Nicholson (2010, 2011, p. 35ff.), Stoodley, Stein (2011, p. 101ff.).
24 See also A. Schmahmann (2004), and, to a limited degree, Glickstein (2007, S.R. 824ff.).
25 See also Piaget and Inhelder, similar as to the stage of formal operations. For a critical review see, Thomas, Schillig (1996, p. 99ff.).
26 The Wikipedia article on so-called "neurodidactics" (last accessed October 19, 2015) contains an overview of critical views on the transferability of neuroscientific insights to pedagogy or with the hope to be able to develop a consistent pedagogy based on such insights.
27 Christian Rittelmeyer contributed to this topic by outlining possible pathways toward understanding.

References

Aronson, Elliot/Wilson, Timothy/Akert, Robin (2008): Sozialpsychologie. *6. Edition. [Social Psychology, 6th edition.]* Weinheim: Beltz.

Barnea, Anat/Pravosudov, Vladimir (2011): Birds as a model to study adult neurogenesis: bridging evolutionary, comparative and neuroethological approaches. In: European Journal of Neuroscience, 34, pp. 884–907.

Barnea-Goraly, Naama/Menon, Vinod/Eckert Mark et al. (2005): White matter development during childhood and adolescence: a cross-sectional diffusion tensor imaging study. In: Cerebral Cortex, 15, pp. 1848–1854.

Bauer, Joachim (2007): Lob der Schule – Sieben Perspektiven für Schüler, Lehrer und Eltern. *[In praise of school – seven perspectives for students, teachers and parents.]* Hamburg: Hoffmann and Campe.

Bauer, Joachim (2015): Selbststeuerung. Die Wiederentdeckung des freien Willens. *[Self-control – The rediscovery of free will.]* Munich: Karl Blessing.

Beaton, Alan/Marien, Peter (2010): Language, cognition and the cerebellum, Grappling with an enigma. Online at: www.culturacientifica.org/textosudc/cerebelo/cerebellum_cognition_languaje_Cortex10.pdf (last accessed: 03.24.2010).

Becker, Nicole (2006): Die neurowissenschaftliche Herausforderung der Pädagogik. *[Neuroscience's challenge to pedagogy.]* Bad Heilbrunn: Klinkhardt.

Bergmann, Olaf/Frisén, Jonas (2013): Why adults need new brain cells. In: Science, 340, No. 6133, pp. 695–696. Online at: www.sciencemag.org/content/340/6133/695.summary (last accessed: 03.24.2016).

Bjork, James M./Knutson, Brian/Fong, Grace W. et al. (2004): Incentive-elicited brain activation in adolescents: similarities and differences from young adults. In: The Journal of Neuroscience, 24, No. 8, pp. 1793–1802. Online at: www-psych.stanford.edu/~span/Publications/jb04jn. pdf (last accessed: 03.24.2016).

Blakemore, Sarah-Jayne/Frith, Uta (2006): Wie wir lernen. Was die Hirnforschung darüber weiß. *[The learning brain: Lessons for education.]* Munich: Deutsche Verlagsanstalt.

Blakemore, Sarah-Jayne/Choudhury, Suparna (2006): Development of the adolescent brain, implications for executive function and social cognition. In: Journal of Child Psychology and Psychiatry, 47, No. 3/4, pp. 296–312. Online at: www.icn.ucl.ac.uk/sblakemore/SJ_papers/BlaCho_jcpp_06. pdf (last accessed: 03.24.2010).

Blakemore, Sarah-Jayne (2012): Imaging brain development. In: The Adolescent Brain, 61, No. 2, pp. 397–406.

Bramen, Jennifer E./Hranilovich, Jennifer Ann/Dahl, Ronald E. et al. (2011): Puberty influences medial temporal lobe and cortical gray matter maturation differently in boys than girls matched for sexual maturity. In: Cerebral Cortex, 21, pp. 636–646.

Brown, Timothy T./Kuperman, Joshua M./Chung, Yoonho et al. (2012): Neuroanatomical assessment of biological maturity. In: Current Biology, 22, No. 18, pp. 1693–1698.

Casey, B.J./Jones, Rebecca M./Levita, Liat et al. (2010): The storm and stress of adolescence, insights from human imaging and mouse genetics. In: Developmental Psychobiology, 52, No. 3, pp. 225–235.

Caviness, V.S. Jr./Kennedy, D.N./Richelme, C. (1996): The human brain age 7–11 years, a volumetric analysis based on magnetic resonance images. In: Cerebral Cortex, 6, pp. 726–736.

Crone, Eveline A./Wendelken, Carter/Donohue, Sarah et al. (2006): Neurocognitive development of the ability to manipulate information in working memory. In: PNAS, 103, No. 24, pp. 9315–9320.

Crone, Eveline (2011): Das pubertierende Gehirn. Wie Kinder erwachsen werden. *[The adolescent brain. How children develop into adults.]* Munich: Droemer.

Damasio, Antonio (1994): Descartes' Irrtum. Fühlen, Denken und das menschliche Gehirn. Munich: Paul List.

Das Manifest *[The Manifesto]* (2004). Elf führende Neurowissenschaftler über Gegenwart und Zukunft der Hirnforschung. Was wissen und können Hirnforscher heute? *[Eleven leading neuroscientists on present and future brain research. What do brain researchers know and what can they do today?]* In: Gehirn & Geist *[Brain and Spirit/Mind]*, 6, pp. 31–37. Online at: www.gehirn-und-geist.de/alias/hirnforschung-im-21-jahrhundert/das-manifest/839085.

Fawcett, Angela/Nicolson, Rod (2010): Dyslexia, The role of the cerebellum. Online at: www.investigacion-psicopedagogica. com/revista/articulos/4/english/Art_4_45.pdf (last accessed: 04.20.2011).

Fawcett, Angela/Nicolson, Rod (2011): In: Electronic Journal of Research in Educational Psychology. 2, No. 2, 35–58. Online at: www.unirsm.sm/media/documenti/unirsm_1992.pdf.

Fend, Helmut (2000): Entwicklungspsychologie des Jugendalters. *[Developmental psychology of adolescence.]* Opladen: Leske + Budrich.

Flammer, August/Alsaker, Françoise D. (2002): Entwicklungspsychologie der Adoleszenz. Die Erschließung innerer und äußerer Welten im Jugendalter. *[Developmental psychology of adolescents. Opening up to inner and outer worlds in adolescence.]* Bern: Hans Huber.

Förstl, Hans (Ed.) (2004): Frontalhirn – Funktionen und Erkrankungen. *[Frontal lobes – Functions and diseases.]* Berlin: Springer.

Frielingsdorf, Volker (2012a): Waldorfpädagogik kontrovers. Ein Reader. *[Controversial aspects of Waldorf education. A reader.]* Weinheim and Basel: Beltz Juventa.

Frielingsdorf, Volker (2012b): Waldorfpädagogik in der Erziehungswissenschaft. Ein Überblick. *[Waldorf education in educational science.]* Weinheim and Basel: Beltz Juventa.

Fuchs, Thomas (2008): Das Gehirn – ein Beziehungsorgan. Eine phänomenologisch-ökologische Konzeption. *[The brain – A relational organ. A phenomenological-ecological concept.]* Stuttgart: Kohlhammer.

Fuster, Joaquin M. (1989): The Prefrontal Cortex. Anatomy, Physiology and Neuropsychology of the Frontal Lobe. New York: Raven Press.

Galvan, Adriana (2008): The adolescent brain. In: Science Direct. Developmental Review, 28, pp. 62–77.

Galvan, Adriana/Hare, Tod A./Parra, Cindy E. et al. (2006): Earlier development of the accumbens relative to orbitofrontal cortex might underlie risk-taking behavior in adolescents. In: The Journal of Neuroscience, 26, No. 25, pp. 6885–6892.

Giedd, Jay N. (1997): Normal brain development: ages 4–18. In: Krishnan, Ranga R. and Murali Doraiswamy (Eds.) (1997): Brain Imaging in Clinical Psychiatry. New York: Marcel Decker.

Giedd, Jay N./Blumenthal, Jonathan/Jeffries, Neal O. et al. (1999): Brain development during childhood and adolescence: a longitudinal MRI study. In: Nature Neuroscience, 2, No. 10, pp. 861–863.

Giedd, Jay N. (2002a): Interview in: Research fact and findings – a collaboration of Cornell University. University of Rochester and the NYS Center for School Safety. Adolescent Brain Development. May 2002. Online at: www.actforyouth.net/resources/rf/rf_brain_0502.pdf (last accessed: 03.24.2016).

Giedd, Jay N. (2002b): Interview: Inside the teenage brain. In: Frontline. Online at: www.pbs.org/wgbh/pages/frontline/shows/teenbrain/interviews/giedd.html (last accessed: 03.24.2016).

Giedd, Jay N. (2004): Structural magnetic resonance imaging of the adolescent brain. In: Annals of the New York Academy of Sciences, 2004, No. 1021, pp. 77–85.

Giedd, Jay N./Keshavan, Matcheri/Paus, Tomáš (2008): Why do many psychiatric disorders emerge during adolescence? In: Nature Reviews Neuroscience, 9, No. 12, pp. 947–957.

Giedd, Jay N./Lalonde, Francois M./Celano, Mark J./White, Samantha L. et al. (2009): Anatomical brain magnetic resonance imaging of typically developing children and adolescents. In: Journal of the American Academy of Child and Adolescent Psychiatry, 48, No. 5, pp. 465–470. Online at: www.ncbi.nlm.nih.gov/pmc/articles/PMC2892679/pdf/nihms-207307.pdf (last accessed: 04.15.2016).

Giedd, Jay N./Lalonde, Francois M./Celano, Mark J./White, Samantha L. et al. (2015a): Adolescent neuroscience of addiction: a new era. In: Developmental Cognitive Neuroscience, 16, pp. 192–193 (last accessed: 04.15.2016).

Giedd, Jay N./Lalonde, Francois M./Celano, Mark J./White, Samantha L. et al. (2015b): The amazing teen brain. In: Scientific American, 312, pp. 32–37.

Glickstein, Mitch (2007): What does the cerebellum really do? In: Current Biology, 17, No. 19, pp. R824–R827.

Gogtay, Nitin/Giedd, Jay N./Lusk, Leslie/Hayashi, Kiralee M. et al. (2004): Dynamic mapping of human cortical development during childhood through early adulthood. In: Proceedings of the National Academy of Sciences, 101, No. 21, pp. 8174–8179.

Götte, Wenzel M. (2006): Erfahrungen mit Schulautonomie. Das Beispiel der Freien Waldorfscs.hulen. *[Experiences with school autonomy. The example of the Independent Waldorf schools.]* Stuttgart: Freies Geistesleben.

Götte, Wenzel M. (2009): Das Jugendalter. *[The age of adolescence.]* In: Götte, Wenzel M., Peter Loebell, and Klaus-Michael Maurer (Eds.) (2009): Entwicklungsaufgaben und Kompetenzen. Zum Bildungsplan der Waldorfschule. *[Tasks and competencies in development. On the curriculum of Waldorf schools.]* Stuttgart: Freies Geistesleben, pp. 214–246.

Götte, Wenzel M./ Loebell, Peter/ Maurer, Klaus-Michael (Eds.) (2009): Entwicklungsaufgaben und Kompetenzen. Zum Bildungsplan der Waldorfschule. *[Tasks and competencies in development. On the curriculum of Waldorf schools.]* Stuttgart: Freies Geistesleben.

Götte, Wenzel M. (2011): Oberstufe und Jugendalter. *[Senior high school and adolescence.]* In: Peter Loebell (Ed.) (2011): Waldorfschule heute. Eine Einführung. *[Waldorf schools today. An introduction.]* Stuttgart: Freies Geistesleben.

Gyseler, Dominik (2006): Problemfall Neuropädagogik. *[Neuro-pedagogy – A problematic case.]* In: Zeitschrift für Pädagogik *[Magazine for Pedagogy]*, 52, No. 4, pp. 555–570.

Hubel, David H. (1989): Auge und Gehirn. Neurobiologie des Sehens. Spektrum der Wissenschaft. *[Eye and brain. The neurobiology of vision. Spectrum of science.]* Heidelberg: Verlagsgesellschaft.

Heusser, Peter (2011): Anthroposophische Medizin und Wissenschaft. Beiträge zu einer medizinischen Anthropologie. *[Anthroposophical medicine and science. Contributions to a medical anthropology.]* Stuttgart: Schattauer.

Hüther, Gerald (2003): Die Bedeutung emotionaler Sicherheit für die Entwicklung des kindlichen Gehirns. *[The significance of emotional security for the development of the child's brain.]* In: Gebauer, Karl and Gerald Hüther (Eds.) (2003): Kinder brauchen Wurzeln. *[Children need Roots.]* 3rd edition. Düsseldorf and Zürich: Patmos, pp. 15–34.

Hüther, Gerald (2004): Kinder brauchen Wurzeln. Zum Verhältnis von Bindung und Bildung. *[Children need roots. On the relationship between attachment and education.]* In: Schavan, Annette (Ed.) (2004): Bildung und Erziehung. *[Development and education.]* Frankfurt am Main: Suhrkamp.

Hüther, Gerald (2006): Die Strukturierung des Gehirns durch Erziehung und Sozialisation. *[Structuring the brain through education and socialization.]* In: Andreas Neider (Ed.) (2006): Wer strukturiert das menschliche Gehirn? Fragen der Hirnforschung an das Selbstverständnis des Menschen. *[Who structures the human brain? Questions posed by brain research regarding the self-concept of the human being.]* Stuttgart: Freies Geistesleben.

Jonas, Hans (1987): Macht oder Ohnmacht der Subjektivität. *[Appendix to: The imperative of responsibility.]* Frankfurt am Main: Insel.

Kalwitz, Bernd (2008): Schneeschmelze im Gehirn. Vom Bauchdenken zum kühlen Nachdenken. *[Snowmelt in the brain. From gut thinking to cool deliberation.]* In: Erziehungskunst *[The Art of Education]*, 2008, 5, pp. 535–544.

Karolinska Institutet (2004): Nachricht des Karolinska Institutet. www.cmb.ki.se/research/frisen/research.html (last accessed: 03.26.2016).

Killgore, William D. S./Oki, Mika/Yurgelun-Todd, Deborah A. (2001): Sex-specific developmental changes in amygdala responses to affective faces. In: Brain Imaging Neuroreport, 12, No. 2, pp. 427–433.

Kranich, Ernst-Michael (1999a): Unterricht im Übergang zum Jugendalter. Anregungen zur Bewältigung einer schwierigen Aufgabe. *[Teaching during the transition to adolescence. Impulses for mastering a difficult task.]* Stuttgart: Freies Geistesleben.

Kranich, Ernst-Michael (1999b): Anthropologische Grundlagen der Waldorfpädagogik. *[Anthropological foundations of Waldorf education.]* Stuttgart: Freies Geistesleben.

Kranich, Ernst-Michael (2003): Der innere Mensch und sein Leib. Eine Anthropologie. *[Inner man and his body. An anthropology.]* Stuttgart: Freies Geistesleben.

Lebel, Catherine/Beaulieu, Christian (2012): Longitudinal development of human brain wiring continues from childhood into adulthood. In: The Journal of Neuroscience, 32, No. 17, pp. 5964–5972. Online at: www.jneurosci.org/content/31/30/10937.full.pdf+html (last accessed: 03.26.2016).

Leber, Stefan (1993): Die Menschenkunde der Waldorfpädagogik. Anthropologische Grundlagen der Erziehung des Kindes und Jugendlichen. *[The study of man in Waldorf education. Anthropological bases for education in childhood and adolescence.]* Stuttgart: Freies Geistesleben.

Lenroot, Rhoshel K./Giedd, Jay N. (2006): Brain development in children and adolescents: Insights from anatomical magnetic resonance imaging. In: Neuroscience and Biobehavioral Reviews 30, pp. 718–729.

Loebell, Peter (Ed.) (2011): Waldorfschule heute. Eine Einführung. *[Waldorf schools today. An introduction.]* Stuttgart: Freies Geistesleben.

Maris, Bart/Zech, Michael (Eds.) (2006): Sexualkunde in der Waldorfpädagogik. *[Sex education in Waldorf education.]* Stuttgart: Pädagogische Forschungsstelle beim Bund der Freien Waldorfschulen.

Marti, Thomas (2012): Ausgehirnte Gehirnkonstruktionen. Über das Verständnis von Hirnforschung und Pädagogik. *[Brainy brain constructions. On the understanding of brain research and pedagogy.]* In: Erziehungskunst September 2012, pp. 51–55.

Meinberg, Eckhard (1988): Das Menschenbild der modernen Erziehungswissenschaft. *[The concept of man in modern educational science.]* Darmstadt: Wissenschaftliche Buchgesellschaft.

Memorandum "Reflexive Neurowissenschaft" *[Memorandum "Reflexice Neuroscience"]*. (2014): In: Psychologie Heute. *[Psychology Today, German ed.]* Online at: www.psychologie-heute.de/home/lesenswert/memorandum-reflexive-neurowissenschaft/ (Last accessed: 03.25.2016).

Morasch, Gudrun (2007): Hirnforschung und menschliches Selbst. Eine erziehungswissenschaftliche Konzeption des Selbst unter Berücksichtigung neurobiologischer Erkenntnisse. *[Brain research and the human self. An educational science concept of self, taking into consideration insights from neurobiology.]* Heidelberg: Universitätsverlag Winter.

Mukamel, Roy/ Ekstrom, Arne D./Kaplan, Jonas et al. (2010): Single-neuron responses in humans during execution and observation of actions. In: Current Biology, 20, No. 8, 2010, pp. 750–756.

Nagy, Zoltan/Westerberg, Helena/Klingberg, Torkel (2004): Maturation of white matter is associated with the development of cognitive functions during childhood. In: Journal of Cognitive Neuroscience, 16, No. 7, pp. 1227–1233.

Nardini, Marko/Bedford, Rachel/Mareschal, Denis (2010): Fusion of visual cues is not mandatory in children. In: PNAS, 107, No. 39, pp. 17041–17046. Online at: www.pnas.org/content/early/2010/09/03/1001699107. full.pdf+html (last accessed: 03.26.2016).

Neider, Andreas (Ed.) (2006): Wer strukturiert das menschliche Gehirn? Fragen der Hirnforschung an das Selbstverständnis des Menschen. *[Who structures the human brain? Questions posed by brain research regarding the self-concept of the human being.]* Mit Beiträgen von *[with contributions by]* G. Hüther, E.-M. Kranich, M. Kollewijn, R. Benedikter. Stuttgart: Freies Geistesleben.

Nitschke, Alfred (1968): Das verwaiste Kind der Natur. *[The orphaned child of nature.]* Tübingen: Niemeyer.

Oerter, Rolf/Montada, Leo (Eds.) (2008) Entwicklungspsychologie. *[Developmental psychology.]* 6th edition. Weinheim, Basel: Beltz.

Oliveri, Massimiliano/Bonni, Sonia/Turriziani, Patrizia et al. (2009): Motor and linguistic linking of space and time in the cerebellum. In: PLoS One, 4, No. 11. Online at: journals.plos.org/plosone/article?id=10.1371/journal.pone.0007933 (last accessed: 03.26.2016).

Pauen, Michael (2004a): Illusion Freiheit? Mögliche und unmögliche Konsequenzen der Hirnforschung. Frankfurt am Main: Fischer.

Pauen, Sabine (2004b): Zeitfenster der Gehirn- und Verhaltensentwicklung: Modethema oder Klassiker? *[Window of opportunity in the development of the human brain and behavior.]* In: Zeitschrift für Pädagogik, 50, No. 4, pp. 521–530.

Pauen, Sabine (Ed.) (2008): Entwicklungspsychologie im Kindes- und Jugendalter. *[Developmental psychology in childhood and adolescence.]* Heidelberg: Spektrum Akademischer Verlag.

Pauen, Michael/Roth, Gerhard (2008): Freiheit, Schuld und Verantwortung. Grundzüge einer naturalistischen Theorie der Willensfreiheit. *[Freedom, guilt, and responsibility. Possible and impossible consequences of brain research.]* Frankfurt am Main: Suhrkamp.

Popper, Karl R./Eccles, John C. (1982): Das Ich und sein Gehirn. *[The self and its brain.]* 2nd edition. Munich: Piper.

Popper, Karl R. (1997): Alles Leben ist Problemlösen. Über Erkenntnis, Geschichte und Politik. *[All life is problem solving. On cognition, history, and politics.]* 3rd edition. Munich: Piper.

Ramsden, Sue/Richardson, Fiona M./Goulven, Josse et al. (2011): Verbal and non-verbal intelligence changes in the teenage brain. Online at: www.nature.com/nature/journal/v485/n7400/full/ nature11113.html (last accessed: 03.26.2016).

Rauthe, Wilhelm (1990): Stufen der Urteilskraft. In: Zur Menschenkunde der Oberstufe (1990). Gesammelte Aufsätze. *[Levels of judgment. In: On the study of man in high school (1990). Collected articles.]* Stuttgart: Pädagogische Forschungsstelle beim Bund der Freien Waldorfschulen.

Raznahana, Armin/Lee, Yohan/Stidd, Reva et al. (2010): Longitudinally mapping the influence of sex and androgen signaling on the dynamics of human cortical maturation in adolescence. In: PNAS, 107, No. 39, pp. 16988–16993.

Rittelmeyer, Christian (2002): Pädagogische Anthropologie des Leibes. Biologische Voraussetzungen der Erziehung und Bildung. *[Pedagogical anthropology of the body. Biological prerequisites for education and formative development.]* Weinheim and Munich: Juventa.

Rittelmeyer, Christian (2010): Warum und wozu ästhetische Bildung? Über Transferwirkungen künstlerischer Tätigkeiten. Ein Forschungsüberblick. *[Aesthetic education – Why and to what purpose? On the transfer effects of artistic activities.]* Oberhausen: Athena.

Rittelmeyer, Christian (2011): Gute Pädagogik – fragwürdige Ideologie? *[Good pedagogy – Controversial ideology?]* In: Peter Loebell (Ed.) (2011): Waldorfschule heute. Eine Einführung. *[Waldorf schools today. An introduction.]* Stuttgart: Freies Geistesleben, pp. 327–347.

Rizzolatti, Giacomo/Fogassi, Leonardo/Gallese, Vittorio (2006): Mirrors in the mind. In: Scientific American, 295, No. 5, pp. 54–61.

Rosenthal, Robert/Jacobson, Leonore (1971): Pygmalion im Unterricht. *[Pygmalion in the classroom.]* Weinheim: Beltz.

Rosso, Isabelle M./Young, Ashley D./Femia, Lisa A. et al. (2004): Cognitive and emotional components of frontal lobe functioning in childhood and adolescence. In: Annals of the New York Academy of Sciences, 1021, pp. 355–362.

Roth, Gerhard (2007): Worüber dürfen Hirnforscher reden – und in welcher Weise? *[What are brain researchers allowed to talk about – and in what way?]* In: Hans-Peter Krüger (Ed.) (2007): Hirn als Subjekt? Philosophische Grenzfragen der Neurobiologie. *[Brain as subject? Philosophical avant-garde questions of neurobiology.]* Berlin: Akademie Verlag, pp. 27–38.

Roth, Gerhard (2011): Bildung braucht Persönlichkeit. Wie Lernen gelingt. *[Education needs personality. How learning succeeds.]* Stuttgart: Klett-Cotta.

Scheunpflug, Annette/Wulf, Christoph (2006): Biowissenschaft und Erziehungswissenschaft. *[Bioscience and educational science.]* In: Beiheft der Zeitschrift für Erziehungswissenschaft *[Supplemental issue of the magazine for educational science]*, 9, *[Supplement]* issue, No. 5, pp. 5–8.

Schmahmann, Jeremy D. (2004): Disorders of the cerebellum: ataxia, dysmetria of thought, and the cerebellar cognitive affective syndrome. In: The Journal of Neuropsychiatry and Clinical Neurosciences, 16, pp. 367–378.

Singer, Wolf (2006): Brain development and education. In: Biowissenschaft und Erziehungswissenschaft. Beiheft der Zeitschrift für Erziehungswissenschaft, 9, No. 5, pp. 11–20.

Skiera, Ehrenhard (2010): Reformpädagogik in Geschichte und Gegenwart. 2., überarb. edition. *[Reform pedagogy in history and present time.]* Wien, Munich: Oldenbourg.

Somerville, Leah H./Hare, Todd/Casey B.J. (2011): Frontostriatal maturation predicts cognitive control failure to appetitive cues in adolescents. In: Journal of Cognitive Neuroscience, 23, No. 9, pp. 2123–2134.

Spalding, Kirsty L./Bergmann, Olaf et al. (2013): Dynamics of hippocampal neurogenesis in adult humans. In: Cell, 153, 6, pp. 1219–1227. Online at: www.cell.com/cell/fulltext/S0092-8674(13)00533-3 (last accessed: 04.15.2016).

Spitzer, Manfred (2004): Selbstbestimmen: Gehirnforschung und die Frage: Was sollen wir tun? *[Self determination: Brain research and the question: What should we do?]* Heidelberg: Spektrum Akademischer Verlag.

Spitzer, Manfred (2006): Lernen. Gehirnforschung und die Schule des Lebens. *[Learning, brain research, and the school of life.]* Heidelberg: Spektrum Akademischer Verlag.

Steinberg, Laurence (2005): Cognitive and affective development in adolescence. In: Trends in Cognitive Sciences, 9, No. 2, pp. 69–74.

Steiner, Rudolf (1987 [1907]): Die Erziehung des Kindes vom Gesichtspunkte der Geisteswissenschaft. *[The education of the child in the light of anthroposophy.]* In: Steiner, Rudolf (1987): Lucifer – Gnosis. Grundlegende Aufsätze zur Anthroposophie und Berichte aus den Zeitschriften «Luzifer» und «Lucifer – Gnosis» 1903–1908. Rudolf Steiner GA 34. Dornach: Rudolf Steiner Verlag, pp. 309–348.

Steiner, Rudolf (1961): Der Goetheanum-Gedanke inmitten der Kulturkrisis der Gegenwart. Gesammelte Aufsätze aus der Wochenschrift «Das Goetheanum» 1921–1925. *[The spirit of the Goetheanum in the context of the contemporary cultural crisis. Collected essays from the weekly "Das Goetheanum" 1921–1925.]* GA 36. Dornach: Rudolf Steiner Verlag.

Steiner, Rudolf (1969): Die gesunde Entwicklung des Leiblich-Physischen als Grundlage der freien Entfaltung des Seelisch-Geistigen. *[The healthy development of the physical body as a basis for free unfoldment of mind/soul and spirit.]* GA 303. Dornach: Rudolf Steiner Verlag.

Steiner, Rudolf (1979): Anthroposophische Menschenkunde und Pädagogik. *[The Anthroposophical Study of Man and Pedagogy.]* GA 304a. Dornach: Rudolf Steiner Verlag.

Steiner, Rudolf (1984): Erziehungskunst. Seminarbesprechungen und Lehrplanvorträge. *[The art of education. Seminar reviews and lectures on lesson planning.]* GA 295. Dornach: Rudolf Steiner Verlag.

Steiner, Rudolf (1986): Menschenerkenntnis und Unterrichtsgestaltung. *[Insight into human nature and lesson design.]* GA 302. Dornach: Rudolf Steiner Verlag.

Steiner, Rudolf (1987): Entsprechungen zwischen Mikrokosmos und Makrokosmos. *[Correspondences between microcosm and macrocosm.]* GA 201. Dornach: Rudolf Steiner Verlag.

Steiner, Rudolf (1990): Erziehungskunst. Methodisch-Didaktisches. *[The art of education. Methods and didactics.]* 6th edition. GA 294. Dornach: Rudolf Steiner Verlag.

Steiner, Rudolf (1993): Erziehung und Unterricht aus Menschenerkenntnis. *[Education and teaching in the light of insights into the nature of the human being.]* GA 302a. Dornach: Rudolf Steiner Verlag.

Stern, Elsbeth (2004): Wie viel Hirn braucht die Schule? Chancen und Grenzen einer neuropsychologischen Lehr-Lern-Forschung. *[How much brain is needed for school? Opportunities and limits of neuropsychological research on teaching and learning.]* In: Zeitschrift für Pädagogik 50, No. 4, pp. 531–538.

Stoodley, Catherine J./Stein, John F. (2011): The cerebellum and dyslexia. In: Cortex, 47, pp. 101–116.

Stoodley, Catherine J. (2012): The cerebellum and cognition: evidence from functional imaging studies. In: Cerebellum, 11, No. 2, pp. 352–365.

Strauch, Barbara (2007): Warum sie so seltsam sind. Gehirnentwicklung bei Teenagern. *[Why are they so weird? What's really going on in a teenager's brain?]* 2nd edition. Berlin: Berlin Verlag.

Sturman, David A./Moghaddam, Bita (2011): Reduced neuronal inhibition and coordination of adolescent prefrontal cortex during motivated behavior. In: The Journal of Neuroscience, 31, No. 4, pp. 1471–1478.

Thomas, Joachim/Schillig, Susanne (1996): Die Entwicklung hypothetisch-deduktiven Denkens im Jugendalter. *[The development of hypothetic and deductive thinking.]* In: Schumann-Hengsteler, Ruth and Hanns Martin Trautner (Eds.) (1996): Entwicklung im Jugendalter. *[Development in Adolescence.]* Göttingen: Hogrefe, pp. 99–118.

Thompson, Richard F. (1990): Das Gehirn. Von der Nervenzelle zur Verhaltenssteuerung. [The Brain.] Heidelberg: Spektrum der Wissenschaft Verlagsgesellschaft.

Tiemeier, Henning/Lenroot, Rhoshel K./Greenstein, Deanna K. et al. (2010): Cerebellum development during childhood and adolescence: a longitudinal morphometric MRI study. In: Neuroimage, 49, No. 1, pp. 63–70.

Ullrich, Heiner (1987): Waldorfpädagogik und okkulte Weltanschauung. Eine bildungsphilosophische und geistesgeschichtliche Auseinandersetzung mit der Anthropologie Rudolf Steiners. 2nd edition. *[Waldorf education and occult worldview. An educational, philosophic and intellectual-historic discussion of Rudolf Steiner's anthropology.]* Weinheim and Munich: Juventa.

Ullrich, Heiner (2011): Rudolf Steiner. Leben und Lehre. *[Rudolf Steiner. Life and teaching.]* Munich: Beck.

Ullrich, Heiner (2015): Waldorfpädagogik. Eine kritische Einführung. *[Waldorf education. A critical introduction.]* Weinheim and Basel: Beltz.

Yurgelun-Todd, Deborah A./Killgore, William D.S. (2006): Fear-related activity in the prefrontal cortex increases with age during adolescence: A preliminary fMRI study. In: Neuroscience Letters, 406, No. 3, pp. 194–199.

Ziemke, Axel (2008): Kann die Pädagogik von der Hirnforschung etwas lernen? *[Can pedagogy learn something from brain research?]* In: Erziehungskunst *[The Art of Education]*, 2008, 1, pp. 31–40.

CHAPTER 4

Learning Theory

INTRODUCTION

Peter Loebell

Waldorf school students have significantly more intense and frequent feelings of joy in learning and an interest in classroom instruction than pupils at public schools (Liebenwein, Barz, Randoll 2012, p. 59). Apparently, Waldorf teachers are more successful in bringing the students to identify with what they are learning. At least some of them have the impression that the way of learning is more quintessential and intense at their schools.

The survey presupposes that researchers, subjects, and recipients of the study understand what *learning* means. But learning has become a "wholesale word" that we use in everyday conversation as well as in scientific discourse, in national economics as much as in politics (Faulstich 2013). That leaves many unanswered questions:

- What do students learn? Is it the school's curriculum content or rather elements of a "secret program of study"?
- How do they learn? Are they engaged in a regurgitation of facts that they do not understand and in producing correct solutions, or are they actively acquiring new insights and competencies? Is new content comprehended with ease or as a result of stressful work?
- Who or what functions as their teacher? Do they acquire new knowledge from teachers or peers? Are there special experiential adversities that trigger a learning process?
- What facilitates their learning? Which of their own activities (listening, reading, writing, practicing, presenting, tutoring their peers, etc.) come into play?
- When, why, and to what purpose do learning happen? In what kind of biographic situation and through what type of meaningful experience do they acquire content?

Answering the question "What is learning?," we notice first that the verb *to learn* always requires an object. But aside from the actual content to be learned (e.g., a dictated text), there is also a kind of indirect objective that indicates the overarching aim of the learning activity (e.g., understanding certain rules of orthography). These indirect objectives can be differentiated depending on their effects: Are they changing the way a learner acts, are they expanding knowledge, or do they aim at eliciting an understanding of connections?

According to Heinrich Roth, we can distinguish the following processes:

1. A type of learning mainly aiming at competencies, generating automatic capability for motoric and mental skills.
2. Learning aimed primarily at problem-solving (thinking, understanding, arriving at insights).

DOI: 10.4324/9781003187431-19

3. Learning with the main goal of memorizing knowledge and keeping it available.
4. Learning predominantly focusing on processes (learning to learn, to work, to research, to look up things, etc.).
5. Learning mainly directed at later transfer to other areas, i.e., increasing capabilities and powers (learning Latin in order to have an easier time learning Romance languages).
6. Learning with the main goal of forming mindsets, values, and attitudes.
7. Learning chiefly concerned with developing a deeper interest in a subject area (differentiating between needs and interests).
8. Learning aimed foremost at a change in behavior (Roth 1969, p. 202).

As we compare these learning goals, we conclude that they appear in no way of equal weight nor are they exclusive of each other. We could consider some of these aims as interim or partial goals. For example, the active work of learning new content can, at the same, time target the overarching goal of practicing certain thinking capabilities (Kluwe 1979, p. 80). Furthermore, the acquisition of new mental skills can also serve to learn how to work more economically. We can think of a variety of ways for how we can create hierarchical orders of the goals listed above, even though the learner may not always be fully aware of them. The learner will often pursue just short-term or midrange goals, which later may be recognized to constitute parts of a comprehensive process. Nevertheless, the subject will assume that his efforts were successful if one of the goals listed by Roth is reached.

If we consider Roth's "learning goals" as being pursued by an autonomously acting subject, we can detect a qualitative leap in this list. The first five objectives describe the expansion of future capabilities for action, while the subject does not have to face any problem of their own personality's peculiarities, preferences, and tendencies. These first five learning goals could even be put under the umbrella of the maxim that they serve to satisfy the subject's own spontaneously felt needs.

Beyond these possibilities, we can think of learning goals that aim to transform the learners' own dispositions and convictions; this fact expresses the specifically human quality of learning.

Here the differentiation becomes fuzzy between the terms *learning* and [the German] *Bildung* [which indicates a simultaneous formative education of both mind and character]. The concepts of *Bildung* and *learning* share a stronger emphasis on the individual learners' own active participation in learning and acquisition processes than the related terms *educating* and *teaching* (Wulf, Zirfas 2014). Bildung aims even more strongly at the normative quality of change, that is, at "an ideal of the human being that provides an orientation for education, learning and teaching and for the process of forming the mind and character of a person" (Wulf, Zirfas 2014, p. 18). Any person who wants to change the structure of his/her own identity based on insight counts on the continuity of a power of individuality that is not plainly apparent at first. Because when I intend to transform my own mindset, I know that I also change the very basis of my current decision. Only a human being who acts freely has this opportunity: to change oneself (identity) in order to find oneself (individuality).

The ideas about learning obviously change as we age (Marton, Booth 2014, p. 80ff.). There are different concepts of learning due to the developmental process, but there are also individual differences. Two main categories emerged in a survey of students who answered questions about their concept of learning. One type of student has a narrow understanding of learning as something "that is closely connected to a task: They describe learning with a focus on the accumulation of building blocks of knowledge and information from a text, and, if applicable, its memorization for later use" (Marton, Booth 2014, p. 63). On the other hand, there are other students who experience learning as a way to arrive at meaning through accomplishing tasks: "They see things in a new light, they refer to their own, earlier experiences and to their environment; they see learning as something that changes them in a certain way" (ibid.). So, what are students talking about when they answer questions about their learning processes?

Pedagogic psychology and learning-teaching research have intensely pursued this line of questioning since the end of the 19th century. Various theories of teaching and learning offer different approaches

Introduction

to understanding human learning. This article aims at exploring how far such theories can offer theoretical clarification for the distinctive features of Waldorf education. Rudolf Steiner expounded his understanding of human learning mainly in his numerous lectures. We will examine where and in what way Steiner's thoughts on this matter offer some connectivity for contemporary educational science.

First, Wolfgang Nieke's article offers a detailed overview of the various scientific positions that developed over the last hundred years. He presents the original models of learning psychology that are indebted to the ideal of natural science and were largely integrated without critical assessment into academic teacher-training courses. He then juxtaposes these models with new definitions of the concept of learning offered by modern educational science. In the context of educational science, Nieke writes: "Learning is deemed the basis for qualification, competency, education and *Bildung* [mind/character formation]." Against this backdrop, Nieke mentions five different approaches, each one referring to a different aspect of learning: phenomenological body experience (Meyer-Drawe), intentionality in connection with the body as the foundation for learning (Faulstich), the special structural relationship between learning and *Bildung* (Marotzki, Nohl), pedagogic theories of learning (Göhlich, Zirfas), and the transformative concept of learning (Koller).

Nieke also lists various reasons for learning (motivation, interest, relevance), points to the differences in types of learning, and mentions the cultural/scientific perspective on learning, illustrated by the example of resistance to learning and the factor of equal opportunity. He goes on to contemplate the relationship between learning and teaching and contrasts it with learning that springs from a ground of freedom, as well as learning processes that happen through group work or in antagonism to groups, before he describes an "educated [*gebildet* referring to the concept of *Bildung*] state of being" as the result of learning. After that section, Nieke discusses whether we should understand learning as content-independent (in the sense of learning psychology) or category-specific (in the sense of the educational sciences). He characterizes experience, experiment, and exploration as the three basic forms of learning and outlines a theory of emergent learning as presented by Faulstich building on Wygotski's work. In closing, Nieke points to three results of learning processes as the pedagogical consequence of his line of thought: Learning requires meaning, learning generates meaning, and learning is also the foundation of health and constitutes individuality.

The next article by Peter Loebell presents different approaches to human learning and contrasts them with the pedagogic concepts of Waldorf education, referencing Steiner's *Study of Man* with special consideration of his relevant legacy of lectures. In the introductory outline of various approaches to understanding the 20th-century concepts of learning, we already find references to Waldorf education, which spread in that same timeframe parallel to the development of the educational [Bildungs-] sciences. Loebell's article mentions the contributions of neurobiology, of learning through exploration, associative learning, and constructionist learning theories as well as first approaches to action theory in contrast to behavioral research. One section deals with the subject-oriented scientific foundation of learning by Klaus Holzkamp. Loebell goes on to introduce the concept of human individuality—in contrast to the concept of the human being as a subject—as the theoretical foundation of Waldorf education.

The next section explains some aspects of human learning that are important for understanding Waldorf education: the concept of "formative powers," learning through thinking, feeling, and willing, the significance of rhythms for learning, imitation, embodied cognition, heterogeneity, and individualization, as well as the importance of the teacher. The article closes with a summary and an outlook toward current and future areas of development for Waldorf education.

In the next article, Jost Schieren develops the epistemological foundations of Waldorf education's concept of learning. He presents a brief sketch of the historic development of the concept of learning, followed by a quick outline of Steiner's epistemology with a complementary addition by the philosopher, Herbert Witzenmann. After that, Schieren adds further depth to his deliberations by discussing Steiner's juxtaposition of "imagination" and "will," which constitute an essential basis for understanding Waldorf education, and he points to the establishment of agricultural/horticultural internships at

Waldorf schools. This line of thought leads to the unfolding of a differentiated understanding of truth that, in turn, leads to participation in the world through the relationships with phenomena and the world. He emphasizes the significance of memory and forgetting in learning and discusses the process of transformation using the example of the [German] fairy tale "Mother Holle." In his summary, Schieren reiterates once again some core aspects of learning such as transformation, forgetting, abilities, wholistic orientation, truth, and meaningfulness.

References

Faulstich, Peter (2013): Menschliches Lernen. Eine kritisch-pragmatistische Lerntheorie. *[Human learning. A critical-pragmatistic theory of learning]* Bielefeld: transcript.

Kluwe, Rainer H. (1979): Wissen und Denken. Modelle, empirische Befunde und Perspektiven für den Unterricht. *[Knowing and thinking. Models, empirical findings, and perspectives for classroom teaching]* Stuttgart: Kohlhammer.

Liebenwein, Sylva/Barz, Heiner/Randoll, Dirk (2012): Bildungserfahrungen an Waldorfschulen. Empirische Studie zu Schulqualität und Lernerfahrungen. *[Educational experiences at Waldorf schools. Empirical study on school quality and learning experiences]* Wiesbaden: VS Springer.

Marton, Ference/Booth, Shirley (2014): Lernen und Verstehen. *[Learning and understanding]* Berlin: Logos.

Roth, Heinrich (1969): Pädagogische Psychologie des Lehrens und Lernens. *[Pedagogic psychology of teaching and learning]* 11th edition, Hannover: Schroedel.

Wulf, Christoph/Zirfas, Jörg (Eds.) (2014): Handbuch Pädagogische Anthropologie. *[Handbook of pedagogic anthropology]* Wiesbaden: VS Springer.

LEARNING FROM THE PERSPECTIVE OF EDUCATIONAL SCIENCE[1]

Wolfgang Nieke

1 Our learning concept model is imported from psychology

For a long time, *learning* was not discussed as an independent concept in educational science, formative educational sciences, and pedagogy, but theoretic models were transferred over from learning psychology, since learning fell within this academic discipline's competency. *Making someone learn, teaching,* and *classroom instruction* were understood as modifiers for learning outcomes (competencies and attitudes) and belonged in the area of instructional psychology (or, more generally, of pedagogic psychology) under the umbrella of academic psychology; this subdiscipline provided orientation for subject-specific methodologies, which have always maintained autonomy from educational science, since they are unavoidably linked to the structure of the teaching content of their academic reference disciplines.[2]

Bildungswissenschaft concentrates on the selection of subject content for the task of intergenerational transmission—or enculturation—and, since 1968, it has focused with a sociological slant on the social conditions under which pedagogy unfolds in the educational process and in school instruction, while accentuating both the explicit power structures and, primarily, those that remain hidden.

Mainly due to the reception of international comparative studies on the capacities of national educational systems from an economic perspective (e.g., PISA of the OECD), the interest of educational sciences turned more intensely toward learning and, implementing the mandate interests of the OECD, it turned within that field to the aspect of building competencies so that all future citizens would function in the best possible way in their work environment and democracy. This approach bundles relevant content areas, domains of knowledge, and the process of learning understood as the reception of information and its transference to long-term memory for future planning and execution of action (which can be generated by competency and should be brought about in performance).

This is bundling is necessary, because the development of competencies in various areas or dimensions of expertise (Nieke 2012) requires such diverse mental representations of the world, which we can obviously construct only through various learning strategies that are adapted to the structures of the content, and only then can we successfully transfer such knowledge to the different areas of long-term memory so that we can, at will, draw on it spontaneously and with certainty. This is by no means a new insight and was not just newly discovered through international comparison studies that evaluate the efficiency in various educational systems from a utilitarian perspective; but, also due to this economic impulse, the concept of learning has received more attention and proved successful for empirical research. Since the beginnings of pedagogy, the obvious and ever-present insight presented itself: Learning a subject's content requires diverse, corresponding methods. This insight appears today in the form of differentiated subject-specific methodology.

DOI: 10.4324/9781003187431-20

Given this fact, it is definitively astounding that, over a long time, practical classroom instruction as well as academic educational science accepted unquestioningly the psychological modeling for learning, because that tries to describe learning as independent of content.

The *reasons [for the acceptance of the psychological model of learning]* can be found in the self-concept of mainstream psychology as it evolved from psychophysics toward the end of the 19th century. Psychology oriented itself by defining a paradigm of the natural sciences (Karl Popper, Thomas Kuhn, Stephen Toulmin), specifically in physics and later also medicine, which understood itself as a natural science. These sciences arrived at true statements about phenomenal, objective reality through both experiments and abstractions, the latter presenting in form of mathematization. Physics expresses its ideal of cognition—which informed also the other natural sciences—through the principle of economy of thought (Ockham, Ernst Mach): We should explain ourselves with as few elements as possible, quite in line with the criterium of elegance in mathematics. This leads to an intentional reduction of elements when describing reality, which we no longer grasp in its fullness but exclusively in the relevant aspects and dimensions, which we define as motion, energy, mass, etc., in order to arrive at precise predictions on the future states of natural systems. The extremely high success of this paradigm and its technical application led to a highly effective domination of nature, which rendered [this paradigm] convincing and unassailable in its explanatory capacities.

This may also explain the fascination that this paradigm held, and still holds today, for any attempt to come up with a model of the human being. Medicine and psychology design their models of the human being according to this paradigm—although that endeavor is not crowned with the same success as in the reliable prognosis of future systemic conditions, or the course of illnesses, or of behavior. However, so far this predicament has not been attributed to any shortcoming of the paradigm's but has been considered to be a result of temporary and surmountable inaccuracies of the descriptive models and the observed variables and their mathematization, which may have to take a very different approach than the algebraization in classical macrophysics in order to find an appropriate model for complex interlinked effects.

Thus, the psychological approach to learning (Hasselhorn, Gold 2006) has been shaped by the natural science paradigm. This model does not see the human being as possibly unique, occupying a special position (in nature), but views man simply as a living being, which makes it possible to explain human learning along the same principles as that of other species. This allows for using animal research as conducted in foundational medical research.

According to this approach, learning is thus a successful adaptation to a changing environment in living beings that have the ability to move (i.e., in animals, including human beings), and learning proceeds by:

- absorbing information from outside;
- building viable internal representational models of the outer world (successfully enabling survival);
- effective storage of such models in memory;
- reliable recall of such memories in moments of orientation and preparation of reactions in corresponding situations.

This is also true for everything that educational science considers its genuine area of research, namely an orientation model of the world formed by adopting collectively shared patterns of orientation that are individually reconstructed as cognition in form of word-image-combinations and stored in memory. The psychologically formulated, content-independent learning patterns are thus complemented by simply pouring content into them. It is therefore only plausible for clinical psychology to include findings of neurology and often even adopt such findings wholesale as its sole foundation.

Neurology supplies information about specific activity patterns in various brain areas through its imaging procedures that detect brain activity based primarily on indirect indicators (oxygen use, sugar levels as indicators for neuronal activities), and only very rarely on direct deductions from electric potentials through implanted electrodes. These results are then correlated with behavioral data—i.e., with the methods of psychology—by applying test apparatus stimuli to the test subject, as was done in psychophysics in the 19th century, or else, the researcher ask the subjects to visualize images and situations with diverse affective charges in order to identify stable correlation patterns. These patterns are then mostly interpreted as uni-causal, in the sense of monistic materialism, as if the physiological process was the primary and sole ontological factor that matters, while thoughts are treated as non-autonomous epiphenomena that can be completely explained within the [materialistic] paradigm. Some research assumes, in the vein of wholistic monism, that there exists a psychophysical parallelism, which interprets both dimensions of the measured data as expressions of one unified entity. At this time, there are practically no experts to voice support for the possible interpretation stemming from a dualistic ontology that nonphysical thoughts engender brain activity and modulate it, so that we can physically see the thought activity. But, in principle, we can imagine a such a causal direction as long as we adopt such a dualistic ontology, which, up to 1900, had served globally as the self-evident basis for all worldviews.

Learning is a modulation of memory, which is why it stands to reason that we consult psychological theories of memory (Markowitsch 2009).

This approach has the advantage—compared with the general biological, content-independent theories of learning—that here content can be categorized according to its storage in partial memory areas with different structure and function, from whence it can be called up again: the very process that describes learning.

2 Reasons for needing a new definition of the concept of learning from a perspective of educational sciences

All definitions of *character- and cognitive development [Bildung]* and *education [Erziehung]* agree that this type of activity (including the special case of self-education and self-development) always results in change in the "target person," who was termed "pupil" in former times, and today are called *educand* (Wolfgang Brezinka), *addressee* (recipient of a pedagogically motivated communication) or—in institutional perspective—*student* or *participant*. From without, we can perceive such changes through modifications of regular behavior (which may also include communication content), or the subjects can report from within their own experiences and perspectives.

Biology, as the relevant science for this task, describes the physical basis of such a lasting change in a "target person" as *learning*, i.e., as an organism's active, permanent adaptation to changeable environmental circumstances, in order to ensure survival. According to this general understanding, all organisms—even those without central nervous systems—can and must learn.

The paradigm of biology describes all life along the categories of a general systems theory, and it suggests that such learning in living organizations can be transferred to any non-living ones, such as social organizations or, mainly, business enterprises. Currently, authors do not yet agree on whether an organization as a system can indeed learn; it remains open as to whether any organization's detectable adaptation to specific surrounding conditions can or must be attributed to the learning of the people who are active within these organizations.

Since 1900, psychology has understood itself as a natural science adopted from biology and the concept of learning as an adaptation by an organism to the organism's environment. This has enabled psychologists to do experimental learning research with simple animal models (rats, pigeons, dogs) to detect law-like patterns and to then, without compunction, transfer the findings of such studies to human beings. Until today, learning psychology has considered the findings of behavioristic psychology to constitute a firm and seemingly unassailable part of its canonical knowledge on learning.

During the early stages of theory development in pedagogy—e.g., by Comenius, Locke, Rousseau, Pestalozzi, Herbart—each theory, of course, contained its respective specific learning theory (Meyer-Drawe 2012), and so educational science relegated this domain of defining learning to psychology, in line with the academic division of labor. This canon was unquestioningly transferred over generations to general pedagogical and subject-specific teacher trainings and the education of future pedagogues.

With the rise of cognitive psychology, the insight gains recognition that general learning in human beings does not and cannot exist, but that, within any given specific domain, learning happens in various ways. We therefore cannot just transfer experience with successful learning in one area (e.g., riding a bicycle) to another area (e.g., learning the vocabulary of a foreign language). By now, the obsolete transfer hypothesis developed by behaviorism can be considered refuted—that learning in one area creates formal structures for comprehending the world, which we can now—at will—apply to other areas of learning. That is why a general, domain-independent *learning how to learn* system can probably never happen. We can only detect domain-specific learning strategies that are successful in their specific areas, and that are, furthermore, strongly dependent on the person's individual learning experiences.

Learning experience is emphasized in constructivist learning psychology, which is a further development of the cognition theory approach. In this framework, learning happens largely through the learner's own activity in constructing and modifying internal representational patterns of the world. This leads to huge inter-individual differences that are inevitable and that we must respect. Teaching and instruction cannot modulate this process according to any plan but can only suggest and inspire it. Furthermore, all formations of homogenous learning groups according to achievement level are questionable; only a strict and uncompromising individualization of learning support can be appropriate.

A theoretic model of *informal* learning ensues: We learn always and everywhere by constructing and reconstructing representational patterns of the world. On that understanding we must base every methodical and institutionalized form of learning. However, the difference between *formal* and *informal* learning dissolves, because it is always then student himself who learns; so we can consider both forms of learning as equivalent.

The biological theory of learning offers interesting aspects through a combination of the psychology and neurophysiology of the brain. Researchers suspect that it is only in certain newly assigned states of sleep that learning occurs as a transfer of content from short-term memory to long-term memory, from whence they can be recalled for purposes of further orientation and targeted action. It appears that something like *intuition* is at work here, which distills the relevant aspects from the plethora of daily impressions and restores the various elements to an overarching meaningful whole [Gestalt] so that the learner can memorize them in this form (Born 2015).

Most recently, there have been new attempts to once again arrive at an autonomous definition of learning from the perspective of educational science. We might find the reason for these efforts possibly in the discomfort caused by psychology's adoption of the natural science model of the human being, particularly when taking into account that mankind has developed a cultural life form that makes him unique among all living creatures. Culture is transmitted intergenerationally, which requires education and formative development. Therefore, it may be called for and hold promise to find a new model of learning that differs from psychology's biology-oriented concept of learning. For this, we need to consider the context in which the concept of learning occurs and where it is needed in educational science, and which theoretical models would—or could—be appropriate in these connections. Such model developments need a contextual reference. Pedagogic psychology meanwhile has already integrated this in recent modeling, for example, when talking about domain-specific learning and referencing its own special forms of intelligence. This differs categorically from older, paler models of a general cognitive competency independent of content.

In a first approximation, we can determine such relevant contexts as follows: *Learning* is a basis for:

a. Qualification, as in building a competency, which can contribute in the form of regulated exchange processes to the achievement-oriented society characterized by division of labor: formalized completion of general education as a prerequisite for starting specialized professional education and—throughout one's life—continuing professional education. All qualifications are determined by content, which differs greatly in volume and formal structure. So far, no convincing concepts have been developed from the attempt to identify content-independent basal qualifications (key qualifications that would allow autodidactic competency building in any content area). This is no surprise, since the structure and the specific requirements of what has to be learned strongly determine strategies for acquiring content and skills.

b. Competency, as in a comprehensive construct for explaining permanently available mental achievement capacity, which we can only understand and measure through performance. This, however, can always only show part of the available achievement capacity that we indirectly access as competency. All these concepts proceed from the assumption of a threefold interdependency of predisposition, incidental learning, and the effect of treatment (instruction) on the measured level of competency; in many studies, researchers attribute no more than 10 percent of the variance factor to treatment.

c. Education, as in successful intentional socialization: We learn to conform to norms and to naturally incorporate them into a firm habit through *incidental learning*, i.e., through role models (especially those communicated via social media), and through expectations, demands, and corrective feedback from our social environment (our family and peer group). This engenders a reliable form of self-management that becomes part of our self-competency; older models called this the development of the will and personality. The second form of learning is that of *defensive* learning, stemming from the intention to avoid unpleasant present situations in future through adaptation to the demands. This type of learning continues into adulthood, demonstrated in the fact that the penal code of the law (down to traffic violation fees) speaks of the intended *educational effects* of the penalization.

d. Education, as a reflected relation to the world and self as enculturation, i.e., the part of our surroundings' culture that we acquire though intentional learning as we deal with objective content areas. Experts agree that predisposition (genetic preconditioning) has no influence on this area of learning, while they assess the influence of concomitant enculturation (milieu of the parental home) as being highly effective.

3 Five approaches to a new definition of *learning* from the perspective of educational sciences

Consequently, the concept of learning must be released from the confines of a psychology whose thinking follows a natural science paradigm, and it must be set in the cultural science context instead, as is done in educational science. Several approaches attempt to do this, and we shall here give a brief outline of five of them.

3.1 Learning as body phenomenology

On the basis of phenomenological body experiences, Käthe Meyer-Drawe (2012) developed a learning concept within educational science that builds on the concept of experience by Günter Buck (1989), connecting the body phenomenology of Merleau-Ponty with Buck's own approach to learning that is in turn based on Husserl. She focuses on the part of learning that enables education as a transformation of previously held worldviews ("experiences").[3]

3.2 Intentional and incidental learning as embodiment learning

In his foundation study on human learning, Paul Faulstich (2013) presents the views of Merleau-Ponty, Waldenfels, Bourdieu, and, first of all, Holzkamp, regarding the specifically human relation to the world.[4] The first two of these authors give a phenomenological description of an elementary pre-orientation toward the sense of learning directly through the body and only indirectly toward the world, society, and culture.

This reasoning can be complemented by a functional point of view. This is also habitually done in anthropological perspectives based on evolutionary biological theory. This approach is predicated on the assumption that essential, basic human orientations can be interpreted as genetic predeterminations in service to survival. From this perspective, there must exist *an intentionality of the body through preserving and expanding existence.*

The *intentionality* of the body (Merleau-Ponty) branches into two elementary vectors—one toward *preserving existence*, and the other toward *expansion*. Not random are the psychic processes of world orientation, of integrating information coming in through the body and reaching our mind, where it is processed and selectively evaluated, brought into meaningful coherences (thinking), and stored in memory, but these processes are directed by this intentionality of the body. According to current natural-science-based anthropological modeling, this is the effect of selective processes in evolution. Such perceptions and action alternatives are affectively encoded in the amygdala; they serve to preserve life and are therefore genetically predisposed.

This intentionality aims at two things:[5]

1. Preservation of existence. This is the elementary striving for security—most recently, Hartmut Rosa (2012, 2016) systematically added this point into a cultural-science theory of society—and the striving to avoid fear. It expresses itself in securing food (hunting prey, storing foods, defending food stores through regulation property, and readiness for combat), and protecting shelter and territory (against being preyed upon by enemies who covet the food, including whole other groups of human beings).[6] Essential for survival is the cooperation within the group to heighten survival capacity down to creating states for preserving inner and outer security, economy, and technology. Therefore, we experience it as a threat to our existence when we are socially ostracized and lose social recognition (the definition of a social misfit).

2. Expansion through reproduction (sexuality, raising children) and exploration—investigating the environment to secure and build effective world orientations that serve to avert dangers (geography, nature studies, history) and to expand possibility realms (religion, philosophy, science, fictional art). The sphere of the sublime also belongs here (to magically banish spirits and the gods), as well as the realm of beauty (order, adornment, a soothing feeling of security when beholding the symmetrical form).

These approaches to body-connected learning fail to mention the influence of the body on learning possibilities and learning effectivity: sleep hygiene,[7] day rhythm, nutrition, permanent sexualization in direct interaction, neuro-enhancement (uppers—from coffee to drugs), as well as disability, illness, and stress. Currently there is some occasional work on these topics, usually addressing specific contexts such as self-optimization—which ALWAYS requires also intentional learning for building the necessary competencies—or the topic of sexual abuse in special education[8] (Werner 2006).

Faulstich developed his educational science theory of learning on the basis of the activity theory of the so-called Russian school of cultural history (Vygotsky, Leontjew). This led him to develop a theory of emergent learning (Faulstich 2013, p. 100), which allows physiological and behavioristic modeling of the elementary learning processes, in which the cognitive, internal representations of the world are superseded in an overarching level of emergence[9] that he describes as societal. Faulstich adopted Leontjew's distinction between sign and meaning which, however, shows that in fact the integration of this emergence level includes culture as collective human memory. This memory presents itself in collectively organized patterns of orientation and their material manifestations,[10] and which individuals employ—and must employ—such patterns in building their orientation to the world. Therefore, we can more precisely describe this step of emergence as *enculturation.*

The distinction between *intended* and *incidental* learning (Faulstich 2013, p. 12) points to the question of whether we can "will" to learn. The daily experiences of forgetting and of failed efforts to learn in school show that obviously willing alone brings about hardly any reliable effects. It appears possible that in dealing with a learning topic we form associations with anticipated and imagined situations of future recapitulation: the praise of the teacher, the in-class exams, the presentations to a peer group, etc. Such intentionally formed associations do have an effect on memorization.

By far the larger part of learning—also of formal learning—occurs incidentally, i.e., along the way and unnoticed while dealing with the subject matter. Successful learning or building memory depends therefore on the specific conditions of the learning activity. Important factors are, e.g., time, acquisition of content through questions and sorting content into already familiar patterns of orientation, astonishment, and assigning relevance to one's own existence. In behavioristic terms, this all fell under the term of "intrinsic motivation." Krapp and Prenzel (1992) called it *interest* in place of the mechanistic concept of motivation, while at the same time giving consideration to the dimension of content.

Currently, there is little attention given to the aspect of allowing sufficient time for an activity that was formerly called "practicing"—a factor that was considered a matter of course in earlier times.

Recapitulations as well as practical applications apply here, i.e., fitting the learned material into an overarching memory-matrix of actions and meanings in such a way that we can reliably recall it. This time-expanded activity includes not only the actual practice period, but, beyond that, also the repeated intake of the learning material, reviewing and working through it again and again. Experience has shown that a one-time reading or presentation in the classroom has only a small effect on the formation of memory.

Faulstich addresses the relevance of *space and time* for sufficiently understanding human learning, but he tarries with maximal abstractions, which are also used in natural science-oriented psychology in connection with the formal, contentless concept of learning that he himself criticized. However, this does not sufficiently explain the peculiarities of formative learning.

From an educational science perspective, *time* is relevant for learning in two areas:

- Consideration of biorhythm—when we can effectively learn in our daily rhythm and throughout our life; and
- Managing time for repetition, practice, application, as incidental learning also cannot reach certain levels of competency.
- *Space* is relevant as:
- The place where we learn: e.g., the school, the place where we apply learning in professional training, immediate demonstration during excursions. Factually, this means positioning learning on a two-dimensional plane (the dimension of height is mostly irrelevant) (Nieke 2015).
- Learning environment: Space can have a stimulating or an obstructive effect. Its effect depends on the concrete and symbolic design (such as the color of the classroom walls).

So far research has paid little attention to this factor, which, however, is considered essential by those exposed to it. Noise can greatly impinge on learning or even obstruct it fully, and noise is basically connected to room design. One can create a virtual simulation of room designs—then we no longer deal with a (three-dimensional) space, but with the visibility and approachability of symbols for amplification (Nieke 2007) of mental activity: research materials (on a specific desk, an encyclopedia), a folder for materials for immediate access (texts, images, videos, etc.), memory symbols for structuring time of intentional learning, access to other learners (for peer education, meaning mutual help through communication and cooperation), and access to teachers, production tools for mind maps, notes, text drafts, etc.

In fact, this process also develops on the two-dimensional plane of the computer screen, and while we can virtually create a third dimension—depth—that only generates an aesthetic effect with no relevance for learning; therefore, the simulation technology term *cyber space* is rather misleading here.

Overall, we can understand the thesis of embodiment learning only after clarifying what it antagonizes, namely a dualistic ontology that differentiates between a body that is assigned to matter and nature, and a substantially different, i.e., immaterial, soul. This idea, stemming from antiquity, expresses the dawning intuition that man, through his own inner efforts, can overcome the dictates of nature—needs, desires, or pains, if necessary. It is in the soul that this possibility of liberation exists. Occidental rationalism followed this insight by forming the implicit view that the body is irrelevant and only a hindrance for all mental activity, and therefore also for learning as the intaking of something new—a concept we already find in Plato's work. Toward the end of the 19th century, with *Sturm und Drang*, the romantic period and modern monistic materialism,[11] the view changed to perceive this concept as possibly being insufficient and one-sided. From this change profited both the phenomenology of the body and Marxist materialism, together with the concepts of learning derived from them. It is interesting that occasionally there are breakthroughs of reminiscences of the old idea that the body hinders the soul in its possibilities of freedom, as it indeed stands to reason in the cases of, for example, physical disability or economic deprivation. We could not even address the formation and dependency of mental activity, or the origin and modification of world orientations (cognitions) as effects of the body, if they never impinged on freedom; in that case, such a cognitive pattern of differentiating between body and soul could not exist at all. Talking about the embodiment of the soul (and thus also of learning) is dangerous, insofar as it could lead to frame this as a unidirectional causal relationship, and this problem has not yet been sufficiently solved. Such causal attribution would implicitly deny the freedom of the soul which was then intuitively adopted—i.e., accepted by many as being correct—and continues to have an effect even today.

The findings of psychosomatics—such as, for example, of psycho-neuroimmunology—also show how the psyche has reverse effects on the body, however psyche may be understood (mostly as an emergent state of autopoiesis in complex organisms that cannot be reduced to processes of physics or chemistry). In such models, even those conceptualized entirely in monistic materialistic ways, the intuitions of freedom and of body-transcending will always found to be denied.

3.3 *The structural relation between learning and education*

[The author here uses Bildung—*meaning comprehensive education of mind and character, including enculturation.]*
In the wake of Gregory Bateson's (1964) philosophical-logical analysis of learning, Winfried Marotzki suggests a structural relationship between learning and education (Jörissen, Marotzki 2009, p. 21ff.).[12] Marotzki distinguishes two stages of learning: learning through rigid stimulus-response reaction and learning of certain conditional reflexes through context sensitizing. These two stages correspond to two levels of education *[Bildung]*. In the first stage of education (education I), the learner forms the construction principles for a progressive world order (schemata contained in culture for the purpose of orientation); these are independent of any empirical testing. The second stage of education (education II) leads to the recognition of the respective limitations of those worldviews that the learner formed—and, in principle, has the ability to form—during the stage of education I.

Arnd-Michael Nohl pointedly summarizes this as follows: We investigate education "as a transformation of self- and world reference, while we consider learning a continuous acquisition of knowledge and skills within a given [orientation] framework of self- and world reference" (2014, p. 156).

3.4 *Learning as a fundamental pedagogical concept*

Based on an interdisciplinary perspective of learning, Michael Göhlich and Jörg Zirfas (2007) are developing a theoretical outline for learning as a fundamental pedagogical concept. This concept reveals itself in a categorically different way from knowledge-learning, life-learning, and learning-learning.

The draft was generated by a review of history and with empirical material and thus raises a claim to plausibility. The draft itself is still brief and awaits further *development and differentiation*.

Learning from the Perspective of Educational Science

3.5 Transformational and transformative education

The term transformation is applied to learning processes that engender fundamental changes in the learner's existing previous knowledge base. The specific educational science perspective allows a better understanding through this categorization than we can gain through psychological learning theories oriented on natural science, not only regarding formal processes, but also to content. This can mean two things:

- First, a change brought about by an encounter that leads us to evaluate our previously held world orientation as insufficient, and, consequently, a better one should take its place. If successful, this kind of educational learning would also be permanent.
- Second, an *eccentric positionality* (Helmuth Plessner), which enables a new and different view—from a fringe perspective—of a subject matter and its mental representation (cognition, patterns of orientation, and interpretation of meaning). Such a change in perspective allows for the construction of a new orientation. In various contexts (e.g., in concepts of cognitive psychotherapy), this is termed *reframing*, deconstruction, or critical theory along the lines of dominance critique.

Hans-Christoph Koller presents a theory of transformational education (2012) that uses and further elaborates on this differentiation. According to his view, education only happens if we substitute a different world orientation that we deem more appropriate for a previous one—a process that inevitably brings with it unease, effort, and a crisis in regard to previous certainty, and that process connects to corresponding resistances against any kind of imposition or any offer to change orientation. Koller explains his theory as mostly deconstructionist, referencing mainly French educational philosophers. But we find there also a strong structural affinity to Kahneman's (2011) theory suggestion of two separate human orientation systems, which he formally divides into system I (routine, intuition, affect control) and system II (reflection, calculation).

It is striking that learning is seen as a sudden change in orientation patterns (cognitions) that alters the overall Gestalt.

Kant had already offered this idea, describing it as a revolutionary process (Meyer-Drawe 2012, p. 14). The essential factor in this conceptualization is the aspect of time: It views learning not as a linear gradual layering and accumulation of orientations (knowledge), but as a sudden turnaround of an existing orientation. The goal is not accumulation of inanimate matter, but an accomplishment of adaptation, as is typical for living organisms. The basic model for this process is extension of the eukaryote's membrane as it engulfs something from without; it is an elementary process of acquisition, of assimilating something external into one's own identity. (In the eukaryote, that material assimilation is, in the case of learning, the immaterial assimilation resulting in a new pattern of orientation.) Jean Piaget's developmental theory already offers such fundamental deliberations using the terms *assimilation* and *accommodation*.

Without this reference to biology, Faulstich points to the relevance of these sudden turning points, bringing up concepts like Kairos (opportune moments) that practical pedagogic reflections have employed in regard to making someone learn (2013, p. 156f.).

Rolf Arnold initiated the translation of Jack Mezirow's *Transformative Adult Education* that had found barely any reception in Germany (1997).[13] In contrast to common patterns of reception, the term *transformation* does not stem from Mezirow himself. In 1984, he talks about his source: He adopted the term from Chet Bowers, who used it to describe the view that we can and must step back from the self-evident facts of socialization (i.e., the world we live in) and recognize that these "facts" are linguistic constructs predicated by their terminology. This approach is very close to deconstructivism, but Bowers traced it back to Dewey, Whitehead, and Freire.

Therefore, *transformation* describes something like reframing but means more than and is different from a simple transition from one worldview to another, because it contains a moment of cognition, of recognizing truth. This understanding is meant to prevent the randomness of change through irritation and reflection, and to orient it toward a truth that can be constructed in discourse (in the sense of Jürgen Habermas's theory).

The paper as well as Bowers' self-description on the web (www.cabowers.net) lacks clarity as to the origin of the certainty criteria for such insight—except in the understanding that everything that we held to be self-evident and unchangeable is only one possible and interested worldview and that there are infinitely more alternatives that we can freely choose from—once they are recognized. This resembles the thoughts of Marx, that insight into the historic origins of conditions allows us to recognize that we can change them.

4 Reasons for learning: Motivation, interest, relevance

Not every encounter leads to an incidental or intentional learning experience, but only such encounters that facilitate the recognition of something relevant. Remarkably, the term relevance (which Max Weber and Alfred Schütz use to describe activity tendencies and to explain the choice of action alternatives) is not used in the psychology of learning, maybe because it is linked too closely to learning content. Instead, a construct is in use that defines learning as an emotionally coded transfer of mental content from short-term to long-term memory—in other words, the effect of learning depends on specific concomitant and preparative emotions. But since there is also an explicitly unenthusiastic kind of learning, namely in the form of defensive learning that aims to avoid future failure, we cannot apply the basic behavioristic scheme of pleasure and displeasure to learning. Therefore, the coding does not proceed along the lines of *pleasurable/unpleasurable*, but rather of *important/unimportant, fascinating/boring,* which means, in fact, the coding proceeds according to relevance.

The old concept of motivation, which is still in frequent use today, follows a mechanistic line of thought. It is based on the elementary physical idea that any change (motion) needs a continuously activated impulse from outside, as Aristotle postulated (and was refuted by Newton with the principle of inertia). In this context, motivation is then viewed as an elementary psychic process of action-oriented decision-making—and that includes learning, insofar as it is implicitly understood as an action, i.e., as intentional learning. The content-related dimension of the material to be learned is expressed in the dichotomy of *extrinsic* and *intrinsic* motivation (Heckhausen 1980):

- *Extrinsic* motivation for an activity (and that means also for intentional learning) follows the principle of means-to-an-end economy. The activity, in itself, is not valuable to the one who engages in it, but it is the means to an end, i.e., a different, more valuable purpose. The paradigmatic example from the area of formal education is intentional learning of a subject matter that the learner may deem irrelevant or difficult but is necessary for successful graduation and for obtaining the certificate or diploma that has barter value in the job market or confers high social status. Such extrinsic motivation often also forms the basis of defensive learning that aims to avert undesirable future consequences of not having learned: being despised, excluded, or punished.
- *Intrinsic* motivation stems from the existential change that an activity brings about, e.g., the knowledge itself that we acquire through learning—a process that is often described as *fascination* (Leonhard 1971). This type of motivation is deemed to have more lasting effects and it is more highly valued. Without doubt, it is unreservedly pleasant when compared to the efforts inevitably connected with intentional and defensive learning. Learning of this type is factually incidental, since it arises as we deal with the subject matter without requiring the meta-cognitive concentration and efforts needed for intentional and defensive learning.

The concept of *interest* comes into play here (Deci, Ryan 2008; Krapp, Prenzel 1992). Such an interest can:

- pre-exist on an elementary level, e.g., in infants;
- have been formed biographically through experiences that we considered positive;
- be newly generated through encountering a subject matter or a text;
- arise due to the suggestions of others, e.g., teachers.

As we immerse ourselves in learning something new and fascinating, incidental learning happens without our noticing or intent. Even an intention to come to know more about the subject matter follows the interest in the subject itself, and therefore we cannot call it truly *intentional* learning.

Most of the time our interest is awakened by randomly coming across something that may or may not be arranged institutionally (school). In this process, a situational fascination can flare up that may just as quickly dissipate again.

Intentional learning only occurs in the mode of means-to-an-end: I do not learn English because I think it is an interesting or pretty language, but I learn it so that I can better communicate in foreign countries or join a scientific discussion.

Since I am not interested in learning the language, but only in its future use, I try to organize the learning process as efficiently as possible and focus on tried and tested strategies of acquiring language skills through intentional learning (learning vocabulary, grammatical exercises) that guarantee success in the shortest time possible, instead of pleasurably immersing myself in the language for a long time, which would lead to incidental learning. This directs the focus to learning strategies rather than to the content of what I learn, i.e., something like a meta-cognition of learning.

In the context of attempting to awaken motivation or interest, we as teachers also search for types of learning that might allow us to methodologically reduce and sequence the content in such a way that most appropriately meets the needs of each respective type. The common typology—e.g., visual or auditory types of learning—has not met the validity criteria in more sophisticated meta-analyses of available studies. In this process, researchers were, however, able to identify more and less *successful learning strategies* (Mandl, Friedrich 2006). Their studies highlighted study strategies and were thus limited to a high level of formal previous education, to young adults, and to complex abstract subject matters to be learned. Probably a broader and different spectrum of strategies would emerge, if research would focus on an entirely different set of learning tasks in early childhood education, elementary school education, or instructive skill-oriented professional education (education here understood as competency building).

Orders of relevance can also appear in *learning styles*, as applied to content and meta-cognitive strategies for successful processing of learning materials (Hasselhorn, Gold 2006, p. 100).

Sociology recognizes the collective effects of *educational distance* in social strata and milieus to be an explanatory variable for the disparity in educational outcomes in an intentionally egalitarian educational system. These collective effects can be more precisely understood to be effects of a *collective learning culture* in these life worlds. This includes the *full range of orientation patterns* for relevance in learning and for effective forms of acquiring knowledge (including learning strategies and necessary sleep hygiene, which enables the transfer of content in the brain from short-term to long-term memory). This term [*orientation pattern*] is preferential to that of *learning habitus*, which Faulstich (2013, p. 165) uses, following Bourdieu and inspired by Herzberg (2004), because the latter term implies reluctance to change, while orientation patterns are always flexible. We know from the observation of educational milieus that these orientations connected to learning are by no means so invariant as is suggested by the term *learning habitus*; rather, these patterns can undergo swift and complex changes due to manifold influences from without and within.

5 Learning—A cultural science perspective, illustrated by the example of learning resistance and equal opportunity

From the viewpoint of a psychology that sees itself as a natural science, learning is a living system's (organism's) successful adaptation to changing environmental conditions through autopoiesis, i.e., through self-generated modifications in form of assimilation and accommodation. It is independent of any specific content. The laws of learning thus formulated can apply to all living beings, in all and any environmental constellations. We can also understand human learning in such terms; however, this approach disregards possible specifications that are then engendered by the content of the subject matter to be learned. We shall demonstrate this using the example of learning resistance.

In his remarks on learning resistances, Faulstich (2013) points out that they occur in vocational, professional education in particular, and that such resistances cannot be explained on an individual level, i.e., psychologically, but only by a view on the imprints received from one's life world, the milieu. Such resistances develop through specific meanings that we attribute to the content and process of learning, and these meanings differ in varying milieus.

From this perspective, we also must rethink the discourse on equal opportunities. This idea implies that the learning ability is the same in all human beings, and in principle the educational institutions can completely level out differences in performance through appropriate support.

This approach is psychologically conceptualized based on an ability to learn, at the same time assuming that this ability is evenly distributed in social groupings, regardless of class or milieu. From a perspective of cultural science, we might possibly see that performance differences do not essentially originate from a combination of generalized learning abilities with formal principles of motivation and instruction (in the educational system), but that they result from finding meaning in the subject matters, meaning also from relevance and interest. The studies so far indicate that milieu is a formative factor here, and it is rather improbable that these lasting imprints could be easily or completely de-activated through educational support given in a narrow time period. A political effort to make equal opportunity a reality would have to complement the support provided in schools with a change in orientation patterns within the surrounding culture, i.e., the life-worlds and milieus. To this end, "parental participation" heads in the right direction but would need to be essentially expanded toward parental education, for which the schools that offer obligatory and general public education presently have no mandate at all, because they are so far constitutionally limited to neutrality in world view and must follow the educational canon defined by the state.

6 Learning and teaching

In all Germanic languages without exception, the word "learning" describes an inseparable connection between receiving something and understanding it, i.e., between learning and teaching (Grimm, Grimm 1885, p. 766ff.). To this day, this connection is alive and commonly understood. Therefore, educational science found that learning, in its form of incidental learning, was only of secondary interest. In observation and theory development, educational science focuses on influencing the learning of groups with assumed deficits in competency and on special manipulations such as guidance, instruction, schooling, motivation, demonstrations, and methodology, all of which are conceptualized differently and lack a streamlined theoretical development and refinement.[14]

A constitutive element in making someone learn is the competency difference between learner and teacher. It gives rise to the teachers' authority: They know more and can do more and therefore they should and must be obeyed and trusted. Only then can the learner change the level of relevance and find different meaning—more precisely: change themselves, regulating the transfer of the material to be learned into memory.

As Dollase points out, this authority has an organic basis in the need for attachment that provides elementary security (2013, p. 87). Accordingly, students expect complete truthfulness from the teacher.

In the societal discourse on the misuse of authority (Nieke 2014), this unconditional view has turned permanently controversial. Today, authority has become fragile and must be re-established time and again through acts of metacommunication. This can proceed either based on the learner's recognition of authority (in the framework of authority-concepts, this is termed *personal authority*) or via threatening sanctions. The latter is termed *authority by office* and brings up the issue of pedagogic power and the constant danger of its misuse (Nieke 2014).

However, aside from intentional learning that comes into focus in teaching, there is inevitably also a large amount of incidental learning that takes place unnoticed. The methodological concepts for teaching so far have completely ignored this type of learning, or, at best, considered it as a possible disturbance. Only sociological studies critical of dominance structures have focused on this aspect of

Learning from the Perspective of Educational Science

institutional enculturation and socialization, calling it the *secret curriculum* (Zinnecker 1975). However, these studies only assume its existence and can only postulate it; it is not yet possible to bring this secret curriculum into plain view, due to the constraints of available means and appropriate research methodology. One reason is the fact that learners are not—and cannot be—experts about their own learning process, because learning happens mainly unconsciously. We can ask students to remember learning situations and concomitantly perceive, mentally and reflexively, what happens in their consciousness during the process of trying to learn intentionally, but this will furnish only trivialities—at any rate, nothing that completely explains the process.

We are coming up against a boundary of epistemology regarding the phenomenological attempt to understand learning; Meyer-Droste points that out by clearly stating that the learning process is in principle unrecognizable for the learner and certainly for any outside observer, while treading this path of cognition.

7 Learning in freedom

Learning in freedom is a common topic that contains different meanings. On one hand, it entails respect for the *freedom of the learner*, who should be coerced as little as possible. He should be as self-directed as possible about content, timing, and, hopefully, also the place where he may learn. This is termed *participatory learning* or *student-oriented teaching*. Without the shackles of predetermination of space and time, new concepts can take form, like distant learning and media-supported (blended) learning.

In contrast to the concept of freedom [of the learner] stands the system of mandated general education for everyone without exception, manifested legally in obligatory attendance of a public school that is regulated by the state. The latter is based on the insight that we can safeguard the level of culture that we have reached (including, in a comprehensive sense, society, economy, technology, and state) only if enough, or, preferably, all people are involved in an obligatory process of intergenerational cultural transfer. That is then the general education for all, which is considered indispensable. Thus, the concept of general education was at first integrated into the canon of required knowledge.

Up until today, this concept of general education has expressed itself in the odd assortment of subjects at public schools, a collection that is not—and can in no way be—systematically justified; rather, it is a result of past power struggles. The titles and content of courses being taught in public schools contain much that is unimportant and lack other areas that would be of high importance for living and survival in present-day culture. In the second half of the 19th century, resistance rose opposing this canon; it resulted from the rapidly increasing body of knowledge in the disciplines that the school subjects referred to. Teachers could no longer convey all this knowledge, not even if they presented it in the briefest way possible. From this quandary arose the principle of teaching by example, which is to this day central in all subject-oriented methodology. Keeping the formal learning goals in mind, the teacher can and must choose which examples are suited best for presenting the subject matter. Here, freedom of choice comes into play for each individual school (in subject-focused conferences) and for each individual teacher; students are also getting involved in the decision-making process on what to choose, which is meant to give them some freedom.

The idea of a wholesale cultural transfer falls away with a limitation on synoptic knowledge and an attempt to establish something like survival competency. But this model of freedom in learning through example does not change the fact that there is an obligatory predetermination of relevance during curriculum development as to what constitutes overview knowledge or survival competency. On the other hand, the theme of *not wanting to know* comes into play, i.e., acceptance of the learner explicitly rejecting learning content. This is distinct from *learning resistances* that result from experiences of being overwhelmed but do not question the relevance of the learning material itself. The context of a beginning discourse on the "right to not knowing" has created the possibility within practical pedagogy and educational science to perceive and discuss such an intentional, and perhaps justifiable wish to remain ignorant. There are two reasons for such a wish:

On one hand, there may be a painful experience of being completely overwhelmed by information, due to an overabundance of readily-available knowledge and the simultaneous claim of a society that holds to the ideal that everyone must make an effort to know everything required and to maintain that level of knowledge through lifelong learning, including updates and changes in the knowledge base; and that such knowledge should be ever newly acquired by applying self-discipline, through one's own effort and without mistakes. Most of us, if not, in principle, all of us, are overwhelmed by this demand. Based on this experience, the claim arises that one has the right to not need to know everything.

It is also possible to justify the right of not-knowing by pointing to the global knowledge base that is accessible and available through internet data banks, or by pointing out that there is a societal division of labor: *What I do not know nor want to know I can ask of someone else, upon whom I can rely to give me trustworthy information.*

On the other hand, the claimed right to not-knowing today mainly refers to information on genetically preconfigured illnesses that cannot be therapeutically treated or cured. The patient experiences and considers such knowledge as unbearable and meets it with rejection. However, the medical concept of *compliance* sees the patient as an emancipated human being who must participate in every therapeutic decision (including a genetic analysis) and requires the physician to inform the patient fully without concealing anything.

The context of learning in freedom encompasses such a wish to remain ignorant in the face of learning requirements. Up to now, such freedom was framed differently: e.g., Faulstich addresses it as freedom of choice and therefore as freedom in decision-making (2013, p. 100). But we must consider that the selection of the learning materials in *intentional learning* (*incidental learning* happens involuntarily or contrary to the will of the learner) and also in *defensive learning* does in not occur in the context of a freedom of choice or through decision-making, but through the selective filters of ranked relevance that steer this process (in the terminology of neurophysiological brain theory, through affective coding, which is the only way to transfer content from short-term to long-term memory). This filter is biographically imprinted, and it exerts a pre-conscious influence on the routine of the world we live in.

We can, however, modify the ranked orders of relevance by reflecting upon them (according to Kahnemann's System II) and changing them. Cognition psychology refers to this process as reframing. It describes the accomplishment of meta-cognition, i.e., an overarching cognition that brings single insights—which are mostly stored in memory in form of a word-image assignation—into a coherent connection, i.e., a subjectively meaningful connection, and that we can also restructure or create new structures, even in spite of mental resistance.

Also, a constructivist theory of learning results in rejecting of all possibilities of outer-directed learning[15] and the full thrust is toward *self-directed learning.*

While the basic assumption of this paradigm entails that learning is a self-directed activity that cannot be stipulated from the outside, this in no way precludes the need for teaching. *Autodidactics*[16] is an approach focused fully on self-directed learning for building competency and acquiring an education, but we have sufficient proof that its effects are questionable, and it is described often as "half-knowledge" (half-knowledge is deadly) and as dilettantism. This kind of freedom in learning fails in principle because it lacks the possibility to correct an incomplete or faulty reception of content to memory. The teacher provides such a corrective function when directing the learner with his instructions; also, the peer group of other students can offer corrections. That leaves only *experience* for the autodidact: trying something out, with the possible outcome of failure in applying the learned material. In some areas of knowledge that is an option, e.g., in mathematics, or when we learn to ride a bicycle, but in other areas it is not possible. In such other areas of knowledge, there are endogen structures that enable such a correction of errors.

8 Learning with the group and against it

The concept of situated learning (Faulstich 2013, p. 141f.) emphasizes the effect of learning happening in a group of learners—that is, learning that would not occur without the interactive dynamics of a peer group and an instructor. However, one must consider that most learning groups are constituted

Learning from the Perspective of Educational Science

due to purely economic necessities and that actually a personal, dyadic relationship could be much more effective, as we can see in the example of training athletes or musicians. We must therefore take into account that in such classes—assembled due to economic necessity—learning has to happen in spite of the disruptions by the group (Winkel 2011), because those occur essentially not in interactions with individuals but rather while dealing with learning content. (*"Please be quiet!"*)

But this reservation is not directed against the concept of situated learning, because that does entail aligning the learner with a recognizable and acceptable context of meaning, which is the most basic prerequisite for human learning. The arranged situation (i.e., in formal learning) should provide exactly that, be it through fascinating learning content or through the attraction of peer interactions—which, however, are obviously systematically overrated regarding the quality and effect of school learning[17]—and the appeal of working with a teacher.

John Locke noticed the conspicuous negative effects that peers [can] have on education and character formation. Today, we find that peers consistently and immediately discriminate against good students, subjecting them to mobbing and calling them "teacher's pet," causing them to conceal their interest in the subject matter and often to not become as intensely involved in the subject matter as their own interest would prompt them to do. The criticizing classmates are motivated by avoidance anxiety; they are afraid that their own lesser achievement capabilities will undergo a worse evaluation in comparison to the high accomplishment of good students. This is a good and accurate observation; indeed, in spite of competency evaluation criteria that are independent of the respective group, German schools still implicitly and explicitly practice grading largely in the context of class comparisons. We can understand this defense against dreaded low evaluations, but it remains problematic that the result of learning in classes of peer groups is an avoidance to learning and achievement in the interested (and therefore in fact highly performing) students. So far, little systematic research has focused on the effects of mutual teaching and learning controls in group instruction settings, but it is likely that they are overrated. This form of peer education is based on the idea that same-aged students can more easily grasp the required cognitive coping strategies for mastering the material to be learned; and that, therefore, peers can more easily offer help and appear more appealing than adult teachers to students who need to ask for help. But observations of peer interactions in common forms of group instruction show that, without special preparations, an immediate and spontaneous division of labor develops, and a dominance structure appears between the few competent and engaged students and those who tag along in their wake.

But this very result contradicts all those approaches that aim at individualization and compensation for initial dissimilarity due to differences in educational milieus.

Therefore, we must not limit *situated learning* to the current parameters of a school class as an externally assembled learning group. This approach could be more effective if the demand for learning also introduced the projection of future usage. When questioned as to why they are interested in something and want to learn it, surveyed students often describe how they imagine using the new knowledge or skill: to please their parents or to master a task, to win recognition, etc. Such an anticipation of a future event is then being reintegrated into the learning situation for establishing an individual meaning of learning, or at least to suggest it.

The term *cooperative learning* often comes up in this context. It bundles disparate factors: On one hand, it means something like dialogue learning, e.g., when a peer takes on the role of the teacher to support the learner—and they can switch these roles later—through appropriate questions in precisely and reliably remembering the content of intentionally learned material in a simulated application scenario. The concept is aligned along the idea of cooperation—a jointly coordinated activity for fulfilling a purpose that one cannot achieve alone—and describes a learning arrangement that facilitates individual intentional learning of agreed-upon and diverse content; then the learners remember it along the division of labor principle in an ensuing application event. Thus, they create a product—a problem-solving process—that they could not have achieved alone. Intentional learning that is set into the framework of cooperative intentional learning achieves the utilitarian relevance of a required means to an end that is external to the process of learning and its content.

Wolfgang Nieke

9 An educated state of being as a result of learning

The term *comprehensive education [Bildung]* is ambiguous insofar as it addresses both a process and its result. The process itself consists of two components, namely one's own activity and an outer arrangement (educational system). We can understand the results only in multidimensional ways, with the dimensions being partly relational and partly not relational. "Being educated" describes primarily a person who has command of knowledge that was not inborn. Such knowledge is more the result of intentional than incidental learning and is rather an effect of a kind of learning that opens up the world than the result of defensive learning.

We can describe "being educated" in four areas of knowledge that differ in structure and categories and for which their origins cannot be traced back to each other nor to an underlying fundamental store of knowledge. An educated person knows:

- what he can or wants to do and how to be successful in that endeavor: *reflexive change-oriented knowledge;*
- why something has to be done in a certain way in order to successfully reach the goal: *condition-oriented knowledge;*
- what could be done: *orientational knowledge* as an expansion of possible space;
- what should be done and for what reasons: *normative knowledge.*

Here we see that orientational knowledge has two components: a normative one and one that refers to an expansion of possibilities also involving condition- and change-relates types of knowledge—or *should* implies *could* (Wolfgang Brezinka). We therefore must examine whether and how goals of action can be realized if they are not to remain merely regulative (Immanuel Kant) or utopian ideas.[18]

In the discussion on building competencies, we often find a distinction between two kinds of competency: knowledge and skills. Indeed, building competency for either of these types happens for each in their own specific way. The respective memory content appears to be stored in topographically different brain areas: one type in the area of declarative memory and in the motoric cortex, and the other in procedural memory. Therefore, it seems imperative that skills should not be treated like knowledge. Skills are un-knowing, as we can see in the example of learning how to ride a bicycle: Someone can do it or not but cannot say how. He does not know what enables him to do it. Skills, therefore, cannot be viewed simply as subcategories of change-oriented knowledge. However, change-oriented knowledge can steer and modify skills.

The four areas of knowledge [*reflexive, condition-oriented, orientational, and normative*] are filled with culture-specific content. Each culture and life world has its own canon of what it expects an educated person to know and of what specializations are possible and expectable within its context.

"Being educated" can *express* itself in different manifest forms that are transverse, as it were, to the areas of knowledge listed above. In social interactions, these forms characterize something like a habitus of responsible use of the knowledge gained. With the concept of manifested forms of expression, we can comprehensively describe the concept of "being educated" from the perspective of learned knowledge, and that sets it apart from conventional notions of "being educated" as the habitus of the educated citizen, a notion that Bollenbeck (1996) had historically reconstructed.

Being educated means:

To be intelligent—Aristotle called this life-intelligence *phronesis*: Someone can do something that others cannot do; he knows many possible ways to get it done.

To be clever—Odysseus is deemed a prototype in occidental intellectual history: the clever one who, even in difficult, seemingly hopeless situations, can find knowledge-based optimal ways to get out through his quick mind and imagination; in this process, he often goes to the limits of, or even beyond, what is permissible.

To be qualified—The educated person reliably performs what others expect of him in the framework of a cooperative division of labor.

To be competent—The educated person can generate new types of performance based on an overabundant structural knowledge (which is exactly how we define competency) and thus successfully complete new kinds of performance tasks.

To be wise—The educated person can take something given and assign it a place in overarching webs of meaning, from which he is able to gain certainty as to which way to take and can communicate that habitually (authority and its recognition).

10 Human learning: Independent of content or category-specific?

10.1 Knowledge and coherence

Having presented above the need for a concept of learning that is specific to the educational sciences, we can now pose the fundamental question of whether a theory of human learning must be categorically specific or whether it can be a concrete realization of a general, i.e., biological, theory of learning.

Our approach here does not attempt to understand or theoretically elucidate effects of learning as behaviors that adhere to rules, which would then—according to the natural science paradigm—allow us to make verifiable prognoses about future systemic conditions, i.e., predictions about the behavior of individuals who have learned something specific.

Instead, we ask how we can explain intentional human behaviors, i.e., actions. For this, we need two categories: *Knowledge* and *Coherence* (*relevance, meaning*).

The theory of knowledge here employed integrates the concept of learning as transfer of content from the stream of consciousness (short-term memory) to long-term memory and the effect of this transition in using competency and performance, i.e., actions. To explain this process, we need structural analyses of

- knowledge,
- memory,
- the encoding processes for the transition from short-term to long-term memory: interest, relevance, meaning, etc., and,
- the renewed actualization of knowledge in competency and performance (actions).

In order to analyze *knowledge*, we must more precisely describe the various types of knowledge mentioned above—*orienting knowledge, conditional knowledge,* and *change-related knowledge*—and we must make clear how they are distinct from each other. We cannot go into detail in that regard here but can only hint at it. Likewise, in this connection, we can only point to how knowledge constitutes itself generally from pieces of *information*. Newly received bits of information (including the construction of new cognitive elements without the processing of external stimuli) are integrated into already existing webs of meaning, i.e., through creating *coherence*. This process produces knowledge that is stored in memory that we can re-actualize through targeted efforts to remember, or that we can call up spontaneously in association with current content of the stream of consciousness. We can then employ that *knowledge* for orienting ourselves and for planning and executing our actions (performance).

Competence, then, denotes the knowledge that we presently remember and employ; those parts of knowledge we draw from the web of coherence and re-actualize. From competence, we generate performance that others can observe. Competency underlying performance is deemed to be always many times greater than the performance that we can see from the outside. Within this framework of understanding, we cannot measure competency directly but only indirectly through measuring performance, and here it is true as well that the substructure of competency is always higher, greater, and more comprehensive than the measurable performance.

The commonly used subdivisions of competency areas according to the type and structure of knowledge go basically back to Heinrich Roth, who builds on the discourse in contemporary American psychology and its suggested threefold division into self-competency, social competency, and subject competency (Nieke 2012). Three forms of knowledge can—but need not—be found in each of these three domains of competency:

While *orientational knowledge* refers to conditional knowledge of physics regarding the origin of the cosmos as an issue of energy and mass from one point (Big Bang), it has no connections to change-related knowledge: There is no practical use for this kind of knowledge. While it can stir us to further deliberations—e.g., on the meaning of one's own existence in view of such an infinitely expanding cosmos—we do not commonly use the term "action" for such movements in thought.

We can speak and write about such things, applying the rules of logic, and that would be something like change-related knowledge (e.g., expressed in philosophy as speech-act theory), but *change-related knowledge* derives not from cosmology but a different area of knowledge, namely that of normative orientation, aimed at differentiating truth from erroneous statements or lies, meaning, from epistemology and ethics.

In understanding learning from the perspective of its content, the process is of the essence, which transfers this content from the stream of consciousness to long-term memory. This happens in two ways:

One part of the transfer of content is not available to intentional remembering. This kind of knowledge we describe as unconscious or pre-conscious. This kind of learning proceeds *incidentally*, i.e., in living, experiencing, or dealing with content, and is not perceived as learning. Likewise, a large part of *defensive* learning cannot be intentionally remembered, as it is aimed at avoiding present dangerous and therefore unpleasant situations from occurring in the future; we will remember such avoidance-related lessons spontaneously in structurally similar dangerous situations and feel correspondingly intense action imperatives to reject and avoid the danger we remember. That gives rise not only to neuroses, but also to corresponding situations that we experience as negative within the framework of formal school education—especially in public mandatory schools—which leads to such defensive learning that sinks down into the unconscious. Biographically, this results in vehement spontaneous reactions to situations that are structurally similar, and the afflicted person can only rarely remember the cause for their reaction, as it lies hidden in a past bad experience in school.

There are reports from adult education that quite a few participants in these courses emphatically reject anything that in its form resembles instruction in school—and this has thus become an integral part of the theory of adult education, under the motto "Adults learn differently"—without the attendees being able to recall concrete memories.

A further example is *implicit knowledge*, that we acquire *incidentally* when we enter an educational institution and which functions as a safe compass for action after an introductory period. This action compass lets attendees of the institution recognize each other as members, but they can give no account to outsiders about the basis for such orientation patterns. Neo-institutionalism bases its description of institutions on these findings and thereby rejects as insufficient older organization theories that try to explain the function of thus regulated social networks—such as organizations and institutions—that rely on explicit behavioral regulations and the correspondingly described assignment of positions and inequalities in power.

Meanwhile it remains unclear what exactly happens in these two variants—incidental and defensive learning. It is certain that the corresponding content of the stream of consciousness are effectively encoded into short-term memory to then transition into long-term memory. We consider the amygdala to be the physiological functional system that causes this encoding process. This process is stimulated hormonally (through chemical signal transduction) and directed not only from the brain but also the entire body. This corresponds to the idea in phenomenological learning theories that learning happens in and through the body.

Another part of the content is encoded in consciousness through *intentional* learning so that it aims at transference to long-term memory: We intend to remember something and never again forget it. Up to now, that is the primary focus modus of school learning and receives the most support. Experience shows that this approach is quite seldom successful. Against the learners' intent—and all too quickly (namely, after six weeks at latest)—they forget most of what they have memorized this way. However, this forgetfulness is not absolute. Many learners complain that in a situation where they need to apply their knowledge, like in an exam, they cannot remember content that they memorized earlier, while they can recall the material shortly before, or again afterward, without a problem. We must be dealing with something like a memory block, rather than a process of complete forgetting. Consequently, the task of intentional learning consists mainly of learners memorizing the content in such a way that they can intentionally and without problems remember them in any future situation requiring recall.

Experts suggest memorizing techniques that mostly rely on forming associations between the content to be learned and a structure of meaning. That points to the basic mechanism of storing knowledge in long-term memory and reliably recalling it through remembering: The available long-term memory incorporates *meaningful* content. Meaning is *coherence*, i.e., the integration of discrete elements of knowledge into an overarching context that is *relevant* to the learner. Apparently, this relevance is not invariant and predetermined like in other non-human species, allowing them to effectively survive in their ecological niche, but it is largely malleable, i.e., it can be modified through learning or deliberation that restructures the orders of relevance.

This is a specific characteristic of human learning and of its result, that is, competency. Depending on experience and remembered life history, this competency is variable memory content and the selection of long-term memories, and it stays changeable throughout one's life. Large parts of such competency (memory content and its availability for intentional re-actualization) are encoded into long-term memory in form of word-image combinations, which is specifically human, because other species cannot avail themselves of such variable and complex kinds of language.[19]

10.2 Three basic forms of human learning

These forms of knowing correspond to three basic forms of human learning:

a. *Experience*—defined as successful survival and overcoming of adverse happenings. The etymology (and thus, imperceptibly, also the semantic aspect) of the German word *Erfahrung* reflects that more directly than the corresponding English word *experience*, which approximates more closely the second and third basic (verb) form. Experience leads to *phronesis*, the worldly intelligence that Aristotle practiced and described. This phronesis is change-related knowledge.

b. *Experiment*—In dealing with nature, we find regular patterns through systematic experiments, which vary with repetition; these patterns are possessed of such a firm structure that they suggest mathematical modeling and enable predictions about future states in the observed and manipulated patterned systems. This generates *conditional knowledge*.

c. *Exploration*—The most basic form of exploration is the reconnaissance of unknown territory to find prey or suitable farmland. This way forms *orienting knowledge*, at first closely tied to orientating oneself in a landscape. From this elementary meaning derives the metaphor of orientation that applies also to non-spatial contexts (Nieke 2015). Orienting knowledge does not primarily refer to concrete practical usage; it serves to gain an overview, detect possibilities and coherences between distinct areas of knowledge.[20]

Forms of reception and processing, as well as personal relevance, are each categorically distinct:

- Regarding *Experience*: *incidental* learning, mostly below the threshold of awareness; *defensive* learning, in avoidance of danger experienced or imagined, and we have known since antiquity that only stupid people learn primarily through their own pain; (Meyer-Drawe 2012, p. 35)

- Regarding *Experiment*: manipulative-operative, repetitive, prognostic viability control (e.g., through hypothesis-testing processes such as falsification);
- Regarding *Exploration*: theoretical curiosity, integration of details into overarching contexts; constitution of meaning, cognitive landscapes in word–image combinations.

10.3 Emergent learning theory: Human learning is tied to culture

Peter Faulstich adopts Vygotsky's learning theory, which can be understood as an emergent theory (Faulstich 2013, p. 100). This term describes a connection between theories where one theory level can arrive at qualitatively new insights—compared to those of lower levels—and we cannot reduce them to the possibilities for insight offered by the lower theory levels (Greve, Schnabel 2011).

Receiving and building upon all the insights of the lower levels and adding a new theory element, we can successfully arrive at such further-reaching new insights. In that context, we call this process emergence.

Faulstich's reception of Vygotsky provides a sketch of such an emergent theory, which provides a categorical and theoretical explanation for the specific characteristics of human learning. I can only note here that the level of social learning described by Faulstich, following Vygotsky, is less social in the sense of power structures but rather describes cultural learning. This becomes apparent when Faulstich adds the concepts of Leontjew (1982). Vygotsky and Leontjew are called the founders of the "cultural-historical school" in Russian psychology, representing the rejection of a natural-science based concept of learning and the soul, taking recourse to the historic materialism of Marx, who is much more comprehensive in his analysis of the social conditions during the power struggles between the working classes and the bourgeoisie.

11 Pedagogical consequence: Learning requires meaning and generates it

We are here pursuing three goals by presenting deliberations and classification attempts regarding the discourse on an understanding based on learning educational science.[21] These goals consist of:

- The attempt to establish coherence between human learning and the different discourses as well as the paradigms of epistemological approaches, theories, and concepts; to seek and construct a meaning in thinking about the basis of pedagogy.
- To direct attention to the neglected connections between information, knowledge, memory, and competency-building as a goal of learning and of pedagogical practice.
- Bringing into focus the existing but mostly ignored *close connection between individual learning and the overall surrounding culture.*

These deliberations not only contribute to developing a theory for the basic concepts of the educational sciences but lead also to practical consequences. Some of them may be trivial, but after all, with all of its insights, educational science does not have to produce new pedagogic practices. But it may be helpful to accurately validate existing daily practices and routines from the abstracting, overarching perspective of its discourses on truth.

In summary, we can highlight five precepts:

a. *Learning requires meaning.* The findings we presented here regarding concepts that include the content dimension of learning allow us to conclude: *Only that which the learner finds relevant can be learned.* Vygotsky already alerts us to this fact. It corresponds to the current mainstream model of memory building (Markowitsch 2009): Content can transfer from short-term to long-term memory only if it has been affectively encoded, through:

- Negative encoding: resulting in defensive learning to avoid endangerment;
- Positive encoding: as expansive learning to explore the world and for orientation within the world, as it engenders it security and recognition.

Both types of learning occur incidentally and intentionally. Intentional learning needs stimulation and challenges through fascination inherent in the subject matter or through an arrangement (teaching, suggestions, etc.).

b. Meaning is engendered by coherence among the multiplicity of aggregate orientation patterns in the collective memory of humanity. In 1997, Antonovsky developed a concept of coherence to explain salutogenesis (Antonovsky 1997). He subdivided coherence into three areas that are structurally identical to the forms of knowledge that we introduced here: *comprehensibility*, which corresponds to conditional knowledge; *manageability,* which corresponds to change-related knowledge; and *meaning*, through integrating our own existence into overarching contexts, corresponding to our category of orienting knowledge.[22]

There are paradigmatic model examples in the great narratives of humanity that are passed on in entirety from generation to generation. But it also happens individually, as an identity forms with its respective orders of relevance that allow different individuals not only to distinguish themselves from each other, but also to find commonalities. This describes the concept of resonance (Rosa 2012, 2016).

c. *Learning generates meaning.* We can only integrate learned material into memory when we can fit it into an overarching whole (Gestalt of meaning). Only then can we reliably remember it again and use it for our world orientation and to prepare for action. We here suggest three categories of knowledge as a foundational figure for such connective constructions:

- ♦ orienting knowledge,
- ♦ conditional knowledge, and
- ♦ change-related knowledge.

While this suggestion for categorization is heuristic, without being random, we base it on insight into the structural identities of these three areas of knowledge, whose differentiation from each other appears meaningful.

d. *Meaningful learning enables successful life management.* Based on empirical evidence, Antonovsky surmises that *effective coherence* offers a reliable protection against stress and thus stabilizes one's health. With learning basically producing coherence, it becomes closely and essentially connected to stabilizing health—as reflected in its institutionalized conveyance through teaching.

So far, the focus has been directed at [effective coherence's] negative aspects only, namely as a threat to health because of high achievement demands in imposed institutionalized learning, within obligatory schooling and professional training, or as illnesses impinging on learning achievements.

e. *Learning constitutes individuality.* The learning concept from the perspective of educational sciences, as we suggest it here, and a pedagogical practice based on this concept affect and stimulate inspiration and support for the individuality of the learner, which has been defined as the task of education since the Renaissance and later—more emphatically—in age of the enlightenment.

We must ever defend this project against anthropologically universalizing approaches in the institutional system of education; Rudolf Steiner did this when he presented his new and unique pedagogy based on the ideas of anthroposophy (Loebell in Chapter 4; Loebell 2000). With his approach, Steiner took a stand against the growing trend of his time to take a biological, curtailed concept of the human being; he postulated that all learning processes are equal for all people so that—accordingly—we can formulate a methodology prompted by learning content, without consideration of the different and just-developing student personalities (this is particularly apparent in Herbartianism, which even now is still powerful in its effects). This task is still highly relevant today.

Notes

1 [Translator's note: Educational sciences are here referred to in a wider sense, not limited to the academic discipline of educational science. The German term used here is "Bildung," which includes knowledge, subject mastery but also formative aspects of enculturation, character building, personal maturation, and elements of specific professional education. The English term *education* translates to "Erziehung," which is more limited to gaining knowledge and subject mastery at the same time it has also a connotation of "raising" a child. In this translation, I will use "educational sciences" (plural) when the German text refers to "Bildungs-" whereas I will apply "educational science" (singular) when there is reference to the academic discipline or education in the narrower sense.]

2 Most recently, the term *formative educational science* [*Bildungswissenschaft*] is also in use as a summary term for educational science, pedagogy, and job-specific parts of teacher training, or, in its plural form, *formative educational sciences* [*Bildungswissenschaften*], side-by-side with the term *educational science*, denoting the academic discipline. The plural "formative educational sciences" extends also to subject-specific didactics and—when applicable—to independent reference sciences such as psychology, sociology, or political science. This terminology is awkward for two reasons: On one hand, it gives rise to constant confusion between the academic discipline and this cluster of various branches of learning; on the other hand, subject-oriented studies are part of the curriculum for teacher trainees and can hardly be cast in opposition to a professionally oriented science. This note is above all supposed to highlight that not everyone who has studied an academic subject area is also able to teach the corresponding subject in a good, effective, and responsible manner—that requires further "professional science" studies, which are presumed to bring about such professional competency.

3 There is no further explanation for this here, as it appears elsewhere in this anthology handbook.

4 The historic materialistic and—as Faulstichs calls it (in a pejorative sense, which is here used to mark his self-concept)—pragmatistic lines of reasoning I will not further deal with, because they do not tie in with other lines of discourse.

5 This replaces Abraham Maslow's hierarchy of needs, which was not plausible in determining its levels and was primarily tied to occidental culture, but it is still referenced often for orientation purposes.

6 This goes as far as becoming overweight to store fat in the body to be prepared for a sudden famine.

7 Jan Born (2015) offers empirically validated results.

8 This term for a subdiscipline of educational science is by now deemed discriminating, but newly suggested terms, such as "supportive pedagogy," cannot remedy the discrimination that hinges on a deficit in competency but can only shift the issue. This is unavoidable in a meritocracy, i.e., a culture and society based on individual achievement and thus differences in individual attainments. It is therefore more honest to allow this discrimination to remain visible, so that we can openly act against its spurious forms.

9 The term *emergence* here indicates a qualitatively new level of being and cognition, which cannot be traced back to elements of the previous level (Greve, Schnabel 2011).

10 On this concept of culture, see Nieke (2008).

11 We can fully explain everything including the realms of the psyche and mind/spirit through principles of coherence and movement that were developed for describing matter. It serves—and should serve—economy of thought to assume the existence of a single principle of being, namely matter. This is not an ontological claim, but only a hypothetical one.

12 Referencing Kant, Lutz Koch attempted to distill a logic of learning (1991) from the analysis of thought processes, which Koch relates to learning; this attempt is similar in categorization but very different in its process. Such a logic of learning must be developed, according to Koch, by means of philosophy and cannot rely sufficiently on the tools of natural science.

13 On the reception in Germany and approaches to further development, see Zeuner (2014).

14 Here and there we find attempts at systematizing mostly based on philosophy, as recently presented by Koch (2013). Professional acceptance of such attempts is secured not so much by derivative argumentation or reasoning as, rather, by an expectation of plausibility, due to references to the canon of philosophy (which would be the argumentative support of authority) and everyday experiences.

15 See for example Horst Siebert on adult education: "Adults Supposedly Cannot Be Taught" (1999, 2011).

16 The history of adult education in Germany's "book-based self-education," based on free access to no-cost libraries, was an important path to emancipation for the working class, allowing them to overcome the barriers that the educated middle class had erected, barring them from access to world knowledge; Wolfgang Seitter (2001) emphasizes this point. But a more precise analysis would bring up the question of whether such self-education could have been successful and inerrant without any basic instruction (in school or in educational workers' associations). As far as we can reconstruct, this self-education through reading was always accompanied by attendance to lectures that may have provided at least some basic orientation.

17 This only refers to the learning process, not to the fact that a majority of students report in their answers to survey questions pertaining to the quality of their school attendance that the critical factor was not the

Learning from the Perspective of Educational Science

classroom instruction and its content, but rather the opportunity to meet the classmates and their friends among them; there was in this type of answer a strong variation according to educational milieu. We find this kind of peer orientation more frequently in so-called educationally distant milieus (Projektgruppe Jugendbüro 1977).

18 This does not mean that regulative or utopian ideas are wrong or useless: They are an important part of world orientation. In this connection, it only is important that normative orientations should be of a kind that can also easily connect with actions geared at possibly reaching the goals that were set.

19 In light of the findings of biology, we can no longer uphold the old viewpoint that only the human being has the faculty of speech, which accounts for his special rank. We find speech and language in many species down to the communication between cells and among cell particles: These forms of language serve only a complex form of signal transmission. The specific difference here lies only in the special characteristics of human languages—their variability in using symbols—and in the complexity of their statements, as well as their storage in memory, namely through word-image combinations.

20 This relegates pragmatism—like that of John Dewey—to its narrow boundaries: Experience that is tied to actuality does not lead to insight in all areas of cognition.

21 This endeavor follows the dictum of Max Weber that science is an intelligent order of facts—and by facts, Weber means not just simply the experience of reality outside of thinking in a sense of naïve realism, but also the constructions for a mental approach to such a reality.

22 The concept of self-determination theory—as a surrogate for the late mechanistic motivation theories by Deci and Ryan (newest edition: 2008)—includes an identical threefold formal classification approach, with the third category limiting integration to social recognition. This is also important in Antonovsky's work, but he uses a wider concept of integration, including also mental integration of world connectivity webs, i.e., that which other concepts call transcendence, e.g., Maslow.

References

Antonovsky, Aaron (1997): Salutogenese – zur Entmystifizierung von Gesundheit. *[Salutogenesis – on demystifying health.]* Tübingen: DGVT.

Bollenbeck, Georg (1996): Bildung und Kultur – Glanz und Elend eines deutschen Deutungsmusters. *[Education and culture – Glamour and misery of a German interpretive pattern.]* Frankfurt am Main: Suhrkamp.

Born, Jan (2015). Lernen lässt sich im Schlaf verstärken, aber es gibt Grenzen. [Sleep can strengthen learning – within limits.] Interview. In: Psychologie Heute [Psychology Today], 2015, 9, pp. 62–66.

Buck, Günther (1989): Lernen und Erfahrung. Epagogik – zum Begriff der didaktischen Induktion. *[Learning and experience. Epagogics – on the concept of didactic induction.]* 3rd edition with the addition of a part III. Darmstadt: Wissenschaftliche Buchgesellschaft.

Deci, Edward L./Ryan, Richard M. (2008): Self-Determination Theory: A Macro-Theory of Human Motivation, Development and Health. In: Canadian Psychology, 49(3), p. 182–185

Dollase, Rainer (2013): Lehrer-Schüler-Beziehungen und die Lehrerpersönlichkeit – wie stark ist ihr empirischer Einfluss auf Leistung und Sozialverhalten? [Relationships between teachers and students and the personality of the teacher – how strong is its empirical influence on achievement and social behavior?] In: Jochen Krautz and Jost Schieren (Eds.) (2013): Persönlichkeit und Beziehung als Grundlage der Pädagogik. *[Personality and relationship as the basis for pedagogy]* Weinheim: Beltz Juventa, pp. 85–94.

Faulstich, Peter (2013) (Ed.): Menschliches Lernen. Eine kritisch-pragmatische Lerntheorie. *[Human Learning. A Critical Pragmatic Theory of Learning.]* Bielefeld: transcript.

Greve, Jens/Schnabel, Annette (Eds.) (2011): Emergenz. Zur Analyse und Erklärung komplexer Strukturen. *[Emergence. On the analysis and explanation of complex structures.]* Frankfurt: Suhrkamp.

Grimm, Jacob/Grimm, Wilhelm (1885): Deutsches Wörterbuch. vol.12. *[German thesaurus.]* Leipzig: Hirzel.

Göhlich, Michael/Zirfas, Jörg (2007): Lernen. Ein pädagogischer Grundbegriff. *[Learning. A Basic Pedagogical Concept.]* Stuttgart: Kohlhammer.

Hasselhorn, Marcus/Gold, Andreas (2006): Pädagogische Psychologie. Erfolgreiches Lernen und Lehren. *[Pedagogic psychology. Success in learning and teaching.]* Stuttgart: Kohlhammer.

Heckhausen, Heinz (1980): Motivation und Handeln. Lehrbuch der Motivationspsychologie. *[Motivation and action. Textbook of motivational psychology.]* Berlin: Springer.

Herzberg, Heidrun (2004): Biographie und Lernhabitus. Eine Studie im Rostocker Werftarbeitermilieu. *[Biography and habitual learning patterns. A study in a Rostock's dock worker milieu.]* Frankfurt: Campus.

Jörissen, Benjamin/Marotzki, Winfried (2009): Medienbildung – Eine Einführung Theorie – Methoden – Analysen. *[Media Education – An Introduction Theory – Methods – Analyses.]* Bad Heilbrunn: Klinkhardt.

Kahneman, Daniel (2011): Das schnelle und das langsame Denken. *[Slow and quick thinking]* Munich: Siedler.

Koch, Lutz (1991): Logik des Lernens. *[The logic of learning.]* Weinheim: Deutscher Studien Verlag.

Koch, Lutz (2013): Lehren und Lernen. Wege zum Wissen. *[Teaching and learning. Pathways to knowledge.]* Paderborn: Schöningh.

Koller, Hans-Christoph (2012): Bildung anders denken. Einführung in die Theorie transformatorischer Bildungsprozesse. *[A different take on education. Introduction to the theory of transformational educational processes.]* Stuttgart: Kohlhammer.

Krapp, Andreas/Prenzel, Manfred (1992): Interesse, Lernen, Leistung. Neuere Ansätze der pädagogischpsychologischen Interessenforschung. *[Interests, learning, achievement. More recent approaches of pedagogic/psychological research on interests.]* Münster: Aschendorff.

Leonhard, George B. (1971): Erziehung durch Faszination. *[Education via fascination.]* Reinbek: Rowohlt.

Leontjew, Alexej (1982): Tätigkeit, Bewußtsein, Persönlichkeit. Köln: Campus. *[Activity, consciousness, personality.]* Stuttgart: Kohlhammer

Loebell, Peter (2000): Lernen und Individualität. *[Learning and individuality.]* Weinheim: Deutscher Studien Verlag.

Mandl, Heinz/Friedrich, Helmut Felix (2006): Handbuch Lernstrategien. *[Textbook learning strategies.]* Göttingen: Hogrefe.

Markowitsch, Hans (2009): Das Gedächtnis. Entwicklung – Funktionen – Störungen. *[Memory – functions – disorders.]* Munich: Beck.

Mezirow, Jack (1997): Transformative Erwachsenenbildung. *[Transformative adult education.]* Baltmannsweiler: Schneider Hohengehren.

Meyer-Drawe, Käthe (2012): Diskurse des Lernens. *[Discourses on learning.]* 2., rev. edition. Paderborn: Fink.

Nieke, Wolfgang (2007): Allgemeinbildung durch informationstechnisch vermittelte Netzinformation und Netzkommunikation. *[General education through information technological web information and web communication.]* In: Gross, Friederike von, Winifred Marotzki and Uwe Sander (Eds.) (2007): Internet – Bildung – Gemeinschaft. *[Internet – education – community.]* Wiesbaden: VS, p. 145–167.

Nieke, Wolfgang (2008): Interkulturelle Erziehung und Bildung. Wertorientierungen im Alltag. *[Intercultural education and character formation. Value orientations in everyday life.]* 3., rev. edition. Wiesbaden: VS.

Nieke, Wolfgang (2012): Kompetenz und Kultur. Beiträge zur Orientierung in der Moderne. *[Competency and culture. Contributions for providing orientation in modern times.]* Wiesbaden: Springer VS.

Nieke, Wolfgang (2014): Pädagogischer Eros – wider die Instrumentalisierung pädagogischer Beziehungen. *[Pedagogic eros – against the instrumentalization of pedagogic relationships]* In: Böllert, Karin and Martin Wazlawik (Eds.) (2014): Sexualisierte Gewalt. Institutionelle und professionelle Herausforderungen. *[Sexualized Power. Institutional and professional challenges.]* Wiesbaden: Springer VS.

Nieke, Wolfgang (2015): Redeweisen über Raum aus kulturtheoretischer Perspektive in ihrer Relevanz für die Erziehungswissenschaft. *[Figures of speech on space from a perspective of culture theory in its relevance for educational science.]* In: Berndt, Constanze and Claudia Kalisch (Eds.) (2015): Bildungsräume erschließen und gestalten. Erziehungswissenschaftliche und pädagogische Perspektiven auf den Raum. *[Developing and designing educational spaces. Views of space from the perspective of educational science and pedagogy.]* Bad Heilbrunn: Klinkhardt.

Nohl, Arnd-Michael (2014): Lernorientierungen: Empirische Analyse und grundlagentheoretische Reflexion. *[Learning orientations: Empirical analysis and foundational theoretic deliberations]* In: Faulstich, Peter (2014) (Ed.): Lerndebatten. Phänomenologische, pragmatistische und kritische Lerntheorien in der Diskussion. *[Learning debates. Phenomenological, pragmatistic, and critical learning theories of discussion.]* Bielefeld: transcript, p. 155–180.

Projektgruppe Jugendbüro (1977): Subkultur und Familie als Orientierungsmuster. Zur Lebenswelt von Hauptschülern. *[Subculture and family as orientation patterns. On the lived-in world of (vocational track) high-school students.]* Munich: Juventa.

Rosa, Hartmut (2012). Weltbeziehungen im Zeitalter der Beschleunigung. Umrisse einer neuen Gesellschaftskritik. *[Relations to the world in the age of acceleration. Sketch of a new social criticism.]* Frankfurt am Main: Suhrkamp.

Rosa, Hartmut (2016): Resonanz. Eine Soziologie der Weltbeziehung. *[Resonance. A sociology of relations to the world]* Frankfurt: Suhrkamp.

Seitter, Wolfgang (2001): Bibliothekswesen. *[Library institutions.]* In: Arnold, Rolf Sisgrid Nolda, and Ekkehard Nuissl (Eds.) (2001): Wörterbuch Erwachsenenbildung. *[Thesaurus of adult education.]* Bad Heilbrunn: Klinkhardt, pp. 47–48.

Siebert, Horst (1999): Pädagogischer Konstruktivismus. Eine Bilanz der Konstruktivismusdiskussion für die Bildungspraxis. *[Pedagogic constructivism. A summary of the constructivism debate on practical education.]* Darmstadt: Luchterhand.

Siebert, Horst (2011): Lernen und Bildung Erwachsener. *[Adult learning and education.]* Bielefeld: Bertelsmann.

Werner, Göran (2006): Von Verflechtungen zwischen Ästhetik und Ethik – verlängert auf die Sterbeproblematik von "Schwerstbehinderten." *[On the intertwining of aesthetics and ethics – extended to thoughts on the problem of dying of "severely disabled persons".]* Rostock: Dissertation.

Winkel, Rainer (2011): Der gestörte Unterricht. Diagnostische und therapeutische Möglichkeiten. *[The disrupted class. Diagnostic and therapeutic possibilities.]* 10th rev. edition. Baltmannsweiler: Schneider Hohengehren.

Zeuner, Christine (2014): "Transformative Learning" als theoretischer Rahmen der Erwachsenenbildung und seine forschungspraktischen Implikationen. *[Transformational learning as a theoretical framework for adult education and its implications for practical research.]* In: Faulstich, Peter (2014) (Ed.): Lerndebatten. Phänomenologische, pragmatistische und kritische Lerntheorien in der Diskussion. *[Learning debates. Phenomenological, pragmatistic, and critical learning theories of discussion.]* Bielefeld: transcript, pp. 99–131.

Zinnecker, Jürgen (Ed.) (1975): Der heimliche Lehrplan. Untersuchungen zum Schulunterricht. *[The secret curriculum. Research on classroom instruction.]* Weinheim: Beltz.

WALDORF EDUCATION AND LEARNING RESEARCH

Convergences and Differences

Peter Loebell

1 Waldorf education in the context of different learning theories

1.1 Learning and education

"Being human is to learn." With this sentence, Heinrich Rombach denotes an anthropological constant (Rombach 1996). It says that all human beings continuously make new experiences and expand their knowledge and abilities throughout lifelong development. The human being can be defined as "*homo discens,* as a learning human being" (Wulf, Zirfas 2014, p. 16). Learning always refers to the process of acquiring knowledge or abilities. So, the concern cannot be to teach learning itself. Rather, we must understand learning processes in the context of the concept of education, that is, as processes that engender lasting change in the learners' understanding of self and finally aim at the learners' emancipation and participation in society. The focus here is on acquiring resources that allow a productive way to deal with unexpected problems, what Koller postulates in his concept of transformative education: We can understand education as a change of fundamental patterns in the human relationship to self and to the world; human beings have to learn "when they are facing new, problematic situations, which they no longer can manage using their previous framework of relations to world and self" (Koller 2012, p. 16). Koller holds the view that educational processes always point toward transformation of the relationship to the world and self when we face new and problematic experiences; they are caused by crisis-like or at least irritating events. At the very least, the structure of the relationship to the world and self must prove brittle so that educational processes can take place: "This brittleness – aside from moments of crisis – constitutes a further possible cause for transformation" (ibid., p. 71).

This ability—to accept new tasks and problems as challenges and to creatively solve them—Steiner calls "Learning from Life." He thus characterizes the goal of Waldorf education as a comprehensive preparation for lifelong learning: "The individual can learn throughout his life and learn from life. But he has to be educated to do so. During his school years he must develop inner powers that can grow strong during this developmental period so that they can no longer break down in later life" (Steiner 1991, p. 195).

1.2 On the concept of learning

A lasting change in the learner as a result of his own activity is the characterizing mark of a learning process. This latter aspect differentiates learning from biological concepts such as growth or maturation. This change can refer to observable behavior, abilities, knowledge, and skills, as well as to feelings or

234

DOI: 10.4324/9781003187431-21

interpretation patterns of the learner. Both outer influences and inner impulses can trigger learning processes. School pedagogy is mainly interested in those learning processes that are initiated from outside, with preset content and goals and with verifiable results. Different learning theories describe processes such as structure formation in the central nervous system, changes in behavior, acquisition of knowledge and skills, and expansion of action competency. These aspects are fundamental for every kind of school-based learning.

Brain research describes factors and processes of neuroplasticity: Permanent changes in knowledge and abilities are accompanied by changes in the human being's neuronal system, particularly in brain structures. Therefore, we can view learning from the perspective of neurophysiology as a "modification of synaptic super-strength" (Spitzer 2002, p. 146). Researchers consider the general goal of such brain restructurings to consist of "an organism's mid- or long-term adaptations to its environment" (Roth 2011, p. 92). Consciously implemented learning processes—or those that lead to a restructuring of the brain—leave their traces in the neuronal structures of the cortex: "Generally, we can say that the cortex is the 'seat' of consciousness because only events that are connected with cortical activity can arise in our consciousness – everything else is in principle non-conscious" (ibid., p. 321f.).

While the brain structures in all their plasticity do reflect an individual's potential, we cannot reduce the human being, as the acting subject, to the functions of the central nervous system. Therefore, neurobiologist Gerald Hüther writes: "Beyond the reality of material, observable and measurable phenomena created by the life itself, there obviously exists an immaterial, invisible and immeasurable spiritual world" (Hüther 2008, p. 35). Waldorf education is rooted in anthroposophy and establishes a relationship between this spiritual world and physically measurable phenomena by understanding human learning as a phenomenon of body, soul, and spirit—in keeping with current scientific findings. On the other hand, Rudolf Steiner emphasizes the fundamental significance of the human body and especially the central role that the brain plays in its formation and development (Steiner 1987, p. 34).

Behavioristic theories emphasize learning by association, especially in the forms of classic and operative conditioning. But even early on, e.g., in prenatal forms of learning, the fetus apparently relies on the elementary associations between spontaneous activity and sensory perception. "Apparently, we can adequately describe a few prenatal learning processes with terms such as *imprinting* or *conditioning*. On a very basic level of experience, the infant possibly connects remembered events with mainly pleasant experiences in the mother's body" (Rittelmeyer 2005, p. 41). The formation of associations most likely happens when several stimuli occur simultaneously (contiguity) as premised in stimulus-reaction types of learning (Hasselhorn, Gold 2013, p. 39ff.). We can see its effect when the newborn baby recognizes prenatally received auditory imprints (voice of the mother, sounds, melodies)—although it happens on an unconscious level (Rittelmeyer 2005, pp. 36f.): "Apparently there is something like an *elementary faculty of learning detectable in the unborn child*, at latest in the last trimester of pregnancy" (ibid., p. 41).

Behavioral changes occur through conditioning—this is true not only for prenatal learning processes but also throughout the entire life of a person. In the context of Waldorf education, therefore, we need to reflect on possible conditioning mechanisms in the close relationship between teacher and students and in the formation of de-stressing classroom habits and rituals. Waldorf education attributes special significance to caring personal attention, which is evidenced, for example, in the special importance of classroom teachers or in the relinquishing of graded evaluation systems. This caring attention may generate positive or negative stimulus effects and thus result in a conditioning of the students. Therefore, we must strive to carefully differentiate between unexamined measures of reward and punishment and an appropriate feedback culture.

Cognitivist and constructivist learning theories allow us to understand the ways knowledge is acquired and how understanding develops. Today, we generally view learning as a process that produces change—not as a result of innate dispositions but rather due to experiences that undergo reflection that our understanding refers to "a reflexive gain or acquisition and the development or gain of changed forms of knowledge" (Wulf, Zirfas 2014, p. 16f.). Consequently, we cannot distinguish human learning by certain kinds of behavior but rather by a more-or-less conscious control of courses of action and by stores of available knowledge. The central focus of cognitivist learning theories is directed at the actual building of concepts and knowledge inventories. Weinert dates the shift in focus in pedagogic psychology to the year 1956 and summarizes: "The study of human behavior fell out of fashion; in its stead began the intense exploration of cognitive structures, contents, processes and products of the individual engaged in action, learning and teaching" (Weinert 1996, p. 2).

Cognitivism is based on the premise that the conscious, thinking human being is facing the world and that his mind contains the representation of the outer world. This approach assumes that the human being forms mental constructions in his own mind. "Human beings attribute [...] meaning to their actions; they do have reasons for doing something and in that, they distinguish themselves clearly from organisms or systems" (Faulstich 2013, p. 55). Thus, we can describe constructivism at its core as an epistemological program that is assembled from various theoretical fragments (ibid., p. 52). Waldorf education is no stranger to cognitivist and constructivist approaches. But Steiner distinguishes himself from constructivism by pointing to a peculiar trait in human sensory perception. He emphasizes that the human being always perceives objects as more than a sensory modality. For example, in visually perceiving the outer world, there "is also a vague, simultaneous sentience of one's own self." The percept evokes a representation of an object in the observer; at the same time—according to Steiner—the sense of equilibrium transmits an unconscious sensation of the reality, the actual existence of the percept (Steiner 1983, p. 147f.). Today we call this synergy "sensory integration"; it provides the foundation for the reality nexus of human action.

Waldorf education furthermore assumes that active thinking creates inner images that are not mere [mental] constructions; rather this type of thinking activity is crucial for producing one's own insights and for accessing reality. "Reason never penetrates as deep into reality as imagination. Imagination can err, but it penetrates into reality; reason virtually always sticks to its surface" (Steiner 1979b, p. 122). Teaching material therefore has to offer content and must be presented in a way that invites the child to individually get involved in the material to be learned. "The teacher must truthfully present the material in such a way that the child can use her imagination and on her own arrive at understanding. This self-generated understanding then leads to an independent creative or verbal processing of the child's experience" (Lindenberg 1987, p. 201).

Action theory directs attention to self-effective, autonomous learning. The theories mentioned above can hardly explain self-intended and self-initiated learning, because behavioral science and cognitivism—regardless of all significant differences—share one common denominator: The learning organism is viewed as the recipient of stimuli or perceptions, which elicit reactions that are either visible or processed internally. In contrast, there is the view of an acting subject experiencing an active, self-initiated reach into the world, e.g., the independent acquisition of reading and writing skills that can occur already during preschool years. Human beings need surroundings where they can freely—without obstructions—learn what they need for their own life. Reform pedagogy coined the term "negative education" for this phenomenon. This approach characteristically views the human being analogous to the image that the scientist has of himself: as a subject that generates and tests hypotheses. According to that view, science would be a special case of general human learning; the learner appears in consciousness as a problem-solving subject. This addresses the human being as an autonomous, self-reflecting subject, who first recognizes a problem as such.

According to Marton and Booth, we can comprehend the actions of people only if we understand how they "*experience* the challenges, situations and world segments that they are dealing with and to which they orient their actions" (Marton, Booth 2014, p. 172). These authors assume that the world is an *experienced* world, and that each person can only be imagined in the context of their own world. According to them, there is to be no separation between "inner and outer," "knowledge and knower," "subject and object" (ibid., p. 215). Based on this assumption, they arrive at the understanding that the object of learning only emerges in the "course of learning" or "learning means constituting the object of learning" (ibid., p. 248). In dissolving the subject-object split, they are in agreement with an essential assumption of Waldorf education: Anthroposophy goes from the premise that the cognitive human being creates inner images through active thinking.

Cognitive thought accordingly is a crucial factor in creating one's own insights and for participating in reality. Steiner sees perception and concept as two sides of the *one* world (Steiner 1978b). "*Re-cognition* is nothing but a merging of the world's two objective sides into one objective reality" (Kallert 1960, p. 54). "Our thinking is not individual like our sensing and feeling. It is universal. It only takes on individual character in each person because it refers back to their individual sensing and feeling" (Steiner 1978b, p. 72). Therefore, the cognitive human being experiences "that his striving does not invoke a process that runs parallel to the world's course, but rather a process that completes this course of the world and makes it whole" (Kallert 1960, p. 72).

Furthermore, Holzkamp's subject-scientific approach forms an important basis for understanding learning processes in the life space of school. The starting point is the subject, who is located in the world; he inhabits a specific location that offers him a special perspective, "a 'view' of the world (including the subject's own person) from precisely that particular standpoint" (Holzkamp 1995, p. 21). The subjective perspective always has intentional character because it comprises the subject's possibilities for action and his intentions. Thus, Holzkamp calls the subject a "center of intentionality." The determination of the standpoint—not at all [only] in a spatial-geographical sense—continues to be significant: "From this standpoint I do not meet the world neutrally. But I relate to it with my senses and body as an *interested* subject. My intentions, plans, and resolutions are characteristics of my intentionality and are *substantial positions and action plans issuing from the standpoint of my life interests*" (ibid.).

To a subject thus situated, the phenomena of the world appear to carry meanings, and within the scope of such meanings, he can actively transform the conditions of his life. Holzkamp transcends constructivist concepts by focusing on the subject and his unavailability and stubbornness (Faulstich 2013, p. 86). In his terminology, "subjective" signifies the "expansion of being able to manage one's own life conditions" (Holzkamp 1995, p. 23). In this sense, the subject can recognize his intentions for action as being more-or-less "justified." While this does not preclude unjustified action, we can still examine the subjective reasons for each action, since we cannot assume a conscious damaging of one's own interests. An essential implication derives from these terminological considerations: The observer cannot give a causal "explanation" of another person's action that at first appears incomprehensible (in the sense of behavioral theory).

He rather surmises that the other person will have good, potentially comprehensible reasons for his action. Central to Holzkamp's deliberations is the criticism that the reality in the public school system is systematically characterized by "defensive reasons for learning." Children learn mainly because it would have adverse effects on their life management and on their quality of life if they would refuse to do so. More precisely phrased: Students learn in order to solve certain everyday problems within the action field of "school." According to Holzkamp, this happens by employing a whole system of coping mechanisms, among which the successful acquisition of preset learning content is only one strategy of many, and, from the perspective of the student, not even the most important one.

Different theoretic perspectives yield essential pointers for the concept of learning that are significant for any school pedagogy. Beyond that, Waldorf education always searches for ways to challenge, stimulate, encourage, and comprehensively support the incomparable individuality of the human being, who is destined for freedom, while always in accordance with their own developmental goals.

2 Learning in the context of Waldorf education

2.1 Subject or individuality

A fundamental element of Waldorf education is the respect from the start for every child as a unique individuality. From the times of Humboldt and Schleiermacher until today, individuality has remained a topos in educational theory and a goal of educational politics. Nevertheless, nowadays it takes a background role, while comparisons and producing comparability, standardization, and quality-control standards have moved more to the foreground (Frost 2008, p. 303). Already in 1919 Rudolf Steiner remarked that there was a trend toward *nivellement*, i.e., the same treatment for different people or an effort to make them equal, "while it must be the innermost aspiration of human beings to strive for individualization" (Steiner 1979a, p. 83). Therefore, Schieren describes Waldorf education accordingly as an "I"-pedagogy with the "I" considered to be a completely autonomous agency that is not determined by anything else and is self-substantiated (Schieren 2015, p. 235). This view of Waldorf education is not identical with Holzkamp's concept of the learning subject. In fact, the pedagogue must clearly know who the subject is if he wants to orient an intended learning process toward the questions of the learner and his "life interests." The very personality he meets as a child or adolescent is not only entitled to act inconsistently and illogically, but that also means to act in a seeking or questioning manner.

This leads to two demands on the teacher. First, he may not take the verbal or behavioral communication of the child as a revelation of her individual nature or intent without having more detailed knowledge of his surrounding conditions. Here we do not mean that a student's communication should be disregarded, but rather that the teacher must make an effort to come to know the underlying intent in an understanding way, so that the child can feel recognized and seen by the teacher. The second demand on the teacher concerns the future development of the child's personality. The task of the teacher is not limited to understanding reactions in regard to the unfolding of the student's personality. To the same degree that it is important to appropriately understand the child's communications and to take them into interactive account, it is also important for the teacher to anticipate the student's opportunities for learning and development in the planning and design of his lessons. In this process, he must not base his preparations on the known attributes of the students alone, without risking limiting their chances of development by identifying them with earlier behaviors—this is also true when dealing with the temperament of a child. When planning his lessons, the teacher must keep in mind an image of the student that is open regarding the future, without neglecting the understanding of the student's personality that he has attained so far.

What is meant here is a tentative or questioning attitude of the teacher when dealing with the individuality and future development of every single child, just like the attitude that should be fostered in child studies at Waldorf schools (Seydel 2009; Wiechert 2012). That means that the teacher counts on there being an aspect—as-yet hidden—of the child's individuality, which will reveal itself fully only in the future. In its experience of self, each individual shows intention that is not exclusively aimed at "the management of one's own life conditions" because being human means precisely also to be open to "non-managed" spiritual experiences (Loebell, Buck 2015). While I am aware of my doing when I act and experience my individuality in its presence, I do know that my "Self" is not fully expressed or exhausted in that action. This "I" or "Self" will be also present tomorrow in different actions and with a change in identity. Thus, I recognize my individuality as the orientation and goal of my actions. As the one who acts, I can grasp intuitively whether I am aligned with my individuality but, because of the individuality's subject character, I cannot describe and recognize it from a perspective of self-distancing.

Individuality is not identical with itself but does not appear—in contrast to "identity"—as a constant factor in specific power constellations of an individual human being; […] rather, it appears in the potential for change and regeneration of the "I" (Rittelmeyer 1993, p. 134).

The term "individuality" is meant to denote "I," i.e., it is the word we use when we sense that we act in full responsibility and freedom. "Learning is a variant of 'I think something' and in this case the 'I' does not signify an abstract agency but the living self, which is called upon in many ways and has to account for itself" (Meyer-Drawe 2008, p. 399). But insofar as children claim their right to act inconsistently and unreasonably, knowing that they are not yet fully responsible, their individuality is present in their perceptible behavior like a possibility of their own true future being.

The experience of this reality is subjective in nature; it is incomprehensible from without and thus also not immediately accessible to scientific description (Frank 1991). We can communicate it only through the power of subjective certainty or self-evidence, surmising that everyone knows it from their own experience. For the "I" is not a sum of attributes, but is a beingness that continuously gives birth to itself through its own creative activity. As acting subject, the "I" is not accessible for self-reflection. Whenever I think about myself, when I become the object of my self-reflection, I can only ever grasp the image I have made of myself. Therefore, Steiner emphasizes that the human being knows of his own self not by thinking, but through a higher level of perception—through intuition (Steiner 1986, p. 18). "This inner experience of intuition provides that sense of self-evidence, which will never again wholly vanish" (Leber 1990, p. 146).

But how then can a teacher come to know anything at all about the actual essence, the individuality of the children in order to reach them with his instruction?

According to Steiner, we can divide the inner development of the human life into three parts. "One of the parts comprises what we sense to be our gifts, talents, and abilities. The second part deals with what we develop in interactions with our fellow human beings and that emerges in the interplay between our consciousness and theirs. And the third part contains our experiences" (Steiner 1980, p. 135). Human individuality does not express itself directly in personal giftedness nor in social interrelations, but in experiences or, more precisely, in becoming more experienced, the individuality finds its expression (ibid., p. 137).

In our quest for the child's individuality during school learning, we find here a significant impulse, if we succeed in describing learning as an individual process *of becoming more experienced*. Steiner's point here is that one-sided support for special giftedness is insufficient for fostering the child's individuality—his "actual essence." Individual impulses throughout a person's life do not necessarily find effective expression, even if schools offer the students opportunities to cooperate in class with other human beings and thus fulfill useful societal tasks.

2.2 *Learning from the perspective of individuality*

There appear to be three achievements or experiences that allow an individual to turn single actions into learning activities: Only the learner himself can muster the attention necessary for absorbing information that is relevant in classroom instruction. Likewise, it is the achievement of individuality to accept a set task and commit to it as a challenge. Finally, only the learner himself can arrive at insights and convictions (Loebell 2000, 2004). The three achievements of individuality in the learning process—attention, commitment, and the experience of self-evidence—correspond to man's relationship with the world. Rudolf Steiner takes these three achievements as the starting point in his essay, "Theosophy": "The human being becomes aware[...] that he is connected with the world in a threefold way. The first way is something he finds, something that he takes as a given. The second way entails that he make the world his own affair, something that has meaning for him. The third way for he regards as a goal toward which he shall strive incessantly" (Steiner 1987, p. 25). According to these three forms of encountering the world, he calls the threefold essential nature of the human being "body, soul and spirit."

Physical existence provides a center for one's individuality in turning toward the spatial world and thus it provides a foundation for any kind of perception. This quality of the learning process is the faculty of *attention,* enabling the learning subject to turn toward the world's phenomena. Social participation appears in the learning process as *commitment* that serves the individuality to recognize a task as one's own to solve and to accept. Allport described this achievement as participation in different steps, e.g., as "task-involvement" and "ego-involvement" (Allport 1970, p. 104f.). In the process of learning, individuality as "its own creation" and incomparable "project" finds a "deep ground" in the form of singular insights and experiences of evidence.

We know that every individual remains ultimately alone with experiences like that; they cannot be fully communicated in all their ramifications. Nevertheless, they form the indispensable basis of every secure orientation: Responsibility and conscience are rooted in this ground of certainty.

Attention, commitment, and the experience of evidence correspond to the three cognitive forms of world participation that Steiner developed in his work *The Study of Man*—in reversal of the classic syllogism—"conclusion, judgment and concept." According to Steiner, we already draw a conclusion "when we look at a simple thing" (Steiner 1992, p. 135). Our earlier experiences cause our attention to lift something out from the general flood of sense impressions. Based on all our previous experiences, we draw conclusions—as Steiner words it—regarding the special characteristics of an object, an event, or an attribute. Following Schütz and Luckmann, we can speak of "lifelong relevance structures" (Schütz, Luckmann 1979). Our attention is captured by the unusual, the contrary; it structures the world of perceptions into an object, a background and its further surrounding, which is temporarily outside of conscious awareness, but from where a sensory stimulus can at any time draw attention to itself. In other places, I called this surrounding field "horizon" (Loebell 2000, p. 71).

With the act of judging, we transcend mere ordering activities and connect our sense impressions with the knowledge of our life world. We take note of essential and unessential aspects of things and evaluate them, e.g., about their usefulness; likes and dislikes occur, because judgments are closely connected with feelings. And vice versa: "Emotions and feelings lead us to assess events, social constellations and people, and they contribute to the structuring of our life world" (Wulf 2014, p. 115). Emotions originate mostly in habits of the soul, and not in the same high conscious awareness as conclusions. It is of the highest importance that during the learning process students are ever again faced with questions and problems in the form of tasks. Judging therefore leads to a loss of indifference for the object; commitment emerges when the students take personal ownership of a given task.

Steiner's third logical category is the concept. "In forming concepts, i.e., in noting the results of human judgments, you have a deep-reaching effect on the sleeping soul, or, in other words, on the body of the human being" (Steiner 1992, p. 138). The deep effect of concepts on the entire life nexus of a human being presents a special challenge to pedagogy: "The educator must strive to communicate such concepts to the children, since they will never again in later life have them in the same original form because these concepts transform themselves in later life" (ibid., p. 139f.).

However, this is possible only if we largely avoid giving definitions in our classes and instead provide a characterization of the things and events. When we form a concept in accordance with Steiner's meaning, we can directly experience the evidence and validity of his insight. Wagenschein describes this process as a "feeling at home" in the subject matter, and the corresponding "exciting" experience then happens "suddenly" and "luminously" (Wagenschein 1968, p. 21f.).

With the three categories of conclusion, judgment, and concept, Steiner points to human perception as an experiential process that moves from being closed to being open. When noticing an object, the perceiver first encounters his own previous experiences. After that, a series of deliberations occurs that leads to substantiated judgment. Finally, the concept comprises the entire essence, the idea of a thing, and thus opens up a new perspective to the observer. Then he no longer experiences the urge to assess the object according to his fears and hopes, likes and dislikes. Rather, he can now recognize the nature of the thing itself, the essential existence, which is the foundation for what is being recognized.

Consequently, according to Steiner, we should, e.g., not offer predefined examples for specific grammar rules. The child's notebook should only be there to write down the rules because: "There is a gigantic difference between the teacher simply asking the child for a grammar rule and prompting him to read out loud the example he copied into his notebook so that he repeats it – and between treating the example as something that was meant to be forgotten and now prompting the child to find his own examples. In finding his own examples, the child engages in an activity that is eminently educational" (Steiner 1990, p. 130f.). That is, Steiner is concerned with children independently handling the rules they learned. In this sense, the logical categories open our eyes for the development of potential of human concepts and encourage creativity and fluid flexibility in thinking.

2.3 Learning through transmuted formative powers

Around the seventh year of life, the child experiences the first signs of school readiness. Rudolf Steiner described this development and noted that the same formative powers that are building the child's physical body in the first seven years of life afterward start to be effective in the realm of the child's soul processes (Steiner 1907; Loebell in Chapter 3).

Piaget took the position that this threshold, in general, marks the onset of concrete-operational thinking when the ability develops to assess spatial relations independent of one's own standpoint (Montada 2002). At the same time, children are starting to differentiate their body scheme in distinguishing right from left. In this process, the development both of the body scheme and of a good spatial orientation appear to be important prerequisites for general progress in learning. In particular, many researchers point out that a lack of right-left orientation is connected with learning disabilities such as dyscalculia and dyslexia (Maier 1994, p. 136ff.).

The understanding that education relies on the learner's actively employing his inner formative powers has far-reaching consequences for curriculum, methodology, and didactics. If the instructor already knows what she has to teach the children, if textbooks contain already didactically processed and pre-determined content, the lesson will lack the necessary openness for initiating an unconditional search impulse [in the students' minds]. The problem constellates itself already in the very first encounter with the world's phenomena; the way we generally pursue science is so-to-say spoiling the pedagogic character. Therefore, Kranich demands that if we want to give our students an understanding of the world, we first must come to know it in a way that moves our soul (Rumpf, Kranich 2000).

Rumpf makes clear that any student who learned to only trust in the knowledge of experts runs the danger of losing the ability to formulate his own questions. A teacher who advocates that kind of knowledge can no longer be believable when he tries to communicate to the children that more effective than any pre-packaged, sterile knowledge are awe and wonder, their own searching, and finally the insights they gain independently. In this framework, Kranich presents four dimensions of thinking suitable for arriving at an understanding of the essential character of things: thinking in causal relations, thinking in images, thinking in reciprocal relations (organic recognition), and thinking in physiognomic recognition (ibid., p. 61ff.). Each of these four activities of the mind relies on fully focused activity of the thinker, guided by his interest and with the goal of independently gaining insight into inner laws—the phenomenal world becomes "mentally [and spiritually] transparent" (ibid., p. 66).

2.4 Learning through thinking, feeling, and willing

Heinrich Roth's concept of learning emphasizes its effect on thinking, feeling, and willing: "From a pedagogical perspective learning signifies the improvement or new acquisition of different forms and contents of behaviors or achievements. Most of the time learning signifies even more, namely change or improvement in the soul's functions of perceiving and thinking, feeling and evaluating, striving and willing, which precede and determine these forms of behavior and achievement; in other words the inner faculties and powers change or improve and thus also a person's inner reservoirs of knowledge, attitudes and interests that are built upon these faculties and powers" (Roth 1969, p. 188). It is not only the knowledge of the students that changes, but also their emotions and dispositions for action.

2.4.1 The polarity of thought and will

In his work, *The Study of Man as the Foundation for Pedagogy*, Rudolf Steiner's bases his deliberations on the dichotomy of thought and will (Steiner 1992). He posits that the imagination produces representations of reality. This is an intentional process, because there is *something* that the human being can consciously grasp in his representations (ibid., p. 31). The human will forms an antithesis to this way of accessing the world, because human action occurs within the realm of physical laws—through his physical strength, the subject brings about a change in the reality of his surroundings. Thinking and acting or imagination and will are according to Steiner the two forces within man, which form the basis for the entire [inner] development of the world; he calls them *antipathy* and *sympathy* (ibid., p. 35). He uses the first term to point to the fact that human thought tends to isolate single phenomena from the undivided stream of experiences and to fix them as static objects. Steiner here speaks of a transfixing, paralyzing power, created in man's soul by conscious perceptions and thoughts. "Abstract imagination is a kind of reality that has been devitalized in ordinary consciousness; it remains below the threshold of awareness in life" (Steiner 1983, p. 140). In contrast, he uses the term *sympathy* to mean that as soon as the human being engages in specific activities, he knows that he is directly and closely connected to his body, in particular to his organs of movement. In employing his will [in physical activity], the human being can have the immediate experience of feeling the aliveness of his body, while at the same time any conscious awareness of his organismic activity diminishes. "Willing completely eludes his awareness because that is only directed at the phenomena *within the soul*. Yet there is something in the *will* that is not based on a decision of the soul, but is the soul's vehicle for participating in the experience of the outer world" (ibid., p. 163). In his phenomenological description of body movements, Merleau-Ponty also describes the unconscious or "sleeping" quality of the will:

I move external objects with the help of my own body; it takes the object from one place in order to put it down in another location. But I directly move the body without help, I do not find it at any given point in objective space and I do not move it to another place, I do not first have to search for it, because it always is already where I am – I do not have to move it myself toward a target – right from the beginning the body is already in contact with me and it propels itself toward the target. The relation between my decision [will] and my moving body is a magical one (Merleau-Ponty 1966, p. 119).

Obviously, the will is inaccessible to human consciousness; we can talk only about our *imaginings regarding the will*. Only the subject, actively engaging in an act of will, can experience its actual effects. That was the reason why modern psychology ignored the concept of will for decades, even though we have trouble explaining human actions without it. The first to revisit this topic was motivation psychologist Heinz Heckhausen in 1987. He views the course of a life as a continuous stream of behaviors, while the individual himself determines a good part of the respective stimuli that meaningfully elicit reactions. Many phenomena in courses of action seem to be directed like that—from within—and stand up against the push and pull of the outer situation. They can be explained only with a capability-oriented psychological construct such as the will. Heckhausen stated that he himself had no qualms using terms such as "to will," "will," or "volition," besides "willing" for the manifold phenomena of action (Heckhausen 1987, p. 121).

In *The Study of Man*, Steiner states that we cannot directly cause a child to use his will. We can only educate the whole person toward developing life habits of body and soul that lead to such a rallying of the will in specific cases. For example, so-called remedial learning targets the students' system of self: It aims at the students learning to attribute their achievements to their own efforts. One study (Reid, Borkowski 1987) showed that targeted support for students, with simultaneous strengthening of the conviction that they themselves earned their accomplishments, led to "higher memory achievements and longer-term recall of the learned strategies, which they also then could transfer to other learning tasks. At the same time hyperactivity in the supported children decreased" (Neber 1996, p. 415).

It is of central significance to Waldorf education that Steiner considers the will to develop first of all through various artistic activities such as drawing, painting, and making music (Steiner 1990, p. 10f.). For Steiner, the methodological task lies in "engaging the whole person" (ibid., p. 11). This thought leads him to the postulate that education and teaching itself must develop as an art form.

2.4.2 The mediatory quality of feeling

Between the two polar opposite—and seemingly incompatible—forces of thinking and willing or "antipathy" and "sympathy," a third quality unfolds, which is human feeling in all its many differentiated, vast forms. Accordingly, these two elementary forces also play a role in the origination of feelings: "We are not immediately and consciously aware of either antipathy or sympathy, but they live in our unconscious and signify our feelings, which compose themselves continuously and rhythmically in an interplay between antipathy and sympathy" (Steiner 1992, p. 35). Steiner calls feeling "restrained will" and defines will as "implemented feeling." Feeling is close to willing and can thus stimulate the tendency for action. However, feelings in the sense of emotional intelligence do not stand in opposition to cognition. Obviously, emotions are a constitutive function of all people in all cultures and at all times (Wulf 2014, p. 112); since early childhood, feelings contribute to building memory (ibid., p. 116). We differentiate emotional memory as the third fundamental form of memory since it shares characteristics with declarative (explicit) memory and procedural (implicit) memory (Roth 2011, p. 106). The three soul activities of thinking, feeling, and willing correspond to these three types of memory.

Any experience that we remember contains mainly "what happened *in us:* the *feeling* triggered by the respective situation" (Morasch 2014, p. 553). The intensity of concomitant feelings shapes our subjective experiences and determines the sustainability of their neuronal anchoring. Moreover, a decisive factor is "the *point in time* when an experience takes place: The significance and impact of experiences on the development of human behavior and personality are proportionally greater [...] the earlier they happen in ontogenesis" (ibid.).

For Steiner, feeling forms the essential basis for human learning, especially between the 7th and 14th years of life, with artistic activities being particularly important. For example, rhythms in music and dance provided early human communities with ways of communicating feelings and representational images. First, art enables transmission of meanings that defy description; second, art offers each individual the opportunity "to use and develop his mental potential in his very own way" (Eisner 2007, p. 117); and, as a third point, art makes a form of experience possible that we call "aesthetic" and "Aesthetic experience is worth remembering" (ibid.).

Eisner goes so far as to state that pedagogy's main goal is to prepare students to become artists: "People, who are able to contemplate their own activities in an artistic way, can use their power of imagination, experience their work as it progresses, make use of the unexpected, and can evaluate the direction of their work on the basis of feelings and of rules" (ibid. p. 118).

2.4.3 The synergy of thinking, feeling, and willing in the development of the child

Basically, children learn through emotional participation, which, according to Steiner, occurs as the polar forces of imagination and will affect each other in mutual interplay. The qualities of the interactive effects change in the course of development. Steiner states that will and feelings are still intimately linked during the first years of school—giving rise to the infectious spontaneity of children just starting school. In this context, thinking unfolds, and it reflects the wholistic quality of the child's experience. We sense the intensity of their immersion in the undivided attention they give to their own activity—be it at play or work. Their affection for others is generally not yet directed at the whole class but—in a school setting—they bond mostly with the person of the teacher or one single child. Apparently, school beginners lack distance to their own subjective standpoint. Lasting change occurs when, in middle childhood, the will starts to detach itself from feeling and the children internalize their self-created images. Experience shows that this happens mostly during the ninth or tenth year of life. This process generates a plethora of soul experiences that no longer urge the child to immediate action or visible expression. Instead, the child contemplates an interesting object, which triggers a felt inner movement: joy and enthusiasm, maybe desire, possibly also defense and disgust. The released formative powers have reached a pinnacle in their soul activity. As feelings detach from the will, children can intensely relish plunging into the powers of their own imagination. But that means children do not yearn for ready-made images, but prefer to practice the use of their own creative powers of imagination. Not only the subject matter is of interest in class, but increasingly also all socially relevant happenings. Viewing the world's phenomena from a distanced standpoint can lead us to manifold new discoveries and explorations.

In this process, the simple spontaneity with which a young child seized upon a task is lost. If the material to be learned is not interesting or puzzling enough, the issue of motivation can push to the foreground. The question arises as to how children can build a solid relationship to the lesson's subject matter and develop commitment in the sense described above. Waldorf schools introduce students to learning content mainly through a lesson plan oriented to the developmental tasks of the children, with foremost emphasis on their own developmentally appropriate, active use of the formative powers. A multitude of mere demonstrations, however spectacular or baffling, allow the child to remain in an observer role, which entails that—after a short stimulus—the inner engagement of the child is in danger of being lost again. Instead, Waldorf schools specifically stimulate the use of the children's own creative powers of imagination, e.g., in nature study classes. We can awaken the child's form-giving activities first through dealing with the natural world because the forces at work there resemble those of their inner thought processes. Rudolf Steiner poignantly expressed this connection in a lecture he presented to medical doctors: "There is a perfect parallel between our inner soul experiences and the formative principles of nature that actively build the outer world" (Steiner 1985, p. 66).

Around the tenth year of life, the child develops a new relation to his surroundings; the phenomena of the world now impact the child's feelings much more directly. Not only joy and enthusiasm, but also annoyance and boredom now determine how the child opens to instruction in the class. The child's relationship to his activity loses some of its intensity; the work is experienced as easier, less committal, so that a trial run or looking for fun satisfaction sometimes determines the work on a task. But the images the child takes in at this age can lastingly shape his thoughts and perceptions, often for his entire life.

In the time of pre-puberty—around age 11 for girls and 12–13 for boys—the possibility arises for students to more strongly direct their own thought processes, aside from dealing with important events in their social life. The students are increasingly trying to look beyond the surface of the phenomenal world. The decisive difference here is their transition from *having* representational images to *forming* thoughts. Based on Steiner's *Philosophy of Freedom*, Schieren describes the special significance of thinking in Waldorf education with the two characteristics of "individual performance" and "universal lawful patterns." He writes: "These are the two central attributes of thinking: It must be produced individually and at the same time it lawfully roots in itself."

In this regard, a dynamic transition and exchange occur between *individual* and *universal* factors (Schieren 2015, p. 230). The urge to form their own thoughts should lead the students to grasp the hidden laws. In classroom instruction, phenomenology is more than recognizing and categorizing phenomena; rather, it deals with the issue of causality. As they first approach this question, most students awaken to the awareness for the distinctions between essential and non-essential phenomena. Of foremost importance here is Steiner's statement that young people are moved by the question of causality. The adolescent is supposed to integrate the phenomena into the world of his imagination and to reconstruct on an inner plane what he has perceived. "This creates a special realm in the inner world of a young person – an inner space for cognition and for truth" (Kranich 1997, p. 53).

2.5 The importance of rhythm for learning

According to Morasch, there are four different factors that influence the occurrence of experiences and their anchoring in the brain: timing, intensity, frequency, and multidimensionality. The earlier in life (starting in utero) we have experiences, the deeper and longer lasting is their effect on cortical structure formation, with puberty as an essential watershed time. "The connectivities that have been activated by then will remain with us throughout our life as a potential that can be activated, while all others are eliminated permanently" (Morasch 2014, p. 555). Strong emotions and repeated occurrence of experiences catalyze lasting changes in the brain. Furthermore, we observe augmented learning effects when an experience "is facilitated on as many levels as possible, i.e., is solidified" (ibid.). For Waldorf education, that means primarily that effective learning processes develop in the rhythmic interplay of feeling, will-directed action, and thought processes. In his work, *The Study of Man*, Steiner attempts to awaken an understanding of the rhythms that correspond to the interplay of these three soul activities and their underlying states of consciousness. He assumes that thinking occurs mainly in waking consciousness, the will happens in a "sleeping" state, and feelings are experienced in an intermediate dreamlike state (Steiner 1992, p. 99).

Attentive concrete consciousness has a tendency to change—on one hand due to the change of perceptible objects and sense modalities, on the other hand due to sliding into states of dreamlike or sleeping-unconscious forms of experience.

A child that perks up and turns to an object with waking consciousness will soon find another target for his awareness or will transition into a quiet, half-conscious dream state. Changes and transitions are constitutive characteristics of consciousness; they are the factors that allow us to experience time with its different components. And so, Rapp recommends applying the principles of (among others) tension and relaxation in dealing with children who have attention deficits. "Already in preparing the lesson, a teacher can plan this alternation [of tension and relaxation], while taking into account his students' ability to cope with pressure. Several factors allow for smoother change: varying the type of activity, using all the senses, facilitating concrete, physical activities, and inserting breaks" (Rapp 1982, p. 108).

Every object, every act of perception, has its own time, an appropriate time of dwelling in human consciousness. We must allow awareness to rise; it must ripen, so to speak, in the consciousness of the child, and then it fades away again in a rhythmic way. This phase of non-conscious dreaming, too, is essential to the unfolding of the lesson. In a one-hour lesson, the teacher has to heighten the tension of cognitive receptivity and then release it again like the movement of a pendulum. That means the teacher must plan the number of teaching objects, their sequence, and inner connection very carefully and sparingly, as if composing a piece of music. The composition can be successful if the lesson design arises from a sense of appropriate rhythms. In that sense, we can indeed speak of teaching as an "art" and of the teacher as an "expert in the art of teaching": "In regard to subjective representation of topic-specific contents in students [...] and on content-related tasks in classroom instruction, cognition-psychology based research has shown that teachers cannot at all make the students learn [...]; the studies showed that the development of learning opportunities in the classroom puts high demands on teachers, precisely because they have only very limited possibilities to influence the learning success of their students" (Bromme 1997, p. 186). Rudolf Steiner makes a connection between rhythmic lesson design and the human breath, pointing out that feelings find their immediate expression in the process of breathing. Kranich shows how the breathing rhythm as a "living physiognomy of our emotional life" influences the activity of the central nervous system and thus causes cognitive realization to become an inner experience. In this process, students can develop a special cognitive attitude: "namely only then to begin thinking about a matter when one has connected with it experientially" (Kranich 1999, p. 178).

On the other hand, the alternation of sleeping and waking significantly affects human learning. In his first lecture in *The Study of Man*, Steiner draws our attention to this point as well (Steiner 1992, p. 26).

Today's research distinguishes different phases of sleep. Simplified, we can contrast the changes of brain activity up to deep sleep with so-called paradoxical sleep, which is characterized by rapid eye movement under the eyelids and therefore called REM sleep. Only recently, newer research has become available: Giulio Tononi's studies show that brain synapses are dismantled during deep sleep and that the remaining synapses are strengthened during paradoxical [REM] sleep (Spork 2011, p. 274f.). But we also know that the content of adults' declarative memory is mainly consolidated during non-REM sleep, i.e., in deep sleep, while the content of procedural and emotional memory, however, is consolidated in REM sleep (Roth 2011, p. 119). The experience of the day obviously undergoes a profound change during sleep. Memory builds up through distinctive patterns of excitation in the brain and can be triggered through specific associations. Sleep also enables procedural memory, i.e., declarative memory turns into abilities. Sleep thus not only solidifies the memory tracks but also changes their quality. Sleep results in gaining an overview and a more facile generalization of solutions to problems.

Steiner portrayed in several lectures how to transmit lesson content in such a way that it can continue to correctly unfold its effects during sleep (Steiner 1973, p. 175ff., 1978a, p. 45ff.). The description of his so-called three-step method—illustrated with the example of physics and history classes—is significant for cognitive instruction (Sommer in Chapter 5): The teacher must stimulate the volitional, comprehending awareness of the child by presenting a natural science experiment or a historical event. In directing their attention to the lesson content, the children in fact continuously draw conclusions:

The children recognize patterns and Gestalt configurations and establish meaningful attributions between action sequences and units of language. It proves helpful to students, if they can integrate the events presented in class into a spatial and chronological order because that appeals to the whole person. According to Steiner, the students must fully connect through their will with the forces and laws of the objective, physical world. The next step now consists of characterizing the facts that were merely presented up to now. The students review the recalled content but only emphasize what is essential, evaluating the relative importance of various details for the overall context. This stimulates the feeling nature of the children before the class is over and they are dismissed. Conclusions and judgments that are formed this way continue to be active during sleep.

The following day, the objects of the initially waking awareness appear as (at first) unconscious images. As the students are prompted next to contemplate the previously introduced events for conceptualization purposes, this review aims precisely at lifting into awareness the patterns and laws of the events. While observing a physical experiment or merely registering historical events, the students proceed to form individual representations in their imagination. They were able to draw conclusions from what their eyes and ears perceived, could recognize, and create order—i.e., judge—based on their personal previous experiences. But the goal of the cognitive process is the *concept* that appertains to the observed, registered fact. This concept emerges in the mind only after the structure-forming forces were active in the brain during the night. And so, it is during sleep that the student makes his cognitive transition from individual representation to meta-personal world comprehension. Therefore, the concept may contain more than the results of initial observation. In the best case, the feeling of self-evidence arises in the student, the certainty of experiencing a truth.

Obviously, this three-step process of concluding, judging, and conceptualizing corresponds again with the above-mentioned three achievements of self during the learning process: attention, commitment, and the experience of evidence. Concluding means to perceive things, a first recognition that relies on the attention of the observer. In judging, the students establish a special relationship with phenomena by attributing importance to them—or denying it. This indicates the degree of commitment they muster regarding things and events. Finally, by forming appropriate concepts, the experience of evidence can emerge in the students as realization.

Steiner presupposed that lasting learning processes take place at night, during sleep, and the findings of modern sleep research largely confirm his assumption. Moreover, Steiner likens falling asleep with forgetting, which has been called a "most important process" by Roth, "however it is as yet little understood by science" (Roth 2011, p. 121). The comparison with sleep suggests that in process of forgetting there is also a catabolism of synapses in the cortex, as a prerequisite to selectively strengthening other, frequently activated neuronal connections. Such a dismantling would not be physically necessary because the brain's capacity is in principle unlimited (ibid., p. 123). Nevertheless, forgetting obviously forms the basis for a transformation of concepts that enables a deeper understanding of the received content—the change from declarative to procedural memory.

We can learn even complex behavioral patterns quickly through imitation (Rauh 2002, p. 155). Newborns can already imitate finger movements, sticking out their tongue, and facial expressions, such as the mouth positions for forming O, E, or A-sounds, eye squinting, head movements, frowning, or even sounds. We can observe delayed imitation still after 24 hours in babies as young as six weeks old. In the first years of life, we master important developmental tasks through learning by imitation. The so-called wolf children, who grew up without the model of other human beings, were unable to learn erect gait or language expression. Even later, in the company of other people, these children demonstrated only imperfect language acquisition (Petermann, Niebank, Scheithauer 2004, p. 121).

Imitation depends on sense perception, but it entails more than mere imitation of gross motoric movements of other people. Like an organ of resonance, the entire body reacts to the inner posture and soul movement of the other person. Kranich therefore cites cases "of children who imitate the soul expression of adults, even down to metabolic processes. Depending on circumstances, the worry and grief of a mother can already in early childhood cause paralysis in the digestive activity of the stomach or even vomiting up the nourishment" (Kranich 1999, p. 81).

After the discovery of so-called mirror neurons, we know today that everybody reproduces with their own body the visible movements and facial expressions of other people. These nerve cells are activated not only whenever a person engages in a purposeful activity, but also when they observe the same process in another person. Most importantly, this activity of the neuronal system makes it possible "to decipher the meaning of observed 'motoric events,' i.e., to understand them directly without any need for the mediating influence of thinking, concepts or speech" (Rizzolatti, Sinigaglia 2008, p. 131f.).

Mirror neurons are characterized by reactivity to movements of living actors, and especially to purposeful actions. They also activate when we imagine an action, but especially when we imitate an observed action (Fuchs 2010, p. 199). These nerve cells also mirror the emotional expression of others (ibid., p. 201). But it is questionable whether we can explain the manifold phenomena of empathy with the function of these neurons alone. We must consider "that the concept of empathy in its full meaning entails an entire complex of perceptions, representations, feelings, and previous experiences and also involves counter-relevancies, which means that empathy is a wholistic, affective and cognitive activity that we can certainly not attribute to any specific neuronal system, however specialized" (ibid., p. 202).

Long before young children begin to speak on their own, they grasp the speech of other human beings within the movements of their own body. The fine nuances in the behavior of adults, their inner attitudes, their language, thoughts, and feelings so move the inner being of young children that they experience them as impulses for their own actions.

Waldorf education accords special significance to imitation as a learning principle. Rudolf Steiner repeatedly emphasized that the young child, up to the seventh year of life, is mainly an imitating being and—to lesser degrees—still during the first two or three school years (Steiner 1998a, p. 19). "The child learns the peculiar way he moves, also his language and even the form of his thoughts, by imitation" (ibid., p. 53). In his lectures, Steiner often presented his theses in a pointed way. His one-sided emphasis on how important imitation is for the developmental period until the seventh year can best serve as advice for the adult educator. Steiner points out that young children "allow themselves to be taught only by that [...] which is visible in the surrounding" (Steiner 1998b, p. 72). Up to the seventh year, therefore, children cannot be educated by admonishments, "but only by example, down to the level of thought" (ibid., p. 215).

Phenomenological philosophy views the human being basically as a corporeal being that feels, perceives, reaches into the world and is at the same time present in time and space (Liebau 2007). In this context, a new branch of research has developed in recent years that Shapiro characterizes like this: "Replacing the old vision of cognition as disembodied symbol processing, beginning with inputs from the sensory system and ending with commands to the motor system, is a new vision of cognition as emerging from continuous interactions between a body, a brain and the world" (Shapiro 2011, p. 156). Against this backdrop rises the awareness of spontaneous self-movement as an essential condition for learning. "Before we discover our capabilities in dealing with objects, we first find out about our kinetic faculties: I can stretch myself, twist, point, grasp, turn, etc. – a multitude of possibilities within certain limits. All this we learn in the first months of life. Spontaneous self-movement leads to body-based concepts that form the basis for our knowledge of the world and ourselves (cognitive concepts)" (Koch 2013, p. 38). Already before birth, a fetus develops many of the activities mentioned.

Besides the perception of outside stimuli, the sensation of one's own spontaneous activity forms an elementary prerequisite for learning. Impressions from without evoke differentiated body states after birth as well. The perception of such body states in other individuals prompts us to bodily imitate them, and the movements in one's own body in turn cause emotional states to arise (ibid., p. 53). In newborn children, muscle activity occurs synchronously with the articulation of talking people and apparently leads to the perception of speech based on their own physical activity.

Modern embodiment research has been able to demonstrate that perceiving and mimicking the movement of another person lead not only to neuronal mirroring, but also to a corresponding activation of one's own movement organs. For example, seeing a sad or joyous facial expression causes a certain tension in the observer's own facial muscles that are needed for producing the observed expression (Rittelmeyer 2013, p. 43). In adults also, imitation relies in principle on a barely visible activity in one's own body that precedes the conscious sensation produced through the neuronal system. "Every muscle activity is being transmitted to the brain via the sense receptors for self-movement; the imitation activity thus in a way mirrors back to the brain. It must be a form of *retroflexed mirroring,* because the impulse for facial micro-imitation originates first in the brain (or the carrier of that organ), and then the observed outer impression mingles with self-motoric impressions in the act of perception" (ibid. p. 43). This form of elementary participatory physical experience could—supposedly—form the basis for the development of compassion or empathy with the soul experiences of others.

We have mentioned that, already before birth, the awareness of one's own movement forms a significant basis for the learning process. Sports scientist Anke Abraham states that from a perspective of neurobiology and brain physiology the traditional dichotomy of body and soul/spirit and the priority of consciousness are no longer a given. She holds that it is becoming ever clearer "that the brain, and thus our thinking, feeling and acting, could not develop at all without the rest of the body, while sensations and feelings form an irreplaceable connecting link between organism and brain" (Abraham 2013, p. 18f.).

As outlined above, the triad of thinking, feeling, and willing forms an elementary foundation for Waldorf education. In 1917, Rudolf Steiner had already emphasized in his essay "Riddles of the Soul" the importance of a synergy between various sense modalities, especially the interplay of outer observation, e.g., by seeing, hearing, tasting, and smelling, and the experience of one's own bodily activities, e.g., through proper motion and the somatic-visceral sense faculty.

According to Abraham, the fact that the human being can experience his surroundings to be real is rooted in the synergy of the outward-directed senses with the simultaneous experience of one's own body as a resonance organ in the vein of sensory integration. Furthermore, the human motoric system forms the foundation for imagination, such as in geometry: "We have to thank the features of our skeletal system for our knowledge of all abstract science" (Steiner 1992, p. 56). Abraham, too, highlights that the body offers opportunities for building practical knowledge that need to be taken seriously as the necessary basis of abstract thinking. Education thus depends on the practice of body movement. "True understanding, in contrast to second- or third-hand knowledge that remains abstract, constitutes an eminently important connection for pedagogy, and it needs an emotional as well as corporeal-affective context. From a perspective of developmental psychology, such a context consists of concrete encounters with things that I meet through my movements and senses and notice due to a resistance or difference. Such encounters trigger sensations and feelings, provoke reactions, and help me to contour and structure the world" (Abraham 2013, p. 27). In this context, we also might understand the significance of eurythmy classes in Waldorf schools. This art form is meant to facilitate awareness of the connection between body movement and one's own thinking and feeling. Steiner attributes great pedagogic and hygienic significance to this movement art, which he inaugurated himself, because "it seeks to find healthy and nature-appropriate connections that must exist between the soul's inner experience, sensing and speech expression and the movement potential of the whole human being" (Steiner 1998b, p. 178).

2.6 Heterogeneity and individualization—the significance of the teacher

According to Ruberg and Walczyk, the current discourse on heterogeneity in school pedagogy can be seen to juxtapose the approach of learning- and teaching research against a perspective of educational theory. Each side focuses on a different dimension of heterogeneity (Ruberg, Walczyk 2013, p. 20): "Differentiating variable characteristics are intelligence, previously acquired knowledge, learning strategies, motivational and affective determinants, as well as structural aspects" (ibid., p. 21).

Here we must consider that within the context of a three-tier school system we can only speak with reservations of heterogenic learning groups after the fifth grade or, at the latest, after the seventh grade. The situation in Waldorf schools appears unusual in face of the current discussion about heterogeneity in the public school system. In fact, the concept of a unified K–12 (or K–13, if the graduation prep year is counted) school is one of the essential characteristics of Waldorf education. This school model is based on the conviction that children of all levels of giftedness and of diverse social backgrounds can in principle benefit most from cooperative learning—a concept that also forms the basis for the demand for inclusiveness issued by the 2009 UN convention on disability rights. The only selection occurs insofar as the parents consciously choose a school for their child from a pool of several offers. However, the first Waldorf school already established smaller special classes for children with greater needs for support, for whom one of the larger classes with often more than 50 children was not an appropriate learning environment. Waldorf pedagogues have thus gained decades of experience in dealing with classes that are mixed with respect to giftedness and achievement capacity, while the learning results, measured in successful graduations, show no evidence of systematic deficits. We can explain this success with certain determining factors and elements of specific [Waldorf] didactics and methods:

- A manageable college teacher (at least at single-track schools) as well as the same classroom and subject teachers over a stretch of many years all make it possible to build intense individual relationships with each child and adolescent.
- A largely stable class community lasting 12 or 13 years creates the social framework in which developing children with varying talents can experience the acceptance and support of their peers.
- The block lesson principle in main lesson classes serves to deepen the daily immersion into an area of learning for several weeks.
- Artistic, rhythmically structured lesson designs meet the demand for a healthy psychosomatic development of children and adolescents.
- The curriculum is age-appropriate and flexible to respond to the student's need for developmentally appropriate learning.
- The diverse cognitive, artistic, and craft-oriented practical classes as well as regular projects in the areas of theater, choir, and orchestra, in addition to various internships, correspond to the diversity in the talents of the students so that everyone of them has the opportunity to experience his or her own strengths and weaknesses.
- The students are assigned individual projects such as the so-called yearly projects on topics they can choose themselves; thus, they can intensely pursue longer-term work in their area of focus, supported by teachers.

The pedagogue must know each single child and adolescent so well that he can support them individually in their development. One essential factor in Waldorf education is the view that, in the last analysis, each individual can only educate and form himself. With their lessons, the teachers create surroundings and learning invitations that are meant to stimulate and motivate each child to work according to their own possibilities. Waldorf education uses its own set of diagnostic tools that it has developed quite independently, apart from the respective discourse in the educational sciences.

The practice of the child study is of crucial importance; it was introduced in the [Waldorf] conferences between 1919 and 1924, and, until today, it has undergone continuous further development as an essential diagnostic tool in Waldorf schools (Seydel 2009; Wiechert 2012). Steiner responded to most questions on how to deal with individual students with concrete tips and advisements. We can arrive at a meaningful interpretation of specific diagnostic terms that he introduced only when we consider their original contextual framework and refer to the respective personalities involved. Terms such as "big-headed" or "small-headed" or "cosmic" and "terrestrial children" have stimulated further deliberations on one hand, but on the other they have also given rise to misunderstandings. On the level of concrete lesson designs, Ruberg and Walczyk consider the teacher to be the core resource for managing diversity (Ruberg, Walczyk 2013, p. 21). The teachers must be competent in four areas that are important for the kind of instruction that supports heterogeneity: professional expertise (to be acquired in academic study of the respective subject area) and methodological, diagnostic, and class-oriented leadership competencies. The three last areas are "the result of extended developmental and learning processes and of dealing with one's own professionality" (ibid., p. 28). There is one type of teacher who is particularly successful in regard to student achievement; Baumreich called that type "authoritative": "He plans his lessons well: He sets clear goals; gives guidance even during illustrative learning; delegates; chooses lesson materials; evaluates achievements and makes sure that behavioral rules are followed in class; he is friendly and offers help when needed" (Mietzel 1993, p. 291).

New Zealand scientist John Hattie arrived at a similar result with his statistical evaluation of more than 800 English-speaking meta-analyses on school learning. He started from the premise that the success of school learning can be measured with appropriate testing procedures and then attempted to determine the factors for successful learning by analyzing the test measurement results. With this approach, he also concluded that the person of the teacher is the critical factor for the learning success of students.

Hattie's differentiated presentation of teacher-specific factors of influence reveals that their subject expertise and academic education are generally less important for learning success. In contrast, he accords much stronger positive effects to practical teaching efforts and their contemplation (micro-teaching). Other factors that are eminently important for learning processes are the quality of the relationship between teacher and student, the clarity of the teachers, abstaining from labeling learners, and teachers going through continuing education and trainings (Hattie 2014, p. 129ff.). Hattie summarizes the essential results of his comprehensive work in six "signposts for excellence in education." His list starts with the thesis that teachers "are one of the most important influences in learning" (ibid., p. 280). They have to be "directive, influential, caring and actively engaged, with a passion for teaching and learning" (ibid.). Moreover, Hattie considers it especially important that the teachers should be aware of what the students think and know, in order to construct for them the kind of experiences that convey purpose and meaning in the light of that knowledge (ibid., p. 280).

Finally, Hattie considers it important to create an atmosphere in which mistakes are welcomed as learning opportunities. His monumental analysis is supported by experiences and results of studies in the area of brain research. The neurobiologist Joachim Bauer states in his book on mirror neurons that the "interpersonal human relationship between learner and teacher is of paramount significance" (Bauer 2006, p. 122f.). He further emphasizes "that personal instruction is a crucially important component in teaching and learning, including demonstrations and modeling by the teacher" (ibid., p. 123). The arguments and insights gained from empirical study, which attribute a significant influence on learning success to the role of the teachers, resonate with an essential core principle of Waldorf education. Steiner emphasized this in his first lecture on *The Study of Man*, which he presented to future Waldorf teachers: "You will not become good teachers of instructors when you pay attention only to what you do, if you do not attend to who you are" (Steiner 1992, p. 27). In this sense, it is the effect of the teacher's personality itself that enables learning processes.

Therefore, it is an essential characteristic of Waldorf schools that a classroom teacher pedagogically accompanies the children throughout the first eight grades and teaches in the mornings a number of subjects in block format.

The authority of the teacher, therefore, does not rely primarily on subject-specific expertise and knowledge. Rather, this authority is rooted in trust—advanced by children and their parents—which has to be ever-newly earned and substantiated during their school years. This is brought about on one hand by the teachers' continuous attendance to their own subject-specific and methodological competency and on the other hand by the different experiences that students and their parents have in dealing with teachers.

- Reliability and flexibility: While, of course, keeping his agreements and following through on his announcements, the teacher retains his flexibility in order to quickly react to unforeseen events with presence of mind.
- Recognition and encouragement: Children need to feel seen by their adult persons of reference. Any individual challenge and praise should always encourage the child and elicit further effort.

- Trust in the leadership of the teacher becomes more solid by repeatedly experiencing that the required work and the suggested pathways to problem-solving lead to success.
- An important pedagogic task is presented at puberty when the adolescents detach themselves from authority and can develop their own capacities for judgment.

3 Summary and outlook

Waldorf education rests on a view of human learning that offers manifold connectivity options for various learning theories that have originated in the 20th century. Waldorf education is based on Steiner's *The Study of Man*, which understands the learner as a being of body, soul, and spirit. It takes into consideration all the fundamental processes that are already significant for the first learning experiences, e.g., for learning the mother tongue: spontaneous activity together with the awareness of the movements in one's own body, sensory perception, and reaction to outer stimuli, exploration, and imitation. On one hand, learning arrangements that take into account rhythmic processes and individualization aim at a broadening of capacity in regard to knowledge, ability, and competency.

On the other hand, each learning process also brings with it a limitation of developmental possibilities and the loss of a sense of unity. Therefore, Waldorf education not only focuses on expanding one's own resources but also places value on spiritual experiences that elude one's grasp and on trust in a comprehensive world order (Loebell, Buck 2015).

As elaborated at the beginning of this article, in Waldorf schools, young people are meant to learn "learning from life." Faced with an acceleration of societal development, students today will be confronted in the future with issues that today's educational plans can hardly anticipate. More than ever before, learning will have to rely on developing personal resources that enable them to deal creatively with unforeseen challenges. In that sense, Waldorf education's overarching goal then resembles the psychological concept of resilience, meaning that vigor of the soul, elasticity, and endurance are capacities that will allow a person to overcome difficult challenges in life in a healthy way (Loebell 2007). As a prerequisite for gaining such resilience when faced with crisis-like situations or life events, Gerald Hüther, from the perspective of neurobiology, calls for a school atmosphere of trust on three levels, which children need for any form of learning:

- Trust in their own potential, capabilities, and skills to overcome problems.
- Trust in being able to resolve difficult situations together with others.
- Trust in the meaningfulness of the world and in feeling protected and comforted within the world (Hüther 2007, p. 53).

Steiner's concept of Waldorf education harmonizes with this demand. It is designed to create the prerequisites for comprehensive, formative human education through long-term, reliable support from certain teachers who are committed to foster every child with mindfulness and esteem; through the stable community of a learning peer group throughout the entire 12 years [of schooling]; through a formative feedback culture that relinquishes any standardized, comparison-based evaluation system; through targeted stimulation of the student's own image-producing activity; through rhythm between effort and relaxation; and last, not least, through a learning atmosphere that enables and values spiritual experiences.

We will illustrate the effects of Waldorf education's qualities as described above with an example of an animal studies lesson. In fourth grade, most children are interested in their natural environment and animals in particular. They hear their teacher explain that most rodents are small, agile, and very flexible in their movements and that many of them dig their burrow in the earth. And, of course, they are familiar with squirrels with their impressive skillfulness. It is no coincidence that of all things the largest European rodent prefers to live in water. The beaver grows over a longer time span than its close relatives; it gains more weight and appears somewhat clumsy when moving around on dry land.

But in the water its body assumes streamlined contours, elegantly sliding through the floods. Its toes are webbed, and underwater it can close the openings of its nose and ears as it dives into deeper waters down to the bottom to seek nourishment there. It can stay underwater for up to a quarter hour without coming up for air, and all the tunnels of its underground burrow end underwater. The children are astonished to learn that more than 12,000 hairs grow in a spot on the beaver's back about the size of a thumbnail, and in the same-sized spot on the belly, there are nearly double as many. The beaver shares with other rodents the trait that its lower incisors grow continuously and have to be used constantly. But its powers of digestion are so strong that it eats huge amounts of wood and bark (4000 kg a year). Particularly mystifying is its paddle-shaped, highly vulnerable tail that it uses to loudly slap the water surface when there is danger. But its most astonishing ability is the communal building of dams and "fortresses" using tree trunks and branches, so that they transform whole river courses and valleys into ecologically diverse, rich landscapes. Thirty-four children listen attentively, ask deepening questions, note down key words for their own essay, and copy a drawing from the blackboard: a beaver in its typical posture, gnawing on a tree log. The homework assignment is: "Write down what you know about the beaver."

The description above clearly shows that the children's attention is first stimulated by the teacher's narrative and a hand-drawn picture on the blackboard. Furthermore, commitment emerges as the whole class is gripped by stirring interest. Single children who are distracted by side events or personal problems are swept up in the mood of their peers. The common interest naturally constellates an assignment, and the variety of the homework presented the next day reflects the children's diversity.

All did their work. Some of them have only been able to produce a few sentences; they still have difficulties articulating themselves in writing, and they are content with a few general phrases. Most children wrote two to three pages; one of them ended up with nine. The teacher's artistic drawing had piqued the children's interest. And in presenting the lesson content, the teacher did not just enumerate abstract facts, but through narrative offered a living portrait of the animal in its natural habitat. The students, in their own imagination, create inner images of a quietly flowing river, and on its banks, beavers are digging their burrows so that the access tunnels are underwater. With their inner eyes, they see the skillful movements of the swimming animals and imagine how they gnaw through thin tree trunks during the night and drag their building material to the right place by the river. The teacher purposely does not show them pictures or video clips, so the children will activate their own powers of imagination and, e.g., reenact how the work of more than 300 animals creates a dam and a lake behind it. The dam is constructed in such a way that the animals can regulate the water level with a few skillful movements: e.g., in winter, they pull out twigs at specific places in the dam's structure and drain as much water as needed to create an air bubble under the ice so that they don't need to climb onto shore to breathe, but can, while swimming, come up for air underneath the ice layer. This type of narrative is meant to stimulate the student's own activity, to motivate them to find further information, to draw, and to write a poem or a short story about a beaver family. Finally, the students can exchange their thoughts and questions in class conversation the next day so that an insight into the animal's special character emerges as an experience of evidence.

Waldorf school classes are of heterogeneous composition, which means we find a wide range of varying talents and capacities in a peer group that learns together over a 12-year time span. It is a matter of course for the children that everyone has different abilities, interests, and ways of working. They do not have to compare themselves with others; they can be happy together, celebrating special achievements of classmates. There are many examples of successful teaching experiences in Waldorf schools, and reports of students and graduates attest to predominantly positive memories (Barz, Randoll 2007; Randoll 1999). But in various contemporary threads of discussion, we can also recognize that the potential of Steiner's impulses for pedagogy has by no means been exhausted yet.

- Orientation toward a final exam still imposes a limit on full wholistic support for the soul development of the human being through art instruction and on the strengthening of the will through practical activity (Schneider 2006; Stöckli 2011). With his concept of "life learning," as a "learning in life and for life," Stöckli reaches beyond the common practice of Waldorf education and creates links over to the concept of the Hibernia school that has joined vocational/professional and general educational elements since 1952.

- The worldwide proliferation of Waldorf schools poses considerable challenges to the culture-specific application of methodic and didactic components. The Friends of Rudolf Steiner's Art of Education coordinate academic education, introductory on-the-job training, and continuous education for teachers in all continents.

- Widespread founding of Waldorf schools occurred during a time of dramatic political and social change, which affected pedagogical practices. This applies to developments in subject-specific disciplines (e.g., physics, technology, history, languages) and also to topical areas that in the first part of the 20th century—unlike today—were not yet considered a necessary part of the curriculum, such as sexual education and media pedagogy.

- Pedagogic challenges result from the close proximity in which different cultures live together in Middle Europe; founding of intercultural Waldorf schools constitutes an important reaction to such societal changes.

- Aside from anthroposophical remedial education, several Waldorf schools have for quite a while taught classes composed of both children with various special needs and "normal" students. In 1994, the UNESCO conference established the guiding principle of inclusion as a standard for national systems of general education, which also impacts Waldorf schools. Even though the latter have pursued the principle of a unified K–12 school format since 1919, inclusive modes of teaching impose higher demands on teachers who, in the course of their education so far, have not been prepared to guide young children with different needs for special support.

Steiner's call for "learning to learn from life itself" concerns also Waldorf education itself, which has to reinvent itself continuously in order to meet new challenges. Because the founding and operation of Waldorf schools in principle result from the initiative of people (mostly parents or teachers), new concepts are developed where the people involved recognize a need for change. The anthroposophical-anthropological foundations of Waldorf education offer opportunities; their realization depends on the needs and efforts of those who bring a Waldorf school into existence.

References

Abraham, Anke (2013): Wie viel Körper braucht die Bildung? Zum Schicksal von Leib und Seele in der Wissensgesellschaft. *[How physical should education be? On the destiny of body and soul in the knowledge society.]* In: Hildebrandt-Stramann, Reiner, Ralk Laging, and Klaus Moegling (Eds.) (2013): Körper, Bewegung und Schule. Teil I: Theorie, Forschung und Diskussion. *[Body, movement, and school. Part 1: Theory, research, and discussion.]* Kassel: Prolog, pp. 16–35.

Allport, Gordon W. (1970): Gestalt und Wachstum in der Persönlichkeit. *[Pattern and growth in personality.]* Meisenheim am Glan: Hain.

Barz, Heiner/Randoll, Dirk (Eds.) (2007): Absolventen von Waldorfschulen – Eine empirische Studie zu Bildung und Lebensgestaltung. *[Waldorf school graduates – an empirical study on education and life design.]* Wiesbaden: Springer VS.

Bauer, Joachim (2006): Warum ich fühle, was du fühlst. Intuitive Kommunikation und das Geheimnis der Spiegelneurone. *[Why I Feel what You Feel. Intuitive communication and the secret of mirror neurons.]* 12. Edition. Munich: Heyne.

Bromme, Rainer (1997): Kompetenzen, Funktionen und unterrichtliches Handeln des Lehrers. *[Competencies, functions, and teachers' instructional actions.]* In: Weinert, Franz E. (Ed.) (1997): Enzyklopädie der Psychologie. *[Encyclopedia of Psychology.]* Themenbereich D. *[Topic area D.]* Series I, vol. 3: Psychologie des Unterrichts und der Schule. *[Psychology of classroom instruction and school.]* Göttingen: Hogrefe, pp. 177–214.

Eisner, Elliot W. (2007): Ästhetisches Lernen. *[Aesthetic learning.]* In: Göhlich, Michael, Christoph Wulf and, Jörg Zirfas (Eds.) (2007): Pädagogische Theorien des Lernens. *[Pedagogical theories of learning.]* Weinheim and Basel: Beltz, pp. 113–118.

Faulstich, Peter (2013): Menschliches Lernen. Eine kritisch pragmatistische Lerntheorie. *[Human learning. A critical-pragmatistic theory of learning.]* Bielefeld: transcript.

Frank, Manfred (1991): Selbstbewusstsein und Selbsterkenntnis. Essays zur analytischen Philosophie der Subjektivität. *[Self-confidence and self-knowledge. Essays on the analytical philosophy of subjectivity.]* Stuttgart: Reclam.

Frost, Ursula (2008): Bildung als pädagogischer Grundbegriff. *[Education as a foundational concept of pedagogy.]* In: Merterns, Gerhard, Ursula Frost, Winfried Böhm, and Volker Ladenthin (Eds.) (2008): Handbuch der Erziehungswissenschaft. *[Handbook of educational science.]* Vol. 1: Grundlagen Allgemeine Erziehungswissenschaft. *[Foundations. General educational science.]* Paderborn: Schöningh, pp. 297–311.

Fuchs, Thomas (2010): Das Gehirn – ein Beziehungsorgan. Eine phänomenologisch-ökologische Konzeption. *[The brain – a relational organ. A phenomenological-ecological conceptualization.]* 3. Edition. Stuttgart: Kohlhammer.

Hasselhorn, Marcus/Gold, Andreas (2013): Pädagogische Psychologie. Erfolgreiches Lernen und Lehren. *[Pedagogic psychology. Success in learning and teaching.]* 3. Edition. Stuttgart: Kohlhammer.

Hattie, John (2014): Lernen sichtbar machen. *[Making learning visible.]* 2. Edition. Hohengehren: Schneider

Heckhausen, Heinz (1987): Intentionsgeleitetes Handeln und seine Fehler. *[Intentional action and its mistakes.]* In: Heckhausen, Heinz, Peter M. Gollwitzer and Franz E. Weinert (Eds.), (2014): Jenseits des Rubikon – Der Wille in den Humanwissenschaften. *[On the other side of the Rubicon – Will in the humanities.]* Berlin: Springer, pp. 143–175.

Holzkamp, Klaus (1995): Lernen. Subjektwissenschaftliche Grundlegung. *[Learning. Subject-specific scientific groundwork.]* Frankfurt am Main: Campus.

Hüther, Gerald (2007): Resilienz im Spiegel entwicklungsneurobiologischer Erkenntnisse. *[Resilience in the light of insights from developmental neurobiology.]* In: Opp, Günther and Michael Fingerle (Eds.) (2007): Was Kinder stärkt. Erziehung zwischen Risiko und Resilienz. *[Making children strong. Education between risk and resilience.]* 2. Edition. Munich, Basel: Reinhard, pp. 45–56.

Hüther, Gerald (2008): Die biologischen Grundlagen der Spiritualität. *[The biological foundations of spirituality]* In: Hüther, Gerald, Wolfgang Roth and Michael von Brück (Eds.) (2008): Damit das Denken Sinn bekommt. *[Injecting meaning into thinking.]* Freiburg: Herder, pp. 25–37.

Kallert, Bernhard (1960): Die Erkenntnistheorie Rudolf Steiners. Der Erkenntnisbegriff des objektiven Idealismus. *[Rudolf Steiner's epistemology. The concept of knowledge in objective idealism]* Stuttgart: Freies Geistesleben.

Koch, Sabine C. (2013): Embodiment. Der Einfluss von Eigenbewegung auf Affekt, Einstellung und Kognition. *[Embodiment. The influence of self-directed motion on emotion, attitude, and cognition.]* Berlin: Logos.

Koller, Hans Cristoph (2012): Bildung anders denken: Einführung in die Theorie transformatorischer Bildungsprozesse. *[Thinking differently about education: Introduction to the theory of transformative educational processes.]* Stuttgart: Kohlhammer.

Kranich, Ernst-Michael (1997): Kausales Erkennen als Phänomenologie – seine Bedeutung für die menschliche Entwicklung nach dem zwölften Lebensjahr. *[Causal cognition as phenomenology – its significance for human development after the 12th year of life.]* In: Kranich, Ernst-Michael (Ed.) (1997): Unterricht im Übergang zum Jugendalter. Anregungen zur Bewältigung einer schwierigen Aufgabe. *[Teaching during the transition to puberty. Suggestions for mastering a difficult task.]* Stuttgart: Freies Geistesleben, pp. 23–56.

Kranich, Ernst-Michael (1999): Anthropologische Grundlagen der Waldorfpädagogik. *[Anthropological foundations of Waldorf education.]* Stuttgart: Freies Geistesleben.

Leber, Stefan (1990): Die menschliche Individualität. *[Human individuality.]* In: Bohnsack, Fritz and Ernst-Michael Kranich (Eds.) (1990): Erziehungswissenschaft und Waldorfpädagogik. *[Educational science and Waldorf education.]* Weinheim and Basel: Beltz, pp. 140–184.

Liebau, Eckart (2007): Leibliches Lernen. *[Body learning.]* In: Göhlich, Michael, Christoph Wulf and Jörg Zirfas (Eds.) (2007): Pädagogische Theorien des Lernens. *[Pedagogic theories of learning.]* Weinheim and Basel: Beltz, pp. 102–112.

Lindenberg, Christoph (1987): Zur Problematik der Individualisierung des Lernens in Theorie und Praxis der Rudolf-Steiner-Pädagogik. *[On the problem of individualizing learning in theory and practice.]* In: Hansmann, Otto (Ed.) (1987): Pro und Contra Waldorfpädagogik. *[Pro and cons of Waldorf education.]* Würzburg: Königshausen and Neumann, pp. 188–204.

Loebell, Peter (2000): Lernen und Individualität. *[Learning and individuality.]* Weinheim: Beltz.

Loebell, Peter (2004): Ich bin der ich werde. Individualisierung in der Waldorfpädagogik. *[I Am, Who I Am Becoming. Individualization in Waldorf education.]* Stuttgart: Freies Geistesleben.

Loebell, Peter (2007): Schule und Resilienz. Konzepte und Erfahrungen in der Waldorfpädagogik. *[School and resilience. Concepts and experiences in Waldorf education.]* In: Die Deutsche Schule 1/2007, pp. 80–91.

Loebell, Peter/Buck, Peter (Eds.) (2015): Spiritualität in Lebensbereichen der Pädagogik. *[Spirituality in life spheres of pedagogy.]* Leverkusen: Budrich.

Maier, Peter H. (1994): Räumliches Vorstellungsvermögen. *[Spatial imagination competency.]* Frankfurt am Main: Peter Lang.

Marton, Ference/Booth, Shirley (2014): Lernen und Verstehen. *[Learning and understanding.]* Berlin: Logos.

Merleau-Ponty, Maurice (1966): Phänomenologie der Wahrnehmung. *[Phenomenology of perception.]* Berlin: Walter de Gruyter.

Meyer-Drawe, Käte (2008): Lernen als pädagogischer Grundbegriff. *[Learning as a basic concept in pedagogy.]* In: Merterns, Gerhard, Ursula Frost, Winfried Böhm, and Volker Ladenthin (Eds.) (2008): Handbuch der Erziehungswissenschaft. Vol. 1: Grundlagen Allgemeine Erziehungswissenschaft. *[Handbook of educational science. Vol. 1 Foundations, general educational science.]* Paderborn: Schöningh, pp. 391–402.

Mietzel, Gerd (1993): Psychologie in Unterricht und Erziehung. *[Psychology in instruction and education.]* 4. Edition. Göttingen: Hogrefe.

Montada, Leo (2002): Die geistige Entwicklung aus der Sicht Jean Piagets. *[Mind and spirit development from the perspective of Jean Piaget.]* In: Oerter, Rolf and Leo Montada (Eds.) (2002): Entwicklungspsychologie. *[Developmental psychology.]* 5. Edition. Weinheim: Beltz, pp. 418–442.

Morasch, Gudrun (2014): Erfahrung. *[Experience.]* In: Wulf, Christoph and Jörg Zirfas (Eds.) (2014): Handbuch Pädagogische Anthropologie. *[Handbook of pedagogic anthropology.]* Wiesbaden: Springer, pp. 549–558.

Neber, Hans (1996): Psychologische Prozesse und Möglichkeiten zur Steuerung remedialen Lernens. *[Psychological processes and possibilities of directing remedial learning.]* In: Weinert, Franz E. (Ed.) (1996): Enzyklopädie der Psychologie. Themenbereich D, Serie I, Vol. 2: Psychologie des Lernens und der Instruktion. *[Encyclopedia of psychology. Theme area D, series I, vol. 2: Psychology of learning and instruction.]* Göttingen: Hogrefe, pp. 403–444.

Petermann, Franz/Niebank, Kay/Scheithauer, Herbert (2004): Entwicklungswissenschaft. Entwicklungs psychologie – Genetik – Neuropsychologie. *[Developmental science. Developmental psychology – Genetics – Neuropsychology.]* Berlin: Springer.

Randoll, Dirk (1999): Waldorfpädagogik auf dem Prüfstand. Auch eine Herausforderung an das öffentliche Schulwesen? *[Waldorf education being tested. Also, a challenge to the public school system?]* Berlin: VWB.

Rapp, Gerhard (1982): Aufmerksamkeit und Konzentration. Erklärungsmodelle, Störungen, Handlungsmöglichkeiten. *[Attention and concentration. Explanatory models, disturbances, possibilities for action.]* Bad Heilbrunn: Klinkhardt.

Rauh, Hellgard (2002): Vorgeburtliche Entwicklung und frühe Kindheit. [Prenatal development and early childhood.] In: Oerter, Rol and Leo Montada (Eds.) (2002): Entwicklungspsychologie. *[Developmental psychology.]* 5. Edition. Weinheim: Beltz, pp. 131–208.

Reid, Molly K., & Borkowski, John G. (1987). Causal attributions of hyperactive children: Implications for teaching strategies and self-control. Journal of Educational Psychology, 79(3), 296–307.

Rittelmeyer, Christian (1993): Individualität und Autonomie. Zur Geschichte und Krise eines pädagogischen Projekts. Einleitung des Herausgebers. *[Individuality and autonomy. On the history and crisis of a pedagogical project. Introduction by the editor.]* In: Bildung und Erziehung, 46, issue 2, pp. 129–137.

Rittelmeyer, Christian (2005): Frühe Erfahrungen des Kindes. Ergebnisse einer pränatalen Psychologie und der Bindungsforschung. *[Early childhood experience. Findings of prenatal psychology and attachment research.]* Stuttgart: Kohlhammer.

Rittelmeyer, Christian (2013): Leibliche Erfahrung und Lernen. Über den Sinn einer allseitigen Sinnesbildung. *[Body experience and learning. On the reason for a well-rounded education through the senses.]* In: Hildebrandt-Stramann, Reiner Ralk Laging and Klaus Moegling (Eds.) (2013): Körper, Bewegung und Schule. Teil I: Theorie, Forschung und Diskussion. *[Body, movement, and school. Part I: Theory, research, and discussion.]* Kassel: Prolog, pp. 36–53.

Rizzolatti, Giacomo/Sinigaglia, Corrado (2008): Empathie und Spiegelneurone: Die biologische Basis des Mitgefühls. *[Empathy and mirror neurons: The biological basis of compassion.]* Frankfurt am Main: Suhrkamp.

Rombach, Heinrich (1996): Anthropologie des Lernens. *[The anthropology of learning.]* In: Willmann-Institut (Ed.) (1996): Der Lernprozeß. *[The learning process.]* Freiburg: Herder, pp. 3–46.

Roth, Gerhard (2011): Bildung braucht Persönlichkeit. Wie Lernen gelingt. *[Education requires personality. How learning succeeds.]* Stuttgart: Klett-Cotta.

Roth, Heinrich (1969): Begabung und Lernen. Ergebnisse und Folgerungen neuer Forschungen. *[Giftedness and learning. Findings and consequences of recent research.]* Stuttgart: Klett.

Ruberg, Christiane/Walczyk, Julia (2013): Zwischen Standardisierung und Individualisierung: Heterogenität in der Schule. *[Between standardization and individualization. Heterogeneity in school.]* In: Beutel, Silvia-Iris, Wilfried Bos and Raphaela Porsch (Eds.) (2013): Lernen in Vielfalt. Chance und Herausforderung für Schul- und Unterrichtsentwicklung. *[Learning in diversity. Chance and challenge for school- and curriculum development.]* Münster: Waxmann, pp. 13–34.

Rumpf, Horst/Kranich, Ernst-Michael (2000): Welche Art von Wissen braucht der Lehrer? *[What kind of knowledge does a teacher need?]* Stuttgart: Klett-Cotta.

Schieren, Jost (2015): Die spirituelle Dimension der Waldorfpädagogik. *[The spiritual dimension of Waldorf education.]* In: Loebell, Peter and Peter Buck (Eds.) (2015): Spiritualität in Lebensbereichen der Pädagogik. *[Spirituality in life spheres of pedagogy.]* Leverkusen: Budrich, pp. 221–242.

Schneider, Peter (2006): Ursprung und Ziel der Waldorfschule: Eine notwendige Besinnung. *[Origins and goals of Waldorf schools: A necessary reflection.]* In: Bauer, Horst Philipp and Peter Schneider (Eds.) (2006): Waldorfpädagogik, Perspektiven eines wissenschaftlichen Dialogs. *[Waldorf education, perspectives of a scientific dialog.]* Frankfurt am Main: Peter Lang, pp. 105–128.

Schütz, Alfred/Luckmann, Thomas (1979): Strukturen der Lebenswelt. *[Structures of the life world]* Vol. 1, Frankfurt am Main: Suhrkamp.

Seydel, Anna (2009): Ich bin Du. Kindererkenntnis in pädagogischer Verantwortung. *[I am you.]* Stuttgart: Pädagogische Forschungsstelle beim Bund der Freien Waldorfschulen.

Shapiro, Lawrence (2011): Embodied Cognition. London and New York: Routledge.

Spitzer, Manfred (2002): Lernen. Gehirnforschung und die Schule des Lebens. *[Learning. Brain research and the school of life.]* Heidelberg and Berlin: Spektrum.

Spork, Peter (2011): Das Schlafbuch. *[The book of sleep.]* Köln: Anaconda.

Steiner, Rudolf (1907): Die Erziehung des Kindes vom Gesichtspunkte der Geisteswissenschaft. *[The education of the child in the light of spiritual science.]* In: Steiner, Rudolf (1987): Lucifer – Gnosis. Grundlegende Aufsätze zur Anthroposophie und Berichte aus den Zeitschriften «Luzifer» und «Lucifer – Gnosis» 1903-1908. *[Lucifer-Gnosis: Foundational essays on anthroposophy and reports from the periodicals 'Lucifer' and 'Lucifer-Gnosis'.]* Rudolf Steiner Gesamtausgabe 34. Dornach: Rudolf Steiner Verlag, pp. 309–348.

Steiner, Rudolf (1973): Gegenwärtiges Geistesleben und Erziehung. 14 Vorträge in Ilkley. *[The spiritual life of the present and education. 14 lectures in Ilkley.]* GA 307. Dornach: Rudolf Steiner Verlag.

Steiner, Rudolf (1978a): Menschenerkenntnis und Unterrichtsgestaltung. *[Knowledge of the human being and the forming of class lessons.]* GA 302. Dornach: Rudolf Steiner Verlag.

Steiner, Rudolf (1978b): Die Philosophie der Freiheit. *[The philosophy of freedom.]* GA 4. Dornach: Rudolf Steiner Verlag.

Steiner, Rudolf (1979a): Die Erziehungsfrage als soziale Frage. Sechs Vorträge vom 9. bis 17. August 1919 in Dornach. *[The question of education as a social question. 6 Lectures held between August 9.-7. 1919 in Dornach.]* GA 296. 3. Edition, Dornach: Rudolf Steiner Verlag.

Steiner, Rudolf (1979b): Die Kunst des Erziehens aus dem Erfassen der Menschenwesenheit. *[The art of education from an understanding of the being of humanity.]* GA 311. Dornach: Rudolf Steiner Verlag.

Steiner, Rudolf (1980): Vergangenheits- und Zukunftsimpulse im sozialen Geschehen. *[Impulses of the past and future in social occurrences.]* GA 190. Dornach: Rudolf Steiner Verlag.

Steiner, Rudolf (1983): Von Seelenrätseln. *[The riddles of the soul.]* TB 637 (GA 21). Dornach: Rudolf Steiner Verlag.

Steiner, Rudolf (1985): Geisteswissenschaft und Medizin. Zwanzig Vorträge, gehalten in Dornach 1920. *[Spiritual science and medicine. Twenty lectures held in Dornach 1920.]* GA 312. Dornach: Rudolf Steiner Verlag.

Steiner, Rudolf (1986): Die Stufen der höheren Erkenntnis. Kosmologie, Religion und Philosophie. Vom Seelenleben. Drei Schriften zum anthroposophischen Schulungsweg. *[Levels of higher knowledge. Cosmology, religion, and philosophy. On the life of the soul.]* TB 641 (from GA 12, 25 and 36). Dornach: Rudolf Steiner Verlag.

Steiner, Rudolf (1987): Theosophie. *[Theosophy.]* GA 9. Dornach: Rudolf Steiner Verlag.

Steiner, Rudolf (1990): Erziehungskunst. Methodisch-Didaktisches. *[The art of education. Methodology and didactics.]* GA 294. Dornach: Rudolf Steiner Verlag.

Steiner, Rudolf (1991): Geisteswissenschaftliche Behandlung sozialer und pädagogischer Fragen. 17 Vorträge in Stuttgart 1919. *[Spiritual-scientific treatment of social and pedagogical questions. 17 Lectures held in Stuttgart 1919.]* GA 192. 2. Edition. Dornach: Rudolf Steiner Verlag.

Steiner, Rudolf (1992): Allgemeine Menschenkunde als Grundlage der Pädagogik. 14 Vorträge, gehalten in Stuttgart 1919. *[General knowledge of the human being as the foundation of pedagogy. 14 Lectures held in Stuttgart 1919.]* GA 293. Dornach: Rudolf Steiner Verlag.

Steiner, Rudolf (1998a): Erziehung zum Leben. *[Education for life.]* GA 297a. Dornach: Rudolf Steiner Verlag.

Steiner, Rudolf (1998b): Idee und Praxis der Waldorfschule. *[The idea and practice of the Waldorf school.]* GA 297. Dornach: Rudolf Steiner Verlag.

Stöckli, Thomas (2011): Lebenslernen. *[Life learning.]* Berlin: Universitätsverlag.

Wagenschein, Martin (1968): Verstehen lehren. *[Teaching understanding.]* Weinheim: Beltz.

Weinert, Franz E. (1996): Für und Wider die "neuen Lerntheorien" als Grundlagen pädagogisch-psychologischer Forschung. *[Pro and con of the "New Learning Theories' as the basis for pedagogic-psychological research.]* In: Zeitschrift für Pädagogische Psychologie, 10 (1996) 1, pp. 1–12.

Wiechert, Christof (2012): "Du sollst sein Rätsel lösen …" Gedanken zur Kunst der Kinder- und Schülerbesprechung. *["You must solve his riddle…" Thoughts on the art of child student reviews.]* Dornach: Verlag am Goetheanum.

Wulf, Christoph (2014): Emotion. In: Wulf, Christoph and Jörg Zirfas (Eds.) (2014): Handbuch Pädagogische Anthropologie. *[Handbook pedagogic anthropoplogy.]* Wiesbaden: Springer, pp. 113–123.

Wulf, Christoph/Zirfas, Jörg (Eds.) (2014): Handbuch Pädagogische Anthropologie. *[Handbook pedagogic anthropology.]* Wiesbaden: Springer.

LEARNING IN WALDORF EDUCATION

Jost Schieren

1 Learning theories

Since the beginnings of Western thought, there have been broad discussions in philosophy, psychology, pedagogy, and, most recently, brain research on the issue of the learning process and its significance for the human being. Based mostly on experience and ideas, the complementary strands of Platonian and Aristotelian thinking in antiquity gave a paradigmatic assessment of the learning process, which medieval thought expanded to include the Christian Gospel's idea of redemption. Learning's goal and purpose lay in closeness to God and deliverance from sin.[1] During the time of the Enlightenment, the idea of the rational individual moved to the foreground and with it, also, the autonomy of the learner. Kant's *sapere aude* ("dare to know" or "have courage to use your own mind") became the imperative for learning. At the same time, the striving for rational orientation called for explicitly rational interpretations of the learning process and thus for a scientific theory of learning. Johann Friedrich Herbart's (1776–1841) theory of formal steps was elevated to become a methodological canon for regulatory teaching and learning, due to the strict fixation of rules by his followers (Herbartians) (Geissler 2007).

The science of learning experienced an empiric breakthrough with Ivan Petrovich Pavlov's (1849–1936) work based on the theory of behavioral science, and with the work of John B. Watson (1878–1958). They arrived at their research findings essentially through animal experiments.

Behaviorism understands learning as a form of conditioning based on a predetermined schema of stimulus and response. Cognition research offers another approach to learning theory. Jean Piaget (1896–1980) and Lev Semyonovich Vygotsky (1896–1934) set the essential impulses for this research. Both authors investigated human structures of understanding and inquired, from a developmental psychology perspective, into how understanding is generated. Piaget focused on logical structures inherent in the human being, while Vygotsky saw the cause for specific forms of understanding and learning in sociocultural factors, especially language.

A further approach to learning theory, distinct from the mechanistic views of behaviorism, emphasizes human *insight* as a crucial component of the learning process. Examples of such a comparatively holistic learning theory are Wolfgang Köhler's (1887–1967) Gestalt psychology and Albert Bandura's (*1925) concept of learning, mainly focusing on social processes. The latter introduced the concept of *self-efficacy* as an important personal aspect in the learning process.

In the context of pedagogic learning theories, we can highlight the approaches of Alfred Petzelt (1889–1967) and Lutz Koch (*1942), who use a philosophical perspective for understanding the process of cognition. "Petzelt sees learning as a process of conferring meaning. He distinguishes it strictly from mere acquisition of knowledge and from behaviorism's […] change of conduct. This view of learning

DOI: 10.4324/9781003187431-22

has influenced a great number of authors, who proclaim a strictly pedagogic view of learning in contrast to psychological-experimental or constructivist approaches to learning" (Meyer-Drawe 2008b, pp. 399–400f.). In this context, Käte Meyer-Drawe references Maurice Merleau-Ponty (1908–1961) in discussing a phenomenological view of learning that "focuses on the productive disruption and delay of learning." Similarly, Alfred Schirlbauer writes, "A learning theory of [school] pedagogical significance must therefore introduce the concept of an 'I' that seeks for truth (Petzelt); it must address insight and error, understanding and lack thereof, comprehension and lack of concepts" (Schirlbauer 2008, p. 205).

Within the various approaches to understanding the learning process, there is no consensual definition of learning. Psychological learning theories still can agree to the following statement: "Learning refers to a relatively sustained change in behavior ... in reference to certain situations, based on repeat experiences with these situations" (Winkel, Petermann, Petermann 2006, p. 12).

In contrast, pedagogical learning theories uphold that such a definition implies a subject who merely *behaves* in a certain way, presupposes a static world of representational objects, and claims to offer a single step-by-step progress in successful learning. (On this and the following, see Breinbauer 2008, pp. 59f.) Some have objected, however, that there are always also irritations and autonomous self-organizing events that characterize the learning process. In learning, there occurs a productive, transformative, (Koller 2012) and dynamic integration of subject and object without any anticipation, a reception of seemingly static situations, stores of knowledge, or unchanging social realities. In that sense, learning is always also inventive. In this vein, Koller argues for differentiating between a concept of *learning,* which he narrows down to the reception and processing of information, and a broader and more basic concept of *education.* "In the terminology of information theory, on one hand we can therefore understand learning as a process of receiving, acquiring, and processing new information without infringing upon the framework itself within which processing occurs. On the other hand, in this perspective, educational processes are also learning processes of a higher order that serve not only to acquire new knowledge but that fundamentally change the mode of information processing" (Koller 2012, p. 15).

Each of the various approaches to understanding learning indicates a different concept of the human being and of the world and thus of the diverse aspects of learning under scientific scrutiny. Even if there may be clear opposing arguments, we are dealing here less with matters of *right* and *wrong,* and more with a *decision:* namely, which understanding of learning (i.e., which concept of the world and man) will we adopt and translate into pedagogic practice accordingly. Even if we have many objections to a one-sided advocacy for behavioristic learning theory, especially in a school context, we still must note that the learning theory of behaviorism corresponds in large part not only to early childhood and childhood forms of learning in particular (such as motoric skills, social learning, enculturation), but also it can apply to habit formation in everyday activities of adults. For example, Waldorf education categorically refuses to generate learning success in children through argumentatively gained insights (Steiner 1990, p. 29f.). We can say that behaviorism *functions* in these cases. However, at the same time, we must not ignore the dangers of authoritarian and possibly also manipulative forms of learning that are implicit in behaviorism. Fixed stimulus response schemata produce, for example, desired learning results in military training contexts. They also prove extraordinarily effective in computer applications, especially in computer games. And the advertising industry also works successfully with a behavioristic concept of man.

It is very different, however, if we favor a concept of the human being that is more oriented toward autonomy, freedom, and insightful action. In that case, we would attempt a more open organization of learning processes and respond more to the personal conditions of learning. This is a point of possible discussion for Waldorf education, which we will more closely consider in the following paragraphs.

2 Rudolf Steiner's teachings on imagination

The learning concept of Waldorf education is based in Steiner's epistemology. In his early philosophical writings, Steiner took a basic epistemological position in regard to man's relationship with reality (Steiner 1918, 1923). He distances himself from a naïve-realistic notion of reality that takes the world phenomena as given and attributes mere mirroring functions to human cognitive processes. He considers reality to be the product and creative result of the process of human cognition. Steiner bases his deliberations on a characterization of human perception, which he understands not as the activity of perceiving but rather as its object, the percept. These percepts are transmitted through the sensory nervous system and at first occur only as isolated and intermittent events. Thinking offers connections and structure to these isolated percepts and allows them to adapt according to their essential nature, which is veiled in the process of perception but then revealed in conceptual penetration (Wagemann, in Chapter 2 of this book). For example, the term *bitter* serves to identify a perception and discloses its intrinsic quality. Of course, many errors occur when we conceptually penetrate percepts, mainly because a subject engaged in cognition can too strongly foist as-yet unknown qualities of perception onto conceptual configurations. Furthermore, the transmitted segments of perception may be too narrow for a valid reception of conceptual contents. For example, if we drive along a country road on a bright summer day, we may at first interpret a mirage appearing on the street as a puddle. This conceptualization is justified, because our past experience has taught us that a water surface has mirroring qualities. In order to arrive at a valid judgment, however, further perceptions and conceptualizations are necessary: When we drive through, there should be splashing water (if there really were a puddle).

Therefore, an additional foundational perception is lacking for making the possible concept of "puddle" real. The error is in fact caused neither by perception nor conceptualization. The error lies in being too hasty and sloppy when connecting the two elements (concept and percept).[2]

In Steiner's epistemology, the conjoining of percept and concept creates reality, an approach that appears kin to constructivism. But actually, Steiner differs fundamentally from constructivism insofar as he, as stated above, interprets the concept's penetration into the sphere of perception not as a subjective construction, but as an objective adoption. Furthermore, from a conceptual-realistic perspective, Steiner considers thought-generated concepts not to be mere subjective human creations, but ontologically rooted entities. Only parts of these entities appear within the limited scope of the respective human thought process, but they are nevertheless based on their very own entelechy *[meaning: a vital agent or force directing growth and life, the actualization of form-giving cause as contrasted with potential existence]*. This entelechy of concepts we may call *logicity*, and mathematics offers a good illustration for it.

Steiner uses the term *imagination* for blending perception and concept. In ordinary consciousness, imagination leads to forgetting its own genesis and thus to a belief in a naïve-realistic worldview. In contrast to the elements that formed it, imagination is accessible to memory, which is significant for a more memory-focused learning process. According to Steiner's epistemology, the learning process extends in two directions, which we may call *universalization* and *individualization*. Individualization denotes the appropriate integration of general concepts into specific perceptions (since their generality is fixed into an individualized Gestalt); universalization denotes a creative interpretation and mental grasp of entelechial conceptual coherences (since the individual act of thinking is integrated into the general thought matrix). Both forms of learning are interdependent, because the conceptual penetration of a percept (individualization) requires an act of creative thinking (universalization). Conversely, the ever-wakeful activity of thinking receives impulses from the mystery of perception. Against this backdrop, we will use an interpretation of Steiner's epistemology to explain this interconnection in the following paragraphs in more detail.

3 Disposition and condition

The philosopher Herbert Witzenmann (1905–1985), in his mostly epistemologically oriented work, makes reference to the philosophical approach of Steiner.[3] In his essay, "Primordial Thought," (Witzenmann 1988) he starts out from the definition of perception: "In the matchless, artful creation of a human sensory nervous system, the world's creation returns to its original state. Our sense organs transmit pure perceptions that represent the disordered material mandate of our self-realization; we create ourselves out of the matrix of the uncreated world and we create the world anew in this process;

we can succeed in fulfilling our mandate to the degree that we can master the organizing task with our thinking. In creating reality, we are realizing our own individual essence" (Witzenmann 1988, p. 10). Witzenmann portrays perception as an epistemological ground zero. The activity of the human sensory nervous system deconstructs ontological connections of the created world. Only then is a free space cleared for a new creation through human cognition. He describes the connectivity-generating function of human thinking as the process of interpreting percepts through "co-individualization of general concepts (universalia) during their metamorphic adaptation to conditions, which they encounter in form of the percepts they have now penetrated" (Witzenmann 1988, p. 11). Once we have engaged in such a process of co-individualization, we can then repeat and eventually optimize it. This forms the basis for the recognition of Gestalt configurations, objects, and processes in the surrounding world and also constellates the ability to appropriately realize one's own intentions for action. *Disposition* is the term that Witzenmann uses to describe this increased ability in man's encounter with the world.

An additional aspect is the other side of the learning process, pertaining to the ability to creatively conceptualize with human thought, which Witzenmann calls *condition*. Referring to *dispositions,* Witzenmann elaborates: "Our *dispositional* freedom is generated by participating in the individualization of spirit in its penetration of perceptions. [Translator's note: The German word *Geist* enfolds many different meanings: spirit, mind, intellect, ghost, distilled essence, and more. In this quote, the meaning centers around spirit/universal mind, so 'spirit' is used as an appropriate translation.] It is a development in *substance*. It is self-realization through co-creation of thought *contents*. Our *conditional* freedom is engendered by our individual (i.e., conditioned) effects on the universal spirit, so that it (the universal mind/spirit) receives this freedom into its own domain. Therefore, this is a freedom of the spirit. It is a grasping of spirit by recalling *acts* of thinking implemented by the self-determining spirit that manifests in these acts (but is not identical to them)" (Witzenmann 1988, p. 13f.). The concept of *spirit* used here may irritate the reader, but it means nothing less than the already mentioned self-originated inner connectivity of concepts. This is the reference for all human acts of thinking and is integrated therein. We can call conscious experience of this connectivity a capability for insight. If we read a complicated text, for example, or try to solve a complicated mathematical equation, we experience the gradual dawning of understanding as an evidential expansion of consciousness in the context of the respective task area. Further, we must take note that here, too, any repetition of such an activity leads to increased abilities and higher capacities for insight.

4 Imagination and will

The material presented so far allows us now to more clearly highlight Steiner's core concern in founding Waldorf education. During 1919 and the following years, Steiner held many—later transcribed—lectures for teachers of the first Waldorf school in Stuttgart; in contradiction to the school system of his time, Steiner emphasized that Waldorf education does not aim to educate the "head" aspect of the human being but should address the "limbic" aspect (1980). These terms are meant to express that Waldorf education does not aim to one-sidedly foster the intellect but primarily focuses on the education of the will. Steiner thus opposed the—in his view—"head-heavy" or overly intellect-focused education of his time. Essentially, his view is in agreement with reform-pedagogical approaches that developed at that same time. In Steiner's understanding, the purpose of school does not lie in solely teaching "to the head." The goal is not to cram as much knowledge content (in form of representations) as possible into the student's head. Steiner criticized the one-sided accumulation and exam-oriented memorization of representational (abstract) contents. In this context, the problem does not lie in representational content itself, which should be learned and memorized meaningfully also in Waldorf education. The problem rather lies in the fact that representations and inner images emerge without any consciousness of their own origination—namely, of the self-initiated, self-creating merging of percept and concept. Thus, in an epistemological sense, they suppress the individual's participation in reality and establish the subject-object dualism in the experience of consciousness. Imaginative, representational consciousness understands the world as "other," that is, as categorically distinct from one's own self.

5 Case study: Agricultural internship

The following example describes a distinctive learning situation that is not representative of everyday learning in school but is suited for clarifying central aspects of the understanding of learning in Waldorf education: 35 students participated in a study at a ninth grade at a Waldorf school that is located in a city in the (German) Ruhr area (traditionally a mining district with a blue-collar worker milieu); there were nearly equal numbers of girls and boys who were sent to participate in a two-week agricultural internship on a biodynamic (organic) farm in Northern Germany. The farm was equipped to provide room and board as well as educational services for the young people. Boys and girls each had a communal room where they slept, and the attending teachers had separate accommodations. The agricultural tasks covered stable work (cows and pigs), cheese dairy, vegetable garden, and orchard, as well as work in fields and forestry. In groups of five, the students worked in each of these areas during this internship. In addition, every day there were small class units highlighting specific aspects of agriculture and forestry. During the first three to four days of the internship, the students needed time to get used to everything. Pulled out of their usual family and school surroundings, they were now integrated into a challenging but appropriate work process and they felt overtaxed. In principle, getting up early every morning (6:30 am) is not different from a normal school day routine, but it is arduous. Since many parents packed a big supply of candy and snacks for their children, they initially barely touched the healthy and nutritious food offered to them at the farm. After only a short time, the students felt exhausted after performing simple tasks that require stamina, such as digging a vegetable bed. Right at the beginning of the internship, the class- and work atmosphere was quite burdened by these experiences.

But then the following happened: During the communal lunch on the fourth day, a student bursts into the dining room and reports that a gate had been left open and one of the farm's horses has escaped from its corral. Suddenly, the students jump up and hurry out to catch the horse. They see it grazing in a meadow not far from the house. When the whole group of students approaches, the horse gallops away, then stops, and resumes grazing. The students fail to get any closer to the horse than about 60 feet, a distance dictated by the horse's behavior itself. Every time the group of students comes closer, the horse moves further away. This goes on for three-quarters of an hour while the students eagerly discuss how to solve the problem. By then the horse has reached a part of the meadow where there is a small valley that has no exit other than the inroad. The students agree to work together: They disband as a group and surround the horse from two sides, always keeping the 60-foot distance. Then they approach it from the other direction. They avoid all talking and sudden movements, and after another half hour they corral the horse back to the gate.

The attending adults notice that the difficult atmosphere of the first days has changed: The work proceeds more effortlessly, the students start to coordinate by drawing lots for who can get up earlier, at 5 am instead of 6:30 am, to milk the cows before breakfast. And, last but not least, now they are eating all of the plentiful meals they are served and returning empty bowls to the kitchen. When they leave the farm at the end of the two weeks, they take tearful leave of each other, the members of the farm family, and also of all the animals they have come to love. During the next vacations, a small group of the students returns to the farm to volunteer as helpers.

6 Aspects of learning

Much of the above example describes a learning process in a special situation (distinct from school learning). In their motivations and actions, the students took ownership of the tasks presented by the whole farm organism.

In this process, they learned about the sources of foodstuffs, the steps required in processing, how to take care of animals and plants, and generally about human foods and nutrition. In this particular farm environment, they learned something about the world and its laws. They learned to overcome their own difficulties and arrived at a good work motivation. In a certain sense, they also gained an ethically based relationship to nature, e.g., by developing respect for nature and especially by being emotionally drawn to the animals; these aspects are also reflected in the acquisition of new action competencies. Last, but not least, the social connectivity of the class markedly improved in regard to mutual attentiveness and consideration.

Accordingly, learning comprises in a wholistic sense the following aspects and action competencies: emotional (sympathetic connection to the farm), motivational and volitional (will to work, stamina), cognitive (agricultural knowledge), ethical and moral (respect for nature), and social (class community).

The learning environment created through the arrangement of the internship was an essential determinant for the benchmarked learning progress. It took place in the real world. Learning did not happen in the classroom under "artificial" conditions created only by the teacher but occurred on the farm itself. Thus, all work processes that the students participated in were the actual, real work processes of the farm enterprise. This is, of course, a situation apart from everyday learning in school, but nevertheless it points to a core intent of Waldorf education, namely, that learning and relation to the world should be relevant to one's life. Even though the agricultural internship is an exceptional situation, it still is indicative of the overall goal of Waldorf education's individual learning arrangements, which is to create life-relevant, intense teaching and learning situations that are rooted in a consistent practical and experiential orientation by offering numerous projects and making many individual methodologic-didactic decisions. We shall take a closer look at this, focusing on the aspects of meaning and truth in learning.

6.1 Truth

Students always accompany each learning process with the question: "Why do I have to learn that?" And we can satisfy no student by answering: "Because you will need that later in life." Learning requires immanent meaning.

For example, as we learn motor skills or gain practical competencies during early childhood development (grasping, walking, speaking, etc.), an immediate learning success follows. The acquired abilities can satisfy different needs. That gives this process meaning. During the school years, the immediate sensory experience of meaning retreats more to the background as learning contents become increasingly abstract. This requires a *didactic of meaning* and a *methodology of meaning* to integrate immanent horizons of meaning into the teaching process in a relevant way; this integration must be appropriate for the respective developmental stage, the students' life-world, and their general human relations. The overarching aim is to establish a relevant relationship with the world that can serve as a gauge for the correctness of what has been learned or acquired. The world is the gauge that measures learning success. Käte Meyer-Drawe calls the significance that our relationship with the world holds for learning the "appeal of things" (2008a).

Alfred Schirlbauer rightfully demands a reference point for truth or correctness of learning: "Without reference to 'truth' or 'correctness,' it would make little or no sense to speak of insight, of understanding or realization" (2008, p. 205). The term *truth* is not used here with any claim to deep philosophical accuracy or to universal and final validity, but it is used in a living, practical sense of a logical coherence, a realization that stands the test of experience and leads to success in action, and as an understanding of the world pertaining to the respective learning material. In reference to the previously listed capacity areas of disposition and conditioning, truth means the object-relational merger between acquired concepts and perceptions (individualization leading to conditionings) and concepts bonding with different concepts (universalization leading to dispositions). Schirlbauer writes, in reference to Theodor Ballauf (1970), "One cannot *will* to think but thinking must receive us, so that we are swept up into a realm of thought when we think" (Schirlbauer 2008, p. 207).

This points to evidential self-determination, which we, in thinking, experience as insight. The learning subject experiences the objective bond between capability and the lawfulness of an object, which in this case is not a thing, but a thought. This insight, however, does not overwhelm or coerce the learner, but capabilities unfold within the matrix of implicit and explicit insights. An insight is not coercive since it is simultaneously a self-determination of the learner (Witzenmann 1992). It would be nonsensical to claim there is coercion at work when we realize that we need to open the door in order to leave the room. The subject's self-determination rests on his actions, based on acquired experiences that appear to be individually valid truths. Against this backdrop, the currently much quoted slogan *learning to learn* is not a meaningful concept, but merely redundant phrasing. Learning is not an end in itself; it always is directed toward something. That is its gauge.

Schirlbauer strictly differentiates such an object- or content-oriented concept of learning from mere methodical training: "The theory of teaching and learning must address the contents of teaching and learning because learning would not exist without it, because ... when we learn, we are taught to think that thoughts themselves can be contents. ... Thoughts in turn refer to *some thing* that is actually the very thing that allows us to gauge the correctness, appropriateness and finally also the truth of a judgment" (2008, p. 205).

The above-described relation to object or world expands the concept of "content-oriented" learning. A retrospective model of what predetermined inventories of knowledge should be acquired is not important—the curriculum takes care of that—but in the vein of the (student internship) example, we see a wholistic form of learning that comprises also an implicit "store of knowledge" (see Polanyi's concept of *tacit knowing*, 1985).

Accordingly, learning leads to participation in the world, to participation in the laws and patterns of the world as mirrored in acquired dispositional and conditional capabilities. Waldorf education strictly implements this model of learning through its experiential and activity-oriented methodology. Everyday school life systematically integrates craft-, art-, and workshop-projects. Waldorf teachers methodically and didactically develop more cognitive-abstract subjects, e.g., mathematics, through demonstrations and in an action-oriented way.

6.2 Remembering

There is one more factor to consider: The process of learning meets success only if the memory of the learned material is not lost right away but is sustained over time. What has been learned must be PRESERVED. In this context, Steiner speaks of "treasures of the past" (1992, p. 52). Learning always is also a process of persevering, lasting over time. The learned material becomes a permanent part of the human personality. To this end, the memory and remembering functions must be operative. Steiner describes the ability to remember as a basic faculty of the human soul. This view functionally describes the *soul as the keeper of the past.*

What is Steiner's understanding of the process of remembering? In his work *Theosophy,* we find a revealing sentence, which draws our attention first to the ephemeral nature of sense impressions, and then directs us to more closely examine the process of remembering: "Corporeality would allow all impressions to sink back again and again into nothingness, if we do not form a *present* image or representation in the act of perceiving. At the same time something happens in the relation between the outer world and the soul that allows the human being to later recall that which was previously the product of an *outer* representation, and appears now as an *inner* representation caused from within" (Steiner 1922, p. 50).

Saying that "something happens between the soul and the outer world" that engenders present representations is a complicated way of expressing himself (Steiner). What is meant here? Steiner points to the process of forming representations. Previously, we pointed out that Steiner views representation or inner image-building as a merging of sensory perceptions with concepts, which thinking itself produced. He emphatically rejects the thought of naïve realism that the phenomena of the world enter perception and are then stored in consciousness as representations.

Man does not encounter the world in a receptive, passive mode, but in a highly active and creative way. We do not just adopt images of a premade world, but our consciousness actively participates in the process of creating reality. However, in the images that we form, we are not conscious of this process-oriented participation. It happens too fleetingly, too quickly. Consciousness awakens only in the already formed image. As an end product of the realization process, the image is already detached from that process. Witzenmann emphasizes: "Our usual consciousness, therefore, is a representational consciousness that does not directly contain reality" (1985, p. 61). Witzenmann differentiates between a primary structure of human cognition that is actively involved in the process of creating reality and a secondary structure that represents this process in conscious images in the form of memories. In Steiner's words, the merging of percept and concept that he calls basic (or primary) structure is that "which happens in the relation between the outer world and the soul and that allows the human being through *inner* processes to regain an image *within* of a representation that was previously produced from *without*" (Steiner 1922, p. 50). Steiner calls these processes that we experience on an inner plane "remembering." He specifies: "Those who are practiced in observing the soul may find that there is something off in the view that today there is one image and tomorrow memory produces this same image after it was in the interim stored somewhere within the human being. No, *this* image that I have *now* is a phenomenon that passes when the *now*, the current moment, passes. In the case of a memory, we experience a process that is caused by something that has happened in the relation between the outer world and myself, *outside* of our recall of the current representational image. Memory calls up images that are new and *not* the same as the old, stored representations. Memory thus consists of the ability to create an image *again*, [recreate in the imagination] not to resurrect an old one. That which emerges *again* is something other than the [original] image itself" (Steiner 1922, pp. 50f.).

Therefore, memory does not reproduce a preformed image but forms a *new* image. This new representation stands in reference to what happened "in the relationship between outer world and myself, *aside from* the process of calling up the current image" (ibid.). This interactive dynamic is in fact nothing else but the primordial self-initiated connection of percept and concept, called basic or primary structure. Steiner thus originates a new concept of memory: Memory refers not solely to preformed images, but whenever we remember something, we, at the same time, become conscious of how we earlier participated in creating these representations. Therein lies, in a certain sense, the *magic* of each memory: In remembering, we surmount object-focused consciousness, which is passive and dualistically framed; I become conscious of my own creative participation in constructing the earlier image and gain awareness of my own self as a being that is dispositionally enabling (the construction of) reality. In various contexts, Steiner calls this process *spiritual remembering*: When an individual remembers, he also evokes a latent memory of his own spiritual being that actively participates in the construction of reality, as he self-realizes himself in that process. That is at the same time also the core of Steiner's concept of spirit: The world of spirit does not exist outside of the human being but is the active self-creation of the human being within reality.

We can get an inkling of this so-called *magic* of memories when, for example, we come back to a childhood place that we have not visited for a long time and we are touched by the faintest of impressions: a smell or a certain quality of light. Then we become aware not only of the momentary impression, but also of our past participation (in constructing the memory images); we remember our past *beingness*.

6.3 *Forgetting*

Steiner's presentation of the process of cognitive remembering is highly active and productive. This has direct consequences for the learning process. Waldorf education understands learning as an active accessing of reality. It is only efficient if the individual participates in the learning process as creatively as possible. Therefore, learning is not a passive reception of material—as illustrated by the so-called Nuremberg Funnel—but is an active, personal, and emotional process. The human personality configures itself in learning, because in that process it finds its own purpose, in congruence with its awareness of reality.

From a perspective of Waldorf education, it is therefore inadvisable to only learn through ready-made images or pre-formed contents of knowledge. These can have an orienting and structuring effect on learning, but it is essential to convey to the student an awareness of their own participation in the construction of reality from the start. To this end, the lessons are arranged in directly experiential and action-oriented ways. Moreover, Steiner emphasizes that it is an essential element of Waldorf instruction that teachers use "images" or "flexible concepts." This also points toward a mandate to avoid teaching preformed representational contents.

But another factor must be added: the aspect of *forgetting*. One of Steiner's special achievements regarding learning theory lies in the fact that he worked out the significance of *forgetting* for the learning process. However, to put it correctly, we must speak here of *volitional* forgetting. Because involuntary forgetting refers to the process of forgetting our own participatory role in constructing reality. Every image engenders forgetfulness of how it was formed and conveys the illusion of naïve realism, i.e., of a pre-existent reality that has been constructed without human participation in the creative process. The human being spontaneously forgets with each image-generating process that he was involved in the creation of that reality. *Volitional* forgetting, in contrast, consists of systematically overcoming the usually dominant consciousness of acquired representational contents, so to speak.

Waldorf education practices this by keeping the representations somewhat more "open," by using images and flexible concepts. Waldorf lessons are arranged in such a way that the class ends with a subject-specific experiential opportunity (often in form of a story) or, even better, with an open-ended question. Waldorf educational jargon expresses that by saying that a subject matter "is taken along into the night." In the following days, the topic is taken up again and deepened. The main lesson blocks are arranged to teach one subject every morning in the first 2 hours of school (about 105 minutes) and over a timespan of three to four weeks; this format provides a suitable form of organizing a day-by-day wholistic immersion into the subject matter involving the phase of night and sleep. At this point, more than 90 years have passed since Steiner developed this approach to learning; today the same topic is also being explored by empirical brain research. Researchers—mainly in the USA—have proved that material learned before sleeping anchors in our memory better than content that we learn when no sleep phase follows (Karni et al. 1994; Plihal, Born 1997; Wilson, McNaughton 1994). This research concept distinguishes *declarative memory,* which mainly stores cognitive information (data, vocabulary, autobiographical, and general knowledge), from *non-declarative,* or *procedural* memory, which applies to skills and sequential action.

Wilson, McNaughton (1994), and Karni (Karni et al. 1994) suggest in their studies that the processing of non-declarative knowledge happens during the REM phase, while declarative knowledge is being processed during deep sleep. Overall, the research shows that sleep has a stabilizing function for memory.

Aside from recognizing the significance that night sleep has for solidifying and securing learning, the principle of the block lesson format also entails that after deep immersion in one subject over three to four weeks, the subject is laid to rest again. This does not imply that the content is forgotten, but it means relaxing the hold that acute consciousness has on the subject. Following the block lesson curriculum, the same subject is revisited after three to six months; now the foreground is no longer taken up by the acute, sharpened references to the subject matter, but rather, the students are encouraged to form *new* representations—as suggested earlier in Steiner's quote. In that process, they can refer back to their own biographical connection with the subject matter. The block-lesson format in Waldorf education systematically aims at accessing and actively participating in reality and not only at passively taking in representations or content. Volitional forgetting plays a crucial role in this process.

6.4 Transformation

Another aspect of learning that was already stated implicitly is *transformation*. This concept plays a central role in the pedagogically oriented learning theories of Rainer Kokemohr (2008), Günther Buck (1981), and especially in the work of Hans-Christoph Koller (2012), who makes reference to the aforementioned authors. According to their approach, the educational value of learning is tied to a *reframing* of one's worldview, based on crisis experiences in connection with respective fields of learning and acting (see Nieke in Chapter 4).

The agricultural internship example showed that the first days at the farm were to a degree characterized by crisis. As learning always involves effort, it must necessarily lead to a crisis. Even good teachers cannot spare their students the effort. Good instruction is not characterized by everything being easy for the students nor by a lack of crises. Rather, the mark of good teaching is good crisis management: The students learn to deal with the struggles and challenges of learning.

Errors and mistakes turn into important and necessary stimuli for consciousness to focus more clearly on what is "right" (Benner 2005). If a student cannot consciously understand what he has done wrong, he cannot develop a feeling for what is right. A pedagogical approach that leads to punishing errors and mistakes (e.g., with bad grades) is, in this sense, counterproductive. The crises that accompany learning bring about a change in the student's familiar view of an object. Rigid representational structures break open; a transformation occurs. The subject undergoes a transformation regarding the object's constraints. That is one direction. But there is also a transformation in another direction, i.e., from object toward subject. In each successful learning process, objects transform themselves into dispositional and conditional capabilities of the subject. The French painter Paul Cézanne used the phrase *sur le motif* to describe this reciprocal transformation of subject and object, and he visualized it in the form of fingers laced together in prayer. When this process occurs, learning is experienced as highly satisfying because the human personality—in its identity as a capable individual—is then connected to a specific object.

7 "Mother Holle"

The collection of Grimms' fairy tales contains the well-known tale of "Mother Holle," which offers many images that we can relate to the learning process described, and, in this vein, we shall interpret it here. It is the tale of a woman who has two daughters. One of them is "ugly and lazy" and does not actively deal with reality. The other is "beautiful and industrious" and goes every day to sit by the well and does her spinning work there. She actively connects with reality by dispositionally *spinning* her concepts into the thread of her perception, and conditionally involving her thinking in the cognitive nexus. She is so active that she bloodies her hands in the process of spinning, i.e., she lets her own self flow into the unfolding reality. She expends a lot of effort; merely observing, representational consciousness does not make for bloody hands. When the girl loses her spindle at the well, this is a kind of crisis, crucial for the learning process, since it transcends the boundary of the subject (the familiar, which is securely anchored in consciousness). Active thinking loses itself in the phenomena of the world; an element of will moves to the foreground, which is not on same level of conscious awareness as representational consciousness. That is exactly what is being transcended. The human being gives itself up to the phenomena of the world.

In our example, this is the moment when the students jump up from the lunch table in order to catch the horse. The girl in the tale jumps into the well to fetch the lost spindle and enters a new world. She is no longer the subject who forms images of things, but the things start to talk to her, the subject. In the language of fairy-tale imagery, the loaves of bread say that they want to be pulled out of the oven and the apple tree asks to be shaken down. The girl does all that and also willingly agrees to become Mother Holle's servant, who—with her large teeth—represents the wisdom and laws of the world.[4] The girl can connect with Mother Holle through her own activity (regarding bread and apple tree). And when she leaves Mother Holle's world, she brings back a gift of gold (that she received for her good services). These are capabilities, faculties, which she has learned because she actively connected with reality. She has been endowed with the gold treasure of her acquired capabilities.

The other girl, the ugly and lazy one, covets the same treasure. So she pricks her fingers with thorns to bloody them. We can see this as a metaphor for a rather mechanistic kind of learning: It is not the spindle of one's own thought activity that bloodies the fingers and hurts her, but a hedge of

Learning in Waldorf Education

thorns—those are unwieldy representational contents. Then the girl also jumps into the well but cannot let go of her habitual way of thinking and, in the end, she cannot actively connect with reality. When she leaves Mother Holle's realm, she is showered with pitch. This illustrates the problem of an education that accumulates knowledge but develops very few genuine capabilities.

8 Summary

A brief summary shall highlight the main aspects of the concept of learning as we have developed it here:

- *Transformation*: Learning means to experience crises in leaving representational consciousness and actively merging with reality. It means mutually integrating the world and the self. Piaget coined the term *equilibration* for this process (1976).
- *Forgetting:* In order to learn, we must forget; i.e., we must again release the tight connection with the world of representations. *Sleep* is part of the learning process.
- *Capabilities:* The golden treasure of learning consists of an increase in one's own capabilities. We form both conditional and dispositional capabilities as we learn.
- *Wholeness:* Learning happens through actively—and as holistically as possible—dealing with reality, which is mainly based on experience. The aim is not a mere accumulation of representational contents.
- *Truth:* In learning, human beings connect with the world and its lawful patterns that express themselves in the capabilities the learners acquire.
- *Meaning:* We experience this capability-based connectivity with the world as the immanent, relevant, meaningful content of learning.

Notes

1 On the development of the concept of learning, see Meyer-Drawe (2008b).
2 Goethe's phenomenological approach bears deeper references to the complex challenges of appropriate judgment formation (Goethe 1975; Schieren 1998).
3 In regard to these and previously cited deliberations, see primarily Herbert Witzenmann (1985, 1987, 1988, 1992), as well as the listed works of Rudolf Steiner.
4 In his interpretation of this fairy tale, Eugen Drewermann calls her "Mother Earth" (2002).

References

Ballauff, Theodor (1970): Systematische Pädagogik. Eine Grundlegung. *[Systematic pedagogy. Fundamental principles.]* Heidelberg: Quelle & Meyer.

Benner, Dietrich (1995): Über pädagogisch relevante und erziehungswissenschaftlich fruchtbare Aspekte der Negativität menschlicher Erfahrung. *[On fruitful aspects of negativity in human experience, as relevant for pedagogy and educational science.]* In: Zeitschrift für Pädagogik, 49. Beiheft *[Journal for pedgaogy. 49. Supplement issue]*, pp. 7–21.

Breinbauer, Ines Maria (2008): Nachhaltiges Lernen. *[Long-term learning.]* In: Mitgutsch, Konstantin, Elizabeth Sattler, Kristin Westphal and Ines Maria Breinbauer (Eds.) (2008): Dem Lernen auf der Spur. *[In pursuit of learning.]* Stuttgart: Klett-Cotta, pp. 51–64.

Buck, Günter (1981): Hermeneutik und Bildung. Elemente einer verstehenden Bildungslehre. *[Hermeneutics and education. Elements of an educational theory based on understanding.]* Munich: Fink.

Drewermann, Eugen (2002): Lieb Schwesterlein, lass mich herein. Grimms Märchen tiefenpsychologisch gedeutet. *[Little sister, my dear – let me in! An interpretation of Grimm's fairy tales from a perspective of depth-psychology].* Munich: dtv.

Geissler, Erich E. (2007): J.F. Herbarts ideengeschichtlicher Beitrag zu einer wissenschaftlichen Unterrichts- und Erziehungslehre. *[J.F. Herbart's contribution to a scientific theory of instruction and education from the perspective of the history of ideas.]* In: Flagmeyer, Doris and Iris Mortag (Eds.) (2007): Horizonte. Neue Wege in Lehrerbildung und Schule. *[Horizons. New pathways for teacher training and school.]* Leipzig: Leipziger Universitätsverlag, pp. 29–51.

Goethe, Johann Wolfgang (1975): Der Versuch als Vermittler zwischen Objekt und Subjekt. *[The experiment as mediator between object and subject.]* In: Goethe, Johann Wolfgang von (1975): Werke *[Works]*. Vol. 13. Ed. E. Trunz. Munich: Beck, pp. 10–23.

Karni, A./Tanne, D./Rubenstein, B. S./Askenasy, J.J.M./Sagi, D. (1994): Dependence on REM sleep of overnight improvement of a perceptual skill. In: Science, 265, pp. 679–681.

Kokemohr, Rainer (2008): Bildung als Welt- und Selbstentwurf im Anspruch des Fremden. *[Education as a sketch of self and the world in the claim of the other.]* In: Koller, Hans-Christoph Winifred Marotzki and Olaf Sanders (Eds.) (2008): Bildungsprozesse und Fremdheitserfahrung. Beiträge zu einer Theorie transformatorischer Bildungsprozesse. *[Educational processes and the experience of the Other. Contributions to a theory of transformative educational processes.]* Bad Heilbrunn: Klinkhardt.

Koller, Hans-Christoph (2012): Bildung anders denken. Einführung in die Theorie transformatorischer Bildungsprozesse. *[Thinking differently about education. Introduction to the theory of transformative educational processes.]* Stuttgart: Kohlhammer.

Meyer-Drawe, Käte (2008a): Diskurse des Lernens. *[Discourses on learning.]* Munich: Wilhelm Fink.

Meyer-Drawe, Käte (2008b): Lernen als pädagogischer Grundbegriff. *[Learning as a fundamental concept in pedagogy.]* In: Mertens, Gerhard, Ursula Frost, Winfried Böhm and Volker Ladenthin (Eds.) (20008): Handbuch der Erziehungswissenschaft. *[Handbook of educational science.]* Vol. 1. Paderborn: Schöningh, pp. 391–402.

Piaget, Jean (1976): Die Äquilibration der kognitiven Strukturen. *[The equilibrium of cognitive structures.]* Stuttgart: Klett.

Plihal, W./Born, J. (1997): Effects of early and late nocturnal sleep on declarative and procedural memory. In: Journal of Cognitive Neuroscience, 9, pp. 534–547.

Polanyi, Michael (1985): Implizites Wissen. *[Implicit knowledge.]* Frankfurt am Main: Suhrkamp.

Schieren, Jost (1998): Anschauende Urteilskraft. Methodische und philosophische Grundlagen von Goethes naturwissenschaftlichem Erkennen. *[Intuitive power of judgment. Methodical and philosophical foundations of Goethe's natural science paradigm.]* Düsseldorf and Bonn: Parerga.

Schirlbauer, Alfred (2008): 37 Elefanten. Oder: Kann man ohne Lerntheorie unterrichten? *[37 Elephants. Or: Can we teach without a theory of learning?]* In: Mitgutsch, Konstantin, Elizabeth Sattler, Kristin Westphal and Ines Maria Breinbauer (Eds.) (2008): Dem Lernen auf der Spur. *[In pursuit of learning.]* Stuttgart: Klett-Cotta, pp. 93–106.

Steiner, Rudolf (1918): Die Philosophie der Freiheit. *[The philosophy of freedom.]* Berlin: Philosophisch-Anthroposophischer Verlag.

Steiner, Rudolf (1922): Theosophie. *[Theosophy.]* Dornach: Philosophisch-Anthroposophischer Verlag am Goetheanum.

Steiner, Rudolf (1923): Grundlinien einer Erkenntnistheorie der Goetheschen Weltanschauung. *[An outline of the epistemology of Goethe's worldview.]* Dresden: Emil Weises Buchhandlung.

Steiner, Rudolf (1980): Allgemeine Menschenkunde als Grundlage der Pädagogik. *[The general study of man as a basis for pedagogy.]* Dornach: Rudolf Steiner Verlag.

Steiner, Rudolf (1990): Die Erziehung des Kindes vom Gesichtspunkte der Geisteswissenschaft. *[The education of the child in the light of spiritual science.]* Dornach: Rudolf Steiner Verlag.

Wilson, M.A./McNaughton, B.L. (1994): Reactivation of hippocampal ensemble memories during sleep episodes. In: Science, 265, pp. 676–679.

Winkel, Sandra/Petermann, Franz/Petermann, Ulrike (2006): Lernpsychologie. *[Learning psychology.]* Paderborn: UTB.

Witzenmann, Herbert (1985): Strukturphänomenologie. Vorbewusstes Gestaltbilden im erkennenden Wirklichkeitenthüllen. *[Structural phenomenology. Preconscious Gestalt formation in the cognitive revelation of reality.]* Dornach: Gideon Spicker Verlag.

Witzenmann, Herbert (1987): Goethes universalästhetischer Impuls. *[Goethe's impulse of universal aesthetics.]* Dornach: Gideon Spicker.

Witzenmann, Herbert (1988): Der Urgedanke. Rudolf Steiners Zivilisationsprinzip und die Aufgabe der Anthroposophischen Gesellschaft. *[Primordial thought. Rudolf Steiner's concept of civilization and the task of the anthroposophical association.]* Dornach: Gideon Spicker.

Witzenmann, Herbert (1992): Intuition und Beobachtung. Bd. I und II. *[Intuition and observation. Vols. I and II.]* Stuttgart: Freies Geistesleben.

CHAPTER 5

The Art of Teaching

TEACHING APPROACHES IN WALDORF EDUCATION

Wilfried Sommer

1 Introduction

1.1 Basic positions

Current educational policy relies on administrative steering functions, using educational standards and centralized final exams while granting greater autonomy to individual schools at the same time. On one hand, curricular decisions are made within a unified framework of central guidelines, but, on the other hand, they have become in a new way part of the responsibility and freedom of teachers. Accordingly, the reflective culture of general teaching would gain greater significance for the individual teacher, since the "theory and practice of learning and teaching" (Jank, Meyer 2009, p. 14) specifically includes curriculum- and lesson-plan issues.

In March 2013, the commission "School Research and General Didactics" of the section "School Education" within the German Association for Educational Science (*Deutsche Gesellschaft für Erziehungswissenschaft*) held a theory conference at Leipzig University; under the topic "Comparative didactics and curriculum research: national and international perspectives," the conference aimed at counterbalancing the fragmentation of theoretical approaches and at exploring the developmental potential that such comparative approaches hold for the science of teaching. Among others, suggested criteria for comparisons were drawn from the philosophy of science, anthropology, and learning theory (Rahkochkine et al. 2013).

The approach of Waldorf education is informed by Rudolf Steiner's programmatic claim that the Waldorf school "will be truly comprehensive in the sense that the education and instruction it offers will be tailored to meet the needs of the whole human being" (Steiner 2020, p. 16). Waldorf education was conceived of from the start with a high anthropological aspiration and its curriculum and general teaching approaches were legitimized on that basis.

At the start of the teacher training course immediately preceding the opening of the first Waldorf school, Rudolf Steiner gave an address—from which we here quote—addressing the future teachers of this new school; in this address, he demanded that the future teachers, while being given much autonomy, should nevertheless "be flexible enough" to synchronize the framework of state guidelines with anthropological aspirations. The field of tension between the autonomy of the individual teacher within the respective school and its administrative governance did then, and does now, inform the way Waldorf schools operate, especially regarding curriculum and teaching in general. The connections with the topics of the above-mentioned theory conference are plain to see: What stance does Waldorf education take, if assumptions taken from the philosophy of science, anthropology, and learning theory are used as criteria for comparison?

DOI: 10.4324/9781003187431-24

The following sections introduce and discuss various aspects of the approach to teaching in Waldorf education. Numerous connections and comparisons emerge in that process, for example to the UNESCO report on "Education for the 21st Century" (German UNESCO Commission 1997) or to Klafki's categorial education (1964), as well as its discussion and further development by Meinert Meyer and Hilbert Meyer (2007), or also to constructivist positions (Varela 2008) or performative education.

1.2 Possible connections to Waldorf education

Waldorf education favors an understanding of education close to the one developed and explained by the authors of the UNESCO report. These authors assume that on one hand "education is an extraordinarily well-suited tool for personal development" (German UNESCO Commission 1997, p. 11) and on the other hand that it is a pillar of learning for life itself, which includes the cultivation of all individual talents of a human being and fosters a person's readiness to assume responsibility for the common goals of humankind (ibid., p. 19).

Connected with this understanding of education are anthropological assumptions that Waldorf education considers to reach beyond the scope of the UNESCO report: in each individual lies the potential for taking a stand in the world and for engaging in it authentically and freely, if they take hold of their autonomy and develop themselves.

Freedom then represents an individual's creative possibility for seizing their own existence and designing it free of formative constraints. Karl-Martin Dietz differentiates further aspects of freedom: It is an acquired "ability to realize tasks that lie within the scope of one's own capacity" and it is "every individual's responsibility for the 'whole.'" Finally, he summarizes: "Thus, freedom means that I do something out of my own volition, which otherwise others would demand of me, and I do it out of my own free will (not because of traditional or instinctive conditioning). Freedom's prerequisite is self-development" (Dietz 2003, p. 19; Chapter 1).

According to Waldorf education, educational processes should catalyze the structural possibility for freedom Dietz refers to. There are parallels between Waldorf education's positions and Peukert's educational theory, which finds it meaningful to presume that such an ineliminable, subjective moment of freedom is operative in the pedagogical practice (Peukert 2000, p. 520).

Steiner himself considers this form of autonomy a basis for the further development and renewal of society: "We should not ask: What knowledge or ability does a person need to benefit the social order such as it is? But rather: What potential lies in them that can be developed? Then it will become possible to infuse the social order with ever new vigor from the rising generations. Then a new order will always manifest what fully individuated young people make happen, who are newly joining the ranks of society; but never should the new generations be molded into something that conforms to the wishes of the existing social organization" (Steiner 1983, p. 8).

Klafki thinks of education as a process that dialectically interlaces its material and formal aspects (Klafki 1964); if we follow his line of thought, we can see how Waldorf education connects the formal side to the self-development processes outlined by Dietz. General teaching questions, and especially those pertaining to curriculum development, lead to a search for specific educational processes that are particularly supportive to students opening up to the world *and* to their own potential for self-development (formal side).

Curriculum development in Waldorf schools, furthermore, has a certain tradition and proximity to Klafki's critical-constructive didactics, because it contains a line of discussion that explores epochal key issues. By and large, though, this is a far more comprehensive tradition, which discusses the anthropological legitimation of curricular decisions (Götte, Loebell, Maurer 2009; Richter 2006). This discussion is mostly based on an education concept that—often implicitly—presumes a dialectic interlacing of material and formal education.

Waldorf education's anthropological approach views many educational processes as achievements of an embodied self. In understanding cognitive learning to be embodied acting, Waldorf education has a certain proximity to constructivism. Two approaches suggest themselves for further exploration of the embodied self or the *embodied mind*: to analyze it along the lines of the internal argumentation in Waldorf education or to view it as construction and to further investigate it from a constructivist perspective. This aspect would, for example, lend itself to modeling the linking of formal and material education as a constructive achievement down to the physical level of the body. Body-oriented aspects here complement Klafki's concept of categorial education.

Another theoretical framework is provided by the phenomenology of corporeal and spatial experience as Fuchs (2000) conceptualized it, with particular regard to "personal space." In the following sections, we shall often refer back to Fuchs's approach to phenomenological anthropology, especially when presenting and anthropologically discussing the main lesson model offered by Waldorf schools (Meyer, Meyer 2007, p. 10). Some epistemological excursions will be necessary, because both Waldorf education and phenomenological anthropology are determined by very specific choices in the philosophy of science.

Finally, many Waldorf schools lay claim to offering artistic instruction, based on some of Steiner's statements (Steiner 1961, p. 288ff.). A further section—containing more recent works of Fischer-Lichte on performative education (2004) as well as the works by Wulf and Zirfas (2007) on performativity—is added so that we can reflect on and discuss possible artistic qualities of instruction and aesthetic educational experiences.

2 Connections and divisions in educational theory

2.1 Klafki's theory of categorial education

Waldorf education's approach of orienting instruction and education to the needs of the "whole human being" (Steiner 2020, p. 16) was from the start accompanied by a parallel discussion: What kind of educational content not only gives the students access to a specific subject matter but also facilitates a differentiation process in their relation to the world that is appropriate and adequate to their "whole being"? Which educational content enables the students to open up their humanity to something new, based on their learning experiences, so that they can find new ways to self-realize and find themselves? These discussions took place during the faculty meetings of the first Waldorf school, often with Steiner's participation (1985). They later continued, for instance during subject-specific symposia or—in Germany—also in meetings of the boards of directors and advisors of the *Pädagogische Forschungsstelle* (Education Research Institute) at the *Bund der Freien Waldorfschulen* (Association of Independent Waldorf Schools). In this context, Zech (2012) has presented an in-depth study on history teaching.

Such a view of educational processes and these lines of argument based on educational theory draw focal attention to the interplay of content and form in education. Within the framework of this discourse, Waldorf education follows traditional lines of reasoning that obviously interface with Klafki's theory of categorial education. His theory distinguishes between a material or objective factor (a reality has categorially opened itself up to the students) and a formal or subjective factor (students have been enabled to open themselves to a reality) and discusses the dialectic interlacing of material and formal education (Klafki 1963, p. 44).

Waldorf education attends to that interlacing process as well. However, other than Klafki, it adds priorities to the formal side. As students open themselves up to a reality, they self-realize in a new way. How are we to understand this self-realization process? Formal education is characterized by emphasis on the personal factor.

In the process of preparing for their lessons, teachers analyze their teaching approach and, if indicated, take Klafki's five basic questions (ibid., 135 ff.) as their starting point; the question about the present-day relevance of a content alludes not just to the significance this content may already have for the spiritual life of the children in this class or what significance it should have from a pedagogical point of view, but rather how can the students grasp their own humanity in dealing with this content? The overall quality of this kind of searching and questioning process is determined by the different ways students can self-realize as individuals in response to this subject matter and how it can stimulate the development of their specific abilities and identity formation processes. This is similarly true for the remaining four questions, which pertain to the significance of the content for the future, to content structure, to its exemplary meaning and its accessibility.

Here is an example: The fact that in math tuition in 11th grade in Waldorf schools Euclidean analytic geometry is complemented by projective geometry means that curricular choices are not only informed by the vertical interconnection of teaching contents but that an anthropological factor also comes into play. What kind of self-development processes are inspired in students as the different aspects of projective geometry again and again evidence the special case that two parallel lines have an infinitely distant meeting point? Which kind of anthropological potential does this kind of math tuition have, when we read what a student writes about the class in retrospect: "To imagine the meeting of two parallels in infinite space is in my mind purely a matter of an agreement that I reach with my own self. If I do not want the two parallels to meet, they will never do so – at least not in my imagination" (Sommer 2010, p. 45).

Students become aware of the fact that they are free to choose to make agreements with themselves and that these free choices are connected to very different geometric contexts. Topics such as multi-perspectivity, one's own participation in the cognitive process, and the role of demonstrability are here intimately connected to the question of parallel straight lines. The geometric subject matter contains within itself the educational content as described. This educational aspect may prove itself to be a meaningful stage in an educational process that has as its goal both to awaken in the 18-year-old students at the end of 12th grade an awareness of their own part in the process of cognition and to activate a courageous free attitude toward their own self—an attitude that is geared toward accessing their own potential and realizing it in life.

Klafki's theory of categorial education thus provides a framework for a fruitful discussion of the educational concept in Waldorf pedagogy and of its references to the science of teaching in general. Waldorf education associates ample anthropological reflections and curricular legitimization with the formal side of education. From this particular perspective, it also brings up the issue of the educational value of an educational content. Teachers are expected to interweave into the creative process of lesson planning general teaching and subject-specific knowledge and a culture of anthropological reflection, and to bring these elements to life, drawing on a broad repertoire of methods. Teachers with that kind of training are in turn accorded the autonomy to try out new curricular ideas, to discuss them with their colleagues, and finally to integrate them into an individual-oriented school culture. As early as 1919, when the Waldorf school was founded, one of the cornerstones of this school, which was to be governed in a republican manner (Steiner 2020, p. 17), was this curricular autonomy, embedded in a culture of anthropological observation and reflection (Steiner 2020, p. 16).

The general approach to teaching in Waldorf education outlined above makes explicitly high demands on the governance of independent Waldorf schools regarding staff recruitment and professional development.

2.2 Klafki's critical-constructive concept of teaching

Klafki gives his didactic "model a new foundation" (Jank, Meyer 2009, p. 230) by further evolving his theory of categorial education toward a critical-constructive approach to teaching and the problem-based method of teaching. As general basic characteristics or teaching goals of a general education for the present and the future, he cites and programmatically adopts the capacities of codetermination, solidarity, and self-determination. These goals are to be realized in dealing with epoch-typical key issues using the problem-based method of teaching that simultaneously fosters the development of diverse interests and abilities. Jank and Meyer (2009, p. 235) and Meyer and Meyer (2007, p. 124) present a clearly arranged, straightforward graphic juxtaposition that we will not discuss further.

Klafki adds four further dimensions of meaning in general education. Aside from the epoch-typical key issues, he identifies a pragmatic dimension and attributes a central role to fostering aesthetic perceptive and creative abilities and to the understanding of trans-epochal issues of humanity (Berg 2003, p. 14).

Jank and Meyer point out that the problem-based method of teaching "can only work, if the teachers, students and parents involved all see themselves as a *learning school*" (Jank, Meyer 2009, p. 239). In developing this hypothesis, they make reference to the consequences for school organization that Klafki himself derives from his concept of problem-based teaching; for example, the need to minimize selective or dividing factors within a school's structure (no repetition of classes, heterogeneity in class composition) or the teaching in subject blocks. Elsewhere, Klafki demands a considerable scope for teachers regarding the creative use of time and content (Berg 2003, p. 28)—another aspect that coincides with Waldorf education.

Waldorf education presents many subjects, especially also those focused on cognitive learning, in the form of lesson blocks. During a period of time, typically stretching over three to four weeks, a specific subject topic is taught daily for about the length of two lessons. These two periods are usually taught at the beginning of the school day, forming for both students and teachers a focal point in their daily activities. This explains why Waldorf schools refer to this teaching period as "main lesson."

Due to the curricular autonomy and free timing choices of the main lesson teachers, many discussions in Waldorf schools on teaching today evidence close proximity to Klafki's critical-constructive approach to teaching and his problem-based method of teaching. These discussions center not only around the role of epoch-typical key issues such as electronic media (Hübner 2008), but also around trans-epochal, overarching motifs of humanity, for instance when (in German Waldorf schools) the epic poem *Song of the Nibelungs* or Wolfram von Eschenbach's *Parzival* is taught (Zech 2002).

To my knowledge, this proximity to Klafki is variously implied, but only rarely has Waldorf education engaged more deeply with these interfaces (Rohde 2003). Gögelein's work on the history and principles of the Waldorf "curriculum" lists several factors as guiding principles: orientation to the human being and development; orientation to world and culture; orientation to childhood and situational factors; and, last but not least, orientation to cognition and practice; however, Gögelein refers to Klafki merely in passing (Gögelein 2007).

2.3 Lines of discussion

Klafki's theory of categorial education and his critical-constructive approach to teaching spark new discussions even today (Arnold, Lindner-Müller 2012; Meyer, Meyer 2007). The following section follows two threads of discussion on positions in Waldorf education and relates them to each other. The first thread of discussion deals with the role of the universal in Klafki's theory of categorial education, and the second one with a quasi-ontological assumption of stability implicit in that theory.

Klafki posits that didactic analysis should reveal the educational value of an educational content, naming principles in this process the fundamental, the exemplary, and the elementary. According to Jank and Meyer, the principle of the exemplary is "actually the only one" that survived (Jank, Meyer 2009, p. 220). In fact, though, this principle includes also the fundamental and the elementary, when, in an impressive and fruitful example, something specific, pointing beyond itself, uncovers something universal, thus allowing access to fundamental insights into our relationship with reality (ibid.).

Meyer and Meyer (2007, p. 61) criticize Klafki's position and argue: "When the 'I' engages with the world for the purpose of learning, that is a process of accessing 'something,' in which what we access can only be something concrete. Whether and in how far this specific 'something' is also something universal, we have to ascertain for each special case – we cannot just postulate it" (ibid.). We could develop something similar, if we assumed as a matter of course that a specific curriculum is appropriately fitted to its educational theory.

It will have to be shown in the following chapter on main lesson teaching that this criticism by Meyer and Meyer in regard to lesson blocks is in fact already heeded in Waldorf schools, where specific problems of "high-density reality" (Wagenschein 2008, p. 101) are identified, which have the potential to reveal the *universal* in Klafki's sense. The phase structure of main lesson blocks is designed to be meaningful only for specific learning contents with the potential mentioned above. In reference to Klafki's terms, Waldorf education's main lesson curriculum is marked by the intent to realize exemplary procedures.

When, for example, a Waldorf school pursues a phenomenological approach in a science main lesson, the lessons focus on a series of experiments designed to enable the students through the inner movement of involved thinking to derive a meaningful order from the phenomena themselves (Østergaard, Dahlin, Hugo 2008). In this process, the students learn to first seek and appreciate sensory and contextual access to the phenomena, and to then systematize their findings into phenomenological patterns. The students then work out the order immanent in sensory phenomena, and, in particular, also the causes compelling a phenomenon to arise.

Jank and Meyer reference Türcke (1986) in directing another criticism at Klafki's theory of categorial education, which is feasible from a philosophical perspective. This critique "contains the reproach that the idea of a two-sided categorial understanding of the world implies the assumption of a quasi-ontological stability of the world, which is no longer acceptable today. The categorial access to the world can only 'work', if a well-ordered, yes, harmonious world exists with comprehensible educational resources, that corresponds to the students' educational needs" (Jank, Meyer 2009, p. 219). Similar criticism could be applied to education in the context of epoch-typical key issues, but this also raises the question as to an epistemology of teaching (Meyer, Meyer 2007, p. 66).

Meyer and Meyer counter this critique with their own teaching-related arguments: "Students can only then successfully access the world, if at least the school offers a sheltered space so that the educational needs of the growing individuals can be met with a corresponding, well-ordered and harmonious world that offers comprehensible educational resources" (ibid., pp. 65f.). They elaborate further: "Even if there were no such things as 'the essential being of a person' or the 'universal contents' of the world, we would need them so that we could support the learning processes of children and adolescents" (ibid.).

The ethical understructure of Meyer and Meyer's line of argument resembles that of Waldorf education in that it values a kind of education and instruction that is oriented to the needs of children and adolescents. From a philosophical perspective though, Waldorf education's general approach to teaching is rooted elsewhere in that it refers to the theory of knowledge Steiner developed in his early works. Chapter 1 of this book is dedicated to this theory of knowledge; in addition, numerous authors have discussed this topos, such as Muschalle (1989), Schieren (2012), Schneider (1997), da Veiga (2006), and Wiehl (2015).

Steiner's theory of knowledge is directly connected with Goethe's phenomenological approach and worldview (Steiner 2011). Briefly said and using Jost Schieren's phrasing, Steiner assumes that thinking brings structuring concepts to the individual percepts and, in doing so, brings the creative source of the world's phenomena into conscious human awareness (Steiner 2012b). For Steiner, cognition thus becomes an act of creating reality. Cognition for him is objective in respect to its appearance in consciousness, but subjective in the form of its occurrence.

From the perspective of Waldorf education, the questions as to the role of the universal and how we relate to reality do not arise as quasi-ontological but as ontological problems: "Based on a conceptually realistic understanding, Steiner does not consider the concepts that have been engendered through thought merely as subjective human creations but as ontologically justified entities, which occur partially in the specific, limited context of one person's thinking, but which are always based on their entelechy" (Schieren 2012, p. 77). In this respect, students experience ontological participation as they find a universal or conceptual principle in the particular example they consciously perceive. This epistemological position of Waldorf education then legitimizes the process of seeking the universal within the particular.

3 The model of main lesson teaching in Waldorf schools

The following sections on the general approach to teaching in Waldorf schools present the example of main lesson blocks as a model, because it offers the opportunity to distill many elements of Waldorf education from the specific traits of this approach. The general teaching approach in the main lessons corresponds to curriculum subjects, which are mostly organized into subject-specific lessons such as languages. Reflecting professional subject knowledge, these lessons accordingly modify universal teaching approaches. Jaffke (1994) and Templeton (2010) have provided detailed accounts of this process for English (as a foreign language). We cannot discuss these modifications in detail here.

Main lesson is taught in blocks in Waldorf schools, which means that a particular subject is taught over a period of three to four weeks for two periods every morning (usually the first 90–110 minutes of the school day). This teaching structure is particularly suitable for introducing new topics and working on broader contexts. However, the organizational structure of continuous subject classes often proves more appropriate when a class aims at incrementally increasing abilities with steady practice or by cultivating routines.

In mathematics, for example, most Waldorf schools introduce wide topics such as analytical geometry or differential calculus in main lesson, while they choose the subject lesson format to address detailed questions and offer corresponding exercises. In contrast, another example are physics classes, which are often scheduled as one annual four-week main lesson and are only during the time of exam preparation complemented with specific subject lessons. Some schools also offer work experience in a laboratory. There are considerable variances from school to school in the number of main lessons devoted to any given subject as well as in their duration and combination with continuous subject lessons.

Waldorf education offers many suggestions on how to create instances of direct encounters for the students as they study a topic within the main lesson model. The term "encounter" here denotes a teaching episode that the students experience as an external stimulation to open up to new and wider horizons of experience and to generate meaning at the same time. It is the event character of educational processes that is important here. These suggestions focus on lesson episodes that constitute experiences for the students in which they immediately participate. Meyer-Drawe describes this process: "Starting to see things in a new light is an event that one participates in as the one to whom it happens" (Meyer-Drawe 2003, p. 505).

Steiner also made a specific suggestion for a phase-oriented lesson structure supported by anthropological arguments.

The main lesson concept is close to Wagenschein's approach of starting with "specific individual problems of high-density reality that simultaneously point to universal laws" (Wagenschein 2008, p. 101). Teachers then should design the students' encounter with the world and with a reality in such a way that the encounter itself stimulates a cognitive process. In this process, the students are enabled to discover universal laws by themselves. The following section illustrates how such an exemplary lesson design in Klafki's sense could manifest, using physics and history lessons as examples. At the same time, these examples serve to clarify in detail what is meant by a *phenomenological approach to teaching*.

3.1 Phenomenological approaches to teaching physics and history

A series of experiments begins with striking different tuning forks so that they sound a chord. Teachers and students pause to linger for a while in the experience of the sound and then touch the tines of some of the forks. As a result, the sound emitted by these forks immediately ceases. Touching a tuning fork near the joint, however, will have virtually no effect, and similarly, a clear sound rings out when striking the fork at the tines, while there is only a muddled sound when striking it close to the joint.

If we strike a tuning fork and swiftly dip it in a glass bowl filled with water, the tone becomes lower at the moment of immersion, and water splashes away—depending on the immersion angle of the tuning fork it splashes to the side (the tines hit the water sideways) or both to the sides and vigorously straight upward (the tines hit the water vertically as a parallel). Finally, the students work in small groups or pairs and strike the tuning forks themselves. They touch each other's nose tips with the tines (it tickles) or strike the forks' tips against a series of objects (they resonate).

The students create a record of the setup, implementation, and observation of the experiments. In this process, the students often also remember what struck them as beautiful, unpleasant, or surprising and they emotionally relive these experiences as they recall them. This creates a situation in class in which the students can connect emotionally more intensely with their experiences.

Up to this point, the series of experiments is designed so that students can engage as directly as possible in the encounter facilitated by the experimental design. They can encounter the phenomena with a lifeworld attitude. The immediacy of their experience is a key factor. A perspective of objectivity still guides the experimental sequences, but it is only implicit in this phase of the lesson.

The next step consists of evaluating the results of the experiments based on the question: "What does the tuning fork do while it emits the sound?" Soon the students will find out on their own that the tuning fork actually moves, and that the two tines must produce juxtaposed lateral oscillations, because that is the only explanation for the water splashing experiments. Next, the students may try to figure out the longitudinal vibration of the fork handle. Maybe the students come up with graphic representations of the various stages of the handle's longitudinal vibration or the lateral vibration of the tines.

The evaluation in class begins with opening questions designed to preserve a close connection with the process, while at the same time challenging the students to distance themselves from the experience. Such an opening question could be "How are sound and movement connected here?" or "What is the link here between sound and motion?" The second question, in particular, would force a transition to an objective standpoint as it directly calls up objectifying, abstract terms. The question "What does the tuning fork do while it emits sound?" is therefore chosen for a reason. That kind of question is central to a phenomenological approach to education. This approach begins with a sensory, authentic experience, and as the students gradually learn to distance themselves from their experiences, they learn to seek inherent order from the more comprehensive viewpoint gained in the distancing process.

In history class, the teacher presents a specific, vivid narrative so that the students can visualize a historical situation in which they can experientially participate. A similar instant of encounter occurs, if here too a lifeworld perspective is prioritized. In contrast to the physics experiment, the students' experience occurs in an inner level through active participation in the teacher's narrative, not on an outer level through sensory observation.

For example, the students can encounter French absolutism through a colorful, vividly detailed narrative about the rising ceremony of Louis XVI and a graphic description of the Versailles palace. To have their story transcend the merely informative level and to evoke tangible inner images, teachers must have detailed knowledge of courtly life, of the persons involved, and of the premises of Versailles. Inner experience marks the onset of historical understanding.

In history class, for example, understanding may dawn through contextualization in a basic historical, anthropological, or philosophical framework. It is therefore important to foster a profound historical consciousness by adopting a detached perspective about where to actively question the content, which the first step of teaching made emotionally accessible—often after a phase of strongly emotional partisanship ("Such a waste of money!").

Initially, this is facilitated by questions aimed at highlighting characteristic parts of the narrative, which in the example described above may be "What does it mean that there is a bedroom at the center of the Versailles palace and no longer a chapel?" Such deliberations tie in with historical facts, and, in ensuing discussion in class, these facts can serve to characterize French absolutism as a cultural, social, and political historical phenomenon; this process in turn will prepare the way for studying the ideas of philosophical Enlightenment and the demands of the French Revolution by raising questions about the concept of the human being and its political and social implications. Deliberations about the present or future relevance of the learned material may follow (Schmelzer 2000, pp. 9ff.).

Similar to what we saw in the physics class example, we see here again that a phenomenon is understood as an intense emotional encounter, which can enable the students to discover immanent structures and future perspectives. These enter into the students' awareness as they gradually distance themselves from the phenomena and adopt a more generalizing standpoint.

3.2 General characteristics of phenomenological teaching

Phenomenological teaching approaches are an essential feature of main lesson teaching in Waldorf schools. They represent a path to the discovery of universal aspects in a fertile specific example that at the same time may also be fundamental to the relationship between us and reality; they therefore tie in with Klafki's thoughts on educational theory. In science teaching, in particular, they have a long tradition. A synoptic article by Østergaard, Dahlin, and Hugo (2008) most recently summarized their origin and orientation.

The authors address the gap that students may experience between the immediate, sensory, corporeal perception of natural phenomena, and the concepts with which these phenomena are explained or scientifically imparted. They discuss in what way phenomenological teaching approaches can bridge this gap in an orderly cognitive process and thereby live up to their claim of presenting scientific subjects in a relatable, interesting, and accessible form and, more generally speaking, foster participatory experiences.

According to Fuchs (2018), this gap is inherent in the reductionist "scientific program begun in early modern times," which divides "original lifeworld experiences" into a "physical, quantitative and a subjective, qualitative component" (Fuchs 2018, p. xvi) and then, for scientific purposes, establishes the constructs of a quantitative explanation as the "actual" reality, which engenders the experience in the lifeworld. The impression of being connected to and embedded in experiences of reality may instead turn into a feeling of alienation, while any real lifeworld or qualitative experience becomes a purely subjective adjunct to the "actual" quantitative version of reality.

Wiesing further explains the gap in the context of the philosophy of mind: Within the framework of "origin stories of perception," people make up "bold occult entities, all of which have in common that they are undetectable building blocks of perception: There is talk about impressions, sensations, percepts, impacts, Lego-blocks, sensory data, and stimuli. [...] But however inventive the tales about the origins of perception may be, they still remain preambles that speak of entities and processes which, although not unsubstantiated, are mere fabrications" (Wiesing 2009, p. 111).

Numerous suggestions for phenomenological approaches to teaching specifically shun the subject/object separation that characterizes the causal construction described by Fuchs and Wiesing. In physics teaching, for example, the transition from an involved to a detached observer's perspective has been established as a teaching model that fosters a different, dialogue-based orientation in judgment attitude (Grebe-Ellis 2005; Sommer 2005). Initially, phenomena are explored experientially through the senses and appreciated (involved perspective) and then systematized into a series of phenomena. In a final step, the class must work out the immanent order of sensory phenomena, in particular the causes that are necessary conditions for a phenomenon to arise (detached perspective).

Theory development proves to be a path for students to gradually distance themselves from their experiences and to learn to seek out immanent patterns, based on the generalizing viewpoint they gained in the distancing process. Participation and contemplation are then complementary factors, characterizing active cognition and its process (Grebe-Ellis 2005, p. 38), which the students can comprehend and integrate in a transparent way. The students are "fully engaged" when they discover the laws. Central to this process are not external causes but cognitive experiences that they distill from direct experiences.

This example drawn from physics teaching illustrates the phenomenological approach, and it also offers a more general perspective: We may generalize participation and observation as complementary process modalities of active cognition so that the transition from a person- and lifeworld-based attitude to a naturalistic-objectifying one can become a characteristic of this approach that can apply across all subjects.

In general, it is all about coming into an experience, in which the students engage earnestly, and about the breakthrough to a comprehensible order that we achieve through reflective observation.

Phenomenological teaching approaches empower students to transition from their subjective experience to objective observation in a specific way. The dichotomy of subject and object no longer marks an insurmountable boundary but a threshold that can be crossed with understanding.

The material side of education unfolding in the phenomenological approach has the potential to be especially closely linked with the formal aspect of education, for it is the formal side of education that is understood as the self-realizing student's cognitive achievement and transition from a lifeworld perspective to an objectifying point of view. Phenomenological teaching approaches, therefore, denote a differentiation of Klafki's concept of categorial education.

The central role of phenomenological teaching approaches in Waldorf education may appear plausible if they are seen in association with Steiner's theory of knowledge: As outlined above, Steiner starts from the premise that thinking brings structuring concepts to individual perceptions, thus producing in the human mind the idea of what forms the phenomena of the world (Schieren 2012, p. 77; Steiner 2012b).

Phenomenological teaching is consequently the attempt to put into practice what corresponds to this theory of knowledge. From this point of view, it is about accompanying students through cognitive movements that do not tie their thinking to preconceptions, premature judgments, or pre-set patterns that have little to do with the phenomena. Rather, their thinking is considered to be able to "adapt to," or as Goethe puts it "to rationally amalgamate" with the world's phenomena (Goethe 1966, p. 24) to such an extent that they can creatively participate in what actively shapes these phenomena. As explained above, this takes on an ontological dimension for Steiner.

Steiner himself took the opposite path. He developed core aspects of his theory of knowledge in studying Goethe's scientific insights. This is also apparent from the title of one of Steiner's epistemological works: "Goethe's Theory of Knowledge – an Outline of the Epistemology of His World View" (Steiner 2011). Goethe himself pursued a phenomenological approach in his scientific studies. Following up on these references, Schieren studied in detail the methodological and philosophical foundations of Goethe's scientific epistemology (Schieren 1998).

While phenomenological teaching approaches are epistemologically linked to Goethe, Steiner, or Schieren, they do not necessarily have to refer to these authors. Varela (2008, p. 120) writes, for example: "It is precisely the agenda of phenomenology that is so crucial for modern cognitive science: To investigate, without prejudice or premature judgment, one's own experiences and perceptions; to include oneself as the researcher in the reflections in order to avoid disembodied, purely abstract analysis" (Varela 2008, p. 120).

3.3 Phase structure

In Waldorf's main lesson teaching, phenomenological approaches are implemented in a specific three-phase structure that refers back to Steiner (Steiner 1986, pp. 45ff.) and further differentiates this teaching model into a structural model of instruction.

The task in the first phase is to unfold one single example or moment of encounter of "high-density reality" (Wagenschein 2008, p. 101). This expository quality has been demonstrated above in the examples taken from physics and history teaching. This teaching approach takes a phenomenological, experiential segment of the world and designs it so that the students can experience it intensely and come to understand it.

These experiences, which are central to main lesson teaching, are discussed in Waldorf education from both epistemological and anthropological perspectives. Waldorf education assumes that students intelligently deal with their perceptions within a phenomenological field by intentionally turning the flow of their thoughts to the world and letting the world and its phenomena work on them. The progress in their thinking and the connections they make in their mind are guided by the perceptions themselves: The tuning fork splashes into the water in this specific way and no other; the palace of Versailles was constructed just so (see the previous section).

Steiner uses the term *perceptual judgment* to describe this process in his early epistemological works: "Perceptual judgment allows us to recognize that a specific sense-perceptible object, by its nature, coincides with a specific concept" (Steiner 2011, pp. 45f.). In his lectures on education, on the other hand, he uses the term *conclusion* instead.

Steiner freely uses this latter term to denote the creative achievement of connecting disordered impressions with interested perception. In this perspective, the *conclusion* represents a connection with the world. Schieren (2010) remarks that the *conclusion* for Steiner "is the connection of a new experience with one's own understanding or comprehension-continuum." Wiehl elaborates further that the phase of concluding and understanding starts out as "a process of becoming aware of a phenomenon through listening and interested perception" (Wiehl 2015, p. 226). A number of Waldorf schools therefore now commonly use the term *conclusion part,* or abbreviated *conclusion,* to denote the first phase of the main lesson.

Waldorf education's anthropological approach aims at awakening the students' awareness of the active part they play in this process that denotes interested human perception, and at addressing and practicing this active participation in class through its teaching methods.

In physics, for example, the students first sequentially strike four different tuning forks with a small mallet so that a chord rings out. Taking the mallet simply by hand and letting it lightly strike the table twice, the students observe, by the way it bounces back, that the mallet is coated with rubber. If the tuning forks are arranged sequentially from left to right, and their height decreases, the students immediately recognize upon striking the fork how size and pitch are connected. Finally, the sound experience ends when the students manually squeeze the two tines of the forks together. This first sequence of an experiment or experimental demonstration is designed to be self-explanatory. The teacher is not required to speak. An attentive atmosphere can be set up before the class even starts, then the encounter with the world can follow an aesthetic design without having to interrupt the student's perceptual process with explanatory comments. The teacher does not verbally explain the property of the mallet, for example, but only demonstrates it.

This example shows how a general objective of Waldorf teaching manifests in a particular subject—using the experiential dimension of a world encounter to demonstrate how our own creative participation is important to the perceptual process. Perceptive presence here takes the place of rapid conceptual categorization, addresses the active aspect of interested perception, and, in doing so, cultivates the students' increased self-activity in the first phase of an encounter between "I" and world. Schieren (2010) discussed the epistemological dimension of this didactic approach in depth.

Wiesing takes an epistemological perspective in investigating the perceptive presence in particular, asking questions about "the consequences of the reality of perception for the subject" (Wiesing 2009, p. 112). He goes on: "A perception is a possible state or an experience for a subject – the state, that is, of deeming a certain describable object to be present and existent. But this state presupposes the existence of the subject as a perceiving subject, for something can only be present if there is someone for whom it is present" (ibid., p. 121). Referencing the categories of having and being, Wiesing notes that the subject does not "have perceptions" but is engaged in the act of perceiving, since it is a presence defined by relationships (ibid., p. 122). The above-used term "perceptive presence" here denotes an educational orientation that reflectively includes this dimension of perception.

In history class, this phase of the main lesson called *conclusion* often consists, for instance, in the teacher describing the Versailles palace, the lavish lifestyle at court, the etiquette, and finally the rising ceremony of Louis XVI (Schmelzer 2000, pp. 9ff.). Where possible, this narrative proceeds without introduction or previous assignments, so that the students can immerse themselves fully in the narrative without any demand for analysis interfering with this experience. The narrative must be aesthetically designed so that it on one hand invites discussion and judgment formation as well as stimulates the study of fundamental historic issues; but, on the other hand, it should not supply an already pre-formed understanding of history. The recommendation is to describe rather than characterize and judge the content. A prerequisite is therefore a good knowledge of details and facts. The choice of what to present is determined by what kind of specialized topics are planned as a follow-up to deepen understanding and knowledge.

The first phase strongly directs the student's intentionality to the outer world: In the centrifugal motion of their attention, they seek out meaningful perceptions. Their conscious mind is dominated from without by their encounters with the world. In comparison, personal previous knowledge, quick associations, etc. retreat to the background.

In the second phase, Steiner provides for the change from the outer perspective of appraising perception to the inner perspective of personal relating. The first relationships to the perceptions develop, perhaps also the first personal evaluations. A process of attribution unfolds. That is why Steiner termed these processes in teaching (and life in general) as *judgment*, using the word once more in a very free sense. Many Waldorf schools are used to calling this second phase *judgment part* or just *judgment*.

The first phase challenges the students to be aware, present, and perceptive as they engage with a range of phenomena. They must "adapt to" the world. In contrast, Steiner envisions for the second phase that the students may emotionally and appraisingly accept what they perceive. This happens, for example, not only when students recapitulate a process and consciously contemplate how one element has given rise to another, but also when they relate to what they have perceived through personal judgments or opinions. The students change from an outward orientation to an inner one, actively taking ownership in their experience. Instruction is especially designed to facilitate this achievement.

After the first—experimental—phase of physics classes at Waldorf schools, it has proved useful to set the experiment equipment aside or to push the table cart with experiment props into the anteroom and then work with the students on integrating and ordering their experiences. From memory, the students take clearly structured notes and evaluate the structure of the experiment, its timing, striking features, or special observations. Providing no direct sensory connection and calling on the students' memory is meant to support and foster the transition to an inner perspective.

The teacher-student dialogue and a drawing on the blackboard can establish the work method, if the class has not yet developed much of a routine in describing experiments. This applies particularly to structuring the description of an experiment into setup, execution, and observation. Experience has shown that as the students gain routine, they can themselves—in individual work or with a partner—implement this process step-by-step, while the teacher merely provides support in the form of new terminology, graphic symbols, or measuring data.

This phase is not designed for the students to immediately discuss and analyze the experiments but rather for them to personally integrate an encounter with the world. In physics, an emotional connection to the experience can be established, for instance, when, after the students have worked individually or in pairs, they are encouraged to have a brief exchange on what was special, surprising, "really good," or "boring"; furthermore, the teacher can assure that the students take well-structured notes that form a basis for the description of the experiment, which may be assigned next as homework.

In history, the presentation of new content is followed by the students working individually, in pairs, or groups to process the new material. The students now order their experiences and relate to them emotionally and intellectually. Unlike in science lessons, the students' self-activity in the humanities does not consist in inwardly detaching themselves from an outer, sensory impression, but in structuring and inquiring into a personal picture that has arisen in them spontaneously as they listened to the presentation. Most of the time, this process relies on complementing the narrative with more primary or secondary sources, which in turn requires a discursive, source-critical mode of working; also, the choice of contrasting materials may direct the students' attention to the fact that evaluations of history depend on the perspective of the author and thus may challenge the students'

Teaching Approaches in Waldorf Education

Teaching phase	Name	Focus within the phenomenological approach
1	Conclusion part	Encounter with a world content
2	Judgment part	Personal engagement with the world content
3	Concept part	Conceptual penetration of world content

Figure 5.1 Phases of the phenomenological approach to Waldorf main lesson teaching

own active evaluating process. A possible homework assignment might then be to write an individual view of the issues raised in class.

But, independently of specific subject-related factors, a general-didactic perspective aims at giving the students an opportunity to personally deal with what they experienced in the vivid encounter with a phenomenon. They should take ownership of their own encounter experience.

The first phase focuses on the encounter with the world, the attention is directed outward, while the second phase is mainly concerned with the personal engagement and integration of this world encounter; the third phase aims to help the students to derive and recognize lawful and conceptual patterns, draw general connections, analyze and evaluate, etc. (Figure 5.1). Instruction in this phase refers mainly to the topics of the first two phases. In the heterogenic learning groups of Waldorf schools, mental or cognitive work therefore crucially refers to content that all of the students encountered. Any diffuse pre-knowledge of the students is relegated to a subordinate role.

In other words, the third phase focuses on the meaning of the class experience and highlights mental connections and abstractions. In accordance with established philosophical terminology, Steiner here uses the term *concept*. Waldorf schools therefore refer to this teaching phase as *concept part* or just *concept*.

Because the third phase mentally processes and deepens the moment of encounter of the first phase, thus meeting a learning target, the term *deepening part* has become customary as well. The general within the particular emerges as a theme; simultaneously, questions arise about what the general aspects point toward and which fundamental issues may come up as a result.

In physics, the third phase is about evaluating and interpreting the experiments. In this phase, the goal is to empower students to discover laws and contexts on their own; teachers mainly pose open questions and increasingly take on the role of moderators in the class discussions. For the series of experiments described above, a fitting question could be "What does the tuning fork do as it rings out?" Based on their experience during the previous phases, the students themselves can come to recognize the lateral vibration of the tines and the longitudinal vibrations of the handle. In particular, the way the water splashes allows them to conclude that the two tines move simultaneously toward and away from each other in a counter-vibration. From the experimental series itself, the students can mentally "distill out" the conceptual connections by themselves.

Schieren in his essay "Conclusion, Judgment, Concept – the Quality of Understanding" highlights the epistemological dimension Steiner connects with this approach: "In this approach […] the term concept has a different connotation. The concept at first does not denote the mental representation a person forms of an outer phenomenon but the lawfulness that governs the phenomena. In the context of the famous *problem of universals* of medieval scholasticism, Waldorf education therefore assumes a decidedly realistic position in regard to concepts and ideas. The Waldorf approach […] is philosoph- ically based on the view that concepts are active in the things of the world as ontological entities" (Schieren 2010, pp. 21f.).

Another cognitive path could have been taken by posing the question in the form of "What is sound?" This would have brought up the idea of air being impacted by the vibration of the tines, how air is compacted and thinned by those vibrations, and, finally, the students could have arrived at an understanding of the inherent molecular impact processes. The students would have been challenged to conceptually construct a model of sound. "We hear the sound of the tuning fork because its vibrations cause the air density to regularly increase and decrease, leading to impact processes in the air molecules. Our ear or brain interprets this as sound," a student might say in answering that challenge.

The students would have developed a physical model, which would have explained their sound experience based on a purely mechanistic process that was presented from without. They could interpret this process as "the actual, essential factor." In that approach, the students' own sound experiences would only represent a subjective add-on to an objective process. Because of the modeling, this explanatory path contains an alienation from nature. Epistemologically, this approach would be one of *metaphysical realism*: The processes behind the phenomena are the actual reality. They themselves give rise to the phenomena.

In contrast, the question "What does the tuning fork do when it rings out?" directly targets the mechanical processes connected to sound. No explanatory meta-level is constructed; instead, one strives for a conceptual description that aligns with *conceptual realism*.

In physics, the phase structure of *conclusion—judgment—concept* aligns with phenomenological approaches to teaching, while it seems questionable with teaching content that centers on the construction of models. Why practice interested perception in the first phase, and an inner order through an interactive encounter with the world in the second, when, in the third phase, the students are asked to construct models that, because of their position of metaphysical realism, are inherently alienated from the phenomena and have no dialogic proximity to them? This question is further discussed elsewhere (Sommer 2010, pp. 59f.).

Changing from the subject-specific perspective of physics to general Waldorf teaching, we note that the phases *conclusion—judgment—concept* aim at understanding through dialogue. This form of interactive understanding does not align with every epistemological position.

In history teaching, this third phase cannot focus on any supposedly universal laws and patterns in cultural phenomena, nor can it entail any conclusive conceptual penetration of connected facts. Conceptualization here can only mean probing the subject matter for anthropological, philosophical, or current societal relevance. Forming comprehensive historical awareness and differentiated understanding in a universal sense is therefore the primary goal of this (third) part of teaching. In class, open questions aim at facilitating the understanding how historic phenomena continue to exert an influence across diverse levels or at recognizing historic phenomena as symptoms of developments within the history of ideas or as facets of human nature. The example of late French absolutism could give rise to a discussion about issues of a metaphysically legitimized understanding of rulership in an increasingly enlightened and secularized world, or the discrepancy between claims of an ideology of absolutistic governance and the social reality.

Especially in the humanities, the students' individual achievements are expressed in two ways: On one hand, they should reach a learning target in the way described. On the other hand, this individually reached learning target should not "only" be a complete, finished concept that conclusively evaluates and categorizes a phenomenon. The aim is rather that the path the students take in this teaching phase in order to generate meaningful content intensifies and solidifies into a learning target. But it is also supposed to be an individual step that the students may want to modify in their life in manifold ways and that transcends the class in the form of farther-reaching interest. Steiner speaks here of "living concepts" (Steiner 1992, pp. 140f.).

The lessons are designed to facilitate individual development of concepts and, at the same time, their individualization. If the teaching is successful, such concepts represent an educational content that the students have both individually developed and individualized and that may be the point of departure for a variety of interests. In that respect, these individualized concepts are characterized by "intentional signatures." The "intentional signature" becomes a goal in both the humanities and sciences as well as in math.

The structure conceived of by Steiner for main lesson teaching distinguishes the three phases as developed above. It is in the third phase that the learning target in a narrower sense is often reached. Many Waldorf teachers working within this model add after the third phase a time of quiet work or

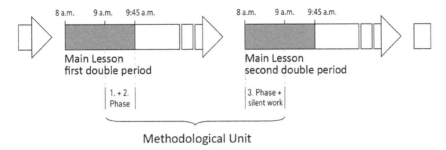

Figure 5.2 Chronological and methodical structure of main lesson teaching

practice, during which the students consolidate what they have learned and apply it or expand it in work assignments.

Figure 5.2 shows how, according to Steiner, the three consecutive phases extend over a two-day period within a main lesson. Many Waldorf schools have main lesson at the beginning of the school day over a time span of 105 minutes. The illustration fixes this main lesson period for the time between 8:00 am and 9:45 am, for example. The period begins by referring back to the previous day, when the first and second phases of a given subject-specific topic took place.

The physics experiments with the tuning forks, for example, would be presented on day one between 9:00 am and 9:25 am (first phase). Afterward, there would be time for ordering, note taking, and personal appraisal (second phase). The students would pass through processes of interested perception or encounter with the world, and they would have the opportunity to internalize what they encountered. The third phase, which aims at evaluating the experiments and contextualizing them conceptually, would then take place on the following day at the beginning of main lesson.

This clearly sets the encounter of the first and second phases apart from the cognitive processes expressed in the form of analyses, evaluations, and explanations. The phase structure cultivates a distinct differentiation between processes of perception/world encounter and processes generative of meaning.

According to Steiner (Steiner 1986, p. 46ff.), it is important for the phase structure concept that the processes of encounter and perception in the first and second phases undergo a process of transformation during sleep before the third phase with its generation of meaning, which follows on from this transformation process and continues it further. "Sleeping on" a content is therefore an integral part of teaching and learning in Waldorf's main lessons.

3.4 Discussions on phase structure

As part of a project on phenomenology and teaching, Grebe-Ellis reviewed practice-reports and studies on main lesson teaching, which were published in the last two decades, providing a summary of first results of his research (Grebe-Ellis 2009, p. 232ff.). He noticed that numerous research questions regarding main lesson teaching in Waldorf schools have not been addressed to this day. Nonetheless, the research project provided him with a basis for discussing and looking into setting up a comparative study on "Main lesson teaching with and without integrating night sleep." The study he envisioned would be of elementary interest to Waldorf education.

In particular, Grebe-Ellis refers to the work of Wagner et al. (2004), who demonstrated in a study titled *Sleep Inspires Insight* that "sleep does not only reinforce declarative and procedural memory but it also 'processes' freshly memorized content and transforms it; this processing can lead to more creative solving of problems that were deeply contemplated before falling asleep" (quoted from Grebe-Ellis 2009, pp. 232f.). The question arises whether the time structure of main lessons in Waldorf schools particularly promotes creative solutions due to the transformative processes that occur during sleep.

Independently of this question, it can be stated that main lesson teaching in Waldorf schools engenders and practices, through thematic structuring of teaching and learning processes, a certain habitus: separating an encounter with a phenomenon from immediate explanation and conceptual categorization. While students already order and internalize the world phenomena experienced in class on the first day, they only move toward explanation and understanding on the following main lesson day. This may cultivate in the students an openness to encounters as distinct from finding their own explanations and generating their own meaning. At the same time, they gain distance to the world encounter that the teacher unfolded for them on the first day. Within a tolerant class atmosphere, the teacher will encourage their individual approach and personal process of understanding, because they will only be asked during the following day's class to express their thoughts in response to the teacher's previous activity.

In teachers' faculties of Waldorf schools or in Waldorf teacher education, discussions often spring up on whether it would be better to include all three phases in the same main lesson period so that a content unit coincides with a time unit and students can follow without interruption the path from encountering a phenomenon to its understanding. That appears plausible under the perspective of simplification and reconstruction as part of a phenomenological teaching approach. The students would then encounter a new content at the beginning of a double period; they would order it and finally explain it. From a mode of being open to experience, they would transition to a mode of reflective distance.

The question nonetheless remains as to what is gained by this rhythmic alternation of modes, if they do not directly follow on from one another but a period of forgetting and sleeping is inserted. Can the freshness with which the students approach the phenomenon anew, after a phase of distancing, benefit the cognitive processes? Could the dynamic change from the proximity of the encounter to the distance of the students' attempts at understanding cultivate a way of approaching the world phenomena? Could this dynamic interplay enhance the students' and teachers' experience of the lessons as vibrant and exciting?

In regard to main lesson teaching, Wagenschein draws attention to "the immense assistance of 'subconscious work'" that is being "mobilized" (quote from Grebe-Ellis 2009, pp. 232f.). Steiner includes subconscious processing through sleep in his concept of main lesson teaching.

Former Waldorf students view main lesson overall in a positive light when looking back. Barz and Randoll found in an empiric study on education and life design of former Waldorf students that 87.6% found the main lesson format positive (Barz, Randoll 2007, p. 209), and in a parallel study in Switzerland, the percentage was even higher at 90.4% (ibid., p. 130). A student survey showed that "80.8% of the 827 student subjects at the time questioned" liked the main lesson "very well or rather well," and about a third of these found them "very good" (Liebenwein, Barz, Randoll 2012, p. 82).

Frielingsdorf (2012, p. 121ff.) offers a brief overview of some discussions within education science on the topic of main lesson teaching in Waldorf schools. Moreover, students and parents were interviewed on this topic (Liebenwein, Barz, Randoll 2012, p. 81ff), and, in a step called "feedback on feedback," the researchers systematized the results of these student- and parent-surveys and also marked themes that would allow Waldorf education to learn from the survey (Loebell, Sommer 2012). These discussions also addressed the question of heterogeneous study groups in main lesson teaching (ibid., pp. 173f.).

A study on the focus on sciences, which was part of the 2006 PISA study among Austrian Waldorf students, provides further empirical findings regarding Waldorf main lesson teaching, because Waldorf schools provide most of their science teaching according to the phenomenological approach described and in the main lesson format.

With regard to science teaching, this research not only found that students experienced a high level of joy in learning and developed strong confidence in their own achievements and competence, but it also revealed that "in Waldorf schools, [...] interactive participation in natural science subjects constituted common everyday practice for over 80% of the students and thus ranged far above the OECD median (47%)." "Interactive class participation" here denotes "a teaching style that facilitates the students' participation in form of giving their own opinions, explanations, and contributions to discussions" (Wallner-Paschon 2009, p. 387ff.). Overall, research findings indicate that the phenomeno-logical teaching approach is in fact successful in main lesson in that it fosters participatory experiences and supports the will to discover and to gain insight.

In the pedagogical discussions and faculty meetings of Waldorf schools, potential problems of the main lesson concept are often addressed, such as the question if the model practices mostly teacher-centered presentations for a particularly long period of time. The term "teacher-centered teaching" is often used wholesale and without differentiating how far there is a passive form of conveying informa-tion or direct teacher-centered instruction that may challenge students to enter into intense inner par-ticipation. The question of the possible "empirical potential" is not usually posed (Helm 2013).

Liebenwein, Barz, and Randoll for example state: "It would indeed be detrimental to ignore the impressions of a minority of parents that there is still a lot of teacher-centered instruction going on. It could actually be true that there are still too many teachers who know only this method" (Liebenwein, Barz, Randoll 2012, p. 76).

It is certainly true that the phenomenological approach applied in main lesson teaching with its phase structure is highly teacher focused. Particularly during the first phase, it is the teacher who facilitates the encounter with the phenomena of the world, but the teacher also generates active participation rather than passive reception of information.

Moreover, as explained above, the format is designed so that the students participate actively in the second phase, and that they arrive at their own insightful connections in the third phase. Once the main lesson got on its way successfully, it is in the third phase that the main activity shifts to the students. So, while the teacher is mainly responsible for facilitating the encounter with the world, it is the task of the students to embrace the encounter with interest and understanding.

In analyzing this process from the point of view of teacher-centered instruction, the change in per-spective and activities that occurs in the transition from the first to the third phase may not be imme-diately apparent. In my view, however, this is precisely what characterizes Waldorf schools: that they provide teaching and learning processes in the main lesson format with the alternation of activities as described above. This alternation can include a wide range of methods. A great number of student-led experiments can be offered, for example, during the first and second phases of a physics main lesson. In the third phase, there are possibilities in addition to a teacher-student dialogue, such as panel discussions, intervals of group work, working in pairs, and individual study. The living process of an interested encounter with the world can be realized in many ways (Sommer 2011). With reference to Wiechmann's distinction of impartation styles (expository/discovering) and direction (teacher-directed/student-directed), it can be characterized as the transition from a directed, expository encounter to a discovering, autonomous facilitation of understanding (Wiechmann 2002, p. 14f.). In fact, in the first phase, it remains a daily challenge for Waldorf teachers to avoid using the moment of encounter, which has expository character, as a legitimization or inlet for continuing teacher-centered instruction.

This chapter presented an explanatory view of the phase structure of the Waldorf main lesson, illustrated by the examples of physics and history classes. This structure offers a general framework for cognitive learning that is filled in specific ways depending on the subject taught. Waldorf education characteristically expands its general teaching approach homogeneously to subject teaching and thus in fact provides an interdisciplinary orientation.

According to Loebell (Chapter 3), the Waldorf curriculum anticipates a clear break in regard to cog-nitive learning in sixth grade. Causal thinking, which seeks to find causes for phenomena, is systemat-ically pursued only from sixth grade on. In a narrower sense, this chapter therefore refers to cognitive learning in main lesson only from sixth grade onward.

However, a phenomenological approach to teaching is employed from first grade. When introducing the letters, for example, the teacher tells a story and one event of the story is then depicted in an evoca-tive chalkboard drawing. This drawing serves to inspire the students to draw their own pictures during the lesson. In the next lesson, the dancing bear transforms into a "B," a fish into an "F," or a mouth into an "M" (Steiner 1997, p. 69ff.). Here, too, from an event vividly presented in the "conclusion" part, semiotic meaning is derived in the "concept" part. Prompted by the immediacy of experiencing the story events, the students internalize them by drawing their own pictures. The next day they move from the image to the abstract sign, the letter. As explained above using other examples, this is, again, a path of interrelating closeness and distance. From the immediacy of the experienced narrative, the letter with its functional significance emerges in a process of increasing distancing. In the local geography lesson in fourth grade, one can proceed similarly, by letting the students experience "the immediate environment of their school – the town or village – in its geographic/spatial and historic/temporal development up to the present time" (Richter 2006, p. 216).

From a perspective of developmental psychology, different authors have discussed what forms of judgment are specifically addressed by the Waldorf curriculum in grades 6–12. They differentiate the phases that are part of the phenomenological approach in a way that highlights different forms of judgment depending on the students' ages and development. Manfred von Mackensen wrote a foundational essay on the ability to judge, depending on the students' ages (Mackensen 2000). He references and modifies previous writings by Rauthe on "stages of judgment" (Rauthe 1990). In addition to this line of discussion, there are also subject-specific ones, such as Zech's analysis of "the stages of judgment formation in the higher grades, with examples from lessons" for history teaching (Zech 2012, p. 259ff.).

3.5 Steiner's anthropological lines of argument

In accordance with Waldorf education's mandate to orient teaching and education to the needs of the "whole human being," (Steiner 2020, p. 16), there are manifold connections between Waldorf anthropology and Waldorf teaching. Particularly conspicuous are parallels that can be drawn between the phases of main lesson teaching and the three ways of encountering the world developed by Steiner in his work *Theosophy* (Steiner 2012a).

In this book, Steiner differentiates "human nature" into body, soul, and spirit. "Body" for him denotes the aspect by means of which "the things in our environment [...] reveal themselves to us" (ibid., p. 24). Through our senses, we become aware of the things around us; we find them and accept them as "given fact" (ibid., p. 23). When we turn what we find into something that "concerns us," allowing impressions of like or dislike, of sympathy and antipathy to arise, these are, according to Steiner, attributes of our inner soul life (ibid., p. 23). Finally, when we bring meaningful order to the impressions of these things, which allows them to reveal to us "the secrets of what they are and how they work" (ibid.), Steiner speaks of "spirit."

We can easily relate the aspects of body, soul, and spirit (ibid., p. 26ff) to the phases of main lesson teaching: conclusion, judgment, and concept, or encounter, emotional connection, and creation of meaning. In physics teaching, for instance, the encounter with the world arising in the conclusion phase can be a sensory and self-explanatory series of experiments; in history, it can be a narrative that vividly describes how an event unfolds to the external observer. In Steiner's terminology, this phase mainly addresses the "body," and the lesson content is accordingly presented "bodily." This includes in particular the students' sensory presence and bodily resonances described by Rittelmeyer (2014) in relation to aesthetic education.

The "soul" aspect moves to the foreground as students get personally involved in this encounter during the "judgment" phase, when they bring order to the observed physics experiments or contextualize a historic event through source text study. In the final "conceptual" part, the physics lesson will focus on evaluating the experiments, while the history lesson strives to develop historic consciousness in the students. The insights envisaged Steiner attributes to the human "spirit."

Looking at these events from a performative perspective gives rise to the question as to how the way of teaching just described can establish a connection between the person and the world.

When, in the "conclusion" part, the students are addressed and the lesson content unfolds at the "bodily" level, this "bodily" unfolding constitutes the material side of the educational process, while the students' "bodily" connection with the content constitutes the formal side of this process.

In the conclusion phase, the material and the formal aspect can be conceived of as interlinking in the "body" dimension. This means that, in the first phase of main lesson teaching, Waldorf education strives toward a (dialectic) interconnection of material and formal education on the "bodily" level, or in "bodily" terms. At the "bodily" level, Waldorf education therefore realizes Klafki's *Theory of Categorial Education* (Klafki 1963, p. 44).

As students get inwardly involved (in their soul) in this educational event by internalizing it, and as they derive insights from it in their mind or spirit, a further interconnection of formal and material education occurs according to Steiner's theory of knowledge, as explained in Section 3.2: In the insights they have gained, the students productively bring to expression what actively forms the phenomena in the world (Steiner 2012b).

Steiner's theory of knowledge is based on conceptual realism and assigns an ontological dimension to concepts (Schieren 2012, p. 77). Therefore, the students unlock the being of the world for themselves as they gain "spiritual" insights—and at the same time they become "spiritually" unlocked for this being in the cognitive act. Through Steiner's epistemological position, Klafki's theory of categorial education becomes a personal, "spiritual" experience of participating in the being of the world.

In his work *Theosophy*, Steiner not only differentiates human nature into "body," "soul," and "spirit"; he also speaks about human self-awareness and about the soul having its center in the "I": "Through this consciousness of self, an individual achieves self-definition as an independent being, separate from everything else, as 'I'. By 'I' a person means the total experience of his or her being as body and soul. Body and soul are the vehicles of the 'I'; it works in them. [...] Our 'I', however, our actual individual essence remains invisible. It is very telling that Jean Paul describes becoming aware of the 'I' as an 'incidence ... veiled in [the] human holiest of holies,' because we are each totally alone with our own 'I'. This 'I' is the self of each human being. We are justified in seeing this 'I' as our true being" (Steiner 2012a, p. 48f.).

Steiner describes the "I" as our personal center that integrates the experiences of body and soul and that participates in the world spiritually in cognition. Based on this, he characterizes, in his lectures on education, someone who encounters the world through the senses, i.e., with their body, as someone whose "I" connects dynamically with their "body" out of an inner motion of interest: The "I" is then fully incarnated in the body: an *embodied mind*. We will now look at this concept in more detail in relation to the phases of main lesson teaching.

As described above, the "conclusion" part addresses the "body" and the lesson content is unfolded during this part at the "bodily" level. In an expansive motion of interest, the students open up to an encounter; their "body" becomes the focal point for their experiences as this encounter unfolds at the level of the "body."

In guided perception, the students adapt the free flood of their thought movements, ideas, and inner images to an unambiguous external phenomenon (Figure 5.1: Phase structure—first phase). According to Steiner (1986, p. 46), the students, as they unfold their inner experiences, attend to what they perceive through their senses. They unite the flooding thought movements with the phenomenon; their advancing thinking connects them with the world, as they seize, in an incarnating movement, their bodily being in the sensory experience.

Steiner's concept of an *embodied mind* therefore links his epistemological concept of perceptual judgment with the anthropological perspective of an incarnating process (Steiner 2011, pp. 45f.). Moreover, the integration of the human body into the gravitational field of the earth plays a central role for him.

Steiner particularly includes, within the totality of bodily sensing, the fact that the students experience the heaviness of their body more or less consciously. He refers to the legs and feet especially, but this heaviness permeates the whole body. This experience is an expression of the fact that the sensed body is also physical object that, as all earthly objects, is drawn toward the center of the earth and weighs down upon it. The earth gives the body's heaviness a clear direction, toward its own center. The students experience this weight through their sensed body as being aligned toward something definite and unambiguous. Their bodily sensing, or the fact that they are, as persons, incarnated in a body, opens up for them the experience of unambiguous relational structures (Steiner 1956, p. 111ff.).

In this view, the bodily sensing of gravity (feet and legs) as an experience of unambiguity and the unambiguous relating of surging inner experiences to concrete phenomena become one in perception. The conclusion, or perceptual judgment, is understood as an achievement of the embodied person who, in forming the conclusion, relies particularly on the support of their legs and feet. Steiner explains: "[...] because we come to conclusions with the 'I', which is supported by the legs and feet" (Steiner 1986, p. 36).

In his morphogenetic contemplations on puberty, Rittelmeyer builds upon this idea of embodiment in the process of cognition and interprets the results of various growth measurements of bones, muscles, and subcutaneous tissue in adolescents (Rittelmeyer 2002). His approach is "to mentally conflate the various morphological events into a whole and to interpret them phenomenologically." He outlines the possibility that the experience of weight in the extremities, which is connected with bone growth, may induce distinct will impulses that challenge the adolescents' "I" due to its slightly modified form of embodiment. This in turn affects the experience of identity and could explain—in the sense of the above considerations—why adolescents at the onset of puberty experience their own opinions and positions to their own lines of rational argumentation as particularly significant.

In Waldorf education, cognitive learning is therefore anthropologically contextualized. At the beginning of the learning process, the embodied self is at the center of the teaching and learning process. In practice, based on this anthropological contextualizing, teachers prepare their teaching methods in advance but examine again and again whether these are still adequate. In physics, for instance, teachers speak as little as possible with the students as they set up an experiment for demonstration, but the individual steps are prepared in a way that makes them largely self-explanatory. This approach aims to maximize both the students' sensory presence and their interested perception. It is meant to support their inner orientation to the unambiguity of an external event. This orientation and interest should not be disrupted or modified through comments. However, it does not mean that teachers cannot explain what cannot be presented in a self-explanatory manner. The teacher strikes the desk successively using different mallets; the task is clear without any comment: The different kinds of impact caused by the mallets are to be examined. Or the teacher moves a lens back and forth on the optical bench so that the image is sometimes blurred and sometimes clear. When the lens is in the right place and a clear image is created, the teacher may say, "That's it" and move on. The intention, as the students observe the experiment, is that they will "find their legs."

In history class, many teachers will not channel and functionalize their presentation by giving assignments beforehand. Explanatory introductions are not required either. The students often don't attend to them in any case. They prefer to dive right into the experience and let the presentation itself work on them. Then, in a second step, they develop from this experience assignments that usually require additional material. Metaphorically speaking, the presentation speaks to the students because of the way it is oriented to outer forms and events; they should be able to bodily enter into resonance with the "secure position of their legs and feet." This is achieved, above all, by providing clear spatial and temporal references.

In math, the students are asked to add up the odd numbers, which are listed in order in a vertical row, always noting down the intermediate results in an adjacent second row. The students notice that the second row shows the square numbers, and they note down in a third row what number has been squared in each case. Once one of the students has put into words what needs doing, the students continue with the task up to a particular, previously announced, number, noting down everything they have observed in setting up this table. Again, this is about inner orientation, in this case toward an unambiguous mathematical phenomenon.

Many of these methodical tools have been developed in practice based on Steiner's anthropology. If one is open to Steiner's anthropological indications and uses them heuristically, they can also be seen as something else: as methodical elements that require the students' alert, embodied presence to

Teaching Approaches in Waldorf Education

a particular degree. Such methodical elements, used in the Waldorf practice, must then be examined as to the constructive achievements they inspire in each student as an embodied self.

The empathy that arises from the centrality of the bodily existence and realizes itself in the conclusion phase always requires a sacrifice of the students: for instance, not to immediately link their personal experiences to their perceptions, or not to let the one or other event resonate emotionally within, or not focus their emotions on something particularly prominent. But it is through such sacrifices that learners take possession of their perceptions. Instead of withdrawing into their own perceptions, they experience themselves in their subjectivity, their emotions, and the wealth of related, previously undergone experiences.

The "judgment" part, in allowing for a phase directly after the experiment or presentation when experiences can be ordered, characterized, and sensitively supported, gives room for the students' inwardly unfolding subjectivity. Their gaze is first directed outward, exhausting the possibilities of their own physical existence, then inward, including their own experiences and feelings. A first distancing occurs, in which the students' own concernedness, experienced in centripetal motion, comes into its own. The dynamic of the centrifugal incarnation process described earlier now abates.

When something affects us personally, our interest is not restricted to the content with which we engage, but our inner feelings are also involved. According to Steiner, feelings therefore play a part in the judging process of this teaching phase. The students begin to weigh things up and search for memories that they can compare them with (Steiner 1986, p. 29). When people perform such thought movements, they often use weighing-up gestures. As embodied persons, we include our bodily experiences into our processes of judgment formation. In Steiner's words, "the judging even happens in the mechanical movements of our arms and hands" (Steiner 1986, p. 29).

Steiner's anthropological contextualization has resulted in different teaching methods in the Waldorf practice. Depending on their point of view, teachers either take these anthropological indications as a foundation for their teaching or they use them heuristically.

The physics teachers' attempt to bring a sense of humor to the characterization of particularly exciting, conspicuous, or also monotonously occurring phenomena in the phase of ordering the experiments goes back to Steiner's indication that this teaching phase is related to feeling. With normal air pressure, the feather in the tube will descend "like a leaf in fall," and with reduced air pressure, it will drop "like a mountain rock." The metal mallet produces a "high, sharp sound," and the rubber mallet "is simply better suited to the tuning fork." The lens is not positioned "any old way" but "exactly right, with these exact measurements ...."

In history class, teachers often strive to enable students to structure and consciously relate to the inner images they formed almost involuntarily as they were listening. The students do this mainly by engaging with sources whose statements, context, underlying perspectives, and intentions they question. Changing the medium alone opens up a different kind of access: Simply by focusing on written or pictorial sources, the students distance themselves from the object of their study. More intensely than during the narration, they experience themselves as facing the presented content, with which they now "engage" sensitively and appraisingly.

In math teaching, the laws discovered in the table of square numbers appear "here, there, and most probably also in the following places." In retrospect, one can be "really amazed that adding up the odd numbers results consistently in square numbers."

In the "judgment" part, the students look for wider contexts and find connections that enhance understanding. To achieve this, they need to distance themselves from the phenomena because they will only gain an overview of how these phenomena relate to each other if they can perceive as many of them as possible and if they are able to reduce them to their essence. They need to move inwardly away from the concrete phenomena and gain reflective distance from them. The dynamic of the incarnating process described earlier is even further reduced in the "judgment" part.

The students enter a different mode. According to Steiner, they no longer take hold of the content of their consciousness out of their direct embodiment down into the feet. Rather, they strive, in the time stream of their thought formations, to create a panorama in which relations become apparent. In a certain way, this panorama forms a closed entity that Steiner localizes in or around the head (Steiner 1986, p. 28ff.).

Steiner explains that the incarnation process of the "I" has changed in that it no longer fully connects with the body's life processes but partially closes itself off and begins to act independently. The life processes are now applied to establish conceptual connections, but they are not permeated to the extent that the fully embodied person turns to the outside world. Steiner assigns to full embodiment the character of being; to the conceptual connections a person establishes in reflective distance, he ascribes image character (Steiner 1992, p. 31ff.). In short, we gain, according to Steiner, immediate bodily presence, with its ontological quality, at the cost of the overall mental picture, and we gain the overall mental picture at the expense of ontological quality. These states reflect different modes of embodiment.

In perceiving, we must adapt our flood of thoughts to the circumstances, constantly trying to concretize. In doing so, we can enjoy the freshness of new impressions and let ourselves be inspired to go toward new encounters. But we have to do without our own reflective movements: One could say, with slight exaggeration, that grasping contexts always alienates us slightly from the immediacy of the phenomenon, and that embracing perception is a gentle renunciation of the profoundly human quality of gaining thoughtful orientation in reflective distance.

Steiner sees this as the expression of two basic "soul" dispositions (Steiner 1992, p. 34ff.): on the one hand, the soul activity with its sympathy for immediate bodily presence; on the other hand, antipathy whose oppositional force is what makes reflective distance possible in the first place.

We have already discussed and explained how these anthropological contextualizations have led to the use of open questions. But they also give rise to other teaching methods.

In physics, for instance, the experimental setup is usually not brought into the classroom, when the experiment is evaluated (third phase), when laws are discovered, and connections are established. This is unusual compared to other approaches to physics teaching. Waldorf physics teachers who don't apply Steiner's anthropological contextualizations dogmatically but heuristically, may question this method: What does the lesson gain from this reflective distance that tries to establish correlating inner images in order to understand the experiment? What does it mean for the students that they no longer directly perceive the experimental setup? What does it mean concretely if one separates perception so strictly from reflection?

In history teaching, this phase is about developing the example character of individual phenomena, or about contextualizing events, in order to enable narrative creation of meaning, which must, however, never claim universal validity.

In math class, it is about grasping the formal side of one's own activity by distancing oneself from the concrete mathematical experience. Inductive reasoning is particularly well suited to this phase.

In Steiner's anthropological contextualizations, the phase structure of the main lesson has proven itself as a way of making the modes of human life described above interact in a way that allows the students to feel increasingly at home in the world.

If teachers enable their students to approach new things with empathy and to observe presentations and experiments first from the outside, and if they initially hold back personal statements and abstract explanations, the students learn to find a center in their body and approach the world openly. Their immediate bodily presence becomes the measure of their encounter with the world. If this encounter can happen in the right way, it will provide stimulation and rich experience, and promote development. Here lies the central importance of phenomenological approaches to teaching.

Abstract concepts are developed from a reflective distance, once rich experience has provided the necessary foundation. The aim is not to see the phenomenon as a special case of abstraction but abstraction as a distillate of lived experiences. This allows students to develop habits of judging that are connected with their embodied presence as individuals. They learn to relate their need for intellectual orientation to themselves as embodied persons and thus develop a thinking that does not alienate them from themselves as persons but that provides a context for their embodied personal existence. What the students conceive in reflective distance will then gain its specific quality based on the strong bodily centeredness that preceded it. Life in reflective distance is not meant to lead to alienation but to life-filled orientation. Intellectual self-finding is not meant to be abstraction but thoughtful, life-filled world connection: The body is not meant to be the vehicle for intellectual potential but a gift through which the intellectual potential can actively connect with the world: world and body as sources of rich experience.

In the heterogeneous classroom community with its different talents, different modes of enacting life are realized. Analysis and reconstructing in teaching aim to enable students to develop judgment through dialogue based on an integral unity of cognitive learning and sensory, bodily experiences.

3.6 The link to phenomenological anthropology

Waldorf education has a differentiated view of the embodied self and sees school as a space of experience and development for the embodied self. It understands teaching and learning as processes in which students can evolve and be active as embodied individuals. However, it does not see the learning process as mere information transfer in which students build up or construct information or thought processes in some kind of inner world. Waldorf education rejects the Cartesian heritage at this point.

Cartesian heritage here refers to the dualist anthropology pioneered by Descartes, who separates bodily experience from soul experience. He sees the material, extended body (res extensa) and separates from it an interior world that is not thought of as bodily or spatial (res cogitans). The sensations and conscious acts occurring in this inner world are seen as projections built up by the inner world as bodily events that are thought to be mechanic (Fuchs 2000, p. 29ff.).

Waldorf education is concerned with the students' embodied existence in its immediacy. The students are persons and as such they are incarnated; they experience their enactments of life, their moods, and conscious processes as embodied beings. This position brings Waldorf education very close to phenomenological anthropology, which has most recently been mainly represented by Fuchs (2000, 2018).

Phenomenological anthropology assumes an embodied subject. This embodied subject inhabits a body, experiencing its acts of life directly and pre-reflectively. The body is a mode of "*être-au-monde,*" of "being toward the world" (Merleau-Ponty 1966) that precedes self-reflectivity. It is "the grounding principle, yet not the object of experience" and "always precedes the act of becoming conscious; the self only experiences itself in the mode of its self-withdrawal. Whatever we plan or do consciously, we live on the basis of an unconscious, bodily background which we are never able to fully reveal to ourselves" (Fuchs 2018, p. 71).

The bodily ground of our experiences therefore constitutes an experience of (in) full immediacy. It is unalienated experience, "it is what it is." Husserl correlates this experience with a "personalistic attitude" (Husserl 1952, p. 63) which, according to Fuchs, "always grounds our common lifeworld and experience of life" (Fuchs 2018, p. 75).

Husserl juxtaposes this with a "naturalistic attitude" (Husserl 1952, p. 63), which objectifies and with which we perceive and order things from an outside perspective. If the body itself is perceived from this outside perspective, phenomenological anthropology speaks of "corporeality." "In that sense, an individual is an objective or *physical body* as the entirety of material-anatomical structures and physiological processes that may especially be objectivized from a medical third-person perspective" (Fuchs 2008, p. 74).

According to phenomenological anthropology, embodied personal existence can be understood from the perspective of a subjective, or lived, body and of an objective, physical body. They are two sides of the same coin. A person is a unity. This unity appears as ambiguity. The subjective and the objective body are not conceived as an either/or but constitute the threshold toward an as-well-as. As a whole, this entity characterizes embodied personal existence. Fuchs speaks of the "dual aspect of subjective and physical body" (Fuchs 2018, p. 74).

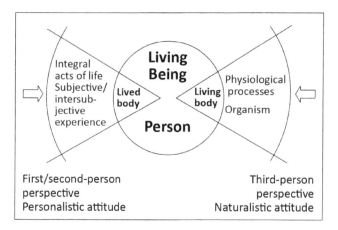

Figure 5.3 "Dual aspect of the living being" developed by Fuchs (Fuchs 2018, p. 79)

Fuchs elaborates further that only a living organism can be "the carrier of unified, conscious acts of life" at the same time as "a complex composition made up of physical matter" (ibid., p. 77). For him, "*the living being itself*" is the "primary entity. […] Its manifestations of life may be regarded, on the one hand, as integral (bodily, emotional, intellectual) acts, which are experienced subjectively and, on the other hand, as physiological processes in any degree of detail" (ibid., p. 79). Figure 5.3 illustrates the dual aspect of living being and person developed by Fuchs (ibid.).

In comparing the phase structure of main lesson teaching with the "dual aspect of living being and person," we notice the particular part played by the personalistic, lifeworld attitude in the first phase of teaching ("conclusion part"). In this part, encounters are facilitated by the teacher through emphasizing the immediacy of the phenomenon and holding back explanations. Similarly to Husserl, who correlates the "personalistic attitude" with the body (Husserl 1952, p. 63), Waldorf education does not only present this teaching phase "bodily" in the sense of Steiner's anthropology (Steiner 2012a, p. 23 ff.; Section 3.5.) but particularly also "bodily" in the sense of phenomenological anthropology. The lifeworld perspective is of primary importance: The students are meant to open up to a phenomenon in a centrifugal motion of interest out of the centrality of their bodily existence. This centrality of bodily existence corresponds to Plessner's "centric position" as the center of a person's enactment of life (Plessner 1975).

In the third teaching phase ("concept part"), the students work out connections and laws in reflective distance. The personalistic, lifeworld attitude now becomes a naturalistic, objectifying attitude. Bodily experiences are analyzed physically. Depending on the subject taught, the terms "bodily" and "physically" are to be used metaphorically here. The metaphorical use of "physical" in particular corresponds to the correlation Husserl establishes between a "naturalistic attitude" and the (physical) body (Husserl 1952, p. 63).

Students confront their experiences, looking from the outside at what they have experienced in centric position. In Plessner's terminology, they relate to their experiences in "eccentric position" (Plessner 1975).

In the phase structure of main lesson teaching, the transition from the first to the third phase therefore corresponds to a transition from the centric to the eccentric position. From the point of view of phenomenological anthropology, the students first realize themselves as persons in the centric position before transitioning to the eccentric position in the cognitive learning process. Successively and in distinct separation, the learning process embraces the different modes that can be assigned to the dual aspect of personal existence. Metaphorically speaking, the teaching structure allows the immediate "bodily" experience to be followed by the self-distancing or reflective distance of a physical standpoint. It therefore assigns a central position to the body as subject at the beginning of the teaching and learning process.

Further examinations are required to show what may be gained from teaching by addressing different modes of personal being in a clear and unmixed manner. Waldorf education addresses both modes by inserting in the second phase of main lesson teaching ("judgment part") a phase in which the students' own connection with "bodily" experiences is in the foreground, when the emotional acceptance of what has been encountered informs the teaching.

From the point of view of phenomenological anthropology, cognitive learning unfolds as follows in the Waldorf main lesson: The students absorb the lesson content in centric position and with a lifeworld approach. This is followed by a phase where the students connect with the lesson content emotionally and appraisingly. This phase facilitates a transition that will allow the students to achieve the cognitive learning target in eccentric position with an objectifying attitude. They do justice to the dual aspect of their personal existence by realizing its different modes separately in subsequent teaching phases.

When through phenomenological teaching concrete problems of "high-density reality" (Wagenschein 2008, p. 101) can be developed in a way that allows students to transition from the centric to the eccentric position, the educational process may, in the sense of Klafki (1963, p. 44), have the potential to closely interlink the material side of education (what is being developed in accordance with the phenomenological approach to teaching) and its formal side (the person's realization in transitioning from the centric to the eccentric position).

Waldorf education is then characterized by the fact that it uses phenomenological approaches to main lesson teaching as a structural model that corresponds to different modes of personal being in their pure form. Students are called upon to newly create their personal existence in pure form again and again. It is a performative education that sees the encounter with the world in lessons as an event and encourages students to newly create themselves continuously as persons, alternating between the centric and the eccentric position.

Waldorf education then has a specific form that can be seen as performative and that interlinks material and formal education.

4 Main lesson teaching as performative education

4.1 *The performative approach*

Waldorf education applies phenomenological methods in its approach to main lesson teaching. This approach does not arise from a theory of knowledge that assumes a logically preceding world—in the form of model structures, for instance—from which the phenomena are to be derived but suggests a performative perspective: It does not seek the meaning or understanding of a phenomenon "only in a world (structure) that lies 'behind,' 'beneath,' or 'above' it" (Wulf, Zirfas 2007, p. 8f.). Instead, it focuses on the reality-constituting aspect of the phenomenon itself as it makes its appearance.

In his early epistemological work, Steiner (2012b) understands ideas as productive, his starting point being, as explained above, conceptual realism. Ideas are for him consequently not logically preceding entities from which phenomena can be derived but the phenomena are a performative act of the ideas themselves.

Waldorf education therefore does not see teaching merely in an anthropological context but also as a performative act. It focuses on the aspects that constitute reality and through which the world is opened up and subjectivity constituted.

The performative character of Waldorf education suggests an inquiry into "the work of the special research area of *performative cultures*" (Wulf, Zirfas 2007, p. 16). This "research illustrates that the performative perspective can be applied not only to ritualized performances but also to *perception, the media, and gender development*. This view leads to a performative concept of perception and of space in education, a concept that enables a new perspective on the rhythmic interplay of order and movement, memory and expectation, participation and distance in educating and teaching processes" (ibid.).

We will now explain and discuss how these interrelations are realized in the individual case, starting with the pedagogical practice in Waldorf schools that arises from the intention to enable intensive moments of encounter in lessons. I will refer repeatedly to the special qualities identified by Fischer-Lichte as being characteristic of performative acts: bodily co-presence, spatiality, corporeality, tonality, rhythm, perception/ creation of meaning, eventfulness (Fischer-Lichte 2012, p. 53ff.).

Waldorf education's aim to promote experiences of participation by providing intensive moments of encounter in lessons does not only go back to the anthropological foundations explained earlier but also to Steiner's view of education as an art: "Teachers should not talk so much of how this or that art is 'useful' in developing this or that competence. Art is an end in itself. Teachers should love art to the extent that they do not wish the growing young person to go without it. They will then see what the growing person, the child, will gain from experiencing art. Rational thinking only comes to life through art. A sense of duty grows when the urge to be active can conquer matter in the freedom of artistic application. Educators and teachers who have artistic understanding bring soul into the school. [...] The rational mind only comprehends nature; experiencing nature requires artistic understanding" (Steiner 1961, p. 291).

We will therefore discuss the need for artistic teaching from the performative point of view in relation to the phenomenological approach of main lesson teaching.

4.2 Bodily co-presence, autopoietic feedback loop, spatiality, and atmosphere

With the physics experiment described earlier, a mood of expectant participation can be achieved in the first phase of main lesson teaching, if the tuning forks are only struck when all students are ready to enter into the experiment, and if both the teacher and the students enjoy the chord produced and are keen to find out how long it will resonate. Depending on the classroom situation, this mood can be further enhanced when the teacher strikes the chord a second time. When only one tuning fork is struck but in different places, one can basically sense how the students' attention becomes more concrete and differentiated (difference between tines and base).

This process is in my view both sensory and analytic. The sensory sound experience of the "tuning fork concert" leads to an experimental analysis of how the individual tuning fork can be made to ring out. The carrying out of the experiment includes the awareness of the students' bodily presence and the atmosphere of sound in the classroom. The experience should encompass the objective sound in the room and the simultaneous subjective presence of everyone involved in this sound atmosphere, and it should unfold as an artistic process.

The phenomenological approach to teaching is designed to allow the encounter with a new content to be particularly intense. This encounter is seen as a performative act. It is similar to history teaching, when the teacher, in presenting the rising ceremony of Louis XVI, also absorbs the atmosphere generated in that moment by the students' bodily presence in the classroom.

In the lesson situation, the focus is on the creative qualities and specifically the bodily co-presence of the actors (Fischer-Lichte 2012, p. 54). In being bodily co-present, the teacher and the students influence each other. The intensity of the presentation is determined by an autopoietic feedback loop (Fischer-Lichte 2004, p. 358). The actors are neither autonomous nor externally determined; their subject-object boundary becomes blurred and destabilized. With reference to Tomasello, one could say that this is typical human communication, where the understanding of attention becomes joint attention and a joint background (Tomasello 2011, p. 117ff.). Fischer-Lichte characterizes this process from a performative perspective.

Similar destabilization occurs in the experience of sound itself, when the students don't just hear the sound "somehow" but live in it. Objective sound and subjective presence then form a whole. The room is not only a vessel for sound waves: A specific sound atmosphere lives in it. The sound of the tuning forks and the students' directed attention come together in this atmosphere.

In more general terms, teachers can, in the rhythm of presenting an experiment or narrative, relate the materiality of their experiment or narrative to their experience of the students' bodily co-presence, which they experience as an autopoietic feedback loop. If the phenomenological approach to teaching is successful in the way described, an aesthetic dimension is added to the educational process. The phenomenal occurrence of a world encounter that stands at the beginning of the teaching process will then assume the aesthetic character of a performance. The teaching then corresponds to what Stenger described and discussed, from a performative perspective, as the event character of aesthetic educational experiences (Stenger 2007). This, in my view, coincides with the claim of Waldorf education that teaching should be artistic.

The qualities of performative acts developed by Fischer-Lichte (Fischer-Lichte 2012, p. 53ff.) relate to bodily co-presence and spatiality. The subject-object boundary between teachers and students destabilizes. It becomes a threshold through which a "space" of joint pedagogical activity is entered and at the same time constituted. The boundary between the persons involved in the pedagogical process and the encounters with the lesson content or with the world unfolded in the lesson also destabilizes. This boundary, too, becomes a threshold through which a space is entered into and constituted. They become immersed in an atmosphere, become "in a certain way part of the atmosphere," rendering "it more intense or weakening, even eliminating, it with their reaction – and thus possibly produce spatiality in a new and different way" (ibid., p. 60). Spatiality is then no longer a vessel for external occurrences but is, as atmosphere, "poured out spatially" and "placeless" at the same time (Böhme 2013).

In the first phase of main lesson teaching ("conclusion part"), the students are addressed in the centric position. Their centrifugal motion of interest and their directed attention flow into the performative processes, where—as described—boundaries destabilize and turn into thresholds. The teacher-student interaction and the encounter with the teaching content aim at the kind of immediacy that Fischer-Lichte has developed for a new aesthetics of the performative.

In the second phase of main lesson teaching ("judgment part"), the ordering of the performed experiment or historical presentation leads over to the students' becoming themselves active and involved. They make what they have experienced their own concern. The immediacy and participation of the first phase give way to a greater distance in the second phase. During the first phase, the expectation of a new encounter flows into the teaching situation, and in the second phase, the students' own memories and attributions become effective.

According to Wulf and Zirfas, the "rhythmic interplay of order and movement, memory and expectation, participation and distance in educational processes" are of particular interest from the performative point of view (Wulf, Zirfas 2007, p. 16). These rhythms are taken hold of in specific ways as has been described earlier.

4.3 Corporeality, perception/creation of meaning

In the third phase of main lesson teaching ("concept part"), the experiments are evaluated and historical events contextualized. This is about generating meaning based on what has been perceived and absorbed in the preceding phases. In transitioning from the centric to the eccentric position, the students unlock new horizons of understanding.

Fischer-Lichte identified both the transition from the centric to the eccentric position and that from perception to creation of meaning as qualities of performative acts (Fischer-Lichte 2012, p. 60ff.), which means that the performative perspective can also be applied to the third phase of main lesson teaching.

Fischer-Lichte introduces and discusses the ambiguity of bodily and corporeal presence and the related centric and eccentric positions in relation to theater, where a distinction is made between the phenomenal and the semiotic body. "We *have* bodies that we can manipulate and instrumentalize like any other object, and that we can use and interpret as signs that stand for something else. At the same time we *are* our bodies, we are body-subjects. This is what Plessner sees as the unique human condition – the fact that we can distance ourselves from ourselves" (ibid., p. 61).

Fischer-Lichte describes the performative act in a theater performance: "In the processes of embodiment, with which actors generate their phenomenal body in their presence, their semiotic body is often generated simultaneously as a sign indicating different symbolic orders" (ibid., p. 62). It has been explained in previous chapters that the processes occurring (almost/again and again) simultaneously in theater are experienced successively in the phases of main lesson teaching. The first phase addresses the phenomenal body in centric position; in the third phase, bodily experiences are observed from the eccentric position as semiotic corporeality. This raises the question whether teaching, like theater, takes hold of one when the oscillating transitions between bodily and corporeal presence are skillfully staged, both in a very concrete and in a metaphorical sense.

The transition from the first to the third phase of main lesson teaching also includes the transition from perceiving new content to analyzing its meaning. This process is comparable to the performative quality of a theater play, when both the audience and the actors realize how the more associative perception of something as something changes to the perception of something as a sign or expression of something (ibid., p. 65). The persons involved may realize at the same time that they are the ones who are changing and who generate meaning. This generating of meaning evokes an experience of participation. They experience themselves as crossing the boundary line that perception draws of something as something. It becomes a threshold and, as this threshold is being crossed, meaning is generated, and one enters a sphere of understanding. This is a performative act.

In teaching, the change from the centric to the eccentric position could have similar performative qualities if it is introduced by a successful open question or other suitable means of initialization. In that case, there is a good chance that teachers succeed in shaping both the encounter with a phenomenal event and the cognitive process for the students in a way that allows them to "fully enter into it." World encounter and creation of meaning then become two sides of the same coin through which participation can be realized in a dialogic approach.

4.4 The event character of teaching

Fischer-Lichte's work on performativity opens up a new perspective for Waldorf education: Its phenomenological approach to teaching, the main lesson model, and its claim of teaching artistically can be subsumed and differentiated in a performative teaching model (Fischer-Lichte 2012). This brings the performative qualities of the teaching practice together with the concept of a phenomenological approach. Regarding the relation to life and the intensity of life, Fischer-Lichte writes: "As a conscious living organism, an embodied mind, we can only become ourselves if we permanently create ourselves anew, if we keep changing, keep crossing thresholds. Performance makes this possible for us, even demands it of us. In this respect, performance can be seen both as life itself and as its model: As life itself in that it really uses up the life time of those involved in it, actors and audience, giving them the opportunity to continually create themselves in new ways; as a model of life insofar as it intensifies the processes and makes them stand out so that the attention of those involved is directed to them and they become aware of them" (Fischer-Lichte 2004, p. 359).

The fact that, with this performative orientation, the processes of life unfold with particular intensity coincides precisely with the claim of phenomenological teaching that it enables lived, bodily, and cognitive participation in the world. This may inspire a habitus in the students of seizing world encounters as an inspiration to become someone else, to newly create themselves. Educational processes would then become transformative processes. The event character of aesthetic educational experiences would be supported by such transformative processes. The boundary experiences described earlier would become thresholds and those crossing them would realize that they themselves are "beings in transition" (ibid., p. 362), and that they are transforming themselves. As well as a distinct experience of self-efficacy, this would inspire and promote free personal development.

Fischer-Lichte derives a perspective for self-development from her aesthetics of the performative. This can also be applied to main lesson teaching: "In marking the limits of enlightenment, which requires dichotomous concepts to describe and govern the world, and in presenting the human being as an *embodied mind,* it [the aesthetics of the performative] reveals itself as the effect of a 'new' enlightenment: It does not call on or urge us to govern nature – neither our own nor that around us – but encourages us to enter into a new relationship with ourselves and the world that is not an either/or but an as-well-as relationship, and to act in life as in artistic performance" (ibid., p. 362).

Waldorf education assumes that education and teaching can support free personality development, that within each of us lives the potential, if we seize our independence and keep developing, to engage with the world authentically and in freedom. Free personality development is enhanced by "artistic teaching" and aesthetic educational experiences. Such experiences can be prompted by intensive world encounters that, as performative events, inspire specific transformative processes in both students and teachers.

5 Conclusion

The reflections on teaching approaches in Waldorf education presented here are based on its anthropology and theory of science.

In a first step, free personality development was presented as a basic anthropological position that assumes that self-development is possible and that it constitutes a resource of social renewal. Waldorf education therefore claims that its teaching and learning processes, and its curricular choices in particular, are attuned to the developmental possibilities of the students, who take hold of their development as embodied individualities.

In a second step, we explained how the anthropology of Waldorf education sees the embodiment of the self as a dynamic incarnation process of an "I" into a "body" (Steiner 2012a). From this premise, Waldorf education derives the phase structure of main lesson teaching. In comparing the anthropology of Waldorf education with phenomenological anthropology, it was possible to call attention to and discuss the proximity of Waldorf education to positions described by Plessner (1975) and Fuchs (2008).

From the point of view of phenomenological anthropology, Waldorf students first absorb the main lesson content, which has been presented to them, from the centric position of their lifeworld. Emotional and appraising involvement with the lesson content is at the center of the next phase. This phase facilitates the students' transition that will subsequently allow them to achieve the cognitive learning target in eccentric position and with an objectifying attitude. This corresponds to the dual aspect of their individual being because it enables them to realize the different modes of being in their pure form in consecutive lesson phases.

The transition, realized by the students in the lesson, from the centric to the eccentric position is tied to a specific, phenomenological approach to teaching. This approach starts with "concrete problems of high-density reality" (Wagenschein 2008, p. 101), which have the potential to reveal something universal in the specific case. The universal contexts that the students work out for themselves in reflective distance and with an objectifying attitude are developed from specific lifeworld experiences.

It emerges that the phenomenological teaching approach can be reflected on and specified on the basis of Klafki's (1964) theory of categorial education: The material side of education, the world that opens up to the students in the phenomenological teaching approach, can potentially be very closely interlinked with the formal side of education, which is seen as the students' self-realization in the transition from the centric to the eccentric position.

All subjects taught in the main lesson format have the potential to be particularly closely interlinked. The teaching approaches they require are suited to the general pedagogical model of main lesson teaching. This subordination of specialist subject teaching to a general pedagogical approach is a specific feature of Waldorf education.

With reference to Türcke (1986), Jank and Meyer criticize that Klafki's theory of categorial education assumed a quasi-ontological stability regarding the condition of the world (Jank, Meyer 2009).

The science theory of Waldorf education makes it not a quasi-ontological but an ontological problem: The thinking students bring structuring concepts to the individual percepts and, in doing so, realize in their conscious mind what forms the phenomena of the world. Waldorf education's epistemological position interprets ideas as productive and performative. Reversing Jank's and Meyer's criticism, phenomenological approaches to teaching can be seen as logically complementing their epistemological position.

The anthropological postulation of a dynamic incarnating of the "I" in the "body" (Steiner 2012a) and of ideas as productive and performative center both on the reality-constituting aspects of personal existence and on the event character of the world with all its phenomena. In the light of Fischer-Lichte's (2004) aesthetics of the performative, the event character of aesthetic educational experiences, which are possible with the phenomenological approach to main lesson teaching, becomes a developmental perspective in Waldorf education: Its claim to "artistic" teaching can be concretized and expanded, especially with regard to the qualities that are intrinsically performative (Fischer-Lichte 2012, p. 53ff.). Bodily co-presence, spatiality, corporeality, eventfulness, perception/generation of meaning, etc. are of decisive interest.

The boundary experiences described by Fischer-Lichte in relation to these qualities also occur in the practice of main lesson teaching in Waldorf schools, often derived from Steiner's request that teaching should be artistic (Steiner 1961, p. 288ff.). These boundary experiences can become thresholds, and in crossing these thresholds, we might realize that we are ourselves "beings in transition" (Fischer-Lichte 2004, p. 362), and that we are transforming ourselves.

What remains is the need to examine the performative character of main lesson teaching in Waldorf education as a transformative educational process in the sense of Koller (2011). Independently of that, this approach, in Fischer-Lichte's words, "does not call on or urge us to govern nature – neither our own nor that around us – but encourages us to enter into a new relationship with ourselves and the world that is not an either/or but an as-well-as relationship, and to act in life as in artistic performance" (Fischer-Lichte 2004, p. 362) — and, one could add from the point of view of Waldorf education— realize ourselves as free beings in the process,.

References

Arnold, Karl-Heinz/Lindner-Müller, Carola (2012): The German tradition in general didactics. Its origins, major concepts, approaches, and perspectives. In: Jahrbuch für Allgemeine Didaktik. Baltmannsweiler: Schneider.

Berg, Hans Christoph (2003): Bildung und Lehrkunst in der Unterrichtsentwicklung. Zur didaktischen Dimension von Schulentwicklung. Schulmanagement-Handbuch, Vol. 106. Munich: Oldenbourg.

Böhme, Gernot (2013): Atmosphäre. Essays zur neuen Ästhetik. Frankfurt am Main: Suhrkamp.

da Veiga, Marcello (2006): Die Diskursfähigkeit der Waldorfpädagogik und ihre bildungsphilosophischen Grundlagen. Ein Essay. In: Bauer, Horst Philipp/Schneider, Peter (2006): Waldorfpädagogik. Perspektiven eines wissenschaftlichen Dialogs. Frankfurt am Main: Peter Lang.

Deutsche UNESCO Kommission (Hrsg.) (1997): Lernfähigkeit: Unser verborgener Reichtum. Bericht der Internationalen Kommission "Bildung für das 21. Jahrhundert". Neuwied: Luchterhand.

Dietz, Karl-Martin (2003): Erziehung in Freiheit. Rudolf Steiner über Selbstständigkeit im Jugendalter. Heidelberg: Menon.

Fischer-Lichte, Erika (2004): Ästhetik des Performativen. Frankfurt am Main: Suhrkamp.

Fischer-Lichte, Erika (2012): Performativität. Eine Einführung. Bielefeld: transcript.

Frielingsdorf, Volker (2012): Waldorfpädagogik in der Erziehungswissenschaft. Ein Überblick. Weinheim: Beltz.

Fuchs, Thomas (2000): Leib – Raum – Person. Entwurf einer phänomenologischen Anthropologie. Stuttgart: Klett-Cotta.

Fuchs, Thomas (2008): Das Gehirn – ein Beziehungsorgan. Eine phänomenologisch-ökologische Konzeption. Stuttgart: Kohlhammer. English translation: Fuchs, Thomas (2018): Ecology of the Brain. The Phenomenology and Biology of the Embodied Mind. Oxford: Oxford University Press.

Goethe, Johann Wolfgang von (1966): Erfahrung und Wissenschaft. In: Goethes Werke. Hamburger Ausgabe. Vol. 13. Hamburg: Wegener, pp. 23–25.

Gögelein, Christoph (2007): Geschichte und Prinzipien des "Lehrplans" der Waldorfschule. Zur Lehrplankonstitution der Pädagogik Rudolf Steiners. In: Hellmich, Achim/Teigeler, Peter (Eds.) (2007): Montessori-, Freinet-, Waldorfpädagogik. Konzeption und aktuelle Praxis. Weinheim: Beltz.

Götte, Wenzel/Loebell, Peter/Maurer, Klaus-Michael (2009): Entwicklungsaufgaben und Kompetenzen. Vom Bildungsplan der Waldorfschule. Stuttgart: Freies Geistesleben.

Grebe-Ellis, Johannes (2005): Grundzüge einer Phänomenologie der Polarisation. Berlin: Logos.

Grebe-Ellis, Johannes (2009): Zeit und Lernen. Erfahrungen mit Epochenunterricht – Eine Recherche. In: Höttecke, Dietmar (Ed.) (2009): Chemie und Physikdidaktik für die Lehramtsausbildung. Gesellschaft für Didaktik der Chemie und Physik. Jahrestagung in Schwäbisch Gmünd 2008. Münster: LIT.

Helm, Christoph (2013): Eine Didaktik empirischer Potenziale. Methodische Didaktik empirisch durchdacht? In: Jahrbuch für Allgemeine Didaktik. Baltmannsweiler: Schneider.

Hübner, Edwin (2008): Imaginationen im virtuellen Raum: Technik und Spiritualität – Chancen eines neuen Jahrhunderts. Frankfurt am Main: Clavis.

Husserl, Edmund (1952): Ideen zu einer reinen Phänomenologie und phänomenologischen Philosophie II. Husserliana. Vol. 4. The Hague: Nijhoff.

Jaffke, Christoph (1994). Fremdsprachenunterricht auf der Primarstufe: Seine Begründung und Praxis in der Waldorfpädagogik. Weinheim: Deutscher Studienverlag.

Jank, Werner/Meyer, Hilbert (2009): Didaktische Modelle. Berlin: Cornelsen.

Klafki, Wolfgang (1963): Studien zur Bildungstheorie und Didaktik. Weinheim: Beltz.

Klafki, Wolfgang (1964): Das pädagogische Problem des Elementaren und die Theorie der kategorialen Bildung. Weinheim: Beltz.

Koller, Hans-Christoph (2011): Bildung anders denken. Einführung in die Theorie transformatorischer Bildungsprozesse. Stuttgart: Kohlhammer.

Liebenwein, Sylva/Barz, Heiner/Randoll, Dirk (2012): Bildungserfahrungen an Waldorfschulen. Empirische Studie zu Schulqualität und Lernerfahrungen. Wiesbaden: Springer VS.

Loebell, Peter/Sommer, Wilfried (2012): "Feedback zum Feedback" – Wie die Waldorfpädagogik die Ergebnisse der Schüler- und Elternbefragung einordnet und was sie lernen kann. In: Liebenwein, Sylva/Barz, Heiner/Randoll, Dirk (Eds.) (2012): Bildungserfahrungen an Waldorfschulen. Empirische Studie zu Schulqualität und Lernerfahrungen. Wiesbaden: Springer VS, pp. 157–175.

Mackensen, Manfred von (2000): Die Urteilsfähigkeit auf den verschiedenen Altersstufen. In: Berichtsheft Lehrerseminar Kassel. Kassel: Bildungswerk Beruf und Umwelt.

Merleau-Ponty, Maurice (1966): Signes. Paris: Gallimard.

Meyer-Drawe, Käthe (2003): Lernen als Erfahrung. In: Zeitschrift für Erziehungswissenschaft 6/4, pp. 505–514.

Meyer, Meinert/Meyer, Hilbert (2007): Wolfgang Klafki. Eine Didaktik für das 21. Jahrhundert? Weinheim: Beltz.

Muschalle, Michael (1989): Das Denken und seine Beobachtung. Untersuchungen zur Beziehung von Epistemologie und Methodologie in der Philosophie Rudolf Steiners. Universität Bielefeld: Dissertation.

Østergaard, Edvin/Dahlin, Bo/Hugo, Aksel (2008): Doing phenomenology in science education: a research review. Studies in Science Education 44/2, pp. 93–121.

Peukert, Helmut (2000): Reflexionen über die Zukunft von Bildung. In: Zeitschrift für Pädagogik 46/4, pp. 507–524.

Plessner, Helmuth (1975): Die Stufen des Organischen und der Mensch. Berlin: de Gruyter.

Rahkochkine, Anatoli/Hallitzky, Maria/Koch-Priewe, Barbara/Kenzhegaliyeva, Makhabbat/Störtländer, Jan Christoph (2013): Vergleichende Didaktik und Curriculumsforschung: nationale und internationale Perspektiven – Call for Papers. www.dgfe-sektion5.de/kom1/dokumente/ 2013-CfP_Leipzig.pdf (accessed on January 6, 2015).

Randoll, Dirk/Barz, Heiner (Eds.) (2007): Bildung und Lebensgestaltung ehemaliger Schüler von Rudolf Steiner Schulen in der Schweiz. Eine Absolventenbefragung. Frankfurt am Main: Peter Lang.

Rauthe, Wilhelm (1990): Stufen der Urteilskraft. In: Zur Menschenkunde der Oberstufe (1990). Gesammelte Aufsätze. Stuttgart: Pädagogische Forschungsstelle beim Bund der Freien Waldorfschulen.

Richter, Tobias (Ed.) (2006): Pädagogischer Auftrag und Unterrichtsziele – vom Lehrplan der Waldorfschule. Stuttgart: Freies Geistesleben.

Rittelmeyer, Christian (2002): Pädagogische Anthropologie des Leibes. Biologische Voraussetzungen der Erziehung und Bildung. Weinheim: Beltz Juventa.

Rittelmeyer, Christian (2014): Aisthesis. Zur Bedeutung von Körper-Resonanzen für die ästhetische Bildung. München: Kopaed.

Rohde, Dirk (2003): Was heißt "lebendiger" Unterricht?: Faradays Kerze und Goethes Pflanzenmetamorphose in einer Freien Waldorfschule. Marburg: Tectum.

Schieren, Jost (1998): Anschauende Urteilskraft. Methodische und philosophische Grundlagen von Goethes naturwissenschaftlichem Erkennen. Düsseldorf und Bonn: Parerga.

Schieren, Jost (2010): Schluss, Urteil, Begriff – Zur Qualität des Verstehens. In: Research on Steiner Education 1/2, pp. 15–25.

Schieren, Jost (2012): Das Lernverständnis der Waldorfpädagogik. In: Research on Steiner Education 3/1, pp. 75–87.

Schmelzer, Albert (2000): Wer Revolutionen machen will. Zum Geschichtsunterricht der 9. Klasse an Waldorfschulen. Stuttgart: Freies Geistesleben.

Schneider, Peter (1997): Einführung in die Waldorfpädagogik. Stuttgart: Klett-Cotta.

Sommer, Wilfried (2005): Zur phänomenologischen Beschreibung der Beugung im Konzept optischer Wege. Berlin: Logos.

Sommer, Wilfried (2010): Oberstufenunterricht an der Waldorfschule: Kognitive Herausforderungen für das verkörperte Selbst. In: Research on Steiner Education 1/1, pp. 33–48 & 1/2, pp. 53–63.

Sommer, Wilfried (2011): Lernen als Lebensvorgang – erst recht in der Oberstufe. Alte wie neue Lernformen haben ihre Berechtigung. In: Erziehungskunst spezial 11/2011, pp. 7–10.

Steiner, Rudolf (1956): Die geistig-seelischen Grundkräfte der Erziehungskunst. Rudolf Steiner Gesamtausgabe (= GA) 305. Dornach: Rudolf Steiner Verlag.

Steiner, Rudolf (1961): Der Goetheanumgedanke inmitten der Kulturkrisis der Gegenwart. GA 36. Dornach: Rudolf Steiner Verlag.

Steiner, Rudolf (1983): Die pädagogische Grundlage und Zielsetzung der Waldorfschulen. GA 298. Dornach: Rudolf Steiner Verlag.

Steiner, Rudolf (1986): Menschenerkenntnis und Unterrichtsgestaltung. GA 302. Dornach: Rudolf Steiner Verlag.

Steiner, Rudolf (1992): Allgemeine Menschenkunde als Grundlage der Pädagogik. GA 293. Dornach: Rudolf Steiner Verlag. English translation: Steiner, Rudolf (2020): The First Teachers' Course. Anthropological Foundations-Methods of Teaching-Practical Discussions. GA 293-295, trans. Margot M. Saar. Bangkok: Ratayakom

Steiner, Rudolf (1997): Erziehungskunst. Methodisch-Didaktisches. Menschenkunde und Erziehungskunst. Zweiter Teil. GA 294. Dornach: Rudolf Steiner Verlag. English translation: Steiner, Rudolf (2020): The First Teachers' Course. Anthropological Foundations-Methods of Teaching-Practical Discussions. GA 293-295, trans. Margot M. Saar. Bangkok: Ratayakom

Steiner, Rudolf (2011): Grundlinien einer Erkenntnistheorie der Goetheschen Weltanschauung mit besonderer Rücksicht auf Schiller. Bremen: Europäischer Literaturverlag.

Steiner, Rudolf (2012a): Theosophie: Einführung in die übersinnliche Welterkenntnis und Menschenbestimmung. GA 9. Dornach: Rudolf Steiner Verlag.

Steiner, Rudolf (2012b): Wahrheit und Wissenschaft. GA 3. Dornach: Rudolf Steiner Verlag.

Stenger, Ursula (2007): Zum Ereignischarakter von Bildungsprozessen. In: Wulf, Christoph/Zirfas, Jörg (Hrsg.) (2007): Pädagogik des Performativen. Weinheim: Beltz.

Templeton, Alec (2010): Teaching English to Teens and Preteens: A Guide for Language Teachers with Techniques and Materials for Grades. Szeged: Hevesim, pp. 4–9.

Tomasello, Michael (2011): Die Ursprünge der menschlichen Kommunikation. Frankfurt am Main: Suhrkamp.

Türcke, Christoph (1986): Vermittlung als Gott. Metaphysische Grillen und theologische Mucken didaktisierter Wissenschaft. Lüneburg: Dietrich zu Kampen.

Varela, Francisco (2008): Wahr ist, was funktioniert. In: Pörksen, Bernhard (2008): Die Gewissheit der Ungewissheit. Gespräche zum Konstruktivismus. Heidelberg: Auer.

Wagenschein, Martin (2008): Verstehen lehren. Weinheim: Beltz.

Wagner, Ullrich/Gais, Steffen/Haider, Hilde/Verleger, Rolf/Born, Jan (2004): Sleep inspires insight. Nature 427, pp. 352–354.

Wallner-Paschon, Christina (2009). Kompetenzen und individuelle Merkmale der Waldorfschüler/innen im Vergleich. In: Schreiner, Claudia/Schwantner, Ursula (Hrsg.) (2009). PISA 2006: Österreichischer Expertenbericht zum Naturwissenschaftsschwerpunkt. Graz: Leykam.

Wiechmann, Jürgen (2002): Unterrichtsmethoden. Vom Nutzen der Vielfalt. In: Wiechmann, Jürgen (Hrsg.) (2002): Zwölf Unterrichtsmethoden. Vielfalt für die Praxis. Weinheim: Beltz.

Wiehl, Angelika (2015): Propädeutik der Unterrichtsmethoden in der Waldorfpädagogik. Frankfurt am Main: Peter Lang.

Wiesing, Lambert (2009): Das Mich der Wahrnehmung. Eine Autopsie. Frankfurt am Main: Suhrkamp.

Wulf, Christoph/Zirfas, Jörg (2007): Performative Pädagogik und Performative Bildungstheorien. Ein neuer Fokus erziehungswissenschaftlicher Forschung. In: Wulf, Christoph/Zirfas, Jörg (Hrsg.) (2007): Pädagogik des Performativen. Weinheim: Beltz.

Zech, Michael (2002): Von gestern oder zeitgemäß? Die Nibelungensage als Unterrichtsstoff. Erziehungskunst 01/2002, pp. 11–18.

Zech, Michael (2012): Der Geschichtsunterricht an Waldorfschulen. Frankfurt am Main: Peter Lang.

THE WALDORF CURRICULUM
Curriculum, Teaching Plan, or Guideline?

M. Michael Zech

The Waldorf curriculum is rather a diffuse object of examination, not only because Waldorf education is rooted in Rudolf Steiner's anthroposophy and because of the schools' heterogeneous pedagogical practice, but also because it does not aim at particular standards but at heterogeneous and individualized application. A certain tension between its curriculum, which is informed by developmental psychology, and the demanded teacher autonomy is inherent in the self-concept of Waldorf education. This specific definition of the Waldorf curriculum, which differs both from curricular teaching programs[1] and from competence-oriented educational programs, will be described and examined with regard to the self-image, genesis, challenges, and perspectives of Waldorf schools.

1 Curriculum and teacher autonomy in Waldorf education

The way Waldorf schools understand curriculum is closely linked to the notion of teacher autonomy and collegially governed schools that arises from Steiner's principle of freedom of teaching and individual ethics. The autonomy concept of Waldorf schools includes:

Free choice of teachers, because this includes the option that a teaching faculty committed to an agreed way of working can integrate in their collaboration teachers who freely decide in favor of this way of working.
Free choice of pupils and parents, based both on the teachers' willingness to support the students entrusted to them and on the trust these students, or their legal guardians, place in the teachers.
Free choice of teaching material and method, which is founded on the individual teacher's freedom and responsibility to competently support the development of the student's personality, and is therefore prerequisite to a child-oriented education (Zech 2013a, p. 16).

As early as 1888, in a critique of the programmatic design of curricula and the lack of teacher education, Steiner hinted at the idea of teacher autonomy that was to become central to the concept of Waldorf education: "A curriculum defined to the smallest detail and regulations prescribing each and every one of a teacher's actions are the death of education. Today [Austria in 1888], teachers are not only told what to teach in every subject but also how to teach it" (Steiner 1989, p. 212 ff.).

In 1919, Steiner counterposed the prevalent curricula, which were content-based and aimed at conveying general knowledge, and which, in secondary education, largely followed the humanistic tradition, with the demand that school education was to be derived from the immediate

DOI: 10.4324/9781003187431-25

teacher-student relationship. This postulate goes further than similar demands expressed by other education reform approaches in that it ascribes to young people an innate intention of their own that teachers have to respect and promote. Steiner explains these individual biographical orientations from the point of view of anthroposophy with a person's gradual individuation over the course of many incarnations (Steiner 1987, p. 61ff., p. 199ff.) Pedagogy, he therefore claims, has to take this individual development into account. While many Waldorf teachers have been doubtful or skeptical of the anthroposophic ideas of reincarnation and karma, they choose to teach in a way that supports the students' self-realization and individuation, and they insist on the school and teacher autonomy required for this. Stefan Leber, who was for many years a board member of the German Waldorf schools' association (*Bund der Freien Waldorfschulen*) and a senior faculty member at Freie Hochschule Stuttgart (an independent university for teacher education), explained this self-concept, which led to the fast-rising number of Waldorf schools in the 1970s and 1980s: "Schools have to respect the autonomy of the evolving individual, which means that their pedagogical practice needs to be oriented to the child's abilities and development. This is not possible if rules and regulations are imposed by an external [state] administration. Teachers will be able to balance the different requirements in a healthy way that does justice to children only if they consider the concrete needs of children, their personal situation, their development as human beings on the one hand and as contemporaries and conscious members of society on the other. This presupposes the right to self-determination. However, not much of the required freedom has been realized in schools so far" (Leber 1991, p. 34). Leber's characterization of school and educational autonomy ties in with a socio-political request made by Steiner after the breakdown of the German Empire with regard to education and in connection with his proposal of a threefold social order: "Young people should grow up supported by educators and teachers who are independent of state and economy, and whose freedom of action enables students to realize their individual abilities in freedom, too" (Steiner 1982, p. 39).[2] These ideas continue to inform the identity of Waldorf schools to this day, presumably because they correlate with modern goals of civic engagement and with the findings of education research (Zech 2013b, p. 30ff.).

The authors of Waldorf curricula have always been committed to this educational approach that promotes individuation and personal development. In 1925, shortly after Steiner's death, Caroline von Heydebrand, a member of the founding faculty of the first Waldorf school in Stuttgart, was the first to describe the field of tension surrounding the implementation of the Waldorf curriculum: "The ideal curriculum must reflect the changing image of the developing human nature at its various ages, but like any other ideal it must face and fit in with the full reality of life. This reality includes many things: It includes the individuality of the teacher facing a class. It includes the class itself with all the peculiarities of each pupil. It includes the world-historical timeline and the particular place on earth with its valid school laws and school authorities. It encompasses where the school stands in the world. All these circumstances demand change and adjustments, reshaping the ideal curriculum. The educational task is given to us by the nature of the growing human being. This can only be solved if the curriculum is constructed with mobility and malleability" (Heydebrand 2009, p. 13). Heydebrand clearly states that education is not a standardized program but that it needs, on the one hand, to be informed by child development, and on the other to consider the circumstances of each individual school. In 1955, Karl Stockmeyer published his commented collection of orally made curricular indications, which continued to be the guiding curriculum of Waldorf education into the 1990s. He also emphasized the importance of teacher autonomy over a strictly defined curriculum: "Trying to press Rudolf Steiner's art of education into a rigid framework would be detrimental to its intention and essence. [...] While a true curriculum may point the teacher's awareness to what is required, it must provide the necessary freedom for teachers to apply their immediate insights and ingenuity. [...] An appropriately assembled curriculum can consequently only be a collection of objective and general requirements arising from the child's gradual development that teachers should consider for the different age groups" (Stockmeyer 2001, p. 6f.). Again, the teacher responsibility postulated in this introduction is linked to a curriculum consisting of recommendations relating to objective child development processes. Tobias Richter, who published the first systematic curriculum in the mid-1990s, also pointed out that "One always needs to see the child behind the teaching content, because the child is the actual 'curriculum' for the teacher" (Richter 2010, p. 41). To this day, the Waldorf concept therefore demands that teaching content and methods consistently serve individuation, and that teachers have the competence to understand and analyze child development to enable them to realize the teaching concept based on their own competence and in accordance with their student encounters.

Even this brief outline shows that the concepts developed in educational science for teaching plans, curricula, and education plans are not simply transferable to Waldorf schools. Although current education plans give more weight to teacher autonomy by granting teachers more freedom to design their own lessons, and although lessons are always influenced by developmental processes, the concept of an ideal-typical and development-based curriculum is still largely rejected in education science, and teacher autonomy continues to be restricted by clearly defined output-oriented standards.

2 Concept continuity and heterogeneity[3]

Before we examine the structure and composition of the Waldorf curriculum, we need to clarify an apparent contradiction in Waldorf education: a noticeable concept consistency that seems to go against the notion of teacher and school autonomy. Up until the 1990s, the Waldorf curriculum served as an orientational tool that was seen as ideal-typical. As such, it was communicated in the above-mentioned publications by Heydebrand and Stockmeyer, as well as in internal teacher conferences, in teacher education, and in the writings of individual Waldorf teachers. It is therefore based on personal tradition, which contributed, on the one hand, to an astonishing concept consistency that has been perpetuated for a hundred years now, and, on the other hand, to widespread diffusion due to its heterogeneous interpretation. The schools united under the umbrella of the German Waldorf schools' association continue to reject mandatory status for their curriculum: No binding agreements or supervisory bodies ensure its implementation. While the designations "Waldorf" and "Rudolf Steiner" are internationally protected brands relating to the schools and the education, they do not include specific curricular content. The quality assurance, for which the International Council for Steiner Waldorf education (Hague Circle) takes responsibility, refers above all to the framework conditions outlined above, which constitute the foundation for the tuition and pedagogy realized in Waldorf schools. To understand the described concept consistency, one therefore needs to inquire into this tradition and the referencing system inherent in it.

Steiner himself referred to the teaching examples he gave, which were mainly derived from his anthropology and developmental psychology and rarely from pedagogical deliberations, as "curriculum." His suggestions were meant as guidelines on how the choice of teaching material, methods, and forms of thinking and judgment could be used to support the students' physical, emotional, and mental maturation. The curriculum that became established in Waldorf schools after Steiner's death is a result of the canonization of these examples and of the interpretation and textualization of oral statements made by Steiner in particular situations: His statements, in other words, received literary status. The first Waldorf curriculum, published by Caroline von Heydebrand, reflects the respect with which the first Waldorf teachers approached these examples provided by their school founder: "The Waldorf School, founded in 1919 by Dr. h.c. [honorary doctor] Emil Molt in Stuttgart, received its spiritual foundations from its educational director, Dr. Rudolf Steiner. He gave the school and its teachers a wealth of explanations about human development from out of his Anthroposophy. He derived the details of Waldorf methods and instruction, of the art of teaching and education, from this knowledge of the human being derived from spiritual science. What the child should learn at each age can be determined only by the developing human nature and its laws. From the nature of the human being alone he derived what is appropriate for the child's development at each age. What Dr. Rudolf Steiner indicated about the way in which the curriculum should be distributed across the individual classes of the Waldorf school was always the culmination of considerations that had as their object the nature of the individual stages of child development. To these considerations, his statements about the curriculum were given as individual examples. [...] In this way, a curriculum has developed which, above all, is free of all programmatic and dogmatic elements." (Heydebrand 2021, p. 8f.).

From today's point of view, we need to question whether the Waldorf curriculum is really free from anything "programmatic or dogmatic." This first curriculum already did much to promote the canonization of statements that were provided as examples: It was to be presumed, was it not, that the examples presented by Steiner himself would reliably reflect the intentions of Waldorf education? A referencing system established itself that was based on respect for the person whose ideas had inspired the curriculum. Anything that can be traced back to or is corroborated by something Steiner once said counts as "Waldorf." This implies the claim that one knows how to interpret Steiner's statements.

After the ban on Waldorf schools in the Third Reich, those schools that reopened or were newly founded initially looked to the first Waldorf teachers for guidance. Because its members had worked directly with Rudolf Steiner, the faculty of the first Waldorf School, the "mother school," was considered particularly legitimate and responsible for preserving the quality of Waldorf education. As a result, Stockmeyer's annotated collection of Rudolf Steiner's "curricular indications" assumed lasting significance. As the man of the hour, he presented an overview of the indications Steiner had given as impulses for an education that was to be individually realized and accounted for by autonomously working teachers, and that as such formed the basis of the teacher-education course founded at the Stuttgart-Uhlandshöhe Waldorf school. While Stockmeyer's introduction points to teacher autonomy and curriculum development as essential conditions for Waldorf education, it also reflects the importance ascribed to Steiner's indications: "It is certainly not a matter of preserving the structures developed between 1919 and 1924 as dogma [...] but one would thoroughly misunderstand Rudolf Steiner's intentions and the insights effective in them if one considered the pedagogical impulse [...] to be obsolete as early as one generation after its inception" (Stockmeyer 2001, preface of 1955, no page reference).

This referencing system continued to inform the development of Waldorf education in the second half of the 20th century, on big teacher conferences, in the internal teacher-education programs, and in numerous publications. As the Waldorf movement grew rapidly in Germany and around the world, this person-based tradition no longer met quality assurance requirements, because it was increasingly difficult to guarantee the quality of teaching, of the schools, or of their adherence to the original intentions of Waldorf education. The teachers, though often state qualified, tended to have no or insufficient training for an educational approach that largely relied on personal responsibility and self-organization. They lacked the competence that is crucial to Waldorf education: to assess the developmental processes of children and make these assessments the foundation for their pedagogical actions. These processes were no longer addressed in professional development based on peer learning. The written curricular guidelines, on the other hand, with their exemplary character, turned out to be too general for this growing group of teachers, who were unable to interpret them without explanation. Within the Waldorf school movement, the concern about teaching quality resulted in a call for a binding curriculum. The following four factors presumably contributed to the steps in that direction in the early 1990s:

- Because of the continuously growing number of Waldorf teachers, the number of teacher training centers also increased. As a result, the number of teachers attending the big annual teachers' conferences dropped. These central conferences, which did much to buttress the Waldorf identity, were therefore under threat.
- Following the German unification, the number of new Waldorf schools increased rapidly, leading to a growing demand for Waldorf teacher education.[4]
- With the spreading of Waldorf schools, political, public, and—to a modest degree—scientific interest in this education also grew. Critical writings that appeared mostly focused on Rudolf

Steiner's anthroposophical ideas but to some extent also on Waldorf education itself. Teachers asked for generally accessible explanations of the intentions of Waldorf education so they would be armed to meet such criticism.

- Waldorf parents also began to ask for some kind of programmatic documentation on Waldorf education that would enable them to gain greater clarity about interpretations that had so far been orally conveyed on parents' evenings, parent council meetings, and parent council conferences.

These challenges not only concerned German Waldorf schools. The demand for binding guidelines for implementing Waldorf education became even more pressing in other countries and cultures that had no Waldorf tradition. The Hague Circle, which coordinates the international Waldorf school movement, decided in the early 1990s, and after intensive debate, to commission the Austrian Waldorf teacher and lecturer Tobias Richter to compose a curriculum (Leber 1995, p. 15; Richter 2010, p. 17ff.). However, Steiner's basic ideas would continue to be the guiding reference in the discourse on the authentic implementation of Waldorf education. At the same time, it was confirmed that the identity of Waldorf education was to be developed on the basis of the diversity of approaches and experiences of practicing teachers. The conflict around the autonomy of schools and teachers as an underlying principle of Waldorf education is also reflected in the introduction to the new curriculum: "The question was if, after 75 years of Waldorf practice, teachers were able to competently comment on their own practice. [...] Would it be possible to develop example-based rather than standardized guidelines that corresponded to the substance of teaching envisaged by Rudolf Steiner for the different age groups and subjects" (Leber 1995, p. 1). Leber goes on to outline the controversial discussion of the draft curriculum within the Waldorf school movement. "The current version has been published by the *Pädagogische Forschungsstelle* (education research institute of the German Waldorf schools' association) as a limited edition, so that experiences and improvements can continue to be collected and integrated later" (Leber 1995, p. 1).

Leber characterizes the 1995 curriculum as a preliminary account, openly discussed by the community of teachers in Germany, of the teaching program applied in most Waldorf schools and presents it at the same time as a practice-based process of continued dialogic development.[5] However, if one disregards the updating of the curricula along with scientific developments, which have always informed the Waldorf practice, one can discern a clear adherence to the basic concept of the first Waldorf school in relation to the content and methods applied for the different age groups (Zech 2012, p. 116ff.).

Richter's curriculum, in its fourth revised edition of 2016, certainly brings clarity to the teaching content of Waldorf schools. By standardizing certain contents and methods, it serves as a quality assurance tool, but, in doing so, it also deprives Waldorf teachers to a certain extent of the need to take responsibility for their own pedagogical choices. In imposing foundations, it contributes to the further canonization of teaching content. It remains to be seen how Waldorf schools can continue to maintain and update their identity under these circumstances, and whether the teachers working there can continue to take individual responsibility for their work given these framework instructions.

This first programmatic curriculum fundamentally changed an over 90-year-old culture that relied on the individual application and passing on of the Waldorf concept, because until then the central goal always had been for teachers to develop their work individually and competently in the concrete pedagogical situation, in the immediate encounter with the child. This was the main reason why the curriculum project was initially highly controversial. Many teachers saw their autonomy under threat and were concerned that the standardization associated with a curriculum would compromise the teaching quality. What these internal critics feared most of all was that their personal freedom and responsibility and their pedagogical creativity, which arises from the immediate educational process, would be undermined. The heated internal discourse was about maintaining the autonomy of schools and teachers, one of the central qualities of Waldorf education.

Up until 2008, curriculum development in Waldorf schools had taken little notice of the curricular discourses in education science in general. Instead, they relied on the founding ideas and the founding concept that were constantly worked on and developed at school level, in regional associations, and by the Research Institute of the German Waldorf schools' association. In this sense, the Waldorf schools, that is, the teachers, who were actively involved in education, pursued their own quality development based on their understanding of collaborative governance and autonomy as civic engagement. This self-reference and internal discourse made Waldorf schools appear to be a hermetic subculture. It developed its own terminology, rooted in Steiner's anthroposophy, which has become rather a hindrance to any discourse with education science and is also the reason why both its conceptual foundations and its practice have long been the object of speculation and often unverified assumptions rather than serious inquiry. Most educationists see in the self-reference, jargon, habitual demarcation, founding myths, and the naïve reception of anthroposophy constituents of Waldorf education that hinder any scientific dialogue. The initially substantial resistance of Waldorf practitioners to a curriculum were allayed through discussions at teachers' and delegates' conferences on the one hand and by involving more subject teachers in the curriculum work to ensure plurality. Despite this communicative and integrative achievement, which was indeed considerable for a self-organizing autonomous school movement, the "Richter Curriculum," once published, continued to be rejected by many teachers.

The tendency to self-referencing holds the additional risk that individual teaching content is not sufficiently reflected or that habitual teaching methods are perpetuated for too long. A tradition-based movement—and the German Waldorf movement is certainly that—always ails from the burden of the habitual, of what has proven successful at one point, and from nurturing its identifying features. Such tendencies are counterpoised by the constantly newly joining, freshly qualified teachers, by the curriculum development work initiated by the Education Research Institute, and by parents and students articulating their needs.

Remarkably, Waldorf teachers also confirm that the teaching program, which has established itself as a result of curricula and tradition, has proven to be sustainable, both in relation to specific subjects and the educational approach with its roots in developmental psychology. The basic concept has never been challenged, although it was often reconsidered at conferences and by curriculum work groups, and although it has been amended and modified numerous times. It also continues to convince new generations of academically and subject-specifically qualified teachers in their professional development. Such sustainable conceptual validity and consistency are both supported and explained by the fact that new scientific insights and social questions are constantly integrated into the basic concept of the Waldorf curriculum.

The fact that, despite frequently changing requirements, Waldorf students have always been prepared successfully for final exams up to university access level also proves that the teaching concept, which has been constantly individualized and updated by the teachers, is indeed practicable. Moreover, the curriculum framework, which goes back to Steiner's recommendations and is an identity-forming feature of Waldorf schools, seems to be able to absorb ever-new knowledge areas such as quantum theory, genetics, fascism theories, globalization.

The recent publication by Götte, Loebell, and Maurer (2009) is a first attempt at locating the Waldorf curriculum within the education sciences. The authors discuss above all topics such as the task of development, developmental psychology, competence orientation, and personality. However, it leaves essential problems unconsidered, such as the difference between the competence discourse in vocational training and schools, subject-specific competences, education science's use of the term "*Bildungsplan*" (education plan) with its normative orientation, the distinction between competence structure models and competence development models, and the problem with using the term "competence" before adulthood.

On balance, curriculum development in German Waldorf schools between 1919 and 2016 has been mostly governed internally, under widely differing political conditions. Inspired by Steiner's idea of teachers taking responsibility for their lessons, and of deriving education directly from the pedagogical process, the autonomy of teachers and schools continues to be a distinctive feature of Waldorf education. However, this self-responsibility was from the beginning interlinked with Steiner's recommendations on teaching content and teaching methods that were given as examples and in particular situations. The canonization of teaching content, which was already apparent in Caroline von Heydebrand's short curriculum, is still evident today in all curricular concepts of Waldorf schools: Many concrete lesson contents and elements have become essential Waldorf features.

3 Attempt at defining the Waldorf curriculum in terms of education science

Depending on type and underlying educational policy, teaching plans or curricula are binding to various degrees in terms of implementation, but they are legally enforceable. Waldorf schools, on the other hand, with their self-concept as autonomous educational organizations, distance themselves from such prescription and insist on the primacy of teacher autonomy and teacher responsibility in education.

3.1 The Waldorf curriculum as an orientational tool and the commitment problem

As the editor of the most recent curriculum, Tobias Richter describes it in his introduction as "having orientation and example character" without being "binding in its details" (Richter 2010, p. 18). It can therefore be seen as an orientational curriculum that is not legally binding but essential and recognized within the internal Waldorf discourse. Even if Richter and his co-authors refer to it as a "framework curriculum" (*Rahmenlehrplan*) (Richter 2010, p. 6 and p. 99), I would, for reasons of hermeneutic clarity, call it an "orientational curriculum," because the term "framework curriculum" is differently connoted in education science (Tenorth, Tippelt 2007, p. 594). Framework guidelines or a framework curriculum convey guidelines and options for realizing particular learning goals previously established in socio-politically sanctioned processes.[6] The Waldorf curriculum, on the other hand, derives all its subject-related curricula from overarching criteria such as developmental psychology or superordinate educational goals, which are determined both by the canon of subjects and by the school's orientation to individuation and personality development (Richter 2010, p. 44 ff. and p. 73ff.). The Waldorf curriculum is horizontal in that each subject is defined in relation to the totality of subjects. "Horizontal curriculum refers to the attempt to describe the mutual attunement of the individual subjects at a particular stage of child and youth development. [...] Because it is interdisciplinary, it is often vague on concrete lesson content and fragmentary by necessity" (Richter 2010, p. 43). This makes both the individual children with their individual developmental tasks and the entire canon of subjects as a peripheral reference the center and starting point of the teacher's curricular orientation. Since no empiric studies are available, the question as to how binding the Waldorf curriculum is can only be answered on the basis of circumstantial evidence. The fact that the Richter Curriculum was soon out of print may indicate that it was in high demand among teachers and maybe even parents.[7] From my own involvement in national and international curriculum development groups within the Waldorf movement, and from lesson observations as a teacher educator, I would conclude that the extent to which the recommended content and teaching methods are implemented varies widely.[8]

3.2 Is the Waldorf curriculum a curriculum?

Unlike teaching plans, the kind of curriculum that has been adapted from the Anglo-American education discourse claims that it contributes to enabling students to cope with life: "From a subjective point of view, education as a process is an equipment for behavior in the world" (Robinsohn, cited in Grießhaber 2002). This approach not only offers indications regarding teaching content, but it also supplies precise operationalizations for the acquisition of qualifications—in other words, pathways to the educational goal as well as the evaluation methods (monitoring) that correspond to this goal. "Curricula are meant to ensure consistent and goal-compliant orientation and to align the different orientation and control mechanisms of educational processes. Curriculum development consequently includes not only the specification of educational goals and contents but also the production of teaching aids and learning materials, of lesson arrangements, and of learning and examination tasks" (Künzli 2009, p. 135). According to this view, curricula encompass the entire framework of school learning and structure this process "in order to enable systematic knowledge acquisition" (Tenorth, Tippelt 2007, p. 138).

The original intention with this approach was to keep up with societal changes by continuously developing the curricula: in other words, by continuously modernizing the teaching and learning process by opening it up to insights on child-appropriate learning, new scientific findings, and new requirement analyses.[9] This claim was never fully met (Künzli 2009, p. 136; Robinsohn 1971, p. 47). The reform process was obstructed not only by increasing bureaucratic standardization that focuses on exam-based entrance qualification, but also by the complex lobbying that always affects curriculum changes, and by the narrowing influence[10] the Anglo-American approach had on the German curriculum tradition.

These developments seem to have had no effect whatsoever on the Waldorf school movement, which does not appear to have engaged explicitly with the operationalization of the curricula, presumably because of its hermetic inward orientation described earlier. This does not mean that the Waldorf schools did not engage with contemporary social and scientific problems, but rather that this engagement always happened against Waldorf education's anthropological/anthroposophical background. The discourses, prompted by the curriculum movement, on method (in particular on the reorientation from receptive to reflected learning processes), on forms of teaching that promote problem awareness, and the debate on overcoming teacher-centered teaching took place without the Waldorf teachers, although the Waldorf practice with its broad range of methods and differentiated underlying anthropology and learning psychology would have had much to offer to this process. On the other hand, many new approaches entered the Waldorf schools informally because every teacher in Germany must have an academic degree, which means that Waldorf teachers have consistently brought with them knowledge acquired at universities or in state teacher-education institutions.

The seemingly logical steps were never taken: that is, to link Waldorf education's view of the nature of curricula to the original Humanistic and Enlightenment conceptions that, in addition to the *curriculum scholasticum* and the *curriculum academicum,* introduced to the European discourse the *curriculum vitae* (Künzli 2009, p. 134f.), which at the time was more than an educational biography (in that it included personality development as a teleological element). These are possible roots of Waldorf education's understanding of education (Bildung) as individuation and personality development.

3.3 Is the Waldorf curriculum a spiral curriculum?

Steiner formulated the principles of his anthropology or developmental theory for the first time in his 1907 treatise *Education in the Light of Anthroposophy* (Steiner 1907). These principles refer to three developmental phases that he also explained, from 1919 onward, in his lectures on education:

a. Early years' education based primarily on learning through participation, imitation, and sensory experiences.
b. The period from the beginning of formal schooling up to the age of 14, usually the class or grades teacher period in Waldorf schools (1st through 8th grades), i.e., all educational processes are guided by a learning specialist who is supported by a team of subject teachers. At this stage, learning processes are always from the stimulation of inner experiences that then form the foundation of cognitive and will-forming educational processes.
c. High school from 9th grade, when the teaching process is guided by specialist subject teachers, from the acquisition of knowledge and skills to the development of independent judgment, to social and communicative maturity, self-determination, and responsibility.

The teaching program in Waldorf schools, which is informed by developmental psychology, follows these stages. Accordingly, the "Richter Curriculum" presents, after a survey of the horizontal curriculum, the vertical curriculum for every subject in its main part (Richter 2010). The curriculum is structured according to age from 1st to 8th and 9th to 12th or 13th grade, because up to 8th grade the main subjects are taught by the class teacher: English (or the students' native language), arithmetic/math, general studies, history, geography, nature studies/biology, physics, and chemistry. From 9th grade, the individual subjects are taught by academically or otherwise qualified specialist teachers. The "grades teacher period" aims to convey cultural techniques and basic knowledge, enabling the children to explore the world and its importance for human beings with their teacher and from the different subject-related perspectives, and to develop independent thinking and judgment. High school, which starts with 9th grade in Waldorf schools, seeks to stimulate young people to develop independent judgment and conceptualization and to build up domain-specific competences in the individual subjects. This means that what was learned in the lower and middle school is now reflected in more complex contexts and in relation to the young people's own participation in the world. A third level is apparent in 12th and 13th grade, because now the curriculum encourages reflection on the individual content, based on overviews and subject-specific epistemological questions (as well as with a view to responsible action), as a way of building up self-reflective awareness toward the individual subjects and their content. This process could have the following structure:

Level 1: From direct participation to causal thinking (introductions/foundations)

> 1st to 3rd grades: reading, arithmetic, art, general studies
> 4th to 8th grades: getting to know the world from the perspective of the different subjects

Level 2: Judgment-forming and conceptualization based on the different subjects

> 9th grade: objective/principal and idealistic judgments
> 10th grade: inferential, causal, and self-orienting judgments
> 11th grade: dialectic, aesthetic, and empathic judgments

Level 3: Self-reflective (subject-related) awareness

> 12th grade: moral and conscious judgments from a wider perspective (Zech 2016, p. 38)

In choosing an antithetic title for the vertical curriculum: Open Curriculum—"Defined Education," Richter reflects on the field of tension described earlier. He cites Steiner as saying, "Our entire curriculum is only defined as far as its underlying spirit is concerned; where their individual actions are concerned, teachers have the greatest possible freedom" (Richter 2010, p. 101; Steiner 1986, p. 265). Richter expands on this with another Steiner citation: "The way we understand the curriculum is that we need to be able to develop it within us in every moment; that we learn to read from the seven-, eight-, nine-, ten-year-old child what we need to do at every stage" (Richter 2010, p. 102). This asks much of teachers in terms of pedagogical assessment skills. But Richter then adds a restriction to this open principle: "Teachers can, on the other hand, not subjectively and arbitrarily change or restructure teaching content that has been derived from anthropology without first conducting thorough and responsible pedagogical research" (Richter 2010, p. 102). This provides an orientational framework both for a curriculum for which individual teachers take responsibility as they accompany and support the young people's maturation and developmental processes in the sense explained in the curriculum, and for the spiral structure of the subject-related curricula. Ultimately, this means that all teaching content and suggested teaching methods in the Waldorf curriculum are determined by developmental steps that are ideal-typical and to be expected at the various ages, and by the students' developmental tasks that are to be supported by the educational process. Teaching content and themes consequently need to be returned to at different levels. The exploring of content in the lower grades through literary-mythical images, which speak to the child soul, through artistic and creative experiences, and through general studies, transitions in 4th and 5th grade to the imparting of skills and knowledge, which aim to increasingly convey reflected basic orientations by building on emotional experiences and aesthetic, creative activities. Through adolescent judgment-forming and conceptualization, this knowledge is transformed into insights when the young people engage with the lessons, bringing in their individual options, competences, and motivation as they unfold their individuality. Analysis of Richter's curriculum reveals how the topics and themes of many subjects that were introduced in the lower classes are systematically revisited in the middle and high school.[11]

The Waldorf curriculum's vertical structure, with its roots in anthropology and developmental psychology, brings it close to the "spiral curriculum" that is defined (in "Lexikon Pädagogik") as a "specific way of arranging learning contents in a curriculum: In addition to subject-related and logical aspects, the students' cognitive, mental, and motor development is also taken into consideration. The contents are revisited repeatedly in the course of the students' education, each time at a more complex level" (Tenorth, Tippelt 2007, p. 686). Waldorf education takes the same approach. How this process works out in practice under the professional responsibility of the individual teachers and in concrete situations is a question that cannot be answered because no empiric studies are available on the matter. Educationists criticize the Waldorf curriculum's underlying ideal-typical concept as a construct that cannot be empirically verified. Waldorf teachers, who draw on this concept in order to understand individual developmental processes and substantiate their teaching choices, have made the experience that a consistent teaching program can be derived from it.

3.4 Education plan rather than curriculum?

The theoretical discourse on competences in education has grown immensely in the last decade. It has become a tool in education policy because it can be used to justify a paradigm shift in learning, or rather in the learning plans that aim at standardized quality assurance in education. On its homepage, the Education Server of the German state of Baden-Württemberg published a definition in 2004 of the education plan that also explains its function. This explanation can serve as an example of the most recent generation of learning plans: "The new education plans herald a paradigm shift with regard to binding regulations for teaching in our schools. While earlier generations of education plans specified primarily what should be taught, the new education plans specify the competences children and young people need to acquire. This implicates a change from input to output orientation. The stages are marked in the different types of school by the proof of educational standards, mostly in a two-year rhythm. They describe the students' subject-specific, personal, social, and methodical competences. Contents are assigned to these competences in the form of a core curriculum. These contents have been chosen so that they can be worked through by the students in around two-thirds of the lesson time they have available. They form the basis for the central examinations. In addition, the attainment of educational standards in secondary schools is assessed through centrally provided comparative tests which are based on the core curriculum" (Education Server Baden-Württemberg 2004).

The standardizations developed in the educational plans derive from competence models and seem to finally make it possible to organize education systematically. A combination of competence measurements and quality management is expected to contribute to optimizing the output aimed for. Only few reservations have been expressed, pointing out that the concept of competence—borrowed from vocational training and developed for adults, because it presupposes self-reflection and dialogue ability—cannot simply be applied to schools and school education[12] (Bohnsack 2006, p. 102 ff.; Bohnsack 2008; Schmidt 2005). Even the fact that competence-oriented standardization is mostly justified by economic goals has hardly been challenged.[13] However, skepticism toward this approach is growing because the competence models for schools presented so far, however different their approaches, are struggling with a number of problems which Bormann and de Haan summarize in the following questions:

- How can competence predisposition be conclusively and clearly identified in definable developmental stages?
- How can an individual's very complex educational environment be assessed with competence descriptions?

- How can competences be measured or assessed?
- Can competences and competence measurements be defined without reference to political and economic interests?
- How can competence measurement evidence sustainable educational progress? Can competences built on specific situations and problems be decontextualized and transferred to new problems? (Bormann, de Haan 2008, p. 8).

Götte's publication on developmental tasks and competences in the education plans of Waldorf schools (Götte et al. 2009) addresses competence- and output orientation on the basis of the Richter Curriculum, introducing the term "education plan" for Waldorf schools in its subtitle.[14] The book focuses on the developmental tasks in different subjects and in relation to different ages or developmental stages that are seen as both a precondition and an indicator for the development or building up of competences. The authors do not so much dwell on content, themes, and procedures but characterize the challenges and tasks that need to be dealt with in order to achieve subject-specific, methodic, social competence, as well as self-competence. The Waldorf education plan is therefore one that assigns school learning to the four-part competence grid explicitly rejected by Klieme in his expert report on national education standards that was commissioned by the German Standing Conference of Ministers of Education and Cultural Affairs (Kultusministerkonferenz/ KMK): "The term 'competences' as applied here needs to be seen as distinctly different from the concepts of subject-specific, methodic, social, and personal competence used in vocational training and in public parlance" (Klieme 2007, p. 22, footnote 3). Supported by the subject-specific sciences, Klieme instead demands that the competences should be derived from the requirements of the individual subjects. This domain-specific approach is not intended in the education plan described.

In her foreword to the commissioned expert reports on the development of national education standards in Germany—*Kerncurriculum Oberstufe* (high school core curriculum)—Doris Ahnen,[15] who was KMK president in 2004, clearly describes their role as performance standards for quality assurance and consequently as a function of socially sanctioned expectations and targets (Ahnen 2001, p. 7). This is precisely what the authors of the Waldorf schools' education plan want to avoid, stating at the very beginning of their publication: "The question why a person should develop particular competences in the first place cannot be answered on the basis of economic or political interests. The development of the individuality alone can be the guiding principle for competence acquisition" (Götte et al. 2009, p. 9f.). The concept of an education plan represented by Loebell, Götte, and Maurer clearly differs from the one that provides the framework conditions for standard-oriented competence acquisition and that is currently discussed by education ministers and scientists. The Waldorf schools are not concerned with the acquisition of competences as a precondition for the successful participation in society. Their primary goal is the optimization of each person's individual potential that then flows into society. Their measures of performance are not standardized expectations but, true to the fundamental concept of Waldorf education, the individual child. Children can only realize their potential if they meet the conditions and challenges that come toward them. The qualifications for this are not gained by meeting admission requirements but by accepting one's own biographical conditions.

Waldorf education ultimately continues to be guided by an understanding of performance and of society that Steiner formulated as early as 1919: "The question cannot be: What does a person need to know or what do they need to be able to do to support the existing social order? The question is: What does a person bring with them that can be developed in them? Then young people will always carry new forces into the social order. The social order can be enriched and enlivened by these fully developed individuals, which is as it should be rather than young people being molded to fit into the existing social order" (Steiner 1982, p. 35). Competence building in Waldorf schools is clearly at variance with the demands of collective educational standards and output control. Waldorf schools seek to make the biographical intentions and the potential dormant in each person fertile for society by promoting individuation.

The extent to which such a shift from input to output orientation can contribute to the decanonization of the teaching content in the Waldorf curriculum is unclear, as is the question whether the traditional content and methods will not only be confirmed as tried and tested but also as a sensible foundation for competence building. The present education plan for Waldorf schools does not suggest any new orientation of Waldorf education, which is probably not something the authors intended anyway.

What is noticeable however is a new overlap between education science and Waldorf education due to the competence-oriented education plans and the definition of competence. The fact that competence building requires self-reflection, self-regulation, and self-organization and conceptually includes agency means that it focuses on the personality of the person who possesses the competences in question. One of the shortcomings in the discourse on competence development has been that the "I," as the entity carrying the competence or the initiative for competent action, is not given epistemological or ontological consideration. The competence concept suggested by the initiative Education for Sustainable Development nonetheless—and this is where it has a meeting point with Waldorf education—relies on maturation and the will to be creative and to assume responsibility. Competences prove themselves in performance and this is ultimately tantamount to agency based on individual awareness.

According to its own motto, Waldorf education's aims to empower students to ask questions and to create in this way the conditions for an increasingly reflected world encounter; it also aims to give young people the possibility to become aware of their interest in the world as an expression of their own biographic impulses. If it succeeds in this, it will meet essential criteria declared by Schmidt to be constitutive to the concept of competence: "As the learning and competence discourse focuses increasingly on lifelong learning, interpreting this as self-regulatory action control, concepts of competence must become reflective: Self-organization is seen as the result of the interplay of cognitive, social, emotional, and motivational resources; as the conscious directing of a person's own learning toward a reflective approach to life" (Schmidt 2005, p. 167).

4 The future of the curriculum and of curriculum development in Waldorf schools

On balance, the possibilities Waldorf teaching offers for competence development, in high school above all, reveal ways for skills and abilities to be dialogically confirmed and evaluated; for personality to not only be included in but also to be seen as prerequisite to the teaching situation; and for the attempt to elicit intrinsic motivation through competently guided processes of world exploration. These possibilities lead to self-regulation and to awareness through reflection and dialogue; they promote interest and motivation, educate young people to ask questions, i.e., to autonomous judgment, and they try to build the bridge from externally prompted learning to biographically motivated learning decisions. Empiric studies are required to examine how successfully these theoretical or ideal-typical ideas of Waldorf education are implemented in practice and how effectively the intended goals of competence building are realized.

Notes

1 In principle, my distinction between "teaching plan" (Lehrplan) and "curriculum" follows Tenorth who defines "Lehrplan" as the programmatic description of a course of instruction, while curriculum locates the teaching program within the wider context of overarching educational goals and therefore also includes statements on conditions required for learning. I will first explore how Waldorf education understands its curriculum before trying to define this curriculum in relation to the concepts of teaching plan/curriculum/guidelines (Tenorth, Tippelt 2007).

2 This practice can also be seen as civic engagement because factors such as the parental initiative to found schools, their co-responsibility for running the school, which includes financial commitment, and the teachers' responsibility for supporting and promoting individuation are based on the taking on of responsibility in the sense of a civil society.

3 The following section is an abridged and revised extract from my dissertation (Zech 2012).

The Waldorf Curriculum: Curriculum, Teaching Plan, or Guideline?

4   In Germany, more than 40 new Waldorf schools were founded in the six years leading up to 1995; between 1990 and 2010, the number of schools almost doubled. It appears to have become impossible to convey to currently over 8000 Waldorf teachers the foundations for their work through professional development and discourse.

5   One should add that teachers from the international Waldorf movement were also involved in this process. The curriculum in the end did not meet all the criteria of the original requirement analysis. It has for instance limited international validity in the humanities (native language/history/art history). Because of its acknowledged comprehensive description of all teaching approaches for the 12-year school concept, it has nonetheless been translated into multiple languages and serves as basis for numerous national Waldorf curricula around the world.

6   "Curriculum development: politically and pedagogically determined process, depends on the specific subject. Learning targets are operationalized and hierarchically categorized so they can be more easily compared. The curriculum is initially constructed by a curriculum panel (curriculum construction), before it is politically administrated and enforced" (Tenorth, Tippelt 2007, p. 471). William F. Pinar (Pinar 2009, p. 149ff.) presents an international overview of curriculum development (Pinar 2009, p. 149 ff.).

7   First manuscript edition of 1000 copies printed by the Research Institute of the German Waldorf schools' association (*Forschungsstelle beim Bund der Freien Waldorfschulen*) in Stuttgart in 1992; a second manuscript edition of 3000 copies in 1995; first edition in book form of 3000 copies published in Stuttgart in 2003, second edition of 2500 copies in 2006, out of print in 2009; new edition of 5000 copies in 2010. Around 12,000 German copies have been sold so far, with currently around 8300 practicing Waldorf teachers in Germany. The 1992 edition was so thoroughly revised that it had to be replaced. The importance of this publication is also reflected in the fact that it was translated into other languages or adapted to other countries. It has established itself as an internationally cited reference work.

8   The Waldorf curricula written by subject teachers in Bavaria and Hamburg, which were submitted and approved by the education authorities in these states, are more binding although they also consider the teacher autonomy based on pedagogical and subject-specific responsibility that is intrinsic to the self-concept of Waldorf education. The specifications in these curricula regarding content and methods therefore have only orientational character.

9   Robinsohn mentions three highest criteria for curriculum innovation: "1 The importance of a subject within the scientific context; 2 the contribution of a subject to understanding the world (i.e. for orientation within a culture and interpreting its phenomena); 3 a subject's function in specific applications in private and public life" (Robinsohn 1971, p. 47).

10 The rejection of curricula that are, as intended by Robinsohn, oriented to general educational goals, in favor of subject-specific segmentation was criticized early on by numerous educationists (Fingerle 1983, p. 118).

11 Similarly to the German mainstream education system, the term "lower school" refers to 1st to 4th grade, the term "middle school" to 5th to 8th grade. "High school" or "upper school" denote 9th to 13th grade (this differs from the German grammar school system). In the internal Waldorf discourse on pedagogical principles regarding 7th to 10th grade, this structure is sometimes called into question.

12 In the preface to their handbook on Competence Measuring, Erpenbeck and Rosenstiel warn against the "adventurous use of the term 'competence,'" expressing their concern that a trivialized and aligned competence concept with the associated high expectation of self-regulation and individuality may "backfire" (Erpenbeck, von Rosenstiel 2003, pp. XII/XIII).

13 Böhm (1997), Messner (2004), Rittelmeyer (2006, p. 9 ff.), Heinemann (2008, p. 52 ff.), Krautz (2007), Liessmann (2006).

14 The term is still under discussion and interestingly not yet included in "Lexikon Pädagogik." Künzli defines it as a conceptually unclear variant of the curriculum concept (Künzli 2009, p. 134). The conceptual connection between "education plan" and "curriculum" is apparent from the fact that the expert report published by Tenorth on behalf of the KMK is entitled "Kerncurriculum Oberstufe." The task of core curricula is to operationalize the target competences prescribed by the education plan into a teaching program, i.e., to assign them to specific teaching-learning contents (Tenorth 2001/2004).

15 Doris Ahnen was still minister for education, science, further training, and culture of the German State of Rhineland-Palatinate in 2014.

Bibliography

Ahnen, Doris (2001): Preface. In: Tenorth, Elmar (Eds.) (2001): Kerncurriculum Oberstufe II. Expertisen – im Auftrag der Ständigen Konferenz der Kultusminister. Band I für die Fächer Mathematik, Deutsch und Englisch. Weinheim: Beltz, pp. 7–9.

Böhm, Winfried (1997): Die Person als Maß der Erziehung. In: Lischewski, Andreas (Ed.)/Böhm, Winfried (1997): Entwürfe einer Pädagogik der Person. Gesammelte Aufsätze. Edited and introduced by Andreas Lischewski. Bad Heilbrunn: Klinkhardt.

Bohnsack, Fritz (2006): Bildungs-Steuerung und Personalität. In: Erziehungskunst. Zeitschrift zur Pädagogik Rudolf Steiners. Sonderheft Bildungsstandards. Schule als Produktionsbetrieb? Oktober 2006, pp. 97–107.

Bohnsack, Fritz (2008): Martin Bubers personale Pädagogik. Bad Heilbrunn: Klinkhardt.

Bormann, Inka/de Haan, Gerhard (Eds.) (2008): Kompetenzen der Bildung für nachhaltige Entwicklung. Operationalisierung, Messung, Rahmenbedingungen, Befunde. Wiesbaden: VS.

Erpenbeck, John/von Rosenstiel, Lutz (Eds.) (2003): Handbuch Kompetenzmessung. Erkennen, verstehen und bewerten von Kompetenzen in der betrieblichen, pädagogischen und psychologischen Praxis. Stuttgart: Schäffer-Poeschel.

Fingerle, Karlheinz (1983): Curriculumstheorien im Bereich von Schulformen und Schulstufen. In: Hameyer, Uwe/Frey, Karl/Haft, Henning (1983): Handbuch der Curriculumsforschung. Übersichten zur Forschung 1970-1981. Weinheim: Beltz, pp. 117–128.

Götte, Wenzel M./Loebell, Peter/Maurer, Klaus-Michael (2009): Entwicklungsaufgaben und Kompetenzen. Zum Bildungsplan der Waldorfschule. Stuttgart: Freies Geistesleben.

Grießhaber, Wilhelm (2002–2008): Curriculumsentwicklung nach Robinsohn 1967 http://spzwww.uni-muenster.de/griesha/fsu/cur/cur-robinsohn.html (accessed 4/4/2016).

Heinemann, Karl-Heinz (2008): Verhindern PISA und Bologna Bildung? In: Pädagogik 04/08, p. 52 ff.

Heydebrand, Caroline von (2009): Vom Lehrplan der Freien Waldorfschule. 11th edition. Stuttgart: Freies Geistesleben. English translation.

Heydebrand, Caroline von (2021): The Curriculum of the First Waldorf School, transl. Daniel Hindes. Longmont, Colorado: Aelzina Books.

Klieme, Eckard (2007): Zur Entwicklung nationaler Bildungsstandards. Eine Expertise. Berlin: Bundesministerium für Bildung und Forschung. Unamended reprint (2009) online at https://www.bmbf.de/pub/zur_entwicklung_nationaler_bildungsstandards.pdf (accessed 4/4/2016).

Krautz, Jochen (2007): Ware Bildung. Schule und Universität unter dem Diktat der Ökonomie. Munich: Diederichs.

Künzli, Rudolf (2009): Curriculum und Lehrmittel. In: Andersen, Sabine/Casale, Rita/Gabriel, Thomas/Horlacher, Rebekka/Larcher Klee, Sabina/Oelkers, Jürgen (Eds.) (2009): Handwörterbuch Erziehungswissenschaft. Weinheim: Beltz, pp. 134–148.

Landesbildungsserver Baden-Württemberg. Der Bildungsplan 2004 kurz vorgestellt. www.bildung-staerktmenschen.de/schule_2004/bildungsplan_kurz (accessed 4/4/2016).

Leber, Stefan (1991): Die Sozialgestalt der Waldorfschule. Ein Beitrag zu den sozialwissenschaftlichen Anschauungen Rudolf Steiners. New revised edition. Stuttgart: Freies Geistesleben.

Leber, Stefan (1995): Geleitwort. In: Richter, Tobias (Ed.) (1995): Pädagogischer Auftrag und Unterrichtsziele einer Freien Waldorfschule. Im Auftrag des Haager Kreises gedruckt. Stuttgart: Pädagogische Forschungsstelle beim Bund der Freien Waldorfschulen, pp. 1–2.

Liessmann, Konrad Paul (2006): Theorie der Unbildung. Die Irrtümer der Wissensgesellschaft. Vienna: Paul Zsolnay.

Messner, Rudolf (2004): Was Bildung von Produktion unterscheidet – oder die Spannung von Freiheit und Objektivierung und das Projekt des Bildungsstandards. In: Die Deutsche Schule. 8. Beiheft 2004, pp. 26–47. Online at kobra.bibliothek.uni-kassel.de/bitstream/urn:nbn:de:hebis:34-2007072619068/1/MessnerBildung.pdf (accessed 4/4/2016).

Pinar, William F. (2009): Curriculumsentwicklung. In: Andersen, Sabine/Casale, Rita/Gabriel, Thomas/Horlacher, Rebekka/Larcher Klee, Sabina/Oelkers, Jürgen (Eds.) (2009): Handwörterbuch Erziehungswissenschaft. Weinheim: Beltz, pp. 149–162.

Richter, Tobias (Ed.) (2010): Pädagogischer Auftrag und Unterrichtsziele – vom Lehrplan der Waldorfschule. 3rd edition. Stuttgart: Freies Geistesleben.

Rittelmeyer, Christian (2006): Probleme der Messung von "Basiskompetenzen" In: Erziehungskunst. Zeitschrift zur Pädagogik Rudolf Steiners. Sonderheft Bildungsstandards. Schule als Produktionsbetrieb? Oktober 2006, pp. 9–13.

Robinsohn, Saul B. (1971): Bildungsreform als Revision des Curriculum und ein Strukturkonzept für Curriculumsentwicklung. Neuwied: Luchterhand.

Schmidt, Siegfried J. (2005): Lernen, Wissen, Kompetenz, Kultur. Vorschläge zur Bestimmung von vier Unbekannten. Heidelberg: Auer.

Steiner, Rudolf (1907): Die Erziehung des Kindes vom Gesichtspunkte der Geisteswissenschaft. In: Steiner, Rudolf (1987): Lucifer – Gnosis. Grundlegende Aufsätze zur Anthroposophie und Berichte aus den Zeitschriften «Luzifer» und «Lucifer – Gnosis» 1903–1908. GA 34. Dornach: Rudolf Steiner Verlag, pp. 309–348.

Steiner, Rudolf (1982): Freie Schule und Dreigliederung. In: Steiner, Rudolf (1982): Aufsätze über die Dreigliederung des sozialen Organismus und zur Zeitlage 1915–1921. GA 24. Dornach: Rudolf Steiner Verlag.

Steiner, Rudolf (1986): Gegenwärtiges Geistesleben und Erziehung. GA 307. Dornach: Rudolf Steiner Verlag.

Steiner, Rudolf (1987): Theosophie. Einführung in übersinnliche Welterkenntnis und Menschenbestimmung. GA 9. Dornach: Rudolf Steiner Verlag.

Steiner, Rudolf (1989): Gesammelte Aufsätze zur Kultur- und Geistesgeschichte 1887–1901. GA 31. Dornach: Rudolf Steiner Verlag.

Stockmeyer, E.A. Karl (2001): Angaben Rudolf Steiners für den Waldorfschulunterricht. Manuskript. 6th edition (with new title). Stuttgart: Pädagogische Forschungsstelle beim Bund der Freien Waldorfschulen.

Tenorth, Heinz-Elmar (2001): Kerncurriculum Oberstufe. Expertisen – im Auftrag der Ständigen Konferenz der Kultusminister. Band I für die Fächer Mathematik, Deutsch und Englisch. Weinheim: Beltz.

Tenorth, Heinz-Elmar (2004): Kerncurriculum Oberstufe. Expertisen – im Auftrag der Ständigen Konferenz der Kultusminister. Band II für die Fächer Biologie, Chemie, Physik, Geschichte, Politik. Weinheim: Beltz.

Tenorth, Heinz-Elmar/Tippelt, Rudolf (Eds.) (2007): Lexikon Pädagogik. Weinheim und Basel: Beltz.

Zech, M. Michael (2012): Der Geschichtsunterricht an Waldorfschulen. Genese und Umsetzung des Konzepts vor dem Hintergrund des aktuellen geschichtsdidaktischen Diskurses. Frankfurt am Main: Peter Lang.

Zech, M. Michael (2013a): Waldorfschulen als Beispiel gelebter Schulautonomie auf dem freien Markt. In: Randoll, Dirk/da Veiga, Marcello (Eds.) (2013): Waldorfpädagogik in Praxis und Ausbildung. Zwischen Tradition und notwendigen Reformen. Wiesbaden: Springer, pp. 11–24.

Zech, M. Michael (2013b): Die Gründungsidee der Waldorfschulen und das Problem der Schul- bzw. Lehrerautonomie im internationalen Kontext. In: Barz, Heiner (Ed.) (2013): Unterricht an Waldorfschulen. Berufsbild Waldorflehrer: Neue Perspektiven zu Praxis, Forschung, Ausbildung. Wiesbaden: Springer, pp. 19–51.

Zech, M. Michael (2016): Urteilsbildung im Oberstufenunterricht an den Waldorfschulen. In: Lehrerrundbrief des Bundes der Freien Waldorfschulen Nr. 104, pp. 35–52.

CHAPTER 6

Theory of Professions

INTRODUCTION

Walter Riethmüller

The dimensions, structure, and development of professional agency in Waldorf teachers have so far only been studied in relation to Ulrich Oevermann's sociological interaction model (Baumert, Kunter 2006, p. 469f.). Of the many different occupational roles Waldorf teachers have, that of "class teacher" or "grades teacher" is the only one that has been analyzed in depth, using Werner Helsper's case reconstruction method. The relation between grades teachers and their students, which occupies a "polar position even within the professional model and theory," was reconstructed as a "modern/de-modernized pedagogical answer to the processes of modernization" and, moreover, as a "strong and pointed variant of the professional model of pedagogical communication" (Helsper 2007, p. 487). Even among reform school models, the Waldorf concept of the grades teacher who, if possible, remains with the same class for the first eight years of formal schooling appears to be a "special case" both from the social and the curricular perspective.

With their diverse dimensions of authority, their diffuse and tendentially unlimited claim to provide a "caring" education, to try to grasp each student's whole individuality, including their home background, grades teachers are said to aim to have a formative effect on the students as "universal spirits" and "guiding role models" (Ullrich 2007, p. 503). Especially in seventh and eighth grades, this has often caused problems for grades teachers if their professional and pedagogical competence should be called into question.

The case reconstructions carried out so far have focused on the upper end of the class-teacher period, mostly eighth grade, since this "fragile" aspect of the class teacher principle with its programmatic eight-year duration was a promising starting point for scrutinizing its educational, social, and professional dimensions.

Based on the empirical study mentioned (Helsper et al. 2007), Walter Riethmüller, in the first contribution, asks how the grades teacher principle envisaged by Rudolf Steiner, the founder of the first Waldorf School, can be justified under today's very different social conditions, including aspects such as the earlier onset of adolescence and expectations of professional competence. According to Steiner, the success of the (ideally) eight-year class teacher concept depends on the ability of teachers to build a relationship with their students. He did not disregard professional competence but rather expected grades teachers to be able to acquire the necessary specialist knowledge. He relied on the willingness of teachers "to self-develop," so as to understand the various stages of child development and to provide, on the basis of that understanding, suitable content conveyed using appropriate methods. Steiner formulated seven "teachers' virtues" that Waldorf teachers should strive for. His understanding of "authority" also needs to be seen in this context. It is not about power but about the educational effect the teacher's self-education has on the students. In summary, Riethmüller formulates eight requirements that need to be met for the class teacher model to remain a relevant principle of Waldorf education.

DOI: 10.4324/9781003187431-27

In the second contribution, Jürgen Peters uses Dirk Randoll's empirical study *Ich bin Waldorflehrer* (I am a Waldorf teacher) (Randoll 2013) to explore the link between teacher competence and professional success. Based on Steiner's "seven teachers' virtues" Randoll asks whether particular competences have a definite correlation with professional success on the one hand and resilience on the other, and whether comparable effects can be discovered with regard to professional competence. Peters concludes that Waldorf-typical competences such as "initiative and personal responsibility" and "imagination and enthusiasm" as well as professional competence are closely connected with the experience of professional success. Students appreciate professional competence and enthusiasm in teachers, as well as "initiative and personal responsibility." Given the reliance on self-management in Waldorf schools, this is not surprising. Peters proves that developing the competences mentioned also affects the teacher's own resilience and mental health. The evidence that professional competence is a particularly important factor for the experience of success *and* for resilience is especially relevant to Waldorf education. These empirical findings, which are relevant to the discussion about the competence of grades teachers, above all in seventh and eighth grades, confirm the research results of Helsper and his colleagues *ex post* (Helsper et al. 2007).

Albert Schmelzer, in his contribution, uses the relevance, confirmed by Hattie (2009), of the teacher's personality and the teacher-student relationship for learning success as a basis for examining the development of personal competences from the point of view of anthroposophy and Waldorf education. He begins by discussing central elements of "mindful education," an approach inspired by Buddhism that is becoming increasingly popular in all kinds of fields, including psychosomatic medicine, psychotherapy, and education. Schmelzer understands mindfulness as the ability to meet events with an open mind and suggests that developing this faculty was associated with awareness, unintentionality, freedom from judgment, and presence in relation to current events. Practicing mindfulness would help teachers to strengthen their own health according to the salutogenic principle and promote a more student-oriented approach to teaching. In this context, Schmelzer discusses aspects of the anthroposophical path of inner development that not only prepare teachers for meeting challenges in their work and encounter with students but that also enhance their social skills and awaken an active interest in current events. Schmelzer then details the quality of Steiner's "subsidiary exercises" that can support teachers on their way to self-development. This approach has implications for education in that it moves the teacher's personality and the teacher-student relationship to center stage. The teacher's personal development gains essential importance for education and teaching and therefore also for the individualization of the students.

References

Baumert, Jürgen/Kunter, Mareike (2006): Stichwort: Professionelle Kompetenz von Lehrkräften. In: Zeitschrift für Erziehungswissenschaft 9, issue 4, pp. 469–520.

Hattie, John (2009): Visible Learning: A Synthesis of Over 800 Meta-Analyses Relating to Achievement. Abingdon: Routledge.

Helsper, Werner (2007): Das Waldorfklassenlehrerkonzept im Feld pädagogischer Kommunikation. In: Helsper, Werner/Ullrich, Heiner/Stelmaszyk, Bernhard/Höblich, Davina/Graßhoff, Gunther/Jung, Dana (2007): Autorität und Schule. Die empirische Rekonstruktion der Klassenlehrer-Schüler-Beziehung an Waldorfschulen. Wiesbaden: VS, pp. 483–489.

Helsper, Werner/Ullrich, Heiner/Stelmaszyk, Bernhard/Höblich, Davina/Graßhoff, Gunther/Jung, Dana (2007): Autorität und Schule. Die empirische Rekonstruktion der Klassenlehrer-Schüler-Beziehung an Waldorfschulen. Wiesbaden: VS.

Randoll, Dirk (Ed.) (2013): *Ich bin Waldorflehrer.* Einstellungen, Erfahrungen, Diskussionspunkte – Eine Befragungsstudie. Wiesbaden: Springer VS.

Ullrich, Heiner (2007): Fachwissen und Bildung der Person. In: Helsper, Werner/Ullrich, Heiner/Stelmaszyk, Bernhard/Höblich, Davina/Graßhoff, Gunther/Jung, Dana(2007): Autorität und Schule. Die empirische Rekonstruktion der Klassenlehrer-Schüler-Beziehung an Waldorfschulen. Wiesbaden: VS, pp. 500–506.

THE PROFESSIONAL IMAGE OF THE WALDORF GRADES TEACHER

Walter Riethmüller

1 Outline of recent research

Current empirical research on Waldorf education focuses almost exclusively on the profession of the Waldorf class or grades teacher. The grades teacher as a specific type of pedagogue that does not exist in other school forms, mainstream or independent, seems to be most suited to scrutinize the reality and implications of Waldorf education.

Besides certain other practical, didactic, and pedagogical specialisms of Waldorf education (such as eurythmy teaching, arts, crafts, and music lessons, two additional languages from first grade, main lesson blocks, no repeating of classes), the grades teacher principle is the most outstanding specialty of this educational system. Waldorf grades teachers generally stay with their classes for eight years. For almost two hours every morning, they teach their classes a variety of subjects in "main lesson blocks" that stretch over three to four weeks (Eller 1998; Röh, Thomas 2015). Because of their close relationship with the students and their parents, grades teachers occupy a special position not only in their own class but also within the faculty of teachers of the self-managed Waldorf schools.

The grades teacher principle has become established in Waldorf schools over the decades although it has been called into question again and again since the 1980s as a result of accounts published by former Waldorf students (Jacob, Drewes 2004; Rudolph 1987). Within the Waldorf discourse, these responses have generally been seen as individual cases rather than as causes for revisiting the reality and consequences of the class teacher principle in theory or practice.

Prompted by the German educationalist Heiner Ullrich, the role of the Waldorf grades teacher has in recent years become the focus of various empirical scientific studies that have resulted in a series of groundbreaking findings. Based on theoretical case analyses, the grades teachers' work on relationship-building and their biographical effect has been examined (Idel 2007). The "authority" principle, an essential element in Waldorf education from first to eighth grades, has been scrutinized using selected examples of teacher-student relationships. As a result, basic considerations and ideas for further research were formulated and addressed directly at the Waldorf school movement (Helsper et al. 2007). The relationship quality of the grades teacher, found by structural theory to be "diffuse" and not clearly framed, which reaches beyond the class context into the students' home background and is therefore tendentially unlimited, was subjected to a detailed case analysis (Graßhoff 2008). Another comprehensive study discussed the professionalization of the grades teacher role as a biographical project (Kunze 2011).

The empirical approach based on structural theory and case analysis has been complemented by Dirk Randoll's surveys and analyses regarding teacher satisfaction in Waldorf schools (Randoll 2013), for

DOI: 10.4324/9781003187431-28

which Randoll asked former Waldorf students about their experiences at school (Barz, Randoll 2007), established an overview of formative experiences in Waldorf schools (Liebenwein, Barz, Randoll 2012), and interviewed thirteenth grade students from Waldorf schools in the German state of Hesse on how effective they found the grades teacher system (Randoll, Graudenz, Peters 2014; Riethmüller, Neal 2014).

A common denominator of the examinations suggested by Heiner Ullrich is that they question the grades teacher system in Waldorf education with its authority concept, mainly because of factors such as the socio-political changes and developments that have marked recent decades, the ever-earlier onset of adolescence and the correspondingly earlier striving of young people for autonomy. The fact that puberty now starts at age 11 or 12 is seen as problematic for the grades teacher system, where the same teacher is responsible for a group of students from first through eighth grade. The students earlier striving for independence and autonomous decision-making was met with more or less professional competence (Ullrich 2007a, p. 91ff.). The professional competence expected of grades teachers in seventh and eighth grades is another bone of contention: The absence of such competence and the pressure to acquire it is said to put grades teachers under excessive stress (ibid.).

In conclusion, these studies specify areas in need of attention and address these directly at the grades teachers. Aside from the "*need for systematic reflection* of the wide range of professional tasks associated with the special role of the grades teacher" (Höblich 2007, p. 531), there was an obvious need for specialist training and professional development, particularly for teaching seventh and eighth grades, as Waldorf teacher education programs did not give the same priority to professionalism and the quality of teaching as state-run teacher trainings (Ullrich 2007b, p. 505). The success of a reflective "dynamic and modification of the authority concept" (Höblich) required cooperative and collegial ways of working such as supervision regarding both the grades teachers' "appropriate use of their own resources" and the "collegial case work" in order to shape the pedagogical relationship at such a critical student age more professionally and appropriately based on a better developed "case understanding." This would also free grades teachers "from their problematic all-round responsibility" and limit their educational intentions. The conditions for the retention and further development of this pedagogical principle, with its elevated grades teacher position, needed to be constantly revisited and adjusted (Höblich 2007, p. 531f.).

The validity of the—only—nine case reconstructions is supported by statements from former Waldorf students who remark on the tendential stress of class teachers caused by the "impartation of content up to eighth grade," and difficulties experienced due to the early onset of adolescence (Barz, Randoll 2007, p. 262ff.). The most recent survey of German Waldorf high school students in the state of Hesse regarding their experiences with the grades teacher system revealed that, while the principle as such is mainly seen as positive, there was a need for advice and action, above all for seventh and eighth grades, in relation to professional, didactic, and methodical requirements (Randoll, Graudenz, Peters 2014). Furthermore, it was suggested that new forms of transitioning from ninth grade to high school should be discussed and implemented so as to take some weight off the grades teachers.

While these research results and suggestions are valuable to the internal Waldorf discourse, it needs to be said that there is no *one way* of being a Waldorf school and that, given the manifold preconditions, possibilities, and routes for becoming a grades teacher in Waldorf schools, there is no one way of being such a Waldorf grades teacher—there can't be.

But the meticulously executed and carefully documented studies cited here reveal a range of questions and problems that those responsible for the development of Waldorf schools and the pedagogy provided there need to address. Volker Frielingsdorf, in his assessment of the empirical studies inspired by Ullrich, also sees them as "valuable suggestions and indications" that were to be understood as "aids for reflection"; they could "encourage Waldorf teachers to look at the grades teacher–student relationship, which was so natural for them, from the outside, analyze it, and feel inspired to critically assess what they think of as certain" (2012, p. 117). Frielingsdorf urges that the questions raised by the research in relation to intellectual-cognitive and social aspects of the grades teacher–student relationship, particularly with 12- to 15-year-olds, should "soon be addressed systematically" (ibid., p. 118).

That scientific studies have so far been limited to grades teachers may seem justified because of the grades teacher's prominent position. However, for subject teachers in Waldorf schools—particularly those who teach specialist main lesson blocks in the high school—a more differentiated and possibly domain-specific model would emerge in the theory of professions, freeing the concept of the "Waldorf teacher" from the "narrow focus on the grades teacher" and resulting in a richer professional image. Focusing on the grades teachers has led to a rather reduced picture of the reality and effectiveness of Waldorf schools. By extending the method of case reconstruction to include the Waldorf subject teachers, the view of the Waldorf school reality, which had become limited by its focus on the grades teacher, could be enriched by the perspective of the educational and formative effect that the many different subject teachers have on the students.

The vibrant diversity of Waldorf schools, especially in the high school, asks for multiple, open questions that are to be adapted flexibly to the individual school profile. Based on the investigative methods mentioned, the grades teacher's prominent position could be better integrated into the school reality and its importance viewed in more differentiated ways. Its dominant role and heightened impact on the individual student's biography could then probably be slightly qualified.

The discussion below focuses on the eight-year duration of the grades teacher period and the grades teacher's authority, two issues that have attracted particular criticism and that can exemplify the whole problem of the professional image of the Waldorf teacher and especially of the Waldorf grades teacher.

2 The Waldorf grades teacher from the point of view of professions theory

The few existing "internal" Waldorf publications confirm that teaching seventh and eighth grades is a rewarding and enriching experience for grades teachers (Riethmüller 1993). Taking a group of students through, if possible, to eighth grade is seen as a successful and satisfying achievement, although it has also been pointed out that a different, pedagogically more fruitful system was conceivable from sixth grade onward (Riethmüller 2011, p. 181; Eller p. 151ff.).

One tried and tested example is that of the "Engelberg model." This model has been in use for almost two decades now and works on the premise that a team of grades teachers take it in turns to teach the different main lesson blocks in seventh to ninth grade. The original grades teacher only stays with his group of children until the end of sixth grade. This middle school team teaching model has mostly been rated as positive by teachers (Brücher 2003). But there are also those who think that students experience more stress during puberty if they do not have the grades teacher support up to eighth grade (Kruckelmann 2014). So far, there are no studies that evaluate the "functioning" of such a model or provide convincing evidence based on comparisons.

Peter Struck does not necessarily agree with the view that the principle of having one grades teacher up through eighth grade is questionable due to a potential lack of professional competence. He thinks that children need scientifically oriented specialists less than they need good grades teachers who "love the children, are committed to their work, and have pedagogical charisma," and who "have time for their students" (Struck 1994, p. 16). Frielingsdorf, while not dismissing the results of the exemplary, phenomenologically descriptive studies based on case reconstructions and systematic reflection, and even explicitly lauding their methodical, objectively hermeneutic approach, warns against the generalization of such case constructions (Frielingsdorf 2012, p. 117). It also seems to be a question of the perspective from which one views the profession of the grades teacher.

If one sees them, as Helsper suggests, as trying "to teach 'everything to everyone' in the various main lessons, in Comenian fashion, as didactic monarchs and universalists [...]" (Helsper 2007, p. 488f.), one may be tempted to compare them to the patriarchal pedagogues of the late 19th century. In that case, the collision of the grades teacher's claim to universality with the "scientific demands of individual subjects" and the "ever earlier demands for autonomy of today's children and young people" (Ullrich 2015, p. 46) is all but inevitable. It is little surprising and only logical that Ullrich sees the grades teacher principle as a "regime," and that he demands it should be limited both in duration and scope

(Ullrich 2015, p. 168). That he now interprets "authority" one-sidedly as power-seeking is remarkable, given his warning that a few years ago that there was a need to clarify the programmatic role of the grades teacher within the Waldorf movement, referring to the discourse conducted between educationalists such as Fritz Bohnsack and Horst Rumpf and Waldorf representatives such as Stefan Leber (Bohnsack 1996; Leber 1996; Rumpf 1996; Ullrich 2007a, p. 92).

The one-sided interpretation and classification of the grades teacher role in the direction of a "universal claim to leadership" does not, however, do justice to the diversity of the grades teacher's demanding duties. It would be more appropriate to refer, as intended in Waldorf education, to a "universal claim to relations" (Riethmüller 2011, p. 174ff.). The capacity to form relationships is the quality Rudolf Steiner requested of grades teachers even before the foundation of the Waldorf school: It was not the testing of easily acquired knowledge that would be at the center of future teacher examinations, but the examinee's ability to establish relationships with children that enabled, supported, and promoted learning. "Then they will not be instructors of reading, arithmetic or drawing and so on, but they will be true formers of evolving human beings" (Steiner 1996, p. 92).

Steiner's request anticipates what has often been confirmed by today's learning research. "In order to learn, children need to feel safe and accepted by their teacher" (Largo, Beglinger 2009, p. 56). Building a relationship needs space and time—something that is made impossible by constant teacher changes and the chopping up of learning content in bite-sized units conveyed breathlessly in 45-minute lessons. Relationships will grow stronger and more stable "if teachers do not only teach the children but enter into their emotional needs and interests. Deeper relationships can often develop outside the lesson" (ibid.), for instance on school trips or during school-based leisure activities. This relationship quality comes into its own during puberty, when students expect (usually without expressing this) that teachers "legitimize their authority through their personality and their social and professional competence" (Largo, Beglinger 2009, p. 122).

For a hundred years now, Waldorf schools have had mostly positive experiences with the grades teacher system and its focus on relationships. The approach is supported by the findings of learning psychology studies into the grades teacher years. Nonetheless, a discourse within the Waldorf movement on a modern professional understanding of the grades teacher role is urgently necessary and is taking place now. The authority issue is being discussed, as is the problem of the often-lacking professional competence in specialized tuition for seventh and eighth grades (sciences, math, English, and history), and the need for a modern understanding of the teacher's social role and tasks as a "lone warrior" or team player.

The need for the German Waldorf movement to engage intensively with the grades teacher question arose in late 2012, when an internal survey was conducted across all German Waldorf schools, asking about their grades teacher systems: Did they adhere to the eight-year principle or use a transitional model from middle to high school? Of the 160 schools that responded, 10 percent stated that they used a middle school model—that is to say, the grades teacher period ends at the end of sixth grade, and, from seventh grade on, main lessons are taught by "specialist teachers." A further 10 percent stated they were considering such a middle school concept. A total of 114 schools used individual flexible solutions to "wean" grades teachers from their classes. Based on these research results, a dynamic discussion on middle school concepts has evolved in many Waldorf schools in Germany. Prompted by developers of Waldorf teacher education programs, the realization or questioning of the grades teacher principle and the conditions for this are being discussed in meetings and conferences. This debate is further driven by current developments, above all in the Netherlands, where, due to official regulations, the grades teacher principle can only be implemented very rudimentarily.

The *eight*-year grades teacher period is nothing "canonical"; in other words, it is not based on explicit statements forwarded by Rudolf Steiner in lectures (Röh, Thomas 2015, p. 170f.). The desirability of the principle, however, can be derived from indications he made and from what had been established as a reality after two years of "Waldorf school history." Systematic reflection on new middle school concepts beyond individual solutions would be a necessary requirement for an experience-based discourse on different middle school models (Frielingsdorf 2012, p. 118).

3 The grades teacher principle

The grades teacher principle as a system for Waldorf grades 1 through 8 that is not to be questioned has so far been supported by a narrative in Waldorf circles of a positive biographical experience (Eller 1998; Röh, Thomas 2015). Current scientific findings are consulted to evidence the necessity of stable relationships for successful learning and a thriving class community (Largo, Beglinger 2009; Riethmüller 2011; Struck 2010). Since the views expressed on the Waldorf side (Eller 1998; Riethmüller 1993, 2011; Röh, Thomas 2015) rather reflect, more or less convincingly, the teacher's perspective, describing the effect on the "addressees" rather in terms of an ideal that one tries to approach without dwelling much on the critical aspects, they cannot really stand up to scientific-critical analyses and scrutiny.

As a way of gaining clarity in this respect, it seems to be indicated to go back to Rudolf Steiner's impulse as the originator of Waldorf education, to introduce the grades teacher principle. Insights into his motives and arguments are central to the question as to the professional role of the grades teacher and the self-image of Waldorf education.

The first Waldorf school operated under Rudolf Steiner's direction from 1919 to 1924, and, during that time, the concept of an eight-year grades teacher period was already established (Zdražil 2013). Steiner knew that this was a clear departure from the common contemporary practice in Wurttemberg, the part of Germany where the school is situated, and where, up until the 1930s, school attendance was compulsory up to seventh grade. Introducing an eight-year school concept was a deliberate step on Steiner's side, as he stated in the preparatory course he gave to the future teachers on August 21, 1919, "The task of the grades teacher is a comprehensive one; [...] Grades teachers remain with their group of children until the final grade and then take on a new first grade" (2020, p. 43). That by "final grade" he meant eighth grade is apparent from a statement he made on August 27, 1919, during the same preparatory course, when he repeated that "Teachers should stay with one class for as long as possible," if possible up to eighth grade and then take a new first grade (2020, p. 146). The wording "as long as possible" opens up the possibility for individual solutions.

There was no doubt in 1923 that the grades teacher period would cover the first eight years. "Eighth grade is the final grade of elementary school. After that the teachers change" (Steiner 1975b, vol. 2, p. 25). This unambiguous announcement arose from the fact that in the first two school years, 1919–1920, the two top grades—seventh and eighth grades—were taught alternately by two teachers. This led to the class "disintegrating" and the students beginning to display challenging behaviors. Steiner saw this as a great danger and his solution was to demand that grades teachers should stay with their class for as long as possible (Steiner 1975b, vol. 2, p. 95).

When founding the Waldorf school, Steiner's intention was not to transfer the patriarchal model of the late 19th century to this school but rather to implement the grades teacher principle mainly for health-related reasons. In the basic preparatory course for the future teachers of the first Waldorf school (Steiner 2020, p. 254ff.), Steiner called attention to the fact that the entire grades teacher period, which covered the elementary school years, enabled teachers to "accompany the children's healthy physiological development down to their speed of growth" (Zdražil 2013, p. 30). This aspect was sufficient justification for an extended grades teacher period and it made "no sense whatsoever for children to have a change of teacher every year" (Steiner 2020, p. 255). In the same lecture, he stressed how important it was for teachers to really get to know their students, especially at the beginning of the transitions "in the seventh, ninth, and twelfth year of life that were so crucial for the children's further development" (ibid.).

That this motive was future-oriented is apparent form Peter Struck's more recent considerations. Struck points out how important it is that teachers and students get to know each other well, as this had an impact even on the students' health and enabled appropriate actions on the part of the teacher. "In addition to subject teachers who have profound knowledge of their subject, schools increasingly need grades teachers who also know something about nutrition, exercise, play, behavioral and learning problems, the prevention of violence and addiction, media education and parenting," because the traditional view that "parents bring children up and school educates them" no longer applied.

While it is possible to portray Steiner's health-related educational intentions as esoteric by refer-ring to the grades teacher as a "spiritual healer" (Ullrich 2015, p. 47f.), one can also see them as an impulse of social health and social reform that he tried to convey to the teachers. Steiner considered it important for teachers to develop a feeling for the fact that they could only fulfill their educational tasks if they acquired a comprehensive understanding of life that went beyond pedagogical, didactic, and theoretical expertise. The education question was for him also a social question, and teachers, rather than being "scholars," should be able to "impart" knowledge to and educate others "in the right way" (Steiner 1975a, p. 124). In a special sense, relating to the socially effective aspects of their position and actions, teachers were "for a comprehensive worldview as much healers as physicians were," for teachers supported healing processes similarly to physicians, but "at a different level" (ibid., p. 125).[1] Waldorf education is therefore also understood as a "healing" influence on the social life. Its main task was not to educate young people to adapt to the existing social order but to develop faculties in them that allow them to "bring ever new forces" to the existing social order (Steiner 1961, p. 37).

How little Steiner's thinking followed traditional patterns is apparent from a lecture he gave in Berlin as early as November 4, 1910. One of his topics there concerned the strengthening of the memory forces. He described how "immensely beneficial" it would be to have a school with seven grades, where the grades on either side of grade four, the central grade, would mirror each other: Fifth-grade motifs would mirror those of third grade, in a different form; sixth-grade content would mirror second-grade content, and so on, the higher grade always taking up the themes of the lower and repeating them but in an advanced and age-appropriate way. "This would immensely enhance" (Steiner 1980, p. 203). One could argue that this can be done successfully only if the same teacher stays with the class for those years.

Around 14 years later, Rudolf Steiner expressed a similar thought, when he pointed out how fruitful and useful it was for teachers "to present a theme to children in their seventh or eighth year in a pictorial way and return to it in some way later, maybe in their twelfth or fourteenth year" (1965, p. 63)—yet another reason for grades teachers to stay with the same children for as long as possible. The transformation of teaching motifs, which are planted in seed-form one year and brought back to life and expanded on at a later level, enriches the lesson content and promotes more differentiated thinking (Zdražil 2013, p. 36).

Regarding the professional, methodical, and also educational deficits evidenced for grades teachers, particularly in seventh and eighth grades, and the hardly manageable demands of lesson preparation and specialist scientific competence, it can be helpful to turn to Steiner's basic ideas. It can only be in the interest of Waldorf education to ask direct questions about professional competence in order to avoid simply calling for perseverance, because more realistic solutions and ways forward that relieve the burden would be much more helpful and more beneficial to the young adolescents. "Professional com-petence" does not mean "one-sided specialization," as that would go against Steiner's understanding of the grades teacher role.

Even before he founded the first Waldorf school in 1919, Steiner formulated in three lectures a forward-looking education program that is remarkable from the point of view of professions theory, because it radically opposes the ideas people held at that time about school and the teaching profession (1996). He envisaged a school for *all* children from all social strata. Its education was to be rooted in a knowledge of the development of the human being from the change of teeth to puberty, since the laws governing that period were the same for everyone. Knowledge of these universal developmental laws, while observing each child's individual peculiarities, leads to an understanding of teaching targets, con-tent, and methods, as well as insight into what children should "achieve" at age 14 or 15 (ibid., p. 91). This radical departure from what school was traditionally meant to be therefore asked for new examin-ation guidelines for the teaching profession, no longer based on specialist knowledge but on the ability of teachers to establish a "productive" relationship with the students (ibid., p. 92). This unambiguous rejection of any subject specialization in favor of relationship specialization described the type of "grades teacher" that Steiner went on to detail in the preparatory courses for the first Waldorf faculty just before the opening of the first Waldorf school.

Steiner did not emulate the idea of the old-style class teacher, who could be found into the 1980s in rural Baden-Wurttemberg, teaching all eight grades in one classroom. Rather, he deliberately replaced specialist teachers who, in their one-sidedness, may easily lose sight of the universally human and cause social problems, by the kind of teacher who could look beyond their specific subjects at the whole. Future teacher examinations would value what the teacher is "as a human being" (Steiner 1996, p. 122). Steiner talked of this often as the first Waldorf school evolved (Zdražil 2013, p. 32ff.). Grades teachers in particular, he suggested, needed to develop from scientists into educational artists, or from the scientific to an artistic way of understanding the world (Steiner 1977a, p. 40). Everything depended on this enhanced humanity of teachers (Steiner 1975b, vol. 2, p. 74). The distinguishing feature of Waldorf (grades) teachers was not, however, that they were more humane while possessing only a superficial knowledge of the world, but that they continued, on the basis of scientific specialist competence, to develop as human beings, constantly widening their horizon and increasing their potential.

Steiner's understanding of the teaching profession is therefore based on the commitment to development with a clear goal in mind. To strive for, and possibly attain, this goal required not small steps but a comprehensive approach to life (Steiner 1975a, p. 123) that literally involved reaching for the stars, "Teachers today should have a thorough understanding of cosmic laws as a background to their teaching"—not, however, as a means of self-education in order to become better persons, but in order to be better able to understand human beings and their relationship, in body, soul and spirit, with the universe (Steiner 2020, p. 67).

These expectations that Steiner continued to develop emphatically in his various lectures on education hold not only impulses but also the potential for excessive workloads and stress. It can lead Waldorf teachers to ask much more of themselves than they can possibly manage in the reality of their professional life with its manifold challenges. There is also the danger of an overblown self-image of grades teachers and their "auratization" affecting the students negatively (Randoll 2013).

For Steiner, the (grades) teacher profession is tendentially risky—not a soft option but one that asks for full responsibility (Steiner 1992, p. 14). In the ideal case, the "art of education" meant reading in the child what needed to be taught and how. "You can read in the children what you have to do – not just each year, but each month, week, and ultimately, with a view to the individual, each day" (Steiner, 1975a, p. 135). Evidently, this can only succeed if teachers enable themselves to not only perceive the students' development but also understand and act on it in a way that is adequate in each individual case (Steiner 1985).

4 The concept of authority in Waldorf education

The concept of authority in Waldorf education, its effectiveness, and "danger of perversion" have been much scrutinized and discussed (Bohnsack 1996; Leber 1996, p. 160 ff.; Rumpf 1996). Continuing to recapitulate the oppositional discourse is hardly fertile since the topic has been largely exhausted and no new arguments can be expected in favor of either side. It is conceivably more promising to look more closely at what Steiner meant by "authority."

Steiner suggests that "the longing for an authority is part of the child's basic forces and feelings between the ages of 6 or 7 and 14 to 15" (1977b, p. 21). The "most essential educational principle, the most essential educational force" at that age was the child's belief "that the authority figure knows what is right and does what is right" (1979, p. 105). With this in mind, recent findings could also be of interest that clearly state the importance of a positive, reliable personality that can relate to children's willingness and ability to learn (Bauer 2007; Largo, Beglinger 2009; Struck 2010). Discussions around this ambiguous and historically problematic issue could relax, if Waldorf teachers, too, recognized that Steiner thought that the authority principle was only really effective between the ages of 9 and 12, because young people after that needed to increasingly develop their own judgment (Steiner 1977b, p. 82; Zdražil 2013, p. 34f.). Extending the authority principle in its pure form into eighth grade was definitely wrong and against the ideal of constant transformation as the only constant in the life of the grades teacher.

Regarding Waldorf-specific professional behavior, one needs to point out that the grades teacher's self-education is the only acceptable educational orientation, particularly when students reach early adolescence and tend to challenge the teacher's authority. The anecdote that Mahatma Gandhi only considered teaching others once he had rid himself of the "weakness" he expected others to rid themselves of can illustrate the educational effect of authority: Anyone who, like teachers, is active in the social sphere requires "two things: loving devotion to one's own actions, understanding for the actions of others" (Steiner 1975a, p. 134).

In order to meet these two requirements, teachers had to "behave around children in a way that enabled them, once the students reached puberty, to consciously experience what these two social mottos entail" (Steiner 1975a, p. 134). This could only happen with a teacher who practiced self-education and who understood what it meant "to stand beside the children in a way that enabled them to educate themselves in the best possible way" (ibid.). Top-down power ambitions are here replaced by the idea of two individuals standing side by side, where the one's striving for self-education is noticed by the other and becomes the latter's guiding image. The concept of the grades teacher's authority can then be defined, as intended by Steiner, as education "in freedom."

The grades teacher's potential and willingness for development have consequently a strong educational and guiding impact, enabling children to develop in freedom and to experience what responsible behavior in adult life means: learning from life and always being ready to change. If this potential role-model effect comes to bear, it casts light on the ideal of the grades teacher principle. Helmut Fend may have had this in mind when he declared that it was more important for young people to find their own identity than to accumulate knowledge. For this, "the young people look for role models, 'successful embodiments of coping with life.' Teachers can be such role models if they present certainty, 'fearlessness,' and resilience in their relation to the young people (one could call it personal authority, as opposed to official authority)" (Bohnsack 2009, p. 89; Fend 2005, p. 462f.).

In opposition to Ullrich's unverified yet repeatedly made allegation that "the anthroposophical dogma of reincarnation and karma" provided the "ultimate justification for holding on to the eight-year destiny community of Waldorf grades with their grades teachers" (2015, p. 48), the grades teacher principle can and should only be seen on the basis of its intended educational effect. It serves the developmental and educational needs young people have, in which the grades teacher endeavors to provide crucial support.

5 Reflections from the point of view of professions theory

Steiner's understanding of the teaching profession is entirely optimistic. He relies above all on the individual teacher's "will for self-development," their sense of responsibility and motivation to educate themselves. Steiner's idea of a self-managed school organism expects teachers to take full responsibility for their teaching and to derive the motives for their teaching, which should always be educational and support development, directly from the encounter with the students. Steiner therefore refrained from presenting a standard "curriculum" in his preparatory course for the first Waldorf teachers. Instead, he restricted himself, then and in the subsequent faculty meetings, to indications and impulses that the teachers could develop further, depending on their individual possibilities.

The "guiding thoughts" that Steiner formulated in 1919, at the end of that preparatory course for the founding faculty of the first Waldorf school, were meant to inspire self-empowerment in the teachers: "Imbue yourself with the power of imagination. Have courage for the truth. Sharpen your feeling for responsibility of soul!" (2020, p. 310). Steiner then presented four further ideals to the teachers: "You must be a person of initiative [...] teachers must have an interest in everything that is going on in the world and that concerns humankind. [...] Never make within yourself any compromises with the truth. [...] Never turn stale and sour" (2020, p. 346).

This "practicing" of reflection on ethical virtues in teaching can, of course, not be prescribed but needs to be chosen by the individual teacher out of their own freedom. If teachers use it, however, and keep drawing strength from it in their daily professional life, this will have an influence on their agency and, as has been demonstrated in studies on "teaching competences and professional success" (Peters in Chapter 6), result in a positive impact not only on their job satisfaction but also on the way they are perceived by their students.

The implementation of Waldorf education clearly depends to a high degree on the teachers' individual "impulse to self-educate." There is not one single way of delivering Waldorf education, and there is no such thing as *the* Waldorf school. Waldorf education is consequently a highly risky undertaking if any form of routine narrows this individual impulse down and hinders it or if it is restricted by external political, economic, and societal demands—or even if Steiner's works are seen as normative (Wiechert 2010). It was Steiner's central concern that each individual teacher should have full responsibility, for the whole and for social balancing in the weekly faculty meetings, so that individual interests could come together in the joint observation of the whole and goals, tasks, and obligations be embraced together. The weekly faculty meetings were a very optimistic creation, introduced by Steiner in 1919 when the first Waldorf school was founded, which he led, corrected, and constantly adjusted up until the fall of 1924 (Steiner 1975b).

As the Waldorf school evolved, signs of fatigue appeared in all areas of its structured, teacher-led self-management. While people are happy with the system in general, decision-making processes are often experienced as onerous (Randoll 2013, p. 159ff.).

In the early years of the Waldorf school movement, the grades teacher position gained ever greater prominence, a process that was enhanced by the role-model effect of important personalities who devoted their individual talents wholly to the development of the Waldorf school and were therefore rightly seen as representing the school's identity (Tautz 1979). It also had the effect, however, that a valuable educational maxim of the school's foundation was ignored and grades teachers attributed an "aura" of specialness (Idel 2007).

As a result, very dominant grades teacher personalities appeared here and there, indeed acting at times like "monarchs" and often being questioned by neither parents nor colleagues. Ullrich and other authors have repeatedly, and with a certain relentlessness, referred to the negative implications of such an unbalanced position of grades teachers (most recently summarized by Ullrich 2015).

The question is whether the entire grades teacher principle needs to be called into question because of this. It is certainly justified to ask for approaches that are more in tune with our time, such as inclusive ways of teaching and inclusive types of school, considering intercultural pedagogical tasks and new forms of collegial collaboration that include everyone involved in the educational process.

As a result of changes in society, what is expected of teachers has become far more complex in the past 30 years. Exposed as they are, grades teachers lose confidence for various reasons, not because they are pedagogical "special cases" of the modern type or relics of a bygone patriarchy, but because they have to possess or develop multiple skills to meet the expectations of a traditional profession. In his analysis in the theory of professions, Helsper mentions diverse expectations that grades teachers are meant to meet. They include the provision of a stress-free environment for children who are stressed by demands, and of learning and social spaces where the children can learn in freedom, in a holistic and community-oriented way, and in accordance with their developmental rhythms. Grades teachers are moreover expected to act as role models and convey orientation and a sense of safety in the face of a plural, uncertain, complicated, and unstable social world. Given the elusiveness and fragility of emotional childhood relationships, grades teachers are also expected to enable trusting and reliable pedagogical relationship as a foundation for children to build their emotional self (Helsper 2007, p. 483).

Tenorth suggests that the main task of the teacher is to enable teaching and to create the conditions for learning in the sense of increasing knowledge (Baumert, Kunter 2006, p. 472). As "universalists," grades teachers will probably, from seventh or eighth grade, reach the boundaries of their subject-related knowledge and of their methodical and didactic skills (Helsper 2007, p. 488f.), but these are problems that cannot be generalized because every grades teacher is different. A considerable number of them studied education or another academic subject at university before adding a Waldorf training and should therefore have the required scientific expertise (Randoll 2013, p. 79ff.).

Helsper's conclusion, which assigns an "explicitly traditional position" to the Waldorf grades teacher concept "with regard to both personal proximity and a canonized knowledge that is to be conveyed in an authoritative way" (2007, p. 488), may be justified in the theory of professions, but it ignores Steiner's differentiated understanding of authority described above, as well as the personal "pedagogical closeness," which is universally rated as a positive stabilizing factor for successful learning.

In addition, such a view fails to recognize the effective understanding of a Waldorf school "curriculum" that does not constitute a rigid canon that is to be understood and implemented. Past editions of the Waldorf curriculum first published in 1992 don't have a very long half-life (Richter 2010). In 2016, a complete new edition of the "Richter Curriculum" was published with learning targets, methods, and tried and tested possible lesson content of Waldorf education, examined and presented, in horizontal and vertical order, by a large group of practicing Waldorf teachers. References to this curriculum as "canonized educational knowledge" (Ullrich 2015, p. 67ff.) are the result of a misunderstanding, perpetuated continuously since the 1980s, of Steiner's curricular indications and how they are to be used. It is interesting in this context that, up until 1992, the only orientation Waldorf schools had, aside from indications Steiner made, which were taken down in shorthand (Stockmeyer 1976), was a small 60-page summary brochure that Caroline von Heydebrand had composed in 1925 (Heydebrand 2009).

However, if the reference to a "canonized educational knowledge" is implicitly used to pay lip service to the technocratic-economic educational model and to use that model as a benchmark, the representatives of Waldorf education should point to the discourse that has flared up since PISA (Programme for International Student Assessment) on what education is meant to be. This discourse does by no means present convincing reasons for the technocratic-economic achievement-oriented kind of school. From that point of view, Waldorf education and its methods are certainly relevant and pertinent today (Rittelmeyer 2007, p. 97ff.).

With his thesis on the particular vulnerability of the grades teacher (Helsper 2007, p. 489), Werner Helsper certainly prompted a discussion at a time of complex pedagogical communication that has, for some years, been conducted intensively and at times also controversially. This has resulted in differentiated models of the grades teacher system, such as grades teachers being in charge of a class from first through sixth grades, after which the class transitions to the high school, where they are taught by subject teachers.

The results of further specific empirical studies in professions theory, which cast light on the relationship between families and grades teachers, for instance (Graßhoff 2008), or use biography research to interpret the professionalization of the grades teacher as a biographic project (Kunze 2011), highlight an array of demands for grades teachers that is inflated and, given finite individual resources, potentially depressing. Surprisingly, and tellingly, the job satisfaction of Waldorf teachers appears to be significantly more positive than that of their colleagues in mainstream schools (Randoll 2013).

Given the requirement, in a self-managed school, for the teachers' full application, the conflict between the desired individualization and collegial demands is basically preprogrammed at present. The work-life balance needs adjusting. Individual de-stressing strategies, such as turning down administrative tasks, quickly end in collegial conflict. The formulating of individual stress boundaries is seen as provocative given the urgent communal tasks that result from the unlimited scope of the pedagogical task (Randoll 2013). But there are also accounts by grades teachers who see their profession with its ups and downs as entirely beneficial for the students, the parents, and their own development (Keller, Loebell 2013).

6 Outlook and conclusions

These considerations will have illustrated that holding on rigidly to the traditional eight-year grades teacher model is no longer tenable, even if one ignores the weighty argument of subject-related deficits. These deficits are, by the way, easily remedied by the professional development options that have been offered for decades by Waldorf teacher education institutions at relatively little financial and personal expense.

Tradition alone can no longer serve as an argument, however. Professional Waldorf school management relies on individual skills and the willingness to undergo continuous professional development to keep educating oneself. The "joy of profession" (Wiechert 2010) is not to be dampened by rules that are informed by the past rather than by the future, by what is evolving, by the children, by rapidly changing childhood, by changing collegial forms of working, and by the dynamic life and relationship habits of families. This is why today conditions need to be created in which the grades teacher system, which is successful despite all the criticisms, and in which the teacher remains with the class "for as long as possible," can survive by being adjusted to the varying social and individual situations and to current results of learning research (Wiechert 2013).

Various conditions are therefore to be established for a successful and future-viable grades teacher model:

- The teaching profession—and the Waldorf grades teacher principle in particular—relies on the ability to form pedagogical relationships. Developing this ability is one of the central tasks of modern teacher education, in which self-education plays a crucial role (Schmelzer, see Chapter 6).
- This foundation is essential for acquiring the specific skills required by teachers for an inclusive and intercultural pedagogy.
- The grades teachers of today do not act like monarchs behind closed doors but as team players in an open collegial context.
- Collegial team building is essential and guarantees the ongoing internal evaluation of the teaching. Asking for and being offered help is integral to the school's culture. Intervision, supervision, and the kind of collaboration that allows for lesson observations by both colleagues and external advisers and mentors are possible forms of a collegial school culture.
- Grades teachers do not have to meet the all-encompassing (Comenian) teaching claim to the point of self-abandonment; instead, they have the possibility to let subject teacher colleagues take on main lessons, particularly in seventh and eighth grades.
- Collaboration with educational partners outside the school is informed by high transparency regarding the intended teaching goals, main lesson content, and learning methods. Accountability, a feedback culture, etc. are a given.
- Continuous professional development is not an obligation but a matter of course. The need for development and lifelong learning are essential parts of the teacher's professional ethos.
- Collegial collaboration and self-management are not restricted to delegations, structures, and forms; they are nurtured by mutual interest, the sense of responsibility for the school organism as a whole.

From the point of view of today's findings in developmental psychology and education science, the eight-year grades teacher system in Waldorf schools can be regarded not only as a very successful but also as a decidedly sustainable system of school education. Problems arise particularly in relation to the rigid insistence on the eight-year principle in some schools.

What is needed today is a more flexible approach with "grades teachers for six or eight years." Reflecting on the original impulse of Waldorf education can help to solve this problem. Studying this original impulse, as intended by Rudolf Steiner in 1919, reveals that there will never be "one" solution. The task of realizing Waldorf education and the Waldorf school depending on individual, regional, and political circumstances is one that falls to free individuals and a self-managed school community and will always lead to different forms and manifestations of the grades teacher concept.

Note

1 On the motif of "healing," cf. Steiner (1977a, p. 124f.) (Available in English as GA 302a, *Balance in Teaching*, SteinerBooks 2007, tr. René Querido, rev. Douglas Gerwin).

References

Barz, Heiner/Randoll, Dirk (Eds.) (2007): Absolventen von Waldorfschulen. Eine empirische Studie zu Bildung und Lebensgestaltung. Wiesbaden: Springer VS.

Bauer, Joachim (2007): Lob der Schule. Sieben Perspektiven für Schüler, Lehrer und Eltern. Hamburg: Hoffmann und Campe.

Baumert, Jürgen/Kunter, Mareike (2006): Stichwort: Professionelle Kompetenz von Lehrkräften. In: Zeitschrift für Erziehungswissenschaft 9, issue 4, pp. 469–520.

Bohnsack, Fritz (2009): Aufbauende Kräfte im Unterricht. Lehrerinterviews und empirische Belege. Bad Heilbrunn: Klinkhardt.

Bohnsack, Fritz (1996): Soziales Lernen als Weg zu einer Sozialkultur der Schule. In: Bohnsack, Fritz and Stefan Leber (Eds.) (1996): Sozial-Erziehung im Sozial-Verfall. Grundlagen, Kontroversen, Wege. Weinheim, Basel: Beltz, pp. 71–143.

Brücher, Gesine (2003): Das Engelberger Mittelstufenmodell. Entstehung, Gestaltung, offene Fragen. In: Erziehungskunst 66, pp. 408–415.

Eller, Helmut (1998): Der Klassenlehrer an der Waldorfschule. Stuttgart: Freies Geistesleben.

Fend, Helmut (2005): Entwicklungspsychologie des Jugendalters. 3rd edition. Wiesbaden: Springer VS.

Frielingsdorf, Volker (2012): Waldorfpädagogik in der Erziehungswissenschaft. Ein Überblick. Weinheim und Basel: Beltz Juventa.

Graßhoff, Gunther (2008): Zwischen Familie und Klassenlehrer. Pädagogische Generationsbeziehungen jugendlicher Waldorfschüler. Wiesbaden: Springer VS.

Helsper, Werner (2007): Das Waldorfklassenlehrerkonzept im Feld pädagogischer Kommunikation. In: Helsper, Werner/Ullrich, Heiner/Stelmaszyk, Bernhard/Höblich, Davina/Graßhoff, Gunther/Jung, Dana (2007): Autorität und Schule. Die empirische Rekonstruktion der Klassenlehrer-Schüler-Beziehung an Waldorfschulen. Wiesbaden: Springer VS, pp. 483–489.

Helsper, Werner/Ullrich, Heiner/Stelmaszyk, Bernhard/Höblich, Davina/Graßhoff, Gunther/Jung, Dana (2007): Autorität und Schule. Die empirische Rekonstruktion der Klassenlehrer-Schüler-Beziehung an Waldorfschulen. Wiesbaden: Springer VS.

Heydebrand, Caroline von (2009): Vom Lehrplan der Freien Waldorfschule. 11th edition. Stuttgart: Freies Geistesleben.

Höblich, Davina (2007): Bewahrung oder Revision des Klassenlehrerprinzips? – Professionstheoretische Perspektiven. In: Helsper, Werner/Ullrich, Heiner/Stelmaszyk, Bernhard/Höblich, Davina/Graßhoff, Gunther/Jung, Dana (2007): Autorität und Schule. Die empirische Rekonstruktion der KlassenlehrerSchüler-Beziehung an Waldorfschulen. Wiesbaden: Springer VS, pp. 527–532.

Idel, Till-Sebastian (2007): Waldorfschule und Schülerbiographie. Fallrekonstruktionen zur lebensgeschichtlichen Relevanz anthroposophischer Schulkultur. Wiesbaden: Springer VS.

Jacob, Sybille Ch./Drewes, Detlef (2004): Aus der Waldorfschule geplaudert: Warum die Steiner-Pädagogik keine Alternative ist. Aschaffenburg: Alibri.

Keller, Ulrike Luise/Loebell, Peter (2013): Der Klassenlehrer an Waldorfschulen – Auftrag, Sternstunden, Herausforderungen. In: Barz, Heiner, ed. (2013): Unterrichten an Waldorfschulen. Berufsbild Waldorflehrer: Neue Perspektiven zur Praxis, Forschung, Ausbildung. Wiesbaden: Springer VS, pp. 89–108.

Kruckelmann, Heinrich (2014): Nachteilige Folgen für die seelische Entwicklung. In: Erziehungskunst 78, issue 1, pp. 17–18.

Kunze, Katharina (2011): Professionalisierung als biographisches Projekt. Professionelle Deutungsmuster und biographische Ressourcen von Waldorflehrerinnen und -lehrern. Wiesbaden: Springer VS.

Largo, Remo/Beglinger, Martin (2009): Schülerjahre. Wie Kinder besser lernen. 4th edition. Munich: Piper.

Leber, Stefan (1996): Gesichtspunkte zur Sozialerziehung. In: Bohnsack, Fritz and Stefan Leber (Eds.) (1996): Sozial-Erziehung im Sozial-Verfall. Grundlagen, Kontroversen, Wege. Weinheim, Basel: Beltz, pp. 160–222.

Liebenwein, Sylvia/Barz, Heiner/Randoll, Dirk (Eds.) (2012): Bildungserfahrungen an Waldorfschulen. Eine empirische Studie zu Schulqualität und Lernerfahrungen. Wiesbaden: Springer VS.

Randoll, Dirk (Ed.) (2013): "Ich bin Waldorflehrer." Einstellungen, Erfahrungen, Diskussionspunkte – Eine Befragungsstudie. Wiesbaden: Springer VS.

Randoll, Dirk/Graudenz, Ines/Peters, Jürgen (2014): Die Klassenlehrerzeit aus der Sicht von Waldorfschülern – Eine Explorationsstudie. In: RoSE – Research on Steiner Education 5, issue 2, pp. 73–96.

Richter, Tobias (Ed.) (2010): Pädagogischer Auftrag und Unterrichtsziele – vom Lehrplan der Waldorfschule. 3rd edition. Stuttgart: Freies Geistesleben

Riethmüller, Walter (1993) Der Klassenlehrer an einer Waldorfschule, in: Leber, Stefan (Ed.) (1993): Waldorfschule heute. Einführung in die Lebensformen einer Pädagogik. Stuttgart: Freies Geistesleben, pp. 251–263.

Riethmüller, Walter (2011): Der Klassenlehrer. In: Loebell, Peter (Ed.) (2011): Waldorfschule heute. Eine Einführung. Stuttgart: Freies Geistesleben, pp. 171–185.

Riethmüller, Walter/Neal, Annette (2014): Kommentar zur Studie von Randoll, Dirk/Graudenz, Ines/Peters, Jürgen: Die Klassenlehrerzeit aus der Sicht von Waldorfschülern – Eine Explorationsstudie. In: RoSE – Research on Steiner Education 5, issue 2, pp. I–IV.

Rittelmeyer, Christian (2007): Kindheit in Bedrängnis. Zwischen Kulturindustrie und technokratischer Bildungsreform. Stuttgart: Kohlhammer.

Röh, Claus-Peter/Thomas, Robert (Eds.) (2015): Unterricht gestalten – im 1. bis 8. Schuljahr der Waldorf-/Rudolf-Steiner-Schulen. Arbeitshilfen für den Hauptunterricht. Überblick über den Fachunterricht, Anregungen zur Klassenführung und zur Elternarbeit. 4th revised edition. Dornach: Verlag am Goetheanum.

Rudolph, Charlotte (1987): Waldorf-Erziehung. Wege zur Versteinerung. Berlin: Luchterhand.

Rumpf, Horst (1996): Einfühlsam vertretene Grenzen … Über Normen, Autorität, Verlässlichkeit in der Sozialerziehung aus psychoanalytischer Sicht. In: Bohnsack, Fritz and Stefan Leber (Eds.) (1996): SozialErziehung im Sozial-Verfall. Grundlagen, Kontroversen, Wege. Weinheim, Basel: Beltz, pp. 227–234.

Steiner, Rudolf (1961): Freie Schule und Dreigliederung. In: Steiner, Rudolf (1961): Aufsätze über die Dreigliederung des sozialen Organismus und zur Zeitlage 1915–1921. Rudolf Steiner GA 24. Dornach: Rudolf Steiner Verlag, pp. 35–44.

Steiner, Rudolf (1965): Der pädagogische Wert der Menschenerkenntnis und der Kulturwert der Pädagogik. Zehn Vorträge, gehalten in Arnheim vom 17. bis 24. Juli 1924. GA 311. Dornach: Rudolf Steiner Verlag.

Steiner, Rudolf (1975a): Die pädagogische Praxis vom Gesichtspunkte geisteswissenschaftlicher Menschenerkenntnis. Acht Vorträge, gehalten vom 15. bis 22. April 1922. GA 306. Dornach: Rudolf Steiner Verlag. English: Steiner, Rudolf (1996): The Child's Changing Consciousness as the Basis of Pedagogical Practice, trans. Roland Everett, Hudson NY: SteinerBooks.

Steiner, Rudolf (1975b): Konferenzen mit den Lehrern der Freien Waldorfschule in Stuttgart 1919 bis 1924. Bd. 1 bis 3. GA 300. Dornach: Rudolf Steiner Verlag.

Steiner, Rudolf (1977a): Erziehung und Unterricht aus Menschenerkenntnis. Neun Vorträge, gehalten für die Lehrer der Freien Waldorfschule in Stuttgart. GA 302a. Dornach: Rudolf Steiner Verlag.

Steiner, Rudolf (1977b): Die Erneuerung der pädagogisch-didaktischen Kunst durch Geisteswissenschaft. Vierzehn Vorträge gehalten für Lehrer und Lehrerinnen Basels und Umgebung, 20. April bis 11. Mai 1920. GA 301. Dornach: Rudolf Steiner Verlag.

Steiner, Rudolf (1977c): Erziehungskunst. Seminarbesprechungen und Lehrplanvorträge, gehalten in Stuttgart vom 21. August bis 6. September 1919 anlässlich der Gründung der Freien Waldorfschule. GA 295. Dornach: Rudolf Steiner Verlag.

Steiner, Rudolf (1979): Erziehungs- und Unterrichtsmethoden auf anthroposophischer Grundlage. Neun öffentliche Vorträge, gehalten zwischen dem 23. Februar 1921 und 16. September 1922 in verschiedenen Städten. GA 304. Dornach: Rudolf Steiner Verlag.

Steiner, Rudolf (1980): Anthroposophie – Psychosophie – Pneumatosophie. 12 Vorträge, gehalten in Berlin, 1909 bis 1911. GA 115. Dornach: Rudolf Steiner Verlag.

Steiner, Rudolf (1985): Notwendigkeit und Freiheit im Handeln (30.1.1916). In: Rudolf Steiner (Ed.) (1985): Elemente der Erziehungskunst: Menschenkundliche Grundlagen der Waldorfpädagogik. Vorträge. Ausgew. und hrsg. von K. Rittersbacher. Stuttgart: Freies Geistesleben, S. 167–187.

Steiner, Rudolf (1992): Allgemeine Menschenkunde als Grundlage der Pädagogik. Vierzehn Vorträge, gehalten in Stuttgart vom 21. August bis 5. September 1919 und eine Ansprache vom 20. August 1919. GA 293. Dornach: Rudolf Steiner Verlag.

Steiner, Rudolf (1996): Geisteswissenschaftliche Behandlung sozialer und pädagogischer Fragen. Siebzehn Vorträge, gehalten in Stuttgart zwischen dem 21. April und 28. September 1919, darunter „Drei Vorträge über Volkspädagogik." TB 733 (GA 192). Dornach: Rudolf Steiner Verlag.

English translation: Steiner, Rudolf (2020): The First Teachers' Course. Anthropological Foundations-Methods of Teaching-Practical Discussions. GA 293–295, trans. Margot M. Saar. Bangkok: Ratayakom.

Stockmeyer, E. A. Karl (1976): Rudolf Steiners Lehrplan für die Waldorfschulen. Versuch einer Zusammenschau für die Arbeit der Lehrerkollegien. Stuttgart: Pädagogische Forschungsstelle beim Bund der Freien Waldorfschulen.

Struck, Peter (1994): Neue Lehrer braucht das Land. Ein Plädoyer für eine zeitgemäße Schule. Darmstadt: Wissenschaftliche Buchgesellschaft.

Struck, Peter (2010): Erziehung und Bildung in einer beschäftigungsärmer werdenden Gesellschaft. Handout eines Bundeskongresses der Evangelischen Schulen vom September 2010. Online at www.schulstiftung-ekm.de/aktuelles/bundeskongress/handouts/ (accessed in May 2016).

Tautz, Johannes (1979): Der Lehrerkreis um Rudolf Steiner in der ersten Waldorfschule. 2nd expanded edition. Stuttgart: Freies Geistesleben.

Ullrich, Heiner (2007a): Der Klassenlehrer in der Freien Waldorfschule. In: Helsper, Werner/Ullrich, Heiner/Stelmaszyk, Bernhard/Höblich, Davina/Graßhoff, Gunther/Jung, Dana (2007): Autorität und Schule. Die empirische Rekonstruktion der Klassenlehrer-Schüler-Beziehung an Waldorfschulen. Wiesbaden: Springer VS, pp. 79–118.

Ullrich, Heiner (2007b): Fachwissen und Bildung der Person. In: Helsper, Werner/Ullrich, Heiner/Stelmaszyk, Bernhard/Höblich, Davina/Graßhoff, Gunther/Jung, Dana (2007): Autorität und Schule. Die empirische Rekonstruktion der Klassenlehrer-Schüler-Beziehung an Waldorfschulen. Wiesbaden: Springer VS, pp. 500–506.

Ullrich, Heiner (2015): Waldorfpädagogik. Eine kritische Einführung. Weinheim, Basel: Beltz.

Wiechert, Christof (2010): Lust aufs Lehrersein?! Eine Ermutigung zum (Waldorf) Lehrerberuf. Dornach: Verlag am Goetheanum. English translation: Wiechert, Christof (2021): Teaching, The Joy of Profession: An Invitation to Enhance Your Waldorf Interest, trans. Dorit Winter, Dornach: Verlag am Goetheanum

Wiechert, Christof (2013): Aspekte eines erneuerten Lehrerbildes in den Waldorfschulen. In: Rundbrief der Pädagogischen Sektion am Goetheanum 49, pp. 39–48.

Zdražil, Tomas (2013): Klassenlehrer über acht Jahre. In: Rundbrief der Pädagogischen Sektion am Goetheanum.

TEACHER COMPETENCIES AND PROFESSIONAL SUCCESS

Ex-post Findings from Dirk Randoll's Waldorf Teacher Study

Jürgen Peters

1 Problem, goals, and method

In the past ten years, the professionalization of teachers has moved increasingly into the focus of research. Hüther's call for the unfolding of educational potential, which is only possible with intrinsic motivation (Hüther 2013), can therefore also be seen in connection with the lifelong development of teacher competences. Steiner's demands of the first Waldorf teachers that they should develop competences (Steiner 2015) are also to be seen as a call for professionalization. They have a characteristic, though not exclusive, relationship with Waldorf education. Steiner mentioned seven competences in all that he saw as particularly relevant to Waldorf teachers (ibid., p. 202 ff.):

- imagination and creativity
- integrity
- social responsibility
- initiative
- positivity
- interest in the world (contemporaneity)
- conscious engagement with compromises

One could also add a pedagogical attitude that expects teachers to acquire a spiritual understanding of the "evolving human being" (Steiner 2015, p. 16). This attitude, which aims at child development, has a particular relation to the unfolding of potential.

This inquiry looks at the relevance of the individual competences mentioned by Steiner in relation to professional success and resilience, in as much as these competences can be operationalized ex post from the questionnaire Randoll used for his Waldorf Teacher Study (Randoll 2012). It is consequently meant as a preliminary exploration to a further inquiry with a wider and more appropriate operationalization. The question here is whether a positive link exists between the competences demanded by Steiner and professional success on the one hand and resilience on the other, and whether similar effects can be found for professional competence. Data from Randoll's Waldorf Teacher Study have been used for this with the author's kind permission. In the course of that study, 1807 teachers in Waldorf schools were asked about working conditions, job satisfaction, stress, about their health, and other aspects (Randoll 2012).

Assessment of the items revealed that the competences "imagination and ability to inspire enthusiasm," "initiative and personal responsibility," and "spiritual orientation" could be established in each

DOI: 10.4324/9781003187431-29

case using three questions. A fourth parameter, "professional competence," was also operationalized as a control:

Operationalization of the competence "imagination and ability to inspire enthusiasm":

- "I can inspire enthusiasm for projects in the students."
- "I can rely on my intuition in lessons."
- "I can also involve difficult pupils in the lessons."

Operationalization for "spiritual orientation":

- "How important is anthroposophy in your job?"
- "I feel stronger when I trust in superordinated perspectives."
- "What is your relationship to anthroposophy?"

Operationalization of the competence "initiative and personal responsibility":

- "I feel that I am involved in shaping the school."
- "I have personal decision-making competences."
- "I can convince even skeptical colleagues of innovative changes."

Operationalization for the control parameter "professional competence":

- "I am equal to the professional demands in the lessons."
- "I am satisfied with the professional level of the content of my lessons."
- "I can apply my knowledge and skills in my work."

Two reference groups were formed in order to identify the relevance of these competences. All questions were assessed on a four-point Likert scale (applies fully—applies somewhat—hardly applies—does not apply at all). The majority of responses were spread across the categories "applies fully" and "applies somewhat." The reference groups were therefore divided as follows: If one of the three items "applies fully" was chosen at least twice and "applies somewhat" once at the most, the competence in question was categorized as "distinctly present." The remainder of the group was summarized as "not distinctly present" regarding the competence in question. Distinguishing purely between the categories "applies fully" and "applies somewhat" would have resulted in the case numbers for the "agree fully" group to be no longer reliable. The division is therefore a compromise and owed to the ex-post design. In a further study, the response scales would have to have more options.

2 General findings

Based on 1807 data sets with the distinctions described above, Randoll's Waldorf Teacher Study (Randoll 2013) showed the following frequency distribution for the distinct presence of the chosen competences:

All findings shown in Figure 6.1 are based on the teachers' self-assessments. The small proportion of teachers who, according to their self-assessment, had fully developed the competence "imagination and enthusiasm" is not to be seen as a negative result because, on the one hand, the group division described above was due to the data structure and, on the other hand, inaccuracy remains as to the benchmarks applied by the individual teachers in their self-assessment. It can therefore not be concluded from Figure 6.1 that the competences specified by Rudolf Steiner are only present to a small degree in Waldorf teachers. This inquiry rather seeks to establish if these two reference groups differ with regard to further distinguishing factors. The relatively low figure of 13.9 percent for the distinct presence of imagination and enthusiasm does, after all, correspond to 251 cases so that the groups are certainly comparable.

Teacher Competencies and Professional Success

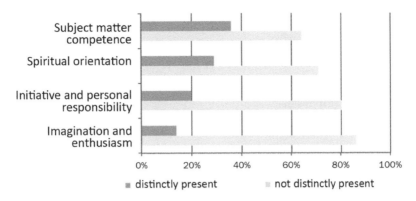

Figure 6.1 Frequencies of distinct presence of individual competences

Teachers in Waldorf schools have undergone different kinds of teacher education. According to the Waldorf Teacher Study, 44.5 percent of Waldorf teachers attended full-time teacher education (Randoll 2013, p. 82); 80.4 percent of the teachers asked said they had done some kind of Waldorf training (Randoll 2013, p. 81). Figure 6.2 shows the presence of the competences depending on full-time Waldorf teacher education:

The bars in Figure 6.2 show the proportion of teachers who, according to their own statements, developed the relevant competence to a high degree. The illustration reveals a (highly) significant deviation for spiritual orientation. Spiritual orientation is more distinctly present in teachers who completed full-time Waldorf teacher education. This does not necessarily suggest that this orientation was developed during their training; it could have been present before and have led to the choice of training.

As is apparent from Figure 6.3, choosing former professional training as a distinguishing feature leads to a remarkable result for the competence "imagination and ability to inspire enthusiasm."

Again, the bars in Figure 6.3 reflect the proportion of teachers who, according to their own assessment, developed the competence in question to a high degree. The significant rise for the distinct presence of the competence "imagination and enthusiasm" suggests that practical professional training enhances the power of imagination or that teachers with a practical professional training evidently find it easier to develop imagination and creativity in their teaching. For spiritual orientation, too, there is a tendentially higher presence for the group of teachers with professional training.

Finally, Figure 6.4 shows how the different competence levels relate to the teachers' self-evaluation, and to what extent teachers feel their training has prepared them well for their job.

Figure 6.4 illustrates that all the competences examined here are related to vocational preparation. This is most evident for "subject matter competence": 69.1 percent of teachers, who developed this

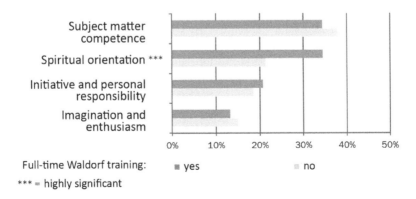

Figure 6.2 Distinct competence development and training routes

339

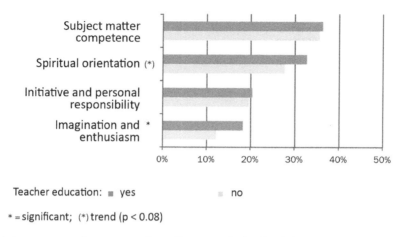

Figure 6.3 Distinct presence of competence depending on professional training

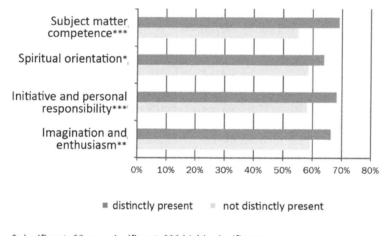

Figure 6.4 Competences and vocational preparation: "Do you feel your training has adequately prepared you for your job?"

competence to a high degree, feel sufficiently prepared for their job as a result of their training, while only 55.2 percent of the comparison group say this of themselves. While this finding is hardly surprising, it highlights the importance of subject matter competence in Waldorf teachers. The differences for the competence "initiative and personal responsibility" are also very marked: 68.2 percent of teachers who developed this competence to a high degree feel they are sufficiently prepared for their work, while only 58.2 percent in the comparison group claim this for themselves. Somewhat lower but still significant are the differences for the competences "spiritual orientation"—63.9 percent and 57.6 percent, respectively—and "imagination and enthusiasm"—66.3 percent (with a strong presence of this competence) and 59.2 percent, respectively.

3 Competences and professional success

The different assessment of the teachers' own vocational preparation suggests that the four competences under consideration are related to the experience of professional success. Experiencing professional success is a multi-dimensional quantity that cannot be expressed in a few parameters. However, for

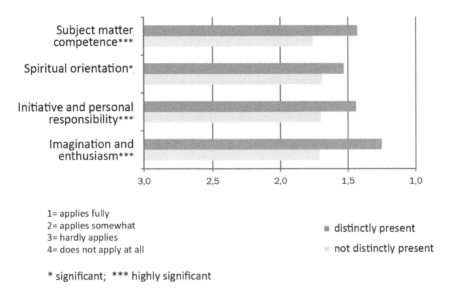

Figure 6.5 Competences and recognition by students: "I feel respected and recognized by my students."

an explorative approach as the one chosen here, selecting a few factors is nonetheless relevant. Again, the variables were chosen as to their ability to be mapped well in a questionnaire. On the one hand, two items were chosen for this which are oriented to the recognition of the teachers' work:

- recognition by the students
- appreciation from colleagues

On the other hand, the factor "experiencing professional success" was examined as one of the constituent features of the AVEM[1] typology. This typology will be discussed in more detail in the next chapter.

Figure 6.5 shows the link between competences and recognition by students. It lists the individual mean values of the comparison groups on a 4-point Likert scale, from 1 = "applies fully" to 4 = "does not apply at all."

Figure 6.5 illustrates that a more thorough development of all four competences corresponds significantly with recognition by students. The differences are most evident for the competence "imagination and enthusiasm": The mean value for the group of teachers who developed this competence to a high degree is 1.25 compared to 1.71 in the other group. For "subject matter competence" (mean values: 1.43 and 1.76) and "initiative and responsibility" (mean values: 1.44 and 1.70), the differences are also highly significant. In percentages: 74.9 percent ("applies fully") of teachers who developed the competence "imagination and enthusiasm" to a high degree felt they were respected and recognized by their students (33.6 percent in the comparison group). For "subject matter competence," the percentages are 54.9 percent (also "applies fully") and 32.6 percent; and for the competence "initiative and personal responsibility," 58.0 percent agree (compared to 34.7 percent). For "spiritual orientation," the results for full agreement, 49.5 percent compared to 35.2 percent, are more closely together. "Subject matter competence," "initiative," and above all "the capacity to inspire enthusiasm" are consequently noticed by the students and mirrored positively to the teachers.

The results showing the appreciation of a teacher's work by their colleagues are shown in Figure 6.6.

Figure 6.6 shows no noticeable link between the appreciation of a teacher's work within the faculty and spiritual orientation. There are obvious differences for the competence "initiative and personal responsibility" (mean values: 1.38 and 1.91, respectively), and for "subject matter competence" (mean values: 1.62 and 1.91, respectively). This means that 64.0 percent of teachers with a high degree of

Jürgen Peters

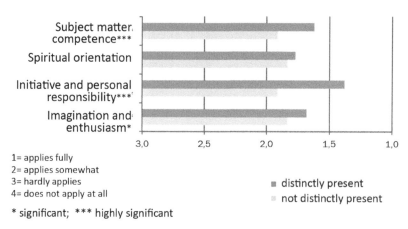

Figure 6.6 Appreciation of the teacher's work within the faculty: "I am satisfied with the appreciation of my work within the faculty."

"initiative" fully agree with the statement, as compared to 35.3 percent in the other group of teachers. For "subject matter competence," 45.8 percent (and 27.5 percent, respectively) express full agreement. For the equally significant "enthusiasm and creativity," 46.4 percent (distinct presence) and 30.8 percent, respectively, agree fully. As well as "subject matter competence," colleagues therefore find "initiative" most important. This is presumably due to the importance of self-management in Waldorf schools.

Appreciation on the part of parents was also investigated. This also increases significantly with distinctly present competences, but the scaling differences are not as pronounced as with the feedback from students and colleagues, because parents tend to generally be appreciative of the work of Waldorf teachers.

The following diagram reflects the link between the competences and the "experience of professional success." This variable is 1 of 11 standardized AVEM features (the AVEM typology will be discussed in more detail in the following section). The 9-point scale follows the presentation of Schaarschmidt (2005) and contains a vocation-specific standardization of teachers. Points 1–3 represent below-average, points 7–9 above-average presence of occupational success experiences. The value 5 corresponds to the mean of 16,000 teachers in regular schools assessed in the Potsdam Teacher Study (Schaarschmidt 2005).

Figure 6.7 demonstrates that the mean values for all four groups with distinctly present competences are clearly above the total mean of 5; for the competences "initiative and personal responsibility" and

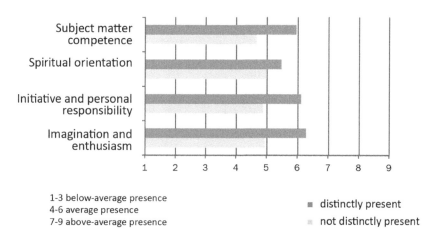

Figure 6.7 Competences and experiences of professional success (AVEM feature)

Teacher Competencies and Professional Success

"imagination and enthusiasm" they are even above 6. All differences are highly significant, although those for "spiritual orientation" are lower than for the other factors. "Subject matter competence," "initiative and personal responsibility," and "imagination and enthusiasm" are therefore clearly connected with the experience of professional success. This is in line with the results presented above regarding preparation for the working life through training.

4 The link between competences and resilience

Randoll's Waldorf Teacher Study also examines the AVEM typology (Peters 2013) introduced by Schaarschmidt (2005), which distinguishes four work-related behavior patterns: the G pattern (for *gesund*, meaning "healthy"), which reflects high commitment and high resilience; the S pattern (for "self-care" or "self-mindfulness"), a type that avoids excessive stress.[2] Then there are two "risk patterns": the A pattern (*Anstrengung* = effort), which describes the classic "workaholic," that is, someone who shows high commitment with low ability to distance themselves; and the B pattern (risk of burnout), which describes behaviors of inner withdrawal and resignation. In Schaarschmidt's Potsdam Teacher Study, the percentage of both risk patterns was 59 percent in state schoolteachers, making teachers the professional group with the highest stress levels.

The proportion of risk patterns within the Waldorf Teacher Study amounted to around 50 percent, that is 9 percent lower than for state schoolteachers. The exact distribution of the individual patterns was: G (healthy) pattern, 17 percent; S (self-care) pattern, 33 percent; A (effort) pattern, 27 percent; and B (burnout) pattern, 23 percent.

Figure 6.8 represents the proportion of risk patterns in connection with the competences.

Figure 6.8 shows considerably lower proportions of risk patterns for higher degrees of subject matter competence, as well as for "initiative and personal responsibility" and for "imagination and enthusiasm." The differences are 19.3 percent for subject matter competence, followed by 17.5 percent for "initiative and personal responsibility," and 13.1 percent for "imagination and enthusiasm." The difference for spiritual orientation is still 5.5 percent. This is a clear result overall, which reveals that subject matter competence, initiative, and the capacity for enthusiasm are closely linked to teachers' mental and physical health. One needs to add that the proportion of the problematic B pattern, in particular, is decreasing. While for the entire sample of Waldorf teachers the B pattern was 23.1 percent, the groups with a high degree of competences only have the following B-pattern proportions: spiritual orientation 16.1 percent; subject matter competence 12.3 percent, initiative 9.0 percent, and, lastly, enthusiasm 7.8 percent. The proportion of the resignation pattern B is therefore clearly decreasing.

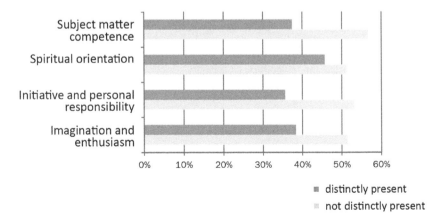

Figure 6.8 Competences and AVEM risk patterns

Jürgen Peters

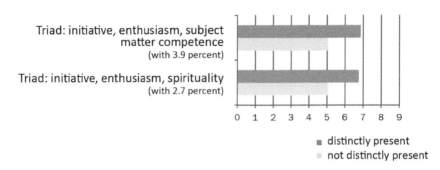

Figure 6.9 Triad of competences and experience of professional success (AVEM)

The final question concerns the modifications that can be observed with simultaneous high degrees of several competences. Two variant groups are being examined for this: firstly, the triad "enthusiasm – initiative – subject matter competence," and, secondly, "enthusiasm – initiative – spiritual orientation." The results in relation to professional success and the experience of stress are presented in the following two diagrams.

Like Figure 6.7, Figure 6.9 is also based on the 9-point scale of the Potsdam Teacher Study. The presence of several competences to higher degrees is closely linked with the experience of professional success; the mean values for these groups are above-average at >6. However, the triad as a whole only applies to 3.9 percent (2.7 percent, respectively) of teachers in Waldorf schools.

It is evident from Figure 6.10 that the proportion of risk patterns is considerably reduced for triads of competences: from around 50 percent to 32 percent and 26 percent, respectively. The proportion of B patterns has been almost fully, or fully, reduced. For the top triad, the proportion of B patterns is down to only 1.6 percent, in the lower one to 0 percent. In comparison, the A-pattern proportion has only gone down slightly.

5 Conclusion

The Waldorf-typical competences "initiative and personal responsibility" and "imagination and enthusiasm" are linked to the experience of professional success. The same is true for subject matter competence. Students relate in a particular way to the teachers' subject matter competence and their capacity to inspire enthusiasm, while colleagues seem to particularly appreciate "initiative and personal responsibility" as well as subject matter competence. The same two factors are especially relevant to the preparation for the job as teachers. There is a significant correlation for "spiritual orientation" with professional success, although that is less marked as for the other factors.

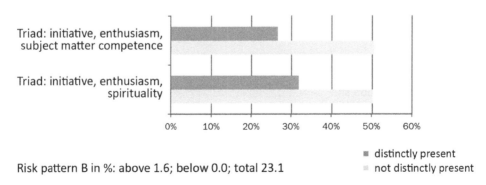

Figure 6.10 Triad of competences and proportions of AVEM risk patterns

Resilience and mental health can also be related to the competences, evidenced by the reduction of risk patterns in the AVEM distribution. Since more distinctly present competences coincide above all with a reduction in the B-pattern proportion, one can assume that there is a lower risk of burnout in this case. This is especially true for a more distinct presence of subject matter competence and of the competence "initiative and personal responsibility," but less so for "imagination and enthusiasm." The link is only very slight for "spiritual orientation." The effects described increase when several competences are present simultaneously to a higher degree. For the triad "initiative – enthusiasm – spiritual orientation," for instance, the B-pattern proportion is 0 percent. However, this combination is only found in 3 percent of teachers and constitutes nothing more than a tendency, given a case number of only 50.

According to this examination, it makes a difference for both professional success and mental health whether or not the four competences under consideration have been developed to average or above-average levels. Even if, due to the available data structure, the assessment of what exactly defines distinct presence and how precisely that differs from average presence can only be preliminary, it has become clear that the examined factors are linked to professional success and resilience. This certainly suggests that further research would be worthwhile.

It also needs to be pointed out that subject matter competence is similarly related to resilience as the two competences "initiative and personal responsibility" and "imagination and enthusiasm." While this may be surprising, it certainly highlights the importance of subject matter competence for teachers in Waldorf schools.

Notes

1 AVEM Arbeitsbezogenes Verhaltens- und Erlebensmuster (work-related behavior and experience pattern).
2 The self-care attitude described by Schaarschmidt, which is based on low commitment and a high ability to self-distance, could not be evidenced in this form for teachers in Waldorf schools, because even the Waldorf teachers allocated to the S pattern show medium commitment. The designation "self-mindfulness" was therefore added (Peters 2013).

References

Hüther, Gerald, (2013): Was wir sind und was wir sein könnten: Ein neurobiologischer Mutmacher. 6th edition. Frankfurt am Main: Fischer.
Peters, Jürgen (2013): Arbeitsbezogene Verhaltens- und Erlebensmuster, in: Randoll, Dirk (2013): "Ich bin Waldorflehrer." Einstellungen, Erfahrungen, Diskussionspunkte – Eine Befragungsstudie. Wiesbaden: VS, pp. 185–222.
Randoll, Dirk (Ed.) (2012): "Ich bin Waldorflehrer." Einstellungen, Erfahrungen, Diskussionspunkte – Eine Befragungsstudie. Wiesbaden: VS.
Schaarschmidt, Uwe (2005): Halbtagsjobber? Psychische Gesundheit im Lehrerberuf – Analyse eines veränderungswürdigen Zustands. Weinheim: Beltz.
Steiner, Rudolf (2015): Allgemeine Menschenkunde als Grundlage der Pädagogik. 9th edition. Dornach: Rudolf Steiner Verlag.

THE TEACHER'S PATH OF DEVELOPMENT
Toward Mindfulness in Education

Albert Schmelzer

1 Introduction

This contribution looks at the development of general personal competences that will be presented from the point of view of anthroposophy and Waldorf education. It first inquires into the discourse in education science that has recently highlighted the importance of the teacher's personality in the pedagogical process. Important basic personal competences are then described, with particular reference to "mindfulness" in education. This will be followed by a presentation of how the teaching profession is seen as a path of inner development in anthroposophically oriented pedagogy, and of personal qualities that seem worth striving for in this context. Finally, some of Rudolf Steiner's guidelines for practicing this inner development will be examined concerning their relevance to the teaching profession.

2 Personal competences in the education science discourse

The current interest in the development of personal skills in the pedagogical practice goes mainly back to the broad reception of John Hattie's (2009) book *Visible Learning*, which contains a synthesis of more than 800 meta-analyses based on over 50,000 empirical studies with around 250 million learners (Hattie 2009). Hattie's study proves impressively how immensely relevant the teacher's personality and the teacher's relationship with the students is for successful learning. The concurrent and subsequent discourse has made apparent that, as well as professional competences related to subject matter knowledge and methodical skills, general human and personal qualities are worth striving for (Krautz, Schieren 2013). Valuable developments have taken place in this respect, particularly in the approach to education based on mindfulness. The concept of mindfulness was inspired by Buddhism but has grown beyond this philosophical context and variously found entrance in psychosomatic medicine, psychotherapy, and education (Dauber 2010). Michael Huppertz' proposed definition describes the essence of this approach succinctly, "Mindfulness is an attitude that is as aware, unintentional, open as possible with regard to the current situation" (2009, p. 23). This characterization includes the following elements:

- *Awareness.* In this context, awareness means self-reflection and presence. Teachers need to be present in the moment, in body, soul, and mind, in the pedagogical process, and develop alertness and sensitivity in their relationship with the students (Dauber 2011, p. 11).
- *Unintentionality.* In education, this does not mean that one gives up on one's own intentions but "letting go inwardly and meeting what comes toward you without preconceptions – openly, receptively, but not at all passively" (Dauber 2010, p. 7).

The Teacher's Path of Development: Toward Mindfulness in Education

- *Openness.* Normally, we tend to constantly judge situations, things, and people we are dealing with in life, finding them helpful or dangerous, useful or useless, pleasant or unpleasant. Mindfulness, on the other hand, is an attitude that creates, for a moment, a space of non-judgmental perception, where the phenomena can speak but where we can also become conscious of involuntary feelings and judgments. Only after that moment do we react.
- *Presence.* Mindfulness means being present in what is going on in and around us: We are willing to give up our ideas of what should and should not be—ideas that come from the past—and to strive to act in ways that are not schematic or automatic but that original and new in each situation.

Given these different characterizations, mindfulness is an attitude worth striving for in teachers, an attitude that should ideally permeate their whole being. The educationist Heinrich Dauber distinguished four modes of consciousness that are relevant here:

- the "conscious perception of external sensory impressions (seeing, hearing, smelling, touching, tasting) in the sensing mode,"
- the "conscious perception of inner processes (feelings, thoughts, associations, visions) in the feeling mode,"
- the "conscious awareness of external situations and contextual conditions from an 'eccentric' observer position in analyzing mode,"
- the "conscious awareness of inner processes in self-reflection/meditation from the eccentric position of the inner witness in reflecting mode" (Dauber 2011, p. 6).

Similarly comprehensive and important as the forms of consciousness in which mindfulness can be effected is its practical application: It aims at the "self-chosen free attention in the relation to one's own history, to the world, and to our fellow humans" (ibid., p. 4). Ethical qualities such as empathy and compassion are guiding values here. In the sense of Erich Fromm's and Ivan Illich's radical humanism, schools as institutions are asked to what extent "they support or hinder the human ability to experience more liveliness and joy" (ibid., p. 12). Mindfulness implicates "respect for life in all our daily activities" (Dauber 2007, p. 135); at the center of mindful pedagogical practice "stands the unlocking of potentials as spaces of possibility" (ibid., p. 139) and the "opening up of new and further horizons of experience and reflection" (ibid., p. 144); "support that is appropriate to age and to the stage of development" (ibid., p. 144) is an essential postulate in this context.

Bearing such goals in mind, certain basic psychosocial competences appear essential for teachers: "the capacity for self-reflection, for empathy, for changing one's inner perspective, for distancing oneself inwardly, and for being mindful of one's inner, especially emotional, processes" (Dauber 2011, p. 11). Studies on salutogenesis in the teaching profession reveal that these competences also "contribute essentially to teacher health and enable teachers to teach in a way that is more oriented to the students" (ibid.). Based on the insight that the "mental resources mentioned need to be seen as an important part of the teacher's professional self" (ibid.), exercises have been developed to promote mindfulness in the context of education. They aim at the development of self-observation and self-reflection in team work, of non-judgmental participation in one's own pedagogical experiences and in those of others, of awareness of one's performance in front of a group of learners, and at practicing the ability to change one's inner perspective in collegial consultation (Dauber 2009).

If one considers these foundations for "mindfulness in education," their broad reception, and their implications for the image of the teacher and for teacher education, one can conclude that there is a growing awareness of the fact that—as well as subject-specific, methodical, didactic, and pedagogical competences such as knowledge of anthropology and developmental psychology, for instance—teachers need human qualities that are not naturally given but need to be acquired, again and again, and applied in the pedagogical process. It is precisely this aspect that, as we shall see, will make it possible to build a bridge from the education discourse to Waldorf education.

3 Anthroposophically oriented education as a path of development

Rudolf Steiner conceived Waldorf education as an "art" and was convinced that it was necessary for "education to become an art" (1977b, p. 12). This would be possible, he thought, if the principles of education science, which were basically correct, were permeated and quickened by the living concepts of anthroposophy (ibid., p. 13). Anthroposophy is for Steiner not a philosophical system, not an anthropology that claims objectivity, but a path on which one embarks to practice becoming conscious of one's own humanity (Steiner 1983, p. 76). In the context of the current discourse, one can see this approach also as an inspiration to develop mindfulness of one's own history, tasks, and potential.

This view has implications for education: In an anthroposophically oriented "art of education," one would "speak less of objective matters, of pedagogy and teaching as a science or art, and more of the children and young people who need to be educated and taught"; one would be more concerned with "knowing better what we are to each other, and particularly what the teacher is to the growing human being, to the child" (Steiner 1979a, p. 65). These words place the teacher's personality and the teacher's relationship with the students at the center of any pedagogical practice. The teacher's path of inner development is consequently crucial in teaching and education.

In 1920, in the first lecture of *Meditatively Acquired Anthropology*, Steiner phrases this thought even more radically: Successful teaching is always a developmental journey. Good teachers do not follow the "best masters of education" and do everything "to put these pedagogical principles into practice" (1977c, p. 18). The best teachers are those who "enter the classroom every morning nervously and hesitantly, who are not so sure of themselves, but who say to themselves at the end of the year: 'I'm the one who has learned most in this time.' [...] In life, not ready-made knowledge is of value but the effort that leads to this ready-made knowledge; and in the art of teaching this effort is particularly valuable. It is basically the same as with art. I don't think one can be a genuine artist, if one does not say once one has completed a piece: Only now am I able to do it" (ibid., p. 18ff.).

Comprehending the fundamental importance and relevance of these statements is essential, because they qualify concepts that see teaching and learning as mechanical processes, that are output oriented, and that rely radically on linear means-end causalities (Meinberg 1988). These concepts work with ideas that are based on past experience. Teaching, on the other hand, is *present encounter*; in the sense of mindful education, it requires presence of mind in conjunction with the willingness to leave past experiences and tried and tested concepts behind in order to open up to what is new and surprising. The education process is not enhanced by the sound confidence of the experienced "doer" but by the more cautious searching of the artist who, though well prepared, knows that it is impossible to plan the "fulfilled moment." Waldorf education is therefore the ever-new and ever-open searching for what Friedrich Copei called the "fertile moment in the educational process" (1950).

The following section looks at the qualities and skills that are important in this context.

4 Personal qualities and skills worth striving for

4.1 Enlivened anthropology

The earlier contributions (cf. Chapters 2 and 3) illustrate how important it is for Waldorf teachers to gain knowledge of anthropology and developmental psychology. This knowledge must, however, not remain purely theoretical; it must be applied in a living way in relation to the diversity of student personalities and pedagogical situations. In this striving for knowledge of anthropology and developmental psychology, Steiner's suggestion can be helpful that gaining an understanding of the different layers of human nature can be considerably enhanced with artistic practice (1974, p. 52ff.). Anatomy and physiology could only explain the physical body, Steiner thought; in order to understand the life body—that is to say, the formative element that carries the life organization and growth processes—it was helpful to enter into sculptural processes. Access to the soul body with its elementary sensations of pleasure and displeasure, joy and pain, and to the multilayered world of feelings could be found through music. And the "I," finally, lived in forces that are expressed in speech: One can think here of the different sound qualities, or orientations arising from the use of the active or passive voice, or of different tenses. It seems essential that such relations are not only considered in theory but that they are also experienced through artistic practice. Subjects such as sculpting, music, speech, and eurythmy are therefore an intrinsic part of Waldorf teacher education. Rudolf Steiner's request that teachers should study and meditate anthropology so that they can remember it in a living way in the lessons (1977c, p. 51ff.) illustrates the purpose of such artistic experiences: They aim to enhance the teacher's capacity for intuition, the ability to do the right thing in the right moment.

4.2 Connecting with the students

According to Steiner, this intense occupation with a living understanding of human nature also enhances the teacher's connection with the students. Teachers who cultivate "thoughts of the evolving human being" make a different impression on students than "those who never think such thoughts" (1973, p. 27). Not considering this aspect would mute "all that is pure personality spirit" (ibid.) and it was through "inner forces that a relationship is established between the students and the teacher" (ibid.).

These thoughts must not be seen as abstract—on the contrary: The Goetheanist Steiner envisaged teachers who develop a subtle perception for the students' physiology, gait, speech, gestures, and behavior. Steiner himself gave examples of such student characterizations, especially in *Education for Special Needs* (1975, p. 90ff.). Based on such examples and indications, "child studies" have been developed that are used both in special needs and regular Waldorf schools.[1] The ability to observe and empathize and use precise imagination with regard to each child's potential are as essential for this as knowledge of anthropology and developmental psychology.

Steiner summarized his ideas of the attitude to be aspired to in working with children succinctly, in a form that considers the temporal dimension of development and enables meditative reflection: "Reverence for what precedes the child's existence, enthusiastic anticipation for what follows the child. Protective gesture for the child's experiences" (1977c, p. 39).

4.3 Interest in and knowledge of the world

In addition to the tasks mentioned, teachers should also develop a lively interest in the world. "Teachers today should have a thorough understanding of cosmic laws as a background to their teaching" (Steiner 2020, p. 67). Lower-school teachers, too, should acquire knowledge of basic questions of cultural history and science, because "particularly in the lower grades, teachers must connect inwardly with humanity's most sublime ideas" (ibid.). In the same lecture, Steiner went on to describe motifs in the humanities and sciences that prevent humans from being seen as spiritual beings, as beings of initiative who can inspire new developments in evolution.

This explains what Steiner meant when he said that teachers should acquire broad general knowledge in order to understand the human being's position in the cosmos. Steiner himself said much about this in his work (Uhlenhoff 2011). Both the phenomenological approach to science and the symptomatologic method in the humanities start with the observing and experiencing person who can gain deeper insights through research and the meditative deepening of exemplary motifs and so develop their own view of the world. This should not be mere theory but "something that can flow like a soul force through the person's whole active being" (Steiner 1974, p. 58) so that "they can draw enthusiasm from it just like artists who are fulfilled by their art" (ibid., p. 59). On the way to developing this worldview, teachers needed—as well as a living interest in the world and joy in research and discovery—concentration, perceptiveness, and flexible thinking.

4.4 Breathing tuition. Preparing and reviewing lessons

The basic attitudes and skills described above are conditions for successful teaching. The wealth of cognitive and artistic skills successful teachers require were discussed in depth in the contributions on professionalism and didactics. Teachers must know their subjects; they should be able to speak, sing, tell stories, and draw chalkboard pictures well; over and above that, it is important that they know how to teach in a way that their lessons breathe, by using an artistic and rhythmic approach, and alternating between seriousness and humor, tension and relaxation (cf. Chapters 5 and 6). In addition to these tuition-related requirements, there are also some personal ones that should be mentioned briefly.

According to Steiner no lesson should be taught that "did not fully go through the teacher's mind before" (1986b, p. 191). It was therefore essential to create external conditions "that allow teachers enough time to fully experience for themselves what they are about to carry into school" ibid.). It seems advisable therefore to prepare lessons over a longer period of time. The Waldorf teacher Heinz Zimmermann suggests distinguishing between long-term, medium-term, and short-term preparation (1997, p. 16). He recommends that grades teachers look at the content of the entire following school year, without any pressure. "Once I have made a connection with it, I will continue to experience it, add to and deepen it over time, in conversations, and faculty studies. Then, during the vacation that precedes the planned main lesson, I work through the material a second time, establishing a plan for possible approaches and structures. Short-term preparation is the one I do day after day in preparing the actual lesson" (ibid.). It goes without saying that this kind of practice requires a high degree of conscious time management and self-discipline.

As well, thorough preparation, consistent reflection, and reviewing of one's lessons also contribute to successful teaching. Experience shows that once one has put something into practice one wishes to do it better, or at least differently, next time (Steiner 2020, p. 92). A very concrete conclusion can be drawn from this for one's lesson review: Teachers should take a moment to look back directly after a lesson. This calls impressions to awareness that would otherwise remain unconscious and that can now be used to enhance the teaching process.

4.5 Self-management as a chance to develop social skills

Waldorf schools are conceived as independent institutions, which mean that Waldorf teachers must contribute to the school's self-management. It is essential for this task that fruitful relations can be established between the individuals and the community. Steiner points out that Waldorf schools are not only characterized by "their real independence, by not even having a principal, but by the fact that the teaching faculty is a truly representative community" (1977a, p. 198). Relations between individuals and the community will not be fertile, however, in a state of unregulated chaos, where covert authorities try to impose their will, or in structures of formalized democratic decision-making, where the will of the whole dominates over individual initiative. The better way is for individual initiatives to be able become effective through delegation: The community gives an individual or a group a mandate for which they take responsibility. Mandate holders should, however, take into account what lives in the community. This approach requires initiative and willpower on the one hand, and objectivity, positivity, impartiality, self-control, and responsibility on the other so that a culture of encounter and cooperation can emerge.

5 How to practice?

The above considerations have taken us to sensitive, if not dangerous, terrain. For hardly anything has as paralyzing an effect as expectations that cannot be met. Soon, one ends up with the type of "ideologically destroyed teacher" that Anton Hügli describes in his critique of the development of virtues in mainstream teacher education: Teachers "who are unable to cope with their idealism in the day-to-day work" (1988, p. 147). Faced with such danger, the first remedy is that to become aware of it oneself; the second to ensure that one does not see striving for the qualities and skills mentioned as an obligation but as an invitation for personal development. The exercises introduced below are therefore not meant as a mandatory program but as guidelines for individual practice, in accordance with the individual teacher's changing biographical situations. They are a selection from numerous indications for practice given by Steiner and have been chosen with a view to their relevance to the teaching profession.

5.1 Developing thinking

The first exercise aims at promoting concentration and helps to develop factual and logical thinking. The idea is to achieve a situation where one is in charge of one's own thoughts and is able to direct one's own thinking. "Over a matter of months, if we can overcome ourselves to the point of being able to focus our thoughts for at least five minutes a day on some ordinary object (for example, a pin, a pencil, or the like), and if, during this time, we exclude all thoughts unrelated to this object, we will have made a big step in the right direction. (We can consider a new object each day or stay with the same one for several days)" (Steiner 1989, p. 330).

Steiner recommends that, when doing this exercise, one contemplates different aspects of the pencil or other object consecutively. One can start with sense-perceptible properties such as form, color, size, weight, or outer shape, then move on to think about the way it was manufactured, its inventor, function, and cultural significance. If necessary, one can consult an encyclopedia to find more information. The importance of this kind of exercise for the teacher's profession is evident. Both for preparing lessons and for teaching, particularly for facilitating conversations, teachers should be able to follow a thread of thoughts and not lose themselves in associations. They need to be objective rather than emotional in every phase of their teaching activity, especially if there are conflicts to deal with. This also includes the ability to tell whether one's own or another person's statement is a logical thought, mere opinion, or even a rationalized wish. In an age where we are increasingly exposed to floods of information, this exercise can help to develop a sense for the beneficial quality of independent thinking. It also enhances procedural thinking: Contemplating different properties of an object consecutively helps to not get stuck in static mental images; our thinking moves from one property to the next and becomes fluid and vibrant. And finally, this exercise of controlling our thoughts is also a will exercise: Doing it daily requires and enhances the power of initiative—thinking becomes permeated with will.

5.2 Strengthening the will

The next exercise concerns the will and aims to promote initiative and perseverance. It also helps to overcome heteronomy in that it prepares us to listen to our own voice rather than relying on instruction from others. Our actions should be guided by "laws of goodness and beauty" that we have recognized ourselves, enabling us to act out of freedom. "A good exercise is to tell ourselves to do something daily at a specific time, over a number of months: Today at this particular time I will do *this*. We then gradually become able to determine what to do and when to do it in a way that makes it possible to carry out the action in question with great precision. In this way, we rise above damaging thoughts, such as 'I'd like this, I want to do that' [...]" (Steiner 1997, p. 312).

It is easy to imagine how important initiative and strength of will are for the teaching profession. Teachers are often expected to be the driving force behind projects, class plays, and class trips. When they notice that students are struggling, they should also intervene early and provide support. The same is true for working with parents and contributing to the teacher-led school management: Apparent shortcomings must be dealt with early on. In independent schools such as Waldorf schools, the capacity for innovation is particularly important. At the same time, the opposite pole to willpower—a sense of duty and perseverance—is also called for. The pedagogue Walter Kling once said that authority was "the sum total of what is reliable minus the sum total of what is unreliable" (cited in Pelzer 1998, p. 39). All teachers and educators know how often this statement is corroborated by experience.

Considering all this, it appears to be essential for teachers to work on their strength of will. In this case, too, practicing the relevant exercise will have a positive side-effect. Carrying out an exercise daily at the same time requires attentiveness; if the ordinary stream of events is interrupted and consciousness arises in the stream of time, a cognitive element enters the will.

5.3 Equanimity

The third exercise concerns the feeling life: It helps to acquire a certain degree of composure rather than be carried away be extreme emotions, positive or negative. The idea is not to become unfeeling but on the contrary, "The soul should indeed rejoice when there is reason to rejoice, and it should feel pain when something sad happens. It is only meant to master its *expressions* of joy and sorrow, of pleasure and displeasure" (Steiner 1997, p. 313). Tranquility and equanimity should permeate the soul. The aim is to cultivate our feelings so that they are not expressions of our inner state but gradually develop into a cognitive organ for the phenomena in the world.

This is not an easy exercise. Florin Lowndes suggests doing it in three steps (Lowndes 1999, p. 96ff.). On the first day, one gains clarity of one's own feelings and their physical expression, such as turning red with anger or sweating when insecure or scared. On day two, one looks back on the previous day, asking which of these feelings one really experienced and in what kind of situation. On the third day, one looks ahead: What challenging situations may be encountered and how can one control one's own expressions of feeling? Doing this exercise makes us aware of how difficult it is to carry consciousness into the wide range of our feelings and the corresponding facial expressions and body language.

It is obvious how important it is for teachers to develop such "inner mindfulness." Involuntary bursts of anger, mood swings, and being caught in one's likes and dislikes—in short, any lack of self-control— are duly noted by the students and not easily forgiven. In fact, if teachers experience provocations and disturbances in their lessons, this can often be a call for them to develop tranquility and inner balance. Students appreciate equanimity in their teachers, especially if it comes with a sense of humor. The more teachers learn to deal with their own emotions, the greater their ability to empathize with others: a valuable quality for interacting with others and for teaching, for instance when it comes to understanding literary or historical figures. Being able to empathize is one of the most important teacher virtues. It requires awareness of one's own feelings and at least a degree of self-regulation.

5.4 Positivity

The positivity exercise follows on from the equanimity exercise. We tend to be quick to judge, classifying the world and others as good or bad, beautiful or ugly, clever or stupid. This attitude leads to a loss of differentiation, a quality that is particularly valuable in education. The positivity exercise helps to remain aware of the complexity of the world phenomena. "The erroneous, the bad, and the ugly must not prevent the soul from finding the true, the good, and the beautiful wherever they are present. [...] We cannot consider bad things good and false things true, but we can reach the point where the bad does not prevent us from seeing the good and errors do not keep us from seeing the truth" (Steiner 1997, p. 315).

As with the equanimity exercise, this one can also be spread over several days by recognizing and anticipating situations to which we tend to respond with marked antipathy, maybe even disgust, and trying to come to a differentiated judgment.

The discovery of the mirror neurons illustrates that education begins long before individual pedagogical measures are put in place. It begins with the way the teacher observes the students (Bauer 2006, 2007, p. 26ff.). It is therefore inevitable that teachers critically assess and, if necessary, change the way they approach the pedagogical process. Practicing positivity is not about acquiring general goodwill and tolerance but about being open and thorough in the cognitive process so that the multiple facets of a person or situation are being taken seriously.

5.5 *Impartiality*

The next exercise, which also relates to the feeling life, promotes impartiality. Previous experiences are essential for orientation, but they can also tie us to the past. The impartiality exercise aims to help us open up to new ventures. This includes the willingness to "examine our view against a new one and to correct it" (Steiner 1992, p. 129) and receptiveness for new impressions. A balance needs to be established between acquired experiences and openness for everything unknown we encounter. Above all, one must beware of the judgment "That is impossible! That can't be!" (Lowndes 1999, p. 114; Steiner 1979b, p. 33). Like the previous exercises, the impartiality exercise needs to be practiced by means of self-reflection and self-transformation and in relation to one's everyday experiences.

The relevance of the impartiality exercise for the pedagogical context is obvious. Every encounter contains surprising or unforeseeable moments. For Martin Buber, this is essential. "In the most important moments of our existence neither planning nor surprise rules alone: In the midst of the faithful execution of a plan we are surprised by secret openings and insertions. Room must be left for such surprises, however; planning as though they were impossible renders them impossible. One cannot strive for immediacy, but one can hold oneself free and open for it. One cannot produce genuine dialog, but one can be at its disposal. Existential mistrust cannot be replaced by trust, but it can be replaced by a reborn candor. This attitude involves risk, the risk of giving oneself, of inner transformation [...] surpassing one's present factual constitution" (Buber 1964, p. 186). Openness to this kind of attitude can be inspired by the impartiality exercise.

5.6 *Harmony*

The sixth exercise consists in practicing two or three of the previous exercises together over several days to bring the respective qualities into harmony.

5.7 *Further exercises*

The exercises presented are merely a selection. Numerous others could be added (1994, pp. 9–28; Steiner 1992). Steiner also recommends exercises for the "Practical Training in Thought" (Steiner 1986a). It was important, he pointed out, to care for one's physical and mental *health* (Steiner 1992, p. 103), and to take the time to inwardly distance oneself from one's experiences and actions, to observe them from the outside, "*like a stranger*" (ibid., p. 31). The exercise he recommended for this is to look back on the day's events at night, in reverse order (Steiner 2001, p. 87; Wiechert 2010, p. 174f.). This *nightly review* allows you to judge your own actions, and, at the same time, it activates the will in thinking because you break through the ordinary chronological order of events. Steiner's meditations, which are based on words, images, or situations, can also enhance individual development. They work with the deepening of thoughts and aim to awaken awareness of the spiritual dimension of reality.[2]

6 Conclusion

This article strives to call attention to the importance of personal inner development in the context of Waldorf education, and to outline ways of acquiring the necessary skills. It relates to the current scientific education discourse by referring to the presently widely discussed "education of mindfulness," where basic psychosocial competences such as creating inner distance, self-reflection, changing perspectives, empathy, and mindfulness to one's own mental health are seen as important aspects of the teaching profession and essential for teacher health. Anthroposophically oriented education follows a similar approach in that it places the personality of the teacher and the teacher's relationship with the students at the center of the pedagogical process. The personal qualities required for this are therefore particularly important. These are not naturally given and available but need to be constantly newly acquired in the pedagogical practice. The Waldorf teacher profession is therefore *a developmental path*.

The skills that need to be developed on this path have been described: entering deeply and in a living way into the anthropology and developmental psychology of adolescence in order to develop *intuition* in the pedagogical practice; fostering basic attitudes such as *reverence, enthusiasm, and empathy* in relation to the children and young people; good *time management* and a broad interest in the world, including all the qualities that enable the building up of an individual worldview, such as joy in *discovery, perceptiveness and concentration*, and *living thinking*. The tasks connected with school management require further skills that are also important in education: *initiative* and *responsibility, the ability to cooperate and to look at a situation from different perspectives*, as well as *objectivity, positivity, impartiality, and self-control*.

These "teacher virtues" are not theoretical postulates. In outlining ways to practice them, Steiner demonstrates that anthroposophy is a practical path of development. It needs to be pointed out again that the exercises for this path were not conceived as a compulsory program by Rudolf Steiner, the author of *Philosophy of Freedom* (Steiner 1995), but rather as an invitation to teachers to embark on an individually chosen, personal, and professional path of development. The diverse indications given by Steiner can be understood as supporting the "mindful education" ideas that are currently widely considered, in that teachers gain awareness of their own health in body, soul, and spirit—not through introspection but through self-transformation.

Notes

1 Ruhrmann, Henke (2008), Seydel (2009), Wiechert (2012).
2 Vandercruysse (2005, p. 118 ff.), Wiechert (2010, p. 175 ff.); Zajonc (2010).

References

Bauer, Joachim (2006): Warum ich fühle, was du fühlst. Intuitive Kommunikation und das Geheimnis der Spiegelneurone. Munich: Heine.
Bauer, Joachim (2007): Lob der Schule. Sieben Perspektiven für Schüler, Lehrer und Eltern. Hamburg: Hoffmann und Campe.
Buber, Martin (1964): Schriften zur Bibel. Werke. Vol. 2. Munich: Lambert Schneider. English: Buber, Martin (1982): On the Bible. New York: Schocken Books.
Copei, Friedrich (1950): Der fruchtbare Moment im Bildungsprozess. Heidelberg: Quelle und Meyer.
Dauber, Heinrich (2007): Achtsamkeit in der Pädagogik – zur Dialektik von Selbstverwirklichung und Selbsthingabe. In: Belschner, Wilfried/Büssing, Arndt/Piron, Harald/Wienand-Kranz, Dorothee (Eds.) (2007): Achtsamkeit als Lebensform. Münster: LIT.
Dauber, Heinrich (2007): Erziehung zu Achtsamkeit und Präsenz. In: Transpersonale Psychologie und Psychotherapie, issue 2, vol. 30, pp. 5–16.
Dauber, Heinrich (2009): Psychosoziale Basiskompetenzen im Lehrerberuf. Ein Modellprojekt am Zentrum für Lehrerbildung der Universität Kassel. In: Bildung bewegt. AfL Hessen, issue 1, 2009, pp. 7–9.
Dauber, Heinrich (2010): Neue Lernkulturen in der Lehrerbildung. Achtsame Erfahrungen und biografische Reflexionen in kollegialen Netzwerken. Amt für Lehrerbildung, Reinhardswaldschule Fuldatal. Online at: www.heinrichdauber.de/uploads/media/Vortrag_RHWS.pdf (accessed on 8-28-2014).
Dauber, Heinrich (2011): Fallstricke und Chancen von Achtsamkeitspraxis in pädagogischen Kontexten. Internationaler Kongress Achtsamkeit. Universität Hamburg. Panel Achtsamkeit und Pädagogik. Online at www.heinrichdauber.de/uploads/media/Achtsamkeit_und_Paedagogik.pdf (accessed on 8-28-2014).
Hattie, John (2009): Visible Learning: A Synthesis of Over 800 Meta-Analyses Relating to Achievement. Abingdon: Routledge.
Hügli, Anton (1988): Von den Tugenden des Lehrers und den Umständen, die den Menschen machen. In: Beiträge zur Lehrerbildung. Hrsg. vom Schweizerischen Pädagogischen Verband (SPV), June 1988, vol. 6, pp. 146–149.
Huppertz, Michael (2009): Achtsamkeit, Befreiung zur Gegenwart. Achtsamkeit, Spiritualität und Vernunft in Psychotherapie und Lebenskunst. Paderborn: Junfermann.

The Teacher's Path of Development: Toward Mindfulness in Education

Krautz, Jochen/Schieren, Jost (Eds.) (2013): Persönlichkeit und Beziehung als Grundlage der Pädagogik. Weinheim and Basel: Beltz Juventa.

Lowndes, Florin (1999): Die Belebung des Herzchakra. Stuttgart: Freies Geistesleben.

Meinberg, Eckhard (1988): Das Menschenbild der modernen Erziehungswissenschaft. Darmstadt: Wissenschaftliche Buchgesellschaft.

Pelzer, Wolfgang (1998): Janusz Korczak. 6th edition. Reinbek bei Hamburg: Rowohlt.

Ruhrmann, Ingrid/Henke, Bettina (2008): Die Kinderkonferenz. Stuttgart: Freies Geistesleben.

Seydel, Anna (2009): Ich bin du. Stuttgart: Pädagogische Forschungsstelle beim Bund der Freien Waldorfschulen.

Steiner, Rudolf (1973): Allgemeine Menschenkunde als Grundlage der Pädagogik. Rudolf Steiner GA 293. Dornach: Rudolf Steiner Verlag. English translation: Steiner, Rudolf (2020): The First Teachers' Course. Anthropological Foundations-Methods of Teaching-Practical Discussions. GA 293–295, trans. Margot M. Saar. Bangkok: Ratayakom.

Steiner, Rudolf (1974): Die Methodik des Lehrens und die Lebensbedingungen des Erziehens. GA 308. Dornach: Rudolf Steiner Verlag.

Steiner, Rudolf (1975): Heilpädagogischer Kurs. GA 317. Dornach: Rudolf Steiner Verlag. English translation: Steiner, Rudolf (2015): Education for Special Needs: the Curative Education Course. Trans. Anna R. Meuss. Forest Row: Rudolf Steiner Press.

Steiner, Rudolf (1977a): Die befruchtende Wirkung der Anthroposophie auf die Fachwissenschaft. GA 76. Dornach: Rudolf Steiner Verlag.

Steiner, Rudolf (1977b): Die Erneuerung der pädagogisch-didaktischen Kunst durch Geisteswissenschaft. GA 301. Dornach: Rudolf Steiner Verlag.

Steiner, Rudolf (1977c): Erziehung und Unterricht aus Menschenerkenntnis. Meditativ erarbeitete Menschenkunde. GA 302a. Dornach: Rudolf Steiner Verlag.

Steiner, Rudolf (1979a): Erziehungs- und Unterrichtsmethoden auf anthroposophischer Grundlage. GA 304. Dornach: Rudolf Steiner Verlag.

Steiner, Rudolf (1979b): Die Stufen der höheren Erkenntnis. GA 12. Dornach: Rudolf Steiner Verlag.

Steiner, Rudolf (1983): Anthroposophische Gemeinschaftsbildung. GA 257. Dornach: Rudolf Steiner Verlag.

Steiner, Rudolf (1986a): Die Beantwortung von Welt- und Lebensfragen durch Anthroposophie. GA 108. Dornach: Rudolf Steiner Verlag.

Steiner, Rudolf (1986b): Gegenwärtiges Geistesleben und Erziehung. GA 307. Dornach: Rudolf Steiner Verlag.

Steiner, Rudolf (1989): Die Geheimwissenschaft im Umriss. GA 13. Dornach: Rudolf Steiner Verlag. English translation: Steiner, Rudolf (1997): An Outline of Esoteric Science. GA 13. Trans. Catherine E. Creeger. Great Barrington, MA: Anthroposophic Press.

Steiner, Rudolf (1992): Wie erlangt man Erkenntnisse der höheren Welten? GA 10. Dornach: Rudolf Steiner Verlag.

Steiner, Rudolf (1994): Erfahrungen des Übersinnlichen. Die drei Wege der Seele zu Christus. GA 143. Dornach: Rudolf Steiner Verlag.

Steiner, Rudolf (1995): Die Philosophie der Freiheit. Grundzüge einer modernen Weltanschauung – Seelische Beobachtungsresultate nach naturwissenschaftlicher Methode. GA 4. 16th edition. Dornach: Rudolf Steiner Verlag.

Steiner, Rudolf (2001): Seelenübungen. Vol. 1. GA 267. Dornach: Rudolf Steiner Verlag.

Uhlenhoff, Rahel (ed.) (2011): Anthroposophie in Geschichte und Gegenwart. Berlin: BWV.

Vandercruysse, Rudy (2005): Herzwege. Von der emotionalen Selbstführung zum meditativen Leben. Stuttgart: Freies Geistesleben.

Wiechert, Christof (2010): Lust aufs Lehrersein?! Eine Ermutigung zum (Waldorf) Lehrerberuf. Dornach: Verlag am Goetheanum.

Wiechert, Christof (2012): «Du sollst sein Rätsel lösen ...». Gedanken zur Kunst der Kinder- und Schülerbesprechung. Dornach: Verlag am Goetheanum.

Zajonc, Arthur (2010): Aufbruch ins Unerwartete. Meditation als Erkenntnisweg. Stuttgart: Freies Geistesleben. English Original: Zajonc, Arthur (2008): Meditation as Contemplative Inquiry: When Knowing Becomes Love. Great Barrington: Lindisfarne Books.

CHAPTER 7

Education Science and Waldorf Education/Education Reform

INTRODUCTION

Peter Loebell

Historically, the education reform movement tends to be assigned to the period between the end of the 19th and the first third of the 20th century: 1880–1930 (Oelkers 2005), 1889–1924/1925 (Skiera 2012), or 1890–1933 (Keim, Schwerdt 2013). The industrial states in Europe first established full general schooling in the late 19th century, a process that was associated with the disciplining of society as a whole. Modern schools switched "public education from conveying knowledge within the immediate environment to the dynamic of knowledge and the related learning achievements" (Oelkers 2005, p. 32). But the almost complete inclusion of all demographic groups by expanding the general education system also led to growing demands for reform. As Jürgen Oelkers pointed out, "In pedagogical reflection, schools are notoriously imperfect" (Oelkers 2005, p. 33). As schools became more widespread, school criticism also increased and became more vehement. Instead of "book school" methods, these critical voices called for object-lessons and an "education that was suitable for children." The Swedish pedagogue Ellen Key deplored the conventionality and alienation of state schools (Flitner 1999, p. 17). The movement was associated with eminent individualities such as Pestalozzi or Rousseau: "It was not the theory but the personal center of the concept that counted" (Oelkers 2005, p. 36). The kinds of educational institution proposed and realized were not based on empirical research results. The origin of the motifs and central ideas of education reform, on the other hand, was "cryptic; they arise from everyday reflections, and receive a theoretical foundation by drawing on theological or metaphysical systems" (Oelkers 2005, p. 34).

While criticism arose within the state school system, conceptions that deviated from this system became a starting point for a number of new school foundations, which today are usually subsumed under the heading of "education reform" or "progressive education." Institutions founded in the late 19th and early 20th century included

- the Laboratory School Chicago, founded in 1896 (John Dewey)
- *Landerziehungsheime* (boarding schools in rural locations), founded in 1898 (Hermann Lietz)
- the *Hauslehrerschule* (home tutor school), founded in 1906 (Berthold Otto)
- *Freie Schulgemeinde Wickersdorf* (independent school community), founded in 1906 (Gustav Wyneken, Paul Geheeb)
- Montessori schools, founded in 1907 (Maria Montessori)
- *Odenwaldschule* (boarding school in Germany), founded in 1910 (Paul und Edith Geheeb)
- Summerhill, founded 1923 (Alexander S. Neill)
- the Jena Plan Concept, initiated in 1927 (Peter Petersen)

DOI: 10.4324/9781003187431-32

Other approaches, which impacted on the curricula and methods of state schools, were

- *Kunsterziehung* (art education), from 1901 (Alfred Lichtwark)
- Freinet education, from 1920 (Célestin Freinet)

The German *Bund für Schulreform* (association for education reform), which was founded in 1908 and whose members included teachers from all types of schools, as well as school administrators, university lecturers, and interested laypersons, was interested in founding comprehensive schools and in reforming academic teacher education. In 1924, Fritz Karsen published 12 reports from experimental reform schools, most of which were state-run elementary schools (Link 2012, p. 25). As early as that, at least 200 reform or experimental schools existed in the Weimar Republic. In his synopsis, Link mentions three main characteristics of these schools: they were "public and democratic," "cooperative and self-critical," and "flexible and competence-oriented" (Link 2012, p. 28).

Oelkers describes the practice of educational reform, using five central motifs that, in his view, determine the reform debate: "Essentially, it is about 'work' and 'teaching to work,' 'imagination' and 'learning' as a means of aesthetic education, 'walking' and 'gymnastics' as an extension and complementation of the school experience, 'internal school reform,' about educating the mind, as well as about reforming teaching methods based on the principle of 'observation'" (Oelkers 2005, p. 40).

Finally, there are also voices in the education reform discourse that call for non-selective comprehensive schools, a direction that has so far only been consistently pursued by Waldorf schools.

In his discussion of the phenomena of education reform, Ullrich describes four different lines of argument (Ullrich 1990). He notices that education reform is trivialized to a "déjà-vu." Oelkers, for instance, argues in his "critical history of dogmas" that since Comenius, and definitely since Rousseau, education was always education reform, because true education was always associated with improving the world (Skiera 2012, p. 50). A second line of discussion consisted in elevating education reform to the status of an epochal global movement. Ullrich cites Hermann Röhrs as a representative who declared internationality to be the defining feature of education reform (Skiera 2012, p. 52). The third line of argument sees education reform as fictitious and regressive. Klaus Prange, for instance, suggests that, from the point of view of social history, Nohl's "pedagogical movement" was mere fiction. He sees "child-oriented education" as the anonymized infantile regression of its protagonists (cited in Skiera 2012, p. 53). Horst Rumpf rejected this view, pointing out that "education reform initiatives aim primarily at humanizing educational institutions, in the school context, for instance, by introducing different, 'subject-sensitive' teaching methods" (cited in Skiera 2012, p. 54). According to Ullrich, a fourth approach to education reform consists in its rehabilitation as a "crisis management pattern" in the process of modernization. Elmar Tenorth speaks of an epochal turning-point in educational thinking, occurring alongside changes in other areas of society. At the core of the education movement, he sees, above all, the attempts at reform within schools that are concerned with the institution as such—with individual subjects, or ways of working. But he also points to the "often murky sources" of education reform's critical impulse (Skiera 2012, p. 55). In this context, the antisemitic tendencies of Hermann Lietz, the founder of the *Landerziehungsheime*, spring to mind, for instance (Röhrs 1986, p. 24). Ullrich finds education reform "paradoxical" because, he says, it responds to the "external" modernization of educational conditions with the "internal de-modernization" of the lifeworld-related educational thinking. In other words, "an idyllic inner world, a life community, is set against the functional fragmentation and disenchantment of the outer world" (Skiera 2012, p. 56).

Skiera contradicts Ullrich, pointing out that education reform was more modern than the talk of the "crisis management pattern" let on. "At an essential level, education reform does not respond to 'outer modernization' with the 'inner de-modernization' of the social context but, on the contrary, updates the social relationships within the school by introducing a near-democratic concept of education and learning" (Skiera 2012, p. 58). Skiera consequently adds a further, topical approach to Ullrich's four points: "Education reform is (also) a form of pedagogical reflection and action which seeks to develop

Introduction

and implement a learning concept that enables learning without fear, in order to counteract unreflected, limiting constraints imposed by the institution" (Skiera 2012, p. 59). The scientific education reform discourse clearly concerns Waldorf schools at multiple levels. There is nonetheless no agreement in the relevant literature on whether Waldorf education constitutes education reform. Many publications on the topic mention it only marginally or not at all (Fitzner, Kalb, Risse 2012; Flitner 1999; Oelkers 2005). Edgar Weiß, on the other hand, argues that "within the history of education, there are good reasons to consider Waldorf education to be education reform" (Weiß 2013, p. 373).

Similarly to Weiß, Keim and Schwerdt also ignore the contributions and empirical research on Waldorf education that have emerged in the past 25 years (Keim, Schwerdt 2013).[1]

Heiner Ullrich has concerned himself with Waldorf education in a much more differentiated way since 1986. He thinks that, formally, Waldorf schools have common ground with the original thinking of education reform but that they add a dogmatic dimension to it (Ullrich 2012, p. 186). As late as 2012, he granted that Waldorf education had advanced from being an outsider to being a "leader of the education reform International" (Ullrich 2012, p. 181). However, in a more recent publication, he suggests that all that Waldorf education had in common with the historic education reform movement was "the time of its emergence in the first third of the 20th century" (Ullrich 2015, p. 173).

The literature classifies Waldorf education, therefore, in different ways in relation to education reform: while some authors find that it is, if at all, only marginally related, others assign it a special reform status. Where Waldorf education is mentioned in the context of education reform, this seems to happen for three reasons that are relevant to a critical inquiry. Firstly, the founding of the first Waldorf School falls historically into the period when various alternative school models emerged, all seeking to change existing state school systems. Secondly, the didactics and method of Waldorf education are oriented in a particular way to the development and needs of the child, similarly to other contemporary concepts that also favored a primarily "paidotropic" approach (Caselmann). Thirdly, alternative educational concepts were born from criticism of the prevalent school system and their arrival therefore constituted a challenge that continues to have an effect to this day. Measured in the number of existing schools, Waldorf education is therefore to be seen as successful and cannot be ignored by the current scientific discourse on education.

The first article in this chapter, by Wolfgang Nieke, therefore looks above all at where Waldorf schools rank in the current scientific debate. In his introduction, Nieke refers to the changing orientation of education reform toward a new image of the human being. He points out that education is generally rooted in anthropological images that are, in turn, embedded in particular views of the world. There is, accordingly, no such thing as education without an underlying worldview. Nieke reconstructs the worldview underlying education reform, its knowledge of change, conditions, and orientation, by taking recourse to Skiera's theoretical argumentation. As regards Waldorf education, he refers to the confusion in the education sciences about the unresolved tension between its application in practice and anthroposophy as its theoretical foundation, a tension that he allocates theoretically with the help of Popper's contrasting of discovery and justification. In his attempt to understand the connection between recognized pedagogical practice and philosophical foundation, Nieke discusses two elements: the school climate and the mindful way teachers deal with students. He concludes that Waldorf education is not only to be seen as part of education reform but that it also needs to be discussed as an independent, topical concept of formation.

In the second contribution, Volker Frielingsdorf systematically compares education reform and Waldorf education. He identifies five commonalities: the historical context, their criticism of the state school system, an elevated view of education, world-life plans, and similar approaches to practice. However, he also describes five apparent differences, where Waldorf schools stand out from other education reform movements or claim specific status: their coherent anthroposophic foundation, their view of the teacher's role, their lesson content and social structure, and their distinction from other pedagogical streams. Frielingsdorf ends with an outlook on possible forms of future cooperation.

Peter Loebell begins his concluding contribution by comparing education reform and Waldorf schools on the basis of three elements they have in common: a "child-oriented education," the importance of development, and the role of experience for learning. In addition to the differences in these three areas, Waldorf education has some characteristic features that distinguish it from other contemporary educational concepts. Some of these features are portrayed in more detail, and the relation between the educational practice and anthroposophy is discussed at various levels. Loebell concludes that, due to the distinctive epistemological quality of its original inspiration, its origin, and its development over the past hundred years, Waldorf education constitutes a multifaceted, incomplete search movement.

Note

1 Cf. Barz and Randoll (2007), Bohnsack and Kranich (1994), or Paschen (2010). See also Frielingsdorf's comprehensive literature review (Frielingsdorf 2012).

References

Barz, Heiner/ Randoll, Dirk (2007): Bildung und Lebensgestaltung ehemaliger Schüler von Rudolf Steiner Schulen in der Schweiz. Eine Absolventenbefragung. Frankfurt am Main: Peter Lang.

Bohnsack, Fritz/Kranich, Ernst-Michael (Eds.) (1994): Erziehungswissenschaft und Waldorfpädagogik. Der Beginn eines notwendigen Dialogs. *[Educational science and Waldorf education. Opening a necessary dialog.]* Weinheim, Basel: Beltz.

Fitzner, Thilo/Kalb, Peter E./Risse, Erika (Eds.) (2012): Reformpädagogik in der Schulpraxis. Bad Heilbrunn: Klinkhardt.

Flitner, Andreas (1999): Reform der Erziehung. Munich: Piper.

Keim, Wolfgang/Schwerdt, Ulrich (2013): Schule. In: Keim, Wolfgang/Schwerdt, Ulrich (Eds.) (2013): Handbuch der Reformpädagogik in Deutschland. Part 2. Praxisfelder und pädagogische Handlungssituationen. Frankfurt am Main: Peter Lang, pp. 657–775.

Link, Jörg-W. (2012): Reformpädagogik im historischen Überblick. In: Barz, Heiner, ed. (2012): Handbuch Bildungsreform und Reformpädagogik. Wiesbaden: Springer VS, pp. 15–30.

Oelkers, Jürgen (2005): Reformpädagogik – eine kritische Dogmengeschichte. 4th edition. Weinheim, Munich: Juventa.

Paschen, Harm (Ed.) (2010): Erziehungswissenschaftliche Zugänge zur Waldorfpädagogik. Diskussion paradigmatischer Beispiele zu epistemischen Grundlagen, empirischen und methodischen Zugängen und Unterrichtsinhalten. Wiesbaden: VS.

Röhrs, Hermann, ed. (1986): Die Schulen der Reformpädagogik heute. Düsseldorf: Schwann.

Skiera, Ehrenhard (2012): Reformpädagogik in Diskurs und Erziehungswirklichkeit. In: Herrmann, Ulrich/Schlüter, Steffen (Eds.) (2012): Reformpädagogik – eine kritisch-konstruktive Vergegenwärtigung. Bad Heilbrunn: Klinkhardt, pp. 47–78.

Ullrich, Heiner (1990): Die Reformpädagogik. Modernisierung der Erziehung oder Weg aus der Moderne? In: Zeitschrift für Pädagogik 36 (1990), pp. 893–918.

Ullrich, Heiner (2012): Reformpädagogische Schulkultur mit weltanschaulicher Prägung – Pädagogische Prinzipien und Formen der Waldorfschule. In: Hansen-Schaberg, Inge, ed. (2012): Reformpädagogische Schulkonzepte, vol. 6. Waldorfpädagogik. Baltmannsweiler: Schneider, pp. 181–219.

Ullrich, Heiner (2015): Waldorfpädagogik. Eine kritische Einführung. Weinheim and Basel: Beltz.

Weiß, Edgar (2013): Entwicklung. In: Keim, Wolfgang/Schwerdt, Ulrich (Hrsg.) (2013): Handbuch der Reformpädagogik in Deutschland. Part 1. Gesellschaftliche Kontexte, Leitideen und Diskurse. Frankfurt am Main: Peter Lang, pp. 363–378.

CHALLENGES TO EDUCATION SCIENCE POSED BY WALDORF EDUCATION AS EDUCATION REFORM

Wolfgang Nieke

1 Education science—The link among orientational, conditional, and transformative knowledge

In education science, Waldorf education is often portrayed as an established education reform movement and treated as canonical orientational knowledge for prospective students (of education, mostly), for instance in Heinz-Hermann Krüger's widely used textbook *"Einführung in Theorie und Methoden der Erziehungswissenschaft"* [Introduction to the theory and methods of education science] (Krüger 2012). In a diagram displaying the theoretical streams of (German) education science, the author lists the following "pedagogical theories" in a separate text box: Montessori, Waldorf, Freinet, anti-authoritarian education, and antipedagogy (ibid., p. 11).

While these teachings continue to be relevant because of their reception and practice, they have, according to Krüger, "not the status of theoretical concepts of education science" (ibid., p. 12).

In the descriptions of education reform (most comprehensively and meticulously presented by Skiera 2010),[1] some authors (Frielingsdorf and Loebell in Chapter 7) count Waldorf education as one of these pedagogies.[2] *Reformpädagogik* (education reform) is usually assigned to the period between 1880 and 1932. The term is generally applied to all conceptions that are opposed to the late-rationalist book schools and the effects of industrialization and open to elements of the late-Romantic[3] life reform movement.

These progressive pedagogies have in common a change of perspective with regard to their object—that is to say, the way the older generation deals with the younger generation in order to build up a socially competent personality (education as intentional socialization) and the successful and lasting absorption of cultural content that is considered relevant (education as intentional enculturation) (Ecarius 2008). This happens both in the schools, which need to be transformed for this purpose, and in the immediate pedagogical relationship (Nohl 1933) outside such institutions: in private tutoring, in the newly emerging youth groups, and in subsequent youth and adult education.

With this change of perspective, young people are perceived in a new way. A new educational image of the human being is developed and applied. This suggests that every pedagogical practice is based, and must be based, on an implicit image of the human being,[4] often unknowingly and without reflection (Meinberg 1988; Schilling 2000). And this image inevitably serves as an orientation for pedagogical actions.

In practice, three forms of knowledge are relevant that differ from each other in structure and content[5]:

a. transformative knowledge arises from experience and possibly a systematic technique for successful changes in the field of the envisaged actions;

DOI: 10.4324/9781003187431-33

b. conditional knowledge for this intended change, again based on biographically accumulated and integrated experiences of the conditions surrounding the action; in scientific[6] societies, this is based throughout on nomothetic knowledge regarding the regularities of changes in systems over time, enabling well-planned and effective actions aimed at bringing about future system changes;

c. orientational knowledge is needed to identify action targets. It consists in normative orientations of society and culture, in views of the world that produce coherence (world orientations; Nieke 2006), and in procedures for the determination of truth in practical and theoretical discourses.

Images of human nature serve primarily to provide orientation for possible actions, for constructing possibility spaces in given action situations; but often they also contain components of a conditional knowledge on how and under what conditions these goals can be realized.

There is, for instance, the assumption that humans can be evil by nature and from birth. This arises from the biblical myth of the original sin that has dominated the Christian view of the human being for a long time: The guilt incurred through the transgression of the first parents, Adam and Eve, was passed on to their descendants, and as a result, every newborn child has, in principle, the ability to be evil. From birth, education and state must do everything to counteract this potential consistently, relentlessly, and under threat of the most severe punishment. Without referring to such a Christian view but taking recourse to the Roman playwright Plautus, Thomas Hobbes (Leviathan, 1651/2011) assigns to the state the important task of working against a naturally evil disposition. This view lives on in the current thesis, fed by biology, action theory, and cultural theory, that human beings need cultural institutions because they are not driven by instincts (Gehlen 1940/2014). Pedagogical action must consequently aim to suppress and, if necessary, transform this innate evilness by means of fully planned days (for idle hands are the devil's tools) and severe punishment, as envisaged, for example, by the philanthropic educational doctrines that have been referred to as "poisonous pedagogy" (Rutschky 1977).

If, reversely, the assumption is that we are good by nature and only become evil as a result of the wrong societal influences (Rousseau, humanist psychology: Cohn, Rogers), the suggestion would be for an education that is as lenient as possible, where the only possible negative sanctions are the natural consequences of one's actions. This polarity was described by Theodor Litt in his antinomy of leading and letting grow (1927/1958). The currently discussed educational theories and scientifically founded educational concepts (education and teaching styles, classroom management, discipline) can also be allocated to this polarity. Arguments to support the correctness of either assumption can, in fact, be found in both of the outlined images of the human being, even if that is often not clearly stated.

Images of human nature are always, if often implicitly, embedded in wider images of the world, or worldviews. They must be coherent in order to be action-guiding, and coherence can, initially, be defined as the possibility to integrate something (not only elements of knowledge, perceptions, cognitions, but also complex orientational patterns such as images of the human being) into an overarching context.

In plural (postmodern) cultures, several or even many such orientations coexist, even if they occasionally contradict each other, some of them explicitly. But because there is no generally accepted criterion to guide any general or individual decisions as to what is true or not true, one (though uncomfortable) consequence is that everything needs to be accepted and tolerated. This agnostic value relativism (explained in more detail in Nieke 2008) is typical of postmodernism.[7]

Despite this basic acknowledgment of any kind of thinking and moral action, there are attempts with value conflicts arising from differences, contradictions, and different world orientations (both within one "culture" and between cultures that perceive each other as different), to come to decisions regarding actions that are morally justifiable and can be accepted by all involved. For this, the model of virtual discourses was introduced, using the example of emerging intercultural value conflicts (ibid.). Here, the validity conditions of the discourse procedure itself (as elaborated by Karl-Otto Apel 1976 and Jürgen Habermas 1983; although with both authors, the validity conditions are determined quasi-anthropologically and withdrawn from the discourse itself) must be included in the discourse. The arguments from the point of view of the different world orientations must also be included, if necessary

Challenges to Education Science Posed by Waldorf Education as Education Reform

virtually, that is to say, by safeguarding the relevant interests, if the real discourse participants do not have the possibility (empirically, a frequent event) to introduce this themselves into the discourse.

The three forms of knowledge mentioned are also part of teachers' professional knowledge, but in this case they no longer appear as routine knowledge absorbed unnoticed from the surrounding culture (or life world in the sense of Alfred Schütz, Thomas Luckmann 2003), but acquired and continuously developed further in the form of reflective professionalism: In scientific studies, the capacity is acquired to justify one's own actions normatively and with a view to the conditional knowledge, including the weighing up of possible alternatives (Harm Paschen's schema for pedagogical arguments can be helpful here, Paschen 1992).

Education reform movements are characterized by a total of transformative knowledge (practice forms and rules), conditional knowledge (above all, the new view of children as subjects of their educational process),[8] and orientational knowledge (late-Romantic life philosophy and life-reform impulse against the evident problematic forms of industrialization). This means that they can be distinguished very precisely from other conceptions, in their attempt to change and innovate schools and education as well as youth and adult education outside schools.[9]

In a wider context, the education reform era and movement can be seen as an oscillation, appearing as a longitudinal wave in the history of education in the antipathy of "book school" versus "life educates," and brought in against the rationalist planning-through of the daily routine and teaching for youth education and enculturation, and for a more intense experience with self-activity on the way to world-appropriation and self-education. The first is informed by an understanding of humanity where children are evil by nature, and the second by one where children are good by nature.

Skiera summarizes the key elements of education reform as an era and pedagogical movement between 1880 and 1932:

- "the rigid domination of the curriculum is opposed by an education oriented to the child's questions, needs, and interests ('child-oriented education');
- the dominance of receptive learning forms and the 'chalk and talk' method of the 'book school' is opposed by a 'new' concept of learning as an activity that is creative, promotes independence, and is practical and 'natural';
- the 'coercive character' of the 'Old School' is opposed by the image of the 'New School,' as a model of a good, harmonious partnership which is to become an educational, socio-ethical, and aesthetic space, an inspirational community;
- the excessive emphasis on intellectual learning is opposed by an education that addresses the 'whole person' with their intellectual, physical, social, and emotional skills and possibilities" (Skiera 2010, p. VII).

The underlying worldview is characterized as follows: "In the education reform discourse, enlightened modern thinking – with its concept of individuality, empirical knowledge, and a humane, child-friendly education – and rational arguments used by civilization, education, and school critics, with irrational, even explicitly antirational theorems and irrational salvation fantasies. [...] The image of the child is, for instance, tied to the belief in redemption and development" (ibid., p. VIII).

To summarize: Education reform is "the attempt to oppose the traditional, fear-inducing 'old' education with a 'new' education that is concerned with the child's happiness and seeks the child's agreement" (ibid.).

In this context, Waldorf education is presented as one of the education reform movements. Education science is, first of all, interested in the visible pedagogical practice in Waldorf schools and the accompanying pedagogical conceptions for shaping the school life, the peculiarities of the curricula and educational programs, as well as lesson design and didactics. The interest therefore focuses on transformative knowledge, which is not related to any conditional or orientational knowledge and seen as sufficient for understanding the observed pedagogical practice.

A twofold interest is noticeable:

a. Education science is, in principle, interested in difference, in showing up, documenting, understanding, and explaining varieties and variance in delivering the basic pedagogical task of enculturation in the interaction of the generations. In diachronic comparison, this happens by following the course of history, in synchronic comparison by examining what exists simultaneously, that is, internationally and, above all, interculturally. This includes taking stock of the diversity within nations and cultural regions. Here, one also finds the currently existing Waldorf schools as preservers or developers of a specific education reform, seen in historical comparison.
b. Education science always seeks ways of optimizing the existing pedagogical practice. It examines them for possible deficits as regards externally imposed and internally developed goals, before looking for alternatives that may be better at achieving the goals than the previous practice. Possible side-effects are considered. Harm Paschen developed this basic picture in his analysis of pedagogical argumentation (1992). This kind of interest is not primarily theoretical, serving to explain the world better and more precisely, it is utilitarian, that is, aiming to improve the practice under examination.

For the second kind of interest, it is sufficient to focus on the observable and conceptualized practice, in other words, on transformative knowledge. This explains the frequent strict separation of Waldorf education and anthroposophy, where the latter is seen as irrelevant to the former. Sometimes this seems like a reflection of Karl Popper's distinction between discovery and justification (Popper 1989), which is common in the empirical sciences: The discovery context is irrelevant for the truth of the theory and relevant only for the psychology and sociology of emerging new insights and possibly their optimization; the justification context alone is relevant and must present itself without the discovery context. Only the visible and measurable effects of Waldorf education would then have to be reconstructed out of this justification context alone (and seen as a remarkable contribution to many diverse pedagogies), while anthroposophy can be disregarded as discovery context that is, as a historical foundation, irrelevant to this evaluation. This implies that any possible criticism of positions within the guiding anthroposophical literature is also entirely irrelevant for evaluating the appropriateness and relevance of Waldorf education.

For the first kind of interest, the coherence of transformative, conditional, and orientational knowledge remains important, not only historically for the reconstruction of the development of Waldorf education from Rudolf Steiner's anthroposophy, but also systematically, because transformative knowledge cannot be acquired and applied in isolation in pedagogical professionalism. It must inevitably be integrated into the wider contexts of conditional and orientational knowledge so it can be action-guiding, which means not only generating simple practice but being able to make an informed selection from a range of possible options. Education science therefore needs to show an interest in the discourse on the link between Waldorf education and anthroposophy. The problem that arises is that anthroposophy is neither a philosophy nor a theory whose arguments are easily accessible to intersubjective scrutiny: It contains elements of esotericism that, although communicable, are not easy to understand without specific ways of access to their validity. Access to this kind of orientational knowledge requires interpersonal communication. It cannot be achieved by merely studying literature that remains incomprehensible and is easily misunderstood if not contextualized. This difficulty may be the reason why this has so far been blanked out by education science that, guided by the second kind of interest, has hardly attempted this access yet.

There is nonetheless a growing interest in Waldorf education and anthroposophy, which is reflected in the fact that, as a whole, they both have been successful around the world for more than a century and continue to be so, with teachers training in Waldorf education, and with parents, and supporters. The causes and reasons for this lasting and growing fascination would be worth investigating.

Educationists are trying to understand and explain the observable specific features of Waldorf schools with their genuine modeling. While the first attempts were made without reference to anthroposophy, which presents itself as esoteric, more recent inquiries sought to understand the indivisible link between this pedagogical conception and anthroposophy because most Waldorf teachers state that this link is important for them. This is facilitated by the more recent publications of Rudolf Steiner's work that focus less on the esoteric elements and more on aspects that make it easier to relate to the thinking of his time and that can be better integrated into the current educational discourse. These possible relations shall be outlined below in connection with two features of Waldorf education: the school climate and the mindful way teachers deal with students and both groups with each other.

2 School climate as a shared orientational pattern

The term "climate" is used in three contexts: to refer to the weather conditions in a particular area, to describe the immediate spatial surroundings, and, metaphorically, arising from the second meaning, to describe the social environment: the tangible but not directly explicable relations of people who interact, mostly within an institutional setting.

With the school climate, the second and third meanings merge when the health of students and teachers is concerned. The description is based on a bipolar subjective rating scale between good and bad. This implies that as a standard the climate should be as good as possible. A school climate that is experienced as good generates well-being; with a bad school climate one needs to look for the causes and find ways of soon removing the sense of discomfort.

Visitors to Waldorf schools often remark on their particularly pleasant climate. This is usually explained with a reference to a visible manifestation of the relationship between teachers and students, or within either of these groups, and to the effect of the unusual interior and exterior architecture of the school buildings, grade rooms, and functional spaces. In contrast to experiences in state schools this is found to be soothing.[10]

Education science is by now interested in the effect both of the school architecture on well-being and of the way people deal with each other in a school. Both elements are often associated with health promotion. It is noticeable that, while the term "school climate" or "lesson climate" is used as an explanatory variable for well-being, school performance, health, school quality, freedom from violence, and democratic habits, there is no explanation of the concept that the various studies or practical guidelines for improvement would relate to. There appears to be a kind of intuitive general perception of well-being, recognition, and safety that can be assessed by asking about subjective estimates and that evidently manifests in statistically coherent judgments for examined units (grade, school).

Helmut Fend tried to describe school climate theoretically as an explanatory variable and operationalize it for empirical measurements (Fend 1977, 1998). School climate arises from "interpretive patterns shared between teachers and students [...]. The content of these interpretive patterns consisted in shared [...] perceptions of what is required in which way, how people deal with each other, how they are accepted and included" (Fend 1998, p. 48). The focus here is on the social climate, the actual surrounding space seems to be irrelevant in this context.

In the model used to explain the performance of an educational system in terms of the student achievements it promotes (diagram, ibid., p. 322), school climate is one of five variables subsumed under "quality and means of educational provision." This operationalizes Fend's independent further development of the underlying model by Haertel, Walberg, Weinstein (1983) to educational productivity. He highlights as a central dimension the qualitative interacting of teachers and students, with particular emphasis on teachers' actions, while the older model, based on 1980s psychology, provides a mechanical explanation of the result.

Fend's school climate model is consequently compatible with the idea of new institutionalism that emerged in the United States and gradually found favor in Germany.[11] While the older institutionalism tried to explain social stability with standardized expectations regarding behaviors and power relations and relied on explanations of these factors as documentation, the new institutionalism conceptualizes the implicit, not conscious, orientation of the members of the institutions on the basis of specific orientational patterns that only apply within an institution.[12] This coincides with Fend's "shared interpretive patterns." But it also enables the more comprehensive concept of school climate that includes the spatial surroundings, because they, too, can (and mostly are unconsciously) included in the orientational patterns, for example in the general perception of a sense of well-being in a situation and in a building that is part of the institution.

With the inclusion of "school climate" as a shared orientational pattern within an institution, this concept could probably be much more relevant and more effective than in Fend's conceptualization, where it constitutes—along with "process characteristics of teacher behavior, teaching methods, school climate, teacher biographies, didactic continuity" (change of teachers, change of grade; cf. diagram ibid., p. 322)—the factor of "quality and manner of provision."

These orientational patterns cannot be explained on the basis of behavior observation or analysis of documents from the institution alone. This requires socio-hermeneutic methods of reconstructing collective orientational patterns, such as those developed in continuation of Karl Mannheim's sociology of knowledge (Bohnsack 2014) or in ethnography, using methods such as "thick description" (Geertz 2003) or "grounded theory" (Glaser, Strauss 1967). Both methods have in common that they refer to human communication as an elementary explanation for the emergence of social life (Nieke 2010a,b).

These kinds of survey are elaborate and do not produce large, standardizable samples with representative statements, which means that they are not usually considered for the currently so highly valued meta-analyses (Hattie 2013).[13]

The special Waldorf school climate that has been perceived and reported on by outside visitors can, therefore, based on Fend's conceptualizations and inspired by the new institutionalism, be seen as a shared interpretative pattern within this specific institution. It can be assumed that the teachers and other specialized staff do orient themselves, implicitly or explicitly, not only to the rules of Waldorf education that are written down and can therefore be reconstructed by outsiders in an intersubjectively verifiable way, but also to the anthroposophic understanding of the human being that has been acquired in training and that is applied concretely and continuously developed in living pedagogical practice.

This living interaction can also explain the perception that the school climate as defined here differs considerably from one Waldorf school to the next. The shared orientation patterns are specific to each institution—in this case: to each school—because of the way the individual agents within the institution relate to each other. In their mutual relations, the individual orientation patterns are constantly adjusted to those of others (the special case of defending one's own position is included in this category of adjusting because of its potential to change to the other's orientation); new patterns are adopted if they are more plausible than the ones adhered to before.

It follows that Waldorf education, as an education reform movement that actually exists and is outwardly perceptible, cannot be understood or explained without considering the orientational effect of engaging with Rudolf Steiner's work. This interdependence is not uniform, however; in other words, it has no dogmatic or dogmatizing implications for the reality of education in Waldorf schools.

This special orientational knowledge can initially only be treated as a closed variable whose effect can be made visible without its inner quality being known or having to be known. Only in future, more detailed analyses can the question be asked as to what parts of this worldview the visible and measurable effects may be ascribed to. Presumably, they can be understood and explained by the fact that teachers look at their students in a different way—because they have studied Rudolf Steiner's pedagogical anthropology, for instance—and that they deal with their students differently based on this conditional and orientational knowledge. The students, on the other hand, who have no such knowledge, develop specific manners in response to this different interaction. These manners contribute to the observed specific school climate, but they can also remain a lifelong characteristic or "habitus" that is observable from the outside.[14]

3 Teachers' mindfulness toward students in Waldorf schools

External observers often explain the special Waldorf school climate with the mindfulness teachers cultivate in dealing with their students. It goes beyond and differs from the efforts teachers make in other schools to promote their students. In other words, it is different from what is currently described and generally demanded as student orientation (against a school's curriculum-oriented enculturation task) and individualization, dealing with diversity (against the kind of class teaching that relies on a homogeneous learning background).

In his synthesis of meta-analyses of highly effective teachers—using as indicators of teaching quality not only the students' successful learning but also the students' assessment of the teachers' professional competence—Hattie identifies as confirmed explanatory factors that they have "a positive classroom climate that fostered learning" and "respect for their students" (Hattie 2009, p. 117). Respect here means recognition of students' personality independently of their cultural background, performance, and health. This is no trivial matter. It requires a professional habitus that goes far beyond everyday attitudes: Routinely, we judge others within a split second of becoming aware of them, based on the social stereotypes of our own life world, associating these conclusions with evaluations, above all on the scales of "likeable – not likeable" and "dangerous – not dangerous" (for details cf. Aronson, Wilson, Akert 2004). Distancing oneself from these involuntary judgments in order not to do an injustice to others requires intensive self-development.

Respect therefore means esteem, but mindfulness is even more than that: The concept has been adopted in the pedagogical practice—but far less so in education science (Zimmermann, Spitz, Schmidt 2012)—from approaches in psychotherapy that use elements of Buddhism. Mindfulness is about focusing one's conscious, concentrated attention on one's present state or on other persons. The effects are immediately noticeable not only to those who practice mindfulness, but also to their social environment, and they can be measured with objectifying methods.

We can therefore distinguish three levels of mindfulness:
Mindfulness as

a. Mental hygiene: Most practical guidebooks are concerned with this, offering teachers help in dealing with themselves, with their students, with developing inner peace and promoting health. Pausing, focusing one's mind on one's inner self and on the outer situation generates inner calmness, reduces stress, and establishes an inner distance from stress-evoking influences so that these can be managed more easily in the future.

b. Enhanced empathy: Being able to empathize with others enables us to better understand them and their actions in everyday life. In exceptional situations, however, especially when we are dealing with individuals with situational or permanent emotional dysregulation, this everyday empathy fails us. In this case, it can help if we widen or deepen our understanding of the unusual emotional situation by mindfully focusing on the other person. However, this does not seem to be as easily possible as the pausing of the first level, because the cognitive barriers against the alien affective state are acting powerfully as a defense against what is perceived as a threat. Mindfulness as enhanced empathy therefore needs to be practiced, essentially by achieving a change in our interpretation of unfamiliar affective states—in other words, by reframing the way we cognitively categorize our perceptions. What used to seem simply pointless, stupid, and dangerous will then become meaningful from the other person's perspective.

c. *Eidetic vision* (perceiving the essence): In Buddhism, enhanced mindfulness does help not only to cope better with everyday problems but also to see or experience things in the world that would otherwise remain hidden. If we don't reject this possibility categorically because we are convinced that nothing hidden exists behind the things (a false conclusion derived from the now dominant paradigm of materialist monism based on the economy of thought), such an attempt can potentially open up a deeper understanding of the object of our mindful attention.

This kind of consideration is not as alien to education science as it may seem at first glance. Unlike other human sciences, education tends to accept a usually highly regarded form of eidetic vision that is essentially not dissimilar to the Buddhist concept: the phenomenological approach with its qualitative research methods, as long as they are not hermeneutically (examining the meaning of texts in the paradigm of philology) but phenomenologically oriented, such as in reconstructive biography research or "grounded theory" of ethnology: In observing matter, something coherent, a form—or the essence—is extracted. The methods all refer to the eidetic vision, or *Wesensschau*, used by Edmund Husserl to explain his phenomenology.

This phenomenologically oriented education science comes quite close to Waldorf education with its anthroposophic image of the human being. The cognitive process in this anthropology is very similar to, if not identical with, the *Wesensschau* known from phenomenology.[15]

The mindful interaction observed by outside visitors in Waldorf schools can be understood as belonging to this third stage of mindfulness as perception of the inner essence. Here could be a potential point of access for the education sciences.

4 Waldorf education is more than and different from education reform

In summary, one can say that, historically speaking, Waldorf education has been, and can be, seen by education science as a variant of education reform. However, the experienced specific effect of Waldorf education—in fulfilling the basic educational task of intentional socialization and intentional enculturation—can also be made accessible to education science with its systematic categories of effect research independently of this historical categorization. This will open up other connections than those that can be made visible on the basis of education reform.

Notes

1 Jürgen Oelkers (2005): Reformpädagogik. In his history of an international movement, Oelkers mentions the term only briefly and pejoratively, referring to a comprehensive reform movement in the United States, Great Britain, and continental Europe. But since he merely lists seemingly arbitrary reform concepts that have so far hardly been noticed, his presentation lacks inner and outer coherence. The concept of *Reformpädagogik* used by Dietrich Benner and Herwart Kemper (2001) in their multi-volume publication differs from the one generally used: He refers to any educational innovation as reform, which gives the term to broad a meaning and trivializes it.

2 Harm Paschen systematically analyzed the—unusual—plural "pedagogies" and proposes systematization (Paschen 1997). It becomes apparent that a difference in quality or status between different pedagogies is not as easily justifiable as often implied, for instance by Krüger, who distinguishes between theoretical concepts and pedagogical theories. In both cases, presentations rely on closed axiomatic systems of values and assumed knowledge that need to be accepted, in other words: believed. This is particularly true for the theoretical approaches and paradigms (cf. Poser 2012; Sandkühler 2009).

3 It is often assumed that the late-Romantic criticism is aimed at industrialism and capitalism, but this view is not doing it full justice. Romanticism was first of all directed against the dominance of reason over body and feeling (as in the *Sturm und Drang* period); in the course of the 19th century, it focused on a fashionably exaggerated rationalism, i.e., mechanic materialism, and toward the end of the century on monistic materialism (Nieke 1980), which claims that everything (including soul, feeling, culture, spirit) can be explained using the principle of "mental economy" (Ernst Mach), in terms of eternally existing and unchangeable matter and its movements (or, in today's parlance, its "system states"). Upheld against this view are intuition and feeling, and the concept of life, since monistic materialism is not (yet) able to explain the scientific phenomenon of life in mechanical terms. This leaves room for an explanatory principle such as the "vital force" or a spiritually conceived life principle, as well as for an increasingly influential life philosophy. Industrialization and capitalism are then particularly conspicuous and effective applications of this thinking, with which humans are (allowed to be) placed, as part of nature, and nothing but nature, in just such end-mean relations as are known from the extremely effective domination of nature, which has resulted from this paradigm, and as are now consequently applied to human beings, too. That this is an alienation can only be claimed once it has been established that human beings are different from nature.

4 The expert information system *Bildung* has 2000 entries on this topic, so it is clearly one that is discussed intensely.

5 This classification is to be understood as a heuristic proposal, which means there is no coherent justification for it yet and it could be changed if expedient.

6 From a descriptive perspective, scientific societies are those where the final decision in case of controversial issues lies with the nomothetic sciences that are able to establish reliable prognoses regarding future system states, based on experiments in which hypotheses are tested. Their material basis consists essentially in applied science—technology—rather than in subsistence production that is based on experience passed on narratively from generation to generation. From a normative perspective, precisely this orientation toward intersubjectively verifiable, rational final decisions is affirmed as right and worth striving for. The critical use of the term calls the sole power of interpretation of (natural-) scientific rationality into question but tends to not have good reasons for this or offer convincing alternatives.

7 Of the many possible definitions of postmodernism, one aspect will be singled out here, which is that it was possible in the modern period, through rational forms of determining truth, to make clear decisions on this, which could be verified intersubjectively and therefore implemented as universally valid—such as human rights as a universally valid reference system for legal, political, and also moral decisions in everyday life. In this view, postmodernism qualifies also these Great Narratives of Modernism, resulting in an agnostic relativism not only in relation to value decisions (practical discourses) but also to all questions of knowledge (theoretical discourses).

8 This is usually attributed to Rousseau: He is seen as the inventor of a new image of the child. But this is only partially true. While his critique of the damaging effects of a (feudalistic and clerical) state society on the child, who is good by nature, is original and also the basis of his revolution-supporting criticism of the feudal state, the thought that children cannot learn through violence and must therefore be respected and supported goes back as far as Plato (Laws [Nomoi], 793 c) and one can assume that Rousseau, who was well conversant with ancient sources, knew of this and absorbed it, possibly indirectly via Augustine.

9 It is therefore understandable that Ullrich and Skiera are skeptical of Oelkers' calling any proposal for change in "educational reform" and of integrating the movement and epoch thus designated historically and internationally in a way that suppresses its unique character disappear.

10 This impression has been systematically confirmed in objective comparison studies on school quality, in which the school climate is included: Weiß (2013), Liebenwein, Barz, Randoll (2012).

11 Meyer (2005); so far mostly received in social pedagogy.

12 Sometimes also called "beliefs." The term here does not refer to religious beliefs or values because the operationalizations often include anthropological views and expectations regarding the effects of particular didactic models, for instance when teachers are asked if they agree with certain items in teacher research surveys. "Beliefs" are therefore shared interpretative patterns that are valid either in the entire life world or in specific institutions.

13 But regarding the measured effect size of formal teacher education for student performance, for instance, Hattie calls attention to the entirely insufficient state of research of the individual studies included in his meta-analysis. This methodical problem is also apparent in many other places and points to desirable future research designs that are more relevant to the subject-matter under examination.

14 Pierre Bourdieu's (1979/2012) habitus theory also explains embodied social and cultural orientation patterns with collectively shared and largely implicitly effective world orientations. It focuses on an existing social inequality that serves to retain the privileges of those who possess excessive cultural capital (which includes money). In a wider, less concrete sense, the habitus concept can also be used to explain "lasting behavioral dispositions" in relation to cultural and societal influences. Personality psychology, on the other hand, models what it measures as the effect of an internal mental processing of innate elements and external stimuli constellations.

15 As a mathematician, Rudolf Steiner drew on geometry to explain his method of gaining knowledge of the essence behind the phenomena. The experience of understanding mathematical truths independently of empirical confirmation connects him with Husserl.

References

Apel, Karl-Otto (1976): Transformationen der Philosophie. Vol. 2. Das Apriori der Kommunikationsgemeinschaft. Frankfurt am Main: Suhrkamp.

Aronson, Elliot/Wilson, Timothy D./Akert, Robin M. (2004): Sozialpsychologie. 4th revised edition. Munich: Pearson.

Benner, Dietrich/Kemper, Herwart (2001): Theorie und Geschichte der Reformpädagogik. Parts 1 and 2. Weinheim: Deutscher Studien Verlag.

Bohnsack, Ralf (2014): Rekonstruktive Sozialforschung. Einführung in qualitative Methoden. 9th revised and extended edition. Opladen: Budrich.

Bourdieu, Pierre (1979/2012): Die feinen Unterschiede. Kritik der gesellschaftlichen Urteilskraft. 22nd edition. Frankfurt am Main: Suhrkamp.

Ecarius, Jutta (2008): Generation, Erziehung und Bildung. Stuttgart: Kohlhammer.

Fend, Helmut (1977): Schulklima: soziale Einflussprozesse in der Schule. Weinheim: Beltz.

Fend, Helmut (1998): Qualität im Bildungswesen. Schulforschung zu Systembedingungen, Schulprofilen und Lehrerleistung. Weinheim: Juventa.

Geertz, Clifford (2003): Dichte Beschreibung. Beiträge zum Verstehen kultureller Systeme. Frankfurt am Main: Suhrkamp.

Gehlen, Arnold (1940/2014): Der Mensch, seine Natur und seine Stellung in der Welt. 16th edition. Wiebelsheim: AULA.

Glaser, Barney G./Strauss, Anselm L. (1967): The Discovery of Grounded Theory. Strategies for Qualitative Research. Bern: Huber.

Habermas, Jürgen (1983): Diskursethik. Notizen zu einem Begründungsprogramm. In: Habermas, Jürgen (Ed.) (1983): Moralbewusstsein und kommunikatives Handeln. Frankfurt am Main: Suhrkamp, pp. 53–125.

Haertel, Geneva D./Walberg, Herbert J./Weinstein, Thomas (1983): Psychological Models of Educational Performance: A Theoretical Synthesis of Constructs. In: Reviews of Educational Research 53, pp. 75–91.

Hattie, John (2013): Lernen sichtbar machen. Baltmannsweiler: Schneider. English original: Hattie, John (2009): Visible Learning. New York: Routledge

Hobbes, Thomas (1651/2011): Leviathan oder Stoff, Form und Gewalt eines kirchlichen und bürgerlichen Staates. Frankfurt am Main: Suhrkamp.

Krüger, Heinz-Hermann (2012): Einführung in Theorien und Methoden der Erziehungswissenschaft. 6th revised edition. Opladen: Budrich.

Liebenwein, Sylvia/Barz, Heiner/Randoll, Dirk (Eds.) (2012): Bildungserfahrungen an Waldorfschulen. Empirische Studie zu Schulqualität und Lernerfahrungen. Wiesbaden: VS.

Litt, Theodor (1927/1958): Führen oder Wachsenlassen. Eine Erörterung des pädagogischen Grundproblems. 7th edition. Stuttgart: Klett.

Meinberg, Eckhard (1988): Das Menschenbild der modernen Erziehungswissenschaft. Darmstadt: Wissenschaftliche Buchgesellschaft.

Meyer, John W. (2005): Weltkultur. Wie die westlichen Prinzipien die Welt durchdringen. Frankfurt am Main: Suhrkamp.

Nieke, Wolfgang (1980): Materialismus. In: Ritter, Joachim (Ed.) (1980): Historisches Wörterbuch der Philosophie. Vol. 5. Basel: Schwabe, pp. 842–850.

Nieke, Wolfgang (2006): Religion als Bestandteil von Allgemeinbildung: Weltorientierung statt Religionslehre. In: Ziebertz, Hans-Georg/Schmidt, Günter R. (Eds.) (2006): Religion in der Allgemeinen Pädagogik. Von der Religion als Grundlegung bis zu ihrer Bestreitung. Gütersloh: Gütersloher Verlagshaus, pp. 191–210.

Nieke, Wolfgang (2008): Interkulturelle Erziehung und Bildung. Wiesbaden: VS.

Nieke, Wolfgang (2010a): Philosophische Traditionslinien. In: Bock, Karin/Miethe, Ingrid (Eds.) (2010): Handbuch Qualitative Methoden in der Sozialen Arbeit. Opladen: Budrich, pp. 39–47.

Nieke, Wolfgang (2010b): Reformpädagogik. Entstehungsgeschichten einer internationalen Begegnung. Seelze: Kallmeyer.

Nohl, Herman (1933): Die Theorie der Bildung. In: Nohl, Herman/Pallat, Ludwig (Eds.) (1933): Handbuch der Pädagogik. Vol. 1: Die Theorie und die Entwicklung des Bildungswesens. Bad Langensalza: Beltz, pp. 3–80.

Oelkers, Jürgen (2005): Reformpädagogik. Eine kritische Dogmengeschichte. 4th edition, fully revised and extended. Weinheim: Juventa.

Paschen, Harm (1992): Aufgaben und Instrumente einer argumentativ disziplinierten Erziehungswissenschaft. In: Paschen, Harm/Wigger, Lothar (Eds.) (1992): Pädagogisches Argumentieren. Weinheim: Deutscher Studien Verlag, pp. 141–153.

Paschen, Harm (1997): Pädagogiken. Zur Systematik pädagogischer Differenzen. Weinheim: Deutscher Studien Verlag.

Popper, Karl Raimund (1989): Logik der Forschung. 9th improved edition. Tübingen: Mohr.

Poser, Hans (2012): Wissenschaftstheorie. Eine philosophische Einführung. 2nd revised and extended edition. Stuttgart: Reclam.

Rutschky, Katharina (Ed.) (1977): Schwarze Pädagogik. Quellen zur Naturgeschichte der bürgerlichen Erziehung. Berlin: Ullstein.

Sandkühler, Hans Jörg (2009): Kritik der Repräsentation. Einführung in die Theorie der Überzeugungen, der Wissenskulturen und des Wissens. Frankfurt am Main: Suhrkamp.

Schilling, Johannes (2000): Menschenbilder in der Sozialen Arbeit. Neuwied: Luchterhand.

Schütz, Alfred/Luckmann, Thomas (2003): Strukturen der Lebenswelt. Konstanz: UVK.

Skiera, Ehrenhard (2010): Reformpädagogik in Geschichte und Gegenwart. Eine kritische Einführung. 2nd corrected edition. Munich: Oldenbourg.

Weiß, Manfred (2013): Schulleistungen an Privatschulen. In: Gürlevik, Aydin/Palentien, Christian/Heyer, Robert (Eds.) (2013): Privatschulen versus staatliche Schulen. Wiesbaden: VS, pp. 227–234.

Zimmermann, Michael/Spitz, Christof/Schmidt, Stefan (Eds.) (2012): Achtsamkeit. Ein buddhistisches Konzept erobert die Wissenschaft. Bern: Huber.

EDUCATION REFORM AND WALDORF EDUCATION

Interpreting a Historically Difficult Relationship

Volker Frielingsdorf

1 Introduction

Just before the beginning of the 20th century, John Dewey foresaw a "Copernican revolution in relation to the child" that would result in an entirely difficult attitude of educators and parents and therefore require totally different forms of school. Dewey likened this event to the revolution inspired by Copernicus: In future, children, with their specific needs, would be at the center of everything related to education (Koslowski 2013, p. 134).

Dewey's dictum did, in fact, signalize the dawn of a new era for schools and for education. Most historians in the German-speaking world place this period of what is usually termed "education reform" in the years between 1890 and 1930/1933 (Keim, Schwerdt 2013a; Skiera 2010). While this new phase in the history of education may be called or categorized differently in other countries,[1] there is general agreement that in the decades leading up to and after the Second World War important pioneers initiated a thorough educational revolution that continues to reverberate today and that led to a reorientation in the entire education system of the industrialized world.

Cecil Reddie, John Haden Badley, A.S. Neill, John Dewey, Helen Parkhurst, Célestin Freinet, Jean Piaget, and Maria Montessori are usually seen as the prominent international figures of that era, while representatives in Germany include Hermann Lietz, Gustav Wyneken, Paul Geheeb, Georg Kerschensteiner, and Peter Petersen. Although Rudolf Steiner is in principle also counted among these luminaries of "progressive education," the attribution is in his case interestingly not as consistent and matter of fact as with the other protagonists.[2]

These difficulties to clearly assign Rudolf Steiner and his anthroposophically oriented education to the education reform movements have continued, if to a less marked degree, to this day. In the German history of education and education reform, Waldorf education has been more or less ignored for a long time, or has at best been mentioned marginally, for the sake of completeness, as it were (Nohl 2002; Röhrs 1998; Scheibe 1999).

This noticeable neglect on the part of education science[3]—which requires explanation—is made up for, however, by the fact that other educationists include Steiner's education in the rather loosely defined category of "progressive education." This seemingly premature inclusion became common in the 1970s (Frielingsdorf 2012; Steinmann 2001) and has led to Waldorf education being mentioned in the same breath with the approaches of Montessori and Freinet (Hellmich, Teigeler 1999), or with the *Landerziehungsheime* (rural boarding schools) and Peter Petersen's Jena Plan Schools (Hansen-Schaberg, Schonig 2006). The same is true for Ehrenhard Skiera's monograph, a justifiably leading study in the history of education reform, past and present. Skiera dedicates an entire chapter to

Waldorf education, including a detailed description and concluding with an ambivalent evaluation (Skiera 2010).

Since around 1975, Waldorf education has been presented as "one of the established orientations in reform education" in teachers' colleges or education studies, and it has been seen as a kind of "canonical orientational knowledge for prospective students" (Nieke in Chapter 7) that was even integrated into the curriculum of education studies in the German state of North Rhine Westphalia. All these incompletely reflected attempts tend to overlook, however, that the relationship between Waldorf education and education reform has not always been as harmonious, or even as dialogical, as the by-now common contextualization and canonization seem to suggest. Rather, with the remarkable exception of the *"Arbeitsgemeinschaft Freier Schulen"* (working committee of independent schools), there have, for many decades and until recently, hardly been any attempts at an open exchange between representatives of education reform movements and of Waldorf education, a fact that gives rise to the impression that the two must, after all, be separate streams.

In the mid-1950s, the educationist Heinz Kloss described Waldorf education as a third and therefore autonomous approach besides the mainstream "learning school" and "progressive education," examining at length whether this "trisection" was adequate and whether Waldorf education "is distinctive enough to justify such a separate position" (Kloss 1955, p. 12). What remains undisputed is that Waldorf schools have always occupied a special status in relation to the educational reform schools (Frielingsdorf 2012, p. 188ff.). Martin Näf confirms this emphatically in his multi-faceted monograph on Paul Geheeb and his wife Edith Geheeb-Cassirer, where he points out that both Steiner's claim to truth and the anthroposophic cosmogony put education reformers off in equal measure. Näf adds, sensitively, that the conceptions of Montessori, Petersen, and Freinet "mixed" more easily with other pedagogies than Steiner's approach to education (Näf 2006, p. 104). This does not mean that Waldorf education and education reform are incompatible. Nonetheless, it needs to be carefully examined whether Waldorf schools practice their own pedagogy or whether they are part of an overarching education reform movement.

How widely views differ on this, even if this has not been explicitly discussed, is apparent from the way Waldorf education is treated by the educationists Jürgen Oelkers and Heiner Ullrich. While Oelkers, in his groundbreaking critical history of dogmas in education reform, mentions Waldorf education and Rudolf Steiner only in passing (Oelkers 2005, 2010a), Ullrich, who has critically studied Steiner's education and anthroposophy since his dissertation was published in book form (Ullrich 1986), even suggests that Waldorf education was no longer, as it used to be, an "outsider" of education reform but had by now, thanks to its astonishing quantitative growth, become its "leader" (Ullrich 1995, 2015).

This remarkable upgrading of Waldorf schools by their most persevering critic comes as a surprise to the unbiased reader, given its implication that Waldorf education has advanced to a particularly prominent position among the education reform movements. Whether this is indeed the case will be examined below, where first the commonalities and agreements of both streams will be discussed, followed by any noteworthy differences and deviations. Five essential aspects will then be presented for each side before the attempt is made to provide a multi-perspective answer based on four theses.

2 Waldorf education and education reform: What they have in common

The inclusion of Waldorf education among the education reform movements suggests itself simply because they emerged around the same time. Rudolf Steiner inaugurated Waldorf education in the summer of 1919, right in the middle of the education reform period that, following its modest beginnings before 1914, found broad reception in the ready-for-change, turbulent times after the First World War. In this climate, which was very susceptive to comprehensive educational reform, Rudolf Steiner and Emil Molt, the director of the Stuttgart Waldorf Astoria cigarette factory, were able to found the first Waldorf School rapidly and without many bureaucratic hurdles. Steiner could work intensely with the teachers he appointed for a period of five years, support and advise them, before serious illness in the fall of 1924 prevented him from traveling to Stuttgart from Dornach (near Basel in Switzerland). His untimely death six months later did not stifle the energy of the Stuttgart faculty of teachers but strengthened their will to continue the work they had started, building on the foundation provided for them.

Steiner's death in March 1925 occurred at a time when education reform had reached its peak. In 1921, the New Education Fellowship (NEF), an international organization of education reform founded in that year, organized a major congress on education in Heidelberg (DE), inviting Martin Buber to give the introductory lecture and C.G. Jung as a guest speaker (Koslowski 2013, p. 66ff.). In 1923, Peter Petersen took over the chair of education science at Jena and spent the following year developing the plan Pedagogy. Around 1925, the social-democratic "German Experimental Schools" met with broad interest, as is apparent from the publications of Fritz Karsen and Franz Hilker (Hilker 1924; Karsen 1923). All these movements could establish themselves in the golden 1920s of the Weimar Republic, before the disastrous consequences of the global economic crisis began to put a damper on any educational experiments in 1929.

It is therefore true to say that the first phase of Waldorf education, which was decisively shaped by Rudolf Steiner, coincided with the heyday of education reform in Germany. Since both movements were critical of the outdated school system and sought to introduce radically new ideas to education and teaching, it seemed only natural to include Waldorf education in the broad education reform movement of that time. That Rudolf Steiner's anthroposophically inspired education was later often lumped together without reflection with the pedagogical approaches of Maria Montessori, Peter Petersen, and others was most likely due to the ever-spresent need for simplification and labeling.

That Waldorf education is usually categorized with the education reform movements is because it shared their vehemently expressed criticism of the prevailing school system. At the end of the 19th century, when industrialization and urbanization were driven relentlessly in the German Reich, the state school system had only just become established. And yet, most schools were seen as repressive cram-and-drill establishments, where children were basically locked up and instructed according to the ideas of a monarchic-authoritarian society.

The "epochal incision at around 1890" cited by Heinz-Elmar Tenorth impacted profoundly on schools and on the teaching in particular, because the ongoing industrial-technological impetus of the era of William II triggered profound social transformation and "rapid change in education" (Tenorth 2000, 183f.). In the years leading up to 1914, in the prevailing mixture of cultural criticism, diffuse fears of socialism, and romanticist expectations of the future, an entirely novel philosophy emerged, introducing a revolutionary educational approach that placed the child in the center.[4]

All the educational reformers mentioned, including Rudolf Steiner, belong to this stream that gained particular momentum after the turn of the century. Steiner had been very critical of the existing school system even before 1900, demanding educational reform. Even if his early philosophical thoughts on education met with little interest at the time and have remained largely unknown, they illustrate that he had been interested in and actively studying educational questions early on. Having studied Friedrich Nietzsche and his work in-depth for many years, Steiner was, as early as 1895, deeply familiar with the critique of culture and education that was rife at that time.[5]

Among the many rejectors of the existing school system were, aside from avantgarde writers and poets, teachers especially, who asked for school reform and who presented alternatives based on their own pedagogical experiments. Hermann Hesse's vehement criticism of education, expressed both explicitly and implicitly in his 1906 novel *Unterm Rad* (Beneath the Wheel, Hesse 1972), can be seen as a kind of *cantus firmus* underlying the protestations and complaints of education reformers.[6]

The teachers of the first Waldorf School, who worked with Rudolf Steiner, certainly agreed with the representatives of education reform, of whatever provenance, in rejecting the predominant school system, which they felt was coercive, indoctrinating, and inadequate.

Education reform and Waldorf education also share a high, sometimes even excessive, estimation of education in general and school in particular. For some education reform groups, "education as redemption" (Baader 2005) became a kind of world-salvation program that lead to the mystification of children and their quasi-divine forces. Such glorification, which was very prominent with Ellen Kay and Maria Montessori, seems strange today in that it assigns an almost religious status to education.

But this kind of elevation also occurs in the anthroposophical movement. Here, too, education—seen in Steiner's intention as an art—is sometimes assigned a certain solemnity, with the teacher playing an almost priest-like role. However, since children, according to anthroposophical developmental psychology, rely on education and on the authority of the teacher, this hypostatizing of students meets natural boundaries. On the other hand, there is the idea of reincarnation in anthroposophy, which opens the possibility for teachers to assume that their students are inhabited by particularly gifted personalities.

One can certainly observe in some elements of both education reform and anthroposophic education the "transformation of religion" into education described in-depth by Meike-Sophie Baader (Baader 2005).[7] The associated powerful cosmogony that can be rather disconcerting for outsiders is also common to both directions. It not only plays a not-to-be underestimated part in Rudolf Steiner's ideas but also in those of Maria Montessori and the schools inspired by the British theosophists around Beatrice Ensor. The alleged dawn of a "New Era"—also the title of the New Education Fellowship's journals since the 1920s—certainly reveals the immense importance for the whole of human evolution, assigned to education in some prominent reform streams.

It was not only in France and Italy that such excessive expectations of salvation were associated with the search for a true *éducation nouvelle* or *educazione nuova*, but in a weakened form even in the pragmatic United States, instilling great motivational power in Waldorf teachers there, too. On the other hand, such expectations always harbor the danger that they cannot be met in the actual teaching reality.

Despite the great potential for disappointment, both education reform and the Waldorf schools' "art of education" are rooted in unwavering pedagogical optimism arising from their profoundly positive view of human nature. As early as 1955, Heinz Kloss cited as the most essential commonality of education reform and Waldorf education "the belief in the primacy of the quality of education:" "quality on the part of the teachers, trust on that of the students, love on both sides; that is the light that illuminates both houses, that of education reform and that of Waldorf education; the light shining out of their windows" (Kloss 1955, p. 35).

This shared view of inwardly affirming the human being and consequently each individual child was to build a bridge that would bring the representatives of both sides together and deeply connect them. The danger of elevating and overestimating education is present on both sides, too, however.

From what has been said so far, it is clear that both education reform and the anthroposophic "art of education" are intended to be more than "mere" pedagogy. They rely on comprehensive world and life plans that concern the most diverse levels of existence. In the widest sense, they can therefore be seen as part of the early 20th century's life reform movement, in as far as that movement saw itself as holistic rather than particularistic. In opposition to sectarian groups whose "life reform" consisted in propagating one particular aspect (such as nudism, vegetarianism, or naturopathy), most projects of education reform or anthroposophy had a holistic orientation. The British garden city movement, for example, included ecological, associative, and, later, also pedagogical ideas. It was similar with its German counterparts, one of which is Hellerau, founded in 1909 as the first German garden city in a suburb of Dresden. That A. S. Neill, who was still largely unknown at that time, was able to work there as a teacher, developing the radical educational ideas he would later become famous for, illustrates how closely the life reform movement of that time was linked with education reform.

Something similar, if in a different way, is also true for the anthroposophic movement. Within the fields of practice inspired by Steiner, there were closely connected initiatives—ranging from biodynamic farming to anthroposophic medicine to special needs education, social therapy and Waldorf education, including also diverse artistic endeavors—that were intended to counteract the fragmentations of modernism. The "social threefolding movement," which also goes back to Rudolf Steiner, even provided a sociopolitical backdrop to these initiatives, manifesting at the microsocial level in the impulse to form life communities.

In contrast to the life reform projects that many reform teachers felt close to and that often existed disparately side by side, the diverse initiatives inspired by anthroposophy had a solid foundation in the worldview created by Steiner that can be traced back to Goethe. This foundation with its esoteric roots connected people, provided an identity to the movement, and created social coherence and stability in times of crisis.

What Waldorf education and education reform consequently also have in common is the fact that they can only be understood against the background of their individual and very comprehensive worldviews and the impulses arising from this worldview for practical life changes. Within this holistic worldview, the striving for genuine community played a central part. The equality of man and woman, respect for the individuality of each child, and the dissolution of hierarchies were as important to both movements as "comprehensive schools" linked inseparably to principles, such as coeducation, collegiality, and collaborative governance.

Because education reform and Waldorf education pursue a holistic approach, it is not surprising that many aspects of practical school life also coincide in both movements. In both, school climate plays a particular part, because it is understood to enable children and young people to "learn in freedom" (Rogers 1984), "free of fear" (Lindenberg 1995), and so they can develop in a pleasant and enjoyable ambience. Peter Petersen's idea of a "*Schulwohnstube*" (school living room) that would inspire students belongs to this endeavor, as do the "free work" group spaces in Montessori's pedagogical concept, and the sympathetically designed classrooms in Waldorf schools that aim to form a protective shell around the students where they can feel at home, especially in the first school years.

Petersen placed much emphasis on school climate and classroom design as essential elements of his Jena Plan, pointing out that they mirrored a school's pedagogic approach and ways of teaching (Klein-Landeck 2009, p. 131). Waldorf education has very similar arguments, focusing additionally on the architectural design of the entire school building (Rittelmeyer 1994).

The education sciences, too, have long understood the importance of school climate for student performance (Fend 1977). Nonetheless, the sober conclusion more than 30 years after Helmut Fend's groundbreaking studies is that, while many Waldorf and educational reform schools feature a particularly pleasant school climate, this can clearly not be said of regular state schools (Nieke in Chapter 7).

That educational reform schools and Waldorf schools are not as different from one another as both are from state schools is apparent if one looks at essential lesson organization and teaching methods in the different types of school. Waldorf schools and educational reform schools reject the tight corset of a rigid timetable with 45-minute lesson units that usually follow randomly on from each other. They either complement this structure or have totally replaced it, with alternatives such as block teaching or project lessons.

When it comes to methods, educational reform schools value forms of independent study in particular, while Waldorf education relies on the ability of teachers to motivate students and inspire interest in them for their subjects. Both reject external pressure and coercion by means of punishments, grades, and end-of-year reports, and both prefer to rely on the students' intrinsic motivation, the inner drive for education (*Bildungstrieb*) that lives in each person and only needs to be stimulated and developed.

The range of subjects offered in Waldorf schools and educational reform schools also differs considerably from that of state schools, especially from the still largely cognitive approach of grammar schools. As a result of their holistic concept, independent schools have always paid particular attention to young people's emotional and social needs. Gardening and handwork lessons, drama, choir, and orchestra are therefore as much part of the curriculum as art and music.

The arts and crafts provision in Waldorf schools I,s in some aspects, a reflection of Georg Kerschensteiner's "activity education" and in others of Alfred Lichtwark's art education movement. Due to the many noncognitive subjects, which in Waldorf education are seen as equivalent to the so-called main subjects, one could even be tempted to see Waldorf schools as the successful integration of all the diverse elements of education reform. This assumption is further corroborated by the fact that the Waldorf principle also includes the social-democratic principle of the life community school and that it has been from the start, in a very radical way, a "comprehensive school" even practicing an early form of inclusion.

Waldorf schools and educational reform schools therefore agree particularly in their ideals of the social aspect of education, their choice of subjects, and their lesson structure. This is not surprising if one knows that both approaches, which did not emerge at the same time by coincidence, are based on a holistic view of the human being and of the world. It is almost inevitable that this has implications for the school design. And it is also inevitable that the reform-oriented schools differ noticeably from schools that continue to hold on to the old paradigm.

3 Differences between Waldorf education and education reform

Having considered the many commonalities between Waldorf education and education reform, one may be led to assume that there cannot be any striking differences. But even with so many similarities, one must not overlook what separates the different approaches. Heinz Kloss stated early on that these commonalities were "sometimes overrated by the reform teachers and overlooked by the Waldorf teachers" (Kloss 1955, p. 33). Reversely, it could be said of the differences that they are being overlooked by reform teachers and many outsiders, while the representatives of Waldorf schools tend to overrate them.

Below, the differences between the two directions are set out in a deliberately accentuated way. Their actual significance will be apparent from the subsequent qualifying conclusion.

3.1 Philosophical foundation

The first fundamental difference between Waldorf education and education reform lies in the former's intrinsically coherent and multilayered philosophical foundation that some find fascinating, while others are alienated or even deterred by it. The complexity of Rudolf Steiner's anthroposophy, which underpins Waldorf education, prevents easy or quick access to it. Because of its claim to truth and its totality, anthroposophy is seen as sectarian and its originator scorned as a seemingly omniscient prophet.[8]

However, Steiner himself never expected his listeners to blindly and uncritically accept his statements but to test them for themselves. The claim to absoluteness raised by many of his followers is therefore not intrinsic to anthroposophy if one sees it, as Steiner did, as a philosophy and opens it up to scientific discourse. Steiner's Philosophy of Freedom, first published in 1894, and his theory of knowledge, which traces back to Goethe, were, however, a quarter of a century old by the time he founded the first Waldorf School. This primarily philosophical early work always remained present to him—a second edition of The Philosophy of Freedom was published in 1918 (Steiner 1973)—but not to many of his followers and to even fewer of those who met Steiner after the First World War as a school reformer, spiritual teacher, or lecturer. His extensive knowledge of so many fields, from Christology to modern science, from agriculture to astrology, made him appear as a revered leader of humanity to some and as an esoteric fantasist or even a charlatan to others.

As a result, Waldorf education, which was founded in 1919, struggled to gain a foothold in public. Many school reformers were probably irritated by the alleged or actual claim to absoluteness raised by many anthroposophists or were not prepared to engage with Rudolf Steiner's ideas on education.

But precisely that would have been helpful. For given its multilayered developmental psychology and its distinction of different levels of existence, the anthroposophic view of the human being constitutes an inspiring and thought-provoking anthropology (Rittelmeyer 1990). For many Waldorf teachers, the *Menschenkunde* (anthropology) developed by Rudolf Steiner continues to be the very heart of his education. This spiritual-scientific anthropology, which is the only one for many insiders, is in fact what distinguishes Waldorf education fundamentally from education reform streams that do not have such a sophisticated foundation. Education reformers did not usually discuss the question of an anthropology of their own explicitly, even though their approach was also based on a particular image of the human being.

In the faculty meetings of Waldorf schools, the content of Steiner's *Meditatively Acquired Anthropology* (Steiner 1993) and other courses on education continue to be intensively studied and reflected upon. That other anthropological approaches are not being considered is another matter.

3.2 The role of the teacher

A second, and probably the most profound, fundamental difference between the anthroposophic "art of education" and education reform arises from its distinct understanding of the role of the teacher, particularly in the phase that is referred to as the "second seven-year period" in Waldorf education. During this period of eight school years, the "class teacher" or "grade teacher" has a very dominant position, teaching all the "main lessons;" that is to say, he or she teaches all the main subjects in blocks of three to four weeks, every morning for the first 2 hours of school. The class teacher is, therefore, during that period, the dominant influence on Waldorf students between the ages of 7 and 14. This predominance is deliberate and constitutes an important pillar of Steiner's pedagogy. In his developmental psychology, Steiner points out again and again how important this "healthy" authority of the teacher is at that age[9] and how harmful premature camaraderie and intellectualization are. In the eyes of Waldorf teachers, premature self-determination is not good for children, particularly because it hinders them from unfolding other soul faculties.

Most education reformers favored the exact opposite approach. For them, it was particularly important, even in elementary school and kindergarten, to encourage children to determine their own activity and take on responsibility. Montessori's "free activity" and John Dewey's pragmatic "learning by doing" follow this ideal that sees the teacher as a companion rather than a figure of authority, as an older friend rather than someone who commands respect, a helper and facilitator rather than a leader or instructor.

Waldorf education does not pursue the old ideal of the authoritarian school master, however. But it knows the danger of awakening children's powers of judgment too early. It therefore seeks to allow school children to grow up for as long as possible in a beautiful, harmonious environment. The "story part" that concludes the classic main lesson in Waldorf schools is an interesting example of this in two ways: First, the simple fact that grade teachers tell a story every day that the children listen to attentively is remarkable. The second remarkable fact is the choice of story material Steiner recommended, starting with folktales, fables, and legends, followed later by the great sagas and folk myths, and from sixth or seventh grade, the biographies of eminent historical personalities.

While Waldorf teachers claim that listening to and inwardly connecting with valuable cultural treasures from the history of humanity is particularly good for children, most education reformers find this less important and choose instead topics from the daily reality for their lessons. The representatives of radical education went even further: like A. S. Neill, trusting in the innate goodness of children, they promoted free development wherever possible, whilst seeking to abolish or at least restrict the influence exerted by parents and teachers.

Waldorf education resolutely rejects precisely this, insisting on the special responsibility of teachers and relying on their success in becoming authority figures for the children, "loved and freely accepted, but an authority nonetheless," who "alone and without discussing this with the students determines what should be done in the lessons" (Kloss 1955, p. 39).

Waldorf education is clearly diametrically opposed to the central principle of many approaches of education reform, resembling in this respect rather more the old learning schools or elementary schools. It may even come across as a fossil of the restoration period from before 1968, because in this respect even most state schools have embraced a certain degree of education reform. While this astonishing conclusion, from which it is a quick step to the judgment that Waldorf education is not appropriate for our time, may be mitigated by pointing out that Waldorf students are at least given more space for independent activity in the arts and craft lessons, it is true that even in that case the self-activity tends to be *guided* and rather constitute a "doing before learning," because the students are expected to first gain experience through all their senses before they really understand and learn with the help of their teachers (ibid., p. 41).

Waldorf education is therefore clearly different from education reform throughout, including in subjects that are strongly based on self-activity. It is also true to say, however, that more and more teachers in Waldorf schools have started in recent years to use forms of group teaching and other elements of a more student-centered method.

This is also why it would be interesting in future for Waldorf and reform teachers to discuss questions of education and teaching connected with the authority principle. This may even open up the possibility of answering the very different views on this question, not with an "either/or" approach but by reflecting together on situations and age groups for which the otherwise diverging teaching styles could be sensibly employed.

Theodor Litt's essay *Führen oder Wachsenlassen* (Leading or Letting Grow, Litt 1927) could prove helpful in this context. As early as the mid-1920s, Litt critically analyzed certain one-sided habits of education reform in his "exposition of the basic pedagogic problem," demonstrating that "leading" and "letting grow" do not necessarily have to be mutually exclusive opposites in teaching and education. He tried to explain that "these two basic orientations are by necessity mutually dependent, dialogically complementary, and constructively exciting moments in each educational process" (Seichter 2009, p. 256). From this point of view, it should be possible to combine responsible authority, which anthroposophically speaking, is always "education toward freedom," with a relaxed laissez-faire approach, so long as the latter is aware that it is its duty to set boundaries.[10]

3.3 Teaching content

As indicated before, education reform and Waldorf education do not only differ with regard to the teachers' role and teaching *method* but also with regard to their teaching *content*. As a rule, the favoring of the teacher-centered approach implicates firm didactic instruction, and this also applies to Waldorf education. It is definitely the teacher who chooses, determines, and is responsible for the lesson material. Most Waldorf teachers take Rudolf Steiner's curricular indications as an orientation, which he only developed in broad strokes, however. Especially in the faculty meetings of the Stuttgart Waldorf School up until 1924, he gave numerous clear indications for the daily practice (Steiner 1975). Many of these indications, presented at the time by Steiner to individual teachers for specific situations with their own classes, were later assigned canonical status in the Waldorf schools, although Steiner never intended them as universally and eternally valid recipes.

In the following years, a clearly set out "curriculum" nonetheless appeared (Stockmeyer 1956/2001; von Heydebrand 1931/2009) which, as a whole, goes back to Rudolf Steiner and is only slightly influenced by some of the first Waldorf teachers. Because this curriculum constitutes something like a *gesamtkunstwerk* (total work of art), it is very difficult not to treat it as a comprehensive whole, because the individual parts relate to and are connected with one another and can therefore hardly be seen in separation. In a way, Steiner's teaching program therefore seems like a composition, impressive in its inner coherence and completeness.

Precisely for this reason, this program can be seen as a problem or even a danger. To representatives of education reform with its thoroughly liberal character, such a complete curriculum may easily appear as an authoritative requirement that the individual teacher has little influence on. Its didactics in particular make Waldorf education easily appear to outsiders as an unchangeable dogmatic structure, willingly accepted by Waldorf teachers.

The choice of material in education reform, on the other hand, is very much left to the teachers, and often the students themselves have a say in it or even decide what is being taught. This approach holds much potential for projects and groups, and for working in teams outside the lessons, but it also exposes its proponents to the accusation of arbitrariness. They see themselves confronted with questions such as how they can do justice to the task of schools to provide general education and whether their lack of clear guidelines and coherent planning did not deprive the students of important educational and cultural assets.

Rudolf Steiner, on the other hand, created a multi-faceted and inspiring curriculum that has been seen from the beginning as universally binding, that, for a long time, no one called into question, and that no student can circumvent, not even in high school because students don't have the ability to select their own courses. Here, too, Waldorf schools therefore come closer to the classic school system that also does not offer much choice.

The impact of Steiner's curricular indications for the teaching practice should, however, not be overrated. This is mostly because most instructions are phrased in very general terms, giving much scope to the individual Waldorf teacher to be creative. If, for example, the instruction for the second-grade teachers is to tell fables, it is left to the individual teacher whether they use Aesop, La Fontaine, Lessing, or others as their source. It also needs to be borne in mind that the Waldorf curriculum as such is not static but has been continually developed further (Richter 2010; Loebell in Chapter 7).

Despite these restrictions, there are fundamental didactic differences between Waldorf education and education reform that illustrate clearly how very different their underlying anthropological concepts are.

3.4 Social structure

The social structures aspired to in education reform and Waldorf education also differ widely. While the principle of collaborative governance is one of the cornerstones of Waldorf education (Götte 2006; Leber 1991), many reform movements—Montessori or Jena Plan schools for instance—saw no problem with establishing themselves within the regular school systems. The *Landerziehungsheime* (boarding schools in a rural environment) have always been private schools creating a certain exclusiveness by demanding rather high school fees.

Right from its foundation, the Waldorf school has seen itself consistently as a "comprehensive school" that welcomed children of all abilities and refrained as much as possible from early tracking. In that respect, it has remained the only comprehensive school where children and young people from 1st to 12th grade are taught without selection. Waldorf education rejects the tripartite school system with its very early tracking (as soon as after fourth grade) that continues to prevail in Germany. To this day Waldorf schools have remained truly comprehensive despite the ongoing pressure from school authorities and ministries of education.

Collaborative governance has consequently been crucial to Waldorf schools: externally, in order to stand up to educational policies and bureaucracy, and internally, as a way of including teachers actively in the running of the school. This possibility for active participation is further enhanced in Waldorf schools by their principle of collegiality. This realization of a "teachers' republic" probably means that Waldorf schools are more liberal-democratic than (German) state schools with their still directorial structure, but also than most educational reform schools, which have traditionally been under the leadership of some authoritative personality.

The social structure of Waldorf schools is also unique due to the way it involves and assigns important roles to parents. Particularly, in the school councils, which are in charge of legal and financial issues, parents are welcome and indispensable representatives, who are involved in decision-making processes as members of the school community.

With this degree of parental involvement, Waldorf schools differ distinctly from the *Landschulheime*, where the parents tend to be far away and teachers assume important aspects of the parental role. Waldorf schools, on the other hand, were never conceived as a "pedagogic province" far away from the city. Having been founded primarily for the children of Stuttgart factory workers, it was clear as early as 1919 that this school was not about bringing up children in some rural idyll. Its intention was, rather, to meet the challenges of the modern age and the educational conditions of the industrial society head-on.

Its city environment and proletarian and bourgeois clientele made sure that the Waldorf school was safe from any elitism. That, despite these egalitarian intentions, the Waldorf concept was not received as an example or model in the social-democratic educational landscape is only surprising at first glance. A closer look reveals that the representatives of that landscape did not look favorably at the Waldorf school's ideas of collaborative self-governance and their striving to escape any centralist interference.

Even this very rough outline and analysis of the specific social structure of Waldorf schools (Leber 1991) illustrates that Waldorf education—although it shares important elements of education reform and of a modern democratic understanding—it embodies these in a particular way that could be seen as a genuine synthesis but is too idiosyncratic to fit in with the concepts of any political provenance.

3.5 Organizational structures

The last of the five points to be mentioned here that speaks against including Waldorf education with the education reform movement may seem to be external, but it conceals an internal contradiction that points to an ongoing conflict. This difference is, first of all, about organizational structure and forms of cooperation (or lack of cooperation) between the two streams.

The NEF mentioned earlier played a key role in this. Like the first Waldorf School, the NEF was born directly after the First World War. Its orientation was from the start international, and it saw itself as a forum for education reform of any kind. At the major congresses that the NEF organized and that, from 1927 onward, were attended by more than a thousand teachers, school leaders, and scientists interested in educational questions (Koslowski 2013, p. 62), the pedagogical concepts of Maria Montessori, Peter Petersen, John Dewey, Célestin Freinet, Paul Geheeb, and many other renowned reform teachers of that time found a receptive audience. Participants further included Jean Piaget, A. S. Neill, and Alfred Adler, the school reformers Franz Hilker and Otto Glöckel, and international luminaries, such as the philosophers of religion Sarvepalli Radhakrishnan and Martin Buber. While psychoanalysis was represented by prominent individuals and was well received, one looks in vain for the names of representatives of anthroposophically oriented education on the lists of attendees. Waldorf education was clearly hardly represented at these international conferences and congresses held in the period between the world wars. Initially, it also failed to be mentioned in the NEF journals that were published in English, French, and German—until 1930, when a supplement came out with contributions from Waldorf teachers.

Given the many commonalities between education reform and Waldorf education, this omission seems remarkable and in need of an explanation. Why was Waldorf education, which was in many respects a radical antithesis to the state school system, largely ignored by other education reform groups? Why was it excluded even in the 1920s, when it was a successful and otherwise widely recognized school form? Did the Waldorf teachers isolate themselves or were they deliberately kept at arm's length?

Since this question has not yet been investigated one can, for the time being, only guess at the reasons why Waldorf education was ignored. Interestingly, the NEF was cofounded, and in its early years substantially informed, by British theosophists. This little-known fact is the more sensitive given that Rudolf Steiner broke with the Theosophical Society in 1912/1913.

This is not the place to go into the reasons for the division between the Theosophical Society and the Anthroposophical Society then founded by Rudolf Steiner. In the context of the questions posed here, it would, however, be interesting to find out what effect this rift had on the relevant pedagogical concepts. The thought suggests itself that it seriously affected the relationships between the anthroposophic groups around Steiner and the representatives of the Theosophical Society, and that any existing ties were severed in 1913. In addition there was, during the First World War, the political-military opposition between the Anglo-American bloc and the Central Powers that also produced strange effects in the relationship between the theosophists following Anni Besant, who decisively supported the idea of Anglo-Saxon world domination, and those around Rudolf Steiner (Osterrieder 2014, p. 937ff.). It is consequently hardly surprising that the NEF initiators were reluctant to even invite representatives of a hostile educational movement to their conferences and congresses.

In any case, there was little or no contact in the 1920s between Waldorf education and education reform, and that state of affairs did not seem to change after the Second World War, for even after 1945, when more than 20 Waldorf schools were founded in quick succession in Germany (Götte 2006), Waldorf education remained largely isolated. With the exception of the *Arbeitsgemeinschaft Freier Schulen* (independent schools' working community), or AGFS for short, Waldorf schools remained isolated in the 1950s and 1960s. And it was precisely the AGFS that was the exception to that rule. While this advocacy group for independent schools, to which Waldorf schools had belonged from the start, also represented the *Landerziehungsheime*, it otherwise only included Catholic and Protestant boarding schools, but not the Montessori or Jena Plan schools.

The main AGFS initiator was the lawyer and solicitor Hellmut Becker who was immensely influential in education policy after the war. Very well-connected and close friends with Georg Picht and the brothers Carl Friedrich and Richard von Weizsäcker,[11] Becker was presumably the most important reformer in the years before and after 1970. Surprisingly, Becker also had close contact with Ernst Weißert, who was for many years head of the *Bund der Freien Waldorfschulen* (Federation of Independent Waldorf Schools). Other than that, he favored the *Landerziehungsheime*, which were consequently received broadly and positively by the wider public and the education sciences in Germany.

There is still need for clarification as to the effect the dominant "Becker system" had on the acceptance of Waldorf schools within the German education landscape. Independently from that, it remains conspicuous why Waldorf education, for decades after the Second World War, continued to be almost entirely ignored by the education sciences in Germany (Frielingsdorf 2012). And given that Waldorf schools were hardly noticed by the representatives of education reform either, the continuous growth of the Waldorf movement is even more surprising. Without much support from academic education and the political establishment, it seems to have made a virtue out of necessity and put all its energy into developing its own organizational structures with active "regional working communities" (*Landesarbeitsgemeinschaften*) and the *Bund der Freien Waldorfschulen* as its umbrella organization.

Thanks to the successful establishment of internal associations and structures, including non-university institutes for research and teacher education, as well as (in recent years) state-recognized universities, something like a parallel educational world has evolved around the Waldorf schools. This has led to the strange paradox of an educational practice that is generally highly esteemed in public on the one hand but shows signs of a tendential ghettoization on the other. Whether this has been caused by the fact that Waldorf teachers isolate themselves to a certain degree or that they are being ostracized by the established school system, including the education sciences and, interestingly education reform as well, will need to be examined in more depth.

Independently of that, it can be said that the Waldorf schools have been successful in building up their own organizational structures and in positioning themselves effectively as an association, which mean that more and more schools can be founded successfully on the basis of anthroposophic education. But this parallel existence also illustrates that, regarding its organization and its networks, Waldorf education cannot be counted as belonging to the education reform movement despite its intensive involvement with the *Arbeitsgemeinschaft Freier Schulen* (independent schools' association).

4 Five theses on the relationship between Waldorf education and education reform

All studies into the history of Waldorf education and its integration in the historical context reveal that the anthroposophic "art of education" is not as unique as many of its followers and representatives continue to think. Rather, it is increasingly apparent that there are a great number of commonalities between Waldorf education and education reform. At the same time, Waldorf education is not simply another alternative educational approach but a differentiated pedagogy in its own right that differs in central points from conceptions of education and teaching reform.

Thesis 1: Waldorf education is assigned to the context of the reform-oriented pedagogical aspirations that flourished from 1918 onward, for instance because of the holistic approach that characterizes the entire anthroposophic movement with its ecological agriculture, holistic medicine, art education, spiritual foundation, etc.

Thesis 2: Waldorf education has much in common with education reform, which was not as unified as it may seem. Both combine strong pedagogical optimism with a profound respect for the individuality of each child. Both agree in their criticism of the state school system and their special validation of community, a holistic approach to education, and the embedding of their schools in practical life.

Thesis 3: Waldorf education and reform education differ profoundly with regard to their anthropology, method, didactic approach, and their understanding of collaborative governance. These principal differences are reflected in very different school realities and in unrelated organizational structures.

Thesis 4: Even given all the similarities, the differences clearly predominate, which is a reason why Waldorf education should not be ranked as "a branch of education reform" but as an independent stream. It is therefore more suitable to call it a third "main branch," of the Central European education system at least (Kloss 1955, p. 157).

Thesis 5: The differences must nonetheless not distract from the fact that both approaches can only benefit from exchange and dialog. Because, in engaging with an entirely different educational concept, one learns to newly appreciate—and qualify—the peculiarities of one's own approach.a

5 Constructive forms of future cooperation

If education reform and Waldorf education accepted and affirmed that they have common ground but that they are nonetheless very different from each other, this could facilitate a dialog between them where the focus on what one has in common could become a foundation for looking at and judging these considerable differences. Such dialog would presumably soon reveal that the transitions are smooth and that the ideas of education reform and Waldorf education are by no means two rigid blocks but conceptions that differ more in their choice of method than in the goals pursued.

Looking back to the beginning of this paper and the "Copernican revolution in how children are seen" proclaimed by John Dewey more than a hundred years ago, it is apparent that both approaches have made highly valuable contributions toward effecting this change of direction in education. For the revolutionizing of education and teaching that has happened in many places since then is owed not least to impulses arising from both the various conceptions of education reform and the anthroposophic "art of education." That much of this has remained fragmentary can and should inspire representatives of both Waldorf education and education reform to embark on a constructive dialog that can help each to appreciate the differences of the other and, on that basis, to continue to develop their own approach in productive ways. Such conversations would certainly reveal that the wish on both sides for a radical new orientation of the education system rests on key issues they have in common: to humanize schools and education and to protect them from economic and political interference.

Notes

1 In the English-speaking world, the term used for this era was "progressive education," sometimes also "radical education," the French referred to it as "*éducation nouvelle*" and Italians as "*educazione nuova.*"

In the USA and Great Britain, the beginning of that period was located around 1880. In these countries, as well as in the French-speaking world, where at the time very important impulses came from Belgium and francophone Switzerland, this development was of course not disrupted in 1933. But from 1930, the consequences of the global economic crisis did cause a loss of such joy in experimentation, particularly in education—both in private and public schools. In Germany and in the other countries mentioned, including Sweden and the still emerging USSR, education reform really flourished directly after the First World War and up to around 1925.

2 It should be mentioned here that, aside from the representatives named, there were many other education reformers who were no less important but have fallen into oblivion. For example, Johannes Trüper, the founder of Sophienhöhe, a then innovative school in Jena for children with special needs, is only known to experts. The same is true for Elisabeth Rotten and Adolphe Ferrière in Switzerland, the Agazzi sisters from Brescia in upper Italy, the British theosophist Beatrice Ensor, the Belgian Ovide Decroly, and the Russian education reformer Pavel Blonsky. Surprisingly, even originators of social-democratic and socialist school concepts, such as Fritz Karsen in Berlin or Otto Glöckel in Austria, have largely been forgotten.

3 Pursuing the reasons for this obvious neglect should be an intriguing task, particularly since the German *Landerziehungsheime*, of all institutions, have always enjoyed a wide and almost exclusively positive reception within the German education sciences. One would, however, also have to examine why the much more wide-spread socially-democratically inspired "experimental schools" (Karsen 1923) were equally ignored.

4 Skiera (2010, p. 76ff.) discussed the close connection between the alienating phenomena of the modern period, the emergence of "life reform" movements, and the related revolutionary educational concepts in great depth.

5 On Nietzsche's immense influence on the youth movement of that time and on 20th-century education, cf. Christian Niemeyer's comprehensive study, where he draws a clear line between the great philosopher and other initiators of education reform such as Paul de Lagarde or Julius Langbehn (Niemeyer 2002). It is not well known that Rudolf Steiner studied Nietzsche's career in great depth as early as the 1890s—that is at the time when the Nietzsche cult first emerged.

6 It is little known that Hermann Hesse and Emil Molt (both born in Calw, Germany) were school friends and that from 1919 onward, Hesse wrote regularly for the "Waldorf News" published by Molt. Even if Hesse was never able to relate to anthroposophy despite this friendship, it shows clearly how close the contact was between the early Waldorf school and the school critics or representatives of school reform.

7 That Baader almost entirely excluded Waldorf education from her otherwise very commendable study is unfortunate, since its inclusion would certainly have resulted in some interesting discoveries.

8 This accusation of an excessive claim to absoluteness was also raised by Skiera (2010, p. 263 ff.).

9 Rudolf Steiner also knew, on the other hand, that the authority of the teacher must not exclude the child's own activity. In a lecture in April 1923, he pointed out that teachers and educators should "merely be the environment of the self-educating child." He added that "we have to be the most favorable environment so that the children educate themselves in it, as they have to educate themselves through their inner destiny" (Steiner 1988, p. 131). As Professor Peter Loebell, Freie Hochschule Stuttgart, Germany kindly pointed out: In his course for young people (CW 217), Rudolf Steiner described this aspect of the student's self-education through the teacher's special individuality, stating in summary that "the children educate themselves through us" (ibid., p. 162).

10 In this context, one should at least mention Martin Buber's *Rede über das Erzieherische* (Speech on Education, 1926), which pointed in a similar direction. Buber presented his contemplations at the time, in 1925, in the opening lecture of the New Education Fellowship's international congress in Heidelberg, Germany. They were felt to be highly critical by the initiators. Interestingly, Buber's suggestions were hardly mentioned in the later congress reports and summaries (Koslowski 2013, p. 67).

11 Becker protected, for example, Heinrich Roth, Wolfgang Klafki, and, not least, Hartmut von Hentig as well as Gerold Becker (not a relative) who would later become head of the Odenwaldschule. Becker's circle of friends and acquaintances included Marion Countess Dönhoff, Ernst Klett, and many important scientists from Helmut Plessner and Alexander Mitscherlich to Theodor Eschenburg, Theodor W. Adorno, and Jürgen Habermas.

References

Arbeitsgemeinschaft, Freier Schulen (Ed.) (1971): Freie Schule. Gesellschaftliche Funktion des Freien Schulwesens in der Bundesrepublik Deutschland. Stuttgart: Klett.

Baader, Meike Sophia (2005): Erziehung als Erlösung. Transformation des Religiösen in der Reformpädagogik. Weinheim and Munich: Juventa.

Barz, Heiner (2010a): Pädagogik groß gedacht. Montessori und Steiner im Vergleich. In: Erziehungskunst, 74, pp. 57–58 (Langfassung: "Montessori und Steiner. Gemeinsamkeiten und Unterschiede" online at www.waldorf-absolventen.de/montessoriundsteiner.pdf).

Barz, Heiner (Ed.) (2010b): Reformpädagogik. Reformschulen im Spiegel empirischer Bildungsforschung. Wiesbaden: VS.

Bast, Roland (1996): Kulturkritik und Erziehung. Anspruch und Grenzen der Reformpädagogik. Dortmund: projekt.

Bauer, Horst Philipp (2006): Zur Ethik selbstverwalteter Organisationen – Anspruch und Realität von Schulen und Einrichtungen in freier Trägerschaft. In: Bauer, Horst Philipp/Schneider, Peter (Eds.) (2006): Waldorfpädagogik. Perspektiven eines wissenschaftlichen Dialoges. Frankfurt am Main: Peter Lang, pp. 129–234.

Benner, Dietrich/Kemper, Herwart (2003): Theorie und Geschichte der Reformpädagogik, Weinheim und Basel: Beltz.

Berg, Hans Christoph (1990): Bilanz und Perspektiven der Reformpädagogik. Vorschlag zum Neuansatz eines Forschungsschwerpunktes "Reformpädagogische und alternative Schulen in Europa." In: Zeitschrift für Pädagogik, 36, issue 6, 877–892.

Böhm, Winfried (1994): Die Reformpädagogik in Italien und Spanien. In: Röhrs, Hermann/Lenhart, Volker (Eds.) (1994): Die Reformpädagogik auf den Kontinenten. Frankfurt am Main: Peter Lang, pp. 87–108.

Böhm, Winfried (2012): Die Reformpädagogik: Montessori, Waldorf und andere Lehren. Munich: Beck.

Böhm, Winfried/Oelkers, Jürgen (Eds.) (1995): Reformpädagogik kontrovers. Würzburg: Ergon.

Bohnsack, Fritz (2003): John Dewey (1859–1952). In: Tenorth, Heinz-Elmar (Ed.) (2003): Klassiker des pädagogischen Denkens. Vol. 2: Von John Dewey bis Paolo Freire. Munich: Beck, pp. 44–60.

Bohnsack, Fritz/Kranich, Ernst-Michael (1990): Erziehungswissenschaft und Waldorfpädagogik. Der Beginn eines notwendigen Dialogs. Weinheim und Basel: Beltz.

Borchert, Manfred/Derichs-Kunstmann, Karin (1979): Schulen, die ganz anders sind. Werkschule Berlin/Freie Schule Essen/Freie Schule Frankfurt/Glocksee-Schule Hannover/Tvind-Schulen in Dänemark. Erfahrungsberichte aus der Praxis für die Praxis. Frankfurt am Main: Fischer.

Borst, Eva (2007): Reformpädagogik. In: Graßhoff, Gunther (Ed.) (2007): Reformpädagogik trifft Erziehungswissenschaft. Mainz: Logophon, pp. 51–67.

Brügge, Peter (1984): Die Anthroposophen. Waldorfschulen, biodynamischer Landbau, Ganzheitsmedizin, kosmische Heilslehre. Reinbek bei Hamburg: Rowohlt.

Buber, Martin (1926): Rede über das Erzieherische. In: Buber, Martin (Ed.) (2005): Schriften zu Jugend, Erziehung und Bildung. Werkausgabe. Vol. 8. Edited by Juliane Jacobi. Gütersloh: Gütersloher Verlagshaus, pp. 136–154.

Carlgren, Frans (1981): Erziehung zur Freiheit. Die Pädagogik Rudolf Steiners, in der Reihe "Perspektiven der Anthroposophie." Stuttgart: Freies Geistesleben.

Dick, Lutz van (1979): Alternativschulen. Informationen, Probleme, Erfahrungen. Reinbek bei Hamburg: Rowohlt.

Döpp, Robert (2003): Jenaplan-Pädagogik im Nationalsozialismus. Ein Beitrag zum Ende der Eindeutigkeit. Münster: LIT.

Fend, Helmut (1977): Schulklima. Soziale Einflussprozesse in der Schule. Weinheim: Beltz.

Flitner, Andreas (1980): Freie Schulen. Ergänzung und Herausforderung des öffentlichen Schulsystems. In: Merkur, 387, issue 34, pp. 772–783.

Flitner, Andreas (1992): Reform der Erziehung. Impulse des 20. Jahrhunderts. Jenaer Vorlesungen. Pieper: Munich and Zurich.

Flitner, Wilhelm/Kudritzki, Gerhard (Eds.) (1995): Die deutsche Reformpädagogik. Die Pioniere der pädagogischen Entwicklung. 5th edition. Stuttgart: Klett-Cotta.

Foitzik Kirchgraber, Renate (2003): Lebensreform und Künstlergruppen um 1900. Basel: Dissertation Basel University. Online at doi:10.5451/unibas-003082110 (accessed on February 23, 2016).

Frielingsdorf, Volker (Ed.) (2012): Waldorfpädagogik kontrovers. Ein Reader mit 33 Beiträgen von Befürwortern und Kritikern. Weinheim: Beltz Juventa.

Füller, Christian (2010): Ausweg Privatschulen? Was sie besser können, woran sie scheitern; unter Mitarb. von Annegret Nill und Wolf Schmidt. Hamburg: edition Körber-Stiftung.

Götte, Wenzel M. (2006): Erfahrungen mit Schulautonomie. Das Beispiel der Freien Waldorfschulen. Stuttgart: Freies Geistesleben.

Götte, Wenzel M./Loebell, Peter/Maurer, Klaus M. (Eds.) (2009): Entwicklungsaufgaben und Kompetenzen. Zum Bildungsplan der Waldorfschule. Stuttgart: Freies Geistesleben.

Graßhoff, Gunther/Höblich, Davina/Idel, Till-Sebastian/Kunze, Katharina/Stelmaszyk, Bernhard (Eds.) (2007): Reformpädagogik trifft Erziehungswissenschaft. Mainz: Logophon.

Hansen-Schaberg, Inge (Ed.) (2005): Die Praxis der Reformpädagogik. Dokumente und Kommentare zur Reform der öffentlichen Schulen in der Weimarer Republik. Bad Heilbrunn: Klinkhardt.

Hansen-Schaberg, Inge (Ed.) (2012): Waldorf-Pädagogik. Reformpädagogische Schulkonzepte. Vol. 6. Neuausgabe. Baltmannsweiler: Schneider.

Hansen-Schaberg, Inge/Schonig, Bruno (Eds.) (2006): Waldorf-Pädagogik. Reformpädagogische Schulkonzepte. Vol. 6. Second corrected and extended edition. Baltmannsweiler: Schneider.

Hansmann, Otto (Ed.) (1987): Pro und contra Waldorfpädagogik. Akademische Pädagogik in der Auseinandersetzung mit der Rudolf-Steiner-Pädagogik. Würzburg: Königshausen & Neumann.

Hellmich, Achim/Teigeler, Peter (Eds.) (1999): Montessori-, Freinet-, Waldorfpädagogik: Konzeption und aktuelle Praxis. 4th revised edition. Weinheim and Basel: Beltz.

Helmchen, Jürgen (1999): Wie viele Geschichten der Reformpädagogik gibt es? In: Oelkers, Jürgen/Osterwalder, Fritz (Eds.) (1999): Die neue Erziehung. Beiträge zur Internationalität der Reformpädagogik. Frankfurt am Main: Peter Lang.

Herrlitz, Hans-Georg/Hopf, Wulf/Titze, Hartmut (2005): Deutsche Schulgeschichte von 1800 bis zur Gegenwart. Eine Einführung. 4th revised and updated edition. Weinheim and Munich: Juventa.

Herrmann, Ulrich (Ed.) (2007): In der Pädagogik etwas bewegen. Impulse für Bildungspolitik und Schulentwicklung. Weinheim and Basel: Beltz.

Herrmann, Ulrich/Oelkers, Jürgen (1994): Reformpädagogik – ein Rekonstruktions- und Rezeptionsproblem. In: Zeitschrift für Pädagogik, 40, issue 4, pp. 541–547.

Herz, Gerhard (2007): Waldorfschulen entwickeln sich. In: Graßhoff, Günther et al. (Eds.) (2007): Reformpädagogik trifft Erziehungswissenschaft. Mainz: Logophon, pp. 115–128.

Hesse, Hermann (1972): Unterm Rad. Roman. Frankfurt am Main: Suhrkamp.

Hilker, Franz (Ed.) (1924): Deutsche Schulversuche. Berlin: Schwetschke & Sohn.

Holmes, Brian (1994): Entstehung und Entwicklung der Reformpädagogik in England. In: Röhrs, Hermann/Lenhart, Volker (Eds.) (1994): Die Reformpädagogik auf den Kontinenten. Frankfurt am Main: Peter Lang, pp. 51–72.

Huber, Joseph (1979): Astral-Marx. Über Anthroposophie, einen gewissen Marxismus und andere Alternatiefen. In: Kursbuch, 55: Sekten. Berlin: Rotbuch, pp. 139–161.

Kallert, Heide/Rothenburg, Eva-Maria/Illert, Christa (1994): Außenansichten der Montessori- und der Waldorfpädagogik. Ein Lesebuch. Frankfurt am Main: Institut für Sozialpädagogik und Erwachsenenbildung.

Karsen, Fritz (1923): Deutsche Versuchsschulen der Gegenwart und ihre Probleme. Leipzig: Dürr'sche Buchhandlung.

Keim, Wolfgang (2013): Friedensbewegung. In: Keim, Wolfgang/Schwerdt, Ulrich (Eds.) (2013): Handbuch der Reformpädagogik in Deutschland (1890–1933). Part 1: Gesellschaftliche Kontexte, Leitideen und Diskurse. Frankfurt am Main: Peter Lang, pp. 135–168.

Keim, Wolfgang/Schwerdt, Ulrich (Eds.) (2013a): Handbuch der Reformpädagogik in Deutschland (1890–1933). Teil 1: Gesellschaftliche Kontexte, Leitideen und Diskurse. Part 2: Praxisfelder und Handlungssituationen. Frankfurt am Main: Peter Lang.

Kerbs, Diethart/Reulecke, Jürgen (Eds.) (1998): Handbuch der deutschen Reformbewegungen 1880–1933. Wuppertal: Peter Hammer.

Klein-Landeck, Michael (2009): Freie Arbeit bei Maria Montessori und Peter Petersen. Münster: LIT.

Kloss, Heinz (1955): Waldorfpädagogik und Staatsschulwesen. Stuttgart: Klett.

Konrad, Franz-Michael (2013): Vorschulerziehung. In: Keim, Wolfgang/Schwerdt, Ulrich (Eds.) (2013): Handbuch der Reformpädagogik in Deutschland (1890–1933). Part 2: Praxisfelder und Handlungssituationen. Frankfurt am Main: Peter Lang, pp. 629–656.

Koslowski, Steffi (2013): Die New Era der New Education Fellowship. Ihr Beitrag zur Internationalität der Reformpädagogik im 20. Jahrhundert. Bad Heilbrunn: Klinkhardt.

Kranich, Ernst-Michael (1971): Die Freien Waldorfschulen. In: Arbeitsgemeinschaft, Freier Schulen (Ed.) (1971): Freie Schule. Gesellschaftliche Funktion des Freien Schulwesens in der Bundesrepublik Deutschland. Stuttgart: Klett, pp. 61–85.

Kranich, Ernst-Michael (1999): Anthropologische Grundlagen der Waldorfpädagogik. Stuttgart: Freies Geistesleben.

Larsson, Yvonne (1987): The World Education Fellowship: Origins and Development with Particular Emphasis on New South Wales, the First Australian Section. University of Sydney.

Leber, Stefan (1991): Die Sozialgestalt der Waldorfschule. Ein Beitrag zu den sozialwissenschaftlichen Anschauungen Rudolf Steiners. 4th updated edition. Stuttgart: Freies Geistesleben.

Leenders, Hélène (2001): Der Fall Montessori. Die Geschichte einer reformpädagogischen Erziehungskonzeption im italienischen Faschismus. Bad Heilbrunn: Klinkhardt.

Lindenberg, Christoph (1995): Waldorfschulen: angstfrei lernen, selbstbewusst handeln. Praxis eines verkannten Schulmodells. Reinbek bei Hamburg: Rowohlt.

Litt, Theodor (1927): Führen oder Wachsenlassen? Eine Erörterung des pädagogischen Grundproblems. Leipzig: Teubner.

Loebell, Peter (Ed.) (2011): Waldorfschule heute. Eine Einführung. Stuttgart: Freies Geistesleben.

Meinberg, Eckhard (1988): Das Menschenbild der modernen Erziehungswissenschaft. Darmstadt: Wissenschaftliche Buchgesellschaft.

Meyer, Claudia (2000): Musikdidaktik bei Maria Montessori und Rudolf Steiner. Darstellung und Vergleich vor dem Hintergrund der anthropologisch-pädagogischen Konzeptionen. Berlin: Mensch & Buch.

Mialaret, Gaston (1994): Die Neue Erziehung in Frankreich. In: Röhrs, Hermann/Lenhart, Volker (Eds.) (1994): Die Reformpädagogik auf den Kontinenten. Frankfurt am Main: Peter Lang, pp. 73–86.

Miller, Damian/Oelkers, Jürgen (Eds.) (2014): Reformpädagogik nach der Odenwaldschule – Wie weiter? Weinheim and Basel: Beltz Juventa.

Müller, Walter (1995): Ver-Steiner-te Reformpädagogik oder: Ist die Waldorfschule trotz Anthroposophie eine gute Schule? In: Böhm, Winfried/Oelkers, Jürgen (Eds.) (1995): Reformpädagogik kontrovers. Würzburg: Ergon, pp. 105–125.

Näf, Martin (2006): Paul und Edith Geheeb-Cassirer: Gründer der Odenwaldschule und der École d'Humanité. Deutsche, Schweizerische und internationale Reformpädagogik 1910-1961. Weinheim and Basel: Beltz.

Niemeyer, Christian (2002): Nietzsche, die Jugend und die Pädagogik. Eine Einführung. Weinheim and Munich: Juventa.

Nohl, Herman (2002): Die pädagogische Bewegung in Deutschland und ihre Theorie. 11th edition. Frankfurt am Main: Vittorio Klostermann.

Oelkers, Jürgen (1994a): Ursprung und Verlauf in Zentraleuropa. In: Röhrs, Hermann/Lenhart, Volker (Eds.) (1994): Die Reformpädagogik auf den Kontinenten. Frankfurt am Main: Peter Lang, pp. 29–49.

Oelkers, Jürgen (1994b): Bruch und Kontinuität. Zum Modernisierungseffekt der Reformpädagogik. In: Zeitschrift für Pädagogik, 40, issue 4, pp. 565–583.

Oelkers, Jürgen (1999): Die "neue Erziehung" im Diskurs der Reformpädagogik. In: Oelkers, Jürgen/Osterwalder, Fritz (Eds.) (1999): Die neue Erziehung. Beiträge zur Internationalität der Reformpädagogik. Frankfurt am Main: Peter Lang, pp. 13–41.

Oelkers, Jürgen (2005): Reformpädagogik. Eine kritische Dogmengeschichte. 4th revised and extended edition. Weinheim and Munich: Juventa.

Oelkers, Jürgen (2008): Probleme der Reformpädagogik am Beispiel von Summerhill. Lecture given at the Pädagogische Hochschule in Zug/CH on October 17, 2008. Online at www.ife.uzh.ch/dam/jcr (accessed on February 23, 2016).

Oelkers, Jürgen (2010a): Reformpädagogik. Entstehungsgeschichte einer internationalen Bewegung. Zug: Klett und Balmer.

Oelkers, Jürgen (2010b): Was bleibt von der Reformpädagogik? In: FAZ (Frankfurt Allgemeine Zeitung) of March 16, 2010.

Oelkers, Jürgen (2011): Eros und Herrschaft. Die dunklen Seiten der Reformpädagogik. Weinheim: Beltz.

Oelkers, Jürgen/Osterwalder, Fritz (Eds.) (1999): Die neue Erziehung. Beiträge zur Internationalität der Reformpädagogik. Frankfurt am Main: Peter Lang.

Oelkers, Jürgen/Osterwalder, Fritz/Tenorth, Heinz-Elmar (Eds.) (2003): Das verdrängte Erbe. Pädagogik im Kontext von Religion und Theologie. Weinheim and Basel: Beltz.

Osterrieder, Markus (2014): Welt im Umbruch. Nationalitätenfrage, Ordnungspläne und Rudolf Steiners Haltung im Ersten Weltkrieg. Stuttgart: Freies Geistesleben.

Osterwalder, Fritz (1999): Deutsche Nation und Volksgeist als reformpädagogische Konzepte. In: Oelkers, Jürgen/Osterwalder, Fritz (Eds.) (1999): Die neue Erziehung. Beiträge zur Internationalität der Reformpädagogik. Frankfurt am Main: Peter Lang, pp. 45–68.

Oswald, Paul (1985): Die Pädagogik Maria Montessoris und Rudolf Steiners. In: Zeitschrift für Pädagogik, 31, pp. 385–396.

Paschen, Harm (1990): Lernen von der Waldorfpädagogik? Zum systematischen Verhältnis von Erziehungswissenschaft und Waldorfpädagogik. In: Bohnsack, Fritz/Kranich, Ernst-Michael (Eds.) (1990): Erziehungswissenschaft und Waldorfpädagogik. Der Beginn eines notwendigen Dialogs. Weinheim and Basel: Beltz, pp. 50–63.

Plake, Klaus (1991): Reformpädagogik. Wissenssoziologie eines Paradigmenwechsels. Münster und New York: Waxmann.

Potthoff, Willy (2000): Einführung in die Reformpädagogik. Von der klassischen zur aktuellen Reformpädagogik. 3rd updated and extended edition. Freiburg: Reformpädagogischer Verlag.

Retter, Hein (Ed.) (2004): Reformpädagogik. Neue Zugänge – Befunde – Kontroversen. Bad Heilbrunn: Klinkhardt.

Richter, Tobias (Ed.) (2010): Pädagogischer Auftrag und Unterrichtsziele – vom Lehrplan der Waldorfschule. 3rd extended and updated edition. Stuttgart: Freies Geistesleben.

Rittelmeyer, Christian (1990): Der fremde Blick – Über den Umgang mit Rudolf Steiners Vorträgen und Schriften. In: Bohnsack, Fritz/Kranich, Ernst-Michael (Eds.) (1990): Erziehungswissenschaft und Waldorfpädagogik. Der Beginn eines notwendigen Dialogs. Weinheim and Basel: Beltz, pp. 64–74.

Rittelmeyer, Christian (1994): Schulbauten positiv gestalten. Wie Schüler Farben und Formen erleben. Wiesbaden und Berlin: Bauverlag.

Rogers, Carl R. (1984): Lernen in Freiheit. Zur Bildungsreform in Schule und Universität. 4th edition. Munich: Kösel.

Röhrs, Hermann (1994a): Die Internationalität der Reformpädagogik und die Ansätze zu einer Welterziehungsbewegung. In: Röhrs, Hermann/Lenhart, Volker (Eds.) (1994): Die Reformpädagogik auf den Kontinenten. Frankfurt am Main: Peter Lang, pp. 11–26.

Röhrs, Hermann (1994b): Die "New Education Fellowship" – ein Forum der internationalen Reformpädagogik. In: Röhrs, Hermann/Lenhart, Volker (Eds.) (1994): Die Reformpädagogik auf den Kontinenten. Frankfurt am Main: Peter Lang, pp. 191–203.

Röhrs, Hermann (1998): Die Reformpädagogik. Ursprung und Verlauf unter internationalem Aspekt. 5th revised and extended edition. Weinheim and Basel: Deutscher Studien Verlag.

Röhrs, Hermann (Ed.) (1986): Die Schulen der Reformpädagogik heute. Handbuch reformpädagogischer Schulideen und Schulwirklichkeit. Düsseldorf: Schwann.

Röhrs, Hermann/Lenhart, Volker (Eds.) (1994): Die Reformpädagogik auf den Kontinenten. Frankfurt am Main: Peter Lang.

Scarbath, Horst/Scheuerl, Hans (1979): Martin Buber (1878–1965). In: Scheuerl, Hans (Ed.) (1979): Klassiker der Pädagogik. Vol. 2: Von Karl Marx bis Jean Piaget. Munich: Beck, pp. 212–224.

Scheibe, Wolfgang (1999): Die reformpädagogische Bewegung. Eine einführende Darstellung. Unaltered reprint of the 10th extended edition with an epilog by Heinz-Elmar Tenorth. Weinheim and Basel: Beltz.

Scheuerl, Hans (1979): Klassiker der Pädagogik. Vol. II: Von Karl Marx bis Jean Piaget. Munich: Beck.

Schmoll, Heike (2010): Die Herren vom Zauberberg. In: FAZ (Frankfurter Allgemeine Zeitung) of March 14, 2010.

Schonig, Bruno (1999): Pädagogik und Politik "vom Kinde aus" – Zum historischen Kontext der Pädagogik bei Freinet, Montessori und Steiner. In: Hellmich, Achim/Teigeler, Peter (Eds.) (1999): Montessori-, Freinet-, Waldorfpädagogik: Konzeption und aktuelle Praxis. 4th revised edition. Weinheim and Basel: Beltz, pp. 17–29.

Schwerdt, Ulrich (2013): Heilpädagogik. In: Keim, Wolfgang/Schwerdt, Ulrich (Eds.) (2013): Handbuch der Reformpädagogik in Deutschland (1890-1933). Part 2: Praxisfelder und Handlungssituationen. Frankfurt am Main: Peter Lang, pp. 777–799.

Seichter, Sabine (2009): Theodor Litt. Führen oder Wachsenlassen. In: Böhm, Winfried/Fuchs, Brigitta/Seichter, Sabine (Eds.): Hauptwerke der Pädagogik. Paderborn: Ferdinand Schöningh, pp. 255–257.

Singer, Kurt (1981): Maßstäbe für eine humane Schule. Frankfurt am Main: Fischer.

Skiera, Ehrenhard (2010): Reformpädagogik in Geschichte und Gegenwart. Eine kritische Einführung. 2nd revised and corrected edition. Munich: Oldenbourg.

Skiera, Ehrenhard (2014): Rezension zu: Keim, Wolfgang/Schwerdt, Ulrich (Eds.) (2013): Handbuch der Reformpädagogik in Deutschland (1890–1933). 2 volumes. In: H-Soz-Kult www.hsozkult.de/publicationreview/id/rezbuecher-21593 (accessed on February 23, 2016).

Steiner, Rudolf (1987): Die Erziehung des Kindes vom Gesichtspunkte der Geisteswissenschaft. In: Steiner, Rudolf (Ed.) (1987): Lucifer – Gnosis. Grundlegende Aufsätze zur Anthroposophie und Berichte aus den Zeitschriften «Luzifer» und «Lucifer – Gnosis» 1903-1908. Rudolf Steiner GA 34. Dornach: Rudolf Steiner Verlag, pp. 309–348.

Steiner, Rudolf (1973): Die Philosophie der Freiheit. GA 4. Dornach: Rudolf Steiner Verlag.

Steiner, Rudolf (1975): Konferenzen mit den Lehrern der Freien Waldorfschule 1919-1924. 3 volumes. GA 300a-c. Dornach: Rudolf Steiner Verlag.

Steiner, Rudolf (1988): Geistige Wirkenskräfte im Zusammenwirken von alter und junger Generation. Pädagogischer Jugendkurs. GA 217. 13 Vorträge, gehalten in Stuttgart vom 3. bis 15. Oktober 1922. Rudolf Steiner Verlag: Dornach.

Steiner, Rudolf (1993): Erziehung und Unterricht aus Menschenerkenntnis. GA 302a. Dornach: Rudolf Steiner Verlag.

Steinmann, Lothar (2001): Reformpädagogik und Waldorfschule. In: Erziehungskunst, 65 (2001), 10, S. 1115–1123.

Stockmeyer, Karl A. (1965/2001): Angaben Rudolf Steiners für den Waldorfunterricht. 6. Auflage. Stuttgart: Pädagogische Forschungsstelle beim Bund der Freien Waldorfschulen.

Tenorth, Heinz-Elmar (2000): Geschichte der Erziehung. Einführung in die Grundzüge ihrer neuzeitlichen Entwicklung. Weinheim und München: Juventa.

Ullrich, Heiner (1986): Waldorfpädagogik und okkulte Weltanschauung. Eine bildungsphilosophische und geistesgeschichtliche Auseinandersetzung mit der Anthropologie Rudolf Steiners. Weinheim und Basel: Juventa.

Ullrich, Heiner (1995): Vom Ausenseiter zum Anführer der Reformpädagogischen Bewegung? Betrachtungen über die veränderte Stellung der Pädagogik Rudolf Steiners in der internationalen Bewegung für eine Neue Erziehung. In: Vierteljahresschrift für wissenschaftliche Pädagogik, 71, S. 284–297.

Ullrich, Heiner (2015): Waldorfpädagogik. Eine kritische Einführung. Weinheim und Basel: Beltz.

von Heydebrand, Caroline (1931/2009): Vom Lehrplan der Freien Waldorfschule. 11th edition. Stuttgart: Freies Geistesleben.

CENTRAL MOTIFS IN EDUCATION REFORM AND WALDORF EDUCATION

Peter Loebell

If Waldorf education is assigned a place in the context of education reform, this usually happens for various reasons: aside from historical proximity, these are a child-oriented approach, the idea of development, and learning through experience. We will first look at how these three topics live in education reform and in Waldorf schools, respectively. This will be followed by the description of some essential features of Waldorf education, before a concluding summary will illustrate its closeness to other education reform aspirations on the one hand and its special position on the other.

1 Education reform and Waldorf education: Common topics

1.1 Child-oriented education

In the pedagogical reflections of school reformers, a distinct and special quality is assigned to childhood. Children are not judged by what they are lacking compared to adults (Flitner 1999, p. 25), but special childhood laws are assumed and considered (Flitner 1999, p. 31) based on a specific anthropology of childhood (Flitner 1999, p. 45). The hopes of these educationists focus on Rousseau's idea that every child is good by nature (Röhrs 1986, p. 15). Maria Montessori applies the concept of "freedom" to young children in the sense of "freeing their life from hindrances that hinder their normal development" (Montessori 1969, p. 71).

The poet Rainer Maria Rilke's review of Ellen Key's book *The Century of the Child*, in which he demands respect for the child's individuality (Rilke 1987, p. 587), is characteristic of the theses proposed by a child-oriented pedagogy. Everyone must only be guided to the point where they are able to work and learn for themselves (Rilke 1987, p. 590). Schools should not think in terms of classes or grades but in terms of individualities (ibid.). Orientation to the child would result in schools without exams or competitions, schools that would not lose sight of life (ibid., p. 591).

The different concepts of education reform strive for these and similar goals but accentuate different aspects. The *Odenwald Schule* and *Jena Plan Education*, for example, advocate individualized teaching where each child is given adequate attention (Röhrs 1998, p. 168ff.). The *Hauslehrerschule* (tutor school) claims that the optimal learning conditions can be read from the young child's learning (Flitner 1999, p. 33; Röhrs 1998, p. 240). The idea that living in the country is most suitable to the way children learn underlies the concept of the *Landerziehungsheim* (rural boarding school). Maria Montessori's school model has a specific approach to individualization in that it seeks to provide the best conditions for the child's self-determined learning (Flitner 1999, p. 38ff.). Other school reformers insist that each child's artistic abilities need to be taken seriously and promoted (ibid., p. 33ff.).

DOI: 10.4324/9781003187431-35

This orientation to the child's needs goes hand-in-hand with the demand for a "natural education" (Lischewski 2015); it also leads some reformers to introduce the question of genetics and the "laws of natural selection." Ellen Key, for instance, postulates each child's right to "good" —that is to say, healthy—genes, while Maria Montessori advocates the "profound intermixture of races" (ibid., p. 40). Great hopes were placed on the newly emerging empirical research and experimental pedagogy. "There was no reform teacher who would *not* have pleaded to support the child-centered approach with methodical research" (ibid., p. 48). Montessori, for instance, sought to substantiate the effectiveness of her natural method by proving that it helps children to learn even the most difficult content more easily and quickly (ibid., p. 49).

In opposition to the calls for a pedagogy based on empirical research, Rudolf Steiner, in his introductory course for the future teachers of the new Waldorf school, discusses the problematic one-sidedness of what he terms "experimental psychology" the methods of which he refers to as "studying the anatomy of the soul." This, he says, will as little result in good teaching as dissecting a beetle will teach you "how to assemble the parts again into a living creature" (Steiner 1990, p. 85). Instead of a defined image of the human being, he creates a general and an individual anthropology. Steiner is not concerned with a particular educational concept or method, with lesson content or classroom material. He thinks that teachers should see themselves as the "environment of the self-educating child." Their starting point is the conscious, reflected observation of the learning individual, and, on the basis of this observation, they practice the art of educating and teaching, deciding on and developing teaching content, learning targets, methods, and materials in direct relation to their students. This way of working without rash interpretations of the world corresponds to the phenomenological approach of Edmund Husserl, who essentially claims that subject and objects are united through the intentionality of the perceiving person. Objects are constituted in the act of conscious perception. What teachers know about children is therefore always based on their own life-world knowledge. They consequently need to exclude any preconceived expectations that would render them unable to perceive what is new and surprising in others. The child appears to the teacher as a riddle; teaching and education are always the result of the teacher's searching.

This seems to be contradicted by the fact that anthroposophy provides premises that are essential for an understanding of Waldorf education. One of these is the spiritual existence of the human individuality. In 1904, in his book *Theosophy*, Rudolf Steiner explained in detail that "we become aware of our interwovenness with the world in three ways. The first is what we find, what we accept as a given fact. The second that we make the world our own, something that concerns us. The third way is to set ourselves a goal that we continually strive toward" (Steiner 1987a, p. 25). These three ways of meeting the world he calls "body, soul, and spirit." It is the second way, where we make the world our concern, that corresponds to the concept of intentionality in phenomenology.

When we assume that children follow their own individual drive for learning and that they ultimately must find their own learning goals, we will no longer see them as objects of adult instruction. There has been agreement since the Enlightenment that human beings should be seen as subjects of themselves or, to use Schiller's term, as their own "project" (Soetebeer 2010). This premise can be interpreted as an expression of our spiritual existence. Based on this assumption, Steiner's categories provide a heuristic tool that Waldorf teachers can explore for themselves and use fruitfully in their teaching. The anthroposophical concepts open up ways of thinking that teachers can try out to sharpen their perceptiveness, develop their pedagogical competence, and to reflect critically on their own pedagogical practice.

Before the first Waldorf school was founded in Stuttgart, Rudolf Steiner gave 14 lectures in which he unfolded his anthropological foundations as the basis of the "art of education" (Steiner 2020) and developed the conceptual polarity of thinking and will: When we think consciously, we tend to withdraw from engaging in the world in order to represent it in ideas and thoughts and understand it. In our will activity we work on our surroundings, we change the objects in their reality, but the clarity and acuity of our consciousness is reduced down to actual unconsciousness when we act routinely or carry out reflexive movements. Thought and will therefore constitute extreme opposites that are connected through the multifaceted world of feelings, which we perceive with a dreamlike consciousness. These feelings constitute our inner soul world, while with our thinking we penetrate into universal laws and with our will we can change the real, intersubjective world. Steiner uses this terminology across his comprehensive body of work to describe general laws of human development and the foundations of education. His concepts of thinking, feeling, and will with their corresponding states of consciousness can be used as a heuristic tool for perception on different levels that are relevant to education.

It is easy to distinguish between reflection or concentrated thinking, active will activity, and compassionate feeling, for instance when children listen to a story. In early child development, when children learn through imitation, we see mostly will activity, while children in the first years of school are primarily led by their feelings. Around the twelfth year, young people begin to seek to develop their own conscious judgment. But even when we observe individual children, these three categories can be useful, for instance when we distinguish between children who have a more intellectual, a more physically active, or a more dreamy disposition. What is crucial with all these applications is that teachers remain open to unexpected expressions and behaviors in the children and that they critically examine their own perceptions and judgments.

Child-centered education also requires that one discusses critically whether standardized assessments may interfere with the learning process. If we teach in a way that focuses one-sidedly on the achievement of prescribed learning targets, we cannot consider how individual children meet the world. We are forced to convey particular competences that can then be measured and assessed through standardized tests. It is hardly surprising then that students often find formal processes (products and ways of assessing learning success) more important than the lesson content (Fölling-Albers, Meidenbauer 2010). This "negative spiral" appears to be particularly problematic in children with learning disabilities: They hardly pay attention to the lesson content, focusing instead on the behaviors of their peers and comparing their own achievements above all with those of children who struggle even more to keep up. In other words, they react exactly as intended by selection-oriented state schools where inequality among the individual age groups is systematically generated by means of comparison and grading (Breidenstein 2010, p. 881). "If one observes the practice of teaching, the use of grades seems to have largely become a separate means that essentially gains importance through the practices and rituals of its application" (ibid., p. 874). This is why Waldorf schools do not use standardized grading but prefer formative evaluation of achievements in the form of permanent feedback and annual descriptive reports. In these reports, which are handed over to parents at the end of the school year, teachers try to describe each child's progress and perspectives of future development. If parents find their own experience with their children reflected in these reports, with added components relating to their school life, this can create a basis of trust that allows for the continued sharing of the educational responsibility (Loebell 2004).

1.2 The idea of development

One of the concepts of education reform is its orientation to the peculiarities of child development, which is seen as a condition for human evolution as such (Lischewski 2015, p. 46). It assumes progressive change over relatively long periods of time, typically described and teleologically reflected with the help of phase- or stage-based models (Oelkers 2005, p. 130f.). Development consequently appears as targeted movement toward perfection (Oelkers 2005, p. 134f.). Added to this is the common view that "mental faculties or forces [cannot be] generated but must be respected in the way they develop by themselves" (Oelkers 2005, p. 137). Developmental psychology focuses on age-appropriate forms of educability, the fact that these are not repeatable, and the danger of premature exposure (Röhrs 1998, p. 52). Each child's developmental potential is to be supported from the outside through the right kind of education.

Maria Montessori holds, for example, that each child has a "natural building plan" that they reveal in their development, supported by surroundings that have been created in the "right" way (Oelkers 2005, p. 143ff.). John Dewey, on the other hand, sees education as "growth" or "development" in the sense of the continuous reorganization of experience. His view is not teleological but sees education as an end in itself (Oelkers 2005, p. 146f.).

More recently, developmental psychology has critically discussed the various features of the traditional concept of development. Because this concept occupies a central place in the "elaborate developmental theory" of Waldorf education (Skiera 2012), it needs to be discussed in more detail. Montada rejects the idea that development progresses toward a definable end, arguing that it was impossible to define a clear end state of human development. It was more a case of describing individual changes with very different objectives. It was also impossible to tell whether the pursued end state was more valuable than the one preceding that end state. Whether or not a developmental state could be seen as highly valuable was ultimately decided by social, ideological, and individual value judgments (Montada 2002, p. 4). Regarding childhood and adolescence, one can reply to this that the acquisition of agency, judgment, and maturity can count as a universally desirable goal. If developmental psychology seeks to assess the entire human biography, including the manifestations of physical decline in old age, the question as to the higher value of later developmental stages becomes particularly relevant. One would have to follow Steiner, who sees the process of dying as the transition to a different spiritual state of existence, to support the assumption of continuous development. However, restrictions are not only found with decreasing performance in old age, but also in in healthy children with regard to spontaneity and creativity. Growth and decline are found at any stage of life. And if one assumes that development is tied to age, one also has to consider that, while lasting changes are clearly related to a person's biography, such as the beginning of a partnership or building a relationship with one's child, many developments are not related to a particular age but to "critical life events" (coping with a separation or unemployment, for instance) that do not affect all people in the same way (Preiser 2003, p. 149f.).

If seen as an external process, development means that we never stay the same but that we are a new, different person in every moment. That is not to say, however, that later states are necessarily to be seen as superior to earlier states. The thought that a young child cannot read yet and is therefore in need of catching up with adults is justified if the mastering of cultural techniques is seen as an important prerequisite for social participation. Not being able to read is a deficit in this view. What it does not consider, however, is that by learning to read and write children lose their natural, immediate access to the world.[1] In considering both sides, one will create an environment for children that awakens and promotes their interest in a writing culture. One will, however, not force learning prematurely according to externally imposed standards, as long as careful assessment shows that the individual children develop in a healthy way. Waldorf education, too, can determine and justify times when children should achieve certain competences so as to be able to master their developmental tasks (Götte, Loebell, Maurer 2016).

How teachers work with the children is not informed by a specific image of the human being but by the general and individual potential for development. Teachers should, therefore, be sensitized to the potential, interests, and developmental requirements of each individual child and of the whole class. Children are susceptible to particular themes; they notice special features around them that they can interpret in relation to their experiences of their environment. They can connect with the objects of their interest in ways that are appropriate to their age. Children explore, investigate, and discover what arouses their curiosity. Gradually, they will also understand how different phenomena relate to each other, and they will form their own theories about the reality. Anthropology forms the foundation for teachers to perceive their students' learning efforts empathically and to support them in a targeted way. Because they work with age-homogeneous groups, teachers can use the elements of the curriculum for orientation that relate best to the developmental age of their students. This is why understanding child development is crucial for Waldorf teachers (Chapter 3).

1.3 Learning through experience

In addition to the concept of childhood and natural development, experience is another central element in education reform. The idea behind this is "that, in order to develop, forces require an object that inspires them to grow" (Lischewski 2015, p. 50). Acquiring knowledge and skills therefore always relies on practical engagement with the world. In order to create a counterweight to the conventional "book school" of the late 19th century, early 20th-century school learning should be based as much as possible on concrete application. Georg Kerschensteiner pursued this goal with the *"Arbeitsschule"* (work school) he integrated into the state school system (Flitner 1999, p. 80), and John Dewey with his Laboratory School in Chicago.

Other approaches, such as Alfred Lichtwark's art education movement, rely above all on the creativity of children, which they aim to promote through esthetic education (Flitner 1999, p. 57). Gustav Wyneken's *Landerziehungsheim* in Wickersdorf (Röhrs 1998, p. 163) and Loheland Gymnastics (Röhrs 1998, p. 119) lay particular emphasis on physical education. Other institutions focus on community life and on special child-appropriate social forms, such as co-education, mixed-age learning groups in Peter Petersen's *Jena Plan* Schools (Röhrs 1986, p. 209) and *Odenwaldschule* (Röhrs 1986, p. 87), children's republics like Father Flanagan's *Boys Town* in Nebraska (Flitner 1999, p. 116), or the German *Landerziehungsheime*, whose main founder was Hermann Lietz. Other goals of education reform are clear presentation and action orientation (Röhrs 1986, p. 49). Lessons should be both humorous and reverent (Röhrs 1986, p. 48).

Learning through experience also means taking the child's environment into account. Berthold Otto's *Hauslehrer-Schule* (tutor school) trusted that "children continually engage with their world and acquire valuable knowledge through everyday experiences that natural tuition can build on" (Oelkers 2005, p. 203). The questions of the students and the teachers' answers result in "cognitive chains" with hardly any need for recourse or repetition. Teachers need to have encyclopedic knowledge that is received by the students.

In John Dewey's "learning by doing," the learners' self-activity is of central importance. Actions arise from problems and tasks that should be pursued in a targeted way and completed effectively so that the actors are enabled to learn from their mistakes (ibid., p. 209). The intention here is not only to support the child's natural development, but rather to "methodically train their ability to have genuine experiences in the interaction of thinking and doing" (Lischewski 2015, p. 60). The children's own actions are thought to enhance attentiveness in the lessons, promote creative thinking, strengthen will activity, and instill essential values such as precision and diligence.

Maria Montessori's concept of active learning goes a step further in that she seeks to generate particular learning experiences with the help of especially constructed or selected materials that promote development, and a "prepared environment." With empirical research, she established "how children use these diverse means, what reactions they provoked in them, how often they used these objects, and, above all, what kind of development they facilitated" (Montessori 1969, p. 112). All properties of the material "were determined through experiments" (ibid.). Montessori assumes, however, "that the acquisition of particular competences and skills follows an inner time plan and that every person has their own 'intrinsic building plan of the soul and certain developmental guidelines'" (Pütz 2015, p. 96). Learning materials and environment therefore support free, spontaneous, and normal child development that manifests in a number of desirable qualities. Impetuous, idle, or stubborn behavior in children, on the other hand, is deviant. Their actions are "unnatural" and need to be prevented. "Even then, people noticed the danger that child-friendly slogans are used here to impose exaggerated cultural standards by means of a subtle control of experiences" (Lischewski 2015, p. 52).

Waldorf education is based on the assumption that the children's experiences in thinking, feeling, and doing (will) form the foundation for all learning processes. The teacher, as the "environment of the self-educating child," has the task to enable students to have the most diverse individual experiences through self-activity. To this end, an environment is created that conveys to the children the protection, trust, and challenges they need for learning at their level of development. Continuity and regularity are characteristic of Waldorf schools and are achieved by the "Main Lesson" that starts every school day, every morning at the same time. Main Lesson is in principle taught by the same class or grade teacher, throughout the first eight years of school. It usually lasts around one-and-three-quarter hours and encompasses artistic exercises, recall of the previous day's work, absorbing of new content, a period of self-directed learning, and a story at the end that is told by the teacher. In the high school, which starts with ninth grade, Main Lesson is taught by alternating specialized subject teachers. Ways of working vary and tend to be more structured in the lower grades and freer in the higher grades, depending on the subjects and the methods they require.

Main Lessons tend to stretch over three to four weeks. During that time, the same subject is taught every morning: English, math, form drawing or geometry, life skills (such as farming and house-building in third grade), local geography, geography, history, anthropology and zoology, botany, geology, astronomy, physics, or chemistry. The group of subjects taught changes from year to year. In the individual Main Lesson blocks, the students create their own Main Lesson book, writing down their main working steps and results, and illustrating them with their own artwork. After Main Lesson, other subjects are on the daily timetable, including two foreign languages from first grade, handwork, music, eurythmy, gym, religion, and—from sixth grade onward—gardening and crafts.

The catalog of subjects and Main Lessons illustrates that Waldorf schools aspire to holistically educate body, soul, and mind. Students' experience of their sense of self-movement in physical activity is an essential part of every school day. This applies as much to Main Lesson as to subjects such as sport or the movement art eurythmy that is taught regularly in Waldorf schools. The musical activities that form part of Main Lesson are complemented by separate music lessons, school choir, and orchestra. In the first eight school years, visual arts are also taught by the grade teacher. Art instruction usually continues in the high school with specialist art teachers. Practical activities have a regular place in the timetable and include handwork, gardening, and crafts such as carving, metalwork, and woodwork. Some schools also offer forging, sculpting, or instrument making.

Storytelling by the teacher is another essential aspect of Waldorf education. In the lower and middle school, above all, the soul life of students can expand as they listen to stories, in addition to their intellectual, active, and social learning experiences. If one witnesses, as a teacher (or student) the interest, engagement, and concentration displayed by the children as they listen devotedly to the imaginatively told stories, one must be convinced of the lasting, stabilizing, and strengthening effect of that experience. The essential educational effect of storytelling is due to the inner freedom with which the young people connect with the narrative stream. It is not the moralizing or admonishing adult who effects the change in the child's inner attitude and values. Only images they can relate to of their own free will, which they can embrace, recognize, and contemplate, can touch them at the deeper level where they form their own values. This effect is most noticeable with stories that teachers invent themselves in relation to occurrences in the daily school life and that can help individual students or groups of students process or transform adverse social experiences or challenges. In the lower school, these "moral stories" reflect in inner images what occurred on the outside. The storyteller creates an open space in the children's soul where they can develop compassion, learn to understand other viewpoints, and develop their own impulses for change.

2 Essential features of Waldorf education

Our contemplations so far have revealed that Waldorf education uses some central elements of education reform, implementing them with special accentuation. Waldorf education also has some inherent features that it shares with education reform but that are, as a whole, more characteristic of Waldorf schools:

- coeducation,
- suspension of the tripartite school system,
- child-oriented curriculum,

- additional languages from first grade,
- grades teacher principle,
- main lesson blocks,
- no textbooks,
- descriptive reports rather than standard grading,
- theater projects,
- emphasis on arts and crafts lessons,
- gardening lessons and agricultural, industrial, and social work experience periods.

These elements are examined in continuous discourse and modified in multiple ways. This applies to individual classes, individual school concepts, the further development of Waldorf education in Germany, but even more so to the practice of Waldorf education in different non-European cultures. Here we see a special feature of Waldorf education that clearly sets it apart from other education reform concepts: It expects of teachers that they consciously engage with both Steiner's educational work and the current scientific discourse. For what is effective in education are not the results of scientific research but the effort invested in striving for knowledge. "Not ready-made knowledge is of value in life, but the work that leads to ready-made knowledge. In education this work is of particular value" (Steiner 1983a, p. 19). Waldorf education therefore needs to be constantly newly developed and shaped. The use of tried and tested pedagogical measures needs as much justification as the introduction of new teaching methods. The foundations provided by Steiner and the secondary literature are no binding canon of content and methods, but a heuristic tool for each individual teacher. Steiner's coherent anthropology thus forms the foundation of a highly differentiated practice that continues to evolve. Only this can explain the great attraction of the Waldorf school that even its critics continue to recognize.

2.1 Waldorf education as a developmental process

Waldorf schools were never tied to a particular lesson content or teaching method. Many approaches that are seen as characteristic have only emerged over the years from faculty meetings, for which Rudolf Steiner, the spiritual originator of the schools, was initially present. More than 230 Steiner Schools in Germany and over 1000 around the world continue to evolve. The faculty of teachers in each individual school is called upon to develop their own school profile in a meaningful way between tradition and innovation. Currently, much-discussed issues include:

- grade teachers staying with their grades all morning in the first school years,
- providing all-day care in the sense of "school as a living environment,"
- block teaching for subjects such as additional languages,
- reducing the grade-teacher period to first to sixth grade, and introducing a middle-school faculty for seventh to ninth grade,
- possibilities for vocational training in the high school,
- smaller classes or support lessons for students with special learning needs,
- an inclusive approach where children with various gifts or support needs are taught together,
- the possibility of offering specific therapies,
- intercultural Waldorf schools,
- creating special learning groups for refugee children or their integration in existing grades.

The classic curriculum of Waldorf schools is close to the traditions of education reform. Its teaching program is not binding, however. It has evolved from Steiner's anthropology and its application is left to the individual schools. Each school develops its own profile, depending on its students and on regional, cultural, and historical conditions. Institutions like the Intercultural Waldorf School in Mannheim, Germany, or schools that offer a combination of general education and vocational training, are examples of this individual profile-building. It is up to the Waldorf schools that have emerged on all continents and in all cultures to develop their own concepts on the basis of Steiner's anthropology (Leber 1997).

It is apparent from the way Waldorf education has spread across different cultures that Waldorf schools have the possibility to combine an education based on specific ethnic values with modern elements of general education. One characteristic of Waldorf schools is their ability to adapt to their environment. This, however, requires teachers to keep developing Waldorf education in relation to concrete life conditions.

2.2 The importance of the teacher's personality

An essential principle of Waldorf education is the special importance attached to the teacher's personality. Recent empirical studies seem to impressively evidence the important role teachers play for a successful education. The teacher's personality has an essential impact, for instance, on the students' loci of control. Persons who believe they have an "internal locus of control" will assume that they can influence the results of their actions and their learning success. A longitudinal study carried out in 1998 of 1600 children from third to seventh grade found that "children who described their teachers as warmhearted, reliable, and predictable in their behavior developed particularly positive patterns of belief in their locus of control. A positive locus of control is associated with more active lesson participation and better school performance" (Hasselhorn, Gold 2013, p. 174f.).

The importance of the teacher's personality for the learning success of students is also shown by John Hattie's statistical analysis of more than 800 English-language meta-analyses on school learning. The sequence of 138 different factors that impact on learning illustrates "that active and guided instruction is much more effective than unguided, facilitative instruction" (Hattie 2014, p. 286). A detailed description of teacher-specific influencing factors reveals that subject matter knowledge and teacher education are hardly relevant for learning success. Hattie ascribes a much more positive effect to practical teaching approaches and their reflection ("micro-teaching"). Additionally, the quality of the teacher-student relationship, clarity on the part of the teacher, refraining from labeling learners, as well as continuous professional development are immensely important for learning (ibid., p. 129ff.). Hattie summarizes the essential findings of his comprehensive study in "six signposts towards excellence in education." His list starts with the thesis that "Teachers are among the most powerful influences in learning" (ibid., p. 280). They need to be "directive, influential, caring, and actively and passionately engaged in the process of teaching and learning" (ibid.). Further signposts concern the teacher's differentiated perception of the students and their learning experiences, and teachers' proficient knowledge and understanding of their subject content (ibid., p. 280f.).

The teacher's personality plays a key role at all levels in Waldorf schools. This applies particularly to the first eight grades, throughout which one grade teacher tends to be in charge of the same group of students. This teacher is the most important attachment figure for the students. Because grades teachers know all their students so well, they are able to support each child individually (together with their subject teachers). The most important pedagogical tools for this are the selection of lesson content and teaching methods.

Steiner's view was that students up to puberty expect their teacher to be a "justified" and "loved" authority. "Naturally, this authority must not be enforced; it must not be imposed externally." Instead, Steiner requests that "children must feel that they can look up with confidence to the teacher or educator as an authority. This tender authoritative relationship must be continued particularly between the seventh and ninth year, generally between the start of elementary school up until the ninth year of age. One needs to foster this, but it will change naturally from the ninth or tenth year onwards" (Steiner 1982b, p. 95f.).

Teachers can gain the children's trust and recognition as an authority through the way they behave and are. Reversely, one can observe that students react with disappointment or aggression when teachers do not prove to be the justified authorities that they are willing to see in them. Steiner's thinking is that an authoritatively oriented approach to education will inspire in the children confidence in the cognitive faculties and morality of adults. Under no circumstances must the children's curiosity be suppressed, but it is important that they are taught in a way that is appropriate to their age. While intellectually highly gifted children and their special requirements must naturally be taken seriously (Götte 2005; Loebell 2005), it is equally important for them to be supported in a holistic rather than one-sided way.

The prominence of the teacher's personality in Waldorf schools has been examined in a survey conducted among high school students in both Waldorf and grammar schools in Germany (Randoll 1999).[2] Evidently, a much higher number of Waldorf students enjoyed learning (81% as opposed to 55%) and found most of the learning content meaningful (73% versus 35%). Only 30% (compared to 63% of grammar school students) felt that too much of the knowledge imparted to them at school was not relevant to their current interests (Randoll 1999, p. 182f.). The percentage of students who stated that they received theoretical subject knowledge at school was about the same (90% and 91%, respectively). The number of Waldorf students who felt they were one-sidedly challenged was considerably lower, however (12% compared to 42%). Striking differences were also found with regard to how the students felt supported and recognized by the teachers (ibid., p. 190) and with regard to personal development.[3] The way Waldorf students judged their teachers' behavior and personality was also more positive in comparison (ibid., p. 231). "While grammar school students learn mostly to get good grades or gain points or because of a test, the learning behavior in Waldorf schools is determined by the students' personal interest in the lesson content" (Randoll 2010, p. 133). Compared to grammar school students, Waldorf students stated that their teachers:

- had better psychological-pedagogical skills,
- had better subject matter knowledge and didactic competence,
- seemed more fun, open to compromise, patient, self-critical, less performance-oriented, and fairer in assessing student achievement (Randoll 2010, p. 137).

"The Waldorf students interviewed found that their schools or teachers did much more justice to the task of supporting personality development than the students from state grammar schools, even though both groups found the promotion of many personality aspects mentioned in the questionnaire equally more important than their actual realization in their schools" (Randoll 1999, p. 338f.). Furthermore, "comparison of the two student perspectives reveals that Waldorf teachers give their students much more space for self-development, self-realization, and self-determination than state school teachers" (ibid., p. 341).

Many high school students in Waldorf schools make use of private coaching, which, on the other hand, gives rise to the question as to whether grade teachers have sufficient subject matter knowledge and adequate methodical and didactic competences. Of almost 46% of interviewees who receive regular or occasional private coaching, almost 73% blame this on learning gaps from earlier years (Liebenwein, Barz, Randoll 2012, p. 138), which can, on the other hand, have a number of causes. It is, for instance, noticeable that children who join Waldorf schools later use private coaching more often than those who attended from the beginning (ibid., p. 137). The greatest need for catching up is in math as one of the important Main Lesson subjects, and the need is mainly among girls (ibid.). Additional languages are next: subjects, in other words, that are not taught by the grade teacher.

Students who were taught by the same grade teacher for eight years have apparently less need for extra coaching (43.2%) than those who have been with a grade teacher for a shorter period of time (51.4%) (ibid.). This means that it cannot be concluded from findings on extra coaching that the grade teacher tuition was particularly deficient. There are nonetheless indicators that suggest that there is room for improvement in middle-school Main Lesson teaching, because almost 60% of interviewees wished they had been taught by high-school teachers in middle school (Keller 2012, p. 110) and more than half find, in looking back, that it was not so good that the same teacher taught so many subjects (ibid.).

Generally, the more recent study of 2012 concludes that "In the light of these findings, Waldorf schools can rightfully claim that they do not only write 'child-oriented' learning on their banners but that they know how to apply it in practice" (Liebenwein, Barz, Randoll 2012, p. 11). Central findings from a survey among more than 800 Waldorf high-school students and from 50 individual interviews with parents and students concern the school climate. Comparatively high figures were found for joy in learning and school satisfaction (79.4% compared to 67.2% in regular schools), and for student interest ("I mostly find interesting what we do in lessons"): 78.6% versus 54.5% in regular schools. Equally, more students see the teacher-student relationship as positive ("Our teachers are interested in the learning progress of each individual student"): 64.8% as opposed to 30.5% in regular schools. Overall, 50.4% of Waldorf students—compared to 23.3% in regular schools—appreciate the quality of teaching ("Our teachers make the lessons interesting and exciting").

Further findings concern the students' personality development: for instance, their perceived self-efficacy. Overall, 83.9% of Waldorf students agree with the statement "It has been conveyed to me at school that I have strengths." The eight-year grade teacher period is seen as appropriate by two thirds (65.5%) of Waldorf students. Overall, 65.9% of the students interviewed are glad that they were taught in Main Lesson blocks, and 87.4% of Waldorf students feel they have very good cultural education (art, music, theater). The figure for support with self-directed learning, on the other hand, is lower for Waldorf schools than for regular schools ("I learned at school how to use reference works"): 65.3% compared to 81.1% of regular school students.

Some scientists around Werner Helsper and Heiner Ullrich have used various studies to examine the relationship between Waldorf grade teachers and their students, using narrative interviews, group discussions, participatory observation, and document analysis (descriptive school reports). Analysis was preferably conducted using the method of "objective hermeneutics." The summary states that "more recent qualitative studies of Waldorf schools document [...] striking quality differences in the teacher-student relationship" (Helsper, Hummrich 2014, p. 14). It needs to be pointed out, however, that for the reconstruction of the teacher-students relationship in three schools, only a few students were targeted and selected in each school to exemplify particular typical relations. The "striking quality differences in the relationships" were therefore determined by the method and cannot count as representative.

Concerning arguments for and against an eight-year grade teacher period, the comprehensive 2007 survey can, therefore, not provide compelling results. On the one hand, it provides positive examples of successful teacher-student relationships over eight years. "Due to the comprehensive personal proximity and moderated by habitual adaptation, grade teachers manage to accompany and sustainably promote the adolescents' socialization and education processes" (Helsper et al. 2007, p. 528). But the authors also mention a few negative examples, including their problematic backgrounds: negative sanctioning by peers, disappointment of the teacher's expectation of closeness, neglecting of cognitive-intellectual learning processes, lack of internal differentiation, or the negation of striving for autonomy. The question is whether these constellations are due to the eight-year grade teacher period or to the teachers' lack of competence, which can, of course, have very serious effects when a grade teacher holds such a prominent authority position for such an extended period of time.

The authors conclude that "no binding recommendation for or against the eight-year grade teacher period can and shall be forwarded here. [...] Generally, it can be stated that the relations with the grade teacher up to eighth grade are accompanied by fewer crises when the teachers achieve a reflective dynamization and modification of the concept of authority in accordance with the student's individual development and resulting striving for autonomy" (ibid., p. 531). The authors describe here one of the central challenges of personality development in grade teachers, who are required to build up astonishing versatility in the eight years they spend with their students.

2.3 Theory of temperaments

Steiner's original concept of psychological personality assessment can be found in the Practical Discussions that form part of the first course for Waldorf teachers, where he also introduces the theory of temperaments and its relevance to education (Steiner 1985a). Misinterpretations are possible because the theory of temperaments goes back more than a thousand years and has been applied in different ways to this day.

The distinction of temperaments was first suggested by the Greek physician Hippocrates (460–377 BCE). It was further developed by the Roman physician Galen (129–199 CE) and has since served as the foundation for distinguishing types of persons, down to their physical appearance.

Around the turn of the 20th century, insights into these typologies was seen as part of general knowledge. Since its inception, modern personality psychology has produced a number of scientific theories that largely use the same terminology even though they derive from different premises. Wilhelm Wundt, in 1903, described four temperaments depending on a person's strength of emotions and how quickly they change (Bartussek 1996, p. 61). Eyseneck, who utilizes a statistical technique known as factor analysis, presents a much more differentiated personality theory. His approach is specific in that he does not derive his "dimensions" from theoretical assumptions but from personality questionnaires. The terminology he uses also goes back to ancient Greece, however.

The same applies to Pavlov, who is known for his animal experiments on conditioning, although his concept works with entirely different premises. He found four types of nervous system in dogs that he thought were also evident in humans: they are either strong or weak, equilibrated or non-equilibrated, mobile or inert (Amelang, Bartussek 1997, p. 392). Strelau (1984) follows in the same tradition. Based on five discriminating features, he distinguishes between temperament from "personality" (Zentner 1998, p. 15).

In the New York longitudinal study that began in 1956 and went on for several decades, Thomas and Chess identified nine different personality traits: activity level, rhythmicity, approach or withdrawal, adaptability, threshold of responsiveness, quality of mood, intensity of reaction, distractibility, and persistence. These can be attributed to three temperaments:

- "Difficult children" have irregular biological routines, avoidance behavior toward unfamiliar persons and situations, struggle to adapt to new situations, respond with high intensity, and display mainly negative moods (Zentner 1998, p. 76).
- "Slow-to-warm" or "shy" children respond with avoidance to new situations and persons; their response is rather moderate, their level of activity low (Zentner 1998, p. 77).
- "Easy children" have very regular biological rhythms and respond by approaching unfamiliar persons and situations; they adapt easily to change and their mood tends to be moderate and mainly positive. "Such children are usually a joy for their parents, pediatricians, and teachers" (ibid.).

Overall 35% of the children examined could initially not be assigned to any of these groups.

Buss and Plomin developed the EAS personality model based on three characteristics: emotionality, activity, and sociability. The model considers the degree of excitability, quickness and energy of behavior, and the tendency to prefer the presence of others to being alone (Rittelmeyer 2010, p. 88). In-depth analysis of this system of temperaments reveals that it appears to be "*compatible* with the four classic temperaments" (Rittelmeyer 2010, p. 91).

These few examples may suffice to illustrate how differently the concept of temperaments is defined. All of them are typologies that reduce the whole complexity of personality to just a few groups of characteristics. The danger here is that one may lose sight of the uniqueness of the individuality. The model of Thomas and Chess is worth mentioning because a third of the test persons cannot be categorized because of the terminology they use, which contains evaluation from the perspective of the adult attachment figures.

The way Steiner expresses himself may suggest that he is trying to separate the children of each grade into the few groups that have been known since Hippocrates: "The distinction between the sanguine, melancholic, phlegmatic, and choleric temperament goes back as far as antiquity. You will always find that a child's character traits can be assigned to one of these temperaments" (Steiner 2020, p. 36).

Steiner's suggestions on how to deal with the temperaments are remarkable. What is most important for him is that each child feels recognized and loved by the teacher. One-sided temperament traits are therefore not to be seen as deficits. It is rather a matter of focusing on and fostering the strengths that each temperament brings with it. Children should have the experience that they have special individual possibilities that become visible in the class community. But teachers also have to help the children to overcome the limitations of their temperament. This cannot be achieved by forcing children to change their innermost being. Rather, Steiner recommends letting children with a similar disposition work closely together so that they notice the weakness of their own temperament in others. Waldorf teachers therefore often apply the "similarity principle," for if children are able to open up empathetically to others, they will be more ready for change and development. Various authors have discussed in detail how methods and content can be used to suit the individual temperaments.[4]

Another element that is crucial to the diagnostic approach of Waldorf education is self-education. Self-education refers to the ability of educators to deal with their own temperament, which can influence both how they perceive children and how they act in their lessons. It is important that teachers recognize their own inner habitus and strive to overcome possible one-sided tendencies and limitations. In order to understand the children, teachers need to know, from experience, the strengths and weaknesses of the individual temperaments, or should at least understand them. "All four temperaments should live harmoniously in the teacher" (Steiner 1965, p. 129).

When Heiner Ullrich states that Steiner did not create a new personality psychology with his theory of the four temperaments but that he drew on the ancient Hippocratic model (Ullrich 2012, p. 230), he fails to recognize Steiner's original approach. Rittelmeyer, on the other hand, derives from his differentiated analysis of temperament models that the EAS system comes probably close to Steiner's concept. He concludes "that a thorough scientific examination of Steiner's theory of temperaments that includes the scientific discourse is still pending" (Rittelmeyer 2010, p. 95). Faced with a way of thinking "that declares the classic temperaments to be unscientific without subjecting this view to rigorous scrutiny," he pleads for "'empirical saturation' and for bringing the statistical findings to life with observations from practical life: this can facilitate the appropriate designation of the factors relating to the temperaments, for instance, which is [...] a *hermeneutic* task" (ibid.). Steiner's multiple and partly disparate statements on the topic do indeed suggest that his indications need to be used very cautiously as heuristic propositions for the pedagogical practice.

2.4 *Anthroposophy and anthropology*

Rudolf Steiner's distinction of anthropology and anthroposophy belongs to the essential theoretical foundations of Waldorf education (Kiersch 2011, p. 435). Anthropology is for him a science that "investigates the realms of the sensory world." It summarizes the facts of the sensory world in the human bodily organism in such a way that "from this summary the consciousness arises that conveys the outer reality as mental representations. Anthropologists see these representations as arising out of the human organism" (Steiner 1983b, p. 30f.). Anthroposophy, on the other hand, observed the spiritual human being "as belonging to the spiritual world. It proceeds to ideas of the human being that reflect the spiritual being within the human body" (ibid., p. 29). If one pursued both paths based on critical argumentation and according to scientific criteria of plausibility, they would "meet in one point [...]. In this meeting a genuinely fruitful understanding between anthroposophy and anthropology is possible. This is inevitable if both evolve into a philosophy of the human being" (ibid., p. 32). The anthroposophic picture of the human being was, however, "painted with entirely different materials" (ibid.) from that of natural science. The understanding of the human being (*Menschenkunde*) of Waldorf education corresponds to this philosophy.

The significance of Steiner's statement on the meeting of anthropology and anthroposophy is reflected in the current discourse between neurophysiology and education science. Brain research, for instance, sees human thinking arising from cortical processes (Fuchs 2010; Roth 2011). Fuchs calls attention to the problem that there are no subjects in the organism that could interpret indifferent neuronal events as meaningful "information." While a person's brain structures with their plasticity mirror his or her potential, it was impossible to reduce the acting subject to the functions of the central nervous system (Fuchs 2010, p. 131).

From Steiner's point of view, the example from neurobiology can characterize the boundary between anthroposophy and anthropology. Stating, for instance, that certain substances "cause negative emotional states in the brain" (Roth 2011, p. 81), or that the brain "has to choose" (ibid., p. 129), gives rise to the question as to who this subject may be that lives in our head. Thomas Fuchs calls attention to the category error underlying such thinking. He holds that the cognitive neurosciences are guided by a metaphysical realism that assumed an objective, material world out there of which there must be a physical description. This world would have to include "everything that happens in the world, that is, also our experience and observation of the world itself. In other words, it would have to include all that could be known about consciousness and its contents. [...] The basic problem of this approach lies in its manifest, though mostly not comprehended, circularity. It is based on the assumption that there could be a position of observation and recognition beyond our lifeworld experience which is, however, always presupposed with the observation. [...] Metaphysical realism or physicalism is thus incoherent insofar as it overlooks its own dependence on the intersubjectively constituted lifeworld" (Fuchs 2018, p. 62).

Neuroscience (as part of anthropology in Steiner's sense) does indeed come to a limit where its questions can no longer be answered with natural-scientific means. "The laws prevailing in logical thinking can no longer be described as those of the physical organization" (Steiner 1983b, p. 31). The neuroscientist Gerald Hüther refers to this boundary: "Evidently, there exists behind the world of material, observable, and measurable phenomena that life produces another, immaterial, invisible, and not measurable spiritual world" (Hüther 2008, p. 35).

Similarly, anthroposophy meets a boundary when characterizing mental representations as arising from inner thinking activity. Exact description of physical processes through which outer reality is represented can only be achieved by anthropology (Steiner 1983b, p. 30f.).

Johannes Kiersch points out that "in Steiner's view, it is not a matter of replacing or overcoming 'anthropology' through 'anthroposophy.' The two should complement each other" (Kiersch 2011, p. 433). While anthroposophy—or to be more precise, "Steiner's esoteric teachers' courses"—with its maieutic character was of high heuristic value, the practice of Waldorf education was based on a pedagogical anthropology, also founded by Steiner, "that is, as any other pedagogical anthropology, accessible in every detail to the evaluating criteria of modern education science" (ibid., p. 436). However, in Steiner's lectures, anthroposophical conceptualizations often transitioned into an empirical-anthropological argumentation without him having explicitly explained the resulting change of perspective (ibid., p. 437). It was therefore not surprising, Kiersch claims, that the different epistemological premises were often not sufficiently considered by either the followers or the opponents of Waldorf education.

2.5 Key aspects of a philosophy on the human being

Waldorf education is informed by different elements which Johannes Kiersch identifies as "key themes of a philosophy on the human being." They include:

- the theory of the fourfold human being,
- the theory of the senses,
- functional threefoldness,
- the autonomous individuality,
- diagnosis and typologies, and
- Goetheanism as natural-scientific hermeneutics.

These themes are only outlined briefly here; they are explained in more detail elsewhere.

Steiner's description of the fourfold human being meets with much interest in the presentations of Waldorf education. Skiera (2010) writes, for example, that according to Steiner, the physical body, the ether body, the astral body, and the "I," are "born" or "set free" in a rhythm of approximately seven years (Skiera 2010, p. 244). If we accept the strict distinction between the two opposite perspectives of anthroposophy and anthropology, we need to consider the anthroposophic origin of the concepts used here. In his book *Theosophy,* Steiner explains that only the "explorer of spiritual life" is able to perceive a creature's "life-filled spirit form" as an "independent, genuine being" (Steiner 1987a, p. 37). Although the effect of the life force at work in a living being can be perceived and empirically verified, it has not been possible yet for natural science to explain the phenomenon of life.

The same is true for the other non-physical constituents of the human organization. While each of us can gain awareness of the existence and mode of working of our soul and "I"-being, and while we can perceive the individuality of another person as a "You," Rudolf Steiner points out that one needs to develop specific organs in order to gain suprasensible perception of these constituent aspects.

Empirical findings appear to confirm the assumption that we have other levels of existence aside from our physical body. Rittelmeyer suggests that Steiner's concept of the fourfold human organization can, in the sense of a heuristic, sensitize us to certain perceptions. "The anthropologic *conceptual categories* make us susceptible for actual phenomena (which is not the same as generally accepting the theory of human fourfoldness itself)" (Rittelmeyer 2011, p. 345).

Insofar as Waldorf teachers use the anthroposophic concepts as guiding, heuristic categories, they can gain from this an extended understanding of the human being that can be made fruitful in education. "If one treats Steiner's anthropology as theory, it seems rather absurd to the scientific way of thinking and perceiving that is typical of our time, because it cannot be evidenced or intersubjectively verified. If one uses it as a heuristic, on the other hand, that is, as an experimental form of looking at illnesses or developmental phenomena in adolescents from a new and unfamiliar perspective, it can unlock an objective, that is, intersubjectively verifiable, new facet of reality" (Rittelmeyer 2011, p. 345; Chapter 8).

Human sense perception is so important to Rudolf Steiner that he introduces the topic at the very beginning of *Anthroposophy*, a (fragmentary) treatise written in 1910: "We shall begin anthroposophy with a contemplation of the human senses" (Steiner 1980, p. 29). Here, it is essential to overcome the subject/object division, "the separation of what is perceptible to the senses into a mechanistically conceived 'objective' outside world (*res extensa*) and an illusionary 'subjective' inner world (*res cogitans*)" (Kiersch 2011, p. 441; Scheurle 1984, p. 65ff.). Giving special consideration to sense perception in education is what links Waldorf education to other concepts of education reform ("learning with all senses") and is, beyond that, highly relevant today (Bilstein 2011). Steiner's theory of initially 10 and later 12 sensory modalities can be seen as essential to Waldorf education (Steiner 1992, p. 124ff., 2020, p. 184ff.). A specific approach to the senses in anthroposophy is the system of three groups of four senses in connection with the threefold functional organization of the human being, and above all the extension of the senses by the "higher" social senses (Kranich 2003; Scheurle 1984). Waldorf education therefore has the possibility to access the scientific discourse on education in this context, by introducing practical considerations regarding the fostering of the senses in the pedagogical practice (Chapter 2).

The threefold structure of the human being is a key motif of Waldorf education. Steiner first discussed it in 1917 in his book *Riddles of the Soul*, having studied the subject in depth over three decades before (Steiner 1983b). According to Steiner, the polarity of the neurosensory system and the system of metabolism and limbs, with the mediating rhythmic processes in between, is essential for understanding the interplay of body, soul, and spirit (Kiersch 2011; Kranich 1994). Crucial elements in the pedagogical practice of Waldorf schools rely on an understanding of this functional coherence, such as alternation between and the mutual complementation of cognitive, volitional, and emotional activities, the rhythm of tension and relaxation, earnest and humorous moments, and the importance of sleep for learning (Chapter 2).

"Education toward Freedom" as the maxim of Waldorf education presupposes an understanding of the human individuality as a subject that is in principle able to act responsibly and on the basis of free decisions, as described by Steiner in his book *The Philosophy of Freedom* (Steiner 1978). From the human capacity for freedom, essential premises can be derived for school learning (Loebell 2000). "Whatever their age, children always educate themselves. Waldorf education can merely try to create an environment that facilitates this and to work on the lower levels of the human organization to ensure that they will not become a hindrance for the child's individuality. What the individuality does of its own accord remains to be seen and cannot be planned" (Kiersch 2011, p. 439; Chapter 2).

Kiersch describes the beginning of a development "which could extend the horizon of scientific didactics, which has been reduced to what Dilthey refers to as 'explaining,' to include the more comprehensive 'understanding'" (Kiersch 1995, p. 214). The forms of thinking of the "exact" natural sciences would then become "part of a holistic hermeneutics, capable of employing all our cognitive faculties" (ibid., p. 214). According to Skiera, "this view of nature focuses on the idea of becoming and of development, of metamorphosis and of the embeddedness of the natural phenomena in their surroundings. Equally important are the original phenomena and ideas that lie behind the phenomena, and the endeavor to consciously grasp beings and phenomena in their entirety (in opposition to dissecting analysis)" (Skiera 2010, p. 239). Possibilities of linking this to general scientific didactics have been discussed in joint symposia and publications (Buck, Kranich 1995; Plestil, Schad 2008; Schad 2007; Chapter 2).

2.6 Education and ideology

In the discourse of education science, the Waldorf schools are mostly portrayed as positive but they are also seen as "ideology schools" (Müller 1999; Ullrich 2015; Winkel 1997). Müller, for instance, finds a number of indications of the "thoroughly normative and dogmatic ideological character of these schools" (Müller 1999, p. 120). Analysis of the pedagogical practice and the positive acknowledgement of Waldorf schools by "renowned educationists and school reformers," on the other hand, lead him to the conclusion that Waldorf schools can be seen as good schools despite anthroposophy (ibid., p. 125).

The question is whether it is possible at all, for any educational institution, to function without any ideological orientation. In order to bring up mature, responsible human beings, it is important to enable students to form their own critical judgment on the epistemological foundations of their tuition. This is precisely what Waldorf education aims for, starting from sixth grade.

According to Barz and Randoll's quantitative and qualitative surveys (2007), Waldorf alumni mostly have a positive picture of their former schools. Between 80% and 90% of interviewees would attend a Waldorf school again if given the choice. A summary of results based on commonalities of content shows that many of the positive statements refer to the education and personality development enabled by the teaching as such (together 59.8%). External conditions such as school climate or atmosphere were mentioned in 16.2% and the social community in 12.8% of statements, with special events such as class plays and class trips being seen as very important. Positive memories of teacher personalities only came in fourth place of the openly expressed views (5.8%). The general impression is that the former Waldorf students generally feel that their whole personality was respected, addressed, and supported.[5] "The data clearly debunk the repeatedly raised accusation that Waldorf schools teach anthroposophy (Prange 1985): the majority of graduates regard it with indifference or skepticism. [...] The graduates hardly ascribe an active role to Waldorf schools in conveying anthroposophic beliefs, but a high degree of religious and philosophical openness" (Barz, Randoll 2007, p. 19).

But even the supporters of anthroposophy and of Waldorf education must admit that various statements by Steiner can be irritating for critical or scientifically trained readers, particularly when Steiner's theses are placed into a historical or theoretical context that was not intended by him. Unbiased scientists should, on the other hand, carefully and critically examine if Steiner's statements can be refuted by their own experiences and by the findings of empirical research. Steiner himself pointed out that his anthroposophic theses were not verifiable by natural science (Steiner 1987a, p. 15). He claims something else: "Just consider the question: Is there a satisfactory explanation of life if the things that are being claimed are true? You will find that each single *life* confirms them" (ibid., p. 21). Neither the anthroposophic nor the anthropological statements therefore escape the scientific criterion of falsifiability; but they must be subjected to the rigorous empirical examination of their compatibility with the lifeworld experience.

Steiner explains his theses differently from the psychologists and educationists of his time. Insofar as his spiritual-scientific statements coincide with empiricism, the commonalities are, to a certain extent, denigrated as "superficial" (Ullrich 2012). It is therefore hardly surprising that Steiner's critics mostly seek to uncover his alleged sources that he himself, they claim, did not reveal.

Steiner's statements have the status of abductive inferences. These differ from inductive inferences in that they cannot be used "to introduce new theoretical concepts in the conclusion that are not included in the premises" (Schurz 2011, p. 52). Rather, we have here the inference from fact that is in need of explanation to hypotheses arising from some background knowledge: one senses a possible explanation for the observed phenomena. The psychologist Harald Walach describes abduction as a "creative act of intuitive insight and cognition. Without it there could be no science" (Walach 2008, p. 95). From a scientific or logical point of view, the validity of such a hypothesis remains preliminary. Its further course would have to "be empirically examined for it to assume the character of a probable hypothesis" (Schurz 2011, p. 53). Anthroposophy therefore constantly demands critical judgment on the part of teachers and empirical examination on that of education science. Steiner himself made it quite clear that he presented his insights in a way that his "listeners or readers were able to form their own judgment on the basis of these facts, because I refrain from influencing this judgment in any way" (Steiner 1989, p. 32).

2.7 Effects of Waldorf education: intentions and expectations

The effects of particular pedagogical measures will usually not become apparent until much later. Steiner poses that the foundations for adults to be able to "learn from life" are laid at school. "We can be learners throughout life, learning from life. But we need to be educated for this. Forces need to be developed in us at school that, only at that time, can grow strong enough to not be broken in later life" (Steiner 1991, p. 195). The demand that schools are there so we learn to learn indicates the practicing of certain learning processes: techniques for acquiring knowledge or problem solving, for example. Steiner means something else when he expects of schools that their graduates should later on be able to learn from life. This ability requires that one acquires living, flexile concepts instead of rigid definitions at school. Growing with our experiences will enable us to expand or totally change our concepts in later life (Steiner 1965).

The prominent position of the teacher personality who, through eight years, guides the students every morning through their lessons clearly has to do with the intention of supporting the development of resilience in young people. Furthermore, an important foundation is laid for the factors "cooperative learning, participation" and "positive peer contacts" because of the stable class community that lasts for twelve years. Since research has found clear evidence for the "importance of the social life and therefore the relevance of education, family, formation, and particularly of social networks for the development of resilience" (Gabriel 2005, p. 213), it seems justified to assume that Waldorf education has this effect. Another essential characteristic of Waldorf education is the close collaboration with parents.

In Barz and Randoll's study of graduates (Barz, Randoll 2007), many of the interviewees have personality traits that come close to the psychological concept of resilience. Some marked findings of this study are evidently linked to resources that are associated with resilience, such as being convinced of one's own efficacy, a positive self-image, a strong sense of self-worth, the ability to self-regulate, an internal locus of control/realistic attribution style, as well as secure attachment behavior (keen to explore): In the open interviews, many interviewees stated they felt they can cope with life and that they were convinced this was due to their schooling. They were referring to "practical skills," "practical thinking," or the "ability to master my own life." "Independence" and acquiring the "basic competences required for professional work" were also mentioned. Almost all interviewees cited their own independence and flexibility as reasons for their job satisfaction. Some also complained that they were not prepared adequately for life in some respects (Barz, Randoll 2007).

Many Waldorf alumni described themselves as self-confident, energetic and vigorous, assertive, and perseverant. Those who took part in the questionnaire-survey said the Waldorf school had a "positive" or "rather positive" influence:

- on their own ability to represent their opinions and views toward others (75.0%);
- on their own self-confidence (in the sense of "I can do that": 64.2%);
- on their own sense of self-worth (in the sense of "I count": 62.1%).

Voluntary activities were remarkably frequent in both the qualitative and the quantitative survey: three-quarters of participants in the former and 47.5% of those who filled in the standardized questionnaire (compared to 37.7% of the general population). One of the reasons given was that they preferred being active to the usual "moaning" and "whining." The attitude apparent from this is that people do not experience themselves as powerless observers but as active agents: an indicator of resilience. People also stated that the foundation for their social values, interest, and the perseverance required for commitment had been laid at school.

The following components of resilience can be attributed to "inner flexibility and creativity": problem-solving skills, active and flexible coping behavior, an optimistic, confident attitude to life, as well as talents, interests, and hobbies. Many former Waldorf students mentioned as an advantage they had over others was their creativity, which they were often convinced was due to their schooling. A greater number of younger than older (over 50) candidates were convinced that their school had a positive effect on their creativity (90.9% compared to 84.3%). Openness to new things, curiosity, and multiple interests were mentioned as advantages of personality-building in the Waldorf school.

If the qualities mentioned were typical of former Waldorf students, this would signify that they had acquired essential prerequisites for "learning from life," one of the aims of Waldorf education. This assumption is corroborated by the participants in the qualitative survey who estimated that their schooling had inspired in them a "positive attitude to life," and fundamental "trust in life," and the ability to "flexibly adjust to adverse conditions." People also stated that the basic competences required for learning, for individual knowledge acquisition, were conveyed to them at school. While some complained that certain specialist subjects had been neglected, or that the subject matter competence of teachers was unsatisfactory, others felt strongly that they had learned to "actively take on tasks, to take charge of life."

3 Summary: Waldorf education—A searching movement

Historically, the first Waldorf schools emerged at the same time as the educational reform schools, and both have in common that they are critical of the state school system. This can explain some of the commonalities they share about central issues. Essential differences, on the other hand, can be found in an idiosyncratic tension that is typical of Waldorf education: While Waldorf teachers are, on the one hand, oriented to Steiner's writings and lectures, which unite all Waldorf schools and give them a coherent foundation, anthroposophy is not a coherent theoretical system from which unambiguous instructions can be derived for teaching and teaching methods.

In Waldorf education, orientation to the child refers to a perceptiveness enhanced by the study of Steiner's Anthropological Foundations (Steiner 2020) for the uniqueness of each individuality and the enigma they present. The idea of development serves primarily to sensitize teachers to changes that are part of the child's maturation and learning. Steiner's references to certain regularities can sharpen the teacher's awareness of the changes that occur in the way young people experience the world, while calling their attention to unexpected forms of behavior.

Peter Loebell

New forms of self-activity that are appropriate for our time can enable students to learn through their own free experiences, which are not determined by prefabricated material, textbooks, or learning programs. Here, too, Steiner's indications can be used as references that, before they can inform lesson content and teaching methods, need to be newly reflected upon by every Waldorf teacher in relation to up-to-date scientific insights. To use an example: Rudolf Steiner encouraged the first Waldorf teachers to base their teaching of zoology on observation of the human form, and from there to distinguish animals with a view to the prevalence in them of characteristics of the human head, torso, or limbs.

Like the suggestions for the teaching of anthropology and zoology, all the fundamentals of Waldorf education were largely developed in lectures, discussions with teachers, and faculty meetings. The various statements therefore need to be interpreted in context and critically reflected. This is particularly important when these statements are transferred to other languages and cultures. In this sense, Waldorf education needs to be seen as an ongoing research movement that needs to be newly shaped to suit different locations and times. While this implies big challenges, it also holds important possibilities for a modern education.

Notes

1 "Children who cannot read and write properly at the age of 14 or 15 – I speak from experience because I was such a child – do not hinder their later spiritual development to the same degree as those who were able to read and write well at the age of seven or eight"(Steiner 1979, p. 34 f.).

2 The grammar school students were interviewed in 1993/1994, the Waldorf school students in 1996/1997. It needs to be considered that the interviewees had not finished school yet; the grammar school students were in thirteenth grade, the Waldorf students between eleventh and thirteenth grade (Randoll 1999).

3 Many more Waldorf students had the experience that their creative faculties were promoted (85% compared to 22%) and diverse interests were inspired in them (76% compared to 47%). They also felt more often that they were taught how to learn (59% compared to 36%) (ibid., p. 192 f.).

4 Bäuerle (1997), Eller (2007), Eltz (1992), Lipps (1998), Schad (1991), Scheer-Krüger (1992), Sixel (1990).

5 The interviewees mostly responded in positive terms ("agree" or "agree somewhat") to the following items: "I had a sense of belonging at school" (87%); "I felt comfortable at school" (86%); "I felt safe at school" (78.8%).

References

Amelang, Manfred/Bartussek, Dieter (1997): Differentielle Psychologie und Persönlichkeitsforschung. 4th edition. Stuttgart: Kohlhammer.

Bartussek, Dieter (1996): Faktorenanalytische Gesamtsysteme der Persönlichkeit. In: Amelang, Manfred (Ed.) (1996): Enzyklopädie der Psychologie, Themenbereich C, Series VIII, Volume 3, Temperamentsund Persönlichkeitsunterschiede. Göttingen: Hogrefe, pp. 51–106.

Barz, Heiner/Randoll, Dirk (2007): Einleitung: Intentionen und Hauptergebnisse der Untersuchung. In: Barz, Heiner/Randoll, Dirk (Eds.) (2007): Absolventen von Waldorfschulen. Eine empirische Studie zu Bildung und Lebensgestaltung. Wiesbaden: VS, pp. 13–23.

Bäuerle, Anna-Sophia (1997): Das Wecken moralischer Kräfte im Blick auf die Temperamente. In: Neuffer, Helmut (Ed.) (1997): Zum Unterricht des Klassenlehrers an der Waldorfschule. Stuttgart: Freies Geistesleben, pp. 1091–1100.

Bilstein, Johannes (Ed.) (2011): Anthropologie und Pädagogik der Sinne. Opladen: Budrich.

Breidenstein, Georg (2010): Überlegungen zu einer Theorie des Unterrichts. In: Zeitschrift für Pädagogik, vol. 56, issue 6, pp. 869–887.

Buck, Peter/Kranich, Ernst-Michael (Eds.) (1995): Auf der Suche nach dem erlebbaren Zusammenhang: Übersehene Dimensionen der Natur und ihre Bedeutung in der Schule. Weinheim: Beltz.

Eller, Helmut (2007): Die menschlichen Temperamente. Stuttgart: Freies Geistesleben.

Eltz, Heinrich (1992): Die menschlichen Temperamente. Bern: Haupt.

Flitner, Andreas (1999): Reform der Erziehung. Munich: Piper.

Fölling-Albers, Maria/Meidenbauer, Katja (2010): Was erinnern Schüler/innen vom Unterricht? In: Zeitschrift für Pädagogik, vol. 56, issue 2, pp. 229–248.

Fuchs, Thomas (2010): Das Gehirn – ein Beziehungsorgan. 3rd edition, Stuttgart: Kohlhammer. English edition.

Fuchs, Thomas (2018): Ecology of the Brain. The Phenomenology and Biology of the Embodied Mind. Oxford: Oxford University Press.

Gabriel, Thomas (2005): Resilienz - Kritik und Perspektiven. Paralleltitel: Resilience –criticism and perspectives. In: Zeitschrift für Pädagogik, 51 (2005) 2, pp. 207–217.

Götte, Wenzel M. (2005): Begabung, Intelligenz und Hochbegabung – aus der Sicht der Waldorfpädagogik. In: Götte, Wenzel M. (Ed.) (2005): Hochbegabte und Waldorfschule. Stuttgart: Freies Geistesleben, pp. 209–312.

Götte, Wenzel M./Loebell, Peter/Maurer, Klaus-Michael (Eds.) (2016): Entwicklungsaufgaben und Kompetenzen. Zum Bildungsplan der Waldorfschulen. 2nd edition. Stuttgart: Freies Geistesleben.

Hasselhorn, Marcus/Gold, Andreas (2013): Pädagogische Psychologie. Erfolgreiches Lernen und Lehren. 3rd edition. Stuttgart: Kohlhammer.

Hattie, John (2014): Lernen sichtbar machen. 2nd edition. Baltmannsweiler: Schneider.

Helsper, Werner/Hummrich, Merle (2014): Die Lehrer-Schüler-Beziehung. In: Schulpädagogik heute, vol. 5, issue 9, pp. 1–22.

Helsper, Werner/Ullrich, Heiner/Stelmaszyk, Bernhard/Höblich, Davina/Graßhoff, Gunther/Jung, Dana (2007): Autorität und Schule. Die empirische Rekonstruktion der Klassenlehrer-Schüler-Beziehung an Waldorfschulen. Wiesbaden: VS.

Hüther, Gerald (2008): Die biologischen Grundlagen der Spiritualität. In: Hüther, Gerald/Roth, Wolfgang/von Brück, Michael (Eds.) (2008): Damit das Denken Sinn bekommt. Freiburg: Herder.

Keller, Ulrike (2012): Klassenlehrerzeit. In: Liebenwein, Sylva/Barz, Heiner/Randoll, Dirk (2012): Bildungserfahrungen an Waldorfschulen. Empirische Studie zu Schulqualität und Lernerfahrungen. Wiesbaden: VS, pp. 101–112.

Kiersch, Johannes (1995): Die Natur "verstehen" lernen – Ein Hinweis auf Owen Barfield. In: Buck, Peter/Kranich, Ernst-Michael (Eds.) (1995): Auf der Suche nach dem erlebbaren Zusammenhang: Übersehene Dimensionen der Natur und ihre Bedeutung in der Schule. Weinheim: Beltz, pp. 213–217.

Kiersch, Johannes (2011): Waldorfpädagogik als Erziehungskunst. In: Uhlenhoff, Rahel (Ed.): Anthroposophie in Geschichte und Gegenwart. Berlin: Berliner Wissenschaftsverlag, pp. 423–476.

Kranich, Ernst-Michael (1994): Anthropologie – das Fundament der pädagogischen Praxis. In: Bohnsack, Fritz/Kranich, Ernst-Michael (Eds.) (1994): Erziehungswissenschaft und Waldorfpädagogik. 2nd edition. Weinheim: Beltz.

Kranich, Ernst-Michael (2003): Der innere Mensch und sein Leib. Stuttgart: Freies Geistesleben.

Leber, Stefan (Ed.) (1997): Anthroposophie und Waldorfpädagogik in den Kulturen der Welt. Stuttgart: Freies Geistesleben.

Liebenwein, Sylva/Barz, Heiner/Randoll, Dirk (2012): Bildungserfahrungen an Waldorfschulen. Empirische Studie zu Schulqualität und Lernerfahrungen. Wiesbaden: VS.

Lipps, Peter (1998): Temperamente und Pädagogik. Stuttgart: Freies Geistesleben.

Lischewski, Andreas (2015): Menschenbilder der Reformpädagogischen Bewegung – Versuch einer klärenden Gliederung. In: Bauer, Horst Philipp/Schieren, Jost (Eds.) (2015): Menschenbild und Pädagogik. Weinheim, Basel Juventa.

Loebell, Peter (2000): Lernen und Individualität. Weinheim: Deutscher Studienverlag.

Loebell, Peter (2004): Ich bin, der ich werde. Individualisierung in der Waldorfpädagogik. Stuttgart: Freies Geistesleben.

Loebell, Peter (2005): Das Erkennen und Fördern besonderer Begabungen in der Waldorfschule. In: Götte, Wenzel M. (Ed.) (2005): Hochbegabte und Waldorfschule. Stuttgart: Freies Geistesleben, pp. 83–151.

Montada, Leo (2002): Fragen, Konzepte, Perspektiven. In: Oerter, Rolf/Montada, Leo (Eds.) (2002): Entwicklungspsychologie. 5th edition. Weinheim: Beltz.

Montessori, Maria (1969): Die Entdeckung des Kindes. Freiburg: Herder.

Müller, Walter (1999): "Ver-Steiner-te" Reformpädagogik oder: Ist die Waldorfschule trotz Anthroposophie eine gute Schule? In: Böhm, Winfried/Oelkers, Jürgen (Eds.) (1999): Reformpädagogik kontrovers. Würzburg: Ergon, pp. 105–125.

Oelkers, Jürgen (2005): Reformpädagogik – eine kritische Dogmengeschichte. 4th edition. Weinheim, Munich: Juventa.

Plestil, Dusan/Schad, Wolfgang (2008): Naturwissenschaft heute im Ansatz Goethes. Stuttgart, Berlin: Mayer.

Prange, Klaus (1985): Erziehung zur Anthroposophie. Darstellung und Kritik der Waldorfpadagogik. Bad Heilbrunn: Klinkhardt.

Preiser, Siegfried (2003): Pädagogische Psychologie. Weinheim: Beltz.

Pütz, Tanja (2015): Kinder sind anders – eine pädagogische Ableitung von Maria Montessoris Bild vom Kind. In: Bauer, Horst Philipp/Schieren, Jost (Eds.) (2015): Menschenbild und Pädagogik. Weinheim, Basel: Beltz Juventa.

Randoll, Dirk (1999): Waldorfpädagogik auf dem Prüfstand. Auch eine Herausforderung an das öffentliche Schulwesen? Berlin: VWB.

Randoll, Dirk (2010): Empirische Forschung und Waldorfpädagogik. In: Paschen, Harm (Eds.) (2010): Erziehungswissenschaftliche Zugänge zur Waldorfpädagogik. Wiesbaden: VS, pp. 127–156.

Rilke, Rainer Maria (1987): Werke. Vol. 5. Frankfurt am Main: Insel.

Rittelmeyer, Christian (2010): Die Temperamente in der Waldorfpädagogik. Ein Modell zur Überprüfung ihrer Wissenschaftlichkeit. In: Paschen, Harm (Ed.) (2010): Erziehungswissenschaftliche Zugänge zur Waldorfpädagogik. Wiesbaden: VS, pp. 75–100.

Rittelmeyer, Christian (2011): Gute Pädagogik – fragwürdige Ideologie? Zur Diskussion um die anthroposophischen Grundlagen der Waldorfpädagogik. In: Loebell, Peter (Ed.) (2011): Waldorfschule heute. Stuttgart: Freies Geistesleben, pp. 327–347.

Röhrs, Hermann (Ed.) (1986): Die Schulen der Reformpädagogik heute. Düsseldorf: Schwann.

Röhrs, Hermann (1998): Die Reformpädagogik. Ursprung und Verlauf unter internationalem Aspekt. 5th edition. Weinheim: Deutscher Studienverlag.

Roth, Gerhard (2011): Bildung braucht Persönlichkeit. Wie Lernen gelingt. Stuttgart: Klett-Cotta.

Schad, Wolfgang (1991): Erziehung ist Kunst. Pädagogik aus Anthroposophie. Stuttgart: Freies Geistesleben.

Schad, Wolfgang (2007): Goethes Weltkultur. Stuttgart: Freies Geistesleben.

Scheer-Krüger, Gerda (1992): Das offenbare Geheimnis der Temperamente. Stuttgart: Freies Geistesleben.

Scheurle, Hans Jürgen (1984): Die Gesamtsinnesorganisation. Überwindung der Subjekt-Objekt-Spaltung in der Sinneslehre. 2nd edition. Stuttgart: Thieme.

Schurz, Gerhard (2011): Einführung in die Wissenschaftstheorie. 3rd edition. Darmstadt: Wissenschaftliche Buchgesellschaft.

Sixel, Detlef (1990): Rudolf Steiner über die Temperamente. Dornach: Verlag am Goetheanum.

Skiera, Ehrenhard (2010): Reformpädagogik in Geschichte und Gegenwart. 2nd edition. Munich, Wien: Oldenbourg.

Skiera, Ehrenhard (2012): Reformpädagogik in Diskurs und Erziehungswirklichkeit. In: Herrmann, Ulrich/Schlüter, Steffen (Eds.) (2012): Reformpädagogik – eine kritisch-konstruktive Vergegenwärtigung. Bad Heilbrunn: Klinkhardt, pp. 47–78.

Soetebeer, Jörg (2010): Selbsttätige Bildungskraft heute. Stuttgart: Pädagogische Forschungsstelle beim Bund der Freien Waldorfschulen.

Steiner, Rudolf (1965): Der pädagogische Wert der Menschenerkenntnis und der Kulturwert der Pädagogik. 10 Vorträge in Arnheim 1924. Rudolf Steiner Gesamtausgabe (= GA) 310. 3rd edition. Dornach: Rudolf Steiner Verlag.

Steiner, Rudolf (1978): Die Philosophie der Freiheit (1894). GA 4. Dornach: Rudolf Steiner Verlag.

Steiner, Rudolf (1979): Die Kunst des Erziehens aus dem Erfassen der Menschenwesenheit. Seven lectures given in Torquay 1924. GA 311. 4th edition. Dornach: Rudolf Steiner Verlag.

Steiner, Rudolf (1980): Anthroposophie. Ein Fragment (1910). GA 45. 3rd edition. Dornach: Rudolf Steiner Verlag.

Steiner, Rudolf (1982b): Die pädagogische Praxis vom Gesichtspunkte geisteswissenschaftlicher Menschenerkenntnis. 8 lectures given in Dornach 1923. GA 306. 3rd edition. Dornach: Rudolf Steiner Verlag.

Steiner, Rudolf (1983a): Erziehung und Unterricht aus Menschenerkenntnis. 9 lectures given in Stuttgart 1920–23. GA 302a. 3rd edition. Dornach: Rudolf Steiner Verlag.

Steiner, Rudolf (1983b): Von Seelenrätseln. TB 637 (GA 21). 5th edition. Dornach: Rudolf Steiner Verlag.

Steiner, Rudolf (1985a): Erziehungskunst. Seminarbesprechungen und Lehrplanvorträge. TB 639 (GA 295). Dornach: Rudolf Steiner Verlag. English translation: Steiner, Rudolf (2020): The First Teachers' Course. Anthropological Foundations-Methods of Teaching-Practical Discussions. GA 293–295. trans. Margot M. Saar. Bangkok: Ratayakom. Steiner, Rudolf (1987a): Theosophie. 1904. GA 9. Dornach: Rudolf Steiner Verlag.

Steiner, Rudolf (1989): Anthroposophische Gemeinschaftsbildung. 10 lectures given in Stuttgart and Dornach 1923. GA 257. 4th edition. Dornach: Rudolf Steiner Verlag.

Steiner, Rudolf (1990): Erziehungskunst. Methodisch-Didaktisches. 14 lectures given in Stuttgart 1919. GA 294. 6th edition. Dornach: Rudolf Steiner Verlag. English translation: Steiner, Rudolf (2020): The First Teachers' Course. Anthropological Foundations-Methods of Teaching-Practical Discussions. GA 293–295. trans. Margot M. Saar. Bangkok: Ratayakom.

Steiner, Rudolf (1991): Geisteswissenschaftliche Behandlung sozialer und pädagogischer Fragen. 17 lectures given in Stuttgart 1919. GA 192. 2nd edition. Dornach: Rudolf Steiner Verlag.

Steiner, Rudolf (1992): Allgemeine Menschenkunde als Grundlage der Pädagogik. 14 lectures given in Stuttgart 1919. GA 293. 9th edition. Dornach: Rudolf Steiner Verlag. English translation: Steiner, Rudolf (2020): The First Teachers' Course. Anthropological Foundations-Methods of Teaching-Practical Discussions. GA 293–295. trans. Margot M. Saar. Bangkok: Ratayakom.

Strelau, Jan (1984): Das Temperament in der psychischen Entwicklung. Berlin: Volkseigener Verlag.

Ullrich, Heiner (2012): Befremdlicher Anachronismus oder zukunftweisendes Modell? – Die Freie Waldorfschule im pädagogischen Diskurs und in der erziehungswissenschaftlichen Forschung. In: Hansen Schaberg, Inge (Ed.) (2012): Reformpädagogische Schulkonzepte. Vol. 6. Waldorfpädagogik. Baltmannsweiler: Schneider, pp. 220–266.

Ullrich, Heiner (2015): Waldorfpädagogik. Eine kritische Einführung. Weinheim, Basel: Beltz.

Walach, Harald (2008): Spiritualität und Wissenschaft. In: Hüther, Gerald/Roth, Wolfgang/von Brück, Michael (Eds.) (2008): Damit das Denken Sinn bekommt. Freiburg: Herder.

Winkel, Rainer (1997): Rudolf Steiner und die nach ihm benannten Schulen. In: Winkel, Rainer (Ed.) (1997): Reformpädagogik konkret. Hamburg: Bergmann und Helbig, pp. 103–119.

Zentner, Marcel R. (1998): Die Wiederentdeckung des Temperaments. Frankfurt am Main: Fischer.

CHAPTER 8

Waldorf Education and Anthroposophy

EDUCATION SCIENCE AND WALDORF EDUCATION

Wolfgang Nieke

1 Waldorf education and anthroposophy

There is not one uniform view of Waldorf education in the German education landscape. Some ideas and descriptions present Waldorf education as one-person-related pedagogical system that, among others, together constitute a part of the textbook knowledge for future teachers: rooted in the past and still effective in practice. Some presentations are more distanced, focusing on the timelessness and continued modernness of Waldorf education, but disconcerted by anthroposophy as its theoretical-philosophical-religious background. Very few (though influential) authors express fundamental criticism of Waldorf education, explicitly not because of its pedagogical theory and practice but solely because of its association with what they think anthroposophy is. They rarely engage profoundly with this system of thought. Instead, they tend to read in it here and there, without due hermeneutic thoroughness. This rejection has been widely absorbed, with the result that the current discourse distinguishes sharply between the pedagogical practice of Waldorf education, which is largely accepted as valuable, and anthroposophy, which is seen as esoteric and, in places, inacceptable due to individual statements made by Steiner. Suggestions are then put forward demanding that Waldorf education should be wholly separated from anthroposophy and classified and recognized as an education reform movement that enriches the pedagogical landscape in valuable ways.

2 What is fascinating about Waldorf education?

There is much that is fascinating about Waldorf education as a pedagogical practice that one can observe from the outside or discover as a visitor.

Almost all visitors to Waldorf schools notice a special school climate that differs markedly from what one finds in state schools or in other private schools. These visitors often don't find it easy to put this special experience into words. Much of it seems to be associated with the way the students deal with each other and with the teachers: more calmly and respectfully, slower in movement and language.

The distinctive school architecture does not have to be understood in its intended expression; it has an immediate effect even without such contextualization. When asked, people describe this effect consistently as an experience of sacredness and of the sublimeness. It seems to suggest to them a hallowing of the child and of education that they find a pleasant contrast to the demonstrative culture of paucity in mainstream school buildings.

What people pick out as positive, as compared to state schools, is that there is no pressure to perform, because of the absence—in the first eight school years—of number-based grades or of the threat

DOI: 10.4324/9781003187431-37

of having to repeat a year if the minimum standard was not attained. They appreciate this particularly in relation to the sizeable number of students who are not, or not yet, able to meet normal learning requirements. Often, this is seen as an expression of the kind of child-centered education reform that exists in other forms but with the same underlying orientation.

Positive comments also refer to the prevalence of arts and crafts compared to the book schools, another motif found in education reform in general.

Those who look more deeply notice that teachers look at their students with different eyes, perceiving each child as infinitely precious and unique, even in the sometimes unnervingly large classes. While outsiders note this, they don't usually associate it with the underlying anthroposophic understanding of human nature that does, however, guide this view of the child.

3 Points of mutual rejection

3.1 *From the point of view of education science*

The different views were briefly outlined at the beginning. Aside from alluding to a romantic, pre-modern orientation of education reform, rejection is usually aimed at anthroposophy, which is seen as inaccessible to scientific scrutiny. Teacher education based on such premises is unacceptable to the basic belief that teachers must be scientifically trained if they are to be admitted to the circle of professions (theology, medicine, law, engineering, etc.).

This rejection could be avoided if anthroposophy could only present itself as a science in the usual sense, by making its insights accessible to intersubjective examination (of which many exist, and many that differ from the natural-scientific experiment). That anthroposophy is a science—a spiritual science—has so far not been compellingly argued.

A promising approach could be to refer to Edmund Husserl's phenomenological reduction, which has similar arguments as Rudolf Steiner: This approach is the basis of the qualitative social, cultural, and educational research that has by now achieved equivalence with the nomothetic approach (quantitative research methods) and hermeneutics. From the point of view of academic science, two ways of presenting anthroposophy must be rejected as a matter of principle:

- esotericism that avoids the need for the intersubjective verifiability of truth claims, by stating that this [anthroposophy] requires initiation;
- dogmatism based on authority.

Although both directions are not denied their right of existence or the claim that they can lead to the truth, they are not truths in the sense of the elementary definition that such truths must be intersubjectively verifiable. These two forms of anthroposophy therefore seem to the outside observer rather like a religion, and religions, with their truth claims, are generally respected in secularized societies.

3.2 *From the point of view of Waldorf education*

Given the thinking underlying their approach, the representatives of an anthroposophically founded Waldorf education must reject the attempt to explain the human being based on physics and chemistry as natural sciences and the use of determinist causal models with linear mathematization. This concerns the empiric education sciences of psychology—to the extent that it sees itself as a natural science—and the nomothetic approaches of sociology.

What lies behind this is the rejection by Rudolf Steiner and many of his contemporaries of monistic materialism (there is only matter and everything can be explained on the basis of matter—not to be confused with the monism represented by Spinoza, Goethe, or Ernst Haeckel, for instance) as an explanation of life and culture (at the time, this sphere was still referred to as *spirit* in the sense of an objectivization of originally subjective insights and creations).

4 Possible meeting points

There are potential meeting points. Two possibilities for a common intellectual search movement are described below.

4.1 *The basic motif of individual freedom*

Observed from my outside position, the fast-growing group of Waldorf teachers that refers, above all, to Rudolf Steiner's early and late work uses this basic motif—individual freedom— as their main orientation in identifying what they expect of anthroposophy. On this basis, Steiner's complete work is then used as a heuristic that can and should give them inspirations for unconventional approaches on which they can build without having to take it literally. However, individual freedom does not mean the kind of unrestricted arbitrariness of individuals toward the interests of others, as propagated by certain liberal and libertarian ideologies. It rather refers to the self-determined way of life that is embedded in and relates to a greater whole: an overarching meaningfulness that informs every individual existence and every well-reflected action. This meaning needs to be sought, found, and constructed, and it can be unique to each person.

From the point of view of education science, there are four possible meeting points:

a. Some concepts of education follow an image of the human being that goes back to Rousseau and that is currently mostly used with reference to humanistic psychology (Carl Rogers, Erich Fromm, Ruth Cohn). According to this concept, we each possess an inherent essence that only needs to develop; this development can either be hindered or promoted by our environment. Because we are basically good by nature, education *merely needs to promote* development. Negative behaviors are seen as being caused by the wrong environmental influences. The central concept of development is clearly informed by an organological picture—that is to say, by the 19th-century biological idea that in every seed the entire form and function of a plant is already contained, and it simply needs the right conditions for them to unfold. It must be pointed out that this concept can be found much more widely in the pedagogical practice than in the academic discourses of German education science. It also needs to be mentioned that this practice is intimately related to psychotherapeutic concepts that are based on humanistic psychology.

b. Since the enlightenment, individualization in subjective freedom has been the central thought in most educational theories. Reference is usually made to Wilhelm von Humboldt, but he only mentioned it aphoristically and unsystematically in his comprehensive and elaborative work, also implying a developmental aspect. It is not the case in this view, however, that everything unfolds by and out of itself. Rather, education can only build on the potential present in every person, albeit in individually different ways, and it must do this by devoting itself to a cause that can be either objective, as in craft lessons, for instance, or, above all, spiritual or cultural, and here it is almost exclusively integrated in the diversity of languages. Teaching, in this sense, does not happen through instruction but in teachers and students together devoting to the cause. The student's education is wholly unavailable to the teacher. The teacher can and should inspire the student but is not responsible for the success of the education. Education happens in solitude and in freedom.

Making recourse to topical discourses in philosophy and psychology, Hans-Christoph Koller, for instance, extends this basic idea toward *transformative education* (Koller 2012). The focus here is on self-education, which does not, according to Koller, take place through continuous new learning and storing of memory content but solely in the confrontation of what one already knows and thinks is right with something new and different. In a process of reflection, this can then be rejected as inadequate or irrelevant, and the former worldview be reaffirmed, or it can be replaced or changed by what is new: transformed into a new worldview. This is strenuous and needs to be achieved by the individual in freedom.

c. The freedom of the individual as an essential general standard can also be found in critical educational science, which rests on three philosophical pillars:

- Marxism, with its rejection of enslavement to the dictate of materialist economics;
- the Frankfurt School's critical theory of society, which extends this perspective by including the dangers of cultural industry;
- the critique of power in contemporary philosophy (Michel Foucault's *dispositives* of power, for instance), calling attention to the subject's disappearance under the overwhelming power structures of big societies.

d. Cultural theory that sees culture as something spiritual—in the sense of spirit objectified from originally individual creation—that cannot be assessed nomothetically or scientifically but only hermeneutically and phenomenologically, manifesting in the qualitative methods of culture-oriented social and educational research.

4.2 *Explaining and understanding*

Despite the largely unchallenged dominance of monistic materialism (there is only matter, and soul and culture, too, can be fully explained by natural science), there is still skepticism as to the correctness of this paradigm. This is apparent, for example, from the routine juxtaposition of *science* and *humanities* in English-speaking universities, which does not simply describe different faculties but two worlds of thinking that mark a fundamentally different access to the world: through explanation on the one hand and through understanding on the other (Toulmin 1981).

The German education sciences have integrated this dualization into their own structures: On the one hand, they conduct explanatory, nomothetic theorizing and the corresponding empirical research, using the quantitative methods also applied in psychology and sociology. On the other hand, they carry out both historical, philosophical research, using the means of hermeneutics (without excluding it as a separate *philosophy of education*), and, at the same time, using phenomenological education research with partly independent methods (of education science biography research).

This should provide plenty of theoretically promising and empirically fruitful possibilities for communication and cooperation.

References

Koller, Hans-Christoph (2012): Bildung anders denken. Einführung in die Theorie transformatorischer Bildungsprozesse. Stuttgart: Kohlhammer.

Toulmin, Stephen (1981): Voraussicht und Verstehen. Versuch über die Ziele der Wissenschaft. Frankfurt am Main: Suhrkamp.

HOW CAN STEINER'S PEDAGOGICAL ESOTERICISM BE OPEN FOR DISCUSSION?

Theses on Avoidable Obstacles to Discourse

Johannes Kiersch

Rudolf Steiner's courses for the teachers of the first Waldorf school served as an introduction to an anthroposophic professional esotericism (Kiersch 2010)—a fact that to this day has eluded rational discussion. Waldorf teachers who value tradition insist that their ideas about human nature, and the didactic principle derived from them, have a scientific foundation in Steiner's anthroposophy. This claim is disputed by representatives of education science. The "esoteric" background remains a taboo for both sides: for the one side, because they fear that critical scrutiny could endanger an intimate inner space whose life conditions must remain alien to outside observers who are not existentially involved; for the other side, because the common, entirely unreflected concept of esotericism, which Steiner's anthroposophy is *a priori* assigned to, seems to discount any rational discussion from the start. Authors who seek a provisional understanding because of the practical success and impressive plausibility of Waldorf education (Paschen 2010; Nieke in Chapter 8) simply ignore this problem. Additionally, outside experts concede that the insistence of Waldorf education on its anthroposophic foundations is one of its essential characteristics (Müller 1999), while it is assumed at the same time that this is associated with totalitarian claims to truth (Skiera 2010). This verdict is supported by self-representations on the part of Waldorf education that, in the effort to clarify Steiner's anthropological "indications," disseminate seemingly dogmatic concepts. In his well-known brief treatise on *The Education of the Child in the Light of Anthroposophy* (1907), which contains a concise summary of his theory of the "fourfold human organization" discussed in more detail in his basic work *Theosophy* (1904), Steiner himself gave cause for such a verdict, since this treatise constitutes a very preliminary work that, compared to the richness of later descriptions, does not sufficiently reflect Waldorf education as it presents itself today (Kiersch 1992). These abstract schematisms are also unattractive to Waldorf school staff who may not be sufficiently familiar with Steiner's anthroposophy, and they seem hardly compatible with the personal responsibility and freedom of the teacher that representatives of Waldorf education have always claimed for themselves.

As a result of this contradiction, the Waldorf practice today sways between anxiously holding on to traditions and fluctuating arbitrariness. What used to provide spiritual support in the past and acted as an innovative force in the first Waldorf school is fading and becomes rather embarrassing. Jost Schieren therefore suggests the pragmatic approach of postponing the scientific solving of the riddles thrown up by the topic of "esotericism" in connection with Waldorf education in the distant future (Schieren 2011). One will have to agree with him in that the time is not ripe yet for an unbiased conversation on this riddle. I am nonetheless convinced that efforts in this direction are possible even now and that they could be rewarding.

A helpful first step in this direction could be the more recent discussion in cultural history on the *concept of esotericism* that has so far remained very diffuse and has largely been trivialized by pejorative

DOI: 10.4324/9781003187431-38

media attention. This discussion has recently begun to take an entirely new direction. While occult spiritual streams in the history of humanity used to be a remote area of study reserved for experts, it now emerges that it touches on fundamental and highly relevant questions regarding our "position in the cosmos" (Scheler, Henckmann 2016), as well as scientific questions discussed currently between holists and reductionists, or the still unexplored field of emergence theories (Greve, Schnabel 2011). Antoine Faivre has prepared the ground with his theses on the thought forms of traditional esotericism (Faivre 2001). Wouter J. Hanegraaff and his colleagues have mapped this new field (Hanegraaff 2006). First attempts are underway to bring the results of these efforts together with the internal anthroposophic discourse (summarized by Dietz 2008). Hanegraaff's recently presented detailed history of the discourse offers a helpful overview of the research questions that need to be addressed (Hanegraaff 2012). How this can cast light on the esotericism of Waldorf schools depends on how the thinking habits, the considerable information deficit, and the unspoken or entirely unconscious reservations can be dealt with, as they prevent an unbiased conversation both on the side of education science and of Waldorf education. Before the relationship of Waldorf education with its "esotericism" can be successfully examined, one needs to identify ways of removing this resistance.

1 Obstacles to discourse

As early as 1935, the Polish physician Ludwik Fleck questioned the concept of "scientific facts," demonstrating how scientific "thought collectives" tended to engender one-sided "thinking styles" that were determined by unconscious preconceptions (Fleck 1980). Thomas S. Kuhn extended these beginnings into his well-known theory of the "paradigm shift"(Kuhn 1976). Joachim Gunther Kitzel has instructively examined the resulting problem of "discussion obstacles" using the reception of Indian philosophemes in the European history of philosophy as an example (Kitzel 1997). Thinking of the remarkable tabooing of esoteric streams of cultural history, including Rudolf Steiner's anthroposophy, by the thought collective of the current scientific mainstream, five obstacles that prevent an open conversation seem particularly noteworthy, even though they are in the process of being resolved and have been widely called into question:

- The Grand Polemical Narrative concerning the struggle of enlightened reason against dark superstition, used by modern science since its gradual rise since the 17th century to consolidate its self-assurance: a problematic construct that goes back to the beginnings of monotheism and that has derived its most effective arguments unreflectingly from the theological debates of the past (Hanegraaff 2005, 2012).
- The current *contingency fetishism*, the mistrust spread down to the popular media against any kind of quest for *meaning* in the world, evoked by antipathy toward ideological usurpations of any kind.[1]
- The tabooing of the phenomenon of transmutation (Faivre 2001), the entirely "normal" process one can observe both in life and in scientific research of the cognizant subject achieving change through practice (acquisition of observation skills, artistic competence, tacit knowledge, empirical knowledge, wisdom of age), and the related holding on to the fiction of the neutral observer who does not change.
- Restriction of the historical perspective to the radical historicism represented, above all, by Otto Gerhard Oexle, one example of which is Helmut Zander's study of Steiner, often considered groundbreaking today (Zander 2007). This narrowing down, although it has been judiciously criticized (Ewertowski 2007; Ewertowski 2008), continues to obstruct any unbiased appreciation of esotericism.
- The current trend toward evidence-based, empirical big science (Nieke in Chapter 8) that seeks to replace any phenomenon-based individual judgment in all areas of life with technocratic, largely automized decision-making processes.[2]

Serious obstacles to a discussion also exist within Waldorf education:

- Steiner's contrasting of anthroposophy and anthropology in his central work of scientific theory, *Riddles of the Soul* (1983b), with its provocative postulate of the full compatibility of two ways of research that seem to have nothing in common at first glance, has not been sufficiently received. Above all, it has been overlooked that, according to Steiner, anthroposophy works "with entirely different means" from empirical research, which relies on sensory data (Steiner 1983b, p. 32; Demisch et al. 2014).
- The fundamental importance for the foundation of Waldorf education of the concept of a "philosophy on the human being," which Steiner characterizes in *Riddles of the Soul* as a mediating factor in the conversation between *anthroposophy* and *anthropology* (Steiner 1983b, p. 30ff.), has not been understood. Such a philosophy would facilitate the ongoing further development in conversation both among friends and with critics and opponents. Instead, preliminary research results by Steiner are claimed as a lasting foundation, leading to a sectarian dogmatism. An openly discussed "philosophy on the human being" as expected by Steiner would be better suited than any kind of prescribed anthroposophy to scientifically explain the main characteristics of Waldorf education: for instance, its interest in phenomena, its great appreciation of life-world knowledge, its body-relatedness, and its openness to the quest for meaning.
- Steiner's rejection of any traditional views of the beyond is being unduly qualified in the internal anthroposophic discourse. The statements in question, posed in the last years of the 19th century (summarized by Hoffmann 2011, p. 95ff.), were not blunders that occurred in an existential trial situation. Steiner never had to take them back. He remained a convinced monist to the end of his life. The "esoteric" statements of the years after 1900 can be seen as approximations to phenomena of *emergence* in the one, undivided perceptual world (Heusser 2011, p. 59ff.).
- For many, probably the majority, of Rudolf Steiner's followers, "anthroposophy has become religion" (Kiersch 2015). This is possibly the weightiest internal obstacle to discourse. For believing anthroposophists, the revelation of higher truths through the initiate Steiner is and remains sufficient. Its contents have by now been largely codified, summarized, and arranged like the theological *summae* of the Middle Ages. This conveys a sense of existential safety to the faithful community, a warm feeling of solidarity and practical efficiency. It also makes it easier to represent the common cause to the outside. At the same time, it generates—in the sense of Steiner's threefold idea—a fateful dominance of the spiritual life over the legal and economic life of anthroposophic institutions, including Waldorf schools; a phenomenon that Steiner refers to as "bolshevism" (Steiner 1980, 2007). (In a critical analysis of the 1993 draft statutes for the International Association for Waldorf Education in Central and Eastern Europe and Countries Further East, IAO, I proposed to use the term "ideocratic system" for this, Kiersch 1993.) Unbiased observers quite rightly see the strange conflict about a new "critical edition" (Clement 2013) of some of Steiner's basic writings as resulting from the fact that these writings are presently seen as "belief texts"(Steinfeld 2014). This *denominationalization* of anthroposophy provokes the kind of dogmatic arguments and fundamentalist tendencies that one finds in the history of all religions, and they are, therefore, the opposite of what Steiner intended with the esotericism of a social model of his "School of Spiritual Science" (Kiersch 2012). One cannot exclude the possibility that "scientific distance and existential proximity" (Ewertowski 2014) are mutually compatible. For the time being, they are, however, caught in an unclear relationship of tension.

As well as Faivre's concept of *transmutation*, Steiner's reflections in *Riddles of the Soul* (Steiner 1983b) on the transition from the sense-bound life of thoughts, in which both the modern-day consciousness and any scientific research are currently moving, to the "suprasensible" perception in the anthroposophic sense, can be a preliminary first bridge to a mutual understanding. Steiner describes how all scientific reflection comes up against questions that cannot be resolved by intellectual thinking. The example he mentions is the resigned *ignorabimus* thesis in Emil Du Bois-Reymond's speech on the "boundaries of scientific knowledge," according to which the essence of matter or that of the simplest phenomenon of consciousness cannot be satisfactorily explained (ibid., p. 20). Steiner suggested that one could either give up any research into such boundary questions or one could try to circumvent them with hypotheses. His anthroposophy avoided both these attempts at evasion. Acting in accordance with anthroposophy meant standing up to the unbearable hopelessness through patient practicing and gradually changing one's own constitution of spirit and soul. The thus-active soul went through a kind of "tactile experience" that could be extended over time into the differentiated perceptions of "suprasensible" phenomena. "And out of the reflected experience it can have with the different boundaries of cognition, the general sense of a spiritual world emerges, resulting in a multifaceted perception of that world" (ibid., p. 22).

What Steiner writes here about scientific research is true for all the meditation exercises he presents in his basic works and consequently also for the exercises in his esoteric teachers' courses. The Point-Circle Meditation from the Curative Education Course[3] and the related motif of the three spheres in Lecture 10 of the First Teachers' Course (2020) (Kiersch 1995, p. 52ff.), the "panacea" motif derived from that in the lectures given in the fall of 1920 (Steiner 1993, p. 39): All these exercises and many others aim at the *reflected experience of the boundaries of cognition*. What may come across as dogmatic instruction, such as statements regarding the existence of the soul before birth and after death, can be seen above all as an encouragement to become more attentive, as a first indication of what would today be termed a *mindfulness exercise*. Such exercises have become very popular independently of Steiner's anthroposophy. Medical experts ascribe a salutogenic effect to them (Büssing, Kohls 2011). The American physicist Arthur Zajonc has developed meditative exercises based on Steiner that emphasize the motif of reflected mindfulness. He speaks of "meditation as contemplative inquiry," clearly referencing Steiner's concept of "reflective experience" (Zajonc 2009). Together with Parker J. Palmer, Zajonc has expanded his approach to astonishingly broad effect to include attempts at reforming academic education (Palmer, Zajonc 2010). It can be assumed that such endeavors will soon also meet with interest and understanding in the field of school education (Schmelzer in Chapter 6).

2 Esotericism between public discourse and secret space

People often overlook how little ideology was involved in the building up of the first Waldorf school under Steiner's personal direction. Fragmented notes from the faculty meetings between 1919 and 1924 cast light on the turbulent conditions surrounding the young faculty, most of whom had little professional experience, and the very heterogeneous student body that grew considerably from one year to the next (Steiner 1975). The book *Riddles of the Soul* (Steiner 1983b), with its basic text on the social threefold theory, had only come out two years before the founding of the school. The teachers' courses, which built on this basic work, made the new context of ideas only gradually, and by no means systematically, available to educational practice. Steiner warmly praised Albert Steffen's summary of his (Steiner's) first public introductory course at the Goetheanum at the end of 1921, beginning of 1922, as a first orientation (Steffen 1983).[4] Only a few sketchy essays had appeared by Steiner himself, without a comprehensive description of his pedagogy. The new school relied on the productivity of each teacher, supported by Steiner's regular visits, his advice on classroom situations, and the faculty meetings with him.

Under those circumstances, the work was carried and supported by the memory of the moral impulse of its foundation in the fall of 1919, which those involved experienced as an overarching existential challenge, as a sacred *inner space*. Something that could not be discussed in public— something difficult to grasp but nonetheless immensely important in its whole preliminary essence— created a special and continually endangered form of what today we would call a *corporate identity*.

At the time, it was not possible for those involved to blithely step into the public. Instead, they kept the (certainly inadequate) transcripts of Steiner's courses and the discussions with him very much to themselves. When, in 1932, Marie Steiner published the first version of the foundation course of 1919 for sale in bookstores, it was not mentioned that Steiner had asked his listeners not to note down a particular passage from his introductory address. Only in the now-used edition of 1992, a note to that effect was included, together with listeners' notes which were added later, revealing what that was about. To this day, Steiner's request to the Anthroposophical Society to unite serious esotericism with the "greatest conceivable openness" (Steiner 1994, p. 92) causes embarrassment for the representatives of Waldorf education, even though the public discussion of all life questions, down to the most private matters, is now widely considered possible and even necessary.

In contrast, it can be helpful to think back to a representative of classic sociology, the philosopher and psychologist Georg Simmel (1858–1918), who explained this newly emerging problem aptly: "Secrets— the concealing of realities by positive or negative means—are among the greatest cultural achievements of humanity. Compared to the infantile state, when every thought is immediately spoken out, every action immediately visible, secrets expand life immensely because many of its contents could not appear if there was full publicity. Secrets, one could say, offer the possibility of a second world next to the apparent one, where the latter intensely impacts on the former. Every relationship between two people or groups is characterized by whether and how much secrecy it contains. The development of society is largely characterized by the fact that what used to be public enters the protection of secrecy while what used to be secret can be without this protection. This is comparable to the other evolution of the spirit: that what was carried out consciously becomes unconscious mechanical practice, while what used to be unconscious and instinctive rises to the bright light of consciousness" (Simmel 1993, p. 317).

We may assume that Steiner was well aware of the dynamic interplay between the secret and the public space, the difficult-to-grasp subtleties of which Simmel described with such ingenious precision. Steiner's treatise on the "former concealment and present publication of suprasensible knowledge" (1918, p. 391ff.) suggests this, as does (to an even greater extent) his impulse in 1923/1924 to found an academic school (*Hochschule*), with which he intended the full individualization of his esotericism, having long distanced himself from the guru principle of his theosophical years (Kiersch 2012).

The "secret" as a space protecting the seeds of an immense expansion of life (Georg Simmel) does not at all contradict the requirements of enlightened rationality. It even has a place in the canon of our basic democratic rights. It should therefore be possible for the representatives of anthroposophy to overcome the widespread sense of embarrassment connected with this topic, and for the education sciences to examine without bias, both in principle and in the everyday practice, the pedagogical efficiency of ever-renewed secret spaces.

3 Helpful questions

As early as October 1905, at the beginning of his esoteric teaching for the Theosophical Society, Steiner pondered an "epistemology of spiritual science" as a methodology for suprasensible knowledge (Steiner 1993, p. 15). As is apparent from corresponding passages in all his later writings and many lectures, he continued to work on this until the end of his life. However, to this day, no full overview exists on these thought processes, their biographical background, and spiritual-scientific context. What research tasks arise from this?

In an esoteric lesson for advanced pupils in 1904, Marie von Sivers already noted down the following astonishing statement by Steiner: "In order to know the truth, one must dogmatize, but one must never see dogma as truth" (Steiner 2001, p. 254). Referring to this, Ulrich Kaiser examined in a fundamental essay the relationship between dogma and truth in anthroposophy (Kaiser 2011). How can this approach be extended and made fertile for both further research and the practice of Waldorf education?

In the fourth appendix to his book *Riddles of the Soul* (1983b), Steiner distinguishes "1) soul processes leading to spiritual perception, 2) spiritual perceptions as such, 3) spiritual perceptions translated into concepts of ordinary consciousness" (Steiner 1983b, p. 143). How can the concept of the *translating* of suprasensible perceptions be reified? (attempted by Bailey 2011).

Ulrich Kaiser tried to look at Steiner's works in the light of more recent research on *performativity* (Fischer-Lichte 2012, Kaiser 2014), opening up a new hermeneutic perspective for understanding the contextuality of many of Steiner's statements, particularly for the confusing multitude of mysterious or even contradicting statements in non-authorized lecture transcripts that also include the texts of the esoteric teachers' courses of 1919–1923. Where could this approach lead?

Wouter J. Hanegraaff drafted a typology of three forms of knowledge based on the criteria of *intersubjective verifiability* and *communicability*. According to this, both criteria apply to scientific knowledge (reason), only the second to faith, and none of the two to the knowledge form of "gnosis" he discovered in texts of the *corpus hermeticum*. This form of knowledge, he thought, could nonetheless be hermeneutically unlocked, even if it has not been sufficiently researched yet. "[We] have yet to begin to develop theoretical frameworks and methodologies capable of making sense of the appeal to 'gnosis' as subjective, experiential, noncommunicable, and nonverifiable/nonfalsifiable knowledge" (Hanegraaff 2008, p. 141). Could anthroposophic esotericism be what Hanegraaff describes as "gnosis"? What conclusions result from this for its description?

In the introduction to Volume 5 of his critical edition of Steiner's writings, Christian Clement discusses Steiner's "idiogenetic" impulse (Clement 2013, p. 42). In his departing lecture on Truth and Science to the Berlin Monists' Association (*Monistenbund*), Steiner himself enthusiastically proclaimed the "original intuition" of the creative human being as the factor that would be essential for further world evolution (Steiner 1983a). When, at Christmas 1923, Steiner introduced the social model of a renewed "Anthroposophical Society" with a school of Spiritual Science as the "heart" in the "blood circulation," he expected individual intuitions at the periphery of the anthroposophical movement to enter into a productive exchange with the center in Dornach (Kiersch 2012). Referring to this, Günter Röschert pointed out that the concept of "moral imagination," as it appears in the ethics of Steiner's *Philosophy of Freedom* (1978), had hardly been researched and implemented in practice (Röschert 2013). What does this mean for an unbiased biographic interpretation of Steiner's motives?

A comment by Christian Clements calls attention to the fact that Steiner's anthroposophy could have been related to the emergence of *existentialism* and that Steiner could probably be seen as a forerunner of Sartre or Heidegger (Clement 2013, p. 260). In his still-eminent biography of Kierkegaard, Johannes Hohlenberg implies a similar connection (Kiersch 2013). The same seems to be true for the monumental new Steiner biography presented by the Norwegian writer Kaj Skagen (Dahl 2014). What does this mean for the comprehension of anthroposophic esotericism?

The considerations presented here prove that Rudolf Steiner did not, as some critics continue to allege, claim absolute truth with the "esoteric" foundation of his pedagogy in his anthroposophical writings and particularly in the Stuttgart teachers' courses. He rather pursued knowledge strategies that were open-ended, both in his own understanding and from a critical-historical perspective, and that were to be fully compatible with the empirical research of different origins, in the sense of the *philosophy on the human being* postulated by him in 1917. Nothing speaks against following Jost Schieren's suggestion to primarily examine, for the time being, matters for which the hoped-for compatibility is already clearly apparent now. But one should nevertheless make use of the more recent research findings and not neglect the more sophisticated question regarding the special riddles of anthroposophic spirituality or Steiner's esotericism.

Notes

1 Examples of counter movements: Nagel (2013) and Metzinger (2013) in philosophy, Gablik (1976) and Donald (2008) in cultural history, Verhulst (1999) and Rosslenbroich (2014) in biology, Paschen (2002) in education science.
2 Cf, in particular, Schirrmacher (2013) and the contrast model to a cognition-based medicine represented by anthroposophically oriented medical scientists (Kiene 2001, Kienle, Kiene, Albonico 2006, Kienle et al. 2013).
3 As Gerhard Stocker (2014) illustrated, based on Dietrich Mahnke (1937), Steiner follows a remarkable tradition here.
4 Albert Steffen was the editor of the weekly journal in Dornach.

References

Bailey, Joseph (2011): Metaphor and imaginative consciousness. Translating the contents of higher consciousness into abstract mental pictures. In: RoSE – Research on Steiner Education 2/2011, p. 121–131. Online at www.rosejourn.com.

Clement, Christian (2013): Introduction. In: Rudolf Steiner: Schriften – Kritische Ausgabe (SKA) vol. 5. Stuttgart-Bad Cannstatt, Basel: frommann-holzboog/Rudolf Steiner Verlag, p. XXV–LXXIX.

Büssing, Arndt/Kohls, Niko (Eds.) (2011): Spiritualität transdisziplinär. Wissenschaftliche Grundlagen im Zusammenhang mit Gesundheit und Krankheit. Berlin, Heidelberg: Springer.

Dahl, Ole Harald (2014): Der norwegische Schriftsteller Kaj Skagen hat eine neue Steiner-Biografie geschrieben. In: Die Drei 3/2014, pp. 49–54.

Demisch, Ernst-Christian/Greshake-Ebding, Christa/Kiersch, Johannes/Schlüter, Martin/Stocker, Gerhard (Eds.) (2014): Steiner neu lesen. Perspektiven für den Umgang mit Grundlagentexten der Waldorfpädagogik. Frankfurt am Main: Peter Lang.

Dietz, Karl-Martin (Ed.) (2008): Esoterik verstehen. Anthroposophische und akademische Esoterikforschung. Stuttgart: Freies Geistesleben.

Donald, Merlin (2008): Triumph des Bewusstseins. Die Evolution des menschlichen Geistes. Stuttgart: Klett-Cotta (first edition: Donald, Merlin (2001): A Mind so rare: The Evolution of Human Consciousness. New York: Norton & Company.

Ewertowski, Jörg (2007): Der bestrittene geschichtliche Sinn. Helmut Zanders Studie "Anthroposophie in Deutschland" in ihrem historistischen Kontext. In: Anthroposophie IV/2007, pp. 292–304.

Ewertowski, Jörg (2008): Die Anthroposophie und der Historismus. Das Problem einer "exoterischen" Esoterikforschung. In: Dietz, Karl-Martin (Ed.) (2008): Esoterik verstehen. Anthroposophische und akademische Esoterikforschung. Stuttgart: Freies Geistesleben, pp. 82–123.

Ewertowski, Jörg (2014): Lesen im Werk Rudolf Steiners. Wissenschaftlicher Abstand und existenzielle Nähe. In: Anthroposophie I/2014, pp. 10–18.

Faivre, Antoine (2001): Esoterik im Überblick. Freiburg: Herder.

Fischer-Lichte, Erika (2012): Performativität. Eine Einführung. Bielefeld: transcript.

Gablik, Suzi (1976): Progress in Art. London: Thames and Hudson.

Fleck, Ludwik (1980): Entstehung und Entwicklung einer wissenschaftlichen Tatsache. Einführung in die Lehre vom Denkstil und Denkkollektiv. Frankfurt am Main: Suhrkamp.

Greve, Jens/Schnabel, Annette (Eds.) (2011): Emergenz. Zur Analyse und Erklärung komplexer Strukturen. Berlin: Suhrkamp.

Hanegraaff, Wouter J. (2005): Anti-Esoteric Polemics and Academic Research. In: Aries 22/2005, pp. 225–254.

Hanegraaff, Wouter J. (2008): Altered States of Knowledge: The Attainment of Gnosis in the Hermetica. In: The International Journal of the Platonic Tradition 2/2008, pp. 128–163.

Hanegraaff, Wouter J. (2012): Esotericism and the Academy. Rejected Knowledge in Western Culture. Cambridge: University Press.

Hanegraaff, Wouter J. (Ed.) (2006): Dictionary of Gnosis & Western Esotericism. Leiden: Brill.

Heusser, Peter (2011): Anthroposophische Medizin und Wissenschaft. Beiträge zu einer integrativen medizinischen Anthropologie. Stuttgart: Schattauer.

Hoffmann, David Marc (2011): Rudolf Steiners Hadesfahrt und Damaskuserlebnis. Vom Goetheanismus, Individualismus, Nietzscheanismus, Anarchismus und Antichristentum zur Anthroposophie. In: Uhlenhoff, Rahel (Ed.) (2011): Anthroposophie in Geschichte und Gegenwart. Berlin: Berliner Wissenschafts-Verlag, pp. 89–123.

Kaiser, Ulrich (2011): "Wann wird das symbolische Gewand fallen?" Dogma und Methode. Zur Hermeneutik des Steinerschen Werks. In: Die Drei 8-9/2011, pp. 41–55. (Also in Demisch, Ernst-Christian et al. (Eds.) (2014): Steiner neu lesen. Perspektiven für den Umgang mit Grundlagentexten der Waldorfpädagogik. Frankfurt am Main: Peter Lang, pp. 71–85.)

Kaiser, Ulrich (2014): Gelingende Worte – sich klärende Gesten. Teil I: Das Konzept der Performativität. In: Die Drei 9/2014, pp. 13–24. Teil II: Das Performative als ursprüngliche Dimension der Anthroposophie. In: Die Drei 10/2014, pp. 11–25.

Kiene, Helmut (2001): Komplementäre Methodenlehre der klinischen Forschung. Cognition-based Medicine. Berlin: Springer.

Kienle, Gunver Sophia et al. (2013): Evidenzbasierte Medizin: Konkurs der ärztlichen Urteilskraft? In: Deutsches Ärzteblatt 2003, 100: A 2142–2146 (Heft 33).

Kienle, Gunver Sophia/Kiene, Helmut/Albonico, Hans-Ulrich (2006): Anthroposophische Medizin in der klinischen Forschung. Stuttgart: Schattauer.

Kiersch, Johannes (1992): Waldorfpädagogik am Beginn ihrer Entwicklung. Zur pädagogischen Erstlingsschrift Rudolf Steiners. In: Erziehungskunst 6-7/1992, pp. 549–561.

Kiersch, Johannes (1993): Die Idee und das Leben. Ein neuer Bund für Waldorfpädagogik? In: Info3, 11/1993, pp. 22–29.

Kiersch, Johannes (1995): Einführung und Kommentar zu Rudolf Steiner: "Allgemeine Menschenkunde." Dornach: Verlag am Goetheanum.

Kiersch, Johannes (2010): "Mit ganz andern Mitteln gemalt Überlegungen zur hermeneutischen Erschließung der esoterischen Lehrerkurse Steiners. In: Research on Steiner Education (RoSE) 2/2010, pp. 73–82.

Kiersch, Johannes (2012): Steiners individualisierte Esoterik einst und jetzt. Zur Entwicklung der Freien Hochschule für Geisteswissenschaft. Dornach: Verlag am Goetheanum.

Kiersch, Johannes (2013): Radikale ethische Praxis. In: Das Goetheanum 26/2013, p. 19.

Kiersch, Johannes (2015): Anthroposophie als Religion. In: Das Goetheanum 6/2015, pp. 6–8.

Kitzel, Joachim Gunther (1997): Thema und Tabu. Über Behandlungshindernisse in der Philosophie. Würzburg: Königshausen & Neumann.

Kuhn, Thomas S. (1976): Die Struktur wissenschaftlicher Revolutionen. Frankfurt am Main: Suhrkamp.

Mahnke, Dietrich (1937) Unendliche Sphäre und Allmittelpunkt. Beiträge zur Genealogie der mathematischen Mystik. Halle: Niemeyer.

Metzinger, Thomas (2013): Spiritualität und intellektuelle Redlichkeit. Ein Versuch. Mainz: Selbstverlag.

Müller, Walter (1999): "Ver-Steiner-te" Reformpädagogik oder: Ist die Waldorfschule trotz Anthroposophie eine gute Schule? In: W. Böhm/J. Oelkers (Eds.) (1999): Reformpädagogik kontrovers. Würzburg: Ergon, pp. 105–125.

Nagel, Thomas (2013): Geist und Kosmos. Warum die materialistische neodarwinistische Konzeption der Natur so gut wie sicher falsch ist. Berlin: Suhrkamp.

Palmer, Parker J./Zajonc, Arthur (2010): The Heart of Higher Education. A Call to Renewal. Transforming the Academy through Collegial Conversations. San Francisco: Jossey-Bass.

Paschen, Harm (2002): Sinnleere, sinnvolle Pädagogiken. Pädagogik und Erziehungswissenschaft im Sinneswandel. Münster: LIT.

Paschen, Harm (Ed.) (2010): Erziehungswissenschaftliche Zugänge zur Waldorfpädagogik. Wiesbaden: VS.

Röschert, Günter (2013): Die Esoterik der moralischen Phantasie. Neukirchen: Novalis.

Rosslenbroich, Bernd (2014): On the Origin of Autonomy. A New Look at the Major Transitions in Evolution. Heidelberg: Springer.

Scheler, Max/Henckmann, Wolfhart (Eds.) (2016): Die Stellung des Menschen im Kosmos. Hamburg: Meiner.

Schieren, Jost (2011): Zum wissenschaftlichen Umgang mit der Anthroposophie. Ein mittelfristiger Lösungsansatz. In: Anthroposophie III/2011, pp. 263–266.

Schirrmacher, Frank (2013): Ego – Das Spiel des Lebens. Münster: Blessing.

Simmel, Georg (1993): Das Geheimnis. Eine sozialpsychologische Skizze. In: Aufsätze und Abhandlungen 1901–1908. Vol. 2. Frankfurt am Main: Suhrkamp, pp. 317–323.

Skiera, Ehrenhard (2010): Reformpädagogik in Geschichte und Gegenwart. Eine kritische Einführung. Munich: Oldenbourg.

Steffen, Albert (1983): Die anthroposophische Pädagogik. Dornach: Philosophisch-Anthroposophischer Verlag/ Novalis.

Steiner, Rudolf (1904): Theosophie. Einführung in übersinnliche Welterkenntnis und Menschenbestimmung. Berlin: Rudolf Steiner Verlag.

Steiner, Rudolf (1907): Die Erziehung des Kindes vom Gesichtspunkte der Geisteswissenschaft. In: Steiner, Rudolf (1987): Lucifer – Gnosis. Grundlegende Aufsätze zur Anthroposophie und Berichte aus den Zeitschriften «Luzifer» und «Lucifer – Gnosis» 1903–1908. GA 34. Dornach: Rudolf Steiner Verlag, pp. 309–348.

Steiner, Rudolf (1918): Frühere Geheimhaltung und jetzige Veröffentlichung übersinnlicher Erkenntnisse. In: Steiner, Rudolf (1965): Philosophie und Anthroposophie. Gesammelte Aufsätze 1904-1923. GA 35. Dornach: Rudolf Steiner Verlag, pp. 391–408.

Steiner, Rudolf (1975): Konferenzen mit den Lehrern der Freien Waldorfschule in Stuttgart 1919 bis 1924. 3 vols. GA 300. Dornach: Rudolf Steiner Verlag.

Steiner, Rudolf (1978): Die Philosophie der Freiheit. GA 4. Dornach: Rudolf Steiner Verlag.

Steiner, Rudolf (1980): Die soziale Frage als Bewusstseinsfrage. GA 189. Lectures of March 2 and 16, 1919. Dornach: Rudolf Steiner Verlag.

Steiner, Rudolf (1983a): Über Philosophie, Geschichte und Literatur. Darstellungen an der "Arbeiterbildungsschule" und der "Freien Hochschule" in Berlin. GA 51. Dornach: Rudolf Steiner Verlag.

Steiner, Rudolf (1983b): Von Seelenrätseln. GA 21. Dornach: Rudolf Steiner Verlag.

Steiner, Rudolf (1993): Die Stufen der höheren Erkenntnis. GA 12. Dornach: Rudolf Steiner Verlag.

Steiner, Rudolf (1993): Erziehung und Unterricht aus Menschenerkenntnis. GA 302a. Dornach: Rudolf Steiner Verlag.

Steiner, Rudolf (1994): Die Weihnachtstagung zur Begründung der Allgemeinen Anthroposophischen Gesellschaft 1923/24. GA 260. Dornach Rudolf Steiner Verlag.

Steiner, Rudolf (2001): Bewusstsein – Leben – Form. Grundprinzipien der geisteswissenschaftlichen Kosmologie. GA 89. Dornach: Rudolf Steiner Verlag.

Steiner, Rudolf (2007): Der innere Aspekt des sozialen Rätsels. GA 193. Dornach: Rudolf Steiner Verlag.

Steinfeld, Thomas (2014): Wie fotografiert man den Allgeist? Für die meisten ist die Anthroposophie nur ein Gerücht – die kritische Ausgabe der Schriften Rudolf Steiners kann das ändern. In: Süddeutsche Zeitung, January 10, 2014.

Stocker, Gerhard (2014): Punkt und Kreis. Ein Leitmotiv mathematischer Mystik und seine pädagogische Metamorphose im Werk Rudolf Steiners. In: Demisch, Ernst-Christian/Greshake-Ebding, Christa/Kiersch, Johannes/Schlüter, Martin/Stocker, Gerhard (Eds.) (2014): Steiner neu lesen. Perspektiven für den Umgang mit Grundlagentexten der Waldorfpädagogik. Frankfurt am Main: Peter Lang, pp. 16–80.

Verhulst, Jos (1999): Der Erstgeborene: Mensch und höhere Tiere in der Evolution. Stuttgart: Freies Geistesleben.

Zajonc, Arthur (2009): Meditation as Contemplative Inquiry. Great Barrington, MA: Lindisfarne Books.

Zander, Helmut (2007): Anthroposophie in Deutschland. Theosophische Weltanschauung und gesellschaftliche Praxis 1884-1945. 2 vols. Göttingen: Vandenhoeck & Ruprecht.

ANTHROPOSOPHY AND WALDORF EDUCATION
A Field of Tension

Jost Schieren

Education science is critical of Waldorf education. The main criticism does, however, not aim at Waldorf education itself but at anthroposophy as its underlying philosophy. Klaus Prange (Prange 1985/2000), Ehrenhard Skiera (Skiera 2009), and not least Heiner Ullrich (Ullrich 1986, 1988, 2015) express, in the strongest terms, their reservations about the ideological "liability" bearing down on Waldorf education because of anthroposophy. In his most recent publication, *Waldorfpädagogik. Eine kritische Einführung* [Waldorf education. A critical introduction] (Ullrich 2015), Heiner Ullrich reintroduces this basic criticism. He demarcates Waldorf education's ideological partiality from other education reform approaches: "The view of human nature and of the world in Rudolf Steiner's anthroposophy form its comprehensive foundation. They not only determine the method of teaching and educating but in many interconnected ways also the content of the curriculum and the lessons. No other school culture from the array of classical education reform approaches is as much informed by ideology as Waldorf education" (Ullrich 2015, p. 173). Ullrich finds it important to point out that anthroposophy is not only the background of an otherwise successful education movement, but that it dominates all its manifestations. A longer citation can illustrate the vehemence of judgment applied to this worldview problem of Waldorf education: "In presenting the specifics of Waldorf schools it has become apparent in many points how important the anthroposophic worldview is. Consider above all the school architecture, designed to reflect the human being, the collegial school constitution based on the idea of social threefolding, the theory of the temperaments in the work of grades teachers that relates to the development in seven-year periods and the fourfold human organization, the method of teaching main lesson blocks that presupposes nightly reincarnations, the curriculum based on cultural periods in the evolution of consciousness, and the Goethean and alchemical science teaching based on the affinity of human beings and nature. [...] After all this, one can conclude that anthroposophy, or anthroposophical spiritual science, provides the master key for understanding the program and practice of Waldorf education. The founder of anthroposophy and, to this day, sole leader for his ideological followers, is Rudolf Steiner (1861–1925)" (Ullrich 2015, p. 91). According to this verdict, Waldorf education is ideologically fully determined by anthroposophy. Ullrich builds his criticism on his own dissertation (Ullrich 1986) and on Klaus Prange's influential publication *Erziehung zur Anthroposophie* [education towards anthroposophy] (Prange 1985). With his book, first published in 1985, the educationist Klaus Prange has for a long time determined the view of Waldorf education by the education sciences. Ullrich follows in the same tradition and does, however, not employ the same aggressive rejection of worldviews or zealous warnings against undermining indoctrination as Prange does in parts of his work (Prange 1985, 2005). Ullrich concludes that Waldorf education is massively ideologically influenced at the personal level (the way teachers think), at the content level (curriculum), and at the methodic–didactic level (image of the human being).

428   DOI: 10.4324/9781003187431-39

Compared to Prange, Ullrich is more ambivalent. He also sees positive aspects in Waldorf education: its aesthetic and humanistic orientation based on experience or sense perception, on personal commitment, and high pedagogical ideals. Qualities such as deceleration, the appreciation of each individual student, and the personal teacher-student relationship are acknowledged. Yet, Prange also decidedly pursues the goal of proving that Waldorf education is ideologically determined by anthroposophy. Unlike Prange, Ulrich does not claim that he needs to warn his readers against a danger but merely that he wishes to enlighten them. This is apparent, for example, in his just rejection of allegations that anthroposophy was racist. "That Steiner was not *the* ethnic-racist anti-Semite his polemical critics like to make him is documented not least by the fact that many Jews were members of the Anthroposophical Society and were able to remain members until the Society was banned by the Nazis" (Ullrich 2015, p. 147). But anthroposophy remains, for him, the problem of Waldorf education. His points of criticism are, in summary (Ullrich 2015, p. 143f.):

- It was mystical and essentially unscientific.
- Rational boundaries were crossed uncritically.
- It was a form of gnosis that suspended the difference between knowledge and faith.
- It was guided by a will "for a totality of knowledge."
- Further critical aspects are the removal of boundaries to the human individuality and the claim of knowledge instead of modesty.
- The lack of cognitive freedom is pointed out because, in the intuition proclaimed by Steiner, human thinking was subjected to world thinking or, in ethical individualism, to the world *plan* (Ullrich 2015, p. 129f.).
- Compulsive causality in the understanding of karma and the idea of reincarnation are highlighted (Ullrich 2015, p. 110).

Anthroposophy rather than Waldorf education is at the center of the criticism by education science as represented by Ullrich. Anthroposophy is presented as a pre-modern dogmatic system that encompassed teachings of a so-called "spiritual world" originating in the (possibly pretended)[1] mystical vision of *one* initiate, which was unverifiable, and which established a metaphysical determinism that contradicted modern humanity's claim to freedom. This view constitutes a devastating verdict that genuinely affects Waldorf education. It cannot develop if, in this view, it depends on, is influenced, and contaminated by a theoretical construct that goes against the consensual demands of modern science. It moreover exposes Waldorf education not only to a theoretical discourse but also to drastic political-legal, personal, and financial implications (accreditation of study courses and universities, teaching permits, access to funding, etc.).

The question is how the relationship between anthroposophy and Waldorf education can be determined, given the critiqued scientific abstinence of anthroposophy. What is the role of anthroposophy in Waldorf education? Are there appropriate and justifiable ways of dealing with it?

1 The worldview problem

First, it needs to be pointed out that Waldorf education's science deficit is not only a problem assigned to it by the established sciences or by a restricted concept of science, as some committed Waldorf defenders like to claim. It is in fact self-inflicted. Many of its representatives have treated and disseminated anthroposophy as a doctrine of salvation. For a long time, a devotional, uncritical, and purely meditative approach was seen as the only legitimate way of receiving Rudolf Steiner's work. Hermetic forms of language and thinking were transported within a purely internal communication without conceptual clarification or critical distance. Rudolf Steiner's "initiation knowledge" was presented as truth and remained unquestioned, often described as "extended" (that is, not materialistically narrowed down) science and apostrophized as a valid theoretical basis of Waldorf education. Up until a few years ago, neither the proponents nor the critics of Waldorf education really considered that this claim was the merely reception-based interpretative attitude of a fellowship that revered its spearhead figure and defended its own views. However, Rudolf Steiner was very much aware of Waldorf education's worldview problem, warning explicitly against allowing anthroposophy to directly inform the Waldorf schools.

Numerous indications and explicit passages can be found in his work that ask for a very different approach and a critical and self-confident form of reception. In a lecture Steiner gave four years after the foundation of the Waldorf School, on August 15, 1923, in Ilkley (Yorkshire, GB), he said, "This principle of the 'universal human' (I described this in terms of various areas of education) is expressed by Waldorf education. It does not in any way promote a particular philosophy or religious conviction. In this sense, as an art of education derived from spiritual science, it has been absolutely essential for Waldorf schools to remove any hint of being 'anthroposophic schools.' They absolutely cannot be anything of this sort. There must be daily efforts to avoid falling into anthroposophic biases, shall we say, because of excessive enthusiasm and honest conviction on the part of the teachers. Such conviction is present in the Waldorf teachers, of course, because they are anthroposophists. But the fundamental question of Waldorf education is the human being as such, not human beings as followers of any particular philosophy" (Steiner 1986, pp. 203f.). Steiner was clearly aware of the problem of a dogmatic and allegedly sectarian anthroposophy and drew a clear line, particularly in relation to Waldorf education. In another address, also given in Britain, in the Welsh town of Penmaenmawr on August 19, 1923, he said, "In education we will merely develop the teaching methods in the best possible way out of the anthroposophic movement. The Waldorf School in Stuttgart, where this pedagogy, this way of teaching, is practiced, is in no way sectarian or dogmatic; it is not at all what the world would like to call an anthroposophists' school. For we do not carry anthroposophic dogma into the school but seek to develop only methods of education and teaching that are universally human" (Steiner 1991, p. 172). This commitment both to ideological neutrality, which would be hard to achieve in any system, and to a distance to anthroposophy in Waldorf education is also shared by the representatives of Waldorf education when it comes to anthroposophy in Waldorf schools. Regarding Waldorf education itself, and particularly to Waldorf teacher education, such commitment to neutrality and distance is rarely recommended.

2 Anthroposophy and science

How can the ambivalent relationship between anthroposophy and science be best described? Rudolf Steiner introduced a concept of *spiritual science* that, in fundamental difference to the usual understanding of the term, does not describe the humanities (with disciplines such as philosophy, history, literature, etc.) in opposition to the natural sciences, but that claims to be a science *of the spirit*. This semantic difference itself causes a problem of communication. Additionally, Steiner requested that his spiritual science should meet the strict criteria of modern natural science. This meant, in essence, that all statements made had to be based on observation or experience. However, because the object of observation relates to something suprasensible, Steiner goes beyond the boundaries of natural science. Steiner's claim to a form of cognition that can be scientifically verified and that meets modern criteria of rationality contradicts the scientific criteria postulated as the boundaries of knowledge.

It has so far not been possible to resolve this dilemma. Anthroposophy is, if anything, accepted as a form of belief but not as a cognitive approach. There have been various attempts on the part of anthroposophy to deal with this problem:

a. *Rejection of modern science and inward orientation of anthroposophy.* More traditional representatives of anthroposophy consider a dialog between anthroposophy and science to be impossible. The materialistic reduction of scientific thinking as applied in universities is, they claim, not capable of appreciating the true dimension of Steiner's work. As a result, such representatives distance themselves resolutely from any attempt to communicate with the world of science; some even consider this an ingratiation at the cost of anthroposophy. Out of this inner circle of these representatives, books are published on anthroposophy—some of which pursue paths of anthroposophic thinking that are sophisticated, reflected, and self-critical, while others treat statements by Steiner uncritically as truth, adding their own considerations to them. The latter group does in fact also touch on esoteric questions without reassuring themselves of the correctness of their insights.

b. *An extended concept of science.* Another approach seeks to argue the limitations of today's science and to establish a new and extended understanding of science. The main protagonists in this group are Helmut Kiene with his publication *Grundlagen einer essentialen Wissenschaftstheorie* [Foundations of an Essential Theory of Science] (Kiene 1984), and Marek Majorek with his dissertation *Objektivität. Ein Erkenntnisideal auf dem Prüfstand* [Objectivity: A Cognitive Ideal under Scrutiny] (Majorek 2002) and his recent book *Rudolf Steiners Geisteswissenschaft: Mythisches Denken oder Wissenschaft* [Rudolf Steiner's Spiritual Science: Mythical Thinking or Science] (Majorek 2015). Trying to introduce and defend a new paradigm of scientific theory is undoubtedly cumbersome. The representatives of established science have so far not acknowledged such efforts. As long as essentialist forms of thinking that claim truth or objectivity are part of such concepts, they not only go against the scientific self-image of our time but also against our modern self-image and approach to knowledge. Modern human beings do not look for rigid truths and unshakeable objectivity. Instead, they have an open, tentative, and investigative concept of cognition that seeks, if anything, an approximation to the object of knowledge. The validity of knowledge, though an evident internal experience, cannot be meaningfully turned outward in argumentation but only integrated into the world encounter as the powerful and dynamic transformation of the subject. For a truth that is claimed and argued with the will to convince is always the "false" truth. Anthroposophy will hardly be convincing in this form.

c. *Esoteric research.* Another attempt at mitigating the conflict between anthroposophy and science, bringing both sides more closely together, consists of including modern esoteric research. Johannes Kiersch (Kiersch 2008, 2011, 2012), Karl-Martin Dietz (Dietz 2008), and Lorenzo Ravagli (Ravagli 2014)[2] see a way of rehabilitating anthroposophy in the scientific realm in the publications of Wouter J. Hanegraaff (Hanegraaff 2005, 2006, 2008, 2012) and Antoine Faivre (Faivre 2001). These authors examine, from the point of view of cultural science, different esoteric streams that are commonly ignored or discredited by the positivist mainstream. They aim to describe the specific forms of knowledge of gnosis and esotericism without disavowing subtext and to assign them a place in cultural science with their idiosyncrasies. This is to say that old esoteric forms are subjected to modern rational examination. While this approach is, as such, laudable and important, and while it is certainly interesting to include anthroposophy in these investigations—freeing it from its scientific isolation in the process—one must ask nonetheless whether anthroposophy's proximity to and affinity with other gnostic streams such as medieval mysticism, theosophy, or Rosicrucianism does justice to its particular intention. Historically, anthroposophy certainly not only shares numerous elements with other esoteric streams, but it also differs from them in significant ways. What anthroposophy shares with esoteric-gnostic views is that it centers around a spiritual understanding of the human being and of the world. It is, however, Steiner's central intention to overcome, with anthroposophy, old forms of consciousness that, in his view, approach spiritual phenomena in rather a passive or solely feeling-related way and also to convey a spiritual worldview that is based on a modern concept of knowledge. Neither the historical forms of gnosis nor the New Age movement with its currently popular need for spirituality meet the requirements of anthroposophy. What sets anthroposophy apart is that it does not replace Enlightenment's liberal subject orientation that distinguishes the modern human being, with metaphysically determining substitute worlds.

The attempt to now look at anthroposophy in the context of current research into esotericism comes with the risk of its reduction to a *mere* esoteric stream among many others and of no longer being sufficiently visible as a modern freedom-based epistemological orientation. Johannes Kiersch therefore emphasizes, referring to Waldorf education, the aspect of an *esoteric pedagogy* by also bringing up the concept of *professional esotericism*. The danger here is that the assumed advantage of seeing anthroposophy scientifically appreciated (even though Faivre's and Hanegraaff's research into esotericism do not relate to education science) comes at a cost, because it means that its specific concern, which is to develop a *modern* spiritual form of consciousness, is no longer clearly enough presented.

d. *A scientific approach to Rudolf Steiner's work.* Another way of approaching the relation between anthroposophy and science has become increasingly apparent recently. It is not about making a case for the compatibility (paragraphs b and c) or the incompatibility (paragraph a) of anthroposophy and science, but about treating anthroposophy itself scientifically and making it an object of scientific discussion. This way, which has been prominently and variously discussed, is represented by Christian Clement[3] who has laid the foundation for a new reception of anthroposophy with his critical Steiner edition. This makes anthroposophy a regular research topic with the required critical distance ensuring that Steiner's statements are not *per se* seen as truths. Approaching anthroposophy scientifically creates a healthy cognitive distance toward Steiner's work without the often unconscious presumption that one can have access to esoteric content out of one's own vision.

The different ways outlined above illustrate how the problematic relationship between anthroposophy and science could be addressed. There are without doubt others that could be mentioned and the individual representatives can certainly not be clearly assigned to the one or other category. Depending on their intentions and attitudes, they will mostly be mixtures of these approaches.

A modern and tenable approach (such as the one described under d) will have to develop a different understanding of anthroposophy that is not informed by a form of consciousness narrowed down by dogma and metaphysical faith but that follows the phenomenological direction of Steiner's early work.

Steiner's early epistemological work (Steiner 1979, 2005b) is based on a phenomenology of consciousness described by him as *"soul observation"* (Witzenmann 1985). He builds this on Goethe's research method of observing judgment (Schieren 1997), which he transfers from natural to mental phenomena. The crucial point is that this philosophical approach does not work with a precritical truth claim but sees human cognition merely in the sense of a modern theory of science (Popper 2003, p. 339f.) as a way of approaching existence. Steiner was able to pursue this approach only to a certain limited extent in his work, a fact he deplores in his *Autobiography* (Steiner 2000, p. 283).

It is interesting that he returns to this philosophical method in his late work, in individual lectures of 1920 and 1921, where he underlines the phenomenological aspect of anthroposophy: "Phenomenology represents the ideal of anthroposophy's scientific endeavor" (Steiner 2005a, p. 318). And, later on, he adds that *spiritual science* "is nothing other than phenomenology [...] which does not content itself with assembling the individual phenomena but reads them in their context. It is phenomenology and it does not commit the sin of speculatively going beyond the phenomena but inquires of them whether they have, not only in their details but in context, something to say about a certain inner activity" (Steiner 2005a, p. 419).

Understanding anthroposophy as phenomenology and accordingly treating it critically and scientifically constitutes an entirely different mode of reception than the one that has become established in the past hundred years in both proponents and critics, resulting in the forming of ideological fronts. This is about a different culture of reception. Official representatives of Waldorf education do therefore not doubt that two things are necessary now and in future: an entirely different tenor and a relatable discussion of the theoretical foundations of Waldorf education. This is not in opposition to anthroposophy, but it is owed to its own claim to knowledge, which is that it is the object of a knowledge-oriented and self-critical discourse in a rational continuum.

3 Anthroposophy in Waldorf education

What does this mean for Waldorf education? In the context of Waldorf education, anthroposophy naturally comes out of its inner sphere: it becomes a social factor and must therefore observe society's criteria and benchmarks. Depending on the laws of the individual countries, Waldorf education has to adhere to the variously stricter or looser regulations and sometimes also accept compromises. In some countries, Waldorf education can be practiced almost in its *pure* form, in others—such as Germany, for instance—the state imposes clear regulations on teaching qualifications and curricula. It is different with medicine, which is another field of applied anthroposophy. Around the world, medicine is subject to strict scientifically defined criteria. Anthroposophic medicine was therefore from the start introduced as a complementary rather than substitutive approach. Every anthroposophic physician, therefore, must undergo regular medical studies. For Waldorf education, there are no such clear prescriptions. There are teacher education centers, but they have traditionally tended to be independent of state regulations and scientific standards. The question of science (in this case education science) has consequently been discussed more controversially in Waldorf education than in anthroposophic medicine, which is naturally more scientifically oriented.

What, then, is the role anthroposophic content plays in Waldorf education? The obvious conclusion could be that the greater the scientific orientation and adaptation to external requirements the less anthroposophy is possible, which in turn would mean that only a less genuine Waldorf education can be practiced. Waldorf education would be sacrificed to mainstream education science. At best, feasible and successful components such as the early introduction of additional languages, a better teacher-pupil relationship, action-based lessons, and so on could be adapted. The incomprehensible anthroposophic ballast would be removed. Many Waldorf representatives see this path as dangerous. In any case, Waldorf education, as it actually exists today in Germany, has been largely secularized. Around 50 percent of teachers in Waldorf schools do not have Waldorf teacher training and are only vaguely familiar with the foundations of the type of school they are teaching in. This is why, within the Waldorf movement, there is an increasingly urgent call for basic anthroposophic studies so that Waldorf education will not lose its authenticity.

Finding a solution is difficult. On the one hand, central anthroposophic themes such as reincarnation, the fourfold human organization, human development, the theory of temperaments, and the path of inner development are not easily accessible and can hardly be conveyed. As a result, Waldorf education will always remain objectionable and open to attacks, seemingly permeated by anthroposophic dogmatism. On the other hand, the loss of anthroposophy would mean a dilution of Waldorf education and the mere technocratic execution of its traditional elements. How can this dilemma be resolved?

4 *Epoché* or the renunciation of anthroposophy

The relation of anthroposophy and Waldorf education is often treated as an absolute, as the attempt is made to present both at the same level. Another approach could be one of weighing up in what form and to what degree it makes sense for anthroposophy to flow into Waldorf education. As mentioned earlier, Rudolf Steiner explicitly spoke of the problem of a dogmatic influence of anthroposophy on Waldorf education. He demanded that Waldorf schools must not be ideological schools. By this, he did not only mean that no anthroposophic content must be taught in Waldorf schools but also that anthroposophy must not interfere in any way with the life of the school. Restraint was called for. Once could also call it the *renunciation of anthroposophy*. This kind of renunciation is of methodic significance.

It is central to phenomenological consciousness that predetermined contents and ideas stand back behind an experiential approach. When cognition critically reflects on its own preconceptions and ways of thinking of its object, this has an educational effect on consciousness. It is initially irrelevant where the preconceptions and ways of thinking come from. In his famous essay *The Experiment as Mediator between Object and Subject*, Goethe writes for instance, "We often take more pleasure in the idea than in the thing itself. Or perhaps we should say: we take pleasure in something in as far as we form an idea of it: it must fit into our way of looking at the world. However high we raise our way of thinking above the everyday one, however much we try to purify it, it usually still remains merely a way of thinking" (Goethe 1988, p. 15). The critical reflection of thoughts that have become or have been formed is a basic feature of phenomenology. Edmund Husserl speaks of *epoché*, the methodical renunciation of content that has become.

As indicated earlier, Rudolf Steiner and anthroposophy follow the tradition of this phenomenological method. Steiner's understanding of art and aesthetics are also informed by this renunciation motif. He is not interested in presenting anthroposophic content figuratively in a work of art. Concerning his aesthetics, he points out that he does not support the idealist statement (which he ascribes to the idealist thinkers of Goethe's time, above all Schelling and Hegel) that beauty was the sensuous appearance of the idea. Rather, beauty, and therefore art, lay in the ideal semblance of the sense-perceptible (Steiner 1889, p. 27f.). He adds that "this is quite different from what the German idealists say. This is not the 'idea in the form of the sensuous appearance;' it is the exact opposite; it is a 'sensuous appearance in the form of the idea.' The content of beauty, its underlying material substance, is always something real, and the form of its appearance is that of the idea. We realize that the exact opposite is true to what German aesthetics says; it has simply turned things upside down" (ibid., p. 32). According to Steiner, art does not serve to convey particular content. It is no vehicle for any kind of ideal but it must convince by itself, by its own aesthetic, sensory power.

With his concept of art, which he developed mainly between 1914 and 1918, Steiner separated himself from the ideology-heavy Theosophical Society. When, in 1918, he began to develop individual fields of practice (anthroposophic medicine, biodynamic farming, Waldorf education), the correspondent conditions and laws were his main focus. These fields did not simply serve to disseminate anthroposophy and apply it in practice. Waldorf education was not only there to realize Steiner's anthropology but also to create the best conditions for children and young people to grow up and unfold their potential. Everything was geared toward the child. Just as art is effective in itself, rather than through transported content, Waldorf education must convince alone through its successful pedagogical work in kindergartens and schools, and in the corresponding teacher education rather than through the representation of dogmatic-ideological content. In Waldorf education, anthroposophy has no value in itself but only *application value*: it *serves* to make good education possible.

Lessing's "ring parable," which is about the value of a religion, can be instructive here (Lessing 1968, p. 90ff.). According to this parable, religions do not carry value within themselves, but they gain their value in that they help someone to become a good or a better person. In this sense, the value of anthroposophy in Waldorf education is only of value in that it helps teachers to better understand their students and to adapt the organization of the school and of the lesson to the students' developmental requirements. Anthroposophy therefore becomes meaningless if it is solely used as a dogmatic conceptual structure.

5 Worldview as a cognitive challenge

The valid way for anthroposophy to be present in Waldorf education is through the form of consciousness derived from phenomenology. The method of "soul observation" developed by Rudolf Steiner constitutes a phenomenology of consciousness where human cognition becomes aware of its participation in the emergence of reality and where it meets the aspect of the world that is observed in the light of a superior cognitive ethics. No preconceived concepts (not anthroposophic ones either) are used but, in an intensive creative effort, the concepts are actualized that give deeper and more genuine access to that aspect of the world. Anthroposophy's true value lies in the fact that it does not follow constrained and preconceived conceptual schemas but that it seeks to generate the most expansive and mobile forms of thinking. Anthroposophy needs to be seen as a method. It does not represent a rigid worldview and it therefore overcomes the constraints of materialistic reductionism without, however, resorting to metaphysical fantasies or spiritual determinism. It relies on self-critical, productive cognition that strives, in a Goethean sense, using mobile forms of thinking and concepts, to adjust to the individual object of cognition according to its (the object's) own conditions. With a view to anthroposophy, a worldview is not a fixed conceptual construct but an expansion of the cognitive capacity, a cognitive challenge. In a Waldorf school, the teachers will not ask about or be guided by anthropological concepts (theory of seven-year periods or of temperaments) with regard to individual students or grades, but use those concepts solely in an heuristic sense (Rittelmeyer 2011) for gaining deeper insights into what action is suitable in a specific pedagogical situation.

6 The teacher's self-development

Another important influence anthroposophy can be seen to have on Waldorf education derives from the many elements of meditative training it seeks to inspire in teachers. Successful teachers need to develop qualities such as patience, emotional balance, good observation skills that are as free from preconceptions as possible, imagination, as well as a sense of humor and a cheerful, encouraging disposition. How such qualities can be acquired, if one does not have them naturally or develops them gradually in everyday professional life, is hardly a central concern of academic teacher education, but in Waldorf education these qualities are essential. Anthroposophy plays an important role in gaining them, again not in a dogmatic and ideological way, but by offering possibilities for personal development through the practice of artistic activities and meditative reflection. Here, too, anthroposophy has merely application value in the sense of the "ring parable."

The importance of anthroposophy in this regard lies solely in the transformative power it has in the teachers' endeavor for self-training or self-development. If teachers succeed, with the help of anthroposophy, in better developing particular personal qualities that are essential for their profession, anthroposophy gains value by that fact alone. In his study *Ich bin Waldorflehrer* (I'm a Waldorf teacher), Dirk Randoll (2012) has provided evidence that many teachers value this aspect of anthroposophy. However, there is a fine line between this *methodical* value of anthroposophy and an uncritical adoption of its *content*. Vigilance and *renunciation* (in the sense explained above) are needed here.

7 Conclusion

In conclusion, an image may illustrate the field of tension between anthroposophy and Waldorf education: Admetus, the Greek hero, who wooed the princess Alcestis, was given the task by the princess' father, the king, to yoke a lion and a wild boar to a chariot. If successful, he would gain Alcestis' hand in marriage. Admetus completed the task.

Anthroposophy and Waldorf education are such a team where antagonistic tendencies must be united to serve a common purpose. Anthroposophy, maybe the lion in this picture, must hold back its ideological content: a renunciation of anthroposophy is required. Anthroposophy has no value in Waldorf education other than as a method: it serves the development of good education. Evaluation of what "good education" means is reserved to empirical research, however. And Waldorf education, the wild boar in this image, because it follows separate factors of time, culture, and science, and is mainly directed at the students, must be taken seriously and respected in its conditions, so that the team can together set off on a successful journey in the service of good education.

Notes

1 Cf. Helmut Zander, who states repeatedly that Rudolf Steiner's alleged original visions are basically disguised citations of other sources (Zander 2007).
2 Cf. Ravagli: www.anthroblog.anthroweb.info
3 Cf. Clement, Christian: Rudolf Steiner: Schriften. Kritische Ausgabe (SKA) im Frommann-Holzboog. Verlag, Stuttgart.

References

Dietz, Karl-Martin (Ed.) (2008): Esoterik verstehen. Anthroposophische und akademische Esoterikforschung. Stuttgart: Freies Geistesleben.
Faivre, Antoine (2001): Esoterik im Überblick. Freiburg: Herder.

Goethe, Johann Wolfgang von (1988): Der Versuch als Vermittler zwischen Objekt und Subjekt. In: Trunz, Erich (Ed.): Goethes Werke. Naturwissenschaftliche Schriften I. Hamburger Ausgabe. Vol. 13. München: Beck, pp. 10–20.

Hanegraaff, Wouter J. (2005): Forbidden Knowledge. Anti-Esoteric Polemics and Academic Research. In: Aries, volume 5, issue 2, pp. 225–254.

Hanegraaff, Wouter J. (2006): Dictionary of Gnosis & Western Esotericism. Leiden: Brill.

Hanegraaff, Wouter J. (2008): Reason, Faith, and Gnosis: Potenzials and Problematics of a Typological Construct. In: Meusburger, Peter/Welker, Michael/Wunder, Edgar (Eds.) (2008): Clashes of Knowledge. Orthodoxies an Heterodoxies. Dordrecht: Springer, pp. 133–144.

Hanegraaff, Wouter J. (2012): Esotericism and the Academy. Rejected Knowledge in Western Culture. Cambridge: University Press.

Kiene, Helmut (1984): Grundlinien einer essentialen Wissenschaftstheorie. Die Erkenntnistheorie Rudolf Steiners im Spannungsfeld moderner Wissenschaftstheorie. Urachhaus: Stuttgart.

Kiersch, Johannes (2008): Vom Land aufs Meer. Steiners Esoterik in verändertem Umfeld. Stuttgart: Freies Geistesleben.

Kiersch, Johannes (2011): "Mit ganz andern Mitteln gemalt." Überlegungen zur hermeneutischen Erschließung der esoterischen Lehrerkurse Steiners. In: RoSE – Research on Steiner Education, volume 2, issue 2, December 2011. Online at www.rosejourn.com

Kiersch, Johannes (2012): Rezension Wouter J. Hanegraaff: Esotericism and the Academy. Rejected Knowledge in Western Culture. In: RoSE – Research on Steiner Education, volume 3, issue 1, pp. 177–180. Online at: www.rosejourn.com

Lessing, Gotthold Ephraim (1968): Nathan der Weise. Ein Dramatisches Gedicht, in fünf Aufzügen. In: Lachmann, Karl (Ed.): Lessing, Gotthold Ephraim (1968): Sämtliche Schriften. 3rd revised and extended edition by F. Muncker. Vol. 3. Berlin: de Gruyter (Reprint), pp. 1–177.

Majorek, Marek (2002): Objektivität. Ein Erkenntnisideal auf dem Prüfstand. Tübingen: Francke.

Majorek, Marek (2015): Rudolf Steiners Geisteswissenschaft: Mythisches Denken oder Wissenschaft. Tübingen: Francke.

Popper, Karl R. (2003): Die offene Gesellschaft und ihre Feinde. Vol. II. Falsche Propheten: Hegel, Marx und die Folgen. Tübingen: Mohr-Siebeck.

Prange, Klaus (1985/2000): Erziehung zur Anthroposophie. Darstellung und Kritik der Waldorfpädagogik. Bad Heilbrunn: Klinkhardt.

Prange, Klaus (2005): Curriculum und Karma. Das anthroposophische Erziehungsmodell Rudolf Steiners. In: Forum Demokratischer Atheistinnen (Ed.) (2005): Mission Klassenzimmer. Zum Einfluss von Religion und Esoterik auf Bildung und Erziehung. Aschaffenburg: Alibri, pp. 85–100.

Randoll, Dirk (2012): Ich bin Waldorflehrer: Einstellungen, Erfahrungen, Diskussionspunkte – Eine Befragungsstudie. Wiesbaden: Springer.

Ravagli, Lorenzo (2014): Polemischer Diskurs. Anthroposophie und ihre Kritiker. In: Heusser, Peter/Weinzirl, Johannes (Eds.): Rudolf Steiner. Seine Bedeutung für Wissenschaft und Leben heute. Stuttgart: Schattauer, p. 332 ff.

Rittelmeyer, Christian (2011): Gute Pädagogik – fragwürdige Ideologie? Zur Diskussion um die anthroposophischen Grundlagen der Waldorfpädagogik. In: Loebell, Peter (Ed.) (2011): Waldorfschule heute. Eine Einführung. Stuttgart: Freies Geistesleben.

Schieren, Jost (1997): Anschauende Urteilskraft. Methodische und philosophische Grundlagen von Goethes naturwissenschaftlichem Erkennen. Düsseldorf, Bonn: Parerga.

Skiera, Ehrenhard (2009): Reformpädagogik in Geschichte und Gegenwart. Eine kritische Einführung. Munich: Oldenbourg.

Steiner, Rudolf (1889): Goethe als Vater einer neuen Ästhetik. In: Steiner, Rudolf (Ed.) (1985): Kunst und Kunsterkenntnis. Grundlagen einer neuen Ästhetik. Rudolf Steiner GA 271. Dornach: Rudolf Steiner Verlag.

Steiner, Rudolf (1979): Grundlinien einer Erkenntnistheorie der Goetheschen Weltanschauung. Mit besonderer Rücksicht auf Schiller. 1886. GA 2. Dornach: Rudolf Steiner Verlag.

Steiner, Rudolf (1986): Gegenwärtiges Geistesleben und Erziehung. Lecture cycle given in Ilkley (UK) from August 5 to 17, 1923. GA 307. Dornach: Rudolf Steiner Verlag. English translation: Steiner, Rudolf (2004): A Modern Art of Education. Tr. Robert Lathe, Nancy Whittaker. Great Barrington, MA: Anthroposophic Press.

Steiner, Rudolf (1991): Das Schicksalsjahr 1923 in der Geschichte der Anthroposophischen Gesellschaft. Vom Goetheanumbrand zur Weihnachtstagung. Ansprachen – Versammlungen – Dokumente Januar bis Dezember 1923. GA 259. Dornach: Rudolf Steiner Verlag.

Steiner, Rudolf (2000): Mein Lebensgang. GA 28. Dornach: Rudolf Steiner Verlag.

Steiner, Rudolf (2005a): Fachwissenschaften und Anthroposophie. Eight lectures, eleven questions and answers, one discussion contribution and a concluding address. Dornach and Stuttgart March 24, 1920 bis September 2, 1921. GA 73a. Dornach: Rudolf Steiner Verlag.

Steiner, Rudolf (2005b): Die Philosophie der Freiheit. Grundzüge einer modernen Weltanschauung. 1918. GA 4. Dornach: Rudolf Steiner Verlag.

Ullrich, Heiner (1986): Waldorfpädagogik und okkulte Weltanschauung. Eine bildungsphilosophische und geistesgeschichtliche Auseinandersetzung mit der Anthropologie Rudolf Steiners. Weinheim, Basel: Juventa.

Ullrich, Heiner (1988): Wissenschaft als rationalisierte Mystik. Eine problemgeschichtliche Untersuchung der erkenntnistheoretischen Grundlagen der Anthroposophie. In: Neue Sammlung. Vierteljahres-Zeitschrift für Erziehung und Gesellschaft. Nr. 28, 1988, S. 168–194.

Ullrich, Heiner (2015): Waldorfpädagogik. Eine kritische Einführung. Weinheim, Basel: Beltz.

Witzenmann, Herbert (1985): Strukturphänomenologie. Vorbewusstes Gestaltbilden im erkennenden Wirklichkeitenthüllen. Dornach: Gideon Spicker.

Zander, Helmut (2007): Anthroposophie in Deutschland. Theosophische Weltanschauung und geselschaftliche Praxis. Vols. I and II. Göttingen: Vandenhoeck & Ruprecht.

THE ANTHROPOSOPHIC UNDERSTANDING OF HISTORY FROM THE POINT OF VIEW OF WALDORF EDUCATION, EDUCATION SCIENCE, AND HISTORY TEACHING

M. Michael Zech

This paper can only draw on a very few academic works. With the exception of the theologian Helmut Zander's comprehensive study (Zander 2007), in which he also takes a critical look at Steiner's understanding of history,[1] there is only one instructive dissertation, by Jens Heisterkamp, who is, however, favorably inclined toward Steiner's anthroposophy from the start. Numerous essays and some more comprehensive publications have been produced within Waldorf education and anthroposophy. This theoretical study draws on works that focus on epistemological and methodical aspects rather than pedagogical implications, such as Christoph Lindenberg's contributions on Steiner's symptomatologic approach to history (Lindenberg 1981, 1982) and André Bartoniczek's two treatises on imaginative historiography (*Imaginative Geschichtserkenntnis. Rudolf Steiner und die Erweiterung der Geschichtswissenschaft*) (Bartoniczek 2009) and on the foundations of history teaching (*Die Zukunft entdecken. Grundlagen des Geschichtsunterrichts*) (Bartoniczek 2014). Both authors interpret Steiner's understanding of history on the basis of lecture transcripts and written essays. They also include epistemological questions. Bartoniczek who, in his most recent publication, focuses on Steiner's way of unlocking historical realities includes in his considerations the discourse on the significance of remembering in anthropology, psychology, and cultural science.

I will attempt to characterize the anthroposophic understanding of history based on a differentiated analysis of Steiner's statements and of their interpretation and contextualization by the authors just mentioned. I will highlight both the obstacles that prevent discourse and potential meeting points between anthroposophy and academic science: an ambitious undertaking given the restricted brief for this contribution, the complexity of the subject matter, and the lack of existing groundwork to build on. I follow this up with a brief look at the importance of the anthroposophic understanding of history for its instruction in Waldorf schools, and an outline that locates this approach to teaching in the discourse on history didactics.

1 Problem description

In investigating the importance of anthroposophy for Waldorf education, one inevitably discovers—as well as Steiner's methodic guidelines on inner development through meditation, i.e., the development of a soul organ capable of greater self-awareness and of extended, differentiated, meditatively supported "inner" perception that transcends the world of sense-perceptible phenomena—his extensive body of work, mostly in the form of lectures, with multilayered descriptions of cosmic and human evolution from the point of view of anthroposophy. They form the foundation of a receptively acquired anthroposophic worldview. Most lectures are introduced in rhetorical style, which prepared Steiner's contemporaneous listeners for the fact that the following presentations would provide guidelines for an active, future-oriented life. In keeping with the central value Steiner ascribes to the human race as continually self-actualizing beings, the development of humanity or humanness is presented as the primary goal (Zech 2012, p. 341ff.). One of the challenges here lies in the paradox that human evolution, according to Steiner, strives toward individuation, while emancipation toward autonomy requires the individuality's self-realization in freedom, out of itself (Steiner 1979, p. 124ff.). This means that the evolutionary concept Steiner assigns to humanity is open-ended. In the anthroposophic reception of these thoughts, this paradox is perpetuated at a different level: people often speak of conditions that are "necessary" for realizing human autonomy. This means that, similarly to Hegel's philosophy, the arguments in the analyses of humankind and society—or in the allusions to actions that are appropriate for human beings—can again and again be received as a salvation-historical narrative.

We realize that history, or change and development at a historical level, are essential to anthroposophy. In seeing itself as a quest for knowledge encompassing areas that are only accessible to spiritual investigation, anthroposophy includes both the past and the future in its efforts to understand human evolution and individuation. This is the reason why most of Steiner's writings and lectures include descriptions and explanations that are based on cultural history.

The emerging content, which needs to be understood historically, confronts its recipients with a number of challenges, which I list below in the form of theses:

Most of Steiner's contemplations on cultural history, and above all those presented in his lectures, are sketches: They don't usually refer to authors or historical sources and are consequently neither bound to any historical discourse nor conclusively evidenced.

Steiner' understanding of history can be examined on at least three levels relating to different phases in his biography. His claim, which is largely accepted in anthroposophic circles, that his lifework, or the development of his ideas, did not contain ruptures but needed to be seen as a unity emerging organically from different working phases, does, however, contradict the obvious tension that exists between statements made by Steiner at different times.

When justifying historical descriptions, Steiner refers to perceptions in realms that are inaccessible to the "non-initiated," but he usually does not make clear if and to what extent his insights are derived from "suprasensory perception" and "spiritual research" (Steiner 1990) or from the study of original texts and materials. Reception is therefore based on trust (the transition to "belief" is seamless) in the initiate; doubts or questioning of Steiner's statements are rejected as inappropriate and critics are reminded of their inability to verify the findings of "suprasensory research." Critics soon become "opponents" and the anthroposophic content the subject of apologies. For many anthroposophically oriented recipients, conflicts arise due to Steiner's chronologic dating, for instance, that often contradicts today's scientific findings: They ask themselves if the initiate is not more likely to know the truth than scientists with their much more specific and therefore restricted view of events.

Because of its implications for an understanding of history, the anthroposophic view of development through repeated reincarnations based on karmic laws constitutes a particular challenge. For scientists, this "idea" is at best a belief, or a cliché borrowed from Eastern philosophy. According to Steiner's basic works, *An Outline of Esoteric Science*, for example (Steiner 1976, p. 103f.), and to his lectures on the same topic, mainly given between 1910 and 1924, human beings take part in the course of history in repeated incarnations. Unless such experiences are called up in reminiscences, past life regression, or meditation, and are experienced or interpreted as reappearing memories of such past lives, we do not tend to have access to these past incarnations in our present life. Preferences or dislikes regarding certain historical epochs or phenomena are interpreted as indications of to such personal participation in history. Against the background of such premonitions and of Steiner's numerous historical presentations, which include "information" on the previous lives of well-known cultural and political (historical) personalities, a tendency toward cultural-historical descriptions has emerged in the anthroposophic subculture. As a result, an anthroposophic history culture has evolved, supported by numerous publications that have, however, hardly been noticed by the relevant sciences.

Anthroposophic recipients tend to treat Steiner's lecture notes and transcripts, which were often not authorized by him, as writings, not considering that they were orally presented in a particular context. It is evident from these presentations that Steiner referred to daily events of that time and, also, that he took into consideration circumstances that concerned the group of people he was addressing, such as previous conversations or lectures. Such references are mostly not directly accessible in the lectures, nor are they sufficiently explained in the commentary. As a result, the actual context or the multiple messages contained in historical statements cannot be understood, leading to distortions and abstruse interpretations, while subtleties such as irony or situational criticism are lost.

Historical references often serve the self-contextualization of anthroposophic initiatives. Waldorf schools, above all, when they were founded, were celebrated as the avant-garde of a "culture of the consciousness soul" that was to be realized in the "fifth post-Atlantean period." The underlying narrative, based on consecutive periods in human evolution, alternates between the periodization used at the time in cultural history (Zech 2012, p. 137f.) and the traditional theosophical concept of evolution that mostly goes back to the Helena Petrovna Blavatsky. Since Steiner tended to develop new concepts and designations depending on context, the changes and differences between them can be established, but explicit corrections or explanations for new designations, referring to new insights, for example, are few and far between. The systematic examination of how concepts change in Steiner's work is therefore very difficult and, from the point of view of historical science, Steiner's concept of anthropology and cultural history remains rather vague.

Steiner's reference, in dating cultural periods, to cosmic-astronomic constellations (such as the vernal point of the sun in the zodiac) that introduces a mathematicized view of evolution and the determination of cultural phases in history (Steiner 1988a, p. 100) adds another problem. The ensuing platonic-cyclical concept serves two purposes: firstly, the description of the evolution of consciousness through a sequence of advanced civilizations that can be systematically explained by referring to the anthroposophic definition of the human organization of body and soul; and secondly, the establishment of a system that encompasses the future (hebdomadal processes) (Steiner 1976, p. 103ff.).

Because, even in the preliminary discussions about founding a Waldorf school, Steiner proposed to use the "post-Atlantic" cultural periods as teaching content (Zech 2012, p. 136), a narrative has established itself as a foundation for today's history teaching that goes back to such statements. Grades teachers, who do not tend to be history scholars, often implement these references naively, aiming to convey a journey "through history" to the students that reflects a coherent understanding of culture as human evolution in progress. Problems arise when actual or alleged anthroposophic content that cannot be supported by reliable sources becomes part of the history presentations (forms of life on Atlantis, the fictional life in Ancient India, etc.); or when terminologies and explanations flow into the lessons that—actually or presumably—go back to statements by Steiner and that can or must be seen as racist and discriminatory (certainly from today's point of view). A number of public scandals relating to Waldorf teaching were fed by such dubious and irresponsible approaches to teaching.

Whatever view one has of Steiner's pronouncements and ideas, one must concede that he—not necessarily systematically but comprehensively—included scientific insights of his time into his (historical) presentations. It is therefore the *reception* rather than the content of Steiner's anthroposophic expositions that is to blame for the fact that the updated and modernized orientation of anthroposophically inspired institutions, Waldorf schools in particular, is not adequately recognized. Interestingly, this is not a problem of history teaching or of the history curriculum, because analysis of their origin reveals that they have been permanently extended and revised informed by scientific findings, terminological changes, and time consciousness (Zech 2012, p. 279f.). A naïve reception that treats Steiner's historical elaborations as verified truths characterizes some anthroposophic publications, and this can also be found within the heterogeneous anthroposophic subculture in lectures and conversations. It lives there in interpretations of the world and its meaning that are passed on, and that develop their own dynamic, claiming Steiner's initiation as evidence of their truth and validity.

Steiner's analyses of historical events can illustrate the difficulty of engaging with him as a historian. Not only must his statements be evaluated within the context of the language and discussions of his time but, because of the lack of references, researchers today also struggle to establish if these statements go back inside political knowledge, the Masonic lodges, analysis of documents, Steiner's own conclusions, or spiritual research. Since Markus Osterrieder's painstaking and comprehensive study, over more than 1600 pages, into Steiner's comments on World War I, what they refer to, and what they are based on, one can no longer simply dismiss Steiner's references, for example, to the activities of some European Lodge members and their impact on the events leading to the outbreak of the war, as speculation or conspiracy theories (Osterrieder 2014). The facts and documents reveal without doubt that Steiner referred to very concrete occurrences. But because these events are always encased in anthroposophic interpretations of the evolution of consciousness and culture, there is again a seamless amalgamation with anthroposophic spiritual science. When Steiner explains Woodrow Wilson's policies as the result of karmic conditions and past incarnations, his statements move to a realm that is not accessible to academic study.

While Steiner's considerations and interpretations of cultural history have not found access to the discourse on history and history teaching, they have attracted polemical comments, mostly in relation to individual statements that were taken out of context. Most scientists refrain from referring to Steiner as an esotericist, or from acknowledging, let alone supporting, his theses and ideas by subjecting them to examination. The theologian Helmut Zander was the first to systematically analyze Steiner's cultural theory at the beginning of the 21t century, in his critical examination *Anthroposophy in Deutschland* (Anthroposophy in Germany) (Zander 2007) that has so far failed to attract any noticeable response from historians. Anthroposophy is only considered in the historical research of esoteric movements that has emerged in the last ten years or so. While Steiner's work on esthetics and philosophy has by now entered the scientific discourse, his contributions to the history of culture have as yet not met with that kind of interest. A number of essays on his understanding of history from within the Waldorf or anthroposophic movement, aiming at access to the relevant discourse, have hardly been noticed. They include in-depth evaluations of Steiner's work and interesting interpretations, but these are informed by a favorable view of anthroposophy.[2]

A problem that has been ignored by anthroposophists and Waldorf teachers is Steiner's diffuse and contradictory attitude toward nationality and racist terminology, particularly because nationalism and racism have no part in the practice of anthroposophic institutions and Waldorf schools. Most people working in these places resolutely distance themselves from that kind of thinking, but they trustfully rely on those of Steiner's ideas that they see as essential for their professional field and therefore ignore or marginalize actual problems. It is this apologetic attitude on the part of those who seek orientation from anthroposophy that exposes them to investigative and polemic journalism. The resulting (often biased and unscientific) revelations, casting suspicion on whole groups of people and on institutions, provoke—against the critics' actual or pretended intentions—a defensiveness in many representatives of anthroposophy and Waldorf education that prevents the necessary unbiased investigations and differentiated discourses. For many scientists, these present yet another reason to not engage with Steiner and his ideas despite the success of Waldorf education and of anthroposophically inspired institutions. Despite the findings of recently presented qualifying, critical-scientific studies (Zander 2007, p. 631ff.; Ullrich 2011; p.196ff.; Martins 2012) and a growing awareness of the existing problems among the anthroposophically oriented (Brüll, Heisterkamp 2008), the necessary clarification continues to be prevented by hardened fronts and polemics.

In the context of history teaching, Waldorf schools have found modest access to the relevant discourse, thanks to individual contributions from Waldorf teachers,[3] but even there, the esoteric background of Steiner's anthroposophy remains something that is to be avoided.

2 The significance of cultural history in Steiner's time

In order to study Steiner's understanding of cultural history, we must look at the political, national, and cultural developments of his time.

As recently illustrated by Franz Beckers in his outline of the cultural concept of cultural history (Beckers 2011, p. 15ff.), cultural history was born from Enlightenment. It emerged as a result of "history turning away from the activities of leaders and states in favor of spheres of life such as religion, ethics, and customs, as well as material culture" (Beckers 2011, p. 16). The view that humanity is evolving and progressing is intrinsic to cultural history. During the period of Idealism, "humanity" not only meant the sum of all human beings but also the species-specific essence: an ideal-typical construct, in other words. Friedrich Schiller, for instance, proposes that individuals can self-responsibly take hold of their humanity, that is, of the potentiality of their humanization. From this educated view of history there emerged in Europe, during the Romantic period at the turn of the 19th century, the nationally oriented cultural histories, partly in competition with the narrative of a cultural history of humankind. They sought to ascertain national identities based on the history of language, literature, customs, traditions, and regional and territorial history. In his outline of the changing self-concept of cultural history, Beckers points out that ethnic or national history tended to focus on the distinction and demarcation of different cultures, while the cultural history of humanity was devoted to "the general progression of human reason" (Beckers 2011, p. 17f.). Nineteenth-century historicism related history—analogously to the political processes and the concerns of the national-liberal citizens' movement—to the state, the fate of which depended on the deeds of great men. Only few eminent historians, such as Jacob Burckhardt, avoided this trend. Toward the end of the 19th century, a sharp opposition arose between nationally oriented political history and humanity-oriented cultural history. In this context, Beckers refers to cultural historians like Kurt Breysig, who saw the dynamics of evolution reflected in the regularly changing, but ultimately not progressing, relation between the individual and the state, or Eberhard Gotheim, who saw any phenomenon arising from human activity, politics included, as resulting from real underlying ideas that the cultural historian had to reconstruct in the attempt to eliminate the contrast between universal and political history (Beckers 2011, p. 19f.).

In the early 20th century, it was mostly Karl Lamprecht who tried to present the evolution of human consciousness by including psychological concepts for collective social processes. His model of an evolutionary theory, which could be presented in images of the world that determine each cultural period, was vehemently attacked because of the factual inaccuracies and simplifications it contains. His view of culture was perpetuated by Johan Huizinga, for example, who saw the reality of a period in the way people lived, worked, and thought, as reflected in testimonials and events. Historians had to develop a sense for this reality (Beckers 2011, p. 23). In the 1920s, the cultural philosopher Ernst Cassirer expressed the view that historical narration depended on the mind of the narrator, thus freeing cultural history from the pursuit of naïve object relations. Up until then, cultural historians had assumed that testimonials were expression of spiritual developments. Beckers holds that Cassirer's concept of cultural history was based on the "dual constructive performance of the historical actors and the investigating historian" (Beckers 2011, p. 24) and that his approach would today be ascribed to the historical consciousness reflected by narrativity theory.

Oswald Spengler's universal historical disquisition (*The Decline of the West*) stands out in that he tries to analyze the historical upheavals of his time in view of the decline of earlier high civilizations. This leads him to a metaphysical theory of history that basically predicts the future decline of European civilization teleologically (Spengler 2014, p. 43). Spengler juxtaposes the cultural histories that are oriented toward constant further and higher development with an epochal view of history that is reminiscent of the cyclic world conceptions of antiquity. Unlike many recipients of his time, Spengler saw this "decline" more optimistically as a natural and meaningful development. Spengler, who explicitly refers to Goethe's morphological nature observations, follows a tradition in cultural history that sees regular natural (not mechanical) processes as the dynamic principle in history.

For Spengler, advanced civilizations were entities of world history: "Cultures are organisms. The history of the world is their biography" (Spengler 2014). He lists eight advanced civilizations in total, each spanning a period of around 1000 years. They are not hierarchical to each other, and each of them has its own underlying founding myth.

- Egypt (from around 3000 BCE, including the Minoan culture)
- Babylon (from around 3000 BCE)
- India (from 1500 BCE)
- Chinese culture (from 1400 BCE)
- Greek-Roman antiquity (since 1100 BCE)
- Arabian culture (from the year 1 CE, includes the early Christian and Byzantine cultures)
- Mexican culture (from around 200 CE)
- Western culture (from 900 CE, includes North America)
- The ninth culture predicted by Spengler for the 3rd millennium in the area that is now Russia.[4]

3 Steiner's approach to cultural history

On the surface, Steiner's understanding of history can initially be seen as following the tradition of cultural history. He explicitly referred to Jacob Burckhardt, whom he recommended to Waldorf teachers for their lesson preparations, although Burckhardt, unlike Steiner, rejected a view of evolution as unfolding in periods (Burckhardt 1978). Steiner is closer to Lamprecht, both in this respect and in seeing history as an expression of collective psychological processes. And like all cultural historians of his time, Steiner distanced himself from the Wilhelmine nationalist concepts of identity-formation. In a series of lectures he gave in Zurich on November 7, 1917, Steiner spoke up explicitly against the 19th-century historicism, when he defended himself against the accusation that anthroposophy was unscientific, by linking it to various other sciences, including history in particular (Steiner 1988b, p. 61). There, he referred to different concepts of development in the history of culture proposed by thinkers and historians from the 18th to the 20th century, clearly locating himself in the tradition of cultural history.[5] At the same time, he distanced himself from those authors' speculative evolutionary concepts which, in his view, did not really penetrate to the true depths of historical processes.

Ultimately, Steiner does not side with Spengler either, even though he studied Spengler's work and mentioned it favorably, and even though Spengler proposed a similar periodic concept, predicted a future cultural center of humanity in the Russian-speaking realm, and derived criteria for historical studies from Goethe's morphology (Steiner 2005, p. 214ff.).

In his study of Steiner's understanding of history, Heisterkamp points out commonalities and differences between Steiner and the cultural historian Karl Lamprecht, because, in his *German History,* the latter also proposed a system of cultural periods based on the idea of anthropological evolution (Heisterkamp 1989, p. 47ff.). Heisterkamp sees Lamprecht's ideas as cause for Steiner to underline the epistemological foundation of his own understanding of history. In his critique of an anthropomorphic interpretation of history, Steiner distances himself from such cultural-historical interpretations, claiming that an approach that went beyond biological-anthropological aspects and focused on the spiritual emancipation of human beings as self-reliant individuals exceeded the initial establishment of historical cause-effect relations (Steiner 1988b, p. 333ff.). Heisterkamp points out that Steiner, rather than deriving historical contexts from the past, from what has become, provides a framework for interpreting history and constructing meaning from a future context, that is, from the human potential for individuation and self-realization. Referring to Chapter 12 of the *Philosophy of Freedom*, he interprets Steiner's historical-cultural understanding of evolution, for instance, as opposite to natural events which are determined by the past. "Temporal-causal events are rather a kind of fabric of human expression, they are cause, condition, and medium of an activity that is genuinely original and belongs to another dimension than time and causality. As causal natural developments are penetrated, they are transformed into history: human expressivity stands 'above' time, as it were; it contemplates what was yesterday and anticipates the tomorrow, leaves behind the temporal ties in making a first decision. [...] Human expressivity is not determined by the past, but is directed toward the present from the future" (Heisterkamp 1989, p. 64ff.).

This suggests that Steiner sees cultural history above all as autopoietic. Closer investigation reveals that his understanding of history is integral to anthroposophy because of its spiritual dimension, its cosmological, anthropological, and psychological integration, and its explanation of comprehensive evolutionary processes (Steiner 1976). By using a specific concept of spiritual science to aim for areas of existence that lie beyond the physical-spatial, sense-perceptible dimension of the world, and that can be unlocked through meditation[6] in order to draw higher knowledge about historical events from additional sources (Akashic records), he renders his view inaccessible to the usual scientific categorization. That Steiner was fully aware of this fact is apparent from comments such as "In my lectures, which deal with occult history, and with historical facts and personalities in the light of spiritual science, I will have to tell you a few rather strange things [...] that will have to rely on your goodwill" (Steiner 1993b, p. 9).

On the one hand, Steiner, with the theosophical approach he developed in his treatise of 1901 *Mysticism in the Dawn of Modernism and its Relationship to the Modern Worldview* (Steiner 1993a), sees himself as part of a cultural stream that seeks contemplative access to the world and that was also represented by Master Eckhart, Nicolas of Cusa, Agrippa von Nettesheim, Paracelsus, Giordano Bruno, Jacob Böhme, and Angelus Silesius. On the other hand, he also postulates a natural-scientific understanding as a foundation for developing his contemplative experiences into grounded and relatable knowledge.[7] By claiming that anthroposophy is a science, he wants to demarcate it methodically from the subjectiveness of mysticism (Steiner 1976, p. 18ff.). He derives his phenomenologically and morphologically informed understanding of science (above all) not only from his Goethe reception but also from his intensive studies of Haeckel's theory of evolution and Nietzsche's philosophy.

By calling Steiner's presentations of history esoteric, established historiography declares them to be inaccessible to factual examination and therefore speculative and fantastic, without any scientific value. Steiner himself was convinced that only through extending the foundations of knowledge by including contemplative experiences that can then be interpreted by natural-scientific means could historiography grow to be a science able to achieve insights into the deeper layers of historical developments and changes. "If one really wants to think historically, one needs to develop spiritual-scientific vision and consciousness in order to understand what cannot be experienced in the ordinary historical processes, what is intrinsic to evolution but not visible in external facts, as little as the soul is visible in a dead body" (Steiner 1988b, p. 80f.).

In his examination of the origin of this theosophic-anthroposophic concept of evolution, Helmut Zander expands on this question in descriptions that evoke countless concrete ideas (Zander 2007). On the whole, he doubts that Steiner draws on spiritual sources in his writings and lectures, and he tries to prove on the basis of numerous details how Steiner drew his insights and concepts from an eclectic jumble of ideas taken from western mysticism, theosophical predecessors, contemporary speculations, and new discoveries. This has remained a highly emotional issue: whether and to what extent can Steiner rightfully claim that his historical-anthroposophical descriptions derive from insights arising from his research in suprasensory realms?

Irrespective of the general doubt in the reliability of Steiner's approach to history and of the problem that there is no real foundation for discourse due to the lack of access to levels of reality that could serve as reference, fundamental cognitive questions arise regarding the origin of his statements on cultural history, even for those who, because of their anthroposophic orientation, have a favorable understanding of Steiner. For there is no doubt, on the one hand, that Steiner was immensely well-read, particularly in history, and many of his views are in fact part of the understanding of culture in his time (*ex oriente lux*; Zech 2012, p. 137ff.). On the other hand, he kept referring to the fact that his historical descriptions were the result of spiritual-scientific research into suprasensory events, especially the Akashic Records (Steiner 1990, p. 21ff.; 1976, p. 106f.). In most cases, it is not clear whether Steiner received contemporary scientific findings, when he, implicitly or explicitly, makes recourse to other esoteric authors,[8] and when he draws directly from his own "suprasensible perception." Additionally, he says himself that he is faced with the hermeneutic problem of putting his spiritual and soul experiences into words and integrating them into known contexts of knowledge (Steiner 1990, p. 22; 1995a, p. 9ff.). The methodical problem Steiner describes here is one that is known from mythological research, where the images described are not interpreted as historical facts but as expressions of inner experiences that may not only relate to inner, psychological—but also to historical—events (Armstrong 2005, p. 7ff.; Kerényi 1982, p. 212ff.).

A brief look at Steiner's presentation of the ancient Indian cultural period can serve as an example. He locates this period between the eight to the sixth millennium before the birth of Christ, that is, in the Neolithic age, before the beginning of the Bronze Age. In the below account, Steiner refers neither to any archaeological nor other knowledge but describes the state of human consciousness in that culture, whose existence is not confirmed by today's scientific insights, from his own spiritual research:

"Then we see the ancient Indian culture evolving, which can be called a culture of unity in the best sense of the word. This is not the culture of the Vedas. The Vedas are but an echo of the true ancient Indian culture. They originated not much longer before our Christian calendar than we live today after its beginning. We could characterize this ancient Indian culture today by saying that its people did not yet sense the difference between the material and the spiritual world when they looked at plants, stones, mountains, fields, and clouds. They did not yet perceive the spiritual as separate from the material world. They generally did not see colors and forms as we do today. For them, the spiritual world was directly adjacent to the material world. For them, the spirit was as real as material colors are: a culture of unity of spirit and matter. They felt that the spirit lived in all things, a principle that was later called Brahman, the World Soul. But this culture, which we meet in ancient times at the starting point of human history, did not yet enable human beings to be active in the material world. [...] This culture was therefore confronted in the North, where the Persian empire would later emerge, by another culture, which is almost its opposite: permeated by the sense that human beings, whilst belonging to the spiritual world, had to work with the material here on earth" (Steiner 1983, p. 339ff.).

In numerous lectures and written works, Steiner described cultural contexts in this and similar ways as real events. The narrative is always about evolving human consciousness. The cultural periods are always presented as examples or as centers of a general cultural development that unfolded in many locations. While Steiner's statements on later historical developments can be verified by today's historical knowledge as to their plausibility, validity, comprehensibility, and relevance, his descriptions of pre-antiquity have so far not been accessible to academic research. While Steiner's chronologic dating and his cultural periodization of human evolution correspond, to a certain extent, to the thinking of cultural history in the early 20th century, his concrete disquisitions on the mentality of ancient cultures, as shown in the example above, cannot be verified by today's academic insights. Verification of such statements could at best be attempted by drawing on ethnology, mythological research, evolutionary biology, or historical anthropology. Points of contact would be possible, above all, by drawing on Steiner's characterizations of early mental qualities for interpreting archaeological testimonials and ethnological insights into pre- and early agricultural communities.[9]

The narrative structure in the last sentences of the above citation reveals that it was not Steiner's intention to present a historical account in the scientific sense. He rather pursued a line of argument by ascribing a certain quality of consciousness to a cultural era that was then overcome or advanced, in the sense of a gradual development, by a following cultural era. Steiner therefore understands the history of the past 10,000 years as a cultural process during which the clan cultures evolved into advanced civilizations. Thus, the ground was prepared—first through the development of mythical, dream-like images, and later through the awakening intellectuality—for the individual self-concept that emerged mainly in Europe from the beginning of modernity. Steiner identifies the following cultural phases in the evolution of consciousness and mentality, wherein the chronological progress also involves a spatial shift of the localities where the various mentalities evolved and from where they spread out further:

- the ancient Indian period (ca. 7200–5100 BCE)
- the ancient Persian period (ca. 5100–2900 BCE)
- the Egyptian-Babylonian-Chaldaean period (ca. 2900–747 BCE)
- the Greco-Roman period (747 BCE–1413)
- the modern period (1413–3573)

If one ignores the drastic change in the knowledge of chronological dating over time, the paradigm shifts—highlighted by Steiner in the transition from pre-agricultural to a settled life, from a farming culture to the myth-based advanced civilizations, to the "Logos cultures" of Israeli, Greek, and Roman antiquity, where scientific-causal thinking moved to the fore, and on to modernity and Enlightenment—can also be found in a similar structure in mainstream 20th-century European historiography, even though Steiner derived his insights from entirely different sources. That Steiner was not, as has been pointed out, interested in historiography as such but in describing the development of the human mind, of human consciousness, is apparent on three levels: Firstly, Steiner explains in relation to a similar description, "What is meant here by 'ancient Indians' does not coincide with the usual meaning of that term. No external documents exist from the time I am talking about" (Steiner 1976, p. 205). Secondly, he explains the historical-cultural phenomena expressed in these cultures in anthroposophic terminology: The mythical consciousness of the theocratic advanced cultures, the "Logos" consciousness of antiquity, and modern individualism are, for instance, described as mental phases of cultivation based on different soul modes—sentient soul (an imaginative, mostly hierarchical understanding of the world in the theocratic high cultures), mind soul (development of logic, science, and self-cultivation in antiquity), and consciousness soul (self-reflecting and oriented to self-motivated activity, from the beginning of modernity). Thirdly, Steiner does not derive the chronological dating and periodization from external historical developments but from cosmic constellations: the progression of the vernal point of the sunrise through the zodiac. This point moves through the entire zodiac in the course of 25,920 years, entering a new star sign on average every 2160 years. In Steiner's interpretation, these cosmic events cause spiritual forces to enter into humanity and initiate or facilitate certain attitudes and mentalities.

Steiner refers to the postglacial cultural process described above as the "post-Atlantean era," separating it from the previous cultural cycles, for which he presents images derived, as he says, from his esoteric research that are meant to evoke in his readers and listeners mental representations of evolution in general and human evolution in particular. Steiner interprets the traditional mythical images as a resonance of these earlier kinds of world experience and draws on them for complementing his own pictorial description (Steiner 1989, p. 83f.; 1976, p. 220). Similarly to C.G. Jung—who assumed archetypes in the collective unconscious that pictorially express evolutionary processes that come to expression again and again in the cultures of humanity, or provide meaningful (mythical) patterns (Jung 2001, p. 7ff.)—Steiner created a topos, for instance, in his repeated references to the myth of the fall of Atlantis. That Steiner sees this fall also a physical-geological event, going back to a time when the individual continents took shape and the cultural transition from the Paleolithic to the Neolithic era took place, is not due to his ignorance or contradictory statements but to his morphological and cyclic-progressive understanding of evolution, where similar developments occur again and again under different conditions (Kaiser 2004, p. 1346ff.). Steiner's way of speaking and writing, which tends to be rather cursory and assertive, constitutes a challenge for his listeners and readers that may give rise to adventurous and untenable interpretations of his ideas, which are, in any case, difficult to assess. With a few embarrassing exceptions, the attitude that has become established in Waldorf schools is to treat the Atlantis story either clearly as a myth or to not touch on it at all, although up into the 1970s it was still naïvely included into the teaching of cultural history (Kaiser 2004, p. 1349).

Heisterkamp concludes his study of Steiner's approach to history by stating that the latter's anthroposophic presentation of evolution and cultural history does not claim an empiric foundation for its periodic and chronological structure, but that it rather offers an ideal-typical structure as a basis for reflecting on the different peculiarities of the individual cultures against the background of anthropological development and the evolution of consciousness. "In engaging with Rudolf Steiner's understanding of history, one will sooner or later find that one, remarkably, comes across the same constant again and again in his historical presentations, however diverse the topics may be. The question regarding a particular complex of events is always about how it relates to the general trend in human evolution" (Heisterkamp 1989, p. 159). It was therefore the purpose of the overarching anthroposophic concept to be a historical-heuristic tool for describing and understanding historical and cultural changes: "[Steiner's] universal history provides ideas, theoretical elements, for evaluating the material differently from how it is usually done. [...] It has been established that Steiner's periodization allows for a coherent view of history. It is, however, not meant as a hypothesis that needs to be verified by empirical examination, but lives essentially from the idea gained through intuition" (ibid., p. 158f.). According to Heisterkamp, one should not consult Steiner—irrespective of the fact that his chronological dating no longer corresponds to today's knowledge—as a historian but rather study the categories for describing and explaining historical change that derive from the interpretive concept. Naturally, one has to conclude with Heisterkamp that "[Steiner's] existential interest in the genesis of humanity, the assumption of a potentially meaningful historical evolution, and the search for a non-sensuous structure arising from it, are clearly opposed to the critically oriented, often closely material-bound way of working in today's business of historical science" (Heisterkamp 1989, p. 160).

4 The importance of the history of culture and consciousness in anthroposophy

Both in terminological and contextual terms, Steiner's historical presentations can only be understood in conjunction with anthroposophy. At the center of this esoteric-spiritual "knowledge of the human being" lies a view of human evolution based on theosophic terminology. In 1904, when he was still active in the Theosophical Society, Steiner summarized its hebdomadal structure as follows, "The seven stages of consciousness are expressed in the course of human evolution in seven planetary developments. At each of these stages, consciousness undergoes seven subordinate conditions, which are realized in the smaller cycles mentioned earlier. [...] Western occult science refers to these subordinate states as 'conditions of life' – in contrast to the superordinated 'conditions of consciousness.' It is also said that each 'condition of consciousness' passes through seven 'realms.' Based on this calculation, we must distinguish seven times seven, that is 49, small cycles or 'realms' in the whole of human evolution. And each small cycle must pass through seven even smaller ones, called 'conditions of form' [...]. For the full cycle of humanity this amounts to seven times 49, or 343, different 'conditions of form.' [...] It will become apparent that in order to truly understand ourselves as human beings we must know our own development" (Steiner 1990, p. 159f.).

The whole evolutionary concept also forms the basis of anthroposophy's sevenfold understanding of the human being and of the human biography as presented by Steiner in his *Theosophy* (Steiner 1995a) and explained against the background of the entire cosmic and human evolution in his book *An Outline of Esoteric Science* (Steiner 1976). The historical dimension, or that of cultural history, down to the terminology, is therefore an elementary part of Steiner's anthroposophy, which is itself presented in this concept as a cultural phenomenon. But the evolutionary and historical concept meets a conflict that is also perceptible from within anthroposophy, for, on the one hand, human evolution—as expressed in the above citation—as well as individual development are explained with a basic ideal-typical, platonically closed, hebdomadal system, thus displaying the characteristics of a teleological, salvation-historical narrative, while Steiner describes this development as a process of emancipation and individuation in which the individual becomes increasingly self-reliant through evolution, particularly in the future. Steiner defines individuality as independent of external determination and sees human beings seizing their freedom as an open, self-defining telos (Steiner 1995b, p. 104 ff., p. 237ff.).

Steiner's accounts of past incarnations of well-known historical personalities and his description of the work of spiritual beings through them constitute a special form of historical observation whose esoteric nature make them totally inaccessible to any usual historical approaches. Such "esoteric contemplations of karmic relations of personalities and events in world history" (Steiner 1993b) already resulted in speculation, conspiracy theories, and elitist demeanor in Steiner's lifetime, even within the anthroposophic community. Their evaluation requires careful and above all complex studies in order to grasp Steiner's contextualizations. A more profound examination of history which, like Lessing in his treatise *The Education of the Human Race* (Lessing 2003, p. 30f.), assumes repeated incarnations that ultimately confront individuals with the consequences of their own history and therefore allows them to develop further, would, consequently, according to its objective, have to ask about the meditative-contemplative foundations of such claims or about the phenomenon of esoteric culture. Only the latter would currently be able to connect with the established scientific understanding of history or the academic discourse of esoteric research (Schmidt 2008, p. 15ff.).

Steiner himself based his karma research on the view that each individual participated in different times and cultures in the past. He therefore concluded that these former incarnations are effective in the depth of each soul and can consequently be investigated. Bartoniczek, extending Steiner's "symptomatologic view of history," concludes that if one intensely studies historical ideas or, rather, if one deeply contemplates historical imaginations, an inner "sense," or soul organ, is activated through inner resonance, leading to the inner experience of the evidence of historical statements. Historical imaginations then become experiences of the reality of the past, from which individual historical insights could be derived (Bartoniczek 2014, p. 300ff.). Heisterkamp explains the problem that arises here, independently of the questions evoked by Steiner's idea of reincarnation, from the point of view of scientific theory: "The method of 'soul observation,' or the direct experience of spiritual phenomena in human cognition, which is essential to Steiner, appears to 'enlightened' science […] as a remnant of idealist philosophy and metaphysics and is consequently not taken seriously" (Heisterkamp 1989, p. 164). A preliminary decision is therefore required: one first needs to engage with Steiner's conceptual realism in order to be able to analyze his statements. Rejecting the reality of these contents means deciding against belief—on the level of belief: a scientific dilemma!

There does not seem to be any methodical awareness in the internal anthroposophic discourse of the question as to whether Steiner assumes a lawfully unfolding course of history that is suited to future prognoses (Steiner 1990, p. 153ff.), or whether he sees history as an open process. What is apparent in the numerous works on history and cultures is the eminent importance of Steiner's authorship for anthroposophy; and it is apparent from a reference model that either provides exegetic evidence of Steiner's statements or that uses them as evidence of an authority to whom access to higher or deeper spheres of consciousness is ascribed (Zech 2012, p. 89f.). But Steiner's understanding of history is in fact discussed controversially in anthroposophic circles. Because its reception is, on the one hand, characterized by the adoption of formulations by Steiner in which he—as in the above citation on the "ancient Indian" cultural period—includes in his narrative consecutive justifications for historical events (Bartoniczek 2014, p. 149). On the other hand, one ascribes to Steiner, referring to his early work, an open, non-teleological understanding of history whose historical and anthropological orientation contrasts with the narratives of national history (Bartoniczek 2014, p. 247f.; Lindenberg, p. 19ff.). For this reason alone, the attempt must be made to examine whether one can assume that Steiner had a consistent historical theory or differing, if not contradictory, concepts.

5 The background of Steiner's historical theory

In the various phases of Steiner's working life, three different methodical approaches to history can be identified:

* History in the epistemological writings before 1900
* Historiography in the theosophical tradition and terminology from 1901
* Steiner's symptomatologic approach to history from 1917

In addition, there are his analyses of contemporary history that permeate almost all of his presentations and lectures but gained particular pertinence during and after World War I. They will not be pursued further here, because they are more relevant for questions of method than of content, such as his view of Marxism, Central Europe, nationalism or *Deutschtum*, war guilt, etc.—topics that continue to be vehemently and controversially discussed even today and that would go beyond the margins of this study. For further reading, I recommend Osterrieder's comprehensive publication and the subsequent controversial discourse (Osterrieder 2014).

Steiner's statements on history and its method in his epistemological writings seem to clearly answer the question as to whether he had a teleological concept of history. In his book *Goethe's Theory of Knowledge*, Steiner expresses his basic view that "the sense-perceptible manifests [...] as a revelation of the spiritual" (Steiner 1979, p. 9). With this adaptation of Goethe's morphological phenomenology, Steiner defines himself as a monist who assumes that the world is reflected in human thinking, ascribing to thinking—as the philosopher Wolfgang Welsch does today (Welsch 2012, p. 150f.)—an affinity with the world and with human beings (since they have immediate experience of it), and therefore their possibility to relate to the processes and effects underlying the phenomena in reflecting on experiences. "Since we experience real lawfulness, ideal determination, only in thinking, the lawfulness of the rest of the world, which we do not experience in the world itself [because it cannot be directly perceived], must already be contained in thinking" (Steiner 1979, p. 48). By relating to the phenomena or experiences directly through thinking, we create reality (ibid., p. 55ff.). In order to free this reality from subjectivity, Steiner follows Goethe who asked that one should interact with the objects repeatedly, without preconceptions and selfish intentions so that these objects can be grasped through thinking and given the opportunity to "realize their lawfulness, to express their laws themselves, as it were" (ibid., p. 56). Perception thus provided "the one side of reality," while the other side was provided by taking hold of the world in thinking (ibid., p. 63). On this basis, Steiner then distinguishes the nature knowledge from scientific knowledge. He sees the former as the "conclusion of creation" since "thinking is the final step in the sequence of processes that form nature" (ibid., p. 115). For the latter, he sees entirely different preconditions: "Here, our consciousness deals with the actual spiritual content: with the individual human mind, with cultural creations, literature, successive scientific convictions, artistic creations. The spiritual is grasped by spirit. Reality already contains the idea, the lawfulness, within itself. [...] What, in the natural sciences, is a product of reflecting on the things is here intrinsic to them. Science plays a different role here. The *essence* is contained in the object even without the scientific effort. We are speaking here of human actions, creations, ideas; of the way we deal with ourselves and the rest of humankind" (ibid., p. 115f.).

Steiner's contemplations on history as a cultural product must be seen in this context. "The spirit only takes up the position within the world as a whole that it gives itself as an individual" (Steiner 1979, p. 117). It was therefore the purpose of the humanities to "carry the idea of the personality" (ibid., p. 117), that is, to do justice to the spirit of the creator of a theory or a scientific insight. Whereas in natural science the law or type explains the specific, in the humanities the universal is derived from, or always contains, the specific. Steiner concludes from this that, "If we can derive universal laws from history, these will only be such laws in that they were intended by historical personalities [those who effect history] as goals, as ideals" (ibid., p. 118). Natural science consequently proceeded from the conditioned to the conditioning, while history, as a spiritual science, proceeded from the conditioning to the conditioned, or the affected. Since what is told as history aims to assess what has been affected by individuals, history had to look for meaning in the intentions of those individuals. Historical events could therefore be seen as expressions of the spirit affecting them. "Therefore in history, which is always the history of the human being, we must not speak of the outer influences of human activity, of contemporary ideas, least of all of an underlying plan. History is nothing other than the unfolding of human activity, views, etc." (ibid., p. 127). Steiner continues, citing Goethe, "In all ages, it has been individuals rather than the age that affected science [...] All *a priori* constructions of plans that are meant to underly history go against *the historical method* that arises from the nature of history. [...] Our science of knowledge excludes the possibility of ascribing a purpose to history" (ibid., p. 127f.).

Steiner agrees with Goethe in rejecting the idea of a teleological concept. But because it is said that our actions as human beings are motivated by our thinking, Steiner continues, citing Goethe, historical facts are "determined by ideas. [...] History is essentially a science of ideas. Its reality consists of ideas. Devotion to the object is therefore the only correct method. Anything beyond that is unhistorical" (ibid., p. 128). According to Steiner, history found its meaning in assessing the motives and ideas of the actors; this is where the spiritual was to be found in history.

While working as a lecturer in rhetoric and cultural history at the Berlin Workers' School, which was founded by Wilhelm Liebknecht, Steiner also began, in 1900, to give lectures in the Theosophical Society in Berlin. His contemporaries, who knew him as the editor of Goethe's natural-scientific writings, an expert on Nietzsche, editor of a literary journal (*Magazin für Literatur*), critic and lecturer in the Giordano Bruno Society (which advocated ideological impartiality), saw him transforming from an intellectual to a spiritual esotericist (Ullrich 2012, p. 48). Steiner now not only adopted and modified the theosophical terminology in his writings and lectures but also presented himself to the public as a spiritual initiate, explaining that his statements were the result of his spiritual research. He kept pointing out that the problems of the time could only be resolved if these spiritual dimensions and the spiritual knowledge of higher worlds were considered. He conveyed to his readers and listeners, first as a theosophist and later, from 1912, as an anthroposophist, numerous insights gained from the spiritual-suprasensory research that, he claimed, was authentic and he himself had conducted it (Steiner 1995a, p. 15). During this phase, Steiner explained development and historical change with the influence of spiritual powers acting through personalities, the link between social and historical processes and ideological conflicts, and karmic conditions. Based on the theosophical terminology, he distinguished between the laws and structures of human and cosmic evolution, including the tasks and requirements for humanity's further advancement, and the announcement of future cultural conditions. Many anthroposophists understood and understand these descriptions as teleological revelations and orientations. Steiner's explanations of cultural history with its hebdomadal rhythms, human development of body, soul, and mind, and the post-Atlantean cultural periods, can be seen as anthroposophic orientation knowledge that has remained effective to this day. Ullrich concludes from these principles that Steiner's explicitly proclaimed evolutionary goal—our emancipation from evolutionary conditions, and the attainment of freedom and self-realization—did not constitute real freedom. Steiner preempts such reservations himself at the end of his central work on this evolutionary concept, *An Outline of Esoteric Science*: "If we believe that human freedom is incompatible with foreknowledge and with predestination of the shape of things to come, we should think of it like this: Our free action in the future will depend as little on what predestined things will be like then as it does on our intention to be living a year from now in a house we design today" (Steiner 1997, p. 396).

The question is whether Steiner did not from the start bring the concept of human evolution with its future-oriented structures together with the option of individual self-realization and therefore with his ideas of ethical individualism which he introduced in the 1890s. One can also follow Heisterkamp's thesis, presented above, and look at Steiner's evolutionary concept as a heuristic tool for describing the phenomena reflected in concrete cultures and events. What speaks for this view is that Steiner developed an anthropology (*Allgemeine Menschenkunde*) that can help to understand individual biographies and processes and to accompany them in education or self-development. Steiner's anthroposophic concepts of development could then be understood as ideal-typical rather than deterministic. Since this would contradict the above Goethe citation, used by Steiner to dismiss any conceptual, predetermined transformation of history as going against the science of history, it could be seen as including spiritual structures and cosmic influences from suprasensory realms as teleological conditions for human development. This teleological character is also noticeable in Steiner's conviction that development and progress underlieboth the events in the world and human self-realization. Steiner's metaphor of the house where, although it has been designed in a particular way, free life can take place, can therefore be interpreted as a dialogical understanding of reality between openness and conditions (*telos*).

On March 14, 1918, Steiner gave a public lecture in Berlin, introducing his symptomatologic approach to history (Steiner 1992a), which can be seen as a third way of looking at the phenomenon of history. On October 17, 1918 he spoke in Zurich, rejecting the kind of superficial anthropomorphism that projects natural laws on history: "When it comes to history, the temptation is particularly strong to project what we find in ourselves onto the historical events. We can overcome this only if we, in studying anthropology, go beyond the narrow boundaries of human nature characterized by the fact that we act directly according to the subjective purposes possible for us in our soul life between birth and death" (Steiner 1988b, p. 334f.). Steiner thus includes this kind of historical philosophy with his view of Goethean science that we first judge the phenomena we perceive on the basis of feeling and purpose, but that we can only achieve true knowledge if we overcome this self-orientation and realize that the phenomena themselves are an expression of their inner lawfulness (Steiner 1995a, p. 24ff.). The study of their appearance will then reveal their spiritual conditions. If we rise above our subjective self-focus, we will realize our spiritual potential (Steiner 1988b, p. 334). This is a direct reference to the idealism of Goethe's time. If we approach historical knowledge from such a supra-personal perspective, "history will no longer be the observation of consecutive facts, but it will be what I would call 'symptomatology.' We don't look at individual facts as they present themselves in the sense life, but we see them as symptoms that allow us to penetrate to the suprasensory, supra-historical events that lie concealed behind them. We will no longer strive for completeness, which can never be achieved anyway (anyone who has studied history will know this), but we will try to use the facts we discover and which we take as symptoms, in order to penetrate to the wider spiritual context that is hidden behind these symptoms" (Steiner 1988b, p. 336f.). Steiner then refers back to anthroposophy, describing its heuristic character: "History, once it has been fructified by spiritual science, will proceed from a purely factual to a symptomatologic science" (ibid., p. 337).

These statements seem to contain a critique of historicism, since Steiner is clearly not interested in outer causal relations or the provision of detailed evidence. He rather assumes that the outer events point to deeper layers of reality where the true events can be found. And these, he said, could be unlocked through knowledge gained from anthroposophy. The knowledge one aims for does not concern the events themselves but the processes of which they are symptomatic. This, he added, any constructivist theory claimed for itself today, but the difference was that these related to conceptual constructs rather than spiritual effects. Heisterkamp identifies this as clear conceptual realism (Heisterkamp 1989, p. 164). The question is where Steiner locates these spiritual processes: in cosmic events or in the motives for human actions that live in each of us as something specific rather than universal.

Six months after this first lecture, Steiner embarks on a series of nine lectures, stating right at the start that we need to see through the outer events, which are symptoms, and to penetrate to "the depths of events where the reality of human evolution will reveal itself" (Steiner 1987, p. 9). Historical events should be seen as something that "can lead to the underlying reality and reveal it if approached in the right way" (ibid., p. 10). This tells us that we need to move on methodically from the event, which is mere picture. Steiner establishes that "Symptomatologic history nonetheless needs to consider the outer facts, simply because the observation and evaluation of the outer facts opens up the possibility to gain insight into the true reality" (Steiner 1987, p. 10). Neither in these nor in later lectures does Steiner discuss his method in greater depth. Instead, he uses early modern events to show how they reflect emancipations away from a medieval worldview, self-directed individual actions, etc., describing them in anthroposophic terms as actions arising from the "consciousness soul," a mentality that reflects on itself and acts out of this consciousness. In stating that this level was characteristic of the fifth post-Atlantean period, he refers to the evolutionary structure outlined earlier in order to evaluate the quality that becomes apparent here. We realize how Steiner uses the results of his "spiritual science" to assign meaning to historical events.

Steiner has another reason for thinking that gaining historical insights is necessary, in that events are, in the Goethean sense, to be seen as expressions of underlying deeper processes. For in the lecture cited earlier, of November 7, 1917, he already stated under the heading of *Anthroposophy and History*, after speaking about other (cultural) historians, and after discussing dreaming as a state of consciousness, "The impulses that work and weave in history do not live in our waking consciousness, even if that sounds like a paradox, but we dream them" (Steiner 1988b, p. 75). He says this because, according to his epistemological explanations, the spiritual aspect of history comes to expression in each person and their actions. But Steiner points out here that we are mostly not fully conscious of our motives, or of the causes and effects of our actions. When children learn to walk and speak, they do this unconsciously without having clear targets in mind. History and its consequences were therefore realized through emotions and half-conscious actions, and only in looking back would it become clear what these tendencies were aiming at. This means that historical events need to be unlocked, similar to the analysis of dreams or research into myths. The events and the stories told about them are images whose complex depths need to be gradually unlocked. Steiner offers a method for this that arises from this anthroposophic schooling and his understanding of Goethe's method: "It is entirely scientific to speak of the dream of becoming. This becomes apparent when we realize that only a visionary consciousness can gain insight into the actual historical impulses: when we permeate these historical impulses with imaginative, inspired, living research" (Steiner 1988b, p. 75).

Steiner suggests here that the depths of important processes can be unlocked gradually and, as mentioned earlier, by historical researchers who develop a special sense for this. With this view, Steiner follows Wilhelm von Humboldt, who was also inspired by Goethe, and who wrote about the historiographer's task: "The events of history are even less open to be read than phenomena of the sensory world [...]. Their comprehension is but the erratic product of their properties and the meaning that the observer assigns to them" (Humboldt 1959, p. 164f.). Humboldt explains first that events gain significance as a result of the meaning the historiographer ascribes to them. Then he goes on to distinguish four layers that their historical consciousness relates to (ibid., p. 164ff.):

- The level of external facts that he calls the secretion and skeleton of the layers.
- The procedural level that he identifies as the contexts or life processes (such as rise and decline).
- The level of the psychological-mental motives of the actors in history.
- The level of ideas expressed in the historical events. These, he thinks, can be described but can never be fully assessed and explained (Zech 2012, p. 161ff.).

Steiner's method presupposes sensory training in the Goethean sense. Once this sense has been developed, which can be done through art, it first perceives historical events as images. "When we truly experience art inwardly, we are permeated by something that enables us to understand human nature in a certain way, we understand its pictorial nature [...]. Once we see through the things of reality, everything sense-perceptible becomes an image of the spiritual" (Steiner 1987, p. 113). What, then, speaks out of these events? Bartoniczek, who has examined Steiner's symptomatologic approach in depth, summarizes this step: "At this point, the need for 'inspired' cognition arises. This corresponds to the character of the symptom: In the phenomenon, the observed object is fully contained; in the symptom it reveals itself as lying behind the phenomenon" (Bartoniczek 2009, p. 177). From this arises, as an experience of evidence, or as an intuitive act in the individual, the relation to the idea that then lends meaning and significance to the historical event.

Bartoniczek interprets this process of deepened unlocking of symptoms in the anthroposophic sense as connecting to the level of soul and spirit, where we also realize ourselves as embodied individualities. He consequently assumes that the symptomatologic approach to history aims at the "will impulses underlying the historical gestures" (Bartoniczek 2009, p. 183) on the one hand, and, on the other hand, at "the individual deeds and destinies that come to expression in the different incarnations" (Bartoniczek 2009, p. 184), including the observer's.

Steiner's symptomatologic approach links his ethical individualism, which defines us as beings that emancipate themselves and become individualized in an open-ended development, to his ideal-typical concept of human and cosmic evolution. This is apparent, on the one hand, from his lectures on historical symptomatology (Steiner 1987), where he explicitly refers to his epistemological writings, and where he, on the other hand, constructs meaning by consulting anthroposophic ideas. The method alternates between consulting the anthroposophic concept of interpretation and the gradual cognitive act that occurs within the observer of history, an act that is meant to lead to historical meaningfulness and the individually experienced historical reality though the individual experience of evidence. We can see this as the kind of dialogic principle that can be inferred from Steiner's early epistemological considerations and the metaphysical framework gained from anthroposophy, his second access to history, that is. In other words: In every historical description, events that are realized openly by individuals, are integrated in a narrative that structures and usually also periodizes them. We can therefore speak of an anthroposophic narrative that goes back to Steiner. Depending on whether its content is received as authentic or epistemologically as reflexive, Steiner's cultural history is either scientifically inaccessible or suited to discussion.

The symptomatologic approach that raises historical events to the level of imaginative expression is realized—like any metaphor or image, and any historical narrative—in the relation between subject and world. Steiner explains the stream of history on the one hand with the spiritual-suprasensory activities of beings that effect evolution, and, on the other hand, with the cultural activities of a humanity that is becoming conscious of itself. The latter can be associated with constructivist approaches, while the former, with its esoteric-anthroposophic references to realms that can be spiritually explored, such as reincarnation, karma, and cosmic memory (Akashic Records), is fundamentally opposed to today's scientific approach.

6 The self-location of anthroposophy and Waldorf education

Before discussing the importance of Steiner's understanding of history for the pedagogical practice in Waldorf schools, I need to point out that Steiner himself located both his spiritual science and the professions and institutions that apply it in practice within his concept of cultural history (Zander 2007).[10] The Waldorf School was founded not only in response to the social and political conditions of the time but also as a cultural contribution, as the realization of a pedagogical concept, in the age of the "consciousness soul" (Zech 2012, p. 18f.). It was intended as an education that takes its cue from the individual child and that promotes individuation; an education that did not aim to serve the demands of societal standards and institutions at meeting but at releasing the potential each individual person can bring to society. "All teaching and education is to be derived from insight into the growing human being and each person's disposition. [...] We will not ask: What knowledge and skills does a person need to support the existing social order, but: What lives in a person and can be developed? Then the younger generation will always be able to bring new forces to the social order" (Steiner 1982, p. 37f.). Young people should not be taught to participate but to unfold their personality out of themselves, out of their spiritual potential, and to contribute to the progress of society. In the address Steiner gave at the foundation of the first Waldorf School, he made it clear that he saw the work of the first Waldorf teachers as one of historical dimensions. "If the Waldorf School is to bring about a renewal of today's spiritual life, it must be a true cultural enterprise" (Steiner 2020, p. 16). On the following day, he said to the first Waldorf teachers, "We must understand how important our task is, and we will understand this [...] if we look at the foundation of this school not as an everyday but as a celebratory act of cosmic dimensions" (ibid., p. 20). Steiner clearly links Waldorf education both with the challenges of his time and with the concept of evolution. The implications of the anthroposophic understanding of history for the Waldorf school therefore need to be examined at two levels, because history teaching is assigned a central role in the school's educational concept and the Waldorf school itself derives its cultural task from this understanding.

7 History in the Waldorf school

In my study of history teaching in Waldorf schools published in 2012, I came to the conclusion that "There is no doubt that Steiner's considerations on cultural history were not only known to the founding teachers of the Stuttgart Waldorf School, but that they informed their understanding of history in the long term. If, therefore, a history syllabus emerged in the first years of the Waldorf School that continues to inform the history curriculum to this day, we must assume that this dialogical curriculum development between Steiner as the main inspiration and the teachers in question referred not only to subject-related aspects but also to anthroposophically inspired concepts and ideas. While Steiner demanded that strictly no esoteric research or theory must flow into the teaching,[11] but that the idea of freedom and autonomy as a precondition for individuation was paramount, a concept of development grew from Steiner's anthroposophic ideas that saw the history of humanity as an ongoing emancipatory process toward individuation. This concept also centrally informs the view of history reflected in the Waldorf curriculum even today" (Zech 2011, p. 135).

In the preliminary discussions about the school foundation, Steiner already recommended to convey to students a cultural history that reflected the evolution of consciousness toward self-awareness and individual self-realization. Stockmeyer, one of the founding teachers, noted down in a meeting on May 25, 1919, "Historical concepts, pre-Christian, post-Christian, Indian, Persian, Egyptian-Chaldean, Greco-Roman culture" (Stockmeyer 1989, p. 658). Steiner clearly intended history teaching in the Waldorf school from the start as cultural history based on his anthroposophic periodization. This basic concept, while faithfully perpetuated, was continually updated in the course of the 20th century, through adaption to new scientific insights and inclusion of prevailing social and political challenges (Zech 2012, p. 276ff.).

In their internal discourse, Waldorf teachers today do not see history teaching as a way toward national or political identity formation but as a cultural task in the history of humanity. The literature and curricula on history teaching reveal that it is meant to inspire students to discover their humanity within the diversity of cultures and in respect for the individuality.[12] Any kind of discrimination or hierarchization of lifestyles, worldviews, and cultures was to be avoided (*Stuttgart Declaration* of German Waldorf School Association of 2007). According to the schools' self-concept, history teaching aimed at promoting individuality by historically exploring the diverse ways of life and global cultural conditions (Esterl 2005, p. 10ff.). This happened currently in the face of social, political, and cultural challenges (interculturality and global interconnectedness) and in the struggle for human dignity and humaneness (Zech 2012, p. 332ff.).

The Waldorf curriculum is informed, on the one hand, by the anthropology and developmental psychology of adolescence, in that content and method are chosen to support the processes of maturation in a way that is appropriate to the young people's age and stage of development (Zech 2012, p. 280ff.), and on the other hand by the goal of supporting the development of individual historical awareness that includes knowledge of the roots of their own culture and the exploration of the global diversity of cultures (Schmelzer 2000, p. 17ff.). According to Lindenberg, history teaching must not lead to defined explanatory models (Lindenberg 1981, p. 33ff.). Instead, it should promote identity formation, openness toward (other) cultures, and a global orientation through the study of earlier and different ways of acting, forms of life, and values (Zech 2014, p. 96f.). This required adolescents to become aware

- of history's temporal dimension and structure,
- of history's truth content (its factual and documented foundation as opposed to fictionality),
- of the historical changes of culture and human consciousness and their diverse global appearance and manifestation,
- of the origin of their own culture and its influence on their self-concept as distinct from that of other and foreign cultures,
- of mutual influences, interdependence, and exchange between cultures,
- of current and previous political conditions,
- of current and previous technological and economic conditions,
- of their narrations' dependence on consciousness-based questions.

Level 1 Historical orientation in space and time

Fifth to eighth grades: Chronology from prehistory to the present time

Level 2 *Historical judgment*

Ninth grade: Early Modern period to the present
Tenth grade: Prehistory to Greek antiquity
11th grade: Roman antiquity to the Middle Ages

Level 3 *Reflection of historical consciousness*

12th grade: Philosophy of history, overviews and analysis of the present

---

Figure 8.1   History curriculum

High school students should realize that history is a human-made narration about the past that tries to grasp and express past contexts and meaning, cites traditional interpretations, seeks to explain the current situation, and to open up perspectives for the expected future. History itself is therefore always subject to change and depends on scientific findings, political interpretation, and the evolving human consciousness. In Waldorf schools, this subject aims to inspire individual knowledge about history as a cultural product in whose origin, interpretation, and continuation students actively participate.[13]

The history curriculum provides the framework for building or enabling this level of differentiation in the students. Two history main lessons per year are envisaged for fifth grade, each lasting two to four weeks, with daily around 105 minutes' exposure. The topics of these teaching blocks usually relate to a historical period or developmental context (such as "The Age of Exploration and Discovery"). Structures follow Stockmeyer's interpretation of Steiner's indications (Stockmeyer 2001, p. 171f.), which means that, between 5th and 12th grade, history is explored on three levels. Building on the local history and life skills periods and the story material of grades 1–4, a first journey through cultural history up to the present time follows from grades 5–8. In ninth grade, the modern period is studied again with a different methodical approach. In 10th grade, history lessons start again with pre- and early history; in 11th grade, these are continued up to the end of the Middle Ages. A second journey through history follows in 12th grade, when a horizontal and vertical overview adds a third level of reflection.

According to the curriculum, high school students should be encouraged to develop their own narration based on their questions and their synopsis of different phenomena in the historical context. This makes them active contributors to the historical culture.[14]

In keeping with the educational concept of Waldorf schools, the entire history curriculum aims to support the students' biographical development toward autonomy, orientation ability, and an open identity concept. In order to promote the independent, increasingly factually founded, and reflected judgment that is necessary for this, there is a specific concept for the gradual building of historical competence (Zech 2012, p. 259ff.).

Numerous internal disquisitions on Waldorf history teaching refer to Steiner's symptomatologic understanding of history. Both Lindenberg and Schmelzer demonstrate, on the basis of concrete lesson content, how teachers—based on their presentation and their exploration of textual and pictorial sources—inspire in students a way of working that leads to historical judgment and conceptualization. The study of these disquisitions shows that this history of culture and of humanity initially followed the 19th-century tradition of universal history, but from the 1970s onward, increasingly took its cue from an understanding of culture that, though still Eurocentric, was oriented toward multivalency and multiperspectivity (Zech 2012, p. 28ff.). Even if Steiner's understanding of history is still sometimes received as teleological and cyclical in the anthroposophic context, the narrative underlying history teaching in Waldorf schools rather follows the historical development toward a society of individuals and therefore the kind of approach to history that is expressed in Steiner's epistemological theses (Steiner 1979, p. 16ff.). In my observation, subject teachers refer to up-to-date research results and materials that convey culture as a multilayered and open process rather than a determined picture of the world.

Waldorf schools place high value on a living impartation of historical content. The teacher-told stories play a particular part in grades 5–8, when history is not usually taught by specialist teachers but by the grades teachers who teach most subjects at that stage. This approach is not only meant to provide a first historical orientation in time and space but, above all, to spark interest in historical change. History is told as the manifestation of human actions and decisions. The historical ideas inspired by this presentation of concrete historical images lead first to an emotional and therefore subjective involvement of the students. This is deepened further in working with source texts, pictures, and maps, and then formulated in the students' own words into a written or oral narrative: The acquisition of historical content manifests in texts, sketches, the drawing of maps, and timelines, which form the foundation for the reflective and narrative skills required later in high school. Instead of approaching history with analytical distance, Waldorf education continues, in grades 5–8, to evoke inner images of history—orientation knowledge, in other words—and, above all, to inspire lasting interest. This is the reason why in Waldorf school— unlike in regular schools—history continues to be a subject that is not negatively connoted.

It should be mentioned that Waldorf schools do not always manage to do justice to the requirement of reflected and (self-)reflexive narration. Even in Waldorf schools, many history teachers see their task primarily in imparting knowledge and hardly reflect on the interpretational authority they establish with their presentations and canonization of content. It becomes particularly problematic when history and Steiner's anthroposophic accounts of history, in particular, are naïvely received by teachers and carried into the lessons (Zech 2014, p. 97). This has fortunately become rare now because teacher education and professional development unambiguously support the application of factual validity, scientific rigor, and reflection. From ninth grade, history is taught by qualified subject teachers who are required to make sure that their students learn to analyze historical presentations and to compose their own historical narrations according to modern narration criteria, rather than merely absorb and reproduce lesson content. This is meant to promote a historical consciousness that observes and reflects the narrative act with regard to its preconditions and structures.

8 History teaching in Waldorf schools

Although history teaching in Waldorf schools is one of few alternatives to the concepts of regular state schools, it has so far not been recognized by the relevant academic discourse. History has been taught in Waldorf schools for more than 90 years and is presently practiced with more than 80,000 students in Germany. It is a subject for which no empirical knowledge is available and whose curriculum has hardly been discussed. The reasons for this have been stated at the beginning and have to do with specific obstacles which prevent discourse. Educationists and history teachers shy away from scientific discourse because Waldorf education cannot be clearly separated from the esoteric-anthroposophic ideas of its founder, Rudolf Steiner. They are afraid that, in looking more closely, they might step on scientifically dubitable terrain. But Waldorf education has been practiced since 1919 based on an intensive internal discourse that has manifested in numerous publications. This discourse does, however, tend to refer to Rudolf Steiner's ideas and, although it has always referred to scientific insights, it hardly ever actively reached the academic level. As a result, by now more than 230 Waldorf schools in Germany, with their teacher education centers and research institutes, have the character of an inaccessible pedagogical subculture, which is also the reason why the history curriculum and history teaching remain largely scientifically unexplored.

It has been established that the Waldorf school curriculum favors an approach based on the history of cultures and of consciousness. This is reflected in 12th and 13th grades in an outline of the history of the world that includes aspects of the philosophy of history and of narration theory, adding a vertical (depth) structure to the horizontal time structure. Based on this goal, links can be established to the discourses on history teaching regarding world history, historical awareness, and historical competences. The following paragraphs are a summary of my more in-depth study regarding connections that could be established between the approach to history teaching in Waldorf schools and the discourse on history teaching at the levels mentioned (Zech 2012).

Hans-Jürgen Pandel and Michele Barricelli recently highlighted the importance of narrative competence. Pandel summarizes his view in the statement "Presentation is the highest discipline in dealing with history" (Pandel 2010, p. 38). He introduces his profound 2010 publication *Historisches Erzählen* (historical narration) with a clarification that seems to be suited to this context, too: "The term 'narration' still causes confusion. For some, it belongs to fiction rather than science, for others it designates a method to be used with young children, who are still at the fairytale stage and who need to be prepared through narration for 'real history.' In high schools, narration that only requires the lowest level of knowledge is not considered adequate. In the science of history, the term is even negatively connoted. Narration, telling stories, is seen as a methodically naïve story of events that lacks theory and reflection, and that modern historical researchers look down upon" (Pandel 2010, p. 7).

Pandel's thesis is that "historiography *is* narration." He points out that every time we create coherence through narration, we also provide interpretation and explanation. History teaching is consequently above all about "the students' narrative competence" (Pandel 2010, p. 8). Referring to Jörn Rüsen's narrativity theory axiom, which states that historical narration is the construction of meaning regarding experiences in time (Rüsen 2001, p. 67), Barricelli, in his study *Schüler erzählen Geschichten* (Students Tell Stories), also defines narrative competence as the most important educational goal of history learning: "Telling stories needs to be learned. Any form of intelligence that paves the way to controlled historical narration and therefore to the special form of knowledge that we call history, shall here be referred to as narrative competence. In analogy to the criterion of meaning in historical thinking, narrative competence acts as a meta-principle or overarching orientation in the scientific practice of history teaching. This is precisely why narrative competence is called the central, even 'highest learning target' of historical learning (and that is fundamentally different from learning from history" (Barricelli 2005, p. 8). In his contribution on *the lasting relevance of narrative competence for historical learning*, he therefore deplores that narrative competence was marginalized, or even substituted, in currently discussed competence models (Barricelli 2008, p. 142ff.). He requests instead that "Above all, history teaching must – to a much greater extent and more intentionally – become, in itself, a narrative event" (Barricelli 2008, p. 148). Even the paradigm of working with source materials, which continues to be well-guarded in Germany, needed to take a backseat, since this—and this is also aimed at Pandel—"much too often stops dead before the step of constructing meaning through the narrative, which is essential for finalizing the learning process" (Barricelli 2008, p. 148; Pandel 2010, p. 9). Bodo von Borries also concludes from his study into the understanding of history: "It is unsettling for evaluation experts when students learn to methodically deal with individual sources and events, but do not acquire themselves the ability to absorb, process, and produce stories about greater contexts. Orientation to method and sources—inevitable as they may be—do clearly not solve the problem of fragmentation and particularization; they may even aggravate it by destroying the great (fictional and mythical) national master stories" (Borries 2008, p. 73).

It has been shown that the reflection and presentation of historical contexts is a declared aim of history teaching in Waldorf schools. It should therefore satisfy the requirements mentioned here. In how far the empirically tested practice results in a different picture from that of the experts in history teaching cited here remains unclear. Skepticism may be recommendable, given that hardly any methodical accounts based on narrativity theory are available in the relevant literature for history teachers in Waldorf schools. But it is also true to say that the history teaching in Waldorf schools does—as described—offer an analyzable curriculum and method for building up narrative competence.

Similar to those who reject national histories as a basis for history lessons and history teaching, the curriculum recommendations and literature for Waldorf schools also state that—not only due to the cultural diversity but also due to the concomitant conflicts and crises of identity—the need for historical orientation must be permanently stimulated. This balancing act, as well as independent learning and the autonomous activation of historical and cultural competence, require above all the ability to pose and pursue questions. This educational goal can be linked to the work within the research project on historical competence, FUER[15] (Zech 2012, p. 319ff.). Susanne Popp, one of the leading experts in history teaching in the discourse on teaching from a global historical perspective, also singles out the competence to question historical presentations as most essential for an independent, reflexive historical consciousness. She concludes that "Learners can only develop perceptual and questioning competence that is oriented to global history and that enables them to contribute ever more actively and independently to the exploration of perspectives of world history, if we enable them to rehearse a particular approach and ensure that contexts become visible that go beyond the individual periods and themes" (Popp 2005, p. 503). This suggests that history can contribute to the self-concept that we are realizing today in the field of divergent perspectives of one humanity, cultural diversity, and our individual uniqueness.

The concept of history teaching in Waldorf schools also emphasizes individuality and seeks to inspire the autonomous construction of meaning in the diversity of cultures and attitudes to life. Dietrich Esterl, for example, writes in his introduction to history teaching in Waldorf schools, "It is important that students develop a sense for the diversity of consciousness and of ways of life in the different cultures that continue to be effective below the surface" (Esterl 2005, p. 33). What he means is that we need to promote an understanding of history based on respect for cultural and individual diversity.

It is tangible how the representatives of history teaching in Waldorf schools and of modern positions in history teaching meet here and this can help to overcome the obstacles to discourse outlined above. For in Waldorf schools, too, the forming of collective and ideological identities is often prevented because of the simplification of complex cultural processes. The currently practiced approach, on the other hand, aims at multiperspectivity, reflexivity, and above all at dialog on stories and on history. At present, this is a requirement that neither Waldorf teachers nor teachers in regular schools are able to do justice to. Since, in Waldorf schools, historical orientation serves the individual's self-concept and personal development, historical consciousness ultimately merges with the individual's general consciousness. In Waldorf schools, the competence to ask questions is consequently not only seen as a starting point for the reconstruction of historical orientation on a new level, but also as an open-ended goal of history teaching.

Standards, insofar as they describe stages and developmental steps in building historical thinking, which includes methodical subject-related competences and the terminological preconditions for interpretive competence, can be derived from the curriculum of Waldorf schools. However, they are not so much used for the purpose of control or performance assessment but rather for dealing with developmental tasks. In my study into history teaching in Waldorf schools, I conclude that "despite the partly differing educational perspectives associated with building competence and developing historical consciousness in Waldorf schools, or in the discourse on history teaching, it is possible to describe the quality of Waldorf lessons, too, with the competence models that are currently developed. It emerges that similar goals are being pursued on different pathways. It would therefore be interesting to continue to examine the quality of the Waldorf-specific concept both theoretically and empirically with a view to building the partial competences that are defined differently in the different competence models" (Zech 2012, p. 363).

In order to develop history lessons that do justice to our hybrid intercultural situation and that also must be suited to inclusive learning, discourse can certainly be fruitful for the didactics of history and for education in general.

Notes

1 Zander's critical study of Steiner's statements on cultural history can be found under the heading *Theosophy*, the concept of the historical self-image of anthroposophy under the subheading *Historism and Theosophy* (Zander 2007, p. 545 ff.).
2 Gabert (1967), Lindenberg (1982), Heisterkamp (1989), Bartoniczek (2009, 2014).
3 Tautz (1969), Lindenberg (1997), Schmelzer (2003a), Zech (2012).

4 Spengler also describes the older cultures as races but does explicitly not use the term in a biological sense but as a "cosmic" category. He clearly distances himself from the antisemitism of this time. The outline is taken from Spengler (2014, p. 599 ff.) and from the time charts on p. 70 ff.

5 Steiner refers to Lessing, Gibbon, Wolff, F. Schiller, Goethe, Hegel, Comte, Schopenhauer, Nietzsche, von Lasaulx, J. Burckhardt, H. Grimm, Mauthner, Spencer (Steiner 1988b).

6 For an in-depth description of the training method that aims at the expansion of consciousness cf. Steiner (1976, p. 222 ff.)

7 His basic epistemological work *The Philosophy of* Freedom (Steiner 1995b), to which he refers frequently in his later writings and lectures, claims in its subtitle that it is the basis of a modern conception of life developed by scientific methods. In the introductions to his basic writings *Theosophy* (Steiner 1995a, p. 15) and *An Outline of Esoteric Science* (Steiner 1976, p. 7 ff.), Steiner also insists that he expects his spiritual scientific findings to be pitted against the thinking and understanding of the natural sciences.

8 Steiner refers, for example, to W. Scott Elliot's description of Atlantis (Steiner 1990, p. 24).

9 Schad, Schmelzer, and Guttenhöfer (2009), Osterrieder and Guttenhöfer (2008).

10 His theses are discussed, and some of them called into question, in Ravagli's reply (Ravagli 2009).

11 Stockmeyer comments on Steiner's demand by saying that "The anthroposophists should adapt method and organization but never teach anthroposophy. First of all we need to understand spiritual freedom. Ideological schools must be avoided most of all" (Stockmeyer 2001, p. 5). The fact that Steiner stated this repeatedly suggests that he had to explicitly point it out to the anthroposophically oriented teachers.

12 Lindenberg (1981), Schmelzer (2000, 2003b), Esterl (2005), Zech (2012).

13 List and text from my contribution on History to the fully revised new edition of Waldorf Curriculum in Richter, Tobias (ed.): Pädagogischer Auftrag und Unterrichtsziele – vom Lehrplan der Waldorfschule. Stuttgart: Freies Geistesleben, published in 2016.

14 A section in this book is devoted to the special character of the curriculum as an orientation for teachers to individually implement a syllabus based on individual competence, and of the tension between curriculum and the teacher's autonomy (Zech 2013a, p. 20 ff.; 2013b, p. 28 ff.). For a more detailed account on the autonomy of Waldorf schools and Waldorf teachers cf. Götte (2006, p. 87 ff.).

15 Among the main contributors to the FUER research project for the promotion and development of reflected historical consciousness are Waltraud Schreiber, Bodo von Borries, Wolfgang Hasberg, and Andreas Körber (www1.ku-eichstaett.de/GGF/Didaktik/Projekt/html/left_ziele.html).

References

Armstrong, Karen (2005): Eine kurze Geschichte des Mythos. Berlin: Berlin Verlag.

Barricelli, Michele (2005): Schüler erzählen Geschichte. Narrative Kompetenz im Geschichtsunterricht. Schwalbach: Wochenschau Verlag.

Barricelli, Michele (2008): "The story we're going to try and tell." Zur andauernden Relevanz der narrativen Kompetenz für das historische Lernen. In: Zeitschrift für Geschichtsdidaktik. Jahresband 2008. Schwalbach: Wochenschau Verlag, p. 142–147.

Bartoniczek, Andre (2009): Imaginative Geschichtserkenntnis. Rudolf Steiner und die Erweiterung der Geschichtswissenschaft. Stuttgart: Freies Geistesleben.

Bartoniczek, Andre (2014): Die Zukunft entdecken. Grundlagen des Geschichtsunterrichts. Stuttgart: Freies Geistesleben.

Beckers, Frank (2011): Umrisse des Kulturbegriffs der Kulturgeschichte von der Aufklärung bis zur Gegenwart. In: Kuhn, Bärbel/Popp, Susanne (Eds.) (2011): Kulturgeschichtliche Traditionen der Geschichtsdidaktik. St. Ingbert: Röhrig Universitätsverlag, pp. 15–37.

Borries, Bodo von (2008): Historisch denken lernen – Welterschließung statt Epochenüberblick. Geschichte als Unterrichtsfach und Bildungsaufgabe. Opladen, Framington Hills: Budrich.

Burckhardt, Jacob (1978): Weltgeschichtliche Betrachtungen. Stuttgart: Kröner.

Brüll, Ramon/Heisterkamp, Jens (2008): Frankfurter Memorandum: Rudolf Steiner und das Thema Rassismus. Schlussfassung, September 2008. Mit Anhängen zur Entstehung und offiziellen Stellungnahmen zum Thema. Online: https://info3-verlag.de/wp-content/uploads/2018/08/Frankfurter_Memorandum_Deutsch.pdf (accessed: October 2022).

Esterl, Dietrich (2005): Was geschieht in Geschichte? Stuttgart: Freies Geistesleben.

Gabert, Erich (1967): Die Weltgeschichte und das Menschen-Ich. Eine Einführung in die Geschichtsauffassung Rudolf Steiners. Stuttgart: Freies Geistesleben.

Götte, Wenzel (2006): Erfahrungen mit der Schulautonomie. Das Beispiel der Waldorfschulen. Stuttgart: Freies Geistesleben.

Heisterkamp, Jens (1989): Weltgeschichte als Menschenkunde. Untersuchungen zur Geschichtsauffassung Rudolf Steiners. Dornach: Spicker.

Humboldt, Wilhelm von (1959): Betrachtungen über die bewegenden Ursachen der Weltgeschichte. Über die Aufgaben des Geschichtsschreibers. In: Rossmann, Kurt (Ed.) (1959): Deutsche Geschichtsphilosophie von Lessing bis Jaspers. Birsfelden-Basel: Schipli-Doppler.

Kaiser, Ulrich (2004): Mythos Atlantis. In: Erziehungskunst. Zeitschrift zur Pädagogik Rudolf Steiners. Dezember 2004, pp. 1344–1353.

Kerényi, Karl (Ed.) (1982): Die Eröffnung des Zugangs zum Mythos. Ein Lesebuch. Darmstadt: Wissenschaftliche Buchgesellschaft.

Jung, Carl Gustav (2001): Archetypen. München: Deutscher Taschenbuch Verlag.

Lessing, Gotthold Ephraim (2003): Die Erziehung des Menschengeschlechts und andere Schriften. Stuttgart: Reclam.

Lindenberg, Christoph (1981): Geschichte lehren. Thematische Anregungen zum Lehrplan. Stuttgart: Freies Geistesleben.

Lindenberg, Christoph (1982): Die symptomatologische Geschichtsbetrachtung Rudolf Steiners. Einführung. In: Steiner, Rudolf (1982): Geschichtserkenntnis. Zur Symptomatologie der Geschichte. Vorträge, selected and edited by C. Lindenberg. Stuttgart: Freies Geistesleben, pp. 145–161.

Lindenberg, Christoph (1997): Geschichtsunterricht an Waldorfschulen. In: Bergmann, Klaus/Fröhlich, Klaus/Kuhn, Annette (Eds.) (1997): Handbuch der Geschichtsdidaktik. 5th revised edition. SeelzeVelber: Kallmeyer'sche Verlagsbuchhandlung, pp. 555–559.

Osterrieder, Markus/Guttenhöfer, Peter (2008): Die Durchlichtung der Welt. Alt-Iranische Geschichte. Kassel: Pädagogische Forschungsstelle beim Bund der Freien Waldorfschulen.

Osterrieder, Markus (2014): Welt im Umbruch. Nationalitätenfrage, Ordnungspläne und Rudolf Steiners Haltung im Ersten Weltkrieg. Stuttgart: Freies Geistesleben.

Pandel, Hans-Jürgen (2010): Historisches Erzählen. Narrativität im Geschichtsunterricht. Schwalbach: Wochenschau Verlag.

Popp, Susanne (2005): Antworten auf neue Herausforderungen. Welt- und globalgeschichtliche Perspektivierung des historischen Lernens. In: GWU 56, issue 9, pp. 491–507.

Martins, Ansger (2012): Rassismus und Geschichtsmetaphysik. Esoterischer Darwinismus und Freiheitsphilosophie bei Rudolf Steiner. Frankfurt am Main: Info 3 Verlagsgesellschaft.

Ravagli, Lorenzo (2009): Zanders Erzählungen. Eine kritische Analyse des Werks "Anthroposophie in Deutschland." Berlin: Wissenschaftsverlag.

Rüsen, Jörn (2001): Zerbrechende Zeit. Über den Sinn von Geschichte. Cologne: Böhlau.

Schad, Albrecht/Schmelzer, Albert/Guttenhöfer, Peter (2009): Der Kulturmensch der Urzeit. Vom Archaikum bis an die Schwelle der Sesshaftwerdung. Kassel: Pädagogische Forschungsstelle beim Bund der Freien Waldorfschulen.

Schmelzer, Albert (2000): Wer Revolutionen machen will … Zum Geschichtsunterricht der 9. Klasse an Waldorfschulen. Stuttgart: Freies Geistesleben.

Schmelzer, Albert (2003a): Prinz und König im Land des Möglichen. Entwicklungspsychologie und Kulturentwicklung, Basisbeitrag. In: Praxis Geschichte 3/2003, pp. 6–11.

Schmelzer, Albert (2003b): Aktuelles Mittelalter. Zum Geschichtsunterricht der 11. Klasse an Waldorfschulen. Stuttgart: Freies Geistesleben.

Schmidt, Robin (2008): Akademische Esoterikforschung und Anthroposophie. Perspektiven eines Paradigmenwechsels. In: Die Drei. Zeitschrift für Anthroposophie in Wissenschaft, Kunst und sozialem Leben, 3/2008, pp. 15–32.

Spengler, Oswald (2014): Der Untergang des Abendlandes. Umrisse einer morphologischen Weltgeschichte. Berlin: Albatros.

Steiner, Rudolf (1976): Geheimwissenschaft im Umriss. TB 601. Rudolf Steiner GA 13. Dornach: Rudolf Steiner Verlag. English translation: Steiner, Rudolf (1997): An Outline of Esoteric Science. Trans. Catherine Creeger. Hudson, NY: Anthroposophic Press.

Steiner, Rudolf (1979): Grundlinien einer Erkenntnistheorie der Goetheschen Weltanschauung mit besonderer Rücksicht auf Schiller. GA 2. 7th edition. Dornach: Rudolf Steiner Verlag.

Steiner, Rudolf (1982): Freie Schule und Dreigliederung. In Steiner, Rudolf (1982): Aufsätze über die Dreigliederung des sozialen Organismus und zur Zeitlage 1915–1921. GA 24. Dornach: Rudolf Steiner Verlag, pp. 35–43.

Steiner, Rudolf (1983): Menschengeschichte im Lichte der Geistesforschung. Sixteen public lectures in Berlin, October 19, 1911 to March 28, 1912. GA 61. 2nd edition. Dornach: Rudolf Steiner Verlag.

Steiner, Rudolf (1987): Geschichtliche Symptomatologie. Nine lectures given in Dornach from October 18 to November 3, 1918. TB (GA 185). 2nd edition. Dornach: Rudolf Steiner Verlag.

The Anthroposophic Understanding of History

Steiner, Rudolf (1988a): Ägyptische Mythen und Mysterien. Twelve lectures given in Leipzig from September 2 to 14, 1908. TB 660 (GA 106). Dornach: Rudolf Steiner Verlag.

Steiner, Rudolf (1988b): Die Ergänzung heutiger Wissenschaft durch Anthroposophie. TB (GA 73). 2nd edition. Dornach: Rudolf Steiner Verlag.

Steiner, Rudolf (1989): Das Christentum als mystische Tatsache und die Mysterien des Altertums. GA 8. 9th edition. Dornach: Rudolf Steiner Verlag.

Steiner, Rudolf (1990): Aus der Akasha-Chronik. TB (GA 11). Dornach: Rudolf Steiner Verlag.

Steiner, Rudolf (1992a): Allgemeine Menschenkunde als Grundlage der Pädagogik. Menschenkunde und Erziehungskunst, erster Teil. 14 lectures given in Stuttgart from August 21 to September 5, 1919 and address given on August 20, 1919. TB (GA 293). Dornach: Rudolf Steiner Verlag. English translation in Steiner, Rudolf (2020): The First Teachers' Course. Anthropological Foundations-Methods of Teaching-Practical Discussions. GA 293–295. Trans. Margot M. Saar. Bangkok: Ratayakom.

Steiner, Rudolf (1992b): Das Ewige in der Menschenseele. Unsterblichkeit und Freiheit. GA 67. Dornach: Rudolf Steiner Verlag.

Steiner, Rudolf (1993a): Die Mystik im Aufgange des neuzeitlichen Geisteslebens und ihr Verhältnis zur modernen Weltanschauung. GA 7. Dornach: Rudolf Steiner Verlag.

Steiner, Rudolf (1993b): Okkulte Geschichte. Esoterische Betrachtungen karmischer Zusammenhänge von Persönlichkeiten und Ereignissen der Weltgeschichte. Six lectures given in Stuttgart from December 27, 1910 to January 1, 1911. TB 707 (GA 126). Dornach: Rudolf Steiner Verlag.

Steiner, Rudolf (1995a): Theosophie. Einführung in die übersinnliche Welterkenntnis und Menschenbestimmung. GA 9. Dornach: Rudolf Steiner Verlag.

Steiner, Rudolf (1995b): Die Philosophie der Freiheit. Grundzüge einer modernen Weltanschauung. Seelische Beobachtungsresultate nach naturwissenschaftlicher Methode. GA 4. Dornach: Rudolf Steiner Verlag.

Steiner, Rudolf (2005): Die Krisis der Gegenwart und der Weg zu gesundem Denken. Ten public lectures given in Stuttgart between March 2 and November 10, 1920. GA 335. Dornach: Rudolf Steiner Verlag.

Stockmeyer, E.A. Karl (1989): Die Entfaltung der Idee der Waldorfschule im Sommer 1919. In: Erziehungskunst 53, issue 8–9, pp. 654–667.

Stockmeyer, E.A. Karl (2001): Angaben Rudolf Steiners für den Waldorfschulunterricht. Stuttgart: Manuskriptdruck der Pädagogischen Forschungsstelle beim Bund der Freien Waldorfschulen (Manuskriptdruck, 6th edition 2006).

Stuttgart Declaration of the German Waldorf Schools' Association of October 28, 2007. Online at www.waldorfschule.de/fileadmin/downloads/erklaerung/StuttgarterErklarung.pdf (accessed: October 2022).

Tautz, Johannes (1969): Zur Methode des Geschichtsunterrichts an der Freien Waldorfschule. In: Mielitz, Reinhard (1969): Das Lehren der Geschichte. Methoden des Geschichtsunterrichts in Schule und Universität. Göttingen: Vandenhoeck & Ruprecht.

Ullrich, Heiner (2011): Rudolf Steiner. Leben und Lehre. Munich: Beck.

Ullrich, Heiner (2012): Befremdlicher Anachronismus oder zukunftweisendes Modell? – Die Freie Waldorfschule im pädagogischen Diskurs und in der erziehungswissenschaftlichen Forschung. In: Hansen Schaberg, Inge (Ed.) (2012): Reformpädagogische Schulkonzepte. Vol. 6. Waldorfpädagogik. Baltmannsweiler: Schneider, pp. 220–266.

Welsch, Wolfgang (2012): Mensch und Welt. Eine evolutionäre Perspektive der Philosophie. Munich: Beck.

Zander, Helmut (2007): Anthroposophie in Deutschland. Theosophische Weltanschauung und gesellschaftliche Praxis 1884 bis 1945. 2 vols. Göttingen: Vandenhoeck & Ruprecht.

Zech, M. Michael (2011): Didaktische Überlegungen zur vertieften Behandlung von Frühgeschichte an der Waldorfschule. In: Hesse, Sibylla/Voß, Thomas/Zech, M. Michael (2011): Göbekli Tepe und der Prozess der Sesshaftwerdung. Von der Archäologie zur historischen Erkenntnis. Kassel: Pädagogische Forschungsstelle beim Bund der Freien Waldorfschulen.

Zech, M. Michael (2012): Der Geschichtsunterricht an Waldorfschulen. Genese und Umsetzung des Konzepts vor dem Hintergrund des aktuellen geschichtsdidaktischen Diskurses. Frankfurt am Main: Peter Lang.

Zech, M. Michael (2013a): Waldorfschule als Beispiel gelebter Schulautonomie auf dem freien Markt. In: Randoll, Dirk/da Veiga, Marcello (Eds.) (2013): Waldorfpädagogik in Praxis und Ausbildung. Zwischen Tradition und notwendigen Reformen. Wiesbaden: Springer VS, pp. 11–24.

Zech, M. Michael (2013b): Die Gründungsidee der Waldorfschule und das Problem der Schul- bzw. Lehrerautonomie im internationalen Kontext. In: Barz, Heiner (Ed.) (2013): Unterricht an Waldorfschulen. Berufsbild Waldorflehrer: Neue Perspektiven zu Praxis, Forschung und Ausbildung. Wiesbaden: Springer VS, pp. 21–51.

Zech, M. Michael (2014): Geschichte als Sinnstiftung und das Wirklichkeitsproblem. In: RoSE – Research on Steiner Education, Vol. 5, Special issue 2014, pp. 90–99. Online at www.rosejourn.com/index.php/rose/article/view/210/219

CHAPTER 9

Individual Topics

INTERCULTURAL EDUCATION AND WALDORF EDUCATION

An Inspiring Encounter

Albert Schmelzer

1 Starting point and research questions

Thanks to the findings of empiric education research in recent decades, a central problem of the German education system has been uncovered: the structural discrimination against children and young people with a migrant background. As recently as June 2014, the education report stated that not much had changed since 2005 in the risk group of "children with a migrant background from uneducated, economically disadvantaged social strata." A third of young adults between 30 and 35 with a migrant background still have no vocational or academic qualification, a figure three times as high as for the same age group with a German cultural background (Autorengruppe Bildungsberichterstattung 2014 [authors' group Education Report 2014]).

Given this difficult situation that has existed since the 1970s, intercultural education established itself as a specific new discipline, and numerous concepts and programs have been developed.[1]

Waldorf schools have largely been bypassed by this debate, for one main reason: While they, too, have children with a migrant background, most of these children belong—like their peers—to the "educated middle classes" (Barz/Randoll 2007). This is presumable mostly due to the school fees that Waldorf schools need to charge because of insufficient state funding, but there is also a cultural threshold: Deciding to send one's child to an independent school requires a considerable degree of educational interest. Faced with this situation, the author co-founded, in 2003, the first Intercultural Waldorf School in Neckarstadt-West, a district in the city of Mannheim, Germany, where more than 50% of the population are migrants. Thanks to partial funding by foundations, the school fees can be kept to a minimum. What is characteristic is the great social and cultural heterogeneity of the by-now almost 300 students. As a school serving a particular borough, it is attended by children from all social strata; around half of them have a migrant background; some come with learning difficulties or conspicuous social behavior.

By now, similar initiatives with a Waldorf background have emerged in Hamburg, Stuttgart, Berlin, and Dortmund. In Hamburg-Wilhelmsburg, three Waldorf classes started in August 2014, integrated into a state school; new classes are added every year (www.waldorfwilhelmsburg.de). Also, a dissertation from 2014 by Mandana Büchele confirmed that Waldorf education is highly compatible with intercultural and transcultural education: It has much in common with these approaches because of Steiner's "anthroposophic view of the human being, his normative cultural-anthropological references, and his individualist, holistic, freedom-oriented pedagogy" (Büchele 2014, p. 311).

These recent developments give rise to the question of how intercultural education and Waldorf education relate to each other. Are there affinities between the two streams? Can they inspire each other?

DOI: 10.4324/9781003187431-42

Might Waldorf education even be able to fill the gap between "pompous theory and pottering practice" in intercultural education, deplored by Joachim Roth (Roth 2002, p. 38)?

I shall try to find answers to these questions in this contribution, which is divided in a theoretical and a practice-oriented part. First, I compare the foundations of intercultural and of Waldorf education before going on to present some essential building blocks in the concept of the Mannheim Intercultural Waldorf School.

2 Intercultural versus transcultural education?

Intercultural education presents itself currently as not very homogeneous. The philosopher Wolfgang Welsch proposes to replace the term by the more modern concept of "transcultural education" (Welsch 1995). A publication by the literary theorist Arata Takeda, *Wir sind wie Baumstämme im Schnee. Ein Plädoyer for transkulturelle Erziehung* (We are like tree trunks in the snow. A plea for transcultural education) has brought the debate to a preliminary climax (Takeda 2012).

Both Welsch and Takeda present a fundamental critique of the concept of intercultural education. Their essential points shall be briefly mentioned here as a kind of introduction. They can be summarized in three statements:

- The concept of intercultural education pursues lofty goals: It seeks ways toward dialog, respect, and tolerance between the cultures. But it is founded on a cultural concept that contributes to causing the problems it strives to overcome. Because it sees the cultures as spheres: isolated from each other, homogeneous, and largely static.
- The consequences of such a concept of culture are pedagogically problematic in several respects.

  First, it leads to an attempted integration of the unknown into one's own; thus students with an immigrant background are classified as different from the norm and if necessary, are given "special treatment" — even if this is well-intentioned language support.

  Second, individuals can often be identified by their own culture of origin and the danger of stereotypical labelling grows. Such *culturalism* can obscure the real problem. Performance deficits. for example, often have environment-specific causes and cannot be tracked back to cultural factors.

  The third problem is a special case of the second: The special focus on cultural affiliations leads to situations in which children with a migration background are expected to function as "experts of their own culture." In this case, children are assigned the role of representing their "own culture," even though they may know very little about it.

- Given these dangers, education is called upon to overcome intercultural in favor of transcultural education. The concept of transculturality assumes that "internally, cultures are not uniform and they cross borders to the outside. [...] There is no longer a strict dividing line between the familiar and the alien, but one finds something of one's own culture in the alien one and vice versa" (Takeda 2012, p. 56). This descriptive statement applies particularly in our time of globalization, and it also applies to ordinary everyday life. Do we still experience Italian cuisine, Swedish furniture, and British music as "foreign" in Germany? Today's cultures are often pluralized inwardly and are open, flexible, and in constant exchange to the outside.

This has several consequences for education: First of all, the concept of integration should be replaced by that of "diversity." This concept puts "individuals in the center, with all their potential for development and their distinctive features" (Takeda 2012, p. 65). "Being different is normal" can be seen as the basic principle of this view. Accordingly, the concept of "intersectionality" replaces that of culturalism. Like everyone else, students find themselves at the intersection of several differential criteria such as gender, religion, language milieu, social stratum, and culture. Dealing with them adequately requires us to consider the diversity of differences and their complex interplay without assigning too much value to the original culture.

Intercultural Education and Waldorf Education: An Inspiring Encounter

Transcultural rather than intercultural competence is required: the ability to deal respectfully and tolerantly with any kind of difference and to see culture in this range of differences as a dynamic, shapeable factor.

If we consider the basic features of transculturality—diversity versus integration, intersectionality versus culturalism, and the striving for transcultural competence—we will easily agree with them.

Nonetheless, the sometimes very curtly presented demarcation from the concept of intercultural education seems to be questionable, for intercultural education no longer assumes a cultural concept that, as Wolfgang Welsch suggests, sees cultures as isolated spheres and that implies "social homogenization, ethnic foundation, and intercultural demarcation" (Welsch 1997, p. 69).

The problem of the culturalization of life situations has been recognized, and leading representatives of intercultural education, such as Georg Auernheimer, Wolfgang Nieke, Paul Mecheril, Alfred Holzbrecher, Ulrike Hormel, and Alfred Scherr reject a rigid concept of culture: "Cultures are imagined to be processual, incoherent, not hermetically closed" (Auernheimer 2012, p. 60).

It is also evident that intercultural education does not aim at integration in the sense of including divergent groups into a standard culture. In other words, it does not aim at assimilation or acculturation. Rather, it sees to find a mode of coexistence in multicultural modern society that is based, in the sense of Karl-Otto Apel's and Jürgen Habermas' discourse ethics, on a political culture that enables participation on the basis of universal rights to freedom and equality, without guaranteeing "cultural species protection" (Nieke 2008, p. 201 ff.; Auernheimer 2012, p. 62ff.). As a consequence of this approach, the concept of "diversity" also has been included; in accordance with the "perspective of egalitarian difference" developed by Annedore Prengel in her book *Pädagogik der Vielfalt* (diversity education) (1995), the aim is to appreciate and promote all minorities (Auernheimer 2012, p. 44ff.).

Prengel points out in this context how important it is for education professionals to be able to assess multiple discriminations (ibid., p. 119ff.). Here, the concept of intersectionality seems to offers itself, because it avoids the exclusive centring on one line of difference. In accordance with a "reflexive interculturality," the "appropriateness of categories has to be examined in the individual case" (Auernheimer 2012, p. 120).

If we look closely at the approaches described, it is evident that intercultural and transcultural competence cannot be separated in the modern view of intercultural education. They need to be seen as transitioning into one another to the point that the "inter" (Latin for in between) can even be interpreted as "a third, a new cultural creation," corresponding to "the idea of the culture-in-between in postcolonial studies" (ibid., p. 24).

Having considered the current discourse, we can hold on to the title "Intercultural Education and Waldorf Education – An Inspiring Encounter." The aim is to examine what intercultural education and Waldorf education are concerned with, how they each deal with cultural diversity, and the goal of achieving intercultural competence.

3 Objectives

The intentions of intercultural education can be fully integrated into general education: It strives to give impulses for the evolving individuality to find their identity, whatever culture they belong to. Intercultural education therefore sees itself as encouraging self-education—as an education of empowerment. Its goal is not to remove deficits but to promote each child's strengths. According to Hans Joachim Roth, "Intercultural education is child-centered education. Its anthropological basis is [...] subject-oriented, in other words it takes its cue from the individual's specific life circumstances, experiences, and needs" (Roth 2002, p. 89). Such an approach naturally avoids premature selection and favors targeted support.

Waldorf education goes in a similar direction, but it describes its concern differently: It aims to develop the individuality. The founder of Waldorf education, Rudolf Steiner, says, "This must be our main ideal: We do not resemble each other. Each of us is unique. [...] Focusing the inner gaze fully on the individuality: That is what education must be about in future" (Steiner 1971, p. 83). Waldorf education consequently also relies on self-education and self-efficacy (Steiner 1982b, p. 131). The impulses differ depending on age: In preschool, we (as teachers) inspire imitation, in the lower and middle school, we encourage a rich inner life of imagination, and in the high school, we encourage independent judgment (Kranich 2011).

The pedagogical implications are radical: Waldorf education rejects grades, the repeating of classes, and selection, and it practices integrated education up to 12th grade, with a varied educational program, including cultural studies and sciences, arts and crafts, so as to allow multiple intelligences to unfold.

4 Ways of dealing with cultural diversity

Intercultural education sees cultural diversity as an enriching element on the way to identity formation (Roth 2002, p. 91). This builds, as Georg Auernheimer points out, on the educational ideas of Herder, Wilhelm von Humboldt, and Hegel.

According to Herder, universal education is only possible if one listens to the "voices of the peoples," the utterances of the diverse cultures. For Wilhelm von Humboldt, the learning of languages, and the change of perspective this required, were both a precondition for respecting difference. Hegel thought that consciously taking hold of what is alien, "alienation," was a precondition for finding oneself (Auernheimer 2007, p. 65ff.).

But compared to the classic traditions, the current concept of culture is more differentiated, dynamic, open: Cultures are no longer seen as monolithic, uniform structures but as a multilayered, evolving fabric made of ethnic, linguistic, religious, philosophical threads that is permanently interacting with other cultures. To put it trivially: What would German cuisine be without Italian influences, European culture without Arab science? Much that was originally alien has become our own, what was our own is now part of other cultures.

Intercultural education thus does not define the relation between individual and culture in the sense that individuals can only find their identity by identifying with a particular culture; rather, they can navigate between cultures and thus create new cultural patterns. Intercultural education therefore does not aim at either assimilation or acculturation; when we speak of integration, we mean accepting constitutionally determined values and procedures.

Respect for cultural diversity has had implications for intercultural education: It sees itself as the "advocate of multilingualism" (Roth 2002, p. 90) and bilingual teaching (Holzbrecher 2004, p. 105). Intercultural education also inspires global learning; arising from the thought of *One* World, many didactic models have been developed for geography, history, and social studies (ibid., p. 108ff.). And, finally, intercultural education also suggests that it is helpful to have more teachers with a migrant background in schools than there have been so far.

Cultural diversity is also a central theme in Waldorf education (Leber 1997). In this respect, Rudolf Steiner continued the tradition of Herder and Humboldt, discovering in them a "striving for cosmopolitism that ennobles and elevates the essence of one's own people by absorbing what can be acquired out of love for all peoples" (Steiner 2005, p. 97). Similarly to Herder and Humboldt, Steiner assumed uniform ethnic cultures—a premise that needs to be called into question in the light of the more recent discourse on cultural theory.

Regarding the relation between individual and culture, Steiner expressed as early as 1917 the view that individuals can decide for a particular culture. In a memorandum on the question of the coexistence of different ethnic cultures in Austria-Hungary in mixed settlement regions, he demanded cultural autonomy within a free spiritual life. There he writes, "The state leaves it to specialist, professional, and national organizations to establish their law courts, schools, churches etc., and to individuals to choose their school, church, judge" (Steiner 1982a, p. 342ff.).

It is therefore not surprising that the striving for cultural diversity has crucially informed the theory and practice of Waldorf education; its agreement with the postulates of intercultural education is

Intercultural Education and Waldorf Education: An Inspiring Encounter

evident: multilingualism from first grade, history teaching based not on national but world history (Zech 2012), the study of world literature and world religions (Richter 2006, p. 144, p. 285ff.), and, also, in recent years, teaching units on the question of globalization. Based on this striving for cultural diversity, an international Waldorf school movement has emerged with over a thousand schools on all continents. One can ask critically if there is enough courage in other countries to include their own culture in the curriculum or if a certain eurocentrism often prevails—a question that will continue to be part of the discourse within the international Waldorf school movement.

5 Goals

Intercultural education strives to promote intercultural competence: the ability to meet other cultures without prejudice or fear, tolerance as active interest and respect for otherness, and the ability to form judgments based on multiperspectivity. Intercultural competence depends on how we deal with what is alien to us. There is an epistemological problem involved in this. In everyday life, our conscious perceptions appear to us as images of reality and we are quick at making judgments: This is nice, that is ugly, etc. Our standpoint is that of naïve realism. More in-depth epistemological analysis reveals that this is not actually the case. We ourselves penetrate the manifold sensory phenomena—colors, sounds, movements, facial expressions—and conceptualize them, but there are always feelings involved. This shows that alienness is a construct that mostly reveals something about ourselves. From the point of view of epistemological constructivism, there is a need for intercultural learning: for finding—beyond rejection or acceptance, separation or assimilation—a way of meeting alienness that is informed by productive curiosity, the overcoming of preconceptions, by active interest and tolerance, and possibly the transformation of what is alien toward new cultural creations.

In this context, Waldorf education does not speak so much of intercultural competence as of the capacity for encounter. And, interestingly, here too the question of how to deal with alienness is an epistemological one. Rudolf Steiner's theory of knowledge overcomes naïve realism. From Steiner's point of view, the human mind is involved in constituting reality and can connect creatively with the world and its phenomena (Simons 2008). This basic epistemological position asks for a careful phenomenology in the search for knowledge: a sensitive, always self-critical approach to the phenomena, in which qualities such as openness, a sense of wonder, and empathy play an important part. This basic phenomenological attitude is important in Waldorf education in two ways: as a way of finding access to the world—in the sciences for instance—and as a basic attitude in the meeting of teachers and students. In his lectures and writings, Steiner encourages us again and again to use characterizations rather than definitions and to look at things from multiple perspectives (Steiner 1973, p. 140), to practice openness and a positive attitude (Steiner 1992, p. 128ff.), and, above all, to become aware of our own preconceptions and to look at ourselves "as from an alien perspective" (ibid., p. 31).

So, while there are different epistemological approaches for comparing intercultural education and Waldorf education—constructivism on the one hand, perspectivist essentialism on the other—there is largely agreement when it comes to the basic attitudes required: Impartiality, active interest, multiperspectivity, overcoming preconceptions, and tolerance are central elements of both intercultural education and Waldorf education.

6 Interim observation

We can now summarize the theoretical part of our contemplation. When we look at the question—how to deal with cultural diversity and the goals of intercultural education and Waldorf education—we see compelling similarities, despite an occasionally disparate terminology: Both seek to encourage children and young people to self-education, beyond their immediate milieu; both see cultural diversity as an enriching element in education, both seek to avoid early selection in schools, and to support individual educational paths. Because they both see cultural diversity as enriching, they both favor multilingualism and global learning. It would therefore be good for Waldorf education to increasingly offer bilingual lessons and to seek to overcome Eurocentric concepts. Regarding the fundamental question as to how to deal with alienness, there may be differing epistemological premises, but both intercultural education and Waldorf education strive for impartiality, multiperspectivity, the overcoming of prejudice, and tolerance as expressions of active interest.

In the second part, I will show how the approaches described have been incorporated in the theory and practice of the Intercultural Waldorf School in Mannheim, Germany.

7 The Intercultural Waldorf School in Mannheim

The Intercultural Waldorf School in Mannheim was founded on September 11, 2003, according to the principles presented at the beginning and with the objective to provide equal chances for *all* children irrespective of their cultural or social background, to realize a "diversity education" (Prengel 1995), and to become a place of active tolerance. It seeks to contribute to "overcoming the hostilities and boundaries between religions, cultures, and social strata, and to discover commonalities where there are differences, enrichment in diversity, the universally human through the specific" (vision statement; Brater/Hemmer-Schanze/Schmelzer 2009, p. 51). I will now introduce some building blocks of the school concept, as well as the findings of an assessment carried out between 2004 and 2006 by the Munich Society for Education Research and Professional Development (GAB) (ibid., p. 208ff.).

7.1 Framework conditions

The neighborhood of the Intercultural Waldorf School reflects its purpose: A discount store, a Turkish supermarket, an Asian goods shop, a call center, and a gym are its immediate neighbors. It is located "right in the middle of it:" in a former furniture store, a drab 1970s box of a building, in the center of Neckarstadt-West, a multicultural microcosm where 50% of people are migrants. But it is also a "deprived district" where the number of unemployed, welfare recipients, and drug addicts exceeds that of any other part of the city (cf. data of the Mannheim statistics office and police).

Most of the currently 300 students come from Neckarstadt-West, just above 50% have a migrant background. More than 30 nations are represented, and children come from all social backgrounds; many families have a low socio-economic status. Social and cultural plurality is seen as important for building up a real comprehensive school and for avoiding further segregation in the district (in some of the schools in the neighborhood, 90% of students come from Turkish families). To what extent the Intercultural Waldorf School, through its profile, also attracts education-oriented and ethnically German parents to this area—as Heiner Ullrich thinks the initiative in Hamburg-Wilhelmsburg could do—is a possible topic for another study (Ullrich 2015, p. 8f.).

The plurality of the student body is reflected in the teaching faculty: Only just over half the teachers have a German cultural background. The faculty is therefore noticeably more diverse and more representative of a migrant society than that of regular state schools. This offers students broad possibilities for cultural exchange and multiple identification and, in a school that is run along the principles of collaborative governance, for the participation of migrants in the local community (Leiprecht/Steinbach 2015, p. 15ff.).

The Intercultural Waldorf School is a *mandatory all-day school*; lessons generally go until 3 pm, with after-school provision until 5 pm. With this comes the challenge of having to create not only a place for learning but also a living space. The school therefore seeks to establish healthy daily rhythms, informed by chronobiological considerations, suggesting that intellectual performance is particularly high in the mornings around 9 am, and clearly decreases toward midday, rising again from 2 pm. One needs to consider, though, that children's circulation is more centered in the morning, with better blood supply to the body core and the head than to the limbs, while this is the other way round in the afternoon (Rittelmeyer 2002, p. 111ff.; Glöckler/Langhammer/Wiechert 2006, p. 34). The timetable is arranged accordingly: In the mornings, during the two-hour "main lesson," the focus is more on intellectual work, followed by artistic subjects and languages. Around midday, there is a longer lunch break, followed in the early afternoon by project lessons with mainly practical activities, including sports and crafts. In this way, the school tries to establish a healthy balance between intellectual, artistic, practical crafts, and sports activities.

7.2 Language promotion

Language promotion both in German and in the students' background language is a central goal of intercultural education. The Intercultural Waldorf School deliberately does not offer separate preparation classes for children with language deficits. Instead, the children are "immersed" in the German language by being allowed to enter into it deeply throughout the day. The daily "rhythmic part" at the beginning of main lesson belongs to this exposure, where speech exercises alternate with poetry recitation, singing, and movement exercises. The story-telling, which concludes the main lesson, is also important for language acquisition. The story told one day is recalled and retold by the students on the following day. By listening to folktales, legends, myths, and biographies, students are exposed daily to an artistically formed language that enhances their feeling for language. Language then becomes more than breathless communication in catchphrases and half-sentences; it becomes an immersion in a multifaceted experiential world. The educationist Christian Rittelmeyer points out that only a "learning culture of emotional participation" can be the basis for real competence development (Rittelmeyer 2010, p. 9). He also speaks of the "astounding successes" achieved by the Intercultural Waldorf School in Mannheim with regard to "immigrant children's acquisition of the German language" (ibid., p. 121).

Children who have longer-lasting language deficits are given "deepening" lessons in classes dedicated to cultivating the German language. In these lessons, appreciation is also shown for the children's original language. A subject called *Begegnungssprache* (language of encounter) has been introduced for this purpose and is offered in the first two years across grades. Migrant children can go to a group where their mother tongue is spoken, and the other children can choose which of these groups they join. This is not so much systematic language teaching than the attempt to facilitate, through language, an encounter with another culture. Songs, verses, little stories, and role plays allow the children to immerse themselves through imitation in everyday aspects of the other cultures, with typical instruments, festivals, food, and dances.

For some migrant children, these lessons are the first official, consciously introduced encounter with their original culture, allowing them to develop love for their cultural roots. Children whose native tongue is German experience these encounters from a slightly different perspective. The other culture comes toward them, without its otherness being experienced as an attack on their own culture that might evoke fear or rejection, but as inspiring, interesting, and enriching. These lessons also have important social implications for both groups of children in that the roles are reversed: In these lessons, the migrant children are the ones who understand everything more easily and can explain it to the children with a German background who need to find their way around in an unfamiliar context: an experience that is fruitful for their social coexistence.

From third grade, the "encounter lessons" are replaced by culture lessons, where the children, again through activities, learn about European, African, American, Asian, and Australian cultures.

All the children learn English (as a foreign language) from first grade. From second grade, they not only can learn French but also have the possibility to deepen their German knowledge during that period.

7.3 Grade teachers and comprehensive school principles

Experience shows how valuable the grades teacher principle is. This principle is characteristic of Waldorf schools and means that the same teacher stays with a group of children from first through eighth grade, teaching main lesson every morning. Grades teachers are at school at least until lunchtime, often longer, giving the children what they need most: reliable orientation. The foundation of this kind of encounter that grades teachers have is learning without fear.

At the Intercultural Waldorf School, there is no segregation according to intellectual ability, as with grading or the repetition of classes. These measures, which are in any case discussed controversially in the pedagogical discourse (Bless et al. 2004), seem particularly counterproductive in a school for children with a migrant background. The Intercultural Waldorf School is proof that such measures are obsolete. The continuity of social relationships that is enabled by children staying together for many years is a crucial support, for weaker students in particular. However, there are school-leaving exams at the end of 10th and 12th grade. The timing of offering the *Abitur* (A-levels, more-or-less SAT equivalents) as an option for graduation depends in part on the financial means of the student. To accommodate this, the Mannheim School works cooperatively with neighboring Waldorf schools.

7.4 *Striving for interculturality*

The search for what intercultural education could be is an ongoing challenge for the school. Cultural differences are not leveled out but appreciated as a part of the school's rich fabric. Festivals play a very important role in this: From first graders' first school day to monthly festivals, carnival celebrations, summer fetes, to the sugar feast to end Ramadan—they allow the cultures to come together. And yet, there are always moments when teachers are confronted with something unexpected and alien.

It is important in such moments to try to understand rather than respond immediately with rejection or even dismay. Developing intercultural competence is ultimately something universally human: the art of encounter. That happens among individuals, however, and every "I" transcends the surrounding culture. This is where transcultural education comes into its own, because it raises awareness of the fact that education and formation aim at the evolving individuality and that education is about respecting and productively dealing with any differences, gender diversity, talents, social milieu, and culture (Takeda 2012; Göhlich et al. 2006). Striving for such an attitude appears to be a process that can never be complete: We come closer to the other, but the riddle of the individuality remains. The philosopher Bernhard Waldenfels put it aptly when he said, "We are always ever on each other's trail" (Waldenfels 1991, p. 53).

7.5 *Assessment*

The Intercultural Waldorf School in Mannheim was assessed between 2004 and 2006. The following is a list of the main findings of that assessment:

- "Based on the 'profile analysis' for second language acquisition (introduced by Prof. Grießhaber, Münster University, Germany), definite improvement was established after two years in almost 90% of children with initial deficits in using the German language. The grades teachers found statistically significant differences for linguistic competence at the beginning of the assessment period between children with and without a migrant background in the lower classes. However, these differences were reduced to such an extent within two years that they were no longer statistically significant. [...]
- The students' learning behavior was also examined. There were no significant differences at *any* time between children with and without a migrant background or between children with a different social background regarding aspects such as 'attention,' 'independent working,' and 'lesson participation.'
- With regard to social integration, or 'popularity with peers,' 'readiness to help,' or 'integration in the class community,' a clearly positive social climate was apparent among the students during the assessment period. There were *no* significant differences between children with or without migrant background, or between children of different social backgrounds [...]

Intercultural Education and Waldorf Education: An Inspiring Encounter

- Two written and oral rounds of interviews with parents revealed high acceptance among parents of the school's intercultural and Waldorf-based concept. The parents interviewed were largely satisfied with their children's progress at school, they felt accepted by the school community, and were motivated to actively support the school. Particularly parents who had experience of state schools, appreciated the active engagement of the teachers at the school, and the open and trustful interaction of teachers, students, and parents" (p. 209ff.).
- The Intercultural Waldorf School's aim to be a local school was also achieved, based on the demand from families in the area: Almost a third of the children attending the school come from the same zip code district or from adjacent neighborhoods. Only a few children live further away. The school has become a well-established institution in Neckarstadt and works closely with many other institutions in the district (ibid., p. 209ff.).

The school has now 12 grades, five classes have taken the exams at the end of 10th grade, three at the end of 12th grade. With one exception, all students passed their exams. One can really speak of an equal opportunities school here. Some students failed to pass the *Abitur*, however, which shows that more steps need to be taken, particularly in implementing a consistent learning concept in the middle and high schools. A preliminary conclusion can nonetheless be established regarding the relation between Intercultural Education and Waldorf education.

8 Conclusion

The comparison of intercultural education and Waldorf education has been an inspiring experience. There are evident affinities between the two educational streams with regard to their intentions, their approach to cultural diversity, and their goals. A case example from the Intercultural School has shown that Waldorf education really has the potential to fill the gap in intercultural education pointed out by Hans-Joachim Roth. This inquiry consequently comes to the same conclusion as Mandana Büchele's dissertation *Culture and Education in Waldorf Schools* (Büchele 2014), which asks to what extent Waldorf education, with its underlying anthroposophic view of the human being, is suited to an environment of cultural diversity. We agree with Büchele's verdict that Waldorf schools, "due to their holistic anthropology and the holistic-aesthetic teaching practice inspired by it, open up diverse possibilities for a student body that is heterogeneous both in terms of languages and cultures, and individual talents," and that they constitute, because of both the "individual education" offered and the "high importance [they] attach to ongoing linguistic education," a meaningful alternative to state education (ibid., p. 312).

Note

1 Auernheimer (2012, p. 38 ff.), Holzbrecher (2004, p. 51 ff.), Mecheril (2004, p. 80 ff.), Nieke (2008, p. 13 ff.)

References

Auernheimer, Georg (2007): Einführung in die Interkulturelle Pädagogik. 5th edition. Darmstadt: Wissenschaftliche Buchgesellschaft.
Auernheimer, Georg (2012): Einführung in die Interkulturelle Pädagogik. 7th edition. Darmstadt: Wissenschaftliche Buchgesellschaft.
Autorengruppe Bildungsberichterstattung (Ed.) (2014): Bildung in Deutschland 2014. Bielefeld: Bertelsmann.
Barz, Heiner/Randoll, Dirk (2007): Absolventen von Waldorfschulen. Eine empirische Studie zu Bildung und Lebensgestaltung. Wiesbaden: VS.
Bless, Gerhard/Bovin, Patrick/Schüppbach, Marianne (2004): Klassenwiederholung. Determinanten, Wirkungen und Konsequenzen. Bern: Haupt.
Brater, Michael/Hemmer-Schanze, Christiane/Schmelzer, Albert (2009): Interkulturelle Waldorfschule. Evaluation zur schulischen Integration von Migrantenkindern. Wiesbaden: VS.

Büchele, Mandana (2014): Kultur und Erziehung in der Waldorfpädagogik. Analyse und Kritik eines anthroposophischen Konzepts Interkultureller Bildung. Frankfurt am Main: Peter Lang.

Glöckler, Michaela/Langhammer, Stefan/Wiechert, Christof (Eds.) (2006): Gesundheit durch Erziehung. Dornach: Verlag am Goetheanum.

Göhlich, Michael/Leonhard, Hans-Walter/Liebau, Eckardt/Zirfas, Jürgen (Ed.) (2006): Transkulturalität und Pädagogik. Interdisziplinäre Annäherungen an ein kulturwissenschaftliches Konzept und seine pädagogische Relevanz. Weinheim: Beltz Juventa.

Holzbrecher, Alfred (2004): Interkulturelle Pädagogik. Berlin: Cornelsen.

Kranich, Ernst-Michael (2011): Das Ich in der Entwicklung des Kindes und des Jugendlichen. In: Loebell, Peter (Ed.): Waldorfschule heute. Stuttgart: Freies Geistesleben.

Leber, Stefan (1997): Anthroposophie und Waldorfpädagogik in den Kulturen der Welt. Stuttgart: Freies Geistesleben.

Leiprecht, Rudolf/Steinbach, Anja (Eds.) (2015): Schule in der Migrationsgesellschaft. Ein Handbuch. Vol. 1. Schwalbach: Debus.

Mecheril, Paul (2004): Einführung in die Migrationspädagogik. Weinheim, Basel: Beltz.

Nieke, Wolfgang (2008): Interkulturelle Erziehung und Bildung. Wertorientierung im Alltag. 3rd edition. Wiesbaden: VS.

Prengel, Annedore (1995): Pädagogik der Vielfalt. Verschiedenheit und Gleichberechtigung in Interkultureller, Feministischer und Integrativer Pädagogik. 2nd edition. Opladen: Leske und Budrich.

Richter, Tobias (Ed.) (2006): Pädagogischer Auftrag und Unterrichtsziele – vom Lehrplan der Waldorfschule. 2nd edition. Stuttgart: Freies Geistesleben.

Rittelmeyer, Christian (2002): Pädagogische Anthropologie des Leibes. Weinheim, Munich: Juventa.

Rittelmeyer, Christian (2010): Warum und wozu ästhetische Bildung? Über Transferwirkungen künstlerischer Tätigkeiten. Ein Forschungsüberblick. Oberhausen: Athena.

Roth, Hans-Joachim (2002): Kultur und Kommunikation. Systematische und theoriegeschichtliche Umrisse Interkultureller Pädagogik. Interkulturelle Studien 10. Opladen: Leske und Budrich.

Simons, Jaap (2008): Phänomenologie und Idealismus. Struktur und Methode der Philosophie Rudolf Steiners. Basel: Schwabe.

Steiner, Rudolf (1971): Die Erziehungsfrage als soziale Frage. Die spirituellen, kulturgeschichtlichen und sozialen Hintergründe der Waldorfschul-Pädagogik. GA 296. Dornach: Rudolf Steiner Verlag.

Steiner, Rudolf (1973): Allgemeine Menschenkunde als Grundlage der Pädagogik. GA 293. Dornach: Rudolf Steiner Verlag.

Steiner, Rudolf (1982a): Aufsätze über die Dreigliederung des sozialen Organismus und zur Zeitlage 1915 bis 1921. GA 24. Dornach: Rudolf Steiner Verlag.

Steiner, Rudolf (1982b): Die pädagogische Praxis vom Gesichtspunkte geisteswissenschaftlicher Menschenerkenntnis. Die Erziehung des Kindes und jüngeren Menschen. GA 306. Dornach: Rudolf Steiner Verlag.

Steiner, Rudolf (1992): Wie erlangt man Erkenntnisse der höheren Welten? GA 10. Dornach: Rudolf Steiner Verlag.

Steiner, Rudolf (2005): Die Krisis der Gegenwart und der Weg zu gesundem Denken. GA 335. Dornach: Rudolf Steiner Verlag.

Takeda, Arata (2012): Wir sind wie Baumstämme im Schnee. Ein Plädoyer für transkulturelle Erziehung. Münster: Waxmann.

Ullrich, Heiner (2015): Waldorfpädagogik. Eine kritische Einführung. Weinheim, Basel: Beltz.

Waldenfels, Bernhard (1991): Der Stachel des Fremden. 2nd edition. Frankfurt am Main: Suhrkamp.

Welsch, Wolfgang (1995): Transkulturalität. Zur veränderten Verfasstheit heutiger Kulturen. In: Zeitschrift für Kulturaustausch 45/1, pp. 39–44.

Welsch, Wolfgang (1997): Transkulturalität. Zur veränderten Verfassung heutiger Kulturen. In: Schneider, Irmela/Thomson, Christian W. (Eds.) (1997): Hybridkultur. Köln: Wienand, pp. 67–90.

Zech, M. Michael (2012): Der Geschichtsunterricht an Waldorfschulen. Frankfurt am Main: Peter Lang.

RELIGIOUS EDUCATION IN WALDORF SCHOOLS IN THE CONTEXT OF THE CURRENT PEDAGOGICAL DISCOURSE

Carlo Willmann

1 Introduction

In Waldorf education, religious education constitutes an integral part of its intended formative processes. Religion is seen as constitutive to the concept of the human being and essential to education. In the theory and practice of Waldorf schools, this is apparent in a general religious education that strives to address and foster the religious dimension irrespective of confession, as well as in the celebration of religious festivals, and in the mandatory—confessional or free Christian—religion lessons. This concept addresses important gaps in religious education that are important in the relevant contemporary discourse. This includes questions such as how important religious education is in society today, the inclusion of religious educational processes into the school context, and ways of providing religious education in the face of social and religious transformation processes that are associated with the departure from tradition, individualization, deinstitutionalization, and religious pluralism.

These questions need to be considered in creating a school culture that is sensitive to religion. I will discuss these three aspects and identify common perspectives of Waldorf education and religious education.

First I would like to point out that the discourse between religious education and Waldorf education has not yet been exhausted, on the contrary: It has only just begun. The reason for this is that the representatives of religious education have not taken sufficient notice of Waldorf education, and that Waldorf teachers are not sufficiently familiar with the tasks and topics of religious education today. That questions of religion teaching are not exactly at the center of Waldorf education is an added factor, even the Waldorf journal *Erziehungskunst* (Art of Education) devotes a special edition to religion and religion teaching in regular intervals[1] or prints individual contributions. In the general religious education landscape, there is not much more to refer to than an entry on Waldorf schools and their way of thinking about religion in the *Lexikon der Religionspädagogik* (Lexicon of Religious Education) (Willmann 2001b). The proportion of publications on religious education in Waldorf schools is rather limited compared to other areas of Waldorf education. Also, the public perception of Waldorf schools tends to focus on aspects other than religion teaching.

The need for information therefore exists on both sides if there is to be dialog between religious education and Waldorf education. This statement refers to religious education as a scientific discipline and concerns both its theoretical discourse and its empirical research. It applies much less to the cooperation, arising from the teaching practice, between confessional religion teachers working in Waldorf schools and Waldorf teachers. Many non-denominational work groups exist at various levels in the field of professional teacher development that are supported by church institutions, or in conferences organized by

DOI: 10.4324/9781003187431-43

them that facilitate exchange and dialog between Waldorf and religion teachers. Theological questions, for example, on the image of Christ in anthroposophy, or on reincarnation and karma, to name just a few central topics, are discussed there, as are more practical issues such as the meaningful contextualization of religion teaching and the Waldorf curriculum, the associated (religious) understanding of learning, or the celebration of religious festivals in Waldorf schools.

2 Religion between plurality and individualism

Today, the situation of religion is informed by two essential components: the plurality of religious options and the growing individualization of religious identities. The non-reversible individualization thrust of the modern period—which goes hand-in-hand with personal choice and freedom of lifestyle decisions—and the multiplicity of views of life and of the world are ultimately mutually dependent. Individuals make use of this possibility, while at the same time generating it by accepting or rejecting, extending, changing, or newly creating possibilities. The availability of religion and religions may not be endless, but the ways of practicing religion, depending on individual inclination, seem to be. One can also say that the religious stability that was perpetuated for a long time under the influence of churches and other religious institutions has given way to the new paradigm of flexibility. The French sociologist Danièle Hervieu-Léger, for example, has identified "movement" as the main feature of modern religion and religiosity and, in an interesting comparison, distinguishes between the tradition-oriented "practitioner" and the "pilgrim," who acts autonomously and individually, as protagonists of different religious landscapes that are presently changing in favor of the "pilgrim." While "practitioners" pursue a religious practice that is institutionally standardized, fixed, localized, and habitual, the religious practice of "pilgrims" is voluntary, autonomous, changeable, and adaptable to their individual needs (Hervieu-Léger 2004, p. 73). This tension among movement, diversity, and subjectivity constitutes a considerable challenge for the theory and practice of religious education. Its response to these developments depends, not least, upon whether the possible danger of eroding confessional profiles is seen as a loss or as a chance for a new authentic and meaningful religious experience rooted in individual freedom.

Individualized religious formats did not find favor even as late as the 1990s. Their sincerity was called into question, and they were dismissed as banal esoteric interpretations of the world, as arbitrary syncretism, or as the longing of the well-situated to "dabble with the infinite" (Höhn 1999, p. 17). Recent studies (Reese 2006; Schnell 2009) have discovered a change in the theological perception and evaluation in that, despite the critical distance, the importance of this change for religious subjectification has been admitted: Individuals are now seen as capable of making their own decision and choosing their education and are therefore "able to cross the boundaries of their own religious or confessional system" (Naurath 2012, p. 90).

While the developments described so far refer primarily to individual biographic experiences, there has also been change sociopolitically concerning the presence of religion in public life. With the strengthening of political Islam, and the regrettable religiously motivated terrorist aberrations, religion has attracted a new media attention, which is, however, mostly focused on Islam. This, too, has had a strong impact on religion teaching. And there is a third level: In society as a whole, we observe not only religious plurality but also the appearance of world interpretation patterns and ways of living that are not related at all to religion and whose representatives consciously distance themselves from religion (and from the church). This asks for efforts to be made toward establishing basic "religious literacy" (Scheunpflug 2006, p. 80), so that religion remains at least communicable in a largely secularized society. Religion can only expect to be accepted and seen as a serious stakeholder in the social discourse if it is transparent—that is to say, if its theory is clearly and comprehensibly conveyed and its practice relatable. What is needed is not only dialog among religious people and institutions of different confessions but also with non-religious, secular forces that are not familiar with religious semantics and for whom a communicable language needs to be found.

In the current discussion on religious education, this situation is primarily observed from the point of view of confessional religion teaching, even if religious education has to consider wider areas of practice. For given the conditions mentioned, religious teaching really does face increased challenges. Religious individualization is not the preserve of adults but a clear mark of self-discovery, particularly in young people who meet institutional church demands with individually formed judgments. It is also important to observe negative developments and deficiencies such as (but not only) religiously motivated radicalization, tendencies toward dogmatism and paternalism, which can appear in all life plans, and to speak openly with students about such developments. At the same time, it is also essential to explain in the public space of schools and education why religion teaching is justified and relevant in a successful quest for meaning.

The heterogeneity of today's religious experiences and ethical value formations therefore constitutes a new situation for the religious practice. Mainstream schools assign this task to confessional religious tuition. In confessional or independent institutions, it is the task of the whole school and can be part of a school's education profile, as is the case with Waldorf schools.

Before we look at the way Waldorf education approaches the teaching of religion, we will present considerations of religious instruction that have emerged from the reflection on religious instruction and learning processes in the modern era. I will focus, in particular, on the theory-guided principal debate on questions of basic religious education in a pluralistic society, the task of interreligious education that has become necessary, and the more practice-oriented demand for a religion-sensitive school culture that is developing into a new key concept in the religious education discourse.

3 Current discussions on religious education

3.1 Basic religious education

In the last ten years or so, religious education has acquired a task that arises from current educational policy rather than immanent educational considerations: the clarification of what is meant by basic religious education. This was prompted by international studies into school performance that, although conducted in entirely different competence areas, claim to not only inquire into school knowledge but also into other skills and competences that are ultimately also relevant for personal, social, and economic thriving. The question of basic religious education is therefore closely connected with the results of the PISA (Programme for International Student Assessment) and IGLU (Internationale Grundschul-Lese-Untersuchung [International Primary School Reading Survey]) studies which, although they exclude religion, ask about basic educational standards that all students are expected to meet. It seems therefore legitimate to ask about such performance standards in religious education, too—an undertaking that meets with considerable difficulties. Because the measurable educational standards required for this can only test cognitive knowledge of (any) religion, they can never do justice to the deep dimension of the religious experience that a person has (or does not have) in the process of religious learning. Essential aspects of religious education cannot simply be turned into evaluable competences. Without suggesting that the discussions or efforts regarding religious education standards are an expression of hasty compliance with a possibly simplified and economized concept of education that needs to be critically scrutinized, especially from the point of view of a humanist religious education or spiritual science (Krautz 2007; Liessmann, 2014), one must not lose sight of the one-sidedness and deficiency of educational standards that fail to do justice to the complex diversity of religious learning. We are therefore less interested here in educational standards but, generally, in what basic religious education should entail and how it can be established and ascertained as a component of general education.

In Germany, different educational approaches to religion are guaranteed by law (Art. 7, paragraph 3 German Basic Law). Recognized religious communities can offer instruction in their faith in schools, whether this is purely confessional, inclusive, or in combination with ethics.

However, religion teaching alone can hardly be seen as the only model for basic religious education. Bernd Schröder, for example, whose considerations, to me, seem fundamental to an understanding of basic religious education, links basic religious education to the question of the degree and kind of religious education graduates of general educational schools in Germany must acquire, irrespective of whether or not they belong to a religious community, and of whether or not they have access to regular religious tuition or to an accepted alternative or substitute (Schröder 2004, p. 13). According to Schröder, basic religious education should not as much be informed by political demands for educational standards as by what is owed to adolescents for their self-actualization and what can guide them toward a critically reflected identity of their religious existence. Beside this didactic task, basic religious education must also transcend confessional restrictions. This is a result of the obvious shift in an increasingly complex religious landscape that is informed by the increasing absence of confessional affiliation, on the one hand, and the increasing presence of foreign religions on the other. Both these factors ask for the development of "religious literacy" and for ways of conveying basic knowledge and experiences of religion that are essential for social and interreligious communication. In addition, the scientific orientation of teaching asks for religious education based on religious science and theology (Schröder 2004, p. 15ff.).

Since Schröder rejects the concept of "basic religious education" for reasons derived from education theory and since he pleads for "minimum standards of religious (school) education" because a "basic religious education" ultimately had to be evaluable (which it can only be if there are measurable standards), competences need to be identified that encompass such basic education or make it describable. In principle, such minimum standards must be justifiable and comprehensible in general pedagogical terms. As a starting point for possible standards, Schröder outlines Christian Grethlein's approach to religion teaching on the Protestant and that of Hubertus Halbfas on the Catholic side. In my view, the difficulty of describing standards is immediately apparent here, because both authors want to move away from one-sidedly intellectual curricula. For Christian Grethlein, religious practices such as celebrating the sacraments, or basic attitudes and rituals such as praying, blessing, and being blessed are as important as the cognitive study of basic Christian religious knowledge. Hubertus Halbfas opens this up even further in that he focuses on the emotional, affective aspect of religion, irrespective of confession, and explores this in the context of symbolic teaching, even though he focuses the teaching on the language-oriented capacity of religious expression. Minimum standards can at best reflect the surface of what is intended with these didactic concepts. Since religion teaching in Waldorf education has strong affinities with symbolic teaching and Hubertus Halbfas' model, this objection applies to it, too.

In recommending the formulating of minimum standards, Bernd Schröder identifies the goals of such religious education as developing a critical understanding of religions, unlocking religious concepts, sensitizing students to experiences that can be religiously interpreted, and, finally, encouraging self-responsibility in the process of clarifying a "general orientation." From this point of view, one would need to look more closely at and describe individual competences: how interpretive competence gains from the experience of religious narrative contexts for orientation in life; expressive competence from the understanding and practice of comprehensible rituals; reflective competence in the factual and appreciative interpretation of religious beliefs; and finally in the agency that teaches students about social responsibility (Schröder 2004, p. 29). The implementation of such "provisional" religious minimum standards must be accompanied, however, by empirical surveys and region- and school-specific methodology. And, lastly, "Aside from the trite old request for interconnecting learning environments both in the practice and theory of religious education, the most urgent need currently is for the religious school life and child- and youth work to be penetrated with and promoted by religion teaching" (Schröder 2004, p. 30).

In his proposed guidelines for the definition of basic religious education, Manfred Pirner also places the self-educating subject at the center of such education. In a religious education that is understood as a dialogical process, individuals should experience a "sense of being touched by objective religious content, so that they are enabled to communicate in religious language and to enter into dialog with other life plans and rationalities as this will lead the practice of basic religious education toward interconnected and intertextual learning." This is, in principle, an experiential approach that needs to be informed by both practical religious impulses and religious knowledge and discourse. It therefore requires "both the encounter with authentic religion and the theological outside-perspective" (Pirner 2004, p. 49).

Both ideas on basic religious education consequently aim at transcending the limitations of religion teaching: Schröder demands basic religious education, which he locates in the general school life; Pirner thinks it can only be guaranteed in the dialog with general education. Both therefore envisage an educational concept that can only be explored and developed in communication with all parties involved in education and in connection with the other—scientific, ethical, aesthetic—educational opportunities. In this context, Pirner rightly points out that confessional religion teaching "has lost its monopoly to define what religious school education actually is" (Pirner 2004, p. 38).

Such a concept can only be realized in a meaningful way when religion is understood and accepted as a part of general education. Wolfgang Nieke in particular points this out while simultaneously expressing valid doubts about the relevance of conventional religious theory to schools. Aside from the fact that the intrinsic values and future performance expectations of the traditional educational canon have been called into question, religious theory in particular has been marginalized by competence-oriented school subjects. "Compulsive, church-bound religious instruction has no place in a catalog of coping strategies for an economically dominated world," Nieke points out, "or in an anthropologic competence model that aims at an autonomous subject, a target that was developed in the age of Enlightenment specifically in rejection of a prescribed and unquestioned religious attachment as (alleged) lack of freedom" (Nieke 2006, p. 196). The first part of the argument can be seen as generally valid, while the second goes against the intentions of today's religious education highlighted by Schröder and Pirner in their subject-oriented approaches: Today, it is the religiously autonomous individual that is at the center of any considerations of religious education. We can still agree with Nieke's view that the unquestioned institutionalization of traditional religion teaching in a plural society requires discussion and with his demand for critical reflection of the concept of religion. Because we will look more closely at Rudolf Steiner's concept of religion later and then briefly touch on this question, we will merely state here that Nieke draws on a wide concept of religion to postulate the idea of schools providing "guidance regarding the diversity of possible world orientations," (Nieke 2006, p. 201) to enable young people to generate and develop their own life plans, including in the field of religion if they are so inclined. This proposal is important in that it even brings up and objectively discusses the possibility of existential life questions, different life plans, and world interpretations, and in that it critically reflects on generally accepted models such as the materialist-scientific image of the world, and in that it trusts people to find "acceptable forms of justification" for themselves. "What counts is not the manner and quality of the justification on the basis of external criteria but the reflexive assurance of its quality for a decision that has been or has to be made" (Nieke 2006, p. 201).

Since the confessional option, because of its binding character, only reaches a small proportion of young people, it could be replaced by *"world orientation,"* which approaches the "question of the meaning of the whole" (Nieke 2006, p. 203) more universally rather than one that is tied to one (Christian) religion. Nieke suggests that the discussion of world conceptions in connection with scientific thinking, philosophical and historical anthropology, and, lastly, aspects of education, theology, and religious science could fruitfully contribute on different levels of reflection, to the universal questions of existence—Where from? Why? What for?—in the study of world religions and mythologies. Nieke does not omit one of the fundamental dilemmas of meaning- and decision-oriented ethical or religious education, which is that, in conveying and dealing with these important topics, the tension becomes apparent between the rejection of any indoctrination on the one hand, and the categories of authenticity and commitment that are essential in education on the other, and which teachers must demand as "conditions for effective pedagogical communication" (Nieke 2006, p. 201). This requires an "attitude of tolerance that, while not denying one's own position, makes it clear that other, opposing, views are also respected" (Nieke 2006, p. 210).

Tolerance and recognition are also necessary for the success of religion teaching and learning, in confessional religion teaching, as well as in interdisciplinary projects or in developing a religion-friendly school culture. Objective presentation, impartation, and personal commitment are not contradictions but engender, in the best case, a mood of curiosity and interest, where diversity and plurality have a place, where individuals can come to a decision in favor or against religious life concepts, and where they can keep examining this decision. The recognition of tolerance and religious freedom is also an important prerequisite for dealing sensitively with students of different religious or cultural backgrounds. In a society determined by pluralism and divergence, with its spiritual, religious, ethical, and ideological diversity, an opening up to social communication on religion and worldviews seems inevitable. This communication is what is needed in religious education for interreligious learning.

3.2 Interreligious learning

Modern European societies have been fundamentally changed by polycausal migrations and the globalization of life contexts, not only in a socio-economic but also in a cultural and religious sense. Christians, Muslims, Jews, Buddhists, and members of other religions live together in Europe more closely than ever before.

This development manifested in religion teaching in different appellations for these religions: The former "foreign religions" was replaced by "world religions," while the commonly used term today is "neighborhood religions." In the educational context, the first two were associated with theological, literary, and methodological concepts, the latter also includes the religious practice in the concrete life environment (Grethlein 2012, p. 404). In parallel to this, the concept of "interreligious learning" has also established itself. K. E. Nipkow, who co-coined this term, postulated as early as 1990 that "Thinking in religiously closed spaces is a thing of the past" (Nipkow 1990, p. 447).

An essential motif of this opening to interreligious learning is dialog. The Catholic theologian Stephan Leimgruber described it as follows: "Interreligious learning in the narrower sense happens in the convivence of members of different religions and through conversations in direct encounters. Dialog is central to any encounter where both sides try to respect and understand one another" (Leimgruber 2007, p. 20f.).

In the school reality, there are some restrictions to the abolishing or giving up of closed spaces. While confessional religion classes can open their doors to a certain degree, extend invitations to (responsible) members of other faiths, design, and realize projects on religious questions together with other confessional religion classes (visiting churches, mosques, synagogues etc.), it is also apparent that this happens only within the margins and from the perspective of the religion in question. This constitutes a certain asymmetry in the desired dialog in the school context (Grethlein 2012, p. 408). Grethlein therefore focuses more on the school life: Schools don't have to form a community, but they have a common task, which is to promote the students entrusted to them. This commonality can be retained and examined despite the differences that are being perceived and respected. Religious festivals and celebrations can therefore be organized together within the school as a "neutral place" where the balance and equivalence of all religions can be established. Because this is about participation rather than usurpation, it also includes non-confessional students.

How difficult it is to establish a conscious and goal-oriented school culture as a foundation for interreligious learning is apparent from the fact that only very few schools have so far devoted themselves to this task. One of these schools is the *Drei Religionen Grundschule* (Three Religions Elementary School) in the German city of Osnabrück. We will briefly look at its concept. The School opened in 2012 and is run by the Catholic school foundation in Osnabrück in cooperation with the Osnabrück Jewish Community, the Islamic Association (Schura) of Lower Saxony, the Turkish-Islamic Union for Religious Affairs (DITiB), and the city of Osnabrück. As an independent school, it is also open to religiously unaffiliated students whose parents support the school program. The school concept, which the cooperating partners developed together, is unique in Germany's educational landscape. It sees itself as a place of learning where religious ways of life are part of the school life and where interreligious, trialogical learning is possible. This vision of a school not just provided *for* Jews, Christians, and Muslims but also "run" by them has been impressively described by Winfried Verburg, the responsible head of department of the diocese of Osnabrück: "The cooperating partners envision a learning community of students, parents, and teachers of the three monotheistic religions, who are more deeply aware of their common foundations and therefore able to meet people of different religious faiths respectfully, and to work and live with them" (Verburg 2011, p. 325).

This program does not aim to exclude differences in a joint educational process, but to develop in the students "identities capable of dialog" (Verburg 2011, p. 326) that can understand and appreciate, on the basis of their own beliefs, the otherness of their peer's religion. Students without confessional affiliation are also welcome.

What makes this possible is, above all, the inclusion of the religious beliefs, lifestyles, and rituals of the three religions represented in the life of the school. Religious tuition is provided by all religious communities, but there are also periods of interreligious learning, which are realized in joint projects, and which are characterized by the development of perceptiveness and (linguistic) expression ("I tell you something about the animals in my religion," November 2014; "I show you my most important book on religion," March 2015), but especially by celebrating religious festivals that are organized by the entire school community. What is special and characteristic of this concept is the inclusion of religious rituals, customs, and rules, which means that the children can have authentic experiences of the ways of life in the different religions, be it the sharing of meals where the different food rules are observed, the rules of everyday communication, or the school calendar that takes the requirements of the individual religions into account.

These high ideals can only be realized if the cooperating partners embark on this journey together and reflect in mutual perception and exchange the conditions of their joined work, and if they develop the school's religious profile together. Parents and teachers together take part in further training that aims at facilitating dialog. A school council consisting of representatives of all cooperating institutions also supports the school's development and has an advisory function regarding the school's religious profile. A scientific committee was asked to conduct an effectiveness study. A first insight into the school's work and the self-concept of the teachers and parents has been published in the Journal for Islamic Theology and Religious Education (Hikma 2014, p. 211ff.).

The example of the *Three Religions School* illustrates that interreligious learning must be able to unfold within the life of the school. If a school culture can evolve that offers the communicative space where religions can present themselves and meet on different levels, the school can fulfill its task of enabling understanding and tolerance as essential principles of humanity. This means fostering a religion-sensitive school culture—a goal of religious education that has been expressed ever more widely and concretely in recent years.

3.3 A religion-sensitive school culture

According to Jürgen Baumert, school has the task of introducing students reflexively to "four modes of meeting the world." These approaches to the world are either cognitive-instrumental (mathematics, sciences), aesthetic-expressive (languages, literature, art, music), normative-evaluative (rights, economy, society), and finally they also include "ultimate questions – that is questions as to the Where from, Where to and What for of human life" (Baumert 2002, p. 108ff.). These "ultimate questions" are usually assigned to religion and philosophy classes. One could also say they are included in these subjects, because reality always has the potential to ask about the Where from, Where to, and What for. And, insofar as reality manifests and is dealt with in specific ways, in all subjects, whether they are natural-scientific, spiritual-scientific, artistic, or practical, they are also open to the question of meaning. We could therefore also say that the modes that Baumert distinguishes must be seen as a whole: The ultimate question is naturally implicated in all other approaches to the world, unless it is artificially excluded. Religious education cannot be presented as a partial phenomenon but needs to be understood, due to its integrative capacity, as a general, transdisciplinary, universal educational principle. Doing justice to this principle requires other, open, and comprehensive conditions.

The publication of Hartmut von Hentig's book *Die Schule neu denken* (rethinking school) (1993) has heralded a paradigm shift that means that school is no longer to be understood and realized simply as a place of learning but also as a living space. As this idea of school has become more concrete, new key concepts have emerged and been politically discussed, such as school autonomy, school development, and school culture. The first two elicit expectations of both improved efficiency in school administration and governance and of higher achievements on all sides involved in the school's learning processes. There is less emphasis on the added pedagogical and human value a school gains in developing its own culture based on social encounter and mutual recognition, on the dialog of cultural and religious differences. Such a school culture can be developed and realized in various forms and in different stages. It can, for example, contribute to a convincing humane school profile with interdisciplinary projects, from the design of rooms and playground, school festivals, work groups, presentations of student work, play performances, orchestra and choir work, class trips and art excursions, sports events, and competitions; and, moreover, it can support the identification of students, parents, and teacher with their school. That this also initiates learning processes and therefore increases learning performance can be seen as a positive side effect. Socially integrative, educational, and learning-oriented functions merge seamlessly with this "learning principle" and the life of the school can be seen as an independent educational sphere of activity.

At a deeper level, school is more than that, though: It cultivates the respectful interacting of teachers, students, of teachers with students, of teachers with parents. This is reflected in the dialog culture, in the possibilities of conflict management, in a positively understood discipline. Cultivating human interaction also extends to the way one deals with objects, such as learning material, books, instruments, rooms, playground, energy, and resources. This refers to a distinctly ethical component of the concept of school culture that encompasses social and ecological aspects. In such attitudes and habits, the school's values and standards are reflected as a crucial mark of its quality that contributes to its profile (Fischer 2009, p. 413).

Given these intentions and endeavors for developing a new school culture, a change has taken place in the religious education of the last 20 years that goes beyond the content, didactics, and methodology of religious education and focuses on the importance and role of religion and of religious learning in the context of the whole school. From this point of view, and in different manifestations, the religious dimension is part of the general educational goal, and it should inform the school culture across the subjects as a component of comprehensive education. From the point of view of educational theory, the approach is justified in that religion is an essential factor of life orientation and of the values held in a holistic educational landscape. Religion as an aid to finding identity, values, and orientation in life within a school also supports individuals and the joint discourse and is, therefore, legitimate and necessary. Despite all this, the role of religion in school development and in the school culture hardly features in the relevant literature. In the usual textbooks about the challenges of a new school organization and a new understanding of school, religion is not considered important or not even mentioned (Blömeke 2009).

The reason for this could be that, while confessional religion teaching is legally guaranteed in German state schools, the situation is more complex with regard to the provision of religious tuition in schools. This has to do with the co-responsibility for education of the churches and is subject to diverging laws in the individual German states (Wermke 2012, p. 109f.).

Recently, Martin Jäggle and Thomas Krobath have critically and comprehensively discussed questions of school development and organizational culture in connection with religion in schools, presenting valuable considerations and clear positions, particularly in relation to the plurality of modern lifestyles: "When we ask whether a school is open to questions of meaning whose reflexive study is, according to the view developed here, crucial to the school's development, we can no longer ignore the question of the status and importance of religion. [...] Schools cannot promote democratic and intercultural life without overcoming their blindness toward religion. The interconnection of cultural and religious differences renders religious education essential to a coexistence based on respect for diversity and particularly for minorities – especially in schools" (Jäggle, Krobath, Schelander 2009, p. 48f.).

It needs pointing out here that the idea of a communicative religious practice embedded in the school life beyond the religion lessons was programmatically formulated and represented by Hubertus Halbfas as early as the beginning of the 1980s (Halbfas 1982). His concept of religious learning, which he discussed in a series of religion books ranging from elementary to secondary school, is inconceivable without the wider school context. We will talk about the approaches he developed later because they come remarkably close to the methods of Waldorf education. Halbfas is one of few authors who is open to considering elements of Waldorf education (Halbfas 1982, p. 34).

As part of the considerations concerning the development of school culture, the relatively new term *religious sensitivity* has become established in the religious education discourse—a concept that certainly asks for a new approach to how religion and religiousness are perceived in the public space of school education. The concept is not easy to define. The endeavors to define "religion" have not even led to convincing, generally binding results (we will come back to this later when I introduce Rudolf Steiner's concept of religion). Similarly to the concept of religion, which is not a radically open one but one that needs to be broadly defined, the concept of sensitivity (to religion) can only be characterized approximately.

Sensitivity to religion is characterized by an openness to basic religious experiences and the willingness to allow these experiences to express themselves in multiple ways. Its role here is not solely a passive one. It is about being actively mindful of the delicate development of religious identity, about being awake to misguided developments of religion (a topical issue currently in connection with young people being seduced to join the Jihad, for instance). It does not serve the particular interests of institutions but focuses on the subject. Martin Lechner, who published a groundbreaking study on religion in youth welfare (Lechner, Gabriel 2009), in which he introduced the concept of religious sensitivity, sees it as an active approach that is "not ecclesiocentric but anthropocentric; that is to say, it starts from the young person and their religiosity. Since this requires the perception of this religiosity, I have called it 'religious sensitivity'" (Lechner, Gabriel 2009, p. 11).

Religious sensitivity is therefore experience-oriented, open to many forms of religious experience and interpretation that extends to all areas of life. Motifs in music and literature, visual arts and film, sports and entertainment can be the object of religious appropriation and engagement, in youth culture above all. Its task is to make it possible to talk of and about religion in a humane context imbued with mutual recognition and appreciation. This has nothing to do, as Harald Schroeter-Wittke points out quite rightly, with sentimentality or the idea that it was about "positivist instrumental knowledge" (Schroeter-Wittke 2011, p. 22). It is not about "pure feeling" or "pure knowledge" but rather about attentiveness to a dimension of human life that, while it exceeds rationality, always wants to be reflected, justified, and becomes accessible to intuition. Religious sensitivity is therefore primarily still a topic of religion teaching and often associated with theological premises, even though reflection in religious education is willing to venture beyond that. This is necessary if it is to be a theme in the general educational discourse and in education science.

Christine Freitag sees a possibility to establish religious sensitivity as a theme of education science in the discussion around the highly trendy concept of school culture, particularly because religious education demands religious sensitivity for the general school life and not only for religion teaching. She calls attention to the fact that school culture mostly describes the special profile of a school, which is mainly discussed in the context of heterogeneity, against the background of performance and migration. This brings the category of interculturality into play, with religion ranking as a subcategory to culture. No development toward religious sensibility can as yet be expected in the current intercultural education sciences, but its attainments can be used for the project of religious sensitivity. They consist, among other things, in exposing negative ascriptions and in identifying disadvantage and discrimination in religion and other fields.

Christine Freitag's proposal can be seen as a useful starting point between religious education and intercultural education. The current debate about the positioning of religion in the school context, given the religious plurality of society, aims at interreligious communication, which is inconceivable without considering deficient forms of religion also, and without evaluating and discussing them in enlightened ways. In addition—and this can also be learned from intercultural research—is it important to neither under- nor overestimate the forms of expression of religious orientations. Religious sensitivity demands awareness of the religious dimension and that due attention is given to religious questions, but it must not be wrongly overstated and become what Freitag terms "religious hypersensitivity" (Freitag 2011, p. 293), where all kinds of phenomena and utterances are categorized as religious and treated accordingly. Hypersensitivity in a wider sense holds a latent danger, particularly in dealing with different religions and their diverging rules and standards, and the related vulnerabilities. The discussion of tendencies that seem questionable, the possibility to objectively question behaviors in a context of active tolerance, nonetheless belongs to the task of any religiously sensitive educational culture.

An essential and critical aspect in the practice of a religion-sensitive school culture is the role of the actors within the school. Religious education has so far been assigned to religion teaching as a specialized field with its coordination of different confessions and interdisciplinary cooperation with other subjects. The demand for inclusion into the school culture breaks up the former restriction to religion teaching. It now concerns everyone involved in shaping the school: teachers, students, and also parents. This is more easily organized in independent or church schools: Teachers act within the (confidently) self-given profile, and parents choose this offer for their children for educational, ideological, or religious reasons. This applies as much to independent Waldorf schools as to church schools or other recognized models with a special profile. For state schools, on the other hand, which are not schools of choice but mandatory, more complex decision-making processes are required, where the school leadership, teachers, and parent councils need to agree to include religious issues into the school life. An essential question to ask is: Do teachers have to be religious in order to work in such a school? Henning Schluss suggests that religiousness cannot be insisted on as a pedagogical competence. It is *one possible* human competence from the infinite range of potentials, but it does not have to be realized, as little as other competences must be realized. Teachers can consequently not be expected to "see themselves as religious, pious, or devoted to a worldview" (Schluss 2011, p. 221). Based on the premise inspired by Schleiermacher—that education should be informed by a diversity from which no area of human life, including religion or religiousness, is excluded—Schluss concludes that "it can be expected of teachers that they are able and willing to support the adolescents entrusted to them in their religious experience and reflection, too, because they must not artificially deprive them of that element of their humanity. This particular pedagogical skill can be described as religious sensitivity and is therefore a pedagogical competence" (Schluss 2011, p. 221f.)

The concepts of basic religious education, interreligious learning, and a religion-sensitive school culture describe three important themes in religious education today. We will now look at the idea of religious education in Waldorf schools in relation to these considerations, focusing on commonalities between religious education and Waldorf education.

4 General religious education in Waldorf schools

4.1 Why religious education?

The religious dimension is represented in multiple ways in the pedagogical portfolio of Waldorf schools. Considered equivalent to science and art, religion is expected to be brought to life in the educational landscape of these schools (Steiner 1975a, p. 17). The schools' whole educational practice should emanate "an ethical-religious atmosphere for the children" (Steiner 1986b, p. 154). Education and teaching are a "moral, religious deed" (Steiner 1986a, p. 209), and teachers must become "inwardly wholly religious" in order to realize "this education" (Steiner 1986a, p. 83).

The full inclusion of religion into the conception of Waldorf education is due, Steiner holds, to the fact that religiousness must be understood as a basic anthropological constant. Religion is a constituent part of our humanity. Religious experience is thus associated with our ontological structure that includes an "original religious disposition" (Steiner 1989b, p. 181).

The view that religiousness is intrinsic to us is indeed a thesis represented in educational anthropology, but it remains an open thesis. Irmgard Bock, for instance, writes in her voluminous handbook on education that "Religiosity is part of the human essence" (Bock 1991, p. 101), although she does not refer to the question again. Volker Ladenthin, too, sees religiosity as a natural dimension of human existence: "We can individually decide on the reception, development, and tradition of our relationship with religion but not on our religiousness as such. That is given to us" (Ladenthin, 2006, p. 115).

The concept of religiousness has become more prominent again in the religious education discourse (Angel 2006). Yet there is no systematic, let alone homogeneous, understanding of the concept. Monika Jakobs presents an often-cited definition based on a functional understanding of religiousness as the biographical processing of religion (Jakobs 2006). This assumes a subjective component that relates to religion as an objective component.

The view that we have a religious disposition has received surprising support from neurobiological findings. Religion-specific or religion-affine phenomena such as prayer and meditation have been studied scientifically for some time now. These studies focus mostly on sociobiological aspects, since people with a religious attitude and lifestyle seem to have better health and resilience, a fact that could point to a certain evolutive justification of religion. These effectively presented findings were recently confirmed by physiological brain examinations that were able to localize neuronal excitation states caused by spiritual experiences. A particular gene was found in persons with a distinct "tendency to self-transcendence," giving rise to the effective but highly imprecise formulation of a "God gene" (Hamer 2006).

Such theses naturally meet with rejection, such as the statement that, given the diversity of religious phenomena, the "question as to religiousness as a basic anthropological constant must remain open" (Hock 2009, p. 402). One can ask, however, whether it is not precisely this diversity of expressive and developmental possibilities that suggests such a "basic constant," particularly since it can be found in all cultures. Even if Benner holds, quite rightly, that religion cannot be innate, as little as one's native tongue can be (Benner 2010, p. 184), it is nevertheless true that the capacity to learn a native tongue must be innate, even if this language can only be learned through imitation in a social context; without this innate capacity such learning would be entirely impossible.

This essay is not, and cannot be, the place to determine whether or not religiousness can only be assigned to humans. The fact is that both positions are still open to debate and that Steiner's ontological view of religiousness cannot simply be rejected. But the definition of what religiousness is must also remain open. This is essentially due to the imprecision of the concept of religion, as shall be shown below. A heuristic approach allows at least to understand religiousness as the subjective side of the phenomenon of religion. It is the subjective experience of our own existence, which is rooted in and connected with a transcendent reality. Religion is then the objectivization, in freedom, of this experienced subject-bound world in symbolic, ritual, cultic forms. Religiousness can then be defined as "the part of religion, realized in freedom, that only exists in religious diversity" (Grümme 2012, p. 456).

4.2 The concept of religion

The discussion about the concept of religion has gained new prominence due to the much-advertised "return of the religions," but it has not been able to produce a compelling definition of religion in the sense of a univocal concept (Schrödter 2013, p. 180). There is, after all, no uniformity or continuity of the phenomenon of religion with its multifaceted traditions that could define religion beyond question, especially in the age of the plurality in all areas of life. Only a differentiated access, characterization more than definition, can therefore contribute to determining the concept of religion. Burkhard Porzelt identifies four aspects of religion (Porzelt 2009, p. 45ff.) which he calls anthropological, substantial, functional, and phenomenological. The anthropological perspective has been touched on in the above characterizations: It starts from the elementary affectedness of the human being as a being oriented toward transcendence. The best-known description is that by Paul Tillich (Tillich 1964), who said religion was "being touched by what deeply concerns us." This widespread and much-cited open concept of religion lacks the specificity that would allow a distinction between quasi- or pseudo-religious and authentic religious content. This weakness of the open concept of religion is contrasted by the comparatively narrow substantial perspective. This focuses on the relationship we have with God or a higher being and is characterized in Thomas Aquinas' statement that "Religion is what offers to God due worship. Two things are therefore considered in religion: first, what religion offers to God [...], and second, to whom it is offered, that is God" (Thomas STh II-II 81.5 c, von Aquin 1934). Porzelt, moreover, refers to theological and sociological aspects. Based on the work of Wilson and Charles Y. Glock, he offers a phenomenological description of the commonalities of the religions, including features such as a reliable connection with tradition, myths, and symbols, concepts of redemption as well as elements of holy order, locations, and objects, writings, and communities (Glock 1969). For the functional perspective, Niklas Luhmann's favored concept of contingency coping is used, according to which religion is a means of coping with life in the face of human mortality and finality, or creates an ordered structure with regard to identity, orientation, and even the cosmic dimension (Kaufmann 1989, p. 84f.).

Within the margins of this essay, it is impossible to consider the whole width of aspects of Steiner's religious ideas (Willmann 2001a, p. 48ff.). But, referring to Porzelt's categories, one can say that Steiner's concept of religion emphasizes the mutually complementing substantial and anthropological perspectives. Steiner says in relation to both categories, "Religion is about venerating the suprasensible. Human nature depends on this veneration. It depends on looking up to theublimee in the suprasensible" (Steiner 1977, p. 131). Steiner characterizes religiousness as a natural human need that seeks concrete forms of expression and realization. Not theories and dogmas are the primary expression of religion and religiosity, however, but an attitude of reverence and respect, built on "attunement to the eternal" (Steiner 1989a, p. 239).

Of particular interest here is what Steiner says about an understanding of religion, which he describes in the context of education and which I would like to call his *pedagogical concept of religion*. "I would like to explain to you [the teachers of the Waldorf school] what religious means in the anthroposophical sense. Religion in the sense of anthroposophy is the sensation, the feelings we absorb in contemplating the world, spirit, and life. The worldview as such is in the head, religion on the other hand always arises from our whole being. This is why a religion based on creed is not truly religious. What makes the difference is that the whole human being, and mainly feeling and will, live in religion. The worldview that lives in religion is just there to exemplify, support, deepen the feeling and to strengthen the will. What religion should instill in us is that we can grow beyond the deepening of feeling and strength of will that the transient, earthly things can give us" (Steiner 1975b, p. 102f.)

Steiner introduces a concept of religion that seeks to break up any theoretical or confessional fixation and that assigns religion to the realm of feeling and will. All religious content must be seen as secondary; it is the product of cognition that serves to present religious knowledge, but it does not reach the depth of the authentic religious dimension. Content is interchangeable; the deeper layers within ourselves, which contain what is religious in us and that precede any concrete religious statement, are not. It is, rather, aesthetic experience and impulses to action that constitute the field of experience of religious people.

Based on this confession-critical and open concept of religion, Steiner develops a general religious education concept for Waldorf schools. This aims primarily at developing a differentiated capacity for feeling, about inspiring and enhancing religious feelings and will impulses, about formal religious abilities, inner attitudes, and ways of thinking, and about religiously motivated interactive processes. The concept of general religiosity suggests no specific religion is meant, but that which is common to all religions, what is elementary to religion as emotional, volitional, and ethical competences, and what can therefore be claimed by all religions. This thought includes a certain universality that allows Waldorf education, as we shall see later, to live in other religious and cultural contexts. Steiner's approach does not aim at religion but at the individual and their religious potential. The concept of universality does not only relate to religion or to the human being, but it also applies to education itself. This form of religious education must be understood as a form of general education.

In his commendable publication on religious education (Schmidt 1993), the theologian and expert in religious education Günther R. Schmidt makes an important distinction between "general religious education" and "Christian religious education." Schmidt's underlying thinking also allows for a categorization of the Waldorf-specific approach to religious education. According to Schmidt, general education cannot be excluded from the questions that form the main themes of confessional education. These include questions and experiences concerning human existence as such, which therefore concern every human being, and which require reflection: for instance, "being affected by the enigma of one's own and others' existence and the question of meaning as the ultimate Where from, Why, and What for of one's own life and of reality as a whole"; the "experience of a possible or real alienation and the longing for authenticity"; "fulfilment in joy and gratitude for a life that is seen as a gift"; and finally the "finiteness of one's own life, the inescapability and eeriness of death" (Schmidt 1987, p. 23). Given this existential aspect of any pedagogical endeavor, any education is "essentially religious education" for Schmidt (Schmidt 1993, p. 86). A strong statement that coincides with Steiner's above cited view that all education is religious.

Schmidt goes on to describe two forms of religious education, a distinction that can be helpful in the positioning of Waldorf education. He distinguishes between instructional and indicative religious education. The instructional variety is rooted in the affiliation with a particular religion or religious group that seeks to convey or transfer its beliefs and values to others so that they identify with its life form, support it, and represent it to the outside. (Schmidt calls attention to antiplural tendencies that counteract individual self-determination). Indicative religious education is independent of positions and aims at an overall orientation in life, the attitude one has to oneself, to others, and to life as a whole, and it seeks to enable an experience of basic trust. It supports the quest for meaning and the related ethical actions. Religiously relevant experiences are discussed rather than suppressed, dismissed, or processed in a sectarian manner. Religion or religions and their structure are explored, and the general sensitization for religious expression and for questions of meaning and value is promoted (Schmidt 1993, p. 142ff.).

For Steiner, religious education that is focused on content and that seeks to guide students toward a particular religion—what Schmidt refers to as instructional education—is not an option in Waldorf education. It is immediately apparent, Steiner says, "how little we can really achieve in ethics and religion, if we confront children with certain religious, or even ethical, matters. At best, we could educate them to become Christians, Jews, Catholics, or Protestants, to the extent that we ourselves practice one of these religions. But we need to exclude from any art of education the attempt to bring up children to be what we are ourselves" (Steiner 1978, p. 297).

The target categories of a general religious education in Waldorf schools are therefore formal-religious: They are about attitudes, feelings, and will formation. Steiner mentions, above all, trust, a sense of wonder, reverence, humility, piety, obedience, universal gratitude, loving devotion, a sense of duty. Children and young people should be enabled to experience that they are the image of God; charity and a love of God can grow from this (Willmann 2001a, p. 249ff.). Teachers are to develop these feelings and this mood in children and create an atmosphere that makes room for these experiences. The development of religious forces, the experience of feeling, and the education of the will are intended, independently of any declared religion.

4.3 Forms of operationalization

How can this concept of general religious education be operationalized? There are two ways: One is by way of a particular didactic and methodical approach, the other on the basis of particular content. The didactic approach involves what Steiner describes as pictorial teaching. In pictorial teaching, the focus is not on finding intellectual solutions to tasks and problems. It rather facilitates the experience and exploration of a deeper reality where feeling and will are included as learning dimensions. It aims at the intuitive, symbolic impartation of content through language, gesture, and activity, through music and images. And it aims at providing children with aesthetic possibilities of reception that lead into the depth of existence and touch on the mystery of the world. For pictures, symbols, and parables do not only address the intellect but also the whole person. Aesthetic-emotional experiences can sensitize children to moral experiences, questions of meaning, and human values. And parables, images, and symbols can awaken a sense for transcendence and the existence of a spiritual world. Special forms of operationalizing the symbolic serve the same purpose: Definition stands back in favor of characterization. Multiple ways of approaching the world are opened up, living and dynamic concepts in a descriptive language replace static, one-dimensional thinking. The implications of this approach are evident: It asks for a sensory, aesthetic education that is supported by a teaching culture based on narration and symbolic presentation.

Steiner's educational thinking anticipates in astonishing ways the motifs of (religious) education that would only be developed decades later in religious education. The concept of symbolic teaching that emerged around 30 years ago and has since gained importance constitutes a model of religious education that comes surprisingly close to Waldorf education, both in its formal justification and methodic intentions. Symbolic teaching addresses not only the rational mind but also the aesthetic sense and the feeling, and it can therefore give wider and deeper access to religion. "Wider" because symbolic teaching does not need to refer to a particular religion; "deeper" because it addresses levels that lie beyond the level of cognitive discourse. It assumes that the religious reality is condensed into symbolic media and that it can therefore also be explored through these. These media represent mainly pictures and myths, parables, folktales and legends, rituals and customs, natural objects, and artistic productions. Symbolic teaching has brought about a crucial shift toward the aesthetic dimension of religion, from which its didactic concept derives. This also includes the prioritization of emotional, affective, and volitional aspects of religion: Image-oriented religion stands against conceptual theology, and dynamic myths against the static Logos. Irrespective of the different objectives that depend on the received symbolic concept (C. G. Jung, A. Lorenzer, E. Cassirer, P. Ricœur) or the specific confessional access (on the Catholic side primarily Hubertus Halbfas; on the Protestant side Peter Baudler), symbolic teaching tries to "guide the tension, arising from the 'breaking with tradition,' between religious tradition and subjective understanding and appropriation, toward a new solution" (Kunstmann 2002, p. 352). Symbolic teaching is consequently also an answer to the crisis of modernity; it is no longer primarily interested in the traditional content of (Christian) religion but in the possibilities of subjective appropriation and interpretation of elementary religious experiences that are also relevant to finding orientation in the context of the loss of traditions and of pluralization.

The aesthetically oriented methodologies of Waldorf education rely on content, too, however. An aesthetic-imaginative education needs material substance for its realization. For religion teaching, a number of elements and motifs can be found in (European) Waldorf schools. These include verses, prayers, and religious songs, and—often inspired by the Christian festivals—seasonal displays in the classrooms with objects from nature. Christian festivals are generally celebrated in the school community: Carol singing, Christmas celebrations, the performing of Christmas Plays by teachers, parents, and sometimes even students, the lighting of the St. John's fire, plays about courage at Michaelmas, and other activities mark the festivals of the year. Around the year, little scenic plays with religious content are performed by second graders (the legends of St. Francis or St. Christopher); in third grade, the opening words of the Book of Genesis are learned in Hebrew; in fifth grade, the beginning of the Gospel of St. John in Greek; in sixth grade, the Lord's Prayer in Latin. Classrooms are decorated with Christian motifs (Raphael's Sistine Madonna, Giotto frescos etc.). The stories told in the first school years have religious themes. Grade teachers tell stories daily; depending on the children's age, these are folktales, legends of saints, stories from the Old Testament, from Germanic, Greek, and Roman mythology, from Zoroastrian religion, legends from Buddhism and Hinduism are told and discussed. The history of Christianity and that of Islam are examples of the story material of sixth grade. In seventh and eighth grade, the focus is on the great themes of Reformation and Enlightenment and also on important biographies. This narrative compendium that stretches across eight school years and encompasses the religious and cultural history of humanity must be seen as a continuous religious foundation of Waldorf education. It does not only serve as information but also, in activating inner images, it develops the capacity for symbolization that can evolve into cognitive capacity in the course of the students' biographical development.

The actualization of general religious education ranges from classroom aesthetics to performances to the narration of religious content, which, depending on the students' age, lead to artistic or discursive reflections. It should also be mentioned that it is easily possible, due to the integrative structure of the Waldorf curriculum, to discuss ethical-religious questions across subjects, particularly in history, literature, art, and music, and that even in subjects that are not close to religion, religious motifs can light up—for instance, in the nature studies in fourth grade where zoology is introduced using the examples of lion, bull, and eagle (the animals that symbolize the three Synoptic Evangelists).

With its emphasis on pictorial and symbolic teaching, the concept of general religious education is open enough to be practiced and realized in religious contexts other than Christianity, on which Waldorf education was originally based.

This thought is also fundamental to a general religious education concept, because such a concept wants to appeal to the religiousness that lives in all people, beyond confessional differences, and develops "the divine-spiritual element that lives in the human soul" (Steiner 1978, p. 309).

4.4 Religious education around the world: Waldorf schools in Israel

As Waldorf schools spread around the world to cultural regions that are further removed from its original context and that have different ideas of religious education, the general religious education approach has become particularly valuable. The question is how the religious education concept of the Waldorf schools can be adapted to other religious contexts and, vice versa, how other religions can be integrated in this concept. Hardly any research has been done on this so far (Willmann 2014; Hofmann 2015), although it is in this context in particular that the relevance and the resilience of Steiner's concept can be tested. The model of the Waldorf schools in Israel is a good example of the successful adaptation of the curricular concept and the simultaneous integration of religious content that is not Christian (Willmann 2014, p. 85ff.): Waldorf teachers in Israel have developed a compelling narration concept to replace the classic story material in Waldorf schools, which contains, as described earlier, numerous Christian elements. This concept, which is also age-appropriate and anthropologically founded, is built wholly on the biblical and Rabbinic literature. The Jewish legends of great rabbis (Rabbi Akiva), for instance, which describe the life and work of these individualities as models of wisdom and courage, replace or complement the legends of Christian saints in second grade. In third grade, teachers tell the stories from Genesis, as they do in all Waldorf schools, introducing the great founding figures of Abraham and Moses. In fourth grade, instead of German mythology, the stories of the judges (Deborah, Gideon, Samuel, Joshua) are used, which relate the dramatic situations of the itinerant and combative Israelites. The story that is central to fifth grade is that of King David, who is also a poet and singer and who seems to anticipate the Greek era that is usually the topic for that age group. The figure of Solomon is dominant in the stories in sixth grade. The building and unfolding of the large Kingdom of Israel and its later division into Israel in the North and Judah in the South are studied and interpreted in parallel to the rise of the Roman Empire and its split into the Western and Eastern Roman Empires. The modern era with its future-oriented projects is reflected, on a different level, in the great prophetic tradition of Israel that heralds a new age of justice.

That in Israeli Waldorf schools the Jewish holidays of Hanukkah, Passover, Purim, or rituals such as Shavuot or Seder are celebrated is also part of the concept of general religious education (Willmann 2014). Here, too, general religious education does not aim to educate students for the Judaic faith but uses its content to sensitize them to religion and inspire feelings and will forces that support community building. The decision to practice the Jewish faith must be made by the young person of their own volition.

4.5 Interreligious education: the Intercultural Waldorf School in Mannheim

Not much experience is available yet of intercultural learning in Waldorf schools, a fact that is linked to the student populations. Only few parents from other cultures, and even fewer from other religions, have discovered or become aware of Waldorf schools as alternative educational possibilities for their children.

The Intercultural Waldorf School in Mannheim is an exception. As the name suggests, it deliberately places an intercultural approach at the center of its education, which means that cultural difference and pluralism are not seen as problems but as chances. Two instructive studies on the school exist: one of them describes the school's intercultural concept (Brater et al. 2007), while the other evaluates the integration of students with a migrant background (Brater et al. 2009). Merely fragmentary results are available at this point on interreligious learning as part of this concept (Willmann 2015, p. 208ff.). Intercultural learning is hardly conceivable without interreligious learning and vice versa.

For interreligious learning, too, both the symbolic teaching approach and the broad and varied content of general religious education are appropriate. In the story material included in the curriculum, diverse religious worldviews are represented, from folktales and legends from around the world through ancient and indigenous mythologies to the great literatures of the present world religions. The open concept of religion is also valuable because, due to its anthropological foundation, it does not accentuate religious divergence but is able to absorb and integrate it. It can be seen as propaedeutic to religious instruction in the different faiths.

The Independent Intercultural Waldorf School in Mannheim was founded in 2003. By early October 2014, the school had 279 students from 34 nations, 149 of them with a migrant background. For a German Waldorf school, this is an unusually high percentage of children with a migrant biography. The faculty is also international, with 40 teachers from 13 nations. The list of religions and faith communities among the students reveals that 116 students belong to the Christian faith (59 protestant, 54 catholic, 3 orthodox), 65 are Muslim, and 3 Jewish; 96 students are either not affiliated to any religion or no information is available.

Given this student population, which is unusual for a Waldorf school, with very different religious affiliations, the faculty decided not to offer confessional religion lessons to start with. The intention was not to emphasize what separates the children but what connects them. In intercultural education, it is important to look at commonalities rather than differences. No "majority religion" should stand out and potentially keep parents of other religions or worldviews from enrolling their children. There are also organizational reasons: Guaranteeing the equivalence of different religious lessons is difficult. Introducing Islamic religion lessons, for instance, would have been very complicated. Nor should religion be seen as a discriminating motif that urges parents to decide in favor of a particular religious tuition that was traditionally viewed critically by many. In keeping with the school's intercultural approach, cultural lessons are therefore offered from third grade in order to gradually familiarize the students with different cultures and their rituals and customs, and to make their own expressions of life, such as language, music, poetry, art, and religion, as well as aspects of everyday life in their cultures accessible to them.

Having described the story material in Israeli Waldorf schools, we will also briefly look at that of the Mannheim Intercultural School. This material has also gone through various changes in that non-European narrative traditions have been increasingly included, the great treasure of Arab-Islamic stories in particular. The treatment of cultural periods was also given a new focus, the aim being to overcome the Eurocentric orientation and to emphasize and honor the achievements of other cultures. Even these few elements of intercultural teaching and practice illustrate how openness, the willingness for dialog, and the recognition of pluralism can contribute to creating a vibrant place of education. At the same time, religious sensitization takes place in that aspects from the life of the different religions are presented. This culminates in the school's interreligious festival culture that demands of everyone involved a sensitive and empathetic attitude during preparation and organization. It is an essential component of the school culture, in that contributions from parents, who also bring their religiousness into the school, are much valued. Organizing festivals also provides an occasion for teachers to engage more deeply with the religions represented at the school. This is discussed and decided in the faculty meetings to the extent that official representatives of the religions from outside the school are invited to the festivals or their preparation. As well as the annual Christian festivals, Jewish, Islamic, and—depending on the student body—other religious festival traditions are included and celebrated.

The concept of a uniting intercultural education is particularly effective in primary school; with the beginning of secondary education, significant aspects of the individual student's religious affiliation gain increasing importance: Islamic and Christian fasting periods, dress codes, confirmation, bar mitzvah, and others need to be explained and discussed.

While this is not the place to go more deeply into the details of this complex situation, we can say that the Intercultural School in Mannheim has achieved remarkable results in terms of religious and interreligious education. Religious sensitization is not just an empty phrase here, but also it is seen as a highly relevant task of education. The survey, which remains fragmentary, has detected one weakness in this concept that seems to ask for the complementation of general religious learning by confessional religion lessons in the higher grades: The transition from the "naïve" religious feelings of childhood to the young person's personal and identity-forming religious positioning needs to be accompanied in more distinct and concrete ways, and the individual-personal and the real societal differentiation of religious and cultural orientations must find clearer ways of expression. Introducing religion lessons in high school, depending on the student's religion and confession, can support awareness-building and lead to new dialogical encounters. Large parts of such religious tuition can be inclusive, with joint projects promoting interreligious learning. It was pointed out in all discussions that all students appreciate being recognized and respected in their religion.

Despite limited space available here, the examples provided can hopefully illustrate that the general religious education program is variable, that the religious, social, and cultural conditions are reflected in this concept, and that religious content and forms of religious learning can be suitably adjusted and developed. This is another future-oriented feature. We need to point out, however, that the focus of religious learning here is not the formulation of religious content, even if that is desirable, but the possibility to experience religion as a resource in life that conveys human values, gives meaning, and enables individual approaches to the space of transcendence.

5 Perspectives

The recent trends in religious education described in this essay in the context of basic religious education, interreligious education, and the development of a religion-sensitive school culture constitute religious education options and needs to which Waldorf schools are well suited. The most obvious advantage is that they are independent; this gives them more freedom regarding religious education and the ability to create religious learning situations even outside the designated religious tuition periods. The same applies to confessional schools.

Waldorf schools are not bound to a particular confession or religion but reflect primarily the religious contents and forms that their students and parents bring to the school. Over and above that, they include contents of all the major religions. This does create some tension since—and this we have not been able to discuss here—Waldorf education is, from a religious perspective, not without preconditions. But it makes itself unconditional through its practice. With its anthropology and its educational thinking that aims at individual freedom, it is rooted in Christian ideas, a fact that is reflected in its trinitarian structure (Willmann 2001a, p. 122ff.). But its approach to religious education and its didactic structures are universal. Its religious education is anthropologically justified, and it therefore derives its methods from human development, which it promotes. Its aim is to educate students toward deepened awareness of themselves and their transcendence in ways that enable a free but fulfilling relationship to God.

This brings us to the question of the necessity of religious education for all involved in the educational processes. Basic religious education is not only a claim everyone can raise but it should also be achievable for everyone. This general possibility, described by Bernd Schröder and others as a require-ment, is made possible in Waldorf schools with their concept of general religious education. Due to its strongly emotional and affective orientation, it does not aim at cognitive evaluability, although it strives to achieve that the experiences students have with it will ultimately enable them to "position themselves autonomously and responsibly in the religious field," as the Protestant theologian Jürgen Heumann said in his appeal for basic religious education (Heumann 2004, p. 71). The demand for reli-gious education for everyone naturally holds the danger of discriminating against those who do not choose a religious way of life. In my view, Steiner's anthropological concept of religion is sufficiently broad that even atheist views, in the sense of Ronald Dworkin's religious atheism, do not have to roundly reject its educational concept. Dworkin's definition of religion emphasizes emotional aspects in the same way that Waldorf schools do with their general religious education. "Religion is a deep, distinct, and comprehensive worldview: It holds that inherent, objective value permeates everything, that the universe and its creatures are awe-inspiring, that human life has purpose and the universe order. A belief in a god is only one possible manifestation or consequence of that deeper worldview" (Dworkin 2013, p. 1).

As Wolfgang Nieke also stated, the conveying of ethical-religious values and the search for meaning in school offering general education require tolerance, a tolerance that needs practicing toward all life plans. This attitude, too, is central to the concept of religious education in Waldorf schools. According to Steiner, Waldorf education can only thrive where there are "tolerance and humanity" (Steiner 1978, p. 311).

Regarding the need for interreligious communication and learning, which gain ever greater urgency given the changes in society described earlier, Waldorf schools have much catching up to do. While they are confronted with the fact that religious beliefs are becoming more diverse and that confessional identities are disappearing, religious heterogeneity is not as prevalent among its students and parents as it is in mainstream schools. Interreligious learning will become more of a challenge for the religious edu-cation concept of Waldorf schools in the future. An institution like the *Three Religions Elementary School*, which we briefly described, stands on more solid and viable ground in this respect than the Waldorf schools. It seems to me that this is owed to the clear religious identity-oriented factors underlying its concept. Supported by the teachers, who belong to the various religions, distinct features of each faith are authentically presented, conveyed, and lived, and on the basis of this, dialog and communication are established with other religions. This is rarely possible in Waldorf schools, within their context of general religious education, not only because of the students' religious background, but also because of the teachers' orientation. The Intercultural Waldorf School in Mannheim is an exception. While there are further initiatives that strive to make Waldorf education more intercultural (Berlin, Hamburg, Dortmund, Stuttgart), these are all in their initial stages. Given the growing demand for intercultural competences in teachers, it is both conceivable and desirable that competences required in religious education will also increasingly be demanded and developed. This could give a more distinct profile to the field of religious education in the Waldorf movement. For interreligious teaching and learning, always ask for the critical reflection of habits and traditions, for a new language, and greater sensitivity to other views, attitudes, and practices.

The greatest strength of the religious education concept of Waldorf schools lies possibly in their multi-faceted potential for religious sensitization. We see this, first of all, in the numerous motifs of religious education that are quickly detected, even for the outside observer. Walking around the grade rooms and looking at the pictures of Christian art, for instance, at the lower grade readers; attending school festivals, where children perform scenic plays based on saints' legends, or listening to high school choirs singing Mozart masses and gospels, one realizes how religious content permeates the entire school. The aesthetics of Waldorf education are not merely illustrative: It is through aesthetics rather than rational logic that children meet the world. World encounter is aesthetic world perception. Sensory perception cannot be replaced by but only complemented by conceptual rationality. Aesthetic experience is where education starts: Images, festivals, rituals and cult, poetry and parables are its language. The forms of religious expression are symbolic, after all. The pictorial, symbolic approach of Waldorf education that is meant to permeate all subjects forms the basis of a sensitivity that can be called religious even if it does not aim at primarily religious content. Any content can be approached from the perspective and in the mood of religious experience, and "every subject [can have] a religious character" (Steiner 1989, p. 178). Religious sensitization can thus become a supporting educational feature that touches all school activities and can therefore, in many ways, unlock and awaken the interpretive, expressive, reflective, and practical competences in students that Bernd Schröder demands of religious education.

In my experience, what can be asked of Waldorf schools, given the high expectations they have of their school culture, is the better integration of religious tuition, in whatever religion or confession, into the general school life, and closer collaboration and communication with the religion teachers. While both Waldorf teachers and religion teachers attend the faculty meetings and consult with one another, they don't organize many projects together. Ecumenic collaboration seems to me to be given more weight in other schools than in Waldorf schools.

The three areas we discussed will not become less relevant in the future and will require action, given current developments. It seems wrong to me to assume that the many questions and problems arising from religious and ideological divergences in an open society can be overcome by reducing religious education in schools. It is essential to seize the chances provided by religious pluralism. This requires more than a superficial minimum knowledge and understanding of, insight in, and tolerance for religion. Religious education and Waldorf education can contribute to this: The perspectives on new forms of religious education described here have great potential both in religion teaching and in Waldorf education.

Note

1 Cf. Erziehungskunst [Art of Education] 11/1993 on Religion and Worldview, and 4/2016 on the question: Why Religion?

References

Angel, Hans Ferdinand (Ed.) (2006): Religiosität. Anthropologische, theologische und sozialwissenschaftliche Klärungen. Stuttgart: Kohlhammer.

Baumert, Jürgen (2002): Deutschland im internationalen Bildungsvergleich. In: Killius, Nelson (Ed.): Die Zukunft der Bildung. Frankfurt am Main: Suhrkamp, pp. 100–150.

Brater, Michael/Hemmer-Schanze, Christiane/Schmelzer, Albert (2007): Schule ist bunt. Eine Interkulturelle Waldorfschule im sozialen Brennpunkt. Stuttgart: Freies Geistesleben.

Brater, Michael/Hemmer-Schanze, Christiane/Schmelzer, Albert (2009): Interkulturelle Waldorfschule. Evaluation zur schulischen Integration von Migrantenkindern. Stuttgart: Freies Geistesleben.

Benner, Dietrich (2010): Religionsunterricht als Ort der Pädagogik und Ort der Theologie. In: Zeitschrift für Pädagogik und Theologie 62, issue 3, pp. 183–193.

Blömeke, Sigrid (Ed.) (2009): Handbuch Schule. Theorie – Organisation – Entwicklung. Bad Heilbrunn: Klinkhardt.

Bock, Irmgard (1991): Pädagogische Anthropologie. In: Roth, Leo (Ed.) (1991): Pädagogik. Handbuch für Studium und Praxis. Munich: Ehrenwirth, pp. 99–108.

Dworkin, Ronald (2013): Religion Without God. Cambridge, Massachusetts, and London: Harvard University Press.

Erziehungskunst. Monatsschrift zur Pädagogik Rudolf Steiners. Vol. 57, No. 11, November 1993.

Fischer, Dietlind (2009): Was ist Schulkultur und wie kann man sie entwickeln? In: Jäggle, Martin/Krobath, Thomas/Schelander, Robert (2009): lebens.werte.schule. Religiöse Dimensionen in Schulkultur und Schulentwicklung. Vienna, Münster: LIT, pp. 413–421.

Freitag, Christine (2011): Religionssensible Schulkultur aus erziehungswissenschaftlicher Sicht. In: Guttenberger, Gudrun/Schroeter-Wittke, Harald (2011): Religionssensible Schulkultur. Studien zur Religionspädagogik und Praktischen Theologie. Vol. 4. Ed. by M. Wermke. Jena: Garamond, pp. 285–306.

Glock, Charles Y. (1969): Über die Dimension der Religiosität. In: Matthes, Joachim (1996): Kirche und Gesellschaft. Einführung in die Religionssoziologie II. Reinbek: Rowohlt, pp. 150–168.

Grethlein, Christian (2012): Pratische Theologie. Berlin: De Gruyter

Grümme, Bernhard (2012): Menschen bilden. Eine religionspädagogische Anthropologie. Freiburg: Herder.

Halbfas, Hubertus (1982): Das dritte Auge. Religionsdidaktische Anstöße. Düsseldorf: Patmos.

Hamer, Dean (2006): Das Gottes-Gen. Warum uns der Glaube im Blut liegt. Munich: Kösel.

Hentig, Hartmut von (1993): Die Schule neu denken. Eine Übung in pädagogischer Vernunft. Munich: Hanser.

Heumann, Jürgen (2004): Religiöse Grundbildung in der öffentlichen Schule. In: Rothgangel, Martin/Fischer, Dietlind (Eds.) (2004): Standards für die religiöse Bildung? Zur Reformdiskussion in Schule und Lehrerbildung. Schriften aus dem Comenius-Institut. Vol. 13. Münster: LIT, pp. 68–81.

Hervieu-Léger, Danièle (2004): Pilger und Konvertiten. Religion in Bewegung. Würzburg: Ergon.

Hikma (2014): Interview mit der Drei-Religionen-Grundschule. Volume 9, Oktober 2014. Online: https://hikma-online.com/wp-content/uploads/2016/04/Hikma-9-interview.pdf (accessed: October 2022), pp. 211–222.

Hock, Klaus (2009): Religiosität. In: Bohlke, Eike (Ed.) (2009): Handbuch Anthropologie. Der Mensch zwischen Natur, Kultur und Technik. Stuttgart: Metzler, pp. 399–402.

Höhn, Hans-Joachim (1999): Erlebnisgesellschaft! Erlebnisreligion? Die Sehnsucht nach dem frommen Kick. In: Hofmeister, Klaus/Bauerochse, Lothar (Eds.) (1999): Die Zukunft der Religion. Würzburg: Echter, pp. 11–22.

Hofmann, Vera (2015): Annual Festivals in Waldorf Schools in multi-religious or non-Christian cultural Settings: "She showed us the fish but didn't teach us how to do the fishing." Master's Thesis. Oslo: Rudolf Steiner University College Oslo.

Jäggle, Martin/Krobath, Thomas/Schelander, Robert (2009): lebens.werte.schule. Religiöse Dimensionen in Schulkultur und Schulentwicklung. Vienna, Münster: LIT.

Jakobs, Monika (2006): Religiosität als biografische Verarbeitung von Religion. In: Angel, Hans Ferdinand (Ed.) (2006): Religiosität. Anthropologische, theologische und sozialwissenschaftliche Klärungen, Stuttgart: Kohlhammer, pp. 116–132.

Kaufmann, Franz-Xaver (1989): Auf der Suche nach den Erben der Christenheit. In: id., Religion und Modernität. Sozialwissenschaftliche Perspektiven. Tübingen: Mohr.

Krautz, Jochen (2007): Ware Bildung. Schule und Universität unter dem Diktat der Ökonomie. Kreuzlingen: Hugendubel.

Kunstmann, Joachim (2002): Religion und Bildung. Zur ästhetischen Signatur religiöser Bildungsprozesse. Gütersloh: Gütersloher Verlagshaus.

Ladenthin, Volker (2006): Religionsunterricht und die Bildung des Menschen. In: Ziebertz, Hans-Georg/Schmidt, Günter R. (Eds.) (2006): Religion in der Allgemeinen Pädagogik. Religion von der Grundlegung bis zu ihrer Bestreitung. Gütersloh: Gütersloher Verlagshaus, pp. 115–125.

Lechner Martin/Gabriel Angelika (Eds.) (2009): Religionssensible Erziehung – Impulse aus dem Forschungsprojekt "Religion in der Jugendhilfe" (2005–2008). Munich: Don Bosco.

Leimgruber, Stephan (2007): Interreligiöses Lernen (Neuausgabe). Munich: Kösel.

Liessmann, Paul Konrad (2014): Geisterstunde. Die Praxis der Unbildung. Eine Streitschrift. Vienna: Zsolnay.

Naurath, Elisabeth (2012): Pluralitätsfähige Religionspädagogik zwischen sozialer Relevanz und religiöser Transfunktionalität. In: Englert, Rudolf/Schwab, Ulrich/Schweitzer, Friedrich/Ziebertz, Hans Georg (Eds.) (2012): Welche Religionspädagogik ist pluralitätsfähig? Kontroversen um einen Leitbegriff. Freiburg: Herder, pp. 89–98.

Nieke, Wolfgang (2006): Religion als Bestandteil von Allgemeinbildung: Weltorientierung statt Religionslehre. In: Ziebertz, Hans-Georg/Schmidt, Günter R. (Ed.) (2006): Religion in der Allgemeinen Pädagogik. Religion von der Grundlegung bis zu ihrer Bestreitung. Gütersloh: Gütersloher Verlagshaus, pp. 191–210.

Nipkow, Karl Ernst (1990): Bildung als Lebensbegleitung und Erneuerung. Kirchliche Bildungsverantwortung in Gemeinde, Schule und Gesellschaft. Gütersloh: Mohn.

Pirner, Manfred (2004): Religiöse Grundbildung zwischen Allgemeinwissen und christlicher Lebenshilfe. In: Rothgangel, Martin/Fischer, Dietlind et al. (2004): Standards für religiöse Bildung? Zur Reformdiskussion in Schule und Lehrerbildung. Münster: LIT, pp. 34–53.

Porzelt, Burkard (2009): Grundlegung religiöses Lernen. Eine problemorientierte Einführung in die Religionspädagogik. Bad Heilbrunn: Klinkhardt.

Reese, Annegret (2006): Ich weiß nicht, wo da Religion anfängt und aufhört. In: Eine empirische Studie zum Zusammenhang von Lebenswelt und Religiosität bei Singlefrauen. Gütersloh: Gütersloher Verlagshaus.

Scheunpflug, Anette (2006): Diskurs zwischen Erziehungswissenschaft und Religionspädagogik. Weltbürgerliche Erziehung, evolutionäre Pädagogik und Religion. In: Ziebertz, Hans-Georg/Schmidt, Günter R. (Eds.) (2006): Religion in der Allgemeinen Pädagogik. Religion von der Grundlegung bis zu ihrer Bestreitung. Gütersloh: Gütersloher Verlagshaus, pp. 76–87.

Schluss, Henning (2011): Religionssensibilität als pädagogische Kompetenz. In: Guttenberger, Gudrun/Schroeter-Wittke, Harald (2011): Religionssensible Schulkultur. Studien zur Religionspädagogik und Praktischen Theologie. Vol. 4. Ed. by M. Wermke. Jena: Garamond, pp. 211–224.

Schmidt, Günther R. (1993): Religionspädagogik. Ethos, Religiosität, Glaube in Sozialisation und Erziehung. Göttingen: Vandenhoek & Ruprecht.

Schmidt, Günther R. (1987): Religionspädagogik zwischen Theologie und Pädagogik. In: Theologica Practica. Zeitschrift für Praktische Theologie und Religionspädagogik (THPR) 22/1987, pp. 21–33.

Schnell, Tatjana (2009): Implizite Religiosität. Zur Psychologie des Lebenssinns. Lengerich: Pabst Science Publ.

Schröder, Bernd (2004): Mindeststandards religiöser Bildung und Förderung christlicher Identität. In: Rothgangel, Martin/Fischer, Dietlind (Eds.) (2004): Standards für die religiöse Bildung? Zur Reformdiskussion in Schule und Lehrerbildung. Schriften aus dem Comenius-Institut. Vol. 13. Münster: LIT, pp. 13–33.

Schrödter, Hermann (2013): Die Religion der Religionen. Umriss eines philosophischen Versuchs. In: Müller, Tobias/Schmidt, Thomas M. (2013): Was ist Religion? Beiträge zur aktuellen Debatte um den Religionsbegriff. Paderborn: Schöningh, pp. 179–194.

Schröter-Wittke (2011): Was ist Religionssensibilität? In: Guttenberger, Gudrun/Schroeter-Wittke, Harald (2011): Religionssensible Schulkultur. Studien zur Religionspädagogik und Praktischen Theologie. Vol. 4. Ed. by M. Wermke. Jena: Garamond, pp. 21–30.

Steiner, Rudolf (1975a): Allgemeine Menschenkunde als Grundlage der Pädagogik. Rudolf Steiner Gesamtausgabe (= GA) 293. Dornach: Rudolf Steiner Verlag.

Steiner, Rudolf (1975b): Konferenzen mit den Lehrern der Freien Waldorfschule. GA 300a. Dornach: Rudolf Steiner Verlag.

Steiner, Rudolf (1977): Soziale Zukunft. GA 332a. Dornach: Rudolf Steiner Verlag.

Steiner, Rudolf (1978): Die gesunde Entwicklung des Leiblich-Physischen als Grundlage der Entfaltung des Seelisch-Geistigen. GA 303. Dornach: Rudolf Steiner Verlag.

Steiner, Rudolf (1986a): Gegenwärtiges Geistesleben und Erziehung. GA 307. Dornach: Rudolf Steiner Verlag.

Steiner, Rudolf (1986b): Was wollte das Goetheanum und was soll die Anthroposophie? GA 84. Dornach: Rudolf Steiner Verlag.

Steiner, Rudolf (1989a): Die Mission der neuen Geistesoffenbarung. Das Christusereignis als Mittelpunktgeschehen der Erdenevolution. GA 127. Dornach: Rudolf Steiner Verlag.

Steiner, Rudolf (1989b): Die pädagogische Praxis vom Gesichtspunkte geisteswissenschaftlicher Menschenerkenntnis. Die Erziehung des Kindes und jüngeren Menschen. GA 306. Dornach: Rudolf Steiner Verlag.

Thomas von Aquin (1934): Summa theologiae. Deutsche Thomas-Ausgabe. Salzburg, Leipzig 1933 ff; Heidelberg, Graz 1941 ff: Pustet.

Tillich, Paul (1964): Religion als eine Funktion des menschlichen Geistes? In: Tillich, Paul (1964): Die Frage nach dem Unbedingten. Schriften zur Religionsphilosophie. Gesammelte Werke. Bd. V. Stuttgart: Evangelisches Verlagswerk.

Verburg, Winfried (2011): Juden, Christen und Muslime machen gemeinsame Schule – Rahmenkonzept für eine trialogische Grundschule. In: Guttenberger, Gudrun/Schroeter-Wittke, Harald (2011): Religionssensible Schulkultur. Studien zur Religionspädagogik und Praktischen Theologie. Vol. 4. Ed. By M. Wermke. Jena: Garamond, pp. 323–34.

Wermke, Michael (2012): Religion und Schulleben. In: Rothgangel Martin/Adam, Gottfried/Lachmann, Rainer (Ed.) (2012): Religionspädagogisches Kompendium. Göttingen: Vandenhoek & Ruprecht, pp. 106–123.

Willmann, Carlo (2001a): Waldorfpädagogik. Theologische und religionspädagogische Befunde. Vienna: Böhlau.

Willmann, Carlo (2001b): Waldorfschulen. In: Mette, Norbert/Rickers, Folckert (Ed.) (2001): Lexikon der Religionspädagogik (LexRP) (2001): Neukirchen-Vluyn: Neukirchener Theologie, pp. 2187–2190.

Willmann, Carlo (2014): Religiöse Erziehung an Waldorfschulen im nichtchristlichen Kontext. Zugänge an Schulen in Ägypten und Israel. In: RoSe – Research on Steiner Education Vol. 5, Special Issue, pp. 80–89.

Willmann, Carlo (2015): Religion am Rande – Fundamentalismus in der Mitte? Ein Plädoyer für eine religionssensible Schulkultur. In: RosE – Research on Steiner Education Vol. 6, Special Issue, pp. 203–213.

WALDORF EDUCATION AND MEDIA
Human and Technological Development in Contrast

Edwin Hübner

1 Introduction

When Waldorf education was founded in 1919, many of the media now dominating everyday life had not yet been invented. People read books and newspapers, cinemas had only just arrived, but radio and TV were still in the early stages of development. No one thought of computers yet. This changed in the course of the 20th century. Mobile communication, and internet above all, changed everyday life so profoundly that it was clear by the end of the century that education needed to change, too, to keep up with the new technologies. "A new revolution," it was said, was required (Der Spiegel 1994, Papert 1994; Sonnenleiter/Jurtschitsch 1994).

In a much-noticed address at the German Education Congress on April 13, 1999, the former German President Roman Herzog said something that moved many people at the time. "Information technology will cause a classroom revolution. But we still *have to invent the education for the information age*. [...] The revolutionary development of information technology confronts us with a totally new situation. Computers will play a central part in the innovation of learning contents and ways of teaching, and must therefore become integral to the methodological concepts for all subjects. [...] We cannot stop halfway now. I am convinced that *computers belong into every classroom!*" (Herzog 1999).

Great efforts were indeed made at the time to equip schools with computers. Within only five years, the Initiative *Schulen ans Netz* (connecting schools) made sure all schools in Germany had internet. These initiatives focused on the technological development, asking how it could inform education. Waldorf education, which is informed by the development of the child (Chapter 3), has a totally different approach.

2 "A Silicon Valley school that doesn't compute"

Waldorf kindergartens and schools exist all around the world now: More than 1,000 are spread across China, Russia, Europe, Africa, and the Americas. As a result of their underlying principle that education must take its cue from child development, they reject the use of computers in the lower grades. This applies to all Waldorf schools worldwide. They consequently go against the widely held view that computers can't be introduced to schools early enough.

A tech-free school therefore calls for a prominently placed newspaper article. On October 23, 2011, the New York Times wrote under the heading "A Silicon Valley School That Doesn't Compute" about a Waldorf school in Silicon Valley. The majority of parents in that school worked for eBay, Google,

496

DOI: 10.4324/9781003187431-44

Apple, Yahoo, Hewlett-Packard, and other high-tech firms, many in leading positions. The article concludes that many parents and teachers at the epicenter of computer technology seemed to think that computers and school do not mix well: They send their children to a school that shuns the use of computers in lessons.[1]

But is an education that focuses on child development and rejects computers in the lower grades not hopelessly antiquated in the information age? Might not this deliberate cultivation of art and craft activities in Waldorf schools cause an unbridgeable divide between them and modern culture? How does Waldorf education see the world of technology and of electronic media?

3 Basic questions

Herzog's statement that an education for the information age first needs to be invented must be taken seriously. Since culture today is dominated by electronic media, any education not considering this fails to meet the requirements of our time. The media experts Daniel Süss, Claudia Lampert, and Christine W. Wijnen are convinced that "Education without media education is inconceivable today" (Süss/Lampert/Wijnen 2013, p. 16), and Heinz Moser goes even further in claiming that "all education is also media education" (Moser 2010, p. 31). They are absolutely right. The question is what kind of media education is sensible.

Waldorf education must ask how media education can be derived from child development. Before this question can be answered, two things need to be clear:

- What concept of media should inform educational considerations? How can one describe media?
- How do children develop? What do children have to deal with as they grow up?

4 Definitions of media

The media concept is multilayered and there has so far not been a generally accepted definition. Some authors wonder if "instead of asking 'What are media?' the question should be 'What isn't a medium?'" (Wiesing 2008, p. 235). Or, even more radically: "What is a medium? The answer is simple: Everything is!" The author then adds, "This answer is good because it is correct, but it is also pointless because it doesn't say anything" (Rauscher 2008, p. 272). The media concept is so complex that the media scientists Lorenz Engell and Josef Vogl wonder whether the first axiom of media theory should not be "There are no media – certainly not in a substantial and historically consistent sense" (Engell/Vogl 2004, p. 10).

Between these polar views lies a wide range of attempts at defining the media concept. The media scientist Hartmut Winkler, for example, proposes a "cumulative definition." He looks at media from different angles, trying to characterize and delimit them (Winkler 2008, p. 11). Bernward Hoffmann divides the multiple meanings of the term "medium" into four groups (Hoffmann 2003, p. 14f.). The media theorists Gerhard Tulodziecki and Bardo Herzig restrict their media concept to "electronically conveyed forms of experience" (Tulodziecki/Herzig 2002, p. 64) because that allows them to examine the properties of electronically mediated experiences while observing other forms of experience, too. They present the diversity of experience made possible by the media in a table (ibid., p. 66). In their introduction to media education, Daniel Süss, Claudia Lampert, and Christine W. Wijnen do not explain at all what they mean by "media" (Süss/Lampert/Wijnen 2013). Neither does Heinz Moser, who eschews a formal definition, characterizing instead our relationship to media and the influence they have on us on the basis of a number of concrete phenomena (Moser 2010). Stefan Hoffmann looks at how the concept has evolved through the past centuries and tries to identify a position that can integrate all the many different aspects (Hoffmann 2002).

5 A phenomenological approach to media

Approaching the media concept phenomenologically promises to be the most successful way from the point of view of Waldorf education.[2] For this, we need to ask: What media forms do we meet in everyday life and how do we use them? We find exactly three forms of media:

- script
- image (static or moving pictures)
- sound (music or speech)

Other media forms such as tactile or olfactory are possible but are less relevant in everyday life. What we are usually dealing with are script, images, and sound or speech. The way we deal with these media is very individual.

In order to access script, we must decipher symbols and develop inner images. We tend to sit still when we read a book, focusing our attention on the text. This is not necessary when we listen to a radio play, for instance. While we have to develop inner images, too, we can do other things at the same time, such as walk, jog, or tidy up. When watching a movie, we must sit still again, but we don't have to develop our own images.

This brief characterization is not about the content conveyed by the different media forms of script, image, and sound, but about the way we actively relate to them, which is determined by the form of media, not their content.

Script, image, and sound do not appear by themselves; however, they require a material (technological) foundation such as paper, a screen, or a loudspeaker. The reading of script can be seen as happening on three levels: first of all, the level of pure content ("What content is conveyed by the script?"), then the level of script itself as a form of medium, and the level of the carrier: paper, monitor, the projection on a screen. The same applies to image (film) and sound. We can therefore distinguish three levels for all media:

- content—what is conveyed to us
- form—the way content is conveyed or presented
- carrier—the material basis on which the "formed" content appears

We relate to the content of media through thinking, as we try to understand the content conveyed through script, image, or sound. With the forms of medium and, above all, the carriers we interact actively: We hold a book in our hands, turn the pages, feel the cover, smell the printing ink, or we hold the mouse, touch the keyboard, etc. We relate consciously to the content, trying to understand what is written on a screen, for instance. The volitional activity we perform in relation to the carrier or device is either merely semi-conscious or even entirely unconscious. We are concerned with the content, not with the device that allows us to perceive the content. But the media forms and the devices nonetheless influence how we take in content and how we then conceptualize it. If we observe ourselves, we notice a clear difference between how a story affects us when we read it or when we listen to a recording of it. The emotional effect of the same content can vary greatly. The difference is also obvious when a book has been made into a movie.

Hartmut Winkler points out that "Media create messages [...] simply by the fact that they provide formats for encoding messages" (Winkler 2008, p. 138). Not all media forms are equally suited to the expression of content. Logical philosophical conclusions are easiest conveyed in script; images would be less suited in this case, whereas the artistic expression of a mood is better conveyed through image and sound and is more difficult to convey in script.

The form of mediums consequently has an influence on both content and on the way the content is received.[3]

The devices we use also have an effect on us in that they require us to use them in a particular way. This produces subtle changes in us as the following example illustrates.

6 Side effects

Wide-spread habits such as searching the internet for information, working on computers, reading texts on a screen often lead to reduced concentration, a phenomenon that has been widely reported in recent publications.[4]

With this reduction of concentration, reading behaviors also change. The American writer Nicholas Carr says of himself, "my concentration often starts to drift after two or three pages. [...] I get fidgety, lose the thread, begin looking for something else to do. I feel as if I'm always dragging my wayward brain back to the text. The deep reading that used to come naturally has become a struggle" (Carr 2010, p. 21f.).

Carr speaks of his friends having the same experience (Carr 2010, p. 23). The German *Stiftung Lesen* (Reading Foundation) conducted studies and found changes in reading behavior.[5] Attention spans have become shorter. People don't like reading long text and no longer have the patience required for in-depth reading.

The internet opens up sheer unlimited access to all the information in the world. This world of available media content is gigantic: a true gain for humanity. The active use of computers or the exposure to computer screens, on the other hand, weakens our ability to read for longer periods of time while remaining concentrated. This is a side effect of the advantage we have gained.

The same is true for media devices as for any technology: It saves us work by doing it for us and by doing it much faster than we could do it. The danger resulting from this is that we lose the ability to do these things ourselves, just as muscles atrophy with lack of use. The German philosopher Günther Anders already called attention to this fact in his examination of how we relate to radio and television (Anders 1994, p. 107).

7 Direct and indirect media education

Because we engage with media in two polar opposite ways, media education must address both poles. It needs to consider how we relate to the media both through *conscious thinking* and through *volitional activity*. This means that we need both a direct and an indirect media education. Direct media education focuses on media *content* and with their different *forms* of presentation: How do we search the internet sensibly? How do we present our own content in public? How do I behave in social networks? How do I best use what Web 2.0 has to offer? What mistakes and dangers need to be avoided? Direct media education also has the task to convey a basic understanding of how the different devices work.

Indirect media education, on the other hand, has the important task of encouraging us to practice all the *skills* we urgently need in the age of media information but that cannot be acquired by using devices or that may even get lost as we increasingly use them.

Indirect media education must consequently aim at providing opportunities to develop and practice focused attention. Its most important task is to make sure that young people develop the ability to integrate the many fragmented pieces of information flooding in on them in daily life into a meaningful whole. Children and young people need to learn how to generate knowledge from information (Sacher 2000, p. 135ff.). In the age of cyberbullying, it is also necessary to teach children how to deal respectfully and mindfully with other people.

How can these educational goals be brought together with an orientation based on human development? To answer this question, we need to cast a brief glance at some basic aspects of child development.

8 Basic gestures of human development

While we each have our unique individuality, we are also members of the human species and therefore subject to general developmental features that characterize this species. The development of motor skills, language acquisition, the maturation of the sense organs, the change of teeth around the age of 6 or 7, entering puberty at the age of 11–13, etc.—they all occur within particular timeframes, providing many criteria for establishing whether or not development is "normal." But what is normal varies greatly depending on the individual person (Schlack 2004, p. 12), so that one can also say that the exception from the rule is the actual rule (Nickel 1974, p. 48). And there are other influences that affect our development, such as our family situation and general environment. Human development relies on many factors and the unique individuality needs to deal with both physical conditions and social influences. Human development is always unique, a unique work of art of the individuality in question.

Looking at the human species in general, one can observe three main developmental phases from birth to the age of 21, despite individual variability:

- Early childhood from birth to the age of 6 or 7
- Childhood from age 6 or 7 to the beginning of puberty at age 11–13
- Youth from age 12 or 13 to around age 18–20

The educationist Dieter Baacke pointed out that, however different the pedagogical approaches were, they largely agreed that the first phase of life can be divided in developmental phases (Baacke 1999, p. 155f.). Baacke himself suggests a division in three broad areas, pointing out, however, that such distinctions must avoid the "error of deriving rigid age groups from the designation of closed blocks" (Baacke 1999, p. 64). Rudolf Steiner also observed three phases of child development, referred to as "seven-year periods" (Steiner 1907; Loebell in Chapter 3).

Each of these developmental phases brings important tasks for the growing child. In early childhood, children learn to use their body and develop its organization. They need to actively acquire the basic human abilities of walking, speaking, and thinking and develop their senses and corresponding neurological structures in a healthy way. At this age, children therefore need an environment that stimulates them to manifold activities, for only through activity do we learn to make ourselves "at home" in our bodies.

Children need to develop their fine and gross motor skills, learn their native language well, and unfold their imagination as a basis for creative thinking. This is essential for later media competence because creativity and the ability to communicate are essential foundations for the information technologies. Without them, we will not be able to make full use of what these technologies have to offer.

When children start school at the age of six or seven, they receive support for their developmental task. Their physical structures have largely been established and they can now focus on acquiring the basic cultural skills: reading and writing, playing an instrument, using simple tools, riding a bike, roller- and ice-skating, swimming, diving, playing soccer, climbing, and many other sporty activities.

By that time, children have gained a certain independence but continue to need protection and support. Their relationship with the world is therefore above all characterized by their relationship with the adults around them. Children need adults whom they experience as authentic and through whom they can learn about the world.

With the beginning of puberty, children become increasingly autonomous. They are keen to get to know the world on their own and, above all, to judge it for themselves. According to Jean Piaget, young people are now ready for formal-operational thinking (Piaget 1970/2003). The Russian psychologist Lev Vygotsky points out that only from the 12th year children are able to think conceptually in the way adults do (Vygotsky 1934/1977, p. 115, p. 157). Insights into brain development corroborate these psychological findings (Blakemore/Frith 2005, p. 160ff.; Strauch 2003, p. 20, p. 39 ff.). Teachers know from practical experience that the period from sixth grade to the end of school can be seen as a time when young people mostly develop the ability to make independent and fact-based judgments by studying the most varied areas of life.

9 Direct and indirect media education in childhood and youth[6]

Technology, computer technology in particular, alienates us from our body, as the psychologist Christal Schachtner impressively illustrated in a study she published some time ago (Schachtner 1993, p. 152ff.). The use of technology relies predominantly on thinking. The ideal is that we will be able to directly control machines through our thinking: that our brain can become an extension of the machine. Sergey Brin, one of the two founders of Google, suggested, "We want to make Google the third half of your brain" (Miller 2010).

Using media alienates us from our physicality. The active will is reduced to representative thinking. This is no problem for adults. All the possibilities of the digital communication networks open up for them and they are able to counteract the detrimental health effects.

Children, on the other hand, are still in the process of building up their body and soul. Media competence expects us to be firmly rooted in life. Only then will we be able to use the chances opened up by the media in a meaningful way and to cope with their dangers.

Indirect media education therefore precedes direct media education. Indirect media education trains the abilities we need to face life and the challenges posed by the high-tech media world.

This is why all education is at present media education, as Heinz Moser points out quite rightly (Moser 2010, p. 31), because education must assume that young people grow up in a high-tech media world. That does not mean, however, that we must follow Roman Herzog's appeal (Herzog 1999) and allow computers to dominate all aspects of teaching and education.

Children's first task is to develop and master their own body. Education needs to support this development first of all. The primary task of education is to offer each child sufficient scope for activity to inspire them to develop their physical skills in a healthy and comprehensive way. This also includes the exclusion, as far as possible, of anything that hinders this development. Indirect media education must consequently ensure in the first years of life, up to the age of six or seven, that electronic media play no—or at least only a minor—part in it.

Childhood before school should be as *media-free* as possible. Children should be stimulated to practice their mobility in many ways in order to strengthen their will. Everything that might prevent this should be excluded. One could even go as far as saying that *later media competence relies on media abstinence at an early age.*

This approach to education is often dismissed as excessively protective (*"Bewahrpädagogik"*), although it should rather be called "enabling education" because it aims to stimulate the most varied self-activity in children, which means children can be more active than is often possible for them in everyday life.

The approach is also said to be unworldly, given that computers are such an essential part of life today. That is true. But this also applies to dishwashers and cars. Merely stating the fact that a technology is important in everyday life is not sufficient justification for children having to be introduced to it at school.

The fact that many children use computers and other electronic media early on at home does not imply either that these devices need to be used more in schools. The opposite is true: Precisely *because* children use these devices so much, kindergartens and schools must make sure to create a balance by involving the children more in activities that they are prevented from at home because of their tech use. The philosopher Gernot Böhme once put it in a nutshell when he said that education "must be anticyclic: It must promote precisely what is not manifest in developmental trends" (Böhme 1999).

In the first school years, indirect media education has priority, even if—and this fact is often overlooked—direct media education begins as soon as children learn to read and write. As children grow older, indirect media education fades into the background and direct media education gains more weight. In this process, the media curriculum must be informed by the child's development. Figure 9.1 shows the main interaction of indirect and direct media education.

10 Direct media education

Direct media education is concerned with media forms and devices. Curricula can be developed for each of the three media forms (script, image, sound), and also for teaching the functioning of devices and the sensible use of media for presenting one's own material.

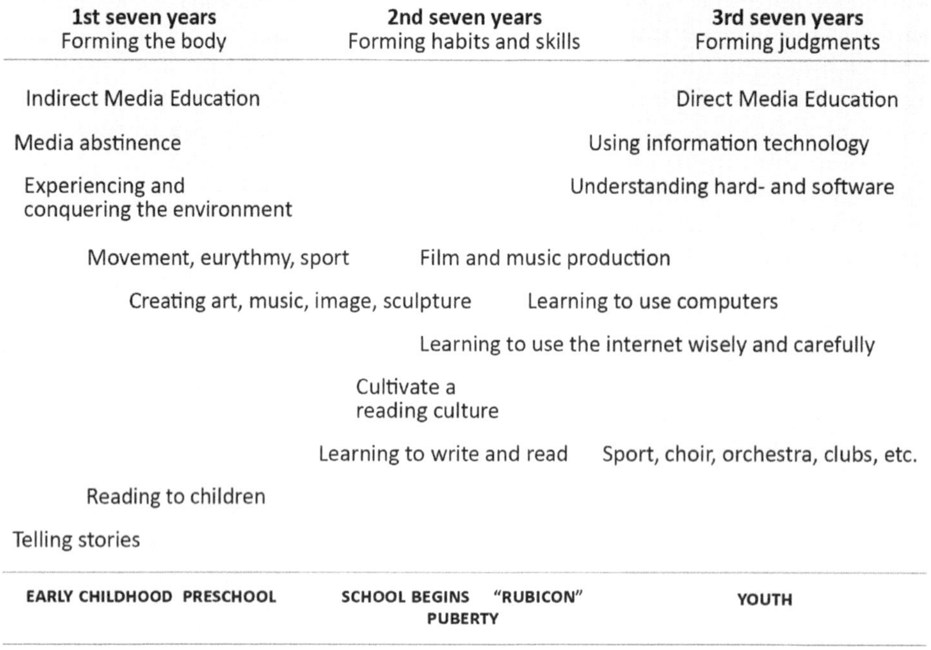

1st seven years Forming the body	2nd seven years Forming habits and skills	3rd seven years Forming judgments
Indirect Media Education		Direct Media Education
Media abstinence		Using information technology
Experiencing and conquering the environment		Understanding hard- and software
Movement, eurythmy, sport	Film and music production	
Creating art, music, image, sculpture	Learning to use computers	
	Learning to use the internet wisely and carefully	
	Cultivate a reading culture	
	Learning to write and read	Sport, choir, orchestra, clubs, etc.
Reading to children		
Telling stories		
EARLY CHILDHOOD PRESCHOOL	**SCHOOL BEGINS "RUBICON" PUBERTY**	**YOUTH**

Figure 9.1 Indirect and direct media education (Hübner 2014)

One of the basic characteristics of any tech-device is that it saves us work and will effort. While this is liberating, it also has its dangers in that it may lead us to practice our own agency insufficiently. Education must introduce a balance by providing activities that are as activity-based as possible.

Especially in the lower grades, this approach supports children's joy in practical activity. In experiencing themselves as active, children develop a deep understanding of what they are doing. This can be illustrated by using the media form "image."

11 Curriculum for the media form "image"

Script needs to be read, as we all know. However, few people are aware that the media form "image" also needs to be "read." In the same way as children need to learn to read and understand words, they also need to learn how images acquire meaning and how they can be understood. A curriculum based on child development will start by allowing children to create images through their own artistic activity. Before formal schooling begins, one can start by letting children draw simple motifs with wax crayons and watercolors. In the lower grades, when children gradually develop aesthetic feeling (Baacke 1999, p. 176), education builds on this: Children learn to distinguish different color nuances and color tones and to judge them aesthetically. As they grow older, their pictures and drawings become increasingly differentiated and multifaceted. At around the age of 12 (sixth grade) is a good time to introduce children to the laws of projection and shadows. Faced with concrete tasks, children learn to apply the laws of perspective in practice, or how to draw two-dimensionally on paper what they see spatially. In high school, this practical understanding can then be applied in the context of descriptive and projective geometry and mathematically deepened. From around ninth grade, young people should learn about the language of films, again by using concrete examples and projects: They should, by reflecting on their practical experience, learn to analyze and understand the processes used in professional filmmaking. Art lessons are also part of this, because they teach the students about the historical development of human creativity from the past to the present, and they invite them to approach the subject through their own artistic activity.

12 Curriculum for the media form "sound"

Schools must also give thorough attention to sound as a form of medium. Both young people and adults are often enveloped all day in a cloud of electronically produced music and language sounds. In 2014, people listened to the radio for 3 hours daily on average. The time spent listening to music on devices needs to be added to that (Media Perspektiven Basisdaten 2014, p. 70). Listening to music is, for the majority of young people, one of the most important leisure activities.

This shows how important it is that children and youngsters are given the chance to form their own judgments about the medium of "sound." This ability is, again, based on active experience. In pre-school, children need adults to sing with and from whom to learn a wide range of songs.

In the lower grades, singing and music are consciously fostered and the repertoire of songs made available to them is continually extended. Children should also learn to play a simple instrument at this time—recorders, for instance—followed by learning a more sophisticated instrument such as the violin or piano, so that they develop as wide a range as possible of musical skills and gain practical experience.

From fourth or fifth grade onward, students begin to penetrate these musical experiences intel-lectually by learning music theory. From eighth or ninth grade, young people should get to know as many aspects as possible of musical culture and learn to understand how music developed through history up to the present time. It is particularly important that they are able to analyze and understand contemporary popular music and to learn how film music is composed and what role it plays in rela-tion to the plot.

There is nothing exotic about art lessons. We are always surrounded by music, images of all kinds. In order to be able to judge all these impressions, we need to have some artistic training.

Art teaching has therefore a prominent role to play in the education that still needs to be invented for the information age according to Roman Herzog's (1999) statement. It is when we practice art or a craft ourselves that we strengthen our will and improve our ability to concentrate—skills that are necessary for, but at the same time subtly undermined by, the use of information technologies.

The importance of artistic work at school goes of course much further than the functional aspect described here. Aesthetic education in school is immensely important. The educationist Christian Rittelmeyer illustrates in his overview of various studies on aesthetic education "that children's and young people's intellectual capacity, creativity, sensitivity to environmental stimuli, social and emo-tional skills are enhanced by artistic activity" (Rittelmeyer 2010, p. 8). Such effects may depend on individuality and on the school as a whole, but they are real (Rittelmeyer 2010, p. 105). The skills inspired and practiced through artistic activity form an important foundation for making sure that our technological capacities remain within the sphere of humanity (Loebell in Chapter 4).

13 Curriculum for the media form "script"

When Rudolf Steiner founded the Waldorf School, he immediately described how writing can be introduced artistically in first grade (Steiner 1975, p. 9ff.).

Before the children actually write, they start with a preparatory activity known in Waldorf schools as "form drawing." When children do form drawing, they first develop a feeling for the forms, while honing their fine motor skills at the same time so that they learn to draw the different forms confi-dently in as balanced a way as possible on blank paper. The objective is that they are inspired to develop an interest in the form qualities. Only when this has been thoroughly practiced will the letters be introduced.

The letters are also introduced artistically. The teacher first tells the children a story—ideally one that she or he invented themselves—so that they can develop an inner picture, of a bear, say, which they then draw into their books during the lesson.

Once the story has been told again on the following day, the teacher develops the letter "B" from the outline of the drawing of the bear, raising awareness in the children of the connection between the letter and the corresponding sound. After that, the children can walk the form of the letter in the classroom, write it into the air with big arm movements, and so on.

This means that, from first grade, children learn through active artistic activity how letters are spelled and how writing can be read.

From second and third grade, the newly learned ability to write and read needs to be practiced continually. Many grades teachers set up a "classroom library" where the children can lend out their books to each other. It also helps when schools have libraries, where children find much inspiration for reading. Reading groups, especially for beginners, do much to support a reading culture.

From fifth or sixth grade, children should be able to develop a concept of what it means to "do research." There are still many things that cannot be found on the internet. Treasures of knowledge, which are not electronically accessible, are hidden away in libraries. This is why it is important that young people get to know libraries and that they have an idea how they can find what they are looking for in the books there waiting to be explored.

In seventh or eighth grade, the students should learn to touch-type—as long as computers are still operated via keyboards at least.

The way script as a medium is introduced—starting with imaginative artistic activity and only deriving the abstract symbol at the end—is an example of how one should proceed generally in media education so as to involve the whole human being: beginning by allowing will and feeling to be active and only forming abstract concepts at the end out of concrete experiences. In other words: Children should first become secure in their actions through practical experience. From this, they will grow to be secure in their understanding and ultimately also in their judgment.

The same basic motif can also be used in the curriculum "Understanding electronic devices"

14 Curriculum "Understanding electronic devices"

In the lectures preceding the founding of the Waldorf School in 1919, Rudolf Steiner spoke of the way human beings relate to technology, pointing out how important it is that we pay attention to our subconscious attitude to it. He said it was essential to understand the principles of the technologies we use in daily life, and that we needed to have the feeling of at least having understood the principle of what is going on around us. "They will be more assured in their actions and in the way they inhabit the world. It will strengthen their will and sense of purpose. People won't bring diligence and initiative to their work if they can't feel they once learned something, however basic, about the world, even if that knowledge does not relate directly to their present job" (Steiner 2020, p. 278).

Steiner concludes from this for education that "We need to make sure that no child leaves school at the age of 14 or 15 without having learned at least some elementary concepts of the most important activities of daily life, so that they develop a curiosity about the world around them and a yearning to widen their knowledge" (ibid.).

It was important for Steiner that children and young people understand their technical environment and Waldorf schools have been true to this impulse. Decades ago, they agreed that the introduction of computer technology must be based on the practical experience of electronic parts and devices. In 10th grade, for instance, they will have a practical main lesson where they use relays and transistors to build and investigate basic computer setups (NOR, OR, NAND, AND gates, half-adders, full adders, flip flops, etc.) before they go on to work out how microprocessors work. Many Waldorf schools offer programming internships in 11th grade.

The goal is to show how computers implement formalized human logic into a series of physical state changes. As students experience this implementation, they realize that these different states and their end result can only be meaningfully interpreted by the human mind. Figure 9.2 outlines the kind of device curriculum that is used in most Waldorf schools:

First school years	Making paper
7th or 8th grade	Bookbinding: Every child binds their own book.
9th grade	Learning to understand the binary system in math.
	Learning how telephones work.
10th grade	Creating AND, OR, and NOT circuits with relays; building an adding system using half and full adders. Learning to understand the basics of building a processor.
	Historical and cultural aspects of computer technology.
11th grade	Programming internship; learning through practice how life processes can be expressed and imitated through algorithms.
	The physical foundations of CRT monitors.
	Wireless technology up to mobile phone systems. The basic principle of digitalizing language and the TDMA process.
12th grade	The internet, history, and basic thoughts on how news, images, sound, etc., travel from one place to another. The physical foundations of flat screens.

Figure 9.2   Curriculum: Understanding electronic devices

15 Curriculum "Sensible media use"

The students should not only understand in principle how electronic devices work, but they should also learn how to use them for their own learning and research. For this, they need to understand how to use books, newspapers, online resources, etc., in a meaningful way in education. Many schools introduce this topic in the lower grades now. Experience in Waldorf schools has shown, however, that students often only have the required inner maturity to want to use the possibilities provided by the internet sensibly from 10th or 11th grade.

This observation is supported by the findings of the 2012 JIM Study (Annual study on youth, information and media in Germany since 1998, JIM 2012, p. 33). When young people were asked what they use the internet for, the answers of 13–15-year-olds suggest that they spend relatively little time looking for information and rather a lot of time playing games. With 17- to 19-year-olds, it is the other way round: The time they spend looking for information increases clearly, while they play games less. So, aside from communication and entertainment, seventh, eighth, and ninth graders use the internet mostly for playing games. From 10th or 11th grade, students use the internet mostly to find information and to do research; in other words, they use it as an educational tool.

Expecting children in fourth grade to use the internet as sensibly as 17-year-olds means starting from the wrong assumptions. The investment put into such tuition is not worthwhile. Targeted instructions on how search machines can be used for meaningful research are possible from seventh or eighth grade. Figure 9.3 shows a possible curriculum for the "Sensible media use" that is used by some Waldorf schools.

16 Underlying paradigms

This outline of possible curricula proves that media education can be derived from human development. Some rethinking is required, however.

The acceleration of everyday life, driven by devices that work ever more smoothly and comfortably, has no place in education where the advantages of a slower pace must be rediscovered, because healthy development always needs time.

It must be understood that children have a totally different experience of the world than adults, and that they have different developmental tasks. That is why they are hopelessly overwhelmed by the demands that self-determined use of the Internet entails. The internet can only be used in a meaningful way from around the age of 11 (Lembke/Leipner 2015, p. 158ff.). There are good reasons why a minimum age applies for recreational drugs such as nicotine and alcohol, or for driving a car. These are

From first grade	Designing a book page attractively.
	Organizing and structuring a main lesson book or project book.
From fifth grade	Finding books to use independently for research. Being able to use the chalkboard or pictures as part of a presentation. Regular small presentations on different topics.
Discuss from eighth/ ninth grades	
Integrate in lessons	
From 10th/11th grades	Online research using search engines; types of search engine; basic procedures and knowledge for internet searches; finding useful resources online.
	Learn to use criteria for the reliability of internet pages.
	The verifying of sources is discussed repeatedly at crucial points in lessons.
	Internet communication. Netiquette. Composing business e-mails. Letters of application. Learning to compose reference lines.
	Security settings for browsers. Network security.
10th grade	Presentation techniques for PC, overhead projectors, flipcharts, boards, etc. are tested in practice and critically discussed.
	Using presentation software, knowing its strengths and weaknesses. Learning to avoid presentation errors. Criteria for organizing files.
	Learning about different file formats.

Figure 9.3 Curriculum "Sensible media use"

even governed by law, but internet use is not. Parents and educators in particular must be aware that the premature independent use of computers is counterproductive and that rules therefore need to be established both at home and at school.

In a high-tech world, schools must educate the intellect and logical thinking less than the will and its employment in practical activity. For the will is weakened by devices that take work away from it. As human beings, we must learn to use the freedom that is gained due to machines to perform will activities and to create a much-needed balance. Using the internet sensibly requires a strong will. Education in the information age must therefore focus on educating and strengthening the will. Brian Knutson, professor of psychology and neuroscience at Stanford University, is quite rightly concerned "that the internet may impose a 'survival of the focused' in which individuals gifted with some natural ability to stay on target, or who are hopped up on enough stimulants, forge ahead while the rest of us flail helplessly in a Web-based attentional vortex" (Knutson 2011, p. 489). The question is how one enables children to develop the strength to inwardly "stay on target." This requires possibilities for strengthening will and concentration. In a media society, education is mainly will education. This can best be done through arts and crafts.

Media competence, which is often said to be essential, is not an isolated skill. It is part of the ability of coping with everyday challenges. The fascination with the new devices must not lead us to overlook the first task of education, which is to help young people find their place in life, to enable them to actively take part in shaping modern life. Media competence is part of that because the media are part of everyday life. They are not our whole life, however, but only a part of it. Human beings and their coexistence are at the center of life.

17 Anthropologic media education compared to other approaches

The media education concept outlined here can be called anthropologic because it focuses on the human being and on human development.[7] How does this concept compare with others? Five main concepts have emerged in the discourse on media education. The media education experts Gerhard Tulodziecki and Bardo Herzig, for instance, distinguish among protective-nurturing media education, aesthetic-culturally oriented media education, functional-system-oriented media education, critical-materialistic media education, and action- and interaction-oriented media education (Tulodziecki/

Herzig 2002, p. 124ff.). Daniel Süss, Claudia Lampert, and Christine W. Wijnen also distinguish five concepts: protective-education concepts, repair-education concepts, enlightening concepts, routine-oriented reflexive concepts, and action-oriented, participatory concepts.[8]

Historically, the concept of protective-nurturing media education, to which Süss, Lampert, and Wijnen refer as protective, first manifested in the 19th-century criticism of "trashy novels." It has been perpetuated in the criticism of unsuitable movies and still exists today. It is apparent in the age-related content rating for films and computer games. It was through the school film movement, starting in 1907, that the view was disseminated that films can be of pedagogical value and contribute to youth education (Hübner 2005, p. 139ff.; Schorb 1994, p. 149 ff.).

Superficially speaking, anthropologic media education could be said to be a kind of "protective education." However, that would mean overlooking that the anthropologic approach is not initially concerned with media contents ("trash") but with the fact that electronic media slow down physical activity in children and that this might cause physical damage in the first years of life. With this difference in mind, we can say that anthropologic media education does take a protective-nurturing-enabling approach at first.

The aesthetic-cultural approach, which emerged in the 1960s in response to the merely protective-educational approach, has the positive impulse to encourage children and young people to develop the ability to critically judge films while also appreciating their aesthetic composition. Aesthetic taste is also developed in that students learn to understand the "language" of images and films, to understand a film's aesthetic worth, and to learn to judge its content about social, ethical, and spiritual qualities (Tulodziecki/Herzig 2002, p. 129).

An aesthetic, culturally oriented approach is clearly immanent in the anthropological media education curriculum. But it implements this approach much more radically: It attaches immense weight to the arts in the *entire* life of the school, including the teaching methods. Aesthetic judgment is therefore developed over many years and can also be applied to the topic of "film" and other media productions once the children have reached the required maturity.

Ideologically informed approaches such as the critical-materialist one, which was influenced by the Frankfurt School, are alien to the anthropologic method, which is in principle concerned with the individual person and how they find their own way in life. Ideological influences—even through anthroposophy, on which Waldorf education is founded—are deliberately avoided. Rudolf Steiner clearly requested this from the start and Waldorf schools have always adhered to this principle (Steiner 1979, p. 216).

The curriculum of anthropologic media education is very close to activity-based approaches throughout. It can therefore, in the sense of Tulodziecki and Herzig, be called action- and interaction-based media education, or in the sense of Süss, Lampert, and Wijnen as an action-oriented participatory concept. The anthropologic approach is essentially about stimulating children's own activity as much as possible and moving on to subsequent reflection based on the experiences of their own activity.

In contrast to other concepts, a wider media concept also includes the historical development of the media. The anthropological approach consequently introduces media education in kindergarten. But it does not start with the final product of technological development, with the computer and internet, that is, but with the beginnings. It allows children to actively experience this development alongside their own development. They can build their understanding of modern technologies on their self-experienced emergence of the media.

Anthropologic media education has therefore much in common with other approaches. The main difference lies in its distinct orientation to child development.[9]

18 Transhumanism and the anthroposophic image of the human being

If one tries to judge the future of technology, there seems to be an essential tendency for our everyday environment to be increasingly dominated by an autonomous technical intelligence. The most visible sign of this is the development of self-driving cars, promoted in many laboratories around the world.

The best known of these self-driven cars is being constructed by Google Inc. and expected to be ready for serialization in 2020 (Klooß 2014). Such cars are basically driving robots and therefore a special case of many independently active devices that are being developed around the globe. Important efforts are made everywhere to build robots that are as intelligent and multiply usable as possible. The Japanese professor Hirohisa Hirukawa, who is working on the Japanese Humanoid Robotics Project, once stated that "just as cars belonged to the most important products of the 20th century, one could expect to find in retrospect that robots were the most important products of the 21st century" (Ichbiah 2005, p. 115).

In experiencing these human-made devices that increasingly resemble us when it comes to "intelligence," we increasingly face the question: *Who am I as a human being?* And as we are in the process of restructuring ourselves technologically, the next question is: *Who will I be in future?*

The protestant theologian and computer scientist Anne Foerst, who is involved with robot development at the MIT, writes at the beginning of her book that we need to start with the most important questions: What does it mean to be human? How can humanity be defined? Will we ever find criteria that distinguish us from animals—or robots? (Foerst 2008, p. 23).

Nine years earlier (1999), the engineer and futurist Ray Kurzweil wrote: "Before the next century is over, human beings will no longer be the most intelligent or capable type of entity on our planet. Actually, let me take that back. The truth of the last statement depends on how we define human. And here we see one profound difference between these two centuries: The primary political and philosophical issue of the next century will be the definition of who we are" (Kurzweil 1999, p. 18).

For others, this is no longer a question at all. Marvin Minsky, one of the founders of the science of artificial intelligence, says bluntly that the brain "is nothing other than a meat machine" (cited in Förster/Pörksen 2001, p. 113; Schirrmacher 2009, p. 14). Klaus Mainzer says it in slightly more genteel terms: As humans we are only a subclass of intelligent systems (Mainzer 2003, p. 10f.).

The views of the human being as a machine, proposed by Descartes and de La Mettrie, are in fact given a new quality by modern biological insights and technological developments. The human being is seen as a mass of biomolecules, as "a machine that acts according to a set of specifiable rules" (Brooks 2003, p. 173). Since humans have emotions and thoughts, there was "no reason, in principle, that it is not possible to build a machine from silicon and steel that has both genuine emotions and consciousness" (Brooks 2003, p. 180).

Given the speed of technological developments, it is only a small step from such views to the thought that humans are only intermediate beings, merely promoting the evolution of intelligence. Humans will, according to such thinking, either merge with their machines and undergo with them an evolution that will spread to the cosmos (Kurzweil 2013, p. 22, p. 368ff.; Moravec 1999, p. 254ff.) or be left behind by an increasingly autonomous technological evolution (Moravec 1999, p. 29, p. 208).

We wouldn't have to take these thoughts seriously that appear in science fiction books and movies (such as Star Trek—The Motion Picture, 1980), if they did not live as firm beliefs in the heads of those who promote technological progress. The leading thinkers at Google Inc., and many engineers doing research and working in Silicon Valley, are convinced of such transhumanist ideas and their long-term vision is to put them into practice (Keese 2014, p. 259ff.).

Creating a super-human artificial intelligence on the internet is the main thought behind the Google search engine. Google's entire research goes into developing a transhuman intelligence that speaks with us through our mobile devices, drives our cars, and organizes our daily life. We routinely meet a view of the human being that has become entirely mechanical. This needs to be understood.

Schools play an important role since they can make sure that, as they grow up, young people learn something about themselves from many different perspectives. The well-known media ecologist Neil Postman once submitted a very notable proposal for school curricula. He asked about the role of school in the present "information age," pointing out that the "most important contribution schools can make to the education of our youth is to give them a sense of coherence in their studies, a sense of purpose, meaning, and interconnectedness in what they learn. Modern secular education is failing not because it doesn't teach who Ginger Rogers, Norman Mailer and a thousand other people are but because it has no moral, social, or intellectual center. There is no set of ideas or attitudes that permeates all parts of the curriculum. [...] In any event, the virtues of adopting the ascent of humanity as a scaffolding on which to build a curriculum are many and various, especially in our present situation. [...] To summarize: I am proposing, as a beginning, a curriculum in which all subjects are presented as a stage in humanity's historical development" (Postman 1993, p. 188ff.). Postman envisages human development as the point of reference for school learning, as the center of the school curriculum.

Rudolf Steiner made a similar postulation. Even before the foundation of the Waldorf School in 1919, he outlined a basic principle of teaching, "All instruction must be related to life. From the age of 15 to 20, everything to do with agriculture, commerce, industry, trade has to be learned, in a sensible and economic way. [...] Also at that age, everything to do with what I would call world affairs must be taught: history and geography, nature studies, but always in relation to the human being so that young people learn about themselves from their knowledge of the world as a whole" (Steiner 1964, p. 98).

Later, when the teachers had started their work, Steiner told them that it was particularly important to use every opportunity in lessons to show how what had been taught related to the human being. "What is of particular importance is that, whenever the occasion arises, you relate what has been taught to the human being. You may teach about an animal, a plant, a warmth phenomenon – there is always an opportunity to relate this to the human being without distracting from the lesson" (Steiner 1978, p. 19).

Not only the anthropologic media education in Waldorf schools focuses on human development. In all subjects, a relation is always established to the human being and human evolution. And this includes technology because technology is nothing other than human thought poured into matter. It is important to discover what is human in technology or, as the philosopher of education Werner Sesink put it, "to find what is human in technology, in other words, to find ourselves again" (Sesink 2004, p. 79). In technology, we meet ourselves, not a hypothetical transhuman intelligence capable of evolving without us.

Notes

1 The author of another *New York Times* article is astonished that Steve Jobs did not let his children have their own iPhones but—like many other prominent CEOs of computer firms—set up strict rules for the use of cell phones and computers (Bilton 2014). Human contact is paramount in Silicon Valley where the new high-tech products are developed. It is seen as essential for the success of new projects. E-mail communication alone is considered inadequate. "Analog work culture: if you're not in, you're out. Being physically present is mandatory; virtual communication is frowned upon. Silicon Valley fosters a cult of extreme intimacy" (Keese 2014, p. 37 ff.).

2 For a phenomenological approach to the media concept cf. Buddemeier (2001).

3 This analytical separation into content, form, and carrier does not mean that the three exist separately side by side: they always work together.

4 Koch (2012), Rühle (2010), Chalupa (2011, p. 88), Kedrosky (2011, p. 90), Metzinger (2011, p. 155), Eno (2011, p. 189), Rheingold (2011, p. 202), Oxman (2011, p. 288), Sanger (2011, p. 534).

5 Boesgen (2001, p. 144), Franzmann (2002, p. 62 f.), Schönbach (2009, p. 57 ff.)

6 The following section is based on Hübner (2015, p. 270 ff.)

7 The same or similar approach is also represented by Schubert (1990), Setzer (1992), Bleckmann (2012), and Patzlaff (2013).

8 Süss/Lampert/Wijnen (2010, p. 61 ff., p. 95 ff.), Swoboda (1994, p. 14 f.), Schorb (1994, p. 149 ff.).

9 This refutes Heiner Ullrich's criticism of the first presentations of the approach outlined here that the "central goal was to protect children from modern media." His second claim—that, given the plurality of today's childhood patterns, "any naturalistic idea of a universally valid model of child development and education must therefore be rejected" is justified in that child development is always individual. But this was said here, too. Ullrich absolutized the thesis of the uniqueness of every human development and failed to notice that the accusation he aims at Waldorf education goes back to his own argumentation. For a view that radically denies any commonalities of child developments is as unrealistic as the one-sided absolutization of commonalities. Ullrich's criticism, which culminates in the verdict that Waldorf education "was to an alarming degree opposed to changes in today's educational reality" (Ullrich 2010, p. 101), can also be applied to educationists who lack practical, everyday teaching experience and are consequently unable to judge the practical relevance of their theses.

Edwin Hübner

References

Anders, Günther (1994): Die Antiquiertheit des Menschen. Vol. 1. Über die Seele im Zeitalter der zweiten industriellen Revolution. Munich: Beck.

Baacke, Dieter (1999): Die 6- bis 12jährigen. Einführung in die Probleme des Kindesalters. Weinheim, Basel: Beltz.

Bilton, Nick (2014): Steve Jobs Was a Low-Tech Parent. In: The New York Times, September 11, 2014, p. E2. Online at www.nytimes.com/2014/09/11/fashion/steve-jobs-apple-was-a-low-tech-parent.html?_r=0 (accessed: May 2016).

Blakemore, Sarah-Jayne/Frith, Uta (2005): Wie wir lernen. Was die Gehirnforschung darüber weiß. Munich: DVA.

Bleckmann, Paula (2012): Medienmündig. Wie unsere Kinder selbstbestimmt mit dem Bildschirm umgehen lernen. Stuttgart: Klett-Cotta.

Boesgen, Gesine (2001): Lesen am Bildschirm: Wer ist "drin," und sind Bücher "out"? In: Stiftung Lesen (Ed.) (2001): Franzmann, Bodo/Neumann, Birgit/Takors, Herbert (Red.): Leseverhalten in Deutschland im neuen Jahrtausend. Eine Studie der Stiftung Lesen. Mainz: Stiftung Lesen, pp. 127–149.

Böhme, Gernot (1999): Bildung als Widerstand. In: Die Zeit 38/1999, September 16, 1999, p. 51 (printed issue).

Brooks, Rodney (2003): Flesh and Machines. How Robots Will Change Us. New York: Vintage.

Buddemeier, Heinz (2001): Von der Keilschrift zum Cyberspace. Der Mensch und seine Medien. Stuttgart: Urachhaus.

Carr, Nicholas (2010): Wer bin ich, wenn ich online bin…. … und was macht mein Gehirn solange? Wie das Internet unser Denken verändert. Munich: Blessing.

Chalupa, Leo (2011): Die größte Ablenkung von ernsthaftem Denken seit der Erfindung des Fernsehens. In: Brockman, John (Ed.) (2011): Wie hat das Internet Ihr Denken verändert? Die führenden Köpfe unserer Zeit über das digitale Dasein. Frankfurt am Main: Fischer, pp. 88–89.

Der Spiegel (1994): Revolution des Lernens. In: Der Spiegel 9/94, February 28, 1994, pp. 96–113.

Engell, Lorenz/Vogl, Josef (2004): Introduction. In: Pias, Claus et al. (Eds.): Kursbuch Medienkultur. Die maßgeblichen Theorien von Brecht bis Baudrillard. Stuttgart: DVA, pp. 8–11.

Eno, Brian (2011): Was mir auffällt. In: Brockman, John (Ed.) (2011): Wie hat das Internet Ihr Denken verändert? Die führenden Köpfe unserer Zeit über das digitale Dasein. Frankfurt am Main: Fischer, pp. 187–190.

Foerst, Anne (2008): Von Robotern, Mensch und Gott. Künstliche Intelligenz und die existenzielle Dimension des Lebens. Göttingen: Vandenhoeck & Ruprecht.

Förster, Heinz von/Pörksen, Bernhard (2001): Wahrheit ist die Erfindung eines Lügners. Gespräche für Skeptiker. Heidelberg: Carl-Auer-Systeme.

Franzmann, Bodo (2002): Die Deutschen als Leser und Nichtleser. Ein Überblick. In: Stiftung Lesen (Ed.): Altenhein, Hans/Franzmann, Bodo (Red.) (2002): Gutenbergs Folgen. Von der ersten Medienrevolution zur Wissensgesellschaft. Baden-Baden: Nomos, pp. 51–74.

Herzog, Roman (1999): Rede von Bundespräsident Roman Herzog auf dem Deutschen Bildungskongress in Bonn, April 13, 1999. Online at www.bundespraesident.de/SharedDocs/Reden/DE/Roman-Herzog/Reden/1999/04/19990413_Rede.html;jsessionid=D34DDD0D29 557B2927A38ED02FA14878.2_cid388 (accessed in May 2016). Also in Frankfurter Allgemeine Zeitung, April 14, 1999, p. 10.

Hoffmann, Bernward (2003): Medienpädagogik. Eine Einführung in Theorie und Praxis. Paderborn: Schöningh/UTB.

Hoffmann, Stefan (2002): Geschichte des Medienbegriffs. Hamburg: Meiner.

Hübner, Edwin (2005): Anthropologische Medienerziehung. Grundlagen und Gesichtspunkte. Frankfurt am Main: Peter Lang.

Hübner, Edwin (2014): Indirekte und direkte Medienpädagogik. In: Kullak-Ublik, Henning (Ed.) (2014): Struwwelpeter 2.0. Medienmündigkeit und Waldorfpädagogik. Hamburg: Bund der Freien Waldorfschulen/Aktion Mündige Schule.

Hübner, Edwin (2015): Medien und Pädagogik. Gesichtspunkte zum Verständnis der Medien. Grundlagen einer anthroposophisch-anthropologischen Medienpädagogik. Stuttgart: Edition Waldorf.

Ichbiah, Daniel (2005): Roboter. Geschichte – Technik – Entwicklung. Munich: Knesebeck.

JIM – Jugend, Information, (Multi-)Media (2012): Basisstudie zum Medienumgang 12 bis 19-Jähriger in Deutschland. Published by Medienpädagogischer Forschungsverbund Südwest. Online at www.mpfs. de/ (accessed in May 2015).

Kedrosky, Paul (2011): Der große Informationsspeicherring, GTG und Ferien von der Schwerkraft am Dienstag. In: Brockman, John (Ed.) (2011): Wie hat das Internet Ihr Denken verändert? Die führenden Köpfe unserer Zeit über das digitale Dasein. Frankfurt am Main: Fischer, pp. 90–92.

Keese, Christoph (2014): Silicon Valley. Was aus dem mächtigsten Tal der Welt auf uns zukommt. Munich: Knaus.

Klooß, Kristian (2014): Google Car. Googles selbstfahrendes Auto verspätet sich um Jahre. In: Manager Magazin, May 14, 2014. Online at www.manager-magazin.de/unternehmen/autoindustrie/google-car-google-roboterauto-verspaetet-sich-um-jahre-a-969411.html (accessed in May 2016).

Knutson, Brian (2011): Gegenwärtiges vs. zukünftiges Selbst. In: Brockman, John (Ed.) (2011): Wie hat das Internet Ihr Denken verändert? Die führenden Köpfe unserer Zeit über das digitale Dasein. Frankfurt am Main: Fischer, pp. 487–489.

Koch, Christoph (2012): ich bin dann mal offline. ein selbstversuch. leben ohne internet und handy. Munich: Blanvalet.

Kranich, Ernst-Michael/Ravagli, Lorenzo (1990): Waldorfpädagogik in der Diskussion. Eine Analyse erziehungswissenschaftlicher Kritik. Stuttgart: Freies Geistesleben.

Kurzweil, Ray (1999): Homo S@piens. Leben im 21. Jahrhundert – Was bleibt vom Menschen? Cologne: Kiepenheuer & Witsch.

Kurzweil, Ray (2013): Menschheit 2.0. Die Singularität naht. Berlin: Lola Books.

Lembke, Gerald/Leipner, Ingo (2015): Die Lüge der digitalen Bildung. Warum unsere Kinder das Lernen verlernen. Munich: Redline.

Mainzer, Klaus (2003): KI – Künstliche Intelligenz. Grundlagen intelligenter Systeme. Darmstadt: Wissenschaftliche Buchgesellschaft.

Media Perspektiven Basisdaten (2014): Daten zur Mediensituation in Deutschland. Edited by Reitze, Helmut. Frankfurt am Main: Media Perspektiven.

Metzinger, Thomas (2011): Öffentliches Träumen. In: Brockman, John (Ed.) (2011): Wie hat das Internet Ihr Denken verändert? Die führenden Köpfe unserer Zeit über das digitale Dasein. Frankfurt am Main: Fischer, pp. 154–157.

Miller, Claire Cain (2010): Google Unveils Tool to Speed Up Searches. In: The New York Times, September 9, 2010, p. B1. Online at www.nytimes.com/2010/09/09/technology/techspecial/ 09google.html?dbk&_r=1 (accessed in May 2016).

Moravec, Hans (1999): Computer übernehmen die Macht. Vom Siegeszug der künstlichen Intelligenz. Hamburg: Hoffmann und Campe.

Moser, Heinz (2010): Einführung in die Medienpädagogik. Aufwachsen im Medienzeitalter. Wiesbaden: VS.

Nickel, Horst (1974): Entwicklungspsychologie des Kindes- und Jugendalters. Vol. 1 Allgemeine Grundlagen. Die Entwicklung bis zum Schuleintritt. Bern: Huber.

Oxman, Neri (2011): Einst war ich verloren, doch nun wurde ich wiedergefunden, oder wie man im Kartenzimmer des Gedächtnisses navigiert. In: Brockman, John (Ed.) (2011): Wie hat das Internet Ihr Denken verändert? Die führenden Köpfe unserer Zeit über das digitale Dasein. Frankfurt am Main: Fischer, pp. 288–291.

Papert, Seymour (1994): Revolution des Lernens. Kinder, Computer, Schule in einer digitalen Welt. Heidelberg: Heise.

Patzlaff, Rainer (2013): Der gefrorene Blick. Bildschirmmedien und die Entwicklung des Kindes. Stuttgart: Freies Geistesleben.

Piaget, Jean (1970/2003): Meine Theorie der geistigen Entwicklung. Hrsg. von R. Funke. Weinheim, Basel: Beltz.

Postman, Neil (1993): Technopoly: The Surrender of Culture to Technology. New York: Vintage Books.

Rauscher, Josef (2008): Unvorgreiflicher Versuch, sich im fragwürdigen Medium der Fragen von der Frage "Was ist ein Medium?" über "Was ist das paradigmatische Medium?" zu "Was sind und leisten (sich) die Medien?" vorzutasten. In: Münker, Stefan/Roesler, Alexander (Eds.) (2008): Was ist ein Medium? Frankfurt am Main: Suhrkamp, pp. 272–284.

Rheingold, Howard (2011): Aufmerksamkeit, Erkennen von Unsinn und Netz-Bewusstsein. In: Brockman, John (Ed.) (2011): Wie hat das Internet Ihr Denken verändert? Die führenden Köpfe unserer Zeit über das digitale Dasein. Frankfurt am Main: Fischer, pp. 202–206.

Rittelmeyer, Christian (2010): Warum und wozu ästhetische Bildung? Über Transferwirkungen künstlerischer Tätigkeiten. Ein Forschungsüberblick. Oberhausen: Athena.

Rühle, Alex (2010): Ohne Netz. Mein halbes Jahr offline. Stuttgart: Klett-Cotta.

Sacher, Werner (2000): Deformationen des Wissens und Lernens in der Informationsgesellschaft. In: Hubert, Kleber (Ed.) (2010): Spannungsfeld Medien und Erziehung. Medienpädagogische Perspektiven. Munich: KoPäd, pp. 135–149.

Sanger, Larry (2011): Blöken Sie für sich selbst. In: Brockman, John (Ed.) (2011): Wie hat das Internet Ihr Denken verändert? Die führenden Köpfe unserer Zeit über das digitale Dasein. Frankfurt am Main: Fischer, pp. 534–537.

Schachtner, Christel (1993): Geistmaschine. Faszination und Provokation am Computer. Frankfurt am Main: Suhrkamp.

Schirrmacher, Frank (2009): Payback. Warum wir im Informationszeitalter gezwungen sind zu tun, was wir nicht tun wollen, und wie wir die Kontrolle über unser Denken zurückgewinnen. Munich: Blessing.

Schlack, Hans G. (2004): Entwicklung – das zentrale Thema der Kinderheilkunde. In: Schlack, Hans G. (Ed.) (2004): Entwicklungspädiatrie. Wichtiges kinderärztliches Wissen über die ersten 6 Lebensjahre. Munich: Marseille.

Schönbach, Klaus (2009): Wertvoller Service. Bücherlesen als "zuverlässige Überraschung." In: Stiftung Lesen (Ed.) Kreibich, Heinrich (responsible) (2009): Lesen in Deutschland 2008. Eine Studie der Stiftung Lesen. Mainz: Stiftung Lesen, pp. 57–63.

Schorb, Bernd (1994): Zwischen Reformpädagogik und Technozentrik – Über Kinoreformer und die "Keilhacker-Schule" zu einer handlungsorientierten Medienpädagogik. In: Hiegemann, Susanne/Swoboda, Wolfgang H. (Eds.) (1994): Handbuch der Medienpädagogik. Theorieansätze – Traditionen – Praxisfelder – Forschungsperspektiven. Opladen: Leske + Budrich. pp. 149–166.

Schubert, Ernst (1990): Erziehung in der Computergesellschaft. Datentechnik und die werdende Gesellschaft des Menschen. Stuttgart: Freies Geistesleben.

Sesink, Werner (2004): In-formation. Die Einbildung des Computers. Beiträge zur Theorie der Bildung in der Informationsgesellschaft. Münster: LIT.

Setzer, Valdemar (1992): Computer in der Schule? Thesen und Argumente. Stuttgart: Freies Geistesleben.

Sonnenleiter, Klaus/Jurtschitsch, Erwin (1994): Nie wieder Schule. Bildungskritiker nehmen die Schule unter Beschuss: "ineffizient, reformunfähig, ungeeignet für das Informationszeitalter." In: Focus 4/94, January 24, 1994, pp. 102–107.

Steiner, Rudolf (1907): Die Erziehung des Kindes vom Gesichtspunkte der Geisteswissenschaft. In: Steiner, Rudolf (Ed.) (1987): Lucifer – Gnosis. Grundlegende Aufsätze zur Anthroposophie und Berichte aus den Zeitschriften «Luzifer» und «Lucifer – Gnosis» 1903-1908. Rudolf Steiner Gesamtausgabe (= GA) 34. Dornach: Rudolf Steiner Verlag, pp. 309–348.

Steiner, Rudolf (1964): Geisteswissenschaftliche Behandlung sozialer und pädagogischer Fragen. GA 192. Dornach: Rudolf Steiner Verlag.

Steiner, Rudolf (1975): Erziehungskunst. Methodisch-Didaktisches. GA 294. Dornach: Rudolf Steiner Verlag. English translation in Steiner, Rudolf (2020): The First Teachers' Course. Anthropological Foundations-Methods of Teaching-Practical Discussions. GA 293-295, trans. Margot M. Saar. Bangkok: Ratayakom.

Steiner, Rudolf (1978): Menschenerkenntnis und Unterrichtsgestaltung. GA 302. Dornach: Rudolf Steiner Verlag.

Steiner, Rudolf (1979): Allgemeine Menschenkunde als Grundlage der Pädagogik. GA 293. Dornach: Rudolf Steiner Verlag. English translation in Steiner, Rudolf (2020): The First Teachers' Course. Anthropological Foundations-Methods of Teaching-Practical Discussions. GA 293-295, trans. Margot M. Saar. Bangkok: Ratayakom.

Strauch, Barbara (2003): Warum sie so seltsam sind. Gehirnentwicklung bei Teenagern. Berlin: Berlin Verlag.

Süss, Daniel/Lampert, Claudia/Wijnen, Christine W. (2013): Medienpädagogik. Ein Studienbuch zur Einführung. Wiesbaden: Springer.

Swoboda, Wolfgang (1994): Medienpädagogik – Konzeptionen, Problemhorizonte und Aufgabenfelder. In: Hiegemann, Susanne/Swoboda, Wolfgang H. (Hrsg.) (1994): Handbuch der Medienpädagogik. Theorieansätze – Traditionen – Praxisfelder – Forschungsperspektiven. Opladen: Leske + Budrich, pp. 11–24.

Tulodziecki, Gerhard/Herzig, Bardo (2002): Computer & Internet im Unterricht. Medienpädagogische Grundlagen und Beispiele. Berlin: Cornelsen Scriptor.

Ullrich, Heiner (2010): Das Konzept der Kindheit – ein aktuelles Problemfeld der Waldorfpädagogik. In: Paschen, Harm (Ed.) (2010): Erziehungswissenschaftliche Zugänge zur Waldorfpädagogik. Wiesbaden: VS, pp. 101–123.

Wygotski, Lev (1934/1977): Denken und Sprechen. Frankfurt am Main: Fischer.

Wiesing, Lambert (2008): Was sind Medien? In: Münker, Stefan/Roesler, Alexander (Eds.) (2008): Was ist ein Medium? Frankfurt am Main: Suhrkamp.

Winkler, Hartmut (2008): Basiswissen Medien. Frankfurt am Main: Fischer.

SCHOOL AUTONOMY AND COLLABORATIVE GOVERNANCE AS CONSTITUTIVE ELEMENTS OF WALDORF SCHOOLS

M. Michael Zech

1 Introduction

"No one gives instructions unless they are actively involved in teaching and educating" (Steiner 2010, p. IV).

Collaborative governance, which is integral to the self-concept of Waldorf schools, presents an ongoing challenge. In the early years, this was compensated for by the authority of its spiritual founder, Rudolf Steiner, who himself took charge of the school from 1919 to 1924. His instructions and advice were largely accepted so that the conflicts about administration and organization could be dealt with that soon emerged not only within the teaching faculty but also between the faculty and the industrialist Emil Molt, who founded the first Waldorf School and initially mainly financed it. After Steiner withdrew from this leadership function at the end of 1924 because of poor health, and even more so after his death in 1925, the faculty of teachers realized that it was not only left to its "own counsel" (Steiner 1997, p. 163ff.) but also greatly challenged by financial crises, teacher development within the school, teacher education courses in general, and its responsibility for ensuring the quality of new Waldorf school foundations. In the field of tension between finding consensus and fighting over power and orientation, a basic trait of the Waldorf movement emerged that remained a determining factor even in the 20th century: Any justifications for educational and institutional steps always referred to Steiner's written or oral (and transcribed) statements. As a result, an internal reference system developed that became a source of self-assurance for those working in Steiner Schools on the one hand, but on the other hand—because of the partly exegetic reception of Steiner's founding ideas—also an obstacle to external discourse.

The collaborative governance culture of Waldorf schools, which will be discussed here from a historical and institutional point of view, has always been at the center of internal conflicts. Authoritative personalities, who were seen as interpreters and experts of Steiner's anthroposophy and were therefore accepted as school leaders, were instrumental in decision-making. The following generations of teachers often experienced them as "Steinerized" conservatives, who met with more-or-less overt resistance in faculty meetings. Former Waldorf teachers talk about the tensions that arose where two or three such luminaries worked in the same school. Waldorf schools that have been around for longer will remember such conflicts and directional struggles. In this context, frequent discussions arose about whether Steiner's instruction that schools should be administrated in a "republican manner" by the teachers (Steiner 2020, p. 16) should be implemented in a direct democratic way or according to the ability and delegation principle. Such debates are, of course, also influenced in each case by the sociopolitical climate (Zech 2013a, p. 33ff.). What has not been investigated yet is the influence of anthroposophic institutions on such conflicts.

DOI: 10.4324/9781003187431-45

It was not until after 1945, and above all from the 1960s, that active parents began to play a more prominent role in the school associations and in the schools themselves (Leist 1998, p. 193ff.). Because Waldorf schools are usually founded by parental initiatives, parents often bring in their hopes and expectations, and therefore influence, in the foundation phase particularly: the development of a school. This requires the constant clarification of a framework or space for the teachers' pedagogical decisions and autonomy. In other words, the interplay between those who work in the school and those who make the school possible needs to be constantly redefined.

Social processes are naturally subject to constant change and require the negotiation of interests. As in all ideologically oriented institutions, one notices a permanent swinging between the need to pursue a vision as freely and self-actively as possible within a community and the need to establish agreements, rules, and transparent standards.

In recent decades, a number of business consultants assisted school communities overwhelmed by these social processes in finding ever-new organizational structures or school cultures. The idea is not to impose concepts on the individuals involved in these processes but to support them in developing together a social form that considers both the existing circumstances and the different wishes and goals. Such transformations and new discoveries should be regarded as belonging to a collaborative governance culture of institutions that see themselves as autonomous. Often it takes less than a decade to identify with a newly established social form. Phases of increased identification with ideas and forms consequently alternate again and again among Waldorf parents and teachers with phases of criticism and discontent, which can lead to divisions, withdrawal, school changes, etc. Needless to say, between 1919 and today, the various prevalent sociopolitical ideas have played a part in the identification and distancing processes. The theory and practice of collaborative governance has hardly been systematically examined so far, leaving much scope for scientific research.

2 History of collaborative governance

The independence of the education system and of schools is crucial to Waldorf education. As early as 1884, in a publication entitled *An Unbiased Look at the Present Time*, Steiner opposed what he saw as an increasing tendency to impose ever more detailed and prescriptive regulations and curricula on teachers, by pointing out that "The state cannot make people free, only education can do this; but the state must ensure that everyone finds the soil on which their freedom can grow" (Steiner 1989, p. 236). This request not only aims at expanding the freedom of teaching claimed by universities to include schools, but it also establishes that this freedom needs a legal framework. When Steiner developed the foundations of Waldorf education 35 years later, placing the promotion of individuation at its center, he did this based on a very realistic estimation of the political process which, informed by a centralist tradition, would certainly not simply agree to such a framework. Referring to the basic goal of school and teacher autonomy, he said: "We have to reconcile two opposing forces. We need to know our ideals and we need to be flexible enough to adapt to requirements that are at odds with these ideals. Reconciling these two forces will present a challenge to each of you and you will need to commit to it from the start, with your whole being" (Steiner 2020, p. 16). The political understanding that speaks from this statement can, in retrospect, be identified as civic engagement. Autonomous individuals work together to realize a task that benefits the whole of society and that itself aims at individual self-realization: "Our concern at this time must be to root the school entirely in a free spiritual life. All teaching and education must only be derived from insight into the evolving human being and its individual dispositions. [...] We shall not ask what a person needs to know and be able to do to support the existing social order, but what lies dormant in a person that can be developed. Then it will be possible to continuously imbue the social order with new forces from the young generation" (Steiner 1982a, p. 37). Institutionally speaking, the realization of Waldorf education is then a sociopolitical act that aims, among other things, to negotiate the envisioned autonomy of education and schools with the world around and to implement it pedagogically on the inside, as a self-governed institution.

Steiner's reasons for this understanding of education have various roots (Zech 2013a, p. 19ff.):

- the philosophical justification of the autonomy of the knowing and acting individual and of ethical individualism in his book *The Philosophy of Freedom* (Steiner 1978),
- the anthroposophic understanding of development that sees individuation as an ongoing process in the field of tension of body, soul, and mind/spirit,
- a social understanding that sees education for everyone as a crucial element in solving the social question at that time.

Historically, the idea to found the Waldorf School arose from Steiner's political engagement for a new social beginning based on the "threefold social organism" derived from the anthroposophic view of the human being (Schmelzer 1991, p. 231ff.). As early as 1917, during World War I, he said, "Consider the total recent suppression of the autonomy of educated learning in suppressing all that is associated with the institutions of learning, and the superimposing of the state principle. [...] The autonomy of spiritual institutions as such has been forced back [...] This is taking a direction that leads away from a spiritual understanding of the world. [...] But the fact that no one pays attention to it is proof of the thoughtlessness of life, of the hatred people even have against the will to think" (Steiner 1982b, p. 195).

Two years later, Steiner sees a free cultural life and, connected with that, the autonomy of schools and of teaching threatened not only by the state but also by economic interests. "There must not be any interference by the state or the economic life. Autonomy, self-governance of the spiritual life, is essential" (Steiner 1979, p. 52).

The struggle for the independence of schools within the legal framework of the state has been a consistent element of Waldorf schools, as Götte has shown in his study on school economy (Götte 2006, p. 7). Steiner's wish to withdraw school education from the political and ideological directives of the state is a logical continuation of the emancipation, in the 19th century, of education from the church to the state. However, his idea is not to privatize or commercialize schools by subjecting them to economic interests; instead. he sees the realization of the individuality as the true goal of education. For Steiner, autonomous individuals are the source both of social and cultural renewal and of ethical responsibility for the common good. This responsibility was no longer informed, Steiner thought, by the moral standards of institutions such as the head of the family, the state, society, or the church, but by a morality arising from individual self-obligation or personal conscience. This ethical individualism (Götte 2006, p. 87ff.) was described by Steiner as early as 1894 in *The Philosophy of Freedom*: "These moral principles manifest in a particular way when we are not told what to do by an external authority but by an inner voice (moral autonomy). We hear this voice within ourselves and have to subject to it. This voice expresses itself as our conscience. That is moral progress: when, instead of simply making the commandment of an outer or inner authority the motive of our actions, we seek to understand the reason why some maxim or other should act as our inner motive for acting" (Steiner 1978, p. 156). For Steiner, the "I" is consequently the source or expression of individual, and ultimately also institutional, autonomy (Steiner 1978, p. 240ff.). These ideas also reflect Steiner's reception of influential representatives of German Idealism such as Herder, Jean Paul, Schiller, Goethe, Fichte, and Wilhelm von Humboldt, from whom he derives that education happens on the basis of rational human autonomy (Zech 2012a, p. 99ff.). As a means of creating the conditions for this educational process, which is a process of individuation, the state had to "make sure that the happiness of the individual does not depend on coincidence and arbitrariness, but that the whole structure, which is built on rational principles, secures the welfare of each person to the extent that they can develop in freedom, both physically and spiritually" (Steiner 1989, p. 236).[1]

Steiner clearly sees his educational concept—or the Waldorf school that was largely inspired by him—as part of process of social renewal. Waldorf education therefore differs from other educational reform approaches that question the authority of the state not only because of its anthroposophic idea of development but also because of its political and social ideas (Schonig 2007, p. 17ff.).[2]

Following the signing of the Versailles Treaty, Steiner concluded that the activities toward social renewal based on the idea of a threefold social order had failed for the time being. They were therefore not continued.[3] But the Waldorf School continued to aim at a society based on social justice, freedom, and individual initiative (Schmelzer 1991, p. 241). Götte describes how, from the beginning of the Waldorf School, the school leadership continued to negotiate the possible framework for autonomy and self-governance with the relevant authorities (Götte 2006, p. 597ff.). After 1933, the protection of this partial autonomy (Zech 2013b, p. 14) continued in Germany, leading to questionable compromises with the school authorities that were by then under Nazi rule. Götte, while pointing out and discussing the now doubtful compromises and adjustments, concludes nonetheless that those in charge of the schools at the time mainly sought to secure the autonomy of Waldorf schools and the survival of its pedagogical ideals at a time when all schools were forced to comply (Götte 2006, p. 542ff.). From today's point of view, not only the motivation of some representatives of Waldorf education but also their goals must be called into question. That their strategy failed—all Waldorf schools were ultimately closed down by the Nazis or decided themselves to close down—may be seen as an indication that autonomous institutions cannot survive in a totalitarian environment.

The dual function of the state in the education system did not change much after 1945, since the state continued to both operate and supervise schools.[4] While a pluralistic school system and the right to provide independent education are legally guaranteed in Germany, the state applies its own standards in practice when approving alternative schools. Waldorf schools consequently continue to have to negotiate conditions for their partial autonomy. Götte illustrates how the self-concept of Waldorf schools, in aiming at conditions that allow for individual initiative and freedom, requires much greater autonomy[5] than achieved by the negotiated compromises (Götte 2006, p. 42). Partial autonomy must therefore always be seen as a compromise that needs to be overcome (Leber 1992, p. 296).

The following diagram shows the framework within which the autonomy of Waldorf schools is currently negotiated in Germany:

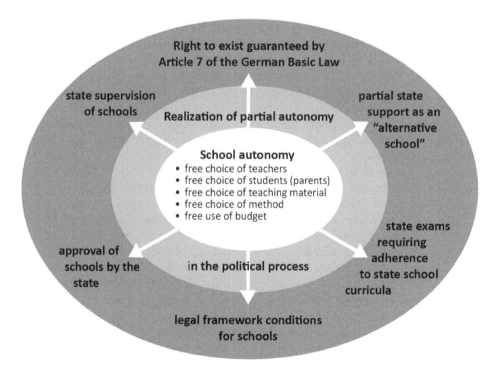

Figure 9.4 Autonomy in Waldorf Schools (in: Zech 2013b, p. 14)

School Autonomy and Collaborative Governance as Constitutive Elements

Today, the claim to autonomy of Waldorf schools not only is an expression of civic engagement, but it also partly coincides with liberalistic demands for deregulation. Such demands are raised rarely in Germany, however, because of its educational system (Zech 2013b, p. 15): The lists of teaching targets contained in the state's education plans, the KMK's[6] standardization concepts, and the centralized examination syllabi are in opposition to the demand for greater teacher responsibility and more individual school profiles as prerequisites for improving school quality.

As mentioned earlier, Waldorf education aims at the consistent promotion of individuation. "Schools must respect the autonomy of the evolving individual, which means that they have to base their pedagogical practice on the child's abilities and development" (Leber 1992, p. 34). Any attempt at socialization must stand back behind this claim. All teaching and learning processes must be informed by the biographic intentions expressed not only in the individual child's interests and talents but also in their struggle for self-extension (by overcoming obstacles). For Steiner, this pedagogy is an educational process that supports the individuality and also secures the social future, because it was his view that the renewing and progress-enhancing impulses can only arise from the individual intentions of the young generation (Steiner 1982a, p. 37). In the 1970s, Leber reinforces this demand for an institutionally and personally guaranteed freedom of teaching as a precondition for this education. "No rules and regulations externally imposed by the (state) school authorities, but solely the concrete needs of the child, insight into the child's personal situation and development on the one hand and the child's experience as a contemporary and member of society on the other can inspire teachers to create a healthy balance between the different requirements that do justice to the child. However, this presupposes the right to self-determination. Not much of the necessary freedom has so far been realized in education" (Leber 1992, p. 34).

Steiner clearly intended the realization of school autonomy at an international level when he said in The Hague in 1921, "A world school association should be founded on an international level by all those who understand what a truly free spiritual life is and what is socially required for the future of humankind. Such an association will gradually inspire in the entire civilized world an understanding that schools must be free; that the teachers in schools must govern themselves. [...] The future demands such free schools" (Steiner 1979, p. 56). Steiner, again, describes how teachers who assume individual responsibility are needed for adolescents to unfold their individual autonomy (Götte 2006, p. 146). This means that, even then, the teachers' work was not seen as depending on the state but as embedded in potentially global civic engagement. "The young person must grow through the power of educators and teachers who are independent of the state and of economic interests; teachers who can enable the free development of individual capacities because their own are allowed to unfold in freedom" (Steiner 1982a, p. 39).

Götte establishes for Waldorf schools the following institutional conditions required for autonomous teaching (Götte 2006, p. 576):

- free choice of teachers (autonomy of the faculty, employees, staff, etc.),
- free choice of students or parents (free parental decision; contract based on trust in the education and in the teachers),
- free choice of teaching content (learning content that serves child development),
- free choice of teaching method,
- freedom of financial self-realization (no influence must be exerted on education and self-governance through money; the autonomous, and therefore adequate and sensible, use of means; parents and teachers together form a "free enterprise community").

The principle of collaborative governance and of the autonomy of teachers is derived from the principle of a "free spiritual life" included in Steiner's social threefolding idea. Regarding education, this is based on the thought that a school's organization and institutional structure are ultimately legitimized and motivated by the direct encounter with concrete students. Stefan Leber, in his treatise on the social structure of Waldorf schools (Leber 1992, p. 22), therefore distinguishes between a "social" and a "pedagogical intention"[7] and proves that Steiner himself gave priority to the pedagogical intention, which he derives from his theory of knowledge, over the socio-political component (Steiner 1982c, p. 266ff.). The primacy of the educational process should not be encroached upon by any ideological targets (of the state or society) nor by economic or administrative categories. "The education and teaching system, from which the entire spiritual life grows, must be governed by those who educate and teach" (Steiner 2010, p. IV). A school's curricular and institutional organization should be informed solely by its directly perceived educational needs, which means that the responsibility for the school, especially for its educational requirements, lies with the teachers who identify with these principles. "What is directly experienced in the lessons also flows into the administration" (ibid.). Collaborative governance is not seen as an additional duty but is an integral part of the Waldorf teacher's professional profile. "Teachers must only spend the amount of time teaching that allows them to also engage in governance in their field. They will be as autonomous in this as they are in their teaching. No one will give instructions who is not also actively involved in teaching and educating" (ibid.). At the institutional level, Waldorf schools tend to form a charitable association or a cooperative based on concrete individual contracts between the students or their legal guardians and the teachers (Leber 1992, p. 195f.).

3 Regional, national, and international collaboration of Waldorf institutions

With the foundation of further Waldorf schools, the teachers in charge carried the idea of collaborative governance beyond the framework of the individual school. In Germany and other countries, a "subculture" emerged, known as the Waldorf movement, which sees collaborative governance as a concentrically expanding system, and which starts from the concrete pedagogical process, growing outward beyond the administration of the individual pedagogical institution through the teachers and parents (students) into the Association of Independent Waldorf Schools (in Germany: *Bund der Freien Waldorfschulen*). Following the experiences with National Socialism, this alliance of Waldorf schools, which had already begun in the 1930s, was reinstituted after 1945, both to represent common political interests and, given the growing number of new school foundations, as a forum for quality assurance. Because of the fast spreading of Waldorf schools and the fact that school legislation produced different financial and legal framework conditions in the individual German states, Waldorf schools began to organize themselves in regional associations (*Landesarbeitsgemeinschaften*). None of these umbrella organizations has authority over the individual schools, which means that all modes of working and quality standards are based on the voluntary self-agreements of the individual schools. The international collaboration of Waldorf schools is even more independent. In view of the social change and a school movement that was growing internationally, too, an exchange on the essential foundations of Waldorf education became necessary. Endeavors in this direction led to an informal alliance called the Hague Circle, which has since become the accepted forum working closely with the Education Section of the School of Spiritual Science at the Goetheanum on questions of quality, support for new foundations, institutional crises, and experiences Waldorf schools have with their claim to autonomy within their own social and political context. The Hague Circle also advises on the right to use of the names "Waldorf" or "Rudolf Steiner" in cases where no regional association oversees such matters. Only a few years ago, an appropriate legal foundation with charitable status was established for the Hague Circle: the International Forum for Steiner/Waldorf Education. Since the 1980s, the Association of Independent Waldorf Schools, which is based in Stuttgart, has been the legal owner of the trademark "Waldorf" and "Rudolf Steiner."

The entire Waldorf movement is based on the idea of autonomously acting entities representing its interests and coordinating its activities in associations as long as that is in keeping with their own intentions. This autonomy concept contains elements of cooperative thinking and of the modern civil society that is founded on initiative, free engagement, and the willingness to assume responsibility for the common good. "It is the perpetuation of the central Enlightenment goals: the idea of the social contract that legitimizes the state and that individuals enter into to safeguard their individual welfare; here, however, at a different level, the aim being to emancipate education from the state" (Zech 2013b, p. 17).

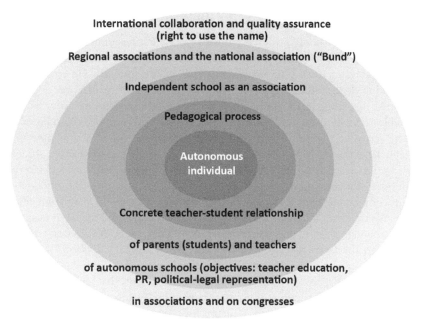

Figure 9.5   Ideal-typical presentation of the concentrically expanding autonomy concept (in Zech 2013b, p. 18)

4 The parents

In looking at the foundation and practice of collaborative governance, we have so far focused on the teachers. In Germany, most Waldorf kindergartens and schools are founded by parents, however. Parents form initiatives, advertise, and talk to others to ensure that enough interested people can be found to carry an educational institution financially. They make contact with the German Waldorf schools or kindergarten associations that send founding consultants to examine the initiative's intentional and material integrity and accompany the development until the school can be founded (land and buildings, funding, teaching staff, legal matters). This is based on the voluntary self-agreements that have been negotiated between the schools in the Waldorf Schools Association ("*Vereinbarung über die Zusammenarbeit im Bund der Freien Waldorfschulen*" of March 27, 2011, presently in the process of being renegotiated).

The parents' engagement for the founding of the school transitions into their assuming co-responsibility for the running of the school, which is expressed in their joining the school association or becoming stakeholders, in active engagement on the school council and in specialist committees, in their financial commitment and active collaboration in contributing specialist competences (legal, financial, architectural, PR etc.). This parental commitment in particular shows that Waldorf schools arise from and are run on the basis of civic engagement.

Parents who choose this kind of active engagement in an alternative or independent school are looking for a contemporary and good education for their children. Their commitment is initially based on good faith that needs to be confirmed over time. This is where parents' evenings and parent-teacher conversations have an important part to play. If school processes and pedagogical or organizational problems are not made transparent, the required trust is soon lost. Parents are important sources of feedback and therefore also of quality assurance. While the parents' view tends to be subjective about their children, it is essential that teachers listen to them. Parents, on the other hand, need to respect the professional competence of the school and of the teachers. Because it is not easy to draw clear lines here, this interface is prone to crises and requires the cultivation of social and communicative competence, especially in collaboratively governed institutions.

5 The students

In the 1970s, some Waldorf schools introduced student representation committees or student councils. In 1974, Leber proposed a student-teacher meeting. He advised against definite rights of co-determination because of the possibly fluctuating interest on the part of the students. He envisaged meetings for sharing and listening to the students and their thoughts about the organization of the school (Leber 1991, p. 301ff.). At that time, teachers often still felt threatened in their authority by such exchanges with, and possible criticism from, the students, but today no one questions the right of students to be heard and to be active on that level. Student representative systems are incorporated in many school statutes, students have the right to address the teachers' meetings and the elected student spokespersons or representatives are granted leave of absence to attend regional, national, and international work meetings with other student representatives (Waldorf SV 2016). In many Waldorf schools, students are also involved in conflict management as appointed and partly trained and qualified mediators.

The German Waldorf Schools' Association supports the meetings and the organization of a national student council, although this organ is not officially mentioned on the Association's official homepage. On its own website, the German national Waldorf student council (*WaldorfSV*) introduces itself as follows:

"WaldorfSV's basic task is to represent the students from schools that are members of the Waldorf Schools' Association. WaldorfSV carries this task as part of the Waldorf Schools' Association because it sees the representation of the needs, interests, questions, perceptions, and problems of students as integral to the development of Waldorf education.

In order to guarantee democratic representation, WaldorfSV gives itself the necessary regulations and structures that are legitimized by the students of the schools represented.

Working together toward an independent education that has at its center the respect for the dignity of the individual and that finds new answers in the careful observation of the current situation is for WaldorfSV the motivation for developing Waldorf education.

Representing students as part of the development of Waldorf education means that WaldorfSV works closely with all Waldorf institutions and associations, with the schools, and with research. Within the Waldorf Schools' Association, WaldorfSV seeks the best possible participation at all levels" (WaldorfSV).

Once a year, the elected councils organize an annual conference of several days, for which speakers are invited and where internal issues as well as particular chosen topics are discussed and deepened.

6 Quality assurance tools

The tension arising in the practice of Waldorf education between curricula and (teacher and school) autonomy is the subject of my essay in Chapter 5, where I discuss how this autonomy relates to the curricular terms developed within the structures of collaborative governance. Klafki's description for the pedagogical practice still applies: "Didactic contemplation is by no means the preserve of curriculum designers and the representatives of the corresponding disciplines in teacher education; it forms the essence of the daily teaching practice" (Klafki 1968, p. 12). So far it has not been systematically examined to what extent the insistence in Waldorf education on the individual teacher's subject-related and pedagogical competence—which far exceeds Klafki's widely cited request that teachers should newly think the thoughts of the curriculum before implementing them—is indeed being met. We therefore don't know whether Waldorf teachers are content with simply implementing the current Waldorf curriculum or whether they implement their own pedagogical conception in personal responsibility. Some initial insights into the teaching practice arise from the studies of Barz and Randoll.[8]

Teacher education was from the beginning included in the development of Waldorf education. The course for teachers given by Steiner in Stuttgart in 1919 before the founding of the first Waldorf School has remained an essential point of reference to this day. The lectures and guidelines provided

School Autonomy and Collaborative Governance as Constitutive Elements

by Steiner in this two-week intensive course were published later based on shorthand notes and notes taken by individual teachers. The series of lectures Steiner gave every morning on the anthropological and anthroposophical foundations of education (published as *"Allgemeine Menschenkunde"*) still forms the basis of every Waldorf teacher education program (Steiner 1992). These morning courses were followed, also on a daily basis, by discussions with the teachers and lectures on the curriculum (Steiner 1984). Steiner continued this teacher education both with the faculty of the first Waldorf School and in public courses in various European cities up to his death in 1925. After his death, the teachers of the Stuttgart Waldorf School set up courses for future Waldorf teachers (Kugler 1981, p. 115). Directly after the war, in May 1945, these courses were reinstated, resulting in the foundation, one year later, of a Waldorf teacher seminar that would later become an independent, university-level institution (*Freie Hochschule für Waldorfpädagogik*) (Leist 1998, p. 63f.).

When, due to the growing number of Waldorf schools, more qualified Waldorf teachers were needed, more Waldorf teacher education seminars were founded in different regions, many of them also offering a variety of further training and professional development opportunities. Correspondent to this culture of self-administration and prompted by the appearance of Waldorf schools around the world, teacher education institutions emerged, which organized exchange and collaboration during conferences or in countries where Waldorf schools were newly founded. With their specific profiles and different interpretations of Waldorf education, these institutions contribute today to a heterogenous teacher education landscape. They work together and compete with each other, and most of them are at least partly funded by Waldorf school associations. They make an essential contribution to the further development or renewal of this education on the one hand and to its conceptual consistency on the other (Zech 2012a, p. 25f.).

7 Conferences

When, after Steiner's death, the first Waldorf School faculty assumed the role assigned to it as guardian of the quality of Waldorf education, it did this without any hierarchical or legal foundation (licensing) (Götte 2006, p. 307 ff.; Esterl 2006, p. 102).[9] It continued the tradition, established under Steiner's direction, of holding annual national or international conferences, where both anthroposophic foundations and specific subject knowledge were presented and discussed. These conferences serve the school movement's ongoing identity formation on the basis of Steiner's ideas (Götte 2006, p. 376ff.). This tradition was only interrupted between 1938 and 1945. Up until the 1990s, the "fall conferences" above all, which were conceived as general conferences for all Waldorf teachers, were well attended. They provided anthropologic and pedagogical lectures on topics such as how to educate the will, inspire imagination, enhance judgment-forming processes, the importance of rhythm for learning and development, strengthening memory, the salutogenic effect of education, and gradual maturation processes. New scientific insights were also communicated at these events and Waldorf education was constantly newly founded against the background of the current wider societal situation. In the 1960s, specific subject-related conferences and study weeks for high school teachers were introduced in addition to these "Internal Teachers' Conferences of the German Waldorf Schools' Association." These conferences and professional development events were and are carried by Waldorf teachers who made a name for themselves with publications on Waldorf education in journals and books, or as lecturers in Waldorf teacher education (Götte 2006, p. 359f.).

Into the 1970s, the Stuttgart Teacher Seminar as the central teacher education center remained the main authority on teaching methods and contents and on the interpretation of the Waldorf curriculum, both in German and international Waldorf schools. Since then it has shared this task with other Waldorf teacher education institutions (Zech 2012a, p. 103f.).[10] The facilitators of teacher education and professional development consequently act as quality guardians of a brand that established its identity in the German-speaking cultural life as "Waldorf Education," "Rudolf Steiner Education," and "Waldorf School" or "Rudolf Steiner School."[11]

8 The function of internal publications

The quality assurance process in Waldorf schools was, from the beginning, supported by the publication of Rudolf Steiner's lectures on education, first in the newsletter of the First Waldorf School, then in Rudolf Steiner's complete works (*Gesamtausgabe* or GA) published by the Rudolf Steiner Estate Administration (*Rudolf Steiner Nachlassverwaltung*) in Dornach, Switzerland. After 1945, the monthly journal *Erziehungskunst* (Art of Education) became the leading publication of the German Waldorf Schools' Association (Leist 1998, p. 140). Further publications, for example on the history of Waldorf education, can be found in the Association's regular reports (*Berichtshefte des Bundes der Freien Waldorfschulen*), which have been published annually since 1965, and in its internal teachers' newsletter (*Lehrerrundbrief*), which is sent out several times a year. Up until the 1990s, books written by Waldorf teachers were mostly published by *Freies Geistesleben* (Free Spiritual Life), a publishing house, in which the Association of Waldorf Schools has, since the 1970s, been a trust company, together with the Anthroposophical Society.[12] One of the main publications to be mentioned in this context is a series on anthropology and education (*Menschenkunde und Erziehung*), with, so far, 77 volumes, edited by the Waldorf Schools' Association's Education Research Institute. Today, many specialist publications on Waldorf education are released within a series called "Edition Waldorf," published by the same institute or by the Education Research Institute in Kassel, Germany, which focuses on specific subjects. The specialist literature on Waldorf education, comprising more than 300 volumes, has initiated an internal discourse which has, however, hardly been noticed by the mainstream academia and can therefore sometimes come across as hermetic. A contributing factor in this may also be that the publications on Waldorf teaching and education, which have increased rapidly since the 1970s, continue to refer mainly to Steiner's anthroposophic justifications of Waldorf education in any questions regarding teaching techniques and methods.

9 The Association of Waldorf Schools' Research Institute

In 1950/1951, Ernst Weißert suggested the founding of a research institute within the Waldorf Schools' Association (Pädagogische Forschungsstelle beim Bund der Freien Waldorfschulen), as a way of systematically promoting quality control and quality development in a fast-growing school movement. This institute has by now organized itself as an independent association (Leist 1998, p. 141ff.). In his book on the history of Waldorf schools since 1945, Leist briefly describes the purpose of this institution: "The Research Institute's main task was to publish books or series that were meant to help teachers in their daily practice" (Leist 1998, p. 141f.). Funded by foundations and donors and with basic equipment provided by the Waldorf schools, the Institute enables the temporary release of individual teachers or lecturers from their teaching obligations for research purposes or project work, following due examination by an advisory committee. This means that this work, which is seen as curriculum work within the Waldorf school movement, has always been funded from the fees paid by Waldorf parents and allocated to the Research Institute by the Waldorf Schools' Association (Leist 1998, p. 141ff.). We see here an expression of the commitment to quality development of a subculture based on collaborative governance and school autonomy. Today, the Education Research Institute constitutes the German Waldorf movement's organ of initiative and coordination that is essential for curricular development.

So far, one can conclude that "after Steiner's death and until the end of the 20th century, curriculum development was indeed based much more on tradition and quality assurance, including the publication activities of many *Waldorf teachers, than on a written standardized general concept*" (Zech 2012a, p. 108).

10 The funding challenge

With their claim to autonomy, Waldorf schools are faced with a funding problem in various respects. On the one hand, the principle of collaborative governance needs to be defended against the conditions linked to financial support that apply to both private and public funds. Steiner's social ideas included the concept of "gift money." According to his view that the spiritual and cultural sphere must not be dominated by economic interests, financial support should be offered as gifts and without purpose limitation. Steiner's justification was that an independent cultural life—and that included the arts, science, and education—releases a higher degree of creativity that then benefits the economic sphere, too, in the form of ideas and research findings. Some of the added value generated should therefore be made available to fund the cultural sphere without specifying particular purposes; in other words, the use of funds within the cultural sphere was to be determined in the sense of collaborative governance. Waldorf schools do indeed receive such "gift moneys" (Leber 1991, p. 160ff.) in the form of donations from foundations, which are used to pay for some of the costs, especially at the institutional level (one-time investments in school buildings and equipment). Parents also contribute to covering costs (if they are not covered by state money), partly in the form of gifts and partly by offering securities for loans. One of the conditions for this kind of support is that those providing it can identify with the institution's ideological principles (Zech 2013b, p. 19). Since such payments are never systematic but always special donations, they do not pay for the school's running costs (staff, operating costs). This must be covered by state funding or the school fees paid by parents.

Waldorf schools also have to defend their autonomy politically, because they try in principle to remain as independent as possible from the influence of the state. This is a complicated matter because German Waldorf schools are, on the one hand, as charities, legally entitled to state funding (German Basic Law, Article 7, paragraph 4), but they try, on the other hand, to keep state influence to a minimum because they see their financial self-realization threatened, especially by the transfer of regular school standards to independent schools (Hardorp 1996, p. 642ff.; Götte 2006, p. 576ff.). In a legal assessment commissioned by the Software Foundation, Hufen states with regard to this problem: "In the Federal Republic of Germany independent schools cannot exist without state funding. The tried and tested state funding system has come under increasing pressure in recent years due to considerable austerity measures. The reason for this is not the lack of public means alone, however. It is becoming increasingly evident that a misguided wish to protect state schools 'from competition' and the misunderstanding that performance can only be enhanced through conformity and centralization also play a part in this" (Hufen 2004, p. 1). This assessment confirms the Waldorf schools' argument that they contribute to the legally guaranteed educational diversity and therefore work in the public interest. "Essentially, this follows from the subjective right to freedom of choice from among different forms of school. This right, too, can in the given circumstances only be made use of if the state compensates independent schools for the competitive disadvantages and enforced conformity requirements they are subjected to compared to state schools. The parents' legally guaranteed right (German Basic Law, Art. 7, paragraph 4, and Art. 6, paragraph 2) is violated if no new independent schools can be founded or if existing ones are under threat even though they meet the necessary requirements" (Hufen 2004, p. 2).

However, the existence of alternative schools cannot simply be transferred to the private sector since this would, in Germany, contradict the law that forbids the restriction of school attendance to the financially privileged. This means that there are limits to the school fees paid by parents. Independent schools therefore do not see themselves as commercially oriented private schools. Hufen says to this: "The picture of the 'private enterprise' that can be expected to cope with the economic demands and the risks associated with founding a private school is false. Independent schools are not founded by profit-oriented entrepreneurs but by idealistic 'founding parents'. The entrepreneurial risk is therefore no legally acceptable argument" (ibid., p. 4). Supported by these arguments, Waldorf schools with their organizations maintain their claim to state funding in negotiations with the authorities, not only in their political work on the legal situation regarding school funding in the different German states, but also in a number of legal disputes (Götte 2006, p. 603ff.). Generally, the German state makes the legally defined funding dependent on student numbers, the number of classes, and the actual teaching provision. Independent schools criticize that the state uses the teaching that is obligatory in state schools as a reference. Moreover, some states make funding dependent on the successful passing of state exams.

Independent schools are therefore faced with restrictions that affect their teaching provision and consequently the implementation of their own curricula, so that "lessons that are seen as pedagogically meaningful can often not be provided for economic reasons. Waldorf schools nonetheless offer, from the beginning, art and craft and cultural activities that differ from the provision of regular state schools" (Zech 2013b, p. 19).

Given their financial situation, Waldorf schools in Germany can indeed only be seen as partly autonomous. While the free contract between a school and the parents is based on the clear acceptance of the teachers' responsibility for the education, there are market laws at work in that parent satisfaction, expressed in the enrolling or withdrawing of their children, has an economic knock-on effect on those working in a school and therefore indirectly on the school's provision. And yet, it is a principle of Waldorf schools that parents cannot buy teaching quality or advantages with their contributions. This is why, in the collaborative governance system, the paying of school fees or the amount of parental contributions to the school is negotiated in confidential parent committees while the teachers have no access to any such information (Zech 2013b, p. 19).

11 Republican and democratic

Arguments concerning the idea of collaborative governance in Waldorf schools tend to be about Steiner's suggestion to manage the schools "in a republican manner." This suggestion, reconstructed from notes taken by those who heard it, is today published in this form: "We have to reconcile two opposing forces. We need to know our ideals and we need to be flexible enough to adapt to requirements that are at odds with these ideals. Reconciling these two forces will present a challenge to each of you and you will need to commit to it from the start, with your whole being. For this reason, our school will be governed from above but administered in a republican manner. In a true teachers' republic, no teacher can hide behind the principal's instructions but each one will take full responsibility for everything that needs doing. Each of us must take full responsibility" (Steiner 2020, p. 16). It can be derived from this source that the process of negotiating a self-governed school's autonomy ultimately relies on the individual commitment of its staff members. They are expected to free themselves from any authoritative thinking, both in relation to external and internal hierarchical structures. Their personal responsibility was to be stimulated by referring to the ideals underlying the education, since that would "replace the need for a principal" (ibid.). Concretely, every administrative act should be legitimized by the educational process rather than outside prescriptions. This is a general principle: "The rejection of hierarchical structures does not only relate to state authorities but also to the national association of schools [Bund der Freien Waldorfschulen] and the regional associations [Landesarbeitsgemeinschaften] that have formed at Federal State level because school legislation differs from one state to the next. These joint activities are purposive and based on arrangements that aim to serve quality assurance, political work, PR, and to establish a solidarity union, particularly in the building up phase of newly founded schools. Here, too, reliability is based on voluntary commitment. Hierarchical structures that restrict the school's autonomy are rejected" (Zech 2013b, p. 18f.).

Every concrete administrative act in Waldorf schools should be legitimized by the educational process rather than external regulations. Faculty meetings consequently take responsibility for the school's leadership and organization. This requires consensus building. According to Steiner, unanimous decisions should evolve from a process of collegial sharing. While this principle includes everyone, it also demands of everyone the ability to make compromises and choose responsibly whether to hold on to or desist from one's own opinion. As long as people can identify with the basic principles and agree that this is a process that needs time, it works and generates collegial identity. The absence of self-discipline or of the will to find consensus, for example in a conflict situation, or attempts to exert pressure on individual colleagues, will result in stagnation and division. Many Waldorf schools have therefore introduced a time element: If no unanimous decision has been achieved within an agreed-upon period of time (within two meetings, for instance), they hold a democratic vote.

School Autonomy and Collaborative Governance as Constitutive Elements

In the first Waldorf School, a democratically legitimated board of directors was soon put in place, still in Steiner's lifetime. The procedure was suggested by Steiner himself: In a secret ballot, six candidates were elected from among the faculty members; these six then chose three final candidates from among themselves through consensus and proposed them to the faculty. When just before the vote, a fourth faculty member was spontaneously suggested, Steiner intervened, pointing out that adherence to chosen forms of deciding and the solidary acceptance of the delegation principle were preconditions for democratic-republican decision-making. The vote then took place on the delegation's proposal (which could also have been democratically rejected). This first conflict with the principle of collaborative governance is not anecdotal but an example that shows that both democratic fundamentalism and the insistence on a consensus-principle without a vote can bring any autonomously governed system to a standstill. Collaborative governance demands pragmatism. In a chapter entitled "Republican *and* democratic," Brüll rejects Lehrs' suggestion of 1956 that the two principles were mutually exclusive (Brüll 1992, p. 51). He interprets "republican" as a concept of collaborative governance based on the delegation principle. The complex tasks involved in running a school can be managed if there are transparent structures that correspond to real life and that are built on the willingness of each person to take on concrete responsibility. This is why Steiner proposed that the lesson load of every teacher should allow for them to actively contribute to the school's administration. But if all the teachers want to discuss everything, they will no longer be able to adequately perform their main task of teaching and the quality of their preparation will suffer. Schools that exploit the strength of their teachers in the social processes of collaborative governance run the risk of losing students due to inferior teaching and, consequently, their foundation. This is why schools have introduced professional administrators to support their organization and to add efficiency to self-government systems by applying the delegation principle. School leadership and legal representation are delegated, directive structures imposed from outside the school are considered contradictory to this pedagogical concept (Leber 1992, p. 24 and 298ff.). Transparency and communicative structures are essential, however, so that each faculty member can support the daily general and administrative decisions and continue to identify with the institution. The organization and structure of faculty meetings play an important role in this. The delegation principle is inevitable in Waldorf schools as a means of coping with the complex regulative and administrative requirements. It will be efficient as long as tasks are delegated sensibly to those who have the competence to deal with them; further training may be necessary for this. If the delegation principle is misunderstood as a field of practice or a mere principle of participation, for instance by faculty members taking on each task once, incompetence will soon become standard, and teachers will wear themselves out in the social process, with dire consequences for the school's main business, which is teaching.

12 Administrative structures

If one analyzes the areas of activity in a self-governed school, it can—on the basis of Steiner's idea of social threefolding—be defined as an institution of the cultural and spiritual life and this justifies its claim to autonomy. However, since such a school has a complex social order that needs to be newly defined again and again, it also operates in the political-legal sphere that means it relies on the active consensus that its agreed-upon and established standards are binding for everyone involved. Its material facilities and operation, on the other hand, belong to the economic life. The commodity character of education as a service is a debatable issue. Solidary-associative structures can be identified in the collaboration of parents and teachers. State support, on the other hand, is always purpose oriented. The allocation of a school's organs and committees to the different social spheres briefly outlined here can be used internally to characterize the different tasks. As a means of penetrating the complex social structure of a collaboratively governed school, I suggest a structure based on the range of tasks:

The first area concerns the pedagogical process that forms the core of every school and includes everything that promotes conscious awareness and understanding of the students' developmental tasks and that supports the organization and quality of the teaching. If, as stated earlier, Waldorf education

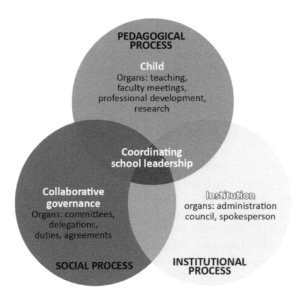

Figure 9.6 Social structure of collaboratively governed schools

sees teaching as enhancing and supporting individuation, the growing young person will always form the center of its activities. Ways of working must therefore be established that enable teachers to study anthropology, developmental psychology, Steiner's anthropological foundations, and general pedagogy, not only to share their specialist competences and make them fruitful in mutual exchange, to perceive new knowledge and social challenges, but also to make use of external opportunities for professional development and feed them into the internal discourse. On this basis, teachers can work on coming to a differentiated understanding of individual students or groups of students in order to promote and optimize their learning achievements; or concrete pedagogical challenges can be discussed and solutions sought. The collaboration with the parents on their children's education and developmental conversations with individual students also belongs to this area of activity.

The second area concerns the school's social process where the self-administration and, therefore, the collaboration of everyone involved in the running of the school are organized. In accordance with the collaborative governance idea and the republican organization of the school, tasks need to be specified at this level, committees and duties established and coordinated, again in accordance with the general running of the school. This is about negotiating in as fair a way as possible who takes on which tasks and usually involves the appointing of committees that are in charge of areas such as timetabling and main lesson plans, lesson delivery, workload coordination and supervision, salaries, remuneration, employee benefits, special school events, playground duties, setting up, maintaining, and fostering certain areas of the school, and care of the building and of rooms. The coordination of delegations is, in principle, regulated by statutes but needs to be constantly adjusted to particular challenges and staff situations. This happens in forums and faculty meetings. In a self-governed school, the goal of an optimal and smooth collaboration constitutes a challenge in that ideas come up in all groups and committees that are partly professionally and partly personally motivated and that always also concern the whole context. The strengths of a collaboratively governed institution quickly turn into weaknesses when people derive from their (positive) identification with and personal commitment to the school the claim that, as co-workers, they are also co-leaders. Crises occur when the social process becomes an end in itself, gains intensity, and pushes the pedagogical process into the background. In the self-concept of Waldorf schools, the social process is in principle subordinated to the pedagogical process (as is the third area of self-governance described below). In other words, the organization of the collaboration within the running of the school always serves the teaching.

The institutional process needs to be considered separately because it encompasses all the tasks that concern the school's relationship with its social, political, legal, and economic environment. It concerns legally binding relations that require professional competence in the individual areas. In most of Germany's federal states, schools are required to name pedagogically adequately qualified principals and deputy principals. They are responsible for the running of the school in accordance with official regulations, which includes the qualification of staff, a transparent complaints procedure for parents, the adherence to safety regulations, the duty of supervision, and the appropriate use of state funding. While the school leadership should in principle not be hierarchical within the Waldorf schools, it must in practice assert its legal responsibility. This includes the relationship with the school council which usually acts as property owner and employer of staff. This requires a systematic relationship between these leadership organs. In practice, they are often staffed with the same persons. In the 1960s, Waldorf schools started to introduce a professionally staffed administration not only to support the school operations but also to coordinate the internal relationship between the school council and the school leadership, a step that has proven successful. Depending on the area and supported by competent parents and committed experts, the school leaders, administrators, or the council foster external relations and negotiate with the authorities, politicians, foundations, and private donors. Committees responsible for institutional stability and external relations are usually staffed with parents and teachers. They include finance or budget, school building, and PR committees. Separate from these is the confidential parents' committee that coordinates the payment of school fees without teacher participation. It belongs to the council or administration.

There is of course, with many tasks, a certain overlap between the three functional areas. Parents' evenings, for example, serve both the pedagogical process and the organization or agreements. The diagram shows that there should be a group or committee that is aware of the duties of all three areas in terms of both intentions and quality, and which can oversee and coordinate the school's core task. Based on the model of the First Waldorf School where, as described above, a board of directors was elected, most schools today have such a central coordinating organ. Its task can either be an entirely internal one or involve the legal or institutional representation of the school to the outside; it can be conceived of purely as a service or as a hierarchically mandated school leadership organ. Today, the autonomy of every Waldorf school reflects a hybrid-diverse, constantly changing culture of collaborative governance.

13 Faculty meetings

The weekly faculty meetings have played an important role in Waldorf education from the very beginning as a central organ of the school and of the pedagogical process. Its task is the ongoing assurance and development of the teaching quality, and its main focus is consequently on the child, on the student body. "In these faculty meetings each child is looked at as an individuality; not at all in any judging way but in relation to what can be learned from this child's particular individuality" (Steiner 1979, p. 180). For education to be implemented in a way that can further this individuation process, it must arise from an understanding of child development, in general and in the concrete case. The pedagogical faculty meetings can therefore be understood as ongoing teacher development and competence acquisition. To put it more subtly: The observation of individual students by the faculty of teachers serves to enhance the relationship with the students and to understand how to best support each of them. In addition, it cultivates pedagogical competence. As with the pedagogical process, this requires study and exchange: "Finding something new for oneself, something new for the whole faculty of teachers, on the basis of which all the experiences and insights gained in teaching are to be shared in the faculty meetings. So that the faculty of teachers is forming a unity inwardly, in spirit and soul; so that each of them knows what the other is doing, what their experiences are, how what they have experienced in the classroom with the children has helped them to move forward. Then the faculty of teachers can become the heart of the school from which the whole blood can stream into the teaching practice, allowing teachers to stay fresh and enthusiastic" (Steiner 1986, p. 241).

Most Waldorf schools divide their meetings: The "pedagogical meeting," which has just been described, and which is usually followed by a brief "technical meeting" for the communication of organizational details, is different from the school leadership meeting (also called "college meeting" in some schools). While all school staff may, or are expected to, attend the first two meetings, the third is only for fully employed teachers or those bearing concrete responsibility for administrative tasks. The underlying principle is that only persons are included in decision-making processes who will in the long term be responsible for the consequences of these decisions. In many schools, a culture has evolved where leadership decisions are prepared in specialist committees (delegation principle) before they are passed by the school leadership meeting or mandated to specialist committees that lead the process to its conclusion. This not only saves time and accelerates processes but also holds the risk that the sense of responsibility of the faculty as a whole is weakened. The expectation of having to create, from a heterogeneous community of parents, teachers, and students, a school identity through identification requires from everyone involved the capacity for communication and consensus building.

14 Outlook

"Within the structures of the state, the spiritual life has grown toward freedom; it cannot realize this freedom if it is not granted full self-governance" (Steiner 2010, p. III).

Waldorf schools look back on over a hundred years of experience with school autonomy, collaborative governance, individual responsibility: structures and elements, in other words, that are linked to civic engagement. Their qualities and weaknesses can be studied in many ways. Prompted by crises and challenges, the schools themselves have continually transformed themselves and, in cooperation with (in some cases anthroposophically inspired) management and social consultants, created analyzing tools and quality development procedures. Discussing these would be a separate topic. Götte shows in his study how Waldorf schools have held on to their claim to self-determination under changing political and social conditions. These experiences make them an interesting field of research, particularly in view of the fact that the taking on of more responsibility is now a standard request in every discussion on education.

The various fields of work and problems in collaboratively governed schools have been discussed. One basic problem shall be mentioned here in conclusion. Mutual respect is naturally a precondition for successful social processes. If, however, the rejection of extra-institutional hierarchies associated with independent schools' understanding of autonomy also includes the rejection of a hierarchy based on competence differences, in other words if faculty members are prevented from contributing and unfolding their particular competence because of concerns over potential power issues, institutions can soon end up in the kind of dead-end situation that arises when a dynamic is suppressed that is essential for a "learning" institution and that is born from new ideas and impulses, and from quality enhancement. A collaboratively governed institution runs the risk of establishing itself as a niche product if it is satisfied with the lowest common denominator and becomes complacent (Zech 2012b).

Notes

1 In his essays and lectures on threefoldness and the Waldorf School, Steiner states as the main conditions concepts such as freedom, individuality, independence, and self-governance. He rarely uses the term "autonomy" that is more common today. For a discussion of the theory underlying this understanding of autonomy and the hermeneutic justification of the concept of autonomy in relation to educational institutions cf. Götte 2007, parts I and II in particular.

2 The skeptical view of progress and technology that also informs educational reform ideas cannot be discussed here. Most discussions regarding the evaluation of these reform ideas focus on this skepticism (Reble 2004, p. 276 ff.). These ideas were widely received in the German-speaking realm because of the book *The Century of the Child* published in 1900 by the Swedish social reformer Ellen Key (Key 1992).

3 Stockmeyer comments: "In the days of his lectures on popular education, Steiner still saw a slight chance of success for the realization of the threefolding idea. However, in August and September 1919, when he gave the lectures for teachers, [...] following the submission of the German government to the Versailles dictate, there

was no longer a chance of directly implementing social threefolding. [...] when the Treaty of Versailles was signed by the German government, Steiner stopped lecturing on threefolding, restricting himself explicitly again to the spiritual-scientific work" (Stockmeyer 1989, p. 265 ff.).

4 After World War II, this partial autonomy was renegotiated for every school, initially with the occupational authorities, later with the department for culture. It was not until the 1970s that this partial autonomy received a legal foundation through regulations, which in some German states refer explicitly to Waldorf Schools.

5 In characterizing the view of autonomy of Waldorf education, Götte refers, among others, to Timmermann (1996), listing three categories that, according to Timmermann, describe a radical model of school autonomy: 1 Decisions are made by each individual school; 2 individual schools meet their need for personal and material resources exclusively through their "clients"; 3 the clients' economic situation must not compromise access to these services.

6 Translator's note: the German *Kultusministerkonferenz*, or KMK, is the Standing Conference of the Ministers of Education and Cultural Affairs of the Länder in the Federal Republic of Germany. According to its own definition, it "plays a significant role as an instrument for the coordination and development of education in the country. It is a consortium of ministers responsible for education and schooling, institutes of higher education and research and cultural affairs, and in this capacity formulates the joint interests and objectives of all 16 federal states" (https://www.kmk.org/kmk/information-in-english.html, accessed May 25, 2022).

7 Steiner characterizes these two intentions in an article he wrote in 1919 for the journal Soziale Zukunft (social future) entitled "The educational objective of the Stuttgart Waldorf School" (Steiner 1982a, p. 266 ff.).

8 Randoll (1999, 2013); Barz, Liebenwein, Randoll (2012).

9 Esterl's documentation includes the letter published by the General Anthroposophical Society's Executive Council on 17 March 1925 on behalf of the school founder, Rudolf Steiner, who at that time was close to his death (30 March). In this letter, Steiner authorized the faculty of the first Waldorf School to take on the "leadership of all [Waldorf] schools in Germany" (Esterl 2006, p. 102).

10 In 1973, the Institut für Waldorfpädagogik was founded in Witten-Annen, Germany, offering four-year teacher education courses. One year later, a similar institute was founded in Stuttgart, gaining university-level status in 1993 and operating today as a recognized university. In 1974, a one-year training course was established at the Nuremberg Rudolf Steiner School. In 1978, another teacher education institute started in Mannheim, Germany, offering full-time study, and the teacher education seminar in Kassel, Germany, began to offer preparation courses and professional development for high school teachers. In addition, a number of part-time courses that work closely with local Waldorf Schools offer further training in Waldorf education (Leist 1998, p. 66 ff.).

11 The designations "Waldorf School," "Rudolf Steiner School," "Waldorf Education," and "Rudolf Steiner Education" have been protected by trademark law since 1981. The licensee (nationally and internationally) is the *Bund der Freien Waldorfschulen* (Waldorf Schools' Association) (Leist 1998, p. 91 f.).

12 The publisher *Freies Geistesleben* was founded in 1947 by the Anthroposophical Society in Stuttgart and the independent Waldorf School Stuttgart-Uhlandshöhe (Leist 1998, p. 144 f.).

References

Barz, Heiner/Liebenwein, Sylvia/Randoll, Dirk (Eds.) (2012): Bildungserfahrungen an Waldorfschulen: Empirische Studie zu Schulqualität und Lernerfahrungen. Wiesbaden: VS.

Brüll, Dieter (1992): Waldorfschule und Dreigliederung – der peinliche Auftrag. Vom Risiko, eine anthroposophische Institution zu sein. Leiden: Lazarus/Nearchus.

Esterl, Dietrich (2006): Die erste Waldorfschule Stuttgart-Uhlandshöhe. 1919 bis 2004. Daten, Dokumente, Bilder. Stuttgart: Pädagogische Forschungsstelle beim Bund der Freien Waldorfschulen.

Götte, Wenzel M. (2006): Erfahrungen mit Schulautonomie. Das Beispiel der Waldorfschulen. Stuttgart: Freies Geistesleben.

Hardorp, Benediktus (1996): Schule als autonomes Unternehmen. In: Erziehungskunst 1996 No. 6, pp. 642–650.

Hufen, Friedhelm (2004): Verfassungsrechtliche Grenzen der Unterfinanzierung von Schulen in freier Trägerschaft. Zusammenfassung der verfassungsrechtlichen Ergebnisse. (Kurzgutachten Prof. Hufen). Online unter: www.software-ag-stiftung.de/fileadmin/Media/Downloads/schuelerkosten_hufen_kurzgutachten.pdf (accessed on April 22, 2016).

Key, Ellen (1992): Das Jahrhundert des Kindes. Unveränderter Nachdruck. Weinheim, Basel: Beltz.

Klafki, Wolfgang (1968): Didaktik. In: Heiland, Helmut (Ed.) (1968): Didaktik und Lerntheorie. Bad Heilbrunn: Klinkhardt, pp. 7–12.

Kugler, Walter (1981): Selbstverwaltung als Gestaltungsprinzip eines zukunftsorientierten Schulwesens dargestellt am Beispiel der Freien Waldorfschulen. Stuttgart: Freies Geistesleben.

Leber, Stefan (1991): Die Sozialgestalt der Waldorfschule. Ein Beitrag zu den sozialwissenschaftlichen Anschauungen Rudolf Steiners. Stuttgart: Freies Geistesleben.

Leber, Stefan (1992): Die Sozialgestalt der Waldorfschulen. In: Leber, Stefan (Ed.) (1992): Die Pädagogik der Waldorfschule und ihre Grundlagen. 3rd edition. Wissenschaftliche Buchgesellschaft Darmstadt, pp. 29–311.

Leist, Manfred (1998): Entwicklungen einer Schulgemeinschaft. Die Waldorfschulen in Deutschland. Stuttgart: Freies Geistesleben.

Randoll, Dirk (1999): Waldorfpädagogik auf dem Prüfstand. Auch eine Herausforderung an das öffentliche Schulwesen? Berlin: Wissenschaft und Bildung.

Randoll, Dirk (Ed.) (2013): "Ich bin Waldorflehrer." Einstellungen, Erfahrungen, Diskussionspunkte – Eine Befragungsstudie. Wiesbaden 2013: Springer VS.

Reble, Albert (2004): Geschichte der Pädagogik. 21st edition. Stuttgart: Klett.

Schmelzer, Albert (1991): Die Dreigliederungsbewegung 1919. Rudolf Steiners Einsatz für den Selbstverwaltungsimpuls. Stuttgart: Freies Geistesleben.

Schonig, Bruno (2007): Pädagogik und Politik "vom Kinde aus"? – Zum historischen Kontext der Pädagogik bei Freinet, Montessori und Steiner. In: Hellmich, Achim/Teigeler, Peter (Eds.) (2007): Montessori-, Freinet-, Waldorfpädagogik. 5th edition. Weinheim: Beltz, pp. 17–21.

Steiner, Rudolf (1974): Erziehungskunst. Methodisch-Didaktisches. Rudolf Steiner Gesamtausgabe (= GA) 294. 5th edition. Dornach: Rudolf Steiner Verlag. English translation: Steiner, Rudolf (2020): The First Teachers' Course. Anthropological Foundations-Methods of Teaching-Practical Discussions. GA 293–295, trans. Margot M. Saar. Bangkok: Ratayakom.

Steiner, Rudolf (1978): Die Philosophie der Freiheit. Grundzüge einer modernen Weltanschauung. GA 4. Dornach: Rudolf Steiner Verlag.

Steiner, Rudolf (1979): Erziehungs- und Unterrichtsmethoden auf anthroposophischer Grundlage. 9 public lectures given in different places between February 23, 1921 and September 16, 1922. GA 303. Dornach: Rudolf Steiner Verlag.

Steiner, Rudolf (1982a): Freie Schule und Dreigliederung. In: Steiner, Rudolf (1982): Aufsätze über die Dreigliederung des sozialen Organismus und zur Zeitlage 1915–1921. GA 24. Dornach: Rudolf Steiner Verlag, pp. 35–43.

Steiner, Rudolf (1982b): Mitteleuropa zwischen Ost und West. Kosmische und menschliche Geschichte. Vol. 6. GA 174a. Dornach: Rudolf Steiner Verlag.

Steiner, Rudolf (1982c): Die pädagogische Zielsetzung der Waldorfschule in Stuttgart. In: Steiner, Rudolf (1982): Aufsätze über die Dreigliederung des sozialen Organismus und zur Zeitlage. Schriften und Aufsätze 1915–1921. GA 24. Dornach: Rudolf Steiner Verlag, pp. 266–276.

Steiner, Rudolf (1984): Seminarbesprechungen und Lehrplanvorträge. GA 295. 4th edition. Dornach: Rudolf Steiner Verlag. English translation: Steiner, Rudolf (2020): The First Teachers' Course. Anthropological Foundations-Methods of Teaching-Practical Discussions. GA 293–295, trans. Margot M. Saar. Bangkok: Ratayakom.

Steiner, Rudolf (1986): Gegenwärtiges Geistesleben und Erziehung. Lectures given in Ilkley from August 5 to 17, 1923. GA 307. 5th edition. Dornach: Rudolf Steiner Verlag.

Steiner, Rudolf (1989): Ein freier Blick in die Gegenwart. In: Steiner, Rudolf (1989): Methodische Grundlagen der Anthroposophie 1884–1901. Gesammelte Aufsätze zur Philosophie, Naturwissenschaft, Ästhetik und Seelenkunde. GA 30. Dornach: Rudolf Steiner Verlag, pp. 232–236.

Steiner, Rudolf (1992): Allgemeine Menschenkunde als Grundlage der Pädagogik. GA 293. 9th edition. Dornach: Rudolf Steiner Verlag. English translation: Steiner, Rudolf (2020): The First Teachers' Course. Anthropological Foundations-Methods of Teaching-Practical Discussions. GA 293–295, trans. Margot M. Saar. Bangkok: Ratayakom.

Steiner, Rudolf (1997): Brief an die Lehrkräfte der Freien Waldorfschule in Stuttgart am 15. März 1925. In: Steiner, Rudolf (1997): Spruchgut für Lehrer und Schüler der Waldorfschule. GA 269. Dornach: Rudolf Steiner Verlag, pp. 162–165.

Steiner, Rudolf (2010): Die Kernpunkte der sozialen Frage in den Lebensnotwendigkeiten der Gegenwart und Zukunft. 1919. GA 23. 4th edition. Dornach: Rudolf Steiner Verlag.

Stockmeyer, E. A. Karl (1989): Die Entfaltung der Idee der Waldorfschule im Sommer 1919. In: Erziehungskunst 53/1989, pp. 265–268.

Timmermann, Dieter (1996): Bildungsökonomisches Abwägen heterogener Argumente zur Schulautonomie. In: Paschen, Harm/Wigger, Lothar (Eds.) (1996): Schulautonomie als Entscheidungsproblem. Zur Abwägung heterogener Argumente. Weinheim: Beltz.

Waldorf SV. Online at: waldorfsv.de/(accessed on April 21, 2016).

Vereinbarung über die Zusammenarbeit im Bund der Freien Waldorfschulen vom 27.03.2011. Online at: www.waldorfschule.de/fileadmin/downloads/erklaerung/Vereinbarung_ZusarbBund._27.03.2011_aktuell.pdf (accessed on April 21, 2016).

School Autonomy and Collaborative Governance as Constitutive Elements

Zech, M. Michael (2012a): Der Geschichtsunterricht an Waldorfschulen. Genese und Umsetzung des Konzepts vor dem Hintergrund des aktuellen geschichtsdidaktischen Diskurses. Frankfurt am Main: Peter Lang.

Zech, M. Michael (2012b): Gibt es Alternativen zu Nischendasein, Anpassung und Durchschnittlichkeit? Ein undiplomatischer Beitrag zur Qualitätsproblematik in den Oberstufen der Waldorfschulen. In: Lehrerrundbrief des Bundes der Freien Waldorfschulen Nr. 97, Feb. 2012, pp. 71–83.

Zech, M. Michael. (2013a): Die Gründungsidee der Waldorfschulen und das Problem der Schul- bzw. Lehrerautonomie im internationalen Kontext. In: Barz, Heiner (Ed.) (2013): Unterrichten an Waldorfschulen. Berufsbild Waldorflehrer: Neue Perspektiven zu Praxis, Forschung, Ausbildung. Wiesbaden: Springer VS, pp. 19–28.

Zech, M. Michael. (2013b): Waldorfschulen als Beispiel gelebter Schulautonomie auf dem freien Markt. In: Randoll, Dirk/Veiga, Marcelo da (Eds.) (2013): Waldorfpädagogik im Praxis und Ausbildung. Zwischen Tradition und notwendigen Reformen. Wiesbaden: Springer VS, pp. 11–19.

EPILOGUE

Volker Frielingsdorf and Christian Boettger

Thinking and doing, doing and thinking, this is the sum of all established wisdom that has ever been recognized and practiced, though not understood, by everyone. Both must eternally ebb and flow in life like in-breath following out-breath; just as there should be no question without its answer. He cannot err, who takes as his law what the Daimon of human understanding secretly whispers into the ear of each newborn: Test doing by thinking and test thinking by doing.
—Johann Wolfgang von Goethe: Wilhelm Meister's Journeyman Years

This anthology extensively documents a cultural change that has occurred throughout the Waldorf education movement during the last 10–15 years. Formerly, critical voices from educational scientists tended to be generally ignored or dismissed polemically. But today these voices are taken seriously, brought into consideration and subjected to discussion, eventually providing the motivation and starting point for this book. The authors of the articles herein demonstrate in manifold ways how stimulating it can be to explore perspectives of educational science and apply them to the field of Waldorf education research.

In the process of preparing the contributions for this book, a surprising fact surfaced: To the degree that it became necessary to answer to external criticism, it became also apparent that we needed to recheck our own theoretic foundations and give them a critical review. Due to its practice orientation, the anthroposophical movement in its many branches of activity shows an understandable abstinence from theory; assuredly that was justified during its pioneer phase and also during the stages of growth and expansion. But for several decades now, Waldorf schools have successfully demonstrated their viability and success in educational practice, and it is time to review our own Waldorf-specific foundations and premises with more vigor. Meanwhile, Waldorf education draws on a wide variety of experiences in its own pedagogic practice. With this experiential background, and taking into consideration the immensely expanded and more differentiated field of educational science, it is now time for review, discussion, and presentation of Waldorf education's theoretical understructure.

We have found it not that easy to work through the pedagogical foundations laid down by Rudolf Steiner in a way that is sound and meets today's academic criteria and demands. On one hand, this difficulty was caused by Waldorf education's long-standing tendency to cast Steiner in the role of a sort of "Uber-father" (Super-dad) of Waldorf pedagogy. As such he was and has been above all critique, and, within the inner realm of Waldorf schools, it was inopportune to approach and evaluate his numerous remarks in a critical way. On the other hand, a thorough review of his educational works shows that we first have to determine the authenticity of part of the statements [attributed to him]. The world of Waldorf schools has based much of its practices on statements that cannot necessarily be traced back to Rudolf Steiner himself, but they firmly adopted them as *fables convenues*, i.e., fictitious but agreed upon "facts."

Epilogue

Discovering such surprising origins of traditions, we gained increasingly the impression that Waldorf education originally was not based on a rigid belief system and certainly was not set in stone by Steiner. Rather, it presents itself as a permanent work in progress that can—and should—never be cast into any final form. The articles in this book show clearly that Steiner was by no means the dogmatic thinker that many of his critics misunderstood him to be, along with many of his followers—like it or not. In contrast to that misunderstanding, Steiner's early works are evidence that his central point of interest consisted of finding foundations and pathways of cognition that would enable individuals to independently gain their own insights and competencies. Steiner's anthroposophical anthropology emerged as the essential core of Waldorf education in the form of his *Study of Man: General Education Course,* which serves as the foundation of its pedagogy. Based on Steiner's understanding of the human being, there emerge didactic and methodological viewpoints, which Waldorf education has variously elaborated on and delineated.

The articles and findings presented in this book call for a renewed critical examination of the contention that Waldorf education is indeed noteworthy and successful in its practice but is based on a highly disconcerting, airy-fairy theory. This argument has been brought forward time and again by educational science. Possibly the allegation of obscurantism misses its mark—if we can further substantiate the finding that Steiner in his early works did indeed develop a true philosophy of freedom; his philosophical approach is precisely not geared toward creating dogmas but toward a liberal attitude that trusts in each individual's finding his or her own way. His approach also relies on educators who will continuously learn and develop and who will create their own suitable forms of teaching and educating. Let me—in the context of the poignant slogan "good practice-dubious theory"—point to Immanuel Kant's treatise "on the popular saying 'good in theory but useless in practice'." In this essay, Kant explains in detail why it is unjustifiable to sever theory from practice, obstructing the development of a true theory. Rather, doing and thinking should not contradict each other, but should "eternally ebb and flow in life like in-breath followed by out-breath," as Goethe described in *Wilhelm Meister's Journeyman Years.*

If, accordingly, we understand the dynamics between theory and practice to be a cross-fertilizing relationship, it makes little sense that a supposedly good practice developed from the matrix of a totally deficient theory. In his treatise of 1793, Kant could not comprehend how one can arrive at the opinion that a good theory might not be valid in practice. He did not even discuss the reverse case of a lastingly successful practice based on a useless theory.

In other words, if we really can know something "by its fruits," educational science would in future need to apply different perspectives to examining the theoretical understructure of Waldorf education with its admittedly generally successful practice. With or without such re-evaluation from the perspective of educational science, the Waldorf school system can only profit from an intensive study of its own roots. In either case, this study will lead to a critical examination of its own heritage, to stronger differentiation, and certainly to deeper conscious understanding.

Fortunately, the Association of Independent Waldorf Schools has, for a quite some time, already set the course toward a stronger academic penetration of Waldorf education. The annual Educational Science Colloquium (*Erziehungswissenschaftliches Kolloqium*) was founded in Stuttgart in 1987 and resulted in a whole series of publications. Moreover, since 2015, a promising Graduate Colloquium for Waldorf Education has been established within the faculty of educational sciences at the Alanus College for Art and Society. Congresses on the positioning of Waldorf education were and are held now and then, attended also by educational scientists and researchers. Furthermore, the Pedagogical Research Institute at the Association of Independent Waldorf Schools initiates and finances projects on the historic development of Waldorf education as well as new editions of Rudolf Steiner's educational works that adhere to current editing standards.

It is now the turn of educational science to decide whether it is meaningful to simply keep ignoring Waldorf education or to recognize it as much too valuable, as the educator Rainer Winkel once said, to leave it exclusively to Waldorf teachers. It may even happen that, in the process of studying Waldorf education and its foundations, one or another scientist may find Rudolf Steiner's views to offer especially valuable new perspectives; precisely because Steiner's views are sometimes cumbrous and go against the grain of mainstream science, they may bring about such broadening of perspectives in the sense of Christian Rittelmeyer's heuristics.

This book remains a work in progress and is in need of further complements, yet it already offers a helpful overview of the current state of discussion and research in Waldorf education. With its publication, the time should be ripe for educational science to determine its own desiderata that emerge for them from Waldorf education. Faced with an alternative school type that has been practiced for so many decades, educational scientists should have no trouble to come up with topics that deserve thorough exploration—not least because this kind of schooling holds important potential for stimulating both educational science and the general school system.

The following bullet points list some of these possible topics:

- Art education as a core concern for schools
- The significance of "authority" in education and classroom teaching
- Inclusive education and integration at Waldorf schools
- Significance and effectivity of the block lesson teaching methodology
- The value of meditative practice for classrooms and for teacher education
- School autonomy as a central demand of a democratic society
- Value and benefits of wholistic education

In its theory and practice, Waldorf education offers a particularly interesting field of research in regard to all these topics precisely because it is so different *[from other school forms]*. Also, comparative studies in educational history beg to be initiated, e.g., on "John Dewey and Rudolf Steiner" or of "A comparison of the concepts of Waldorf education and those of Jena-Plan schools."[1]

In conducting concrete research on Rudolf Steiner's work, some educational scientists may come to the surprising discovery that he was in fact a most stimulating thinker and educator—a pragmatist who definitively did not hand down his information ex cathedra. In reverse, some Waldorf insiders may notice in the course of this intercollegiate exchange that it can be very fruitful to simply look at Steiner's statements as working hypotheses that are worth contemplating but that may prove false at some point in time.

Educational science could readily seize on the openness for dialog and discussion that characterizes the tenor of this volume and could, for example, form research teams recruited from conventional and alternative school types. Most likely team members would soon discover that educational scientists and Waldorf educators share a variety of fundamental tenets; these could form a connective mental matrix for a humane school that strives to offer a multifaceted education to as many students as possible. Probably team members would then recognize that their core values and goals are actually not so different. In our times, education and schooling face so many threats from the outside—due to an overpowering media industry, imposing demands of growing commercialization, and standardization of the educational system.

Humanistically oriented educators—no matter of what color or stripe—would be well advised to focus more on their commonalities than on their differences—especially in view of the pervasive oversimplification of complex issues as presented in politics and society and, often enough, also by scientists. In the treatise cited above, Immanuel Kant sounded a note of caution not to disdain the possibilities of reason to connect theory and practice. He explicitly warned of looking at the world only "through mole's eyes" and to thus reduce the manifest word in a "conceit of wisdom."

Maybe both sides would benefit from heeding this warning of the "old man of Königsberg" in order to open up a dialog that would be, as much as possible, open ended and free of prejudices.

Note

1 *Translator's note:* Jenaplan (or Jena Plan) schools are based on a teaching concept conceived and founded by the German pedagogue Peter Petersen from 1923–1927.

CONTRIBUTORS

Bettina Berger, Ph.D., born 1967; studied theology and cultural sciences; earned her doctorate with a dissertation on the intersection of medicine and educational sciences for the development of patient competency trainings; coordinator of a department for qualitative research in public health agencies; developed and implemented an academic study course for complementary medicine and cultural sciences; since 2010 study coordinator at the academic department for medical theory, integrative and Anthroposophical medicine at the University of Witten/Herdecke; here she works from a patient and client perspective, developing and evaluating interventions for the benefit of self-development and self-management (with focus on patients with chronic illnesses, Rubicon).

Axel Föller-Mancini, Prof., Ph.D., born 1956; studied Waldorf pedagogy in Witten-Annen and philosophy at the University of Bochum; studied Educational Action Research in Oslo, Norway (M.Ed.); afterward earned his doctorate in the field of pedagogic casuistic and action research at the Norwegian University of Life Sciences; between 1990 and 2014 teacher at the Ita Wegman school at the community hospital in Herdecke; since 2014 junior professor for qualitative methodology in education research at the Alanus College in Alfter. *[Note of the Translator: Meanwhile this author was promoted to full tenure as a professor at Alanus.]*

Volker Frielingsdorf, Prof., Ph.D., born 1958; studied social sciences and history at the University of Cologne; he worked for many years as a high school teacher and administrator at the Waldorf School Schopfheim/SüdBaden, teaching history and German language; author of several school text books; publications among others on history of Anthroposophical remedial education and on Waldorf pedagogy from the perspective of educational science; since 2014 professor for Waldorf pedagogy and its history at Alanus University for Art and Social Sciences in Alfter; freelance associate at the pedagogic research center at the Association of Independent Waldorf Schools (Bund der Freien Waldorfschulen).

Wenzel M. Götte, Prof. (ret.), born 1942; studied Newer and East European history, political science, and Slavistics in Tübingen, Berlin, and Freiburg; worked for many years as classroom- and high school teacher as well as in self-government at the Waldorf School Freiburg-St. Georgen; since 1990 lecturer for Waldorf pedagogy at the Waldorf Teacher Training College in Stuttgart; earned his doctorate at the University of Bielefeld with a dissertation on "Experiences with School Autonomy. The Example of Independent Waldorf Schools"; various publications on Waldorf pedagogy; since 2009 professor for didactics in the fields of history, giftedness research, and anthropology of adolescence; retired 2012.

Contributors

Edwin Hübner, Prof. Dr. habil., born 1955; studied mathematics and physics in Frankfurt/Main and Stuttgart; since 1985 teacher for mathematics, physics and religion at the Waldorf school in Frankfurt/Main; 2003–2004 research associate at the University of Paderborn; earned his doctorate in 2004 with a dissertation on "Anthropological Media Education – Foundations and Perspectives"; habilitation in 2009 on the topic of "Individuality and Artistic Design – Becoming Human in Technical Spaces"; since 2015 professor for media pedagogy at the Free University Stuttgart, department of Waldorf pedagogy.

Johannes Kiersch, born 1935; studied Anglistics, history, and pedagogy in Berlin, Tübingen, and Jugenheim an der Bergstrasse; worked as a teacher at the Rudolf Steiner School in Bochum; since 1973 involved in the development of the Institute for Waldorf Pedagogy in Witten/Ruhr; served several years on the board of directors of the Association of Independent Waldorf Schools (Bund der Freien Waldorfschulen); several publications on Waldorf pedagogy and on the history of Anthroposophical esotericism.

Peter Loebell, Prof., Ph.D., born 1955; studied communication science, sociology, and linguistics in Cologne and Hamburg; 1981 M.A. in sociology; studied Waldorf pedagogy in Stuttgart and worked from 1985 to 1996 as a classroom teacher at a Waldorf school; since 1996 lecturer for anthropology, pedagogy, and classroom-teacher methodology at the Waldorf Teacher Training College in Stuttgart; earned his doctorate at the University of Göttingen with a dissertation on "Learning and Individuality"; since 2008 at the Free University Stuttgart, professor for learning psychology and school development with working focus on individualization in the classroom, developmental tasks, and competencies.

Wolfgang Nieke, Prof. em., Ph.D., born 1948; studied educational science, philosophy, psychology, sociology, and Germanistics in Münster; Ph.D. 1976 and habilitation 1991 at Essen University; worked at the Universities of Münster, Bielefeld, and Essen; from 1993 to 2013 founding professor for the chair of general pedagogy at the philosophy department of the University Rostock; focal points of research: pedagogical professionality, intercultural pedagogy; 1994–1996 pro-rector for study and teaching at the University Rostock, 2006–2010 president of the Association of Educational Science Departments (Erziehungswissenschaftlicher Fakultätentag).

Jürgen Peters, Ph.D., born 1955; studied mathematics and physics at the Ruhr University Bochum; worked as a teacher for mathematics and physics at the Waldorf school in Witten-Annen and at the Waldorf teacher training program in Wilton, N.H., USA; since 2009 scientific assistant at Alanus University; earned his doctorate 2013 with a dissertation on "Work-related behavior patterns of Waldorf teachers"; since 2013 faculty member for special tasks at the Alanus University in Alfter.

Walter Riethmüller, born 1948; studied Byzantine history, East- and Southeast-European history, Slavistics (MA); scientific research assistant at the history department of the East European Institute in Munich; Waldorf teacher training; for 13 years was classroom teacher in Freiburg and Stuttgart; 1990–2013 lecturer at the Free University Stuttgart department for Waldorf pedagogy; since 2013 lecturer and adjunct professor at the Free University Stuttgart at the department for Waldorf pedagogy in Berlin; 2007–2014 on the board of directors of the Association of Independent Waldorf Schools (Bund der Freien Waldorfschulen); since 2007 chairman of the Educational Council of the Association of Waldorf Schools and chairman of the Institute for Pedagogical Research.

Christian Rittelmeyer, Prof., Ph.D., born 1940; studied psychology, sociology, and biology in Marburg and Hamburg; M.A. in psychology; until 2003 professor for educational science at the Institute for Educational Science of the Georg-August-University in Göttingen with focus on pedagogical psychology, pedagogical anthropology, history of education, and research methods of educational science.

Contributors

Jost Schieren, Prof., Ph.D., born 1963; studied philosophy, Germanistics, and art history in Bochum and Essen; guest student in Ann Arbor, MI (USA); earned his doctorate with a dissertation on "The Intuitive Power of Judgment. Methodological and Philosophical Foundations of Goethe's Approach to Natural Science"; from 1996 to 2006 he taught German at the Rudolf-Steiner-School in Dortmund; 2004–2008 as scientific research assistant at the University of Paderborn; since 2008 professor for school pedagogy with a focus on Waldorf pedagogy and head of the department for educational science at Alanus University in Alfter.

Albert Schmelzer, Prof., Ph.D., born 1950; studied romance linguistics, theology, and sociology at the Universities of Münster, Angers/France, and Tübingen; high school teacher for German, history, art history, and religion at the Waldorf School Mannheim; earned his doctorate at the Ruhr-University Bochum with a dissertation on "The Threefold-Organization Movement 1919. Rudolf Steiner's Efforts Toward School Self-Government"; since 1990 involved in the training of Waldorf teachers, co-founder of the Intercultural Waldorf School Mannheim; since 2012 professor for general pedagogy at Alanus University's study center in Mannheim with focus on Waldorf pedagogy and interculturality.

Wilfried Sommer, Prof., Sc.D., born 1967; studied physics in Stuttgart, graduating with an M.S. in physics; earned his doctorate in didactics at the Johann Wolfgang Goethe University in Frankfurt/Main with a dissertation "On the Phenomenological Description of Diffraction in the Concept of Optical Pathways"; professional work at the intersection of school and university: high school teacher for mathematics and physics at the Waldorf School Kassel, and head lecturer at the Waldorf Teacher Training College in Kassel; professor for school pedagogy with a focus on phenomenological instruction methods at the Alanus University for Art and Society in Alfter.

Johannes Wagemann, Prof., Ph.D., born 1967; studied electrical engineering in Berlin; research on digital image processing (H. Hertz Institute, Berlin); teacher training for mathematics and physics; since 2000 Waldorf teacher at the Waldorf School Essen; while teaching, he wrote his dissertation on "Brain and Consciousness" (Ph.D. 2010 University Witten-Herdecke [UWH]); adjunct professor at the psychology department (UWH); since 2014 junior professor for consciousness research at Alanus University in Alfter with focus on structure phenomenology; focal points of research: methods of introspective and meditative consciousness research, history of consciousness, theory of cognition and science, social aesthetics.

Carlo Willmann, Prof., Theol. Dr., born 1956; studied catholic theology in Freiburg, Frankfurt/Main, and Vienna and studied art history in Vienna and Waldorf Pedagogy in Mannheim; dissertation on "Waldorf Pedagogy – Religious Pedagogy and Theological Concepts in Rudolf Steiner's Pedagogy"; teacher for religion, history, and art history at the Waldorf School Darmstadt and the Rudolf Steiner Countryside School Schönau close to Vienna; since 2001 lecturer at the Center for Culture and Pedagogy in Vienna; since 2009 professor for religious pedagogy and ethics at Alanus University in Alfter; director of the master study course for Waldorf pedagogy at the Danube (Donau-)University in Krems (Austria).

M. Michael Zech, Prof., Ph.D., born 1957; academic teacher training for teaching German, history, and social studies at high schools graduating with the second teacher state exam *[German High School teaching certificate]*; 1986–2001 Waldorf teacher in Prien/Chiemsee; since 1991 adjunct faculty for teacher training programs; since 1998 member of advisory council at the Center for Pedagogical Research of the Association for Independent Waldorf Schools (Bund der Freien Waldorfschulen); 2001–2006 executive director and lecturer for the International Association for Waldorf Pedagogy in Middle- and Eastern Europe (IAO); since 2006 member of the teacher seminar for Waldorf pedagogy in Kassel; since 2009 member of the Haager Kreis International Conference; 2012 dissertation on "Teaching History at Waldorf Schools" graduating with a Ph.D. from University Göttingen; 2012 junior professor for history didactics at Alanus University in Alfter.

INDEX

Note: Page references with "n" denote endnotes.

Abraham, Anke 248
Ach, Narziss 111
Adler, Alfred 97, 383
Adorno, Theodor 25, 59
Ahnen, Doris 313, 315n15
Ainsworth, Marie 152
Allport, Gordon W. 239
Alsaker, Françoise D. 191
Ament, Wilhelm 99, 125
Anaxagoras 25–26
Anders, Günther 499
Antonovsky, Aaron 229
Apel, Karl-Otto 364, 467
Aquinas, Thomas 486
Aristotle 27, 218
Arnold, Rolf 217
Auernheimer, Georg 467, 468

Baacke, Dieter 500
Baader, Meike-Sophie 377
Bacon, Francis 21, 27
Badley, John Haden 374
Ballauf, Theodor 262
Bandura, Albert 110, 257
Barricelli, Michele 457
Bartoniczek, André 438, 448
Barz, Heiner 4, 5, 98, 119, 121, 124, 286, 287, 405, 406
Bateson, Gregory 216
Baudler, Peter 488
Bauer, Horst Philipp 5
Bauer, Joachim 141, 178, 191, 250
Baumert, Jürgen 481
Becker, Hellmut 384
Becker, Nicole 190–191
Beckers, Franz 442
Benner, Dietrich 485

Berger, Bettina 99, 125
Berk, Laura 109, 112
Besant, Anni 383
Binet, Alfred 121
Blakemore, Sarah-Jayne 191
Blavatsky, Helena Petrovna 121, 440
Blonsky, Pavel 385n2
Bock, Irmgard 485
Boettger, Christian 7, 9
Böhm, Winfried 98, 123–124, 125
Böhme, Gernot 63, 69, 501
Böhme, Hartmut 69
Böhme, Jacob 444
Bohnsack, Fritz 5, 326
Bois-Reymond, Emil du 23, 422
Bollenbeck, Georg 224
Bollnow, Otto Friedrich 59, 61
Booth, Shirley 236
Bormann, Inka 312
Bourdieu, Pierre 60, 371n14
Bowers, Chet 217–218
Bowlby, John 104, 106, 152
Braun, Anna Katharina 190
Brecht, Bertolt 41
Breysig, Kurt 442
Brin, Sergey 501
Bruno, Giordano 444
Buber, Martin 353, 376, 383
Büchele, Mandana 465, 473
Buck, Günter 213, 265
Bühler, Charlotte 104
Burckhardt, Jacob 443

Caesar, Julius 158
Carr, Nicholas 499
Cassirer, E. 442, 488
Cézanne, Paul 266

Index

Chomsky, Noam 109
Clement, Christian 424, 432
Cohn, Ruth 417
Copei, Friedrich 348
Copernicus 18
Crone, Eveline 189, 191, 196

Dahlin, Bo 4, 279
da Veiga, Marcello 276
Decroly, Ovide 385n2
de Haan, Gerhard 312
de La Mettrie, Julien Offray 508
Del Giudice, Marco 169–170
Descartes, René 293, 508
Dewey, John 18, 91, 374, 380, 383, 385, 394, 395
Dietz, Karl-Martin 272, 431
Dreher, Eva 191
Dworkin, Ronald 492
Dwyer, Kathleen 169

Ebbinghaus, Hermann 99, 121, 126
Eccles, John 178
Ellert, Christa 120
Elsner, Birgit 99, 146
Empedocles 25–26
Engelhardt, Frank 9
Ensor, Beatrice 385n2
Erikson, Erik H. 99, 105, 108, 110, 169
Eschenbach, Wolfram von 275
Esterl, Dietrich 458, 529n9

Faivre, Antoine 420, 421, 431–432
Faulstich, Paul 213, 215, 219, 220, 222
Faulstich, Peter 228
Fegert, Jörg M. 169
Fend, Helmut 191, 367–368
Ferrière, Adolphe 385n2
Fichte, Johann Gottlieb 15, 17, 28–32, 34, 515
Fischer-Lichte, Erika 273, 296–298, 300
Fisher, Ronald 22
Flammer, August 124, 191
Fleck, Ludwig 26
Fleck, Ludwik 420
Flitner, Andreas 59–60
Flohr, Hans 23
Foerst, Anne 508
Föller-Mancini, Axel 99, 125
Foucault, Michel 68, 418
Freinet, Célestin 374, 375, 383
Freitag, Christine 483–484
Freud, Sigmund 99, 109, 110, 121, 122, 126
Friedrich, Carl 384
Frielingsdorf, Volker 6, 9, 286, 324–325, 361
Frith, Uta 191
Fromm, Erich 347, 417
Fuchs, Thomas 152, 177–178, 273, 279, 299

Galen 401
Galileo Galilei 18, 21

Gandhi, Mahatma 330
Garnitschnig, Karl 4
Gebser, Jean 19–20, 22–23
Geheeb, Paul 374, 375, 383
Geheeb-Cassirer, Edith 375
Gehlen, Arnold 61
Gesell, Arnold 104, 111
Giedd, Jay N. 177, 180, 181, 184, 188
Glock, Charles Y. 486
Glöckel, Otto 383, 385n2
Goethe, Johann Wolfgang 8, 15, 17, 25–32, 43n23, 74–75, 80, 86, 159, 276, 280, 378, 379, 416, 432, 434, 443, 449–452, 515, 532, 533
Gögelein, Christoph 275
Göhlich, Michael 216
Gollwitzer, Peter Max 158
Göppel, R. 135
Gotheim, Eberhard 442
Götte, Wenzel M. 7, 8–9, 100, 308, 313, 515, 516–517, 528, 529n5
Graßhoff, Gunter 4
Grebe-Ellis, Johannes 285
Grethlein, Christian 478
Grosse, Rudolf 120
Guardini, Romano 124

Habermas, Jürgen 364, 467
Haeckel, Ernst 416
Haertel, Geneva D. 367
Halbfas, Hubertus 478, 483, 488
Hall, Granville Stanley 159–160
Hall, Stanley 100
Hanegraaff, Wouter J. 420, 424, 431–432
Hattie, John 250, 322, 346, 369, 398
Heckhausen, Heinz 158, 242
Hegel, Georg Wilhelm Friedrich 28, 146, 434, 439, 468
Heidegger, Martin 424
Heisterkamp, Jens 438, 443, 446–448, 451
Helsper, Werner 4, 165, 321, 325, 331–332, 400
Hentig, Hartmut von 482
Herbart, Johann Friedrich 87, 257
Herrmann, Ulrich 190
Hervieu-Léger, Danièle 476
Herzberg, Heidrun 219
Herzig, Bardo 497, 506–507
Herzog, Roman 496–497, 501, 503
Hesse, Hermann 376, 386n6
Hetzer, Hildegard 104
Heumann, Jürgen 492
Heydebrand, Caroline von 304, 305, 309, 332
Hilker, Franz 376, 383
Hippocrates 401
Hirukawa, Hirohisa 508
Hobbes, Thomas 364
Hoffmann, Bernward 497
Hoffmann, Stefan 497
Hohlenberg, Johannes 424
Holzbrecher, Alfred 467

Index

Holzkamp, Klaus 207, 237–238
Horkheimer, Max 25
Hormel, Ulrike 467
Hubel, David H. 180
Hufen, Friedhelm 523
Hügli, Anton 350
Hugo, Aksel 279
Huizinga, Johan 442
Humboldt, Wilhelm von 237, 417, 452, 468, 515
Hume, David 22
Huppertz, Michael 346
Husserl, Edmund 293–294, 370, 416, 433
Hüther, Gerald 141, 177, 190, 192, 235, 337

Idel, Till-Sebastian 4
Illich, Ivan 347

Jaffke, Christoph 277
Jäggle, Martin 482
Jakobs, Monika 485
Jank, Werner 275, 299–300
Jobs, Steve 509n1
Jonas, Hans 178
Jung, C.G. 446, 488

Kahneman, Daniel 217
Kaiser, Ulrich 423–424
Kallert, Heide 119, 120
Kalwitz, Bernd 192
Kamper, Dietmar 62
Kant, Immanuel 15, 23, 29, 38, 54–56, 62–63, 74–75, 217, 257, 533
Karni, A. 265
Karsen, Fritz 360, 376, 385n2
Kay, Ellen 377
Keim, Wolfgang 361
Keller, Heidi 108, 111
Kepler, Johannes 42n8
Kerschensteiner, Georg 374, 378, 395
Key, Ellen 359, 391–392
Kiene, Helmut 21, 431
Kierkegaard, Søren 424
Kiersch, Johannes 86, 120, 403, 405, 431
Kitzel, Joachim Gunther 420
Klafki, Wolfgang 272–276, 277, 289, 295, 299, 520
Kling, Walter 351–352
Kloss, Heinz 375, 377, 379
Knutson, Brian 506
Koch, Lutz 230n12, 257
Koch, Sabine C. 63n6
Kohlberg, Lawrence 99, 101, 138
Köhler, Wolfgang 257
Kokemohr, Rainer 265
Koller, Hans-Christoph 217, 234, 258, 265, 300, 417
Korczak, Janusz 99, 128
Kranich, Ernst-Michael 28, 51, 122, 146, 148, 150, 192, 193, 241, 245
Krapp, Andreas 215
Krautz, Jochen 4
Krobath, Thomas 482

Kroh, Oswald 111, 123, 160
Krüger, Heinz-Hermann 363
Kuhn, Thomas P. 26
Kuhn, Thomas S. 420
Kunze, Katharina 4
Kurzweil, Ray 508

Ladenthin, Volker 485
Lampert, Claudia 497, 507
Lamprecht, Karl 442, 443
Langeveld, Martinus Jan 53–54
Largo, Remo 131
Lay, Wilhelm August 99, 125
Leber, Stefan 192, 193, 304, 326, 517, 520
Lechner, Martin 483
Leimgruber, Stephan 480
Leist, Manfred 522
Lenroot, Roshel K. 179, 184
Leontjew, Alexej 228
Lewin, Kurt 104, 111
Lichtwark, Alfred 378, 395
Liebau, Eckart 71
Liebenwein, Sylvia 4, 287
Liebknecht, Wilhelm 450
Lietz, Hermann 360, 374, 395
Lievegoed, Bernard 111
Lindenberg, Christoph 121, 146, 438, 454
Lischewski, Andreas 2
Litt, Theodor 364, 381
Loch, Werner 60
Locke, John 223
Loebell, Peter 7, 8, 99, 146, 148, 207, 287, 308, 313, 361–362
Lorenz, Konrad 109
Lorenzer, A. 488
Lowndes, Florin 352
Luckmann, Thomas 240, 365
Luhmann, Niklas 486
Lütjen-Drecoll, Elke 112

Mackensen, Manfred von 288
Mailer, Norman 508
Mainzer, Klaus 508
Majorek, Marek 431
Malaguzzi, Loris 149
Mannheim, Karl 368
Marotzki, Winfried 216
Marti, Thomas 146, 192
Marton, Ference 236
Marx, Karl 218, 228
Maurer, Klaus-Michael 308, 313
McNaughton, B.L. 265
Mecheril, Paul 467
Meier, Michaela 190
Meister Eckhart 444
Merleau-Ponty, Maurice 213–214, 242, 258
Meumann, Ernst 97
Mey, Günter 102
Meyer, Hilbert 272, 275, 276, 299–300
Meyer, Meinert 272, 276

Index

Meyer-Drawe, Käte 213, 258, 262
Mezirow, Jack 217
Mill, John Stuart 22
Minsky, Marvin 508
Moll, Emil 51
Molt, Emil 375, 386n6, 513
Montada, Leo 105, 191
Montessori, Maria 2, 374, 375–376, 377, 380, 383, 391–392, 394, 395
Morasch, Gudrun 244
Moser, Heinz 497, 501
Müller, Walter 405
Müller-Wiedemann, Hans 101, 163
Muschalle, Michael 276

Näf, Martin 375
Neider, Andreas 192
Neill, A.S. 374, 377, 380, 383
Nettesheim, Agrippa von 444
Newton, Isaac 21
Nickel, Horst 110
Nicolas of Cusa 444
Nieke, Wolfgang 4, 207, 361, 467, 479, 492
Niemeyer, Christian 386n5
Nietzsche, Friedrich 376, 444, 450
Nipkow, K. E. 480
Nohl, Arnd-Michael 216, 360

Oelkers, Jürgen 370n1, 375
Oerter, Rolf 102, 105, 191
Oevermann, Ulrich 162, 166–168, 172n12, 321
Oexle, Otto Gerhard 420
Østergaard, Edvin 279
Osterrieder, Markus 441
Otto, Berthold 395

Palmer, Parker J. 422
Pandel, Hans-Jürgen 457
Pannitschka, Sophie 7, 9
Papoušek, Mechthild 152
Paracelsus 444
Parkhurst, Helen 374
Paschen, Harm 5, 366, 370n2
Patzlaff, Rainer 146, 151
Pauen, Sabina 99, 146, 190, 191
Paul, Jean 289, 515
Pavlov, Ivan Petrovich 257
Peirce, Charles S. 18, 32
Peters, Jürgen 3
Petersen, Peter 374, 375, 376, 378, 383, 395
Petzelt, Alfred 257
Petzold, Hilarion G. 147, 149
Piaget, Jean 99, 101, 104, 108, 110, 120–121, 123, 125, 131–132, 137–138, 146, 164, 217, 241, 257, 374, 383, 500
Picht, Georg 384
Pirner, Manfred 478–479
Plautus 364
Pleines, Jürgen-Eckhard 60
Plessner, Helmuth 61, 299

Pollack, Guido 4
Popp, Susanne 458
Popper, Karl 26, 32, 178, 366
Porzelt, Burkhard 485–486
Postman, Neil 508–509
Prange, Klaus 1, 4, 98, 119–120, 121, 122, 125–126, 159, 360, 428–429
Prengel, Annedore 467
Prenzel, Manfred 215
Preyer, Wilhelm 97, 99, 100, 159

Radhakrishnan, Sarvepalli 383
Ramge, Hans 102
Randoll, Dirk 4, 124, 286, 287, 323–324, 337–338, 343, 405, 406, 435
Rapp, Gerhard 245
Ravagli, Lorenzo 122, 431
Reddie, Cecil 374
Rein, Wilhelm 88
Remplein, Heinz 111
Richter, Tobias 305, 307, 309, 311
Ricoeur, P. 488
Riethmüller, Walter 7, 8, 99, 321
Rifkin, Jeremy 63n3
Rilke, Rainer Maria 391
Rittelmeyer, Christian 7, 52, 86, 87, 98–99, 145, 190, 288, 290, 402, 534
Rizzolatti, Giacomo 179
Rogers, Carl 417
Rogers, Ginger 508
Rohen, Johannes W. 112
Röhrs, Hermann 360
Rosa, Hartmut 214
Rosslenbroich, Bernd 81
Roth, Gerhard 177, 190, 246
Roth, Hans-Joachim 466, 467, 473
Roth, Heinrich 60, 69, 205, 206, 241
Rotten, Elisabeth 385n2
Rousseau, Jean-Jacques 54, 68, 417
Ruberg, Christiane 248, 249
Rumpf, Horst 5, 55, 326

Sartre, Jean-Paul 424
Saßmannshausen, Wolfgang 146
Schaarschmidt, Uwe 345n2
Schachtner, Christal 500
Scheler, Max 18
Schelling, Friedrich Wilhelm Joseph 434
Schenk-Danzinger, Lotte 102, 104, 132, 150
Scherr, Alfred 467
Scheuerl, Hans 60–61
Scheunpflug, Annette 190
Schieren, Jost 7, 8, 52, 207–208, 238, 276, 281, 283, 424
Schiller, Friedrich 56, 58, 75, 442, 515
Schirlbauer, Alfred 262–263
Schirrmacher, Frank 424n2
Schleiermacher, Friedrich Daniel Ernst 484
Schleuning, Eva Maria 120
Schluss, Henning 484

Index

Schmelzer, Albert 7, 8, 52, 98, 322
Schmidt, Günther R. 487
Schneider, Peter 4, 276
Schneider, Wolfgang 98, 105, 122, 123, 124, 125
Schopenhauer, Arthur 88
Schröder, Bernd 478–479, 492–493
Schröer, Karl Julius 15
Schroeter-Wittke, Harald 483
Schütz, Alfred 218, 240, 365
Schwerdt, Ulrich 361
Sears, Robert E. 111
Sesink, Werner 509
Silesius, Angelus 444
Simmel, Georg 423
Singer, Wolf 24
Sivers, Marie von 423
Skagen, Kaj 424
Skiera, Ehrenhard 2–3, 44n52, 98, 123, 124, 125, 193, 365, 374–375, 403–404, 405, 428
Skinner, Burrhus 109, 111
Sommer, Wilfried 7, 8
Spengler, Oswald 442–443, 459n4
Spinoza, Baruch 15, 416
Spitz, René 104, 106
Spitzer, Manfred 113n19, 138, 141, 177, 190
Steffen, Albert 422
Steiner, Marie 423
Steiner, Rudolf 2, 5–7, 15, 17–18, 25–41, 44n47, 51, 52, 58, 61, 63, 71–78, 80–81, 85–88, 90–91, 97–103, 106, 109, 112, 119, 120, 124–125, 128–131, 138–142, 148, 158–166, 168, 176, 182, 188, 192, 193, 194–195, 207, 229, 234, 235, 238–248, 250–251, 258–259, 264–265, 271, 277, 280, 282, 284–285, 288, 289–292, 295, 303–306, 313, 321, 322, 326–331, 333, 337–338, 346, 348–350, 351, 366–368, 371n15, 374, 375–376, 377–378, 379–383, 386n9, 392–394, 397, 398, 400, 401–408, 415, 416, 419–424, 428–435, 442–456, 458n1, 459n7, 468–469, 500, 503, 513–518, 524–525, 529n7
Stern, Daniel N. 99, 146, 151
Stern, Elsbeth 188, 190
Stern, William 97
Stockmeyer, Karl 304–306, 454–455, 459n11, 528n3
Störich, Hans-Joachim 88
Strauch, Barbara 191
Strelau, Jan 401
Struck, Peter 325, 327
Süss, Daniel 497, 507

Takeda, Arata 466
Tausch, Reinhard 104
Templeton, Alec 277
Tenorth, Heinz-Elmar 2, 59, 331, 360, 376
Thorndike, Edward Lee 121
Tillich, Paul 486
Timmermann, Dieter 529n5

Tinbergen, Niko 109
Tippelt, Rudolf 2
Traub, Hartmut 15–16, 18
Trüper, Johannes 385n2
Tulodziecki, Gerhard 497, 506–507
Türcke, Christoph 299

Ullrich, Heiner 1–2, 4, 82n4, 98, 119, 120–123, 124, 146, 193, 323, 324, 330, 360, 361, 375, 400, 402, 428–429, 509n9

Varela, Francisco 280
Verburg, Winfried 481
Vygotsky, Lev Semyonovich 109, 228, 257, 500

Wagenschein, Martin 240, 286
Wagner, Hans-Josef 166, 285
Walach, Harald 406
Walberg, Herbert J. 367
Walczyk, Julia 248, 249
Waldenfels, Bernhard 43n33
Watson, John B. 257
Weber, Max 172n12, 218
Weinstein, Thomas 367
Weiß, Edgar 361
Weißert, Ernst 522
Weizsäcker, Richard von 384
Welsch, Wolfgang 449, 466, 467
Werner, Heinz 111
West-Eberhard, Mary Jane 170
Wiehl, Angelika 9, 276
Wiesing, Lambert 279, 281
Wijnen, Christine W. 497, 507
Wilken, Etta 119, 120
Wilson, M.A. 265
Wilson, Woodrow 441
Wimmer, Michael 69
Winkel, Rainer 533
Winkler, Hartmut 497, 498
Wittgenstein, Ludwig 32
Witzenmann, Herbert 34, 44n45, 73–74, 207, 259–260, 264
Wulf, Christian 59, 273, 297
Wulf, Christoph 60, 190
Wundt, Wilhelm 99, 100, 121, 122, 125, 126, 159
Wyneken, Gustav 374, 395

Zajonc, Arthur 422
Zander, Helmut 18, 72, 124–125, 159, 420, 435n1, 438, 441, 444, 458n1
Zech, Michael 273, 288
Zellmer, Svenja 170
Ziemke, Axel 193
Ziller, Tuiskon 88
Zimmermann, Heinz 350
Zirfas, Jörg 60, 69, 216, 273, 297